Components of Emotional Meaning

Series in Affective Science

Series Editors: Richard J. Davidson, Paul Ekman and Klaus R. Scherer

The Evolution of Emotional Communication Eckart Altenmüller, Sabine Schmidt, and Elke Zimmnermann (eds.)

The Neuropsychology of Emotion John C. Borod

Persons, Situation, and Emotions: An Ecological Approach Herman Brandstätter and Andrzej Eliasz

Handbook of Emotion Elicitation and Assessment James A. Coan and John J.B. Ellen (eds.)

Anxiety, Depression, and Emotion Richard J. Davidson

What the Face Reveals: Basic and Applied Studies of Spontaneous Expression Using the Facial Action Coding System (FACS) 2e Paul Ekman and Erika L. Rosenberg (eds.)

The Nature of Emotion: Fundamental Questions Paul Ekman and Richard J. Davidson

The Psychology of Gratitude Robert A. Emmons and Michael E. McCullough (eds.)

Who Needs Emotions? The brain meets the robot Jean-Marc Fellous and Michael A. Arbib (eds.)

Emotions in Psychopathology: Theory and Research William F. Flack and James D. Laird (eds.)

Shame: Interpersonal Behaviour, Psychopathology, and Culture Paul Gilbert and Bernice Andrews (eds.)

Pleasures of the Brain Martin L. Kringelbach and Kent C. Berridge

Infant Chimpanzee and Human Child: A Classic 1935 Comparative Study of Ape Emotions and Intelligence N.N. Ladygina-Kohts (deceased) and Frans B.M. de Waal (eds.) Boris Vekker (translator)

Feelings: The Perception of Self James D. Laird

Cognitive Neuroscience of Emotions Richard D. Lane and Lynn Nadel (eds.)

The Development of Social Engagement: Neurobiological Perspectives Peter J. Marshall and Nathan A. Fox (eds.)

Science of Emotional Intelligence: Knowns and Unknowns Gerald Matthews, Moshe Zeidner, and Richard D. Roberts (eds.)

Affective Neuroscience: The Foundations of Human and Animal Emotions Jaak Panskepp

Nonverbal Behaviour in Clinical Settings Pierre Philippot, Robert S. Feldman, and Erik J. Coats (eds.)

Emotion in Memory and Development: Biological, Cognitive, and Social Considerations Jodi Quas and Robyn Fivush (eds).

Memory and Emotion Daniel Reisberg and Paula Hertel (eds.)

Emotion Explained Edmund T. Rolls

Emotion, Social Relationships, and Health Carol D. Ryff and Burton Singer (eds.)

Oxford Companion to Emotion and the Affective Sciences David Sander and Klaus Scherer

A Blueprint for Affective Computing: A sourcebook and manual Klaus R. Scherer, Tanja Bänzinger, and Etienne Roesch

Appraisal Processes in Emotion: Theory, Methods, Research K. Scherer, A. Schorr, and T. Johnstone (eds.)

Bodily Sensibility: Intelligent Action Jay Schulkin

Boo! Culture, Experience, and the Startle Reflex Ronald C. Simons

Thinking and Feeling: Contemporary Philosophers on Emotions Robert C. Solomon

Components of Emotional Meaning

A sourcebook

Edited by

Johnny J.R. Fontaine

Klaus R. Scherer

Cristina Soriano

OXFORD

UNIVERSITY PRESS

Great Clarendon Street, Oxford, OX2 6DP,
United Kingdom

Oxford University Press is a department of the University of Oxford.
It furthers the University's objective of excellence in research, scholarship,
and education by publishing worldwide. Oxford is a registered trade mark of
Oxford University Press in the UK and in certain other countries

© Oxford University Press 2013

The moral rights of the authors have been asserted

First Edition published in 2013
Impression: 1

Published in the United States of America by Oxford University Press
198 Madison Avenue, New York, NY 10016, United States of America

British Library Cataloguing in Publication Data
Data available

Library of Congress Control Number: 2013938573

ISBN 978–0–19–959274–6

Printed and bound by
CPI Group (UK) Ltd, Croydon, CR0 4YY

Oxford University Press makes no representation, express or implied, that the
drug dosages in this book are correct. Readers must therefore always check
the product information and clinical procedures with the most up-to-date
published product information and data sheets provided by the manufacturers
and the most recent codes of conduct and safety regulations. The authors and
the publishers do not accept responsibility or legal liability for any errors in the
text or for the misuse or misapplication of material in this work. Except where
otherwise stated, drug dosages and recommendations are for the non-pregnant
adult who is not breast-feeding

Links to third party websites are provided by Oxford in good faith and
for information only. Oxford disclaims any responsibility for the materials
contained in any third party website referenced in this work.

Preface

Klaus R. Scherer

The idea that gave rise to the research reported in this book is, as is often the case in science, due largely to serendipity and chance events. However, as is also frequently the case, the time had to be ripe for serendipity to play its role. What had slowly ripened as the idea was born was the conviction that emotion was best defined as an episode during which different subsystems of the organism are tightly coordinated (and can thus be considered as *components* of emotion) in order to allow optimal adaptation to environmental contingencies. This definition emerged during the development of a new breed of appraisal theories (following the pioneering work of Arnold and Lazarus; see Schorr, 2001), as the theorists in this tradition converged on the claim that emotions were to be seen as processes that are elicited and differentiated by the appraisal of relevant events (see Scherer, 1999a, 2005a). This influential theoretical development occurred at a time when a group of European emotion researchers created, with the help of the Maison des Sciences de l'Homme in Paris and its director, Clemens Heller, a consortium of their laboratories, designed to facilitate collaboration on different projects and jointly train their young researchers. During one of the meetings of the consortium, I happened to discuss the thorny issue of emotion labels and the differences between languages (an issue which is directly related to the question of how many emotions are distinguished in different languages and cultures, and what counts as a "real" emotion) with Nico Frijda. Both of us had an inkling that the key to the question might have to do with the fact that different emotion labels (especially across languages) reflect the different components of emotion, as postulated by both of us, to a different degree. For example, some words seem to focus on the cognitive appraisal configuration that gives rise to an emotion (e.g., irritation), whereas others might focus more on physiological manifestations, expressions, or action tendencies (e.g., rage). This led to the idea that this approach might provide a royal road to defining and potentially measuring the meaning of emotion words in different languages.

Like many good ideas that are generated while drinking wine, this one was not immediately pursued, as other priorities determined our research agendas. But, also like other good ideas, this one lingered in my mind and I decided to pursue the goal of measuring the meaning of emotion words empirically via component ratings in a cross-cultural and cross-language setting. I had been encouraged in this by the success of a large cross-cultural study on the self-report of emotion experiences (ISEAR, Scherer & Wallbott, 1994) and of an expert system allowing the differentiation of emotion (GENESE, Scherer, 1993), which had demonstrated the feasibility of differentially assessing the different emotion components through self-report. Having generated the idea of an empirical study, I published the first formal proposal for this work (Scherer, 2005a), suggesting the use of a design feature approach to create a *grid* of features and emotions. This proposal included a first version of a profile of features for different components and a set of emotion words.

But a plan is not enough. It took a second chance event for it to be put into action. During a meeting on cross-cultural psychology in Budapest in 2003, an old friend, Ype Poortinga, introduced me to Johnny Fontaine, who had carried out a series of extremely interesting culture-comparison studies of emotion (Fontaine et al., 2006). Johnny came to visit our group in Geneva and we discovered a great deal of overlap in interests, as well as complementary skills and approaches, and decided to work together. In the meanwhile, we had received funding from the Swiss federal government to form a National Center of Competence in Research (NCCR) in the Affective Sciences (the Swiss Center for Affective Sciences). With the support of the NCCR and of the University of Geneva, we were able to found, with the help of Pierre Dasen, an International Consortium on Cross-Cultural Research on Affect to serve as an organizational framework for a "GRID study."

The ensuing research activity was greatly facilitated by a third happy coincidence, namely the presence of a competent cognitive scientist with extensive computer skills in our group, Etienne Roesch, and the collaboration with interested colleagues in the European HUMAINE (Human Machine Interaction and Emotion) network of excellence. The first version of the GRID questionnaire (via controlled web administration) was run in Geneva, Gent, and York/Belfast, and the results published by Fontaine, Scherer, Roesch, and Ellsworth (2007). The initial phase of the collaborative research was greatly enhanced by Phoebe Ellsworth's precious input, largely on the occasion of a cross-cultural psychology conference on the Greek island of Spetses in 2006, which also served as a launching pad for securing the collaboration of research teams from many different countries.

A final propitious event was the arrival of Cristina Soriano, a cognitive linguist who had worked on metaphoric expressions of emotion, as a consequence of our Center recruiting a postdoctoral fellow for an interdisciplinary research focus on Language and Culture. She organized the data collection with over 20 teams in as many countries and also enriched the conceptual and theoretical background of the study with pertinent input from linguistics.

Without these serendipitous and chance effects, neither the GRID research nor this book would exist. However, the most important factors for the success of this ambitious endeavor have been the competence, enthusiastic interest, and hard work of all those concerned, in particular the large number of collaborators in this intercultural study in over 25 countries and almost as many languages. Many of them are also co-authors of this book and have contributed to the data collection, several meetings and symposia, and the writing of the book in a truly interdisciplinary spirit. As one might imagine, the editorial process of bringing together contributions of scholars raised in very different scientific traditions was not an easy matter, especially given the fundamental differences between qualitative and quantitative approaches and different habits of establishing evidence. Despite these circumstances, the reviewing and resubmitting process went very smoothly, thanks to the interdisciplinary background of the editorial team and the strong spirit of cooperation on the part of the various groups of authors.

In concluding, I want to thank, in the name of the editors of this volume, all of the contributors to this ambitious research enterprise, including the collaborators who, for various reasons, could not write a chapter in this volume. Our special thanks go to Anna Ogarkova for recruiting many research collaborators for the Slavic language families and writing a chapter that makes a central contribution to the review of the literature and the theoretical foundation of the work reported in this volume. We also thank Etienne Roesch for programming the initial version of the GRID instrument, the technical staff of the NCCR (Natascha Michel, Urs Richle, Olivier Rosset and Julien Savary) who supported the smooth running of a multilingual questionnaire online, Christelle Gillioz and Samidh Shrestha for their help in manuscript preparation, and the staff at Oxford University Press for a stellar editing and publishing effort.

Last but not least, we very gratefully acknowledge the financial support from a number of institutions who have made this ambitious research and the preparation of this book possible: the Swiss National Science Foundation (SNSF), the Swiss Network for International Studies (SNIS), the Research Foundation Flanders (FWO), the University of Geneva, Ghent University, and the European Research Council (ERC).

Geneva, July 2013

Contents

PART VIII **Taking stock and further development of the GRID paradigm**

List of contributors

Gülcan Akçalan Akırmak
Istanbul Bilgi University (Turkey)

Paola Alarcón
University of Concepción (Chile)

Itziar Alonso-Arbiol
University of the Basque Country UPV/EHU
(Spain)

Guglielmo Bellelli
University of Bari (Italy)

Hale Bolak Boratav
Istanbul Bilgi University (Turkey)

Seger M. Breugelmans
Tilburg University (The Netherlands)

Cecilia Chau Pérez-Aranibar
Pontificia Universidad Católica del Perú
(Peru)

Let Dillen
Ghent University (Belgium)

Michael Eid
Free University of Berlin (Germany)

Phoebe Ellsworth
University of Michigan (USA)

Johnny J. R. Fontaine
Ghent University (Belgium)

Dario Galati
University of Turin (Italy)

Hans Groenvynck
Ghent University (Belgium)

Shlomo Hareli
University of Haifa (Israel)

Ahalya Hejmadi
University of Maryland (USA) & Utkal
University (India)

Ursula Hess
Humboldt University (Germany)

Svetlana Ionova
Volgograd State University (Russia)

Keiko Ishii
Kobe University (Japan)

Cara Jonker
North-West University (South-Africa)

Efthymia C. Kapnoula
University of Iowa (USA)

Liisi Kööts-Ausmees
University of Tartu (Estonia)

Spike W. S. Lee
University of Toronto (Canada)

Manon Levesque
Omar Bongo University (Gabon)

Barbara Lewandowska-Tomaszczyk
University of Łódź (Poland)

Deon Meiring
University of Pretoria (South-Africa)

Claudia Mejía Quijano
University of Antioquía (Colombia)

Lerato Mojaki
North-West University (South-Africa)

Marcello Mortillaro
Swiss Center for Affective Sciences—
University of Geneva (Switzerland)

Yu Niiya
Hosei University (Japan)

Anna Ogarkova
Swiss Center for Affective Sciences—
University of Geneva (Switzerland)

Penny Panagiotopoulou
University of Patras (Greece)

Nataliya Panasenko
University of SS Cyril and Methodius in
Trnava (Slovakia) – Kiev National Linguistic
University (Ukraine)

Irina Prihod'ko
Kyiv National Taras Shevchenko University
(Ukraine)

Athanassios Protopapas
University of Athens (Greece)

Anu Realo
University of Tartu (Estonia)

Pio E. Ricci-Bitti
University of Bologna (Italy)

Annekathrin Schacht
University of Göttingen (Germany)

Klaus R. Scherer
Swiss Center for Affective Sciences—
University of Geneva (Switzerland)

Viktor Shakhovskyy
Volgograd Socio-Pedagogical University
(Russia)

Yuh-Ling Shen
National Chung Cheng University
(Taiwan)

Ching-Fan Sheu
National Cheng Kung University (Taiwan)

Vera Shuman
University of Lausanne (Switzerland)

Mari Siiroinen
University of Helsinki (Finland)

Mia Silfver-Kuhalampi
University of Helsinki (Finland)

Cristina Soriano
Swiss Center for Affective Sciences—
University of Geneva (Switzerland)

Diane Sunar
Istanbul Bilgi University (Turkey)

Marina Terkourafi
University of Illinois at Urbana-Champaign
(USA)

Pascal Thibault
Cégep Saint-Jean-sur-Richelieu (Canada)

Heli Tissari
University of Helsinki (Finland)

Eddie M. W. Tong
National University of Singapore
(Singapore)

Fons J. R. van de Vijver
Tilburg University (The Netherlands),
North-West University (South Africa),
& University of Queensland (Australia)

Steven J. E. Van den Eede
Ghent University (Belgium)

Yvette van Osch
Tilburg University (The Netherlands)

Elke Veirman
Ghent University (Belgium)

Yana Volkova
Volgograd Socio-Pedagogical University
(Russia)

Paul A. Wilson
University of Łódź (Poland)

Sowan Wong
City University of Hong Kong (China)

Zhengdao Ye
The Australian National University
(Australia)

Dannii Y. Yeung
City University of Hong Kong (China)

Julia Zakharova
Internal Affairs Ministry Academy
(Ukraine)

Marcel Zeelenberg
Tilburg University (The Netherlands)

Aïda Zitouni
University of Jendouba (Tunisia)

List of GRID collaborators (dataset owners)[1]

Gülcan Akçalan Akırmak
Istanbul Bilgi University (Turkey)

Paola Alarcón
University of Concepción (Chile)

Itziar Alonso-Arbiol
University of the Basque Country UPV/EHU (Spain)

Guglielmo Bellelli
University of Bari (Italy)

Cecilia Chau Pérez-Aranibar
Pontificia Universidad Católica del Perú (Peru)

Joana Dimas
INESC-ID and Instituto Superior Técnico, Universidade Técnica de Lisboa (Portugal)

Michael Eid
Free University of Berlin (Germany)

Phoebe Ellsworth
University of Michigan (USA)

Johnny J. R. Fontaine
Ghent University (Belgium)

Dario Galati
University of Turin (Italy)

Shlomo Hareli
University of Haifa (Israel)

Ahalya Hejmadi
University of Maryland (USA) & Utkal University (India)

Ursula Hess
Humboldt University (Germany)

Keiko Ishii
Kobe University (Japan)

Cara Jonker
North-West University (South-Africa)

Zoltan Kövecses
Eötvös Loránd University (Hungary)

Barbara Lewandowska-Tomaszczyk
University of Łódź (Poland)

Deon Meiring
University of Pretoria (South-Africa)

Marcello Mortillaro
Swiss Center for Affective Sciences—University of Geneva (Switzerland)

Yu Niiya
Hosei University (Japan)

Anna Ogarkova
Swiss Center for Affective Sciences—University of Geneva (Switzerland)

Marina Palazova
International Psychoanalytic University Berlin (Germany)

Nataliya Panasenko
University of SS Cyril and Methodius in Trnava (Slovakia)—Kiev National Linguistic University (Ukraine)

Hu Ping
Renmin University of China (China)

Athanassios Protopapas
University of Athens (Greece)

---

[1] Contact information for all GRID collaborators is available on the GRID website at http://www.affective-sciences.org/GRID

Anu Realo
University of Tartu (Estonia)

Pio E. Ricci-Bitti
University of Bologna (Italy)

Klaus R. Scherer
Swiss Center for Affective Sciences—
University of Geneva (Switzerland)

Yuh-Ling Shen
National Chung Cheng University (Taiwan)

Ching-Fan Sheu
National Cheng Kung University (Taiwan)

Mari Siiroinen
University of Helsinki (Finland)

Cristina Soriano
Swiss Center for Affective Sciences—
University of Geneva (Switzerland)

Diane Sunar
Istanbul Bilgi University (Turkey)

Heli Tissari
University of Helsinki (Finland)

Eddie M. W. Tong
National University of Singapore
(Singapore)

Yvette van Osch
Tilburg University (The Netherlands)

Sowan Wong
City University of Hong Kong (China)

Dannii Y. Yeung
City University of Hong Kong (China)

Aïda Zitouni
University of Jendouba (Tunisia)

General introduction: A paradigm for a multidisciplinary investigation of the meaning of emotion terms

Johnny J. R. Fontaine, Klaus R. Scherer, and Cristina Soriano

Understanding the meaning of emotion terms is a shared interest across the different disciplines that study emotions, such as psychology, linguistics, cultural anthropology, sociology, history, and multidisciplinary cross-cultural research.

It goes without saying that emotion words play a central role in psychological emotion research. Frequently emotion words are used directly as stimuli or indirectly as response scales. But even when no emotion words are used, the stimuli have often been selected on the basis of ratings by experts on emotion words. An implication of this widespread direct and indirect use of emotion terms is that the results of most psychological emotion research depend on the meaning of the terms used. This dependence is often overlooked. It is implicitly assumed that people react to the meaning of emotion words just as intended by the emotion researcher. However, this assumption is highly problematic because emotions can be defined by focusing on different psychological phenomena, including well-observable facial and vocal expressions, overt bodily reactions, as well as internal changes in motivational orientation that might or might not translate into observable behavior.

Comparative research between cultures in psychology, sociology, and anthropology has shown many cultural and linguistic specificities in the respective emotion lexica. When they go unnoticed, these specificities may bias cross-cultural emotion research, especially as English is generally used as the source or reference language in these studies. Moreover, some theorists claim that emotions are culturally constructed phenomena that fundamentally differ between cultural groups. According to this constructivist account, emotion words represent the result of this conceptualization process and they play a key role in passing on these culturally specific constructions.

Several linguistic research traditions focus on what emotion terms mean. Some traditions decompose the meaning of words into basic semantic features, whereas others look at the figurative uses of those words, and still others analyze the lexico-grammatical contexts in which emotion terms appear, in an attempt to define their meaning by looking at the company the words keep. In all of these cases, linguists try to derive the meaning of emotion terms from an analysis of actual language use.

Understanding the meaning of emotion words is thus a cross-disciplinary concern. Unfortunately, there is little exchange between the different disciplines involved. While they deal with the same problems at a conceptual level, their theoretical and methodological approaches are often so diverse that a fruitful exchange seems impossible. The present book reports a project that aims to create an instrument (the "GRID") to study the meaning of emotion terms jointly from psychological, cultural comparative, and linguistic perspectives, encouraging a genuine exchange between these different disciplines and the different theoretical approaches within them. The GRID project is presented here in eight parts.

Part I. Disciplinary perspectives and theoretical approaches to the meaning of emotion words

The first part of the volume presents the disciplinary perspectives and the theoretical approaches in which the development of the instrument has been embedded. In the first chapter, the componential approach to emotion definition, represented by the Component Process Model (CPM, Scherer 2001, 2005a), is presented (Chapter 1). The CPM, which forms the basis for the development of the GRID instrument, postulates that emotions are processes triggered by goal-relevant events and consist of synchronized activity in several human subsystems (cognitive appraisal, action tendencies, bodily reactions, expression, and feeling) in order to prepare the person for rapid action. Although the CPM represents only one theoretical account of emotion processes in psychology, it lends itself to developing an instrument for multidisciplinary use. Its integrative orientation and its open, dynamic architecture make it suitable to address the issues raised by very different theoretical approaches in the relevant disciplines. The remaining chapters present systematic overviews of the major issues and theoretical models put forward from psychological (Chapter 2), cultural-comparative (Chapter 3), and linguistic perspectives (Chapter 4) in the study of emotion words.

Part II. The GRID instrument: Hypotheses, operationalization, data, and overall structure

The second part of the volume describes the construction, data collection, and overall results obtained with the new instrument. This instrument is called the GRID because it simply consists of a grid of 24 commonly used emotion terms and 142 features that refer to cognitive appraisals, bodily reactions, expressions, feelings, and action tendencies that potentially define emotion terms. The GRID instrument measures the perceived probability of each of these features to substantially contribute to the meaning of a given emotion word. The first chapter in this part (Chapter 5) describes and justifies the central hypotheses and related questions generated by the CPM and by other work in the psychological, cultural-comparative, and linguistic perspectives on emotion outlined in the first part of the volume. The chapter also provides an overview of the procedures that have been chosen for data analysis. The second chapter (Chapter 6) provides a detailed description of the extensive cross-cultural data collection with the GRID instrument. The final chapter in this part (Chapter 7) presents an overall analysis of the data with respect to the internal meaning structure of the emotion domain spanned by 24 major emotion terms, as measured by the GRID instrument, and examines the compatibility of this structure with componential, categorical, and dimensional approaches to the study of emotion.

Part III. Decomposing the meaning of emotion terms: Analysis by emotion component

The third part of the book focuses on the separate emotion components. In the GRID instrument, each of the five emotion components has been operationalized by one or more major theories. The contribution of each of the individual emotion components to the meaning of emotion terms is investigated and discussed step by step in five chapters dealing with one component each: Feeling (Chapter 8), Bodily reaction (Chapter 9), Expression (Chapter 10), Action tendency (Chapter 11), and Appraisal (Chapter 12). A final chapter attempts to integrate the results across components (Chapter 13).

Part IV. **Psychological perspectives**

The fourth part of the book further reports different subanalyses of the GRID dataset from a psychological perspective. The replicability and relevance of the overall structure identified by the GRID instrument is investigated with different psychological (Chapters 14 and 15) and neuroscientific methods (Chapter 16). Moreover, this part demonstrates that the GRID instrument can be used to define the meaning of specific emotions (Chapter 17) and how it can contribute to the construction of theoretically well-grounded psychological assessment instruments in the emotion domain (Chapters 18 and 19).

Part V. **Cultural-comparative perspectives**

The fifth part of the book presents the use of the GRID instrument for cultural and linguistic comparative purposes. This part demonstrates how similarities and differences in the meaning of emotion terms between two or more cultural/linguistic groups can be identified with the GRID instrument (Chapters 20–22 and 24–26) and how the GRID instrument can be used to clarify the meaning of language-specific emotion terms (Chapter 23).

Part VI. **Linguistic perspectives**

In the sixth part, the GRID methodology is compared with approaches classically used in the linguistic analysis of the meaning of emotion words, namely the Natural Semantic Metalanguage approach (Chapter 27), the Conceptual Metaphor approach (Chapter 28), and the Cognitive Corpus Linguistic approach (Chapters 29 and 30).

Part VII. **Special topics**

The seventh part of this volume consists of short, focused chapters on specific topics proposed by collaborators of the GRID project. These issues concern the challenge of applying the GRID instrument in non-Western groups with little experience in web-based testing (Chapter 32), the country-specific findings on the meaning structure of emotion terms (Chapters 31, 33–38, and 41), and the exploration of promising research avenues in which the GRID can be applied (Chapters 39, 40, 42, 43).

Part VIII. **Taking stock and further development of the GRID paradigm**

The last part of this book starts by presenting two shortened versions of the GRID instrument available for future use, namely the CoreGRID and the MiniGRID (Chapter 44). The CoreGRID captures the essential information in each of the emotion components, but with less than half of the features of the original instrument (68 items). The MiniGRID assesses the overall structure of the emotion domain with 16 features. Finally, the book ends (Chapter 45) with a discussion of the insights generated by the GRID study for the main disciplines involved in the study of emotion words and their various theoretical approaches, as well as with a reflection on future developments of the paradigm, pertinent for emotion research in each of these fields and theoretical approaches.

In conclusion, the GRID paradigm, and the associated research program, presented in this book are intended for researchers and scholars who consistently rely on everyday emotion terms in their work. Emotions are elusive phenomena as evidenced by the lack of convergent agreement among emotion researchers on how to define the class as a whole and individual members of the class. At the same time, emotion words from everyday language are continuously used to refer to these phenomena both in daily discourse and in scientific work—largely because there are few alternatives to describe the fuzzy multicomponential episodes they refer to. This volume advocates the use of profiles of features selected on the basis of a domain specific approach—treating emotion in terms of synchronized changes in major components—as a promising framework to approach these elusive phenomena in a systematic way.

Part I

Disciplinary perspectives and theoretical approaches to the meaning of emotion words

## Chapter 1

Measuring the meaning of emotion words: A domain-specific componential approach

Klaus R. Scherer[1]

First, words are our tools, and, as a minimum, we should use clean tools: we should know what we mean and what we do not, and we must forearm ourselves against the traps that language sets us. Secondly, words are not (except in their own little corner) facts or things: we need therefore to prise them off the world, to hold them apart from and against it, so that we can realize their inadequacies and arbitrariness, and can relook at the world without blinkers. Thirdly, and more hopefully, our common stock of words embodies all the distinctions men have found worth drawing, and the connexions they have found worth marking, in the lifetimes of many generations: these surely are likely to be more numerous, more sound, since they have stood up to the long test of the survival of the fittest, and more subtle, at least in all ordinary and reasonably practical matters, than any that you or I are likely to think up in our arm-chairs of an afternoon – the most favoured alternative method *(Austin, 1956, p. 8).*

Austin's famous quote about the world knowledge being embodied in ordinary language words is often cited as a justification for the lexical approach to personality (often referred to as the lexical sedimentation hypothesis; John, Angleitner, & Ostendorf, 1988; Saucier & Goldberg, 1996). In fact, very early on, a pioneer of personality assessment made the assumption "that all aspects of human personality which are or have been of importance, interest, or utility have already become recorded in the substance of language. For, throughout history, the most fascinating subject

[1] Corresponding author: Klaus R. Scherer. Swiss Center for Affective Sciences—University of Geneva. 7, Rue des Battoirs, CH-1205 Geneva, Switzerland. Klaus.Scherer@unige.ch

of general discourse, and also that in which it has been most vitally necessary to have adequate, representative symbols, has been human behavior" (Cattell, 1943, p. 483). Given the importance of emotion in human social interaction, as well as in literature, this is equally true for the emotion domain. In consequence, it seems largely justified to adopt a lexical approach and to examine the lexical sedimentation hypothesis for emotion words in ordinary language. Assuming that language primarily serves social communication, the question is, what elements of meaning must be present in the emotion lexicon to serve the function of reliably and accurately conveying the emotional reactions of individuals to significant events and their behavioral intentions?

Adopting this approach requires, if one takes Austin's caveats literally, that we should know exactly what we mean by the word "emotion" and by the different emotion words in ordinary language and that we have to prise them off the phenomenon, and hold them apart from, and against it. This is exactly what we propose to do in this book, contrary to the general tendency of taking emotion words as a given in emotion research, a tendency that transcends all theoretical traditions in this domain.

The starting point for the approach advocated here is that the features of the meaning of all emotion words must be determined by the specific nature of emotion as a biopsychosocial phenomenon. In consequence, first the nature of "emotion" is examined in order to determine the constitutive aspects of this joint characteristic of meaning in emotion terms. This will serve as a baseline to explore the specific meaning of words for specific tokens of the general type "emotion," as well as to investigate ways to measure and represent this meaning. To this effect, three potential theoretical frameworks are explored and, as a componential framework is judged to be most promising for the task, the architecture of the Component Process Model of emotion (Scherer, 2001, 2009a) is presented. The question concerning the number of different emotions and the role of emotion words in categorizing them is then breached, including a consideration of the underlying mechanisms. This is followed by an argument for using, following Austin, emotion words in ordinary language, to learn more about the folk concepts of emotion built into the semantics of these labels. Finally, encouraged by the ideas of design feature analyses, the GRID paradigm is proposed, which is specific for the emotion domain and operationalized by feature profiles encompassing all components of the emotion construct.

1.1 **What is an emotion?**

Ever since William James rhetorically asked this question in 1887, his answer and many alternative suggestions have been hotly debated. After more than a century of debate, there is still no consensus on a scientific definition of the phenomenon under discussion or on questions such as: How many emotions are there? Are some more basic than others? Are there natural kinds? Should they be represented as regions in dimensional space rather than discrete categories? The amount of discord between emotion scholars is surprising, as the basic facts are uncontroversial: There are certain types of events or situations (such as loss, frustration, danger, success) that tend to elicit specific affective responses in organisms. These responses are characterized by physiological changes (in cardiovascular activity, blood flow, respiration, temperature, and muscle tension); expressions in the voice, face, and body (such as laughing, crying, shouting, gesticulating, and cringing); and shifts in behavioral intention and direction. The life episodes characterized by such response patterns to salient events, generally, produce a conscious feeling of a particular quality in the person concerned that constitutes a unitary experience over a certain period of time. Importantly, these episodes and the associated experiences can be, and often are, labeled with a specific word, a brief expression, or a metaphor, both by the experiencing person and by observers. Such expressions exist in all languages of the world and generally show sufficient translational equivalence to allow intercultural communication.

Frijda and Scherer (2009) have attempted to summarize the constitutive features of a definition of emotion that seem to be shared by a majority of emotion theorists and researchers in different disciplines: 1) Emotions are elicited when something relevant happens to the organism, having a direct bearing on its needs, goals, values, and general well-being. Relevance is determined by the appraisal of events on a number of criteria, in particular the novelty or unexpectedness of a stimulus or event, its intrinsic pleasantness or unpleasantness, and its motivational consistency, that is, its conduciveness to satisfy a need, reach a goal, or uphold a value, or its "obstructiveness" to achieving any of those (Scherer & Ellsworth, 2009; Scherer, 2001). 2) Emotions prepare the organism to deal with important events in their lives and thus have a strong motivational force, producing states of action readiness (Frijda, 2007a). 3) Emotions engage the entire person, urging action and/or imposing action suspension, and are consequently accompanied by preparatory tuning of the somatovisceral, and motor systems. This means that emotions involve several components, subsystems of the organism that become synchronized to different degrees during the emotion episodes, maximizing the organism's capacity to adapt to the contingencies of the situation (Scherer, 2001, 2005a). 4) Emotions bestow control precedence (Frijda, 2007a) on those states of action readiness, in the sense of claiming (not always successfully) priority in the control of behavior and experience.

The authors argue that it is these four central features that jointly define what is generally meant by emotion, both in lay and scientific terminology. From these considerations, emotion can be defined as a *bounded episode* in the life of an individual that is characterized as an emergent pattern of *synchronization between changing states of different subsystems* of the organism (which are considered as components of the emotion), preparing *adaptive action tendencies to relevant events* as defined by their behavioral meaning (as determined by recurrent appraisal processes), and thus having a *powerful impact on behavior and experience*. This definition provides a working hypothesis for a meaning feature set that is common to all emotion words and is capable of distinguishing emotions from other affective states such as preferences, moods, attitudes, interpersonal stances, and affective dispositions (Scherer, 2005a, 2009c). In other words, if someone is described with an emotion adjective (e.g., angry, sad, fearful), this means that the person has evaluated an event, behavior, or situation as being relevant for his/her well-being or goal attainment, and that an appropriate action readiness or behavioral tendency has been prepared through synchronized changes in different mental and somatic subsystems (with a sizable effect on the person's experience and behavior).

More recently, Mulligan and Scherer (2012) have proposed an argued list of elements for a working definition of emotion, justified by the inclusion of elements from philosophy and psychology. Concretely, they propose the following working partial definition:

> **X** is an emotion **only if X** is an affective episode, which has the property of intentionality (i.e., of being directed), AND contains bodily changes (arousal, expression, etc.) that are felt, AND contains a perceptual or intellectual episode, **Y**, which has the property of intentionality (the intentionality of **X** being inherited from the intentionality of **Y**), AND is triggered by at least one appraisal, AND is guided by at least one appraisal.

While one perceives increasing convergence on these central elements of a definition of emotion, and thus presumably also on the shared semantic features of the class of emotion terms, there is disagreement about the precise set of terms that references affectively charged states in the widest sense and that should be included in the class of bona fide emotion words. Thus, whereas joy, anger, sadness, and fear are included in everybody's emotion list, this is not the case for interest, regret, amusement, or stress. The reason is that scholars disagree about the extent to which the central design features of emotion, as outlined above, apply to the states or episodes referenced by the respective words (for example: Is there a relevant object in "contentment"? Do physiological changes occur in "guilt"? Is an action tendency produced in "joy"?). The answer to the question as to how many different emotions there are depends on basic theoretical assumptions about the mechanisms underlying emotion elicitation and differentiation. In consequence, we need to first briefly survey the assumptions made by different emotion theorists.

1.2 **Theories of emotion**

While there are many types of emotion theories (Moors, 2009; Scherer, 2009b), three major currents can be identified—basic emotion, dimensional/constructivist, and appraisal theories. These theories differ with respect to the definition of the basic units of emotional experience, the underlying mechanism that is assumed, and the role of the verbal emotion labels in ordinary language in relation to the psychobiological emotion process. *Basic (or discrete) emotion theories* have been developed in the wake of Darwin's (1872/1998) pioneering work on the expression of emotion, in particular by Tomkins (1962), Ekman (1972, 1984), and Izard (1977, 1992). These theorists postulate clearly separated categories of emotions, assuming that specific types of events trigger specific affect programs corresponding to one of a limited number of basic emotions, and producing characteristic expression patterns and physiological response configurations. More recently, both Ekman (1999) and Izard (2007) have modified their earlier accounts by emphasizing the flexibility of the emotion system, the difference between basic and complex (or primary and secondary) emotions, the influence of sociocultural context, and the interactions of different emotion components. The discrete categories of basic emotions and their expression programs are referred to by distinctive labels (although variations within emotion families are acknowledged; Ekman, 2003).

Dimensional/constructivist emotion theories have emerged from the confluence of two different traditions. The dimensional aspect was pioneered by Wundt (1905) who, based on introspection, proposed that feelings varied in three dimensions—valence (positive–negative), arousal (calm–excited), and tension (tense–relaxed). These three dimensions have been further developed, in modified forms, to show the dimensionality of facial expressions (Schlosberg, 1954), dimensions of semantic meaning (Osgood, Suci, & Tannenbaum, 1957), and the similarity structure of feelings (Russell, 1980). The constructivist bend took its origin in William James' claim "that the bodily changes follow directly the perception of the exciting fact, and that our feeling of the same changes as they occur is the emotion" (James, 1884, p. 190), which has led to a "century of debate" (Ellsworth, 1994). To counter some of the opposition to James' theory, Schachter and Singer (1962) proposed a two-factor theory in which increased arousal (the first factor) is perceived by an individual as requiring an explanation that is generally achieved by a cognitive analysis of context features (the second factor), resulting in a differentiated feeling state. More recently, Russell (2003) suggested that the first factor is not just arousal, but a valence by an arousal composite (core affect), with the second factor, as in Schachter/Singer's case, consisting of cognitive categorization. Barrett (2006a) adopted this position, but proposes a variant that assumes that core affect is differentiated by a "conceptual act," which constitutes the emotion. In this theoretical tradition, emotional experience is seen as being organized in low-dimensional spaces, rather than in discrete categories. Little effort is made to propose concrete mechanisms for the elicitation and differentiation of emotional experience. Most importantly for the purposes of this book, the emotion words in ordinary language are seen as belonging to a separate sociocultural domain, being "constructively" applied by each individual on the basis of a myriad of motivational and situational factors.

Appraisal theories of emotion are deeply rooted in philosophical traditions. Aristotle, Descartes, Spinoza, and Hume have all assumed that the major emotions (as indexed by the respective words in the language) are differentiated by the type of evaluation or judgment a person makes of the eliciting event. The recent history of establishing the term *appraisal* as the central constitutive of the approach started with Arnold (1960) and Lazarus (1968) and was further developed in the early 1980s (see Schorr, 2001; Scherer, 1999a). Ellsworth and her students (Smith & Ellsworth, 1985; Roseman, 1991; Roseman & Smith, 2001) and Scherer (1982, 2001, 2009a) independently developed theories suggesting that people's subjective *evaluation or appraisal* of the significance of events for their well-being and goal achievement elicits the emotion process, and determines the response patterning. Despite large conceptual overlap, different appraisal theorists have proposed divergent accounts of the temporal organization of appraisal checks, and the nature of the underlying mechanism, as well as the nature of valence appraisal, the number and nature of emotion categories, including emotion blends, and the role of consciousness (Grandjean, Sander, & Scherer, 2008).

Several other theorists share some of the major assumptions of appraisal theories, but differ in scope, focus, or underlying architecture: Weiner (1985) stresses the attribution of agency and control; Ortony, Clore, and Collins (1988) focus on the cognitive or situational structure of emotion concepts; Oatley and Johnson-Laird (1987) highlight the evaluation of current goal states on non-propositional and propositional levels of representation; and Frijda (1986, 2007a) considers "action readiness" and the meaning and function of motor response processes as the defining core of emotional response.

With respect to the units of emotional experience, appraisal theories occupy a middle ground. They acknowledge the existence of discrete categories, but do not see them as rigidly defined and constrained as basic emotion theories. They also acknowledge the existence of dimensions of emotional experience, but see the dimensions as emerging from the underlying categorical organization, a mapping of the huge diversity of emotional experiences into a lower-dimensional space. Contrary to the other two positions, appraisal theories give precedence to an elaboration of the mechanisms that govern the elicitation and differentiation of the emotions, in particular the appraisal of relevant events, generating testable hypotheses. They see the labeling of emotional experience by ordinary language words as being intimately tied to the emergent patterns of appraisal and responses characterizing specific emotion episodes.

The differences among the three theoretical traditions can be summarized as follows. The basic emotion model is deterministic on a macro level—a given stimulus or event will determine the occurrence of one of the basic emotions (through a process of largely automatic appraisal). In contrast, appraisal theories are deterministic on a micro level—specific appraisal results or combinations thereof are expected to determine, on a more molecular level, specific action tendencies and the corresponding physiological and motor responses. Most importantly, appraisal theorists espouse emergentism (in the sense of John Stuart Mill); they assume that the combination of appraisal elements in a recursive process unfolding over time, and the ensuing reactions, will form emergent emotions that are more than the sum of their constituents and more than instantiations of rigid categories. As one might expect, constructivist theorists shun determinism in any shape or form and generally espouse a more ideographic than nomothetic model of science (Scherer, 2010a).

Which of these theories is best suited to guide investigations into the meaning of emotion terms? A central concern is the presumed number and type of emotions. On one extreme, we find the notion of a limited number of evolutionarily continuous adaptive emotion systems (held by many basic emotion theorists) and on the other, that of fuzzy, unpredictable state changes that achieve coherence only by their place in a valence/arousal space and by conceptual classification, as espoused by some constructivists. In this debate, appraisal theorists are somewhere in the middle—they accept neither the idea of a limited repertoire of basic, homogeneous emotions with highly prototypical characteristics, nor the idea of emotions being individually labeled points in two-dimensional affect space. Rather, while assuming that there are widely varying types of emotions, they postulate the existence of modal emotion families (Scherer, 1994) with typical, frequently occurring appraisal profiles that have adaptive functions in dealing with quintessential contingencies in animal and human life.

This approach seems well suited to conceptually and empirically address the issue of the development of fuzzy emotion categories and the corresponding lexical labels in different languages and cultures, as well as the construction of a framework to compare the respective semantic fields. Before dealing specifically with this issue, one of the appraisal theories, the component process model (CPM) of emotion, will be described in more detail, with specific emphasis on the categorization and labeling of felt experience. This discussion will highlight the importance of different components of emotion and their synchronization toward a certain degree of coherence that defines the emotion episode, a dynamic process rather than steady state.

1.3 The component process model (CPM) of emotion mechanisms

The CPM is based on the conjecture that during evolution, emotion replaced instincts in order to allow for more flexible responding to events in a complex environment, and it did so by introducing an interruption into the stimulus-response chain to allow for more ample information processing. It also contends that emotion has been optimized to serve the following functions: (a) evaluation of objects and events, (b) system regulation, (c) preparation and direction of action, (d) communication of reaction and behavioral intention, and (e) monitoring of internal state and organism–environment interaction (see Scherer, 2001). Specifically, the model suggests that efferent effects of sequentially accrued appraisal results cumulatively constitute the unique, context- and individual-specific response pattern for a given emotion episode.

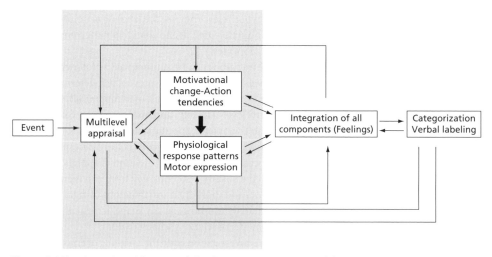

Figure 1.1 The dynamic architecture of the Component Process Model.
Reproduced from Philosophical Transactions of the Royal Society, Series B, 364, (1535), Emotions are emergent processes. They require a dynamic computational architecture, Scherer, K. R. pp. 3459–3474 © 2009, The Royal Society, with permission.

Figure 1.1 shows the basic architecture of the model, highlighting the dynamic, recursive emotion processes following an event that is highly pertinent to the needs, goals, and values of an individual. Briefly put, the CPM suggests that the event and its consequences are appraised with a set of criteria on multiple levels of processing, producing a motivational effect or action tendency that often changes or at least modifies the status quo. Specifically, the appraisal results and the concomitant motivational changes will produce efferent effects in the autonomic nervous system (in the form of somatovisceral changes) and the somatic nervous system (in the form of motor expression in face, voice, and body). All of these components, appraisal results, action tendencies, somatovisceral changes, and motor expressions are centrally represented and constantly fused in a multimodal integration area (with continuous updating as events and appraisals change). Parts of this central integrated representation may then become conscious and subject to assignment to fuzzy emotion categories, as well as being labeled with emotion words, expressions, or metaphors. Given the interdisciplinary nature of this volume, the following section provides only a brief outline, restating some of the major elements of the theory based on the earlier publications. More detailed treatments of these issues can be found elsewhere (Scherer, 2001, 2004a, 2009a).

The nature of the appraisal process

The CPM proposes that the organism evaluates events and their consequences on a number of appraisal checks, with the results reflecting the organism's subjective assessment of consequences and implications on a background of personal needs, goals, and values (which may well be unrealistic or biased). Figure 1.2 shows the processes within the gray-shaded panel in Figure 1.1 in greater detail. In particular, the horizontal panel labeled "Appraisal processes" shows the different

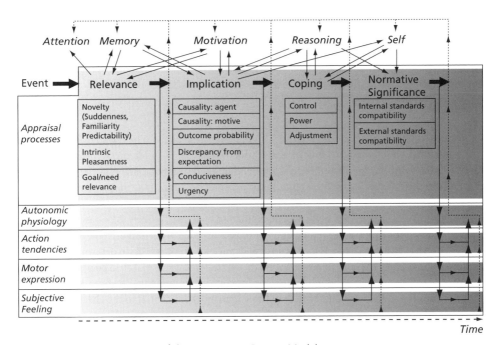

Figure 1.2 Schematic summary of the Component Process Model.
Reprinted from Neural Networks, 18 (4), David Sander, Didier Grandjean, and Klaus R. Scherer, A systems approach to appraisal mechanisms in emotion, pp. 317–52, Copyright (2005), with permission from Elsevier.

groups of appraisal criteria (with the individual checks within the respective group) organized in the theoretically expected sequence (see Scherer, 2001, 2009a), together with the respective cognitive structures that are recruited in these appraisal processes (with the downward-directed arrows representing the input of the different cognitive structures into the appraisal process, e.g., retrieval of past experiences of a similar kind from memory, and the upward-directed arrows representing a modification of the current content of these structures by the appraisal results, e.g., attention being redirected by a relevance appraisal). The horizontal panels below the appraisal level show three response components and the final integration of all changes in the feeling component. The bold downward-directed arrows illustrate the central assumption of the model in each phase of the process: the appraisal results sequentially and cumulatively affect all response domains. The dotted upward-directed arrows represent the changes induced in this fashion (which are fed back to the appraisal module and the cognitive structures subserving and regulating the appraisal process). The appraisals are expected to unfold sequentially over time. Each type of assessment receives input from other cognitive and motivational mechanisms, such as attention, memory, motivation, reasoning, and the self-concept, which provide stored information and evaluation criteria that are essential for the appraisal process. Further details of the specific appraisal criteria or checks are provided in the next section of this chapter.

1.4 **Appraisal criteria**

The outline of the appraisal criteria provided below is based on Scherer's CPM (Scherer, 2001, 2009a), but there is a great deal of overlap with other appraisal theories that have proposed a set of criteria or dimensions for appraisal (see Ellsworth & Scherer, 2003; Roseman & Smith, 2001; Scherer, 1999a). The appraisal checks are grouped into four functional classes: detection of the relevance of an event, inference of the probable implications or the consequences of an event for oneself, determining one's potential or power to cope with these consequences, and an evaluation of the normative significance of the event (i.e., its compatibility with social values and one's self-image).

Relevance detection

Novelty check. At the most primitive level of sensory-motor processing, any sudden stimulus (characterized by abrupt onset and relatively high intensity) is likely to be registered as novel and deserving attention. Beyond this low-level detection of novelty or suddenness, the assessment of novelty may vary greatly for different species, individuals and situations, and may depend on motivational state, prior experience with a stimulus or expectation. One of the most important mechanisms might be matching it to schema to determine the degree of familiarity with the object or event. On a still higher level of processing, the evaluation of novelty is likely to be based on complex estimates of the probability and predictability of the occurrence of a stimulus.

  Intrinsic pleasantness check. It is of central relevance for an organism to determine whether a stimulus event is likely to result in pleasure or pain (in the widest sense). Intrinsic pleasantness is a feature of the stimulus and, although preference for certain stimuli may have been acquired from previous experience, the momentary state of the organism is not central to the check. In contrast, the evaluation of stimuli that help to reach goals or satisfy needs (see goal relevance check below) depends primarily on the relationship between the significance of the stimulus and the organism's motivational state.

  Goal relevance check. This check establishes the relevance, pertinence, or importance of a stimulus or situation for the momentary hierarchy of goals/needs. A stimulus is relevant for an individual if it results in outcomes that affect major goals/needs. Relevance is likely to vary continuously from low to high, depending on the number of goals/needs affected and their relative status in the hierarchy. For example, an event is much more relevant if it threatens one's livelihood or survival than if it just endangers one's need to listen to a piece of music.

Implication assessment

Causal attribution check. One important factor in determining the potential implications or consequences of an event is to determine who or what caused it. This is of course a subjective evaluation, which is the reason for the term causal attribution (phenomena studied in much detail by attribution theory; Weiner, 1985). The important issues concern the responsibility for causing the event, that is, the agent who brought it about, which means attributing responsibility to oneself, another person/other persons, or supernatural powers. It is also possible that no agent can be identified, leading to an attribution of chance occurrence. Another important issue is to determine whether the likely agent has caused the event inadvertently or intentionally, as this will have an impact on potential implications (for example, if someone wants to hurt me intentionally, it is likely that he or she will persist).

Outcome probability check. Some types of events, such as the death of a close person, have fairly predictable implications and the probability of specific consequences can be established with certainty (i.e., no further interactions are possible, the relationship ends). In other cases, the implications might be much more difficult to determine. Thus, it is difficult to determine what the ulterior consequences of a sudden drop in the stock market are for the development of my portfolio—the probability of further losses, or potential recovery, are difficult to assess.

Discrepancy from expectation. In most cases, we have specific expectations as to what kinds of outcomes we expect at certain points in a goal-plan-action sequence, either because of our own behavior or because of our prior knowledge of the evolution of certain events. Thus, specific outcomes of an event can be more or less congruent or discrepant with what we expected at this point in time.

Goal/need conduciveness check. Most importantly, the organism needs to check the conduciveness of a stimulus event to help attain one or several of the current goals/needs. The consequences of acts or events can constitute the attainment of goals/needs, or progress toward attainment, or facilitate further goal-directed action (see Oatley & Duncan, 1994). The more directly that the outcomes of an event facilitate or help goal attainment and the closer they propel the organism toward reaching a goal, the higher the conduciveness of an event.

Urgency check. Adaptive action in response to an event is particularly urgent when high priority goals/needs are endangered, and the organism has to resort to fight or flight. Urgency is also likely to increase when delaying a response will make matters worse. Urgency is evaluated on a continuous scale: the more important the goals/needs and the greater the time pressure, the more urgent the action becomes. Urgency depends not only on the relevance of an event for an organism's goal/need, but also on temporal constraints.

Coping potential determination

This group of checks determines to what extent the organism can deal with a particular object or event. One can distinguish three different objectives in checking one's coping potential—control, power, and adjustment capacity.

Control check. A central determinant of coping potential concerns the degree of control possible in a particular situation. In many cases, this depends on the nature of the agent responsible for having caused the event. For example, an act of nature is something for which no control attempt can possibly succeed. In other cases, more or less control might be possible, for example, in the case of critical phases during which events can still be influenced.

Power check. If control is possible, the question becomes how much power or how many resources one has to influence the consequences of an event. These may be personal resources such as physical, intellectual, financial, and social-relational resources. In other cases, it might be the possibility of calling on help from others (such as summoning one's elder brother in a fight in the school yard).

Adjustment capacity check. Finally, if consequences cannot be changed, coping potential depends on how well one can live with the consequences of an event, that is, how well one can adjust to the consequences or implications of the event.

Normative significance evaluation

In socially living species, there are two more checks that take into account how the majority of the other group members evaluate an action and the significance of an emotion-producing event for one's self-concept and self-esteem. Obviously, this appraisal objective is—by definition—only relevant in socially organized species capable of a self-concept and of a mental representation of sociocultural norms and values. This type of appraisal is served by the following two checks (see Scherer, 2001).

Internal standards check. This check evaluates the extent to which an action falls short of or exceeds internal standards, such as one's personal self-ideal (desirable attributes) or an internalized moral code (obligatory conduct). These can often be at variance with cultural or group norms, particularly in the case of conflicting role demands or incompatibility between the norms or demands of several reference groups or persons. For example, a failed student will react with a different emotion if s/he has an ideal self-concept of being a brilliant scholar in the respective field as compared to a self-ideal of being a financial wizard.

External standards check. Social organization in groups implies shared values and rules (norms) concerning status hierarchies, prerogatives, desirable outcomes, and acceptable and unacceptable behaviors. The existence and reinforcement of such norms depends on the emotional reactions of group members to behavior that both violates and conforms to norms. The most severe sanction a group can use against someone who violates norms—short of actual aggression—is the relegation of this person to the status of an outsider or a reject. Therefore, evaluating the significance of a particular action in terms of its social consequences is a necessary step before deciding on appropriate behavioral responses. This check evaluates to what extent an action is compatible with the perceived norms or demands of a salient reference group in terms of both desirable and obligatory conduct. Our student would appraise his/her failure quite differently on this check, depending on whether s/he applies the intellectual expectations and study performance standards of a group of junior scientists or those of the university football team.

Before turning to the results of the appraisal process, a note on the importance of a general valence dimension underlying appraisal is in order. While all of the appraisal checks described above evaluate different criteria, these are all *valenced* (i.e., the outcome of the check will be considered as more or less positive or negative, or good or bad, by the organism). The two classic valence checks are of course intrinsic pleasantness and goal conduciveness (a distinction that is unfortunately rarely made in the literature, even though it can be shown that the basis of the evaluation and in part also its consequences can be different, see Aue & Scherer, 2011). But the other checks also involve valenced outcomes. Thus, it is generally considered as positive and desirable for an organism to be strong, powerful, and dominant, whereas being weak and submissive is, generally, seen

Table 1.1 Varieties of valence and dimensions of the affective space

Evaluation checks	Evaluation outcomes	Type of valence/feeling dimensions
Novelty	Newness—familiarity	Valence as predictability
Intrinsic pleasantness/beauty	Pleasure—displeasure	Valence as pleasure
Goal/need relevance	Satisfaction—frustration	Valence as satisfaction
Coping potential	Power—weakness	Valence as power/dominance
Compatibility self-concept/standards	Achievement—failure	Valence as self-worthiness
Compatibility social norms/values	Virtue—vice	Valence as moral worthiness

Reproduced from The component process model: a blueprint for a comprehensive computational model of emotion, Scherer, K. R., In: K. R. Scherer, T. Banziger, & E. Roesch (Eds.), A blueprint for affective computing: A sourcebook and manual (pp. 47–70) (c) 2010, Oxford University Press.

as negative. Behavioral outcomes that are consistent with one's self-image and feeling of self-worth are evaluated as positive, whereas failure to live up to one's standards is seen as rather negative. Similarly, behavior that is consistent with social values or norms is almost universally considered as good, whereas a violation of norms and values is seen as bad. The situation is a bit more complicated for the novelty check. Here, a curvilinear relationship seems to hold—too much suddenness and unpredictability may be dangerous and thus bad; on the other hand, too much familiarity and predictability breeds boredom, which is also bad. Thus, a safe amount of novelty and unpredictability is good. Table 1.1 illustrates these six types of valence in relation to the appraisal criteria.

1.5 Response patterning

Component patterning

For each sequential stage of assessment based on the appraisal checks outlined above, there are two types of output: (1) a *modification* of the cognitive and motivational mechanisms that have influenced the appraisal process; and (2) *efferent effects* on the periphery, in particular the neuroendocrine system and the autonomous and somatic nervous systems. In this model, emotion differentiation is predicted as the result of the net effect of all subsystem changes brought about by the outcome profile of the appraisal sequence. Thus, as shown in Figure 1.2, the fundamental assumption of the CPM is that the appraisal results drive the response patterning in other components by triggering efferent outputs designed to produce adaptive reactions that are in line with the current appraisal results (often mediated by motivational changes). Thus, emotion differentiation is the result of the net effect of all subsystem changes brought about by the outcome profile of the appraisal sequence. These subsystem changes are theoretically predicted on the basis of a componential patterning model, which assumes that the different organismic subsystems are highly interdependent and that changes in one subsystem will tend to elicit related changes in other subsystems. As illustrated in Figure 1.2, this process, similar to appraisal, is highly recursive, which is what one would expect from the neurophysiological evidence for complex feedback and feedforward mechanisms between the subsystems. As shown in Figure 1.2, the result of each consecutive check is expected to differentially and cumulatively affect the state of all other subsystems.

The CPM makes specific predictions about the effects of the results of certain appraisal checks on the autonomic and somatic nervous systems, indicating which somatovisceral changes and which motor expression features are expected, based on both the general functions of the emotion components and the specific functions of each appraisal check. In particular, specific motivational and behavioral tendencies are expected to be activated in the motivation component in order to serve the specific requirements for the adaptive response demanded by a particular appraisal result. In socially living species, adaptive responses are required not only for the internal regulation of the organism and motor action for instrumental purposes (organismic functions), but also for interaction and communication with conspecifics (social functions).

Integration and central representation

The CPM assigns a special status to the feeling component in the emotion process, as it monitors and regulates the component process and enables the individual to communicate its emotional experience to others. If subjective experience (the feeling component) is to serve a monitoring function, it needs to integrate and centrally represent all information about the continuous patterns of change and their coherence in all other components. Thus, feeling is an extraordinarily complex conglomerate of information from different systems. Figure 1.3 shows how the different components of the emotion process might be integrated and represented in a unitary fashion in what philosophers have described as qualia (see Scherer, 2009a). As shown on the left side of Figure 1.2, the autonomic physiology, the motivation, and the motor expression components are driven by the appraisal component (which is, in turn, influenced by the changes that occur in these other components and which may be in part the results of component-specific factors). The current state of each of these components is then represented in an integrated fashion in the feeling component. Quality, intensity, and duration of the feeling are determined by these integrated inputs. Appraisal results will be represented by the patterning of the appraisal check results and the weights that are assigned to individual appraisal checks. Both autonomic physiology and motor expression changes will be represented as a function of the respective response patterns and their amplitude. Finally, the motivation component will be represented by the nature of the action tendencies that have been elicited, as well as by the estimated urgency of action.

Scherer (2004) describes in detail which integration tasks need to be achieved in the process. Information needs to be integrated in the cognitive component, as different appraisal results may vary greatly with respect to the nature of the outcome. Information integration is also required for the response components, as the response modalities, for example, physiological variables and expressive behaviors, vary greatly with respect to their underlying metric. Finally, multicomponent

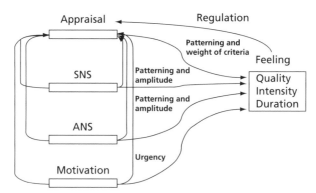

Figure 1.3 Integration of emotion components.

integration is required to bring all the separate information channels together. In addition, temporal integration has to be achieved to create the impression of a coherent episode.

1.6 **Emotion words and modal emotions**

In the preceding description of the architecture of the CPM, the issue of the number, nature, and qualities of the tokens of the "emotion" category type (i.e., the individual emotions) and in particular the issue of verbal labels for these tokens, has not been addressed. This issue is of course linked to the debate about the definition of emotion and is just as controversial. Basic emotion theories are resolutely based on the claim that a limited number of affect programs for a limited number of discrete emotions exist, such as anger, fear, joy, and sadness, a number that varies, depending on the theorist, between 5 and 15. However, most adherents to that tradition concur that there are also other emotions, often called "secondary," as evidenced by the existence of respective labels (e.g., Ekman, 2003). Dimensionalist/constructivist theories see emotions as a sociocultural construction defined by the available labels that individuals bestow on "conceptual acts" in rudimentary states of "core affect" (described as points in a two-dimensional valence × arousal space). The emphasis of the research in this approach seems to be to identify, in an ideographic fashion, motivational or contextual factors (such as salience or situational priming) that are seen to determine the "constructive" choice of a label (e.g., Lindquist & Barrett, 2008; see also Deonna & Scherer, 2009). In both of these cases, emotion words have a different, but secondary function. In the case of basic emotion theories, they just name the response patterns produced by the psychobiologically defined affect program. In the constructivist case, emotion words serve as arbitrary labels that individuals can use to conceptually categorize rudimentary affective states of positive or negative arousal. A central discussion between the adherents to these two theoretical traditions concerns the question of whether the emotions referred to by the verbal labels are natural kinds (Bird & Tobin, 2008). Obviously, basic emotion theories, assuming the evolutionary continuity of a small number of affect programs, tend to assume that the emotions are indeed natural kinds (Griffiths, 2004), whereas constructivists attempt to show that there is no evidence for this assumption (Barrett, 2006a).

The CPM takes a very different approach to this issue by assuming that many different combinations of appraisal check results are possible (especially since evaluation is thought to occur in a graduated fashion, determining not only the type but also the intensity of the emotional arousal). In consequence, the number of potential emotional states (as defined by the process of synchronized patterning of all components in the emotion episode time window) is virtually infinite. However, some major patterns of adaptation in the life of animate organisms reflect frequently recurring patterns of environmental evaluation results (Scherer, 1994). All organisms, at all stages of ontogenetic development, encounter blocks that need satisfaction or goal achievement at least some of the time. Thus, frustration in a general sense is universal and ubiquitous. Equally universal are the two major reaction patterns fight and flight. Consequently, it is not surprising that the emotional states that often elicit these behaviors, anger and fear, respectively, seem universal and are present in many species. In terms of the model proposed here, it is highly likely that, if one were to compile a frequency distribution of appraisal check patterns, some combinations of check results would be found to be frequently encountered by many types of organisms, giving rise to specific, recurring patterns of state changes.

Early on, the term *modal emotions* was suggested to refer to the states resulting from these predominant appraisal check outcomes that are due to general conditions of life, constraints of social organization, and similarity of innate equipment (Scherer, 1984a). Just as certain appraisal check outcomes in response to certain types of situations are more frequent, the patterning of elements in the other emotion components would also occur more frequently. Modal emotions are characterized, then, by a prototypical pattern of appraisals and the corresponding patterning of expression, autonomic arousal, action tendencies, and feeling states. This would account, it seems, for the evidence for universal prototypical patterns mentioned at the outset. However, it is important to highlight the central difference of the modal emotion concept to the postulate of basic emotions: no effort is made to find or define a definite number of homogeneous, integral categories or mechanisms that justify an a priori definition of basic or fundamental phenomena. Instead, the modal emotion concept proposes empirically studying the frequency with which certain patterns of sequential, synchronized changes in the different components of emotion episodes occur.

The study of verbal labeling plays a special role in efforts toward an empirical assessment of modal frequency or "bunching." Given the prominence and the frequency of occurrence of these episodes of highly similar emotional experiences, it is not surprising that they have been labeled with a short verbal expression, mostly a single word, in most languages of the world. This would be predicted on the basis of a principle of economical verbal coding of objects of communication (see Clark & Clark, 1977, pp. 552–557; Whorf, 1956; Zipf, 1949). Thus, discreteness is—at least in part—bestowed by linguistic categorization and the cultural prototypes that these categories reflect (see Shaver, Schwartz, Kirson, & O'Connor, 1987). Linguistic categories conceptually order the world for us in many domains and they do so for emotion. Among the many advantages of this categorical organization are cognitive economy and communicability of the underlying referents. One can venture specific theoretical predictions as to the patterns of appraisal check results that are likely to produce such modal emotions, as they are labeled in many different languages of the world (see Scherer, 1986a). In fact, we can show that a simple expert system allows prediction of the use of verbal labels for emotional experiences on the basis of the subject's recalled appraisal processes (Scherer, 1993; Scherer & Meuleman, 2013).

It is important to keep in mind that the activity of labeling is independent of the emotion process and of emotional experience as a whole (Scherer, 1994). Depending on the communication intentions of the language users, it is to some degree arbitrary which aspects of the emotion process are selected and labeled by a word in the language. Thus, there are some words that mainly select out the physiological reaction component, such as "aroused" or "tired." Some are cognitive, such as "bewildered" or "curious." Others focus on specific sociomotivational antecedents, such as "jealous." Still others emphasize the action tendency aspect, such as "hostile." Thus, the special importance of the "basic emotion words" may reside in the fact that they refer to a more global set of changes in many of the subsystems of our emotion construct (see Scherer, 1984b).

It is important to note that the existence of a specific emotion label in one, or even several languages, does not yet establish the existence of a corresponding, frequently occurring pattern of appraisal check results with respective componential response patterning, that is, a modal emotion. This would seem to be a matter for empirical investigation. Consequently, a verbal emotion label cannot be used as an explanans (as it often is in the psychology of emotion); rather, it is an explanandum. Emotion labels may in part be based on typical reactions of the social environment, which may be similar for different emotions (cf. the constructionist view held by Averill, 1980; see also Mesquita & Frijda, 1992). Consequently, empirical investigation is required to determine how patterns of event appraisal and the nature of the subsequent subsystem responses result in the use of a particular emotion word or expression by the experiencing subject.

On the basis of an emergent notion of emotion, as defended by certain appraisal theories, it can be reasonably argued that there are as many different emotions as there are discriminably different profiles of appraisal with corresponding response patterning (Scherer, 1984b)—and these are likely to generate different forms of qualia, even though they will obviously be categorized into larger classes for labeling. Using the definition proposed above, in particular the necessary criterion of response synchronization, the number of different emotions could, in principle, be determined empirically by analyzing the response profiles of a very large number of emotion experiences and determining the number of clusters that have similar profiles. However, this proposal is only of academic interest as, in addition to conceptual problems such as the criterion for a sufficient level of response synchronization, problems of access to a vast range of naturally occurring, everyday emotional episodes and problems of measurement render such an empirical assessment impracticable.

1.7 **Categorization and verbalization of feeling**

How do qualia emerge into consciousness and what is the nature of the categorization and verbalization process? The CPM model offers a conceptualization of the problem, as shown in Figure 1.4, using a Venn diagram in which a set of overlapping circles represents the different aspects of feeling. The first circle (A) represents the sheer reflection or representation of changes in all synchronized components in some kind of monitoring structure in the central nervous system (CNS). This structure is expected to receive massive projections from both cortical and subcortical CNS structures (including proprioceptive feedback from the periphery). The second circle (B), only partially overlapping with the first, represents that part of the integrated central representation that enters awareness and thereby becomes conscious, thus constituting the feeling qualities, the qualia that philosophers and phenomenologically minded psychologists have been most concerned with. Thus, this circle corresponds most directly to what is generally called "feelings." The conscious part of the feeling component feeds the process of controlled regulation, much of which is determined by self-representation and socio-normative constraints. It is hypothesized that it is the degree of synchronization of the components (which might in turn be determined by the pertinence of the event as appraised by the organism) that will generate conscious experience.

Although a richly textured conscious feeling that fits the situation that a person experiences like a glove is highly functional for fine-tuned adaptation and regulation, it is less well suited to cognitive manipulation, memorization, or communication. Of course the same is true for all of perception, which is why categorization plays such a major role in all of cognitive processing.

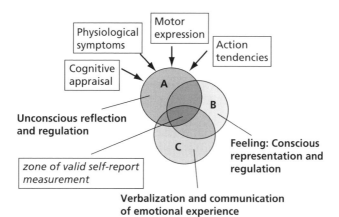

Figure 1.4 The reflection of component emotion processes in a monitor system (circle A), the emergence of consciousness (circle B), and categorization and verbalization (circle C). Reproduced from Scherer, K. R., What are emotions? And how can they be measured?, Social Science Information, 44(4) (c) 2005, SAGE Publications Ltd. All rights reserved.

Unfortunately, all we can currently measure is the individual's verbal account of a consciously experienced feeling, represented by the third circle (C) in Figure 1.4. Drawing this circle as only partially overlapping with the circle representing conscious experience (B) is meant to suggest that the verbal account of feelings captures only part of what is consciously experienced. This is so for two reasons: (a) verbal report relies on language and thereby on the emotion categories and other devices (at any level: phonetics, morpheme choice, words, phrase construction, sentence structure, text structure) available to express the qualia that are consciously experienced. Apart from capacity constraints (the stream of consciousness cannot be completely described by a discrete utterance), it is unlikely that these linguistic devices are capable of completely capturing the incredibly rich texture of conscious experience. In other words, language can only represent part of the complexity of conscious thought (and the accompanying emergent experience of feeling). Furthermore, (b) contextual constraints (cultural, situational) *unconsciously* limit what we become aware of and can attempt to express linguistically. In addition, there can be a desire to control the expression of emotion and to suppress the tendency to label or report certain aspects of one's innermost feelings.

How can one envisage the process of feeling categorization on the basis of the component process architecture? A more detailed recent suggestion on this issue (Scherer, 2009a), of central importance for this book, starts with the important early contribution to this domain made by Rosch (1973a), who proposed two general principles for the formation of categories that have been widely accepted: (a) cognitive economy, reducing the infinite differences among stimuli to behaviorally and cognitively manageable scope; and (b) reflection of perceived structures and regularities in the world. The author also distinguished between vertical (inclusiveness of a category) and horizontal (differentiation of categories at any one layer) levels of categorization and proposed that the use of prototypes, containing the most representative attributes inside a category, will increase the flexibility and distinctiveness of categories along the horizontal dimension. Shaver and his collaborators (Shaver, Schwartz, Kirson, & O'Connor, 1987) have shown the utility of this approach for understanding the emotion vocabulary, distinguishing between superordinate (positive, negative emotions), basic (joy, fear, anger, sadness), and subordinate (irritation, rage) category levels.

As categorization occurs before verbalization (e.g., in very young children, Hamlin, Wynn, & Bloom, 2007; Hirschfeld, 2001), preverbal categories for emotional feelings are likely to be formed by the observation of regularity in the differential patterning of different emotional experiences. Thus, one would expect prelinguistic categories to precede verbalization (on the ontogenetic and microgenetic levels). It is reasonable to assume that the lowest level of inclusiveness, as defined by Rosch, is that of the preverbal qualia, as they represent qualitative types of experiences that can be recognized and remembered. This level can be expected to be idiosyncratic and fuzzy. More inclusive categories might be formed through a constraint satisfaction procedure between cognitive economy optimization and the practical importance of certain structures and regularities encountered during emotion episodes. Even though the content of the qualia is likely to consist of an integrated representation of the individual components, one might imagine that some components, especially those that best differentiate types of qualia, are more important than others in determining categorization beyond the first preverbal categories.

One candidate for determining category formation is somatovisceral feedback, which was highlighted by the peripheralist tradition founded by James and Lange (Mandler, 1975; Schachter & Singer, 1962) and which has currently been revived under the concept of embodiment (Barrett, 2006a; Prinz, 2004). As postulated by the CPM, somatovisceral feedback, as part of the representation of the efferent effects of appraisal results, is indeed one of the central determinants of categorization. However, other factors are needed to further differentiate bodily feedback, as certain types of physiological activation occur in a similar form in several emotions. For example, an increase in heart rate and in muscle tension generally occurs because sympathetic activation serves urgent action preparation, a feature shared by several emotions. In consequence, it seems unlikely that this modality is the *only* determinant of category formation (as many critics of the James/Lange position have argued over the last century). The "perception of bodily changes" may well add color to the emotional experience (as James, 1890, argued), for example, concerning the intensity and vividness of the feeling, but it is unlikely to account for the bulk of differentiation and categorization of feelings. One can reasonably argue that appraisal configurations (Scherer, 2001), core relational themes (Lazarus, 1991a; Smith & Lazarus, 1993), or action tendencies (Frijda, 1986, 1987) are more promising candidates. This is one of the claims to be discussed in this volume.

It is thus likely that qualia clusters, representing integrated appraisal configurations and action tendencies that occur relatively frequently and are of central importance to the individual's well-being (modal emotions), will serve as the basis for categorization into more inclusive categories on Rosch's vertical dimension. As suggested early on (Scherer, 1984b, p. 311), one would expect that it is those modal categories that are generally labeled with a single word or a brief expression in most languages of the world. The availability of such linguistic labels (corresponding to both the subordinate and basic levels of categorization in Shaver's system) imposes a large degree of separateness and discreteness to particular types of experiences.

An interesting question is whether the act of categorization that is implied by verbal labeling, which will undoubtedly affect the representation of the emotional experience, may impoverish the rich qualia experience and mold it into socioculturally determined schemata.

A requisite to investigate this issue is to fully understand the semantic content of the verbal labels. While dictionary definitions in different languages, as well as thesaurus entries, may be useful, reflecting the learned intuitions of the language experts responsible for the respective entries, this approach is neither sufficiently comprehensive nor consensual enough to be appropriate for scientific profiling of emotion terms. Chapter 4 describes a variety of linguistic methods to describe emotion lexical meaning, which are currently used in lexical semantics. However, many of the underlying approaches are underspecified in that they are not domain-specific and do not take into account the specific nature of the signified concepts, that is, the construct of "emotion." This is particularly serious, as emotions are unlikely to represent "natural kinds," in philosophical parlance. An interesting alternative option would be to conceptualize, measure, and compare the semantics of emotion terms in a *domain-specific* manner, taking into account the unique construct of emotion.

For that purpose, we propose to use the current state of knowledge about the elicitation and differentiation of emotion to deduce what elements would need to be represented in the semantic content of different emotion words in different languages. The approach advocated here is based on componential emotion theories, in general, and the CPM model in particular.

Additionally, since languages differ with respect to emotion vocabulary, in order to improve the model, it is imperative to better understand the nature and origin of the differences between the semantic fields of emotion terms in different languages across the world. Chapter 3 describes the current state of the art in linguistics and anthropology with respect to this question.

1.8 Design feature analysis of affect concepts

Before addressing the measurement of the meaning of terms representing individual emotions, one needs to define the domain from which to draw the respective exemplars. This is all the more necessary since, as described above, there is widespread disagreement as to which states qualify as an emotion. In consequence, it seems useful to first define how emotions differ from preferences, moods, attitudes, interpersonal stances, and other types of affective phenomena that populate the domain that used to be called the "sentiments." One can use Hockett's (1960) notion of *design features* (see Hauser, 1996) to distinguish words that designate emotions (fearful, sad, ashamed, happy, angry) from those that refer to other types of affective states (liking, ironic, depressed, hostile, cheerful, cranky). Scherer (2005a) has suggested five such types of affective phenomena that should be distinguished from emotion proper, although there may be some overlap in the meaning of certain words: preferences, attitudes, moods, affect dispositions, and interpersonal stances. Table 1.2 shows these design features and how they can be used to disambiguate different affect terms and differentiate two types of emotion—utilitarian and aesthetic.

In particular, bona fide emotions must possess the following characteristics or design features:

Event focus. The definition given above suggests that emotions are generally elicited by stimulus events; that is, something happens to the organism that stimulates or triggers a response after the event has been evaluated for its significance. Philosophers talk about emotions having an *object* (Deonna & Scherer, 2009; Mulligan & Scherer, 2012). Such objects can consist of natural phenomena such as thunderstorms, the behavior of other people or animals that may have significance for our well-being, one's own behavior, sudden neuroendocrine or physiological changes or even memories or images. The need for emotions to be somehow connected to or anchored in a specific event, external or internal, rather than being free-floating, resulting from a strategic or intentional decision, or existing as a permanent feature of an individual, constitutes the event focus design feature.

Appraisal driven. The eliciting event and its consequences must be relevant to major concerns of the organism, as determined by a complex, yet very rapidly occurring appraisal process that can occur on several levels of processing ranging from automatic and implicit to conscious conceptual or propositional evaluations (Leventhal & Scherer, 1987; van Reekum & Scherer, 1997).

Table 1.2 Design feature differentiation of different types of affective phenomena

Design features / Type of affect	Event focus	Intrinsic appraisal	Transactional appraisal	Synchronization	Rapidity of change	Behavioral impact	Intensity	Duration
Preferences	VH	VH	M	VL	VL	M	L	M
Attitudes	VL	L	L	VL	L	L	M	H
Moods	L	M	L	L	M	H	M	H
Affect dispositions	VL	L	VL	VL	VL	L	L	VH
Interpersonal stances	H	L	L	L	VH	H	M	M
Aesthetic emotions	H	VH	L	M	H	L	L-M	L
Utilitarian emotions	VH	M	VH	VH	VH	VH	H	L

Note: VL = very low, L = low, M = medium, H = high, VH = very high

Response synchronization. This design feature of the proposed emotion definition is implied by the adaptational functions of emotion. If emotions prepare appropriate responses to events, the response patterns must correspond to the appraisal analysis of the presumed implications of the event, resulting in massive mobilization of resources coordinated by response synchronization (Scherer, 2001).

Rapidity of change. Events, and particularly their appraisal, change rapidly, often because of new information or re-evaluations. As appraisal drives the patterning of the responses in the interest of adaptation, the emotional response patterning is also likely to change rapidly as a consequence. Although we are in the habit of talking about "emotional states," these are rarely steady states. Rather, emotion processes are undergoing constant modification, allowing rapid readjustment to changing circumstances or evaluations.

Behavioral impact. Emotions prepare adaptive action tendencies and their motivational underpinnings and thus have a strong effect on emotion-consequent behavior, often interrupting ongoing behavior sequences and generating new goals and plans. In addition, the motor expression component of emotion has a strong impact on communication, which has important consequences for social interaction.

Intensity. Given the importance of emotions for behavioral adaptation, one can assume the intensity of the response patterns and the corresponding emotional experience to be relatively high, suggesting that this may be an important design feature in distinguishing emotions from moods, for example.

Duration. Conversely, as emotions imply massive response mobilization and synchronization as part of specific action tendencies, their duration must be relatively short in order not to tax the resources of the organism and to allow behavioral flexibility. In contrast, low intensity moods that have little impact on behavior can be maintained for much longer periods of time without showing adverse effects.

It should be noted that the widely used term *feeling* does not figure in the list of affective states to be distinguished from emotion. As shown above, the CPM reserves the use of this term for the *subjective emotional experience component of emotion*, presumed to have an important monitoring and regulation function. In fact, it is suggested that "feelings integrate the central representation of appraisal-driven response organization in emotion" (Scherer, 2004), thus reflecting the total pattern of cognitive appraisal, as well as motivational and somatic response patterning, that underlies the subjective experience of an emotional episode. Using the term feeling (a single component denoting the subjective experience process) as a synonym for emotion (the total multimodal component process) produces serious confusions and hampers our understanding of the phenomenon. In fact, it can be argued that the long-standing debate generated by William James' peripheral theory of emotion is essentially due to James' failure to make this important distinction: When he asked "What is an emotion?" in 1884, he really meant "What is a feeling?" (see Scherer, 2000a). Unfortunately, it seems difficult to convince emotion researchers to reserve feeling exclusively as the term for the experience component of emotion and to combat the tendency to use feeling as a synonym for emotion. As the feeling component is the gateway to consciousness of an emotion episode, and thus to classification and verbalization, the emotion words are in fact *also* words for *emotional feelings*, used by the person experiencing the emotion episode to label and communicate the felt experience. However, the same words are also used by observers, including scientists, who have no access to the person's internal feeling state to refer to the complete package of component changes in the emotion episode that are observable (for example, verbal utterances, facial and vocal expression, signs of physiological arousal such as blushing or heavy breathing, or cues for action tendencies such as raising one's arm in preparation of hitting), or that can be inferred (with more or less accuracy) from situational and contextual cues. Thus, emotion words function at the same time as markers for emotion episodes with special qualities of the synchronized components (the full package) and for the special quality of the conscious feeling.

There are, of course, other kinds of feelings, as philosophers do not tire of pointing out (see Mulligan & Scherer, 2012). Thus one can feel warm, self-assured, combative, weak, tired, aroused, good or bad, and so on. One can also feel pain in the right foot, a warm breeze, or pity with someone else's plight. Feeling is a general term for the subjective experience of sensory stimuli or internal states. Thus, feeling terms, or more generally, feeling expressions, constitute a special class of lexical units that are semantically marked by their special mode of reference to a subjective experience as internally felt by a person. In each case, the nature, object, or domain of the feeling needs to be specified, such as bodily sensations or mental states. The canonical emotion words, on which this volume is focused, are special in that a coherent package of changes in several domains or components, including the feeling component, is referenced. However, there are also feeling terms that refer to subjective experiences linked to individual subsystems, which may be involved in affective reactions. In these cases, the degree of synchronization with other subsystems may vary and thus it might not be justified to use an emotional term that requires a high degree of synchronization of several subsystems. Thus, feeling hot or tense, or feeling one's heart racing, refers to the experience of bodily reactions. Feeling one's jaw drop or one's voice quiver is part of the expression component. Feeling combative or listless belongs to the action tendency component. Feeling confident or righteous is part of the appraisal component. In contrast, words for emotional feelings, such as feeling angry, sad, shameful, or proud, refer to the full, synchronized emotion "package," as described above. There are some special cases, in particular the terms used by dimensional emotion theorists, such as feeling good or bad, strong or weak, or more or less aroused. These represent a low-dimensional descriptive level of the emotional feeling component, which integrates the changing states of the other components. The terms used for the dimensions in this low-level mapping of the complex packages may reflect the contributions of individual components or of a coherence of several components. Thus, feeling good or bad is likely to be a direct consequence of a valence appraisal, but may, in some cases, also reflect pleasurable bodily sensations. Feeling calm or aroused probably represents the overall level of autonomic activity in the bodily reactions, but may also reflect more or less turbulence in mental operations. Finally, feeling strong or weak is likely to reflect the outcome of a differentiated appraisal of how well one can cope with the consequences of a particular event, but may also indicate the feeling of bodily condition. In contrast to the emotional feelings that are part of the emotion packages, these feeling terms are more diffuse, indicating broad regions of affective space rather than precise coordinates, as marked by emotion terms.

1.9 Developing a feature profile to measure the semantics of emotion words—the GRID

The design feature analysis described above suggests that the uniqueness of the emotion construct, apart from its episodic nature, consists in its *multi-componentiality*, the packing together of complexly organized profiles that reflect temporary synchronization of subsystems (a proposal that seems to find approval with emotion researchers from different traditions; see the commentaries on Scherer, 2005a, in Frijda, 2007b). Having clarified how the term "emotion" can be differentially defined as a specific category type of affect, the next issue is to construct a framework that can be used to differentiate the different tokens of that special category of affect, that is, the individual "emotions," in a principled fashion.

Scherer (2005a) proposed a variant of the design feature approach outlined above to establish semantic feature profiles of folk concepts of emotions represented by emotion terms from natural languages. The underlying idea is that whereas all emotion terms share features pertaining to the synchronized components, *the profile of appraisal check results and the specific response profiles across the components are different for qualitatively different emotions*. This amounts to defining the meaning of emotion words as the *specific pattern of appraisal and response changes in all components that are implied when a specific word is used to describe an emotion episode*. This form of representation of qualitative differences between emotions can be directly applied, for example, to differentiate terms within an emotion family (e.g., irritated, angry, mad) and to examine the semantic overlap of translationally equivalent words across different languages.

How can such meaning profiles be empirically assessed? Scherer (2005a) suggested having emotion words rated by native speakers of different natural languages with respect to a large number of features for each of the emotion components described above. For example, one can ask participants to imagine a person whose emotional experience at a particular point in time is consensually described by observers as "irritated." Then raters are asked to evaluate the typical eliciting and response characteristics that would warrant the description of the person's emotional state with this label. This would include items on the eliciting event, the type of appraisal the person is likely to have made of the event and its consequences, the response patterns in the different components (e.g., bodily reactions, facial and vocal expressions), the behavioral impact (action tendencies) generated, and the intensity and duration of the associated experience. For this procedure, the name *semantic grid profiles* was proposed, as the ratings on the component features for different emotions can be arranged in a grid with the respective emotion words as columns, as shown in Table 1.3. In this volume, this approach will be referred to more briefly as the *GRID paradigm*.

Semantic grid profiles for different emotion terms allow, at least if there is reasonable agreement between raters (in the sense of inter-rater reliability), to define the meaning of an emotion term in the respective language. In addition to facilitating the examination of subtle differences in the meanings of different emotion terms and providing similarity-of-profile data that can be

Table 1.3 A simple example of a component-based semantic grid

Emotions	Anger	Fear	Shame	Guilt
Features				
Event is novel	2	7	6	2
Caused by other	8	2	5	2
Outcome is negative	7	4	5	1
Heart beats faster	7	9	4	2
Feel hot	6	2	8	2
Smile	1	1	4	1
Feel like attacking	7	3	1	1
Try to hide feeling	2	4	6	8
Last long time	4	2	3	7

Note: The numbers in the cells indicate the probability of the respective feature being applicable to an emotional experience labeled with the respective emotion word.

used to statistically determine the relationships between members of emotion families and the overall structure of the semantic space for emotions, such data for different languages inform us about potential cultural and linguistic differences in emotion encoding. This aspect, apart from the scientific interest, is of great value to ensure comparability of instruments in intercultural studies.

It should be noted that Table 1.3 suggests a parametric precision that is unlikely to be attained in reality. It is plausible that, apart from the fact that there will be a range of variation in the assessment between different speakers of a language, the semantic profiles constitute fuzzy sets in the sense that not all conditions need to be met for the meaning of a word to be recognized (cf. prototype semantic concepts described in Chapter 4). Apart from the probability that there will be different configurations that are acceptable to justify the use of a word, it is to be expected that different sets of weights that are applied to different components. This is one of the more probable reasons for the differences observed across languages and cultures. For example, in languages that favor a "somaticized" emotion lexicon (see Chapter 3), it is likely that a stronger emphasis on and weighting of physiological features will be found.

It is interesting to speculate what has determined the central and most strongly weighted feature configurations in the semantic profiles in the development of a language—is it that individuals share similar emotional experiences and thus develop similar semantic representations, or is there social pressure in a linguistic community to reach consensus on semantic profiles? As is often the case with such questions, both factors have probably played a role. One can argue that the individual experiences are extremely variable and that there is no need for precise labels unless one is required to provide one—as in responding to questionnaires. In fact, even when communicating or sharing an emotional experience, individuals rarely use emotion category labels in a spontaneous fashion when describing emotional episodes; rather, they often refer to these in terms of situations or events and the resulting response patterns. Thus, people can simply refer to one of the components, whichever is most salient in their representation of the situation. For example, to the question "how did you feel?", people may say "abused" (appraisal of event), "I couldn't stand still" (expression), "my heart was racing" (physiology), "I was upset/deeply affected" (feeling), "Like I didn't know how to react" (action tendency), etc. The specific emotion felt in each case (sadness, fear, anger, joy?) is left to be inferred (e.g., "abused" = sad? angry?; "upset" = sad? angry? worried?; "deeply affected" = sad? concerned? shocked?). The context can disambiguate different potential meanings. This suggests that labeling may not be necessary for emotion memory. In consequence, it may be the case that social conventions for emotion labels are more determinative and that these may be based to a large extent on externally noticeable emotion manifestations that can serve to obtain agreement on the meaning of labels. Such shared definitions could consist of shared appraisal inferences from typical situations by personality interactions, as well as visible or audile manifestations of emotional arousal, such as externally visible signs of physiological changes (e.g., blushing or shaking) and facial, vocal, and bodily expressions that may indicate action tendencies.

1.10 **Cognitive mechanisms of emotion encoding and decoding through words**

Given the architecture outlined above, especially with respect to the categorization and verbalization of prototypical forms of emotion processes with widely different qualities, one might ask exactly which mechanisms could be involved in the matching of a word that has a specific meaning in ordinary language with the fuzzy multicomponent profile likely to constitute the qualia entering consciousness. Based on the preceding discussion, a first hypothesis can be ventured. Starting from a model of appraisal registers for the sequential cumulative integration of the appraisals (see Figure 5.3 in Scherer, 2001), one can imagine an expanded model that includes the categorization and verbalization process. Concretely, in addition to the appraisal registers, one would include response registers for all components receiving efferent input from appraisal results. These registers, part of short-term working memory in executive space, contain the current state of the features in the different components in time (*current experience vectors*, corresponding to the component features in the GRID instrument). Lexical memory would be added to the model and each emotion word would be represented by *meaning prototype vectors* (again corresponding to the component features in the GRID instrument). In addition, the episodic long-term memory component would contain *past experience vectors* in which memory traces of past personal emotion experiences would be represented (again corresponding to the component features in the GRID instrument, and thus including somatic markers, but also stored appraisal configurations). On the basis of such architecture, one can envisage that the encoding of an emotional experience into an emotion word works through a matching algorithm. The latter would compute the respective distances between the current experience vector and the different meaning vectors for each of the emotion words that are salient in lexical memory, resulting in the choice of the most appropriate word on the basis of minimal distance. In the decoding process, an inverse matching process would take place, finding the minimal distance between the meaning vector of the given emotion word and the past experience vectors of the different memory traces of personal emotion experiences. These profile matching processes could be optimized by constraining the respective input profiles to particular regions of a multidimensional affective space generated in a similar fashion by both the individual experience vectors and the prototypical meaning vectors.

1.11 Conclusion: The promise of the GRID paradigm

The differences between the three major theoretical approaches (basic emotion, dimensionalist/constructivist, and componential appraisal theories) systematically outlined above were discussed with respect to the implications of each theoretical stance for our understanding of the semantics of emotion words in general and the semantic sedimentation hypothesis in particular. While the three theories agree about the existence of the components of emotion, they disagree with respect to their organization in emotion episodes. Constructivist theorists do not seem to envisage much organization of features within and across components. In contrast, basic emotion theorists assume a tight preordained organization as part of evolutionary stable affect programs, and appraisal theorists postulate a more flexible organization that emerges on the basis of specific configurations of appraisal results within social and environmental constraints and affordances. All three traditions agree that a central component is conscious feeling. Dimensionalist/constructivists see feeling as the first form of organization, the basic building block, arguing for "core affect," which consists of the location of a feeling in two-dimensional valence × arousal space. For basic emotion theories, the primary emotions triggered by affect programs are represented in feeling as packages (which may be represented in dimensional space because of similarities and differences). The CPM assumes that feeling consists of an integrated representation of all component patterns in the episode in the form of nonverbal qualia that can be directly mapped into multidimensional affective space.

While all three theories postulate some form of categorization and labeling of conscious feeling, the presumed mechanisms are different. For constructivist theories, emotion terms are largely independent of the underlying affective processes—they are cultural constructs that are used to make sense of continuous changes in valenced arousal. Their application is seen as subject to a multitude of motivational and contextual variables. Basic emotion theorists assume that the felt basic emotion is given its appropriate label in the respective language, assuming a large degree of universality. As described above, the CPM assumes that the feature profile representing the multicomponent appraisal-response patterning is matched with an array of labeling options with prototypical semantic feature profiles. In summary, whereas basic emotion theories could be said to define the role of emotion terms as "program descriptors" and constructivist theories to see them as "meaning constructors," the CPM views emotion terms as "modal response markers," that is, marking a frequently occurring multicomponent configuration of appraisals and associated response patterns. In the current book, the CPM is taken as a point of reference to assess the meaning of emotion words.

The major claims made in this chapter on the basis of the CPM can be summarized as follows:

- Emotions are tightly organized packages of synchronized multicomponent response patterns driven by appraisal.
- These packages become available to consciousness in the form of nonverbal qualia that can be mapped into a multidimensional affective space.
- Some of these packages occur more frequently than others, given the pervasiveness of situations producing frustration, loss, achievement, etc., resulting in *modal emotions*.
- Most linguistic communities have given discrete labels to such modal emotions, which, due to the human condition, are often universal (although there may be specific emotions reflecting particular interpersonal relations in some societies).
- Given the modal response marking function of such lexical expressions, it can be expected that the semantics of the respective terms reflect the synchronized patterns of appraisal and response configurations in the underlying package.
- Feature profiles measuring the quality of the respective patterns can be used to empirically measure the meaning of specific nouns or other lexical units and to determine the differentiation as well as the similarity relationships between different terms and their translational equivalence across different languages.

In this chapter, the groundwork for a functional, psychological account of the nature of emotion words is laid—based on the CPM. In particular, the relationships of emotion words to the underlying sociopsychobiological processes were examined and potential mechanisms proposed that may be involved in the categorization and verbalization of the emotion process, including a preliminary architecture for encoding and decoding. The central claim is that the multicomponential nature of emotion requires a domain-specific approach that integrates the componential structure of emotion into semantic representation.

As a first step in using this framework, a proposal is made to measure the meaning of different emotion words through profiles of features that represent all of the components of the emotion construct. The utility, and future promise, of this proposal is to be assessed in the bulk of this volume, which describes a massive multiculture and multilanguage study using the proposed *GRID paradigm* to investigate the likelihood that the semantics of emotion words are grounded in specifiable profiles of component features that are stable across individuals and languages.

Chapter 2

Dimensional, basic emotion, and componential approaches to meaning in psychological emotion research

Johnny J. R. Fontaine[1]

The present chapter focuses on the meaning of emotion words from the perspective of the discipline of psychology. In most psychological studies, the meaning of emotion words is not made explicit. Emotion terms are either indirectly used to construct stimuli (e.g., when actors are asked to display a certain emotion and the displays are then used in recognition tasks), or directly used as stimuli (e.g., when people are asked to recall and describe emotional episodes) or as response scales (e.g., when people are asked to rate their emotional experience on a list of emotion terms). The presumed meaning of emotion terms has to be inferred from the theoretical framework on which the research is based and from the context in which the terms are applied. It is not feasible in the current chapter, though, to give a comprehensive overview of psychological emotion research and the different, often implicit, assumptions made about the meaning of emotion words. Therefore, the chapter focuses on those approaches that have led to explicit psycholinguistic research on the meaning of emotion terms. The two theoretical approaches that have dominated psycholinguistic research on emotion terms, the dimensional and the basic emotion approach, are at the center of this chapter. Moreover, a third psychological approach, the componential emotion approach, will be discussed. The GRID paradigm, which was presented in the previous chapter and forms the basis for studying the meaning of emotion words throughout the current book, is rooted in the componential emotion approach. The componential emotion approach therefore also receives attention in the current chapter, although this approach has resulted in virtually no psycholinguistic research in the past.

The current chapter is organized into five parts. As most psycholinguistic research on emotion words has been rooted in the dimensional approach, this approach is presented first and most extensively. The basic emotion approach is discussed second. The componential approach to emotion and its implied conceptualization of the meaning of emotion words is examined in the third part. The fourth part focuses on the compatibilities and incompatibilities between the dimensional, basic emotion, and componential approaches with respect to the meaning of emotion terms. The

---

[1] Johnny J. R. Fontaine. Department of Personnel, Work and Organisational Psychology. Faculty of Psychology and Educational Sciences. Ghent University. Henri-Dunantlaan 2, 9000 Gent, Belgium. Johnny.Fontaine@UGent.be

chapter ends with a discussion on how the GRID paradigm can be informed by and be informative for the dimensional and the basic emotion approaches.

2.1 **The dimensional approach**

According to the dimensional approach, an emotion, as well as the meaning of an emotion term, can be represented by a specific position within the continuous space that is defined by a small number of underlying dimensions. This approach has an honorable origin. Aristotle (Rhetorica) considered the hedonic tone ranging from highly positive to highly negative as a key characteristic of the emotional experience. More dimensions were proposed by the 17th century philosopher Spinosa (1677), who theorized that a key source of variability between the emotions was that they ranged from weak to strong and from less to more persistent. Moreover, the dimensional framework was present in scientific psychology right from its origin. On the basis of introspection, Wilhelm Wundt (1896) proposed the dimensions pleasure–displeasure, arousal–calming, and tension–relaxation (Lust–Unlust, Erregung–Hemmung, and Spannung–Lösung). Ever since its introduction into scientific emotion psychology, the dimensional approach to emotions has played (e.g., Schlosberg, 1952), and continues to play, a prominent role, especially in the assessment of affective experiences and in psycholinguistic research on the meaning of emotion words. The following section begins with a discussion of the four most important dimensional models for representing emotional experiences. Subsequently, the psycholinguistic research on the meaning of emotion words from a dimensional approach is introduced. A comparison between the dimensional structure of emotional experiences and the dimensional structure of the meaning of emotion words is next presented. The section then concludes with a note on the labeling of the emotion dimensions.

Dimensional approaches to emotional experiences

Dimensional approaches play a central role in the assessment of emotional, and more broadly, affective experiences. In studies that apply this approach, participants are typically asked to report the degree to which a number of emotion and affect terms describe their own affective experience. The way that people use these terms to describe their own affective experiences, and possibly those of others, can throw an important light on their meaning. Very different models have been proposed to represent self-ratings on a number of affect terms. They share, however, a two-dimensional view on the affective space. The presentation here is restricted to the four most important models in the literature, the positive affect–negative affect model (Watson & Tellegen, 1985), the pleasure–arousal model (Russell, 1980), the pleasantness–activation model (Larsen & Diener, 1992), and the tense arousal and energetic arousal model (Thayer, 1989). The defining characteristics of these four models are first presented, which is followed by a discussion of the two central issues that differentiate these models: the bipolarity of valence and the relevance and dimensionality of arousal.

   Four two-dimensional models of emotional experience. The positive affect–negative affect model (Watson & Tellegen, 1985) is the most well-known model, both within and outside emotion psychology. It is often used in theoretical and in applied research. Originally, it was an inductively developed model. According to Watson and Clark (1997), affect measurement reveals three replicable empirical findings: (1) self-ratings on positive affect terms are mutually positively correlated, (2) self-ratings on negative affect terms are mutually positively correlated, and (3) self-ratings on positive affect terms are virtually uncorrelated with self-ratings on negative affect terms. From this observation, Watson and Clark (1997) concluded that although positive and negative affect terms are opposite in meaning, they refer to two distinct and largely unrelated affective systems. The

Positive and Negative Affect Schedule (PANAS) (Watson, Clark, & Tellegen, 1988), which is one of the most widely used affect scales, is based on this model. It contains a scale for positive affect and a scale for negative affect, with both scales being virtually uncorrelated.

Russell's pleasure-arousal model (Russell, 1980) proposes two very different dimensions in the affective domain. According to this model, the first factor is a bipolar pleasantness factor on which positive and negative emotions are opposed to one another. The second factor represents the arousal dimension on which high arousal (e.g., nervous) and low-arousal (e.g., calm) affective experiences are opposed to one another.

The pleasantness–activation model of Larsen and Diener (1992) is close to Russell's pleasure–arousal model, although it uses slightly different terms and slightly different labels. It also assumes that positively valenced experiences are opposed to negatively valenced experiences on the first dimension. Moreover, high-activation experiences (e.g., aroused) are opposed to low-activation experiences (e.g., quiet) on the second dimension, which is comparable to Russell's arousal dimension.

The tense arousal and energetic arousal model (Thayer, 1989) is yet another model. This model has the arousal system as its central focus. According to Thayer's theorizing, there are two arousal systems: one system that regulates energetic arousal (which ranges from being sleepy to being energized) and the other that regulates tense arousal (which ranges from being calm to being tense).

The bipolarity of the valence dimension. The first and most important source of disagreement between the four models is the bipolarity of the valence dimension. According to the positive affect–negative affect model (Watson & Tellegen, 1985), positive and negative affect are two virtually uncorrelated dimensions. In this model, it is possible for human emotional experiences to not only be high on positive affect and low on negative affect, or high on negative affect and low on positive affect, but also high on both positive and negative affect at the same time. The second and third models, however, assume that valence is a single bipolar factor. These two models assume that the higher the positive affect during an emotional experience, the lower the negative affect and vice versa. There have been vigorous debates between the proponents of both views. In the course of the debate, the role of methodological factors in the dimensional representation of the emotion domain has been extensively demonstrated (e.g., Feldman-Barrett & Russell, 1998; Green, Goldman, & Salovey, 1993; Green, Salovey, & Truax, 1999; Russell & Carroll, 1999; Yik, Russell, & Barrett, 1999). The five most important methodological factors are unreliability due to random measurement error, acquiescent response style leading to systematic measurement error, the selection of the affect terms, the formulation of the response scales, and shared method variance. As these methodological factors are also potentially relevant when the meaning of emotion terms is studied, these factors are presented in more detail.

One methodological factor is random measurement error that affects the reliability of the measurement (e.g., Green, Goldman, & Salovey, 1993; Green, Salovey, & Truax, 1999). As is well known in validity research, the reliability of scales determines the upper limit of the observable validity coefficients. The lower the reliability, the more the observed correlations will tend to be closer to zero. Thus, negative correlations will become less negative and positive correlations will become less positive.

A second methodological factor is non-random error that is caused by response styles (e.g., Green, Goldman, & Salovey, 1993; Green, Salovey, & Truax, 1999). Acquiescence, in particular, has a systematic effect on the observed correlations. Acquiescence means that participants differ systematically in the tendency to agree with questions or to systematically give a higher or lower score irrespective of the content of the items. This response tendency forces the observed correlations upward. Positive correlations will become more positive, and negative correlations will become less negative.

A third methodological factor is the selection of the terms in the instrument. For bipolarity to be observed, affective terms are needed that are genuinely opposite in meaning. This is not the case in the PANAS, which is the most widely used instrument to assess positive and negative affect. Most items from both the positive and negative affect scales share a high level of arousal (e.g., enthusiastic and nervous) (e.g., Feldman-Barrett & Russell, 1998).

A fourth methodological factor is the formulation of the response scale (Russell & Carroll, 1999). A response scale can be formulated from unambiguously unipolar through to unambiguously bipolar. In an unambiguously unipolar response scale, the lowest score means that the affect is absent and the highest score means that the affect is strongly present (e.g., the response categories: 1 "not," 2 "slightly," 3 "moderately," 4 "extremely"). In an unambiguously bipolar scale, the response scale is defined by two opposite affect terms (e.g., "sad" 1 2 3 4 5 "happy"). The range of correlations that can be observed between affect items is determined by the kind of response scale that is used. The unambiguously unipolar response reduces the size of negative correlations between affect terms. It can be demonstrated psychometrically that when the underlying latent correlation between two affect terms is −1, the strongest negative correlation that can be observed empirically is only −0.46 with an unambiguously unipolar response scale. This effect is due to a highly skewed distribution of the responses with unambiguously unipolar scales (for a detailed account, see Russell & Carroll, 1999). In affect measurement, the use of unambiguously unipolar response scales is most popular, probably because that response scale sounds natural. However, it also reduces the possibility of observing bipolar factors.

A fifth more general methodological effect is shared method variance. Items that are formulated in the same way and that have to be answered in the same way induce common method variance, and this also forces correlations upward (e.g., Feldman-Barrett & Russell, 1998). Combined, these five methodological factors have the same effect on negative correlations: they all lead to less negative correlations. Note that this is not the case for positive correlations: some method effects will make positive correlations less positive (e.g., unreliability) and others will make positive correlations more positive (e.g., acquiescence). It has by now been extensively demonstrated that when all of these methodological factors are controlled for (multimethod approach to counteract acquiescence and shared method variance, not using unambiguously unipolar scales, working with affective terms that are really opposite in meaning, and using confirmatory factor analysis to model unreliability), a high negative correlation is observed between positive and negative affect (e.g., Feldman-Barrett & Russell, 1998; Green, Goldman, & Salovey, 1993; Green, Salovey, & Truax, 1999; Russell & Carroll, 1999; Yik, Russell, & Barrett, 1999). Thus, on the basis of extensive psychometric and empirical research, the psychometric debate has been closed in favor of the unidimensional bipolar view on valence.

The nature of arousal. The second issue of debate is the presence and the nature of the arousal experience. Russell's pleasure–arousal model (Russell, 1980) and Larsen and Diener's pleasantness–activation model (Larsen & Diener, 1992) assume one bipolar arousal factor, while Thayer's tense arousal and energetic arousal model (Thayer, 1989) supposes two different bipolar arousal factors. Moreover, Watson and Tellegen's positive affect–negative affect model (Watson & Tellegen, 1985) does not even consider arousal as a basic dimension in the affect domain. Extensive empirical research has, however, demonstrated that the discrepancies between these four models are only seeming differences (Yik, Russell, & Feldman-Barrett, 1999). Once the methodological factors that affect bipolarity have been taken into account, the differences between the four affect models can

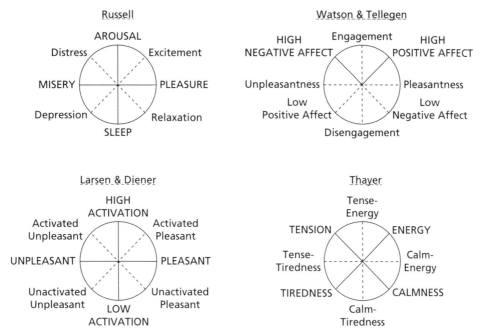

Figure 2.1 Four schematic descriptions of affect as represented by Yik, Russell, & Feldman-Barrett (1999). Reproduced from Journal of Personality and Social Psychology, 77 (4), Yik, M. S. M., Russell, J. A., & Feldman-Barrett, L., Structure of self-reported current affect: integration and beyond pp. 600–619 © 1999, American Psychological Association, with permission.

be accounted for by a simple rotation of the dimensions in a two-dimensional representation (see Figure 2.1). Although using a different conceptualization, the four models are thus empirically interchangeable. Russell's pleasure–arousal model and Larsen and Diener's pleasantness–activation model refer to the same rotation of axes, but they use slightly different items and labels for their dimensions. Thayer's tense arousal and energetic arousal model corresponds to a 45° rotation of the axes of Russell's pleasure–arousal model, with energized arousal corresponding to a combination of pleasure and high arousal, and tense arousal corresponding to a combination of misery and high arousal (see Figure 2.1). Moreover, Thayer's tense arousal and energetic arousal model corresponds closely to Watson and Tellegen's positive affect–negative affect model, with positive affect closely relating to the energized arousal pole, and negative affect to the tense arousal pole. Thus, although working with slightly different items (or using only a subset of items) and using different terminology, these four models assess highly similar psychological phenomena. Next to a bipolar valence factor, a bipolar arousal factor has also been identified in the most widely used models to assess affective experiences.

The debate now centers on the most adequate rotation to represent the internal structure of the affect domain. Some researchers favor the valence-arousal orientation because of the fundamental role of the valence in psychological functioning in general (e.g., Russell & Carroll, 1999). Others favor the positive and negative affect rotation because they assume that this rotation would be congruent with the expected brain architecture (e.g., Watson, Wiese, Vaidya, & Tellegen, 1999). In support of the latter claim, circadian rhythms have been shown to have an effect on positive affect, but they are not related to negative affect. As there is rotational indeterminacy from a psychometric point of view, analyses of the internal structure of the instruments alone cannot further contribute to this debate. The most important conclusion for the purpose of the current chapter is that when persons are asked to rate their own emotional experiences on sets of emotion and affect terms from the four most widely used models, their responses can be represented by a bipolar valence and a bipolar arousal dimension, or a rotation thereof.

Dimensional models in psycholinguistic research

Not only have interindividual differences in emotional experiences been studied from the dimensional emotion approach, but so, too, has the meaning of emotion words. This psycholinguistic research has been heavily inspired by Osgood's research on the connotative meaning dimensions in language. Because of its impact, Osgood's findings are presented first, with the psycholinguistic research on the meaning of emotion terms subsequently presented.

Connotative meaning dimensions. In linguistics, a distinction has been made between denotative and connotative meaning (e.g., Osgood, Suci, & Tannenbaum, 1957). While the denotative meaning refers to what a word points to in the world, the connotative meaning refers to the affective loading of a word. In the 1950s, Osgood and colleagues (1957) found that the connotative meaning of English words can be represented in a three-dimensional space, and they developed an instrument to assess the connotative meaning in a standardized way. The basic principle was simple. They identified a set of bipolar pairs of adjectives that people often use in daily language to describe the quality of things (such as big–small, fast–slow, soft–hard). Moreover, they observed that people can easily apply these bipolar adjectives in a metaphorical way to things for which they are not used by default (e.g., to evaluate "house" on the bipolar pair "fast–slow"). More importantly, they found that the ratings of objects and nouns on these bipolar pairs can be represented in a three-dimensional structure in which the dimensions have been interpreted as evaluation (good–bad), potency (strong–weak), and activation (active–passive). Osgood and colleagues thus demonstrated that connotation in English can be represented in a three-dimensional structure.

In an extensive cross-cultural research program, he and his colleagues further investigated the connotative meaning dimensions across many languages and cultural groups (Osgood, May, & Miron, 1975). Rather than just translating the English instrument, they went to great lengths to identify the specific connotative meaning structure within each language. They first identified the bipolar pairs of adjectives that were frequently used within a language (without taking into account the pairs that were identified in other languages). While working with culture- and language-specific bipolar adjectives, they revealed the same underlying universal dimensions of connotative meaning across different languages. Although Osgood and colleagues did not directly study emotion terms, their findings have been considered relevant for the emotion domain. The connotative meaning dimensions are interpreted as affective dimensions. They represent the feelings that are typically associated with words and nouns.

Similarity studies with emotion words. Besides the connotative meaning tradition, there is also a large tradition in psycholinguistics that directly focuses on the meaning of emotion words. In these studies, the perceived similarity between pairs of emotion terms is investigated. Participants are asked either to sort a (presumed) representative set of emotion terms into groups of similarity (e.g., Shaver, Schwartz, Kirson, & O'Connor, 1987), or to directly rate the similarity between pairs of emotion terms. It is an ecologically valid (participants can work with the affective words they use in daily language) and easy-to-use research method (it is an intuitively understandable task that can be easily explained across cultural groups). Both research designs lead to a similarity matrix; within each cell is the number of times that two emotion terms were sorted in the same group or the average direct similarity score. The observed similarities between the emotion terms are represented as distances between points in a geometrical space by means of multidimensional scaling. This approach has been very popular in Western psychological (e.g., Gehm & Scherer, 1988), cross-cultural psychological (e.g., Russell, Lewicka, & Nitt, 1989), and anthropological research (e.g., Lutz, 1988).

A valence dimension differentiating positively from negatively valenced emotion terms has been identified in all studies that used this approach. There is disagreement, though, about the dimensions beyond valence. Some studies found only a two-dimensional representation (e.g., Church, Katigbak, Reyes, & Jensen, 1998; Russell, 1983; Russell, Lewicka, & Nitt, 1989), while others found a three-dimensional representation (e.g., Fontaine et al., 2002). Moreover, among those studies that found only a two-dimensional representation, there is disagreement about the nature of the second dimension. In some of those studies, the second dimension was an arousal or activation dimension on which high-arousal emotions, such as anger and fear, were differentiated from low-arousal emotions, such as sadness (e.g., Russell, Lewicka, & Nitt, 1989). In other such studies, the second dimension was a power or potency dimension on which emotions such as anger and fear were differentiated (e.g., Gehm & Scherer, 1988; Herrmann & Raybeck, 1981). Those studies in which three dimensions emerged, these three dimensions could be interpreted as valence, power, and arousal (e.g., Fontaine, Poortinga, Setiadi, & Markam, 2002; Shaver, Schwartz, Kirson, & O'Conner, 1987; Shaver, Wu, & Schwartz, 1992).

An important question is what causes these different dimensional representations. A cultural account can be excluded: studies using exactly the same procedure in different cultural and linguistic groups recover the same dimensional structure. For instance, Russell, Lewicka, and Niit (1989) stably identified the valence–arousal structure across different languages, while Herrmann and Raybeck (1981) stably identified the valence–power structure across linguistic groups; Fontaine et al. (2002) and Shaver et al. (1987, 1992) stably recovered all three dimensions in languages as different as Dutch, English, Italian, Chinese, and Indonesian.

Two methodological factors constitute good candidates to account for the observed differences, namely the selection of emotion terms and the reliability of the similarities (see also Chapter 14). For the first candidate, Russell (1991a) has hypothesized that which of the two dimensions emerges (first) over and above valence depends on the nature of the emotion words included. When more intrapersonal emotion terms are included, an arousal dimension would emerge. When more interpersonal emotion terms are included, a power dimension would emerge. A second likely methodological candidate is the number of participants. The more participants there are, the more reliable the similarity estimations. The studies that worked both with a large sample of emotion terms and a large sample of participants recovered all three dimensions of evaluation, potency, and activation (e.g., Fontaine, Poortinga, Setiadi, & Markam, 2002; Shaver, Schwartz, Kirson, & O'Conner, 1987; Shaver, Wu, & Schwartz, 1992). Studies that worked with a small set of emotion terms and/or with relatively small sample sizes usually found only two dimensions (e.g., Gehm & Scherer, 1988; Herrmann & Raybeck, 1981).

It can be concluded that there is strong evidence for three affective dimensions in the psycholinguistic domain. Those studies that went to great lengths to identify a large and representative set of emotion terms, and that relied on a large sample of participants to compute the similarities, stably found three dimensions. Moreover, the three-dimensional structure of valence, power, and arousal emerges both when participants are asked to rate objects and nouns on a representative set of bipolar adjectives and when participants directly judge emotion terms on their meaning similarity.

Comparing dimensional models of emotion experiences with dimensional models of the meaning of emotion words

In psycholinguistic research, there is thus converging cross-cultural evidence for the three dimensions of valence, power, and arousal. When these psycholinguistic findings are contrasted with the four affect models that dominate self-report research, a highly substantial divergence is observed. The power dimension, which is very important in the psycholinguistic approaches (and is even the second dimension in Osgood's connotative meaning structure), is completely absent in the four most popular self-report models.

A possible explanation for the divergence between psycholinguistic and self-report models lies in the selection of the emotion terms. As discussed previously, Russell hypothesized in 1991 that a power dimension would emerge if more interpersonal emotion terms are sampled and that an arousal dimension would emerge if more intrapersonal emotion terms are included. It could be hypothesized that the most important current affect models work predominantly with intrapersonal affect terms. The fact that Kitayama, Markus, and Kurokawa (2000) have identified a two-dimensional model, which is structured according to the dimensions of valence and what they call "engaged" versus "disengaged" emotions in a cross-cultural context, seems to support this explanation. Within cross-cultural psychology, it is assumed that the interpersonal aspects of the emotional experience are much more salient in non-Western than in Western groups (see also Chapter 3). In developing their emotion instrument, Kitayama et al. carefully represented interpersonal emotions and affects. When these interpersonal affect terms are well represented, the second dimension looks very much like Osgood's power dimension in that anger and pride (disengaged/high power) are opposed to tenderness and shame (engaged/low power). While this observation is suggestive, it has not yet been demonstrated that the three dimensions of valence, power, and arousal can be jointly identified in self-ratings of emotional experiences when a representative set of emotion terms is rated by a large number of participants.

It can thus be concluded that there is converging evidence that valence and arousal both structure the domain of emotional experiences and the meaning of emotion terms. For power, the results are less clear-cut. Power is evidently a dimension in the meaning of emotion terms, next to valence and arousal; it still has to be demonstrated, however, whether power can be identified as a separate dimension in emotional experiences next to valence and arousal (see Chapter 15 for an empirical investigation of this issue).

Labeling the emotion dimensions

Before completing this discussion of dimensional models, the labeling of dimensions should be addressed. As can be seen, the three dimensions have been labeled differently by the various theoretical and empirical traditions. Despite these differences, however, comparable emotion terms are differentiated. The most important labels that have been given to the first dimension are evaluation, valence, hedonic tone, pleasantness, and pleasure. They all refer to the observation that positive emotion terms such as joy and happiness are opposed to negative emotion terms such as sadness, fear, and anger. For the second dimension, the most important labels have been potency, power, control, and dominance. On this dimension, anger terms are opposed to fear and sadness terms. The labels arousal and activation have been the most popular for the third dimension. Fear and anger terms are typically differentiated from sadness terms on this dimension. Although these labels each carry their particular meanings, which can be important for differentiating them in specific contexts, they have been used interchangeably because they all refer to a common core in each of these dimensions.

For the remainder of this book, the labels *valence*, *power*, and *arousal* will be used. For the first dimension, the label *valence* is preferred because valence can best be used to refer to all aspects of the emotion process. The other labels either strongly focus on the appraisal component (evaluation) or on the feeling component (hedonic tone, pleasantness, or pleasure). For the second dimension, the label *power* is further used because it best captures potency/strength, control, and dominance, which have been identified as key facets of the second dimension. For the third dimension, the label *arousal* has been chosen. Arousal and activation are often used interchangeably in the literature. However, arousal refers more to the bodily aspect of the emotional process than does activation. As bodily activation is considered a defining aspect of this dimension, we prefer to label this dimension arousal.

2.2 **The basic emotion approach**

The emotion approach that dominated much of emotion research in the second half of the last century and that has remained influential until today is the basic emotion approach. The key assumption of this approach is that there exists a limited number of qualitatively different, hardwired, and universal emotion processes. It is claimed that these processes are internally coherent and characterized by, for instance, distinctive universal signals (expressive behavior), distinctive physiology, an automatic appraisal focused on distinctive universal antecedent events, and a distinctive subjective experience (e.g., Ekman, 1999). The basic emotion approach can be traced to the ground-breaking work of Charles Darwin on emotions in humans and animals (1872) and has been strongly elaborated in psychology by Tomkins (1962) and later by Izard (1977) and Ekman (e.g., Ekman & Oster, 1979). The most well-known basic emotion theory is that of Ekman (e.g., Ekman, 2003), who postulates the existence of seven evolutionary developed basic affective programs: happiness, surprise, contempt, sadness, fear, disgust, and anger. Much of the research in the basic emotion tradition has focused on the facial and vocal expression of emotions, which are assumed to be hardwired manifestations of the basic emotion process. In the typical research paradigm, participants are shown facial expressions or have to listen to vocal expressions and are then asked to identify the expressed emotion from a list of emotion terms. Using this standard paradigm, it has been demonstrated that the recognition for each presumed basic emotion was above chance level across cultural groups for vocal expression and even more so for facial expression (e.g., Ekman & Friesen, 1971; Scherer, Banse, & Wallbott, 2001).

From the basic emotion approach, emotion terms refer to a limited number of categorically different basic emotion processes. The basic emotion approach thus has a categorical view on the meaning of emotion terms. This view on meaning is often assumed in daily emotion talk and when emotion words are used in psychological research. Within the basic emotion approach, a core set of emotion terms is assumed to have the basic emotions as their referents, and therefore the existence of these terms is expected to be (nearly) universal. Beyond these basic emotion terms, the variability of terms in the emotion lexicon is accounted for by three factors in traditional basic emotion theorizing: intensity, context, and blending (e.g., Fontaine et al., 2002; Plutchik, 2001). The first factor is related to the fact that different intensities of the same basic emotion can have been encoded in language, such as irritation and rage to refer to a low- and high-intensity form of anger. Regarding the second factor, emotion words could imply information about the specific context in which the emotion is experienced. For instance, bliss can be seen as intense joy in a spiritual context. The third factor, blending, follows from the fact that a single situation can elicit more than one basic emotion and that, although basic emotions are qualitatively different processes, their incidence is not mutually exclusive. Emotion terms could thus refer to blends of basic emotions, such as distress, which shares properties of sadness and fear. Thus, according to the basic emotion approach, a distinction can be made between two types of emotion words: emotion words that have a basic emotion as their referent and emotion words that qualify the basic emotion in terms of intensity, context, or blending with other basic emotions. In more recent basic emotion theorizing, other types of non-basic emotional phenomena are also allowed for, for instance on the basis of emotion schemas that are culturally and developmentally more malleable (e.g., Izard, 2007).

The assumption that the emotion lexicon is organized around basic emotion terms has been psycholinguistically investigated in conjunction with Rosch's natural language theory (Rosch, 1973a, 1978) (see also Chapter 1). According to this theory, natural language categories are organized hierarchically in a superordinate, a basic, and a subordinate level of categorization. These three levels differ in terms of informativeness and cognitive economy. A high level of categorization is economical, as only a few words are needed to categorize a domain, but it is not very informative (e.g., the category mammal). The basic level of categorization has an optimal trade-off between informativeness and cognitive economy (e.g., the category of cats or dogs). A lower-level category is very informative, but not cognitively economic, as many terms are needed to categorize a domain (e.g., a golden retriever). As the basic level offers the best trade-off between informativeness and cognitive economy, basic categories are encoded in language by single and typically short words, which come to mind first when someone is asked to categorize an object, and are learned first in language acquisition. When Rosch's natural language theory is applied to emotions, it is assumed that the basic emotions correspond to the basic level of categorization. In line with this assumption, it has been observed that terms for presumably basic emotions are almost universally found across cultural groups and languages (with some exceptions, Russell, 1991; Chapter 3). As predicted by Rosch's natural language theory, these basic emotion words are mostly encoded by single and short words and come to mind first (e.g., Fehr & Russell, 1984). Moreover, these basic emotion words are learned first by children (e.g., Bretherton & Beeghly, 1982). Although not yet empirically confirmed, these observations raise the expectation that emotion words for the basic emotions have a much more stable meaning, both within and across cultures, than do the other emotion words that qualify the basic emotions in terms of intensity, context, or blending.

The empirical investigation of the hierarchical structure in the emotion domain relies on exactly the same similarity sorting or rating procedures as those that are used by the dimensional approaches. However, instead of representing the similarities in a dimensional space by means of multidimensional scaling, the similarities are represented categorically by means of hierarchical cluster analysis (e.g., Shaver, Schwartz, Kirson, & O'Connor, 1987). Applying hierarchical cluster analyses to similarities between emotion terms reveals four clusters that stably emerge across languages and cultural groups: joy, anger, sadness, and fear (see, for instance Figure 2.2 from a study in The Netherlands by Fontaine et al., 2002). Depending on the sample and the language, more clusters can emerge. For instance, it was found that instead of one broad joy cluster, a more narrow joy cluster and a love cluster emerged in the US (Shaver et al., 1987), Italy (Shaver, Wu, & Schwartz, 1992) and Canada (Storm & Storm, 1987). In the US and Italy, a separate surprise cluster emerged (Shaver et al., 1987; Shaver et al., 1992). In China, a separate shame and a separate sad love cluster emerged (Shaver et al., 1992). These other clusters, however, are not replicable across samples and languages. Thus, when it comes to meaning, the basic emotion approach has revealed at least four universal basic emotion clusters, joy, sadness, anger, and fear.

2.3 **The componential approach**

One of the most striking characteristics of the emotion domain is its variability in theoretical approaches. These theoretical approaches not only differ in their view on how emotions function, but they vary even more with respect to the very phenomena that are at the center of their theorizing. Some approaches focus on psychophysiological changes, in line with the theorizing of William James, who defined emotion as the awareness of bodily changes (e.g., James, 1894). Building on Darwin's evolutionary approach to emotions (Darwin, 1872), many emotion theorists have focused on facial and vocal expressions (e.g., Ekman & Oster, 1979; Izard, 1977). Others have treated feelings as key to the emotion-related processes (e.g., the core affect theory of Russell, 2003). Furthermore, motivational changes that have precedence in ongoing behavior have been proposed as the essence of emotions (Frijda, 1986). Still other theorists have built on the early work of Arnold (1960) and have focused on the cognitive basis of emotion. In this view, cognitive appraisal of the emotional situation is seen as the driving force for the emotion processes (e.g., Lazarus, 1991a; Roseman, 2001; Scherer, 2001).

The componential emotion framework, of which the Component Process Model presented in the previous chapter is a typical example, proposes an integrative framework for the diversity of empirical phenomena that have been studied under the umbrella of the emotion concept. According to this framework, an emotion is not a specific state or any one type of phenomenon, but a process in which these different phenomena interact in a coordinated fashion. The componential emotion framework proposes that these phenomena refer to basic subsystems of human functioning (named components) that start to interact in a coordinated way in goal-relevant events in order to prepare the person for adequate action.

The aim of the research program of the componential emotion framework is to identify the number and nature of features in each component and how they interact in a coordinated way in goal-relevant events. For instance, Scherer and Wallbott (1994) identified feeling, physiological, and motor expression profiles from daily experienced episodes of each of seven emotions in 37 countries. Another example is the study of Frijda, Kuipers, and ter Schure (1989), who studied how 23 appraisal dimensions relate to 29 action tendency dimensions for 32 emotional states.

The componential emotion approach is characterized by a *feature profile view* of the meaning of emotion terms. That is, it decomposes the meaning of an emotion term into a profile of features. This feature profile view has received little attention in psycholinguistic studies. A notable exception is the work of Tzeng, Hoosain, and Osgood (1987), who investigated the denotative meaning of 22 emotion concepts in 23 cultural groups by identifying their respective feature profiles with regard to 10 features: pleasantness, activation, control, ego orientation, cognitivity, overtness, dominance, time orientation, terminality, and sociality. These features were especially selected from the cognitive approach to emotion, which, according to Tzeng et al. (1987), defined an emotion word denotatively. The researchers asked experts in the 23 cultural groups to rate each of the 22 emotion concepts on these 10 features. They observed that the feature profiles were stable across cultural groups and could differentiate the 22 emotion concepts. Despite its innovative character and its extensiveness, this study had no impact on the psycholinguistic study of the meaning of emotion words.

The GRID paradigm, which was introduced in the previous chapter and was developed independently from the research of Tzeng et al. (1987), can be considered as a further elaboration of their feature profile approach. It differs from their approach with respect to the selection of the features. Whereas Tzeng et al. (1987) selected their features on the basis of the cognitive approach to emotion, the GRID paradigm is rooted in the componential emotion approach. In this approach, an emotion corresponds to a process elicited by goal-relevant events in which several components interact in coordinated ways. Thus, according to the GRID paradigm, the features of each of these emotion components, which change in response to goal-relevant events, are needed to convey the denotative meaning of an emotion word.

2.4 The incompatibilities and compatibilities between the dimensional, the basic emotion, and the componential emotion approaches

Incompatibilities. At first sight, the dimensional, the basic emotion, and the componential emotion approaches are incompatible, both with respect to the processes that they propose to account for the emotional phenomena, and with respect to their views on what constitutes the meaning of an emotion term. From a theoretical point of view, the dimensional and the basic emotion approaches conflict. The affective experience, which continuously varies in a two-dimensional space, forms the essence of the emotion construct according to the dimensional approach (e.g., Russell's core affect theory, Russell, 2003). All the other phenomena that are studied in the emotion domain can become associated with, can be affected by, or can affect this continuous affective experience. From the basic emotion approach, though, the essence of the emotion domain consists of a limited number of qualitatively different affect programs.

The dimensional approach also conflicts with the componential emotion approach. The former puts the two-dimensional affective experience at the heart of emotion (e.g., Russell, 2003). According to the latter, the (possibly dimensional) affective experience is considered as an outcome of coordinated activity between emotion components in response to goal-relevant events. The emotion process is only brought to consciousness in order to facilitate the regulation of the process (e.g., Scherer, 2009).

The views in the basic emotion approach also conflict with those in the componential emotion approach. According to the basic emotion approach, there exist a few qualitatively different affect programs that determine the emotion domain, while the componential emotion approach assumes that patterns of appraisals with respect to ongoing events will drive an appropriate synchronized activity in all emotion components (cf. previous chapter).

In line with these different presumed processes, these three approaches also have different views on how the meaning of an emotion word has to be defined. The meaning of an emotion term is defined by a set of coordinates on a small number of dimensions (dimensional approach), by a reference to one or more internally coherent affect programs (basic emotion approach), or by a pattern of features representing the activity in each of the emotion components (componential approach).

Moreover, there is still another important source of incompatibility between the dimensional approach on the one hand, and the basic emotion and componential emotion approach on the other hand, with respect to the terms that belong to the domain of investigation. The dimensional approach works with a much more extensive domain of reference than the two latter approaches. All terms that are studied from the basic emotion and feature profile approaches qualify in principle for the dimensional approach as well (such as joy, anger, sadness, and fear). The reverse, however, is not necessarily true. Many dimensional models make abundant use of terms such as "sleepy," "strong," and "jittery," which are not considered bona fide emotion terms by many researchers. They neither refer to a basic emotion (or a combination of basic emotions), nor to coordinated activity in the different subsystems of the human organism. These terms can be considered feeling terms that describe the general quality of the emotional experience, rather than emotion terms. The three approaches of meaning can only be directly investigated in relationship with one another with respect to the same domain of reference, that is, only on the basis of emotion words that belong to the domain of reference for the three approaches.

Compatibilities. Although the views on the underlying emotion processes are certainly different and in many respects even conflict with one another, the information that these approaches do reveal or can reveal about the meaning of emotion terms is not incompatible. While each of these approaches has its own favorite focus of research (subjective experiences for the dimensional approach, facial and vocal expression for the basic emotion approach, and appraisals for the componential approach), they are not restricted to it. The three approaches do agree, in general, that cognitive (appraisal), psychophysiological (bodily reactions), motivational (action tendencies), expressive (facial, vocal, and gestural expressions), and experiential (feelings) aspects are all phenomena that are to be investigated within the emotion domain. Thus, empirical evidence on how these phenomena are related is relevant across emotion approaches.

Moreover, although the views about what constitutes meaning seem incompatible, the empirical investigation of meaning from these different approaches is perfectly compatible. This has already been demonstrated for the dimensional and basic emotions approaches. In psycholinguistic research, both approaches work on the same data, that is, with perceived similarities between emotion terms. Depending on the theoretical approach, the same data are represented differently. From a dimensional approach, multidimensional scaling is applied, and the emotion words are represented as points in a geometrical space. From the basic emotion approach, cluster analysis is applied and the similarities are represented by hierarchically organized categories. These two representations are perfectly compatible, as they are based on the same similarity data. Moreover, there is a mathematical relationship between both representations, as any set of K points can be represented in a K-1 dimensional space. In line with this relationship, it has been observed that the four replicable basic emotion clusters are systematically differentiated in a three-dimensional space, with the joy cluster being opposed to the other three clusters on the first dimension, the anger cluster being opposed to the fear and sadness cluster on the second dimension, and the sadness cluster being opposed to the anger and fear cluster on the third dimension (e.g., Fontaine, Poortinga, Setiadi, & Markam, 2002; Shaver, Schwartz, Kirson, & O'Conner, 1987; Shaver, Wu, & Schwartz, 1992) (see Figure 2.2 for an example). It has thus already been well established in the empirical literature that the dimensional and the basic emotion approaches offer two complementary representations of meaning in the emotion domain.

Although not yet empirically validated, the study of meaning from the componential emotion approach is perfectly compatible with the study of meaning from the dimensional and the basic emotion approaches. From the componential emotion approach, an emotion term is characterized by a specific feature profile that represents the typical coordinated activity in each of the components for that emotion. These feature profiles also allow computation of similarities between pairs of emotion terms. Profile similarities can be computed and these profile similarities can either be dimensionally represented using multidimensional scaling, or can be categorically represented using hierarchical cluster analysis. Thus, a feature profile representation, a categorical representation, and a dimensional representation of the meaning of emotion terms are just alternative representations of the same data and are compatible.

It can be concluded that although the underlying emotional mechanisms proposed by the three theoretical approaches are substantially different (and in many respects incompatible), the three approaches are compatible when it comes to the meaning of emotion terms, at least for those terms that belong to the more narrow category of emotion terms. The same data can be represented in different ways, depending on the specific emotion approach. This means that the GRID paradigm, which is rooted in the

Average Distance Between Clusters

1.3 1.2 1.1 1.0 0.9 0.8 0.7 0.6 0.5 0.4 0.3

PLE = Pleasantness
ARO = Arousal
DOM = Dominance

Basic And Lower-Order Emotion Clusters

Cluster	PLE	ARO	DOM
Positive Emotion			
passie [passion]: aantrekking [attraction], verlangen [longing], bewondering [admiration], fascinatie [fascination], begeerte [desire]	**1.67** / 1.63	**-0.05** / 0.93	**0.33** / -0.05
verliefdh. [in love]: *liefde [love]*, gevleidh. [flattered], vriendschap [friendship], genegenh. [affection], tederh. [tenderness], geluk [happiness]	1.91	0.27	-0.18
ontroering [moved]: overgave [surrender]	1.21	0.20	-0.36
verbazing [amazement]: moed [courage], *trots [pride]*, verwachting [anticipation]	1.33	0.59	0.67
berusting [resignation]	0.73	-1.07	-0.42
opluchting [relief]: *tevredenh. [satisfaction]*, kalmte [calmness], *vredigh. [peacefulness]*	1.73	-0.85	-0.07
blijheid [joy]: *plezier [pleasure]*, opgetogenh. [elation], uitbundigh. [exuberance], vreugde [joy], opgewekth. [cheerfulness], uitgelatenh. [elation], verheuging [joy], *verrassing [surprise]*, meligh. [corny], *optimisme [optimism]*, enthousiasme [enthusiasm], vrolijkh. [gaiety], hoop [hope], verrukking [delight]	1.77	-0.51	0.89
Anger			
walging [disgust]: agressie [aggression], vijandigh. [hostility], *haat [hate]*, wraakzuchtigh. [vengefulness], afschuw [disgust], *woede [fury]*, afkeer [aversion], nijd [envy], wrok [resentment], afgrijzen [horror], verachting [contempt]	**-1.11** / -1.33	**0.57** / 0.88	**1.11** / 1.18
wroeging [remorse]: belediging [insult], *jaloezie [jealousy]*	-0.72	0.75	0.63
boosheid [anger]: ergernis [irritation], *irritatie [irritation]*, kwaadh. [anger], geprikkeldh. [irritation], ongeduldigh. [impatience]	-0.87	-0.14	1.21
Fear			
angst [fear]: bevreesdh. [apprehension], onzekerh. [uncertainty], *zenuwachtigh. [nervousness]*, bangh. [fear], *nervositeit [nervousness]*, schrik [terror], verwarring [confusion], verontrusting [alarm]	**-0.38** / -0.60	**0.77** / 0.59	**-0.85** / -1.29
schaamte [shame]: schroom [diffidence], *schuld [guilt]*, spijt [regret], berouw [remorse], zondigh. [sinfulness], onderwerping [submission]	-0.11	1.39	-0.49
paniek [panic]: vernedering [humiliation], wantrouwen [suspicion], ontzetting [horror], huivering [shiver]	-1.25	0.80	-0.25
medelijden [compassion]: *bezorgdh. [worry]*, medeleven [sympathy]	0.78	-0.17	-1.33
verlegenheid [shyness]	0.57	0.60	-0.91
Sadness			
bedroefdheid [sadness]: droefh. [grief], treurigh. [sorrow], triesth. [melancholy], *eenzaamh. [loneliness]*, zielígh. [pitifulness], leegte [emptiness], verlorenh. [feel lost], gemis [miss], verdriet [sadness], heimwee [homesickness]	**-0.92** / -0.62	**-0.83** / -1.04	**-0.43** / -1.07
teleurstelling [disappointment]: depressiviteit [depression], *pessimisme [pessimism]*, neerslachtigh. [dejection], somberh. [gloominess], ongelukkigh. [unhappiness], teneergeslagenh. [dejection]	-1.01	-1.08	-0.49
gekwetstheid [hurt]: *gefrustreerdh. [frustration]*, stress [stress], gekweldh. [torment]	-1.24 / -1.10	-0.21 / -0.23	0.01 / -0.81
wanhoop [desperation]: hopeloosh. [hopelessness], *lijden [suffer]*, minderwaardigh. [inferiority], onmacht [impotence]			
het beu zijn [fed up]: onverschilligh. [indifference], verveling [boredom], chagrijn [feel chagrined], humeurigh. [moodiness], ontevredenh. [dissatisfaction], onstemming [put out], ongesteldh. [indisposition]	-0.98	-1.02	0.51

Note. Emotion words printed in italic have a translation-equivalent counterpart in Indonesian.

Figure 2.2 Hierarchical cluster analysis on 120 Dutch emotion terms and cluster position in a three-dimensional space.

Reproduced from Cognition and Emotion 16 (1) Fontaine, J. J. R., Poortinga, Y. H., Setiadi, B., and Suprapti, S. M., Cognitive structure of emotion terms in Indonesia and The Netherlands, pp. 61–86 © 2002, Taylor and Francis Ltd, http://www.tandf.co.uk/journals.

componential emotion approach and which was presented in the previous chapter for studying the meaning of emotion terms, can be directly linked to the meaning of emotion terms from the dimensional and basic emotion approaches. The expected links are presented in the last part of this chapter.

2.5 **The GRID paradigm and the psychological perspective on meaning**

The essence of the GRID paradigm is the feature profile approach to meaning. The GRID paradigm proposes to identify the meaning of emotion terms through the profile of features that describe the emotion process according to the Component Process Model (Scherer, 2005a, 2009c, Chapter 1). The GRID paradigm should not, however, be restricted to identifying the profiles that define the meaning of each emotion term. The GRID paradigm also allows one to take a dimensional and a basic emotion approach at the same time. Compared to these existing psycholinguistic approaches to the meaning of emotion terms, the GRID paradigm makes explicit the very features on the basis of which emotion terms are related to one another. Thus, if the Component Process Model indeed identifies the features that define the psychological meaning of emotion terms, the GRID paradigm makes explicit the basis of the perceived similarities between emotion terms. Under that condition, the profile similarities derived from the component features will be highly comparable with the perceived similarities between emotion terms collected through similarity tasks. It can then be expected that a categorical representation on the basis of the feature-based similarities will also generate the four major clusters of joy, anger, fear, and sadness terms, and that a dimensional representation of these feature-based similarities will also generate the three dimensions of *valence*, *power*, and *arousal*. Thus, although the GRID paradigm is rooted in one particular theoretical model, the Component Process Model, it is useful for all three meaning approaches to emotion words. At the level of meaning, it does not contradict the fundamental assumptions of the other two approaches. Rather, it can help to provide a better understanding regarding the source of the perceived similarities between emotion terms as they have been observed in the dimensional and basic emotion approaches.

Chapter 3

Folk emotion concepts: Lexicalization of emotional experiences across languages and cultures

Anna Ogarkova[1]

3.1 **Introduction**

In the context of the "affective revolution" in human sciences of the last few decades (Davidson et al., 2003), a burgeoning research field has emerged that focuses on lexicalized emotion (i.e., the words labeling emotional experiences). Multiple directions can be singled out in this research domain (cf. Chapters 2 and 4). Among others, many studies address the *contextualized* use of emotion labels, and the ways it varies as a factor of age (Dunn, 2003; Fivush, 1989; Planalp, 1999), gender (Cervantes & Callanan, 1998), cultural background (Cervantes, 2002), socioeconomic status (Burger & Miller, 1999), race (Weathers et al., 2002), or language proficiency (Dewaele & Pavlenko, 2002). Others use emotion words as *stimuli* and investigate how they are processed as regards the access to word meaning, contextual integration, or memory encoding (Jay & Janschewitz, 2007; Kissler et al., 2006).

The present chapter aims to overview a distinct research field in this area—the one where emotion words in various languages are thought to be referents of culture-embedded cognitive categories, or *"folk" emotion concepts*. The key premise here is that language plays an important role in establishing categories, both culturally and developmentally (Neisser, 1987: vii), and that the ways in which emotions are represented in language can provide an insight on emotion conceptualization, categorization, and even experience in different cultural groups.

This perspective can be broadly termed as "cognitive" because it assumes that the relationship between the emotional experiences people have, on the one hand, and (arbitrary) linguistic signs (emotion words), on the other hand, is not purely referential, so that no inference can be drawn from each of the areas (Kanner, 1931: 24; Watson, 2004). Instead, it is assumed that not only affective experiences are constitutive for the meaning of emotion words labeling those experiences in a language, but also that the emotion vocabulary of a language provides its speakers with the default ways of categorizing emotional reality (Harré, 1986; Soriano & Ogarkova, 2009).

Two main factors contributed to the emergence of this perspective on emotion lexis. The first is the dissatisfaction among cultural researchers with the skepticism about the relevance of language evidence for the study of emotions *per se*. In philosophy, this skepticism includes arguments against the "linguistic thesis," that is, the one-to-one correspondence between linguistic forms and

[1] Correspondence concerning this chapter should be addressed to Anna Ogarkova, Swiss Center for the Affective Sciences, 7 Rue des Battoirs, CH-1205, Geneva, Switzerland, e-mail: Anna.Ogarkova@unige.ch

the ways in which such phenomena ought to be classified (Wollheim, 1999: 20), or claims that "ordinary language is not a good place to look if one wants to develop a theory of feeling" (Charland, 1995: 296). In anthropology, the "theory of resonance" is formulated (Wikan, 1992), which posits it is insufficient to consider indigenous emotion lexicons to understand the specific ways of feeling in local communities. In social sciences, strong claims are made that language "is not suited to represent emotional experiences at all" (Halberstadt, 2005: 19), and that the diverse vocabularies of emotion developed in many societies are wrong about the feelings they purport to describe (Needham, 1981: 23, quoted in Lutz, 1986: 295).

The second factor is the scholarly opposition to the body of research where emotion words (e.g., English *anger*[2], *fear, sadness*, or *pride*), as well as generic terms (e.g., English *emotion, feeling, sentiment*, or *affect*) have undergone the semantic process of terminologization (Weinreich, 1962: 149; Werner, 1965), and are used in reference to *scientific*, rather than *culturally-embedded*, or "experience-near" (Geertz, 1984) concepts. As a result, both generic labels and the emotion terms proper are assumed to be devoid of culture- and language-specific connotations and are viewed upon as classical concepts (susceptible to cross-culturally viable definition). This terminological use of emotion labels has been found unsatisfactory by anthropologists and linguists (Lutz, 1985: 38–39; Wierzbicka, 1999b, 2009; but see Ekman, 2003; Griffiths, 1997) who assert that English words like *fear* or *anger* refer to essentially American ethnopsychological concepts and cannot thus be used as culture-free analytical tools in analyses of any disciplinary orientation.

The aim of this chapter is two-fold. Firstly, we aim to briefly outline the main theoretical approaches to the relationship between emotion words, concepts, and experiences, specifically through highlighting the degree of significance ascribed by them to language in emotion conceptualization and categorization (see Section 3.2). The second goal is to overview the available empirical evidence on emotion lexicalization in the light of both similarities and differences of how emotional experiences are labeled in different languages (see Section 3.3). The chapter concludes with the discussion of the implications of the overviewed evidence for large-scale cross-cultural research on emotion lexis undertaken with the GRID approach presented in this volume (see Section 3.4).

3.2 **Theoretical approaches to emotional experiences, concepts, and words**

While all studies within the "cognitive" view on emotion lexis assume the existence of an interrelationship between the experiential, the conceptual, and the linguistic in the emotion domain, there is considerable variation in how this interrelationship is theorized. Most of this variation lies along the continuum of views about the extent to which language is thought to be involved in human cognition (Carruthers, 2008; Gleitman & Parafragou, 2005). Overall, two major positions—each including studies of various disciplinary orientations—can be discerned. On the one hand, there is a view that language determines, or guides emotion conceptualization (and sometimes even experience); on the other hand, there is a view that the emotional experiences and their (pre-linguistic) conceptualizations determine, or guide lexicalization. The latter position typically focuses on the role of culture.

In its extreme formulation, the former opinion can be illustrated by a radical (and largely theoretical rather than empirical) position labeled by some as the "nominalist" view (Fernandez-Dols

---

[2] Throughout this paper, italics (*anger*) will be used for lexemes, inverted commas ('anger') will be used for emotion categories and concepts, no marks (anger) will be used to refer to emotional experiences.

et al., 2001: 123). Here, the crucial role that language plays in creating conceptual categories is emphasized, and the emotion concepts are thought to derive from the existence of emotion words, rather than from emotional experiences. This is believed to be so because the states to which emotion words point to are so highly variable that they lack universal psychological reality and distinctiveness. Thus, it is only due to emotion words used with reference to certain (vaguely similar) psychological events that distinct emotion categories emerge.

Similar views—often loosely referred to as "strong Whorfian"—assert that emotion words do not only reflect, but also guide and even determine emotion perception, recognition, conceptualization, categorization, and experience. In semantics, linguistic determinism has been advocated by the *Natural Semantic Metalanguage* (henceforth NSM) theorist Anna Wierzbicka, who, ever since the publication of *Semantic Primitives* (1972), has insisted that emotion vocabularies—the lexical "grids" provided by natural languages—not only impose certain constraints on classifying the emotions, but also can bias the speakers to interpret emotional experiences through the prism of a particular language (Wierzbicka, 1992c: 456, 1995b: 236, 1999b: 31).

In psychology, deterministic views have been articulated in the "*language-as-context*" hypothesis and *the conceptual act model* (Barrett, 2006a, 2006b, 2009; Barrett et al., 2007). Deriving from the evidence that emotion terms are involved in disambiguation of facial affect perception (Barrett et al., 2007), the proposal is that emotion words serve as anchors for emotion concepts acquisition through infancy and childhood (Lindquist & Barrett, 2008). Moreover, "emotion language, or cognitive categories it expresses, plays a role in creating conscious emotional experience" (Barrett & Russell, 1999: 13). Thus, having an emotional experience is seen as conditional on one's conceptualization of this experience as an instance of emotion (Barrett, 2006a, b; Lindquist & Barrett, 2008). This categorization happens as a result of communal (social and cultural) agreement to parse the mental activity in a specific way, allowing thus for cross-cultural differences in how different societies "carve up" their affective spaces. Similarly to the "nominalist" view, the conceptual act model submits that no emotion label has a stable referent. Instead, it is thought to refer to a wide range of experiential states, and the variance of experiential states to which one and the same emotion word refers to is not substantially lower than the variability between the states labeled by different emotion words (Barrett, 2009: 1288). Therefore, "emotion words serve as 'conceptual glue' that holds a category together. Without words, these categories would not exist" (Barrett, 2009: 1292).

Deterministic views have also been voiced in linguistic anthropology (e.g., Wilce, 2009) where (broadly conceived) emotion language is deemed to not only have an impact on emotion concepts, but also to exert influence on emotional experiences themselves: "more than straightforwardly revealing psychological processes, [. . .] genres of so-called emotional expression help *constitute* social understandings and apparently *internal processes*" (Wilce, 2009: 5; emphasis added).

A common (though not always explicitly formulated) assumption in the "language-first" view is that the absence of an emotion label in the lexicon of a language might preclude its speakers from entertaining the "lacunal" emotion concept. Without straightforwardly equating the lexical lacunae with the conceptual ones (criticized in anthropology as a "nominalistic fallacy," see Goodie, 2002, cf. Caplan, 1992; Carruthers, 2008; Paradis, 1997), culture researchers assert however that the lexical gaps can limit speakers' power to manipulate the respective concepts, or impede the elaboration of these concepts in oral and written genres of a culture (Gordon, 2004, 2005; Goodie, 2002: 24).

In sum, "language-first" approaches assume the existence of a causal link going from language to the conceptualization: the way people think is strongly biased by the languages (and lexicons) they have. The second group of approaches reverses the causal arrow between lexicalization and conceptualization: by contrast, it is the cultural architecture of a lingual community (feeling rules, values, norms, salient concepts, focal concerns) that is assumed to drive lexicalization and have both qualitative and quantitative impact on the lexical resources of a language (Nida, 1958; Gordon, 2004, 2005). Said plainly, this is a "culture-first," rather than a "language-first" position.

In the culture-first view, the cultural elaboration of an emotion as focal or, alternatively, as "muted" (cf. Levy, 1973, 1982 on *hyper-* and *hypocognition*) is thought to underlie the ubiquitous lexicalization of some emotion concepts, like "shame" in Chinese (Ho et al., 2004; Li et al., 2004), or, conversely, the scarce lexicalization of others, like "sadness" and "guilt" in the Tahitians (Levy, 1982), or "depression" and "anxiety" in Yoruba and Chinese (Jadhav, 1996; Leff, 1973). Thus, the vocabulary relating to the focus of a culture is assumed to be directly proportionate to its cultural relevance (Nida, 1958)[3].

The language-first and culture-first approaches are not incompatible but rather reflect a different focus. Both approaches submit that linguistic representations are reliable signposts to conceptual categories. For example, the fact that an emotion word is recorded in dictionaries of a language is taken to provide definite evidence about the presence of the respective emotion category in the cultural group (Hupka et al., 1999).

Another premise shared by both approaches is that the properties of emotion labels can serve as evidence about the properties of the respective emotion concepts. For example, the finding that most frequently used emotion terms from different historical periods and across countries are the labels for the emotions known in the literature as "basic" (Ekman, 1999; Ortony & Turner, 1990; Plutchik, 1980a) is considered to support the claim on the "basicness" of the emotions referred to by these words (Delgado, 2007).

In social psychology, two main methodological frameworks based on this approximation of the semantic with the conceptual have evolved. The first is the *prototype approach* to emotion lexicons (Fehr & Russell, 1984; Shaver et al., 1987, 1992, 2001, see also 3.1). It is based on the assumption that the outcomes of emotion conceptualization and categorization (that could inform on the place of an emotion concept in the domain hierarchy) are accessible through elicitation of emotion labels from native speakers and testable through various categorization tasks on these words (Iaccino, 1989; Niedenthal et al., 2004).

The second methodological framework is the *dimensional approach* (see Chapters 2 and 7), which derives from the cross-culturally validated empirical research on the structure of connotation underlying various semantic domains in natural languages (Osgood et al., 1957). The Osgoodian dimensions—Evaluation/Valence, Potency/Power, and Activity/Arousal—instantiate three deemed universal types of evaluation: good vs bad, strong vs weak, and active vs passive. Unlike the studies on the connotative meanings of words[4], however, the dimensional models for the emotions frequently imply that the dimensions do not only capture the evaluation of the verbal stimuli (emotion *words*), but also represent the evaluative attitudes to emotion *concepts* or, in several interpretations, also capture the intrinsic qualities of emotional *experiences* themselves.

---

[3] The centrality of an emotional concept reflected in its more extensive lexicalization does not necessarily entail that this emotion is frequently experienced in the society where it is 'hypercognized'. Rather, an emotion could be 'hypercognized' by a cultural group because it is greatly feared (Levy 1983; cf. Solomon 2003: 139).

[4] Many studies replicated a similar set of dimensions with emotional stimuli other than words, including pictures (Remington et al. 2000), affective scripts (Panayiotou 2008), or autobiographical memories cued by emotions (Rubin & Talarico 2009). The same, or similar dimensions emerge when one uses extensive language databases (Samsonovich & Ascoli 2007), corpora (Sinclair 1991; Stubbs 2001), or segments of texts longer than a word, as in the phenomenon of the 'semantic prosody' (Partington 1998). Finally, affective dimensions have also been shown to drive lexical choice in context (Corrigan 2007).

For example, Ekman's (1955) study of 23 Swedish emotion words explicitly declares to explore "the degrees of qualitative differences between the emotional *states* represented by the stimulus words" (1955: 280; emphasis added). Likewise, the circumplex model (Barrett & Russell, 1999; Russell, 1980, 2003) proposes that "the descriptive structure of affect represents *both* language and conscious affective experience" (Barrett & Russell, 1999: 13, emphasis added), and that the dimensions are the "core processes" that constitute the primitive basis of an emotional experience.

In summary, four key premises underlie the cognitive perspective on emotion lexis discussed above. The first is the assumption that the very fact of lexicalization of an emotional experience points at the existence of the respective concept in the conceptual system of people speaking that language. Secondly, although concessions are made that language speakers can have all kinds of emotional experiences (and entertain emotion concepts without lexical designations in their languages), emotion lexicons are assumed to offer default matrices for conceptualization, categorization, and interpretation of emotions in respective cultural groups. Thirdly, the qualitative and quantitative differences in emotion lexicalization in different languages reflect culture-motivated differences in feeling rules, values, norms, salient concepts and concerns of the cultural groups at stake. The fourth and final premise is methodological: in the cognitive perspective on emotion lexis, linguistic evidence—both experimental (e.g., categorization tasks with language speakers), and analytical (e.g., analyses of emotion word use in corpora)—is assumed to provide a viable access to "folk" emotion conceptualization.

3.3 Emotion lexicalization across languages and cultures

In this section, we will give an overview of the state-of-the-art evidence on the similarities and the divergences in emotion lexicalization in different languages. On the cognitive approach to emotion lexis presented above, both types of evidence can highlight both the common and the specific aspects of how emotions are conceptualized across cultures.

Cross-lingual similarities in the linguistic representation of emotions

There are five general loci of similarities in how emotions are lexicalized in different languages. Firstly, although the differences in the size of emotion vocabularies are pronounced (Pavlenko, 2005; Russell, 1991a; Soriano & Ogarkova, 2009), the vast majority of languages investigated to date are reported to have specific words or expressions to name what would be labeled as "emotional states" in academic English. One of the most representative studies (Hupka et al., 1999) found dictionary translations of English emotion terms in 64 languages that represent 60 major geographical and linguistic groupings of the world's languages, complemented with four languages with fewer than one million speakers (Dehu, Mazahua, Toaripi, and Walpiri). That every world language would have "emotion terms" (i.e., terms for cognitively-based feelings) has been formulated as a working hypothesis for a cross-lingual emotional universal (Wierzbicka, 1999b: 36), and has been supported by NSM research on five language families, including Indo-European (e.g., Polish, Spanish, Russian, Portuguese), African (e.g., Hebrew and Amharic), Austronesian (e.g., Melayu-Papua, Malay, Filipino, Alamblak), Native American (Cree), and Sino-Tibetan (e.g., Chinese).

The second area of cross-lingual similarity in emotion lexicalization relates to specific emotion categories. The study by Hupka and associates (1999) looked into a generalized sequence of how emotion categories emerge in language and established that "anger" is the first emotion category to evolve in any language that has emotion words, followed by "shame/guilt" (Hupka et al., 1999). This finding is also corroborated by NSM research: relying on the evidence from a wide array of languages, Wierzbicka hypothesizes that all languages have words overlapping (though not identical) in meaning with the English words *angry, ashamed*, and *afraid* (Wierzbicka, 1999b: 36). Agreeably, our own inquiry into which emotional experiences are lexicalized in the languages with the smallest emotion vocabularies—Chewong, Fante, and Dagbani—suggests that they overlap in lexicalizing four emotional experiences, and these words are the glosses of English *anger, fear/ fright, shame/disgrace*, and *jealousy/envy* (see Table 3.1).

The third cross-lingual similarity in emotion lexicalization is that, alongside with the abstract psychological language (i.e., emotion words), in a huge variety of languages emotions can be represented via somatic sensation expressions and somatic metaphors (Mumford, 1993, see also "Partial semantic overlap" in Section 3.3), that is, body-part phrases referring to both literal and imaginary processes taking place inside, or with the body (e.g., English *she blushed, his hair stood on his head*, or *his heart sank*) (cf. Russo, 2010; Sharifian et al., 2008 for overviews). With very few exceptions (e.g., Michelson, 2002), the possibility to codify emotions in somatic terms is reported for Arabic (Seidensticker, 1992), Basque (Ibarretxe-Antunano, 2008), Chinese (Ye, 2002; Yu, 2002), Chocktaw (Mithun, 1984), Dholuo (Reh, 1998), Estonian (Vainik, 2007), Hebrew (Kuzar & Kidron, 2002), Hmong (Jaisser, 1990), Indonesian (Siahaan, 2007), Irianese and Papua New Guinean languages (McElhanon, 1977), Japanese (Hasada, 2002; Kuwabara & Smith, 2007), Ponorogo Javanese (Weiss, 1977), Kambera (Klamer, 1998), Kaytetye (Turpin, 2002), Kuot (Lindström, 2002), Korean

Table 3.1 Chewong, Fante, and Dagbani emotion words

Chewong	Fante	Dagbani	English gloss
Chan	Ebufo	Suli/Suhiyigsili	anger
Hentugn	Akomatu	Dhem	fear/fright
Lidya	Aniwu	Anyimguase	shame/disgrace
Meseg	Ahowoyaw	Jelinsi Nyuli	jealousy/envy
Hanrodn	–	–	proud
Punmen	–	–	like
Osayagn	–	–	fond of
–	Ayemhyehye	Ninimooi	worry/anxiety
–	Anika	Nyagsim	joy/contentment
–	Yawdzi	Suhisajingu	sorrow/sadness
–	Ahobo	–	surprise
–	Anyito	–	guilty/ashamed
–	Ahobrase	–	humility
–	Brɛ	–	tired, weiry
–	Basa	–	agitated, irritable
–	Asomdwee	Suhidoo	peace
–	Anibre	–	determined/jealous
–	–	Suhipelli	happiness
–	–	Bomma Nyuli	admiration/positive envy

Note: summarized from Howell, 1981: 133–43 and Dzokoto & Okazaki, 2006: 128–9.

(Kyung-Joo Yoon, 2008), Malay (Goddard, 2001; Oey, 1990), Old Koromu (Priestley, 2002), Selepet (McElhanon & McElhanon, 1970), Thaayorre (Gaby, 2008), Thai (Diller & Juntanamalaga, 1990), Tunisian Arabic (Maalej, 2004), Wolof (Becher, 2003; Bondeelle, 2011), and Zulu (Taylor & Mbense, 1998). The same tendency is recorded for ancient languages, such as Gothic, old Hebrew, old Greek, and Latin (Chamberlain, 1895; Mumford, 1993). Agreeably, the contention that, in all languages, people can describe their emotions using both literal and metaphoric body-part expressions has been put forward as a putative universal emotion (Wierzbicka, 1999b: 36).

Fourthly, reports on crosslingual similarity in the emotion domains come from the dimensional studies. Here, comparable (although not identical, see "Emotions as internal states vs relational phenomena" and "Aspects of variation in emotion term semantics" in Section 3.3) dimensions are reported to emerge in the analysis of emotion vocabularies in over twenty languages, including, among others, Swedish (Ekman, 1955), Norwegian (Block, 1957), Hebrew (Fillenbaum & Rapoport, 1971), Woleaian spoken by the Ifaluk (Lutz, 1982), German (Abele-Brehm & Brehm, 1986; Gehm & Scherer, 1988), English, Spanish, Vietnamese, Greek, Haitian Creole, Hong Kong Chinese (Herrmann & Raybeck, 1981), Gujarati, Croatian, Japanese (Moore et al., 1999; Romney et al., 1997; Russell, 1980; Russell & Sato, 1995), Polish and Japanese (Russell, 1980), English, French, and Dutch (Fontaine et al., 2007), Italian, French, Catalan, Portuguese, and Romanian (Galati et al., 2008).

Finally, the entirety of the prototype approach studies shows that comparable (but see "Aspects of variation in emotion term semantics" in Section 3.3) emotion categories are found at the basic level of categorization (Rosch, 1978) in typologically distant languages, such as English (Fehr & Russell, 1984; Shaver et al., 1987), French (Niedenthal et al., 2004), Tagalog (Church et al., 1998), Samoan (Gerber, 1985), Bahasa Indonesia (Shaver et al., 2001), Basque (Alonso-Arbiol et al., 2006), Woleaian (Lutz, 1982), Chinese (Shaver et al., 1992; Li et al., 2004), Italian (Galli & Zammuner, 2006; Zammuner, 1998), Czech (Slaměník & Hurychová, 2006), Estonian (Vainik, 2004), Turkish (Smith & Smith, 1995), and Palauan (Smith & Tkel-Sbal, 1995).

Five types of similarities outlined above are subject to both quantitative and qualitative limitations. Quantitatively, while almost 7 thousand languages (Crystal, 1997; Ethnologue) have been cataloged in the world (of which 82% are spoken by fewer than 100 thousand people and 8% are nearly extinct), the best exemplars of research on lexical universals consider the evidence from a maximum of 500 languages, and concerns have been voiced about the representativeness of any specific selection (Evans & Levinson, 2009). In emotion research proper, the widest selection of languages considered within a single study is 64 (Hupka et al., 1999).

Qualitatively, the similarities outlined above do not inform on two important issues. The first one relates to the variation in emotion lexicalization at *the generic level*, where the pertinent questions are whether "emotion" emerges as a cross-linguistically stable category that can serve as a common denominator on which languages can be compared, what lexical items qualify as "emotion words" in different languages, and what these divergences tell about the indigenous ways to conceptualize emotions. The second issue relates to the variation at the *term level*, where the central questions are how specific emotion words compare across languages, whether satisfactory translational correlates can be found for comparative analyses, and what aspects contribute most to variation in emotion term semantics. Relevant evidence on these two issues will now be overviewed in more detail.

Variation at the generic level: "emotion" as a non-universal cognitive category

Although in scientific discourse the cognates of the English word *emotion* (e.g., French *émotion*, Italian *emozione*, or Spanish *emoción*) are generally used in a sense "modeled on that of the English *emotion*" (Wierzbicka, 1995a: 22), in ordinary use, these superordinate terms are argued to have somewhat different meanings compared to the English term (Wierzbicka, 1995a: 22). In this context, an even more pronounced divergence between non-Western indigenous terms and English *emotion* can reasonably be expected.

Indeed, research in anthropology, linguistics, and cross-cultural psychology shows that not all languages classify the words to denote emotional experiences into a distinct category of experiential states. Firstly, there is evidence that some languages lack a superordinate term for emotional experiences, which is the case of Dagbani (Dzokoto & Okazaki, 2006), Tahitians (Levy, 1973), Bimin-Kuskusmin (Poole, 1985), Gidjingali (Hiatt, 1978), and Chewong (Howell, 1981).

Secondly, in languages where superordinate terms are available, these terms are qualitatively different from the English word *emotion*. On the one hand, the superordinate terms can be narrower in their referential scope than English *emotion*, so that more than one term is needed to capture all relevant words. This is the case of Turkish and Indonesian where several terms are used to speak generically about emotional states: three in Turkish – *duygu* "feeling," *heyecan* "excitement, enthusiasm," and *his* "feeling" (Smith & Smith, 1995: 105), and two in Indonesian –*perasaan hati* "feelings of the heart"[5] and *emosi* "(negative) emotions" (Beatty, 2005; Heider, 1991; Shaver et al., 2001).

On the other hand, generic-level affect terms in non-Western languages can have a wider referential scope than English *emotion* and thus apply to the states that do not normally qualify as affective in English. For instance, indigenous categories roughly equivalent to English *emotion* can embrace both emotion terms and the lexemes denoting character traits and affective-cognitive dispositions. For example, alongside the emotions words proper, the Japanese category of *jodo* "emotion" includes also the equivalents of English *considerate, motivated, lucky*, and *calculating* (Matsuyama et al., 1978). In other languages, emotion words fall into one category with the labels for the physiologic, or somatic states, such as hunger or thirst, as in the Fante and Anlo indigenous categories of *atsinka* and *seselelame* (Dzokoto & Okazaki, 2006; Geurts, 2002). Thirdly, in several languages emotion words appear to be grouped together with the words denoting mental states, as in the Balinese category *keneh* "feeling-thought" (Wikan, 1992: 463), the Shuar category *anentaimia* (Boster, 2005), or the Ifalukian category *nunuwan* (Lutz, 1985: 17). As a result, emotion vocabularies in these languages include words with cognition, rather than affect, as their referential focus, such as, for instance, Woleaian *filengaw* "discomfort/indecision," *komayaya* "incapability," or *yeyewal* "indecision/doubt" (Lutz, 1982: 116).

Obviously, these differences in the generic-level labeling of emotional experiences have an impact on what language items qualify as "emotion words" in various languages. In English, several attempts to formulate the criteria for "emotion terms" have been made. Wallace and Carson (1973) suggested using the words that would fit both syntactic contexts of "*He feels X*" and "*He has a feeling of X*" (so that both *sad* and *sadness* qualify as emotion terms). Clore et al. (1987) argued that an emotion word has to express emotions in two contexts, *feeling X* and *being X* (so that, e.g., *sad* qualifies as an emotion word but *ignored* does not). A most influential and common approach however is the one suggested by Ortony and associates (1987, cf. Church et al., 1998) where the following criteria were formulated: (1) the terms should refer to internal and mental conditions; (2) they should describe a momentary state; (3) they should have affect as opposed to behavior or

---

[5] More precisely, *perasaan hati* is uncommon compound of *rasa*, meaning 'feeling-tone', and *hati*, literally meaning 'liver' (the seat of emotions) (Beatty 2005: 28). Goddard (2001: 170) argues that *perasaan hati* 'designates feelings that are relatively longstanding, involve evaluation, and are directed at other people (as opposed to transient or impersonal feelings such as *terkejut* 'being startled' and *takut* 'fear')'.

cognition as a predominant (rather than incidental) referential focus. With these criteria as the reference point, the evidence on several alternative ways to conceptualize emotions in non-Western cultures will now be overviewed.

Emotions as internal states vs relational phenomena

Rich ethnographic literature reports that in many non-Western cultures – for example, Ifaluk (Lutz, 1986), Balinese (Wikan, 1990), Fula (Riesman, 1977), Ilongot (Rosaldo, 1980), Kaluli (Schieffelin, 1985), Pintupi (Myers, 1979), Samoan (Gerber, 1975, 1985), and A'ara (White, 1978, 1980) – emotions are seen as relational phenomena, embedded in social situations and taking place between people rather than "inside" them. As a result, emotion words in those cultures function as "statements about the relationship between a person and an event (particularly involving another person), rather than as statements about one's introspection on one's internal states" (Lutz, 1986: 267). Thus, the *types of emotion-eliciting events* are a central factor involved in emotion categorization in those cultures (see also "Aspects of variation in emotion term semantics" in Section 3.3).

A classical example of this alternative emotion conceptualization comes from the hierarchical clustering study of the emotion words in the Woleaian language spoken by the Ifaluk (Lutz, 1982). This study shows that Ifalukian affect-related vocabulary does not cluster into groups of near-synonymous items around a prototype word (like English *anger* or *fear*), but forms clusters of words denoting states elicited by similar *types of situations*, such as those of good fortune, danger, human error, connection/loss, or inability (Lutz, 1982). Therefore, *metagu* "fear/anxiety," *lugumet* "discomfort/guilt," and *ma* "shame/embarrassment" cluster together because all of them happen in situations "when one must go someplace where respectful behavior is required" (Ibid: 116).

Comparable findings come from a study on emotion categorization in Turkish (Smith & Smith, 1995): despite explicit discouragement in a free-listing task, Turkish participants listed *situations* as instances of "emotion" nearly as frequently (48%) as names for emotional states proper, and 80% of the participants used a situation label at least once. This suggests that the Turkish perceive emotions "holistically, such that they do not consider subjective states independent of the situations that elicit them or the behaviors that result" (Ibid: 110).

Conceptualizing emotions as situation-embedded phenomena rather than as inner states is also captured by the dimensional studies. Whereas in the Western languages the distinction between positive and negative emotions concerns primarily the differences in the perceived (un)pleasantness of a particular emotional experience ("simple hedonic tone," see Davitz, 1969; Russell, 2003), in Ifalukians this contrast pertains to the differences in the evaluation of the *consequences of the emotion-eliciting situations* (Lutz, 1982: 124). Likewise, for Samoans the pleasantness dimension sets apart "socially virtuous" and "socially non-virtuous" emotions, which might not be "pleasurable" in the Western sense, as they require submissiveness: for example, *lotomama* "a socially approved feeling of happy passivity and willingness to agree with the desires of others" (Gerber, 1985).

Emotions as somatic vs psychological states

Another alternative type of emotion conceptualization stems from the observations that many non-Western languages do not differentiate between emotion and bodily sensation to the same extent that the Western languages do. On the one hand, multiple studies in cross-cultural psychiatry conclude that patients from non-Western cultures tend to "somatize" their emotions, while Western patients tend to "psychologize" them (Mumford, 1993). Thus, the emotional and the somatic appear to be less differentiated in China (Kleinman & Kleinman, 1985; Tsai et al., 2004; Tung, 1994), Kenya and Tanzania (Ice & Yogo, 2005; Kaaya et al., 2002; Pike & Young, 2002), India (Saxena et al., 1988), and Saudi Arabia (Racy, 1980; see also Mumford, 1993 for an overview).

On the other hand, anthropologists and linguists report a higher representation of somatic expressions in the emotion vocabularies of African languages (e.g., Ameka, 2002; Dzokoto & Okazaki, 2006; Dzokoto & Adams, 2007; Geurts, 2002; Nida, 1958; Taylor & Mbense, 1998), as well as in the languages of several Asian and indigenous South and Central American cultures, such as Chewong (Howell, 1981: 139), Malay (Goddard, 2001: 167), Twaka Indians (Chamberlain, 1895: 590), and Tiribi Indians (Gatchet, 1894: 217).

Although the tendency to codify emotions in somatic terms may well be a universal feature of the majority of the world's cultures (as discussed in "Cross-lingual similarities in the linguistic representation of emotions" in Section 3.3), three aspects of cross-lingual variation can nevertheless be singled out.

Firstly, languages differ in the extent to which the connection between the affective and the somatic is elaborated and nuanced. While languages have been classified into predominantly *cardiocentric* (e.g., Germanic and Romance languages, Japanese, Hausa), where the heart is the "seat" of emotions (Batic, 2011; Ikegami, 2008; Niemeier, 1997, 2008; Occhi, 2008; Pérez, 2008), and *abdomen-centric*, where emotions are figuratively localized in either the belly/guts (as in Nigerian English, Tahitian, Thaayorre, and Tigre; see Bauer, 1973; Gaby, 2008; Lemaître, 1995; Littmann & Hoeffner, 1962) or the liver (as in Malay and Kambera; see Goddard, 2001; Klamer, 1998; Siahaan, 2008), some languages make fairly nuanced associations between specific body parts and specific emotions. For example, in Wolof, an African language spoken in Senegal, heart (*xol*) is the seat of grief, anger, joy, and jealousy (e.g., *dafa xett xolam* "it pierced his heart," it made him jealous), mind (*xel*) is the seat of contentment, worry, and disappointment (e.g., *suma xel bi tilim* "my mind is dirty," I am disappointed), body (*yaram*) is the seat of sadness and pity (e.g., *suma yaram bi yepp dee* "my whole body died," I am sad), and skin (*der*) is associated with shame (e.g., *danga yàq suma der* "you destroyed my skin," you made me feel ashamed) (Becher, 2003: 13). Likewise, while all emotions (both positive and negative) are associated with the heart (*bihotz*) in Basque, only negative emotions (e.g., *gibelbeldur* "distrust," *gibelgogo* "aversion," or *gibelondo* "disdain") are associated with the liver (*gibel*) in this language (Ibarretxe-Antuñano, 2008).

Secondly, languages differ quantitatively in *the proportion of the body-part phrases in their emotion vocabularies*, which overall signals the salience of embodied imagery in language representation of emotions. Here, in contrast to English (a cardiocentric language) where *heart*-imagery is less frequent than literal emotion denominations (Geeraerts & Gevaert, 2008), in Anlo-Ewe, Ewe, Anuak, Fante, Dagbani, as well as in Anuak and Niasan, somatic expressions constitute around a half of the emotion vocabularies (Beatty, 2005; Dzokoto & Okazaki, 2006; Nida, 1958: 286). For example, in Wolof one literal rendering of "anger" (*dafa mer* "she is angry") is paralleled by at least five body-part phrases that label "anger" experiences of various shades of intensity, ranging from *sama xol bi neexul* "my heart is not sweet" to *sama xol bi fuur* "my heart is boiling" (Becher, 2003: 15).

Thirdly and most importantly, languages differ in the *possibility to lexicalize emotions in abstract psychological language as compared to codifying them somatically*. While in many Western languages figurative body-part expressions (e.g., *it made my blood boil*) exist in parallel to literal renderings (e.g., *anger* or *fury*), in many indigenous languages no such possibility has been attested. McPherson and Prokhorov (2011: 39–40) note the near-total absence of emotion-specific vocabulary in nine Dogon languages of Mali where emotions are encoded by idiomatic expressions containing the word "liver." Likewise, in Wolof, both "sadness" and "disappointment" can exclusively be codified through body-part phrasals—*dafa tilimal suma xel* "my mind is dirty" and *suma yaram bi yepp dee* "my whole body died," respectively (Becher, 2003: 13–14). A pidginized term *bel i-nogut*, "belly no good" is the only recorded item to mean "disappointment" in Neo-Melanesian (Hupka et al., 1999: 250); *sānītlwīne* "bad-hearted he-is" is the only gloss for *angry* in the Kootenay Indian language of British Columbia (Chamberlain, 1895: 394). Lacking a one-word label for *guilt*, Niasans use a somatic metaphor *itegu dödögu* "my heart is pressed/nagged" instead (Beatty, 2005: 24).

Taken together, these findings suggest that somatic expressions tend to be a basic mode of emotion labeling in many non-Western languages. This, from the cognitive perspective on emotion lexis, can be assumed to have impact on how emotions are conceptualized in respective cultural groups. Being substituted by a body-part term and appearing only as a possessor attributed to this body-part, people undergoing emotional experiences are seen as inactive participants in the emotional process. In other words, emotions are conceptualized as processes upon which an experiencer has no, or very little control (cf. Becher, 2003; Matisoff, 1986). Furthermore, since somatic metaphors are intrinsically linked with literal expressions conveying somatic sensations (cf. Mumford, 1993), the evidence overviewed above also suggests that somatic symptoms are a salient aspect in emotion term semantics (see "Aspects of variation in emotion term semantics" in Section 3.3).

Variation at the term level: commensurability of specific emotion words

Alongside with the generic-level differences in emotion labeling outlined in previous sections, considerable cross-lingual variance is also observed at the word level, that is, in the comparisons of deemed equivalent, or comparable words in different languages.

The very concept of semantic equivalence resides on a fairly straightforward idea that two emotion words should share the same/very similar meaning to be considered equivalent. Clearly, the way meaning is defined largely depends on the discipline: some of the psychological approaches assume that the meaning of an emotion word can be derived from the position that word takes on a set of evaluative dimensions; others assess semantic similarity through a degree to which an emotion term shares in the prototypical characteristics pertinent to a specific emotion category. In linguistics, semantic equivalence requires a significant overlap in both the referential and the connotative aspects (Besnier, 1990), or in the referential, the affective and the social (cf. Lyons, 1977). This latter convergence presupposes that the two compared items are used in the same social contexts.

Regardless of a specific approach, however, semantic equivalence is never taken to be an absolute value. Agreeably with a common view that no word can ever mean the same in two different utterances (Ariel, 2002) or for two different speakers (see Chapter 4.), the lack of exact correspondences between comparable words in different languages is one of the fundamental presuppositions in most semantic analyses (Nida, 1958). So, our discussion will be henceforth limited to considering various types of (sometimes very) relative semantic overlap between translation correlates in different languages.

Lexical lacunae

An extreme case of the lack of equivalence at the level of specific emotions words comes from the rich literature on lexical lacunae. With few exceptions (e.g., Beatty, 2005), English is a most frequent language used in comparative work, therefore two types of findings are most common: (1) English terms are said to not have one-word equivalents in other languages; (2) other languages are attributed "culture-specific" terms that do not have one-word correlates in English.

Examples of the former include Tahitians lacking a word equivalent to English *sadness* (Levy, 1973), Nyinba lacking a word for *love* (in its Western sense of "romantic love," Levine, 1988), Fante and Dagbani not lexicalizing *loneliness* (Dzokoto & Okazaki, 2006), or Greek, Arabic, and Russian having no satisfactory correlate of *frustration* (Panayiotou, 2004a; Pavlenko, 2008; Russell, 1991a). Particularly exuberant reports are available for the lack of correlates of English *guilt* and *depression*. Among the languages reported not to lexicalize *guilt* are Sinhala (Obeyesekere, 1981), llongot (Rosaldo, 1984), Pintupi (Morice, 1978), Samoan (Gerber, 1975), and Niasan (Beatty, 2005). The data from Hupka and associates' (1999) study show that in 32, that is, a half of the languages studied, no equivalent of English *guilt* is recorded. Likewise, English *depression* has no equivalents in several indigenous Indian languages of North America (Termansen & Ryan, 1970), Malay (Resner & Hartog, 1970), Chinese (Chan, 1990; Tseng & Hsu, 1969), Eskimo (Leff, 1973), Fulani (Riesman, 1977), Kaluli (Schieffelin, 1985), and Xhosa (Cheetham & Cheetham, 1976), as well as in 35 other languages from Hupka et al.'s study (1999).

Conversely, many languages are reported to have names for the emotional experiences without one-word designations in English. Among others, these include Chinese *chou* "sorrow, worry, melancholy" (Ye, 2001), Bengali *obhiman* "sorrow caused by the insensitivity of a loved one" (Russell, 1991a: 426), Javanese *sungkan*, "an inhibition of one's desires before a superior" or *iklas* "a state of pleasant/indifferent frustration" (Geertz, 1959), and Japanese *ijirashii*, "a feeling associated with seeing someone weak but praiseworthy overcoming an obstacle" and *amae* "a pleasurable sense of dependence" (Araki, 1994; Doi, 1981). Several widely-known examples come also from European languages, such as Polish *przykro* (Wierzbicka, 2001), Czech *dojetí* and *lítost* (Slaměník & Hyruchová, 2006), Russian *toska* (see Chapter 23) and *perezhivat'* (Pavlenko, 2002a), as well as Spanish *cariño* (Altarriba, 2003), Portuguese *saudade* (Farrell, 2006), German *Schadenfreude* (Wierzbicka, 1998b), and Greek *stenahoria* (Panayiotou, 2004b; 2006).

It is important to note, however, that alongside the frequently reported "cultural untranslatability," many of the deemed "culture-specific" emotion words are nevertheless translatable linguistically. Firstly, context-dependent renderings can in most cases be found for "lacunal" emotion words: for instance, Polish culture-specific word *żal* does share some (although not all) elements with the English *grief, sadness*, and *sorrow* (Besemeres, 2006); Greek *ntropi* can be rendered, depending on the context, as *shyness, shame, embarrassment*, or *discomfort* (Panayiotou, 2006). Contextual translational correlates of the salient Russian emotion word *toska* are "sadness," "anxiety," and "boredom" words in other languages, Germanic, Romance, and Slavic alike (see Chapter 23). Depending on the contexts of use, the Woleaian word *fago* can be defined in English as *compassion, sad love*, or *sadness* (Lutz, 1982: 123).

Secondly, there is evidence that the meanings lexicalized in a mono-lexemic way in one language can however be rendered in another language in a linguistically more complex way (e.g., as a multiword expression). For instance, *enthusiasm* and *enthrallment* have no one-word denominations in Luganda, but vernacular expressions meaning "the person is working hard" and "the person left us with our mouth open," respectively, are commonly used instead (Hupka et al., 1999: 248). *Depression*, a lacunal word in Yoruba, can be rendered in this language as "the heart goes weak" and "the heart is not at rest" (Leff, 1973). Psychologists working in the regions where Luo, Turkana, and Datoga are spoken (languages that lack a correlate of English *stress*) conventionally use the local idioms meaning "thinking too much" (Ice & Yogo, 2005; Pike & Young, 2002).

Taken together, these reports corroborate the so-called "Strong Effability/Translatability" hypothesis in linguistics (Katz, 1976) which asserts that anything that can be said (i.e., is effable) in one language can be translated into another language (von Fintel & Matthewson, 2008) and that "every useful meaning can be verbalized" (van Benthem, 1991: 25, cf. Katz, 1976). However, what can be expressed by a word in one language might require a rather complex expression in another language.

It is important to note that a transition from one language level to another, or from one morphological word class to another, can impact the semantic and conceptual structure of verbalized emotions (cf. Chapter 4). For instance, while emotion adjectives (e.g., *joyful*) are commonly held to be more easily associated with immediate emotional experience (Plutchik, 1980a), emotion nouns (e.g., *joy*) refer to an abstract store of representations separated from contextual elements (Conway & Bekerian, 1987). Nouns, rather than verbs or adjectives, are assumed to increase the psychological similarity of emotions to "objects" (Shaver et al., 2001: 203) and therefore they are used in emotion categorization research (Fehr & Russell, 1984; Shaver et al., 1987, 1992, 2001). In turn, verbs—the dominant way of emotion lexicalization in Igbo, Hindustani and Russian (Agbo, 2011; Semin et al., 2002; Wolfson, 2005), and the only morphological class to label emotions in East Cree, Amharic, and Alamblak (Amberber, 2001; Junker & Blacksmith, 2006; Bruce & Bruce, 2010)—encode emotions as processes and relationships, highlighting thus their procedural aspects.

Partial semantic overlap

A much more common relationship between emotion terms in different languages is, however, that of a partial overlap in meaning, for which several types are commonly reported. Firstly, there are cases where an emotion word in one language represents only a part of the referential scope of a comparable word in another language. This is the case of correspondence between Ukrainian *kohannya* "a deep affection felt toward a person of the opposite sex" (SUM; Grygorash, 2006, 2007) and English *love*, which has a much wider referential scope (Ogarkova, 2003, 2005); or Russian lexeme *revnost'* which correlates with English *jealousy* only in the sense of "the state of mind arising from the suspicion, aggression, or knowledge of rivalry" (OED), but not in the sense of "unhappiness or anger about other people's possessions" (OED, cf. Pavlenko, 2008: 152).

Secondly, sometimes emotion concepts referred to by a single term in one language are lexically differentiated in (an)other language(s). On the one hand, an indigenous term in one language can correspond to two or more distinct labels from *different emotion categories* in another language, as does the Gidjingali word *gurakadj* which combines "fear" and "shame" (Hiatt, 1978, cf. Wierzbicka, 1999b), Samoan *alofa* that spans together the meanings of "love/liking" and "sympathy/pity" (Gerber, 1975: 3), Amharic *azzənnə* which combines "sadness" and "sympathy" (Amberber, 2001: 45), or Woleaian *rus* that integrates "panic/fright" and "surprise" (Lutz, 1982: 116). A frequently attested pattern here is the conflation of "anger" and "sadness" in several African languages (Leff, 1973) such as, for instance, in Luganda, where the verb *okusunguwala* ("to get angry") also means "to get sad" (Orley, 1970: 3)[6].

On the other hand, many reports show that an indigenous term in one language can correspond to two (or more) *same-category words* in other languages. For instance, the meanings of Polish *pogarda* or Swedish *förakt* correspond to two French "contempt" nouns, *mépris* and *dédain* (Koselak, 2005: 21), or the Gidjingali word *gurakadj* can be rendered into English as *terror, horror, dread, apprehension*, and *timidity* (Hiatt, 1978). A frequently mentioned cross-lingual pattern here is the conflation of "shame" and "embarrassment": while the two emerge as distinct emotion concepts in English (cf. Wierzbicka, 1999b), they "seem to be a lexically unified cluster in many or perhaps most parts of the non-Western world" (Levy, 1983: 131). Indeed, ethnographic accounts suggest that the lexical distinction between "shame" and "embarrassment" is not made in Alamblak (Bruce and Bruce, 2010), Amharic (Amberber, 2001: 53), Indonesian (Keeler, 1983: 153), Japanese (Lebra, 1983: 194), Javanese (Geertz, 1959: 233), Kanuri (Hupka et al., 1999: 276–277), Pintupi (Myers, 1979: 361), Tahitian (Levy, 1973), Tamajaq (Rasmussen, 2007: 238), and Woleaian spoken by the Ifaluk (Lutz, 1988: 209).

---

[6] For many more relevant cases, see Hupka *et al.* (1999), Appendix D, pp. 276–278, where 117 words in 64 languages referring to more than one of the English emotion categories are catalogued.

Aspects of variation in emotion term semantics

While the body of work overviewed in previous sections reveals a complex network of (sometimes, very relative) correspondences between emotion words in different languages, the final issue that still needs to be addressed in this chapter concerns the *aspects of variation* that contribute most to the differences in emotion term semantics. Here, the salience of several such aspects, or components, can be highlighted.

First of all, differences in the meanings of comparable words across languages frequently derive from the differences in the ***typical antecedent events*** of emotional experiences labeled by the words. For instance, Malay *malu* refers to an emotional experience that typically happens not only in the situations that would be easily recognized as prototypically shame-eliciting by speakers of English (e.g., having done something wrong or foolish), but also in response to being teased, even in a relatively mild way (Goddard, 1996, 2005). *Yirufa*, one of the "shame/embarrassment" words in the Alamblak language, is reported to arise in response to a public insult (Bruce & Bruce, 2010). Another study of English *shame* and Spanish *vergüenza* shows that while most typical antecedent events of *shame* (and least typical of *vergüenza*) are moral transgression, humiliation, and wrongdoing, most typical elicitors of *vergüenza* (that are simultaneously not characteristic of *shame*) are ridicule and the presence of others (Hurtado, 2007, 2008).

Typical antecedent events can also underlie lexical differentiation of larger groups of words within a language: for instance, each of the over thirty East Cree "anger" verbs are reported to refer to an emotion elicited by a distinct event, such as an insult, mutual ill feeling, taking leave of an individual on a walk, offensive visual sights, and so on (Watkins, 1938: 284–285). Likewise, the exuberant "shame" vocabulary in Chinese falls into two smaller subcategories: the lexemes denoting shame varieties arising from appraising of one's own behavior ("self focus" shame), and the words referring to shame experiences elicited by the actions of others ("other-focus" shame, Li et al., 2004).

Centrally important here are the *social aspects* of emotion-eliciting situations. Overall, five types of them appear to be most salient in this regard, namely:

1   *The social status* of agents involved in an emotional episode. In Woleaian, for instance, a distinct cluster of words denotes experiences involving interactions with higher-rank people, such as *nguch* "the frustration engendered by the obedience required to those of higher rank" (Lutz, 1982: 119). Conversely, other emotion terms emerge to label the emotions one has (or is expected to have) with regard to people of a lower rank, such as Utku *naklik*, "the love for those who need protection" (Russell, 1991a).

2   *The in-group or out-group membership* of the person(s) causing an emotion in the experiencer. In contrast to the typical "self–other" dichotomy in the Western world, researchers of non-Western cultures contend that many indigenous constructs—such as Filipino *kapwa* (Enriquez, 1992), Korean *woori* (Choi et al., 1993; Choi & Han, 2008), Zulu, Shona, and Runyakitara *ubunti* (Forster, 2006; Louw, 2001), as well as Pintupi *walytja* (Myers, 1979)—conceptualize the social universe differently. In Pintupi, for instance, the social world is divided into (a) those who are "kin," "relations," or "family" (*walytja*), and (b) those who are not kin—often described as "not men," or "different men" (*munuwati*) (Myers, 1979: 351). Consequently, same emotion experienced toward either an in-group or an out-group person implies different modes of emotional expression. For example, when used in reference to the emotion one feels toward the kin, Filipino *galit* "anger" presupposes free and open anger manifestation; when referring to an emotion felt toward outsiders, however, it denotes an anger-like experience accompanied by the culturally-prescribed tendencies to hide, keep quiet, and show indifference (Lorenzano, 2006: 5).

3   *The focus of the appraisal of a person* who causes an emotion in the experiencer. Alongside with the behavior, two more aspects—people's inherent characteristics and possessions—appear to be important. The former is felicitous to discriminate between English *anger* and its Chinese correlate *nu*, which, unlike *anger*, can be caused by "observing certain striking characteristics of someone whom we cannot habitually stand (*taoyan*), for example, especially tall or short, fat or thin, big-eyed or with a pock-marked face" (Kornacki, 2001: 263). The latter aspect—material possessions—is a defining semantic feature of a distinct class of words in Woleaian which unites the emotions of "good fortune" and where many of the emotions occur when a person has a valuable object (Lutz, 1982: 115-116).

4   *Social sharing/reciprocity*, that is, possibility of the emotional experiences referred to by emotion terms to be more typically experienced by, or about a group of people at a time. Inherently reciprocal are many Palauan emotion words, such as *klsiberreng* "mutual bad or hurt feelings," *kaubtikerreng* "mutual fondness," and *kltareng* "mutual trust" (Smith & Tkel-Sbal, 1995: 91). Likewise, Chinese "anger" lexeme *fen* is not only typically used to refer to a "collective" emotion experienced by many people at a time, but is also typically experienced about a group people (esp. in authority positions) rather than a single individual (Kornacki, 2001: 277).

5   *Attribution*, which refers to the possibility that in some cultures (e.g., collectivistic) specific emotional experiences (e.g., negative other-directed emotions) are more readily attributed by their experiencers to others than to themselves. Such reluctance in self-attribution of negative other-directed emotions is indeed attested for Ifalukians: "*gasechaula* ('hate') [is] the only emotion that people would not say, even in private conversation, they had experienced" (Lutz, 1983: 251). Ifalukians are also reluctant to acknowledge several emotions that result from the acquisition of material goods, sexual relationships, or other valued objects, given "the primary danger in an admission of *chegas* 'pride/self-confidence' or *ker* 'happiness/excitement' because one might be seen as showing-off one's good fortune" (Ibid.: 251).

The second important source of semantic variation between comparable emotion terms is the ***subjective feelings*** associated to the labeled emotional experiences. For example, given the evidence that Portuguese *saudade* is frequently used in the constructions *estar com* + N (lit. "to be with +N") designating afflictions or ailments in Portuguese, as well as in the construction *morendo de* "die of," *saudade* is said to denote a more afflictive emotional experience than its closest English correlates *nostalgia* and *missing* (Farrell, 2006). A contrastive analysis of Russian *zhalost'* and its English counterpart *pity* amounts to similar observations: deriving from the evidence that *zhalost'* is centrally (metaphorically) construed as physical pain, this Russian lexeme is argued to denote an experience associated with more suffering on part of its experience compared to *pity* (Danaher, 2002: 8).

The salience of subjective feelings as a source of semantic variation can extend beyond individual comparisons and differentiate between clusters of words in different languages: in Chinese, a distinct cluster of "sad love" words emerges (Shaver et al., 1992), suggesting that "love" is viewed upon as a negative rather than a positive emotion in Chinese—a contention at least in part corroborated by further analysis of the metaphorical (Na, 2007) and discursive construction of love in Chinese vs American English (Rothbaum & Tsang, 1998). Similarly, Indonesian "love" words are reported to focus more on yearning and desire compared to the words in the analogous American English category (Shaver et al., 2001).

Thirdly, cross-lingual glosses have been shown to refer to emotional concepts that differ with respect to the emotion component of ***physiological symptoms***. For instance, Greek *stenahoria* is reported to be typically accompanied by a feeling of suffocation which is not implied in *frustration*, its rough English gloss (Panayitou, 2004a). The salience of physiological symptoms as part of emotion term semantics appears to be applicable at a more general level as well. For example, a dimensional scaling study of several Neo-Latin languages (Galati et al., 2008) shows that in Romanian and Portuguese the factor that explains most of the variance between emotion terms is Activation/Arousal (which signals that the somatic aspects of emotions linked to the "physiological activation" are more important in these languages), whereas in Italian, French, Catalan, and Castilian the most salient factor is that of Potency/Power (which the authors relate to the influence of the Latin and Greek rationalist tradition where the cognitive aspects of mental activity have always enjoyed privileged attention) (Galati et al., 2008: 217).

Finally, the deemed equivalent emotion words in different languages can vary with regard to *expression, action tendencies*, and *regulation*. Many of these reports touch on the translation equivalents of English *anger* in German (Durst, 2001), Biblical Hebrew (Myhill, 1997), Chinese (Kornacki, 2001), Arrente (Harkins, 2001), Woleanian (Lutz, 1982), Malay (Goddard, 1996), or Shuswap (Kuipers, 1974). For example, while English *anger* is generally taken to imply a negative judgment of someone's action and a desire to do something about this action which is directed at the offender (Lazarus, 1991a; Russell, 1991a; Wierzbicka, 1999b), several "anger" words in the above mentioned languages do not imply similar retribution tendencies. In Woleanian *song*, as argued by Lutz (1988: 301), the direction of the expression of *song* can be towards the anger experiencer rather than the perpetrator, therefore *song* can manifest itself instead in its experiencer's sulking, refusal to eat, or an attempted suicide. The same directness at the experiencer, rather than the perpetrator, is attested for Chinese *qi* (Kornacki, 2001: 268). Similar evidence is available for Malay *marah*, which is associated with sullen brooding rather than aggression (Goddard, 1996), and Arrente *akiwarre* in which the retribution is not expected to happen immediately, as *akiwarre* contains the notion of "latent revenge" (Harkins, 2001: 208). As with all emotion components discussed above, the discriminative power of action tendencies, expression, and regulation can go beyond the comparison of translation equivalents across languages and differentiate between the same-category labels within a language. For example, "to be angry-faced" has a distinct *lexical* designation in Shuswap, in contrast to comparable Shuswap lexemes meaning "making somebody angry," "becoming angry," and "being angry at somebody" (Kuipers, 1974).

3.4 The cross-cultural and cross-linguistic perspective on the GRID paradigm

This chapter has overviewed the research domain that focuses on emotion vocabularies and assumes that representation of emotions in language can provide a valuable insight into emotion conceptualization and categorization in various cultures of the world. A review of relevant theoretical proposals in the field has shown that many and varied ways to theorize the relevance of language for the emotion research can be assigned to two broad positions: the one that emphasizes the ultimate impact of language on conceptualization of experience (the "language-first" view), and the other that typically focuses on the role of culture in both emotional experiences and linguistic representations of emotions (the "culture-first" view). Despite some differences in emphasis, these two positions share an important set of common assumptions, which, taken together, highlight the importance of linguistic evidence in the study of "folk" emotion conceptualization.

It is in the light of this exigency to consider language data that the anthropologic, ethnographic, psychological, and linguistic evidence has been further considered in this chapter. Relevant cross-lingual commonalities and divergences have been our two major concerns. The GRID paradigm can build on these commonalities and has to deal with the divergences in order to function as a multidisciplinarily viable paradigm to study the meaning of emotion terms.

With regard to the common aspects, our overview has revealed five general similarities in emotion labeling across languages. Firstly, there is reliable evidence that all natural languages studied thus far have terms referring to what is conventionally defined as "emotional states" in academic English. These emotion categories emerge in different languages in approximately the same order. Furthermore, in most languages of the world emotions can be represented, alongside with the abstract psychological language, via literal and figurative body-part expressions. Finally, there is robust evidence that a sizable part of variance in the emotion vocabularies can be captured by a few meaningful dimensions, and that the hierarchical structures of the emotion domains are similar across the many and various cultures studied to date. Thus, as emotion words have been found to be universally encoded in language, the aim of the GRID paradigm to study the meaning of emotion words can be considered universally valid. Moreover, it is important for the GRID paradigm to accommodate for the dimensional and the categorical perspectives (see also previous chapter), as they have revealed very comparable structures across cultural and linguistic groups.

At the same time, our review also suggests that emotion lexicalization can go along somewhat different lines in different languages. On the one hand, considerable cross-lingual variation is observed with regard to individual emotion words, with some emotion words emerging only in one language, and with sometimes very sizable shifts in meaning between deemed translation equivalent terms across languages. On the other hand, substantial differences between cultural and linguistic groups have been observed with respect to the features characterizing these terms. There are two sources of variation in meaning that have received special attention. First, relative differences in salience between the psychological and the somatic aspects of emotions have been suggested. Second, it has been proposed that in Western cultural groups emotions are more intrapersonally focused, while they are more interpersonally focused in many non-Western groups.

A multitheoretical and multidisciplinary approach to study the meaning of emotion terms has to take these cultural and linguistic differences into account and has to further elucidate them. The GRID paradigm lends itself very well for this task. Within the GRID paradigm emotion terms are not defined in terms of other emotion terms, but in terms of their componential profiles. This implies that there is no *a priori* assumption about the equivalence of emotion terms. The GRID paradigm only assumes that emotion terms can be identified in each of the groups. Moreover, the differences that have been reported in cross-cultural and cross-linguistic studies can be very well framed within the componential emotion approach, or can at least be easily incorporated into this approach. Some of the proposed cultural and linguistic differences can be reframed as differences in the salience of particular emotion components, with, for instance, the somatic component being much more salient in some cultural groups than in others. Other suggested cultural and linguistic differences can be conceptualized as differences within specific emotion components. For instance, which appraisals and which action tendencies are salient can be expected to depend on the cultural intrapersonal versus interpersonal focus. The more the interpersonal focus becomes salient, the more it can be predicted that events are appraised in terms of their interpersonal relevance, and that actions are prepared to enhance or restore interpersonal functioning.

It can thus be concluded that the GRID paradigm builds further on the universal observation of emotion words across cultural and linguistic cultural groups. At the same time, it offers a coordinating framework for studying cultural and linguistic differences in the meaning of these terms. These can either be conceptualized as differences in the salience of whole emotion components or as differences in the salience of specific features within specific emotion components.

Chapter 4

Linguistic theories of lexical meaning

Cristina Soriano[1]

4.1 Introduction

Emotion is a multifaceted phenomenon affecting many and varied areas of human experience, which calls for a multidisciplinary approach in its investigation. The GRID project presented in this volume offers one such approach, integrating psychological, anthropological, and linguistic insight into a unified research agenda. Previous chapters have contextualized the GRID from a number of disciplinary orientations relevant to the paradigm, but since the study is first and foremost a linguistic one, given that it aims to describe the meaning of emotion words across languages and cultures, the goal of this chapter is to provide a theoretical framework for the paradigm and an explanation of its contribution from the point of view of linguistics and, more specifically, lexical semantics. The approach will also be compared with other methodologies available in the field for the study of lexical meaning. Among them the GRID is the only paradigm specifically designed to describe the meaning of emotion terms.[2]

The chapter is divided in two sections devoted to theories and methodologies, respectively. In the first one, we give an overview of three main areas of concern in lexical semantics and how they have been addressed by modern theories of lexical meaning. This will allow us to point out the advantages and disadvantages of each theoretical stance for the study of emotion, as well as to identify which one lends itself better to interdisciplinary research. In the second section, we give an overview of four of the most productive methodologies currently employed in the study of emotion term semantics. This will be important to identify in what sense and to what extent the GRID methodology can complement already existing approaches to the study of emotion words.

But before we proceed, two caveats need to be considered. First, this chapter focuses on the meaning of lexical units. Larger units of meaning, like the phrase or the sentence, will not be dealt with. Second, we will focus on *decontextualized* meaning, that is, off-line semantic representation. These two decisions are based on the nature of the GRID paradigm itself, designed to investigate the meaning of decontextualized lexical units (see Chapter 5).

4.2 Issues in lexical semantic theories

Although word meanings have been discussed in Western literature since antiquity, lexical semantics only evolved as a discipline in the 19th century (Paradis, 2012). Various schools of thought

---

[1] Cristina Soriano. Swiss Center for Affective Sciences—University of Geneva. 7, Rue des Battoirs, CH-1205 Geneva, Switzerland. Cristina.Soriano@unige.ch

[2] Emotion words and emotion terms are used as synonymous expressions in this chapter. They refer to lexical labels like the English *love*, *fear*, or *anger*.

in linguistics since then have provided different answers to the two basic questions in the field: what is lexical meaning and how is it best studied. According to Dirk Geeraerts (2002, 2009), four main theories or schools of lexical semantics can be distinguished. The first is the pre-structuralist school, represented by the work of Brèal, Paul, Sperber, or Stern, interested in historical semantics. The second, governing most of the 20th century is the structuralist school, spurred by the work of Saussure and represented by Trier, Weisberger, Pottier, or Lyons, as well as by their contemporary "neostructuralist" heirs (like Coseriu, Cruse, or Halliday). Structuralists and neostructuralists view language as a system of interdependent constituents and are interested in the syntagmatic (i.e., combinatorial) and paradigmatic (i.e., substitutional/oppositional) relationships between the words in the language system. Toward the end of the century, the third school developed under the influence of Chomskian linguistics; it was the generativist semantic school represented by Katz and Fodor (Katz & Fodor, 1963), which has found continuation in the "neogenerativist" works of Pustejovsky and to a certain extent Jackendoff (see Geeraerts, 1997, 2002). Generativist semantics relies on the notion of (universal) rules that the speaker of a language needs to master to construct and decode meaning in a unit (e.g., rules for semantic extensions from core meanings). Finally, the cognitive school emerged in the late 1970s and 1980s, with the works of Fillmore, Lakoff, and Johnson on semantic/conceptual representation.

These schools reflect different concerns in linguistic research and, consequently, different conceptions about the nature and organization of word semantics. In order to review in more detail the definition and description of lexical meaning endorsed by each theory, we will organize the discussion around three issues addressed by each of them (cf. Geeraerts, 2002):

1   the nature of lexical meaning itself (the scope of linguistic meaning and its cognitive status)

2   the temporal frame in the study of lexical meaning

3   the preferential object of study in lexical semantics.

According to Geeraerts (2002), the last two are dimensions articulating lexical semantic research at large. In his view, a third dimension would be the interest that different scholars assign to referential vs non-referential types of meaning, that is, to the study of the denotation (concepts and referents) vs connotation (associated values) of words. Such dimension is not included in this chapter because the GRID instrument was designed to investigate denotation, not connotation. Studying non-referential aspects of meaning, like the affective connotations associated to everyday words, informs us of how language "expresses" emotion, rather than how language "represents" emotional experience by means of specific emotion labels (cf. Foolen, 1997, 2012; Grondelaers & Geeraerts, 1998; Reh, 1998), and it is only the second issue the GRID paradigm is interested in. Additionally, as Geeraerts himself explains, "non-referential types of meaning (like the emotive or stylistic value of words) have never occupied a central position within the actual research activities of lexical semanticists" (p. 8).

In the following sections we will describe the position of each theory/school with respect to issues 1–3 introduced above, and illustrate them with studies on the meaning of emotion words. We will also highlight the advantages and limitations of each approach in the context of interdisciplinary research.

The nature of meaning

A first aspect of lexical semantics cutting across different theories is the relationship between semantic and conceptual content: are they the same, related, or intrinsically different? This is one of the most debated issues in linguistics and a full consideration of its implications exceeds the scope of this paper (but see e.g., Nuyts & Pederson, 1997, for an introduction). For that reason here we will merely provide a brief account of the two main positions, how they relate to the various schools in lexical semantics, and their main implications for emotion research.

Two main stances can be adopted with regard to the relationship between semantic and conceptual representation. The first one contends that semantic meaning need not be the same as conceptual representation and should not be treated in the same way. This confers true disciplinary independence to linguistics, an ideal of the structuralist paradigm, which pursues the study of linguistic units only with respect to other linguistic units, explicitly refusing to make use of "non-linguistic" constructs like conceptual representation and extralinguistic reference to explain the meaning of words. The speaker's knowledge of the world is considered independent from the language system. Structuralist approaches would sustain that meaning depends on intra-system oppositions and the range of combinatorial possibilities that a word can entertain with the rest of the words in the language system. That is to say, the description of meaning can only be done in the framework of grammatical templates. For example, the meaning of the word *anger* should be defined by establishing which other words could occupy the same slot in a sentence, and which words it can combine with. The main problem with this approach is that studies that define meaning strictly by means of intra-system relations cannot say anything about the ability of a language to represent the world, although it is experientially obvious that languages allow us to communicate about and interact with the external reality we inhabit. As Anolli puts it: "knowing that *zeffo* is the opposite of *zoffo*, a pejorative of *zaffo*, and the superlative of *ziffo* does not enable anybody to know the meaning of *zeffo* at all" (2005: 29).

Unlike structuralism, the generativist approach thinks of linguistic categories as psychological entities, but linguistic skills are nevertheless considered different from other cognitive skills and processes. Chomsky (1980) defends the existence of autonomous "cognitive modules" with system-specific principles, the linguistic module being one of them. For this reason, according to the generativist school, semantic representation should be described independently of other forms of conceptual representation. Therefore, the goal in generativist lexical semantics is to create an independent logical formalism to describe word meaning and its generation (a formalized grammar of meaning). This is mostly pursued through semantic feature decompositions: identifying the conceptual units (e.g., Place, Manner, Action, Event, Thing, Property, Cause, etc) out of which the meanings of linguistic items are built and the rules that combine them. The ultimate goal is to create predictive models susceptible of being implemented computationally.

An alternative position, defended by the cognitive approach (and coherent with the pre-structuralist school), submits that lexical meaning *is* conceptual representation, and is therefore affected by the same mechanisms and principles studied in psychology for other mental abilities like categorization and perception. The approach also implies that linguistic categories are particularly privileged as a "source of information" on conceptualization (Pederson & Nuyts, 1997: 4), although not all concepts are lexical, and important questions remain open, like whether conceptualization is derived or at least heavily influenced by language (the Sapir-Whorf hypothesis), or the other way round.

Another feature of the cognitive paradigm is that meaning is thought to be "encyclopedic," rather than "dictionary-like"; that is, word meaning is believed to reflect world knowledge, as opposed to a limited number of minimal and sufficient features of the sort one would find in a dictionary entry. The latter is the view of meaning endorsed by the structuralist and generativist schools. The reason for an encyclopedic view of meaning is that meaning in the cognitive paradigm is not understood as something self-contained in the word, but rather dependent on large networks of knowledge cued by the use of the word, which can be differentially activated depending on the context of use.

From the previous discussion it transpires that interdisciplinary communication between psychology, anthropology, and linguistics is better developed within the cognitive paradigm, where lexical meaning is seen as conceptual representation. Without this basic stance, linguistic categories and their relations could not be expected to reveal anything about the way we represent the world. Another advantage of the cognitive paradigm for interdisciplinary communication is that the view of meaning as encyclopedic world-knowledge can account for the role of culture in shaping and changing word meanings, as illustrated by Lakoff's (1987) seminal study on radial categories and how culture shapes categorization.

The temporal frame in the study of lexical meaning

This section looks at the two temporal frameworks that the study of lexical meaning can adopt: synchronic and diachronic. *Synchronic* studies investigate the current meaning of words, whereas *diachronic* studies focus on the evolution of their meaning. Each school of thought in lexical semantics has adopted a different temporal framework.

Modern linguistics starts with the pre-structuralist school's focus on diachronic semantics, that is, with an interest in etymology and the reasons why word meanings change over time (Geeraerts, 2002: 23–24). This interest in temporal processes is strongly contested by the structuralist school, which advocates a change of focus from diachronic to strictly synchronic phenomena. Their goal is to make linguistics a science, which, in their opinion, requires the study of meaning to be circumscribed to the observable phenomena taking place "here and now." The focus on synchronic phenomena is also shared by the generativist school, and it is only with the development of cognitive linguistics at the end of the 20th century that diachronic studies have flourished again.

The two temporal approaches are not mutually exclusive, though. It is generally accepted that both accounts of meaning are useful and complementary. Even if one is only interested in the current meaning of words, looking back at their semantic evolution is highly desirable because "the more or less coherent sets of concepts that cultures use to structure experience and make sense of the world are not reinvented afresh with each new period in the culture's development. [. . .] It is only by investigating their historical origins and their gradual transformation that their contemporary form can be properly understood" (Geeraerts & Grondelaers, 1995: 176; cited in Gevaert, 2002: 275).

An example of diachronic research on emotion words is Gevaert's (2002) investigation of the concept ANGER[3] in Old and Middle English. She explains how the conceptual domain of ANGER in both periods is fairly stable, but a Latin influence can be observed around the years 850 to 950 because of a strong biblical influence, whereas a return to more Germanic concepts takes place between 950 and 1050.

Another example of the diachronic orientation in emotion lexical semantics from a cognitive linguistic perspective is Tissari's work on the semantic evolution of the lexemes *affection*, *friendship*, *passion*, and *charity* in English since the fifteenth century (Tissari, 2001). Tissari explains how the semantic changes are due to general cognitive processes of generalization and specialization, as well as metonymic and metaphoric thinking (see "Conceptual metaphor and metonymy" in Section 4.3 on the latter two concepts). For example, the word *passion* in Early Modern English used to refer to a strong emotion for which the symptoms were often explicitly described; on the

---

[3] In the remainder of this chapter, italics are used for specific lexemes in a language (e.g., English *anger*) and small capitals for the overall concepts (e.g., ANGER), which can have several lexicogrammatical instantiations (e.g., *anger, to annoy, furious*, etc.).

contrary, the current use of the term is mostly concerned with emphasizing intensity at the expense of a specific characterization of the emotion. Tissari suggests this semantic development is metonymy (PART FOR WHOLE) because one of the original components of the meaning of the word (i.e., "intensity") becomes foregrounded and takes up most of the space in the current meaning of the word. Tissari also describes the secularization of the term, which used to be heavily associated to Christ's suffering, but has currently acquired the new sense of "loving *things* intensely" (e.g., *a passion for opera*), a sense that was absent in Early Modern English.

In spite of the recent interest in diachronic studies, most modern works on emotion lexical semantics adopt a synchronic approach. Indeed, all studies referred to in the remaining of this chapter illustrate this orientation, so no specific example is necessary at this point. Although both temporal frameworks are useful and could be said to complement each other, for the sake of interdisciplinary collaboration a synchronic approach may be preferable. The reason is that linguistic studies of the *current* meanings of words can be immediately compared with the work from psychology or neuroscience, whose findings are necessarily time-bound to the features and circumstances of the current speakers of a language.

The preferential object of study in lexical semantics

A third transversal topic of concern in modern lexical semantics is the orientation in the study of meaning. In other words, how should the relationship between conceptual/semantic domains and the meanings of specific words be tackled? Should we study how concepts are labeled, or rather focus on the meaning of specific words? Studies that focus on how the lexis of a language captures a given concept or area of semantic space are said to adopt an *onomasiological* approach, from the Greek noun ὄνομα, "name" (since one focuses on the "names" that a language has for conceptual entities). On the contrary, studies that focus on the characterization of the meaning of specific words adopt a *semasiological* orientation, from the Greek word σημασία, "meaning."

As in the previous case, the approaches are not mutually exclusive, and the different theories in lexical semantics mostly reflect a degree of preference for one or the other approach, rather than an absolute commitment to any of them. According to Geeraerts (2002), the pre-structuralist and neogenerativist schools are mainly characterized by a semasiological orientation, while the rest endorse an eminently onomasiological approach (although cognitive semantics can be said to commit to both). In what follows we illustrate a few types of semasiological and onomasiological studies of emotion terms.

Semasiological studies of emotion terms

Linguistic research with a focus on the meaning of words (semasiology) concerns itself with issues like the number and types of meanings (i.e., senses) a word can have and the relationships between them. That is to say, typical semasiological studies look at polysemy (the fact that words may have several related meanings) and word meaning structure.

The study of polysemy applied to emotion words tells us, for example, that in many languages the names of body parts and body substances are used to refer both to the body and to certain affective states (Enfield & Wierzbicka, 2002; Sharifian, Dirven, Yu, & Niemeier, 2008). A good example is the English noun *bile*, which refers both to the secretions of the liver and to anger (cf. Geeraerts & Grondealers, 1995 for an account of bile-anger in the framework of the Medieval physiology theory of the "four humors"). Another example is the word "heart," which is cross-culturally considered one of the most typical metaphorical seats of emotion (e.g., Kövecses, 2000; Taylor & Mbense, 1998; Yu, 1995).

A second type of semasiological study is the description of the semantic structure of words. This is classically done by means of semantic features—a concept developed by the structuralist school. For example, *man* can be decomposed into the features "animate" + "human" + "male" + "adult" (cf. e.g., Jackendoff, 1983, Chapter 7 for a review of feature-based theories of meaning). Notice, however, that although the notion of "feature" is useful for semantic analysis, it is a matter of open debate whether lexical meaning can be reduced to a limited set of *necessary and sufficient* features or conditions capable of distinguishing the meaning of a word from any other in the system. The structuralist school defended this idea, also endorsed by generativists like Katz (1966: 72–73, Katz & Postal, 1964) and Fodor (Katz & Fodor, 1963). Another supporter is the anthropological linguist Anna Wierzbicka (e.g., 1972, 1996), who defends the existence of a limited number of semantic universals that can be used as metalanguage to describe the meaning structure of any word, including emotion terms (see "Natural Semantic Metalanguage" in Section 4.3 for details on this approach). The same idea is implicit in the work on the emotion lexicon by some emotion psychologists. For example, for Johnson-Laird and Oatley (1989) HAPPINESS, SADNESS, FEAR, ANGER, and DISGUST are emotional primitives (non-decomposable semantic concepts) used to build the remaining emotion categories in a language by adding propositional content to them. In their account, *disappointment* could be defined as "sadness by a failure to achieve a goal" (Ibid, p. 112) and *relief* as "happiness as a result of something that brings to an end fear or sadness" (Ibid., p. 118).

Other works in psychology remain agnostic about the existence of sufficient and necessary conditions for category membership in the affective lexicon (Ortony, Clore, & Foss, 1987), while this possibility is explicitly denied in studies endorsing a prototype approach (e.g., Fehr & Russell, 1984; Russell & Fehr, 1994). The same idea would also be rejected by neogenerativist linguists like Jackendoff (1983) and above all by cognitive semanticists (e.g., Taylor, 1995). For Jackendoff certain meaning features are necessary, but they are not sufficient, because another parameter is needed to represent meaning: preference rules (like the rules that govern gestalt perception). Cognitive semantics in turn rejects the existence of necessary and sufficient conditions on the grounds that meaning is organized in terms of prototype structures with fuzzy boundaries, containing more and less typical or defining features for any given word, none of which are *necessarily* indispensable, nor sufficient, to define the meaning of the term. This position is supported by the observation that most features central for the meaning of a word can be negated or cancelled without significantly changing the meaning of the unit (see, for example, Geeraerts' (1989) analysis of the English word *bird*). Consider, for example, the emotion concept ANGER. The perception of injustice seems to be a recurrent feature in the experience of the emotion (Mikula, Scherer, & Athenstaedt, 1998). Yet, the feature is not necessary for all the variants of the emotion, like *irritation* or *annoyance* (we can be *irritated* or *annoyed* about something that is not intrinsically unfair, but simply tedious). The existence of prototype representation does not preclude the possibility that, occasionally, there may be "essential" or "constitutive" features shared by all members of a category (cf. e.g., Cruse, 1986; Violi, 2001; Teroni & Deonna, 2008).

Whether a universal set of necessary and sufficient features exists that is capable of defining *emotional* meaning in particular is a matter of empirical research that still requires investigation within linguistics (but see Shaver, Schwartz, Kirson, & O'Connor, 1987; Fehr, 1988; Fehr & Russell, 1984; Russell & Fehr, 1994 for a psychological account). Additionally, to our knowledge, no works exist to date within linguistics adopting a prototype perspective of the sort described above to study the meaning features of emotion terms in the same category (e.g., the place of English *rage* vs *indignation* vs *irritation* within a prototype broad ANGER category, and the patterns of features responsible for their relative position within the prototype).

Onomasiological studies of emotion terms

In the study of emotion, an onomasiological approach (i.e., a focus on the wording of concepts) concerns itself with relationships of similarity, hierarchy and, in general, interdependence between the words in a given domain. For example, within the structuralist/neostructuralist tradition, the approach is illustrated by studies on paradigmatic semantic (dis)similarity (i.e., synonymy, antonymy), paradigmatic semantic relations (e.g., hyponymy, hyperonymy), and syntagmatic relations and restrictions (Geeraerts, 2002). Synonymy refers to (near) equivalence in meaning (e.g., *good* ≈ *positive*). Antonymy refers to oppositions in meaning (e.g., *good* vs *bad*). Hyponymy and hyperonymy are category-inclusion relationships. For example, *anger* would be a hyponym of *emotion* (i.e., a more specific kind) and *emotion* would be a hyperonym of *anger* (i.e., a more generic, overarching category including *anger*). The onomasiological approach, with its interest in similarity and hierarchical structures, also characterizes psychological studies of the emotion lexicon based on word similarity ratings, cluster analysis, and hierarchical modeling, which aim to reveal the underlying structure of the affective domain (see Chapter 2 for examples).

A good example of onomasiological research within linguistics is Miller & Fellbaum's *WordNet* Project (Fellbaum, 1998). WordNet is an online lexical database in which English nouns, verbs, adjectives, and adverbs are grouped into synonym sets or "synsets" representing the same overarching lexical concept (e.g., the lexical items *anger, choler,* and *ire* are grouped into the concept or synset ANGER). The relations between the various synsets (hyperonymy, hyponymy, etc.) are also spelled out. The WordNet project has now been expanded in a way particularly relevant for emotion research by including additional details in the meaning of emotion terms specifically, and affective information in the meaning of regular words. For example, *SentiWordNet* (Esuli & Sebastiani, 2006; Baccianella, Esuli, & Sebastiani, 2010) is a lexical resource that assigns three "affective scores" to each synset of WordNet: positivity, negativity, and objectivity. The same can be done for individual words instead of synsets (Esuli & Sebastiani, 2005). For example, high scores in objectivity for a word indicate that the term is not a marker of opinionated content (e.g., the noun *computation*), whereas high scores in positivity or negativity indicate that the term involves a subjective judgment, or affective connotation (e.g., the nouns *honesty* and *offense*). The scores are assigned in an automatic fashion based on the analysis of the glosses (definitions) given to the terms in WordNet. The main application of SentiWordNet at the moment is automatic opinion mining.

Another interesting development of WordNet is *WordNet-Affect* (Strapparava & Valitutti, 2004; Valitutti, Strapparava, & Stock, 2004), a lexical resource that assigns additional labels with affective information to the WordNet synsets representing affective concepts. Examples of new classificatory labels include "emotion" (e.g., *anger*), "trait" (e.g., *aggressiveness*), "emotion-eliciting situation" (e.g., *awkwardness*), "attitude" (e.g., *intolerance*), and "emotional response" (e.g., *cold sweat*). Then, within the elements tagged as "emotion," additional tagging is provided about their valence (positive, negative, neutral, or ambiguous—i.e., context dependent) and the causative/stative nature of the lexemes, specifically adjectival lexemes. An emotional adjective is considered "causative" if the noun it modifies causes the emotion referred to by the adjective (e.g., *amusing movie*: movie that causes amusement). Conversely, an emotional adjective is considered "stative" if the noun it modifies experiences the emotion referred to by the adjective (*happy boy*: boy who feels happy).

The onomasological approach is also typical of much of the emotion work carried out in corpus linguistics. For example, collocational analysis is a direct heir of the general interest in syntagmatic relations of the structuralist tradition. Collocations are words that co-occur more frequently than would be expected by chance (typically in a fixed order). A salient exponent in this field of research is Halliday, although not much of his work has focused on emotions. In one of his studies, however, Halliday (1998) uses corpora to study the lexicogrammar of *pain*, concluding that this emotion is conceptualized in English as a process (in fact, various kinds thereof), as a quality, and as a thing, being impossible to ascribe it to any one single semantic domain.

Many types of onomasiological studies are also available within the cognitive linguistic tradition. They include basic-level categorization studies, metaphor research, and prototype semantics. A well-known case is Lakoff and Kövecses' work on the general concept of ANGER in English (in Lakoff, 1987), in which they explain what features are most central in the prototypical representation of the emotion and what makes some anger variants less central members of the category (see "Frame and prototype semantics" in Section 4.3). But Lakoff and Kövecses's work on ANGER is more famous for its illustration of another eminent approach in onomasiological (cognitive) lexical semantics: the study of conceptual metaphor (see "Conceptual metaphor and metonymy" in Section 4.3).

Both approaches reviewed so far are compatible with interdisciplinary research on emotion and they are both individually valuable. Yet, the most interesting insight does not emerge from one or the other orientation, but rather at the intersection of the two, when cumulative analyses of the meaning of individual emotion words reveal information about the broader underlying concepts. In this sense, a valuable contribution for the future would be to investigate the relative centrality of various semantic features across emotion words and languages (e.g., the most defining features for the lexemes in the category ANGER in English, or in Japanese, or cross-culturally). It would also be interesting to empirically determine whether a core set of features exists for *all* members of the category EMOTION in a language (and across languages) (cf. Fehr and Russell's (1984) analysis of English). These remain open questions in emotion lexical semantics at the intersection between semasiological and onomasiological research.

4.3 Current methods in emotion lexical semantics

Four main trends can be observed nowadays in the linguistic study of emotion lexicons. They correspond to four methodologies and their corresponding theoretical backgrounds. They commit to a view of lexical meaning as conceptual representation and they mostly adopt a semasiological synchronic approach, although some of them also allow for diachronic and onomasiological research. In these approaches, the goal is to provide a description of the meaning of words independent of any particular context, although their proposals are always based on the systematic analysis of those terms in context. These approaches are Anna Wierzbicka's Natural Semantic Metalanguage, the corpus semantics approach, and two paradigms within cognitive linguistics: conceptual metaphor theory and frame semantics. They will all be discussed in the following sections.

Natural Semantic Metalanguage (NSM)

The Natural Semantic Metalanguage (NSM) is a methodology for semantic analysis developed by Anna Wierzbicka (1972, 1992b, 1992c, 1996) and her colleagues (Goddard, 1998; Goddard & Wierzbicka, 1994, 2002). It attempts to describe semantic representation in a language-independent way (i.e., unbiased by the semantic structures of any given language). To achieve this goal, it uses a small inventory of semantic universals, that is, lexically-expressed concepts claimed to exist in all languages. The proposal of these semantic universals is what makes NSM a semantic theory, in addition to a methodology. The semantic universals include notions like "feel," "good," "bad," and "do," which are, therefore, candidate building blocks of semantic content for any word (including emotion ones) in any language in the world. NSM claims that the 60 (or so) identified semantic universals (also called semantic primes) reflect irreducible universal concepts, which can be considered the core of human thought and are "intuitively clear (and presumably innate) and do not require any explanations" (Wierzbicka, 2006: 17). Additionally, NSM claims that these primes combine in the same way in all languages, which means that there is also a universal grammar in language. The methodology further describes meaning as implicit scripts made of the semantic universals when combined by means of the universal grammar. The approach has also been applied to the characterization of cultural models (Goddard, 1997; Wierzbicka, 1994a, 2006).

There are many examples of this line of research applied to emotion in a number of languages, like German (Durst, 2001), Russian (Gladkova, 2010), Japanese (Hasada, 2008; Travis, 1998), Chinese (Ye, 2001, 2006a), Greek (Athanasiadou, 1998), Amharic (Amberber, 2001), Mbula (Bugenhagen, 2001), East Cree (Junker & Blacksmith, 2006), Malay (Goddard, 1998), Australian aboriginal languages (Harkins, 1990, 2001), Biblical Hebrew (Myhill, 1997), and English (e.g., Goddard, 2002a; Wierzbicka, 1992b, c, 1999). For example, Wierzbicka (1999a: 51–53) describes the difference between English *happiness* and *joy* in the following terms: *joy* is characterized by the assessment that "something very good is happening" and "I want this to be happening." *Happiness*, on the other hand, implies an evaluation about the past (not the present) concerning more than one event, and affecting *me* specifically; therefore, it is defined by the features "some very good things happened to me" and "I wanted things like this to happen." Additionally, unlike *joy*, *happiness* includes the idea that "I can't want anything else," which makes it closer to *contentedness*.

One of the major advantages of the NSM paradigm is that the semantic primes constitute a systematic common language to identify cross-linguistic differences or, conversely, combinatorial regularities in the emotion scripts. Another advantage of the method is that, according to Wierzbicka, "the NSM formulae are open to verification (they can be tested against native speakers' intuitions)" (2006: 17). This would indeed be a necessary step in NSM research. The GRID methodology presented in this volume offers a way to achieve that goal (cf. Chapter 27).

Conceptual metaphor and metonymy

Conceptual Metaphor and Metonymy Theory (CMT) is the most typical paradigm for the study of emotion terms within cognitive linguistics. It was initiated by the realization that we talk about abstract concepts in fairly systematic ways. Emotions, for example, seem to be associated to a fairly limited number of recurrent themes, or semantic domains, like FIRE or PHYSICAL FORCES. These associations are observed in the figurative expressions used in a language to refer to the emotions and in the words surrounding literal emotion terms. For example, an association of ANGER with the domain of FIRE is implicit in the figurative verb *fuming*, in the collocation "*kindle* somebody's *anger*" and in more creative expressions like "to see smoke coming out of somebody's ears." What we observe in all cases is an underlying implicit representation of anger as fire. These associations are captured in CMT by formulas like "ANGER IS FIRE" and they are referred to as conceptual metaphors.

The main idea is that conceptual metaphors are conceptual representations of one domain in terms of another, i.e. stable associations in our representation of the world that guide reasoning and influence behavior. For example, if anger is conventionally thought of as a fire, one is invited to infer that the emotion causes an increase in body temperature and is generally dangerous, because – like fire – it is depleting for the experiencer (it can "consume" him/her), it can harm others, and it can easily propagate.

Conceptual metonymies are a similar phenomenon. In this case, the two domains at stake are already related because they are members of a more general one, or because one contains the other.

A typical case of conceptual metonymy is the relationship PART-FOR-WHOLE, where we refer to a thing by mentioning one of its parts (e.g., "we need new *blood* in the team," instead of "we need new people"). This casts the thing referred to in a new light, by highlighting the features of the entity actually mentioned (e.g., in the example above we do not need just "people," but specifically the things associated to people's *blood*: their personality, their idiosyncrasies, and thus the variety they will bring into the team). In the emotion domain many expressions used to label affective experiences are metonymic in this sense because they refer to one of the components of emotion only. For example, in the lexical representation of ANGER in English, we find expressions like "*offended*" that refer to the emotional experience foregrounding only the appraisals concerning its cause. Other examples include "*hot under the collar*" (bodily reaction), "*aggressive*" (action tendencies), or "*upset*" (general feeling). In metonymic expressions, the profiling of one of the components backgrounds the remaining ones.

In CMT, conceptual metaphors and metonymies are sometimes used to characterize the meaning of specific emotion words (for example, English *happiness* vs English *joy*—Stefanowitsch, 2004), but most studies adopt an onomasiological stance and focus on broad emotion concepts. For example, they may study the general category ANGER looking at the metaphors entertained by words like *anger, fury*, and *indignation*, as well as at other phrases and idioms like *blow your top* or *let off steam*.

The studies in this paradigm span a full palette of emotion concepts and languages. They include the work by Barcelona on Spanish and English sadness (1986, 1989) and romantic love (1992, 1995), Kövecses on English pride and love (1986, 1990), happiness (1991), and anger in several languages (1995a, b, Lakoff & Kövecses, 1987), Matsuki (1995) on anger in Japanese, Mikołajczuk (1998) on Polish anger, Ogarkova on English love (2004), jealousy and envy (2007), Soriano on Spanish and English anger (2003, 2005), Taylor, & Mbense (1998) on anger in Zulu, Yu (1995) on Chinese anger and happiness, etc. Some of them have a diachronic orientation (Tissari, 2001, 2006; Györi, 1998). A widespread trait in the field is to use corpora as a source of the linguistic expressions to be analyzed (e.g., Stefanowitsch, 2004, 2006; Ogarkova, 2007). The most recent trend is to look at specialized discourses (e.g., Berger & Jäkel, 2009). Lately some of these findings are also being explored experimentally by psychology (Casasanto & Dijkstra, 2010; Gibbs, 1994; Meier & Robinson, 2004; Nayak & Gibbs, 1990; Williams & Bargh, 2008; Willowski et al., 2009; Zhong & Leonardelli, 2008, etc—for a review of experimental research on emotion conceptual metaphors see Crawford (2009) and Meier & Robinson (2005)).

CMT is a versatile methodology that continues to spur numerous studies on emotion semantics cross-culturally. However, it also entails two limitations. The first is that most studies focus on broad emotion categories, rather than specific emotion concepts; an approach sensitive to lexical variation would be useful to complement these broad onomasiological observations. The second limitation is that CMT uses linguistic patterns to make claims on how emotions are understood by the speakers of a language; as with NSM, a necessary step for the approach would be to contrast the insight provided by language patterns with that provided by the speakers themselves (see Chapers 28, 30, and 36 for examples of how this could be done).

Frame and prototype semantics

Frame and prototype semantics are two typical paradigms for semantic research within cognitive linguistics, although their application to emotion research is less widespread than (the also cognitive) CMT just discussed.

In both approaches, and coherent with the cognitive stance in meaning, concepts are believed to be organized as coherent sets of world knowledge. Semantic frames are representations that capture one part of those conceptual domains (Fillmore, 1975, 1985). More specifically, semantic frames are schematic representations of situations based on repeated experience that are captured by language. They can be characterized in terms of a limited number of interdependent participants (frame elements), necessary in the representation of the frame. For example, the "feeling" frame contains the frame elements Emotion, Emotional State, Experiencer, Evaluation, and Cause. The frame elements are typically realized by lexemes in the sentence. It is assumed that words in use evoke specific frames of knowledge and realize one of the frame roles. For example, the word *angry* in "*Martha feels angry*" realizes the role Emotional State of the "feeling" frame.

The FrameNet Project (https://framenet.icsi.berkeley.edu) is the most important development of this approach. FrameNet is an online database of semantic frames and lexical units associated to them, developed on the basis of linguistic corpora analysis. The frame database "contains, for each frame, its name and description, a list of frame elements, each with a description and examples, and information about relations among them" (Fillmore, Baker, & Sato, 2002: 2). The lexical database is a collection of nouns, adjectives, and verbs with indication of the frames to which their meaning can be related. For example, the noun *anger* is associated to the frame "emotion_directed." According to FrameNet, "the adjectives and nouns in this frame describe an Experiencer who is feeling or experiencing a particular emotional response to a Stimulus or about a Topic." In sentences like (1), *Beth* would be the Experiencer, *Max* the Stimulus, and *intervention* the Topic. Experiencer, Stimulus, and Topic are core elements in the frame "emotion_directed."

1 *Beth* repressed her anger at *Max* about *his intervention*

Other core elements of the frame "emotion-directed" are the Event (the occasion in which Experiencers participate) (2) and the Expressor (3) (body part, gesture, or other form of expression that reflects the Experiencer's emotional state). Non-core elements include the Circumstances (4) (conditions under which the Stimulus evokes its response), the Degree (5) (degree to which the Experiencer feels the emotion), and the Reason (6) (explanation for why the Stimulus evokes a certain emotional response).

2 Some sympathetic bystanders joined the anger *parade.*

3 He could see the anger *in her eyes.*

4 She feels the anger rise *whenever he enters the room.*

5 There is *little* anger left.

6 They can't get over their anger at the company *for how they were treated.*

Different emotion nouns instantiate different types of frame. For example, "Emotion_directed" also applies to *sadness, interest,* and *despair.* By contrast, words like *disgust* and *surprise* instantiate the frame "Stimulus_focus," in which the attention is on the Stimulus and its capacity to bring about a particular emotion in the Experiencer. Another group is formed by words like *compassion* or *pleasure,* which instantiate the frame "Experiencer_focus," where the Experiencer (rather than the Stimulus) is profiled.

An example of FrameNet applied to emotion research is Subirats and Petruck's (2003) analysis of SURPRISE in Spanish and English, or Crocket's (2002) account of Russian SHAME, RESENTMENT, ENVY, and PITY. The goal in both cases is to investigate the various lexicogrammatical realizations of a general affective category, rather than the meaning of any one single term. For example, Subirats and Petruck (2003) notice that, for the expression of emotion predicates in general, English and Spanish share the grammatical frame "Experiencer_subject," in which the Experiencer of the emotion is construed as the subject of the sentence (e.g., *Max panicked/Max se alarmó*). However, while English only has one lexical option for the specific lexicalization of SURPRISE according to this frame, namely the adjective *surprised* (e.g., *Max is/got surprised*), Spanish has two lexicalization possibilities: the adjective *sorprendido* (i.e., "surprised," as in English) and the verb *sorprenderse* (to "undergo-surprise"). As the example illustrates, FrameNet is useful to study cross-linguistic differences in the lexicalization patterns of the same emotion concepts.

Frames often have a temporal dimension, which turns them into a kind of script. The same idea is voiced in psychology for example by Russell (1991a), who in his early work emphasized the process (vs object) nature of emotions and characterized emotion prototypes as scripts. Additionally, frames are to be understood as prototypes. In other words, these temporal frames or scripts are not made of sufficient and necessary features, but prototypical ones (i.e., statistically likely to be present). Following the insight of Wittgenstein (1953) in philosophy and Rosch (1973b, 1975) in psychology, within cognitive linguistics prototypical elements of a category are not assumed to exhibit features that are common to (and indispensable for) the members of the category. Since no features are a priori deemed essential (necessary and sufficient), the central or most prototypical member of a category is defined as the member that shares the largest possible number of features with the rest of the members of the category and the smallest possible number of features with the members of the neighboring ones. Prototypical features are those most frequently shared by the members.

The link between frame/script and prototype semantics had already been suggested by Lakoff (1987) in his "Idealized Cognitive Models" (ICM), which can be defined as prototypical temporal scenarios. One of the best studied ICMs is the ANGER one (Lakoff & Kövecses, 1987), very similar to Shaver's (Shaver et al., 1987) prototype, but defined in terms of ontological elements (e.g., Self, Wrongdoer, Anger, etc) and predications (e.g., Wrongdoer is at fault, Anger exists, there is damage to Self, etc). Lakoff and Kövecses explain what features are most central in the representation of the emotion in English and how deviations from the prototypical script account for less central members of the category. Some of these deviations from the prototype are lexicalized in English by means of a noun (*wrath*), others by means of an adjectival phrase (*cold* anger, *redirected* anger), others by means of a metaphor (*slow burn*) or even an idiom (*don't get mad, get even*), and in many cases the non-prototypical instances of anger are not encapsulated by any specific lexical label, and can only be named indirectly by means of paraphrases or description, like the emotional variants "anger with controlled response" or "anger with an indirect cause." Even in cases where there is no specific "name" (lexical unit) for the emotion variant, the category seems to exist in our conceptualization, because it underlies many of our conventional ways to talk about the emotion. For example, "anger with controlled response" is a non-prototypical form of anger in English, manifested in expressions like *venting one's anger, letting off steam*, or *channeling anger* (a slightly different interpretation of these examples is offered in Lakoff, 1987: 402). In the case of "anger with an indirect cause," the emotional variant seems to be coded grammatically: if the anger is caused by the consequences of an act, rather than by the act itself (i.e., "indirect cause"), English prefers the preposition "about" (angry about something), rather than "for" (angry for something) (Lakoff, 1987: 403).

Frame semantics and the broader domain of prototype semantics offer a valuable framework to study emotion semantics. However, to the best of our knowledge they have not been thoroughly applied to the study of specific emotion words. They are preferred for onomasiological studies (e.g., lexicalization patterns in a general semantic domain, like SURPRISE or ANGER), although their application for semasiological research is possible too.

For example, the frame approach contributes a rich inventory of aspects of the experience referred to by a word (the frame elements) that can be used as an ontology of the domain. Additionally, the approach can reveal differences between similar words in the conceptual frames they prototypically evoke. In turn, prototype-based analyses of emotion concepts allow us to identify the most salient features of a domain and provide a framework to account for the less salient ones.

Corpus-based approaches

Corpus-based methodologies advocate the use of large compilations of naturally occurring discourses from written and oral sources in order to study language. General or reference corpora like the British National Corpus (BNC) tend to include at least 100 million words and are designed to reflect what a language is like at a given period in time.

Within corpus linguistics emotion words are studied as elements in grammatical constructions; hence this approach is said to look at the "lexicogrammar" of the emotion domain. The underlying assumption is that grammatical structure reflects conceptualization: the grammatical shape that concepts acquire in discourse is supposed to reflect how the concepts are mentally represented or construed.

The meaning of specific emotion words can be studied using corpora in a number of ways. First, one can look at the phrases in which a specific emotion term appears (e.g., "*sick with* fear," "*buy* happiness," "*fall in* love"), which are frequently metaphorical. These metaphorical phrases are called "metaphorical patterns" by Stefanowitsch (2004, 2006) and they can help us distinguish the meaning of close synonyms. For example, *happiness* and *joy* are typically considered members of the same emotion category and they are often interchangeable in a sentence. However, the relative frequency of some metaphorical patterns over others for those words tells us that one emotion is more saliently represented in language as a desirable object (we "seek *happiness*", rather than *joy*), while the other is more saliently seen as a substance filling the body (we "overflow with *joy*", rather than *happiness*) (Stefanowitsch, 2004).

A second corpus-based methodology would be to look at the preferred semantic functions that an emotion word adopts in the sentence. For example, emotion nouns could preferentially appear as agents or as patients therefore suggesting that the emotion is more typically conceptualized as a trigger of reactions (emotion does something) or as a state affected by external forces (agent does something to emotion).

A third methodology would be to look at the collocates of an emotion term, i.e. at the words that co-occur with it more often than would be expected by chance. But notice that, defining the meaning of an emotion word in terms of "the company it keeps" through lists of co-occurring terms does not describe explicitly what the word actually means, only the fact that those words are related.

Finally, another corpus approach would be to look at the general lexicogrammatical shape of the sentence in which the emotion term appears. This analysis allows us to identify recurrent lexicogrammatical patterns and it reveals that emotions tend to be represented in complex mixtures (complex emotions), rather than individual types (see Dziwirek & Lewandowska-Tomaszczyk, 2010).

For the onomasiological study of general emotion concepts, it is also interesting to look at their preferred grammatical realization: as nouns, verbs, or adjectives. For example, Wierzbicka (1992b, 1999) has suggested that, for emotion talk, English favors the adjectival construal, while Russian prefers the verbal one. This was corroborated by Pavlenko (2002b) in a study of oral narratives in both languages. Grammatical construals of this sort are referred to by Halliday (1994) as "grammatical metaphors," because a lexical root realized as a noun reflects a cognitive construal as "thing" (e.g., the emotion becomes a metaphorical "object"), whereas the same root as a verb reflects a representation as "process"; adjective construal, in turn, reflects "property or circumstance" (see Chapter 30). Additional detail can be obtained from the grammatical features of those emotion lexemes. For example, SADNESS is preferentially expressed through "active" vs "passive" emotion verbs in Russian, as opposed to English (Wierzbicka, 1995b: 39–40). Finally, word counts in a domain can also tell us about the centrality of a given emotion term in a culture and suggest basic-level candidates in categorization.

The use of linguistic corpora and their annotation for affective features has contributed decisively to the burgeoning study of the ways in which languages represent and express feeling states. The study of emotion term semantics is only a small part in this field. However small, though, the use of corpora in the study of emotion terms has at least three important advantages. First, it provides access to authentic language data representative of large populations. Secondly, it allows for a varied set of methodologies and insights, including quantitative and statistical measures. Third, it makes it possible to consider the role of grammatical form in the meaning of a word. Finally, corpora are an ideal platform for the study of the modulating role of context in word meaning.

4.4 The place of the GRID paradigm among the theories and methodologies

To the extent that the research based on the GRID paradigm aims to investigate the meaning of emotion words, the endeavor is eminently a linguistic one. Therefore, it is important to characterize its position with respect to the theoretical and methodological options discussed in the previous sections.

As stated at the beginning of this chapter, a characteristic feature of the GRID paradigm is that it investigates decontextualized words. This, to a certain extent, constitutes a limitation. The importance of context in the study of meaning is obvious, since words may have a default meaning, but when used in a specific discourse they always adopt a specific sense (cf. sense vs meaning, Vygotsky, 1986). Yet, people seem to be able to say what a word "means," even without a context. A useful concept to account for this ability to pin down (some kind of) meaning in the absence of context is the concept of "modal meaning" defined by Anolli (2005, p. 41) as "the standard outcome of the semantic and pragmatic synchrony process, that is, the prevailing and recursive meaning throughout conventionally given situations within a certain cultural community. [. . .] modal meaning is the preferred (or default) one, regularly predominating in a given set of contexts". This is the definition of semantic meaning endorsed in the GRID study. A similar concept, "modal emotions," has been proposed by Scherer (1994, see Chapter 1) for emotional experiences as well. Modal emotions would be the states resulting from predominant or prototypical appraisal patterns, and the subsequent physiological effects, expressive behaviors, action tendencies, and feeling states that stem from them. Since, arguably, lexical labels capture experiences that are relevant for a particular community, and emotional experiences that recur in a community are more likely to be relevant than infrequent ones, the meaning profiles captured by the GRID can be profitably described as modal meanings reflecting modal emotional experiences in the lingual communities at stake.

With respect to the three main orientations in lexical research, the GRID stands as follows. First, it assumes that word meanings reflect world knowledge, because features deemed relevant by emotion psychology to characterize the emotional experience are used to characterize the meaning of the emotion words that label those experiences. Second, it adopts a synchronic approach for the study of meaning, since it relies on the judgment of native speakers on the current meaning of words in their language. Finally, it adopts both a semasiological and an onomasiological perspective. The starting point is clearly semasiological (feature-based description of the meaning of specific words), but the subsequent identification of the underlying semantic dimensions structuring the semantic space is closer to an onomasiological concern. Additionally, one can investigate the lexicalization of a specific broad concept (e.g., ANGER) identifying the featural profile of the various lexemes (*anger, irritation, fury*, etc) instantiating the overall category and the semantic dimensions articulating the space covered by them (cf. Chapter 22).

The GRID also exhibits some advantages and some limitations with respect to the four methodologies discussed in previous sections. The main advantage with respect to NSM is its capacity to investigate meaning with an empirical, replicable methodology based on quantifiable observations amenable to statistical analysis. It also provides more richness of information in the description of the meaning of words. The main limitation compared to NSM is that, in spite of having been effectively translated into more than 20 languages, the features chosen for the GRID questionnaire may reflect some degree of cultural of language bias, or even ambiguity. By contrast, the features used in the NSM approach should be free of these risks, since they are constructed on the basis of a very limited vocabulary claimed to reflect universal concepts.

The main advantage of the GRID paradigm over frame semantics for the description of specific words out of context would be the amount of featural detail provided. But frames, in turn, reveal in a more explicit fashion the main constituent elements of the emotional scene coded by language (Experiencer, Stimulus, Reason, Result, etc) and they afford us interesting insight about the broad conceptual scenes a particular lexeme typically entertains (e.g., "directed emotion": *anger, sadness*; "stimulus focus": *disgust, surprise*; "experiencer focus": *compassion, pleasure*).

The GRID also offers advantages with respect to metaphor and corpus studies. The main one is its capacity to explicitly spell out the features that differentiate the meaning of two terms. By contrast, in the study of metaphor one needs to infer what the various metaphorical patterns reveal about key semantic aspects like the causation or intensity of the experiences described in figurative terms. Similarly, corpus studies also depend on interpretation to characterize what the various grammatical and co-occurrence patterns of a lexeme tell us about the way a particular emotion is represented. But both metaphor and corpus-based methods offer other advantages over the GRID. The principal one is their ability to generate hypotheses. The nature of the GRID makes it necessary to have a priori predictions about the aspects that may be relevant in the meaning of an emotion word, so that they can be formulated as questions and tested. Conceptual metaphor, corpus studies, and any other approach that looks at the way words are used in language are better suited to generate those predictions to begin with.

In spite of their differences, none of these features make the various approaches incompatible, but rather complementary. There is only one fundamental aspect in which they are intrinsically different: the GRID uses elicited data, while the remaining methodologies rely on observed language use. This may seem unproblematic from a psychologist's point of view. Ortony, for example, explicitly states the following: "if people's *concepts* of emotions have cognitive content, how can we find out what it is? The answer is surely 'Ask them'" (Ortony, 1988: 99). But the matter is not completely uncontroversial for some linguists like Wierzbicka, for whom meaning "can only be established by systematic study of the way words are used (including an investigation of common collocations)" (Wierzbicka, 1995b: 32). She goes on to argue that "to think that untrained native speakers can tell us what a word (e.g., *rabbia*) means, or how it differs in meaning from another word (e.g., *anger*), would be as naïve as to think that an untrained patient can make the best diagnosis of his or her own illness" (Ibid: 32). It seems indeed rather unlikely that people can produce comprehensive accounts of the meaning of a word if simply cued to "describe what it means." However, it is equally unlikely to suppose that they cannot make judgments when presented with specific questions. However partial or inhomogeneous it may be, native speakers of a language have an awareness of what a word entails in their language. Verbal communication would not be possible otherwise. Determining just how comprehensive or homogeneous that knowledge is remains a question for empirical scrutiny and the GRID paradigm is capable of addressing exactly this issue (see Chapter 5). If the semantic profiles emerging from native speakers' judgments of the meaning of emotion words are homogenous (see Chapter 6), the next step will be to compare those profiles with the insight afforded by language use observations (see Chapters 27 to 30). Arguably, the final step would be to compare accounts of the meaning of emotion words with accounts of actual emotional episodes, to ascertain to what extent linguistic representations resemble our representation of experience (see Chapter 15).

4.5 **Final discussion and conclusions**

Emotions are complex phenomena whose nature and functioning cannot be fully accounted for by any one single discipline. Linguistics contributes to this research agenda by looking at the way emotions are represented and expressed in language. The contribution is extremely valuable, given the centrality of language in the experience and communication of emotion, and its relevance in the methodologies employed by other disciplines (notably psychology). In this chapter we have focused on one salient area of research, the emotion lexicon, and we have reviewed the main theories of lexical meaning of the past century and their take on three crucial aspects of inquiry: the nature of meaning versus concept, the optimal temporal scope in semantic research, and the orientation to adopt in the semasiological-onomasiological axis.

Some stances on these issues are preferable over others if one is to pursue cross-disciplinary research. For example, a synchronic approach is preferable to a diachronic one because the experimental sciences are naturally bound to the here and now of their human participants. Both a semasiological and an onomasiological perspective are desirable, in order to provide detailed descriptions of the meaning of emotion words, as well as accounts of the ways in which broad domains of knowledge are represented in language. Finally, an indispensable condition for interdisciplinary collaboration will be to agree with Ortony, Clore, and Collins (1988: 8) that "emotions are not themselves linguistic things, but [that] the most readily available nonphenomenal access we have to them is through language." This perspective assumes that semantic structure is conceptual structure and that semantic categories reflect the way we represent the world. The question remains whether these semantic concepts observe a prototype structure, as defended in cognitive linguistics, or are susceptible to classical definitions by means of a small number of minimal and sufficient features, as proposed by the generativist school. The answer may lie in between. It may be that prototype categorization is sometimes accompanied by the presence of necessary but non-sufficient features in some categories. The GRID study may help us shed light in this respect.

As an instrument for linguistic inquiry, the GRID paradigm offers an empirical, quantitative, replicable approach to the study of emotion word semantics. It also responds to a pressing need for methodological triangulation in emotion research. Russell put it this way: "We need further evidence of all kinds, but we especially need new methods. Conclusions drawn from current methods need to be subjected to empirical tests that are based on other methods" (Russell, 1991a: 445). This is a crucial idea for the GRID. Linguistics is well equipped to provide accounts of emotion semantics, as illustrated by the four methodological approaches described in this chapter. As we saw, they all have individual advantages. However, they also illustrate two main overall limitations with respect to the GRID paradigm. NSM and frame semantics could be said to offer too skeletal an account of meaning. Metaphors and corpora studies, on the other hand, can only offer indirect information about the meaning of specific words, based on the systematic associations of those words to others in language. For both reasons, a new methodology capable of providing both explicit and detail-rich accounts of lexical content would be a desirable contribution in the field of lexical semantics. The GRID paradigm presented in this volume aims to offer such an approach.

This is not to say that the GRID methodology is devoid of limitations. The most important one may be that it aims to investigate words outside of context. Naturally, the study of decontextualized lexemes is always a partial account of linguistic meaning, to be complemented with studies of the senses acquired by the words in use. This, however, does not undermine the validity or the importance of the decontextualized approach. A methodology like the GRID provides us with *averaged default meanings* (featural and dimensional) of the emotion words, which can be considered a baseline against which to compare meaning modulation in different contexts. Finally, the componential GRID paradigm, built on the basis of psychological and anthropological theoretical principles in the study of emotion, provides a common framework for the comparison of findings across disciplinary domains.

The GRID instrument: Hypotheses, operationalization, data, and overall structure

Chapter 5

The why, the what, and the how of the GRID instrument

Johnny J. R. Fontaine,[1] Klaus R. Scherer, and Cristina Soriano

In the present chapter, we present the operationalization of the GRID paradigm proposed in the first part of the book. The paradigm suggests defining the meaning of emotion words on the grounds of features pertaining to the various components of emotion investigated by several theories in the field. Consequently, the "GRID instrument" was designed as a simple grid table with rows representing the emotion words and columns representing pertinent emotion features. First, we summarize the issues raised and the hypotheses proposed in the first part of the book by the GRID paradigm in terms of different disciplinary perspectives: the psychological perspective (componential, dimensional, and basic-emotion approaches in the study of emotion), the cultural-comparative perspective, and the linguistic perspective. Then we present the development of the GRID instrument and how the various disciplinary perspectives and theoretical approaches have been taken into account. Third, we present the data-analytic procedures that have been used to investigate the research questions and hypotheses addressed in Part II and Part III, as well as in many of the chapters in the remaining parts of the book. A comprehensive overview of the issues and the hypotheses, as well as how they have guided the construction of the GRID instrument and the selection of the analysis procedures can be found in Table 5.1.

5.1 Multidisciplinary perspectives

Psychological perspectives: The GRID paradigm

The GRID instrument is directly based on the GRID paradigm as proposed by Scherer in Chapter 1. The GRID paradigm entails applying the Component Process Model of emotions (CPM) to the feature profile view on the meaning of emotion terms (see Fontaine, Chapter 2). The feature profile view implies that the meaning of emotion terms is decomposed into a set of features that describe the emotion process. Which features describe the emotion process is determined by the CPM. According to the CPM, emotion is defined as *an episode of interrelated, synchronized changes in the states of all or most of the five organismic subsystems in response to the evaluation of an external or internal stimulus event as relevant to major concerns of the organism* (Scherer, 1984b, 2001, 2009c). Based on the CPM, the features that define the meaning of an emotion term should

[1] Correspondence on this paper can be address to Johnny J. R. Fontaine. Department of Personnel, Work and Organisational Psychology. Faculty of Psychology and Educational Sciences. Ghent University. Henri-Dunantlaan 2, 9000 Gent, Belgium. Johnny.Fontaine@UGent.be

Table 5.1 Embedding the operationalization of the GRID instrument and selection of data-analytic strategies into multidisciplinary perspectives on emotion

Disciplinary perspective	Issues/hypotheses	Operationalization via GRID instrument	Analysis strategy for GRID data
Psychological: Componential approach, GRID paradigm	All emotion components are involved in the meaning of emotion terms	Operationalization of all emotion components by specific theories	Comparing emotion components with respect to the standard deviations of their respective features across the 24 emotion terms
	Each emotion component is characterized by its own internal organization because each subsystem has its own function	Where possible, theories are operationalized that allow predicting the internal structure	PCA's per emotion component on component-specific features
	Each emotion component is systematically related to the other emotion components due to synchronization		Regression analyses per emotion component of rest factors (in which the respective emotion component was removed) on component-specific factors
Psychological: Dimensional approach	Three overall dimensions span the emotion domain		PCA on all features from all emotion components
	The three overall dimensions are stable		Per emotion component PCA's on all features except the features from the respective emotion component, and comparing the resulting rest factors with overall factors
	Impact of type of response scale on bipolarity	Implicit bipolar response scale	
	Distinction between emotion terms and feeling terms that represent the general quality of the emotional experience	Emotion terms are rated on features. Feeling terms that represent the general quality of the emotional experience are treated as features that operationalize the Feeling component	Check that the overall emotion structure is not dependent on the feeling features

Table 5.1 (continued) Embedding the operationalization of the GRID instrument and selection of data-analytic strategies into multidisciplinary perspectives on emotion

Disciplinary perspective	Issues/hypotheses	Operationalization via GRID instrument	Analysis strategy for GRID data
Psychological: Basic emotion approach	Basic emotion terms have a more stable meaning across languages and cultures	Guarantee that basic emotion terms are included	Comparing emotion terms with respect to the stability of their feature profiles
	Emotion terms cluster into four basic emotion categories: a joy, an anger, a fear, and a sadness cluster		Hierarchical cluster analysis on average pattern similarities between emotion terms
	Profiles of features differentiate emotion terms		Discriminant analyses on overall and component-specific feature patterns
Cultural-comparative	Interpersonal emotion features	Adding interpersonal features in Appraisal and Action tendency components, and in regulation	
	Interpersonal emotion words	Adding interpersonal emotion words from cross-cultural free listing tasks	
	Overall and component-specific internal structures are stable across cultural and linguistic groups		PCA's on four language groups (Germanic, Latin, Slavic, and East-Asian) and Procrustes rotations of resulting structures toward overall structure
	Exploring differences in meaning of emotion words		Bootstrapping and ANOVA on emotion features
Linguistic	Studying decontextualized meaning of emotion words	Focus instructions on decontextualized meaning	
	Reliable identification of the meaning of words by lay persons		Reliability (Cronbach's alpha) of feature patterns per emotion word

thus describe the state of each organismic subsystem (or emotion component) during the emotion (Scherer, 2005a).

Three related hypotheses about the features that define emotion words arise from the GRID paradigm. The first hypothesis is that the features from all five human subsystems are constitutive of the meaning of emotion terms. Thus, emotion terms are hypothesized to refer at the same time to Appraisals (cognitions), Bodily reactions, Expressions (facial and vocal), Action tendencies, and Feelings. The second hypothesis is that the features from each subsystem are characterized by their own internal organization, because each component is assumed to fulfill its own function. However, this does not mean that the features are unrelated across subsystems. On the contrary, because of the assumption of the CPM that the subsystems react in an organized, synchronized way during an emotion episode, the third hypothesis is that, within the emotion domain the features from the different subsystems are substantially related.

Psychological perspectives: The dimensional approach

The most important hypothesis from the dimensional approach to the study of emotion in psychology is that the emotion domain can be robustly represented by a three-dimensional structure, with valence, power, and arousal as the three main dimensions (e.g., Fontaine et al., 2002; Osgood, May, & Miron, 1975; Shaver et al. 1987; 1992).

Moreover, two other issues require attention. A first issue is the nature of the response scale that is used to judge emotion terms. As explained in Chapter 2, the response scale itself can have a substantial impact on whether or not bipolarity between positively and negatively valenced emotion terms will be observed (Russell & Carroll, 1999). For bipolarity to emerge a bipolar, rather than a unipolar response format, should be used. The bipolar and unipolar response formats differ with respect to the neutral point on the response scale. In a unipolar response scale one end is defined by the neutral point (which refers to the absence of the emotion) and the other end by the presence of the emotion (e.g., not happy to happy). In a bipolar response scale the neutral point is in the middle, while one end refers to the presence of the emotion and the other end to the presence of an opposite emotion (e.g., sad—neutral—happy, strong disagreement to strong agreement). If the underlying construct is bipolar, unipolar response scales lead to highly skewed distributions that reduce the possibility to observe negative correlations between opposite emotions.

A second issue is which terms belong to the domain of emotion words. A comparison between the dimensional, the basic emotion, and the componential approaches to the study of the meaning of emotion terms revealed that the dimensional approach considers a broader domain of words as relevant by including feeling terms that define the overall quality of the emotional experience, like *calm* (e.g., Russell, 1983) or *strong* in the PANAS (Watson, Clark, & Tellegen, 1988), instead of only those that can be more narrowly defined as "emotion" terms (see the design feature definition in Chapter 1).

Psychological perspectives: The basic emotion approach

According to the basic emotion approach in the study of affect, emotion terms refer to a few categorically different and evolutionary selected emotion programs (e.g., Ekman, 1999; Izard, 1977, 2007). Within this approach, a distinction can be made between basic emotion terms that have these basic emotions as their referent and non-basic emotion terms. In older theorizing in the basic emotion domain, these "non-basic" emotions would be variations of the basic ones in terms of intensity, in terms of context, or in terms of blending with other basic emotions (e.g., Fontaine et al., 2002;

Plutchik, 2001). In more recent theorizing also other types of non-basic emotions are allowed for, for instance on the basis of emotion schemas (e.g., Izard, 2007). The first hypothesis stemming from this line of theorizing is that basic emotion terms will have a more stable meaning across cultural groups and languages, as they refer to universal, biologically rooted affect programs. Conversely, cultural and linguistic factors are assumed to have a substantial impact on the other emotion terms, as they refer to specific intensity differences, specific contexts, and specific forms of blending that get encoded in language (e.g., Shaver et al., 1992), or to emotion schemas that are developed in a specific cultural context.

A second hypothesis, based on existing similarity research with emotion terms, is that it is possible to identify four basic clusters of emotion terms, namely a joy, a sadness, a fear, and an anger cluster (e.g., Fontaine et al., 2002; Shaver et al., 1987; 1992). Joy, sadness, fear, and anger are also identified as basic emotions by all basic emotion theories.

Not only basic emotion theory predicts the existence of key emotion categories in language. The CPM framework (Scherer 1994, Chapter 1), also predicts the existence of key emotion categories reflecting "modal emotions". The assumption is that typical, frequently occurring appraisal profiles exist that have adaptive functions in dealing with quintessential contingencies in life. The emotion processes these frequent appraisal profiles trigger are called modal emotions, and are likely to have been encoded in language. According to this framework, emotion words are expected to have a well-defined position in the emotion domain, as they mostly refer to (quasi-)universal contingencies of life. This implies that it should be possible to identify an emotion term on the basis of its feature profile.

Cultural-comparative perspectives

Two broad issues have been raised by cultural studies on the emotion words around the world. The first issue has to do with the features different cultural groups employ to represent emotions. According to some anthropological and cross-cultural perspectives, emotions are anything but natural kinds (e.g., Lutz, 1988). Emotion processes are seen as culturally construed. The organizing principles of the emotion domain are assumed to differ between cultural groups. Two cultural differences have received particular attention in the anthropological and cross-cultural domain. First, it has been suggested that some cultural and linguistic groups define the emotional experience primarily in somatic terms and others more in psychological terms (e.g., Mumford, 1993). Another, and probably even more important, difference concerns the interpersonal nature of emotions. In non-Western cultural groups emotions would be conceptualized as interpersonal processes, whereas in Western cultural groups the intrapersonal aspects of emotions would be much more salient. This cultural difference in the emotion domain has been linked to broad cultural dimensions of collectivism (versus individualism) and interdependent (versus independent) constructions of the self (e.g., Markus & Kitayama, 1991).

A second, frequently raised issue in cross-cultural research is the existence of language-specific emotion terms. Taking English as a point of reference, it has been demonstrated that English emotion terms exist that cannot be translated into other languages (e.g., *sadness* into Tahitian), that there are emotion terms that cannot be translated into English (e.g., Portuguese *saudade*), and that there can be shifts in meaning even for translation equivalent words (e.g., Russell, 1991a).

An instrument that studies the meaning of emotion words from a multidisciplinary perspective should take into account that there can be cultural differences in the relative salience of the emotion features that define an emotion, and even that the emotion domain itself is possibly structured in a different way. Moreover, no translation equivalence can be a priori assumed, and it should be possible to investigate the meaning of language-specific emotion terms. In terms of the GRID paradigm this means that there can be cultural differences in the features that define emotions and how they are related to one another, as well as differences in the meaning of translation equivalent emotion terms.

Linguistic perspectives

As an instrument to study meaning, the GRID is essentially a psycholinguistic tool. Many of the issues and hypotheses formulated in the previous sections are linguistic in nature, since they deal with the meaning of emotion terms. Here we want to draw attention to two issues that are particularly relevant for the GRID from a linguistic methodological perspective. A first issue concerns the object of the questions asked. In psychological research, people are typically asked to report on their own (and sometimes on others') emotional experience. A shared understanding of the meaning of emotion words is taken for granted. Instead, in the GRID instrument people are asked to report on the meaning of emotion terms, and not on their own emotional experiences. A second very important issue is the utility of "lay" people to define the meaning of words. The GRID instrument works with a typical psychological methodology, namely a sample of persons from a cultural group is asked to answer survey questions. This is not a traditional methodology in linguistics, which typically relies on language use observations. The question that needs to be addressed is thus whether lay people can be used to reliably identify the decontextualized meaning of emotion words.

5.2 The development of the GRID instrument

The fundamental design of the GRID instrument is extremely simple: It is a simple grid table with rows representing the emotion words and columns representing the emotion features that are assumed to define these emotion words. The operationalization of this simple design into a usable instrument, however, is the result of a complex process in which the issues from the different theoretical approaches and the different disciplines have been taken into account. The operationalization of the GRID instrument is a further elaboration of the proposal by Scherer (2005a) to use the Component Process Model to study the sematic fields of affect words (see Chapter 1). We first present the selection of the emotion terms, then the operationalization of the emotion features, then the response scale participants used to rate the features with respect to each of the emotion terms, and we end by presenting how the research is framed for the participants in the instructions.

The selection of emotion words

The general aim of the selection process was to select a set of emotion terms that could be universally considered as relevant for and representative of the emotion domain. The selection of words took into account the issues raised by the dimensional, basic emotion, and componential approaches to the study of emotion in psychology, as well as the concerns voiced by cultural-comparative studies, as illustrated above. First, in keeping with the basic emotion approach it had to be assured that those emotion words that are consensually considered to refer to basic emotions were included in the set (e.g., *joy*, *sadness*, *fear*, and *anger*). Secondly, only words could be selected that are considered emotion words by all three theoretical approaches in psychology. For that reason, feeling words that only refer to the general quality of the emotional experience were not included. Finally, consistent with the cultural-comparative perspective, it had to be guaranteed that not only intrapersonal, but also interpersonal emotion terms were represented in a balanced way.

In total, 24 emotion terms (nouns) were selected, which were representative and relevant for both emotion research and daily language use of emotion words, on the basis of three criteria. First,

12 emotion words were selected that are often used in emotion research, namely *anger, contempt, disgust, fear, guilt, interest, joy, pleasure, pride, sadness, shame,* and *surprise*. With this selection criterion it was guaranteed that the terms that are consensually considered as basic emotion terms were included in the research, as they attracted most research in the past decades. Second, eight terms were added that were reported with some frequency by at least 2% of the respondents in a large scale study carried out in Switzerland (Scherer, Wranik, Sangsue, Tran, & Scherer, 2004); the terms were *anxiety, compassion, contentment, despair, disappointment, happiness, irritation,* and *stress*. This criterion contributed to the representativeness of the set of emotion terms. Third, *being hurt, hate, jealousy,* and *love* were added, four typical interpersonal emotion terms that have been reported with some frequency in free-recall and prototypicality rating tasks across very different cultural groups (e.g., Fehr & Russell, 1984; Fontaine et al., 2002; Shaver et al., 1987; Shaver et al., 1992; Shaver et al., 1987, 1992; Van Goozen & Frijda, 1993). This criterion ensured that the set of terms was representative of the emotion domain across cultures. In total, eight of the 24 emotion terms were explicitly interpersonal in nature (namely, *contempt, guilt, shame, compassion, being hurt, hate, jealousy,* and *love*).

Moreover, to further contribute to the cultural relevance of the emotion terms, collaborators were offered the possibility to add emotion terms (in blocks of four) that they considered particularly relevant in their cultural group (or in which they were personally interested). The ratings obtained for these additional words are not included in the cross-cultural analyses reported in the present part of the book, but they are reported in the chapters that specifically focus on those languages and cultural groups.

Emotion concepts can be lexically encoded as nouns, adjectives or verbs across languages. In the GRID instrument only one form was used, namely the nouns. This is also the form that has been mostly used in psycholinguistic studies on categorization of emotion words across languages (e.g., Fehr & Russell 1984; Fontaine et al., 2002; Shaver et al., 1987, 1992).

For reasons of feasibility, participants were invited to rate the meaning of only four of the 24 emotion terms in a single session (see also Chapter 6). To assure that the heterogeneity of the emotion terms to be rated was more or less comparable between participants, the set of 24 emotion terms was divided into four a priori groups of terms: *contempt, disgust, anger, irritation, hate, jealousy* (group 1); *fear, anxiety, stress, despair, surprise, interest* (group 2); *joy, pleasure, pride, happiness, contentment, love* (group 3); and *disappointment, compassion, guilt, shame, sadness, being hurt* (group 4). Each participant received, at random, one term from each of these four groups.

The selection of emotion features

The Component Process Model (CPM) was operationalized into 142 emotion features. These features represent the five human subsystems (or emotion components) that constitute the emotion process according to the CPM: (1) *Appraisal* (cognitive evaluation on different levels of processing), (2) *Bodily reaction* (physiological changes or symptoms), (3) *Expression* (face, voice, gestures), (4) *Action tendency* (motivational changes), and (5) *Feeling* (subjective experience). Features referring to intensity, duration, and the possibility of lasting changes in the experiencer, as well as to the *regulation* of the expression and experience of the emotion were also included.

The relevance of the GRID instrument for the different disciplinary perspectives and theoretical approaches was guaranteed by the operationalization of the emotion components. Their operationalization was based on very different theories from the dimensional, the basic emotion, and the componential approaches to the study of emotion in psychology. The cultural-comparative perspective was also taken into account. By merely relying on the CPM some cultural issues were automatically addressed. For instance, the CPM includes somatic, as well as psychological features, allowing us to investigate whether there are cultural differences in the salience of the somatic component. Moreover, in the operationalization of the emotion components additional interpersonal features were formulated over and above the features suggested by each of the component-specific psychological theories, particularly in the Appraisal component (see Chapter 12), Action tendency component (see Chapter 11), and with the inclusion of regulation features (see Chapter 10).

In the selection of relevant features and their operationalization a number of constraints had to be taken into account. The most important one was the necessity to formulate the chosen features in such a way that the description would be comprehensible to laymen in the cultures to be studied. This excluded the use of *technical terms* as they abound in physiology, psychology, acoustics, and other sciences involved in the study of emotion.

We will now present the theoretical frameworks that were used to operationalize each emotion component. For more in-depth information about the theoretical background and the operationalization of each specific component, the reader is referred to the component-specific chapters of part III in the volume (see Chapter 8 for Feeling, Chapter 9 for Bodily reaction, Chapter 10 for Expression and regulation, Chapter 11 for Action tendency, and Chapter 12 for Appraisals). A complete version of the full GRID questionnaire is reproduced in Appendix 2 of this volume.

For the operationalization of the *Feeling component* we have relied on the dimensional approach to the meaning of emotion terms. Special care was taken to differentiate feeling terms that refer to the general quality of the emotional experience from emotion terms. It was already indicated that the dimensional approach typically treats both types of terms as belonging to the same category. Within the CPM, these terms are clearly differentiated: according to the CPM, emotion terms refer to the whole process of synchronization between emotion components, while feeling terms that represent the general quality of the emotional experience refer to a low-level mapping of these complex emotion processes into (sub)consciousness. The Feeling component was thus only operationalized by "feeling" terms that represent the general quality of the emotional experience, and not by emotion terms (which would lead to tautological results). Given the diversity of dimensional models in the literature, an attempt was made to present all important dimensional models in the operationalization of the Feeling component. Thus, six models were taken into account: the one-dimensional hedonistic model (e.g., Frijda, 1986), four two-dimensional affect models (namely, positive–negative affect (Watson & Tellegen, 1985), pleasure–arousal (Russell, 1980), pleasantness–activation (Larsen & Diener, 1992), and tense arousal–energetic arousal (Thayer, 1996)), and the three-dimensional evaluation–potency–activation model (Fontaine, Poortinga, Setiadi, & Markam, 2002; Osgood et al., 1975; Shaver, Schwartz, Kirson, & O'Connor, 1987). The Feeling component was operationalized by 20 feeling features representing the valence dimension (e.g., felt good), two arousal dimensions (e.g., felt nervous and felt energetic), and the power dimension (e.g., felt strong).

For the operationalization of the *Bodily reaction component* we looked at the psychophysiological emotion literature (e.g., Stemmler, 2003b). We especially based the operationalization of this component on earlier cross-cultural emotion research by Scherer, Wallbott, and Summerfield (1986). They made a distinction between three types of bodily reactions in an emotion process, namely reactions with ergotropic arousal elicited by the sympathetic system, reactions with trophotropic arousal elicited by the parasympathetic system, and more general reactions referring to sensations of warmth and coldness. The Bodily reaction component was operationalized in 18 features (e.g., had the feeling of a lump in his/her throat, felt his/her heartbeat getting faster, felt cold).

For the operationalization of the *Expression component* the basic emotion literature was taken into account (e.g., Ekman, 1972, 1984). The operationalization of the features was based on the extensive cross-cultural study of Scherer, Wallbott, and Summerfield (1986). Facial expressions were operationalized in nine features (e.g., frowned, smiled). For vocal expressions, there were 12 features (e.g., changed the melody of his/her speech, spoke louder). The gestural component was operationalized by five features (e.g., made abrupt body movements, moved toward people or things).

The work of Frijda, on action tendencies, was used as the basis to operationalize the *Action tendency component* (Frijda, 1986, 1987; Frijda, Kuipers, & ter Schure, 1989; Frijda, Markam, Sato, & Wiers, 1995). The 16 action tendencies proposed by Frijda (approach, avoidance, being-with, attending, rejection, indifference, antagonism, interruption, dominance, submission, apathy, excitement, exuberance, passivity, inhibition, and helplessness) were operationalized in 40 action tendency features (e.g., wanted to do damage, hit, or say something that hurt; wanted to sing and dance). Of the 40 action tendency features, 12 included an explicit reference to interpersonal motivations (e.g., wanted someone to be there to provide help or support).

The appraisal theory proposed in the CPM (Scherer, 2001) (see Chapter 1 for a detailed description) formed the basis for the operationalization of the *Appraisal component*. Despite minor differences in terminology, there is a large degree of convergence between a core set of appraisal theorists, and thus the choice for the appraisal features of the CPM is representative for the core group of appraisal theories (see Ellsworth & Scherer, 2003; Scherer, 1999). Each appraisal check of the CPM was operationalized by at least one feature: 22 features (e.g., caused by the person's own behavior, consequences predictable) operationalized the CPM appraisal model. In addition to the features representing the appraisal checks, two more global situation descriptors were added in the form of core relational themes (Lazarus, 1991a) (irrevocable loss and being in danger). Finally, seven interpersonal Appraisal features were added to represent the interpersonal nature of emotions (e.g., had negative consequences for somebody else, was in the center of attention), in order to address the hypothesis from the cultural-comparative perspective that emotions are more interpersonally oriented in non-Western cultural groups.

As indicated above, some features were also selected concerning *regulation*. The selection was made on the basis of Ekman and Friesen's model (1969, 1975), which distinguishes neutralization, deamplification, amplification, masking, and qualification as possible regulatory strategies of emotion. Moreover, the effort to regulate both the internal experience of the emotion and the expression of the emotion were taken into account. The regulation of expression focused on the interpersonal aspect of emotion regulation. Regulation was operationalized by four features (tried to control the intensity of the emotional feeling; showed a stronger degree of emotion than he/she actually felt; showed the emotion to others more than s/he felt it; and hid the emotion from others by smiling).

To complete the picture, participants were asked to rate the *intensity* (the person was in an intense emotional state), the *duration* (the person experienced the emotional state for a long time), and the potential *lasting impact* of the emotional experience (the person will be changed in a lasting way due to the emotional experience).

Finally, two items were added to the set of 142 features about the *cultural prevalence* (how frequently is this state generally experienced in your society), and the *social acceptability* of the emotion (to what extent is it socially accepted to experience this emotional state in your society) in their own cultural group. As these two last features do not describe the emotion process itself, they were not included in most of the analyses reported in this book.

The response scale

Because it has been empirically and statistically demonstrated that the response scale itself has a decisive impact on the observation of bipolarity in the emotion domain, special attention was devoted to its construction. The response scale has been designed as an implicit bipolar response scale (Russell & Carroll, 1999), because it offered the possibility of observing strong bipolarity in the emotion domain (unlike unipolar response scales), while not imposing bipolarity on the data (unlike explicit bipolar scales).

Participants were asked to rate each emotion word on how likely it was that each of the features would apply if a speaker of their language used the emotion word to describe an emotional experience. Participants were asked to evaluate this likelihood on a nine-point response scale ranging from: 1 "Extremely unlikely", through 5 "Neither unlikely, nor likely", to 9 "Extremely likely."

The instructions

Special attention was paid in the instructions to clarify that the study was about the meaning of emotion terms, and not about what people experience themselves. It was made clear that they should rate how likely each feature was when a speaker of their language (thus somebody else) uses the emotion terms to describe an emotional experience. Participants were informed at the beginning of the study that questions would follow about each of the five emotion components, as well as about regulation (plus some extra questions). Each component was briefly described. Participants were first asked to rate the features of the Appraisal component, then the Bodily reaction component, followed by the Expression component, the Action tendency component, the Feeling component, and finally they were asked to evaluate the regulation features and the two general questions.

5.3 Data-analytic procedures for the GRID data

In this last section, we present the data-analytic procedures that have been applied to analyse the GRID data. Like the design of the GRID instrument, the data-analytic procedures have been selected in order to deal with the issues and to test the hypotheses raised by the very different disciplinary perspectives and theoretical approaches that have guided the construction of the GRID instrument. Because a key goal of the GRID is to be useful and understandable by emotion researchers from very different backgrounds a decision was made to select well-known and easy to grasp analytic procedures. We start by introducing the data that have been used for most of the analyses reported in this and the next part of the book, as well as in many other parts of the book. Then we present the analysis procedures that have been used to deal with the hypotheses and issues put forward by the dimensional, the basic emotion, and the componential approaches in the psychological study of emotion, as well as by the, cultural-comparative and linguistic perspectives. Because it is characteristic for the GRID instrument to jointly take these disciplinary perspectives and theoretical approaches into account, it is not always possible to neatly separate the data-analytic procedures according to disciplinary perspectives and theoretical approaches. Therefore cross-references are made regularly.

Format of the GRID data

For each emotion word in each sample the data consisted of a matrix of N rows, with N corresponding to the number of participants that evaluated the meaning of that emotion word, and 142 columns representing the 142 features rated. Two additional features, which referred to cultural prevalence and social acceptability, were not included in the analyses, as they did not describe the emotion process itself. As the focus of the GRID instrument is meaning, an average profile was computed for each emotion word across all the participants that at least moderately agreed on its feature profile. The ratings of a participant were taken into account for the computation of the mean profile if the correlation of the participant's profile with the average profile of the other participants was at least 0.20. Moreover, in order to control for differences in acquiescent response styles between participants within samples, but especially across samples and cultural groups, the data were centered per emotion term: across the 142 features an average score was computed for each emotion term and that average score was substracted from all 142 feature scores of the respective term.

Three data-levels were distinguished for the analyses, namely the sample level, the language family level, and the overall level including all samples. At the sample level, the analyses were executed on the sample-specific two-way matrix consisting of 24 rows representing the 24 emotion terms and 142 columns representing the 142 features, with each cell containing the average centered likelihood score of an emotion feature for an emotion word.

Across the 34 samples analysed (cf., Chapter 6), four larger language families could be identified with at least four student samples, namely the Germanic language family consisting of English-, German-, and Dutch-speaking samples; the Latin language family consisting of French-, Spanish-, and Italian-speaking samples; the Slavic language family consisting of Russian-, Ukrainian-, Polish-, and Slovak-speaking samples; and the East-Asian language family consisting of Chinese- and Japanese-speaking samples. The intermediate level of language families was taken into account for reasons of stability. A sample-specific matrix consists of 3408 (24 × 142) cells, which are on average estimated on the basis of 120 to 150 participants. The sample-specific matrices can thus not only differ because of meaning differences in the emotion domain, but also because of random sampling fluctuation, as well as because of differences in motivation to collaborate and because of the composition of the specific samples (ranging from exclusively linguistics or psychology students, to students from all possible majors at university, as well as a few non-student samples). The language family level was considered a good trade-off between cultural and linguistic variability on the one hand and stability and replicability of the 3408 emotion by feature estimates on the other hand. Per language family, one average two-way matrix was computed with 24 rows representing the 24 translation equivalent terms, and 142 columns representing the 142 features, with the averaged centered score for an emotion term on an emotion feature, across the student samples in that language family, in each cell.

Third, there is the overall level of analysis in which all 34 samples are included. For these analyses a large matrix was constructed consisting of 816 rows representing the 24 emotion terms in the 34 samples and 142 columns representing the 142 features. Thus, in the overall analyses no assumption was made about translation equivalence of the 24 emotion terms, as each term in each sample was treated as a separate observation.

To summarize, most analyses were executed on three types of data sets, namely: on (one or more of) the 34 sample matrices (24 terms by 142 features); or on the 4 language family matrices (24 terms by 142 features); or on a single overall matrix consisting of 816 terms (24 by 34 samples) and 142 features.

Analysis procedures from a linguistic perspective

As already indicated, the GRID instrument is essentially a psycholinguistic instrument and all analyses have been designed to reveal information about the meaning of terms. There is, however, one very basic question, already raised above, which is particularly important from the linguistic perspective, namely whether lay people are capable of identifying the meaning of emotion terms. This amounts to the question of whether lay people agree on the meaning profile of an emotion term and can jointly generate a consensual meaning pattern. From an assessment perspective this question refers to the reliability of lay people's assessment of meaning. This was investigated in a simple way by computing the internal consistency (Cronbach's alpha) of the meaning profile of a term across all participants that evaluated the term in a specific sample. Moreover, the agreement of a participant with the other participants was computed as the correlation of the participant's profile with the average profile of the other participants. Only when the correlation was at least 0.20 was the participant included for the final computation of the mean profile of a term. Reliabilities of 0.80 and higher were considered as good. All reliabilities are reported in Chapter 6.

Analysis procedures from a CPM pattern profile approach

The most basic and most central hypothesis arising from the CPM is that all emotion components define the meaning of emotion terms. This implies that the involvement of the emotion components changes depending on the specific emotion a word refers to. Thus, the more an emotion component is involved in defining the meaning variation within the emotion domain, the more the scores on the features of that component will change across the 24 emotion terms. For each feature the standard deviation was computed across the 24 emotion words in each of the 34 samples. It was first investigated whether that standard deviation differed from zero for each component. Then a repeated measures ANOVA was executed with the emotion components as the between-subjects variable and the samples as the within-subjects variable in order to test whether or not each component differentiates the 24 emotion terms to the same extent. Moreover, using Tukey's pairwise comparisons, it was investigated on which emotion component the emotion terms were most differentiated. This analysis is reported in Chapter 7.

If all components are involved in defining the meaning of the 24 emotion terms, then the second hypothesis can be investigated, namely that each emotion component is characterized by its own internal structure. This hypothesis was investigated by looking at the internal structure of each emotion component in the overall data matrix. The internal structure was investigated by applying a Principal Component Analysis on all features of the respective component across all 816 observations. Principal Component Analyses were applied instead of Exploratory Factor Analyses in order to use the same internal structure analysis for all structural questions at all levels. Because in a single sample there are more features than terms for most emotion components, an exploratory factor analysis could not be executed on the sample-specific data. In the sample-specific data there are less observations than variables (which leads to a non-positive definite data matrix). A Principal Component Analysis, which is in essence a data reduction technique, does not require a positive definite data matrix and can thus be applied in an analysis with more variables than observations (e.g., Tabachnick & Fidell, 2007). Often Principal Component Analysis and Exploratory Factor Analysis converge, especially on the most important factors of a domain (which form the focus of the current study). Moreover, although 24 observations (namely the 24 emotion terms) look small for executing Principal Component Analyses, it can be well defended for the current data because the 24 terms have been selected in a highly systematic way to represent the variability in the emotion domain. Moreover, the feature scores for these 24 emotion terms are very reliable for most samples (see Chapter 6). For the overall analyses, there is no problem as there are 816 observations (24 terms in 34 samples), which implies that there are 5.7 times more observations than the total number of features (142).

The number of factors that has been retained was jointly decided on the basis of three, and where available four, criteria: (1) the scree plot of the eigenvalues (Cattell, 1966), (2) the replicability of the structure across the four language families (see section entitled "Analysis procedures from a cultural-comparative perspective," for details of this criterion), (3) the interpretability of the resulting structure, and (4) where available, the a priori expectations about the structure.

When there was no a priori theory available about which feature had to load on which factor, the factor structure was VARIMAX rotated[2]. However, when an a priori theory was available, the factor structure was orthogonally Procrustes rotated toward the a priori expected structure and it was investigated whether each feature had its highest loading on the predicted factor.

For some components, a first general factor or superfactor of valence emerged on which most features of that emotion component had either a substantial positive or negative loading, an observation that is not uncommon in psychology (e.g., "g" in intelligence, Sternberg & Grigorenko, 2002; or extraversion and neuroticism in personality, Strelau & Zawadzki, 1997). For two emotion components, namely the Appraisal and the Action tendency components, it was further explored whether the general factor concealed interesting residual variation. To that end, residual feature scores were computed in which the features that defined the general factor were partialled out. The remaining relationships among these residualized features were further explored.

The internal structures of the Feeling component, the Bodily reaction component, the Expression component, the Action tendency component, and the Appraisal component are reported in Chapters 8, 9, 10, 11, and 12, respectively.

The third hypothesis stemming from the CPM, namely that each component is substantially related to all other components because of the synchronization during the emotion process, was investigated by regressing each component-specific factor on the four overall factors in which the component itself had been removed (see section "Analysis procedures from the dimensional approach"). The regression analyses for the Feeling component, the Bodily reaction component, the Expression component, the Action tendency component, and the Appraisal component are reported in Chapters 8, 9, 10, 11, and 12, respectively.

Analysis procedures from the dimensional approach

The key hypothesis from the dimensional approach is that the meaning of emotion terms can be represented in a three-dimensional space, with *valence*, *power*, and *arousal* spanning this space. To investigate this hypothesis a Principal Component Analysis was executed on the 142 features across the 816 terms. As in the case of the PCA's on the individual emotion components, the number of factors was jointly decided on the basis of four criteria: (1) the scree plot of the eigenvalues (Cattell, 1966), (2) the replicability of the structure across the four language families (see section "Analysis procedures from a cultural-comparative perspective" for details of this criterion), (3) the interpretability of the resulting structure, and (4) the a priori expected

---

[2] To improve interpretation and meaningfulness of the factors and factor scores, bipolar factors have been systematically oriented according to their common interpretation in the literature. For instance, the valence factor has been systematically scored in such a way that the positive pole referred to positive valence and the negative pole to negative valence.

three-dimensional structure. As there was no a priori theory available to accurately predict for all features which one had to load on which factor, the resulting structure was VARIMAX rotated. The results of this analysis are reported in Chapter 7.

An important research question is whether and to which extent the overall structure is sensitive to removing the indicators of specific emotion components. If an emotion process consists of a synchronization between five human subsystems, then it can be expected that information about four of these subsystems would already convey most of the information about the overall structure. This was investigated by applying five times a Principal Component Analysis on all features except the features of the Appraisals, Bodily reaction, Expression, Action tendency, and Feeling component, respectively. These five reduced structures were then orthogonally Procrustes rotated toward the full overall structure. The stability of the reduced structures was investigated by means of both the congruence between the factor loadings and the correlations of factor scores in the reduced and the full structures. The results of these analyses are reported in Chapter 7.

Analysis procedures from a basic emotion perspective

A hypothesis stemming from basic emotion theory is that the meaning of basic emotion terms will be more stable than the meaning of non-basic emotion terms. The stability of the meaning of a term was investigated by correlating the meaning profile of a term in each of the 34 samples with the average meaning profile for that term (thus generating 34 correlations). Subsequently, it was investigated which emotion terms differed in stability on the basis of paired-sample t-tests. This analysis is reported in Chapter 7.

The second hypothesis stemming from basic emotion theory is the existence of four basic clusters of emotion, namely a joy, an anger, a sadness, and a fear cluster. This was investigated by first computing an average dissimilarity matrix between the 24 emotion terms on the basis of their emotion profiles (average Euclidian distances were computed on the basis of the standardized features). An average linkage hierarchical cluster analysis was executed on this dissimilarity matrix. This analysis is reported in Chapter 7.

Based on the categorical meaning perspective in general, emotion words are not just considered arbitrary points in an emotion space, but categories that take a well-defined position in the emotion domain. This implies that it should be possible to identify an emotion term on the basis of its feature profile. This was investigated through discriminant analyses where the classification accuracy was investigated for the 24 emotion terms across the 34 samples. With 24 terms, complete random classification would lead to a classification accuracy of only 4.2%. Four types of discriminant analyses were executed: (1) on the basis of all 142 features; (2) on the basis of the factor scores on the overall factors that represent the major sources of variability across the 142 features; (3) on the basis of the features of each component separately; and (4) on the basis of the factor scores on the factors that represent the major sources of variability in each emotion component separately. We only report the cross-validated classification accuracy. In cross-validation each emotion term from each sample is classified on the basis of discriminant functions that are derived from all other emotion terms in all samples (thus in which the respective emotion term is not included).

Analysis procedures from a cultural-comparative perspective

A first question from a cultural-comparative perspective is whether the internal structure of a language family or of an individual sample is comparable with the overall structure across all samples and emotion terms. This is investigated by Principal Component Analysis on each language family or on a sample-specific data matrix with the same number of factors as in the overall structure. The specific structure is then orthogonally Procrustes rotated toward the overall structure and the congruence between the factors is investigated (e.g., Fischer & Fontaine, 2011). To interpret the congruence, the following rules of thumb are used: A Tucker's phi of at least 0.85 is considered acceptable, one of at least 0.90 is good, and at least 0.95 is excellent. Next to the congruence measures, it is also investigated whether each feature has its highest loading on the predicted factor after Procrustes rotation.

Finally, there is the issue of comparing profiles of terms between different samples and between different languages. Often no a priori hypotheses exist about the differences in meaning of trans-lation equivalent terms (and of pairs of terms more generally), and the feature profiles of two terms are just exploratively compared in order to generate hypotheses about possible meaning differences. In order to take sampling fluctuations into account when identifying potentially rel-evant features, we have worked with 99% confidence intervals computed on the basis of a simple bootstrap procedure with replacement (e.g., Davison & Hinkley, 1997; Efron & Tibshirani, 1993; Manly, 1997). Furthermore, a visual approach was used to identify those features that differed be-tween two terms. This approach is referred to as the "Visual Hypothesis Testing with Confidence Intervals" in the remainder of this book. When the confidence intervals are non-overlapping, it has been demonstrated that means can be considered significantly different (e.g., Cumming, 2008; Cumming & Finch, 2005; Schenker & Gentleman, 2001). When the mean of at least one of the terms is within the other's confidence interval, it has also been demonstrated that the means do not differ significantly (e.g., Cumming, 2008; Cumming & Finch, 2005; Schenker & Gentleman, 2001). There is, however, debate about the situation when the confidence intervals are overlapping, but the means themselves are situated outside the other mean's confidence interval. According to some, this condition is sufficient to consider the means as statistically different (Smith, 1997). However, it has been shown that the size of the overlap between the confidence intervals has to be taken into account. The rule of thumb that has been proposed is that the proportion of overlap of the margins of error (one half of the confidence interval) has to be smaller than 0.50 for the difference to be significant (Cumming, 2008; Cumming & Finch, 2005; Schenker & Gentleman, 2001). As we often deal with non-normal distributions and compare the means of emotion terms that have been judged by a different number of participants (non-balanced design), it is not clear to what extent the proposed rule of thumb applies to the current data. Therefore, we decided to use the visual testing approach in a conservative way. The difference between means is considered significant only if the confidence intervals were non-overlapping. In cases where the confidence intervals were overlapping, but the means were outside the other term's confidence interval, the difference is only considered interesting for further exploration. For instance, it could be investi-gated whether features with a comparable content all differed in the same direction, which would then substantiate an interpretation of a real difference in meaning. When the mean of one of the terms was within the confidence interval of the other term, the difference was not further considered.

5.4 **Conclusion**

The GRID instrument is based on a straightforward idea: it is possible to describe the meaning of words as a grid table where the rows contain emotion words and the columns emotion fea-tures, and where the cells contain a score indicating the likelihood of each feature to describe the meaning of each word. While the basic idea is simple, its operationalization and the selection of data-analytic procedures is more complex and has taken into account very different perspectives from the major disciplines working on or with emotion words. The goal was to study the hypoth-eses and issues raised by each discipline using a unifying theoretical framework and a common empirical tool.

Chapter 6

Cross-cultural data collection with the GRID instrument

Cristina Soriano,[1] Johnny J. R. Fontaine, Klaus R. Scherer, Gülcan Akçalan Akırmak, Paola Alarcón, Itziar Alonso-Arbiol, Guglielmo Bellelli, Cecilia Chau Pérez-Aranibar, Michael Eid, Phoebe Ellsworth, Dario Galati, Shlomo Hareli, Ursula Hess, Keiko Ishii, Cara Jonker, Barbara Lewandowska-Tomaszczyk, Deon Meiring, Marcello Mortillaro, Yu Niiya, Anna Ogarkova, Nataliya Panasenko, Athanassios Protopapas, Anu Realo, Pio E. Ricci-Bitti, Yuh-Ling Shen, Ching-Fan Sheu, Mari Siiroinen, Diane Sunar, Heli Tissari, Eddie M. W. Tong, Yvette van Osch, Sowan Wong, Dannii Y. Yeung, and Aïda Zitouni[2]

The GRID project described in this volume was conceived as a large international collaboration. Previous chapters have detailed how the GRID instrument was carefully developed as an instrument for the assessment of the meaning of emotion terms. The current chapter elaborates on the steps necessary to use the instrument in different languages and countries around the world and describes the process of data collection.

6.1 Translation of the instrument

The GRID instrument was first developed in English and administered in the UK. Collaborators from different countries were then contacted to represent a variety of cultures and languages in the study. Each collaborator was responsible for the translation of the instrument into his/her mother

[1] Cristina Soriano. Swiss Center for Affective Sciences—University of Geneva. 7, Rue des Battoirs, CH-1205 Geneva, Switzerland. Cristina.Soriano@unige.ch

[2] The authors of this chapter are the dataset owners in the GRID project whose data has been used for the cross-cultural analysis. For further details on their affiliation and contact information please see the list of GRID collaborators at the beginning of this volume and on the GRID website (http://www.affective-sciences.org/GRID).

tongue. They were instructed to follow a translation–backtranslation process (e.g., van de Vijver & Leung, 1997), whereby the instrument was first translated into the target language by a translator and then back-translated into the original language by a second one. Both translators were required to be bilingual or have near-native competence in the two languages involved. Discrepancies between the versions were solved through discussion using a committee approach. The GRID instrument exists at the moment in the following languages:

- *Indo-European family*
  - *Romance group*: French, Italian, Portuguese, Romansh, Spanish
  - *Germanic group*: Afrikaans, Dutch, English, German
  - *Slavic group*: Bulgarian, Czech, Polish, Russian, Slovak, Ukrainian
  - *Greek group*: Greek
  - *Indo-Iranian*: Hindi
- *Afro-Asiatic family*
  - *Semitic group*: Arabic, Hebrew
- *Altaic family*: Turkish
- *Uralic family*
  - *Finno-Ugric group*: Estonian, Finnish, Hungarian
- *Japonic family*: Japanese
- *Sino-tibetan family*: Chinese, Burmese
- *Niger-Congo family*: Sepedi
- *Unclassified*: Basque

A translation of the GRID words into the currently available languages can be found online at http://www.affective-sciences.org/GRID (cf. Appendix 1 to this volume for further details on the availability of the different GRID materials).

6.2 **Questionnaire administration**

The GRID questionnaire was administered in a controlled web study (Reips, 2000, 2002). All language versions were hosted at the site of the Swiss Center for Affective Sciences (http://grid.unige.ch). When necessary, paper versions of the questionnaire were also provided, and the data were then manually introduced into the database by the collaborators. Because of the practical inconvenience of this second approach, it was only implemented in cases when the technological resources of the location precluded electronic administration.

Each data sample was identified by a different study code. This was provided by the collaborator to the prospective participants, who registered in the study using an e-mail account to receive a personal password. Study code and password granted them independent access to the secure interface of the study, in which they could fill in the questionnaire at their own pace. Participants were given the chance to log out of the study and log back in if necessary, but they were always encouraged to fill in the questionnaire in one session, which typically lasted one hour.

To ensure that it would take no more than one hour to fill in the questionnaire, each participant was assigned four emotion terms only, randomly selected from 4 groups: *contempt, disgust, anger, irritation, hate,* or *jealousy* (group 1); *fear, anxiety, stress, despair, surprise,* or *interest* (group 2): *joy, pleasure, pride, happiness, contentment,* or *love* (group 3); and *disappointment, compassion, guilt, shame, sadness,* or *being hurt* (group 4).

They were then asked to rate the likelihood, using a 9-point scale (ranging from "extremely unlikely (1)" to "extremely likely (9)"), that each of the 142 emotion features could be inferred when a person from their cultural group used the emotion terms to describe his or her emotional experience. Each of the 142 emotion features was presented on a separate screen, and participants rated the four emotion terms at the same time. Participants validated their answers by clicking a "Continue" button, and could not navigate at will between the screens of the questionnaire.

In addition to the 142 feature ratings, participants were asked to evaluate the cultural prevalence and the social acceptability of each emotion. Moreover, they were required to provide some background information with regards to their sex, age, mother tongue, the country where they had spent most of their life, where they lived at the time, their level of education, their academic field (if they were students), and their country of origin (if they, their parents, or their grandparents had migrated to the country where they resided at the time). Participants were also asked to list the five languages of which they had at least some passive knowledge, and to rate the frequency ("on a daily basis," "at least once a week," "at least once a month," "several times a year," "(almost) never") with which they would speak, read, and write in those languages[3].

The collaborator responsible for data collection was also the administrator of the study. Prior to launching the study, collaborators were requested to test-run the questionnaire interface in their language. During the study, a specific interface and independent password allowed them to monitor the development of the data collection at all times, and to download the results at the end.

A copy of the full text of the GRID questionnaire (in English) can be found in an appendix to this volume (see Appendix 2).

6.3 **Samples and participants**

In total, 40 samples have been collected so far with the GRID instrument. Of these 40 samples, only 34 were selected for the cross-cultural GRID database reported in this volume, and are further described below. Three samples (Hungarian, Bulgarian, and Portuguese) were not included because their data collection was not complete at the time of the final analyses for the book. Moreover, three samples that were complete were not included because of their very poor interrater reliability and/or uninterpretable structural deviations in a preliminary analysis of the data; these were the Gabon, the Sepedi (South-Africa), and the Hindi (India) samples. The average interrater reliability in the French Gabon and the Sepedi South-African samples was lower than 0.70. Additionally, their internal structures clearly deviated from the other samples, most likely because of the low reliabilities. The Hindi Indian sample exhibited reasonable interrater reliabilities (Cronbach's alpha on average 0.87 per emotion term), but demonstrated a clearly deviant internal structure in the preliminary analysis. As it consisted of a convenience sample of mainly postal workers, and it was unclear to what extent the results of this sample could be generalized to Hindi speakers in general, this sample was also removed from the database.

The final cross-cultural GRID database comprises 34 datasets from 27 countries covering a total of 23 different languages (see Table 6.1). In some cases several languages were collected in one country (e.g., Basque and Spanish in Spain), several countries were sampled for a single language (e.g., English in the USA, UK, and Singapore), or several regions were sampled within the same

---

[3] Additionally, participants were required to choose from two personality profiles, that which described them best. The two options were as follows: (Person A) "Likes languages a lot, reads a lot, expresses herself or himself clearly, likes games like cross-words, does not like numbers." (Person B) "Is good at Maths, is at ease with abstract symbols, likes strategy games like chess, does not pay much attention to her or his writing style."

Table 6.1 GRID dataset description

Language	Country	Region	N	F	M	Age range	Mean age	SD age	Format	Compensation
Afrikaans	South Africa	Potchefstroom	184	130	54	19–41	21.11	2.11	online	course credit
Arabic	Tunisia	Tunis	120	62	58	20–61	27.79	9.28	paper	none
Burmese	Burma	various	66	27	39	16–54	26.32	8.20	online	remuneration
Chinese	China	Beijing	247	201	46	18–28	19.70	1.25	online	course credit
Chinese	China	Hong Kong	151	96	55	17–34	20.18	1.87	online	course credit
Chinese	Taiwan	Chia-Yi	211	159	52	17–30	20.16	1.59	online	course credit/remuneration
Czech	Czech Republic	Zlín	120	43	77	17–55	19.28	3.91	online	none
Dutch	Belgium	Gent	118	61	57	18–27	20.95	1.50	online	course credit
Dutch	Netherlands	Tilburg	178	142	36	17–38	19.76	2.78	online	course credit
English	Singapore	Singapore	103	85	18	18–26	20.03	1.58	online	course credit
English	UK	Belfast & York	201	124	77	18–49	21.51	4.43	online	remuneration
English	USA	Michigan	182	129	53	16–22	18.51	0.77	online	course credit
Estonian	Estonia	Tartu	192	160	32	18–52	23.15	5.80	online	remuneration
Euskera	Spain	Basque Country	130	91	39	18–54	23.27	5.58	online	remuneration
Finnish	Finland	various	120	101	19	19–68	32.75	11.61	online	raffle
French	Canada	Montreal	96	71	25	17–80	25.96	11.59	online	course credit
French	Switzerland	Geneva	140	101	39	18–48	23.79	5.86	online	course credit
German	Germany	Berlin	120	92	28	18–57	24.47	6.15	online	course credit
Greek	Greece	various	199	159	40	18–50	26.04	5.65	online	none
Hebrew	Israel	Haifa	81	42	39	24–59	38.99	8.63	online	none
Italian	Italy	Bari	191	166	25	18–50	20.08	3.71	online	course credit
Italian	Italy	Bologna	122	95	27	19–43	21.70	4.16	online	course credit
Italian	Italy	Turin	168	150	18	18–50	21.41	5.63	online	course credit
Japanese	Japan	Sapporo	129	56	73	18–34	19.40	1.69	online	remuneration
Polish	Poland	Lodz	124	95	29	15–55	23.17	6.32	online	none
Romansch	Switzerland	various	175	110	65	16–65	23.18	11.08	online	remuneration
Russian	Ukraine	Kiev	135	90	45	16–57	24.97	9.11	online/paper	none
Slovak	Slovakia	Trnava	128	107	21	18–28	22.20	1.59	online	none
Spanish	Chile	Concepción	88	65	23	18–38	20.17	2.61	online	course credit

Table 6.1 (continued) GRID dataset description

Language	Country	Region	N	F	M	Age range	Mean age	SD age	Format	Compensation
Spanish	Peru	Lima	220	138	82	16–36	19.84	2.96	paper	course credit
Spanish	Spain	Basque Country	159	99	60	18–55	22.99	6.00	online	remuneration
Spanish	Spain	various (South)	98	67	31	16–64	33.45	13.72	online	none
Turkish	Turkey	Istanbul	135	117	18	19–34	21.49	2.81	online	course credit
Ukrainian	Ukraine	Kiev	116	82	34	17–59	24.23	9.27	online	none

country (e.g., Italian in the North and South of Italy). The entire database included 4948 participants (1434 males and 3514 females), with a mean age of 23.29 (mean SD 5.31).

The pool of participants varied across studies. Most of our samples were collected among university students who took part in the collaborators' courses, but in some cases participants were also recruited through mailing lists or fliers. Most participants received course credit or remuneration in the form of an individual monetary compensation (or a gift) or the right to participate in a lottery. Collaborators were instructed to recruit 120 participants for their studies, gender balanced to the extent possible. In most cases the participants filled in the questionnaire autonomously, at school or at home. In some cases, though, the collaborator arranged for a computer room and supervised the data collection. After the study, the collaborators could download the collected data from the administrator's interface.

6.4 **Interrater reliabilities**

Interrater reliabilities were computed for each emotion term in each sample. The interrater reliability was computed as a Cronbach's alpha, with the participants rating the same emotion term being treated as variables and the 142 features being treated as observations (see Table SM 1 and Table SM 2).[4] For each emotion term within each sample, a participant was removed from the computation of the average feature scores if the correlation between the participant and the average of the other participants rating the same term was smaller than 0.20. Thus, only those participants that converged at least to some extent with the other participants were used to compute the average feature scores per term (see Table SM 3 and 4 for the interrater reliabilities with only the converging participants).

In Table 6.2, the average interrater reliabilities across emotion terms per sample are reported, based on all the converging participants. Each emotion term was on average rated by 24.72 participants leading to an average interrater reliability of 0.91. On average about two participants (or about 8%) did not converge with respect to the meaning of the emotion term. When the nonconverging participants were removed, the reliability reached 0.92.

In Table 6.3, the average interrater reliability across samples per emotion term is reported both for all participants and for the converging participants only. Differences were observed between the

---

[4] All supplementary materials (SM) are available at the GRID website: http://www.affective-sciences.org/ GRID. See Appendix 1 ("Availability") for further details.

Table 6.2 Average interrater reliability (Cronbach's alpha) and average number of participants across emotion words per sample with all (A) and with only converging (C) participants

Language	Country (region)	Alpha$_A$	N_A	Alpha$_C$	N_C
Afrikaans	South Africa	0.93	30.42	0.93	27.67
Arabic	Tunisia	0.84	19.42	0.86	16.92
Burmese	Burma	0.76	10.83	0.79	9.63
Chinese	China (Hong Kong)	0.84	24.42	0.87	20.17
Chinese	China	0.96	40.79	0.96	37.46
Chinese	Taiwan	0.96	34.83	0.96	33.00
Czech	Czech Republic	0.78	19.42	0.86	12.83
Dutch	Belgium	0.96	33.04	0.96	31.46
Dutch	Netherlands	0.96	29.50	0.96	29.25
English	Singapore	0.90	16.83	0.91	15.96
English	UK	0.94	32.58	0.95	30.04
English	USA	0.93	29.75	0.94	26.58
Estonian	Estonia	0.96	31.88	0.96	31.46
Euskera	Spain (Basque Country)	0.91	21.58	0.93	19.83
Finnish	Finland	0.95	20.08	0.95	19.96
French	Canada	0.90	16.00	0.91	14.92
French	Switzerland	0.94	23.17	0.94	22.58
German	Germany	0.93	20.00	0.94	19.58
Greek	Greece	0.95	33.04	0.96	34.71
Hebrew	Israel	0.89	13.42	0.89	12.88
Italian	Italy (Bari)	0.95	31.46	0.95	30.25
Italian	Italy (Bologna)	0.95	31.46	0.95	30.25
Italian	Italy (Turin)	0.94	27.96	0.95	27.29
Japanese	Japan	0.93	21.17	0.93	20.58
Polish	Poland	0.92	20.42	0.92	19.67
Romansch	Switzerland	0.76	28.87	0.85	16.79
Russian	Ukraine	0.90	21.71	0.92	17.42
Slovak	Slovakia	0.89	21.29	0.90	19.29
Spanish	Chile	0.85	14.67	0.87	13.38
Spanish	Peru	0.91	36.67	0.92	32.75
Spanish	Spain	0.91	16.17	0.91	15.50
Spanish	Spain (Basque Country)	0.93	26.42	0.94	25.04
Turkish	Turkey	0.92	22.33	0.93	20.58
Ukrainian	Ukraine	0.86	18.92	0.89	15.38
Total		0.91	24.72	0.92	22.68

Note: *Alpha$_A$*: Average Cronbach's alpha across all participants; N_A: Average number of participants per emotion word; *Alpha$_C$*: Average Cronbach's alpha with only converging participants (participant-rest correlation ≥0.20); N_C: Average number of converging participants.

Table 6.3 Average interrater reliability (Cronbach's alpha) and average number of participants across samples per emotion words with all (A) and with only converging (C) participants

Emotion words	Alpha$_A$	N_A	Alpha$_C$	N_C
joy	0.95	24.29	0.95	23.09
happiness	0.94	24.35	0.94	22.76
fear	0.94	25.24	0.94	23.59
sadness	0.93	24.71	0.94	23.32
contentment	0.93	24.21	0.94	22.41
pleasure	0.93	24.47	0.94	22.82
shame	0.93	24.65	0.93	23.35
being hurt	0.92	26.85	0.93	25.38
love	0.92	23.47	0.93	22.21
despair	0.92	24.15	0.93	22.15
anger	0.92	23.79	0.93	22.53
stress	0.92	24.47	0.92	22.82
anxiety	0.91	24.71	0.93	22.74
disappointment	0.91	23.94	0.92	22.12
irritation	0.91	24.50	0.92	22.26
guilt	0.90	24.56	0.92	22.56
pride	0.90	27.59	0.92	24.06
hate	0.90	24.50	0.91	22.65
disgust	0.90	25.15	0.91	22.79
interest	0.89	26.06	0.91	23.15
surprise	0.87	24.00	0.89	22.09
jealousy	0.86	26.65	0.88	23.82
compassion	0.82	23.71	0.85	19.91
contempt	0.82	23.29	0.85	19.68

Note: *Alpha$_A$*: Average Cronbach's alpha across all participants; *N$_A$*: Average number of participants per emotion word; *Alpha$_C$*: Average Cronbach's alpha with only converging participants (participant-rest correlation ≥0.20); *N$_C$*: Average number of converging participants.

emotion terms with respect to their reliability. Two emotion terms in particular, *compassion* and *contempt*, are characterized by a lower interrater reliability and by a larger number of participants that did not converge in their ratings (more than three people, rather than the two on average).

The mean feature scores were centered around the grand mean across all features per emotion term. This centering was done to reduce the impact of interindividual differences in response tendencies, as well as sample and cultural differences in them (see Chapter 5).

A trend was observed for non-Western samples to show less convergence between raters on the meaning of emotion terms. For instance, two of the least reliable samples were Black African samples. Unfamiliarity with a web-based testing design (or its paper and pencil version) constitutes a very likely explanation for this observation. A comparable effect was also observed between Western samples that differed in their familiarity with a web-based testing design. For instance, the average Cronbach's alpha among French-speaking students in Switzerland was 0.94, but it dropped to 0.76 in a sample of Romansch-speaking Swiss older adults that were not so familiar with the web-based testing environment.

As already mentioned, differences were observed not only between samples, but also between emotion words, especially for *compassion* and *contempt*, which showed a lower interrater reliability. A possible explanation for *compassion* could be that the meaning of the term depends on the emotion felt by the person for whom one feels compassionate. Depending on whether one thinks the other is undergoing a more or less negative experience, a different feature profile will emerge for *compassion*. It is less clear why *contempt* showed less interrater reliability than the other emotion terms, as it has even been proposed that contempt is an evolutionarily developed basic emotion (e.g., Ekman & Friesen, 1986).

In general, however, it can be concluded that with only 25 participants on average per term, very reliable feature patterns emerged. Thus, lay people are, on average, capable of identifying the decontextualized meaning of emotion words in their languages.

Chapter 7

The global meaning structure of the emotion domain: Investigating the complementarity of multiple perspectives on meaning

Johnny J. R. Fontaine[1] and Klaus R. Scherer

The present chapter provides a first overview of the meaning structure of the emotion domain on the basis of the GRID database. With the multidisciplinary perspectives that have guided the construction of the GRID instrument and the extensive data collection, an extremely rich database has been generated that can be analysed in many different ways and that can be used to answer very different research questions. This chapter focuses exclusively on the global or overall meaning structures that emerge from the GRID research across all languages, countries, and samples, as well as across all emotion terms and all emotion components. By doing this, the present chapter takes a universalistic stance: it aims at identifying the common denominator of meaning in the emotion domain. It is, however, important to interpret the results of the present chapter together with the results reported in the subsequent parts of the book, which focus on specificity of each emotion component (Part 3), on the relationship between meaning and psychological processes (Part 4), on cultural differences in the meaning in the emotion domain (Part 5), on linguistic issues in the study of meaning of emotion terms (Part 6), as well as on the specific issues that have been raised by the contributors of the GRID project (Part 7). Searching for both general and culturally, linguistically, and psychologically specific aspects are not mutually exclusive, but complementary aims. The general patterns of meaning can be used as a point of reference to identify specificity, and vice versa, the identification of specificity clarifies the boundaries of general tendencies.

The analysis of the overall structure is guided by the hypotheses and research questions that were developed in the first part of this book (see Chapters 1 to 4), and that have been made explicit in Chapter 5. In the current chapter, we systematically restate those hypotheses and research questions, organized in terms of the three theoretical approaches from the psychological perspective on meaning that have guided the construction of the GRID instrument, namely the componential, the dimensional, and the basic emotion approach.

[1] Corresponding author: Johnny J. R. Fontaine. Department of Personnel, Work and Organisational Psychology. Faculty of Psychology and Educational Sciences. Ghent University. Henri-Dunantlaan 2, 9000 Gent, Belgium. Johnny.Fontaine@UGent.be

7.1 **The componential approach**

Based on the Component Process Model of emotion (CPM; Scherer, 1984b; 2001; 2005b; 2009c; Chapter 1) the feature profile view on meaning suggests that the meaning of an emotion term can be decomposed into a profile of features. The CPM has been used to identify the components and features that are needed to define emotion terms. According to the CPM, an emotion is a process that is elicited by goal-relevant events and that consists of coordinated, synchronized changes in five emotion components, namely Appraisals, Bodily reactions, Feelings, Expressions, and Action tendencies, in order to prepare the organism to react adaptively to the event. According to this definition, an emotion term can be decomposed into features that represent the coordinated and synchronized changes in each of these five components. This implies the fundamental hypothesis of the GRID, namely that *features from ALL emotion components play a constitutive role in the meaning of emotion terms (Hypothesis 1),* for the very reason that it is the synchronized activity between these components that constitute the emotion. If confirmed, the question arises *how salient each of these emotion components are in defining the meaning of emotion words (Research Question 1).* The CPM predicts that features from all emotion components will be involved in the meaning of emotion terms, but does not specify the relative role or weight of individual components or features in the process. The additional hypothesis from the componential approach presented in Chapter 5, namely that each emotion component will be characterized by its own internal structure, is not investigated in the current chapter, but will be treated in the next part of this volume (see Chapters 8 to 13).

7.2 **The dimensional approach**

According to the dimensional approach, the emotion domain can be represented by a small number of dimensions. This approach has been very popular in psychological assessment of emotions and affects, as well is in psycholinguistic research on the meaning of emotion words (see Chapter 2). In psychological assessment there are four frequently used two-dimensional models for which it has been demonstrated, empirically, that they consist of a VALENCE and an AROUSAL dimension, or a rotation thereof (Yik, Russell, & Feldman-Barrett, 1999). Psycholinguistic research looking either at the connotative meaning structure of words in general (e.g., Osgood, May, & Miron, 1975; Osgood, Suci, & Tannenbaum, 1957) or at the psychological similarities between more narrowly defined emotion words (e.g., Fontaine, Poortinga, Sediadi, & Markam, 2002; Shaver, Schwartz, Kirson, & O'Connor, 1987; Schaver, Wu, & Schwartz, 1992) has identified a three-dimensional structure across languages, namely a VALENCE, POWER, and AROUSAL dimension. In consequence, when the *meaning* of emotion words is studied, three rather than two dimensions are to be expected.

A low-dimensional representation of the emotion domain is compatible with the CPM, because of the presumed synchronization of the emotion components. Related emotions will share comparable forms of synchronization and their respective feature profiles will overlap. If the CPM represents a plausible model of the emotion process, it can be expected that the overlap between the respective feature profiles will correspond to the psychological similarities between the emotion terms. This implies that the relative degree of overlap between the feature profiles can also be *represented by the three dimensions of VALENCE, POWER, and AROUSAL (Hypothesis 2).*

In a preliminary study with the GRID instrument in three western languages (English, French, and Dutch), a fourth well-interpretable dimension was observed over and above the three dimensions of VALENCE, POWER, and AROUSAL (Fontaine, Scherer, Roesch, & Ellsworth, 2007). The fourth dimension particularly differentiated the term *surprise* from the other emotion terms. The dimension was characterized by Appraisals of suddenness and unpredictability, and by facial expressions of jaw drop and opening eyes widely. This early observation raises the research question of *whether the fourth dimension can be replicated across a broad range of languages and cultural groups (Research Question 2a)*.

A subsequent research question concerns the stability of the dimensional structure after omitting individual emotion components. According to the CPM, each emotion component forms an integral and constitutive part of the emotion process. However, as the dimensional representation is based on the overlap between patterns of features defining the synchronized activity in each emotion component, it could be expected that four of the five components will be largely sufficient to identify the overall dimensional structure. It will thus be investigated *whether the overall dimensional structure is stable when only relying on four of the five emotion components* (namely, after removing the features representing the Appraisal, Bodily reaction, Expression, Action tendencies, and Feeling components, respectively) *(Research Question 2b)*.

A particularly important question from the dimensional approach is why self-report assessment studies and psycholinguistic studies differ in the dimensionality they find empirically in the emotion domain (two versus three dimensions). Because the GRID instrument decomposes the meaning of emotion terms into an extensive pattern of 142 features, it is possible to *investigate more precisely how the three dimensions of* VALENCE, POWER, *and* AROUSAL *relate to one another, as well as to investigate their relative importance in defining the meaning structure of the emotion domain (Research Question 2c)*.

7.3 **The basic emotion approach**

The basic emotion theories (e.g., Ekman, 1999; Izard, 1977) propose the existence of a few universal, biologically rooted, and categorically different emotion processes. There is little agreement between the different basic emotion theories about the exact number of basic emotions, except for four recurring families—joy, sadness, fear, and anger. The same four basic emotion clusters emerge in psycholinguistic research using emotion terms, namely a joy, a sadness, a fear, and an anger cluster (e.g., Fontaine, Poortinga, Sediadi, & Suprapti, 2002; Shaver, Schwartz, Kirson, & O'Connor, 1987; Shaver, Wu, & Schwartz, 1992). Thus one can reasonably hypothesize that *four basic clusters of emotion terms can be identified in the emotion domain on the basis of their feature profiles (Hypothesis 3a)*.

The universality assumption in basic emotion theories implies that *terms for basic emotions can be expected to have a more stable meaning across languages and cultural groups than other emotion terms (Hypothesis 3b)*. As basic emotions are assumed to be evolutionary developed modules that are triggered by well-defined stimulus configurations, the expectation is that they tend to be encoded first and in the same way across languages and cultural groups. Much more linguistic and cultural variability is expected with respect to which specific intensity differences, blendings, contexts, or broader emotion schemata's that have been additionally encoded in emotion words (e.g., Izard, 2007; Plutchik, 2001).

All of the hypotheses and research questions described above start from emotion terms in natural languages and concern both the feature profiles that are associated with these terms and the associations between the emotion terms on the basis of their respective feature profiles. It is also meaningful to reverse the question and start with the feature profiles. The fact that it was possible to identify a set of translation equivalent words for each of the 24 emotion words across languages and cultural groups seems to indicate that these 24 emotion words are differentiated from one another in similar ways. This observation also fits the concept of modal emotions within the CPM framework (Scherer, 1994; Chapter 1). Modal emotions are emotions that are triggered by typical, frequently occurring appraisal profiles that have adaptive functions in dealing with quintessential contingencies in life. Many of these contingencies are relevant across cultural and linguistic groups and are thus likely to be encoded in similar ways across cultural groups. If the meaning of emotion terms indeed consists of changes in each of the emotion components, and these patterns of processes are comparable between cultural and linguistic groups, then the feature profiles should allow the associated emotion term to be identified. The last research question of the present chapter is then *how well it is possible to identify the specific emotion words on the basis of the profiles of features (Research Question 3)*.

For a description of the samples that have been used in the current chapter the reader is referred to the previous chapter (see Chapter 6). For a description of the design, the instrument, and the data-analytic methods, the reader is referred to Chapter 5.

7.4 **Results**

The componential approach

The role of each emotion component in defining the meaning of the 24 emotion terms (Hypothesis 1) was studied in a very simple way: the variation in the likelihood ratings of the features of each component was investigated. Participants were asked to rate to what extent a feature was likely to be inferred if a certain emotion term was used. We can expect that those components that are relevant for differentiating emotion terms from one another will show a large variation in the likelihood of their features. In contrast, those components that are irrelevant will not show any variation at all. For each feature, the standard deviation has been computed across the 24 emotion words in each of the 34 samples. When these standard deviations are averaged per emotion component across all samples, it is indeed observed that each emotion component is involved in defining the meaning of emotion terms as predicted by Hypothesis 1. The average standard deviations range from 1.33 to 1.98: $M_{\text{expression component}} = 1.33$, $M_{\text{appraisal component}} = 1.35$, $M_{\text{bodily sensation component}} = 1.35$, $M_{\text{action tendency component}} = 1.60$, and $M_{\text{feeling component}} = 1.98$. It is thus observed that the emotion terms differ from the average score at least 1.33 scale points per component on average across samples and across features that define the respective component. To better interpret the meaning of these standard deviations, the Expression component can be taken as a point of reference. This can be justified given the long-standing tradition that treats expression as the hallmark of emotion because of its communicative function (Darwin, 1872). It can be observed that ALL emotion components differentiate emotion terms at least to the same extent as the Expression component.

To investigate whether some emotion components were more salient than others in defining the meaning of emotion words (Research Question 1), a repeated measures ANOVA was executed on the standard deviations of the features across the 24 emotion terms with the components as the between-subjects variable and the samples as the within-subjects variable. There was a significant effect of the emotion component [$F(4,130) = 7.79$, $p < 0.000$, *partial* $\eta^2 = 0.19$]. Tukey's post hoc pair-wise comparison tests, however, revealed that only the Feeling component was characterized by significantly more variation across the 24 emotion terms than the other four components. The other four emotion components did not differ significantly from one another.

The dimensional approach

First, the dimensional representation of the emotion domain on the basis of the feature profiles was investigated (Hypothesis 2 and Research Question 2a). Then, it was investigated how stable the overall emotion structure is with only four of the five emotion components (Research

Question 2b). Finally, the relative importance of the three dimensions of VALENCE, POWER, and AROUSAL as well as their mutual relationships were investigated (Research Question 2c).

The dimensional representation of the emotion domain. To investigate the dimensional structure of the emotion domain a principal component analysis (PCA) was executed on the 142 emotion features across all 24 terms in all 34 samples. Four criteria were relied upon to identify the number of factors, namely: (1) the a-priori expected structure, (2) the scree plot, (3) the replicability of the factor structure in the Germanic, the Latin, the Slavic, and the East-Asian language families (see Chapter 5 for more information), and (4) the interpretability of the resulting factor structure.

Based on the literature from the dimensional approach, three dimensions were expected (Hypothesis 2). The scree plot pointed to three larger factors and a few smaller factors (see Figure SM 1)[2]. Three solutions, three-, four-, and five-factorial, turned out to be replicable between the Germanic, the Latin, the Slavic, and the East-Asian language families (see Table SM 1 for the congruence measures of the four-factorial structure). The factor structures that were stable across the four language groups were closely inspected. In the five-factorial solution only Action tendency features uniquely defined the fifth factor. Rather than cross-cutting the emotion domain, the fifth factor was a specific motivational factor. As the four-factorial solution could be well interpreted and was also stable across language families, the four-factorial solution was selected. The four-factorial solution accounted for 65.27% of the total variance in the database.

A close inspection of the factor loadings of the 142 emotion features on the four VARIMAX rotated factors (see Table 7.1) as well as of the average factor scores of the 24 emotion terms on these four factors (see Figure 7.1 to Figure 7.3, Table SM 2) confirmed the a priori expected structure. The first factor is clearly a VALENCE factor. The negative pole is characterized by negatively valenced Appraisals (e.g., "consequences are negative for the person"), Feelings (e.g., "felt negative"), Expressions (e.g., "frowned"), Action tendencies (e.g., "wanted to break contact with others"), and to a lesser extent Bodily reactions (e.g., "stomach troubles"). The positive pole is defined by positively valenced Appraisals (e.g., "in itself pleasant for the person"), Feelings (e.g., "felt good"), Expressions (e.g., "smiled"), Action tendencies (e.g., "wanted to sing and dance"), and to a lesser extent Bodily reactions (e.g., "muscles relaxing"). Anger, fear, and sadness terms are opposed to joy terms on this factor. Both *surprise* and *compassion* take a neutral position on this dimension. We will further refer to this factor as VALENCE.

The second dimension is a POWER factor. This factor is mainly defined by Expressions (e.g., "increased volume of the voice"), Action tendencies (e.g., "wanted to hand over the initiative to someone else"), and Feelings (e.g., "felt submissive") that imply that the person has POWER over the situation and the people in the situation. There was also one Bodily reaction that defined the negative pole of this dimension, namely "felt weak limbs." Moreover, the features that define POWER refer to the three facets that have been identified in the literature factor, namely control versus lack of control ("wanting to control the situation"), potency/strength versus weakness ("felt weak limbs"), and dominance versus submissiveness ("felt dominant"). On this second dimension anger terms are opposed to fear and sadness terms. Moreover, *love* is opposed to *pride* and *interest*. We further refer to this factor as POWER.

The third dimension can be clearly interpreted as an AROUSAL dimension. Most of the features defining this dimension stem from the Bodily reaction component. "Heartbeat slowing down"

---

[2] All supplementary materials (SM) are available at website: http://www.affective-sciences.org/. See Appendix 1 ("Availability") for further details.

Table 7.1 Loadings of all features in a four-factorial VARIMAX rotated structure

GRID features	VALENCE	POWER	AROUSAL	NOVELTY
felt good	0.95	0.23	−0.09	0.07
consequences positive for person	0.95	0.21	−0.07	0.05
in itself pleasant for the person	0.95	0.18	−0.06	0.09
felt positive	0.94	0.26	−0.09	0.07
smiled	0.94	0.20	−0.06	0.07
felt at ease	0.94	0.25	−0.14	0.05
wanted to sing and dance	0.93	0.21	−0.05	0.10
wanted the ongoing situation to last or be repeated	0.93	0.24	−0.11	0.08
wanted to be tender, sweet, and kind	0.93	−0.07	−0.15	−0.04
wanted to be near or close to people or things	0.89	0.00	−0.08	0.01
consequences positive for somebody else	0.87	0.24	−0.10	0.04
wanted to get totally absorbed in the situation	0.86	0.23	−0.10	0.02
wanted to go on with what he or she was doing	0.85	0.33	−0.16	−0.03
felt calm	0.85	0.10	−0.39	−0.04
important and relevant for person's goals	0.85	0.16	−0.03	0.02
felt in control	0.83	0.42	−0.21	−0.05
felt energetic	0.82	0.50	0.09	0.05
in itself pleasant for somebody else	0.82	0.25	−0.12	0.10
important and relevant for goals of somebody else	0.79	0.16	−0.13	0.02
wanted to take care of another person or cause	0.79	−0.02	−0.10	−0.18
felt strong	0.78	0.54	−0.04	−0.01
consequences able to live with	0.77	0.13	−0.18	−0.07
felt powerful	0.77	0.55	−0.05	−0.04
wanted to submit to the situation as it is	0.76	−0.08	−0.18	0.08
wanted to be seen, to be in the center of attention	0.76	0.54	−0.06	−0.01
muscles relaxing (whole body)	0.75	−0.05	−0.35	0.05
center of attention	0.73	0.11	0.14	0.06
confirmed expectations	0.72	0.23	−0.21	−0.20
wanted to comply to someone else's wishes	0.72	−0.22	−0.08	−0.10
wanted to show off	0.71	0.52	−0.08	−0.06
familiar	0.65	0.14	−0.18	−0.23
moved toward people or things	0.61	0.36	0.11	0.17
felt warm	0.59	0.31	0.34	−0.08
felt an urge to be active, to do something, anything	0.58	0.42	0.26	−0.15
felt an urge to be attentive to what is going on	0.58	0.28	0.16	0.03
produced a long utterance	0.57	0.52	−0.03	−0.02

Table 7.1 (continued) Loadings of all features in a four-factorial VARIMAX rotated structure

GRID features	VALENCE	POWER	AROUSAL	NOVELTY
consequences predictable	0.49	0.18	−0.30	−0.30
caused by the person's own behavior	0.48	−0.03	−0.11	−0.28
consequences avoidable or modifiable	−0.34	0.01	−0.10	−0.24
produced a short utterance	−0.38	−0.17	−0.17	0.24
hid the emotion from others by smiling	−0.41	−0.33	−0.14	−0.23
tried to control the intensity of the emotional feeling	−0.42	−0.13	0.00	−0.19
inconsistent with expectations	−0.52	−0.09	0.01	0.50
a lump in throat	−0.52	−0.51	0.16	−0.05
produced speech disturbances	−0.54	−0.39	0.42	0.15
felt restless	−0.55	−0.04	0.40	−0.06
wanted to do nothing	−0.56	−0.51	−0.38	−0.02
lacked the motivation to pay attention to what was going on	−0.58	−0.36	−0.33	−0.04
felt cold	−0.59	−0.51	−0.13	0.17
moved against people or things	−0.61	0.43	0.09	−0.06
wanted to be hurt as little as possible	−0.62	−0.46	0.05	−0.18
muscles tensing (whole body)	−0.63	0.19	0.58	0.08
in itself unpleasant for somebody else	−0.65	−0.17	−0.23	0.03
felt nervous	−0.66	−0.17	0.46	−0.11
lacked the motivation to do anything	−0.66	−0.49	−0.30	−0.05
consequences negative for somebody else	−0.68	−0.22	−0.21	0.02
felt weak	−0.69	−0.65	−0.03	−0.07
felt tired	−0.69	−0.38	−0.18	−0.15
got pale	−0.70	−0.53	0.16	0.21
had stomach troubles	−0.72	−0.36	0.29	0.01
felt out of control	−0.72	−0.06	0.39	0.03
wanted to withdraw into her/himself	−0.76	−0.54	−0.09	−0.17
felt exhausted	−0.76	−0.42	−0.03	−0.13
in danger	−0.77	−0.14	0.16	0.24
irrevocable loss	−0.78	−0.32	−0.05	0.07
wanted to disappear or hide from others	−0.80	−0.51	−0.01	−0.12
felt powerless	−0.80	−0.49	0.00	−0.07
violated laws or socially accepted norms	−0.81	−0.08	0.00	0.05
withdrew from people or things	−0.81	−0.33	−0.10	−0.10
wanted to run away in whatever direction	−0.82	−0.41	0.13	−0.01
wanted to undo what was happening	−0.84	−0.30	0.01	−0.15
wanted to flee	−0.84	−0.44	0.09	−0.05

Table 7.1 (continued) Loadings of all features in a four-factorial VARIMAX rotated structure

GRID features	VALENCE	POWER	AROUSAL	NOVELTY
wanted to keep or push things away	−0.84	−0.24	0.01	−0.06
felt inhibited or blocked	−0.86	−0.36	0.09	−0.04
wanted to do damage, hit, or say something that hurts	−0.86	0.31	−0.02	−0.10
pressed lips together	−0.87	0.04	0.04	−0.19
frowned	−0.88	0.18	−0.08	−0.05
wanted to oppose	−0.88	0.28	−0.01	−0.13
incongruent with own standards and ideals	−0.89	−0.09	−0.07	0.06
wanted to prevent or stop sensory contact	−0.89	−0.29	−0.04	−0.06
felt the urge to stop what he or she was doing	−0.89	−0.27	0.05	−0.05
wanted to destroy whatever was close	−0.89	0.19	0.02	−0.09
felt bad	−0.91	−0.33	0.00	−0.11
wanted to break contact with others	−0.91	−0.15	−0.08	−0.17
in itself unpleasant for the person	−0.92	−0.16	−0.05	0.04
treated unjustly	−0.92	−0.03	−0.09	0.10
consequences negative for person	−0.92	−0.19	−0.02	0.03
felt negative	−0.93	−0.22	−0.03	−0.15
increased the volume of voice	0.10	0.82	0.24	0.24
had an assertive voice	0.29	0.76	−0.15	−0.10
felt dominant	0.64	0.64	−0.09	−0.07
spoke faster	0.26	0.63	0.56	0.17
wanted to be in command of others	−0.18	0.61	−0.01	−0.29
wanted to take initiative her/himself	0.53	0.60	0.01	−0.18
wanted to act, whatever action it might be	0.10	0.55	0.32	−0.16
wanted to be in control of the situation	−0.11	0.51	0.19	−0.32
wanted to move	0.41	0.49	0.37	0.01
wanted to tackle the situation	0.27	0.48	0.09	−0.25
showed the emotion to others more than s/he felt it	0.39	0.42	−0.10	0.25
caused intentionally	0.10	0.35	−0.21	0.00
felt alert	0.01	0.34	0.29	−0.01
changed the melody of her or his speech	0.23	0.27	0.09	0.26
showed the emotion to others less than s/he felt it	−0.20	−0.32	−0.18	−0.23
showed tears	−0.04	−0.56	−0.04	−0.01
had a trembling voice	−0.46	−0.59	0.28	0.10
felt submissive	−0.45	−0.60	−0.08	−0.18
wanted to make up for what she or he had done	−0.27	−0.62	−0.12	−0.32

Table 7.1 (continued) Loadings of all features in a four-factorial VARIMAX rotated structure

GRID features	VALENCE	POWER	AROUSAL	NOVELTY
spoke slower	−0.03	−0.62	−0.57	−0.13
wanted someone to be there to provide help or support	−0.45	−0.63	0.06	−0.10
wanted to hand over the initiative to someone else	−0.15	−0.64	0.01	−0.09
closed her or his eyes	−0.04	−0.65	−0.18	0.00
felt weak limbs	−0.30	−0.68	0.30	0.25
fell silent	−0.43	−0.70	−0.23	−0.06
decreased the volume of voice	0.02	−0.76	−0.31	−0.21
breathing getting faster	−0.07	0.28	0.83	0.18
heartbeat getting faster	0.25	0.25	0.83	0.15
perspired, or had moist hands	−0.32	−0.12	0.79	−0.05
sweat	−0.33	−0.06	0.76	0.00
felt hot	0.04	0.21	0.75	−0.11
produced abrupt body movements	−0.07	0.46	0.54	0.41
felt shivers	−0.04	−0.17	0.48	0.35
blushed	0.36	0.16	0.47	−0.13
required an immediate response	−0.06	0.14	0.40	0.39
was in an intense emotional state	0.12	−0.01	0.40	0.03
did not show any changes in face	0.03	0.09	−0.63	−0.28
did not show any changes in vocal expression	0.27	0.05	−0.63	−0.23
breathing slowing down	0.38	−0.28	−0.64	0.02
did not show any changes in gestures	0.07	−0.07	−0.67	−0.25
heartbeat slowing down	0.05	−0.38	−0.69	0.07
had no bodily symptoms at all	0.23	0.10	−0.77	−0.06
unpredictable	0.00	−0.10	0.21	0.75
suddenly	0.15	0.00	0.24	0.69
had the jaw drop	0.14	0.00	−0.01	0.64
caused by chance	0.42	0.03	0.11	0.62
opened her or his eyes widely	0.32	0.45	0.36	0.53
caused by a supernatural POWER	0.48	−0.06	−0.02	0.51
had eyebrows go up	0.20	0.46	0.03	0.48
caused by somebody else's behavior	−0.16	0.30	−0.12	0.40
enough resources to avoid or modify consequences	−0.02	0.08	−0.15	−0.27
will be changed in a lasting way	0.24	−0.27	−0.21	−0.31
wanted to overcome an obstacle	0.13	0.25	0.19	−0.34
experienced the emotional state for a long time	0.24	−0.25	−0.14	−0.49

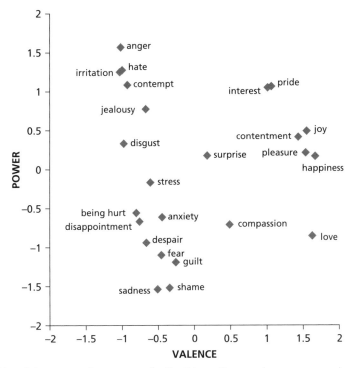

Figure 7.1 Plot of the average factor scores for the 24 emotion words on VALENCE and POWER.

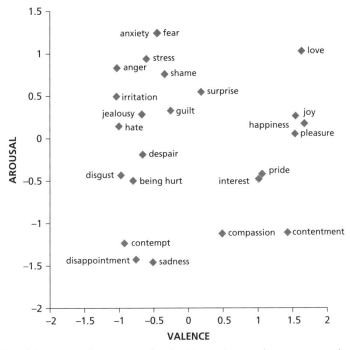

Figure 7.2 Plot of the average factor scores for the 24 emotion words on VALENCE and AROUSAL.

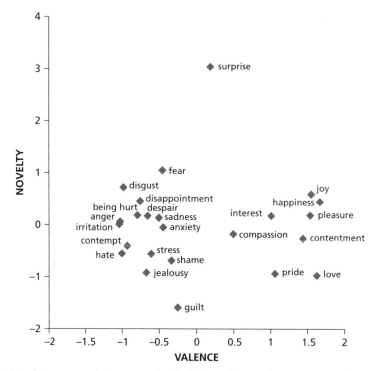

Figure 7.3 Plot of the average factor scores for the 24 emotion words on VALENCE and NOVELTY.

and "breathing slowing down" are opposed to "heartbeat getting faster" and "breathing getting faster" on this dimension. Moreover, the absence of facial, vocal, and gestural expressions defined the negative pole of this factor, while the appraisal "required an immediate response" also loaded positively on this factor. On this factor anger and fear terms are opposed to sadness terms. For the positively valenced terms, mainly *love* is opposed to *contentment* on this factor. This factor is referred to as AROUSAL.

The fourth factor is defined by Appraisals (e.g., "unpredictable" and "sudden") and facial expressions ("jaw drop" and "opening eyes widely") that are triggered by the experience of a novel event. Moreover, "experiencing an emotion for a long time" loads negatively on this factor. On this factor the emotion word *surprise* is strongly differentiated from all the other emotion words (a difference of about two standard deviations with *fear,* which is the second highest scoring emotion word on this dimension). The fourth dimension thus represents a short-lived emotional reaction to novel events. Therefore we label this factor as NOVELTY.

Thus, as predicted, the three most important dimensions in the emotion domain are VALENCE, POWER, and AROUSAL (Hypothesis 2). Moreover, a fourth NOVELTY factor, which had already been identified in a preliminary study with three languages, could also be identified across all languages, countries and samples (Research Question 2a). When VALENCE, POWER, AROUSAL, and NOVELTY written in small capitals are used in the remainder of this chapter and the remainder of this book, it means we refer to these factors as they have been measured by the GRID instrument.

The stability of the overall dimensional structure with only four of the five emotion components. To probe the stability of the overall four-factorial structure, we have investigated whether and to what extent the structure is stable on the basis of features from only four of the five emotion components (Research Question 2b). This was investigated in five separate analyses, after removing the Appraisal, the Bodily reaction, the Expression, the Action tendency, and the Feeling features, respectively. Each of the "reduced" four-factorial structures was orthogonally Procrustes rotated toward the full four-factorial structure. The stability of these Procrustes rotated, reduced structures was investigated in two ways. First, the congruence measures (Tucker's phi's) between the full and the Procrustes reduced factors were computed (see Table 7.2). Second, bivariate correlations were computed between the factor scores based on all emotion components and the factor scores based on only four of the five components (see Table 7.2). In total 19 of the 20 congruence measures (Tucker's phi) and 18 of the 20 bivariate correlations were higher than 0.95 indicating a very high congruence between the full and the reduced factor structures. AROUSAL was a bit less stable when the Bodily reaction features were removed: After removal, the correlation of the factor scores was 0.84. Moreover, NOVELTY was somewhat less well represented when the Appraisal features were removed. The congruence measure between the full and the reduced NOVELTY factor was 0.82, and the correlation of the factor scores before and after removal of the Appraisal features was 0.70. The four-factorial structure is thus by and large independent from the individual emotion components that constitute the emotion domain and can thus be considered as a very stable and robust structure of the emotion domain.

The relationships between, and the relative importance of, VALENCE, POWER, AROUSAL, and NOVELTY. Given the vigorous debates between adherents to different dimensional models in the literature, and the failure to identify the POWER dimension in self-report models, alternative dimensional representations of the meaning structure were investigated. The goal was to further probe the relationships between and the relative importance of VALENCE, POWER, AROUSAL, and NOVELTY (Research Question 2c).

We started by comparing a four-dimensional representation with orthogonal (VARIMAX) and oblique (PROMAX) rotation. The obliquely rotated factors could be interpreted in exactly the same way as the orthogonally rotated factors, namely as VALENCE, POWER, AROUSAL, and NOVELTY. The correlations between the obliquely rotated factors additionally revealed a substantial correlation between the VALENCE and the POWER factor ($r = 0.48$). The correlations among the remaining factors were small (VALENCE–AROUSAL $r = -0.16$, VALENCE–NOVELTY $r = 0.07$, POWER–AROUSAL $r = 0.15$, POWER–NOVELTY $r = 0.08$, and AROUSAL–NOVELTY $r = 0.23$). In an oblique rotation, the

Table 7.2 Stability (Tucker's phi on factor loadings and Pearson correlation between factor scores) of the overall factor structure after removing the features from each component, respectively

Removed component	VALENCE		POWER		AROUSAL		NOVELTY	
	φ	r	φ	r	φ	r	φ	r
Feeling	1.00	1.00	1.00	1.00	1.00	1.00	1.00	1.00
Bodily reaction	1.00	1.00	1.00	1.00	0.94	0.84	0.98	0.94
Facial expression	1.00	1.00	0.99	0.99	0.99	0.99	0.99	0.97
Vocal expression	1.00	1.00	1.00	0.98	1.00	0.99	1.00	0.94
Action tendency	1.00	0.99	1.00	0.98	1.00	0.98	0.99	0.96
Appraisal	1.00	0.99	1.00	1.00	1.00	0.98	0.82	0.70

first VALENCE factor accounted for 43.20% of the total variance, the POWER factor accounted for 23.30%, the AROUSAL 9.80%, and the NOVELTY factor for 5.30% compared to 39.11%, 13.45%, 8.26%, and 4.45%, respectively in the VARIMAX rotated solution. Thus, although the oblique rotation revealed a substantial correlation between the VALENCE and the POWER factor, they did not coincide. POWER clearly emerged as the second strongest factor in a structure with four orthogonal factors.

To further investigate the relative importance of each of these four dimensions, the one-, the two- and the three-factorial solutions have been studied and compared with the four-factorial solution. Factor scores were computed for a one- up to a three-factorial representation (after VARIMAX rotation) and these factor scores were correlated with the factor scores in the four-factorial solution (see Table 7.3). We only discuss the correlations larger than 0.30. The one-factorial model accounted for 44.41% of the total variance. The single factor correlated with VALENCE ($r =$ 0.93) and to a lesser extent with POWER ($r = 0.38$). The two-factorial model accounted for 55.82% of the total variance. The first factor again related mainly to the VALENCE factor ($r = 0.95$), and to a lesser extent to the POWER factor ($r = 0.30$). The second factor was about as strongly related to the POWER factor ($r = 0.67$) as to the AROUSAL factor ($r = 0.70$). A plot of the average coordinates of the terms in the two-dimensional solution showed that the positive emotion terms are opposed to the anger, sadness, and fear terms on the first factor (see Figure 7.4). Moreover, anger terms are opposed to sadness terms on the second factor, with the fear terms being closer to the anger than to the sadness terms. Thus, in a two-factorial solution, the first dimension is basically a VALENCE dimension and the second dimension is a combination of POWER and AROUSAL. The three-factorial solution accounted for 61.72% of the total variance. After VARIMAX rotation the first two factors corresponded very closely to the VALENCE ($r = 0.99$) and the POWER ($r = 0.98$) factors, respectively. The third factor was both related to the AROUSAL ($r = 0.88$) and NOVELTY ($r = 0.48$) factors.

We thus observed that the one-factorial solution represents mainly the VALENCE factor. In the two-factorial solution the second dimension was a mixture of POWER and AROUSAL. It was only in the three-factorial solution that POWER was fully separated from AROUSAL. In the three-factorial solution the third factor was still a combination of AROUSAL and NOVELTY. It was in the four-factorial solution that these two last factors got fully separated.

Table 7.3 Pearson correlations between the factor scores in a VARIMAX rotated four-factorial solution with the factor scores in a one, a two-, and a three-factorial solution after VARIMAX rotation

Factors	VALENCE	POWER	AROUSAL	NOVELTY
One-factorial solution				
Factor 1	0.93	0.38	−0.04	0.04
Two-factorial solution				
Factor 1	0.95	0.30	−0.13	0.01
Factor 2	−0.11	0.67	0.70	0.22
Three-factorial solution				
Factor 1	0.99	0.01	−0.06	0.10
Factor 2	0.01	0.98	0.14	−0.12
Factor 3	0.01	−0.07	0.88	0.48

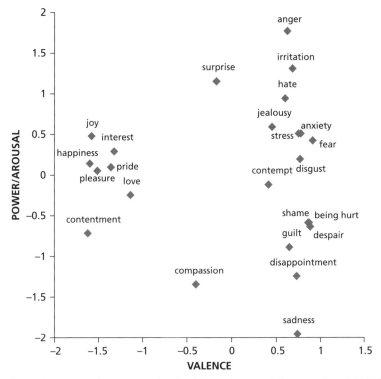

Figure 7.4 Plot of the average factor scores for the 24 emotion words in a two-factorial VARIMAX rotated structure.

The basic emotion approach

The categorical structure of the terms, which was predicted from the basic emotion approach was investigated with hierarchical average linkage cluster analysis (Hypothesis 3a). Then, the stability of the emotion profiles was studied for all emotion terms. It was investigated whether the stability was different for basic and non-basic emotions (Hypothesis 3b). Finally, it was investigated how well it was possible to identify the correct emotion term on the basis of the profiles of features across samples and languages (Research Question 3).

The hierarchical cluster structure of the emotion domain. To investigate which clusters of emotion terms could be identified, an average linkage hierarchical cluster analysis was executed on the averaged squared Euclidean distances between the 24 emotion terms, which were computed on the basis of the standardized profiles across the 142 emotion features (see Figure 7.5). The hierarchical cluster analysis revealed two higher-order clusters (a positive and a negative emotion cluster) and four major basic emotion clusters, namely: (1) a joy cluster consisting of the emotion words *joy*, *happiness*, *pleasure*, *pride*, *love*, and *interest*; (2) a fear cluster containing the words *fear*, *anxiety*, *stress*, and *disgust*; (3) a sadness cluster consisting of the words *sadness*, *disappointment*, *being hurt*, *despair*, *guilt*, and *shame*; and (4) an anger cluster containing the words *anger*, *irritation*, *hate*, *jealousy*, and *contempt*. Moreover, *surprise* and *compassion* each formed a separate basic cluster in their own right at this level.

Stability of feature patterns. The expectation that basic emotion terms have a more stable feature pattern than other emotion terms (Hypothesis 3b) was investigated by computing, for each

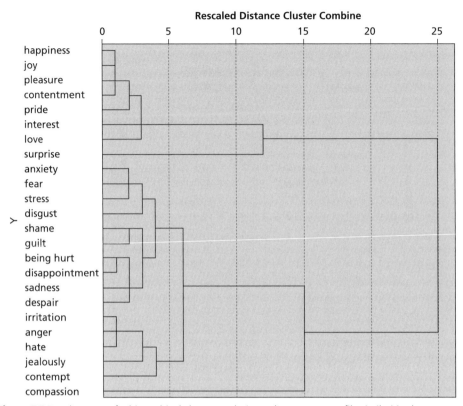

Figure 7.5 Dendrogram of a hierarchical cluster analysis on the average profile similarities between the 24 emotion words.

emotion term, the correlation between the average feature pattern and the sample-specific feature pattern. Across the 34 samples the pattern correlation was on average 0.93 for joy, 0.92 for happiness, 0.92 for fear, 0.92 for shame, 0.91 for sadness, 0.91 for pleasure, 0.91 for interest, 0.91 for anger, 0.90 for being hurt, 0.90 for pride, 0.90 for guilt, 0.90 for love, 0.90 for stress, 0.89 for disgust, 0.89 for disappointment, 0.89 for irritation, 0.89 for hate, 0.89 for despair, 0.88 for anxiety, 0.87 for jealousy, 0.86 for surprise, 0.86 for contentment, 0.78 for contempt, and 0.72 for compassion. Paired-sample t-tests indicated that only *contempt* and *compassion* had a significantly less shared meaning compared to the other 22 terms (at a significance level of 0.01). Except for two terms, there was thus very little evidence for differences in the stability of the meaning of the 24 emotion terms across languages and cultural groups (Hypothesis 3b).

Identifiability of 24 emotion categories. The identification of the emotion terms on the basis of their respective feature profiles (Research Question 3) was investigated by executing two multiple discriminant analyses (MDA), one on the basis of the 142 emotion features and one on the basis of the four overall factors (see Table 7.4). On the basis of the 142 features it was possible to correctly identify 82.1% of the emotion terms (after cross-validation). Confusions (larger than 15%) were observed between joy, happiness, and pleasure, as well as between anger and irritation. More importantly still, 69.4% could be correctly identified (after cross-validation) when only using the scores on the four overall factors of VALENCE, POWER, AROUSAL, and NOVELTY.

Table 7.4 Classification accuracy (in percent) for the 24 emotion words in discriminant analyses based on the four overall factors and on all features

Emotion words	Classification based on the four factors	Classification based on all features	
	Accuracy	Accuracy	Confusion > 15% with
being hurt	41.2	85.3	
sadness	82.4	88.2	
shame	79.4	91.2	
guilt	97.1	94.1	
compassion	79.4	94.1	
disappointment	76.5	85.3	
love	97.1	97.1	
contentment	67.6	73.5	
happiness	58.8	38.2	joy
pride	82.4	91.2	
pleasure	38.2	67.6	joy
joy	67.6	44.1	happiness
interest	79.4	97.1	
surprise	100	100	
despair	35.3	91.2	
stress	70.6	91.2	
anxiety	50.0	76.5	
fear	82.4	94.1	
jealousy	73.5	91.2	
hate	67.6	79.4	
irritation	11.8	58.8	anger
anger	67.6	70.6	irritation
disgust	94.1	88.2	
contempt	64.7	82.4	
Total	69.4	82.1	

7.5 Discussion

Of the hypotheses formulated on the basis of the componential, the dimensional, and the basic emotion approaches, all but one (namely greater stability of basic emotion terms) were confirmed. We discuss the results per approach.

The componential emotion approach

The fundamental assumption of the CPM is that emotions are not affective states, but rather multicomponential processes that are triggered as a reaction to concrete events, which are relevant for the person's needs, goals, and values. The present study clearly confirmed that all the emotion components included in the GRID instrument, namely Appraisals, Bodily reactions, Action tendencies, Expressions, and Feelings contribute substantially to the meaning of emotion terms. Across all languages, countries, and samples people not only infer information about a feeling state, but also about the probable meaning of the event, the probable bodily reactions, the probable expressions, and the probable motivational changes when emotion words are used. Thus, emotion words convey very rich information as predicted by Hypothesis 1. It is clear that the first hypothesis has only been investigated in a very rudimentary way in the current chapter. The specific internal structures for each separate emotion component, which are reported in Part III (see Chapters 8 to 13), further contribute to the confirmation of Hypothesis 1.

Four of the five emotion components contribute to the same extent to the meaning of emotion words. Only the Feeling component is comparatively more important in differentiating the meaning of emotion words (see Research Question 1). This could be explained by the very nature of the Feeling component in the emotion process according to the CPM. In the CPM, the Feeling component is a read-out system that brings the emotion process to (sub)consciousness (Scherer, 2009c; see also Chapter 1). Thus, the Feeling component can be expected to be the most accessible during the emotion process, and is therefore probably also most strongly related to the differentiation of emotion terms in language.

The dimensional approach

It was confirmed that the meaning of emotion terms, which was evaluated on 142 different features can be represented rather well in a low-dimensional space. As already observed in the seminal work of Osgood and colleagues (Osgood, May, & Miron, 1975; Osgood, Suci, & Tannenbaum, 1957), who used a very different methodology, the three most important dimensions are VALENCE, POWER, and AROUSAL in that order of importance (Hypothesis 2). Moreover, the existence of a fourth smaller factor was replicated, which had already been observed in the first preliminary study using the GRID instrument with three languages (Research Question 2a) (Fontaine, Scherer, Roesch, & Ellsworth, 2007).

The first factor, replicated across all 25 languages, is a very salient VALENCE factor. This factor alone accounts for 1.5 times more of the total variance than the three other factors together. This factor is also clearly bipolar. Thus, when it comes to the meaning of emotion terms, the positive and negative VALENCE are mutually exclusive qualities. The importance of the VALENCE factor in the emotion domain can be attributed to the fundamental evaluation that affects all emotion components: do the consequences of the eliciting event match the needs, concerns, or values of the person or not. A positive or negative outcome for this fundamental appraisal issue has profound consequences for the functioning of each of the components.

The second dimension is the POWER dimension. The lost child of the dimensional approach to emotion has been found again in this GRID study. As extensively explained in Chapter 2, early research by Osgood and colleagues established that POWER was the second dimension in the affective structure of language (e.g., Osgood, May, & Miron, 1975; Osgood, Suci, & Tannenbaum, 1957). In the current literature on the dimensional approach to emotion, however, the POWER dimension has almost fully disappeared. The four most popular affect models do not contain any reference to the POWER factor. The rediscovery of the POWER factor in the GRID study is, therefore, highly relevant: the features in the GRID instrument were selected because of their theoretical relevance for operationalizing each of the emotion components. They were not intended to operationalize the POWER factor. An inspection of the factor loadings shows that the second factor is to an important extent an interpersonal factor. It is a well-known and robust finding in social psychological research that interpersonal orientations can be represented in two dimensions that closely correspond to our VALENCE and POWER dimensions (e.g., Wiggins, 1979). However, the POWER dimension is not restricted to the interpersonal realm. Also having or wanting control over the situation, or just the opposite having no control defines this dimension. Furthermore, a plausible set of Bodily reaction features that imply weakness define the second dimension, an observation that is further developed in Chapter 9 on Bodily reaction. Thus, when people across the world use emotion words they convey information about POWER, as was already pointed out by Osgood and colleagues (1957). Moreover, this dimension integrates the three different facets of POWER that have been proposed in the literature, namely control, strength/potency, and dominance.

The third factor represents the classic AROUSAL dimension. Although not exclusively, this factor is predominantly defined by Bodily reaction features. It fits the conceptualization of this factor in the self-report tradition as an AROUSAL factor.

The last factor is a NOVELTY factor. It is the smallest factor, but throws new light on *surprise* and serves as an important differentiator for other emotions. *Surprise*, occupying an extreme position on the NOVELTY dimension, is not an emotion like the other emotions, as it is generally very short and is often rapidly succeeded by another emotion reflecting the VALENCE aspect of the situation. When we first discovered this factor in our preliminary study, we proposed to label it with the term "unpredictability", which is also one of the features loading highly on this fourth dimension (Fontaine et al., 2007). However, we have decided to relabel this factor to NOVELTY, as unpredictability seems too technical and narrow as a descriptive label for this dimension. NOVELTY reflects better the breadth of this factor and is also an established term in other areas of psychology. One may ask why this dimension emerges for the first time in the GRID research. One possible explanation is that *surprise* is rarely included in emotion research (although it is considered as a basic emotion by many basic emotion theorists). Moreover, even if *surprise* is included but is the only term reflecting the NOVELTY dimension, it is unlikely to yield a separate dimension in similarity ratings. Probably the most important explanation is that the GRID instrument is the first instrument to have (unintendedly) sufficiently operationalized the NOVELTY dimension by its defining Appraisals and Facial expressions. Still, when only taking the results with the GRID instrument into account, the question remains whether this factor is due to the specific features included in the GRID instrument, or is a genuine factor in the meaning structure of the emotion domain. In Chapter 14, we present evidence that it is also possible to identify the NOVELTY dimension using a very different methodology, which supports the interpretation of the NOVELTY dimension as a genuine dimension in the representation of the emotion domain.

We observed that the four-factorial structure is a rather robust structure. Even after removing each of the five emotion components one-by-one, we observed a very robust overall four-factorial structure (see Research Question 2b). This confirms the expectation that most of the information on the synchronization between the emotion components can already be identified if only a part is known about the emotion process. The VALENCE and the POWER dimension are not at all affected by the removal of a single emotion component. The AROUSAL dimension is somewhat affected by removing the Bodily reaction component, and the NOVELTY factor somewhat by the removal of the Appraisal component. One possible explanation for the latter observation is that conscious attention is automatically triggered in a NOVELTY reaction, and that, in consequence, the emotional reaction to NOVELTY is more defined by the Appraisal component than is the case for the other emotions. This fits the notion that the reaction to NOVELTY is by its very nature short-lived. From the moment the novel situation is interpreted, the emotional reaction either disappears because the event is eventually interpreted as irrelevant for the concerns and goals of the person, or turns into another emotion depending on the precise meaning of the event.

The comparison of different dimensional representations of the meaning structure allows hypotheses to be generated as to why the second most important dimension in the emotion domain did not manifest itself more forcefully in self-report models (see Research Question 2b). As the oblique rotation revealed, VALENCE and POWER features are conceptually related: having positively valenced experiences may produce feelings of POWER. Most importantly, POWER itself is positively valenced (see Chapter 1). The GRID data clearly shows though that VALENCE and POWER cannot be reduced to one another. Another relevant observation is that POWER only emerges as the second factor in a three- or four-factorial solution. When the emotion structure is based on only two factors, the second factor contains information about both AROUSAL and POWER. Based on these empirical findings we can conclude that the emotion terms, used in typical self-report instruments, clearly refer to the POWER dimension. This generates the hypothesis that in the two-factorial models that dominate the current literature VALENCE and AROUSAL are confounded with POWER.

The basic emotion approach

The present results offer clear support for the position that a dimensional and a categorical representation of emotion information are compatible rather than conflicting. While a very coherent dimensional structure is stably identified, a categorical representation also fits the meaning data. As was already well demonstrated in similarity sorting research (Fontaine et al., 2002, Shaver et al., 1987), there are two superordinate clusters of positive and negative emotion terms and four major basic emotion clusters distinguishing joy, anger, fear, and sadness terms as expected (see Hypothesis 3a). Moreover, *surprise* and *compassion* form two separate basic clusters of their own. With the dimensional structure in mind, the reason for why these two terms each form separate clusters is very different. *Surprise* is identified in the dimensional structure as a term that is really differentiated from the other emotion terms, especially on the NOVELTY dimension. Moreover, *surprise* is probably a possible antecedent for the other emotions, and can thus turn into positive or negative emotions depending on the interpretation of the novel situation. *Compassion*, however, just takes an intermediate position between positive and negative emotion terms, possibly because it is inherently defined by both positive and negative emotion features. On the one hand, it is triggered by the suffering of others which is inherently negatively valenced. On the other hand, it implies an interpersonal bound with the suffering person and a tendency to help and control the situation, which both have a more positive VALENCE. These opposing valences may create ambivalence.

No evidence was found for the hypothesis derived from the basic emotion theories that the meaning profile of basic emotions should be more stable than the meaning profile of non-basic emotion terms (see Hypothesis 2b). On the contrary, we found that emotion terms that are not considered as basic emotions by any basic emotion theorist (like *being hurt*) had a very high stability of their meaning pattern, and that *contempt* which is considered basic according to some, like Ekman (1999), showed significantly less stability than so-called non-basic emotion terms. A possible explanation is that the basic emotion approach is far less focused on the interpersonal context of emotions than a linguistic approach. The need to label emotional experiences and to use emotion words is emerging particularly in communication contexts, which are inherently social in nature. We observed that emotion processes that are typically experienced in social contexts, like shame, guilt, pride, and being hurt have meaning profiles that are as stable as those of emotion terms that are not specifically interpersonal in nature.

Two of the 24 terms have a considerably less stable meaning, namely *compassion* and *contempt*. For *compassion* there is a plausible explanation. As compassion inherently merges positive and negative features, slight differences in the salience of the positive or the negative features will create substantial differences in the profile correspondence due to the importance of the VALENCE factor in the emotion domain. The lack of stability of *contempt*, however, is difficult to explain. It is unlikely that there are systematic differences in the meaning of *contempt* across languages and cultural groups, as we observe both for *contempt* and for *compassion* that the patterns are not only less stable across samples, but are also the least reliable within samples both within western and non-western languages (see Chapter 6). It is a matter for future research to identify why the meaning of *contempt* is so unstable both within and across linguistic and cultural groups.

The most impressive evidence for the categorical view stems from the discriminant analyses (see Research Question 3). The feature profiles across all 142 features allowed to correctly identify the matching emotion term (out of a set of 24) for over 80% of the 816 profiles (compared to a random correct assignment of 4.2%). Moreover, when the feature profile was reduced to only the scores on VALENCE, POWER, AROUSAL, and NOVELTY, almost 70% of the corresponding terms could still be correctly identified. The latter finding excludes random hits due to the sheer number of features as an explanation for the high identifiability. The odds of correctly versus incorrectly classifying an emotion term on the basis of the four overall factor scores was 54.4 times larger than what can be expected on the basis of random classification. This finding clearly supports the idea that emotion words do refer to rather clearly defined subdomains across languages and language groups.

7.6 Conclusions

The results described in this chapter offer strong support for our position that the three emotion approaches in psychology are not mutually exclusive when it comes to the meaning of emotion terms. The confirmation of hypotheses from one approach did not imply a disconfirmation of hypotheses stemming from the other emotion approaches. In fact, when studying the meaning of emotion terms, these three emotion approaches are complementary. Being able to represent the emotion domain in a low-dimensional space does not imply that a variation on these underlying dimensions is all there is. It does not exclude that the emotion process consists of changes in each of the emotion components, as predicted by the componential approach. The low-dimensional space just represents the coherence of changes in the emotion components. In the CPM this overlap is attributed to the synchronization process. The low-dimensional representation does not exclude a categorical representation as proposed by the basic emotion approach neither. We can clearly identify the four basic emotion clusters of joy, sadness, anger, and fear on the basis of emotion profiles. Moreover, it is possible to identify the correct emotion label among a set of 24 labels on the basis of the feature profiles, even if the latter consist only of the scores on the four factors of VALENCE, POWER, AROUSAL, and NOVELTY. We conclude that, while the three emotion models that underlie the three dominant approaches in psychology on meaning may disagree as to the mechanisms underlying the emotion process, they are complementary when it comes to the meaning of emotion terms.

## Part III

Decomposing the meaning of emotion terms: Analysis by emotion component

Chapter 8

From emotion to feeling: The internal structure of the Feeling component

Johnny J. R. Fontaine[1] and Klaus R. Scherer

It is self-evident for emotion experts, as well as for laymen, that to have an emotion means to "feel" the emotion. Emotions and feelings are considered inextricably linked with one another. There is a consensus that feelings play a key role in emotions, but confusions loom large about their defining and differentiating characteristics, as well as about their role in the emotion process. In daily language, people use these terms in an interchangeable way. Also, in the scientific literature there have been, and still are, vigorous debates about what feelings precisely are and how they are to be differentiated from emotions. Probably the most notorious example is the debate started by William James who stated that: "the bodily changes follow directly the *perception* of the exiting fact, and that our feelings of the same changes as they occur *is* the emotion" (James, 1884, pp. 189–190). This statement has been severely criticized for defining emotion as the subjective, conscious experience of an ongoing process in the organism (e.g., Ellsworth, 1994).

Before presenting the meaning structure of the Feeling component, we first present how feelings and the differentiation between feelings and emotions have been conceptualized in the Component Process Model, which formed the basis of the GRID paradigm. We further discuss the operationalization of the Feeling component in the GRID instrument. Then we present the dimensional emotion theories that were used to hypothesize about the structure of the Feeling component. We finally present the features that were used in the GRID instrument to operationalize the Feeling component.

8.1 The differentiation between emotions and feelings in the Component Process Model

According to the Component Process Model (CPM) (Scherer, 1984b, 2009c, Chapter 1), an emotion process consists of synchronized activities between five emotion components, namely the Appraisal, the Bodily reaction, the Action tendency, the Expression, and the Feeling component. In the emotion process, each of these subsystems is characterized by a particular function, namely evaluation of objects and events for Appraisal, preparation of the bodily system for reacting, preparation and direction of action for the Action tendencies, and communication of behavioral intentions for the Expression component. The function of the Feeling component within the CPM is to make the person aware of the ongoing emotion process with the purpose to monitor it. From an

[1] Correspondence on this paper can be addressed to Johnny J. R. Fontaine. Department of Personnel, Work and Organisational Psychology. Faculty of Psychology and Educational Sciences. Ghent University. Henri-Dunantlaan 2, 9000 Gent, Belgium. Johnny.Fontaine@UGent.be

evolutionary perspective, emotions developed out of action programs triggered by characteristic stimulus configurations that were adaptive for survival. However, for the survival of humans who have complex concerns and who live in complex (social) environments, a rigid execution of these action programs would be maladaptive in many concrete situations as they would interfere with the various personal goals of the individual (e.g., it is not adaptive to run away from each exam one fears to fail) and the requirements of the environment (e.g., it is not adaptive to aggress one's boss if one feels unjustly treated). The assumption is that these action programs triggered by characteristic stimulus configurations have developed evolutionarily into open and flexible mechanisms that can be adapted to situational constraints and to the complex concerns of the organism.

Because of its presumed role as a monitoring system, the Feeling component is hypothesized to be an emerging component during the emotion process. The Feeling component receives information about the synchronized activity in the other four emotion components and brings this to conscious awareness of the person (or the information can at least easily be made conscious). As explained in Chapter 1, Scherer proposes this process to consist of three strongly interrelated parts, namely: (1) a centralized representation of the synchronized activity in all subsystems in the central nervous system; (2) a conscious, but preverbal awareness of this process, and; (3) finally a verbal categorization of the experience which allows communication. Thus, it is hypothesized that feelings do not drive the emotion process. This is done by the Appraisal component evaluating the ongoing event. Through the Feeling component, the person becomes only aware of the emotion process, which allows him or her to actively regulate it, for instance by reappraising (e.g., the hurt was unintentional), masking (e.g., covering disgust by a smile), relaxation (e.g., in a stressful situation), or suppressing an action tendency (e.g., count till 10 when really angry).

Within the CPM, the concept of emotion and the concept of feeling can be clearly differentiated. Emotion IS the synchronization of activity in the five organismic subsystems that prepare the person to deal (in principle) in an adaptive way with an event that is relevant for its concerns. Feeling IS AN AWARENESS of this process. There is thus a part-whole relationship between the two concepts, with the concept "emotion" referring to the whole, and the concept "feeling" referring to a part of it. Moreover, feelings do not necessarily represent the ongoing emotion processes adequately. In the course from a central representation of the emotion process in the central nervous system to a verbalization of the subjective experience, information from the original process might get lost and new information might become added. Thus, the fact that the Feeling component has the emotion process as its object does not mean it is the emotion process. While many parts of the emotion process can and often are unconscious, feelings are (sub)conscious. Each of the emotion components can in principle be studied independently from one another and independently from the person who experiences the emotion. Furthermore, when an observer infers an emotion process in others, he or she has no access to their feelings. The emotion process is inferred on the basis of a coordinated activity between those components that are observable (e.g., the inferred appraisal from the antecedent situation, the expression, the motivated behavior, and possibly bodily reactions). When emotions and feelings are defined and differentiated according to the CPM, it becomes clear that emotions are eminently transactional. Their goal is to prepare the individual for action in a goal-relevant situation. Feelings are in the first place internal. They reveal information to the person about his or her internal functioning.

A huge variability can be identified within the Feeling component with respect to the complexity and richness of the verbalization of the (sub)conscious experience of the emotion process (Frijda, 2005; Scherer, 2009). We summarize this variability in three hierarchically ordered levels of verbalization. At the highest level, detailed descriptions can be given of what the person experiences in several or all emotion components during the emotion process. At an intermediate level the use of emotion words is likely. Emotion words represent recurrent types of synchronization between the emotion components. By using emotion words information about what happens specifically in each of the components is lost. However, emotion words are very economical as they convey information about the most salient aspects of the synchronization process that is taking place. At the lowest level only the general quality of the emotional process one is experiencing, is verbalized. These three levels of complexity and richness correspond to the three views on meaning that can be found in psycholinguistic emotion research (see Chapter 2). The highest level corresponds to the feature profile view: the rich verbalization consists of how each of the emotion components are involved in the emotion process. The second level corresponds to the categorical view. The person categorizes the subjective experience of the emotion process into an emotion category, and thereby focuses on what his or her experience shares with typical and recurrent types of synchronization between the emotion components. The lowest level corresponds to the dimensional view. The dimensions correspond to the general quality of the emotional experience.

8.2 The representation of the Feeling component in the GRID

Theoretically, a very clear distinction can thus be made between the concept of "emotion" and the concept of "feeling" within the CPM, with feeling being the specific component of the emotion process which brings the emotion process into consciousness at different levels of richness and complexity. When this approach is applied to emotion language and the use of words to describe other's and one's own emotions, it becomes clear why there has been so much confusion between the concept of emotion and the concept of feeling both in daily life and in psychological theorizing. The very same words can be used to describe "objectively" (aspects of) an emotion process and to describe the "subjective experience" of (aspects of) that emotion process. Just like one can see someone hurting his toe and the person feels his toe being hurt. This implies that an instrument that studies the meaning of emotion words from a componential emotion approach cannot operationalize the Feeling component completely independently from the other emotion components and the emotion words themselves. The emotion features that operationalize the Appraisal, the Bodily reaction, the Action tendency, and the Expression components can be used to denotatively describe an aspect of the emotion, but can also be used to refer to the subjective experience of that process. Moreover, the emotions words that constitute the GRID instrument are words that can be used to denotatively describe and categorize the emotion process, but can also be used to describe one's own personal experience of the emotion process. Still, with the emotion words and with the operationalization of the Appraisal, the Bodily reaction, the Action tendency, and the Expression components, one aspect of the Feeling component is not being represented, namely the low level representation of the emotional experience in terms of its general quality. Therefore we have operationalized the Feeling component in the GRID instrument exclusively in terms of this low level representation of the subjective experience. As already presented, the general quality of the emotional experiences has been most extensively studied by the dimensional approach to emotion. This approach has therefore been used to operationalize the Feeling component in the GRID.

8.3 Dimensional approaches

There is a long-standing dimensional tradition in the emotion literature that can be traced back to Aristotle (Rethorica), who considered VALENCE as a key characteristic of the emotional experience, and to Wundt (1896) at the beginning of psychology as a discipline, who proposed the dimensions of pleasure–displeasure, AROUSAL–calming, and tension–relaxation (Lust–Unlust, Erregung–Hemmung, and

Spannung–Lösung). In current emotion psychology, the dimensional models are very prominent in assessment approaches and in psycholinguistic approaches to emotion. From an assessment approach, different dimensional models have been proposed. The four most important models are the positive affect–negative affect model (Watson & Tellegen, 1985), the pleasure–AROUSAL model (Russell, 1980), the tense AROUSAL and energetic AROUSAL model (Thayer, 1989), and pleasantness–activation model (Larsen & Diener, 1992). While being very different at first sight, it has been demonstrated that they are psychometrically equivalent (Yik, Russell, & Feldman Barrett, 1999). They consist of a VALENCE and an AROUSAL dimension, or of a rotation of these two dimensions.

Osgood and colleagues (Osgood, May, & Miron, 1975; Osgood, Suci, & Tannenbaum, 1957) have demonstrated that it is possible to assess the connotative meaning of nouns in a language with simple bipolar adjectives across cultural groups. They found evidence for three overarching affective dimensions, namely evaluation (from bad to good), potency (from weak to strong), and activation (from deactivated to highly activated). These three dimensions have also been identified in the cognitive structure of emotion terms across cultural groups (e.g., Fontaine, Poortinga, Setiadi, & Markam, 2002; Shaver, Schwartz, Kirson, & O'Connor, 1987; Shaver, Wu, & Schwartz, 1992). The assessment models and the psycholinguistic models agree that the emotion domain is structured according to a VALENCE and an AROUSAL dimension. They disagree about the existence of a third dimension, POWER.

For the operationalization of the Feeling component in the GRID instrument we decided to start from each of the four dominant assessment models that have been proposed in the assessment literature, as well as the three-dimensional VALENCE, POWER, and AROUSAL model that was identified in psycholinguistic research. Before introducing the specific features that operationalized the Feeling component in the GRID instrument, we briefly present these models (see Chapter 2, for a more detailed discussion on these models). According to the positive affect–negative affect model (Watson & Tellegen, 1985), positive and negative feelings are not organized along a single bipolar dimension, but according to two rather independent unipolar dimensions. Positive VALENCE and negative VALENCE are considered to vary rather independently from one another. This model is robustly identified by factor analyses on intensity and frequency ratings of positively and negatively valenced feeling and emotion terms. Not a bipolar, but two uncorrelated or slightly negatively correlated unipolar factors typically emerge from this assessment procedure (e.g., Watson & Clark, 1997). The contention of proponents of this model is that positive and negative VALENCE, while being conceptually opposite, are being registered by two different mechanisms in the emotional architecture (e.g., Watson, Wiese, Vaidya, & Tellegen, 1999).

The pleasure–AROUSAL model (Russell, 1980) and the pleasantness–activation model of Larsen and Diener (1992) are highly comparable. They recognize the centrality of the hedonic quality of the feelings, but add a second, bipolar dimension to it, namely AROUSAL or activation. Feelings would also vary from low AROUSAL or deactivation to high AROUSAL or activation. These models receive empirical support from both self-reports and similarity sorting of feeling and emotion terms.

The fourth two-dimensional model is the tense AROUSAL and energetic AROUSAL model of Thayer (1989). Thayer has exclusively studied the feeling domain from the perspective of AROUSAL, and identified two independent AROUSAL systems. They are represented by two bipolar AROUSAL dimensions, namely a tense AROUSAL dimension where feelings of tenseness are opposed to feelings of relaxation and an energetic AROUSAL dimension where feelings of energy are opposed to feelings of exhaustion.

The last model that was taken into account is the three-dimensional model of VALENCE, POWER, and AROUSAL that emerges from psycholinguistic research. As already presented, this model is based on the seminal work of Osgood and colleagues (Osgood et al., 1957, 1975), who studied not feelings, but the connotative meaning structure of words. The relevance of the three dimensions of VALENCE, POWER, and AROUSAL for the emotion domain was further confirmed by similarity research with emotion terms (e.g., Fontaine et al., 2002; Shaver et al., 1987, 1992). On the VALENCE dimension, positive emotion terms are opposed to negative emotion terms; on the POWER dimension, anger terms are opposed to fear and sadness terms; and on the AROUSAL dimension, sadness terms are opposed to fear and anger terms. Moreover, it has been demonstrated that the POWER dimension consists of three facets, namely control, strength, and dominance (e.g., Russell, 1978).

It is important to note the difference between how these models have been operationalized and investigated in the emotion and assessment literature, and how they have been operationalized in the GRID instrument. In the emotion and assessment literature, emotion terms, which are assumed to describe the process of synchronization between various emotion components (e.g., angry and sad), and feeling terms that describe the general quality of the emotional experience (e.g., strong and nervous) are used interchangeably. In the GRID, a very strong distinction is made between these two types of words. Only the feeling words that describe the general quality of the emotional experience have been used to operationalize the Feeling component of the GRID instrument. Only these words could be conceptually distinguished from the emotions words as well as from the features of the Appraisal, Action tendency, Bodily reaction, and Expression components.

According to the CPM, the Feeling component receives information on the synchronization in all other components, and integrates that information into conscious representation. It is therefore expected that the dimensions that structure the emotion domain will also structure the general quality of the emotional experience. It is thus hypothesized that the feeling words that describe the general quality of the emotional experience, represent the three dimensions of VALENCE (pleasantness, pleasure), POWER (potency, strength, dominance, control), and AROUSAL (activation).

8.4 Operationalization of the feeling features

The Feeling component was operationalized by means of 20 features that represent general feelings according to the positive affect–negative affect model (Watson & Tellegen, 1985), the pleasure–AROUSAL model (Russell, 1980), pleasantness–activation model (Larsen & Diener, 1992), the tense AROUSAL and energetic AROUSAL model (Thayer, 1989), and the evaluation–potency–activation model of Osgood (Osgood et al., 1957, 1975).

The VALENCE dimension was operationalized by the terms:

- felt good
- felt positive
- felt bad
- felt negative.

Besides the AROUSAL dimension (Russell, 1980) and the activation dimension (Larsen & Diener, 1992), the two AROUSAL dimensions proposed by Thayer (1989), namely tense AROUSAL and energetic AROUSAL, were also taken into account. As the tense and the energetic AROUSAL dimensions also include items that fit the general AROUSAL or activation dimension, it was decided to operationalize AROUSAL by the two Thayer dimensions. The tense AROUSAL was operationalized by the terms:

- felt restless
- felt nervous
- felt at ease
- felt calm.

The energetic AROUSAL was operationalized by the terms:

- felt energetic
- felt alert
- felt exhausted
- felt tired.

The POWER dimension was operationalized using the three facets of strength, control, and dominance (e.g., Russell, 1978). The terms for the POWER dimension were:

- felt dominant
- felt powerful
- felt strong
- felt in control
- felt out of control
- felt powerless
- felt weak
- felt submissive.

8.5 **Intensity and duration**

Besides the 20 feeling features, we investigated also two more general aspects of feeling, namely intensity and duration. Emotions are defined as dynamic episodes of subsystem synchronization (see Chapter 1) and are thus extended in time. Subjectively, an emotion episode is delimitated in the flux of experience as a discrete entity (often categorized and labeled as such) with a certain duration. In addition, again subjectively, there is a felt intensity associated with the experience that individuals experiencing an emotion often report spontaneously. In consequence, duration and intensity are two central aspects of emotional feeling. Despite some early work (Frijda, Mesquita, Sonnemans, & Van Goozen, 1991; Sonnemans & Frijda, 1994), there has been little systematic work on these issues, except for a few emotion recall studies (see Verduyn, Delvaux, Van Coillie, Tuerlinckx, & Van Mechelen, 2009; Verduyn, Van Mechelen, Tuerlinckx, Meers, & Van Coillie, 2009; Verduyn, Van Mechelen, Tuerlinckx, & Scherer, 2013). In the context of the GRID study, we were interested in examining to what extent differential intensities and durations are encoded in the semantic profiles of emotion words. To this effect, we included the following two features in the feeling section of the GRID instrument:

- was in an intense emotional state
- experienced the emotional state for a long time.

8.6 **Results**

The analyses on the Feeling component have been executed on data from 34 samples representing 27 countries and 24 languages (see Chapter 6, for a detailed account of the samples). For a description of the design, the instrument, and the data-analytic methods, the reader is referred to Chapter 5. Moreover, the same steps were taken as with the analyses of the overall structure, which were presented in the previous chapter (see Chapter 7). We first report on the factor structure of the Feeling component. We then present the relationships between the feeling factors and the overall factors that have been identified across all emotion components. We continue by investigating how well the Feeling component allows the differentiation of the 24 emotion terms from one another across languages, countries, and samples. We end by presenting the results on duration and intensity.

The internal structure of the Feeling component

In preliminary factor analyses, the feature "felt alert" behaved very differently from the other 19 feeling features. Therefore, the analyses on the Feeling component reported in this chapter were executed on the remaining 19 feeling features. In a first factor analysis on the feeling features across all emotion words and all samples, the scree plot pointed to a single dominant factor (see Figure SM 1)[2]. The first factor alone accounted for 77.30% of the total variance. However, the investigation of the stability of the factor structure across the German, Latin, Slavic, and East-Asian language groups (see Chapter 5, for a detailed explanation of the language groups) pointed to four stable factors (see Table SM 1) that accounted for 90.68% of the total variance. Given the stability of the first four factors, we investigated the one- up to the four-factorial solution.

The first factor opposed positively valenced feelings to negatively valenced feelings (see Table 8.1). All features either had substantially positive or substantially negative loadings on this factor (the lowest absolute loading was 0.587).

As the four self-report models that are dominant in the literature expect a two-factorial VALENCE–AROUSAL structure, the two-factorial structure was orthogonally Procrustes rotated toward a VALENCE–AROUSAL structure, with the VALENCE and the POWER features only loading on the first factor and the tense and energetic AROUSAL features only loading on the second factor. The rotated structure, however, did not confirm the expectation of a two-factorial VALENCE–AROUSAL structure. Of the eight a priori AROUSAL features, only one feature had its highest loading on the second dimension, namely "felt restless" (see also Table SM 2).

As there was a clear theoretical expectation that the three dimensions of VALENCE, POWER, and AROUSAL would structure the Feeling component, the three-factorial structure was orthogonally Procrustes rotated to the a-priori VALENCE, POWER, AROUSAL structure. The orthogonally rotated structure, however, did not confirm the a priori expectation. Of the 19 features, only nine features had the highest loading on the predicted factors (see also Table SM 3).

As a four-factorial structure was not expected, the four-factorial structure was VARIMAX rotated (see Table SM 4). In that structure, most POWER features had their highest loadings on the first factor, most VALENCE features had their highest loadings on the second factor, "felt tired" and "felt exhausted" had their highest loadings on the third factor, and "felt nervous" and "felt restless" had their highest loadings on the fourth factor. This structure thus most resembled the a priori construction of the feeling features which operationalized VALENCE, POWER, tense AROUSAL, and energetic AROUSAL. The structure was, however, not optimal because many features where characterized by cross-loadings.

Thus, the inspection of the one- up to a four-factorial structure could not confirm the a priori VALENCE, POWER, AROUSAL structure, with each indicator representing one of these dimensions. Moreover, the four-factorial VARIMAX solution suffered from many cross-loadings. A close inspection of these structures indicated that independent of the number of factors, all features tended to have

---

2 All supplementary materials (SM) are available at the GRID website: http://www.affective-sciences.org/ GRID. See Appendix 1 ("Availability") for further details.

Table 8.1 Loadings of the feeling features in a one-factorial structure

Feeling features	BAD VS GOOD
felt positive	0.97
felt good	0.96
felt at ease	0.96
felt strong	0.95
felt in control	0.95
felt energetic	0.95
felt powerful	0.95
felt dominant	0.88
felt calm	0.85
felt restless	−0.59
felt submissive	−0.67
felt out of control	−0.73
felt nervous	−0.73
felt tired	−0.81
felt exhausted	−0.90
felt weak	−0.91
felt negative	−0.93
felt powerless	−0.94
felt bad	−0.96

their highest, or second still, very high loading on only one factor. Thus, the original model, where each feature formed an indicator of only one of the four feeling factors, was disconfirmed. The model, which was suggested by the data, was a model with one main bipolar factor on which all features have a high loading and additional subsidiary factors on which specific features load. This model was of course already suggested by the fact that the one-factorial structure accounted for more than three quarters of the total variance.

To investigate whether a model with a general feeling factor and additional subsidiary factors could describe the feeling structure, the two-, three-, and four-factorial structures were rotated to a theoretical structure with all features loading, either positively or negatively on the first strong VALENCE factor, and with cross-loadings on one of the other subsidiary factors. The two-factorial model was orthogonally Procrustes rotated toward a general VALENCE factor and a subsidiary AROUSAL factor (see Table 8.2). Still, the AROUSAL factor was not confirmed. Of the seven a priori AROUSAL items, only three had a cross-loading exceeding 0.30 (or −0.30) on the subsidiary factor, namely "felt restless," "felt nervous," and "felt calm." Moreover, two POWER items ("felt submissive" and "felt out of control") also had a cross-loading exceeding 0.30 (or −0.30) on the subsidiary factor. The second orthogonally Procrustes rotated factor is thus not an AROUSAL factor, but a combination of tense AROUSAL and POWER.

The three-factorial structure was orthogonally Procrustes rotated toward a structure with a first general VALENCE factor, a subsidiary POWER factor, and a subsidiary AROUSAL factor (see Table 8.3).

Table 8.2 Loadings of the feeling features in a two-factorial Procrustes rotated structure

Feeling features	BAD VS GOOD	LOW VS HIGH AROUSAL
felt positive	**0.97**	−0.10
felt good	**0.96**	−0.12
felt strong	**0.96**	0.16
felt in control	**0.95**	−0.08
felt powerful	**0.95**	0.15
felt dominant	**0.88**	0.20
felt submissive	**−0.67**	−0.47
felt out of control	**−0.72**	0.44
felt weak	**−0.91**	−0.28
felt negative	**−0.93**	0.04
felt powerless	**−0.94**	−0.13
felt bad	**−0.96**	0.01
felt restless	−0.58	**0.61**
felt nervous	−0.73	**0.41**
felt energetic	0.95	**0.18**
felt exhausted	−0.90	**−0.10**
felt at ease	0.96	**−0.14**
felt tired	−0.81	**−0.23**
felt calm	0.85	**−0.40**

Note: bold font indicates the feature was expected to have its highest loading or a secondary loading on this factor.

That structure fitted reasonably well. Of the eight POWER items, seven also had a cross-loading exceeding 0.30 (or −0.30) on the subsidiary POWER factor. Only the feature "out of control" loaded higher on the third factor. On the subsidiary AROUSAL factor, four of the seven a priori AROUSAL items had a cross-loading exceeding 0.30 (or −0.30). "Felt at ease" and "felt exhausted," however, only loaded on the first overall factor and the feature "felt energetic" only had a cross-loading on the POWER factor.

The four-factorial structure was orthogonally Procrustes rotated toward a structure with a general VALENCE factor and three subsidiary feeling factors, namely a POWER factor, a tense AROUSAL factor and an energetic AROUSAL factor (see Table 8.4). The rotated structure fitted the subsidiary model very well: of the 19 features, only three features did not display the expected cross-loading. "Felt out of control" had no cross-loading on the POWER factor, but had a cross-loading on the tense AROUSAL factor. "Felt at ease" only loaded on the first VALENCE factor and had no cross-loading on any of the three subsidiary factors. "Felt energetic" did not display the expected cross-loading on the energetic AROUSAL factor. Instead, it had a cross-loading on the POWER factor. Because of this latter observation, it is problematic to continue calling the fourth factor "energetic AROUSAL." It is basically a unipolar factor defined by "felt tired" and "felt exhausted." Therefore this factor was reversed and labeled TIRED.

Table 8.3 Loadings of the feeling features in a three-factorial Procrustes rotated structure

Feeling features	BAD VS GOOD	WEAK VS STRONG	LOW VS HIGH AROUSAL
felt good	0.96	0.19	−0.02
felt positive	0.96	0.21	−0.02
felt bad	−0.93	−0.27	−0.05
felt negative	−0.94	−0.16	−0.08
felt dominant	0.70	0.62	0.03
felt powerful	0.81	0.53	0.05
felt strong	0.83	0.50	0.08
felt in control	0.87	0.37	−0.11
felt out of control	−0.80	0.05	0.31
felt powerless	−0.85	−0.41	−0.10
felt weak	−0.75	−0.58	−0.15
felt submissive	−0.43	−0.73	−0.21
felt restless	−0.61	−0.04	0.61
felt nervous	−0.65	−0.33	0.55
felt energetic	0.86	0.40	0.18
felt at ease	0.95	0.20	−0.06
felt exhausted	−0.86	−0.28	−0.15
felt calm	0.88	0.09	−0.32
felt tired	−0.80	−0.17	−0.37

Note: bold font indicates the feature was expected to have its highest loading or a secondary loading on this factor.

Because the orthogonally Procrustes rotated four-factorial structure fitted the a priori selection of the feeling features the best and was stable across language groups, this structure was finally selected. We labeled these four factors BAD VS GOOD, WEAK VS STRONG, CALM VS RESTLESS, and TIRED.

After orthogonal Procrustes rotation, BAD VS GOOD accounted for 64.47%, WEAK VS STRONG accounted for 14.05%, CALM VS RESTLESS for 7.42%, and TIRED for 4.79% of the total variance of the feeling features. When we compare the importance of each feeling factor with the factors in the global structure (in which the feeling features were removed, see Chapter 7), it is clear that the VALENCE factor is much more important in the Feeling component than in the other components. In the overall structure with all features except the feeling features, the VALENCE factor accounted for 36.58% of the total variance, the POWER factor accounted for 13.20%, the AROUSAL factor for 8.92%, and the NOVELTY factor for 4.97%. Thus, in the Feeling component, the VALENCE factor (BAD VS GOOD) accounts for about double the amount of the variance than in all the other components combined.

To further investigate the meaning of the four Procrustes rotated feeling factors, plots were made with the average factor scores of the 24 emotion terms on the four factors (see Figure 8.1 to Figure 8.4). The plots of the terms fit the interpretation of the features very well. On the first factor, positively valenced emotion terms are opposed to negatively valenced emotion terms (with *surprise* and *compassion* in the middle). On the second factor, anger terms (and *pride*) are opposed to fear

Table 8.4 Loadings of the feeling features in a four-factorial Procrustes rotated structure

Feeling features	BAD VS GOOD	WEAK VS STRONG	CALM VS RESTLESS	TIRED
felt good	**0.96**	0.19	−0.12	0.06
felt positive	**0.95**	0.21	−0.12	0.06
felt bad	**−0.93**	−0.26	0.06	−0.11
felt negative	**−0.94**	−0.16	0.03	−0.10
felt dominant	0.67	**0.61**	−0.12	0.21
felt powerful	0.79	**0.53**	−0.09	0.16
felt strong	0.81	**0.50**	−0.07	0.20
felt in control	0.87	**0.37**	−0.19	0.01
felt out of control	−0.80	**0.06**	0.31	0.19
felt powerless	−0.83	**−0.41**	0.04	−0.18
felt weak	−0.73	**−0.58**	0.01	−0.25
felt submissive	−0.47	**−0.74**	−0.19	−0.02
felt restless	−0.46	−0.03	**0.82**	−0.22
felt nervous	−0.61	−0.32	**0.58**	0.17
felt at ease	0.95	0.20	**−0.15**	0.03
felt calm	0.86	0.09	**−0.37**	−0.09
felt energetic	0.85	0.40	0.01	**0.26**
felt tired	−0.75	−0.17	−0.09	**−0.56**
felt exhausted	−0.80	−0.28	0.09	**−0.42**

Note: bold font indicates the feature was expected to have its highest loading or a secondary loading on this factor.

and sadness terms (and to *love*). The positions on the third and the fourth factor look very much alike: anger and fear terms (and *surprise*) are opposed to sadness terms (and *compassion*), as can be expected from AROUSAL dimensions. To explore the differences between the two AROUSAL dimensions, the 24 emotion terms were also plotted separately on these two dimensions in Figure 8.4. It is observed that the fear and the self-conscious emotion terms are the most differentiated on these two AROUSAL factors. *Fear*, *anxiety*, and *stress*, all score very high on the CALM VS RESTLESS factor. However, they vary hugely on the TIRED factor: *fear* scores low on TIRED, *stress* scores high, and *anxiety* is situated in between. The two self-conscious emotion terms, *guilt* and *shame*, score equally high on the CALM VS RESTLESS factor (at the restlessness pole of the factor, but less extreme than the fear terms). However, they are differentiated on the TIRED factor: *shame* scores low on TIRED, while *guilt* scores almost one and a half standard deviation higher on this factor.

Mapping the feeling structure onto the overall structure

To further explore the relationships between the overall factorial structure and the internal structure of the Feeling component, we have regressed the four feeling factors on the four overall factors (after omitting all feeling features). Table 8.5 shows the standardized regression weights and R² of the factors regressed on the four overall factors. The values for R² show that VALENCE is predicted most accurately (mainly by the BAD VS GOOD feeling factor), followed by POWER (mainly by the

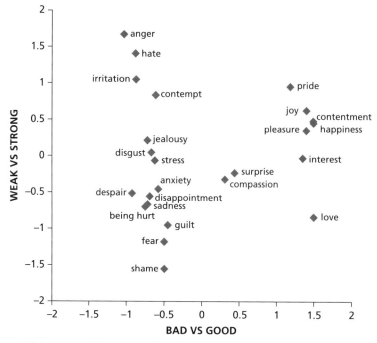

Figure 8.1 Plot of the average factor scores for the 24 emotion words on BAD VS GOOD and WEAK VS STRONG.

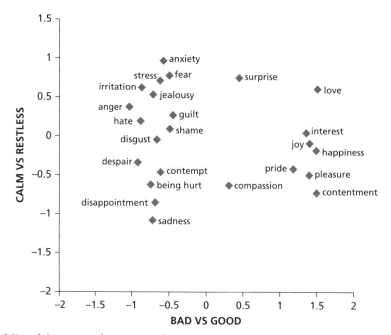

Figure 8.2 Plot of the average factor scores for the 24 emotion words on BAD VS GOOD and CALM VS RESTLESS.

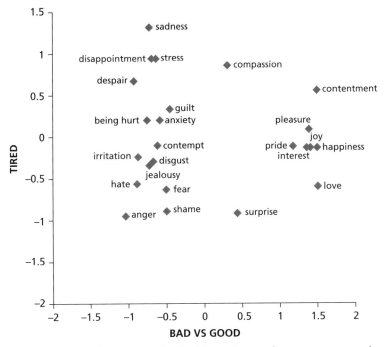

Figure 8.3 Plot of the average factor scores for the 24 emotion words on BAD VS GOOD and TIRED.

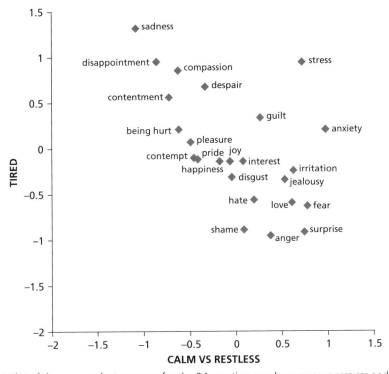

Figure 8.4 Plot of the average factor scores for the 24 emotion words on CALM VS RESTLESS and TIRED.

Table 8.5 Standardized regression weights and R² of the feeling factors regressed on the four overall factors

Overall factors	$\beta_{\text{BAD VS GOOD}}$	$\beta_{\text{WEAK VS STRONG}}$	$\beta_{\text{CALM VS RESTLESS}}$	β_{TIRED}	R^2
VALENCE	0.95***	0.02	−0.10***	0.00	0.91
POWER	0.12***	0.75***	0.11***	−0.28***	0.66
AROUSAL	−0.07*	−0.02	0.58***	−0.42***	0.52
NOVELTY	0.05	0.00	0.05	−0.09*	0.01

Note: * p < 0.05, ** p < 0.01, *** p < 0.001. The feeling features were removed from the four overall factors.

WEAK VS STRONG feeling factor) and AROUSAL (mainly by both the CALM VS RESTLESS and the TIRED feeling factors), which largely confirms expectations. The NOVELTY factor is virtually unrelated to the feeling factors (R^2 is only 0.013). NOVELTY relates slightly negatively to TIRED.

Emotion category differentiation based on the Feeling component

Having identified the factorial structure for this component, we now examine to what extent the four feeling factors in isolation allow the discrimination of the 24 emotion terms, that is, classify them correctly on the basis of the four feeling factor scores (as compared to classification success based on all 19 feeling features). The classification accuracy is shown in Table 8.6 Using the four feeling factor scores as independent variables, 47.2% of cross-validated grouped cases could be correctly classified, which is far above chance level (which is 1/24 or 4.2%). In comparison, the results for the MDA classification that used all 19 feeling features as dependent variables achieved a correct classification of 58.5% of cross-validated grouped cases. This is an improvement of 11.3% in classification accuracy. The last column of Table 8.6 allows inspecting the patterns of the most frequent classification errors in the classification based on all features. There were particularly frequent confusions among *happiness, joy, pleasure,* and *contentment* for the positive emotions. For the negative emotions there were frequent confusions among a) *anger, irritation, hate,* and *contempt*; and among b) *disappointment, sadness, being hurt,* and *despair*. The confusions thus occurred within three of the four major emotion clusters (positive emotion cluster, anger cluster, and sadness cluster). There were no major confusions within the fear cluster.

Intensity and duration

The effects of intensity and duration have been investigated in two ways. First, it has been investigated whether the four major emotion clusters (joy, sadness, fear, and anger) differed from one another in intensity and duration using an ANOVA randomized block design with the emotion cluster being the independent factor and the sample the block factor. Second, it has been investigated whether and to what extent the 24 emotion terms differed from one another also using an ANOVA randomized block design with the emotion terms being the independent factor and the sample the block factor. The differences between the emotion terms have then been further investigated with Tukey's pairwise comparisons.

The four emotion clusters differed from one another significantly in intensity, but the effect was small [$F(3,711) = 6.41, p < 0.001, partial\ eta^2 = 0.03$]. Post-hoc pairwise comparisons showed that sadness terms ($M = 1.78$) and fear terms ($M = 1.82$) are a bit less intense than positive emotion terms ($M = 2.03$) and anger terms ($M = 2.05$). There was a significant and larger difference, in duration, between the emotion clusters [$F(3,711) = 39.24, p < 0.000, partial\ eta^2 = 0.14$]. The post-hoc

Table 8.6 Classification accuracy (in percent) for the 24 emotion words in discriminant analyses based on the four feeling factors and the feeling features

Emotion words	Classification based on *feeling factors*	Classification based on *feeling features*	
	Accuracy	Accuracy	Confusion > 15% with
being hurt	26.5	47.1	disappointment
sadness	50.0	52.9	disappointment
shame	64.7	70.6	
guilt	47.1	58.8	
compassion	70.6	70.6	
disappointment	20.6	38.2	sadness
love	76.5	82.4	
contentment	61.8	55.9	
happiness	26.5	20.6	joy
pride	55.9	91.2	
pleasure	23.5	32.4	joy, happiness, contentment
joy	14.7	38.2	happiness, pleasure
interest	44.1	82.4	
surprise	88.2	94.1	
despair	47.1	52.9	sadness
stress	61.8	82.4	
anxiety	44.1	61.8	
fear	61.8	64.7	
jealousy	47.1	47.1	disgust
hate	17.6	38.2	anger, irritation
irritation	26.5	44.1	anger
anger	64.7	58.8	hate
disgust	41.2	61.8	
contempt	50.0	55.9	hate
Total	47.2	58.5	

comparisons revealed that fear terms ($M = 0.55$) and anger terms ($M = 0.69$) were associated with a shorter duration than sadness terms ($M = 1.20$) and positive emotion terms ($M = 1.27$).

The differences between the 24 emotion terms were significant and much larger than the emotion cluster differences for both intensity [$F(23,759) = 19.16$, $p < 0.000$, *partial eta*$^2 = 0.37$] and duration [$F(23,759) = 44.72$, $p < 0.000$, *partial eta*$^2 = 0.58$]. The pairwise comparisons revealed gradual differences between emotion terms in intensity. Table 8.7 shows the means and standard deviations of the mean centered scores (see Chapter 5 for more information on the centering of the scores) for the 24 emotion words sorted from low to high intensity. Moreover, significant differences were observed within emotion clusters. In the joy cluster, *happiness, love, joy,* and

Table 8.7 Intensity means and standard deviations for the 24 emotion words

Emotion words	Mean	Standard deviation
interest	0.83	0.68
disappointment	1.23	0.74
compassion	1.35	0.79
contempt	1.46	0.83
stress	1.49	0.53
contentment	1.54	1.13
guilt	1.55	0.52
pride	1.69	0.90
surprise	1.71	0.65
shame	1.75	0.62
irritation	1.77	0.74
anxiety	1.81	0.62
disgust	1.87	0.69
sadness	1.96	0.92
being hurt	2.03	0.64
fear	2.10	0.81
despair	2.14	0.77
jealousy	2.22	0.61
anger	2.32	0.64
pleasure	2.35	0.73
joy	2.47	0.71
hate	2.47	0.60
love	2.66	0.47
happiness	2.68	0.77

pleasure were more intense than *contentment*, and *contentment* more intense than *interest*. In the anger cluster, *hate* was significantly more intense than *irritation* and *contempt*, with *anger* and *jealousy* in between. *Fear* was significantly more intense than *stress*, with *anxiety* in between. In the sadness cluster, *despair* was significantly more intense than *disappointment* and *guilt*. *Being hurt* and *sadness* were significantly more intense than *disappointment*, with *shame* and *guilt* in between.

The pairwise comparisons revealed that *surprise* had a significantly shorter duration than all the other 23 emotion terms. Table 8.8 shows the means and standard deviations of the mean centered scores (see Chapter 5) for the 24 emotion words sorted from short to long duration. Moreover, significant differences were observed between terms within the same emotion cluster. *Love* had a significantly longer duration than *happiness*, and *happiness* had a significantly longer duration than *interest*, with *contentment*, *pleasure*, and *joy* being in between. In the anger cluster, *jealousy*, *hate*, and *contempt* had a significantly longer duration than *anger* and *irritation*. *Stress* had a significantly

Table 8.8 Duration means and standard deviations for the 24 emotion words

Emotion words	Mean	Standard deviation
surprise	−1.38	0.79
irritation	0.11	0.61
disgust	0.12	0.77
anger	0.22	0.59
shame	0.32	0.82
fear	0.34	0.72
anxiety	0.76	0.57
contempt	0.80	0.67
interest	0.87	0.60
disappointment	0.87	0.68
pride	0.94	0.74
stress	0.99	0.61
joy	1.08	0.78
hate	1.09	0.62
pleasure	1.11	0.71
contentment	1.14	0.77
compassion	1.22	0.79
despair	1.24	0.94
jealousy	1.26	0.57
being hurt	1.30	0.65
happiness	1.46	0.75
guilt	1.54	0.80
sadness	1.91	0.64
love	2.30	0.50

longer duration than *fear* and *disgust*, with *anxiety* in between. In the sadness cluster, *sadness* had a significantly longer duration than all the other sadness terms (except *guilt*); *guilt* had a significantly longer duration than *disappointment* and *shame*.

8.7 Discussion

The internal structure of the Feeling component

On the basis of the theoretical assumption that the Feeling component receives input from the other four components and transforms that information at a low level into consciousness, it was hypothesized that the Feeling component would mimic the overall structure across all emotion components, which was reported in the previous chapter. This hypothesis was only partly confirmed. While evidence was found for a VALENCE, a POWER, and an AROUSAL factor in the Feeling component, the structure differed in substantial ways from the overall structure.

As predicted, the first factor that structures the feeling domain is a bipolar VALENCE factor. Thus, when it comes to meaning, there is no evidence at all for a model with separate positive and negative feeling factors. The more an emotion word refers to feeling good, the less it refers to feeling bad, and vice versa. While a VALENCE factor was expected, its overwhelming salience was not. VALENCE was not only the most important factor, but it accounted for almost double the variance in the Feeling component compared to the four other components taken together. Moreover, only a model with a general bipolar VALENCE factor and subsidiary factors described the factor structure of the Feeling component well. All feeling features had a very high (or even their highest) loading on the VALENCE factor, and loaded only then on the predicted factor. This effect was particularly strong for the positively valenced items of the tense AROUSAL factor. "Felt at ease" turned out to be a mere VALENCE item. It gave no information on tense AROUSAL. "Felt calm" still loaded negatively on the tense AROUSAL factor, but this loading was far less important than expected. The VALENCE factor thus overshadowed the other factors.

The fact that the VALENCE factor is twice as important in the Feeling component than the three other components taken together, calls for an explanation. From the perspective of the lexical sedimentation hypothesis, which assumes that genuine differences in emotion processes have been encoded in language, the current findings could indicate that the information about what is going on in the Appraisal, Action tendency, Expression, and Bodily reaction components is not only registered and summarized at a low level of representation in the Feeling component, but that the information is also weighted with the VALENCE aspect receiving much more weight than the other aspects of the emotional experience. The centrality of VALENCE could be accounted for by the hypothesized function of the Feeling component, namely becoming aware of the emotion process in order to monitor and regulate it. Given the fact that many sources of information constantly compete for conscious attention, only a clear signal is likely to enter consciousness easily. By amplifying VALENCE, the Feeling component would give a clear signal about the nature of the ongoing emotion process.

A separate POWER factor emerged that was defined by feelings of dominance, strength, and control as predicted. Still, two notable deviations from the expectations were observed. First, "felt out of control" did not define the WEAK VS STRONG factor, but loaded on the CALM VS RESTLESS factor. The opposite of control on the POWER dimension is probably "lack of control" rather than "out of control." "Out of control" likely refers to hectic activity that tries to ward off an unwanted situation. Second, "felt energetic" systematically defined the WEAK VS STRONG factor and not the hypothesized energetic AROUSAL factor. Taken together, these deviations seem to indicate that the WEAK VS STRONG factor can be best interpreted as the subjective experience of having the POWER to proactively realize one's goals versus having to surrender oneself to the situation.

In the three-factorial solution, an AROUSAL factor emerged. However, this factor was mainly defined by tense AROUSAL features. One AROUSAL factor did not suffice to represent the AROUSAL items. Not one, but two AROUSAL factors could be stably identified in the four language groups as predicted by Thayer (1989). These two factors were not just a rotation of a general VALENCE and a general AROUSAL factor, as the two AROUSAL factors emerged after a general VALENCE factor was identified. The first AROUSAL factor could be very well interpreted as Thayer's tense AROUSAL factor. The second AROUSAL factor, however, could not be interpreted as energetic AROUSAL. The two features, namely "felt alert" and "felt energetic," that were a priori hypothesized to define the positive pole of the energetic AROUSAL factor did not do so. Except for its VALENCE, "felt alert" turned out to be very different from all the other features. Alertness is probably not a feeling at all, but is rather a form of attention. "Felt energetic" defined the WEAK VS STRONG factor, and not the second AROUSAL factor. This excludes an interpretation of the second AROUSAL factor as energetic AROUSAL. That factor was only defined by "felt tired" and "felt exhausted." Given the fact that feeling awake is the antonym of feeling tired, it could be hypothesized that the second AROUSAL factor just refers to a wake-sleep dimension.

From the perspective of the lexical sedimentation hypothesis, the question arises what the existence of two AROUSAL factors, which emerge even after an overwhelming first VALENCE factor and a POWER factor were identified, means. It could mean that two separate AROUSAL systems exist, although somewhat different than the one proposed by Thayer (1989). Based on the more narrow interpretation of the second AROUSAL factor as a sleep-wake factor, a hypothetical interpretation of the two AROUSAL systems could be in terms of a constant AROUSAL system and an ad hoc AROUSAL system. The constant AROUSAL system would take care of the wake-sleep cycle. It would be characterized by circadian rhythms and would be thus constantly in a state of change. It is reasonable to expect that this AROUSAL system would not be triggered by the emotion, but would only be influenced by it. For example, when intensely sad, one does not want to wake up in the morning, or the experience of a threatening event in the evening suddenly chases away sleepiness. The ad hoc AROUSAL system would be elicited when particular action is needed. In the present study, we see that the two AROUSAL factors are especially differentiated in the fear and the self-conscious emotion terms. They point to the duration of the emotion process as a key difference between the two AROUSAL factors. If a high-arousal emotion is a short-lived emotion (like in fear), both forms of AROUSAL would complement one another: the sleep-wake cycle would be interrupted, and additional activation would be freed. However, if the emotion process is extended over longer time periods (like is the case for stress and guilt), both AROUSAL systems could get dissociated. The constant AROUSAL system would then indicate that the transition from wake to sleep cannot be further postponed, while the hoc AROUSAL system would remain active.

While feeling factors were observed that corresponded to the VALENCE, POWER, and AROUSAL factors in the overall structure, no feeling factor was identified that corresponded to NOVELTY ("felt alert" had a zero correlation with the NOVELTY factor). An obvious explanation is that such a factor was not identified, because it was not operationalized. Three factors were a priori expected and only those were operationalized. However, a deliberate attempt to identify feeling terms for the NOVELTY dimension (see the research reported in Chapter 14) could neither come up with convincing candidates. A possible explanation is that there is no need in NOVELTY for general feelings that represent the overall quality of the emotional process, because it directly triggers the conscious attentional system. Surprise cannot be dealt with in an automatic way, unlike for instance fear. A threatening object can be automatically detected and an action program can be automatically started to avoid the danger. The awareness can come later, when the fear process has already started. With surprise the persons conscious attention is drawn to the source of NOVELTY, because the nature of the event is unclear. The organism first has to identify what is going on and this requires the full attention of the organism. Thus, rather than signaling that an important process is occurring that possibly needs regulation, attention is immediately and consciously drawn to the source of NOVELTY. Once the meaning of the novel event has been identified, the surprise emotion can convert into another emotion with its accompanying feelings (what happened is positive, threatening, unjust, . . .).

Mapping the feeling structure onto the overall structure

The relationships of the four feeling factors with the overall factors spanning the emotion domain, further confirm the interpretation of the feeling factors. BAD VS GOOD was strongly related to VALENCE, WEAK VS STRONG to POWER, and both CALM VS NERVOUS and TIRED to AROUSAL in the overall structure. Thus, in the feeling structure the overall AROUSAL factor splits up in two separate AROUSAL factors.

Emotion category differentiation based on the Feeling component

Despite the fact that the Feeling component was operationalized by feeling terms that only conveyed information about the general quality of the emotion process, it was still reasonably easy to identify an emotion term on the basis of its respective feeling profile. Almost half of the emotion terms could be correctly identified on the basis of their feature profile on the four feeling factors. Thus, just knowing the feeling pattern substantially constrains the number of possible emotions a person can experience. Becoming aware of the general quality of the ongoing emotion process gives already good indications about the nature of the process. The general feelings thus form a good starting point to further explore one's emotional experience.

Intensity and duration

The analyses on intensity and duration clearly indicate that prototypical duration and intensity differences are encoded in language. A comparison between the data reported here and earlier results from some of the cross-cultural recall studies (e.g., Ricci-Bitti & Scherer, 1986; Scherer & Wallbott, 1994; Scherer, Wranik, Sangsue, Tran, & Scherer, 2004) suggests a great deal of convergence. In previous cross-cultural studies, differences in duration were found to be substantially more pronounced than differences in intensity. Moreover, for the four basic emotions of joy, sadness, anger, and fear, comparable differences were observed with joy and sadness being subjectively experienced much longer than fear and anger. Furthermore, differences in duration and intensity differentiate emotion terms much more within language families than between language families. Because information about duration and intensity is encoded in language, it can be hypothesized that the precise emotion label that is used for recalling emotions will have a substantial impact on the reported intensity and duration of the recalled episodes.

8.8 **General discussion**

The operationalization of the Feeling component was based on a conceptual distinction between emotion terms, which represent the synchronization between different components, and general feeling terms that represent the subjective quality of the emotion process. The current results confirm that both types of terms do not convey the same information, and should therefore not be used interchangeably. Two findings are especially important for the Feeling component, namely: (1) that the VALENCE dimension is much more salient in the Feeling component than in the other emotion components; and (2) that the overall AROUSAL factor splits up into a CALM VS RESTLESS and a TIRED feeling factor. A final observation is that the Feeling component, even at this general level is more complex than the two-dimensional feeling and affect models that dominate the assessment literature. The present findings raise the hypothesis that each of these models assesses the four feeling dimensions in a confounded way. In the present study, the scree plot only pointed to one big and a second smaller factor, and the second factor in the two-factor solution was a combination of POWER, tense AROUSAL, and tiredness. At least when it comes to the meaning of emotion terms, the four feeling models do not just differ from one another in terms of the rotation of the factors, but also in the dimensionality in which they have to be represented. There are already indications in the literature that this does not only hold for the feeling structure in language, but also holds for interindividual differences in emotional experience. The current results are in line with the empirical observation of Schimmack and Reisenzein (2002) that energetic AROUSAL and tense AROUSAL could not be fully reduced to a combination of VALENCE and activation. The present findings call for further and focused research on the dimensionality of interindividual differences in feelings.

Chapter 9

Embodied emotions: The Bodily reaction component

Klaus R. Scherer[1] and Johnny J. R. Fontaine

Changes in the physiological support systems of an organism are an important component of emotion episodes, given that they help to prepare for adaptive responses to emotion eliciting-events. These physiological changes are generally perceived in the form of bodily reactions which, ever since William James (1884) insisted on their constitutive role for emotional experience, are considered a central component of emotion (see Chapter 1). However, there are only a limited number of verbal descriptions of bodily reactions in ordinary languages that are likely to be reliably used in everyday speech and that therefore qualify as features for the GRID questionnaire (it should be noted that reliable use does not mean that people are able to actually perceive the underlying physiological functions correctly; see Vaitl, 1996).

For the selection of the bodily reaction features, we relied on two sources. On the one hand, we looked at the work of Stemmler (2003) on psychophysiological reactions in emotion episodes. On the other hand, we looked for verbal expressions of bodily emotional reactions that are widely used in different languages. We adopted a set of bodily reaction descriptions that were successfully used in a large scale cross-cultural study of recalled emotional experiences in which self report data about typical patterns of bodily reactions, such as cardiovascular activity, tension of the striated musculature, gastric motility, and skin temperature were obtained (Scherer, Wallbott, & Summerfield, 1986). The results were used to formulate concrete predictions of the expected bodily reactions for four major emotions (Scherer, 1986, p. 185). Based on these data, in a second cross-cultural experience recall study, which was run in 37 countries on five continents (Scherer & Wallbott, 1994), the following items were used to obtain a self report of bodily reactions: "lump in throat, change in breathing, stomach troubles, feeling cold/shivering, feeling warm/pleasant, feeling hot/cheeks burning, heart beating faster, muscles tensing/trembling, muscles relaxing/restful, perspiring/moist hands, other symptoms." Based on the physiological literature, these physiological patterns were grouped into three major groups for the data analysis: sympathetic, parasympathetic, and felt temperature symptoms (Scherer & Wallbott, 1994, p. 314–5).

In line with prior work on physiological response patterning during emotion episodes, the bodily reaction descriptions in the GRID instrument were selected using the 18 features listed below. As we expected to replicate the structure of categorizing bodily reactions that was found in the earlier recall studies, this list is organized accordingly, differentiating between sympathetic, parasympathetic, and felt temperature reactions. However, it should be noted that this is a heuristic categorization without any claim about the underlying mechanisms. This is particularly true for

---

[1] Corresponding author: Klaus R. Scherer. Swiss Center for Affective Sciences—University of Geneva. 7, Rue des Battoirs, CH-1205 Geneva, Switzerland. Klaus.Scherer@unige.ch

the parasympathetic category (see Jänig, 2003), which we paraphrase here as "non-sympathetic, non-adrenergic AROUSAL," to avoid making any claims as to underlying regulation systems.

Sympathetic AROUSAL:

- heartbeat slowing down
- heartbeat getting faster
- muscles relaxing (whole body)
- muscles tensing (whole body)
- breathing slowing down
- breathing getting faster
- perspiring, or having moist hands
- sweating

Parasympathetic AROUSAL (non-sympathetic, non-adrenergic AROUSAL):

- had stomach troubles
- a lump in throat
- felt shivers
- felt weak limbs
- got pale

Felt temperature:

- felt cold
- felt warm
- felt hot
- blushed

None:

- had no bodily symptoms at all

9.1 **Results**

The internal structure of the Bodily reaction component

In a first factor analysis of the bodily reaction features across all emotion words and all samples, the scree plot (see Figure SM 1) pointed to two main factors.[2] However, the investigation of the stability of the factor structure across four language groups showed three stable factors (see Table SM 1), accounting for 75.5% of the overall variance. Given the stability of the first three factors, we adopted this solution. The Procrustes rotated factor loadings toward the expected three-factorial structure are shown in Table 9.1.

The results generally confirmed the expectations based on earlier findings reported above. The first factor is constituted by items that we have described above as "non-sympathetic, non-adrenergic AROUSAL" ("got pale, felt weak limbs, had stomach troubles, a lump in throat, shivers"). To avoid the problems involved in the distinction between the sympathetic and the parasympathetic

---

[2] All supplementary materials (SM) are available at the GRID website: http://www.affective-sciences.org/GRID. See Appendix 1 ("Availability") for further details.

Table 9.1 Loadings of the bodily reaction features in a three-factorial Procrustes rotated structure

Bodily reaction features	DISTRESS SYMPTOMS	AUTONOMIC AROUSAL	BODY TEMPERATURE
felt weak limbs	**0.87**	0.09	−0.10
got pale	**0.75**	0.26	−0.51
felt shivers	**0.65**	0.19	0.34
had stomach troubles	**0.65**	0.42	−0.42
a lump in throat	**0.60**	0.16	−0.37
muscles tensing (whole body)	0.25	**0.85**	−0.15
breathing getting faster	0.13	**0.77**	0.42
perspired or had moist hands	0.45	**0.75**	0.21
sweat	0.43	**0.73**	0.21
heartbeat getting faster	0.09	**0.58**	0.70
muscles relaxing (whole body)	−0.12	**−0.77**	0.53
heartbeat slowing down	0.24	**−0.80**	−0.25
breathing slowing down	0.09	**−0.91**	0.08
felt warm	−0.37	0.11	**0.75**
blushed	−0.12	0.26	**0.74**
felt hot	0.05	0.63	**0.61**
felt cold	0.63	−0.01	**−0.65**
had no bodily symptoms at all	−0.40	−0.63	−0.26

Note: bold font indicates the feature was expected to have its highest loading on this factor.

branches of the autonomous nervous system (ANS) mentioned above, we chose more descriptive labels for the factors in this emotion component. Thus, we will refer to this factor as DISTRESS SYMPTOMS. The second factor shows high loadings for sensations that are usually perceived in cases of high AROUSAL of the ANS ("muscles tensing, heartbeat and breathing getting faster, sweating and perspiring") and will be labeled AUTONOMIC AROUSAL. The third factor is a temperature factor ("felt hot, felt warm, blushed") and thus labeled as BODY TEMPERATURE.

It should be noted that high cross-loadings indicate that the features "felt hot" and "heartbeat getting faster" are jointly contributing to the AUTONOMIC AROUSAL and the BODY TEMPERATURE factor. The mechanisms and subdivisions of the ANS have been much debated in physiology and there is little work on the relationship between self report of physiological symptoms and actual physiological measurement (due to the fact that it is difficult to induce strong emotions with marked physiological changes in the laboratory). In consequence, the labels used to refer to the factorial structure reported above should be considered in a heuristic sense rather than a description of the underlying physiological processes, until more theoretically anchored empirical studies using precise physiological assessment are available.

The means of the bodily reaction factor scores for the various emotions are reproduced in Table SM 2 and plotted in Figure 9.1 and Figure 9.2. The graphs allow examining the relative position of the 24 emotions in the three-dimensional space formed by the bodily reaction factors. Figure 9.1 shows that especially anger and fear terms score high on AUTONOMIC AROUSAL,

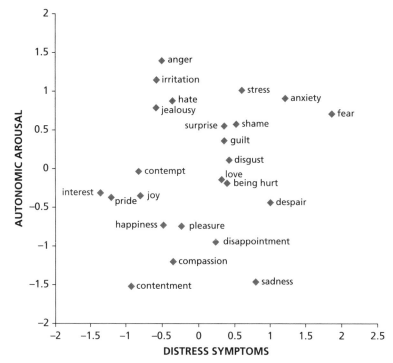

Figure 9.1 Plot of the average factor scores for the 24 emotion words on DISTRESS SYMPTOMS and AUTONOMIC AROUSAL.

while sadness terms (e.g., sadness and disappointment) score low on this factor. Sadness and fear terms (e.g., sadness and fear) score high on DISTRESS SYMPTOMS, while anger, and especially positive emotion terms, tend to score low on this factor (e.g., interest and pride). Figure 9.2 shows a separation between positive and negative emotions at a middle range of autonomic involvement, suggesting a central role of BODY TEMPERATURE in distinguishing them. Here the emotions of sadness and disappointment are of interest, being rather cold and having very low values on the AUTONOMIC AROUSAL factor.

Mapping the bodily reaction structure onto the overall structure

To further explore the relationships between the overall factorial structure and the internal structure of the Bodily reaction component, we regressed the three bodily reaction factors on the four overall factors (after omitting all bodily reaction features). Table 9.2 shows the standardized regression weights and R^2 of the bodily reaction factors regressed on the four overall factors. The values for R^2 showed that VALENCE was predicted best (mostly by BODY TEMPERATURE), followed by POWER (by absence of DISTRESS SYMPTOMS) and AROUSAL (by AUTONOMIC AROUSAL symptoms).

Emotion category differentiation based on the Bodily reaction component

Having identified the factorial structure for this component, we examined to what extent the three bodily reaction factors allowed the discrimination of the 24 emotion terms, that is, classify them

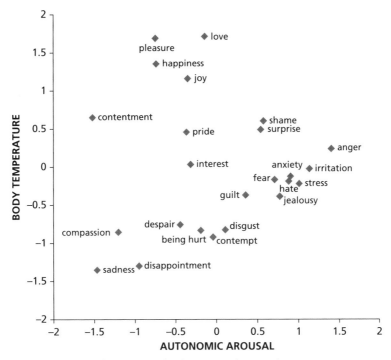

Figure 9.2 Plot of the average factor scores for the 24 emotion words on AUTONOMIC AROUSAL and BODY TEMPERATURE.

Table 9.2 Standardized regression weights and R^2 of the bodily reaction factors regressed on the four overall factors

Overall factors	$\beta_{\text{DISTRESS SYMPTOMS}}$	$\beta_{\text{AUTONOMIC AROUSAL}}$	$\beta_{\text{BODY TEMPERATURE}}$	R^2
VALENCE	−0.32***	−0.46***	0.63***	0.70
POWER	−0.60***	0.30***	0.20***	0.49
AROUSAL	0.21***	0.61***	0.21***	0.46
NOVELTY	0.26***	0.04	0.22***	0.11

Note: * $p < 0.05$. ** $p < 0.01$. *** $p < 0.00$. The bodily reaction features were removed from the four overall factors.

correctly on the basis of the three factor scores (as compared to classification success based on all 18 bodily reaction features). The results of a Multiple Discriminant Analysis (MDA) revealed three discriminant functions, explaining 73.1%, 20.7%, and 6.3% of the variance, respectively. Each of these functions showed correlations with more than one bodily reaction factor, making it difficult to label them unequivocally. The classification accuracy is shown in Table 9.3. Using the three factor scores as independent variables, 45.1% of cross-validated grouped cases can be correctly classified, a result that is far above chance level (1/24, or 4.2%). The results for the MDA classification that uses all 18 component features as independent variables achieved correct classification of 62.4% of cross-validated grouped cases. This represents a clear improvement (an increase of 17.9%) in

Table 9.3 Classification accuracy (in percent) for the 24 emotion words in discriminant analyses based on the bodily reaction factors and the bodily reaction features

Emotion words	Classification based on *factors*	Classification based on *features*	
	Accuracy	Accuracy	Confusion > 15% with
being hurt	17.6	38.2	disappointment
sadness	61.8	76.5	
shame	44.1	91.2	
guilt	67.6	73.5	
compassion	58.8	76.5	
disappointment	52.9	61.8	
love	70.6	73.5	
contentment	61.8	55.9	
happiness	11.8	35.3	joy
pride	38.2	73.5	
pleasure	52.9	64.7	joy
joy	47.1	26.5	happiness, pleasure
interest	52.9	79.4	
surprise	11.8	82.4	
despair	38.2	58.8	disappointment
stress	55.9	73.5	anxiety
anxiety	41.2	50.0	stress, fear
fear	79.4	82.4	anxiety
jealousy	17.6	44.1	hate
hate	20.6	47.1	irritation
irritation	20.6	47.1	hate, anger
anger	58.8	47.1	irritation
disgust	50.0	79.4	
contempt	50.0	58.8	
Total	45.1	62.4	

classification accuracy. The last column of Table 9.3 allows the inspection of the patterns of the most frequent errors in the classification based on all features. There are particularly frequent confusions between happiness and joy, and pleasure and joy for the positive emotional reactions. For the negative emotional reactions there are frequent confusions between a) stress and anxiety, and fear and anxiety, b) jealousy and hate, and hate, anger, and irritation. Being hurt and despair are frequently confused with disappointment. Thus, all major confusions in the MDA classification occurred between emotional reactions that share at least some emotion family resemblance. However, not all emotion family members are mutually confused, but generally only a specific subgroup of emotional reactions.

9.2 **Discussion and conclusions**

We conclude that the data for the Bodily reaction component confirm earlier assumptions about the internal structure of this component. The three predicted factors could be almost perfectly identified across the four language groups.

When looking at the relationships between the bodily reaction factors and the overall factors (from which the bodily reaction features have been removed), it is striking that all four overall factors are related to bodily reactions (although NOVELTY only to a limited extent). The fact that the overall AROUSAL factor is best predicted by the AUTONOMIC AROUSAL factor was to be expected. The features that define AUTONOMIC AROUSAL, also defined the AROUSAL factor in the overall structure. Even when the bodily reaction features are removed from the overall structure (see also Chapter 7), the third factor still refers to emotional reactions that imply a strong bodily activation or deactivation. It was surprising, however, that overall POWER and overall VALENCE would be related as much or even more strongly to bodily reactions, respectively. The substantial relationship of DISTRESS SYMPTOMS with the overall POWER factor (in which the bodily reaction features have been removed) throws a new and important light on the interpretation of the overall POWER factor. The POWER dimension has been interpreted, by many emotion researchers, as a social psychological submissiveness–dominance dimension (e.g., Russell & Mehrabian, 1977) or as an interpersonal engagement–disengagement dimension (e.g., Kitayama, Markus, & Kurokawa, 2000). While we find clear evidence that interpersonal features (such as feeling submissive and feeling dominant) do define the overall POWER factor, this factor is clearly not restricted to interpersonal features, but is as well defined by pure bodily experiences. The fact that overall VALENCE is also strongly related to bodily reactions, throws an interesting light on the debate in psychology about the origins of VALENCE and AROUSAL. Some authors consider VALENCE to be mental and AROUSAL to be psychophysiological, while others hold that VALENCE and AROUSAL have both mental and psychophysiological origins (e.g., Russell, 2003). For the three major dimensions in the emotion domain, we find evidence for the latter perspective. VALENCE, POWER, and AROUSAL are all related to both mental and to psychophysiological features.

Overall, the 24 emotional reactions are well differentiated by individual bodily reaction features. Using the three component factors for classification causes a decrease of accuracy, but still allows for a relatively good differentiation. These results support the classic idea that there is some degree of emotion specific patterning of bodily reaction features, at least as far as shared semantic meaning of emotion words is concerned. So far, empirical research on psychophysiological variables of emotional reactions has failed to demonstrate emotion specific physiological response patterning, except for anger (Levenson, 2003; Stemmler, 2003). However, most of the psychophysiological experiments have been conducted in laboratory settings as they require psychophysiological measurement equipment and experimental control of unwanted factors. These requirements make it unlikely that the psychophysiological patterns of strong emotional reactions can be studied in a laboratory setting. In consequence, it remains an open research question to determine to what extent bodily reaction specificity is a stereotype represented by semantic meaning structure, or whether semantic meaning represents at least a part of the underlying mechanisms and response patterns of emotional reactions.

## Chapter 10

The "mirror of the soul": The Expression component

Klaus R. Scherer[1] and Johnny J. R. Fontaine

One finds abundant quotes in the literature that describe the bodily expression of emotion as the "mirror of" or "a window to" the heart or the soul, implying that they reveal the innermost feelings of a person to the public at large. In the affective sciences, the Expression component of emotion has always been considered part and parcel of the emotion episode package, probably largely due to the (sometimes) dramatic nature of the display, the ease of observation, and finally the important value as a social signal of reaction and action intention. Historically, expression, starting with Darwin's (1872) pioneering volume "The expression of the emotions in man and animals," has been the origin of a revival of the interest in the behavioral analysis of the emotions and has greatly influenced the work of discrete emotion psychologists (Tomkins, 1962; Ekman, 1972, 1992; Izard, 1971, 1994) who have been instrumental in establishing the "basic emotions" tradition, which is largely based on the assumption that a small number of fundamental, evolutionary old emotions have unique prototypical facial expressions.

In consequence, there now exists a huge amount of literature on facial expression. Much of it is concerned with the recognition of posed expressions for basic emotions, which is not a very good test of the unique prototype hypothesis, as recognition can be achieved on the basis of only a partial aspect of a configuration (*pars pro toto*-principle). So far, one finds only very few studies in which the *production* of facial expressions in emotion episodes is systematically studied (see Scherer, Clark-Polner, & Mortillaro, 2011, for a comprehensive review). In consequence, while the assumption of marked differences in facial expression patterns for different emotions is highly plausible, strong empirical evidence remains to be established. The same is true for vocal expressions, which have been studied much more rarely.

If different emotions were indeed to have unique expression signatures, the internal representation of these features are likely to form a part of the semantic meaning of emotion words. To investigate this possibility it is important, in the context of the GRID study, to examine the extent to which expression features in different modalities, especially the face and the voice, differentiate emotion terms.

Facial expression. The problem we faced in constructing the facial expression component part of the instrument is that there is no established vocabulary for emotion specific facial expressions other than "to make an angry, sad, happy, etc. face" which is not very useful for our purposes. There is a widely accepted scientific classification of expressive facial movements, the Facial Action Coding System (FACS, Ekman & Friesen, 1978) which proposes more than 40 so called *action*

---

[1] Corresponding author: Klaus R. Scherer. Swiss Center for Affective Sciences—University of Geneva. 7, Rue des Battoirs, CH-1205 Geneva, Switzerland. Klaus.Scherer@unige.ch

units which consist of groups of muscle contractions. This complex system requires expert training and is clearly not appropriate for our purpose. We thus had to resort to identifying the most frequently used descriptions of facial movement in everyday language that are relevant to emotional expressions (many of which have also been used by Ekman and his collaborators to refer to the action units designated by numbers or anatomic muscle descriptions; see Ekman & Friesen, 1978). Below is the list of features we chose to cover the facial part of the Expression component (with brief illustrations of the major muscles involved in the movements referred to by the popular description):

- smiled (m. zygomaticus)
- felt his/her jaw drop (m. masseter)
- pressed his/her lips together (m. orbicularis oris)
- felt his/her eyebrows go up (m. frontalis)
- frowned (m. corrugator)
- closed his/her eyes (m. orbicularis oculi)
- opened his/her eyes widely (m. levator palpebrae superioris)
- had tears in his/her eyes
- did not show any changes in his/her facial expression

We chose those movements that were frequently shown by actors enacting different emotions in expression portrayals (Scherer & Ellgring, 2007a) and the verbal descriptions of which are frequently used in everyday contexts. We consider these partial movements of the face as building blocks, which may not be unique for certain emotions, but can occur as building blocks in different configurations for different emotions.

Vocal expression. Even though Darwin (1872) also mentioned the great importance of the vocal expression of emotion, often highlighted in classic treatises of rhetorics, there is—compared to facial expression—a dearth of empirical study (see Scherer et al., 2011, for a detailed review). Here the situation for the choice of verbally descriptive features is even more complicated, as vocalizing and speaking are continuous phenomena, which, contrary to a facial expression, cannot be identified as a static configuration (and shown in a photo). Furthermore, the scientific description of the emotional modulations of the voice have mostly used acoustic variables such as fundamental frequency, harmonics, formants, and energy distribution in the spectrum (see Juslin & Scherer, 2005) that are not accessible to lay raters. However, there have been some efforts to develop rating systems for voice quality and vocal expression using verbal descriptions from natural languages such as high-pitched, rough, or breathy (see Gobl & Chasaide, 2003; Laver, 1980). While many of these voice descriptors are also quite technical and require training, there are some that seem, more or less, in popular use and thus ideally suited for our purposes. We chose the following set of features that comes closest to the acoustic variations generally found for vocal emotion expressions (Scherer, Johnstone, & Klasmeyer, 2003), indicating the major acoustic-phonetic dimension involved.

Intensity/energy:
- spoke louder
- spoke softer.

Phonation regularity:
- had a trembling voice
- had an assertive voice.

Vocalization length:

- fell silent
- produced a short utterance
- produced a long utterance.

Intonation:

- changed the melody of his/her speech.

Motor disturbance:

- had speech disturbances.

Tempo/speech rate:

- spoke faster
- spoke slower.

None:

- did not show any changes in his/her vocal expression.

Gesture, posture, and body movement. Gestural expression of emotion, also a favorite topic of ancient treatises on rhetoric, has been studied even less frequently. In particular, attempts to create descriptive coding systems have not yet converged on an easily applicable set of descriptive categories (but see Dael, Mortillaro, & Scherer, 2012; Wallbott, 1998). We have therefore refrained from attempting to propose features for hand and arm gestures but have included a number of features that are frequently referred to in connection to emotional expressions in posture or body *movements*. These were not meant to describe actual purposeful behavior, such as aggression, but rather reflecting action tendencies as expressed in posture or body movements such as leaning forward or backward (all implying a strong motivational component). In addition, we included one item on the quality of movement—abruptness. The chosen features are:

- moved toward people or things
- withdrew from people or things
- moved against people or things
- made abrupt body movements
- did not show any changes in gesture or movements

Emotion regulation. In addition to asking about the nature of the expressive behaviors that are considered to be characteristic for the emotional states designated by the 24 words studied here, we also included four features to cover typical patterns of emotion regulation, especially expression regulation, for the different emotions. The following items were used to assess these features:
How likely is it that the person

- tried to control the intensity of the emotional feeling
- showed a stronger degree of emotion than he/she actually felt
- showed a weaker degree of emotion than he/she actually felt
- hid the emotion from others by smiling

We decided to analyse facial, vocal, and body movement expression ratings separately and to then compare their respective contribution to emotion term differentiation. Below we first examine the internal factorial structure of these three feature domains and their mapping into the overall structure. We will then compare the relative contribution of these factor sets on the discrimination of the 24 emotion words, followed by a brief discussion of the role of emotion regulation.

10.1 **Results and discussion**

The internal structure of the Expression component

Facial expression. The scree plot (see Figure SM 1)[2] resulting from the factor analysis of the facial expression features across all emotion words and all samples pointed to two or three main factors. As the investigation of stability of the factor structure across four language groups confirmed the presence of three stable factors (see Table SM 1), we chose this solution. The three factors account for 74.6% of the overall variance. The VARIMAX rotated three-factorial solution is shown in Table 10.1.

Factor 1 is constituted by items generally representative of a positive (smiling; signaling agreement or social approach tendency) vs negative (frown, indicating incomprehension and disagreement, or lip pressing, showing aggression tendencies) facial reaction syndrome. Factor 2 is made up by items related to unexpected stimulation (jaw drop) often followed by information search (opening eyes widely and eyebrow rise), as suggested by Darwin (1872). Factor 3 clearly reflects withdrawal into oneself (closing eyes) and weeping (tears). We will refer to these three factors as FROWN VS SMILE, JAW DROP/EYEBROWS UP, and EYES CLOSED/TEARS; high values indicate a higher proportion of the respective expression. It should be noted that there are fairly high negative cross-loadings on the third factor for "eyes wide" and particularly "eyebrows up" which is due to the fact that these facial actions are not compatible with "closing eyes."

The mean facial expression factor scores for the 24 emotion terms (listed in Table SM 3) are plotted in Figure 10.1 and Figure 10.2. These graphs allow examining the relative position of the 24 emotions in the three-dimensional space formed by the facial expression factors. As one would expect, Figure 10.1 shows a clear separation between positive emotion terms characterized by smiling, and negative emotion terms characterized by the absence of smiles and a tendency toward frowning. Within each of these valenced clusters there is a spread on JAW DROP/EYEBROWS UP dimension with respect to the likelihood that the respective emotion has been elicited by new and possibly unexpected events. Thus, the terms joy and happiness seem to be used more frequently in the case of somewhat unexpected good news, whereas contentment is a reaction to an expected or

Table 10.1 Loadings of the facial expression features in a three-factorial VARIMAX rotated structure

Facial expression features	FROWN VS SMILE	JAW DROP/EYEBROWS UP	EYES CLOSED/TEARS
frowned	0.93	−0.07	−0.13
pressed lips together	0.92	−0.16	0.03
smiled	−0.93	0.08	−0.21
had the jaw drop	−0.14	0.76	−0.09
opened her or his eyes widely	−0.27	0.74	−0.41
had eyebrows go up	−0.17	0.64	−0.58
did not show any changes in face	−0.12	−0.63	−0.42
closed her or his eyes	−0.02	−0.18	0.76
showed tears	0.02	0.02	0.82

[2] All supplementary materials (SM) are available at the GRID website: http://www.affective-sciences. org/GRID. See Appendix 1 ("Availability") for further details.

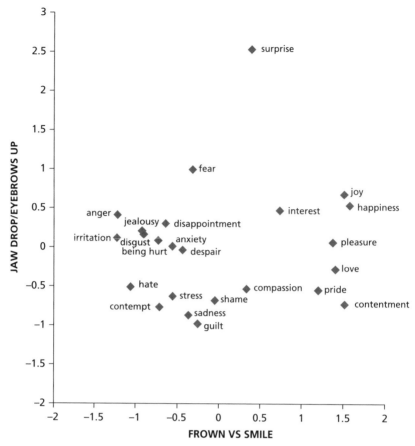

Figure 10.1 Plot of the average factor scores for the 24 emotion words on FROWN VS SMILE and JAW DROP/EYEBROWS UP.

enduring state of affairs. A similar distinction can be made on the negative side, with fear, anger, disappointment and jealousy being elicited generally by new and possibly unexpected events whereas sadness, guilt, shame, and contempt seem to consist of enduring reactions to events that have happened some time ago or were at least, in part, predictable. As expected, surprise (which has a neutral position on the VALENCE dimension) occupies an extreme position on the dimension related to new information to be processed. Figure 10.2 again shows the clear separation of positive and negative emotion terms with the large spread of the negative emotions on the EYES CLOSED/TEARS dimension being attributable to a control factor—more withdrawal and tears in the case of events that are difficult to control, particularly in the case of sadness, despair, fear, and being hurt, as compared to contempt, hate, anger, and irritation where an individual usually feels at least some POWER over the source of the negative event.

Vocal expression. We now turn to the factorial structure of the vocal expression. The scree plot (see Figure SM 2) pointed to two main factors and the investigation of stability of the factor structure across four language groups also showed two stable factors (see Table SM 2). The rotated factor structure for this solution is shown in Table 10.2. The two factors account for 65.4% of the total variance. Factor 1 contrasts a comparatively loud voice (spoke louder) and fast speech

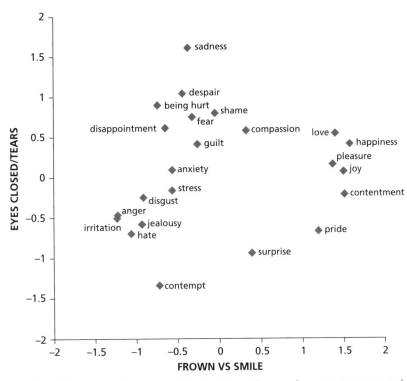

Figure 10.2 Plot of the average factor scores for the 24 emotion words on FROWN VS SMILE and EYES CLOSED/TEARS.

Table 10.2 Loadings of the vocal expression features in a two-factorial VARIMAX rotated structure

Vocal expression features	VOCAL ENERGY	FIRM VS PERTURBED SPEECH
spoke faster	0.89	−0.17
increased the volume of voice	0.86	−0.29
changed the melody of her or his speech	0.46	0.01
fell silent	−0.74	0.52
decreased the volume of voice	−0.85	0.20
spoke slower	−0.87	0.06
produced speech disturbances	−0.06	0.88
had a trembling voice	0.18	0.86
produced a short utterance	0.26	0.35
did not show any changes in vocal expression	0.50	−0.65
produced a long utterance	−0.42	−0.65
had an assertive voice	−0.43	−0.69

(spoke faster) with soft voice (spoke more softly) and slow speech (spoke slower), as well as "fell silent." This factor is best characterized by an underlying factor of energy or dynamism in voice and speech, varying between low (soft and slow speech) and high (loud and fast speech). Factor 2 is mostly determined by "trembling voice" and "speech disturbances," indicating a high degree of phonation and articulation irregularity. The item "had an assertive voice" loads in the opposite direction on this factor, suggesting an underlying quality of regularity of phonation, which gives the impression of a firm, smooth voice as compared to trembling or stuttering voice and speech. In consequence, we will refer to these two factors as VOCAL ENERGY and FIRM VS PERTURBED SPEECH.

The mean vocal expression factor scores for the 24 emotion terms (listed in Table SM 4) are plotted in Figure 10.3. The figure shows the positive emotions in a cluster that is characterized by a firm voice and medium vocal energy. The negative emotions, clustered together in the upper half of the graph (marked by a tendency toward more speech perturbation), are horizontally aligned on the VOCAL ENERGY dimension in the sense of more or less control and POWER, being characterized by higher or lower vocal energy, respectively. Presumably, fear has higher vocal energy than sadness because while POWER is low, there is some control (e.g., the possibility to flee). In contrast, in sadness there is little control or POWER.

Body movement. As we could not find commonly understood gesture descriptors likely to be applicable to the emotion concepts studied here and as bodily movement is represented by only four items, the analysis of the internal structure for the domain is of more limited interest in this case

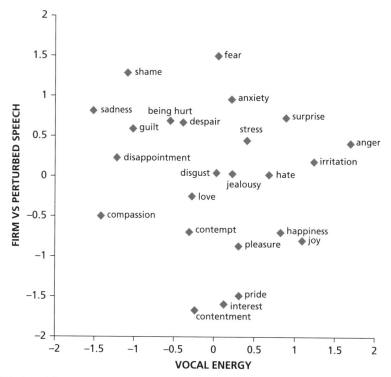

Figure 10.3 Plot of the average factor scores for the 24 emotion words on VOCAL ENERGY and FIRM VS PERTURBED SPEECH.

(with respect to variable reduction) than in the case of vocal and facial expression. A PCA points to two factors accounting for 72.5% of the variance (see Table SM 5). The first factor reflects the classic approach vs avoidance dimension and is labeled MOVING TOWARD VS WITHDRAWING. The second factor consists of a juxtaposition of no movement vs abrupt movement and is labeled NO VS ABRUPT MOVEMENT. The item "antagonistic movement against people or things" has cross-loadings on both factors. Moving toward is characteristic for compassion and all positive emotions (except pride), whereas withdrawing is particularly pronounced for sadness, shame, guilt, disappointment, and being hurt. While the low AROUSAL emotions like compassion or sadness imply very little movement, abrupt movement is frequent for anger, irritation, hate, contempt, and jealousy. As the body movement category is only sparsely represented, and as the features included are rather similar to some of the features for the Action tendency component, we decided to use only the facial and vocal features of the Expression component in further analyses reported in the present and future chapters.

Mapping the Expression component factors onto the overall structure

To further explore the relationships between the overall factorial structure and the internal structure of the facial and vocal expression domains, we have regressed the respective factors on the four overall factors (after omitting all expression features).

Facial expression. Table 10.3 shows the standardized regression weights and R^2 of the facial expression factors regressed on the four overall factors. The values for R^2 show that VALENCE is exclusively predicted—as suggested by Figure 10.1 above—by the FROWN VS SMILE distinction. The R^2 of 0.95 for this prediction is extremely high, suggesting that observing frowning vs smiling faces is in itself sufficient to estimate the degree of VALENCE of an emotion. In the commentary on Figure 10.2, it was suggested that the EYES CLOSED/TEARS dimension is strongly linked to low POWER. This suggestion is supported by the fairly good prediction of the overall POWER factor by this facial expression dimension. Finally, the overall NOVELTY dimension is predicted by high JAW DROP/EYEBROWS UP values. The R^2 for this dimension is relatively low, probably because we have only one emotion word, surprise that carries much of the effect. The AROUSAL dimension is not predicted by facial expression factors.

Vocal expression. The equivalent predictions for vocal expression are shown in Table 10.4. The strongest R^2 is found for the prediction of the overall POWER factor by a high degree of VOCAL ENERGY and absence of PERTURBED SPEECH (see comments on Figure 10.3). The overall AROUSAL factor is also well predicted, although with a somewhat lower R^2, mostly due to high VOCAL ENERGY and strongly PERTURBED SPEECH. Finally, there is a somewhat weaker link between FIRM VS PERTURBED SPEECH and the overall VALENCE factor, with firm voice being characteristic of positive emotions (see comments on Figure 10.3). NOVELTY is not related to the vocal expression factors.

Table 10.3 Standardized regression weights and R^2 of the facial expression factors regressed on the four overall factors

Overall factors	$\beta_{\text{FROWN VS SMILE}}$	$\beta_{\text{JAW DROP/EYEBROWS UP}}$	$\beta_{\text{EYES CLOSED/TEARS}}$	R^2
VALENCE	0.95***	0.07***	−0.05***	0.90
POWER	−0.06*	0.13***	−0.64***	0.44
AROUSAL	−0.08*	0.38***	−0.02	0.15
NOVELTY	0.06	0.55***	0.02	0.31

Note: * p <0.05. ** p <0.01. *** p <0.001. The expression features were removed from the four overall factors.

Table 10.4 Standardized regression weights and R^2 of the vocal expression factors regressed on the four overall factors

Overall factors	$\beta_{\text{VOCAL ENERGY}}$	$\beta_{\text{FIRM VS PERTURBED SPEECH}}$	R^2
VALENCE	0.07*	−0.59***	0.35
POWER	0.65***	−0.47***	0.64
AROUSAL	0.52***	0.41***	0.44
NOVELTY	0.23***	0.19***	0.09

Note: * p <0.05, ** p <0.01, *** p <0.001. The expression features were removed from the four overall factors.

These results confirm the conclusion reached by researchers in the area of facial and vocal expression analysis, based on the findings in recognition studies, that facial expression is best suited for communicating emotional VALENCE (for which there does not seem to be many valid cues in vocal expression). Conversely, vocal expression is much better able to convey the affective dimensions of AROUSAL and of POWER (which are less well signaled by the face; see Bänziger, Grandjean, & Scherer, 2009; Scherer et al., 2011).

Emotion category differentiation based on the Expression component

We now examine, separately for facial and vocal expression, to what extent the respective internal factors allow the discrimination of the 24 emotions, that is, classify them correctly on the basis of the factor scores, in comparison to classification success based on the features for the respective expression modality.

Facial expression. In the case of facial expression (see Table 10.5), the results of the MDA based on factor scores shows that 44.5% of cross-validated grouped cases were correctly classified. In contrast, for the MDA, based on all nine facial features, 62.7% of cross-validated grouped cases were correctly classified. Classification success clearly exceeds chance level (1/24; 4.2%) and although accuracy is rather higher for the complete facial feature set, the three internal factors do reasonably well. Table 10.5 also shows the most frequent confusions in the feature-based classification. Except for one case, all confusions occur within emotion families.

Vocal expression. Table 10.6 reports the MDA data for vocal expression. Results show that for the MDA based on factor scores, 33.1% of cross-validated grouped cases were correctly classified. For the analysis based on the 12 vocal features 53.2% of cross-validated grouped cases were correctly classified. Again, classification success is better than chance although accuracy is somewhat lower than for facial expression. The last column in Table 10.6 also shows the major confusions, most of which again occur within emotion families.

Integration of facial and vocal expression. Having discussed the discrimination and automatic classification of the 24 emotions via MDA separately for facial and vocal expression, we now turn to an integrative assessment of the Expression component. The results of an MDA for the total of five expression factors (facial plus vocal) reveals that the five discriminant functions, explaining 60.3, 22.2, 10.3, 5.3, and 2.0% of the variance, respectively, show correlations with more than one expression factor, making it difficult to label these functions. The only exception is the first discrimination function, which exclusively reflects the facial FROWN VS SMILE factor, which is entered first into the equation and explains most of the variance (60.3%). The classification accuracy for the MDA based on the five factor scores is shown in column 1 of Table 10.7—57.0% of cross-validated

Table 10.5 Classification accuracy (in percent) for the 24 emotion words in discriminant analyses based on the facial expression factors and the facial expression features

Emotion words	Classification based on facial expression *factors*	Classification based on facial expression *features*	
	Accuracy	Accuracy	Confusion > 15% with
being hurt	50.0	47.1	despair
sadness	79.4	82.4	
shame	20.6	67.6	
guilt	52.9	76.5	
compassion	35.3	47.1	pride
disappointment	35.3	70.6	
love	58.8	73.5	
contentment	41.2	47.1	pleasure
happiness	35.3	41.2	joy
pride	55.9	73.5	
pleasure	20.6	58.8	
joy	52.9	50.0	happiness
interest	88.2	91.2	
surprise	97.1	94.1	
despair	17.6	35.3	disappointment, being hurt
stress	32.4	50.0	
anxiety	17.6	35.3	
fear	76.5	94.1	
jealousy	23.5	55.9	
hate	44.1	55.9	irritation
irritation	20.6	50.0	anger
anger	44.1	61.8	
disgust	17.6	85.3	
contempt	50.0	61.8	
Total	44.5	62.7	

grouped cases were correctly classified. Column 2 of Table 10.7 shows the results of the MDA based on all individual expression features (excluding body movement) and the confusions of which there are only very few in this case (occurring only with very close emotion family members). Here, 73.0% of cross-validated grouped cases were correctly classified. This constitutes a rather impressive hit rate for a single emotion component (expression).

Overall, our results show that facial expression features seem to carry somewhat more discriminative cues (yielding 62.7% accuracy) than vocal features (53.2%). When all expression features from all modalities are used in the MDA, a very respectable rate of 73% accuracy is reached. While the classification based on all expression features reaches the highest accuracy rate, as is to

Table 10.6 Classification accuracy (in percent) for the 24 emotion words in discriminant analyses based on the vocal expression factors and the vocal expression features

Emotion words	Classification based on vocal expression *factors*	Classification based on vocal expression *features*	
	Accuracy	Accuracy	Confusion > 15% with
being hurt	14.7	47.1	despair
sadness	41.2	70.6	
shame	52.9	82.4	
guilt	29.4	70.6	
compassion	52.9	76.5	
disappointment	47.1	64.7	being hurt
love	20.6	82.4	
contentment	47.1	44.1	
happiness	14.7	32.4	joy
pride	41.2	64.7	
pleasure	23.5	35.3	happiness
joy	44.1	32.4	happiness, interest
interest	26.5	47.1	contentment
surprise	55.9	67.6	
despair	5.9	29.4	being hurt, disappointment
stress	14.7	55.9	
anxiety	20.6	50.0	stress
fear	70.6	52.9	anxiety
jealousy	23.5	38.2	
hate	32.4	50.0	anger
irritation	17.6	23.5	anger
anger	61.8	64.7	irritation
disgust	5.9	50.0	
contempt	29.4	44.1	
Total	33.1	53.2	

be expected, the combination of the three facial and two vocal factors is doing comparatively very well with 57% accuracy. We started this chapter by highlighting the emphasis placed on emotional expression as a faithful mirror of internal feelings. The current data confirm the important role that is generally assigned to the Expression component with respect to differentiating emotional states.

The regulation of emotional expression

In constructing the feature profile for the GRID study, we had decided to include a number of items related to the regulation of emotion and in particular the strategic control of expression. Given the

Table 10.7 Classification accuracy (in percent) for the 24 emotion words in discriminant analyses based on both facial and vocal expression factors and both facial and vocal expression features

Emotion words	Classification based on facial and vocal expression *factors*	Classification based on facial and vocal expression *features*	
	Accuracy	Accuracy	Confusion > 15% with
being hurt	55.9	64.7	despair
sadness	82.4	79.4	
shame	61.8	82.4	
guilt	67.6	85.3	
compassion	55.9	76.5	
disappointment	70.6	82.4	
love	85.3	91.2	
contentment	52.9	61.8	
happiness	38.2	41.2	joy
pride	58.8	88.2	
pleasure	29.4	67.6	
joy	58.8	50.0	happiness
interest	88.2	91.2	
surprise	100	100	
despair	26.5	41.2	disappointment
stress	64.7	73.5	anxiety
anxiety	47.1	58.8	stress
fear	79.4	88.2	
jealousy	29.4	79.4	
hate	50.0	64.7	
irritation	17.6	47.1	anger
anger	55.9	52.9	irritation
disgust	32.4	82.4	
contempt	58.8	67.6	
Total	57.0	71.6	

importance of emotion regulation, particularly with respect to its function in interpersonal interaction, there has been a tendency in the literature to consider regulation as an emotion component in its own right. However, if the emotion episode is considered as a dynamic unfolding of changes in different organismic systems driven by appraisal (as in the CPM model described in Chapter 1), regulatory processes, from homeostatic and unconscious to strategic or intentional, are ubiquitous and become part and parcel of the complex recursive processes that constitute the emotion. As much of regulation concerns its manifestation in observable expression, we discuss the data pertaining to the four regulation items listed at the beginning of the chapter as part of the Expression component. A factor analysis of the regulation items across all emotion words and all samples,

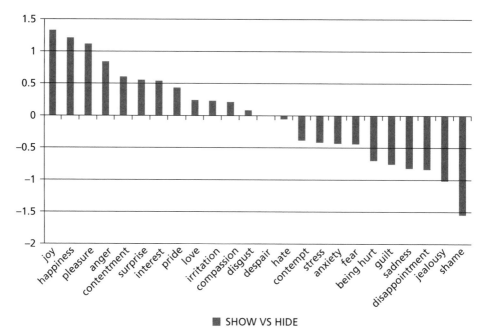

SHOW VS HIDE

Figure 10.4 Plot of the average factor scores for the 24 emotion words on SHOW VS HIDE.

yields a single factor accounting for 53.6% of the overall variance. The factor loadings, shown in Table SM 7, can be easily interpreted in the sense of a continuum from up-regulation, in the sense of showing more expression than warranted by the feeling, to down-regulation in the sense of hiding the expression (e.g., using a poker face), masking an incipient expression by a smile, or even down-regulating the felt emotion altogether to avoid or decrease expression tendencies. This factor will be referred to as SHOW VS HIDE. Figure 10.4 shows the sorted estimated marginal means for the emotions (listed in Table SM 8). While joy, happiness, pleasure, and also anger are rarely masked (and there may be even a tendency to express these emotions more strongly than they are felt), being hurt, guilt, sadness, disappointment, jealousy, and particularly shame are strongly censored and often hidden or masked.

It should be noted that the ratings of the type and degree of up- or down-regulation of different emotions by the participants in this study, have to be taken as estimates of modal tendencies to regulate certain emotions. Given the sensitivity of regulation to situational factors that may impose display rules for certain emotions or strategic concerns of individuals in particular interaction situations, there is likely to be an enormous amount of variance in the amount of regulation exercised in a particular emotion episode. Yet, the data reported here are highly consistent with other data sets in the literature in which differences in regulation attempts for different emotions have been reported (Matsumoto, 1990; Scherer & Wallbott, 1994). However, it is difficult to maintain that such differences in modal tendencies to regulate different emotions are actually part of the *constitutive* meaning of an emotion term. Rather, the ratings of our participants might reflect everyday knowledge about such modal tendencies and thus represent ecological correlations. Moreover, as the regulation tendency has only been operationalized by a few items, it was decided to not include the emotion regulation features and factor in further analyses in this book.

10.2 **Conclusions**

Overall, these results show that, as expected, the GRID paradigm is useful to extract the mental representation people have about emotional expression, representations that form the basis of emotional communication. Given the difficulty of specifying facial and vocal expressions with words alone, the results for the Expression component are rather remarkable. The factorial structure extracted from the data is very clear and appropriate, and, together with the regressions on the overall factors, confirms the differential capacities of the two modalities suggested in the literature—facial expression being better suited to differentiate emotions on the VALENCE and NOVELTY dimensions and voice being more discriminative on the POWER and AROUSAL dimensions. Given these complementary capacities, it is not surprising that emotional expressions can be best recognized in multimodal presentation (Bänziger et al., 2009). What is more surprising is how clearly this important specialization is reflected in the semantics of the emotion words via their position in four-dimensional space. We have also been surprised by the remarkable POWER of the combined set of facial and vocal expression features to successfully discriminate the set of 24 emotion categories, even at the level of the factor scores.

Chapter 11

Emotion is for doing: The Action tendency component

Johnny J. R. Fontaine[1] and Klaus R. Scherer

The function of emotions is to prepare the organism for adaptive behavior in specific situations. Emotions are thus for doing. The functional approach to emotions has been especially elaborated in evolutionary perspectives on emotions (e.g., Plutchik, 2003). Evolutionarily, the preparation of behavioral reactions, in situations that are regularly experienced by the organism, increases its survival chances. The behavioral preparation system has been shaped gradually to be responsive to a more diverse set of situations that have survival value (e.g., Nesse, 2004). Across living organisms, the preparation of either appetitive (approach) or defensive (withdrawal) reactions can be observed (Frijda, 2010; Maxwell & Davidson, 2007; Schneirla, 1959). At a very rudimentary level, this is already present in single cell organisms that move toward or move away from an object depending on the situation. It is hypothesized that in higher organisms, this very rudimentary behavioral preparation has been gradually differentiated into more specific and complex behavioral preparation patterns, such as aggression, fleeing, apathy, or reparative behavior. Moreover, to increase its adaptiveness an increasing flexibility has been brought into the system. An evolution is observed from a fixed behavioral reaction to a fixed stimulus constellation in reflexes to very variable behavioral reactions based on an ongoing evaluation of the situation in the emotion process – not only in terms of what is directly observed, but also in terms of what the situation entails for the needs, goals, and values of the person.

In all three major theoretical approaches to human emotions in psychology, namely in the dimensional, the basic, and the componential emotion tradition, it is assumed that the preparation of behavior can form a part of the emotion process. These approaches differ, however, in the role they ascribe to behavioral preparation in the emotion process, as well as in the differentiation between action tendencies they propose.

The role of action tendencies is the least elaborated in the dimensional tradition (e.g., Russell, 2003). Action preparation is seen as just one of the possible consequences of changes in core affect and these changes have been conceptualized in broad behavioral tendencies. Given the central role of the VALENCE dimension in this tradition, special emphasis has been placed on the basic differentiation between appetitive and defensive tendencies (e.g., Nesse, 2004).

In the basic emotion tradition, each basic emotion is characterized by the preparation of a specific behavioral pattern (e.g., Izard, 1977). For instance, the four basic emotions recognized by all basic emotion theories, namely joy, fear, anger, and sadness, are hypothesized to prepare approach

[1] Correspondence on this paper can be addressed to Johnny J. R. Fontaine. Department of Personnel, Work and Organisational Psychology. Faculty of Psychology and Educational Sciences. Ghent University. Henri-Dunantlaan 2, 9000 Gent, Belgium. Johnny.Fontaine@UGent.be

(moving toward), fleeing (moving away), aggression (moving against), and apathy (ceasing of behavioral tendencies), respectively.

The motivational aspect has received the most theoretical attention in componential emotion tradition, and more particularly in appraisal theories. The term "action tendencies" was coined by Magda Arnold (1960), who laid the foundations for the modern appraisal theories. In appraisal theories, an intimate relationship is postulated between the appraisal of the situation and the activation of action tendencies. It is assumed that a differentiated appraisal of the situation with respect to the needs, goals, and values of the individual is made in order to activate a differentiated adaptive response. Appraisal theorists differ with respect to their assumptions about the nature of the adaptive responses that are prepared. For instance, in 1987, Frijda proposed 18 modes of action readiness. Lazarus proposed specific action tendencies for 17 core relational themes (Lazarus, 1991a). A motivation to take revenge is, for instance, assumed in reaction to an appraisal of an offence against me or mine. Roseman (2001) proposed the elicitation of 17 emotional motivational goals (which he calls emotivational goals) such as "stop moving toward it" and "move toward other" in reaction to appraisals that can be represented on seven major appraisal dimensions. Scherer (2001, Chapter 1) proposed continuous effects of the unfolding appraisal process on the motivational component of emotion, assuming that the specific form and temporal unfolding of action tendencies depend on situational factors.

Despite the theoretical centrality of the Action tendency component in the emotion process, almost no empirical research has been done on this component from the vantage point of any of the three broad approaches to emotions. This probably has to be explained by the inherent difficulty of investigating action tendencies. Whether or not an action tendency is translated into observable behavior does not only depend on the preparation of that behavior, but also on the physical and cultural constraints of the situation as well as on the regulation mechanisms used by the person at a particular point in time. It is thus difficult to attribute observable behavior to an inner drive that is instigated by the emotion process. The behavior in question can also be accounted for by regulatory mechanisms or even general motivational processes (e.g., aggression does not necessarily point to the presence of anger, but can also be the result of an instrumental use to attain one's goals). It is thus very difficult to empirically disentangle emotional from non-emotional accounts of observed behavior.

An exception to the rule that the preparation of behavior has only received scant empirical attention is the work of Frijda and colleagues. Frijda put action tendencies, and more generally *action readiness*, at the heart of the emotion concept in his landmark book *The Emotions* in 1986. He defines action readiness as "readiness to engage in action for establishing, maintaining or breaking the relation with particular aspects of the environment ("action tendency"), or as readiness to engage in relational action generally ("activation mode")" (Frijda, 1987, pp. 132). In 1986, he proposed 17 different modes of action readiness. In his very latest theorizing, Frijda postulated the existence of 18 modes of action readiness considered as "Ur-emotions" that are the basic building blocks of our emotional processes (Frijda & Parrott, 2011).

As Frijda and colleagues were some of the few to systematically conduct empirical research on the motivational component of emotion, we took Frijda's approach as the basis for operationalizing the Action tendency component of the GRID instrument. Only the more narrowly defined action tendencies were used as a point of reference. Frijda's action readiness concept also refers to emotion expressions and, to some extent, to bodily reactions. Frijda and colleagues have, for instance, investigated how facial expression patterns can be interpreted as modes of action readiness (Frijda & Tcherkassof, 1997). The GRID instrument, on the contrary, is based on a clear conceptual differentiation between action tendencies, expressions, and bodily reactions. From a psycholinguistic perspective, the differentiation between expressions, bodily reactions, and action tendencies is supported by the fact that they refer to different semantic primes (Goddard, 2002b; Wierzbicka, 1996). The Expression component refers to the semantic primes of "to see" and "to hear," the Bodily reaction component refers to the semantic prime "to feel," while the Action tendency component refers to the semantic prime "to want." Thus, in language these three components seem to be universally encoded by different verbs.

Because of our narrower conceptualization of the Action tendency component, we based the operationalization of this component on the three empirical studies that had action tendencies as their main focus (Frijda, 1987; Frijda, Kuipers, & ter Schure, 1989; Frijda, Markam, Sato, & Wiers, 1995). In these studies, participants were asked to rate episodes from their own life in which they experienced a particular emotion on the presence of action tendencies or modes of action readiness. In a first study of Frijda in 1987, it was demonstrated that 57 different operationalizations of action readiness modes (of which most could be considered more narrowly as action tendencies) could both conceptually and empirically be well represented by 16 categories, namely approach, avoidance, being-with, attending, rejection, indifference, antagonism, interruption, dominance, submission, apathy, excitement, exuberance, passivity, inhibition, and helplessness. The two additional action readiness categories that were proposed, namely "blushing" and "rest," are not included in the current study as they have other emotion components as their focus according to the GRID framework. "Blushing" is taken into account in the Bodily reaction component. "Rest" refers mainly to rest and relaxation, which is taken into account in the Bodily reaction component. In the subsequent studies of Frijda and colleagues (Frijda, Kuipers, & ter Schure, 1989; Frijda, Markam, Sato, & Wiers, 1995) the list of action readiness items was further elaborated (with up to 36 action readiness items), the list of emotion terms was extended (up to 32 emotion words), and the research was applied in very different cultural groups, such as in Japan and in Indonesia. Factor analyses on the action readiness items across the studies and the culturally diverse samples revealed, three recurrent factors and up to seven additional factors that either differed between the studies or between the cultural groups. The recurrent factors represented tendencies to move toward, to move away, and to move against.

For the operationalization of the Action tendency component in the GRID instrument, the 16 categories proposed by Frijda in 1987 were taken as a point of reference. The action readiness items of the three studies (Frijda, 1987; Frijda, Kuipers, & ter Schure, 1989; Frijda, Markam, Sato, & Wiers, 1995) were used as a source of inspiration for the construction of the action tendency features in the GRID instrument. For each category, at least one feature was formulated in such a way that the feature referred as close as possible to an action tendency, and was not confounded with the other components (especially the Bodily reaction and the Expression component). Moreover, as the action tendencies to move toward, to move away, and to move against were systematically recovered across studies and cultural groups, these three tendencies were operationalized more extensively. Furthermore, as it has been theorized in cross-cultural research that interpersonal aspects of emotions are more salient in non-Western cultural groups (e.g., Markus and Kitayama, 1991) compared to Western cultural groups, explicitly interpersonal action tendencies were also well represented. The 16 action tendency categories were eventually operationalized by the following 40 action tendency features.

Approach:

- wanted to submit to the situation as it is
- wanted to get totally absorbed in the situation
- wanted the ongoing situation to last or be repeated
- wanted to go on with what he or she was doing.

Avoidance:
- wanted to flee
- wanted to run away in whatever direction
- wanted to disappear or hide from others
- wanted to withdraw into her/himself
- wanted to be hurt as little as possible.

Being-with:
- wanted to be near or close to people or things
- wanted to be tender, sweet, and kind
- wanted to take care of another person or cause.

Attending:
- felt an urge to be attentive to what is going on.

Rejection:
- wanted to keep or push things away
- wanted to prevent or stop sensory contact
- wanted to break contact with others.

Indifference:
- lacked the motivation to pay attention to what was going on.

Antagonism:
- wanted to do damage, hit, or say something that hurt
- wanted to oppose
- wanted to destroy whatever was close
- wanted to tackle the situation
- wanted to overcome an obstacle
- wanted to take initiative her/himself.

Interruption:
- felt the urge to stop what he or she was doing
- wanted to undo what was happening.

Dominance:
- wanted to show off
- wanted to be seen, to be in the center of attention
- wanted to be in command of others
- wanted to be in control of the situation.

Submission:
- wanted to comply with someone else's wishes
- wanted to hand over the initiative to someone else
- wanted to make up for what she or he had done.

Apathy:
- lacked the motivation to do anything.

Excitement:
- felt an urge to be active, to do something, anything
- wanted to move
- wanted to act, whatever action it might be.

Exuberance:
- wanted to sing and dance.

Passivity:
- wanted to do nothing.

Inhibition:
- felt inhibited or blocked.

Helplessness:
- wanted someone to be there to provide help or support.

11.1 **Results**

The internal structure of the Action tendency component

The scree plot in a factor analysis (Principal Component Analysis, see Chapter 5 for a more detailed explanation) on the action tendency features across all emotion words and all samples pointed to three factors (see Figure SM 1[2]). The three-factor solution, which was stable across the four language groups (see Table SM 1), accounted for 76.36% of the total variance. The stability analysis also showed the four-factorial solution to be stable across the four language groups. The fourth factor accounted for an additional 3.08% of the total variance. As the fourth factor could not be well interpreted, we decided to select the three-factor solution.

We first investigated the internal structure using VARIMAX rotation (see Table 11.1). On the first factor, aggression and opposition were contrasted with tendencies to be with and submit to others. We labeled this factor ATTACK VS AFFILIATION. The second factor was labeled WITHDRAW VS SHOW OFF as it opposed tendencies to flee, to withdraw, and to want help from others with tendencies to show off and be in the center of attention. The third factor contrasted tendencies to actively change the event with tendencies towards apathy and was therefore called APATHY VS ACTION. While the three-factorial VARIMAX rotated structure was well interpretable, the structure was not fully satisfactory. Most of the items that had a high loading on the first factor, had a substantial cross-loading on the second factor, and vice versa. Also, cross-loadings were observed with the third factor, although to a lesser extent. The three factors seem not to be well differentiated empirically.

We investigated the cause of this substantial overlap by inspecting the unrotated factor solution. The first unrotated factor revealed a strong contrast between appetitive and defensive action tendencies, with positive emotion terms being characterized by appetitive and negative emotion terms by defensive action tendencies. The first factor showed high loadings for rather diverse action tendencies. These shared either an appetitive (e.g., *wanting to show off* and *wanting to be tender, sweet, and kind*) or a defensive (e.g., *wanting*

---

[2] All supplementary materials (SM) are available at the GRID website: http://www.affective-sciences. org/GRID. See Appendix 1 ("Availability") for further details.

Table 11.1 Loadings of the action tendency features in a three-factorial VARIMAX rotated structure

Action tendency features	ATTACK VS AFFILIATE	WITHDRAW VS SHOW OFF	APATHY VS ACTION
wanted to do damage, hit, or say something that hurts	−0.94	−0.03	−0.01
wanted to destroy whatever was close	−0.91	−0.14	−0.09
wanted to oppose	−0.91	−0.15	0.08
wanted to break contact with others	−0.81	−0.40	−0.28
wanted to prevent or stop sensory contact	−0.73	−0.53	−0.31
felt the urge to stop what he or she was doing	−0.71	−0.58	−0.20
wanted to keep or push things away	−0.71	−0.48	−0.27
felt inhibited or blocked	−0.66	−0.61	−0.23
wanted to run away in whatever direction	−0.64	−0.58	−0.35
wanted to go on with what he or she was doing	0.68	0.58	0.22
wanted to get totally absorbed in the situation	0.71	0.54	0.15
wanted to sing and dance	0.76	0.59	0.10
wanted to submit to the situation as it is	0.76	0.29	−0.13
wanted the ongoing situation to last or be repeated	0.76	0.58	0.14
wanted to comply to someone else's wishes	0.83	−0.08	0.12
wanted to take care of another person or cause	0.83	0.06	0.32
wanted to be near or close to people or things	0.86	0.24	0.23
wanted to be tender, sweet, and kind	0.93	0.22	0.13
wanted someone to be there to provide help or support	−0.14	−0.84	−0.11
wanted to make up for what she or he had done	0.06	−0.80	−0.15
wanted to undo what was happening	−0.61	−0.68	−0.10
wanted to withdraw into her/himself	−0.52	−0.67	−0.42
wanted to be hurt as little as possible	−0.42	−0.67	−0.18
wanted to disappear or hide from others	−0.57	−0.67	−0.40
wanted to hand over the initiative to someone else	0.16	−0.66	−0.32
wanted to flee	−0.63	−0.64	−0.33
wanted to show off	0.44	0.70	0.30
wanted to be seen, to be the center of attention	0.49	0.72	0.34
wanted to do nothing	−0.36	−0.39	−0.69
lacked the motivation to pay attention to what was going on	−0.43	−0.30	−0.62
lacked the motivation to do anything	−0.44	−0.49	−0.59
wanted to be in command of others	−0.42	0.32	0.48
felt an urge to be attentive to what was going on	0.51	0.21	0.55
wanted to move	0.20	0.38	0.56
wanted to take initiative her/himself	0.30	0.47	0.63

Table 11.1 (continued) Loadings of the action tendency features in a three-factorial VARIMAX rotated structure

Action tendency features	ATTACK VS AFFILIATE	WITHDRAW VS SHOW OFF	APATHY VS ACTION
wanted to be in control of the situation	−0.29	0.12	0.65
felt an urge to be active, to do something, anything	0.40	0.31	0.69
wanted to act, whatever action it might be	−0.08	0.21	0.70
wanted to overcome an obstacle	0.10	−0.18	0.72
wanted to tackle the situation	0.15	0.14	0.72

to flee and *wanting to oppose*) nature, respectively. This first factor accounted on its own for 57.78% of the total variance, which is three-quarters of the 76.36% of variance accounted for by the full three-factorial solution.

As the first factor was very salient and theoretically well interpretable, we further explored the residual internal structure after controlling for the overall appetitive versus defensive action tendencies in three steps. In a first step, we identified those features that most generally captured the appetitive versus defensive tendencies. These were *wanted to go on with what he or she was doing, wanted the ongoing situation to last or be repeated, felt an urge to stop what he or she was doing,* and *wanted to undo what was happening.* These four features were mutually highly correlated. In a factor analysis a single factor accounted on its own for 91.56% of the total variance in these four features. In a second step, we controlled for this appetitive vs defensive action tendency factor and computed residual feature scores for the remaining 36 action tendency features. A new factor analysis was then executed on these 36 residual feature scores. The scree plot pointed to a two-factor solution that accounted for 45.23% of the total residual variance (see Figure SM 2). A VARIMAX rotation of these two residual factors revealed two well interpretable factors (see Table SM 2). On the first residual factor, apathy, withdrawal, and fleeing tendencies were opposed to features that implied taking initiative to change the situation. We labeled this factor DISENGAGEMENT VS INTERVENTION. On the second residual factor aggressive and opposition tendencies were contrasted with tendencies to be with others and submit oneself to others. This factor is labeled SUBMIT VS ATTACK. In the third step, the original three-factor solution was orthogonally Procrustes rotated toward a structure with a DEFENSIVE VS APPETITIVE factor, a DISENGAGEMENT VS INTERVENTION factor, and a SUBMIT VS ATTACK factor. There was a very high convergence with the target solution (see Table 11.2). The congruence measures (Tucker's phi) were 0.99, 0.93, and 0.96 for the three factors, respectively. Thus, the Action tendency component could also be represented by a general action tendency factor on which almost all action tendencies had a substantial loading and two subsidiary action tendency factors. Because the general action tendency factor corresponded to the evolutionarily basic appetitive versus defensive action tendencies, and because there were very few cross-loadings between the two subsidiary factors, this Procrustes rotation was finally selected to represent the factorial structure of the Action tendency component.

A plot of the 24 emotion terms shows that negatively valenced emotion terms are opposed to positively valenced terms on the first factor (see Figure 11.1). On the second factor, sadness emotion terms are opposed to anger and fear terms for the negatively valenced emotion terms (see Figure 11.1). For the positively valenced terms, it is especially *interest* that scores high on this factor. The third factor opposes anger terms to *guilt* and *shame* in particular (with fear and sadness

Table 11.2 Loadings of the action tendency features in a three-factorial Procrustes rotated structure

Action tendency features	DEFENSIVE VS APPETITIVE	DISENGAGEMENT VS INTERVENTION	SUBMIT VS ATTACK
wanted to undo what was happening	−0.92	−0.08	0.01
felt the urge to stop what he or she was doing	−0.91	−0.19	0.15
wanted to flee	−0.90	−0.31	0.05
felt inhibited or blocked	−0.90	−0.21	0.09
wanted to prevent or stop sensory contact	−0.88	−0.29	0.20
wanted to disappear or hide from others	−0.88	−0.39	−0.01
wanted to run away in whatever direction	−0.86	−0.33	0.10
wanted to withdraw into her/himself	−0.85	−0.41	−0.05
wanted to break contact with others	−0.85	−0.26	0.35
wanted to keep or push things away	−0.83	−0.26	0.22
wanted to be hurt as little as possible	−0.78	−0.17	−0.13
wanted someone to be there to provide help or support	−0.72	−0.11	−0.45
wanted to submit to the situation as it is	0.72	−0.15	−0.37
wanted to be near or close to people or things	0.75	0.21	−0.49
wanted to show off	0.82	0.29	0.13
wanted to be seen, to be the center of attention	0.87	0.33	0.11
wanted to get totally absorbed in the situation	0.87	0.14	−0.17
wanted to go on with what he or she was doing	0.89	0.20	−0.12
wanted to sing and dance	0.94	0.09	−0.18
wanted the ongoing situation to last or be repeated	0.94	0.13	−0.19
wanted to do nothing	−0.54	−0.69	0.02
lacked the motivation to pay attention to what was going on	−0.52	−0.61	0.13
lacked the motivation to do anything	−0.67	−0.58	0.01
felt an urge to be attentive to what was going on	0.50	0.54	−0.26
wanted to move	0.42	0.56	0.09
wanted to take initiative her/himself	0.56	0.63	0.08
wanted to be in control of the situation	−0.09	0.66	0.29
felt an urge to be active, to do something, anything	0.50	0.68	−0.11
wanted to act, whatever action it might be	0.11	0.71	0.19
wanted to overcome an obstacle	−0.06	0.72	−0.21
wanted to tackle the situation	0.22	0.72	−0.03
wanted to comply to someone else's wishes	0.49	0.10	−0.67
wanted to take care of another person or cause	0.60	0.31	−0.59
wanted to make up for what she or he had done	−0.56	−0.15	−0.57
wanted to hand over the initiative to someone else	−0.40	−0.32	−0.55

Table 11.2 (continued) Loadings of the action tendency features in a three-factorial Procrustes rotated structure

Action tendency features	DEFENSIVE VS APPETITIVE	DISENGAGEMENT VS INTERVENTION	SUBMIT VS ATTACK
wanted to be tender, sweet, and kind	0.78	0.11	−0.55
wanted to be in command of others	−0.04	0.49	0.52
wanted to oppose	−0.71	0.10	0.58
wanted to destroy whatever was close	−0.71	−0.07	0.59
wanted to do damage, hit, or say something that hurts	−0.65	0.01	0.68

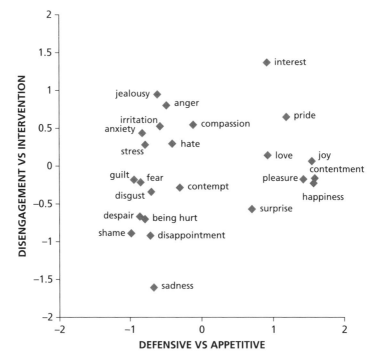

Figure 11.1 Plot of the average factor scores for the 24 emotion words on DEFENSIVE VS APPETITIVE and DISENGAGEMENT VS INTERVENTION.

terms in-between) for the negatively valenced terms, and opposes *pride* to *love* for the positively valenced terms (see Figure 11.2).

Mapping the action tendency structure onto the overall structure

To further explore the relationships between the overall factorial structure and the internal structure of the Action tendency component, we regressed the three action tendency factors on the four overall factors (after omitting all action tendency features). Table 11.3 shows the standardized regression weights and R^2 of the action tendency factors regressed on the four overall factors. The R^2

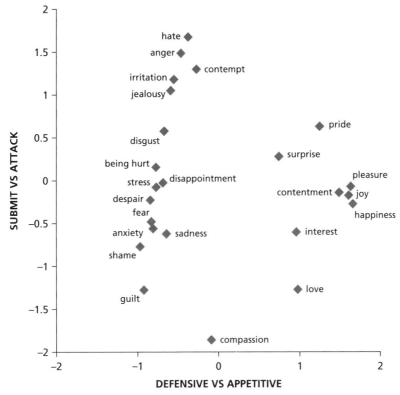

Figure 11.2 Plot of the average factor scores for the 24 emotion words on DEFENSIVE VS APPETITIVE and SUBMIT VS ATTACK.

values show that VALENCE and POWER are very well predicted, while AROUSAL and NOVELTY factors are not at all well predicted by the action tendency factors. The most important predictor of VALENCE is the DEFENSIVE VS APPETITIVE factor, but also the SUBMIT VS ATTACK factor predicted VALENCE. The more submissive action tendencies related to a higher VALENCE. POWER was best predicted by the two subsidiary factors, but also the first DEFENSIVE VS APPETITIVE factor contributed to the prediction of POWER: more attacking action tendencies, more intervention action tendencies, and more appetitive action tendencies related to a higher score on POWER.

Table 11.3 Standardized regression weights and R² of the action tendency factors regressed on the four overall factors

Overall factors	$\beta_{\text{DEFENSIVE VS APPETITIVE}}$	$\beta_{\text{DISENGAGEMENT VS INTERVENTION}}$	$\beta_{\text{SUBMIT VS ATTACK}}$	R^2
VALENCE	0.89***	0.07***	−0.35***	0.91
POWER	0.32***	0.51***	0.61***	0.73
AROUSAL	−0.09**	0.24***	0.09**	0.07
NOVELTY	0.13***	−0.11**	0.01	0.03

Note: * p <0.05. ** p <0.01. *** p <0.001. The action tendency features were removed from the four overall factors.

Differentiating the 24 emotion terms on the basis of the Action tendency component

The action tendencies allow for a greater than chance classification of the emotion words into one of the a priori defined 24 emotion categories (at random, a correct classification of 4.2% can be expected) (see Table 11.4). On the basis of the factor scores on the three action tendency factors, 46.1% of the cross-validated terms could be correctly classified in one of the 24 categories. This percentage rose to 67.6% when the classification was executed on the basis of the 40 action

Table 11.4 Classification accuracy (in percent) for the 24 emotion words in discriminant analyses based on the action tendency factors and the action tendency features

Emotion words	Classification based on action tendency factors	Classification based on action tendency features	
	Accuracy	Accuracy	Confusion > 15% with
being hurt	35.3	67.6	
sadness	52.9	70.6	
shame	47.1	85.3	
guilt	76.5	91.2	
compassion	85.3	91.2	
disappointment	29.4	52.9	being hurt
love	76.5	85.3	
contentment	17.7	50.0	pleasure
happiness	35.3	26.5	pleasure, joy
pride	70.9	91.2	
pleasure	14.7	47.1	contentment
joy	20.6	29.4	happiness, pleasure
interest	85.3	91.2	
surprise	94.1	94.1	
despair	17.7	58.8	disappointment
stress	41.2	70.6	
anxiety	44.1	41.2	stress
fear	29.4	85.3	
jealousy	35.3	76.5	
hate	38.2	61.8	anger
irritation	11.8	44.1	anger
anger	41.2	52.9	hate, irritation
disgust	67.7	82.4	
contempt	38.2	76.5	
Total	46.1	67.6	

tendency features. In the latter case, confusions occurred between (1) *disappointment, despair*, and *being hurt*; (2) *pleasure, joy, happiness*, and *contentment*, (3) *stress* and *anxiety*, and (4) *anger, hate*, and *irritation*.

11.2 Discussion

The internal structure of the action tendency domain

The internal structure analysis revealed a first general factor on which most action tendency features loaded substantially, either in a positive or a negative direction. The opposition between negatively and positively loading action tendencies could be interpreted in terms of the evolutionarily basic distinction between appetitive and defensive action tendencies (e.g., Frijda & Parrott, 2011; Nesse, 2004). The appetitive action tendencies imply that one wants to be in the ongoing event and wants it to continue. The defensive action tendencies imply an urge to stop what is happening and a tendency to withdraw or, to whatever extent possible, change the ongoing event. These two clusters of action tendencies are the motivational consequence to the evaluation of whether the event is intrinsically pleasant and/or goal-conducive or intrinsically unpleasant and/or goal-obstructive.

While the distinction between appetitive and defensive action tendencies is conceptually straightforward, the concrete action tendencies that either have positive or negative loadings on the first dimension lead to incompatible behavior. For instance, *showing off* and *complying with somebody else's wishes* both imply that one wants the event to continue, but it is difficult to do both at the same time. This is even clearer for the defensive action tendencies. For instance, *running away in whatever direction* or *hitting and saying something that hurts* both imply a motivation to change the ongoing situation, but one cannot run away and attack at the same time. The fact that very different action tendencies that imply very diverse and ultimately incompatible behaviors emerge at the same pole of a single factor calls for an explanation. The question is whether this observation only applies to meaning of emotion words, or reveals something about the actual functioning of the motivational component during an emotion process (e.g., the presence of decision conflict).

A first alternative is a pure linguistic explanation. It could be that emotional information in language is systematically organized in terms of the VALENCE it entails, rather than in terms of its actual occurrence in specific emotion processes. Running away and aggressive action tendencies would then share the same highly negative loading on the first dimension because they both refer to a negatively valenced emotional process, and not because they actually co-occur during actual emotion processes. Although this linguistic explanation cannot be ruled out on the basis of mere linguistic data, the fact that such a dominant general factor is not observed for the Bodily reaction and the Expression components renders this account less plausible (see Chapters 9 and 10, respectively).

The second alternative is based on the lexical sedimentation hypothesis. The overall action tendency factor is thought to reveal a genuine property of the emotion processes, namely that action tendencies that imply incompatible behavior (such as fleeing or attacking) are activated jointly when they share either an appetitive or a defensive motivation. This account would make sense from an evolutionary perspective, and fits the conflicting freeze-flight-fight reactions in prey. While freezing, fleeing, and fighting are incompatible behaviors that lead to a very different relationship between prey and predator, they are all activated in a situation where the prey perceives the predator as a threat to its physical integrity (even though they cannot be carried out simultaneously). The prey will show one of these different reactions depending on the distance to the predator (e.g., Blanchard, Blanchard, & Takahashi, 1977). It would thus be evolutionary adaptive that freezing, fleeing, and fighting action programs are prepared jointly in a threat situation so that depending on one additional specific appraisal, namely the distance to the predator, the prey can switch quickly from one action program to the other.

While the general action tendency factor is robust, a least two additional factors can be identified that do indicate further differentiations over and above an appetitive or defensive orientation. A clear interpersonal factor is identified which differentiates tendencies to aggress and dominate others from tendencies to submit oneself to others and to serve others. These action tendencies play a role in affirming or enforcing one's hierarchical position in the group and in maintaining affiliative relationships (e.g., Blanchard & Blanchard, 2005). The strong interpersonal nature of this dimension is confirmed by the emotion terms that are differentiated on it, namely anger terms are differentiated from *guilt* and *shame*, and *pride* is differentiated from *love*.

The third factor is a more intrapersonal motivational factor that opposes tendencies to actively deal with the situation to tendencies that leave the situation unaffected. This factor not only opposes sadness terms to anger and fear terms, but also differentiates within the anger and fear clusters. *Anger* and *jealousy* score much higher on this dimension than *contempt*. In *contempt* little can be done to change the source of contempt, while in *anger* and *jealousy* the person is motivated to take action. A comparable distinction is observed within the fear cluster: in *stress* and *anxiety* the person is instigated to undertake an action to do something about the situation that causes these emotions; however, in *fear* the person is just driven to flee the danger.

The relationships with the overall four-factorial structure

The strong prediction of the overall VALENCE factor by the DEFENSIVE VS APPETITIVE action tendency factor further fits the evolutionary view of action tendencies (e.g., Frijda & Parrott, 2011; Nesse, 2004). A basic issue for a living organism is whether the situation matches its needs and goals or whether there is a mismatch between both. When there is a match, appetitive and approach behavior is adaptive. When there is a mismatch, defensive and withdrawal behavior is adaptive. Thus, the VALENCE dimension is as much about doing as it is about feeling and appraising.

The most remarkable finding, however, is that the two subsidiary action tendency factors both independently predict the overall POWER factor. The action tendencies thus reveal two independent pathways to achieve POWER, namely either by actively working toward a goal or by aggressing people that infringe on one's position and goals. Vice versa, there are also two ways to be weak and submissive: either by not doing anything or by actively putting oneself at the service of others.

In the chapter with the overall analysis of the emotion structure (see Chapter 7), a positive correlation between the VALENCE and the POWER factor was observed with an oblique rotation, indicating that more powerful emotions are perceived as more positive and vice versa. The relationships between the three action tendency factors and the overall VALENCE and POWER factors provide a more complex picture. Appetitive action tendencies contribute positively to POWER. The reverse, however, is not necessarily true. Action tendencies that imply POWER relate in very different ways to the VALENCE factor. DISENGAGEMENT VS INTERVENTION is slightly positively related to VALENCE. The SUBMIT VS ATTACK factor, however, is negatively related to VALENCE. A possible explanation is that these two POWER-related action tendency factors relate differentially to basic human needs. In the self-determination theory proposed by Deci and Ryan (2002), three basic human needs are distinguished: need for competence, for autonomy, and for relatedness. It can be hypothesized that an intervention orientation meets the needs for competence and autonomy, while disengagement is conflicting with it. The action tendency items that define an intervention orientation imply that the person actively takes the initiative to change the situation. To the extent that the (future) change is perceived as feasible, these action tendencies are thus compatible with the basic need for competence and autonomy. By contrast, doing nothing and possibly fleeing the situation imply a lack of competence and autonomy. On the other hand, it can be hypothesized that attacking has a conflicting relationship with the basic need for relatedness. Aggressive behavior might guarantee one's dominant position, but it hurts social bonds. Actively submitting to others has the opposite effect: it contributes to the development and, when needed, restoration of interpersonal relationships. Although the submissive action tendencies can be triggered by negatively valenced situations, they also can contribute to basic need satisfaction.

Virtually no relationships were observed between the action tendency factors and the overall AROUSAL factor. It could be that we insufficiently operationalized those aspects of the Action tendency component that relate to AROUSAL, for instance by not operationalizing Frijda's action readiness factor of rest. Still, the 40 features used here represent the action tendency domain reasonably well. Furthermore, the operationalization of some action tendency features to imply a clear differentiation in terms of AROUSAL. For instance *wanted to destroy whatever was close* and *wanted to run away in whatever direction* imply a high level of AROUSAL, while *lacked the motivation to do anything* and *wanted to withdraw into her/himself* are typically associated with a low level AROUSAL. A possible post-hoc explanation is that the action tendency factors represent general motivational orientations, rather than the preparation of specific behaviors. The general motivational orientation can then be implemented by very different behaviors that can vary substantially in terms of AROUSAL. For instance, taking the initiative can lead to command others about what to do (requiring little AROUSAL) as well as to frantic activity to get control over the situation (requiring a high level of AROUSAL). Also, submission could just imply accepting the POWER of someone who is in a hierarchically higher position (requiring little AROUSAL), as well as the preparation of concrete behavior to support the other (implying higher levels of AROUSAL).

The very limited relationships between the action tendency factor and the NOVELTY factor can be accounted for by the nature of the NOVELTY factor. A situation that is novel, is a situation whose meaning is not clear. The organism does not know yet whether the situation is goal-conducive or not. Only when the meaning of the situation becomes clear, it can be decided whether and which appetitive or defensive action tendencies must be prepared. Thus, the only action tendency is the interruption of ongoing behavior in order to focus one's attention on what is happening.

The results reported in this chapter show clearly that the action tendency structure does not just mimic the overall structure of VALENCE, POWER, AROUSAL, and NOVELTY. Three different action tendency factors underlie the overall VALENCE and the POWER factors, and show very limited relationships with AROUSAL and NOVELTY.

Discrimination of terms

The very substantial discriminability of the 24 emotion terms on the basis of their action tendency profiles counterbalances the observation that the first general DEFENSIVE VS APPETITIVE factor accounts on its own for more than half of the variance. On the one hand, we observe that very different appetitive and very different defensive action tendencies are all related to positive and negative emotion terms, respectively. On the other hand, being able to correctly classify almost half of the terms on the basis of the three action tendency factors and about two-thirds of the terms with the 40 action tendency features implies that specific emotion terms can be differentiated on the basis of their profile of action tendencies.

The breadth of the Action tendency component

The operationalization of the Action tendency component in the GRID instrument was strongly embedded in the theoretical and empirical work of Frijda (1986, 1987). However, there is an important difference between his approach and the operationalization in the GRID instrument. In the GRID, action tendencies were defined more restrictively as tendencies to execute or not execute action. Bodily reactions (e.g., relaxation) and expressions (e.g., crying) that belong to the action readiness concept proposed by Frijda were clearly differentiated in the GRID instrument. The empirical results of the GRID study show that action tendencies, expressions, and bodily reactions are structured in very different ways (see also Chapters 9 and 10). While action tendencies were characterized by a general DEFENSIVE VS APPETITIVE factor and two subsidiary factors, there was no such dominant factor in the Expression or the Bodily reaction components. Moreover, the component specific structures related very differently to the four overall factors. The expression factors related to all four overall factors (see Chapter 10), the bodily reaction factors predominantly related to the first three overall factors (VALENCE, POWER, and AROUSAL) (see Chapter 9), while the action tendency factors related predominantly to the first two overall factors (VALENCE, and POWER). The differences in structure for the three emotion components support a more restrictive approach to the Action tendency component taken in the development of the GRID instrument.

At the same time, a further elaboration of the level of abstraction at which the action tendency factor is organized is called for. In the emotion literature, the action tendency factor has been conceptualized at various levels of abstraction, going from very concrete behavior being prepared up to a change in the general motivational orientation of the person (such as in the concept of emotivations of Roseman, 2001). In the GRID, the operationalization of the action tendency features only ranged from the very concrete behavioral level (e.g., wanting to sing and dance) up to an intermediate level of abstraction (e.g., wanting to make up for what he or she had done). The observation that very different action tendencies had high loadings on the first factor and that the three action tendency factors showed almost no relationships with the AROUSAL dimension seem to indicate that the Action tendency component is encoded in language at the higher motivational level. The structure is compatible with the induction of general motivational changes that can be implemented by very different concrete behaviors depending on the concrete situation. We will use the freeze, flight, fight reaction pattern of prey to illustrate this possibility. The fact that it is adaptive to be able to quickly switch between these concrete action programs depending on the distance between prey and predator does not mean that underlying motivational orientation switches accordingly. The motivation to keep the predator away drives the three very different reactions. They just allow achieving the general goal in the light of the precise characteristics of the situation. Similarly, it does not mean that because a predator withdraws from the prey (e.g., because the prey reacted aggressively), the predator loses the overall motivational orientation to catch the prey. Thus, the same behavior can be driven by opposite motivational orientations (e.g., attacking can be observed in an attempt to keep the predator away or in an attempt to catch the prey) and very different behaviors can be driven by the same motivational orientation (as is demonstrated by the freeze, flight, fight reactions). It would be interesting for future research to jointly investigate the concrete behavioral preparations and the more general motivational orientations that are triggered in an emotion process.

If it is correct that emotion processes not only prepare specific behavior, but have also an impact on broad motivational orientations, then straightforward relationships can be expected between the action tendency dimensions and the dimensions that represent the general motivational orientations people have in life. Conceptual correspondences can indeed be identified between the three action tendency factors and broad motivational dimensions that have been proposed in the personality and social psychological literature. The DEFENSIVE VS APPETITIVE dimension at the emotion level shows correspondences with the interindividual differences in approach-avoidance orientation (e.g., Higgins, 1997). Some people are motivationally more geared toward realizing wanted outcomes, which relates to positive affect. Others are more motivated to avoid negative outcomes.

This latter tendency is positively related with negative affect. The other two action tendency factors can be linked to the value dimensions of the Schwartz's value model, which has received substantial support across cultural groups (e.g., Fontaine, Poortinga, Delbeke, & Schwartz, 2008; Schwartz, 1992). He distinguished in his model two value dimensions, namely self-enhancement versus self-transcendence and openness to change versus conservation. The first dimension opposes values that are self-focused and imply a striving for a high hierarchical position to values that focus on the well-being of others. This dimension shows clear overlap with the SUBMIT VS ATTACK action tendency dimension, where action tendencies to take care of others are opposed to action tendencies to dominate others. The second value dimension opposes values of following one's own plans to values that imply an acceptance of the social structure. This value dimension shows conceptual correspondences with the DISENGAGEMENT VS INTERVENTION action tendency factor. In intervention one actively pursues one's own goals, in disengagement one accepts the situation as it is. Whether the overlap between the three action tendency dimensions and these broad motivational dimensions are more than coincidental will have to be empirically investigated.

11.3 **Conclusions**

The present chapter demonstrates for the first time a stable three-factorial action tendency structure across four very different language groups. At least in the semantics of emotion words, a general defensive versus appetitive action tendency factor emerges, as well as two subsidiary factors. One of these is more intrapersonally focused, namely preparation for disengagement versus preparation for intervention. The other is clearly interpersonally focused and opposes a tendency to submit to a tendency to attack. Emotion is indeed for doing (or, more precisely, for preparing the doing).

## Chapter 12

Driving the emotion process: The Appraisal component

Klaus R. Scherer[1] and Johnny J. R. Fontaine

Having reported the data analyses concerning the Feeling, Bodily reaction, Expression, and Action tendency components of emotion, we now address the component that has been considered the central defining element of emotion by philosophers across the centuries and that is increasingly seen as the key to understanding emotion by most theorists in this domain—the Appraisal component. A detailed description of this cognitive emotion component, responsible for the evaluation of events that trigger emotion, and in particular of the nature of the major appraisal checks and their function in the emotion process, has been provided in Chapter 1. In consequence, here we focus on the selection of the items to represent this component in the GRID instrument and on the presentation and interpretation of the results.

12.1 Operationalization of the Appraisal component

As for the other components, we first describe how the Appraisal component has been operationalized in the GRID instrument, more precisely, how the features have been chosen and how the concrete items were formulated. An effort was made to represent the major streams in the literature.

Component Process Model. As explained in Chapter 1, Scherer's Component Process Model (CPM; 1984b, 2001, 2009c) was chosen as the theoretical framework for the selection of the features representing the different appraisal checks in the GRID instrument and the formulation of the specific items. These features represent the suggestions of the major appraisal theorists concerning the central criteria or dimensions that determine the elicitation and differentiation of emotion episodes. Despite minor differences in terminology, there is a large degree of convergence among appraisal theorists and thus the choice of appraisal features can be considered as representative for a core group of appraisal theories (see Ellsworth & Scherer, 2003; Scherer, 1999a).

Based on the CPM, we selected 13 appraisal features, organized in four superordinate classes of appraisal criteria: relevance, implications, coping potential, and normative significance of the situation for the person (see Chapter 1 for a detailed discussion; also Scherer, 2001, pp. 94–99 and Table 5.4 in that chapter, reproduced in Table SM 1[2]). The CPM postulates that the appraisal system sequentially and recursively processes these appraisal checks in order to achieve a comprehensive account of the situational antecedents and the potential consequences for the person, which drives

---

[1] Corresponding author: Klaus R. Scherer. Swiss Center for Affective Sciences—University of Geneva. 7, Rue des Battoirs, CH-1205 Geneva, Switzerland. Klaus.Scherer@unige.ch

[2] All supplementary materials (SM) are available at the GRID website: http://www.affective-sciences.org/GRID. See Appendix 1 ("Availability") for further details.

the changes in the other emotion components. In other words, the dynamically evolving profile of appraisal results is expected to determine, in a sequential-cumulative fashion, the nature and quality of the emergent emotion episode. If this assumption is correct, we expect that the appraisal results will determine, to a large part, directly or mediated by the corresponding response patterns, the label an individual will chose to describe the nature of the emotional experience. In consequence, appraisal features should be a central constituent of the differentiated semantic profiles of emotion words.

The formulation of the appraisal items in the GRID instrument was largely informed by the questions in a computer-based expert system predicting emotion labels on the basis of user input of appraisal profiles (Scherer, 1993; Scherer & Meuleman, 2013) and the Geneva Appraisal Questionnaire (GAQ, http://www.affective-sciences.org/system/files/page/2636/GAQ_English.PDF; see also the preliminary formulation of the pertinent items in Table 3 of Scherer, 2005a). Table 12.1 shows the final formulation of the appraisal features in relation to the individual appraisal criteria or stimulus evaluation checks postulated by the CPM (indicated by an X in the respective column). In general, only a single item was chosen to represent a specific appraisal check, given the need to constrain the total number of features in the instrument. However, in a few cases (NOVELTY, intrinsic un/pleasantness, causal attribution, and goal conduciveness/obstructiveness), we formulated several items to represent different aspects or outcomes of the same check.

In addition to the features covering the 13 standard appraisal criteria, we added some features to acknowledge specific elements of appraisal highlighted in alternative theoretical approaches to emotion. These items are identified in the last two columns of Table 12.1.

Social appraisal. One set of additional items concerns the social aspects of appraisal. While the CPM focuses on the consequences of an event for the *self*, cross-cultural psychologists and anthropologists have emphasized that cultures differ in the relative focus on the individual or on the group

Table 12.1 List of appraisal features organized by class of appraisal criteria

Appraisal features	Relevance detection	NOVELTY	Intrinsic pleasantness	Goal relevance	Implication assessment	Causal attribution	Outcome probability check	Discrepancy from expectation	Goal/need conduciveness	Urgency	Coping potential determination	Control	POWER	Adjustment	Normative significance evaluation	Internal standards	External standards	Other traditions	Social appraisal	Core relational themes
suddenly		X																		
familiar		X																		
unpredictable		X																		
confirmed expectations								X												
inconsistent with expectations								X												
in itself pleasant for the person			X																	
in itself pleasant for somebody else																			X	

Table 12.1 (continued) List of appraisal features organized by class of appraisal criteria

Appraisal features	Relevance detection	NOVELTY	Intrinsic pleasantness	Goal relevance	Implication assessment	Causal attribution	Outcome probability check	Discrepancy from expectation	Goal/need conduciveness	Urgency	Coping potential determination	Control	POWER	Adjustment	Normative significance evaluation	Internal standards	External standards	Other traditions	Social appraisal	Core relational themes
in itself unpleasant for the person			X																	
in itself unpleasant for somebody else																			X	
important and relevant for person's goals				X																
important and relevant for goals of somebody else																			X	
caused by chance						X														
caused by the person's own behavior						X														
caused by somebody else's behavior						X														
caused by a supernatural POWER																			X	
caused intentionally						X														
consequences predictable							X													
consequences positive for person									X											
consequences positive for somebody else																			X	
consequences negative for person									X											
consequences negative for somebody else																			X	
required an immediate response										X										
consequences avoidable or modifiable												X								
enough resources to avoid or modify consequences												X								
consequences able to live with														X						
incongruent with own standards and ideals																X				
violated laws or socially accepted norms																	X			
center of attention																			X	
treated unjustly																			X	
in danger																				X
irrevocable loss																				X

(e.g., Markus & Kitayama, 1991). In order to take into account this major dimension of cross-cultural variability, for two of the VALENCE features—pleasantness and goal conduciveness, we added two items capturing the VALENCE of an event for *another person* (referring to both a person's own goals and appraisal items that referred to the goals of other persons). In addition, the items "center of attention" and "treated unjustly" were included to represent two different aspects of social appraisal. We felt that these additional features might facilitate the use of the GRID instrument in cross-cultural research by providing a more comprehensive coverage of the relevant appraisal criteria.

Core relational themes. Furthermore, two additional items were added to represent Lazarus' appraisal theory postulating that appraisals establish an integrative meaning of the eliciting situation defined as *core relational themes* (Lazarus, 1991a; Smith & Lazarus, 1993). To evaluate the role of such integrated meanings, the core relational themes of two major negative emotions of fear (danger theme), and sadness (loss theme) were added to the list of appraisal features. A total of 31 features were finally chosen to represent the Appraisal component (see Table 12.1).

12.2 **Theoretical expectations**

Predictions about internal structure. Most of the appraisal features are represented by a single item (or by qualitatively different alternative results of a check). Therefore we do not attempt to examine the overlap or redundancy of items to identify, in a psychometric fashion, sets of items that measure the same underlying dimension or factor (as in scale construction). Rather, each appraisal item is expected to represent an independent feature that, in specific configurations with other features, characterizes a specific emotion (see Chapter 1). As for the other components, we used factor analysis to identify potential superordinate structures. As shown in the introduction to this volume (specifically in Chapter 1), there is reason to assume that each appraisal check is valenced, representing different *types of VALENCE*, such as VALENCE as predictability, as pleasure, as satisfaction, as POWER/dominance, as self-worthiness, or as moral worthiness (see Chapter 1, Table 1.1). Given the pervasiveness of VALENCE in appraisal, one would expect the emergence of a general factor, broad factor, or superfactor of VALENCE (similar to "g" in intelligence, Sternberg & Grigorenko, 2002; or extraversion and neuroticism in personality, Strelau & Zawadzki, 1997).

Predictions about relationships with the four overall factors. Based on the appraisal literature (Ellsworth & Scherer, 2003; Scherer, 2001; see Chapter 1), we developed a number of hypotheses concerning which Appraisal component factors should correlate with each of the four overall factors. Specifically, as mentioned above, we expected a VALENCE superfactor that should correlate highly with the overall VALENCE factor. We also expected a strong correlation between the NOVELTY appraisal checks with the overall NOVELTY factor, given their strong impact on the emergence of NOVELTY in the overall structure (see Fontaine et al., 2007). The items expected to measure coping potential, presumably loading on an Appraisal component coping factor, were expected to correlate to some extent with the overall POWER factor, even though the broad coping potential concept also includes other facets, not related to POWER, such as the ability to adjust to or live with a changed situation. No detailed predictions were made for the AROUSAL factor, as we expected this dimension to primarily qualify responses in the sense of greater intensity or activation, rather that differentiate categories of emotion. However, judging from past work on two-dimensional mapping of emotion words (see the literature reviewed in Chapter 2), it is likely that some emotion words imply a higher degree of intensity or activation within one emotion family. The choice of these words may well be determined by certain configurations of appraisal results (e.g., goals being seriously threatened, having little POWER, or urgent need for action might all require a high degree of AROUSAL).

Predictions about discrimination. Given the fundamental claim of most appraisal theories, and particularly the CPM, that appraisal causes emotional responses and drives the changes in the other emotion components, we hypothesize that individual appraisal features and Appraisal component factors will permit highly accurate classification of the 24 terms in multiple discriminant analyses (MDA). However, as appraisal theorists expect the results for different appraisal criteria to interact, in the case of the CPM even in a cumulative sequential fashion, configurational and nonlinear effects can be expected (Scherer, 2000b, 2009a). It should be noted that such effects cannot be easily identified with standard linear statistical methods (e.g., MDA) and thus only a few illustrations for the existence of such effects will be provided below.

12.3 **Results**

The analyses on the Appraisal component have been executed on data from 34 samples representing 30 countries and 25 languages (see Chapter 6, for a detailed account of the samples). For a description of the design, the instrument, and the data-analytic methods, the reader is referred to Chapter 5. Moreover, the same steps are taken as with the analyses of the overall structure (see Chapter 7). We first report on the factor structure of the Appraisal component. We then present the relationships between the appraisal factors and the overall factors that have been identified across the remaining emotion components. We end by investigating how well the Appraisal component allows the differentiation of the 24 emotion terms from one another across languages, countries, and samples.

The internal structure of the Appraisal component

Standard internal structure analysis. The scree plot (see Figure SM 1) pointed to two to four factors. The investigation of the stability of the factor structure across four language groups showed that only the first two factors are stable across groups (see Table SM 2). The two factors account for 60.7% of the overall variance.

The VARIMAX rotated factor structure for this solution is reproduced in Table 12.2. It shows that Factor 1 is constituted of many items that in one form or another represent a general VALENCE factor. We will refer to this factor as GENERAL VALENCE APPRAISAL below. Factor 2 shows high loadings for items related to the suddenness and unpredictability of events. This factor will be called NOVELTY APPRAISAL.

In order to visualize the position of the 24 emotion words in the two-dimensional space constituted of the GENERAL VALENCE APPRAISAL by NOVELTY APPRAISAL factors, we plotted the means of the appraisal factor scores for the 24 emotion words (listed in Table SM 3) in Figure 12.1. Visual inspection of the plot confirms that the emotions chosen for the GRID study, with the exception of surprise and compassion, are highly valenced, occupying rather opposite regions on the GENERAL VALENCE APPRAISAL dimension, suggesting a clear divide between the positive and negative emotions in our set of 24 emotion words. As to the exceptions, surprise is a very brief reaction in response to a suddenness/unpredictability appraisal of an event that can turn out to have either positive or negative consequences (determined by the ensuing relevance checks). As to compassion, one can empathize with either a positive or a negative emotion experienced by another person.

As far as the NOVELTY APPRAISAL dimension in the plot is concerned, it is dominated by surprise, which, as expected, clearly marks this dimension. However, the spread-out positions of the other emotion words demonstrate that there is also an important amount of variation on the NOVELTY APPRAISAL dimension, suggesting that this dimension contributes significantly to the overall differentiation between the emotion words.

Table 12.2 Loadings of the appraisal features in a two-factorial VARIMAX rotated structure

Appraisal features	GENERAL VALENCE APPRAISAL	NOVELTY APPRAISAL
consequences positive for person	0.97	0.04
in itself pleasant for the person	0.96	0.07
consequences positive for somebody else	0.93	0.07
important and relevant for person's goals	0.88	0.09
in itself pleasant for somebody else	0.88	0.11
important and relevant for goals of somebody else	0.84	0.07
confirmed expectations	0.81	−0.26
consequences able to live with	0.79	−0.11
center of attention	0.73	0.12
familiar	0.70	−0.28
consequences predictable	0.53	−0.48
caused by the person's own behavior	0.47	−0.36
inconsistent with expectations	−0.55	0.48
in itself unpleasant for somebody else	−0.72	−0.09
consequences negative for somebody else	−0.76	−0.12
in danger	−0.81	0.26
violated laws or socially accepted norms	−0.83	0.01
irrevocable loss	−0.86	0.05
incongruent with own standards and ideals	−0.91	0.02
treated unjustly	−0.92	0.05
in itself unpleasant for the person	−0.93	0.02
consequences negative for person	−0.94	0.01
unpredictable	−0.04	0.84
suddenly	0.15	0.76
caused by chance	0.42	0.64
required an immediate response	−0.07	0.56
caused by a supernatural POWER	0.44	0.49
caused by somebody else's behavior	−0.09	0.34
caused intentionally	0.19	−0.23
consequences avoidable or modifiable	−0.35	−0.37
enough resources to avoid or modify consequences	−0.03	−0.41

Overall, the GENERAL VALENCE APPRAISAL dimension, due to the convergence of different types of VALENCE, explains the bulk of the variance. This confirms the overwhelming importance of the generic VALENCE dimension in any kind of dimensional analysis of emotion words (i.e., in similarity research, see also Chapter 14, as well as the results shown in Chapter 7 reporting the overall analysis).

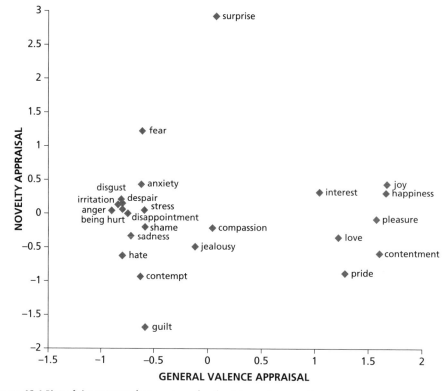

Figure 12.1 Plot of the average factor scores for the 24 emotion words on GENERAL VALENCE APPRAISAL and NOVELTY APPRAISAL.

As mentioned in the theoretical predictions above, it could be expected that specific appraisal factors might be facets of a general superfactor of VALENCE, similar to the superfactor "g" in intelligence research, a general factor underlying various types of competencies. Indeed, the central role of VALENCE in the current data, represented by the first factor on which most of the different appraisal features loaded, strongly suggests the presence of a superfactor "VALENCE." To further examine the structural information in the Appraisal component that is not accounted for by this VALENCE superfactor, we took recourse to alternative exploratory analytic strategies, namely a) separate factor analyses for positive and negative emotion terms, and b) factor analysis on appraisal features after partialling out intrinsic pleasantness and goal conduciveness.

Separate analysis of positive and negative emotion terms. The strong effect of VALENCE in our data set is largely due to the predominance of the clear division between words denoting positive and negative emotions in the set of 24 words studies, as only surprise and compassion can be considered as more neutral. If one looks at the mean ratings on the appraisal features separately for positive and negative emotions (see Table 12.3) it becomes apparent that there are very systematic differences between the two emotion sets with negative emotions having less predictable outcomes, lower coping potential, and lower moral and self-standard compatibility. Most of the differences shown in the table are all very highly significant in a multivariate ANOVA. This confirms the claim that most appraisal checks are valenced and suggests that, in general, the different types of valences tend to go into the same direction for positive and negative emotions. The

Table 12.3 Mean appraisal ratings of positive and negative emotion words

Appraisal features	Negative emotion words	Positive emotion words
suddenly	0.62	0.84
familiar	−0.44	1.21
unpredictable	0.57	0.50
confirmed expectations	−0.63	1.47
inconsistent with expectations	0.76	−0.24
in itself pleasant for the person	−2.61	2.76
in itself pleasant for somebody else	−1.30	1.42
in itself unpleasant for the person	1.57	−1.96
in itself unpleasant for somebody else	0.47	−1.11
important and relevant for person's goals	−0.89	2.27
important and relevant for goals of somebody else	−0.89	1.09
caused by chance	−0.12	0.83
caused by the person's own behavior	0.29	1.31
caused by somebody else's behavior	1.05	0.86
caused by a supernatural POWER	−1.15	0.15
caused intentionally	0.30	0.70
consequences predictable	−0.33	0.81
consequences positive for person	−2.56	2.82
consequences positive for somebody else	−1.55	1.48
consequences negative for person	1.62	−2.06
consequences negative for somebody else	0.45	−1.28
required an immediate response	0.25	0.14
consequences avoidable or modifiable	0.33	−0.32
enough resources to avoid or modify consequences	0.10	0.11
consequences able to live with	−0.83	1.09
incongruent with own standards and ideals	1.24	−1.61
violated laws or socially accepted norms	0.93	−1.57
center of attention	−0.28	1.79
treated unjustly	1.59	−2.37
in danger	0.91	−2.32
irrevocable loss	1.31	−2.41

amount of variance accounted for by this VALENCE superfactor, exacerbated by the fact that we have several items for intrinsic pleasantness and goal conduciveness, can account for the fact that remaining differences between the appraisals was drowned out and only NOVELTY emerges as the second factor in the overall factor analysis.

We therefore computed separate factor analyses for the positive and negative emotion words. As we are interested in examining the extent to which the internal structure of the appraisal ratings reflects the theoretical predictions of the CPM (see Chapter 1) and to obtain Appraisal component factors that represent this theoretical structure, we decided to exclude the features that were added on the basis of alternative theories (the items marked in the last two columns of Table 12.1) from this factor analysis. In other words, only the values for the appraisal features that are explicitly postulated by the CPM were included in the factor analysis (we did include the item concerning "relevance for another person's goals" as a second item for the goal relevance check to capture an aspect that is important for altruistic emotions, such as compassion). The resulting VARIMAX rotated structures are shown in Tables 12.4 and 12.5. For the negative emotion terms a seven factorial

Table 12.4 Loadings of the theoretically predicted appraisal features in a seven-factorial VARIMAX rotated structure for the *negative* emotion terms

Appraisal features	F1	F2	F3	F4	F5	F6	F7
in itself unpleasant for the person	0.78	0.05	0.07	0.02	0.11	0.24	−0.03
consequences negative for person	0.74	0.20	0.24	0.00	−0.02	0.10	−0.03
inconsistent with expectations	0.69	−0.03	0.30	−0.03	0.00	0.06	0.12
consequences positive for person	−0.66	0.12	−0.01	0.12	0.35	0.05	0.14
in itself pleasant for the person	−0.65	0.08	0.08	0.31	0.02	0.02	0.35
enough resources to avoid or modify consequences	0.10	0.83	−0.12	−0.06	−0.12	0.06	0.19
consequences avoidable or modifiable	0.00	0.82	−0.04	0.07	−0.03	0.27	0.12
consequences able to live with	−0.06	0.64	0.03	0.27	0.28	−0.04	−0.06
consequences predictable	0.06	0.54	−0.17	0.44	−0.12	−0.19	0.14
suddenly	0.12	−0.07	0.85	0.01	−0.04	−0.10	−0.05
unpredictable	0.28	−0.19	0.75	−0.14	−0.05	0.01	−0.09
caused by chance	0.08	−0.02	0.67	0.02	0.13	0.06	0.09
required an immediate response	−0.12	0.32	0.56	−0.43	0.08	0.10	−0.36
familiar	−0.06	0.11	0.01	0.76	0.15	−0.12	0.03
confirmed expectations	−0.26	0.09	−0.08	0.72	0.19	0.02	−0.11
caused intentionally	0.13	0.17	−0.11	0.50	−0.34	0.31	−0.21
important and relevant for person's goals	−0.02	−0.02	0.13	−0.03	0.85	−0.03	0.01
important and relevant for goals of somebody else	−0.01	0.01	−0.07	0.23	0.78	−0.12	−0.10
violated laws or socially accepted norms	0.07	0.07	0.05	−0.11	−0.17	0.87	0.11
incongruent with own standards and ideals	0.53	0.15	−0.07	0.04	0.03	0.71	−0.05
caused by the person's own behavior	0.00	0.32	−0.04	0.03	−0.02	0.13	0.79
caused by somebody else's behavior	0.43	−0.03	0.05	0.30	0.09	0.05	−0.66

Table 12.5 Loadings of the theoretically predicted appraisal features in a five-factorial VARIMAX rotated structure for the *positive* emotion terms

Appraisal features	F1	F2	F3	F4	F5
consequences negative for person	0.83	−0.12	−0.20	−0.08	0.11
incongruent with own standards and ideals	0.78	−0.02	−0.24	−0.18	0.17
in itself unpleasant for the person	0.77	−0.06	−0.19	0.08	0.02
violated laws or socially accepted norms	0.75	0.11	0.14	−0.01	0.03
in itself pleasant for the person	−0.62	0.23	0.52	0.15	0.13
required an immediate response	0.50	0.50	0.09	0.12	0.23
unpredictable	−0.05	0.85	0.07	0.00	−0.11
suddenly	−0.05	0.78	0.18	0.20	0.03
caused by chance	−0.13	0.72	0.36	0.03	−0.03
caused by somebody else's behavior	−0.05	0.65	0.06	0.19	0.05
inconsistent with expectations	0.11	0.64	−0.33	−0.16	0.16
important and relevant for goals of somebody else	−0.04	0.18	0.81	−0.01	0.04
important and relevant for person's goals	−0.14	0.12	0.73	0.22	0.00
consequences positive for person	−0.55	0.12	0.61	0.24	0.16
confirmed expectations	−0.15	−0.11	0.59	0.58	−0.07
caused by the person's own behavior	−0.05	0.11	0.07	0.85	0.04
caused intentionally	0.07	0.32	0.15	0.69	0.13
consequences predictable	−0.01	−0.01	0.40	0.68	0.29
familiar	−0.41	0.04	−0.14	0.53	0.27
enough resources to avoid or modify consequences	0.15	0.02	−0.19	0.20	0.82
consequences able to live with	−0.20	0.01	0.30	0.04	0.77
consequences avoidable or modifiable	0.37	0.08	0.05	0.16	0.71

structure accounting for 68.09% of the total variance could be well interpreted. In the case of the positive emotion terms the best interpretation was provided by the five-factorial structure, which accounted for 67.12% of the total variance. The pattern of factor loadings is well interpretable in the light of the CPM predictions described in Chapter 1. Thus, for the negative emotion terms the factors can be interpreted as F1 VALENCE, F2 coping potential, F3 NOVELTY, F4 expectedness, F5 relevance, F6 incongruity with standards, and F7 causality (see Table 12.4). The factor structure for the positive emotions is comparable except that the incongruity with standards and the causality features load on other factors (see Table 12.5). Thus, the analysis of the superordinate structure, after the VALENCE superfactor was neutralized through separating positive and negative emotions, provides a solution that is highly compatible with theoretical expectations about the internal structure of the appraisal criteria.

This solution to controlling the dominant effect of the VALENCE superfactor has the disadvantage that two different sets of factor scores would be required for the two types of emotion for further analyses, which is not compatible with many of the methods used in this study. We therefore chose yet another approach.

Internal structure analysis on residuals. To obtain a single factor structure that represents the differentiation beyond the VALENCE factor, we partialled VALENCE out of the original feature scores (see Chapter 5). For both conceptual and empirical reasons (size of the loadings on Factor 1 in Table 12.2) the meaning of VALENCE in the Appraisal component can be defined by the four central appraisal features "in itself pleasant," "in itself unpleasant," "positive consequences," and "negative consequences." These features have in common that they reflect the hedonic significance of the situation created by the eliciting event—the generally positive or negative outcome engendered by the event. A factor analysis on only these four features yielded a single factor accounting for 95% of the total variance. We further refer to this factor as VALENCE APPRAISAL. This VALENCE factor was then partialled out of the 18 remaining appraisal features that are explicitly postulated by the CPM using linear regression.

These 18 residual features were then submitted to a factor analysis. Figure SM 2 shows the scree plot. The scree criterion suggests a cut-off at five or six factors. The replicability of the residual structure for the six factor solution, which provided the clearest interpretation, was investigated. While not all congruence coefficients reached the cut-off value of 0.85, probably because unreliability had comparatively more effect in the residual structure, all items had the highest loadings on their respective factor after orthogonal Procrustes rotation in each of the four language groups, except for three cases (one feature in the German and two features in the East-Asian language groups loaded on a different factor). In consequence, the resulting six-factor configuration can be interpreted in the same way across language groups. The six factors accounted for 69% of the overall variance in the selected set of residual appraisal variables.

Table 12.6 shows the rotated factor loadings for the six-factor solution. Overall, we find a very similar structure to the separate factor analyses for positive and negative emotions (except for the absence of the VALENCE factor), which demonstrates the stability of this solution given the different analysis approaches. The first factor represents the suddenness and unpredictability aspects of the theoretically postulated NOVELTY check in the early relevance detection phase. However, in contrast to the two-factor solution discussed above, where only the suddenness and unpredictability items of this early check loaded on the NOVELTY APPRAISAL factor, we now also find a strong loading for "inconsistent with expectations," which is part of the theoretically postulated discrepancy from expectation check (see Table 12.1). Most likely, this is due to ecological correlations as described above—if events are unpredictable they are likely to be inconsistent with expectations. Ecological correlations may also be responsible for the loadings of two additional items that were expected to represent separate checks on this factor: "caused by chance" (causation subcheck) and "required an immediate response" (urgency subcheck). Unexpected and unpredictable events often occur by chance and require an urgent reaction. As it would be difficult to clearly separate conceptually postulated and ecological correlations and as we used the factor analysis as an empirical discovery method, we decided to include all five items in the definition of this factor that will be referred to as NOVELTY/CHANCE CAUSE.

The second factor represents the three appraisal checks that make up the theoretically postulated coping potential assessment phase—control, POWER, and adjustment (enough resources to avoid or modify consequences, consequences avoidable or modifiable, consequences able to live with). We call this factor COPING ABILITY. It should be noted that the third feature (consequences able to live with) originally loaded very highly on the VALENCE superfactor (with almost zero correlations with the two other items) and joined the COPING ABILITY group only after VALENCE was partialled out.

The third factor represents a blend of elements from three different theoretically postulated checks in the CPM: 1) the "event is familiar" feature of the NOVELTY check, 2) the "consequences predictable" feature of the outcome probability check, and 3) the "confirmed expectations" part

Table 12.6 Loadings of the theoretically predicted appraisal features after partialling out VALENCE APPRAISAL in a six-factorial VARIMAX rotated structure

Appraisal features	NOVELTY/CHANCE CAUSE	COPING ABILITY	EXPECTED/ FAMILIAR	GOAL RELEVANCE	NORM VIOLATION	SELF VS OTHER CAUSE
suddenly	0.87	−0.10	0.02	0.01	−0.04	0.02
unpredictable	0.85	−0.17	−0.12	−0.01	0.02	0.13
caused by chance	0.75	−0.08	−0.05	0.15	0.08	0.03
inconsistent with expectations	0.64	0.07	−0.11	−0.10	0.11	0.32
required an immediate response	0.63	0.19	−0.25	0.16	0.09	−0.11
enough resources to avoid or modify consequences	−0.05	0.85	0.12	−0.12	0.06	−0.16
consequences avoidable or modifiable	−0.05	0.79	0.17	−0.02	0.25	−0.16
consequences able to live with	−0.01	0.71	0.14	0.31	−0.09	0.20
caused intentionally	0.05	0.14	0.73	−0.19	0.22	0.13
confirmed expectations	−0.28	0.00	0.67	0.38	−0.05	−0.15
familiar	−0.17	0.15	0.63	0.16	−0.26	0.04
consequences predictable	−0.23	0.38	0.62	0.11	−0.09	−0.20
important and relevant for person's goals	0.15	0.00	0.06	0.83	−0.04	−0.14
important and relevant for goals of somebody else	0.04	0.07	0.09	0.81	−0.01	0.25
violated laws or socially accepted norms	0.09	0.01	−0.01	−0.10	0.85	−0.24
incongruent with own standards and ideals	0.07	0.17	−0.06	0.05	0.81	0.24
caused by somebody else's behavior	0.33	−0.02	0.33	0.15	0.05	0.69
caused by the persons own behavior	−0.02	0.26	0.39	0.02	0.09	−0.67

of the discrepancy from expectation check (the extent to which the personal expectations for this point in time are matched) all load on the third factor. In addition, an item originally considered to be part of the causal attribution check, "caused intentionally," also loads highly on this factor. The latter might reflect the fact that expectations are more likely to be met if intentional causation, rather than chance occurrence, is involved and may also be due to ecological correlations. As before, irrespective of the theoretical definitions, we combined these items, which represent a highly plausible appraisal constellation, under the label of EXPECTED/FAMILIAR for this factor.

Factor 4 represents the theoretically postulated goal relevance checks with high loadings on "important and relevant for person's goals" and "important and relevant for goals of somebody else" (the items added to represent relevance in the case of altruistic emotions such as compassion). We call this factor GOAL RELEVANCE.

Factor 5 represents the norm and self compatibility evaluation phase postulated by the CPM with high loadings of "violated laws or socially accepted norms" and "incongruent with own standards and ideals." The factor will be referred to as NORM VIOLATION.

Finally, Factor 6 covers the personal causation part of the causal attribution check represented by high opposite loadings of "caused by the person's own behavior" and "caused by somebody else's behavior." Appropriately, the factor will be called SELF VS OTHER CAUSE.

The factor analysis reported above was computed on the basis of standardized residuals of the appraisal ratings. In consequence, the resulting factors will be referred to as "residual factors" below, highlighting the fact that they represent only residual variance after the VALENCE APPRAISAL factor had been partialled out. Table 12.7 shows the factor score profiles for the individual emotion

Table 12.7 Average factor scores per emotion word for VALENCE APPRAISAL and the six residual appraisal factors

Emotion words	VALENCE APPRAISAL	NOVELTY/CHANCE CAUSE	COPING ABILITY	EXPECTED/ FAMILIAR	GOAL RELEVANCE	NORM VIOLATION	SELF VS OTHER CAUSE
anger	−0.85	0.41	0.07	0.56	−0.37	0.29	−0.02
anxiety	−0.61	0.19	0.03	−0.87	0.60	−0.23	−0.69
being hurt	−0.84	0.07	−0.14	0.47	−0.18	−0.11	0.77
compassion	0.15	−0.39	0.47	−0.03	0.45	−0.53	0.95
contempt	−0.53	−1.18	−0.10	0.61	−0.40	1.36	0.89
contentment	1.49	−0.33	0.31	0.78	0.35	−0.08	−0.33
despair	−0.80	−0.04	−0.48	−0.42	0.10	−0.68	−0.58
disappointment	−0.82	0.15	0.47	0.12	0.57	0.27	0.58
disgust	−0.79	0.07	−0.46	0.24	−0.27	0.58	0.47
fear	−0.64	0.89	−0.77	−0.56	−0.15	−0.93	−0.59
guilt	−0.46	−0.94	0.82	−0.25	−0.51	0.79	−2.07
happiness	1.63	0.35	−0.09	0.19	−0.12	−0.25	0.11
hate	−0.73	−0.99	−0.54	0.44	−0.30	0.59	0.67
interest	1.09	0.40	0.63	−0.16	0.80	0.79	−0.15
irritation	−0.88	0.48	0.47	0.31	−0.25	0.13	0.15
jealousy	−0.43	−0.82	−0.61	0.14	0.04	−1.46	0.82
joy	1.57	0.78	−0.03	0.63	−0.01	−0.39	0.03
love	1.38	−1.15	−0.29	−1.15	−0.42	−0.52	0.64
pleasure	1.56	0.14	−0.11	0.67	−0.21	0.26	−0.09
pride	1.25	−0.78	−0.11	0.13	0.29	−0.18	−0.91
sadness	−0.86	−0.09	0.18	0.82	0.36	−0.80	0.11
shame	−0.65	0.29	0.15	−0.33	−0.47	0.64	−1.14
stress	−0.63	0.12	0.49	−0.74	0.45	−0.50	−0.72
surprise	0.39	2.38	−0.39	−1.59	−0.34	0.95	1.09

categories on these six residual factors as well as, in the first column, the scores for the VALENCE APPRAISAL factor that was separately computed on the four appropriate items.

Even a cursory perusal of the profiles for the individual emotions confirms the high degree of plausibility of the differentiation afforded by the VALENCE APPRAISAL factor and the six residual factors. The scores for VALENCE APPRAISAL clearly separate the emotions into a positive and a negative group, with the exception of surprise and compassion which are in a somewhat neutral zone. Surprise and fear are high on the NOVELTY/CHANCE CAUSE factor whereas contempt and hate are low (indicating that these two emotion words may refer to more enduring affective dispositions toward a particular person than a spontaneous emotion episode). The factor COPING ABILITY, somewhat unexpectedly, does not show a very large degree of variation between emotions which might be due to the fact that the items are worded in a fairly technical way, closely approaching psychology terminology. It is also possible that people normally do not analyze their coping potential in a very conscious and precise fashion. However, despite their small size, the differences are meaningful. Thus, low coping potential characterizes fear and despair (and interestingly jealousy), whereas in irritation, interest, and particularly guilt, there is more of a feeling of being able to master the consequences of the eliciting event or behavior. In the case of guilt, this might be due to the possibility of repairing the wrongs one has caused. On the EXPECTED/ FAMILIAR factor, contentment and sadness are high (probably because the eliciting event happened at some temporal distance), whereas surprise is, not surprisingly, low. Interestingly, love also has a low score on EXPECTED/FAMILIAR, suggesting that it may be related to somewhat rare and unexpected events (especially if one thinks of "falling in love" as an event rather than love in the sense of an enduring relationship).

The GOAL RELEVANCE factor does not seem to be very useful for differentiating the 24 emotions, as only interest has a somewhat higher than average factor score here. One possibility for the lack of differentiation could be the fact that all 24 emotions designated by the words chosen for this study imply personally relevant goals. Another possible explanation is that, as for the coping potential features, the notion of "goal relevance," which, while being a central psychological concept, might be somewhat opaque to the layperson. In any case, in popular parlance the meaning of the word goal seems very constrained in the sense of an immediate conscious intention (like pursuing a specific interest) and not normally generalized to fundamental, unconscious needs and desires (see Scherer, 1993). NORM VIOLATION, in contrast, is very important, both for someone else's behavior, as for contempt and hate (but not being hurt), and one's own behavior, having violated one's own internal standards, for guilt and shame. Other negative emotions such as sadness and fear are very low on this factor, presumably because they have low values on personal causation, and moral evaluation is thus not very pertinent. The sixth factor, bipolar SELF VS OTHER CAUSE mainly separates self-reflective emotions such as shame and guilt, due to one's own behavior, from those elicited by the behavior of others or chance.

Mapping the appraisal structure onto the overall structure

Regression analysis with two general appraisal factors. Table 12.8 shows the results of the regression of the appraisal two-factor solution on the four overall factors computed *with the appraisal features excluded*. As expected, the GENERAL VALENCE APPRAISAL factor in the two-factor solution explains a very high proportion of the variance of the overall VALENCE factor. As argued above, the predominance of a general VALENCE dimension, here demonstrated by a convergence of different types of VALENCE, is probably at the basis of the extraordinary importance of the VALENCE dimension in any kind of dimensional analysis of feelings, and affective words, explaining the bulk of the variance (see Chapter 1 as well as the results shown in Chapter 7).

Table 12.8 Standardized regression weights and R^2 of the two VARIMAX rotated appraisal factors regressed on the four overall factors

Overall factors	$\beta_{\text{GENERAL VALENCE APPRAISAL}}$	$\beta_{\text{NOVELTY APPRAISAL}}$	R^2
VALENCE	0.93***	0.06***	0.87
POWER	0.20***	−0.03	0.04
AROUSAL	−0.06	0.37***	0.14
NOVELTY	0.04	0.40***	0.16

Note: * p <0.05, ** p <0.01, *** p <0.001. The appraisal features were removed from the four overall factors.

The presence of the NOVELTY items in the appraisal feature list may have been a major reason for the emergence of a stable fourth factor representing NOVELTY in the overall PCA of emotion words across cultures and languages (see Chapter 7). This would explain why this fourth factor has not emerged in earlier dimensional analyses of the emotion domain which were based solely on self-report of feeling or motor expression. Given that the second factor in the initial two-factor solution for the Appraisal component could be reasonably defined as a NOVELTY factor, one would assume that it predicts the fourth NOVELTY factor in the overall structure rather well. This expectation is indeed borne out by the data in Table 12.8. However, the relationship is not quite as strong as one might have thought. This probably means that the overall NOVELTY factor is to a large extent defined by appraisals of NOVELTY. In Chapter 7, it was observed that the NOVELTY factor was weakened by removing appraisal features from the global structure.

Regression analysis with residual appraisal factors. Table 12.9 shows the same kind of analysis for the two-phase factor PCA solution (first identifying a superfactor and then partialling it out of the remaining variables) with the VALENCE APPRAISAL factor and the six "residual factors" based on the appraisal features after partialling out VALENCE APPRAISAL. As in the two-factor solution, the VALENCE APPRAISAL factor provides an almost perfect prediction of the overall VALENCE factor. The NOVELTY/CHANCE CAUSE factor predicts the overall NOVELTY factor, although less strongly. In addition, we find a reasonably strong prediction of the overall AROUSAL factor by the two residual appraisal factors NOVELTY/CHANCE CAUSE (positive direction) and EXPECTED/FAMILIAR (negative direction), suggesting that sudden, unexpected events are very likely to generate AROUSAL especially when an urgent response is required. As mentioned above, this is very plausible from an evolutionary point of view, suggesting that unexpected events should generate attention and activation to allow a rapid adaptive response. The remaining beta coefficients in Table 12.9, while often significant, are of less importance—in and of themselves, they are unlikely to explain much of the variance in the overall factors. As shown by the rather low R^2, none of the local Appraisal component factors contributes substantially to predict the overall POWER factor.

Exploring the prediction of the POWER and the AROUSAL factor. While the regression analyses confirmed the expectation for the overall VALENCE, and to an important extent for the NOVELTY factor, they did not confirm the expectation for the overall POWER and the overall AROUSAL factor. If the appraisal process is driving the emotion process, one might expect that variation in POWER and AROUSAL can also be well predicted on the basis of the Appraisal component. Therefore, we systematically investigated possible explanations for the fairly modest prediction of the AROUSAL and particularly the POWER factor by the appraisal features. We could identify four possible explanations, namely problems of operationalization, the importance of individual appraisal checks, statistical suppression effects, and interaction effects.

Table 12.9 Standardized regression weights and R^2 of VALENCE APPRAISAL and the residual appraisal factors regressed on the four overall factors

Overall factors	β VALENCE APPRAISAL	β NOVELTY/CHANCE CAUSE	β COPING ABILITY	β EXPECTED/FAMILIAR	β GOAL RELEVANCE	β NORM VIOLATION	β SELF VS OTHER CAUSE	R^2
VALENCE	0.94***	0.06***	0.07***	−0.03*	0.08***	−0.07***	−0.03**	0.91
POWER	0.20***	−0.02	0.00	0.20***	−0.02	0.19***	0.20***	0.16
AROUSAL	−0.04	0.34***	−0.08**	−0.32***	−0.08*	−0.11***	−0.13***	0.26
NOVELTY	0.08**	0.40***	−0.27***	0.14***	−0.28***	0.09**	0.13***	0.36

Note: * p <0.05, ** p <0.01, *** p <0.001. The appraisal features were removed from the four overall factors.

First, the items formulated to represent the coping ability features (especially "consequences avoidable or modifiable" and "enough resources to avoid or modify consequences") may not have captured the essence of the personal POWER and control aspects that are part of the theoretical coping potential construct (as postulated by the CPM, see Scherer, 2009c). The *item formulation* may have been too indirect or too close to the adjustment check so that the meaning may not have been sufficiently clear to the participants. The fact that the coping features showed much less variance across the 24 emotion words than the other appraisal check features, points in the direction of a problem with the wording of the items.

Second, there is the possibility that important information is lost by *working with factors* rather than with the individual appraisal checks. According to the CPM, each of the appraisal checks, independently and consecutively, contributes to the unfolding of an emotion episode. Thus POWER, control, and adjustment checks are considered as separate checks, here operationalized by a single feature each, even though they are conceptually subsumed under the term "coping potential." In order to estimate how much information may be lost by working with appraisal factors rather than individual appraisal features, we investigated this possibility by testing an a priori theoretical prediction with the data of this study. Scherer (2001) predicted that the AROUSAL dimension would be based on the need to urgently undertake action in the situation. This appraisal check was operationalized by one feature, namely "required an immediate response." In the factor analyses described above, that feature loaded on the NOVELTY factor. According to the theoretical expectation, it is not so much the NOVELTY of the event that causes the AROUSAL, but more specifically the need to intervene. To investigate this possibility we compared the regression model for AROUSAL with all seven appraisal factors (see Table 12.9) with a regression model where the individual feature "required an immediate response" was added as a predictor. The simple addition of this single predictor lead to an increase in the variance accounted (R^2) for from 26% to 35%. Moreover, if the feature "required an immediate response" was included as the only predictor, it accounted on its own for 22% of the total variance, which is almost as much as the seven appraisal factors (the VALENCE APPRAISAL factor plus six residual appraisal factors) together.

Third, combined with the second account, there is a possible problem of *suppression effects* in the prediction of the POWER and AROUSAL factors. Statistically, a suppression effect means that the predictive value of a predictor increases when another predictor is included (or that its predictive value is suppressed in the absence of that other variable; see the review in MacKinnon, Krull, & Lockwood, 2000). As we found that many of these appraisal checks share a strong VALENCE component, it is possible that their contribution to the prediction of variance gets suppressed. In the data we observed a clear suppression effect for the following two appraisal features, namely the features "treated unjustly" and "irrevocable loss," on the POWER factor. When they were each entered separately as predictors they accounted for less than 1% and 11% respectively of the variance in POWER. However, when they were entered together as predictors they jointly accounted for 26% of the variance. Only when entered jointly with "irrevocable loss" "treated unjustly" predicts the POWER factor positively (beta increasing from −0.045 to 0.652). Another suppression effect could be observed for the appraisal checks "familiar" and "consequences negative for somebody else." When each of these appraisal checks were entered separately as predictors of the AROUSAL dimension, they each explained about 3% of the variance respectively. However, when they were jointly entered as predictors, they accounted for 10% of the variance. This means that their joint effect was about three times as large as their individual effects. For instance when "familiar" was entered as single predictor its beta weight was −0.186, however, together with "consequences negative for somebody else," it increased to −0.304.

The fourth possible account is that the regression analyses have only looked at *linear relationships* between the emotion components and the overall factors. However, the CPM, as described in Chapter 1, is a sequential and cumulative model which predicts different emotions by specific configurations of appraisal results over time, yielding *nonlinear* effects. This is to say that while each check will have an effect of its own, it is the cumulative results of a specific configuration of the different checks that produce the essential impact of appraisal on the other components (often in a nonlinear fashion; see Scherer, 2000b, 2009a). In technical terms, this means that the appraisal checks do not determine the emotion process in a linear (additive) way, but that it is the specific *interaction* (configuration) between them that accounts for the final result.

In what follows, we provide a few exemplary illustrations for such effects. We find clear and theoretically interpretable evidence for such interaction effects with just three appraisal checks, namely "caused by the person's own behavior," "caused by somebody else's behavior," and "with consequences that were positive for the person." A linear model with just these three appraisal check predictors accounted for 13% of the variance in the POWER factor. A regression model with just two interaction effects included (namely between self-cause and positive consequences, and between other cause and positive consequences), accounted for an additional 10% of the variance. Thus, the predictive value was almost doubled. In situations where you yourself are responsible for positive consequences, POWER goes up. However, in situations where someone else is responsible for positive consequences for you, POWER goes down. With only three appraisal features and two interaction effects more variance is accounted for in POWER than with the linear effects of the seven appraisal factors.

These examples demonstrate that the simple linear regression model with appraisal factors as predictors is indeed insufficient to represent how the Appraisal component allows for the prediction of POWER and AROUSAL. We found clear evidence for the need to work with individual appraisal features, to be aware of suppression effects and to look at interaction effects. However, here we can do little more than illustrate the relevance of these issues for understanding the Appraisal–other component links. A comprehensive investigation of a model that would fully represent these links would be necessarily complex (including individual appraisal checks and multiple theoretical interaction effects). The development and appropriate testing of such a complex model is beyond the scope of the current chapter.

Differentiating emotion terms on the basis of the Appraisal component features

Ultimately, the ability to correctly classify emotion words on the basis of feature profiles, as measured through multiple discriminant analyses (MDA; see Chapter 5) provides evidence for our claim that appraisal features constitute a central element of the component feature profile, allowing the differentiation of the semantic fields of the emotion words chosen for the GRID study.

MDA based on the two general appraisal factors. First, we computed an MDA based on factor scores resulting from the two-factor solution (shown in column A of Table 12.10). In this case, only 33% of cross-validated grouped cases were correctly classified, showing the enormous loss of discriminative POWER entailed by a reduction of the information to only the two higher order factors accounting for most of the variance.

MDA based on the residual appraisal factors. We then computed an MDA on the basis of the VALENCE APPRAISAL factor scores together with the factor scores for the six residual factors (resulting from the factor analysis in which the VALENCE APPRAISAL factor was partialled out; see section on the internal structure of the appraisal component above). The first five of the seven discriminant functions were clearly identifiable due to strong and unique correlations between the predictor

Table 12.10 Classification accuracy (in percent) for the 24 emotion words in discriminant analyses based on different sets of appraisal factors, CPM predicted features, and all appraisal features

Emotion words	A	B	C	D	
	Classification based on two factors	Classification based on two-phase 1 + 6 factors	Classification based on CPM predicted features	Classification based on all appraisal features	
	Accuracy	Accuracy	Accuracy	Accuracy	Confusion > 15% with
being hurt	0.0	38.2	47.1	61.8	
sadness	8.8	55.9	64.7	79.4	
shame	8.8	73.5	88.2	91.2	
guilt	76.5	88.2	85.3	88.2	
compassion	20.6	41.2	58.8	85.3	
disappointment	5.9	35.3	55.9	67.6	
love	26.5	82.4	94.1	91.2	
contentment	38.2	55.9	52.9	52.9	pleasure
happiness	17.6	38.2	44.1	47.1	joy
pride	52.9	67.6	82.4	94.1	
pleasure	29.4	38.2	55.9	52.9	joy
joy	44.1	58.8	50.0	47.1	happiness
interest	73.5	85.3	79.4	88.2	
surprise	94.1	94.1	97.1	94.1	
despair	2.9	44.1	55.9	79.4	
stress	14.7	41.2	50	73.5	anxiety
anxiety	32.4	35.3	35.3	50.0	stress
fear	76.5	76.5	82.4	85.3	
jealousy	52.9	79.4	76.5	88.2	
hate	38.2	64.7	64.7	70.6	
irritation	0.0	32.4	32.4	38.2	anger
anger	29.4	20.6	26.5	32.4	irritation
disgust	14.7	35.3	58.8	67.6	
contempt	29.4	67.6	67.6	70.6	
Total	32.8	56.3	62.7	70.7	

factors and the respective discriminant functions. A stepwise analysis was used and the first five predictors entered in the following order (with the percentage of the variance accounted for in parentheses): VALENCE APPRAISAL (73), NOVELTY/CHANCE CAUSE (11), SELF-OTHER CAUSE (8), NORM VIOLATION (5), EXPECTED/FAMILIAR (2). The last two discriminant functions were multiply determined (1.2 and 0.3). In this case 56% of cross-validated grouped cases were correctly classified. These results are shown in column B of Table 12.10.

MDA based on the a priori CPM appraisal features. Next we computed an MDA based on the appraisal features that had been predicted a priori by the CPM (i.e., excluding the features that were added based on socio-cultural and core relation theme approaches; marked in the last two columns in Table 12.1), entering all features at the same time. The results (see column C in Table 12.10) show an overall hit rate of 63% (cross-validated). The profile of hit rates for the individual emotions are slightly higher than those in column B for the MDA based on seven factors, but the pattern is highly comparable, suggesting that the factors represent the information in the theoretically predicted features rather well.

MDA based on all appraisal features. Finally, we computed an MDA using all individual appraisal feature items (column D in Table 12.10). Results show that now 71% of cross-validated grouped cases were correctly classified. Again, the profile of hit rates for the individual emotions, while slightly higher than those in columns B and C, show the same pattern across most emotions. The emotions of sadness and despair constitute an exception, as their hit rates greatly increase in this condition. A detailed analysis suggests that this might be due to the core relational theme "irrevocable loss" which Lazarus (1991a) proposed for sadness and despair. A similar increase is seen for compassion. Upon analysis it can be surmised that this might be due to events with positive or negative consequences happening to *other* people (appraisal features added to represent socio-cultural approaches), which is of course central to the meaning of the word "compassion".

It is instructive to consider the major confusions, allowing the determinatin of the emotion words that seem to have somewhat similar appraisal profiles. Particularly frequent confusions occur between: a) happiness and joy, contentment and pleasure, and joy and pleasure; b) stress and anxiety; and c) anger, and irritation. It comes as no surprise that these are the emotion groups that are generally considered as parts of larger emotion families. This can be demonstrated by using the profile of hit rates for the individual emotion words for the best MDA solution, based on all appraisals (column D in Table 12.10), to categorize the emotions with respect to how well they can be classified on the basis of the appraisal feature profiles (in ascending order of accuracy):

Below 50% accuracy: anger, irritation, happiness, joy

Between 50–75% accuracy: anxiety, contentment, pleasure, being hurt, disappointment, disgust, hate, contempt, stress

Above 75% accuracy: sadness, despair, compassion, fear, guilt, interest, jealousy, shame, love, pride, surprise.

Clearly, the emotion words classified with less than 50% accuracy are members of two emotion families, the anger and the happiness family. In fact, the latter could also include contentment and pleasure, from the next group, as there are many confusions between the four words. If we run the MDA with these terms combined into families, both the family accuracies and the overall accuracy increase substantially.

If one compares the accuracy coefficients for the individual emotions across the different MDAs described above, on the basis of the compilation of the respective percentages shown in Table 12.10, one sees in general a gradual increase without major jumps except in the case of moving from the two-factor solution scores (column A) to the seven factor MDA in column B, where there is a very sharp increase. Once the composite scores based on the VALENCE APPRAISAL factor and the six residual factors obtained after partialling out VALENCE APPRAISAL is used, accuracy improves dramatically. This suggests that while VALENCE is a very important factor for affect, in and of itself, it does not allow taking account of the high degree of differentiation in the meaning of a major set of emotion labels. Only surprise is classified accurately, given that the second factor represents

NOVELTY. Interestingly, fear, guilt, and interest have relatively high accuracy scores, possibly because of a special combination of VALENCE and NOVELTY scores.

In general the discrimination results based on only the appraisal items show a rather impressive accuracy of classification. This underlines the claim made in Chapter 1 that it is subjective appraisal that elicits and differentiates emotions, in part through driving the changes in all other emotion components. The comparison in Table 12.10 shows that the VALENCE APPRAISAL factor and the six residual factors capture much of the variance in the theoretically predicted features. However, five emotions reach a satisfactory classification accuracy only when all features are used in the MDA: being hurt, compassion, pride, stress, and fear. This suggests that for some emotions, very specific, configurational appraisal profiles seem to be required to correctly reflect the meaning of the respective label.

Looking at the individual profiles. We reviewed the results of Table 12.7 by column, that is, by appraisal dimension. However, it can also be read by row, looking at the specific appraisal configuration for each emotion. These configurations can be compared with the detailed predictions for 13 of the 24 emotions studied here (see Table 5.4 in Scherer (2001) and Table SM 1). These predictions attempt to specify the appraisal profiles that will lead a person to categorize and label an emotion episode with a specific word. While at this stage, the comparison is limited to eyeballing and approximation, especially as the factors reported here often combine items from different appraisal checks that are treated as independent in the theory, the degree of fit is encouraging. There is only one emotion—anger—in which there are major discrepancies between prediction and factor score configurations. Anger was theoretically predicted to be generally elicited by events that are sudden and unpredictable, discrepant from expectations, often involving violation of norms and standards but in situations in which the individual judges to have relatively high coping potential. The data reported here (see row 1 in Table 12.7) do not bear this out. Instead, the word anger has a rather flat profile across the six appraisal factors. One possible explanation is that the anger family consists of a rather large number of members with very different characteristics, ranging from mild irritation to violent rage, and that in consequence the meaning of the category name *anger* must cover many different alternatives, resulting in a somewhat diffuse semantic profile.

One important function of the current data set is to help fill the many cells in the prediction table (Table 5.4 in Scherer, 2001; reproduced in Table SM 1) that were designated as "open," in the sense that, at the time, no prediction was ventured. We believe that the current data set on the semantic profiles of emotion words defined by appraisal feature profiles is sufficiently robust to serve as the basis for specific hypothesis as to the likelihood that certain appraisal check profiles will engender the use of certain emotion terms.

12.4 **General discussion and conclusion**

Internal structure

The impact of VALENCE. One can argue that the appraisal process in and of itself is fundamentally valenced–it is essential to know what is happening in relationships to my needs/goals and whether something is primarily good or primarily bad for me. Our analysis of the internal structure of the appraisal process shows, as expected, that VALENCE clearly dominates. The fact that only two factors were stable across the four language families and that the first and by far the strongest of these gathers virtually all items, except the NOVELTY-related ones, confirms the earlier suggestion that the outcomes of most of the major appraisal checks are indeed *valenced*, that is, are considered as positive or negative in and of themselves (see Table 1.1; see also Sacharin, Sander, & Scherer, in press). Supporting this theoretical claim, we find high loadings (both positive and negative) for VALENCE (the first factor) as pleasure (in itself un/pleasant for self and someone else), VALENCE as satisfaction (consequences positive/negative for self and someone else), VALENCE as self-un/worthiness (incongruent with own standards and ideals), VALENCE as moral un/worthiness (violated norm/laws, unjust treatment). There is only limited confirmation for VALENCE as POWER or coping ability in the sense that only coping through adjustment (predictable consequences and able to live with consequences) loads highly on the first factor. The items intended to tap the POWER or control aspect (enough resources to modify consequences, consequences avoidable or modifiable) did not load on this VALENCE superfactor. This may be due to the fact that the respective items do not reflect a type of POWER or dominance which is highly context independent (and it is this type of POWER that is likely to be positively valenced), but rather a type of control POWER that is afforded by the situational contexts. For example, if an event has positive consequences, the issue of coping with the consequences is not relevant. It remains an issue for further research to determine under which circumstances positive VALENCE based on POWER or dominance is generated in appraisal. Specifically, items will need to be generated that reflect this type of positive POWER, guaranteeing access to resources, and protection from harm.

Given the impact of the VALENCE superfactor across separate appraisal checks, we decided to remove the effect due to this dominating, superordinate factor by partialling out its contribution to the variance. This allows the identification of the additional contribution of other (underlying) factors on a lower level of this VALENCE generality. As shown above, the six factorial solution is eminently interpretable. It is important to stress the point made in the earlier description of the factors, namely that the factor analysis does not distinguish between conceptual similarity between different features (i.e., measuring similar content as in test items) and ecological correlations (i.e., high common loadings on a factor due to co-occurrences of certain conditions in the real world, such as expected outcomes being more probable for intentional behavior than chance occurrence). Therefore, the factor analysis results cannot be used to confirm the justification of theoretical distinctions. However, the detailed interpretation of the factors computed on the residual variables allows the formulation of hypotheses for further research.

The case of the NOVELTY and expectation checks is particularly interesting. The NOVELTY subchecks of familiarity and predictability (familiar, consequences predictable), as well as the item "confirmed expectations" are very positively evaluated as suggested by high loadings on the GENERAL VALENCE APPRAISAL factor. In contrast, the suddenness and unpredictability subchecks are apparently not positively or negatively valenced. Rather, they constitute the second, orthogonal factor in the PCA solution, together with the item "caused by chance." This pattern suggests that the appraisal criteria might be organized according to a hierarchical structure with two orthogonal "superfactors"—GENERAL VALENCE APPRAISAL and NOVELTY APPRAISAL. The existence of an appraisal subprocess that specifically processes sudden and unpredictable events, which can be either positive or negative, is plausible from an evolutionary point of view as it alerts the organism to potentially relevant consequences. The resulting state, surprise, is not even considered as an emotion by many theorists because it generally constitutes only a first reaction to something sudden and completely unexpected. However, even though this emotional reaction is generally very brief, it may have quite a strong impact on other components, such as inducing search for additional information, a momentary surge of AROUSAL, and specific forms of expression.

Congruence with overall factors

As expected the VALENCE APPRAISAL factor predicted the overall VALENCE factor almost perfectly. The relationship between the NOVELTY/CHANCE CAUSE factor and the overall NOVELTY factor was somewhat less strong than expected but still rather sizable. However, the NOVELTY/CHANCE CAUSE factor (as well as the EXPECTED/FAMILIAR factor) did substantially contribute to the prediction of the AROUSAL factor.

The overall POWER factor was least well predicted by the appraisal factors. We had expected that one or more appraisal factors, especially the COPING POTENTIAL factor (which should represent control and POWER features according to the CPM), would at least partly predict the overall POWER factor but this was not the case. This is probably largely due to the fact that the two coping potential features may not have been worded in an appropriate manner. As mentioned above, we had formulated the items "consequences avoidable or modifiable" and "enough resources to avoid or modify consequences" in a somewhat indirect way to avoid mentioning the concepts of control and POWER. Both the ratings on these items for the different emotion words, the correlations and factor analyses showed that this strategy did not work. Consequently, we will formulate more explicit items to operationalize the control and POWER appraisals for the future use of the GRID instrument (see Chapter 44). Apart from this methodological issue, the current results also plead for an independent role of the appraisal checks of POWER, control, and adjustment. Conceptually, they can all be seen as contributing to "coping potential" in a very broad sense. However, the current data suggest that a combination of these three checks, as in the coping potential factor described below, might not have been useful–either for the prediction of the overall factors or emotion discrimination. One of the reasons might be that the situational context may be a much more important determinant of one's ability to live with an outcome than one's personal potential to adjust to it.

Discrimination and classification

The central claim of our approach is that the meaning of major emotion words can be defined, largely by the appraisal process underlying the respective emotion episodes. How well do the results of the discriminative structure of the appraisal process support this claim? In sum, we have shown that the 24 emotion words in the GRID study can be differentiated with approximately 70% accuracy by the 31 appraisal features alone. This suggests that the differential meaning of different emotion terms is largely carried by the specific appraisal configurations that are predicted to determine the respective emotion episodes. The predictors in the total appraisal set include 10 features that were added to represent appraisal dimensions that have been suggested by sociocultural approaches and the notion of core relational themes. Even if these 10 items are excluded and the prediction is exclusively based on the appraisal checks explicitly postulated in the CPM, the accuracy drops only by about 7% to 63%. This means that the bulk of the variance is explained in the appraisal checks that are part of the architecture of the CPM. The loss of 7% is partly explained by the appraisal that "other persons" experience a positive or negative outcome (important to classify compassion) and relational themes like "loss" (important to classify sadness and despair) are not part of the CPM. However, as has been shown in several places in this chapter, at least some of the information content of these appraisal criteria can be captured by using appropriate interactions or configurational variables based on the individual checks postulated by the CPM. For example, the theme "danger" is represented by a configuration of an expected obstructive event with negative consequences, high goal relevance, insufficient POWER, control, and adjustment, and possibly the need for an urgent response.

Some limitations should be noted. The CPM postulates appraisal mechanisms that intervene in a recursive (sequential and cumulative) *process* of appraisal whereas the raters in the GRID study evaluated which appraisals can be jointly considered to be responsible for the elicitation of a state that is normally labeled with one of the emotion words provided. Clearly, the latter can only provide a very rough assessment of the underlying processes, all the more so as laymen generally are not conscious of these appraisal processes and we had to formulate the respective features in an easily understandable, nontechnical fashion. Clearly, the rating procedure as well as the type of linear statistical techniques used in our analyses cannot capture the complexity of the appraisal criteria and the dynamic nature of the appraisal process, particularly the complex interactions between appraisal checks in the cumulative sequence of their checking. This is particularly true for the factor analysis approach which focuses on identifying a minimal number of factors explaining a maximum of variance. Despite these shortcomings, the discrimination of the emotion terms on the basis of the VALENCE APPRAISAL factor and the six residual factors obtained after partialling out VALENCE APPRAISAL still allow a classification with 56% accuracy, more than 13 times higher than chance.

Future development

Theoretical efforts and the associated research activity need to focus on the reliable measure of the individual appraisal checks and their role in the elicitation of specific emotions–or the semantic differentiation of the respective emotion terms. Of central importance is attention to the hitherto neglected issue of the multiple interactions between appraisal criteria. We have shown that most of the variance in the meaning of emotion terms can, in principle, be captured by modeling the multiple interactions of the appraisal criteria as postulated by the CPM and similar appraisal theories. In consequence, the priority in theoretical and methodological development, as well as empirical investigation, should be given to identifying the specific appraisal criteria interactions that are likely to represent constitutive elements of the meaning of major emotion terms.

Chapter 13

The meaning structure of emotion terms: Integration across components

Klaus R. Scherer[1] and Johnny J. R. Fontaine

Now that we have reported the empirical results for each of the major components of emotion (viz. Appraisal, Action tendencies, Bodily reactions, motor Expression, and Feeling), we will briefly summarize the main results and attempt to integrate findings across the different emotion components. As we used a standard sequential organization of the analyses in each of the preceding chapters, we will maintain this sequence here. First, comparing the internal structure of the different emotion components (reviewing the underlying dimensionality of the component features and discussing the way in which each local structure helps to describe the specificity of the emotion words). Second, using regression to map the local structures into the overall structure of four major, cross-culturally stable factors (VALENCE, POWER, AROUSAL, and NOVELTY). Third, using Multiple Discriminant Analyses (MDA) to evaluate the capacity of the GRID features (and the emotion component factors) to correctly classify the 24 emotion words under study.

Before embarking on this enterprise, a few general comments are in order:

1 As outlined in Parts I and II of this book, the GRID study has a rather explicit theoretical background—both the GRID paradigm and the GRID instrument have been based on a specific type of componential emotion theory, the Componential Process Model of emotion (CPM; see Chapter 1 and Scherer, 1984a, b, 2001, 2009c). The CPM is a process model of emotion elicitation and differentiation. The reason why its architecture is germane to addressing issues concerning the meaning of emotion words, is that its architecture invites this type of generalization (see Chapter 1 for details). It is thus unavoidable that, in what follows, we will in several places draw conclusions about the fit between the data reported and theoretical assumptions made by the model. Generally, we claim that the data are compatible with the CPM, that there is *indirect* support for the model or that the *plausibility* of the model is strengthened by particular patterns of results. We want to make it perfectly clear that we do not make any claims concerning causal inferences implied by the CPM model from the data reported here. We have reported a large set of data on reliable judgments of semantic features of emotion terms in many different languages and these data can be interpreted in an inferential sense with respect to what members of a linguistic community believe about the semantic content of emotion terms. Any links to issues of diachronic language development, for example, the lexical sedimentation hypothesis or the degree to which semantic structure and content mirror structures and processes within the phenomenon under study, in this case emotion, remain

---

[1] Corresponding author: Klaus R. Scherer. Swiss Center for Affective Sciences—University of Geneva. 7, Rue des Battoirs, CH-1205 Geneva, Switzerland. Klaus.Scherer@unige.ch

obviously highly conjectural. The data reported here cannot provide empirical evidence for actual emotion processes and cannot be used for causal inference. However, we believe that such conjectures are useful for the interpretation of data patterns and for the development of more sophisticated hypotheses for future research.

2   As explained in more detail in Chapter 5, the analysis techniques used in this volume are for the most part intended to serve descriptive and exploratory purposes. Given that we entered fairly uncharted terrain, requiring highly interdisciplinary approaches, we felt it would be useful to first provide an inventory, to survey the lay of the land, before using the more sophisticated tools available in the statistical tool box (e.g., multilevel analysis, nonlinear techniques, etc.) to test specific hypotheses. For example, we restrict our analysis and discussion of the results largely on main effects of individual features and factors, rather than including the myriad of possible interactions.

3   We see this book as the beginning rather than the end of the exploitation of an extremely rich data set. It is precisely the hunches and conjectures presented here that are to serve an incentive to other researchers, as well as to ourselves, to develop more detailed and focused hypotheses that can be tested with the current GRID data set or new data to be collected with the instrument.

4   As described at the outset (see Chapter 5, the multicomponent GRID paradigm has been designed to integrate diverse approaches to the study of emotion from many different disciplines. Thus, wherever possible we advocate using this tool as a tertium comparationis, a sort of litmus test that can help to impartially discuss the relative merits of differential assumptions about the mechanisms and processes underlying emotion labeling.

13.1 **Comparing emotion component structures**

How similar are the emotion component factor structures described in Chapters 8 to 12 and what are their respective contributions to the overall structure as reported in Chapter 7? Theoretically, one might expect two diametrically opposite possibilities: 1) the local structures prefigure the overall structure (*duplication model*), or 2) each emotion component structure is unique, depending on its specificity, that is, the function it serves to facilitate adaptive responses or the nature of the organismic subsystem it is based on, and thus providing an independent input to the overall structure (*additive contribution model*). We will show that the answer lies somewhere in the middle between these extreme models. Whereas we have covered the individual components in a didactic order in the preceding chapter, proceeding from the more established (Feeling, Bodily reaction, Expression) to the more recently highlighted emotion components (Action tendencies, Appraisal), we will now reverse the order, following the theoretically proposed causal sequence as described in Figure 1.1 of Chapter 1.

Appraisal component. According to appraisal theories, and the CPM in particular, the appraisal process initially triggers the emotion episode and continually drives the changes in the other components in a recursive process (see Chapter 1, for further detail). Thus one might expect the internal structure of these components to correspond to a duplication model. This is partially true at a first level of analysis as a factor analysis of the appraisal features yielded two factors that are very similar to the first and the last factor of the overall structure: GENERAL VALENCE APPRAISAL and NOVELTY APPRAISAL. However, as the detailed analysis in Chapter 12 showed, the VALENCE factor in this analysis is a powerful superfactor that needs to be decomposed to show the underlying structure of the appraisal feature domain. This is consistent with the assumption (described in

Chapter 1; see Table 1.1 in the chapter) that almost all of the appraisal criteria are valenced, with different types of VALENCE corresponding to the nature of the appraisal checks. Another, statistical, reason for this initial structure is that most appraisal criteria were operationalized by a single feature. A hierarchical analysis, partialling out the VALENCE superfactor and resubmitting the residual appraisal features to a subsequent factor analysis, revealed that the underlying appraisal structure can be best represented by seven factors, including the VALENCE APPRAISAL factor, to represent the 13 theoretically postulated appraisal criteria shown in Table 12.1 of Chapter 12.

The set of six factors obtained after partialling out VALENCE APPRAISAL showed little in the way of duplication of the overall structure–most importantly, the AROUSAL factor was absent and the factors are strongly focused on the eliciting event. The empirically found structure largely corresponds to the theoretical structure suggested by the CPM in terms of the logical interdependence of the appraisal criteria in the evaluation process. Furthermore, a detailed analysis of the factor loadings suggested that the grouping of features on a factor is likely to be, in part, determined by ecological correlations rather than conceptual overlap. All in all, it seems fair to conclude that the appraisal structure, in terms of one-to-one correspondence of factors, strongly contributes to the overall structure, especially in terms of VALENCE and to a lesser degree to NOVELTY, but does not completely duplicate it.

Action tendency component. Most of the work on this emotion component has been performed by Frijda and his collaborators (Frijda, 1986, 1987) and we have borrowed heavily from his work in selecting the items for this component (see Chapter 11). As Frijda has only provided a very high level structure, distinguishing appetitive from defensive action tendencies (see Chapter 11), our factor analyses were largely exploratory. As in the case of appraisal, we found a very strong superfactor which fits Frijda's proposed distinction rather well. In consequence, this superfactor is labeled DEFENSIVE VS APPETITIVE. Using the same strategy as in the case of the Appraisal component, partialling out the superfactor and running additional factor analyses, we identified two reliable subsidiary factors: DISENGAGEMENT VS INTERVENTION and SUBMIT VS ATTACK. Again, the internal structure of this component does not duplicate the overall structure. While the DEFENSIVE VS APPETITIVE superfactor bears resemblance to the overall VALENCE factor, appetitive tendencies being positive and defensive tendencies negative, it does have a distinctive motivational orientation. SUBMIT VS ATTACK and DISENGAGEMENT VS INTERVENTION both contribute to the overall POWER factor. The factorial solution we found shows interesting similarities to dimensional social interaction and personality models. Thus, Scholl (2013), in a large scale review of dimensional research about the perception of feelings, non-verbal and verbal communication, behavior, and personality, reveals in each domain three very similar dimensions: 1) general positive versus negative evaluation (e.g., happiness–disgust or friendliness–hostility); 2) a strong versus weak characterization (e.g., anger–fear or dominance–submission); and 3) an active versus passive impression (e.g., ecstasy–boredom or high-low arousability). The author suggests that these three dimensions might correspond to an evolutionary need for coordination between individuals.

Expression component. As we had been unable to find prior work on the factorial structure of this domain on a molecular level (individual facial movements and voice/speech qualities), we chose a number of expressions in both modalities that have been repeatedly studied in the expression literature and for which there are common expressions in natural language. The internal structure of these items was determined empirically–separately for facial and vocal expressions as we expected that domain-specific groupings would be masked if both modalities were combined (see Chapter 10). The factor analyses yielded the following factors for each modality: FROWN VS SMILE, JAW DROP/EYEBROWS UP, and EYES CLOSED/TEARS for the facial domain and VOCAL ENERGY and FIRM VS PERTURBED SPEECH for the vocal domain. The organization of these factors is unlikely to be generated by facial or vocal subsystems or mechanisms, as factors are based on elements from different substructures. In fact, it seems that elements of expression are grouped together that consistently co-occur in specific social situations and during certain emotional episodes: smiles during pleasant experiences or friendly contact; jaw drop and eyebrows up when encountering an unexpected object or event; closing the eyes and tears in the situation of loss; and high vocal energy in the case of emphasis or stances of dominance. These local expression factors additively contribute to the overall factors (to VALENCE and NOVELTY in the case of facial expression, and POWER and AROUSAL for vocal expression) and do not directly mirror the overall factors (as a duplication model would predict).

Bodily reaction component. In selecting the features to measure this emotion component we drew on elements of questionnaires used in earlier intercultural studies of emotion experiences. We expected to find a similar factor structure, reflecting some of the classic distinctions in autonomous nervous system (ANS) functioning and their respective signature patterns (see Chapter 9). This is indeed what we found: a three-factorial structure, which we labeled the factors as DISTRESS SYMPTOMS, AUTONOMIC AROUSAL, and BODY TEMPERATURE. The confirmation of the earlier cross-cultural results underlines the stability of the bodily reaction factor structure. The latter is completely different from the overall structure, being mainly determined by differences in the activation of different subsystems of the ANS. Thus, again, the emotion component factors for this emotion component seem to additively contribute to the overall structure (AUTONOMIC AROUSAL to overall AROUSAL, DISTRESS SYMPTOMS to overall POWER, and BODY TEMPERATURE to overall VALENCE), but do not duplicate it.

Feeling component. This component comes closest to a duplication of the overall structure, as the overall VALENCE, POWER, and AROUSAL factors are clearly discernible in the adopted four-factorial feeling structure (see Chapter 8). This is a direct consequence of our selection of features to be included for this component on the basis of the major contributions to the literature (see Chapter 8). There are two exceptions to this overall fit: 1) the overall AROUSAL factor is represented by two separate feeling factors: CALM VS RESTLESS and TIRED. A similar distinction has been proposed and empirically demonstrated by other researchers in the domain of feeling research (e.g., Thayer, 1989). In the GRID data set, it emerges in the Feeling component only; as it is not sufficiently supported by similar distinctions in other components to affect the overall factor structure accordingly. 2) The overall factor NOVELTY does not have an equivalent in the Feeling component ratings. This is entirely due to our not having included items designed to measure this dimension. As described above, we followed the rule of choosing only features firmly established in the literature, which, in the case of affective feelings, has so far recognized only three dimensions. NOVELTY was first proposed as an important overall factor on the basis of our own preliminary work with the GRID instrument (Fontaine et. al., 2007). Apart from these two differences, the internal structure of the Feeling component comes closest among the components to the overall structure. This close correspondence confirms the plausibility of the assumption that the Feeling component consists of an integrated representation of the changes occurring in all other components, and serves monitoring functions.

In conclusion, we note that the internal structures of all components, with the exception of feeling, are inherent in the components' nature and function and do not prefigure or duplicate the overall structure. This suggests that while there is direct correspondence between local component and overall structures in some cases, the bulk of the evidence supports an additive contribution model.

For three emotion components, there is a VALENCE superfactor although in each case the VALENCE takes a distinct form: for appraisal, we observe as many types of valences as there are major appraisal criteria, for Action tendencies, VALENCE is represented by APPETITIVE VS DEFENSIVE motivation, and for feeling, VALENCE is captured by the distinction between positive vs negative feeling states.

The Feeling component is special in that it comes closest to the four-dimensional overall structure. This is expected as this component provides a central conscious representation of the other emotion components, which is subsequently categorized and labeled to make meaning out of the experienced emotional episode. Yet there are major differences too and the overall dimensions cannot be considered as simple duplicates or instantiations of the dimensions in the Feeling component. On the contrary, as we saw in Chapter 7, the overall dimensions are firmly and reliably anchored in a wide diversity of synchronized changes pertaining to all five components, not just the emergent feeling, and they provide a much more comprehensive and a much richer reflection of the meaning of the emotion words as lexical encapsulations of emotion episodes.

13.2 How well are the overall factors predicted by emotion component factors?

In this section, we evaluate how well each of the four overall factors are predicted by the emotion component factors. In contrast to the previous section where we focused on emotion components, in this section we focus on the overall factors, discussing each of them in detail. Table 13.1 summarizes the results of the regression analyses reported in the emotion component chapters (Chapters 8 to 12). The table shows the results of regressing *the emotion component factors (shown in rows) separately* on each overall factor computed without including the respective emotion component features for greater independence (shown in columns). If one uses an arbitrary cutoff point of 50% ($R^2 = 0.50$) for the percentage of variance accounted for in the overall factors by the emotion component factors in the respective components, the results can be summarized as follows (excluding the Feeling component as the features were chosen in such a way as to represent the overall factors, as recalled above): 1) the overall VALENCE factor is extremely well predicted by all components except vocal expression (the percentage accounted for generally exceeding 90%). This shows that each of the components reflects valenced reactions. 2) The overall POWER factor is reasonably well predicted (60–70%), mostly by the Action tendency and the vocal part of the Expression component. 3) Neither the overall AROUSAL nor the overall NOVELTY factor is well predicted by any of the emotion component factors (the best prediction being achieved by AUTONOMIC AROUSAL for the overall AROUSAL factor).

To complement the analyses, we computed stepwise regressions of *all emotion component factors together* on each of the four overall factors. The results are shown in Table 13.2. The table lists, separately for each overall factor, which additional emotion component factors (in the order of entry) were automatically entered into the model until the cutoff criterion of R^2 change of at least 0.03 was reached. It should be noted that these regressions do not represent an independent prediction as the overall factor scores here were necessarily based on all 142 items, as well as the emotion component features on which the emotion component factors (used as predictors) were computed. Given the large number of features, this is the only way in which the relative predictive validity of the emotion component factors can be directly compared. While the results are useful for the purpose of illustrative comparison, they cannot be used as exact estimates.

As shown in the preceding section of this chapter, the overall VALENCE factor is very successfully predicted with factors from all emotion components, with the exception of vocal expression. However, as shown in Table 13.2 the appraisal superfactor VALENCE APPRAISAL *alone* is sufficient to predict the overall VALENCE factor with a level of explained variance of over 90% ($R^2 = 0.92$). Only

Table 13.1 Summary of the regression analyses of the emotion component factors on the four overall factors

	VALENCE	POWER	AROUSAL	NOVELTY
Appraisal component factors				
VALENCE APPRAISAL	***			
NOVELTY/CHANCE CAUSE			*	*
COPING ABILITY				*
EXPECTED/FAMILIAR			*	
GOAL RELEVANCE				*
NORM VIOLATION				
SELF VS OTHER CAUSE				
R²	0.91	0.16	0.26	0.36
Action tendency component factors				
DEFENSIVE/APPETITIVE	***	*		
DISENGAGEMENT/INTERVENTION		**	*	
SUBMIT VS ATTACK	*	***		
R²	0.91	0.73	0.07	0.03
Facial expression component factors				
FROWN VS SMILE	***			
JAW DROP/EYEBROWS UP			**	**
EYES CLOSED/TEARS		***		
R²	0.90	0.44	0.15	0.31
Vocal expression component factors				
VOCAL ENERGY		***	**	*
FIRM VS PERTURBED SPEECH	**	**	**	
R²	0.35	0.64	0.44	0.09
Bodily reaction component factors				
DISTRESS SYMPTOMS	*	***	*	*
AUTONOMIC AROUSAL	**	*	***	
BODY TEMPERATURE	***		*	*
R²	0.70	0.49	0.46	0.11
Feeling component factors				
BAD VS GOOD	***			
WEAK VS STRONG		***		
CALM VS RESTLESS			**	
TIRED		*	**	
R²	0.91	0.66	0.52	0.01

Note: symbols representing size of beta coefficients: * $\beta > |0.20|$, ** $\beta > |0.40|$, *** $\beta > |0.60|$.

Table 13.2 Summary of the regression analyses of overall factors on emotion component factors

Overall factors	Emotion component factor	ΔR^2	R^2	β
VALENCE	VALENCE APPRAISAL (appraisal)	0.92		0.91
	SUBMIT VS ATTACK (action tendency)	0.04	0.96	−0.20
POWER	EYES CLOSED/TEARS (facial expression)	0.52		−0.22
	SUBMIT VS ATTACK (action tendency)	0.22		0.44
	DISENGAGEMENT VS INTERVENTION (action tendency)	0.11		0.22
	DISTRESS SYMPTOMS (bodily reaction)	0.07		−0.33
	VOCAL ENERGY (vocal expression)	0.03	0.95	0.22
AROUSAL	AUTONOMIC AROUSAL (bodily reaction)	0.57		0.83
	BODY TEMPERATURE (bodily reaction)	0.23		0.47
	DISTRESS SYMPTOMS (bodily reaction)	0.09		0.25
	SUBMIT VS ATTACK (action tendency)	0.05	0.93	−0.23
NOVELTY	NOVELTY/CHANCE CAUSE (appraisal)	0.60		0.54
	JAW DROP/EYEBROWS UP (facial expression)	0.08		0.37
	DISENGAGEMENT VS INTERVENTION (action tendency)	0.11		−0.42
	SELF VS OTHER CAUSATION (appraisal)	0.04		0.18
	EYES CLOSED/TEARS (facial expression)	0.03	0.86	−0.19

Note: predictor factors were entered into the table as long $\Delta R^2 \geq 0.03$.

one additional factor is added, the action tendency factor SUBMIT VS ATTACK, which adds only 4% to the variance explained. In contrast, it takes five factors from different emotion components to reach a comparable level of explained variance for the POWER factor ($R^2 = 0.95$). All of these predictors make a contribution of approximately comparable size as shown by the beta coefficients (strength of contribution of a predictor in the regression model), which vary between 0.22 and 0.44 in absolute size. The most important contribution is due to the action tendency SUBMIT VS ATTACK, even though it is not the first to enter the model (it follows the facial expression factor EYES CLOSED/TEARS which has a lower beta value once all predictors are in the model). As described above, the overall AROUSAL factor is strongly predicted by the body reaction factor AUTONOMIC AROUSAL accounting for 60% of the variance by itself and maintaining a very high beta coefficient (followed by the body reaction factor BODY TEMPERATURE). Finally, overall NOVELTY prediction is largely due to the NOVELTY APPRAISAL, which accounts by itself for 60% of the variance, but is closely followed by the facial expression factor JAW DROP/EYEBROWS UP and the action tendency factor DISENGAGEMENT VS INTERVENTION, which reach beta coefficients of similar size. In consequence, except in the case of overall POWER, some components seem to provide a particularly strong contribution to certain overall factors, appraisal to overall VALENCE and overall NOVELTY, and bodily reaction to overall AROUSAL.

Given the general assumption in the underlying theory (CPM) that appraisal drives the reaction patterns in the other emotion components one might wonder why the appraisal factors did not show a stronger effect in predicting the overall factors. The main reason is that the effect of appraisal on the overall factors is likely to be mediated by its effects on other components. As shown in Figure 1.1 of Chapter 1, the assumption is that the appraisal process triggers a chain of sequential-cumulative reactions in several other components which are then centrally integrated. It is thus possible that one of the appraisal-caused changes in one of the components is strongly weighted in the integration process and thus obtains a better proximal prediction for an overall factor. Another reason is that, as mentioned in Chapter 12, combination of appraisal check results might produce an efferent effect in a configurational fashion, rather than having a direct linear effect. As our regression analyses only contain the main effects of the appraisal factors and no interactions, such configurational nonlinear effects will not show up in our results. We will return to this issue in the next section.

13.3 Classification of emotion terms through discriminant analysis

In this part of the chapter, we present a series of analyses that are designed to understand how the 24 emotion terms in the GRID study can be differentiated in a way that ensures both high accuracy and reasonable economy with respect to the number of predictors. We first examine the MDA solution for all 22 emotion component factors that have been identified in the preceding chapters as predictors. This is followed by a systematic comparison of the classification hit rates with MDA solutions based on either features or factors as predictors, both separately per emotion component and across emotion components. We then inquire into the possibility of empirically identifying a small set of "best" predictors among the emotion component factors. In this case, we discuss details of the MDA parameters that provide interesting leads on the accurate recognition of specific emotions. In the next step, we examine the stepwise contributions of different emotion components (represented by their emotion component factors) to accurately classify and examine the degree of fit with theoretical explanations. To conclude, we turn to the role of the four overall factors in differentiating the emotions, first showing the positions of the 24 terms in the four-dimensional space and then investigating the role of each overall factor in classification using MDA techniques.

Discrimination based on emotion component factors. The viability of our proposal to measure the semantics of emotion words by profiles of component features can be assessed by the respective success of discriminating the 24 emotion words on the basis of these profiles. As demonstrated in Chapters 8 to 12, the GRID paradigm fares extremely well on this challenge on a component by component basis. After having identified the internal structures of each emotion component and having computed the scores for the emotion component factors, we can now enter *all of the 22 emotion component factors together* into an MDA to determine the degree of classification accuracy that can be obtained on the basis of the emotion component factor predictors. The results in Table 13.3 show a high degree of classification success with an overall accuracy hit rate of 78.8% (cross-validated), which compares extremely favourably with the hit rate based on all 142 features of 82.1%, given that the latter is based on a much larger number of predictors and thus provides much richer information (see Chapter 7). The small number of confusions that do occur represent mainly within-family confusions. These results suggest that the component factors capture most of the information.

Summary of discriminant analyses. Table 13.4 summarizes the cross-validated accuracy percentages for all discriminant analyses reported in this part of the volume, based on the individual features and on the factors extracted for each of the emotion components and the overall set of features. Surprisingly the feature sets in the individual components (set size ranging from 18 to 40 items) allowed successful classification at a rate of 60–70%, which is quite extraordinary given the chance level of 4.2% (1/24). This hit rate compares also rather favourably with the hit rate of 82.1%

Table 13.3 Classification accuracy (in percent) for the 24 emotion words in discriminant analyses based on all 22 and the 10 best predicting emotion component factors

Emotion words	Classification based on 22 emotion component factors	Classification based on the 10 best predicting emotion component factors	
	Accuracy	Accuracy	Confusion > 15% with
being hurt	73.5	52.9	
sadness	97.1	85.3	
shame	88.2	88.2	
guilt	91.2	88.2	
compassion	88.2	91.2	
disappointment	85.3	73.5	
love	97.1	94.1	
contentment	67.6	67.6	
happiness	32.4	41.2	joy
pride	88.2	91.2	
pleasure	61.8	55.9	joy
joy	64.7	67.6	
interest	88.2	91.2	
surprise	100	100	
despair	67.6	67.6	
stress	85.3	79.4	
anxiety	67.6	52.9	stress, fear
fear	91.2	94.1	
jealousy	97.1	91.2	
hate	76.5	85.3	
irritation	50.0	44.1	anger
anger	67.6	64.7	irritation
disgust	85.3	73.5	
contempt	79.4	79.4	
Total	78.8	75.9	

obtained by entering the complete set of features across all components, that is, all 142 items, as predictors. These results suggest a high degree of redundancy of the information differentiating emotional meaning across the features in the different components. This seems consistent with our theoretical assumption that modal emotion episodes, labeled with specific words, tend to consist of experiential episodes with a high degree of synchronization among the components driven by appraisal results. For example, if the appraisal results encourage the preparation of an avoidance reaction, the type of ensuing synchronization of the autonomic nervous system and the motor expression system might well express shared aspects of affective meaning.

Table 13.4 Summary of classification accuracy (in percent) in discriminant analyses per emotion component and across emotion components with feature and factor scores

Component features/ factors	Number of features	Accuracy based on feature scores	Number of factors	Accuracy based on factor scores
Appraisal	31	70.7	7	56.3
Action tendency	40	67.6	3	46.1
Expression	21	71.6	5	57.0
Bodily reaction	18	62.4	3	45.1
Feeling	19	58.5	4	47.2
All emotion components	129	82.5	22	78.8
All emotion features	142	82.1	4	69.4

Table 13.4 also provides an answer to the question to what extent the emotion component *factors* (ranging from three to seven factors) capture the essential information in the respective emotion component *features* (ranging from 18 to 40 items): on average, the hit rate drops by only 15%. This is quite astounding, given the drastic reduction in the number of predictors from approximately 25 to around 5 +/−2 per component. This again confirms that the emotion component factors capture the essential emotion differentiating information in each of the components. On the level of the complete instrument, the hit rate of 78.8% obtained with the 22 emotion component factors compares to a hit rate of 69.4% obtained by entering the *four overall factors* as predictors. The latter figure is quite remarkable given the reduction in the number of predictors (from 22 to 4). It points again to a fairly high degree of redundancy among the component factors.

Set of best predictors. One would like to know which of the emotion components (and of the factors within these components) make a stronger contribution to accurate classification than others. To this end, we computed a discriminant analysis using stepwise entry of the 22 emotion component factors and deciding on a cutoff point in terms of the additional variance explained with the entry of each new factor into the model. This is only an approximate method to decide on the relative importance of predictors as the sequence of entry may be affected by sampling error and by multi-collinearity in the dataset. Adopting a cutoff criterion of approximately 1% of added variance, either nine or ten emotion component factors could be reasonably chosen under this criterion (the ambiguity being due to instability at the cutoff point in the stepwise entry procedure with earlier predictors removed and then reentered). We decided that the safest procedure was to choose the solution with ten emotion component factors (which the regression algorithm entered into the model in the following order): VALENCE APPRAISAL (appraisal); SUBMIT VS ATTACK (action tendency); EYES CLOSED/TEARS and JAW DROP/EYEBROWS UP (facial expressions); AUTONOMIC AROUSAL, DISTRESS SYMPTOMS, and TEMPERATURE (bodily reactions); and, SELF VS OTHER CAUSATION, NOVELTY APPRAISAL, and NORM VIOLATION (appraisals).

These ten factors were then used as the "best" predictor set in a new MDA, yielding 75.9% correct classification after cross-validation (the hit rates for the 24 emotions and the most frequent confusions are shown in Table 13.3). This result is remarkable for two reasons: 1) despite a reduction of the predictor factor set from 22 to 10, the hit rate drops by less than 3%, again pointing to a certain amount of redundancy in the information in the different components, and 2) all of the components, except feeling, are represented among this set of best predictors. This shows that despite a certain degree of redundancy, the unique information provided by specific components is required to define the meaning of the emotion terms in sufficient detail for correct classification. Most likely the Feeling component factors (the only component not represented in the set) are not required because of the important point made earlier in this section, namely that the Feeling component is already an integration of changes that occur in the other emotion components and is thus completely determined by the latter (this is also the reason why the internal feeling structure comes closest to a duplication of the overall factors).

We now examine some of the detailed parameters in the MDA with the 10 best predictors in order to better understand the bases for the emotion classification by this predictor set. The structure matrix is shown in Table 13.5. The structure matrix represents the correlations between the discriminant functions (which are linear combinations of the 10 predictors) that maximally differentiate the emotion terms and each of the 10 predictors. Table 13.6 shows, for each of these functions, the mean score per emotion term (also called "centroid" in MDA). This information allows seeing which emotions have similar values on a specific function and are thus grouped together. For example, the first column in Table 13.6 shows a clear separation between positive and negative emotions. Consistently, function 1 can be described as a "VALENCE distinction function," an inference which is supported by the high correlation of the VALENCE appraisal factor. The correlations in Table 13.5, which were used to interpret the respective functions, are shown in bold.

Importantly, four of the ten best predictors are appraisal factors. Two of these define functions that are directly related to two of the overall factors, functions 1 and 4. Function 1 represents the

Table 13.5 Structure matrix in discriminant analysis with the 10 best predicting emotion component factors

Component factors	Functions									
	1	2	3	4	5	6	7	8	9	10
VALENCE APPRAISAL (appraisal)	**0.88**	−0.06	−0.07	0.05	0.12	−0.32	0.00	0.25	−0.06	0.20
SUBMIT VS ATTACK (action tendencies)	−0.11	**0.71**	0.02	−0.24	0.34	0.11	−0.34	0.42	−0.01	−0.04
EYES CLOSED/TEARS (facial expression)	−0.08	**−0.49**	0.07	−0.20	**0.47**	0.44	−0.16	0.14	−0.46	0.21
NOVELTY APPRAISAL (appraisal)	0.02	0.03	0.18	**0.58**	0.21	0.44	−0.41	−0.24	0.39	0.15
SELF VS OTHER CAUSATION (appraisal)	0.02	0.19	**0.39**	−0.04	0.19	0.25	**0.82**	0.10	0.09	0.14
NORM VIOLATION (appraisal)	0.00	0.14	−0.03	0.12	**−0.54**	0.23	−0.08	**0.72**	−0.12	0.28
JAW DROP/EYEBROWS UP (facial expression)	0.04	0.14	0.19	**0.52**	0.32	0.19	0.00	−0.15	**−0.71**	−0.03
AUTONOMIC AROUSAL (bodily reaction)	−0.17	0.28	**−0.48**	0.32	0.19	0.09	0.13	−0.29	−0.14	**0.64**
DISTRESS SYMPTOMS (bodily reaction)	−0.18	−0.31	−0.04	0.29	**0.41**	0.00	0.01	**0.53**	−0.06	**−0.58**
BODY TEMPERATURE (bodily reaction)	0.32	0.04	**−0.44**	0.16	0.36	0.43	0.02	0.28	−0.13	**−0.52**

Note: correlations used to interpret the discriminant function are in bold.

Table 13.6 Emotion word centroids in discriminant analysis with the 10 best predicting emotion component factors

Emotion words	Functions									
	1	**2**	**3**	**4**	**5**	**6**	**7**	**8**	**9**	**10**
being hurt	−3.4	−0.7	1.9	−0.7	0.5	0.7	0.3	0.2	−0.2	0.3
sadness	−3.5	−3.6	3.0	−1.9	0.5	0.2	−0.6	0.0	0.5	−0.1
shame	−2.1	−2.4	−3.1	0.2	−1.2	2.2	−0.4	−0.1	0.2	−0.2
guilt	−2.4	−3.3	−3.1	0.0	−2.3	−0.7	−0.8	0.1	−0.8	0.3
compassion	1.1	−3.6	2.3	−0.7	−1.3	0.2	1.8	−1.0	0.2	0.3
disappointment	−3.0	−0.7	3.5	−0.4	−0.7	0.4	−0.3	0.1	−0.5	−0.1
love	5.3	−2.6	−2.5	−0.5	0.9	0.1	2.6	0.5	−0.3	−0.2
contentment	6.4	−0.4	0.8	−1.7	−0.3	−0.4	−0.9	0.2	0.5	−0.3
happiness	6.9	−0.6	0.3	−0.2	1.0	0.6	−0.4	0.1	−0.3	0.1
pride	4.7	1.6	−0.8	−1.8	0.2	−1.6	−1.4	0.0	−0.2	0.3
pleasure	6.6	−0.3	−0.7	−0.3	0.6	0.8	−0.3	0.8	0.1	−0.3
joy	6.7	0.1	0.3	0.4	1.0	0.5	−0.6	−0.4	0.0	0.5
interest	4.9	1.8	0.7	2.3	−2.8	−1.2	0.1	−0.8	0.2	−0.3
surprise	1.8	2.4	2.3	5.1	0.2	0.8	0.2	0.4	−0.1	0.1
despair	−3.6	−2.1	1.0	−0.4	0.7	−0.5	−0.9	−0.1	−0.4	−0.4
stress	−3.2	−0.5	−2.2	0.7	0.6	−0.9	−0.1	−0.2	1.0	0.2
anxiety	−3.3	−1.5	−1.9	1.9	0.4	−1.0	0.2	0.2	0.3	0.0
fear	−3.7	−2.0	−0.3	2.7	2.0	−1.1	−0.4	0.1	−0.2	−0.1
jealousy	−1.7	3.0	−0.1	−1.5	1.6	−1.1	1.0	−1.3	−0.4	−0.2
hate	−3.1	3.8	−1.1	−1.7	0.2	0.0	0.7	0.8	0.0	0.1
irritation	−2.8	3.1	−1.0	−0.3	0.0	1.4	−0.3	−0.8	0.3	0.0
anger	−2.8	3.7	−1.5	−0.2	0.2	1.5	−0.5	−0.6	−0.2	−0.1
disgust	−3.5	1.1	1.3	0.5	−0.2	−0.3	0.1	0.8	0.1	0.0
contempt	−2.2	3.6	0.8	−1.5	−1.7	−0.6	0.8	1.1	0.1	0.0

strong VALENCE superfactor (separating the positive from the negative emotions; as shown in column 1 of Table 13.5). Function 4 is defined by NOVELTY APPRAISAL (together with the consequent facial expressions JAW DROP/EYEBROWS UP; separating surprise, fear, anxiety, and interest from the other emotions in column 4). The SELF VS OTHER CAUSATION appraisal factor defines function 3 (together with cold BODY TEMPERATURE and low AUTONOMIC AROUSAL; separating self-reflective emotions from those in which other persons tend to cause the event) and function 7 (separating love and compassion from the other emotions). The NORM VIOLATION appraisal factor defines function 8 (separating contempt, disgust, and hate from the other emotions). Function 10 combines all Bodily reaction component factors, and is obviously related to AROUSAL, but the emotion differentiation is difficult to explain by the patterns in the centroid values. However, the fact that all three body factors entered in the stepwise discrimination suggests that these predictors play an important role, possibly in the fine-grained discrimination within emotion families. Functions 5 and 6 are difficult to interpret in a straightforward fashion.

Function 2 is particularly interesting because it is related to the overall POWER factor as defined here by the action tendency SUBMIT VS ATTACK (together with absence of CLOSED EYES/TEARS; separating emotions with high perceived coping potential from those where the outcome is more uncertain).

Appraisal is not directly involved here (the COPING POTENTIAL factor did not enter the group of the ten best predictors), probably due to the fact, documented in detail in Chapter 12, that the POWER factor is particularly sensitive to interactions between different appraisal checks, requiring configurational interaction analysis (rather than the linear analysis of main effects used here). However, as mentioned in Chapter 12, the definition and computation of variables measuring these configurations in future research may well allow showing the effect of appraisal on the POWER factor. To illustrate this approach for the present case, we attempted to predict the SUBMIT VS ATTACK action tendency with a set of four appraisal factors (i.e., VALENCE, confirmed expectations, norm violation, and self vs other causation). The stepwise regression procedure produced a model with all four of these factors (all yielding significant contributions), with equivalent strength (beta weights around 0.25) and an R^2 of 0.22. This suggests that appraisal is also involved in this potency-related discriminant function, most likely mediated by the emergence of the action tendency of attacking, together with situational context factors. As mentioned in the preamble to this chapter, the detailed analysis of the myriad of interactions between appraisal variables that are possible and meaningful require further hypothesis development, assisted by the current results, and need to be addressed in further work.

Although no direct causal inferences are possible on the basis of our data on the meaning of emotion words, the results obtained with the set of ten best predictors (especially the large number of Appraisal component factors in the set) are highly compatible with our central theoretical proposal–the notion that the appraisal results drive and synchronize the changes in all other components.

Cumulative analysis of emotion component contributions. To further examine the role of appraisal in defining the meaning of emotion terms, we ran a series of cumulative MDAs, adding one emotion component after another based on the theoretical assumptions shown in Figure 1.1 of Chapter 1. The sequence prediction holds that appraisal results first produce specific pattern changes in action tendencies (adaptive reactions to relevant events) and in the Expression and Bodily reaction components. The exact sequence and interactions between these components are not theoretically specified, as they probably consist of a series of recursive adjustments. Finally, the Feeling component should be modified as a result of all preceding modifications because it is expected to integrate the synchronized changes in the other components (and allow access to conscious awareness of an emotion episode). In line with this theoretical prediction, we decided to enter the Appraisal component first, then the Action tendency component, followed by the combined Expression and the Bodily reaction components, as it can be argued that action tendencies lead to physiological preparation and expressive signals (however, it is also possible that bodily symptoms and expressions occur spontaneously and at least partly independently of action tendencies). The Feeling component was entered last.

The results are shown in Table 13.7. In the first step of the successive MDAs, the Appraisal component features alone reached a hit rate of 70.7%. Including action tendencies added 4.7% to the total cross-validated accuracy (effect on individual emotions: the hit rates for being hurt, anger,

Table 13.7 Classification accuracy (in percent) and change in classification accuracy in discriminant analyses with a theory-based sequential entry of emotion component features

Emotion words	Accuracy and change in accuracy				
	Only appraisal features	Plus action tendency features	Plus bodily reaction and expression features	Plus feeling features	All emotion component features
being hurt	61.8	**14.7**	2.9	5.9	85.3
sadness	79.4	−2.9	5.9	**14.7**	97.1
shame	91.2	0.0	0.0	0.0	91.2
guilt	88.2	3.0	2.9	0.0	94.1
compassion	85.3	5.9	2.9	0.0	94.1
disappointment	67.6	8.9	**11.7**	0.0	88.2
love	91.2	2.9	3.0	0.0	97.1
contentment	52.9	3.0	**17.6**	0.0	73.5
happiness	47.1	**−11.8**	−2.9	2.9	35.3
pride	94.1	0.0	0.0	0.0	94.1
pleasure	52.9	0.0	**14.7**	0.0	67.6
joy	47.1	−5.9	8.8	−5.9	44.1
interest	88.2	5.9	3.0	0.0	97.1
surprise	94.1	5.9	0.0	0.0	100.0
despair	79.4	3.0	5.8	5.9	94.1
stress	73.5	5.9	5.9	5.9	91.2
anxiety	50.0	8.8	3.0	5.8	67.6
fear	85.3	2.9	5.9	3.0	97.1
jealousy	88.2	0.0	0.0	0.0	88.2
hate	70.6	−3.0	8.9	2.9	79.4
irritation	38.2	8.9	**14.7**	2.9	64.7
anger	32.4	**29.4**	−5.9	**14.7**	70.6
disgust	67.6	8.9	**11.7**	0.0	88.2
contempt	70.6	**17.6**	0.0	−5.8	82.4
Total	70.7	4.7	5.0	2.2	82.5

Note: change in accuracy larger than 10% in bold.

and contempt rise disproportionately). The bodily reactions and the facial and vocal expressions further added 5% (with love, contentment, pleasure, irritation, and disgust benefitting). Finally, including the Feeling component features to the prediction set adds only an additional 2.2% (with anger and sadness profiting) to attain the total of 82.5%.

Obviously, the exact numbers of the percentage accuracy added with each step must be interpreted with care. Given the redundancy between components that we have demonstrated in this chapter, it automatically follows that whatever component will be entered first will show the highest percentage of classification success, with ever declining percentage amounts for each successive step. If the Feeling component would be entered first and the Appraisal component last, the picture would be quite different. This would indeed be the case for any order chosen. However, testing all possible orders of entry would seem quite meaningless as it is extremely unlikely that, for example, the Feeling component precedes the Appraisal component. While the stepwise procedure reported here cannot be used to empirically establish the relative importance of a component for classification success, it serves to illustrate what the relative contribution of each component might be if the theoretically suggested sequence of effects were correct. This remains to be shown in future experimental work.

Cumulative analysis of overall factor contributions. The three-dimensional plots shown in Figures 13.1 and 13.2 illustrate the distribution of the 24 emotion terms in the four-dimensional space spanned by the overall factors. We have performed a similar series of successive or cumulative MDA analyses with these four overall factor predictors of the 24 emotion terms, to estimate the respective contribution of each of the factors. As reported in Chapter 7, using only those four overall factors to classify the terms results in a cross-validated hit rate of 69.4%, which, quite surprisingly, is only about 10% less than the hit rate obtained with all 142 items.

The results of the cumulative MDAs are shown in Table 13.8. In the first step, the VALENCE factor alone reached a hit rate of 24%, showing that, while VALENCE is very important, it is not very useful for discrimination of emotion terms. Entering the POWER factor into the model added 20.4% to the

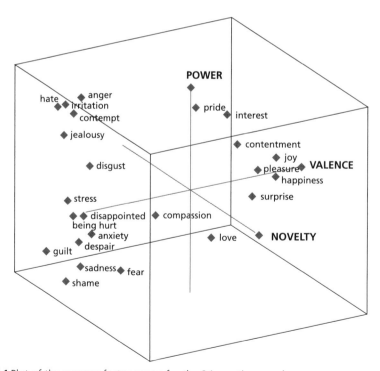

Figure 13.1 Plot of the average factor scores for the 24 emotion words on VALENCE, POWER, and NOVELTY.

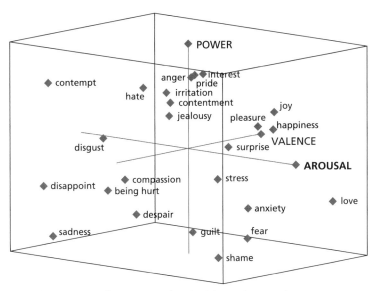

Figure 13.2 Plot of the average factor scores for the 24 emotion words on VALENCE, POWER, and AROUSAL.

total accuracy hit rate; entering the AROUSAL FACTOR further added 15%, and the NOVELTY factor finally added another 10%. As expected, the order of entry and the size of the contribution to the hit rate reflect the proportion of variance accounted for by the respective factors in the original factor analysis (see Chapter 7). Nevertheless, it is instructive to see how important the respective factors are for the correct classification of individual emotions. Most of the 24 emotions rose sizably in their hit rate once the POWER factor was added. The same is true when the AROUSAL factor is added; interestingly, disappointment and contentment had a major increase of hit rate increase at this point. Upon the entry of the NOVELTY factor, there is a particularly strong rise for the emotions of pride and interest. In both of these emotions, the respective factors may help to disambiguate the clouds of positive emotions for which POWER differences do not play a major role. However, there is little further increase in accuracy for surprise—the prediction is already very good after the second step, much before the NOVELTY dimension is entered in the fourth step. Most likely, this can be explained, as in the preceding analysis, by the fact that surprise is located in a mid-position on the VALENCE factor.

As a final illustration of the analyses reported in this section, we provide, in Figures 13.3 and 13.4, the profiles on both the 21 component factor scores and the four overall factor scores for the five emotions that are most frequently studied. These five emotions are generally considered as "basic" emotions, supposed to represent quintessential representatives of a universal emotion system. The graphs allow us to obtain a quick overview of the major similarities and differences between these emotions on the structures we have identified in this section.

Overall, expressing all due caveats about the inappropriateness of drawing causal inferences from our data, we suggest that the findings from this series of successive MDAs provide *indirect* support, in the sense of suggesting high plausibility, for the theoretical claim that appraisal checks

Table 13.8 Classification accuracy and change in classification accuracy in discriminant analyses with a sequential entry of the four overall factors

Emotion words	Accuracy and change in accuracy				
	VALENCE	**Plus POWER**	**Plus AROUSAL**	**Plus NOVELTY**	**Four overall factors**
being hurt	17.6	8.9	8.8	5.9	41.2
sadness	11.8	**38.2**	**26.5**	5.9	82.4
shame	35.3	**11.8**	**23.5**	8.8	79.4
guilt	67.6	**−11.7**	**20.6**	**20.6**	97.1
compassion	26.5	**35.3**	**20.6**	−3	79.4
disappointment	8.8	3	**61.7**	3	76.5
love	11.8	**79.4**	0	5.9	97.1
contentment	26.5	**−11.8**	**52.9**	0	67.6
happiness	61.8	−3	0	0	58.8
pride	20.6	**11.8**	0	**50**	82.4
pleasure	2.9	3	**11.7**	**20.6**	38.2
joy	11.8	*32.3*	*17.7*	5.8	67.6
interest	55.9	−3	−8.8	**35.3**	79.4
surprise	47.1	**38.2**	8.8	5.9	100
despair	8.8	**41.2**	**−11.8**	−2.9	35.3
stress	20.6	**38.2**	**11.8**	0	70.6
anxiety	17.6	5.9	0	**26.5**	50
fear	8.8	**29.4**	**29.4**	**14.8**	82.4
jealousy	8.8	**58.8**	0	5.9	73.5
hate	11.8	0	**23.5**	**32.3**	67.6
irritation	58.8	**−41.2**	3	−8.8	11.8
anger	2.9	**58.9**	5.8	0	67.6
disgust	11.8	**64.7**	**11.7**	5.9	94.1
contempt	20.6	0	**44.1**	0	64.7
Total	24	**20.4**	**15**	**10**	69.4

Note: change in accuracy larger than 10% in bold.

trigger the elicitation and drive the differentiation of emotional states–and encourage the assumption that this process may be partially mirrored in the semantic profiles of emotion words. By far the greatest amount of variance explained is due to the profile of appraisal results, leaving only little room for independent effects in other components. Not surprisingly, the central causal role of appraisal underlying the differentiation of emotion episodes, and also the labels used to refer to them, as a consequence, is now accepted by the large majority of emotion theorists (including discrete or basic emotion theorists, see Ekman, 2004).

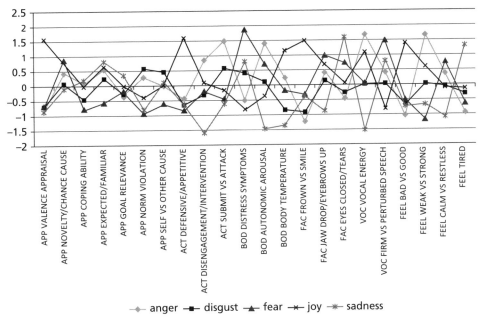

Figure 13.3 Profiles on emotion component factors for five "basic" emotions (APP, appraisal; ACT, action tendencies; BOD, bodily reaction; FAC, facial expression; VOC, vocal expression; FEEL, feeling).

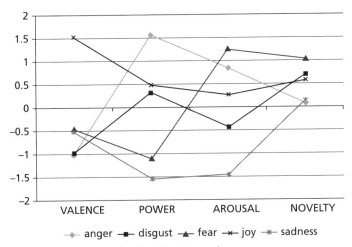

Figure 13.4 Profiles on overall factors for five "basic" emotions.

13.4 **Conclusions**

This concludes the overview of the major empirical findings of the GRID study across all 34 data-sets from 27 countries covering a total of 24 different languages and provides a first opportunity to take stock. With respect to the issues discussed and the questions posed in Part I of this volume, the results of the first wave of analysis of the massive data set collected in this study, suggest the following conclusions:

- the judgments of the 142 GRID features representing the five components of emotion show a high level of agreement between judges in the different language communities and across the different cultures studied. This suggests that semantic profiles of major (translationally equivalent) emotion words are shared in a stable fashion within and across many different cultures

- the data from 27 countries with 24 different languages clearly replicate a preliminary finding with the GRID instrument in three Western countries (Fontaine et al., 2007) showing that the emotional space, as established on the basis of the similarities between the profile based on all 142 items, spans four dimensions—VALENCE, POWER, AROUSAL, and NOVELTY—in this order of importance

- separate factor analyses for each component show a unique dimensional structure for each emotion component, adapted to the specific function of the component in the emotion episode

- regression analyses show that the emotion component factors differentially contribute to, and allow partial prediction of, the overall factors without duplicating or mirroring the overall structure

- in addition to the specificity of the contribution of each component to the overall structure, there is a certain degree of redundancy of emotion specific information across the components

- using the semantic profiles based on all 142 semantic features the 24 emotion words can be correctly differentiated (in an automatic classification by MDA) to more than 80%

- due to the partial redundancy of information available in different components, it is possible to differentiate the 24 emotion categories rather accurately by several emotion component factors in isolation—in particular on the basis of the Appraisal component. A combination of only the ten best predictors drawn from several components allows the differentiation of the categories with approximately 70% accuracy.

These results confirm a fundamental tenet of the GRID paradigm, which is that the semantics of emotion words can be best defined in a domain-specific way–that is by considering many aspects of all the emotion components that emotion episodes consist of. Obviously, definitions are free, and so other scientists may prefer different ways of defining meaning. However, one generally accepted requirement for the meaning of words is that it must be specific to the word in order to allow effective communication. Whatever definition of meaning one chooses, it must be possible to describe the specificities of word meanings with the elements of the architecture proposed by the definition. Consequently, this description must permit the differentiation of the words concerned on the basis of the elements of the definition. In this section, we have been able to demonstrate, in favour of our definition proposal, that feature profiles with representative items for all five major components of emotion do in fact allow a statistical discrimination and classification that exceeds 80% of accuracy in cross-validated MDAs. We believe that this exceptionally high hit rate, which vastly exceeds the chance level of 4.2%, still underestimates the capacity of component feature profiles to encapsulate the meaning of emotion terms and allow discrimination of them, reliably. As explained at the outset of this chapter, in this volume we have reported first descriptive and exploratory analyses of the rich data set constituted by the GRID study results. We feel confident that further theoretical, empirical, and methodological work will allow both us and groups of other researchers to go beyond what has been reported here, particularly with respect to the relationships between emotion components, the interactions between features, especially in the appraisal domain, and the use of multilevel and nonlinear analysis techniques.

In introducing the theoretical basis of the GRID paradigm in Chapter 1, we have pointed out that the three major theoretical traditions in emotion research, apart from differing with respect to the definition of emotion and the presumed nature of the underlying mechanism, disagree on the role assigned to the verbal labels of emotional experience. It has been suggested that basic emotion theories could be said to define the role of emotion terms as "program descriptors," constructivist theories to see them as "meaning constructors," and the CPM viewing emotion terms as "modality identifiers," that is, marking a frequently occurring multicomponent configuration (and synchronization) of appraisals and associated response patterns. As pointed out at the beginning of the chapter, the kind of data collected in the GRID study do not allow the drawing of any causal inferences with respect to the nature of the underlying mechanism, as only judgments on semantic profiles have been collected. However, if one accepts that emotion words are not sheer figments of imagination or culturally shared stereotypes without any kernel of truth, the findings reported here can be interpreted in terms of their compatibility with fundamental theoretical assumptions and their plausibility. Specifically, the following tentative conclusions concerning the disagreements between the three theoretical currents may be drawn from the results reported here:

- the similarity of semantic profiles across languages and cultures seem to point in the direction of a certain grounding of the semantics of emotion words in the underlying phenomena, suggesting that there are certain modal patterns of emotional experience that are relatively universal and that have comparable semantic markers
- the independent contributions of features from different components, confirm the notion that emotions have to be seen as multicomponential processes
- the redundancy of information across different components is compatible with the assumption that emotions emerge from a synchronization of specific subsystems
- the important role played by the Appraisal component in discriminating the emotions is compatible with the assumption that the synchronization is driven by the pattern of appraisal results.

Thus, apart from empirically confirming the utility and plausibility of the GRID paradigm to define the meaning of emotion terms in natural languages, the results reported in this section also help to advance the debate about some issues concerning the definition and the empirical study of emotion. Most importantly, however, the results reported in this section establish the GRID instrument as a comprehensive (given the findings on internal structures), reliable (given the strong agreement between judges), and valid (given the high accuracy of category differentiation) tool to measure semantic meaning. The remainder of the volume will explore the utility of the instrument as a tool in basic research on emotion processes, as an assessment of interesting differences in the meaning of major emotion words across languages and cultures that illustrate the important variation around the core of widely shared modal organization, and as a valid tool for a variety of applied uses.

13.5 **Outlook**

The focus of this third part of the book was to explore the meaning structure of emotion terms across samples, languages, and cultural groups for each of the emotion components. Therefore the cross-cultural aspect, which is one fundamental aspect of the GRID project, has not received much attention in this part. Cultural similarities and differences only explicitly played a part in the investigation of the stability of the factor structures. Still, the results of the present section do constrain the role of cultural and linguistic factors on the meaning structure of the emotion domain. The current results do not fit an extreme constructionist approach. For each of the components a stable structure emerged across four language groups, of which one is very different in nature from the other three, namely the East-Asian language family. Moreover, it was observed that between 70%

and 80% of the terms can be correctly classified based on their profile. We both observed a sizable stability in the meaning of the emotion features and as in the meaning of the emotion terms. This suggests that there is stability in the internal organization of the emotion domain, as well as in the subdomains the emotion terms refer to. These findings are compatible with the lexical sedimentation hypothesis, which states that salient characteristics of our emotional functioning have been encoded in similar ways across languages and cultural groups (see Chapter 1). The stability we found, however, is not incompatible with the existence of important and salient differences in the meaning of emotion terms and of emotion features. With the structures described in this section we have created an empirically validated set of reference points that allow us to look for and interpret cultural and linguistic differences. The chapters in the following parts will provide many examples of the possibilities to use the GRID paradigm to capture fine-grained differences in the meaning of emotion terms between languages and cultural groups.

Part IV

Psychological perspectives

Chapter 14

The new NOVELTY dimension: Method artifact or basic dimension in the cognitive structure of the emotion domain?

Johnny J. R. Fontaine[1] and Elke Veirman

The most surprising finding of the GRID project is the identification of a NOVELTY dimension (see Chapters 7 and 13). This dimension is predominantly defined by appraisals of unpredictability and suddenness, and facial expressions of a jaw drop and a wide opening of the eyes. Moreover, it is by and large the emotion term "surprise" that is differentiated from the other emotion terms on this dimension. The identification of this dimension is remarkable because it has not been identified before in studies on the dimensional representation of the cognitive structure of emotions (see Chapter 2). The VALENCE dimension on the contrary has always been observed as the most prominent dimension in previous research. A second dimension has often been identified, but differs depending on the study. In some studies, POWER is the second dimension (e.g., Gehm & Scherer, 1988; Herrmann & Raybeck, 1981), and in other studies it is AROUSAL (e.g., Russell, Lewicka, & Niit, 1989). Some studies found all three dimensions: VALENCE, POWER and AROUSAL (e.g., Fontaine, Poortinga, Setiadi, & Suprapti, 2002; Shaver, Schwartz, Kirson, & O'Conner, 1987; Shaver, Wu, & Schwartz, 1992). The emergence of a NOVELTY dimension, however, is completely new. This raises the important question as to why the NOVELTY dimension clearly emerges in the GRID study, but was not identified in previous studies on the cognitive structure of emotions. Two opposite explanations are possible, namely: 1) that the NOVELTY dimension is a method artifact caused by the GRID methodology; or 2) that it is a genuine dimension that cross-cuts the emotion domain which the GRID methodology was able to reveal.

   The NOVELTY dimension as a method artifact. One explanation is that the NOVELTY dimension is not a major dimension in the emotion domain, but is a consequence of the specific characteristics of the GRID methodology. The internal structure of the GRID has been identified by means of a factor analysis on a large set of emotion features which vary across 24 emotion terms. One can be confident about the relevance and representativeness of the GRID features. The construction of the GRID instrument was embedded in a strong theoretical framework, as major theories were operationalized for each of the components and the terms were selected with the utmost care to represent the emotion domain. The GRID instrument is a multi-theory loaded instrument that

[1] Corresponding author: Johnny J. R. Fontaine. Department of Personnel, Work and Organisational Psychology. Faculty of Psychology and Educational Sciences. Ghent University. Henri-Dunantlaan 2, 9000 Gent, Belgium. Johnny.Fontaine@UGent.be

represents the various aspects of the emotion domain quite representatively (see Chapter 5). However, a structure that results from a factor analysis depends on the nature of the items (or features in this case) that have been included in the instrument. So, it cannot be excluded that the selection process of features and terms has given a disproportionate weight to issues of NOVELTY, causing factor analysis to identify a fourth dimension. This position would be consistent with previous studies that did not reveal a NOVELTY dimension.

The NOVELTY dimension as a genuine dimension in the emotion domain. The opposite account is that the NOVELTY dimension is a genuine dimension that cross-cuts the emotion domain. While surprise is recognized by basic emotion theorists as a basic emotion (e.g., Ekman & Oster, 1979; Izard, 1977), comparatively little research attention has been devoted to this emotion. Maybe the GRID method was able to identify the significance of the NOVELTY dimension just because the instrument was so carefully developed in order to study the emotion domain in a representative way. If the NOVELTY dimension is indeed a genuine dimension in the emotion domain the question arises why this dimension has not been identified before. Previous studies that investigated the dimensional representation of the cognitive structure of the emotion domain (of which the study of Shaver, Schwartz, Kirson, and O'Conner in 1987 offers a prototypical example) share with the GRID paradigm a focus on the meaning of emotion terms. However, they differ from the GRID paradigm with respect to their reference points. Whereas the GRID paradigm considered a set of preselected emotion features as reference points, the traditional studies on the cognitive emotion structure considered the emotion terms themselves as reference points. The meaning of emotion terms was studied by investigating their mutual relationships. In the most commonly used design participants are asked to sort emotion terms in piles based on their perceived similarity (e.g., Shaver, Schwartz, Kirson, & O'Conner, 1987). The pairwise similarity between emotion terms is derived from the proportion of participants that have put the terms into the same pile. The criteria that participants use to evaluate similarities are not made explicit. Participants implicitly decide on what basis they evaluate the emotion terms. If the NOVELTY dimension is a genuine dimension that cross-cuts the cognitive representation of the emotion domain, one has to expect that people also use this dimension implicitly to judge the similarity in meaning of the emotion terms. Thus, if the NOVELTY dimension is a genuine dimension in the emotion domain, then the NOVELTY dimension should also emerge on the basis of the perceived similarities between emotion terms. The fact that this dimension did not emerge in similarity studies until now has then to be attributed to methodological factors.

Methodological characteristics affecting the dimensional representation of similarity judgments. We see four different possible methodological explanations for why the NOVELTY dimension has not been identified before in similarity judgment studies. A first explanation is the selection of the emotion terms. It has already been hypothesized in 1991 by Russell that the selection of the emotion terms will determine the second dimension in the emotion domain. Russell predicted that the AROUSAL dimension would emerge with predominantly intrapersonal affect terms and that the POWER dimension would emerge with predominantly interpersonal affect terms. If the selection of the emotion terms can determine what will be the second dimension, the selection of emotion terms will as well affect whether a fourth dimension can be identified. So, the NOVELTY dimension is highly unlikely to emerge if the cluster of surprise terms is not (or only marginally) represented.

A second and related methodological account is that the similarities between pairs of emotion terms are mutually dependent in a similarity sorting task. The pairwise similarity is computed as the number of times a pair of terms is sorted in the same pile. How often a pair will be sorted in the same pile does not only depend on the perceived similarity between the two terms, but also directly depends on the other terms that have been included in the similarity task. Whether a separate pile is likely to emerge, depends on how many terms with a related meaning have been included. For instance, while being *amazed* and being *shocked* share a strong unpredictability meaning, they might as well be sorted with high aroused positive terms (such as *enthusiastic*) and fear terms (such as *fear* and *anxiety*), respectively. The NOVELTY dimension might be hidden because other meanings that also characterize surprise terms have a stronger effect on the sorting.

A third methodological account lies in the partial lack of differentiation between the pairwise similarities derived from a similarity sorting task. Pairs of emotion terms that are opposite in meaning as well as pairs of emotion terms that are unrelated in meaning tend to be represented by a zero similarity because both pairs are highly unlikely to be sorted in the same pile. A zero similarity can thus represent a whole range of cognitive (dis)similarities. Smaller dimensions in the emotion domain will be most affected by the lack of information in the similarity sorting data.

A fourth methodological issue is the reliability issue. Until now, little attention has been paid to the reliability of the pairwise similarities that have been computed on the basis of similarity sorting tasks. The reliability of the pairwise similarities will also affect the resulting structure. The less reliable the similarities, the less likely smaller dimensions will be recovered by a multidimensional scaling. As the NOVELTY dimension is the fourth dimension in the emotion domain according to the GRID project, it is the dimension that is most likely to be affected by unreliability in the data.

Thus, the fourth dimension might not have been identified in previous similarity sorting research because (1) surprise terms were not, or were insufficiently, represented; (2) other meaning dimensions overshadowed the NOVELTY dimension due to the mutual dependence of the pairwise similarities; (3) no differentiation was made between unrelated and opposite pairs of emotion terms; and (4) the pairwise similarities were insufficiently reliable. Moreover, a combination of these factors can have played a role in the lack of identification of the fourth dimension. The goal of the present study is to investigate whether the NOVELTY dimension can be identified in the cognitive representation of the emotion domain when these four possible methodological issues are taken into account.

The central question of the present research is to investigate whether a fourth dimension can be found in the cognitive structure of the emotion domain on the basis of emotion terms if (1) surprise-related terms are sufficiently represented in the set of emotion terms, (2) the pairwise similarities are independent from one another so that the NOVELTY dimension can surface even if other meanings are present, (3) a distinction can be made between unrelated and opposite meanings, and (4) the pairwise similarities are sufficiently reliable.

14.1 **Method**

Materials

Emotion list. In total, 85 Dutch terms[2] were selected for the similarity task in three steps. In a first step the 24 emotion terms from the GRID instrument were included. In a second step, 53 terms were added from a recently developed emotion list by Veirman and Fontaine (2011). This emotion list was developed on the basis of an extensive free-listing task. In total, 5071 children and adolescents from primary and secondary schools (53.2% females, mean age of 13.6 years) in Dutch-speaking private and state schools in Belgium were asked to write down as many words or expressions that refer to emotions and feelings as they could think of during ten minutes. Two lists

---

[2] No more terms have been selected because of the feasibility of the pairwise similarity rating task. With each additional term, the pairwise similarities with all previous terms have to be rated.

were derived from this free-listing task, namely a full list with all expressions produced and a specific list with only emotion terms (which was a subset of the full list). An expression was considered an emotion term if it consisted of a single word that referred to more than one emotion component as proposed by the componential emotion theory of Scherer (2005a). So terms that only referred to a single emotion component, like "crying" (Expression) or "cold" (Bodily reaction), or terms that referred to the antecedent situation, like "friend" and "school," were not included in the specific list with emotion terms. Whether or not a term was included in the specific emotion list, was independently judged by three emotion researchers. In case of doubt, two additional emotion researchers were consulted to make the final decision. The selection of the 53 terms from this new emotion term list was based on their frequency: the 53 most frequently reported emotion terms that were not yet included in the list of GRID terms were selected. This new emotion list of Veirman and Fontaine (2011) was particularly interesting for two reasons. First, it consisted of well-known emotion terms in the Dutch-speaking Belgian population as they were generated by children and adolescents. More important, for the present purpose, was that five surprise-related terms were found to be frequently reported by children and adolescents, namely *verrast* (surprise), *gechoqueerd* (being shocked), *verwonderd* (amazed), *geschrokken* (being frightened), and *verbaasd* (astonished). These five surprise terms are thus fully part of the cognitive representation of the emotion domain in Dutch.

In a final step, eight feeling terms that described the general quality of the emotional experience were added to support the interpretation of the emotion dimensions. For the VALENCE dimension, *goed* (good) and *slecht* (bad) were used as marker feelings. *Sterk* (strong) and *zwak* (weak) were added for the POWER dimension. Four terms were included for the AROUSAL dimension, namely *nerveus* (nervous), *actief* (active), *ontspannen* (relaxed), and *rustig* (calm). No genuine feeling terms could be identified for the NOVELTY dimension that were different from the surprise emotion terms. Therefore, no separate marker feeling terms were included for the NOVELTY dimension.

All terms were presented as adjectives. Since no adjective form existed in Dutch for 15 of the 85 terms, for example, for *liefde* (love) and *walging* (disgust), these terms were presented with the qualifier "full of" (e.g., *vol van liefde* (full of love) and *vol van walging* (full of disgust)).

Pairwise similarity rating task. To assure that the pairwise similarities were independent from one another, the similarity of individual pairs of terms had to be rated independently by the participants. Combination of the 85 terms resulted in 3570 pairs. As it would be a daunting task for a single participant to rate all these pairs, 14 different lists were created with each 307 pairs of terms. Each of these lists consisted of 251 randomly assigned unique pairs and 56 overlapping pairs. The overlapping pairs were mutual combinations of *bang* (afraid), *boos* (angry), *blij* (joyful), *verdrietig* (sad), *eenzaam* (lonely), *vol van liefde* (full of love), *geïrriteerd* (irritated), and *zenuwachtig* (tense) and the mutual combinations of *goed* (good) and *slecht* (bad), *sterk* (strong), *zwak* (weak), *nerveus* (nervous), *actief* (actief), *ontspannen* (relaxed), and *rustig* (calm). These overlapping terms formed the common base across all participants.

To allow for a differentiation between emotion terms that are unrelated in meaning and that are opposite in meaning an implicit bipolar response scale was used (Russell & Carroll, 1999). The participants had to rate to what extent they agreed that two terms were *alike* on a 6-point response scale ranging from "*do not at all agree*" to "*fully agree*". For example, the pair *jaloers* (jealous) and *gekwetst* (hurt) was presented in the following statement: "*jealous and hurt are alike.*"

Procedure

The 14 lists with the emotion pairs were presented in a web-based testing environment. The participants were directed to a website which was set up for this study. The allocation to one of the

14 lists of emotion pairs was made randomly by the computer program behind the website. Each of the pairs was presented on a separate screen. The participants had to rate the presented pair before going to the next screen.

Participants

In total, 178 second year Dutch-speaking Belgian (Flemish) psychology students, of which 150 (84.3%) were female, participated on a voluntary and anonymous basis in the research. The mean age was 20.2 years old. To check whether the participants adequately executed the task, their response pattern across the 307 pairs was inspected. Those that made very few differentiations in their similarity judgments (namely when they used the same response category in more than 90% of the subsequent pairs) were removed for the final analyses. Using this criterion, five students were removed.

Data analyses

First, for each version, the reliability of the pairwise similarity judgments was investigated by means of a Cronbach's alpha. The 307 pairs of terms were treated as the observations and the participants judging the same list of pairs as the variables.

Non-metrical multidimensional scaling (MDS) was applied on the average similarity data across versions and participants. MDS represents psychological stimuli (emotion terms in case of the present study) as points in a geometrical space in such a way that the distances between the points reflect as well as possible the empirical similarities between the terms (e.g., Borg & Groenen, 1997). MDS was executed with the PROXSCAL procedure of SPSS Statistics 19.

14.2 **Results**

Across the 14 lists the reliabilities of the similarities (Cronbach's alpha's) ranged from 0.91 to 0.97 with an average of 0.94. Thus the profile of similarities across the 307 pairs of terms was highly reliable for each of the 14 administered lists.

First the adequate dimensionality of the configuration was selected using three criteria, namely (1) the fit indices, (2) the scree plot[3], and (3) the interpretability of the dimensions (Borg & Groenen, 1997). One stress measure and one fit measure were taken into account, namely the normalized raw stress (which is minimized by the PROXSCAL algorithm) and the proportion of variance accounted for in the observed similarities by the distances between the points in the geometrical space. The normalized raw stress for the one- up to the ten-dimensional space was 0.10, 0.05, 0.03, 0.02, 0.02, 0.01, 0.01, 0.01, 0.01, and 0.01, respectively. The proportion of variance in the observed similarities accounted for was 0.61, 0.71, 0.77, 0.82, 0.83, 0.84, 0.85, 0.85, 0.85, and 0.85, respectively. The expected four-dimensional structure thus fitted the data very well with a very low normalized raw stress (0.02) and a high proportion of variance accounted for (0.82). Little information was gained by adding more dimensions to the configuration over and above the fourth dimension. Moreover, the fifth dimension could not be meaningfully interpreted as very different emotion terms were close on this dimension, like "full of pity" and "enraged" or "ashamed" and "full of contempt."

---

[3] Note that the adequate number of dimensions corresponds to the inflection point and not before the inflection point as is the case with factor analysis (e.g., Borg & Groenen, 1997).

Table 14.1 Coordinates of the 85 emotion words in a four-dimensional representation

Dutch emotion words	English translation	VALENCE	POWER	AROUSAL	NOVELTY
vol van plezier	full of pleasure	0.80	0.14	0.01	0.03
vol van geluk	full of bliss	0.80	0.03	−0.02	0.02
vol van vreugde	delighted	0.79	0.05	0.09	0.00
blij	joyful	0.78	0.07	−0.04	0.01
content	content	0.77	0.14	−0.10	−0.17
vrolijk	cheerful	0.77	0.09	0.09	−0.10
euforisch	euphoric	0.76	0.19	0.16	0.02
gelukkig	happy	0.76	0.00	−0.03	0.01
tevreden	satisfied	0.73	0.04	−0.03	−0.30
goed	good	0.72	−0.24	−0.05	0.08
trots	proud	0.70	0.12	−0.25	0.08
opgewekt	lively	0.69	0.11	0.18	−0.14
fier	proud	0.68	0.31	−0.24	−0.03
ontspannen	relaxed	0.67	−0.12	−0.36	−0.28
vol van vertrouwen	full of trust	0.66	0.15	−0.33	−0.30
enthousiast	enthusiastic	0.65	0.22	0.22	−0.01
opgelucht	relieved	0.65	0.06	−0.43	−0.03
hoopvol	hopeful	0.65	−0.22	0.14	0.07
vol van liefde	full of love	0.63	−0.21	0.08	−0.15
geïnteresseerd	interested	0.60	−0.12	0.30	−0.13
vol van energie	energetic	0.54	0.34	0.08	−0.03
verliefd	in love	0.53	−0.17	0.27	0.00
rustig	calm	0.50	−0.17	−0.49	−0.35
actief	active	0.48	0.37	0.25	0.00
sterk	strong	0.45	0.39	−0.28	0.01
vol van verlangen	longing	0.44	−0.06	0.17	−0.38
afgunstig	envious	−0.41	0.30	−0.35	−0.35
angstig	fearful	−0.43	−0.25	0.38	0.17
droevig	sorrowful	−0.44	−0.32	−0.27	−0.10
chagrijnig	miserable	−0.45	0.43	0.05	−0.30
triest	triste	−0.45	−0.28	−0.28	−0.17
kwaad	mad	−0.46	0.38	−0.09	0.00
hopeloos	hopeless	−0.46	−0.40	0.13	−0.29
gefrustreerd	frustrated	−0.47	0.22	0.15	−0.12

Table 14.1 (continued) Coordinates of the 85 emotion words in a four-dimensional representation

Dutch emotion words	English translation	VALENCE	POWER	AROUSAL	NOVELTY
gekwetst	hurt	**−0.48**	−0.04	−0.26	0.19
geïrriteerd	irritated	**−0.48**	0.36	0.25	0.01
vol van walging	disgusted	**−0.48**	0.36	−0.39	0.34
vol van spijt	full of regret	**−0.48**	−0.34	−0.24	0.28
boos	angry	**−0.49**	0.36	−0.05	0.11
verdrietig	sad	**−0.50**	−0.33	−0.19	−0.01
wanhopig	desperate	**−0.50**	−0.28	0.16	−0.20
treurig	mournful	**−0.51**	−0.33	−0.22	−0.10
ongelukkig	unhappy	**−0.54**	−0.21	−0.18	−0.14
ontgoocheld	disillusioned	**−0.55**	−0.05	−0.25	0.06
depressief	depressed	**−0.55**	−0.25	−0.10	−0.40
neerslachtig	dejected	**−0.58**	−0.29	−0.13	−0.20
ontevreden	dissatisfied	**−0.59**	0.02	−0.15	−0.02
teleurgesteld	disappointed	**−0.59**	−0.12	−0.19	0.06
schuldig	guilty	**−0.59**	−0.08	0.48	0.05
<u>slecht</u>	<u>bad</u>	<u>**−0.60**</u>	0.29	−0.14	−0.23
woest	fuming	−0.39	**0.57**	−0.08	0.12
furieus	furious	−0.38	**0.56**	−0.07	0.28
razend	raging	−0.39	**0.56**	−0.04	0.17
vol van haat	full of hate	−0.46	**0.53**	−0.27	0.04
woedend	infuriated	−0.41	**0.50**	−0.08	0.21
nijdig	cross	−0.41	**0.49**	0.01	−0.11
vol van minachting	full of contempt	−0.45	**0.45**	−0.44	−0.14
ontroerd	moved	0.36	**−0.42**	−0.22	0.32
bezorgd	worried	−0.12	**−0.44**	0.26	0.27
vol van heimwee	homesick	−0.20	**−0.49**	0.08	−0.43
beschaamd	ashamed	−0.30	**−0.52**	0.02	0.41
<u>zwak</u>	<u>weak</u>	−0.27	<u>**−0.58**</u>	−0.13	−0.32
vol van medeleven	full of sympathy	0.25	**−0.65**	−0.19	0.03
verlegen	shy	0.12	**−0.68**	0.28	0.12
zenuwachtig	flustered	−0.03	0.06	**0.59**	0.06
<u>nerveus</u>	<u>nervous</u>	−0.16	0.09	<u>**0.57**</u>	0.02
nieuwsgierig	curious	0.43	0.01	**0.55**	0.08
gestresseerd	stressed	−0.29	0.09	**0.53**	0.04

Table 14.1 (continued) Coordinates of the 85 emotion words in a four-dimensional representation

Dutch emotion words	English translation	VALENCE	POWER	AROUSAL	NOVELTY
ongeduldig	impatient	−0.09	0.28	**0.52**	−0.31
ongerust	anxious	−0.28	−0.25	**0.52**	0.04
vervelend	uncomfortable	−0.39	0.32	**0.45**	−0.32
bang	afraid	−0.32	−0.30	**0.36**	0.33
vol van twijfel	doubtful	−0.35	−0.33	**0.36**	0.09
vol van medelijden	full of compassion	−0.02	−0.49	**−0.50**	0.41
onschuldig	innocent	0.33	−0.31	**−0.54**	−0.03
geschrokken	scared	−0.15	−0.07	0.05	**0.63**
gechoqueerd	shocked	−0.19	0.26	−0.07	**0.59**
verbaasd	astonished	0.17	0.00	−0.03	**0.59**
verwonderd	amazed	0.34	0.00	−0.18	**0.56**
verrast	surprised	0.43	0.12	0.08	**0.51**
verontwaardigd	indignant	−0.32	0.05	−0.32	**0.40**
verward	confused	−0.21	−0.10	0.29	**0.38**
jaloers	jealous	−0.36	0.26	0.18	**−0.37**
eenzaam	lonely	−0.28	−0.25	−0.15	**−0.54**
verveeld	bored	−0.35	0.03	0.07	**−0.67**

Note: for each emotion word the highest (absolute) coordinate is in bold. For each of the eight marker terms the expected highest (absolute) coordinate is underlined.

The first four dimensions were well interpretable. The first dimension is labeled VALENCE, opposing positively to negatively valenced emotion terms (see Table 14.1). All marker feelings were differentiated on this dimension, with *goed* (good), *ontspannen* (relaxed), *kalm* (calm), *sterk* (strong), and *actief* (active) on the positive side and *slecht* (bad), *zwak* (weak), and *nerveus* (nervous) on the negative side of the dimension. The second dimension could be interpreted as POWER opposing, for instance, *verlegen* (shy) to *woest* (fuming). With respect to the marker items, *sterk* (strong) and *zwak* (weak) were most strongly opposed on this dimension. The third dimension represented AROUSAL opposing, for instance, *gestresseerd* (stressed) to *onschuldig* (innocent). *Nerveus* (nervous), *ontspannen* (relaxed), and *kalm* (calm) were the marker items that were most differentiated on this dimension. *Actief* (active), which was also predicted to be a marker item for the AROUSAL dimension, however, had a higher coordinate on the POWER dimension (and the VALENCE dimension) than the AROUSAL dimension. The final dimension was clearly NOVELTY. All surprise terms, namely *verrast* (surprise), *gechoqueerd* (being chocked), *verwonderd* (amazed), *geschrokken* (being frightened), and *verbaasd* (astonished) were located at the most extreme positive pole of this dimension. At the opposite pole the items *verveeld* (bored), *eenzaam* (lonely), and *jaloers* (jealous) were situated. None of the marker items had the highest or second highest coordinate on the fourth dimension, but *slecht* (bad), *zwak* (weak), *kalm* (calm), and *ontspannen* (relaxed) were situated at the negative pole of this dimension.

When we take the salience of these dimensions into consideration, we see that VALENCE strongly dominates the structure. Its accounts for almost three times more variance in the observed similarities than the other three dimensions taken together (61% versus 20%). POWER accounts for an additional 10%, followed by AROUSAL that still accounts for an additional 6%. The last NOVELTY dimension, accounting for 5%, is almost as important as the third, AROUSAL dimension.

14.3 **Discussion**

The present study has focused on the methodological issues that could have prevented the NOV-ELTY dimension from emerging in the cognitive structure of emotions in previous studies reported in the literature. First, in the current study surprise-related terms were adequately represented in the list of emotion terms. Surprise terms were not underrepresented, neither artificially overrepresented. They corresponded to the most frequently used emotion terms, which were identified on the basis of an extensive probing of the emotion domain among children and adolescents. Second, the similarities were not derived through a similarity sorting task, but via direct similarity ratings of pairs of terms. Pairwise similarity ratings require a much more extensive data collection, but guarantee the advantage of mutual independence of the pairwise similarities. Third, a distinction could be made between unrelated and opposite meanings of pairs of emotion terms by using an implicit bipolar response scale. Fourth, the reliability of the pairwise similarity judgments was empirically checked. With Cronbach's alpha's exceeding 0.90 the average similarity profiles were highly reliable. When these four purely methodological issues are taken into account, a NOVELTY dimension that cross-cuts the emotion domain clearly emerged. Participants thus implicitly use a NOVELTY dimension to judge the meaning of emotion terms.

Not only the NOVELTY dimension, but the full four-dimensional structure confirmed the GRID structure. VALENCE, POWER, AROUSAL, and NOVELTY of the GRID structure emerged in the same order in the current similarity structure. Thus, also here we observe that POWER and not AROUSAL is the second dimension of the emotion domain. The differentiation between anger emotion terms on the one hand, and fear and sadness emotion terms on the other hand, comes to the fore as a more fundamental differentiation than between high and low aroused terms. Still, slight differences could be observed with respect to the importance of each of these dimensions between the GRID and the similarity structures (see also Chapter 7). VALENCE turned out to be much more salient in the similarity structure than in the GRID structure (accounting for three times more variance than the other three dimensions in the similarity structure, but accounting for less than double as much of the variance than the other three dimensions in the GRID structure). NOVELTY was comparatively more important in the present similarity structure than in the GRID structure. In the similarity structure, NOVELTY accounted for about as much of the variance as AROUSAL. In the GRID structure, NOVELTY accounted for only half of the variance that AROUSAL accounted for. If anything, the comparison of the salience of the dimensions between the GRID structure and the similarity structure indicates that the NOVELTY dimension is certainly not overrepresented in the feature-based GRID structure.

The fact that no appropriate feeling terms could be identified to underpin the interpretation of the NOVELTY dimension requires special attention. The observation is in line with the empirical GRID research. In that research, 20 subjective feeling terms were included from very different theoretical frameworks and none of them characterized the NOVELTY dimension well (see also Chapter 8). A possible explanation is that surprise, by its very nature, is a prototypically short-lived emotion. The key feature is the lack of anticipation of the event that causes surprise. Once psychological meaning is given to the event, surprise either disappears (something irrelevant to one's goals and needs happened), or turns into another emotion (e.g., if the unexpected event is threatening, panic can follow). This implies that surprise can only refer to a prototypical emotion, and not to more extended affective states. The other prototypical emotions, such as joy, fear, anger, and sadness, can be prototypical short-lived emotions, but can also gradually evolve into long-term affective phenomena like moods and personality characteristics. They can eventually become stably associated with objects and persons and give rise to the connotative meaning of words (e.g., Osgood, May, & Miron, 1975). This basic difference between surprise and the other emotions seems to be mirrored by a differential generalizability of the four affective dimensions. The first three affective dimensions structure prototypical emotion episodes, but can be generalized to very different kinds of affective phenomena (from moods to the connotative meaning dimensions of words). By contrast the NOVELTY dimension is probably only structuring the emotion domain: it is only relevant when prototypical emotional processes are contingent upon the experienced events. If correct, this means that there are not only methodological explanations for why the NOVELTY dimension was not identified before in dimensional studies. The lack of generalizability of the NOVELTY dimension from the prototypical emotion domain to the broader affective domain forms the fifth possible explanation for why the NOVELTY dimension was not recovered before.

14.4 **Conclusion**

We can conclude that the current findings offer clear support for the second interpretation, which was proposed in the introduction: the NOVELTY dimension is a genuine emotion dimension that cross-cuts the emotion domain. The dimension has not been caused by the specific characteristics of the GRID instrument. Even when participants are not explicitly asked to judge the meaning of emotion terms on NOVELTY features (as they do in the GRID study), a NOVELTY dimension emerges in the cognitive structure of emotions.

Chapter 15

From meaning to experience: The dimensional structure of emotional experiences

Johnny J. R. Fontaine,[1] Elke Veirman, and
Hans Groenvynck

The design of the GRID study has been informed by two long-standing traditions of psycholinguistic research on emotion words, and more broadly on affective information. The first tradition directly investigated the cognitive representation of emotions by studying the perceived similarity between emotion words (e.g., Ekman, 1955; Shaver, Schwartz, Kirson, & O'Connor, 1987). The second tradition focused on the connotative meaning dimensions in language by having nouns rated on a representative sample of bipolar adjectives (e.g., Osgood, May, & Miron, 1975; Osgood, Suci, & Tannenbaum, 1957). Both approaches have identified three dimensions across cultural and linguistic groups, namely evaluation or VALENCE, potency or POWER, and activation or AROUSAL in the affective domain. The GRID study subsumes both traditions. On the one hand, it works with single emotion words like in the word similarity tradition. On the other hand, these emotion words are rated on features like in the connotative meaning tradition. Most importantly, the contribution of the GRID paradigm is that it is grounded in a strong theoretical framework. The features to be rated have been systematically chosen on the basis of the Component Process Model (CPM), which assumes that an emotion episode consists of a certain degree of synchronization between five basic subsystems of human functioning, namely Appraisals, Bodily reactions, Expressions, Action tendencies, and Feelings (e.g., Scherer, 2005a; see also Chapter 1 and Chapter 5). The GRID study confirms that VALENCE, POWER, and AROUSAL, which were already identified by these two earlier traditions, are the three most important dimensions of the emotion space. Moreover, it finds evidence for a fourth dimension—NOVELTY—which explains less variance, but also occurs reliably across cultures (Fontaine, Scherer, Roesch, & Ellsworth, 2007; see Chapter 7). Although the GRID study takes a more psychological approach, it remains essentially a psycholinguistic study. It is limited to the investigation of the shared cognitive representation of the meaning of emotion words among native speakers, rather than studying episodes of actual emotional experiences.

The central question of the current chapter is whether, and to what extent, the meaning structure (i.e., semantic structure) of the emotion domain mirrors the underlying experience structure of the emotion domain. Can the daily experiences that people label with emotion terms be

[1] Corresponding author: Johnny J. R. Fontaine. Department of Personnel, Work and Organisational Psychology. Faculty of Psychology and Educational Sciences. Ghent University. Henri-Dunantlaan 2, 9000 Gent, Belgium. Johnny.Fontaine@UGent.be

represented by the same four dimensions of VALENCE, POWER, AROUSAL, and NOVELTY? The lexical sedimentation hypothesis would indeed predict such a correspondence (e.g., John, Angleitner, & Ostendorf, 1988; Saucier & Goldberg, 1996). According to this hypothesis, psychological experiences precede the emergence of words in language. It hypothesizes that recurrent psychological experiences that are of significance for human interaction get encoded in language to facilitate communication about these experiences. Thus, from the perspective of the lexical sedimentation hypothesis, emotion words and their associated meaning structure represent the structure of the actual emotional experiences.[2]

This prediction from the lexical sedimentation hypothesis seems to be disconfirmed by the existing empirical research on emotional experiences. It is common practice in psychological emotion research to ask people to describe their emotional experiences by using emotion words (e.g., *sad* and *afraid*) and feeling words that describe the general quality of the emotional experience (e.g., *good* and *weak*). The four most widely used models that use this approach have only identified a two-dimensional structure, rather than a three or even a four-dimensional structure, as would be expected on the basis of the lexical sedimentation hypothesis. The first model, the positive affect–negative affect model (e.g., Watson & Tellegen, 1985), claims that positive and negative affect are two unipolar dimensions that are virtually uncorrelated, rather than the opposite poles of a single VALENCE dimension. Moreover, the model assumes that both dimensions reflect two separate psychobiological mechanisms. In consequence, this tradition supposes a strong difference between meaning and psychological experience. The second and the third model, namely the pleasure–AROUSAL model (e.g., Russell, 1980) and the pleasantness–activation model (e.g., Larsen & Diener, 1992), partially correspond with psycholinguistic approaches. Both models assume a first bipolar VALENCE dimension and a bipolar AROUSAL dimension. According to these models, however, neither the POWER nor the NOVELTY dimension are needed to represent emotional experiences. The fourth model, the tense AROUSAL and energetic AROUSAL model (e.g., Thayer, 1989), takes again a very different stance: it does not assume a VALENCE dimension, but instead supposes that the psychological experience of emotions is based on two AROUSAL systems.

Although these four affect models differ fundamentally in the conceptualization of the dimensions that span the psychological experience of emotions, it has been empirically demonstrated that they are psychometrically equivalent, basically differing only with respect to the rotation of the dimensions in the two-dimensional space (Yik, Russell, & Feldman Barrett, 1999; see also Chapter 2 for a more detailed account). There is thus convergent evidence for a VALENCE–AROUSAL structure (or different rotations thereof) in the psychological emotion and affect literature. The results obtained in this work thus seem to indicate that daily emotional experiences differ systematically from one another only in terms of VALENCE and AROUSAL, but not in terms of POWER or NOVELTY.

The fact that only the two dimensions of VALENCE and AROUSAL (or a rotation of these dimensions) are found in current empirical research on emotional experiences is insufficient to reject the lexical sedimentation hypothesis, which predicts that also the POWER and the NOVELTY dimensions are needed to represent the actual emotional experiences. There are many different methodological factors that can potentially account for the observed differences between meaning and experience

---

[2] It has to be noted that this prediction holds in general, and does not mean that every individual emotion label used in a specific situation by a particular person forms an accurate representation of the underlying emotional experience.

studies in the literature. In the present chapter we focus on three such methodological factors. The most obvious methodological explanation for the observed differences is the type of selection of emotion words for the assessment of emotional experiences. It can indeed be observed that the terms that are typically used in psycholinguistic emotion research and in psychological affect research are often only partially overlapping. In psychological affect research, feeling words that represent the general quality of the emotional experience (such as *good* or *bad* and *weak* or *strong*) are frequently used, while psycholinguistic emotion research is much more restricted to proto-typical emotion words (such as *anger* and *fear*). Moreover, early on Russell (1991a) hypothesized that POWER would be the second dimension in similarity research if predominantly interpersonal emotion terms were used, and AROUSAL would be the second dimension if predominantly intrapersonal emotion terms were used.

Another obvious explanation is unreliability of the data. Unreliability reduces the likelihood of identifying smaller dimensions in a dataset. As demonstrated in Chapter 14, the fourth NOVELTY dimension can also be identified with perceived similarity ratings between emotion words if the perceived similarities are reliably measured. It could be hypothesized that more sources of unreliability play a role in experience than in meaning research. For instance, interindividual differences in the understanding of emotion terms will introduce unreliability in both types of research, but interindividual differences in the accuracy of the conscious representation of one's ongoing emotional experience will only affect experience research.

A third methodological explanation is provided by the way in which the dimensions have been interpreted. In the existing similarity and experience research, the dimensions only reflect the associations between emotion terms. Such research gives no insight into why these associations emerge. There is no additional simultaneous information available about the underlying emotion processes that can confirm or falsify the interpretation of the dimensions. It is thus very well possible that there is more convergence on the nature of the underlying dimensions in meaning and experience research than is suggested by the labels used in both types of research. The GRID paradigm lends itself very well to investigate this last methodological account. In the GRID study, the dimensional representation of emotion words is identified on the basis of their reference to the underlying emotion processes. The dimensions do not only derive their meaning from the position of the emotion terms in the geometrical representation, but as well from the emotion features that define these dimensions. For instance, in the GRID study the first dimension is not only interpreted as a VALENCE dimension because positively and negatively valenced emotion terms are opposed on this dimension (e.g., *joy* and *anger*), but because this dimension is defined by Appraisals (e.g., intrinsically pleasant), Bodily experiences (e.g., felt warm), Expressions (e.g., frown), Action tendencies (e.g., wanting to sing and dance), and Feelings (e.g., felt bad) that define VALENCE (see Chapter 7). Thus, before it can be concluded that there is a fundamental difference between the meaning structure of emotion words and the experience structure of emotions, it has to be demonstrated that the dimensions in both approaches indeed do not refer in the same way to Appraisals, Bodily reactions, Expressions, Action tendencies, and Feelings.

In the present study, the experience structure of the emotion domain is investigated by using the GRID paradigm. Special attention is given to the three methodological issues that might have caused the observed divergence between research on the meaning structure and research on the experience structure of emotions, namely (1) to the selection of emotion terms and feeling terms that describe the general quality of the emotional experience, (2) to the reliability of the assessment of emotional experiences, and (3) to the interpretation of the experience dimensions in terms of the underlying emotion processes.

15.1 **Method**

Participants

Second-year bachelor students in psychology received course credits for participating in the research, as well as for asking two adult, non-student acquaintances to participate. Both students and acquaintances participated on a free and anonymous basis. In total, 964 Dutch-speaking Belgian adults between 19 and 56 years (M_{age} = 31.28 years) completed the study (62.24% women). Most participants described four emotional episodes, but some reported only three or two. In total, 3648 emotion episodes were described.

Procedure

All participants logged on a protected website five times during nine days. On the first day, they were asked to give demographic background information and to fill out questionnaires on general emotional functioning (such as alexithymia). The latter information is not used in the current chapter which is focused on the use of emotion words to describe actual emotional experiences. Subsequently, participants were asked to report, each second day, the most important emotional experience of that day.

Instrument

The instrument used to assess the most important emotional experience of the day consisted of two parts. First, on a web questionnaire the participants were asked to describe the recalled emotional episodes, qualitatively (e.g., where it happened, who was present, how they reacted in the situation) in order to make the recollection of the event as vivid as possible. Moreover, they were asked to generate three labels that best represented their emotions and feelings during each of the episodes. Both "emotions" and "feelings" were mentioned in the instructions to allow for a comparison with the existing psychological research on emotional experiences, which also uses both types of terms. Only the qualitative emotion and feeling labels of the first part are further analysed in the current chapter. Second, they were asked to rate to what extent 137 emotion features[3] stemming from the GRID instrument (see Chapter 5; Fontaine et al., 2007) represented their own emotional experience on a 7-point bipolar scale (1 = *completely disagree*, 7 = *completely agree*). The features referred to Appraisals, Bodily reactions, Expressions, Action tendencies, and Feelings.

15.2 **Results**

The qualitatively reported emotion and feeling labels in each episode were first coded into emotion categories based on the word stem of the main word in each response. All words that shared the same stem and the same meaning, like *blijheid*, *blijdschap*, and *blij* (which all mean joy), were coded into a single category. All terms that were mentioned in at least 18 episodes (which corresponds to about 0.5% of the reported episodes) were selected for further analyses, which resulted in a total of 95 emotion and feeling terms (see Table 15.1). Eleven emotion terms were reported in more than 5% of the episodes, namely *blijheid* (joy), *geluk* (happiness), *verdriet* (sadness), *frustratie* (frustration), *kwaadheid* (anger), *opluchting* (relief), *boosheid* (anger), *angst* (fear), *woede* (rage), *tevredenheid* (contentment), and *teleurstelling* (disappointment).

---

[3] Accidentally five action tendency features were lost in the construction of the experience website.

Table 15.1 Frequency of emotion words used to label the emotional experiences and reliability (Cronbach's alpha) of the corresponding componential experience profiles

Dutch emotion words	English translation	N	Cronbach's alpha
blijheid	joy	625	1.00
geluk	happiness	437	1.00
verdriet	sadness	326	0.99
frustratie	frustration	309	0.99
kwaadheid	anger	272	0.99
opluchting	relief	256	0.99
boosheid	anger	250	0.99
angst	fear	248	0.99
woede	rage	227	0.99
tevredenheid	contentment	209	0.99
teleurstelling	disappointment	196	0.98
vreugde	delight	171	0.99
onmacht	incapacity	168	0.98
ergernis	annoyance	166	0.98
trots	pride	148	0.99
machteloosheid	powerlessness	145	0.98
ontgoocheling	disillusionment	144	0.98
rust	quietness	142	0.99
irritatie	irritation	138	0.98
voldoening	satisfaction	132	0.99
verrassing	surprise	120	0.99
medeleven	sympathy	116	0.98
ongeloof	disbelief	115	0.97
verbazing	astonishment	109	0.97
opwinding	excitement	106	0.98
liefde	love	103	0.99
schuld	guilt	102	0.97
medelijden	compassion	98	0.97
ontspanning	relaxation	99	0.99
spanning	tension	96	0.97
moeheid	tiredness	92	0.94
plezier	pleasure	85	0.99
stress	stress	84	0.96
zenuwachtigheid	agitation	84	0.95
ontroering	being moved	76	0.98

Table 15.1 (continued) Frequency of emotion words used to label the emotional experiences and reliability (Cronbach's alpha) of the corresponding componential experience profiles

Dutch emotion words	English translation	N	Cronbach's alpha
onzekerheid	uncertainty	73	0.96
droefheid	sorrow	72	0.95
bezorgdheid	concern	71	0.97
nervositeit	nervousness	70	0.95
schaamte	shame	70	0.94
spijt	regret	66	0.94
onbegrip	incomprehension	65	0.96
twijfel	doubt	63	0.95
vrolijkheid	gaiety	62	0.98
verliefdheid	being in love	60	0.98
ongerustheid	worry	58	0.95
warmte	warmth	59	0.98
fierheid	pride	58	0.98
genot	enjoyment	55	0.98
verwarring	confusion	58	0.94
enthousiasme	enthusiasm	57	0.98
goed gevoel	good feeling	57	0.98
triestheid	dejection	55	0.93
verlangen	longing	54	0.96
verwondering	amazement	52	0.94
gemis	to miss	51	0.89
nieuwsgierigheid	curiosity	51	0.96
euforie	euphoria	47	0.97
geschrokken zijn	being startled	46	0.94
ongeduldigheid	impatience	46	0.94
verontwaardiging	indignation	47	0.96
vriendschap	friendship	45	0.98
eenzaamheid	loneliness	44	0.93
tederheid	tenderness	43	0.97
genegenheid	affection	42	0.98
schrik	terror	42	0.90
hoop	hope	41	0.93
pijn	pain	41	0.88
paniek	panic	40	0.95
ongemak	discomfort	39	0.91

Table 15.1 (continued) Frequency of emotion words used to label the emotional experiences and reliability (Cronbach's alpha) of the corresponding componential experience profiles

Dutch emotion words	English translation	N	Cronbach's alpha
kalmte	calmness	36	0.95
onrust	unrest	34	0.90
verveling	boredom	34	0.90
verveeldheid	being bothered	33	0.90
energiek	energy	29	0.97
verbondenheid	solidarity	28	0.96
vrijheid	freedom	28	0.96
opgewektheid	cheerfulness	27	0.97
opgejaagdheid	being routed	26	0.92
vertrouwen	trust	26	0.96
zorgeloosheid	carefreeness	26	0.97
bewondering	admiration	25	0.89
gezelligheid	cosiness	24	0.97
bangheid	fear	23	0.82
dankbaarheid	gratitude	22	0.92
geruststelling	reassurance	21	0.93
hulpeloosheid	helplessness	21	0.89
samenhorigheid	being together	21	0.96
verlegenheid	shyness	21	0.84
wanhoop	despair	21	0.85
vredigheid	peacefulness	20	0.96
jaloezie	jealousy	19	0.83
amusement	amusement	18	0.94
interesse	interest	18	0.95
opgetogenheid	elation	18	0.94

Subsequently, we computed, for each emotion and feeling term, the corresponding experienced feature profile across the 137 GRID features. The average of the features was computed across all episodes in which the respective emotion or feeling term was spontaneously used to describe the experience. The reliability of the profile of each term was investigated by means of a Cronbach's alpha with the 137 features being treated as observations and the experiences that were labeled with that term as the variables. The reliability of the average experience profiles ranged from 0.82 to 1.00 with an average of 0.95 (see also Table 15.1).

The experience structure was investigated on the average feature profiles of the 95 terms, namely on a matrix with 137 columns corresponding to the 137 GRID features, and 95 rows corresponding to the 95 emotion terms that were used in at least 18 episodes. A factor analysis (Principal

Component Analysis) was executed on the 137 GRID features across the 95 emotion terms. The scree plot pointed to four factors with the first ten Eigenvalues being 71.407, 13.793, 9.040, 6.707, 3.998, 3.526, 3.015, 2.570, 2.117, and 1.875 (see also Figure SM 1[4]). The four-factor solution accounted for 73.68% of the total variance.

The four-factor experience structure was orthogonally Procrustes rotated toward the GRID meaning structure (see Table 15.2). The congruence measures (Tucker's phi) were 0.90 with the VALENCE meaning factor, 0.86 with the POWER meaning factor, 0.86 with the AROUSAL meaning factor, and 0.59 with the NOVELTY meaning factor. As the congruence coefficients only exceeded the value of 0.85 for the first three factors, only these factors could be considered reasonably congruent (Fischer & Fontaine, 2011). The first experience factor is labeled EXPERIENCE VALENCE. This factor opposes negative to positive valenced features (Appraisals, Feelings, Action tendencies, Bodily reactions, and Expressions). The second experience factor is labeled EXPERIENCE POWER. On this factor especially, expressions of high and low POWER are opposed to one another. The label of the third experience factor is EXPERIENCE AROUSAL. This factor opposes absence of bodily reactions and absence of expressions to sympathetic AROUSAL features. As the fourth factor was clearly not congruent between the meaning and the experience structure, this factor was further explored. Despite the low congruence, the highest loading features were still the appraisals "unpredictable" and "suddenly" and the facial expressions "had the jaw drop," "opened her or his eyes widely," and "had eyebrows go up," which does point to a clear NOVELTY component in this fourth factor. The three features that differed most between the meaning and the experience structure were "felt an urge to be attentive to what is going on," which only defined the fourth factor in the experience structure; "experienced the emotional state for a long time," which only defined the negative pole of the fourth factor in the meaning structure; and "wanted to take care of another person or cause," which only defined the fourth factor in the experience structure. Only the last feature conceptually changed the meaning of the last experience factor.

As the emotion terms formed the observations on the basis of which the factor analysis was executed, just as was the case in the GRID project, it was possible to investigate the position of the 95 emotion terms in the Procrustes rotated four-factorial structure (see Table 15.3). Negatively and positively valenced emotion terms are opposed to one another on the first experience factor. On the second experience factor mainly anger terms are being opposed to sadness terms, and to a lesser extent to fear terms. On the third experience factor, fear terms, and to a lesser extent anger terms, are opposed to being bored, peacefulness, and to lesser extent sadness. On the last experience factor all surprise terms have very high coordinates, namely *verwondering* (amazement), *verbazing* (astonishment), *verrassing* (surprise), and *geschrokken* (being startled) scored very high on the fourth factor. However, not only surprise terms, but also terms that imply empathy with somebody else had very high coordinates on this factor: the terms *bezorgdheid* (concern), *medelijden* (compassion), and *medeleven* (sympathy) were among the highest scoring emotion terms on this factor. Thus both the loadings of the features and the coordinates of the terms on the fourth experience factor imply that next to NOVELTY, also interpersonal care is referred to. Therefore, we will descriptively further label the fourth experience factor as EXPERIENCE NOVELTY/CARE.

After orthogonal Procrustes rotation, EXPERIENCE VALENCE accounted for 46.85% of the total variance, EXPERIENCE POWER for 10.87%, EXPERIENCE AROUSAL for 10.90%, and EXPERIENCE NOVELTY/CARE for 5.06%. Thus, while POWER was clearly more important than the AROUSAL

---

[4] All supplementary materials (SM) are available at the GRID website: http://www.affective-sciences. org/GRID. See Appendix 1 ("Availability") for further details.

Table 15.2 Factor loadings of GRID features in four-factorial experience structure after orthogonal Procrustes rotation toward GRID meaning structure

GRID features	EXPERIENCE VALENCE	EXPERIENCE POWER	EXPERIENCE AROUSAL	EXPERIENCE NOVELTY/CARE
smiled	0.97	0.18	−0.06	−0.09
felt positive	0.97	0.19	−0.11	−0.06
wanted to get totally absorbed in the situation	0.97	0.08	−0.01	−0.06
in itself pleasant for the person	0.97	0.17	−0.09	−0.07
consequences positive for person	0.96	0.18	−0.05	−0.14
felt good	0.96	0.19	−0.11	−0.08
wanted to submit to the situation as it is	0.95	−0.09	−0.15	−0.04
felt at ease	0.95	0.17	−0.20	−0.08
in itself pleasant for somebody else	0.94	0.21	−0.10	−0.07
consequences positive for somebody else	0.93	0.21	−0.06	−0.12
wanted to be tender, sweet, and kind	0.91	−0.20	−0.14	0.17
felt in control	0.91	0.27	−0.16	−0.07
felt strong	0.91	0.35	−0.07	−0.07
wanted to sing and dance	0.91	0.19	0.11	−0.12
muscles relaxing (whole body)	0.87	−0.06	−0.22	−0.14
wanted to be near or close to people or things	0.86	−0.11	−0.09	0.18
felt energetic	0.86	0.45	0.03	−0.07
felt calm	0.85	0.00	−0.42	−0.01
moved toward people or things	0.78	0.33	0.18	0.07
consequences able to live with	0.77	0.27	0.17	−0.15
important and relevant for person's goals	0.75	0.23	0.05	−0.29
caused intentionally	0.75	0.35	−0.06	−0.15
felt powerful	0.73	0.49	0.09	−0.20
caused by the person's own behavior	0.72	0.14	0.16	−0.46
familiar	0.67	0.17	−0.26	−0.45
wanted to be seen, to be in the center of attention	0.66	0.39	0.24	−0.20
confirmed expectations	0.65	0.06	−0.36	−0.44
important and relevant for goals of somebody else	0.57	0.31	−0.06	0.29
breathing slowing down	0.56	−0.42	−0.29	−0.19
wanted to comply to someone else's wishes	0.55	0.04	0.13	0.09
consequences predictable	0.48	0.20	−0.12	−0.44
wanted to hand over the initiative to someone else	0.40	−0.06	0.03	0.11
inconsistent with expectations	−0.51	0.19	0.36	0.31
hid the emotion from others by smiling	−0.53	−0.13	0.19	−0.22

Table 15.2 (continued) Factor loadings of GRID features in four-factorial experience structure after orthogonal Procrustes rotation toward GRID meaning structure

GRID features	EXPERIENCE VALENCE	EXPERIENCE POWER	EXPERIENCE AROUSAL	EXPERIENCE NOVELTY/CARE
moved against people or things	−0.55	0.02	0.36	−0.20
felt weak limbs	−0.57	−0.54	0.45	−0.10
suddenly	−0.57	−0.15	0.39	0.51
produced a short utterance	−0.57	−0.09	0.34	0.30
wanted to take initiative her/himself	−0.58	0.49	0.24	−0.16
had a trembling voice	−0.64	−0.51	0.45	0.11
produced speech disturbances	−0.65	−0.32	0.54	0.06
in danger	−0.67	−0.13	0.53	0.06
required an immediate response	−0.68	0.13	0.46	0.36
got pale	−0.68	−0.48	0.41	0.05
wanted to make up for what she or he had done	−0.69	−0.11	0.28	−0.17
felt tired	−0.70	−0.23	−0.04	−0.50
felt cold	−0.70	−0.54	0.18	0.07
had stomach troubles	−0.72	−0.41	0.29	−0.09
lacked the motivation to pay attention to what was going on	−0.73	−0.34	0.01	−0.40
wanted to disappear or hide from others	−0.73	−0.37	0.35	−0.24
withdrew from people or things	−0.74	−0.36	0.21	−0.30
had eyebrows go up	−0.75	0.19	0.21	0.41
showed the emotion to other less than s/he felt it	−0.75	−0.25	0.28	0.06
muscles tensing (whole body)	−0.76	−0.05	0.56	−0.02
consequences avoidable or modifiable	−0.76	0.19	0.31	−0.23
lacked the motivation to do anything	−0.77	−0.41	0.03	−0.29
wanted to withdraw into her/himself	−0.77	−0.49	0.21	−0.21
felt submissive	−0.78	−0.29	0.20	−0.30
felt exhausted	−0.79	−0.26	0.10	−0.36
wanted to be hurt as little as possible	−0.79	−0.32	0.32	−0.13
tried to control the intensity of the emotional feeling	−0.79	−0.15	0.29	0.10
wanted to run away in whatever direction	−0.81	−0.22	0.35	−0.26
wanted to flee	−0.81	−0.28	0.34	−0.27
felt nervous	−0.81	−0.03	0.46	−0.04
wanted to overcome an obstacle	−0.81	0.13	0.30	−0.10
wanted to prevent or stop sensory contact	−0.82	−0.23	0.28	−0.11

Table 15.2 (continued) Factor loadings of GRID features in four-factorial experience structure after orthogonal Procrustes rotation toward GRID meaning structure

GRID features	EXPERIENCE VALENCE	EXPERIENCE POWER	EXPERIENCE AROUSAL	EXPERIENCE NOVELTY/CARE
irrevocable loss	−0.82	−0.38	0.18	0.07
wanted to destroy whatever was close	−0.83	0.01	0.16	−0.19
wanted to do damage, hit, or say something that hurts	−0.84	0.10	0.10	−0.09
wanted to tackle the situation	−0.85	0.26	0.17	0.04
wanted to keep or push things away	−0.85	−0.27	0.30	−0.17
wanted to break contact with others	−0.85	−0.15	0.23	−0.24
treated unjustly	−0.86	0.12	0.22	−0.03
felt weak	−0.86	−0.40	0.21	−0.08
violated laws or socially accepted norms	−0.87	0.08	0.16	0.16
wanted to be in command of others	−0.87	0.20	0.18	−0.05
felt restless	−0.88	−0.03	0.36	−0.07
felt out of control	−0.89	−0.18	0.34	−0.06
pressed lips together	−0.90	−0.15	0.17	0.06
wanted someone to be there to provide help or support	−0.90	−0.22	0.23	0.00
wanted to be in control of the situation	−0.91	0.08	0.27	−0.13
wanted to oppose	−0.92	0.03	0.18	−0.01
consequences negative for somebody else	−0.93	−0.08	0.09	0.19
frowned	−0.93	0.00	0.06	0.14
felt powerless	−0.93	−0.26	0.11	0.12
felt inhibited or blocked	−0.93	−0.23	0.24	−0.07
felt bad	−0.94	−0.26	0.14	0.02
in itself unpleasant for somebody else	−0.95	−0.10	0.07	0.16
incongruent with own standards and ideals	−0.96	−0.01	0.10	0.04
consequences negative for person	−0.96	−0.14	0.18	−0.01
felt negative	−0.96	−0.17	0.13	−0.05
in itself unpleasant for the person	−0.97	−0.16	0.11	0.02
felt dominant	0.03	**0.82**	0.15	−0.13
had an assertive voice	0.50	**0.72**	−0.08	−0.03
felt an urge to be active, to do something, anything	0.11	**0.69**	0.31	0.01
increased the volume of voice	−0.19	**0.65**	0.48	0.05
felt alert	0.09	**0.64**	0.29	0.24
wanted to move	0.37	**0.55**	0.34	−0.28

Table 15.2 (continued) Factor loadings of GRID features in four-factorial experience structure after orthogonal Procrustes rotation toward GRID meaning structure

GRID features	EXPERIENCE VALENCE	EXPERIENCE POWER	EXPERIENCE AROUSAL	EXPERIENCE NOVELTY/CARE
wanted to show off	0.26	**0.42**	0.31	−0.17
showed the emotion to others more than s/he felt it	0.29	**0.39**	−0.01	0.06
produced a long utterance	0.19	**0.38**	0.33	−0.03
caused by somebody else's behavior	0.08	**0.37**	0.08	0.18
caused by a supernatural POWER	0.25	**−0.37**	−0.05	−0.04
spoke slower	−0.11	**−0.45**	0.05	0.09
heartbeat slowing down	0.29	**−0.49**	−0.26	−0.14
experienced the emotional state for a long time	0.38	**−0.50**	0.27	0.05
felt shivers	−0.35	**−0.54**	0.53	0.20
decreased the volume of voice	−0.13	**−0.62**	0.10	0.11
wanted to do nothing	−0.31	**−0.63**	−0.20	−0.34
a lump in throat	−0.47	**−0.68**	0.21	0.35
fell silent	−0.56	**−0.71**	0.04	0.15
showed tears	−0.29	**−0.71**	0.04	0.28
closed her or his eyes	−0.01	**−0.74**	−0.06	−0.18
felt hot	−0.30	−0.10	**0.79**	−0.18
heartbeat getting faster	−0.47	0.02	**0.78**	0.12
sweat	−0.41	−0.19	**0.75**	−0.13
blushed	0.03	−0.12	**0.73**	−0.18
breathing getting faster	−0.54	−0.05	**0.73**	0.16
perspired, or had moist hands	−0.49	−0.24	**0.71**	−0.15
produced abrupt body movements	−0.04	0.26	**0.69**	−0.04
spoke faster	−0.41	0.47	**0.67**	0.08
center of attention	0.34	0.11	**0.64**	−0.29
felt warm	0.54	−0.09	**0.60**	−0.17
opened her or his eyes widely	−0.09	0.27	**0.59**	0.45
changed the melody of her or his speech	−0.19	0.26	**0.56**	0.29
was in an intense emotional state	0.02	−0.47	**0.55**	0.26
enough resources to avoid or modify consequences	−0.04	0.44	**0.48**	−0.34
wanted to act, whatever action it might be	−0.21	0.39	**0.40**	−0.07
caused by chance	−0.26	−0.22	**0.32**	0.32
did not show any changes in face	0.20	0.33	**−0.47**	−0.42
did not show any changes in gestures	−0.18	0.01	**−0.50**	−0.07

Table 15.2 (continued) Factor loadings of GRID features in four-factorial experience structure after orthogonal Procrustes rotation toward GRID meaning structure

GRID features	EXPERIENCE VALENCE	EXPERIENCE POWER	EXPERIENCE AROUSAL	EXPERIENCE NOVELTY/CARE
did not show any changes in vocal expression	0.44	−0.04	**−0.53**	−0.40
had no bodily symptoms at all	0.37	0.45	**−0.66**	0.02
had the jaw drop	0.00	0.11	0.29	**0.64**
unpredictable	−0.52	0.03	0.33	**0.61**
felt an urge to be attentive to what is going on	0.43	0.13	0.34	**0.56**
wanted to take care of another person or cause	0.35	−0.18	−0.12	**0.53**

Table 15.3 Coordinates of the 95 emotion words in the four-factorial experience structure after orthogonal Procrustes rotation toward the GRID meaning structure

Dutch emotion words	English translation	EXPERIENCE VALENCE	EXPERIENCE POWER	EXPERIENCE AROUSAL	EXPERIENCE NOVELTY/CARE
ongeduldigheid	impatience	−0.87	1.73	−1.08	−0.37
opgetogenheid	elation	1.17	1.53	0.55	0.09
verontwaardiging	indignation	−1.34	1.53	0.20	1.40
irritatie	irritation	−1.61	1.49	−0.80	−0.84
enthousiasme	enthusiasm	1.12	1.47	0.55	0.35
amusement	amusement	0.86	1.44	−0.02	−0.86
interesse	interest	0.70	1.33	−0.86	0.67
ergernis	annoyance	−1.47	1.27	−0.84	−0.60
boosheid	anger	−1.36	1.21	0.45	−0.04
onbegrip	incomprehension	−1.23	1.16	0.27	0.56
energie	energy	1.17	1.05	0.78	−0.95
opgejaagdheid	being routed	−1.16	1.03	0.82	−0.78
kwaadheid	anger	−1.42	1.02	0.21	0.09
frustratie	frustration	−1.43	0.97	−0.43	−0.55
voldoening	satisfaction	0.75	0.85	−0.20	−0.81
trots	pride	0.93	0.83	0.04	−0.24
opgewektheid	cheerfulness	1.17	0.80	−0.14	0.33
samenhorigheid	being together	1.04	0.79	−0.05	0.58
plezier	pleasure	1.01	0.77	0.40	0.18
vrolijkheid	gaiety	1.08	0.67	−0.01	0.15
ontgoocheling	disillusionment	−1.21	0.66	0.00	−0.43
vreugde	delight	1.11	0.57	0.19	0.13

Table 15.3 (continued) Coordinates of the 95 emotion words in the four-factorial experience structure after orthogonal Procrustes rotation toward the GRID meaning structure

Dutch emotion words	English translation	EXPERIENCE VALENCE	EXPERIENCE POWER	EXPERIENCE AROUSAL	EXPERIENCE NOVELTY/CARE
teleurstelling	disappointment	−1.17	0.54	−0.03	−0.18
nieuwsgierigheid	curiosity	0.49	0.45	0.11	0.11
blijheid	joy	1.00	0.44	0.33	0.36
fierheid	pride	1.12	0.43	0.29	−0.26
vertrouwen	trust	0.98	0.38	−0.37	−0.33
verwarring	confusion	−0.66	−0.54	0.48	0.05
genegenheid	affection	1.58	−0.70	0.13	0.01
genot	enjoyment	1.44	−0.76	0.00	−0.58
warmte	warmth	1.44	−1.13	0.07	−0.39
liefde	love	1.57	−1.18	0.45	0.12
verliefdheid	being in love	1.75	−1.44	1.19	0.41
bewondering	admiration	0.41	−1.51	−1.17	0.81
ontroering	being moved	1.16	−1.55	−0.32	1.02
triestheid	dejection	−0.58	−1.87	−0.70	0.49
droefheid	sorrow	−0.58	−1.87	−0.86	0.26
gemis	to miss	−0.01	−2.15	−0.59	−0.17
verdriet	sadness	−0.66	−2.42	0.10	0.53
eenzaamheid	loneliness	−0.70	−2.77	0.29	−1.12
pijn	pain	−0.65	−2.80	0.52	−1.06
verlegenheid	shyness	−0.03	−0.70	3.66	−1.54
paniek	panic	−0.88	−0.58	2.56	0.83
bangheid	fear	−0.60	−1.60	2.00	0.00
opwinding	excitement	0.56	1.18	1.90	0.45
euforie	euphoria	1.14	1.40	1.77	−0.53
schrik	terror	−0.58	−0.52	1.73	0.76
wanhoop	despair	−1.10	−0.24	1.64	−0.19
angst	fear	−0.67	−1.16	1.61	0.04
zenuwachtigheid	agitation	−0.20	−0.19	1.37	−1.16
woede	rage	−1.48	1.00	1.27	−0.07
schaamte	shame	−0.73	−0.77	1.23	−0.83
nervositeit	nervousness	−0.55	0.51	1.04	−0.78
spanning	tension	0.04	0.46	0.94	−0.67
zorgeloosheid	carefreeness	1.52	0.32	0.79	−0.62
opluchting	relief	0.31	0.48	0.56	0.11

Table 15.3 (continued) Coordinates of the 95 emotion words in the four-factorial experience structure after orthogonal Procrustes rotation toward the GRID meaning structure

Dutch emotion words	English translation	EXPERIENCE VALENCE	EXPERIENCE POWER	EXPERIENCE AROUSAL	EXPERIENCE NOVELTY/CARE
geluk	happiness	1.30	−0.08	0.17	0.06
machteloosheid	powerlessness	−1.27	−0.23	−0.38	0.34
twijfel	doubt	−0.64	0.37	−0.55	−0.24
goed gevoel	feeling good	0.59	0.69	−0.84	−0.29
tevredenheid	contentment	0.79	0.36	−0.93	−0.80
hoop	hope	−0.22	0.14	−1.05	0.99
gezelligheid	cosiness	1.06	0.39	−1.10	−0.65
spijt	regret	−0.89	−0.09	−1.38	0.11
geruststelling	reassurance	0.50	0.48	−1.82	−0.01
vredigheid	peacefulness	1.32	−1.09	−1.87	−0.94
kalmte	calmness	0.44	−0.51	−2.02	−1.34
verveling	boredom	−1.37	0.05	−2.84	−2.19
geschrokken	being startled	−0.86	−0.39	0.39	2.61
medeleven	sympathy	−0.24	−1.20	−1.36	2.59
verrassing	surprise	0.79	0.70	0.51	2.20
verbazing	astonishment	−0.39	0.81	−0.29	2.12
medelijden	compassion	−0.71	−0.45	−1.31	2.11
verwondering	amazement	0.03	0.18	−0.33	2.03
bezorgdheid	concern	−0.46	0.13	−0.68	2.01
ongeloof	disbelief	−0.86	−0.07	0.05	1.95
hulpeloosheid	helplessness	−1.05	−0.85	−0.77	1.28
ongerustheid	worry	−0.91	0.20	−0.52	1.06
tederheid	tenderness	1.37	−0.80	0.07	1.04
verbondenheid	solidarity	1.22	−0.20	−0.15	0.74
vriendschap	friendship	0.99	0.64	−0.65	0.74
dankbaarheid	gratitude	0.71	−0.49	−0.16	0.71
onmacht	incapacity	−1.18	−0.01	−0.13	0.64
schuld	guilt	−0.85	−0.26	0.32	−0.43
onzekerheid	uncertainty	−0.69	−0.16	−0.19	−0.45
onrust	unrest	−0.91	−0.39	0.10	−0.68
ongemak	discomfort	−0.84	−0.19	0.34	−0.74
verlangen	longing	0.63	0.18	−0.33	−0.77
ontspanning	relaxation	1.10	0.09	−0.86	−0.92
stress	stress	−0.82	0.28	0.40	−0.97

Table 15.3 (continued) Coordinates of the 95 emotion words in the four-factorial experience structure after orthogonal Procrustes rotation toward the GRID meaning structure

Dutch emotion words	English translation	EXPERIENCE VALENCE	EXPERIENCE POWER	EXPERIENCE AROUSAL	EXPERIENCE NOVELTY/CARE
rust	quietness	1.02	−0.50	−1.03	−1.06
verveeldheid	being bothered	−1.32	0.16	−0.90	−1.11
jaloezie	jealousy	−1.40	0.01	−0.60	−1.52
vrijheid	freedom	0.83	−0.21	−0.88	−1.60
moeheid	tiredness	−0.44	−1.03	−0.47	−2.59

in the GRID meaning structure, EXPERIENCE POWER and EXPERIENCE AROUSAL were of equal importance in the experience structure.

15.3 **Discussion**

The present chapter investigated whether the meaning structure of emotions, which formed the focus of the GRID project, could be generalized to the structure of actual emotional experiences. Based on the lexical sedimentation hypothesis a parallelism was expected between the emotion processes inferred from emotion terms and the actual emotional experiences that are labeled with these emotion terms, and thus that VALENCE, POWER, AROUSAL, and NOVELTY would also structure daily emotional experiences. However, based on the dominant psychological research that asks people to rate their own emotional experiences on emotion and feeling terms, it could be expected that daily emotional experiences were only systematically structured according to the dimensions of VALENCE and AROUSAL. In the current chapter, special attention was paid to three methodological factors that could account for the divergence between the psycholinguistic and the current psychological experience research, namely (1) the selection of terms that are used to study the experience structure, (2) the reliability of the assessment of the emotional experiences, and (3) the interpretation of the dimensions in terms of the underlying emotion processes. The findings in the current research, with respect to each of these three methodological factors, are discussed.

By asking people to qualitatively label their emotional experiences by three emotion and/or feeling terms, these terms can be considered relevant and representative for the actual emotional experiences of the participants. Moreover, by explicitly asking for both emotion and feeling terms, the terms are not only relevant for a psycholinguistic perspective that works with prototypical emotion terms (e.g., *angry* and *sad*), but are also relevant for the dominant self-report research in psychology that additionally relies on feeling terms that describe the general quality of the emotional experience (e.g., *good*, *strong*, or *tense*).

By looking at the average experience patterns across the 137 emotion features, it was possible to identify highly reliable experience patterns. Although there was substantial variability between episodes that were labeled with the same term, there was still sufficient resemblance with an average profile to allow for the identification of reliable experience patterns. Contrary to what has been claimed by constructivist authors (e.g., Lindquist & Barrett, 2008), the current results indicate that people tend to choose emotion labels in a systematic way as a function of the underlying emotion process.

By using the GRID features, it was possible to look at the constituting parts of the emotional experiences. Information on the global interpretation of the emotional experience (included in emotion and feeling words) could be related to the experience of Appraisals, Bodily reactions, Feelings, Expressions, and Action tendencies that constitute the emotion. This allowed us to interpret the meaning of the emotion dimensions on the basis of the processes that constitute the emotions. The expectation from the lexical sedimentation hypothesis was by and large confirmed. A factor analysis pointed to a four-factorial structure. These four experience factors shared basic properties with the meaning factors from the GRID project. The first experience factor could also be interpreted as VALENCE, the second as POWER, and the third as AROUSAL. The fourth experience factor and the fourth meaning factor shared NOVELTY appraisals and facial expressions that are typical for surprise. Moreover, the freely generated emotion terms were differentiated in almost the same way on these four experience factors as was observed on the meaning factors: anger, fear, and sadness terms were opposed to joy terms on the first factor; anger terms were opposed to sadness (and fear) terms on the second factor; fear (and anger) terms were opposed to peacefulness (and sadness) terms on the third factor; and surprise terms scored high on the fourth factor. Thus, the prediction on the basis of the existing literature on emotional experiences that the actual emotional experience is structured exclusively along VALENCE and AROUSAL can be discarded: There is very clear evidence that POWER and NOVELTY do play an important role in actual daily emotional experiences.

Still the experience structure did not perfectly mirror the meaning structure. There were two major differences. First, it was observed that the AROUSAL dimension is much more important in the experience structure than in the meaning structure. EXPERIENCE AROUSAL and EXPERIENCE POWER were equally important in the experience structure, while POWER was clearly more important than AROUSAL in the meaning structure. Three related and not-mutually exclusive explanations are plausible for this observation: (1) AROUSAL is just more important in the actual experience of emotions than in the meaning of terms per se; (2) the current experience research worked with many more emotion terms (95) than the GRID meaning study (with 24 terms) did, which implies that the emotion domain is more profusely represented in this experience study than in the GRID study. We observe for instance that people report very high intensity terms that were not included in the GRID study, such as *paniek* (panic), *woede* (rage), and *euforie* (euphoria); (3) we asked people to use emotion *and* feeling labels. While most spontaneously reported terms were emotion terms, also typical feeling terms that describe the general quality of the emotional experience such as *moeheid* (tiredness) and *goed gevoel* (good feeling) were reported. As it was found in the GRID study that the AROUSAL factor was more salient in the Feeling component compared to the overall emotion structure (see Chapter 8), it is possible that these feeling terms have contributed to the importance of the AROUSAL factor in the experience structure.

The second important difference between the experience and the meaning structure was observed for the fourth factor. While this factor was characterized by NOVELTY appraisals and facial expressions of surprise, and surprise terms have high scores on this factor, the experience structure showed an additional tendency toward terms that imply taking care of another person and terms of sympathy and compassion. A possible post hoc explanation for this observation is that there is an asymmetrical relationship between surprise and compassion in daily emotional episodes. While it makes, theoretically, no sense to assume that surprise would imply compassion, it is very well possible that the experience of compassion is often unexpected in daily life.

15.4 **Conclusions**

The current chapter reports data that lend strong support for the lexical sedimentation hypothesis: There is a high correspondence between the meaning structure and the experience structure in the emotion domain. Both are defined by an interplay between Appraisals, Bodily reactions, Expressions, Action tendencies, and Feelings. Moreover, not only VALENCE and AROUSAL structure daily emotional experiences, but also POWER and NOVELTY. This implies that the meaning structures that have been identified in the GRID project are not only relevant for psycholinguistic research on the meaning of emotion words, but also offer a solid basis for hypothesis development about the emotion processes themselves.

Chapter 16

Reviving a forgotten dimension—potency in affective neuroscience

Annekathrin Schacht[1]

16.1 Introduction

Most of the recent studies in the field of affective neuroscience, investigating the differences in processing of emotional compared with non-emotion (neutral) stimuli, relate to the assumption that emotional concepts have a dimensional structure. In this context, two aspects become obvious. First, even though the assumption of a dimensional affective space was initially suggested on the basis of linguistic analysis (e.g., Osgood, Suci, & Tannenbaum, 1957), most of emotion research focused on biologically determined domains such as affective pictures or facially expressed emotions. Only recently, the question of how emotional words are processed and about their underlying (neural) mechanisms has been addressed. Second, even though early work on the dimensions that constitute the affective space revealed a three-dimensional structure, the majority of recent studies in this field considered only differences in VALENCE and AROUSAL when contrasting processing differences between emotional and neutral stimuli of different domains. In contrast, the potency[2] dimension was not taken into account, neither in studies on neural correlates on or peripheral changes to emotion processing.

In this chapter, first I will briefly introduce the most dominant dimensional models of emotion (see also Chapter 2) that have evidently influenced the neuroscientific study of emotion processing. Major findings of this line of research will be briefly reviewed in the following, focusing on studies on electrophysiological and peripheral correlates of emotional VALENCE and AROUSAL. Motivated by both the core findings of the GRID study and some early investigations of event-related brain potentials (ERPs) in response to the three dimensions as suggested by Osgood's work (e.g., Osgood, 1964), a re-analysis of originally VALENCE/AROUSAL-related ERP data in terms of potency differences will be reported. The findings clearly suggest a significant contribution of the potency dimension to emotion-related ERP components that have consistently been related to differences in emotional VALENCE and thus to generally enhanced AROUSAL. Against this background, the chapter will conclude with assumptions for future research on emotional processing, particularly, in the verbal domain.

[1] Annekathrin Schacht. CRC Text Structures, University of Göttingen, Nikolausberger Weg 23, 37073 Göttingen, Germany, e-mail: aschach@uni-goettingen.de

[2] The dimension referred to as potency in this chapter generally corresponds to the POWER dimension identified in the GRID study.

16.2 **A brief outline of dimensional models of emotion**

Dimensional models have a long history in psychology. Based on introspection and early experimental work, already Wundt (1896) suggested that all affective states can be described by their specific position in a three-dimensional space, depending on their qualities: pleasant/unpleasant, arousing/subduing, and strained/relaxed.

Osgood, Suci, and Tannenbaum (1957) provided the first systematic study, which revealed that the connotative (or emotional) meaning of any verbal term can be described on three dimensions. These dimensions are marked by polar adjectives and together form the so-called "Semantic Differential". The first dimension was named "evaluation" which in general corresponds to the VALENCE dimension in current dimensional models (e.g., Russell, 1980; Lang & Bradley, 2010). The "evaluation" dimension of the Semantic Differential is presented by adjective pairs like fair–unfair, good–bad, pleasant–unpleasant, nice–awful. The second dimension was called "potency" and is characterized by pairs of adjectives like small–large, light–heavy, weak–strong. This dimension is strongly related to dimensions reported by others as "dominance–submissiveness" (Russell & Mehrabian, 1977), "control" (Averill, 1975), or "potency–control" obtained in the GRID study (cf. Fontaine, Scherer, Roesch, & Ellsworth, 2007). The third dimension of Osgood's Semantic Differential is called "activity" and characterized by pairs of adjectives as slow–fast, passive–active, dull–sharp. Similar as for the other two dimensions, "activity" might be directly linked to the AROUSAL dimension in most of current models (but see Ertel, 1964 for a critical discussion of a synonymous use of activity and AROUSAL).

The most dominant dimensional models of emotion that strongly impacted neuroscientific studies on the processing of emotional stimuli—such as affective pictures, emotional facial expressions, and emotional words—within the last three decades have been Russell's "Circumplex Model of Affect" (Russell, 1980) and the motivational model by Lang, Bradley, and co-workers (e.g., Lang & Bradley, 2010, see also Hamm, Schupp, & Weike, 2003). Both models suppose that emotions arise from two fundamental systems, one related to hedonic VALENCE (pleasure–displeasure continuum) and the other to AROUSAL, and, further, that each emotion can be understood as a linear combination of these two dimensions, or as varying degrees of both VALENCE and AROUSAL. Interestingly, both accounts differ in their assumption regarding the dependence of the two dimensions. While in Russell's work both dimensions are seen as independent systems, Lang and colleagues assume a strong dependence between VALENCE and AROUSAL. Within his framework, Russell (1980) proposed that emotions are arranged in a circular structure in which attributes (1) correlate highly with those attributes nearby on the circumference of the circle, (2) correlate near zero with those attributes one quarter way, and (3) correlate inversely with those attributes directly opposite the circle (for a review, see Larsen & Diener, 1992). Affects will always fall between the two axes drawn through the two-dimensional (pleasantness and AROUSAL) space. Per definition, very high or very low values at the pleasantness dimension are accompanied by low values at the AROUSAL/activation dimension and vice versa.

In the second and possibly most influential model in the field of affective neurosciences, both dimensions are seen as reflecting motivational activation (e.g., Lang & Bradley, 2010). Here, affective VALENCE is defined as determined by the dominant of two motive systems in the brain: the appetitive system and the defensive system. Whereas the appetitive system is seen to be primarily activated in contexts that promote survival and to produce positive affect, the defensive system would be activated in contexts that involve threat and prompts negative affect. Both systems are suggested to be implemented by neural circuits in the brain. Their activation provides the source of experienced emotions and triggers several functions in the service of adaptive behavior, such as enhanced sensory attention, organismic mobilization and motor action. Affective AROUSAL is not seen as having a separate substrate but is thought to reflect the intensity of motivational activation (e.g., Bradley, Codispoti, Cuthbert, & Lang, 2001), that is, the specific degree of activation of either the appetitive or the aversive system (Lang, Bradley, & Cuthbert, 1998).

The strong relationship between affective VALENCE and AROUSAL has been shown in several rating studies that revealed a boomerang-shaped distribution of the "affective space" formed by covarying VALENCE and AROUSAL judgments. That is, for affective pictures (Lang, Bradley, & Cuthbert, 1998), words (Bradley & Lang, 1999), and tones (Bradley, Cuthbert, & Lang, 1998), emotionally highly valenced stimuli, being either very negative or very positive, also tend to be highly arousing, whereas stimuli of intermediate (neutral) VALENCE tend to be low in AROUSAL. According to Lang and co-workers, the obtained two "arms" within the affective space reflect the bi-motivational foundation of affective judgments due to the degree to which stimuli engage one of the motivational systems in the brain.

Despite the differences in their basic assumptions concerning the structure of the affective space, both the circumplex model and the motivational model of emotions are consistent in the proposal of two affective dimensions being sufficient to describe emotions. One might wonder about the neglect of a third dimension in consideration of the historical development of dimensional emotion models and, particularly, several pieces of evidence that underscore the relevance of at least one additional dimension building the affective space. Lang and associates directly link their two-dimensional model to the early work of Osgood et al. (1957), but do not even mention the third dimension, that is potency or dominance, of the Semantic Differential (e.g., Lang et al., 1998, pp. 1248–9; Lang & Bradley, 2010, pp. 437–8). This becomes especially surprising since the huge database of normative ratings for the International Affective Picture System (IAPS; Lang, Bradley, & Cuthbert, 2005) does not only provide rating values for affective VALENCE and AROUSAL but also on a third dimension, which is called dominance. The IAPS was developed to provide a set of normative emotional stimuli for studies of emotion and attention and is, in fact, one of the databases most frequently used, particularly, in neuroscientific studies of emotion processing. Applying the so-called Self-Assessment Manikin (SAM; Bradley & Lang, 1994; Lang, 1980) for dominance, participants had to judge each picture on a dimension of "controlled vs in-control", ranging from "feelings characterized as completely controlled, influenced, cared for, awed, submissive, guided" to "completely controlling, influential, in control, dominant, autonomous" (Lang et al., 2005, p. 5). Values of these dominance ratings are reported in the IAPS manual and also in the context of some studies (e.g., Bradley, Codispoti, Cuthbert, & Lang, 2001; Bradley, Codispoti, Sabatenelli, & Lang, 2001). However, they were neither taken into account in the discussion of central findings nor in the theoretical considerations by these authors.

In contrast, Russell (1980) mentioned evidence for at least one additional dimension beside pleasantness/VALENCE and AROUSAL/activation, but strongly argues to skip the potency dimension from his model because of the small proportions of variance they account for or inconsistencies in their interpretations, respectively. However, there is evidence from several studies showing (1) that similarities and differences of emotional qualities cannot sufficiently be explained by a two-dimensional structure (e.g., Osgood, 1966; Russell & Mehrabian, 1977; Morgan & Heise, 1988; Gehm & Scherer, 1988) and (2) that the potency/dominance dimension explains more variance as compared to the AROUSAL dimension as, for instance, provided by the GRID study (cf., Fontaine et al., 2007), but also by some earlier work in the tradition of Osgood (e.g., Ertel, 1964; Osgood, May, & Miron, 1975; Shaver, Schwartz, Kirson, & O'Connor, 1987; Traxel, 1962; Traxel & Heide, 1961). Furthermore, ignoring a construct because of its inconsistent definitions would have seriously hampered past attempts at understanding human behavior, cognition, and affect, in general. Nevertheless, in the majority of studies investigating the neural mechanism underlying emotional processing and their peripheral correlates only the two affective dimensions—VALENCE and AROUSAL—were incorporated, as will be shortly reviewed in the following sections.

16.3 **Effects of emotional VALENCE and AROUSAL on peripheral indicators**

Even from a lay perspective, no one would doubt that emotions are accompanied by complex, more or less consciously noticeable changes in the body. From a theoretical perspective, there is still no consensus about the nature and differentiation of somatic and autonomous activation patterns accompanying emotional processing or experience. However, there is copious evidence for specific psychophysiological responses such as muscular, cardiovascular, electrodermal, gastrointestinal, or pupillometric activity in the context of emotional processing or affective behavior (for an overview, see Cacioppo, Tassinary, & Berntson, 2000; cf. Kreibig, 2010, for a review). In line with the framework of Lang and colleagues (e.g., Lang & Bradley, 2010), these peripheral components of emotion are assumed to reflect the preparedness of the body for action (Hamm, Schupp, & Weike, 2003). The preparatory function of emotion involves general AROUSAL, which triggers the whole organism for an action and VALENCE-dependent AROUSAL in service of adaptively specific behavior (e.g., approach or avoidance). A variety of studies using standardized emotional stimuli, such as provided by the IAPS, have shown that normative ratings on the AROUSAL and VALENCE dimensions reliably covary with psychophysiological measures.

For instance, facial muscle activity, as measured by electromyography (EMG), is strongly related to emotional VALENCE ratings. Thus, EMG activity of the corrugator muscle increases linearly as stimuli are rated as more unpleasant; conversely, zygomatic EMG increases with judged pleasantness (Lang et al., 1998; Lang, Greenwald, Bradley, & Hamm, 1993). These activation patterns have not only been shown for affective pictures (Bradley, Codispoti, Cuthbert, & Lang, 2001; Cuthbert, Schupp, Bradley, Birbaumer, & Lang, 2000), but also for emotional words and tones (e.g., Larsen, Norris, & Cacioppo, 2003).

Electrodermal and cardiovascular activity, and changes of the pupil size are probably the most prominent indicators for enhanced emotional AROUSAL. However, like facial EMG measures neither indicator discriminates between positive and negative hedonic VALENCE. In several studies, both unpleasant and pleasant pictures elicited greater skin conductance responses than neutral pictures (e.g., Bernat, Patrick, Benning, & Tellegen, 2006). Recently, Bradley and associates (Bradley, Miccoli, Excrig, & Lang, 2008) replicated these findings showing larger skin conductance responses to high-arousing affective pictures, regardless of their specific VALENCE. In addition, they measured pupillometric responses which covaried with skin conductance responses. Although the pupil is innervated by both branches of the autonomous nervous system—the parasympathetic and the sympathetic part—this data supports the hypothesis that dilations of the pupil reflect enhanced sympathetic activity (Bradley et al., 2008; see further Critchley, Tang, Glaser, Butterworth, & Dolan, 2005).

Like the pupillary system, the heart is dually innervated by both parasympathetic and sympathetic parts of the autonomous nervous system. Changes in heart rate responses to affective pictures appear with a triphasic pattern of initial deceleration, subsequent acceleration, and secondary deceleration (Hamm et al., 2003). The first phase appears to reflect an effect of enhanced AROUSAL, as both pleasant and unpleasant elicit greater initial cardiac deceleration. Consecutively, the heart rate waveform clearly differed between both valences, as the initial deceleration sustained to unpleasant but change to relative acceleration to pleasant pictures (e.g., Bradley, Codispoti, Cuthbert, & Lang, 2001; Bradley et al., 2008).

All the studies mentioned above measured autonomous or skeletomuscular changes in response to affective pictures. In contrast, the impact of emotional aspects in words on these peripheral systems appears to be smaller (Larsen et al., 2003) or even absent (Bayer, Sommer, & Schacht, 2011) as compared to affective pictures. This is probably caused by the fact that reading words requires the translation of arbitrary symbols and thus provides a less direct source of emotional meaning. Interestingly, recent studies using ERPs provide evidence for a rapid activation of emotional content during word processing, even if the emotional content is not in the focus of attention, leading to similar effects at the level of the central nervous system as has been shown for emotional pictorial stimuli.

16.4 VALENCE, AROUSAL, and potency in the brain—evidence from event-related potentials

The processing of emotional stimuli has also been studied with ERPs, where emotion effects have been shown as early as 100 ms post-stimulus (Junghöfer, Bradley, Elbert, & Lang, 2001; Smith, Cacciopo, Larsen, & Chartrand, 2003; Smith et al., 2006). Initially, ERP studies focused on affective picture processing, but recently the focus has been broadened to the processing of emotional words. Two emotion-related ERP components, distinguished by their time course and distribution over the scalp surface, have been suggested to reflect distinct stages of emotion processing: the early posterior negativity (EPN; Junghöfer, Bradley, Elbert, & Lang, 2001; Schupp, Hamm, & Weike, 2003) and the late positive complex (LPC; e.g., Cuthbert, Schupp, Bradley, Birbaumer, & Lang, 2000; Schupp et al., 2000).

The EPN consists in an early difference wave with negative polarity at temporo-occipital electrode sites around 200 and 320 ms, in response to both positive and negative compared to neutral pictures (e.g., Schupp et al., 2004). On the basis of its similarity in latency and scalp distribution to ERP components elicited by voluntary orientation of attention to non-emotional, the EPN is suggested to result from reflex-like visual attention, facilitating sensory encoding processes, and to reflect a transitory phase in which task-relevant stimuli are selected for further, more elaborate processing (see Potts & Tucker, 2001). Recent studies have also shown EPN effects to emotional words (e.g., Herbert, Kissler, Junghöfer, Peyk, & Rockstroh, 2006; Kissler et al., 2007; Schacht & Sommer, 2009a, 2009b). The EPN to words is highly similar to the EPN elicited by affective pictures and emotional facial expressions, indicating at least partially shared or overlapping brain systems involved during this early stage of emotion processing, even though it appears at longer latencies (Schacht & Sommer, 2009a). In a series of experiments (Palazova, Mantwill, Sommer, & Schacht, 2011; Schacht & Sommer, 2009a, 2009b), we have consistently shown that the EPN to emotional words coincides with or follows ERP components that reflect lexical access, indicating that the emotional connotation of written words is part of their semantics.

Sustained elaborate processing of emotional stimuli is presumably reflected in augmented amplitudes of the LPC, which have been shown for affective pictures of both positive and negative VALENCE (e.g., Cuthbert et al., 2000; Schupp et al., 2000; Schupp et al., 2004), as well as for emotional words (e.g., Herbert et al., 2008; Naumann et al., 1992; Schacht & Sommer, 2009a, 2009b). The LPC typically develops in the time range of the P300 component—that is, around 300 ms—and lasts for several hundred milliseconds. The P300 to non-emotional stimuli increases when the eliciting stimulus is attended (e.g., Johnson, 1988), infrequent, or task relevant (e.g., Picton & Hillyard, 1988), and therefore, presumably reflects processes of stimulus evaluation and memory updating (for reviews, see Bashore & van der Molen, 1991; Polich, 2007). Given that processes similar to those in the P300 are reflected in the LPC, it has been suggested that increased LPCs to emotional stimuli are caused by continued perceptual and elaborate analysis that are initiated by their higher intrinsic relevance.

Since the effect of positive emotional VALENCE on both the EPN and LPC amplitudes is similar, this effect is interpreted as being due to the emotional stimuli's larger AROUSAL value (Hamm et al., 2003; Kayser et al., 1997; Schupp et al., 2000). For the LPC, this interpretation has been challenged by studies showing LPC effects of VALENCE, although the AROUSAL level of stimuli had been controlled for pictures (Conroy & Polich, 2007; Yuan et al., 2007) and words (Bayer, Sommer, & Schacht, 2010). In addition, a number of studies reported differing ERP modulations for positive and negative pictures (Delplanque, Silvert, Hot, & Sequeira, 2005; Delplanque, Silvert, Hot, Rigoulot, & Sequeira, 2006; Ito, Larsen, Smith, & Cacioppo, 1998) and words (Herbert et al., 2008). These results do not support an equivocal conclusion about the influences of emotion on LPC amplitudes, but suggest a more complex modulation than by mere variations of AROUSAL.

Moreover, a few studies on emotional word processing indicate that not only the LPC but also the EPN reflect more than pure effects of enhanced general AROUSAL. For instance, Schacht and Sommer (2009a) reported EPN effects for positive but not negative German verbs in a lexical decision although the latter revealed higher AROUSAL ratings. This finding was recently replicated by Palazova et al. (2011), showing larger EPN effects to positive verbs and adjectives as compared to negative words under same task demands.

Evidence for potency effects on ERPs in emotional word processing is scant. Only a few, particularly early studies, implemented the three dimensions of Osgood's (1964) Semantic Differential—evaluation, potency, and activation—in their investigations of ERP correlates of word processing. For instance, Chapman, McCrary, Chapman, and Martin (1980) recorded ERPs while participants loudly repeated words or judged their semantic meanings on rating scales that predominantly loaded on one of the three semantic dimensions. Based on classification functions, the authors report ERPs to reflect differences between the three dimensions as well as between high and low rating values along each dimension. However, since in this study, only recordings from three midline electrodes are reported, a comparison to more recently reported ERP effects to emotional VALENCE and AROUSAL, is impossible. A more differentiated picture about the influence of Osgood's dimensions on ERPs to single words is provided by two studies by Skrandies (Skrandies, 1998; Skrandies & Chiu, 2003). In the first study (Skrandies, 1998), participants were presented with German single words, which significantly differed on one of the three semantic dimensions and had to be visualized and memorized for subsequent recognitions. Here, three parameters of ERP components—latency, amplitude strength, and distribution over the scalp surface—were analysed according to words classified as high or low on the dimensions. Findings indicate influences of all dimensions on several ERP components in these ERP parameters. For instance, differences on the potency and the evaluation (i.e., VALENCE) dimension prolonged the latency of the visually evoked P 100 component in comparison to differences on the activation (AROUSAL) dimension. In the time range of the EPN (around 220 ms), a component of enhanced posterior negativity appeared with significantly shorter latency for stimuli differing on the potency dimension as compared to stimuli differing on the other two dimensions. This finding indicates that the EPN—which in most recent studies has been strongly related to AROUSAL—might also be sensitive to differences at the potency dimension. In contrast, the amplitudes of this posterior negativity did not differ between the word classes, that is differences on each of the dimensions. More evidence for such early effects of these semantic dimensions has been provided by a study using Chinese two-character words with comparable task demands (Skrandies & Chiu, 2003). Results show differences in the above-mentioned parameters of, particularly, early ERP components elicited by differences on the three dimensions. However, both studies revealed somewhat contradictory findings when looking at their results in detail. Therefore, a clear conclusion beyond the specific impact of not only emotional VALENCE and AROUSAL, but also of potency on visual word recognition, as reflected in ERPs, can not be drawn. Further, a direct comparison to more recent studies on emotional word processing can only be made indirectly because of several differences in ERP recordings and analyses. In the following, I will try to provide a first approach to bridge this gap.

16.5 Potency in emotional word processing—a first approach

In a recent study, Palazova and co-workers (Palazova et al., 2011) investigated the functional locus of emotion effects in the processing of single emotional words. Participants performed lexical decisions on emotionally positive, negative, and neutral German nouns, verbs, and adjectives while ERPs from 61 electrode sites were recorded. In line with previous studies (e.g., Schacht & Sommer, 2009a, 2009b), emotional words elicited an EPN and enhanced amplitudes of the LPC. Interestingly, these effects were more pronounced for emotionally positive adjectives and verbs as compared to negative words, even though emotionally positive words were judged as less arousing in pre-experimental ratings. As in the majority of recent studies in this field, the selected emotional words used in this study were not controlled for potency. Motivated by the main findings of the GRID study, showing that emotion terms differ not only on the VALENCE and AROUSAL but also on the potency and expectancy dimensions, a re-analysis of the original ERP data was performed in order to get first answers to the following questions. (1) Is there an impact of potency on the processing of *emotional* words? (2) Do differences on the potency dimension contribute to standard ERP components, that is, EPN and LPC, which have consistently been related to differences in emotional VALENCE and AROUSAL? (3) Are there other or additional ERP effects, respectively, of potency and if so, when in time do they appear during word processing?

In a first step, a subset of emotional words from Palazova et al. (2011) was selected, consisting of 103 word stimuli for which potency ratings were available in the literature. These rating values were taken from a database provided by Schwibbe, Räder, Schwibbe, Borchardt, and Geiken-Pophanken (1992) containing judgments of VALENCE, AROUSAL, and potency for single German verbs, adjectives, and nouns. Judgments of VALENCE and AROUSAL were comparable between the database by Schwibbe et al. (1992) and the study by Palazova et al. (2011) $r = 0.975$ and $r = 0.807$, $ps < 0.001$. Examples for selected words are *schwach* (weak), *faul* (lazy), *leiden* (to suffer), which revealed low potency ratings, and *erfolgreich* (successful), *stark* (strong), *zwingen* (to constrain), which revealed high potency ratings. Interestingly, emotionally negative words ranged from low to high potency ratings, whereas emotionally positive words were mostly characterized by high potency ratings, reflected in a positive correlation between VALENCE and potency ratings, $r = 0.325$, $p < 0.01$ (see Figure 16.1a for the distribution of selected words on the dimensions of VALENCE and potency).

In a next step, ERPs to the selected subset of emotional words from Palazova et al. (2011) were analysed in several ways[3]. First, ERP mean amplitudes were re-calculated item-wise across participants, allowing a classification according to their potency values, and segmented into consecutive 50 ms time windows after stimulus onset. Figure 16.1b depicts the global field POWER (GFP; Lehmann & Skrandies, 1980) of grand averaged ERPs, contrasted for words of high versus low potency as defined by median split. GFP reflects the overall ERP activity across all single electrodes over the scalp at any given moment and thus a measure of amplitude strength. As can be seen

---

[3] In the original study, ERPs were recorded from 20 university students while performing lexical decisions on correct German words and—randomly intermixed—pseudowords. All stimuli were presented in black letters on a dark-gray background until button press.

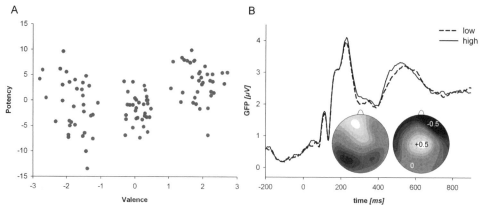

Figure 16.1 a Distribution of ratings on the potency (Schwibbe et al., 1992) and VALENCE (Palazova et al., 2011) dimensions. **b** Global field POWER (GFP) of ERPs to words of high versus low potency. Significant differences were obtained between 250 and 250 ms and 400 and 550 ms. Embedded maps depict the scalp distributions of ERP differences between words of high minus low potency within these time intervals.

in Figure 16.1b, words of high potency elicited larger GFP amplitudes at two different processing stages: around 300 ms and between 400 and 550 ms. This impression was verified by overall ANOVAs on mean ERP amplitudes, including the factors electrode (61) and potency (2), that revealed significant interactions[4] between these factors in the time windows between 250 and 350 ms, $Fs(60,1140) > 3.1$, $ps < 0.01$, $\eta_p^2 > .140$, and between 400 and 550 ms, $Fs(60,1140) > 2.8$, $ps < 0.01$, $\eta_p^2 > .127$. Importantly, the scalp distributions of these potency effects (see Figure 16.1b) clearly resemble the distributions of the EPN and LPC components as shown for positive and negative words in previous studies (e.g., Schacht & Sommer, 2009a, 2009b), and particularly, for emotionally positive words when ERPs were classified for emotional VALENCE in the original analyses by Palazova et al. (2011) and appeared in the same time windows. No further effects of potency were found within the other time segments.

Since the distribution of potency values differs within each of the three VALENCE categories (positive, negative, neutral; see Figure 16.1a), additional ANOVAs on mean ERPs were conducted, including the factors electrode (61), potency (2—high, low), and VALENCE (3—positive, negative, neutral). Here, potency values were divided into two bins for each VALENCE category separately. An additional selection of the word material was made, in order to control for non-emotional, linguistic factors. Finally, 15 words per potency by VALENCE condition contributed to the data analyses, which did not differ in terms of word length (number of letters, number of syllables), word frequency, and imageability ratings between the conditions. ANOVAs revealed significant potency by electrode interactions within the time window of the EPN, between 250 and 350 ms, $Fs(60,1140) > 2.8$, $ps < 0.05$, $\eta_p^2 > 0.126$, but no effects of VALENCE appeared. In contrast,

---

[4] Please note that ERPs were offline transformed to average reference. By definition, the average reference sets the mean amplitude across electrodes to zero for each condition. Therefore, in ANOVAs including all electrodes, only interactions with the electrode site are meaningful. To adjust the degrees of freedom of the F-ratios for violations of the sphericity assumption, the Huynh-Feldt correction was applied. Corrected p-values and uncorrected degrees of freedom values are reported.

between 400 and 550 ms (LPC), both potency and VALENCE significantly affected ERP amplitudes, $F_S(60,1140) > 3.0$, $ps < 0.01$, $\eta_p^2 > 0.140$, whereas no interaction between these two factors appeared. Also in these analyses, no further effects of potency or VALENCE, respectively, have been obtained in other time windows.

Despite the constraints raised by such re-analyses as realized here, the present data indicate that potency actually contributes to ERP effects in emotional word processing. Importantly, these effects appear with both similar latencies and scalp topographies as ERP components that have been previously related to enhanced AROUSAL or positive and negative VALENCE, respectively.

16.6 **Conclusions**

Words definitely provide a special origin of emotion. For instance, they help humans to label and communicate their emotional states and thus play a crucial role in social interactions. From another perspective, many texts elicit emotions in readers since they provide descriptions of emotional situations or states of figures and are appreciated for pleasure or excitement given in the reader. Whereas a lot of research aimed to investigate the mechanisms underlying the preferential processing of emotional stimuli such as affective pictures or emotional facial expressions, the study of processing emotion words and emotional words, respectively, has just recently received more attention. Most of the studies on emotional word or affective picture processing measured behavioral, peripheral, and electrophysiological responses to stimuli that maximally varied on the VALENCE and the AROUSAL dimension, that is, responses to high-arousing positive or negative compared to low-arousing neutral stimuli, presumably, since they have been more or less directly linked to the two-factor model suggested by Lang and colleagues (e.g., Lang & Bradley, 2010). Despite a few studies, the potency dimension had not been taken into account, even though it was considered as a highly relevant dimension of affective space in the pioneering work in this area (e.g., Osgood, 1964).

In the present chapter, a re-analysis of ERP data is provided that aimed to shed light on the question whether and how potency differences might contribute to emotion-related ERP effects. In fact, when ERPs to emotional words differing in their potency values were contrasted, two well-known ERP components were obtained with larger amplitudes to words with high, as compared to words with low, potency ratings. Both components, the EPN and the LPC, have previously been related to the AROUSAL dimension (e.g., Schupp et al., 2007), although there is evidence for VALENCE-specific effects, particularly, in emotional word processing (e.g., Herbert et al., 2008; Schacht & Sommer, 2009a; Palazova et al., 2011). Interestingly, these studies reported some kind of "positivity bias", that is, a larger effect of positive than negative VALENCE on the EPN and/or LPC components, which has also been reflected in facilitated processing of positive words. Given the fact that positive words are characterized also by high potency values, one might speculate whether this processing advantage of positive words is—at least to some extent—derived from potency effects. In contrast, the selected emotionally negative words varied across the whole potency dimension, indicating a larger diversity of emotional meanings within unpleasant concepts. This is, in my opinion, at variance with the assumption that all kind of negative stimuli might activate one unitary motivation system as suggested by Lang and co-workers (e.g., Lang & Bradley, 2010). Future research is needed to differentiate between different sub-types of negative VALENCE and to specify their potentially varying effects in emotion processing.

The present data do not only support the idea that more than two dimensions constitute the semantic space of *emotion terms*, as proved by the GRID study. Moreover, it extends this assumption to the processing of *emotional words*. Recently, Pavlenko (2008) proposed the necessity for such differentiation between linguistic concepts based on differences in their functions: emotion words (equivalent to *emotion terms* used here) are words that directly refer to particular affective states or processes (e.g., "happy," "to rage"); emotion-laden words (equivalent to *emotional words* used here) do not directly refer to emotions, but instead express or elicit emotions from the "interlocutors" (e.g., "loser," "cancers"). Thus, emotion words have the specific function to directly describe ("he/she is sad") or express emotions ("I feel sad"), which is not the case for emotional words. Pavlenko further suggests excluding "emotion-related" words, that describe behavior related to particular emotions but not naming the actual emotions themselves ("tears" and "to scream") from the category of emotion words. Within emotion-laden words, there are different subcategories, which are unclearly demarcated, since words may cross or overlap the subcategories or receive or change emotional connotations in some contexts. As yet, all studies on ERP correlates of emotion effects in language, intermix these different types of words, ignoring potential differences in their semantic representation.

A last remark concerns the most important dimension of emotional meaning: emotional VALENCE. While dimensional models as introduced in this chapter consider emotional VALENCE as a pleasantness dimension, it has been suggested to differentiate between different types of valences (Scherer, 2010a). In his approach, Scherer assumes the existence of different types of VALENCE and that their involvement is defined by the specific type of the appraisal criterion (stimulus evaluation check, SEC). Based on the major classes of SECs, four types of VALENCE criteria are assumed: VALENCE as pleasure (intrinsic pleasantness), VALENCE as satisfaction (goal/need conduciveness), VALENCE as self-worthiness (compatibility with self-standards), and VALENCE as moral worthiness (compatibility with norms/moral standards). One might assume that these different types of VALENCE, which apparently differ in their complexity, might be reflected in ERP components distinguishable in their time course. While early ERP components, as for instance, the EPN might indeed reflect differences in intrinsic pleasantness, components appearing with longer latencies, as for instance, the LPC, might reflect VALENCE differences that are involved in more complex SECs as compatibility with moral standards.

To sum up, in the present chapter, a first attempt was made to investigate the contribution of potency on emotion-related ERP components, which usually are suggested to reflect emotional VALENCE and/or AROUSAL. A re-analyses of ERP data from a study of Palazova and co-workers (Palazova et al., 2011) indeed revealed significant potency effects on both the EPN and the LPC component. Future research should take this second-most important dimension of emotional meaning into account and aim to specify the interplay between potency, AROUSAL, and VALENCE and its impact on language processing. In addition, a specification of linguistic differences between emotion terms and emotional words and their subcategories may help to understand the structure of the human semantic system.

Acknowledgments

The author thanks Marina Palazova for assistance in data analyses and Mareike Bayer, Klaus Scherer, and Werner Sommer for helpful comments and discussions on the present chapter. This research was funded by the German Initiative of Excellence and the "Prize of the Berlin-Brandenburg Academy of Sciences and Humanities for the Support of Young Scholars" awarded to A.S.

Chapter 17

Maggots and morals: Physical disgust is to fear as moral disgust is to anger

Spike W. S. Lee and Phoebe C. Ellsworth[1]

Disgust is a puzzling emotion. In some ways it seems to be more primitive and biological than most other emotions, but it is also extremely variable across cultures. On the biological side, there is a universal facial expression of disgust (Darwin, 1872; Tomkins & McCarter, 1964) and it is one of the few expressions already present in newborns (in response to bitter tastes). It is elicited by putrid food, fetid smells, unclean bodily products such as vomit and feces, death and disfiguring disease, and other threats of contamination (e.g., Bloom, 2004, Chapter 6; Curtis & Biran, 2001; Olatunji et al., 2007; Royzman & Sabini, 2001; Rozin et al., 1999, 2000; Tybur et al., 2009), and these elicitors are very general cross-culturally, perhaps universal. Disgusting things are warm, wet, soft, sticky, slimy, and bestial (Angyal, 1941; Miller, 1997).

On the other hand, every culture also finds certain practices *morally* disgusting, and there is enormous cultural, historical, and individual variability in these elicitors: young children sleeping in the same bed as their parents vs sleeping alone in a separate room (Shweder et al., 1995); blowing one's nose in public vs spitting in public; women wearing shorts vs punishing women who wear shorts; interracial epithets vs interracial marriage. Practices that are seen as disgusting in some times or places are unnoticed or even approved in others.

Is there a single emotion underlying responses to physically disgusting phenomena and the dizzying range of morally disgusting phenomena? What is the relation between the universal response to feces and the highly variable response to women's clothing?

17.1 Two kinds of disgust?

Theorists disagree about whether the term *disgust* defines a single emotion, or more than one. Many researchers treat disgust as a homogeneous emotion with a set of prototypical experiential, expressive, physiological, and functional features. Particular examples of disgust may deviate from the prototype, but are seen as variations on the same basic theme. This assumption is often implicit, for example, in recent studies of the effects of physically disgusting stimuli on moral judgment and behavior (e.g., Jones & Fitness, 2008; Schnall et al., 2008; Wheatley & Haidt, 2005) and on the corresponding effects of moral behavior on disgust-related choices (Lee & Schwarz, 2009; Zhong & Liljenquist, 2006).

[1] Contact authors: Phoebe C. Ellsworth (pce@umich.edu), Department of Psychology, University of Michigan, East Hall, 530 Church Street, Ann Arbor, MI 48109–1043, USA or Spike W. S. Lee (spike.lee@utoronto.ca), Department of Marketing, Rotman School of Management, University of Toronto, 105 St. George Street, Toronto, ON M5S 3E6, Canada

According to some researchers, only physical disgust is a true emotion, and the use of the word "disgusting" to refer to moral violations is nothing but a metaphorical extension of the term as a means of expressing extreme disapproval or indignation (e.g., Jones, 2007; Nabi, 2002). Royzman and Sabini (2001) argue that "purely" sociomoral cues cannot evoke disgust and that people simply use the term *disgust* metaphorically to underscore the strength of their disapproval or indignation. They note that the original version of the Disgust Sensitivity (DS) scale included items with sociomoral elicitors of disgust, but these items were later removed due to a lack of correlation with the overall DS score (cf. Haidt et al., 1994). In a similar vein, Moll et al. (2005) explicitly pointed out the moral connotation of disgust, which they thought should be properly labeled as *indignation* and considered as a moral emotion *affiliated with* disgust (rather than being part of disgust). By implication, *disgust* was reserved for its physical sense. Using written statements as stimuli, they found that self-reported physical disgust could be evoked with or without indignation. But interestingly, disgust and indignation activated both distinct *and overlapping* brain areas.

Other scientists propose the two broad clusters of "primary disgust," "core disgust," or "pure disgust" on the one hand, and "complex disgust" or "(socio)moral disgust" on the other (e.g., Curtis & Biran, 2001; Izard, 1977; Haidt et al., 1997; Marzillier & Davey, 2004; Miller, 1997; Moll et al., 2005; Rozin et al., 2000; Tomkins, 1963). These two clusters correspond to what we would like to call *physical disgust* and *moral disgust*. They conceptualize complex, moral disgust as a more general extension or elaboration of basic, physical disgust through cultural development. Curtis and Biran (2001) speculated that disgust as "an aversion to physical parasites . . . may have come to serve an extended purpose, that of an aversion to social parasites," whose overly selfish behaviors harm societal health, much as germs harm personal health. In physical disgust, we kill germs and avoid contamination; in moral disgust, we punish, avoid, and ostracize social parasites. Offering some empirical support for this idea, Chapman et al. (2009) found that physical contamination and immoral acts elicited the same facial response of oral-nasal rejection.

By far the most common methodological approach to examining the two kinds of disgust has been to compare different elicitors. In a review of the empirical literature on elicitors of disgust, Rozin et al. (2000) identified what they called core disgust, animal-reminder disgust, interpersonal disgust, and moral disgust (see also Barker & Davey, 1997; Haidt et al., 1994; Marzillier & Davey, 2004). Borg et al. (2008) elicited disgust with pathogen-related acts, incestuous acts, and nonsexual acts. They found that participants' self-reported disgust reactions were considerably stronger to pathogen-related and incestuous acts than to nonsexual acts. The three categories of elicitors entrained both common and unique brain networks, revealing discriminant validity at both phenomenological and neurological levels. This distinction holds up in patients with Huntington's disease, who show impairments in generating examples of situations that elicit physical disgust but have no trouble generating examples that elicit moral disgust (Hayes et al., 2007).

This careful attention to differences in *elicitors* does not extend to research on differences in the *experience* or *consequences* of physical and moral disgust. Many researchers seem to assume that the two kinds of disgust, once elicited, are qualitatively the same and involve the same components and processes. Challenging this assumption, Marzillier and Davey (2004) showed that physical disgust and moral disgust were not only elicited by different clusters of stimuli, but also showed different emotional profiles. Moral disgust recruited other negative emotions such as sadness, contempt, fear, and anger, but physical disgust showed no evidence of heightened ratings for any of these negative emotions. Simpson et al. (2006) also found that physical and moral disgust were associated with different self-reported emotional responses, and showed different time courses and gender effects. Taken together, these prior findings suggest that physical disgust and moral disgust are two rather different emotional experiences.

The goal of our research is to add to this analysis an exploration of the *other* components of physical and moral disgust: the appraisals, the action tendencies, and the subjective experience. We begin with the assumption that different kinds of elicitors almost certainly involve different appraisals. We argue that from an appraisal theory point of view (e.g., Frijda, 1986; Scherer, 1984b; Smith & Ellsworth, 1985), the two kinds of disgust involve different appraisals and thus different experiences, physiologies, action tendencies, and motivations to regulate expression. We hypothesize that moral disgust is characterized by a constellation of features—most notably the attribution of agency to another person—that overlaps with the elements of anger; physical disgust is closer to fear. The distinction may be appreciated by comparing physically disgusting situations (e.g., *drinking a glass of milk and discovering a cockroach at the bottom; seeing a man with his intestines exposed after an accident*) with morally disgusting situations (e.g., *hearing a banker say to a Black man, "We don't serve niggers in this bank"; seeing a doctor fondle an anesthetized female patient's breasts before an operation when he thinks no one is around;* Lee & Ellsworth, 2009).

Of course, physical disgust and moral disgust are not mutually exclusive. There are plenty of situations where they co-occur and indeed their intensities may correlate or mutually reinforce each other. But our goal in this chapter is to highlight their distinctive features, as opposed to the usual focus on their shared features or lack of distinction. In so doing, we highlight disgust–fear commonalities and disgust–anger commonalities in addition to the disgust–fear differences and disgust–anger differences emphasized in studies of facial expression (Susskind et al., 2008; Whalen & Kleck, 2008).

17.2 Appraisals, action tendencies, subjective experiences, and regulation of physical disgust and moral disgust in relation to fear and anger

Morality is social. It describes "a code of conduct put forward by a society" (Gert, 2008). Forces of nature, inanimate objects, and animals do not commit immoral acts. People do. The experience of moral disgust, therefore, *necessitates* (a) the presence of an *agent* (b) who behaves in a way that *violates societal norms or personal standards*. These conditions characterize the prototypical morally disgusting situations we mentioned earlier (e.g., seeing a doctor fondle an anesthetized female patient's breasts), but are not necessary to evoke physical disgust (e.g., drinking milk with a roach in it). Contrasts between the two kinds of disgust for these situations have important implications.

The presence of a specific agent in moral disgust provides a target (the wrongdoer) to whom perceivers can attribute responsibility and blame. The social and personal norms by which agentic behavior is judged are generally value-laden, providing perceivers with a sense of justification and righteousness when they feel disgusted by immorality. In order to communicate their moral superiority and their support of community norms, people may be likely to exaggerate their expression of moral disgust. In contrast, physical disgust is less likely to provoke value-laden judgments and censure, because there is no clearly blameworthy human agent. There is no obvious reason for exaggerating the expression of physical disgust.

If the social standards of a group are to be maintained, violations cannot be overlooked. It follows that moral disgust should prompt perceivers to change the agent or the situation by means of reprimands, punishment, or other corrective actions. Thus there is a motivation to approach the transgressors and deal with them. This motivation is likely to be coupled with a subjective feeling of POWER that prepares the person to take action. The absence of perceived agency in physical disgust makes these action tendencies unlikely. Instead, elicitors of physical disgust (e.g., vomit, feces, other bodily excretions) pose physical or biological threats that prompt avoidance. One cleans up a loved one's vomit reluctantly, because one must, not because one wants to. If a stranger vomits, one hurries away. "The behavior associated with [physical] disgust is typically a distancing from the disgusting situation or object. Distancing may be accomplished by an expulsion or removal of an offending stimulus (as in spitting out or washing) or by a removal of the self from the situation (turning around, walking away) or by withdrawal of attention (closing or covering the eyes, engaging in some distraction or changing the topic of a conversation)" (Rozin et al., 1999, p. 430). This avoidance orientation may be accompanied by the subjective experience of weakness and vulnerability.

We argue that in the appraisals of agency and norm violation, the corresponding sense of justification, the action tendencies of approach and punishment, and the subjective experience of dominance, moral disgust resembles anger (Ellsworth & Scherer, 2003; Kuppens et al., 2003); in the absence of perceived agency and sense of justification, the action tendencies of avoidance and withdrawal, and the subjective experience of weakness and dependence, physical disgust resembles fear (Ellsworth & Scherer, 2003; Öhman, 2000). These hypotheses, derived from an appraisal theory framework, go beyond simply proposing a disgust–anger association (which has been found in emotion-similarity sorting tasks in several languages; Fontaine et al., 2002; Shaver et al., 1987; Shaver et al., 1992) or a disgust–fear association (Nabi, 2002; Olatunji et al., 2005; Simpson et al., 2006). We explore the appraisals underlying these associations, as well as the corresponding action tendencies, subjective experiences, and motivations to regulate expression. Our conceptual hypothesis, in its most general formulation, is that (a) moral disgust differs from physical disgust; (b) moral disgust resembles anger; and (c) physical disgust resembles fear. We are not saying that physical disgust and moral disgust have nothing in common, only that there are distinctive components and processes that have not been emphasized in previous work.

We explore our conceptual hypothesis using the GRID dataset. This dataset contains a single term for disgust and does not differentiate physical and moral disgust. In some ways it might have been better (and a more direct test of our hypothesis) if the GRID stimuli included *physical disgust* and *moral disgust* as separate emotions; however, many languages have only one term for disgust, and using two terms might have imposed a distinction on the respondents that was not natural to them. We felt that we could still use the GRID data to explore our hypotheses a little less directly. Our logic was as follows.

We hypothesized that some of the attributes that people chose for *disgust* would overlap with their responses to *anger*, whereas other, different attributes would overlap with their responses to *fear*, suggesting two distinct kinds of disgust. Emotion features that characterize moral disgust, but not physical disgust, should be reported for *disgust* but not for *fear*. Therefore, they should be rated higher for *disgust* than for *fear*. Emotion features that characterize physical disgust, but not moral disgust, should be reported for *disgust* but not for *anger*. Therefore, they should be rated higher for *disgust* than for *anger*. In seeking to extract as much conceptual utility as possible from the GRID data, we believe that our current approach can provide suggestive, although far from definitive, evidence for two kinds of disgust. In the Discussion section, we briefly describe supportive data from studies using different methods.

17.3 **Method**

Participants

One hundred and eighty-two college students at the University of Michigan completed the GRID questionnaire in English. Each participant rated four emotions randomly chosen from a pool of 24, resulting in slightly different sample sizes for disgust, fear, and anger ($n = 35, 33$, and 34).

Analytic strategy and predictions

To test our conceptual hypothesis that (a) moral disgust differs from physical disgust insofar as (b) moral disgust resembles anger, and (c) physical disgust resembles fear, we conducted "per-feature pairwise comparisons" among disgust, fear, and anger in the GRID dataset. We focused on the mean ratings for appraisals, action tendencies, and subjective experience ("emotion features") for which we had a priori predictions. Features on which both emotion terms in the pairwise comparison were rated below 4 (on a 9-point scale) were considered inapplicable to the emotions (e.g., "feeling good" is irrelevant to fear, anger, and disgust) and excluded from analysis.

Since the common term in English (*disgust*) is used in both physical and moral senses, it would obviously have associations with both. Using Smith's (1997) rule-of-thumb for interpretation (see Part II of this volume), we ran four sets of per-feature pairwise comparisons to test the following predictions:

1 Features on which disgust had significantly higher ratings than fear should be features we predicted to characterize moral disgust.

2 Features on which disgust had ratings similar to fear should be features we predicted to characterize physical disgust.

3 Features on which disgust had significantly higher ratings than anger should be features we predicted to characterize physical disgust.

4 Features on which disgust had ratings similar to anger should be features we predicted to characterize moral disgust.

17.4 **Results**

Comparison 1. Differences between disgust and fear: Moral disgust

People found several appraisals more characteristic of disgust than of fear. As can be seen in Table 17.1, disgusting situations were seen as significantly more likely to involve violation of social norms, unjust treatment, and more generally, conflicts with one's own standards and ideals. All of these reflected an evaluative sociomoral judgment. Because morality and social evaluation pre-suppose the existence and involvement of human agents, these mean differences also imply more human agency involved in disgust. Contrary to our expectations, there were no significant differences among fear, anger, and disgust on the direct measure of another person as agent, although the means were in the expected direction. However, the differences between appraisals of human and situational causes did show significant results. The difference between "caused by someone else's behavior" and "caused by chance" was greater for anger than for disgust, and greater for disgust than for fear. The difference between "caused by someone else's behavior" and "caused by a supernatural POWER" were similar for anger and disgust, and greater than for fear. These analyses suggest that human agency was seen as playing a greater role than situational forces in anger and disgust, but not in fear.

The consequences of disgusting situations were seen as more modifiable, possibly because the operation of human agency presents clearer opportunities for reprimands and repairs. When feeling disgusted, people expected to have a stronger urge to hurt and command others. Such tendencies to both *act against* and *act upon* mapped nicely onto their appraisals that *something/someone is wrong* and their evaluative judgment that implied *I know what is right*. Disgust was also consistently higher than fear on such destructive motives as hurting others and destroying whatever is close.

Table 17.1 Empirical and further hypothesized differences between physical disgust and moral disgust in relation to fear and anger

Aspect	Physical disgust (resembling fear)	Moral disgust (resembling anger)		Means		
				Disgust	Fear	Anger
		Results				
Appraisal: agency, value judgment, or morality	Usually not involved	Involved (caused by someone else's behavior[1]†, more violation of social norms[2], unjust treatment[3], and incongruence with one's own standards and ideals[4])	1	6.86	6.23	7.34
			2	6.91	6.06	6.75
			3	7.89	6.32	7.78
			4	6.8	5.9	6.81
Appraisal: consequence	Less modifiable	More modifiable[1]	1	5.23	4.39	5.69
Action tendency	Avoidance and dependence (stop current action[1], prevent sensory contact[2], hide from others[3])	Approach and punishment (oppose[4], be in command of others[5], destroy[6], do damage, hit, say things that hurt[7])	1	7.91	7.71	6.44
			2	7.11	6.71	5.97
			3	6.57	7.55	5.5
			4	7.4	6.32	7.38
			5	5.49	4.45	6.75
			6	6.94	4.77	7.78
			7	7.23	5.23	8.06
Subjective experience	Weaker[1], more submissive[2]	Stronger, more powerful, dominant	1	5.8	7.52	4.03
			2	5.17	6.16	3.75
Regulation: exaggerated expression	Less likely	More likely[1]	1	5.77	5	6.22
		Exploratory hypotheses				
Social complexity	Simpler	More complex (multiple perspectives, multiple interpretations, multiple feelings)				
Intensity (not direction) of physiological response, subjective experience, action tendency, and expression	More intense (because more concrete, experientially direct, sensory, and perceptual; more personally immediate; evolutionarily older)	Less intense (because more abstract, conceptually mediated, ideational, and evaluative; less personally immediate; evolutionarily more recent)				

Note: within each aspect, each superscript corresponds to an item in the GRID questionnaire. For example, superscript 1 within the *Appraisal: agency, value judgment, or morality* aspect corresponds to the item "violated laws or socially accepted norms." † Mean values for this item were in the expected directions but not significantly different from each other.

Taken together, the appraisals and action tendencies that distinguished disgust from fear depict a kind of disgust that is grounded in sociomoral judgment and that motivates people to act in ways that resemble anger, a point also addressed in Comparison 4.

Comparison 2. Similarities between disgust and fear: Physical disgust

Disgust and fear were similar in motivating people to stop whatever they were doing and prevent sensory contact. The tendencies to *withhold* and *move away* were accompanied by a tone of helplessness, as people also wanted to pass on the initiative to others and simply comply with their wishes. They felt weak, powerless, submissive, negative, and bad.

The contrasts between the action tendencies in Comparison 1 (act against, act upon, destroy) and Comparison 2 (withdraw, repel, comply) are striking. Comparison 1 showed that disgust differed from fear in that it prepared people to act in more dominant and approach-oriented ways, tendencies that were predicted to characterize moral disgust and anger. Comparison 2 showed that both disgust and fear involved avoidance and dependence, tendencies that fit well with accounts of physical disgust as a behavioral mechanism to avoid contamination or disease (Curtis & Biran, 2001; Oaten et al., 2009; Rozin & Fallon, 1987). Escaping from physical stimuli such as toxic objects or substances, contagious people, or an environment plagued with contaminants makes functional sense and gives physical disgust its behavioral similarities to fear.

Comparison 3. Differences between disgust and anger: Physical disgust

Disgust was seen as similar to fear (Comparison 2) on features that at the same time distinguished it from anger (Comparison 3). Compared to anger, disgust involved stronger urges to stop whatever one is doing, prevent sensory contact, and disappear or hide from others. Tellingly, in disgust people felt weaker, more submissive, and negative than in anger—the features that captured the similar subjective experiences of disgust and fear. These divergences between disgust and anger matched the convergences between disgust and fear in Comparison 2, arguing for a kind of disgust that feels and functions less like anger but more like fear. By implication, they suggest that disgust is not merely an extreme form of anger.

Comparison 4. Similarities between disgust and anger: Moral disgust

Some of the features in which disgust resembled anger were the same ones that set it apart from fear (Comparison 1). Anger-eliciting and disgust-eliciting situations both involved appraisals of violation of social norms, unjust treatment, and incompatibility with one's own standards and ideals. People considered both kinds of situations as likely to be caused by somebody else's behavior and to have consequences that were bad for themselves and for others but nonetheless modifiable. These appraisals suggest the importance of human agency in the kind of disgust that has more to do with social behaviors than with physical causes, especially those implicating moral values. This kind of disgust prepares people to take the initiative and oppose, acting as though they were angry and ready to punish others.

Exploratory analyses

In addition to these results that supported our a priori predictions, a few other features emerged as more characteristic of disgust than of fear and anger. People's expression of disgust was more likely to be exaggerated than their expression of fear. There may be a communicative dynamic that is particularly relevant to moral disgust. Because moral disgust implies that "something is wrong" and "I know it is wrong," an exaggerated expression ensures clear communication of this message and may serve as evidence of one's righteousness. The communicative function becomes more obvious when we imagine the converse, that is, expressing moral disgust less than we actually feel. If a brutal case of incest comes up in conversation and I say, "I think it's understandable. I mean, yeah, raping his daughter is wrong, but human desires are hard to control," people are likely to be repelled by my perverse moral sense. Exaggerating the expression of disgust confirms one's membership in the moral community.

Disgust resembled anger in this exaggerated expression, but differed in that it prompted a somewhat more reparative action tendency. The hallmark behavioral response in anger is to approach and punish. Disgust shared these, but it also involved a stronger urge to undo what is happening, presumably to restore what was before, possibly making it a more constructive emotion than anger. The difference in action tendency between disgust and fear is also interesting. People were more likely to break contact with others and push things away when disgusted than when scared, suggesting a subtle distinction between the fear response that is more about removing oneself from the scene and the disgust response that is more about removing other people or the disgusting object.

Summary

As summarized in Table 17.1, the term *disgust* elicited two separate, coherent clusters of appraisals, action tendencies, subjective experiences, and modes of expression regulation. The ones we associate with moral disgust involve more value-laden judgments, sociomoral concerns, and modifiable consequences. These appraisals imply the presence of human agency. Although differences among fear, anger, and disgust on the direct measure of agency did not reach significance, human agency was seen as more important than situational forces for anger and disgust, but not for fear. They also fit with people's stronger urges to approach and punish, accompanied by exaggerated expression and subjective experience of POWER and dominance. The ones we associate with physical disgust, in contrast, are seen as involving less modifiable consequences, less value judgment, stronger urges to avoid and comply, diminished expression, and a sense of weakness and submissiveness.

17.5 **Discussion**

Exploratory analyses of the GRID dataset support the distinction suggested by earlier researchers between physical disgust and moral disgust, but also suggest that moral disgust is not simply an extension of physical disgust to a wider range of elicitors. Instead, moral disgust involves distinct appraisals such as incompatibility with personal or social standards (Scherer, 1984b) and changes the dominant action tendency from the withdrawal and avoidance characteristic of physical disgust (e.g., Rozin et al., 2000) to approach and attack, from flight to fight. Physical disgust shares appraisals with fear, moral disgust with anger. These findings are preliminary because the presence of one term (*disgust*) instead of two (*physical disgust* and *moral disgust*) in the present dataset allows only an indirect test of the hypotheses and must be supplemented by other methodological approaches to testing the physical–moral distinction. They also suggest several potential avenues for research.

Agency

Human agency is seen as more important than situational factors in the experience of moral disgust but not physical disgust. How does agency come to be associated with disgust? Developmentally, physical disgust precedes moral disgust. Danovitch and Bloom (2009) found that both kindergarteners and fourth graders respond with disgust to physically disgusting situations, but the kindergarteners are less likely to be disgusted by moral violations. Of course, even physical disgust develops over time: very young children have no qualms about putting food picked up from the floor or even insects and worms into their mouths until their horrified parents teach them that it is disgusting (Bloom, 2004, Chapter 6). It may be that once children have internalized physical disgust, they react with disgust to other children who have not. When they see another child put a worm into his mouth, they are disgusted not just by the behavior but by the child, the agent of the disgusting behavior. They blame the child and feel superior, and with the attribution of agency comes anger. At this point our reasoning is sheer speculation, but it is a promising avenue for future work.

It is also important to remember that agency is not an all-or-none appraisal. When an action is seen as relatively uncontrollable or unintentional, the perceiver is likely to attribute less agency and thus less responsibility to the wrongdoer, feel less morally disgusted or angry, and call for less severe punishment. A person can be seen as lacking control for a variety of reasons, such as stupidity, ignorance, or youth. If a mentally retarded person is pedophilic or voyeuristic, people may still find the behavior unacceptable but feel less disgusted or angry at the offender. If the purpose of punishment is to change behavior, then an actor whose problematic behavior is unmodifiable may be seen as less worthy of punishment (and elicit less moral disgust and anger). The law of homicide recognizes different degrees of agency, differentiating premeditation, heat of passion, recklessness, negligence, and action under duress, and adjusts punishment accordingly. Children, and people suffering from mental illness or deficiency, are held less responsible than adults. Our results suggest that the perception of agency is implicated in moral disgust and the motivation to punish. Of course it is rare that we see people as having absolutely no control over their behavior. The fact that human action is generally seen as controllable may explain why the co-occurrence of moral disgust and anger is the rule rather than the exception.

Emotional complexity

Another promising future direction is the emotional complexity afforded by the presence of multiple parties in morally disgusting situations—at least two (the wrongdoer and the perceiver), often more (a victim or victims). Perspective can powerfully shape emotional experience (e.g., Cohen et al., 2007; Kross et al., 2005). We suggest that when the real eye or the mind's eye attends to different people in a complex social scene, different appraisals become salient, and different processes ensue in the emotion components. Multiple perspectives afford multiple interpretations that generate multiple feelings. Focusing on the perpetrator elicits disgust; focusing on the victim elicits sympathy; focusing on the whole situation elicits frustration; focusing on the self as a perceiver often suggests "I am different from the perpetrator" and elicits a sense of superiority. People's descriptions of their personal experiences of moral disgust reveal such shifting perspectives and emotional changes (Lee & Ellsworth, 2009). Earlier we cited Marzillier and Davey's (2004) finding that morally disgusting events evoke several negative emotions. When people turn the focus onto themselves, their emotion can even change VALENCE from negative to positive as they now feel righteous and superior.

Physically disgusting situations are typically less socially complex and thus less emotionally complex (Marzillier & Davey, 2004). Maggots, rotten meat, and feces, no matter how you look at them, are disgusting. Whether the focus is on the elicitor itself, on the whole situation, or on yourself as a perceiver, the appraisals seem similar, as does the tendency to simply leave the scene and avoid contact with it. Other data suggest that people's descriptions of their feelings in physically disgusting experiences are relatively simple (Lee & Ellsworth, 2009).

Beyond English—potential of cross-linguistic, cross-cultural analysis

This chapter provides an indirect, preliminary exploration of features common to physical disgust and fear on the one hand and to moral disgust and anger on the other. These associations have proven to be coherent and replicable in our subsequent research using multiple methods, correlational and experimental, to provide evidence that physically disgusting situations and experiences are distinct from morally disgusting ones and have different psychological consequences (Lee & Ellsworth, 2009). For example, analyses of people's self-reported emotional reactions to a variety of situations show that people react with strong fear to the most physically disgusting situations but with strong anger to the most morally disgusting situations. In physically disgusting situations, people who feel more disgusted also feel more fear, even controlling for anger. In morally disgusting situations, people who feel more disgusted are also angrier, even controlling for fear.

Altogether these convergent findings deepen our understanding of the two kinds of disgust and their very different appraisals, action tendencies, subjective experiences, and expression regulation. At the same time, it is noteworthy that all of the observed effects are based on a language where the term *disgust* applies to both physical and moral stimuli. Although the same is true in many languages, we are cautious about hasty generalization across languages. The GRID dataset may provide examples of languages where the term *disgust* is applicable only at the physical level or only at the moral level (though this seems less likely), or languages that have two or more distinct terms for disgust. Inquiries to GRID investigators reveal that in some languages the vocabulary for disgust is much more finely differentiated than it is in English. In the future, we plan to follow up our investigation with a more detailed examination and comparison of the connotations of disgust in languages that have one, two, or several different terms for this cluster of emotional experiences.

Acknowledgments

This research was supported by an RC Lee Centenary Scholarship to the first author and by a University of Michigan Distinguished University Professorship to the second.

We thank Klaus R. Scherer, Johnny J. R. Fontaine, and Cristina Soriano for their support with data analysis and helpful comments on this chapter.

Chapter 18

The GRID meets the Wheel: Assessing emotional feeling via self-report

Klaus R. Scherer,[1] Vera Shuman, Johnny J. R. Fontaine, and Cristina Soriano

The GRID study has provided a wealth of new data of high relevance to understand the semantics of emotion terms. This data can be profitably applied to create new tools for emotion research, or to further develop the existing ones. Here, we illustrate one such application by describing how the GRID paradigm was used to improve and further validate a popular tool for emotion assessment, namely the Geneva Emotion Wheel (GEW), a self-report measure of feelings.

Componential theories define emotion as a process during which several components such as physiological responses, motor expression, and cognitive representations (of both eliciting events and self-perceived response patterns) become synchronized over a limited period of time (see Chapter 1). One of these components is Subjective Feeling, a holistic cognitive representation that integrates the temporally coordinated changes of the other components into a succinct, well formed Gestalt, allowing the individual to reach awareness of his/her state and label it—stating that he/she "has" or "feels" a particular emotion. In order to study the feeling component of emotion, psychologists need to rely on self-report. There is no other means but to ask the individual to report on the nature of his/her experience, since feeling is defined as a subjective cognitive representation of the emotional state which reflects a unique integration of mental and bodily changes in the context of a particular event (see Chapter 1). Emotion researchers currently use various paradigms for self-report, including the more recently developed GEW, to be reviewed below.

18.1 Classic self-report emotion assessment methods

Psychologists sometimes ask the participants in a study to describe their feelings in their own words. While this procedure may yield interesting information, it is fraught with problems. For example, people differ with respect to their verbal ability and richness of vocabulary (e.g., Gohm & Clore, 2000), which makes it difficult to compare reports across individuals or to rely on their accuracy. This is a major problem in controlled experimental research where fine-grained scalar measurement for a circumscribed number of specific feeling states is required. In consequence, psychologists generally use forced-choice self-reports of emotional experience. There are two major approaches: (1) the discrete emotion labels approach, and (2) the dimensional rating approach. The following section, based on Scherer (2005a), reviews these two traditions.

[1] Corresponding author: Klaus R. Scherer. Swiss Center for Affective Sciences—University of Geneva. 7, Rue des Battoirs, CH-1205 Geneva, Switzerland. Klaus.Scherer@unige.ch

The *discrete emotion labels approach* is used by scholars and laymen alike to categorize the stream of emotional experience into separate states profiting from the existence of specific emotion words and expressions in language (the type of words used in the GRID study). As shown in Chapter 3, while there are differences between languages with respect to the richness of the emotion lexicon and the meanings of related words, there is also a high degree of overlap. Darwin (1872) has used this convergence to postulate the evolutionary continuity of a set of fundamental emotions and the observable physiological and expressive symptoms that accompany them. This approach has been revived by Tomkins (1962), and has been popularized by Izard (1971; differential emotions theory) and Ekman (1972; basic emotion theory). In this tradition, categorizing emotional experiences according to the emotion words available in natural languages, it is typically assumed that the language-based categories reflect unique appraisal and response patterns (facial, vocal, and physiological) driven by typical event appraisals.

Researchers adopting the discrete emotion approach to assess emotional experience use scales with nominal, ordinal, or interval characteristics. Typically, respondents are presented with a list of emotion terms and are asked (1) to check the terms that best describe the emotion experienced (nominal scale); (2) to indicate on a scale (generally with 3 to 7 points) whether the emotion was experienced "a little," "somewhat," or "strongly" (ordinal scale); or (3) to use an analog scale (e.g., an underlying dimension from 0 to 100) to indicate exactly how much or how intensely the emotion was experienced (interval scale). Methods vary on whether respondents are to respond choosing only the most pertinent emotion category, two or more categories to indicate possible blends, or all categories in a list (replying with "no" or "0" for the emotions that are not at all appropriate to describe the experience). Some standardized instruments of this kind have been proposed in the literature (e.g., the Differential Emotion Scale; Izard, 1991). However, most researchers create ad hoc lists of emotion categories that seem pertinent for a specific research aim, without worrying too much about the representativeness of the chosen list or how well results obtained with the specific list may compare to results obtained with other emotion lists.

The results obtained with the emotion label approach are generally highly plausible and easily interpretable, given that widely shared and frequently used natural language labels tend to be employed. However, it is often difficult or even impossible to compare results across different studies in which widely different sets of emotion labels have been used. In addition, the statistical analysis of these data is hampered by the abundance of missing data and the difficulty to analyze and interpret the frequently reported emotion blends (Larsen et al., 2009; Scherer, 1998; Scherer & Ceschi, 2000). Often, problems are encountered of differential familiarity of respondents with particular emotion words, as well as differential interpretation of the meaning of the terms provided by the researcher. In addition, there are other problems with a discrete emotion response format, such as confusions (e.g., in the case of very extensive word lists), order effects, and other types of artifacts such as demand characteristics (e.g., the choice of specific emotion words may give away the research aim).

The *dimensional approach* in the self-report assessment of emotional experience was pioneered by the German psychologist Wilhelm Wundt (1896), who used introspection to develop a structural description of subjective feelings consisting of their position in a three-dimensional space formed by the dimensions of VALENCE (positive–negative), AROUSAL (calm–excited), and tension (tense–relaxed). This proposal has had a strong impact, both on the measurement of feeling (e.g., Schlosberg, 1954) and on the assessment of emotional connotations of language concepts in general (e.g., Osgood, Suci, & Tannenbaum, 1957). The theoretical foundations of this approach and its recent research development are discussed in detail in Chapter 2 of this book, showing that this domain of inquiry is currently dominated by a two-dimensional VALENCE × AROUSAL model.

To obtain a self-report of feeling with this approach, respondents are typically asked to indicate how positive or negative and how excited or aroused they feel (either in two separate steps, or by providing a two-dimensional surface and asking the respondent to determine the appropriate position in it; Larsen et al., 2009). As a result, the emotional feeling of the person is described by a point in this VALENCE × AROUSAL space. In some cases, respondents are also asked to separately evaluate the positive and negative parts of the VALENCE scale (see Chapter 2). In other cases, three dimensions (VALENCE, AROUSAL, and dominance) are assessed (e.g., Self Assessment Manikin Test, Bradley & Lang, 1994). This simple and reliable method lends itself to advanced statistical processing due to the general use of interval scaling. However, the information obtained is limited to the degree of positive or negative feeling and the degree of felt bodily excitation. Furthermore, the dimensional approach does not allow differentiating intensity of feeling from bodily excitation, which are clearly different constructs. For example, while intense anger is likely to be characterized by high AROUSAL, intense sadness is often characterized by very low AROUSAL. Thus, mild sadness and intense sadness could not be differentiated based on a VALENCE × AROUSAL space alone, as the AROUSAL level is low in both cases. This is a problem for researchers who are interested in clearly differentiating emotions like sadness and depression or grief. Obviously, any attempt to reduce positions in a multidimensional space to a two-dimensional representation will face this problem.

Another disadvantage is that, while most lay persons have little problem evaluating the positivity or negativity of a feeling (or event) and the approximate degree of their felt AROUSAL, the resulting point in two-dimensional space has no specific meaning for them and cannot be communicated to others. It would seem very strange to tell someone that I feel 2.3 positive and 1.6 aroused. Emotional sharing (Rimé, 2009) is an important social phenomenon, directly linked to the adaptive function of emotion communication through expression, and this function would not be well served by a two-dimensional metric.

Most importantly, however, in the two-dimensional VALENCE × AROUSAL space several rather different emotions are close neighbors. Figure 18.1 reproduces the mapping of the terms Russell (1983) used as markers for his emotion circumplex in two-dimensional VALENCE-AROUSAL space (original terms used by Russell in capital letters). In this figure, emotions as different as anger and fear, and other related terms, appear located in the immediate vicinity, as they all share high negative AROUSAL. In consequence, dimensional ratings on the VALENCE × AROUSAL space by themselves do not seem advisable if a researcher is interested in diagnosing the *quality* of a particular feeling. Reisenzein (1994) reviews this problem and suggests using appraisal theory to disambiguate the quality of neighboring states in VALENCE × AROUSAL space (Gehm & Scherer, 1988). As shown in this volume, the use of a discrete emotion label provides at least probabilistic information on the prototypical appraisal patterns differentiating the respective emotions. While appraisal profiles obviously provide the means for a more fine-grained differentiation (Scherer, Schorr, & Johnstone, 2001; and Chapters 1 and 12), this alone does not solve the problem of the lack of an appropriate self-report instrument that is precise, valid, and economical.

Clearly, the two classic self-report approaches reported above have both advantages and disadvantages. Given the central role of emotion self-report in emotion research, it is surprising that relatively few attempts have been made so far to develop new instruments to avoid some of their shortcomings. In particular, it might be worth investing in the development of an instrument capable of combining the advantages of the precise differentiation provided by natural language labels with the simple organizational structure afforded by a two-dimensional space. One possibility would be to use discrete emotion labels and arrange them graphically in a two-dimensional affect space, allowing the user to rapidly orient in this space. Such an instrument would be useful for a wide range of research goals.

Figure 18.1 Alternative dimensional structures for the semantic space of emotions.
Reproduced from Social Science Information, 44(4), What are emotions? And how can they be measured? Scherer, K. R., pp. 695–729, Figure 1 © 2005, Sage Publications, with permission.

18.2 The Geneva Emotion Wheel—design features

Based on these considerations, the Geneva Emotion Wheel (GEW) was designed to combine a discrete and a dimensional approach in the self-report assessment of emotion. It consists of a theory-based circular arrangement of discrete emotion terms in two-dimensional space according to the following design criteria (Scherer, 2005):

1 Two dimensions form the underlying structure of the instrument—VALENCE and control/POWER

2 The instrument uses standard emotion labels from natural languages to capitalize on respondents' intuitive understanding of the semantic field of emotion terms

3 Emotion terms are displayed in a systematic fashion by aligning them with respect to the underlying dimensional structure

4 The instrument allows the systematic assessment of the intensity of feelings

5 The instrument's user-friendly graphical design allows the respondent to rapidly understand the principle and use the instrument in a reliable fashion.

Below we describe how each of these design criteria was addressed in the development of the GEW:

1 **Choice of dimension.** There can be little doubt that VALENCE (positive–negative or pleasant–unpleasant), separating positive and negative emotions, constitutes the most important

dimension of affective space. The decision on the second dimension is less obvious. Despite the fact that, as shown above, the advocates of activation or AROUSAL as the second major dimension have dominated the scene for the last few decades, there are a number of drawbacks to this choice. As shown above, an AROUSAL dimension is very limited in its usefulness to differentiate between emotions due to the fact that most emotion families have several members that differ with respect to their degree of AROUSAL. Furthermore, it is not always clear exactly what is meant by the terms "AROUSAL" and "activation." While *AROUSAL* generally refers to sympathetic AROUSAL in the sense of the dominance of the sympathetic branch of the autonomous nervous system, *activation* is often used in connection with motivation or action tendencies, not necessarily requiring a high degree of sympathetic AROUSAL.

Beyond AROUSAL/activation, there are of course alternative dimensions that can be chosen as a second dimension after VALENCE. For example, Wundt (1905) proposed "tension–relaxation" and Schlosberg (1954) "attention–rejection." Most importantly, Osgood and collaborators (1957) highlighted the importance of a *potency* (or POWER, dominance) dimension in their seminal work on the semantic differential, placing this dimension second after *evaluation* (VALENCE), and before *activity* (activation, AROUSAL). This fits very well with an appraisal account of emotion. If emotions are indeed elicited and differentiated by appraisal patterns (see Chapter 1), the structure of the emotional space should be largely determined by the major appraisal dimensions. The close link between the appraisal checks "intrinsic (un)pleasantness" and "goal (in)consistency" or "goal conduciveness/obstruction" on the one hand, and the VALENCE dimension on the other, is obvious. The same is true for the link between the POWER/potency dimension and the coping potential check (which determines the degree of control available to the individual in a situation, as well as the POWER available to exercise that control; see Scherer, 1984b). As shown by numerous studies (see reviews in Ellsworth & Scherer, 2003; Scherer, Schorr, & Johnstone, 2001), the appraisal dimensions that seem to have the strongest impact on emotion differentiation are indeed goal conduciveness (representing VALENCE) and coping potential (control/POWER), corresponding to Lazarus' (1968) pioneering distinction between primary and secondary appraisal. Obviously, differences in AROUSAL/activation and intensity are also important determinants of feeling but they are more likely to define differences within an emotion family rather than between emotion families. In consequence, it was decided to use a two-dimensional affect space including the dimensions of VALENCE (based on pleasantness and goal conduciveness appraisals) and POWER/potency/control (based on coping potential appraisals) to organize the discrete emotion labels to be measured by the GEW.

Scherer (2005) further justified this theory-driven decision by arguing that this two-dimensional structure fits the organization of emotion terms in the two-dimensional space obtained, for example, through the analysis of similarity ratings. He provides an example, reproduced in Figure 18.1, in which a two-dimensional structure (conducive/obstructive × high/low control–POWER) found for 80 German terms (reported in Scherer, 1984b, pp. 47–55) is superimposed on the item distribution of English terms obtained by Russell (1983). The figure shows that both a classic VALENCE by AROUSAL structure (as postulated by Russell) and a VALENCE (conducive/obstructive) by control/POWER structure (as based on an appraisal model) can be justified, as the respective axes are just rotated by 45°. The latter structure provides a theoretically more homogeneous solution, as both factors represent the two major appraisal criteria.

2 **Choice of emotion families.** It is difficult to decide a priori, on purely theoretical grounds, which words, labels, or expressions should be chosen to represent the discrete states within the different regions of the continuous two-dimensional space spanned by VALENCE and POWER/potency. In the interest of replicability of results across studies, it was attempted to choose a

standard set of emotion families that met three conditions: (1) having been frequently used in past research (to ensure their utility in the assessment instrument), (2) covering most of the regions or segments of the two-dimensional space (to be able to map most positions in affective space), and (3) affording an arrangement of the terms around the rim of the wheel in approximately equal distances. As one might imagine, it is virtually impossible to find a set of emotion terms that equally satisfies all three conditions. In consequence, a pragmatic approach was adopted in the design of the GEW, giving greater weight to the first criterion to achieve a compromise that was satisfactory from the standpoint of potential users. Note that to accommodate users with specific needs, it is accepted that they replace part of the standard terms with terms of their choice, provided that the terms used are differentiated by VALENCE and control/POWER and can be reasonably represented on a circle in this space.

3 **Circular arrangement of emotion terms.** In the GEW, emotion terms representative of major emotion families are arranged in a circle (see Figure 18.3). The two underlying dimensions, VALENCE and control/POWER, separate the wheel into four quadrants: Negative VALENCE–low control/POWER, negative VALENCE–high control/POWER, positive VALENCE–low control/POWER, and positive VALENCE–high control/POWER. The position of the emotion terms in these clusters should correspond to their values on the VALENCE and control/POWER dimensions.

4 **Intensity ratings.** Members of any one specific emotion family can be expected to vary among each other with respect to intensity (e.g., irritation–anger–rage), which, as argued above, may correlate with, but is not the same as, physiological AROUSAL. It was, therefore, decided to map intensity on the distance between the rim and the hub of the wheel, representing the intensity of a specific emotional experience as the distance of its position from the central point in the VALENCE–control/POWER space (see also Reisenzein, 1994; Russell, 1980, p. 1170).

5 **Ease of use.** The wheel interface is easy to understand. Participants are asked to identify an experienced or imagined emotion among the various options provided. They are also asked to rate its intensity on the basis of the distance from the hub of the wheel, which implies choosing one of the answer circles increasing in size from the hub to the rim (the larger the circle, the more intense the emotion is reported to be). Thus, the meaning of the response options is quite intuitive. Also, in the interest of reading ease, the number of emotion families is limited. Finally, the alignment of the emotion terms based on the underlying dimensions should facilitate the usability of the GEW.

Note that the resulting instrument, although conceived in a very different fashion and for a rather different purpose, corresponds in several aspects to the various proposals of personality assessment instruments based on the notion of an "interpersonal circumplex", with the dimensions of "warmth vs hostility" or "love vs hate 'on the one hand and' dominance vs submission" on the other (Leary, 1957; Wiggins & Trobst, 1997). The two dimensions of nurturance/hostility (or warmth/coldness) and dominance/submission are highly comparable to VALENCE and control/POWER (which has often been called dominance in the literature). The arrangement of words in the GEW turns out to be also very similar to the emotion distribution in Plutchik's (1980b) emotion circumplex color wheel (see Figure 18.2), even though this theorist started from the notion of adaptation-oriented basic emotions. One might almost surmise that he arranged the emotions around the circumplex with an implicit VALENCE by POWER structure in mind.

In what follows, two stages of the development and of the investigation of the structural validity of the GEW will be described.

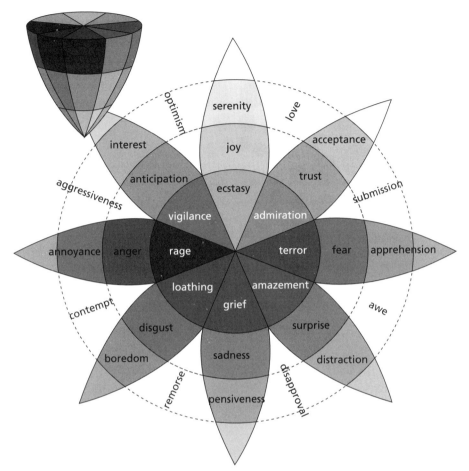

Figure 18.2 Plutchik's emotion circumplex.

Reproduced from American Scientist, 89, Plutchik, R., The nature of emotions: Human emotions have deep evolutionary roots, a fact that may explain their complexity and provide tools for clinical practice, pp. 344–350 © 2001, The Scientific Research Society. Reprinted by permission of American Scientist, magazine of Sigma Xi, The Scientific Research Society.

18.3 Stage 1: Development and structural validation of prototype versions of the GEW

The first prototype (Version 1.0) of the GEW (see Figure 18.3) was developed as a tool for the verbal report of emotions in a study of email communication (financed by the Gottlieb Daimler and Karl Benz Foundation). In this version, four emotion families were presented per quadrant, yielding a total of 16 emotions in the wheel (which seemed reasonable considering that the number of "basic emotions" is often considered to be somewhere between 6 and 14). In this version, a separate word (adjective) was proposed for each level of intensity response option within one emotion family (e.g., vexed, irritated, angry, enraged for the anger family; these are not visible in Figure 18.3, they appeared when the mouse cursor passed over the circles). The choice of the concrete families

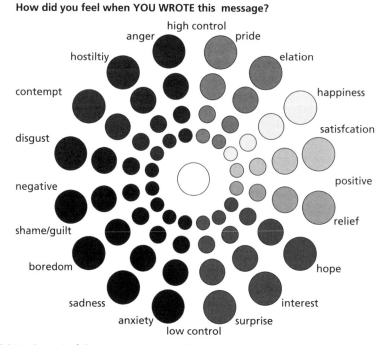

Figure 18.3 Version 1.0 of the Geneva Emotion Wheel. Reproduction of a VisualBasic screen dump; intermediate labels occurred when the mouse cursor passed over the circles.

Reproduced from Social Science Information, 44 (4), What are emotions? And how can they be measured? Scherer, K. R., pp. 695–729 © 2005, Sage Publications, with permission.

was largely determined by what are generally considered to be basic or fundamental emotions, frequently studied in the field.

Based on pilot studies with Version 1.0 of the GEW, a second version (Version 2.0, see Figure 18.4) was developed with two words (relatively close synonyms) referring to each of the 20 emotion families; the goal was to emphasize that each response option represented an emotion *family* rather than individual emotions. Furthermore, as the gradation of intensity levels by four different adjectives from the semantic field of the emotion family in the prototype Version 1.0 proved problematic (in terms of reliability and translatability of the gradation differences; Bänziger, Tran, & Scherer, 2005), in Version 2.0 the different intensity response options within one emotion family were therefore represented only with unlabeled circles of different sizes. Also, some emotions were placed in slightly different positions based on the results of the initial studies (e.g., "interest" passed to a somewhat higher position on the control/POWER dimension).

In several studies, the structural validity of placing the emotion terms in the GEW Versions 1.0 and 2.0 was assessed (see Bänziger, Tran, & Scherer, 2003, 2005; Sacharin, Schlegel, & Scherer, 2012). The results of these studies for the respective GEW Versions address similar issues and are, therefore, presented together below. Additionally, studies performed in our lab and other labs examined how well the GEW Versions 1.0 and 2.0 fared compared to other measurement tools (Caceido & van Beuzekom, 2006; Tran, 2004).

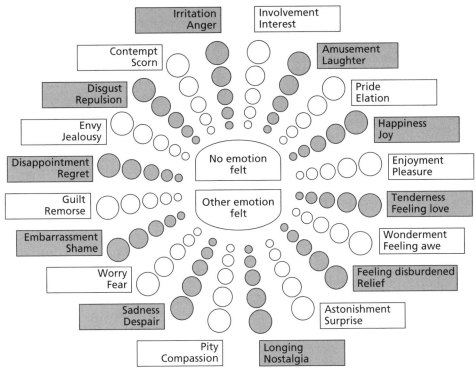

Figure 18.4 Template of Version 2.0 of the GEW (distributed until March 2013 via the website http://www.affective-sciences.org/researchmaterial and replaced by the new version 3.0 described in this chapter).

18.4 **Methods**

Two paradigms were used to assess the validity of the structure of the original version of the GEW: (1) similarity ratings of emotion words, and (2) direct ratings of the position of these words on the VALENCE and control/POWER dimensions. For Version 1.0, Bänziger et al. (2005) performed several validation tasks with a sample of 28 native English and 31 native French speakers. In a first task, respondents performed pair-wise similarity ratings of the 16 emotion family nouns positioned around the circumference of the wheel. In a second task, the 64 adjectives (16 × 4) representing the intensity gradations within families were sorted into the 16 family categories. In a third task, a subsample of 14 English and 15 French speakers rated the 16 emotion family nouns and 64 adjectives by using a dedicated graphic interface (enlarging a circle on the screen to rate intensity and moving markers within a two-dimensional space to rate VALENCE and control/POWER). Another subsample (14 English and 16 French speakers) rated the intensity, VALENCE, and control/POWER associated with each of the 16 emotion nouns and 64 adjectives on continuous rating scales using a mouse-operated slider. For Version 2.0, Sacharin et al. (2012) examined ratings of VALENCE and control/POWER on 11-point scales in an online study with 40 native English speakers. In this study, VALENCE was defined as follows: "the situation is experienced as (un)pleasant and enjoyable (disagreeable) and/or is likely to have positive and desired (negative and undesired) consequences for the person." In turn, control/POWER was described as "the person believes that he/she can (cannot) influence the situation to maintain or improve it (if desired)."

To examine the usability of the GEW, Tran (2004) compared the emotion assessment—first by using the GEW with ratings of emotions presented as word lists in a sample of 80 business school students, and later by administering the GEW in a simulation study with 106 managers attending executive development seminars in four to seven person teams. Caceido and van Beuzekom (2006) directly compared the utility of the GEW with the utility of the PrEmo (Desmet, 2003), a graphical measure for the assessment of discrete emotions.

18.5 **Results**

With regard to the structural validity of the GEW Version 1.0 (Bänziger et al., 2005), the categorization task showed that the adjectives representing intensity differences within an emotion family were almost all correctly classified. However, the agreement on the intensity gradation was less than perfect. With regard to the placement of the main emotion family labels in the VALENCE and POWER space, the ratings of similarity were submitted, for each language sample separately, to multidimensional scaling (MDS) analyses, using an ordinal model and Euclidian distances. The following fit measures for a two-dimensional solution were computed: English sample, stress = 0.34, RSQ = 0.52; French sample, stress = 0.34, RSQ = 0.39. The arrangement of the 16 emotion families in the two dimensions largely confirmed the theoretical prediction with respect to the overall clustering of the emotions in high/low POWER and high/low VALENCE. Exceptions were "interest" in the English sample and "relief" (soulagement) in the French sample, which were empirically found to be placed in the high control/POWER quadrant rather than the predicted low control/POWER quadrant. Similar to the MDS analyses, the data from the direct ratings of VALENCE and control/POWER supported the differentiated alignment of the emotions along the wheel very well for the VALENCE dimension. However, the empirical alignment of the emotions on the POWER/control dimension corresponded less well to the theoretical predictions. This was particularly true for the negative emotions. These emotions were also rated less reliably on the control/POWER dimension as indicated by large standard deviations.

The results of the Sacharin et al. (2012) study can be summarized as follows: for the VALENCE ratings, 19 out of 20 negative emotions and 15 out of 20 positive emotions were rated as predicted. Among the negative, only "compassion" was rated as more positive than expected. Among the positive, "nostalgia," "longing," "feeling disburdened," "astonishment," and "involvement" were not significantly different from the expected position. The results for the control/POWER ratings are more problematic—only 8 out of 20 high control/POWER emotions (all positive emotions) and only 1 out of 20 low control/POWER emotions ("sadness") were rated as predicted. After computing the mean VALENCE and control/POWER ratings for each word across raters, control/POWER and VALENCE were positively associated as reflected in a positive correlation of VALENCE and control/POWER ratings across the 40 word ratings, $r(40) = 0.718$, $p < 0.001$. Furthermore, control/POWER ratings had greater standard deviations than VALENCE ratings (2.89, 1.51), $t(39) = 11.68$, $p < 0.001$. This is in line with the findings reported by Bänziger et al. (2005) with respect to the difficulty of finding the predicted arrangement for the negative, low control/POWER emotions.

Studies examining the usability of the GEW for emotion assessment compared with other measures showed that the same feelings are associated with different vignette scenarios when using the nouns in GEW Version 1.0 as word lists (Tran, 2004). For the use with managers in a quasi-naturalistic environment, very high response rates were obtained in daily assessments for 8 to 10 days, providing an indicator of the managers' strong involvement in the emotion assessment task. The GEW was judged to be a particularly useful measurement instrument under time pressure and with repeated measurements (Tran, 2004). Furthermore, in Caceido and van Beuzekom's (2006) study, respondents overall preferred the GEW over the PrEmo, and judged the GEW as clear to understand, useful to differentiate between emotions, and appealing in its visual design.

18.6 **Discussion**

The studies examining the structural validity of the emotion terms in the VALENCE–control/POWER space showed that for GEW Versions 1.0 and 2.0 the placement of the emotion terms along the VALENCE dimension generally corresponded to prediction. To improve the representation, "compassion," which had been rated as a positive emotion, was to be moved from the negative to the positive side of the GEW.

In contrast to the findings for the VALENCE dimension, the alignment of emotion terms on the control/POWER dimension differs depending on the response paradigm. In the similarity study with MDS analyses, though the model fit was not very good and the sample size was small, the placement of the emotion terms corresponded well to the predicted alignment. In contrast, the empirical data derived from rating studies tend to deviate from the predictions, especially in the negative—low control/POWER quadrant. Inspection of means and variance suggest that, to some extent, the rating results could reflect a response bias in the use of the control/POWER dimension by some participants, resulting in a large variance (Bänziger et al., 2005; Sacharin et al., 2012).

Using a larger sample size or re-wording the description of what control/POWER means might ameliorate this problem. The discussion of the results for the appraisal component in the GRID study (see Chapter 12) also showed that the wording of the control/POWER features in the questionnaire may not have been optimal, and changes are proposed for the CoreGRID and further studies with the full instrument (see Chapter 44). However, it remains to be seen if the changes in wording produce the desired effect. It may well be that the abstract notions of "control" and "POWER" in connection to emotions are not easy to grasp for non-psychologists, and that it is thus difficult to obtain explicit and reliable ratings for these concepts.

An alternative explanation for the observed difficulty in obtaining the theoretically predicted alignment on the POWER dimension (especially for negative high-power and positive low-power emotions) is provided by the strong association of VALENCE with control/POWER ratings (Sacharin et al., 2012). Indeed, it has recently been suggested that control/POWER appraisals are valenced (Shuman, Sander, & Scherer, 2013; Scherer, 2010b). High POWER is associated with positive affect and low POWER with negative affect (e.g., Keltner, Gruenfeld, & Anderson, 2003). A similar correlation was found in the results of the GRID study, as shown in Chapters 8 and 12, suggesting a strong ecological correlation between negative VALENCE and low control/POWER.

Thus, even with a larger sample size and revised wording, it may not be possible to obtain independent and fine-grained ratings of emotions on the control/POWER appraisal criterion alone. To empirically grasp the notion that negative and positive emotional experiences can be associated with more or less control/POWER, other methods may be needed that measure not only control and POWER, in general, or specific appraisals related to it, but additional components of the emotional experience, such as action tendencies.

A further substantiation of the structure of the GEW is timely because the GEW is increasingly used due to its user-friendliness in comparison with other instruments (Caceido & van Beuzekom, 2006). The GEW has been applied in a variety of contexts, such as consumer attitudes to internet videos and industrial design products (e.g., Bardzell, Bardzell, & Pace, 2009; Caceido & van Beuzekom, 2006), the affective evaluation of body movements and vocalizations (e.g., Beck, Stevens, & Bard, 2009; Pammi & Schröder, 2009), emotions during learning in virtual environ-ments and in virtual environments with different illumination (e.g., Longhi, Pereira, Brecht, & Behar, 2009; Santos, 2008), and experience sampling studies of emotions in everyday life (e.g., Tschan, Semmer, Messerli, & Janevski, 2010).

Furthermore, the GEW has been applied to assess emotions at different levels of analysis rang-ing from the individual and the team level emotions of managers (Tran, 2004) to the emotional climate in a hospital (Wittgenstein, 2008). Specifically, Tran (2004) found that the emotions re-corded in the different quadrants of the GEW differentially influence team decision making and cohesion. For example, negative–low control/POWER emotions were positively associated with team cohesion, and negative–high control/POWER emotions were negatively associated with team cohesion. Furthermore, differentiating between the different intensity levels within an emotion family in the GEW contributed important information. For example, moderate levels of positive–low control/POWER emotions were positively associated with alternative evaluation (a key com-ponent of decision making), whereas high intensity positive–low control/POWER emotions were negatively associated with alternative evaluation. Finally, Tran's work showed that the GEW can be used as a means to help develop team processes. Over the course of her study, it was observed that participants often used the GEW ratings as a basis to discuss their emotions with their colleagues, yielding self-awareness and awareness at the group level. In addition, by mapping their emotions on the GEW on a regular basis, all group members can see the evolution of the emotional climate and can proactively manage it (Tran, Páez, & Sánchez, 2012).

To conclude, the existing studies on the GEW Versions 1.0 and 2.0 underscore the utility of the instrument. The placement of the emotion terms in each quadrant of the GEW, however, could not be satisfactorily justified to date. MDS analyses of similarity ratings indicate that the placement of the emotions predicted in each GEW quadrant are valid, but direct rating studies of the VA-LENCE and control/POWER of the same terms were unable to yield the expected placement on the control/POWER dimension. Ratings of control/POWER, it seems, have to be worded in drastically different ways to obtain results that reflect the MDS results.

18.7 Stage 2: Development of a standard version of the GEW based on structural validation with the GRID instrument

After the first results of the GRID study had confirmed that the two major dimensions of the se-mantic emotion domain are indeed VALENCE and control/POWER (Fontaine et al., 2007), it became obvious that the GRID paradigm could constitute a royal road to finalize the validation of the GEW for a set of major emotion terms. As demonstrated in the chapters of Part III of this volume, the GRID results clearly establish the existence of a four factor structure for the emotion space, with activation/AROUSAL and NOVELTY being essential additional factors for a satisfactory mapping of major emotion terms with respect to their discriminability in low-dimensional space. However, we decided to stick to a two-dimensional representation of the emotion terms in a wheel structure for the assessment instrument, as a three-dimensional representation on a two-dimensional paper or screen surface is confusing, and a four-dimensional representation would require a series of inde-pendent two-dimensional graphs. Such formats are inacceptable for a self-report instrument that needs to be immediately obvious to use and economical in terms of time investment. As the two first dimensions emerging in PCAs of the GRID data, VALENCE and POWER also explain the largest percentage of the variance between emotions, this solution seems well justified.

The GRID study described in this volume provides an ideal framework to obtain similarity metrics for emotion words. The GRID provides a very comprehensive feature profile consisting of 142 features covering all components of emotion. In consequence, the assessment of similarity is based on a very rich set of criteria. Furthermore, the information is obtained for a very large set of languages and cultures using sizable groups of native speakers. In consequence, all requirements to obtain a definitive validation of the placement of the emotion terms around the circumference of the wheel are fulfilled. Most importantly, the POWER dimension emerges as the second strongest dimension from the PCA and is clearly identified even if the appraisal component is not included in the analysis. This consistent with the original choice of control/POWER as the second factor in the two-dimensional structure of the GEW (in contrast to AROUSAL in dimensional theories). It is also consistent with the assumption that the appraisals of control and POWER strongly affect the other components producing clear changes, such as dominant action tendencies and loud voice that are sufficient to determine a clear, overall POWER factor. In consequence, the use of VALENCE and POWER coordinates derived from the GRID data seem to be an ideal solution to solve the issue of validating the predicted arrangement of the GEW emotion terms in two-dimensional VALENCE by control/POWER space.

To this end, it was necessary to obtain additional ratings for words used in the GEW that were not rated in the basic GRID study. The list of 24 GRID emotion words (see Chapter 5 for the criteria of choice) already contained 16 of the 20 items that had been regularly used with the previous versions of the GEW. Four words were missing: "amusement," "admiration," "relief," and "regret." Therefore we contacted the different collaborators in the GRID study and asked them whether they would be willing and able to have these words judged on the 142 features in the same way and using similar groups of participants as for the regular GRID questionnaire. Groups in ten different countries—Switzerland (French), United Kingdom (English), Belgium (Flemish), China (Mandarin Chinese), Germany (German), Estonia (Estonian), Finland (Finnish), Italy (Italian), Japan (Japanese), Poland (Polish)—agreed to participate and collected the data using exactly the same procedures as described in Chapters 5 and 6 (see Table 18.1 for sample characteristics).

Table 18.1 Sample characteristics

Language	Country	Region	N			Age			Format	Compensation
			Total	F	M	Range	Mean	SD		
French	Switzerland	Geneva	20	12	2	20–45	29.21	8.285	online	course credit
English	UK	Belfast & York	19	10	9	18–22	19.32	1.416	online	course credit
Dutch	Belgium	Gent	15	9	6	21–23	21.87	0.640	online	course credit
Chinese	China	Hong Kong	19	6	11	19–25	21.24	1.602	online	course credit
German	Germany	Berlin	20	19	1	19–37	22.10	4.241	online	course credit
Estonian	Estonia	Tartu	15	8	7	22–29	25.67	1.759	online	course credit
Finnish	Finland	various	18	17	1	18–37	25.33	5.087	online	course credit
Italian	Italy	Bologna	19	12	2	19–26	23.36	1.946	online	course credit
Japanese	Japan	Sapporo	15	9	6	18–21	18.87	1.125	online	course credit
Polish	Poland	Lodz	14	7	7	19–38	23.36	4.749	online	course credit

In consequence, the new standard version of the GEW presented here contains the following 20 emotion words (the asterisks indicating the four words rated specifically for the GEW validation):

- admiration*
- amusement*
- anger
- compassion
- contempt
- contentment
- disappointment
- disgust
- fear
- guilt
- hate
- interest
- joy
- love
- pleasure
- pride
- regret*
- relief*
- sadness
- shame

We first analyzed the reliability of the rating data for the four new terms for each country (following the procedure described in Chapter 6). These data were then combined with the data for the 16 GEW terms that were part of the basic GRID study and for which the reliability had been assessed previously. Then, dissimilarity matrices were produced for each of the country samples by computing the distances between the feature profiles of the different words. These matrices were then combined and submitted to MDS (using Proxscal) across countries. Proxscal computes solutions for different dimensionalities. As we are interested in a two-dimensional arrangement of the emotion terms for the GEW instrument, here we report only the results for the two-dimensional solution. The stress and fit measures for the two-dimensional solution are as follows: Normalized Raw Stress 0.00481, Stress-I 0.06939, Stress-II 0.13588, S-Stress 0.00503, Dispersion Accounted For (D.A.F.) 0.99519, Tucker's Coefficient of Congruence 0.99759. These fit indices can be judged as quite satisfactory in the light of the levels expected according to the MDS literature. Table 18.2 shows the respective coordinates for the 20 words on the two dimensions (shown as a two-dimensional plot in Figure 18.5).

The two dimensions underlying the plotted coordinates of the 20 GEW words can be readily interpreted—the horizontal dimension corresponding to a general VALENCE dimension (highly comparable to the VALENCE dimension in the overall GRID analysis—see Chapter 7), separating the group of positive emotions from that of the negative ones. The vertical dimension is not as immediately obvious, but comes very close to the POWER dimension in the overall GRID analysis (see Chapter 7). Both of these dimensions correspond directly to the dimensions that have been theoretically

Table 18.2 Coordinates of the 20 GEW emotion words in two-dimensional VALENCE by POWER space

Emotion words	VALENCE	POWER
admiration	0.66	−0.09
amusement	0.67	0.19
anger	−0.37	0.47
compassion	−0.05	−0.55
contempt	−0.55	0.43
contentment	0.77	−0.03
disappointment	−0.77	−0.12
disgust	−0.68	0.20
fear	−0.61	0.07
guilt	−0.57	−0.27
hate	−0.45	0.43
interest	0.61	0.25
joy	0.68	0.07
love	0.58	−0.16
pleasure	0.71	0.02
pride	0.72	0.15
regret	−0.70	−0.19
relief	0.66	−0.36
sadness	−0.68	−0.35
shame	−0.61	−0.16

postulated for the GEW. They seem to be closely related to two types of appraisal: on the one hand, appraisals of unpleasantness and obstructiveness vs pleasantness and conduciveness (underlying the VALENCE dimension), and on the other hand, appraisals of high vs low control/POWER (for the POWER dimension) (see Chapter 12). We also computed a PCA of these data to compare the MDS plots to factor score plots. Essentially, the PCA extracted four factors, the first two of which again correspond to VALENCE and POWER. The two-dimensional factor score plot yielded coordinates for the 20 emotion words that were very similar to the MDS solution. A comparison of the positions of the 20 emotion words in the two-dimensional MDS space shows that the patterning is very comparable to the placement of the same words in the previous Version 2.0 of the GEW shown in Figure 18.4, thus empirically confirming the earlier arrangement, which was based exclusively on theoretical considerations.

Based on these results, a new version (3.0) of the GEW was constructed. Concretely, the two-dimensional coordinates shown in Table 18.2 and Figure 18.5 were projected onto the rim of the circle that represents the wheel structure and arranged equidistantly around the circumference of the wheel. The result of this empirical GRID-based circular ordering of the 20 terms, GEW Version 3.0, is shown in Figure 18.6.

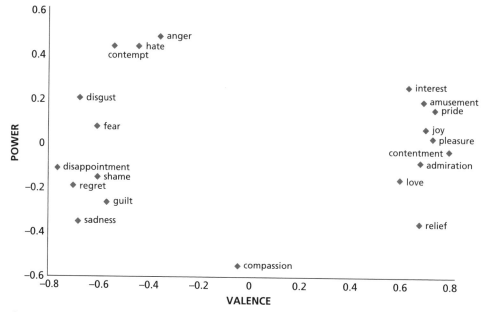

Figure 18.5 Representation of the 20 GEW emotion words in a two-dimensional VALENCE by POWER space.

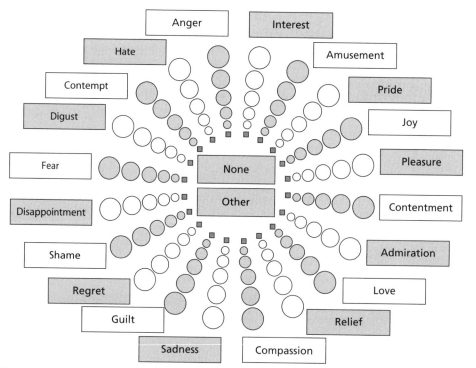

Figure 18.6 Template of Version 3.0 of the GEW as based on the GRID validation described in this chapter.

18.8 **Availability and analysis procedures**

The most recent version of the GEW (Version 3.0) shown in Figure 18.6 is now available for non-commercial use by academic researchers interested in self-report assessment of emotion. The recommended instructions, the final version of the wheel interface, and further information (about adaptation and translation into other languages and licensing for commercial use of the instrument) are available on the GEW web page (http://www.affective-sciences.org/gew). There, the wheel can be downloaded in Word format that can be easily adapted to the needs of different researchers. The web page also shows information about the currently available versions for different languages and computer applications of the wheel.

The 20 items currently used in the wheel, like the 24 items in the GRID study, have been chosen on the basis of an extensive selection process based on theoretical and empirical considerations. They represent a fair sampling of the more frequently used emotion terms in different languages (see Chapter 5 in this volume for the GRID choices). However, they may not constitute an optimal choice for *all* possible applications in different fields of research. For example, an event sampling of emotions occurring in families may require a different selection of emotion categories than an experimental study with a limited set of emotion manipulations. Given the huge diversity of research interests and needs in the field, it would be illusory to propose the use of the current standard version for all kinds of application.

It should be noted that the specific choice of emotion words is not constitutive for the GEW and the advantages its use confers to researchers. Rather, the fact that the arrangement of the terms in two-dimensional space is theory-based and empirically confirmed makes the instrument much easier to use than the usual lists (especially in repeated applications, as participants will find the appropriate terms much more rapidly and precisely). The use of the instrument is also facilitated by the anchoring of the meaning of the chosen emotion terms with respect to their position in the underlying, theoretically determined, affective space. In consequence, users are invited to construct their own wheel if the choice of terms in the standard version is not optimal for the respective research aim (see instructions for adaptation on the GEW web page provided above). However, we would like to stress that, whenever possible, it is advantageous to use the standard version shown in Figure 18.6 to allow for replication by other researchers and to build up cumulative databases.

Finally, we provide a brief overview of the analysis procedures. The GEW can be analyzed in two different ways:

1 Using the classic discrete emotion approach, the ratings on different emotion families in the GEW structure can be analyzed in a very similar fashion to the procedures used with standard questionnaires in which emotion terms are listed one below the other and participants are asked to rate the intensity with which they have experienced each of the emotions on a five-point ordinal scale. Depending on the purpose of the study, participants can be asked to (a) select only one emotion family (the strongest they experienced), (b) choose several emotions they may have experienced simultaneously or in close succession (producing mixed emotions), or (c) give a response to each emotion scale, with a special category for "did NOT experience this emotion" (a format that has desirable psychometric characteristics).

2 Using a dimensional approach allows the researcher to obtain continuous dimensional values by profiting from the explicit arrangement of the emotion terms in two-dimensional VALENCE by control/POWER space. Concretely, each emotion term can be represented by its two coordinates in the space (provided in Table 18.2) with the respective intensity as a third variable. These

three values can then be analyzed separately or in the form of a composite scale. In the case of mixed emotions, with several emotions rated, the respective coordinates and intensities can be combined using statistical measures of central tendency. Alternatively, all ratings within one or more of the four quadrants of the wheel can be combined with the help of statistical measures of central tendency.

18.9 **Conclusion**

The GEW is a theory-based instrument for the assessment of emotional experience through self-report. It combines a dimensional orientation with ratings of intensity for a number of major emotion families, rated in a categorical fashion. The instrument has been used for many years by emotion researchers in many different applications. Earlier studies with multidimensional analyses of similarity ratings of emotion words (Bänziger et al., 2005), designed to validate the theoretical structure that underlies the arrangement of the emotion families on a wheel-like circle, have essentially confirmed the predicted placement of the emotion families in a two-dimensional space formed by VALENCE and control/POWER. However, attempts to use direct ratings of the appraisals that are thought to determine the differentiation of emotions on the control/POWER dimension have met with mixed success. Two of those studies (Bänziger et al., 2005; Sacharin et al., 2012) have been reviewed and it is suggested that it might be useful to use a different approach to validate the position of emotion words in a VALENCE × POWER structure, abandoning the exclusive reliance on coping potential appraisals in favor of a more comprehensive representation of POWER.

The GRID paradigm has been found to be ideally suited for this purpose, given that it anchors the four fundamental dimensions of emotional space in feature profiles based on all emotion components, and given the remarkable stability of these factors over many different languages. The four dimensions reliably emerge even when individual components (also appraisal) are removed from the data set (see data reports in Part III of this volume). The analysis of the 20 GEW words with the GRID instrument in 10 countries with 10 different languages has allowed us to firmly validate the theoretical structure used in the development of the wheel. The precise data provided by these GRID results have allowed recalibrating the positioning of the emotion categories on the rim of the emotion wheel. Based on this recalibration, a new version of the GEW, 3.0, is presented in this chapter and is made available to interested researchers. While the theoretical structure of the GEW has been validated in this research, an empirical construct validation remains to be done.

Apart from providing a combination of a dimensional and a categorical approach to emotion assessment through self-report, the GEW provides an alternative to the dominant VALENCE × AROUSAL model in dimensional approaches. We hope that the new Version 3.0 of the GEW will see widespread use in the future and will help standardize the self-report assessment procedures in the psychological investigation of emotion and in the interdisciplinary domain of the affective sciences more generally. We believe that systematic use of a standard version of the GEW would constitute important progress with respect to replicating results across studies, and, most importantly, allow increased collaboration in designing empirical studies and sharing the data in the emotion domain. These activities, in turn, would greatly contribute to our effort to better understand the semantics of emotion terms and their role in the categorization and communication of emotional experience.

Chapter 19

Assessing interindividual differences in emotion knowledge: Exploring a GRID-based approach

Steven J. E. Van den Eede and Johnny J. R. Fontaine[1]

Emotion knowledge is considered a core aspect of emotional intelligence and plays a central role in its assessment. It is thought to be an essential element in the recognition and interpretation of emotional situations, expressions, and behaviors (e.g., Mayer, Salovey, & Caruso, 2008). Understanding Emotions forms one of the four constituting branches in the currently golden standard for the measurement of emotional intelligence, namely the Mayer-Salovey-Caruso-Emotional-Intelligence Test (MSCEIT, Mayer, Salovey, & Caruso, 2002; Mayer, Salovey, Caruso, & Sitarenios, 2003). The Understanding Emotions branch is represented by two subtests, namely Changes and Blends, which assess knowledge about how one emotion can transform into another and about how different emotions can merge into complex emotions, respectively.

The Understanding Emotions subtests, and the MSCEIT more generally, have been criticized for not having a strong theoretical background (e.g., MacCann & Roberts, 2008). Neither the construction of the items, nor the scoring of the item responses is embedded in an explicit emotion theory. Two types of scoring keys have been developed for the MSCEIT, namely consensus-based and experts-based scoring keys (MacCann, Roberts, Matthews, & Zeidner, 2004; Mayer, Salovey, & Caruso, 2000). In the consensus-based key a response is scored according to the proportion of respondents in a representative sample that have selected that response as the correct one. In the expert-based key, the consensus between judgments of experts in the field is relied upon (MacCann et al., 2004). Both methods result in highly comparable emotional intelligence scores with the difference that expert judgments have been found to be more consistent and reliable than lay judgments (Mayer, et. al., 2003). From the perspective of maximum performance testing, however, both scoring keys are problematic. The scientific literature on human judgment has extensively demonstrated its fallibility. Sometimes the majority chooses the demonstrably wrong answer, and even experts in statistics can be as susceptible to biases in their daily judgment as lay persons (e.g., Gilovitch, Griffing, & Kahneman, 2001). Thus, neither the consensus in a representative sample, nor expertise in a field guarantees the correctness of a response.

One of the most important developments in the assessment of emotion knowledge that deals with the lack of theoretical grounding of both the items and the responses is the development of the Situational Test of Emotional Understanding (STEU) by MacCann and Roberts (2008). Rather

[1] Corresponding author: Johnny J. R. Fontaine. Department of Personnel, Work and Organisational Psychology. Faculty of Psychology and Educational Sciences. Ghent University. Henri-Dunantlaan 2, 9000 Gent, Belgium. Johnny.Fontaine@UGent.be

than starting from an intuitive understanding of the construct of emotion knowledge, they took Roseman's appraisal theory (Roseman, 2001) as a point of reference. According to this theory, emotions are triggered by a combination of seven appraisal dimensions, such as appraisals about the situational state (motive consistency vs motive inconsistency), the expectedness (expected vs unexpected), and the causal agency (caused by self, by others, or by circumstances) that people make in an emotional situation. According to this theory, 17 discrete emotions can be triggered depending on the profile of appraisals. In the STEU, Roseman's appraisal theory is operationalized by 42 multiple choice knowledge questions or items that assess whether respondents can identify the appraisals that characterize an emotion in general situations, in situations in one's personal life, or and in situations at the workplace. The responses are scored according to Roseman's theoretical framework.

The internal consistency of the STEU has been found to range from low ($\alpha = 0.48$ in the study of Austin, 2010) to moderate ($\alpha = 0.71$ in the study of MacCann & Roberts, 2008). Research on the internal structure revealed one well interpretable factor across the 42 items. This factor, however, accounted for only 5.9% of the total variance (Ferguson & Austin, 2011). While from the perspective of the internal structure, the evidence in favour of the new approach is moderate, the relationship of the STEU with other measurements of emotion knowledge and emotional intelligence, as well as with other constructs, such as verbal intelligence and psychopathology do support the new approach (Austin, 2010; MacCann & Roberts, 2008; Ferguson & Austin, 2010). The STEU is positively correlated with verbal intelligence and the MSCEIT, especially the Understanding Emotions branch, and is negatively correlated with psychopathology.

Because of its theoretical grounding, the development of the STEU means an important improvement in the assessment of emotion knowledge. Its limitation, however, is that it only operationalizes one aspect of the emotion process, namely the appraisals that trigger emotions. In the present chapter, we propose a new approach to the assessment of interindividual differences in emotion knowledge based on the theoretical framework of the GRID study, the GRID instrument, and the data of the GRID study. They can contribute to the further development of assessment procedures for interindividual differences in emotion knowledge in four important ways. The GRID study offers: (1) a comprehensive theoretical framework with respect to the defining characteristics of the emotion knowledge construct; and (2) it throws a new light on the debate about the identification of the correct response. Moreover, it offers a rich source for: (3) the operationalization of emotion knowledge items, as well as for (4) the operationalization of a scoring key for these items.

Defining the emotion knowledge construct. The Component Process Model (CPM), which formed the basis of the GRID instrument, offers a strong basis for defining the emotion knowledge construct. According to the CPM, an emotion is a process that is elicited by a goal-relevant event and that consists of a synchronization between the five basic human subsystems, also called emotion components (namely Appraisal, Bodily reaction, Expression, Action tendencies, and Feeling) in order to prepare the person for rapid adaptive action (e.g., Scherer, 2005a; see Chapter 1). If the concept of emotion is defined in this way, then **knowing an emotion** means **knowing the Appraisals, Bodily reactions, Expressions, Action tendencies, and Feelings that synchronize in that emotion**. Taking this definition, knowing Changes and Blends, which is assessed in the Understanding Emotions branch of the MSCEIT, is relevant for, but does not belong to the core of construct of emotion knowledge. The STEU does assess one core aspect of emotion knowledge, namely knowing the appraisals that trigger the emotion. However, the STEU underrepresents the emotion knowledge construct by only focusing on Appraisals. For a full representation of the emotion knowledge construct, also knowledge about Bodily reactions, Expressions, Action tendencies, and Feelings needs to be assessed.

Scoring emotion knowledge responses. From the perspective of the GRID study, which focused on the meaning of emotion terms, the problem of scoring emotion knowledge responses can be approached in a very different way than has been done in the consensus or expert scoring applied in the MSCEIT, or in the a priori theoretical scoring applied in the STEU. In line with the GRID, one can consider the linguistic meaning of a term as the point of reference. Instead of evaluating whether people know the "correct" answer, one can evaluate to what extent people know the meaning of an emotion term as it has been encoded in language. Most people have little or no access to scientific theorizing or empirical studies about emotions. The particularity of emotions, however, is that all persons are confronted with them regularly both within themselves and in others they interact with. People learn to label these recurrent emotional experiences, and learn the meaning of emotion words from the way others communicate about their emotional experiences. The meaning of emotion words captures what a community thinks is pertinent in emotional experiences. For instance, the meaning of the word "anger" represents what a community thinks the experiences of anger are about (see Chapter 4). The GRID study has demonstrated that all theoretically defined emotion components, namely Appraisals, Bodily reactions, Expression, Action tendencies, and Feelings, universally define the meaning of emotion terms. The GRID study has, moreover, demonstrated that the references to these five components do not fluctuate at whim, but show replicable meaning structures across languages and cultural groups. It is thus, in principle, possible to identify the "correct" meaning of emotion terms.

The GRID study moreover qualifies the idea of correctness. The meaning of emotion terms is not defined by a set of necessary and sufficient features (which would mean that a feature either belongs or does not belong to the meaning of an emotion term), but in terms of features that are assumed to be more or less prototypical (cf., the prototype theory on natural language concepts of Rosch, 1978; see also Chapters 1 and 2). In line with this theorizing, it is universally observed that features gradually differ in terms of the likelihood with which they define an emotion term. This implies that a person who has a high level of emotional knowledge should be able to identify the likelihood of features to belong to an emotion concept (rather than differentiate between correct and incorrect features).

Operationalizing the concept of emotion knowledge. From a validity perspective, the first and foremost criterion for the validity of an assessment instrument is the relevance and representatives of its stimuli with respect to the domain one intends to assess (e.g., Messick, 1989). The GRID instrument and study offer a solid base for operationalizing the construct of emotion knowledge in a relevant and representative way. The GRID instrument consists of a set of 24 emotion terms which represent the variability of types of experiences in the emotion domain and of 142 features which operationalize each of the five basic emotion components based on important theories in the emotion literature. The GRID study has revealed that these 24 emotions are organized into four large emotion clusters (namely a joy, an anger, a sadness, and a fear cluster) and also two small clusters of which one is particularly salient (namely surprise, which is also differentiated from the other emotion terms on the fourth dimension in a four-dimensional representation) (see Chapter 7). Thus, based on the GRID study, the emotion domain can be divided into 25 major facets, with each facet defined by a combination of one of five emotion clusters (joy, anger, sadness, fear, and surprise) and one of five emotion components (Appraisals, Bodily reactions, Expressions, Action tendencies, and Feelings). Moreover, the GRID study has generated information about how each of the 142 features that represent the five basic subsystems relate to these 24 emotion terms. Thus, each facet can be operationalized by combining GRID emotion terms with GRID emotion features.

Operationalizing the scoring key for emotion knowledge items. The GRID study has identified an estimation of the likelihood that each of 142 features define the meaning of each of the 24 emotion terms. These estimations can be used to score the "correctness" of responses of emotional knowledge items. The more a participant is capable of identifying the likelihood that an emotion feature defines an emotion term, the higher his/her emotion knowledge.

In the present study, a new instrument for assessing interindividual differences in emotion knowledge on the basis of the GRID study is presented. With the GRID emotion terms and GRID emotion features a new knowledge instrument is constructed that represents the emotion domain in a relevant and representative way. Moreover, a scoring key is developed on the basis of the likelihood with which emotion features define the meaning of emotion terms as observed in the GRID study. Furthermore, a preliminary empirical investigation of the internal consistency (reliability) and internal structure (an important aspect of the construct validity) of the new instrument is presented. More specifically, it is investigated whether emotion knowledge items about Appraisals, Bodily reactions, Expressions, Action tendencies, and Feelings all empirically define the emotion knowledge construct and lead to a reliable scale. Moreover, the GRID-based scoring key is further investigated by comparing it with a consensus scoring key.

19.1 Method

The construction of the emotion knowledge instrument. The new emotion knowledge instrument, further referred to as EKI, consists of 25 different facets of emotion knowledge items with each facet combining one of the five emotion clusters (joy, anger, sadness, fear, and surprise) and one of the five emotion components (Appraisal, Bodily reaction, Action tendency, Expression, and Feeling). For the four large emotion clusters (namely joy, anger, sadness, and fear), three items were constructed for each combination with the five emotion components. For the surprise cluster, which is a small cluster, only one item was constructed per emotion component. Thus, the EKI consists of 65 items, which represent 25 possible combinations between one of the five emotion clusters and one of the five emotion components. Each item consisted of an emotion term and four features stemming from the same emotion component. Participants were asked to rank the four features with respect to their likelihood during an emotion episode that could be labeled with the respective emotion term. A ranking procedure was used instead of a rating procedure in order to avoid the impact of random interindividual differences in scale use. When using a Likert scale, respondents can differ systematically in how they use the response scale irrespective of the content of the items. For instance, some respondents score systematically higher than others across items, and some respondents prefer more extreme response categories than others. In a ranking procedure, these differences in scale use are avoided.

For instance, item 58 was one of the three operationalizations of the anger by bodily reaction facet: Item 58 – If someone experiences **hate** with respect to someone or something, then s/he would: (a) feel hot; (b) feel his/her heartbeat slowing down; (c) feel cold; (d) feel weak limbs.

Participants were instructed to rank the four bodily reactions from the least likely to the most likely Bodily reaction. Two scoring keys were developed, namely a GRID scoring key and a consensus scoring key. For the GRID scoring key, the likelihood scores of the features in the Dutch-speaking Belgian sample in the GRID study were taken as a point of reference. Because also language-specific and cultural-specific meanings have been identified in the GRID study, besides the overall cultural and linguistic stability of the meaning structures, the likelihood scores of the linguistically and culturally matching sample in the GRID study were used. Each item was scored by computing the Pearson-correlation between the rank order proposed by the participant and the likelihood scores of the features in the Belgian sample (for instance, the average likelihood scores for the features in item 58 were 6.35 for "feel hot," 2.74 for "feel his/her heartbeat slowing down," 4.68 for "feel cold," and 4.41 for "feel weak limbs"). The item scores could thus vary between −1 when the participant chose the opposite order and 1 when the participant chose exactly the same order as in the GRID. In the consensus scoring key, the rank order of the respondent was scored according to the proportion of respondents with the same rank order.

Procedure

A web-based study was conducted. Participants were invited to log onto a protected website. First, they completed the general background questions, and subsequently they solved the 65 items. Participation was anonymous and voluntary.

Participants

A heterogeneous convenience sample of adults was selected through snowballing. In total, 233 Belgian Dutch-speaking adults participated in the research: they ranged between 17–64 years, with a mean age of 34.7 years, 59.7% were female. The sample consisted of 17.6% participants who did not finish their secondary education or had a technical and vocational training, 36.5% finished high school or senior technical school, and 45.9% of the participants had at least a bachelor degree. Of the total sample 54.5% was employed, 33.9% was studying, 2.1% was unemployed, and the remaining group consisted of housewives and people on early retirement.

19.2 **Results**

First, the analyses were executed on the GRID-scored responses and then on the consensus-scored responses.

GRID scoring key

The internal consistency of the total score across the 65 items was computed. With a Cronbach's alpha of 0.87, the scale was sufficiently reliable (>0.80, e.g., Lance, Butts, & Michels, 2006). In an ANCOVA with educational level and sex as independent variables and age as covariate, the age and the educational level of the participants was not significantly related to emotion knowledge. There was a small, but significant difference between men and women [$F(1,226) = 10.56, p < 0.001$, partial $\eta^2 = 0.05$], with women slightly outperforming men.

The internal structure of the new instrument was investigated with a factor analysis (principal component analysis). The scree plot clearly revealed a one-factorial solution with the first ten eigenvalues being 9.9, 2.3, 2.2, 2.0, 1.8, 1.8, 1.7, 1.7, 1.5, and 1.5. Moreover, higher-factorial solutions could not be well interpreted. Therefore a one-factorial solution was selected. The one-factorial structure accounted for 15.2% of the total variance across the 65 items with almost all items having a positive loading on this general factor. The factor loadings revealed a large variation ranging from a high 0.70 down to a low and even negative loading of −0.20, with a median loading of 0.35 (see Table 19.1).

As all items were a priori constructed on the basis of the GRID study with the same principles and the same design, the large variability of loadings was unexpected. Therefore, this large variability in loadings was further investigated. In a first step, it was investigated whether emotion clusters, emotion components, or their combination differed in defining the overall general factor. An ANOVA was executed with the factor loadings as a dependent variable and the emotion cluster

Table 19.1 The mean score and the factor loadings of the 65 emotion knowledge items in a one-factorial solution

Item	Emotion cluster	Emotion component	Mean score with GRID scoring key	Factor loadings with GRID scoring key	Factor loadings with consensus scoring key
I31	Joy	Bodily reaction	0.921	0.704	0.507
I62	Joy	Action tendency	0.845	0.679	0.265
I61	Sadness	Feeling	0.871	0.642	0.344
I38	Anger	Expression	0.733	0.631	0.370
I25	Fear	Feeling	0.878	0.612	0.367
I45	Joy	Feeling	0.902	0.589	0.325
I35	Joy	Appraisal	0.733	0.571	0.432
I47	Sadness	Bodily reaction	0.820	0.551	0.440
I16	Fear	Appraisal	0.699	0.533	0.444
I54	Fear	Expression	0.768	0.532	0.250
I39	Sadness	Bodily reaction	0.673	0.525	0.344
I51	Fear	Appraisal	0.696	0.521	0.420
I60	Joy	Appraisal	0.754	0.508	0.506
I44	Fear	Action tendency	0.696	0.504	0.415
I59	Joy	Action tendency	0.761	0.500	0.189
I26	Joy	Appraisal	0.767	0.495	0.325
I56	Sadness	Feeling	0.589	0.485	0.508
I64	Fear	Expression	0.847	0.479	0.273
I13	Joy	Expression	0.842	0.466	0.409
I37	Fear	Feeling	0.697	0.453	0.388
I17	Fear	Bodily reaction	0.706	0.444	0.362
I43	Sadness	Appraisal	0.646	0.434	0.387
I36	Fear	Action tendency	0.515	0.422	0.357
I58	Anger	Bodily reaction	0.614	0.419	0.416
I22	Joy	Bodily reaction	0.751	0.418	0.362
I29	Anger	Action tendency	0.721	0.414	0.347
I32	Sadness	Expression	0.463	0.411	0.325
I20	Anger	Feeling	0.729	0.405	0.294
I55	Joy	Action tendency	0.556	0.385	0.348
I23	Sadness	Expression	0.887	0.382	0.169
I4	Sadness	Action tendency	0.701	0.378	0.323
I1	Anger	Appraisal	0.679	0.375	0.369
I3	Joy	Expression	0.873	0.346	0.308
I65	Sadness	Appraisal	0.548	0.337	0.373

Table 19.1 (continued) The mean score and the factor loadings of the 65 emotion knowledge items in a one-factorial solution

Item	Emotion cluster	Emotion component	Mean score with GRID scoring key	Factor loadings with GRID scoring key	Factor loadings with consensus scoring key
I21	Fear	Appraisal	0.753	0.332	0.365
I28	Sadness	Expression	0.496	0.311	0.201
I50	Fear	Action tendency	0.529	0.301	0.298
I14	Sadness	Action tendency	0.654	0.288	0.395
I27	Joy	Bodily reaction	0.504	0.284	0.148
I10	Sadness	Action tendency	0.701	0.277	0.337
I42	Anger	Expression	0.397	0.275	0.168
I30	Surprise	Appraisal	0.614	0.264	0.284
I53	Anger	Bodily reaction	0.404	0.260	0.241
I34	Fear	Feeling	0.459	0.257	0.238
I41	Sadness	Bodily reaction	0.625	0.253	0.153
I46	Anger	Expression	0.667	0.252	0.301
I12	Surprise	Bodily reaction	0.693	0.244	0.191
I33	Anger	Action tendency	0.361	0.241	0.367
I57	Fear	Expression	0.577	0.234	0.315
I24	Surprise	Action tendency	0.487	0.223	0.257
I49	Joy	Feeling	0.231	0.203	0.282
I19	Anger	Action tendency	0.393	0.194	0.255
I11	Anger	Feeling	0.680	0.185	0.270
I8	Anger	Appraisal	0.204	0.181	0.046
I63	Anger	Bodily reaction	0.598	0.173	0.224
I15	Anger	Feeling	0.537	0.172	0.234
I9	Joy	Expression	0.806	0.151	0.252
I52	Joy	Feeling	0.272	0.127	0.200
I6	Surprise	Expression	0.237	0.124	0.204
I18	Surprise	Feeling	0.057	0.107	0.158
I2	Fear	Bodily reaction	0.375	0.080	0.151
I48	Anger	Appraisal	0.219	0.077	0.233
I5	Sadness	Feeling	0.078	0.022	0.200
I7	Fear	Bodily reaction	0.346	−0.049	0.324
I40	Sadness	Appraisal	−0.15	−0.20	−0.24

and the emotion component as independent variables. Neither the effect of emotion cluster was significant [$F(4,40) = 2.19$, $p = 0.09$], nor of emotion component [$F(4,40) = 0.11$, $p = 0.98$], nor of the interaction between emotion cluster and emotion component [$F(16,40) = 0.91$, $p = 0.57$]. So the variation of the loadings could not be accounted for by the design of the EKI. In a second step, a visual inspection of the properties of the items and the factor loadings revealed a strong relationship between the average item scores and the factor loadings of the items: the higher the average item score, the higher the item loading. This relationship was further explored using a regression analysis with the factor loadings as criterion and the mean item scores as predictors. About two thirds of the variance in the item loadings (64%) could be accounted for by variation in the mean item scores, which was statistically significant [$F(1,63) = 110.71$, $p < 0.001$]. Thus, the easier an item, the better it defined the overall emotion knowledge factor.

The consensus scoring key

A principal component analysis on the consensus-scored items also revealed only one dominant and interpretable factor. However, this factor accounted for only 10.2% of the total variance. Moreover, with a maximum loading of 0.51 and a median loading of 0.32 the consensus-scored items tended to load lower on the overall factor than the GRID-scored items (see also Table 19.1).

With a Cronbach's alpha of 0.83, the internal consistency of the consensus-scored items is only slightly lower than the internal consistency based on the GRID-scored items. Moreover, the total consensus-based scores and the total GRID-based scores across the 65 items were highly correlated ($r = 0.89$) and thus resulted in highly comparable estimations of the interindividual differences in emotion knowledge.

19.3 Discussion

The goal of the present study was to construct a new assessment instrument for emotion knowledge based on the GRID study. The GRID study, and the theoretical framework on which the GRID study was based, allowed (1) the rigorous definition of the construct of emotion knowledge as the knowledge about how each of the five basic emotion components function in a coordinated way during a particular emotion, (2) the rigorous operationalization of this definition in terms of 25 possible combinations between emotion clusters and emotion components, (3) the definition of the "correctness" of responses in terms of the meaning of emotion words, and (4) the development of a scoring key that quantifies the correspondence between responses of participants and the meaning of emotion words as they emerge in the GRID study.

A first empirical investigation of the internal structure of the newly constructed emotion knowledge instrument by and large confirmed the predictions made on the basis of the GRID study. First, it was predicted that not only questions about Appraisals, but also about Bodily reactions, Action tendencies, Expression, and Feelings would assess emotion knowledge. In line with this prediction, only one dominant factor could be empirically identified across items for Appraisals, Bodily reactions, Action tendencies, Expression, and Feelings. Moreover, there was no significant difference in how well knowledge of each of these five emotion components defined the overall emotion knowledge factor. Furthermore, the total score based on all 65 emotion knowledge items demonstrated good internal consistency.

Second, it is possible to score emotion knowledge items on the basis of the results of the GRID study. A GRID-based scoring key demonstrated better psychometric properties than a consensus-based scoring key. This was especially clear in the factor analysis. The single factor accounted for about one third more variance with the GRID-based than with the consensus-based scoring key (15.2% versus 10.2% of the total variance). Most items loaded (substantially) higher with the GRID-based scoring key. The internal consistency across the 65 items was, however, only slightly better with the GRID-based scoring key. The total score based on the GRID scoring key was also highly correlated with the total score based on the consensus scoring key. Thus, although the psychometric properties of the GRID-based scoring key are better, both scoring keys lead to very comparable estimations of emotion knowledge. This observation mirrors the earlier observation made with the MSCEIT that the consensus and the expert scoring keys eventually lead to the same results, but that the expert scoring key is more reliable. It is also observed that the psychometric properties of the new instrument are better than the psychometric properties of the STEU, to which it most closely resembles. Not only the internal consistency is higher, which can be partially explained by the higher number of items (65 in the EKI versus 42 in the STEU), but more importantly the first dominant factor accounted for about three times more variance in the new instrument than in the STEU (15.2% in the EKI versus 5.9% in the STEU).

One observation was not anticipated, namely a large variation of the items in terms of their loadings on the general factor. As all items were constructed in the same way on the basis of the GRID results, no substantial differences in factor loadings were anticipated. When this phenomenon was explored post hoc, a very strong positive linear relationship emerged between the average item score and the loading of the item on the general factor. Thus, the easier the item, the better the item functioned as an indicator of the emotion knowledge factor. This means that items that probe insight into subtle differences in emotional reactions that are difficult to differentiate are not very good indicators of the emotional knowledge construct. Thus, from an empirical perspective, the scale does not really measure how good a person can identify subtle differences in emotion processes, but it captures not being able to identify obvious relationships in the emotion domain. A possible explanation for this counterintuitive observation is that difficult items which probe insight into subtle differences in emotional reactions are more ambiguous and are therefore less valid indicators of the emotion knowledge construct. This would be in line with Trentacosta's and Fine's (2010) definition of discrete emotion knowledge, as *the ability to understand relatively unambiguous cues of discrete emotions expressed in traditional channels* (Trentacosta & Fine, 2010, p.2).

There are two important limitations to the current study. The first limitation is the convenience sample that was not representative for the Dutch-speaking population in Belgium. It remains to be demonstrated that the results can be replicated in representative samples. It is especially likely that the psychometric properties of the consensus scoring will improve with representative samples. A second important limitation is that the current study only investigated the internal structure of the new knowledge instrument. It did not investigate its relationships with alternative assessments of emotion knowledge (like the MSCEIT and the STEU) or with other constructs to which it should be related, such as intelligence and psychopathology. Without this additional evidence, no strong conclusions can be drawn about the validity of the new instrument.

19.4 **Conclusions**

Despite its limitations, the current study offers first empirical evidence that an assessment instrument for emotion knowledge should not be restricted to the Appraisal component, but should include items about the Bodily reaction, the Expression, the Action tendency, and the Feeling components of emotion. Moreover, the present results support the use of the GRID study to construct a scoring key for emotion knowledge items.

Part V

Cultural-comparative perspectives

Chapter 20

The conceptualization of despair in Basque, Spanish, and English

Itziar Alonso-Arbiol,[1] Cristina Soriano, and Fons J. R. van de Vijver

20.1 Introduction

One of the most relevant emotions to the clinical field is despair. When this emotion becomes an enduring emotional state of an individual, it may lead to the development of major depression or other affective disorders. In the Anglo-Saxon clinical literature, despair has been described as an emotion in which an individual is "overcome by a sense of futility or defeat or having an utter lack of hope" (McDougall, Blixen, & Suen, 1997, p. 280). The question we address in this chapter is to what extent the same psychological meaning is covered by the three translation-equivalent terms in English ("despair"), Spanish ("*desesperación*"), and Basque ("*etsipena*").[2]

Russell (1991a) noted already that translation equivalence does not imply equivalence of psychological meaning. He asserted that a translation back-translation procedure does not guarantee the exact semantic equivalence of the source and target terms. Some examples have been observed in languages as diverse as Dutch (Fontaine, Poortinga, Setiadi, & Markam, 2002) and Filipino (Church, Katigbak, Reyes, & Jensen, 1998), where a priori equivalent translations of some emotion terms showed semantic dissimilarity using multidimensional scaling procedures.

Several studies have addressed the lack of semantic equivalence between the terms used to refer to despair (or depression, as a closely related concept) in different languages. Thus, Marsella (1980) drew attention to the absence of terms conceptually equivalent to the English "depression" in several non-Western cultural groups, such as Nigerians (Leighton et al., 1963), Chinese (Tseng & Hsu, 1969), and Canadian-American Indians (Termansen & Ryan, 1970). Conceptual non-equivalence has also been found in some Western groups, such as among French Canadians (Benoist, Roussin, Fredette, & Rousseau, 1965), Australians, and Puerto Ricans (Brandt & Boucher, 1986). Similar results were observed by Tanaka-Matsumi and Marsella (1976) among Japanese. Even though the choice of "*yuutsu*" as the closest Japanese term for the American English term "depression" was beyond dispute, differences were found in the description of their meaning by the Japanese and American groups. Generally speaking, presumed equivalent terms do not seem to be expressing the same idea in all cultures. In fact, when words that convey the concept of depression were

---

[1] Corresponding author: Itziar Alonso-Arbiol, Faculty of Psychology, University of the Basque Country UPV/EHU, E-20018 San Sebastián, Spain. E-mail: itziar.alonso@ehu.es

[2] Quotation marks ("") will be used for linguistic terms denoting emotions (e.g., "*etsipena*," "despair") to distinguish them from concepts (e.g., despair).

analyzed in eight different countries, the only pan-cultural similarities obtained by Brandt and Boucher (1986) were the absence of positive affect and an intimate association with sadness. All in all, the above studies suggest that the cross-culturally shared core of the concept of depression (and hence, of despair as a closely related emotion) is limited.

In this chapter, we examine the semantic meaning (conceptualization) of the despair emotion as captured by the Spanish "*desesperación*," the Basque "*etsipena*", and the English "despair" terms (the latter is used as a useful comparison reference), which are the most representative terms to designate the target emotion in each language[3]. We first analyze the meaning of the English term "despair" from both a linguistic and a psychological viewpoint; we briefly describe the studies and theories that have dealt with this emotion. Second, we address the concept of despair in other languages, paying special attention to the terms that best instantiate the category in Spanish and Basque, and introducing two types of despair (active and passive) that may underlie the emotion terms in these two languages. Third, we outline two types of despair (active and passive) that have been identified in historical analyses of European culture, and which may underlie the emotion terms in Basque and Spanish. Fourth, we present empirical findings of a study that compares the conceptualization of despair in Basque, Spanish, and English. Finally, main conclusions about the reported data are summarized.

20.2 **The meaning of English "despair"**

Etymologically, the English term "despair" derives from old French "*desperer*," itself derived from Latin "*desperare*" (*de-* "without" + *sperare* "to hope"), which means absence of hope. The New Oxford Dictionary of English (Pearsall, 1998) gives practically the same definition: "the complete loss or absence of hope." From a psychological point of view, Nesse (1999) also acknowledged the intertwined relationship between hope and despair: both emotions arise from the expectations about future outcomes of a goal. Thus, events that suggest that our efforts will succeed are likely to trigger hope, whereas events suggesting that our efforts are pointless are likely to elicit despair.

In general, the description of despair has been closely linked to the concept of depression. Although clinicians distinguish between both terms (Cowling, 2004, 2008; Manley & Leichner, 2003; Olney & Lomen-Hoerth, 2005), Oatley (2004) identified "despair" as the ordinary term used to refer to the clinical concept of depression. Both emotion theorists and laypeople (when describing their emotions) have sometimes used the label "depression" to refer to a temporary or more general emotional mood instead of to the clinical syndrome (e.g., Hupka, Lenton, & Hutchison, 1999; Russell, 1980). Depression refers in that case to a low activated and negatively evaluated affect (Russell, 1980), precisely where the basic sadness emotion concept would be located. The classification of "depression" and "despair" as subtypes of the sadness domain has been empirically supported in studies employing hierarchical cluster procedures. Using a comprehensive list of 135 English emotion terms rated by American college-students, Shaver, Schwartz, Kirson, and O'Connor (1987) were able to map all emotion terms into clusters. The clustering was based on the semantic similarities and differences of the terms as perceived by another sample of students. The authors observed a distinction between positive and negative emotion terms at the superordinate level. At a second,

---

3 The term "depression" is also found in every day use to refer to an intense form of sadness, rather than a true clinical state. In this sense the meaning of "depression" is very close to that of "despair," and both terms could have been chosen for the questionnaire. However, it is likely that "despair" was preferred over "depression" because some of the intended participants (psychology students) may be more likely to understand the term "depression" from a clinical perspective.

lower level, five basic emotion categories (anger, sadness, fear, happiness, and love) derived from the previous two, while a sixth one—surprise—could have both a positive and negative meaning at the superordinate level. Emotion terms at the lowest, subordinate level were derived from these basic emotions. Emotion terms appeared semantically grouped at this level with other terms. "Despair" was sorted in the cluster of sadness terms, as were "sadness," "depression," "hopelessness," "gloom," "glumness," "unhappiness," "grief," "sorrow," "woe," "misery," and "melancholy."

In light of the above (clinical observations, descriptions from emotion theorists, and studies on emotion lexicon), it can be tentatively concluded that the English term "despair," as an emotion included in the sadness clustering, denotes an emotion of negative value, characterized by low levels of activation. Scherer (2001) made further predictions regarding the appraisal of despair that help understand its distinctiveness, among others, from the more general emotion of sadness. Thus, in terms of NOVELTY, despair would be an emotion with a high level of suddenness, a somewhat lower level of familiarity, and a low level of predictability (as opposed to a higher level of predictability in sadness). The implications would also vary in three aspects. First, while the cause of sadness is open, the cause of despair is natural or comes from another external source. Second, in despair there is a dissonance with previous expectation, which is not the case for sadness. And third, the level of urgency in sadness is low, but it is high for despair. As for the coping potential, while the level of adjustment is medium for sadness, it would be very low for the person experiencing despair. More specific features of "despair," such as other appraisal elements, feelings, body sensations (physiological features), action tendencies, and expressive behaviors, have not been explored so far. Furthermore, generalizations to other languages, like the ones addressed in the present chapter, have not yet been reported.

But to what extent do these features of English "despair" apply to other languages? Current thinking in cross-cultural psychology suggests that high-level abstract features of psychological functioning are universal and that the closer we get to actual behavior, the more cross-cultural differences are likely to emerge (Berry, Poortinga, Segall, & Dasen, 2002). This universality position may hold in the emotion domain. Sadness (and other basic emotions) would then reveal more cultural similarity than variability (e.g., Matsumoto, Nezlek, & Koopmann, 2007; Scherer & Wallbott, 1994), probably because of its biologically rooted nature (Poortinga, 1992). However, by stepping down to the subordinate level (i.e., despair), cultural specificity in antecedents and expression of emotions become more likely (Alonso-Arbiol et al., 2006; Shaver et al., 1987), and hence, linguistic equivalence is less likely.

20.3 The concept of despair in other languages

While the meaning of "depression" has been more often investigated in the study of emotion lexicons (e.g., Brandt & Boucher, 1986; Benoist et al., 1965; Hupka et al., 1999; Tanaka-Matsumi & Marsella, 1976), there are also a handful of studies in which "despair" has been considered. Fontaine, Scherer, Roesch, and Ellsworth (2007) examined the dimensional structure underlying several emotion terms in English (UK), Dutch (Belgium), and French (Switzerland) using the GRID instrument. In their four-dimensional solution, dimensions were graphically compared two by two; in the comparison of VALENCE by AROUSAL, "despair" (and the equivalent terms in the other languages) showed the second highest variability out of the 24 investigated emotion terms. Some other studies have also studied the lexicalization of despair across languages. Following Shaver et al.'s (1987) methodology to sort emotion lexicons, possibly equivalent terms of "despair" were observed as subtypes of sadness in Dutch ("*hopeloos*") (Fontaine et al., 2002), Bahasa Indonesia ("*putus asa*") (Fontaine et al., 2002; Shaver, Murdaya, & Fraley, 2001), and Basque ("*etsipena*")

(Alonso-Arbiol et al., 2006). In the following subsections we discuss the Basque terms in some more detail and introduce the Spanish ones.

Basque "etsipena" and "desesperazioa"

Before explaining the Basque term for despair, we introduce some explanation of the language and the geographical and cultural context where it is spoken. The Basque language (Basque or *Euskara*) is spoken in the Basque Country (*País Vasco* or *Euskadi*), a region with several provinces in the North of Spain, and in several areas in the South of France. Basque has important differences with respect to Spanish (and to French) from both a semantic and a grammatical viewpoint. As for its origins and relations to other languages, Basque is considered to be a unique non-Indo-European language in Western Europe, with an ancient history and characterized by being genetically isolated from other languages (Trask, 1996). While many words (including emotion names) currently used are of Basque origin and were coined a long time ago, there are some others that have been borrowed from other languages in contact with Basque, such as Latin, Spanish, and French (Alonso-Arbiol et al., 2006). Basque is a co-official language in the Basque Country, where some inhabitants are Spanish monolinguals and some others are Basque–Spanish bilinguals. The language is probably one of the most characteristic expressions of the rich Basque culture, which has some distinct features as compared to the more widely known culture from the south of Spain (often portrayed as the prototypical Spanish culture).

The most widely used and most commonly recognised term to refer to despair in Basque nowadays is the ancient word "*etsipena*." Alonso-Arbiol et al. (2006) found that "*etsipena*" was closely related to two other terms: "*desesperazioa*" and "*gogogabetasuna*." The former is a loan word from the Spanish despair term "*desesperación*." "*Gogogabetasuna*," on the other hand, means "indifference, lack of will-power" (Morris, 1998) and points to a certain state of apathy or passiveness.

The meaning of the two despair terms "*etsipena*" and "*desesperazioa*" is not well distinguished in the dictionaries. The Morris English–Basque Student Plus Dictionary (Morris, 1998) defines "*etsipena*" as "disillusion, resignation, despair, pessimism," or "consent, acceptance." "*Desesperazioa*" is not included in this dictionary, but Sarasola's (2007) *Euskal hiztegia,* one of the most recognised monolingual Basque dictionaries, describes "*desesperazioa*" in terms of "*etsimena*" (another form for "*etsipena*") and "*ernegazioa*" (translated into English by the Morris dictionary as "curse, swearing").

An important feature to differentiate between the two is that "*etsipena*" has come to replace two older expressions currently out of use: "*etsi ona*" and "*etsi gaiztoa*" (*ona* meaning "good," and *gaiztoa* meaning "bad"). According to Sarasola's (2007) dictionary, "*etsi ona*" (the "good despair") means to "give up, accept a situation that one does not like" (p. 370, our translation), whereas "*etsi gaiztoa*" (the "bad despair") means to "despair, situation of having lost hope completely" (p. 370, our translation). An example provided for this latter term is "*etsi gaiztoz oihuka*" (literally, shouting/crying due to bad despair). The meaning of "*etsipena*" could be said to lie between the two (J. K. Igerabide, personal communication, June 11, 2009), but may be closer to the passiveness and melancholy expressed by "*etsi ona*." In fact, "*etsipena*" involves a lower AROUSAL-activity[4] profile than "*etsi gaiztoa*," since the latter more easily brings the person to take an active (and dramatic) action,

----

[4] In this chapter, when we refer to an "AROUSAL–activity" pattern, we imply not only the more physiological aspect of AROUSAL, but other active behaviors as well. To refer to mere physiological activation (as in the Bodily reaction component factor AUTONOMIC AROUSAL described in Chapter 9), we use the terms "AROUSAL," or "aroused."

such as committing suicide or bombing (J. K. Igerabide, personal communication, June 12, 2009). The active non-conformity implicit in "*etsi gaiztoa*" is better captured by the loanword borrowed from Spanish, "*desesperazioa*;" "*etsipena*," the most frequent word, does not seem to carry this active profile. The less aroused and less active conception of Basque despair captured by "*etsipena*" would resemble the features described for the English term "despair."

Two Spanish terms: *"Desesperación"* and *"desesperanza"*

The most common translation equivalent of English "despair" in Spanish is "*desesperación*." It derives from the verb "*desesperar*" (literally, to "remove hope"), which means "to despair" (intransitive) and "to exasperate" (transitive). Because of the polysemy of the verb, the noun is itself ambiguous. As the two examples below from the Spanish CREA Corpus[5] illustrate, "*desesperación*" can refer either to hopelessness (1) or hot exasperation (2). Context is key in these cases to understand if the individual is feeling an emotion of high or low activation:

1 "Julián a su vez le hablaba de París, de lo difícil que estaba resultando todo, de lo solo y desesperado que se sentía" (Julian in return would tell him about Paris, about how difficult everything was turning out to be, how lonely and "despaired" he felt) (Carlos Ruiz Zafón, 2001, La Sombra del Viento. Barcelona, Editorial Planeta, p. 447; emphasis added; our translation).

2 "Hay días que algún vecino, desesperado por el bullicio que forman estos jóvenes, tira sobre ellos cubos de agua" (there are days when some neighbor, "despaired" by the noise these youngsters make, throws buckets of water on them) ("El Mundo" newspaper, El Mundo, 06/10/1994; emphasis added; our translation).

Another related term is "*desesperanza*" (hopelessness). Unlike "*desesperación*," it does not derive from a verb, but from the combination of a suffix (*des-*, without) and another noun ("*esperanza*," hope). It has a more static tone, as it means "lack of hope," rather than "loss of hope." Contrary to "*desesperación*," its current meaning only refers to a low AROUSAL-activity emotion (Real Academia Española, 2003).

If "despair" is characterized by low levels of AROUSAL–activity, one might argue that "*desesperanza*"— rather than the ambiguous "*desesperación*"—may be a better translation equivalent. However, "*desesperación*" is much more frequently used and—unlike "*desesperanza*"—it can be found in adjectival form as well. Therefore, it is the only form available in the language to translate the English adjective "despaired."

20.4 **Aroused–active and deactivated–passive despair**

The terms in Basque and Spanish for despair have a duality—AROUSAL–activity and deactivation–passivity—that is not present in English. Where do these markedly different meanings found in dictionaries come from? Are they rooted in a possible dual tradition of understanding the concept of despair?

Some cultural manifestations point in this direction. Barasch (1999) studied the artistic representation of despair in European history. He noticed that at the end of the Middle Ages and in the early modern times, both artists and audiences recognised two kinds of despair: a passive or apathetic type (which he called "melancholy") and a more active or violent one. The apathetic type of despair was a more commonly applied cultural symbol in the arts, but the active or violent type was

---

5 Corpus de Referencia del Español Actual (CREA). Real Academia Española. Available online at http://corpus.rae.es/creanet.html. Retrieved on August, 10, 2009.

also represented. The representation could take two forms: images portraying some exaggerated motion or showing actions of self-destructiveness (i.e., hanging or stabbing oneself). These exaggerated movements may arise from an intense physiological activation, which could lead to specific action tendencies (as previous movements of actual behaviors) and would come to the surface as extreme behaviors. The question that comes to mind immediately is whether there is any reminiscence of this Medieval and Renaissance double vision of despair (passive melancholy vs active violence) in the modern Western European culture. And more explicitly, does the Mediterranean Latin culture, as manifested in the (peninsular) Spanish language, capture this active and high-arousal manifestation of despair?

Rimé and Giovannini (1986) examined the physiological features associated with different emotions in countries of the north and the south of Europe. The hot-blooded reputed Southerners (including Spaniards), as they were referred to by the authors, showed more blood pressure changes in sadness as compared to people from northern European countries. If we focus specifically on the concept of despair, we may expect that a higher internal activation would also apply to the Spanish "*desesperación*" term. Furthermore, Barasch's (1999) accounts of active despair may suggest that such emotion concept (to be captured by the Spanish "*desesperación*") could be associated not only with a more physiological activation, but also with stronger subsequent action tendencies and expression. Therefore, Spanish "*desesperación*" would convey a specific profile of both higher AROUSAL and activity in its expression, when compared to the Basque "*etsipena*" and to the English "despair."

20.5 **The present study**

The present study tests the hypothesis that the English, Basque, and Spanish prototypical despair terms have different meanings. A recent work by Alonso-Arbiol, Gorostiaga, and Balluerka (2008) showed that the Spanish and Basque despair terms differ considerably on the AROUSAL dimension (and to a certain extent also on the POWER dimension), which may indicate that they are not completely equivalent in meaning. In an effort to identify this semantic variation, it is interesting to study the use of the Spanish term by Spanish-Basque bilinguals. This group has been exposed to the everyday use of both the Spanish and the Basque despair terms. Their understanding of the Spanish term "*desesperación*" may be more similar to the Basque "*etsipena*" due to the cultural effect of language contact, a phenomenon that has been termed by anthropologists and linguists as lexical acculturation (Brown, 1989; Salzmann, 1954). For comparative purposes, two other samples from Spanish-speaking regions different from the Basque Country (south of Spain and Chile) were also analyzed. The English term "despair" was used as a standard reference.

Hypotheses

Linguistic equivalence was measured both at a general level (semantic profile of the emotion) and at component level (Appraisal, Feeling, Bodily reaction, Action tendency, and Expression). Regarding linguistic equivalence, and based on the principles of lexical acculturation (Brown, 1989; Salzmann, 1954) and the definitions of Spanish "*desesperación*" (Real Academia Española, 2003) and Basque "*etsipena*" (Morris, 1998; Sarasola, 2007), we tested the following hypotheses at both general and component level:

1 The three Spanish profiles of "*desesperación*" are equivalent.

2 Northern Spanish is more similar to Basque than are the other two Spanish varieties.

3 Basque and English terms tap equivalent concepts.

We relied on the component level to examine the salience of the differential pattern of AROUSAL–activity. Beyond the behavioral aspect, all terms for despair should convey a core concept of appraisal and feelings common to all languages: a negative emotion, caused by feelings of inability to cope with present and future events, in which the individual feels negative and has a pessimistic outlook on what the future holds for her/him. However, the internal and external manifestations of AROUSAL–activity (body responses, action tendencies, and expression) are expected to show cross-language differences, as observed with other emotion terms too in Basque and Spanish (Alonso-Arbiol et al., (2008)). Therefore, we tested the following additional hypothesis:

4 High AROUSAL–activity features of Spanish are more salient than those of Basque and English for the Bodily reaction, Action tendency, and Expression components, but not for Appraisal and Feeling.

Finally, at the more general level, we posit a series of hypotheses of the differential pattern of Spanish as related to Basque, as suggested by the meanings of the terms in the dictionaries of each language (Morris, 1998; Real Academia Española, 2003; Sarasola, 2007):

5 Basque "*etsipena*" is characterized by a state of apathy or passiveness, with specific features denoting inactivity and low AROUSAL.

6 Spanish "*desesperación*" has more aroused–active character than Basque "*etsipena*" and English "despair."

Methods and analytical procedure

The respondents ($N = 103$) come from five gender-balanced subsamples in four different locations: a sample of native speakers of Basque in the Basque Country ($N = 23$), a sample of native speakers of Spanish in the Basque Country ($N = 26$), a sample of native speakers of Spanish in the south of Spain ($N = 17$), a sample of native speakers of Spanish in the central region of Chile ($N = 13$), and a sample of native speakers of English in the United States of America ($N = 24$). All participants had at least completed secondary studies. Their ages ranged between 18 and 64; mean ages (and SDs) for the subsamples were as follows: 23.0 (3.07) (Basque); 24.2 (7.50) for "North," native Spanish-speakers in the Basque region of Spain; 32.06 (13.90) for "South," native Spanish-speakers in the south of Spain; 20.4 (1.45) for Chilean speakers; and 18.6 (0.68) for US English speakers. There was a significant effect of the age of participants on the linguistic group [$F(4, 96) = 10.17$, $p < 0.001$, $\omega^2 = 0.27$]. Post-hoc analyses (Tukey) revealed that the participants' age was higher in the Spanish-speaking group from the South than in the other groups. We inspected whether this difference may have affected the results in the direction of observing significantly less aroused–active features in the South group than in the other Spanish-speaking groups, but this was not the case. Neither main effects of age nor interaction effects between group and age were observed. Therefore, the age difference was not addressed in the remaining analyses. Participants completed the online version of the GRID questionnaire (see Chapter 5) in their own language, describing the likelihood of each of the 144 emotion features of despair (and three other emotion words not studied here) to be prototypical in their cultural group according to a nine-point Likert scale, where 1 = "Extremely unlikely" and 9 = "Extremely likely." The items (features) belonged to five semantic components (Appraisal, Bodily reaction, Expression, Action tendency, and Feeling) and regulation strategies. Three additional items inquired about other aspects, such as frequency and social acceptability. Further information about the instrument, the back-translation process, and the data collection procedure is provided in detail in Chapters 5 and 6.

Linguistic (dis)similarity and area differences of despair terms

In order to examine the equivalence of despair terms (Hypotheses 1 to 3), we calculated the correlations between their profiles in each of the four samples (composed by the mean scores on the 142 features). The rule of thumb of having correlations above 0.80 has been employed as indicative of equivalent emotion profiles. Yet, because the question of equivalence was central in the present study, we also calculated the correlations along with their confidence intervals following Fisher's z transformation procedures. This procedure enables us to make (statistical) inferences about the similarity/dissimilarity of the various despair terms. From this approach, we consider that two correlations are similar when the z comparing them is statistically non-significant.

The comparison of the general profiles by means of correlations (see Table 20.1) shows that the three Spanish-speaking groups are more alike, and they seem to refer to the same concept of despair, hence confirming Hypothesis 1. Moreover, when the z statistics are computed, these values are statistically significant for the comparison pairs of Basque-North and Basque with other Spanish-speaking samples, supporting the hypothesis that Northern Spanish is more similar to Basque than the other two Spanish varieties (Hypothesis 2) (all the results regarding the Fishers' z differences between correlation coefficients of the samples can be obtained from the first author).

In order to get a more accurate picture of the (dis)similarity of the despair concepts in the different language groups, we used weighted multidimensional scaling (WMDS) procedures. In general, multidimensional scaling procedures are techniques for data analysis that allow us to explain similarities or dissimilarities (distances) between the objects under study in a low-dimensional space with meaningful underlying dimensions. Using the correlation matrices of Table 20.1, the WMDS analysis (INDSCAL) yielded a one-dimensional solution with a relatively good fit (Kruskal's stress = 0.12). This means that the dissimilarities between the pairs of individuals (cultural groups) are best explained as points across a single dimension. The coordinates for each language group along that dimension are shown in Table 20.1. The Spanish-speaking sample from the north of Spain was in between the other two Spanish-speaking samples (south of Spain and

Table 20.1 Correlations of the despair overall profile among different samples (N = 144) and coordinates in the one-dimensional space

Languages and location of participants	1	2	3	4	Coordinates
Spanish					
1. Chile					1.02
2. South Spain	0.89** (0.85–0.92)				1.01
3. North Spain (Basque Country)	0.87** (0.82–0.90)	0.90** (0.86–0.93)			0.22
Non-Spanish					
4. American English (USA)	*0.70** (0.61–0.77)*	*0.67** (0.57–0.75)*	0.85** (0.80–0.89)		−0.71
5. Basque (Basque Country)	*0.50** (0.37–0.61)*	*0.48** (0.34–0.60)*	*0.70** (0.61–0.77)*	0.82** (0.76–0.87)	−1.54

Note: confidence intervals for the correlations are provided in parentheses. The correlations whose intervals are below 0.80 are shown in italics. ** p <0.01, two-tailed.

Chile) at one end, and the Basque sample at the other (a new confirmation of Hypotheses 1 and 2 using a different statistical analysis). The greater closeness of the concept described in the North Spanish-speaking sample to the Basque concept of despair might be a consequence of the cultural diffusion or lexical acculturation effect of the Spanish "*desesperación*" in the Basque region. In fact, 17 out of 24 participants of the north sample declared having some knowledge of Basque, and four of them even spoke the language on a daily basis. Moreover, Hypothesis 3 was also supported. The Basque "*etsipena*" and Northern Spanish "*desesperación*" are more similar to American "despair" than the other two Spanish varieties, which suggests that the concepts as captured in the Basque and Northern Spain samples are fairly similar. Our three hypotheses were, therefore, confirmed at this (general) level: as expected, we found linguistic similarity in Spanish-speaking samples, more similarity between Basque and North than between Basque and other Spanish-speaking samples, and equivalence between the English and the Basque concepts of despair.

This general picture was examined in more detail at the component level. We compared the profiles for the Appraisal, Feeling, Bodily reaction, Action tendency, and Expression components (control/regulation was not analyzed at this level because only four items measured this aspect of emotion). We calculated the correlations between the component features for the different despair terms (see Table 20.2). In this case, the z statistics of the differences between two r values were not calculated, due to the smaller number of items (from 18 to 40). The three Spanish-speaking samples showed again the highest rate of agreement among them for all components. In this regard, the criterion of language similarity seems to prevail over the cultural distance.

The most similar component across the examined languages and cultures involves feelings. Feeling was the only component that showed equivalence across all cultures (all correlations are above 0.80). These results indicate that all three terms seem to have a common pattern of feelings, despite the lack of full equivalence of the Spanish "*desesperación*" with the Basque and English counterparts.

On the other hand, the Bodily reaction component shows the most dissimilar profile for the Basque-speaking group. There is no equivalence between Basque and the rest of samples, as evidenced by the low or lack of correlation between Basque and the other four groups, including the North Spanish sample ($r = -0.05$). This confirms our predictions regarding the non-equivalence of Basque "*etsipena*" and Spanish "*desesperación*," especially when it comes to physiological activation.

Weighted multidimensional scaling (INDSCAL) was again used to analyse the distances (similarities/dissimilarities) among the language groups. The matrices of correlations shown in Table 20.2 were independently examined for each component, and in all five cases the analyses yielded one-dimensional solutions with a very good fit (values of Kruskal's stress were between 0.00 and 0.05). The coordinates for each language group along that dimension, as well as the stress values, are displayed in Table 20.3. As we found for the general profile, Hypotheses 1 to 3 were also confirmed at the component level. The Spanish-speaking sample from the north of Spain is again placed between the other two Spanish-speaking samples (south of Spain and Chile) and the Basque sample. Furthermore, the American English group is positioned near the Basque-speaking group, and the nearest Spanish-speaking group is the one from the north of Spain. This pattern of results lends additional support to the equivalence of the Basque "*etsipena*" and the English "despair" terms.

In sum, both at a general and at a component level, analyses revealed three major findings, which are in line with our expectations: (1) the three culturally-distinct Spanish-speaking groups are alike and refer to the same concept when using the term "*desesperación*"; (2) the Spanish-speaking group from the north of Spain shares more similarities with the Basque "*etsipena*" than the other

Table 20.2 Correlations of despair components among different samples

Languages and Location of Participants	Appraisal (N = 31)				Feeling (N = 22)				Bodily reaction (N = 18)				Action tendency (N = 40)				Expression (N = 26)			
	1	2	3	4	1	2	3	4	1	2	3	4	1	2	3	4	1	2	3	4
Spanish																				
1. Chile																				
2. South Spain	0.90**				0.98**				0.92**				0.84**				0.91**			
3. North Spain	0.85**	0.93**			0.95**	0.95**			0.94**	0.96**			0.91**	0.82**			0.85**	0.91**		
Non-Spanish																				
4. US English	0.87**	0.90**	0.95**		0.83**	0.84**	0.95**		0.74**	0.64**	0.75**		0.78**	0.61**	0.90**		0.38	0.43*	0.69**	
5. Basque	0.63**	0.75**	0.83**	0.82**	0.80**	0.80**	0.90**	0.93**	−0.06	−0.18	−0.05	0.37	0.63**	0.47**	0.79**	0.89**	0.19	0.26	0.53**	0.82**

Note: * p <0.05, ** p <0.01, two-tailed.

Table 20.3 Coordinates of samples for the despair components on the one-dimensional space

Language Groups and Location	Coordinates				
	Appraisal ($S^2 = 0.01$)	Feeling ($S^2 = 0.01$)	Bodily reaction ($S^2 = 0.00$)	Action tendency ($S^2 = 0.01$)	Expression ($S^2 = 0.05$)
Spanish					
1. Chile	−1.33	−1.03	1.38	−0.67	−1.08
2. South Spain	−0.59	−1.03	0.39	−1.44	−0.89
3. North Spain	0.12	−0.17	0.39	−0.02	−0.37
Non-Spanish					
4. US English	0.10	0.70	−0.59	0.73	0.90
5. Basque	1.70	1.53	−1.57	1.40	1.45

Note: S^2 = Kruskal stress for the one-dimensional solution in each component.

two Spanish-speaking groups, which provides an interesting demonstration of lexical accultura-tion; and (3) Basque "*etsipena*" and English "despair" seem to be equivalent terms, as evidenced by the similarity of their profiles. Finally, an important prediction about the components was also borne out; whereas a similar affective pattern of feelings could be traced for all terms, there are marked differences in the physiological concomitants of the varieties of despair across languages, with the Basque and Spanish terms in the opposite poles of the continuum, and the English term between them.

Defining features of despair terms

The correlational profile discussed in the previous section provided us with a measure of semantic distance between the three despair terms, but a more nuanced picture can be obtained by analyzing the most salient features in their profiles (note that a comparison of the scores of specific features across samples is not intended here; instead, we wanted to see the general profile of the despair words in each sample). The most salient features were defined as those whose confidence interval fell above six or below four on the nine-point Likert scale; an overview is presented in Table 20.4. The cutoff values offer valuable information about which features are most relevant (salient) to define the concept of despair in the different linguistic groups. These boundary values were chosen, as the values of 4 and 6 have anchors in the response scale that point to a low and high likelihood of occurrence. Those in the upper end of the scale, marked by a positive sign, are positive salient features (i.e., likely to occur). Negative salient features, marked by a negative sign, are those least likely to occur. Features salient across all three Spanish varieties are marked by gray cells. Shared saliency in the English-Basque semantic cluster is also marked this way.

In line with Hypothesis 4, a more salient AROUSAL–activity profile was observed for Spanish "*desesperación*," whereas fewer salient AROUSAL–activity features were mentioned by English speakers, and even fewer by Basque speakers (see Table 20.4). Regarding the specific components, this pattern of AROUSAL–activity can be seen in the Bodily reaction component; here the Basque language did not exhibit a marked profile, whereas the three varieties of Spanish showed various AROUSAL–activity features (e.g., heartbeat faster, not breathing slower, and breathing faster) that were absent in Basque and English. The Expression component also reflected a quantitative differ-ence in AROUSAL–activity salient features in Spanish (especially in the South group) in comparison

Table 20.4 Characteristic features of despair in different samples

	Item	Spanish			Non-Spanish	
		Chile	South	North	USA	Basque
Appraisal	Pleasing for self		–	–	–	–
	Consequences positive for self			–	–	–
	Consequences negative for self		+	+		
	Needing immediate response		+			
	Treated unjustly			+	+	
	In danger	+	+	+	+	
	Irrevocable loss		+	+		
Bodily reaction	Feeling shivers					–
	Feeling weak limbs	+			+	
	Getting pale				+	
	Lump in throat			+	+	
	Stomach troubles		+		+	
	Heartbeat faster	+	+	+		
	Muscles relax			–		
	Muscles tense		+			
	Breathing slows	–		–		
	Breathing faster	+	+			
	Feeling warm	+	+			
	Perspiring		+			
	Sweat	+	+			
	Feeling hot		+			
Expression	Smiling		–	–	–	–
	Pressing lips		+			
	Frown				–	
	Showing tears	+	+	+	+	+
	Not changing face		–	–	–	
	Abrupt body move	+	+			
	Not changing gestures	–		–		
	Loud voice	+	+			
	Trembling voice		+			
	Falling silent				+	
	Speech disturb		+	+		

Table 20.4 (continued) Characteristic features of despair in different samples

	Item	Spanish			Non-Spanish	
		Chile	South	North	USA	Basque
	Speaking faster	+	+			
	Speaking slower		–			
	Not changing vocal		–			
Action tendency	Continuing what one was doing		–			–
	Wanting situation to last	–	–	–	–	–
	Stopping what one was doing		+	+	+	+
	Undoing what is happening	+	+	+		
	Feeling inhibited	+	+	+		
	Accepting situation as it is	–				
	Needing help or support	+	+	+		
	Urge to be active		+			
	Wanting to move		+			
	Lack motivation				+	+
	Doing nothing				+	
	No motivation to pay attention				+	
	Wanting to flee	+		+	+	
	Pushing things away			+	+	+
	Stopping sensory contact			+		
	Hiding from others	+		+	+	
	Withdrawing into self			+	+	
	Avoiding hurt		+		+	
	Damage or hurt		+			
	Breaking contact with others		+			
	Tackling situation		+			
	Being tender, kind	–				
	Running away	+	+	+	+	
	Destroying close things		+	+	+	
	Singing and dancing		–	–	–	–

Table 20.4 (continued) Characteristic features of despair in different samples

	Item	Spanish			Non-Spanish	
		Chile	South	North	USA	Basque
Feeling	Intense emotional state		+	+	+	
	Feeling good	–	–	–	–	–
	Feeling tired			+		
	Feeling submissive				+	
	Feeling at ease	–	–	–		–
	Feeling powerless		+	+	+	+
	Feeling negative			+	+	+
	Feeling energetic			–	–	–
	Feeling in control	–	–	–	–	–
	Feeling restless	+	+			
	Feeling powerful	–	–	–		
	Feeling positive	–	–	–	–	–
	Feeling exhausted			+	+	+
	Feeling strong	–		–	–	–
	Feeling calm	–	–	–		
	Feeling out of control	+	+	+		
	Feeling bad		+	+	+	+
	Feeling dominant	–	–	–		–
	Feeling nervous	+	+	+		
	Feeling weak				+	+
Other	How frequently experienced	+				
Total number of characteristic features		32	53	45	39	23

to Basque, but not in comparison to the American English group. Likewise, the number of salient AROUSAL–activity features in the Action tendency component was higher in the Spanish groups (again much more evident in the South one) than in the Basque group. Also in line with our expectations, the Feeling and Appraisal components (less related to the AROUSAL–activity nature of the emotion in the latter case) did not show divergent patterns in the salience of this aspect for the five groups.

The following results were obtained for the specific defining features in the various linguistic groups. We first analyze the English term, which has been used as an (arbitrary) standard or starting point for comparison. As could be expected from theoretical descriptions made in the literature, the English "despair" is characterized by negative VALENCE and low AROUSAL–activity. Defining elements with a clear negative VALENCE included the experience of an irrevocable loss, being in danger, being treated unjustly, not feeling good, not feeling positive, and feeling bad. Defining elements suggesting low AROUSAL–activity were a desire to do nothing, lacking motivation to react, and not feeling energetic.

Basque shows a similar profile, therefore confirming Hypothesis 5. The characteristic elements of "*etsipena*" refer to the Feeling component (feeling powerless, negative, bad, weak, and exhausted; not feeling good, at ease, energetic, in control, strong, or dominant) and to the Action tendencies (lacking motivation, pushing things away, stopping what one was doing, and not wanting the situation to last). Many of these features are common to the English "despair," and as in English, they reflect a more passive and deactivated experience of despair, as well as a more intimate and calm way of suffering.

In contrast, the features in the three Spanish-speaking groups compose a very activity-like profile for "*desesperación*," which gives support to Hypothesis 6. This higher activity and also higher AROUSAL is reflected in specific signs of agitation in the Feeling component (not feeling calm, feeling out of control, and feeling nervous), and some revealing Action tendencies that oppose passivity (wanting to run away in whatever direction and wanting to undo what is happening). Moreover, the defining body sensations or physiological changes that imply high AROUSAL in "*desesperación*" are not only more numerous in Spanish than in Basque or English, but in most cases also more intense (higher intensity of fast heartbeat, fast breathing, tense muscles, feeling warm, and feeling hot). This suggests more similarity of "*desesperación*" to anger (or fear) than to sadness.

The profile of defining features provides an additional intralinguistic insight; the emotion in the south of Spain seems to be generally more intense than in the other two Spanish samples. Although participants did not explicitly report feeling a more intense emotion, the specific pattern of body sensations, action tendencies and expressive behaviors in the Southern group tells a different story. There are several characteristics that only show up clearly in this sample, such as stomach troubles, tense muscles, perspiration, and feeling hot (Bodily reaction features); an urge to be active, wanting to move, avoiding being hurt, desire to damage or hurt, breaking contact with others, and wanting to tackle the situation (Action tendency); and pressed lips, trembling voice, changing one's vocal expression, and not speaking slower (Expression features). The salience in intensity of the Southern sample is fully in line with the Mediterranean stereotype of more exaggerated experiences and expressions of emotions.

But is this higher activity and AROUSAL only characteristic of "*desesperación*" or can it also be found in other Spanish emotions? At least three studies (Moltó et al., 1998; Redondo, Fraga, Padrón, & Comesaña, 2007; Vila et al., 2001) have provided supportive evidence for the latter position with Spanish populations. Thus, Redondo et al. (2007) compared the responses given by Spaniards to those of Americans to 1,034 words of a wide nature (the complete list of the Affective Norms for English Words). Rated by participants according to three emotional dimensions (VALENCE, AROUSAL, and dominance), these authors found that the Spanish words were evaluated as being more arousing than those of the (American) English version. Moltó and colleagues (1998) and Vila and colleagues (2001) also obtained a similar pattern of higher AROUSAL for Spaniards using the images of the International Affective Picture System (IAPS). Apart from the data obtained from Spanish populations, similar results can be mentioned regarding other Southern Europeans. In fact, comparable data have been found for Italians in the IAPS; their AROUSAL ratings for the pictures were significantly higher than those of Germans (similar to Americans), whereas Swedish ratings of AROUSAL were lower than those of any other group (Bradley, Greenwald, & Hamm, 1993). These data match the general cultural stereotype commonly attributed to Southern Europeans (e.g., Italians and Spaniards), who are perceived to be more "hot blooded," as Rimé and Giovannini (1986) already suggested in their study. Nevertheless, extant data are not sufficient and/or convincing enough to unquestionably confirm or reject this admittedly tentative line of thinking.

20.6 **Conclusions**

We have provided evidence for the confirmation of hypotheses regarding: (1) (in)equivalence of despair terms across languages and cultural groups, both at a general and a component level, and (2) the specific AROUSAL–active pattern of the Spanish "*desesperación.*" The most salient finding of the present study is that it is impossible to compose a coherent portrait of despair by combining the three linguistically most comparable terms in English ("despair"), Spanish ("*desesperación*"), and Basque ("*etsipena*"). A single combined profile would only have five features in common (showing tears, not wanting the situation to last, not feeling good, not feeling in control, and not feeling positive), which are not much more than the broad picture of a negative emotion. Our analysis suggests that the three words do not refer to a unitary concept, but rather to two different ones. The English and Basque could be considered to be equivalent terms and instances of a more general sadness category, whereas the Spanish "*desesperación*" differs from the other two in a consistent way across all emotion components, except for Feeling. Our study does not imply that despair is a fundamentally different emotion among speakers of Spanish, Basque, and English. However, we assert that the most common word in these languages denoting despair show important differences, both in terms of general meaning of the emotion word and in terms of components associated with the word. Moreover, our study cannot address the question whether the two different types of despair that we found can be identified in all cultures or is a more indigenous concept that can be found in one or a few cultures.

Spanish "*desesperación*" is not just a subtype of sadness (as English and Basque despair terms seem to be), but rather a combination of sadness and the anger elements of frustration/exasperation. The cross-cultural and cross-linguistic divergence is not surprising. It has been argued that basic emotions have clearer adaptive functions, not susceptible to cultural variation, than non-basic emotions (e.g., Poortinga, 1992). Therefore, the cultural influence would be more pronounced in non-basic emotions, where we would include despair, but also depression, an emotion in which despair is a key characteristic and whose meaning has been observed to vary across cultures. The expected larger variability of despair has already been observed in English, Dutch, and French (Fontaine et al., 2007). We tentatively propose that this is also the case for Spanish, as the meaning of the term seems to reflect a cultural tendency to experience and/or express emotions in a more activated manner. Such tendency appears common to other Mediterranean societies as well (Rimé & Giovannini, 1986), where higher AROUSAL levels have been obtained, for example, in the emotionality ratings of pictures (Bradley et al., 1993). Further study of the underlying dimensions and emotion features relevant to the meaning of despair terms in French ("*désespoir*") or Italian ("*disperazione*") may help to shed light on the topic, as well as a systematic study involving more than one emotion.

Another important finding is that the three Spanish cultural groups have more in common with one another than with the speakers of the other two languages, despite the cultural differences in psychological functioning or any other domain there may be. Therefore, it could be asserted that in this case the linguistic similarity effect prevails over the possible cultural differences. Yet, the imprint of lexical acculturation or cultural diffusion is evident here in the greater similarity found between Basque and the Spanish spoken in the Basque region (Northern Spain). A similar effect has been noticed by Davitz (1969), Levy (1973), or Pavlenko (2008), who observed that bilingual individuals applied the characteristics of one emotion in a language when they spoke in the second language, even though the meaning differed slightly between them.

Translation issues arise in the cross-cultural communication of emotion if the terms chosen in the second language do not yield the same concepts expressed in the first one. However, in the back-translation procedure, we run the risk of selecting terms that do not capture the essence of the emotional representation in the target language or cultural context. Efforts to obtain linguistic similarity may lead to a content-biased outcome; studies from an indigenous perspective help to identify this bias (Kim, Yang, & Hwang, 2006). By choosing "*desesperación*" as a translation equivalent for "despair," the native Spanish-speaking linguists and psychologists involved in the GRID back-translation process adopted this indigenous perspective. Our study showed that if we want to maximize comparability of scores, we can only use a limited part of the construct. If, on the other hand, we want to maximize the ecological validity, comparability of scores cannot be achieved. There is no preferred solution to this dilemma. What in the end will constitute a better choice will depend on the aim of the study.

Acknowledgments

We would like to thank Paola Alarcón and Phoebe Ellsworth for allowing us using data collected in Chile and in USA, respectively.

Preparation of this chapter was supported by a mobility grant from the Spanish Ministry of Education (JC2008-00012) and a grant from the Research Council of the University of the Basque Country (GIU08/09) to the first author, and the ELIN Project grant awarded by the Swiss Network for International Studies to the second author and her team.

Chapter 21

Finno-Ugric emotions: The meaning of anger in Estonian and Finnish

Anu Realo,[1] Mari Siiroinen, Heli Tissari, and Liisi Kööts-Ausmees

We cannot say anything about "anger" if we don't know what we are talking about, and to know what we are talking about we must first analyse the meaning of the word anger (Wierzbicka, 1999a, p. 28).

Anger appears to be one of the most thoroughly studied basic emotions both in the field of psychology and that of cognitive linguistics. There are equivalents for the word "anger" in nearly all major languages of the world (Mesquita, Frijda, & Scherer, 1997). In a study that sought emotion nomenclature universals, it was found that emotion categories were added in a relatively similar generalized sequence in most languages, with anger being among the first labeled (Hupka, Lenton, & Hutchison, 1999). To our knowledge, there is only one society—the Utkuhikhalingmiut ("Utku") Eskimos—that does not have a special word for anger (Briggs, 1970).

Furthermore, lexically equivalent words for anger have been shown to involve comparable appraisal patterns in languages and cultures as diverse as Dutch, Japanese, and Indonesian, which could be summarized as "the experience of something unpleasant and that has obstructed one's reaching one's goals, which event was felt to be unfair but inevitable, and for which someone else is to blame" (Frijda, Markam, Sato, & Wiers, 1995, p. 139). If one becomes angry, one should experience body heat, internal pressure, redness in the face and neck area, agitation, and interference with accurate perception (Lakoff, 1987; Lakoff & Kövecses, 1987). The central conceptual metaphor for "anger" appears to be that "anger is the heat of a fluid in a container" (Lakoff, 1987, p. 383; Lakoff & Kövecses, 1987, p. 198). The suggestion is that we see people as containers for emotions and the process of anger as the build up of heat in a fluid in these containers, which may then explode.

However, when someone becomes angry, he or she may express anger within the limits of a variety of culturally prescribed scenarios. Cultures may differ from one another in the degree of anger that is allowed to be expressed (e.g., "anger out") compared to how much anger one is meant to keep to oneself (e.g., "anger in"). For instance, it has been suggested that the expression of anger is

[1] Correspondence concerning this article should be addressed to Anu Realo, Department of Psychology, University of Tartu, Tiigi 78, Tartu 50410, Estonia. email: anu.realo@ut.ee.

quite acceptable in individualist cultures but more suppressed in collectivist cultures (Chon, Kim, & Ryoo, 2000).

Situations that induce anger have also been found to be rather universal (Mesquita & Frijda, 1992). Wherever and whenever something happens that is felt to be unfair and for which someone else is to blame or which keeps people from reaching their desired goal, anger is likely to occur. For instance, perceived injustice was found to play a key role in the elicitation of negative emotion, including anger, in 37 countries (Mikula, Scherer, & Athenstaedt, 1998). Furthermore, anger has a facial expression (Ekman, Sorenson, & Friesen, 1969) as well as a nonverbal emotional vocalization (Sauter, Eisner, Ekman, & Scott, 2010) that can be recognized across cultures. Thus, anger appears to be one of the most fundamental human emotions to have emerged consistently across time and culture (Chon, 2002).

In the present study, we explore differences in the meaning of anger between representatives of two linguistically and culturally similar countries, Estonia and Finland. Anger (*viha*) proved to be the most typical Estonian example for this emotion category (Vainik & Orav, 2005) and the third most frequent emotion term in Finnish (Tuovila, 2005).

21.1 **Languages studied**

The Estonian and Finnish languages belong to the Finnic group of the Finno-Ugric language family.[2] They are the largest of the Finnic languages, with the smaller ones being Karelian, Veps, Votian, Ingrian, and Livonian. These languages are descendants of a common protolanguage probably spoken until about 2,000 years ago. Approximately one million people speak Estonian as a native language today. Most of them live in the Republic of Estonia, which lies on the southern shore of the Gulf of Finland, the eastern most part of the Baltic Sea. Finnish is spoken to the north of the Gulf of Finland, in an area extending some 1,300 kilometres north from the shores of the Baltic Sea and has about five million native speakers (Abondolo, 2006; Laakso, 2001).

Metslang (2009) compared Estonian to Finnish and both languages to the Standard Average European (SAE) languages, the nucleus of which includes French and German, as well as all the Romance, Germanic, Slavic, and Baltic languages, Albanian, Greek, and Hungarian. These languages each include at least five out of twelve SAE features. The main characteristics of SAE can be said to be only modestly represented in Estonian and Finnish; with both languages revealing no more than two features, they do not really belong to the SAE language group (Haspelmath, 2001). However, in spite of the fact that the grammars of Estonian and Finnish are very similar in terms of their principal features and that they also share a great deal of lexis, Estonian—most likely due to historical twists and turns—has drifted somewhat away from Finnish and the rest of the Finnic languages (Metslang, 2009). As such, being closely related, yet somewhat different, Estonian and Finnish provide an interesting case to study in the framework of emotion analysis.

21.2 **Anger in Estonian and Finnish**

The English word "anger" translates into Estonian and Finnish as *viha* (Estonian) and *suuttuminen* (Finnish). However, the word "hate" translates into Estonian and Finnish as *vihkamine* and *viha*, respectively. So, one can see that the same word *viha* appears in both languages but it is used to translate different English emotion terms (i.e., "anger" in Estonian and "hate" in Finnish).

---

2 There are three other language groups in Finno-Ugric family, one being Ugric, in which the biggest language is Hungarian.

Being close relatives, one would expect at first sight that if there are words in both languages that are etymologically of the same origin, like the word *viha,* the meaning would also be the same. Etymologically, the word *viha* came to these languages long ago from the Proto-Aryan word **viša* meaning "poison, bile." Its meaning has actually been, until very recently, "bitter" or "acrid." Yet, although *viha* is the most cognitively salient emotion term in both Estonian and Finnish (Tuovila, 2005; Vainik, 2002a, 2002b)—it comes up most frequently and most prominently when informants are asked to attempt free listing of some emotion category—it appears to carry somewhat different meanings in the two languages.

According to the *Dictionary of the Estonian Language* (*Eesti keele seletav sõnaraamat*), *viha* is "an intense feeling which is mixed with hostility and irritation; strong distress or intolerance."[3] However, Vainik and Orav (2005, p. 12) propose that the Estonian word *viha* could, in fact, have two meanings. The first meaning, which they translate as "anger," they believe to be "a relatively short-term intrapersonal state of mind (not necessarily targeted at a human object, as the object might be e.g., a situation, an incidence or quasiliving)." It stands in opposition to *rõõm* "joy," another relatively short-term and basically intrapersonal emotion, and is synonymous with *vihastamine* "growing angry" or "getting frustrated." The second meaning of the word *viha* they translate as "anger, hate." It is said to stand in opposition to *armastus* "love" and be synonymous with *vihkamine* "hate, hatred." This meaning is defined as being long-term or infinite and the emotion is probably also more interpersonal, that is, targeted at or related to a live human object. In the current project, *hate* was translated as *vihkamine* in Estonian.

In Finnish, however, the simple underived emotion term *viha* was chosen as the translational equivalent of the term "hate". The *Dictionary of Modern Finnish* (*Nykysuomen sanakirja*) defines *viha* as follows: "an intense and lasting feeling of antipathy or anger toward something or someone."[4] This clearly approximates the second meaning given by Vainik and Orav (2005) for the Estonian word *viha*. As the word *viha* was chosen as the translational equivalent for the GRID term "hate" in Finnish, we had to find another word for the term "anger". We chose *suuttuminen,* the exact meaning of which is "to fall into sudden and heated (sometimes unrestrained or blind) indignation or anger, to get angry"[5] (*Nykysuomen sanakirja*). The choice of Finnish term was based on the assumption that "anger" involves a sudden release of internal pressure (Lakoff, 1987), while "hate" lasts longer and tends to be more profound.

21.3 **Aims of the study**

In the present paper, we compare the meaning of the emotion term "anger" (*viha* in Estonian; *suuttuminen* in Finnish) in the two languages across different components of emotions (e.g., action tendencies or emotion regulation). Because the term *viha* was the translational equivalent of "anger" in Estonian and "hate" in Finnish, another aim of the study was to examine the extent to which the Estonian and the Finnish *viha* actually correspond to each other. Finally, we are interested in finding out the emotion features most likely related to the experience of anger in both Estonian and Finnish.

---

[3] The translation is ours, the original being "vaenulikkuse ja ärritatusega seotud tugev tunne, äge pahameel v. sallimatus."

[4] The translation is ours, the original being "jotakuta tai jotakin kohtaan tunnettu voimakas ja kestävä vastenmielisyys tai suuttumus."

[5] The translation is ours, the original being "joutua äkillisen, kiivaan (joskus hillittömän, silmittömän) pahastuksen, suuttumuksen valtaan, suutuksiin."

21.4 **Questionnaire**

We used a questionnaire originally constructed in English, the GRID instrument (see Chapter 5, cf. also Fontaine, Scherer, Roesch, & Ellsworth, 2007). The GRID is based on the componential emotion theory; the basic assumption of this is that an emotion is to be conceptualized as a process that consists of a synchronization of activity in several emotion components as a response to specific events, with the aim of preparing the organism quickly for optimal reaction (Scherer, 1987). The GRID consists of 24 emotion terms and 144 emotion features. The 24 terms are prototypical emotion terms commonly used in both emotion research and daily language: being hurt, sadness, shame, guilt, compassion, disappointment, love, contentment, happiness, pride, pleasure, joy, interest, surprise, despair, stress, anxiety, fear, jealousy, hate, irritation, anger, disgust, and contempt.

The 144 emotion features operationalize activity in each of the five emotion components. Thirty-one features refer to appraisals, 18 to physiological/bodily experiences, 26 to expression, 40 to action tendencies and 22 to subjective feelings. Additional four features refer to regulation and three more ("general") represent other qualities, such as frequency and social acceptance. The English GRID instrument was translated into Estonian and Finnish using the translation/back-translation procedure (see Chapter 6).

The GRID questionnaire was administered by way of a controlled Web study in which each participant was given four emotions randomly chosen from the set of 24 and was asked to rate each in terms of the 144 emotion features. Participants were asked to rate the likelihood that each of the 144 emotion features would be inferred when a speaker of their native language, as spoken in their country or region, uses the emotion term to describe an emotional experience, using a nine-point scale ranging from *extremely unlikely* (1) to *extremely likely* (9).

21.5 **Participants**

Estonian sample. The Estonian sample consisted of 179 participants (152 women and 27 men), most of whom (93%) were undergraduate or graduate students from the University of Tartu. The mean age of the participants was 22.9 years ($SD = 5.7$). One hundred and seventy participants (95%) spoke Estonian and nine participants Russian as their first language. Twenty-eight respondents (22 women and six men; mean age, 22.8 years; $SD = 4.0$) were asked to rate "anger" (*viha*) and 28 respondents (22 women and six men; mean age, 26.3 years; $SD = 8.4$) were asked to rate "hate" (*vihkamine*) in terms of the 144 emotion features.

The instructions were given in Estonian and the participants completed the Estonian version of the GRID questionnaire. The online survey was advertised via email and was posted on Internet electronic mailing lists for students of the University of Tartu. Data were collected from March until October 2008.

Finnish sample. The Finnish sample consisted of 120 respondents (101 women and 19 men) with a mean age of 32.8 years ($SD = 11.6$). The youngest respondent was 19 and the oldest was 68 years old. The questionnaire was sent to as many university email lists as possible. These included lists for students at various departments and two for research units (The Research Unit for Variation, Contacts, and Change in English and the Helsinki Collegium for Advanced Studies) at the University of Helsinki, a list for psychology students at the University of Tampere, and a domestic "Linguist List" called Kitu. The questionnaire was advertised until 120 people had completed it. The data were collected from April to June 2008. Fourteen respondents (12 women and two men; mean age, 33.6 years; $SD = 13.7$) were asked to rate "anger" (*suuttuminen*) and

23 respondents (21 women and two men; mean age, 27.7 years; $SD = 7.3$) were asked to rate "hate" (*viha*) in terms of the 144 emotion features.

21.6 **Results**

How similar are the meanings of the emotion terms "anger" (*viha* vs *suuttuminen*) and "hate" (*vihkamine* vs *viha*) in Estonian and Finnish? To answer this question, we calculated profile agreements between the Estonian and Finnish samples for both emotion terms across five emotion components: appraisal, physiological/bodily experiences, expression, action tendencies, and subjective feeling.

Profile agreement was calculated as the intraclass correlation (ICC) across category items, using the double entry method (Griffin & Gonzalez, 1995). Double-entry intraclass correlations are similar to Pearson correlations, but they are sensitive to differences in profile elevation as well as shape (McCrae, 2008). The *p* value is based on the nondoubled *n*.

For the emotion term "anger," intraclass correlations (ICCs) between the Estonian and Finnish samples were all positive, ranging from 0.77 (action tendencies) to 0.94 (subjective feeling), with a median value of 0.86. In the case of "hate," ICCs ranged from 0.85 (bodily experiences and action tendencies) to 0.91 (subjective feeling), with a median value of 0.86. All ICCs were statistically significant at *p* <0.001. For both "anger" and "hate," the differences between the Estonian and Finnish samples appear to be biggest for the emotion component action tendencies and smallest in the case of subjective feeling (see Table 21.1; first two columns).

However, ICCs between the Estonian and Finnish samples for *viha* ("anger" in Estonian vs "hate" in Finnish) were even higher, ranging from 0.87 (action tendencies) to 0.97 (bodily experiences), with a median value of 0.94. These high correlations show that profiles of emotion meanings in Estonian and Finnish are indeed very similar for the word *viha*. Ratings of the word *viha* in Estonian and Finnish across the most similar (i.e., bodily experiences) and most different (i.e., action tendencies) emotion categories are depicted in Figure 21.1 and Figure 21.2, respectively.

To investigate the differences between the words we used visual hypothesis testing with confidence intervals as described in Chapter 5. For both the words for "anger" (*viha* in Estonian and *suuttuminen* in Finnish) and for *viha* ("anger" in Estonian and "hate" in Finnish), there were only seven ratings out of 144 for which the confidence intervals for the Finnish and Estonian means did not overlap. In other words, there were only seven rating features for both emotion terms for which the means were different at the *p* <0.01 level. The means of those features are shown in Table 21.2.

Table 21.1 Anger and hate: Profile agreement (ICC) between Estonian and Finnish Samples

	n	Anger	Hate	*Viha vs viha*
Appraisal	31	0.86	0.90	0.94
Bodily reaction	18	0.91	0.85	0.97
Expression	26	0.87	0.87	0.89
Action tendency	40	0.77	0.85	0.87
Feeling	22	0.94	0.91	0.94
Median		0.87	0.87	0.94

Note: ICC = Intraclass correlation (double entry method). *n* = number of individual features in an emotion component. All correlations are significant at *p* <0.001. "Anger" – *viha* (in Estonian), *suuttuminen* (in Finnish). "Hate" – *vihkamine* (in Estonian), *viha* (in Finnish).

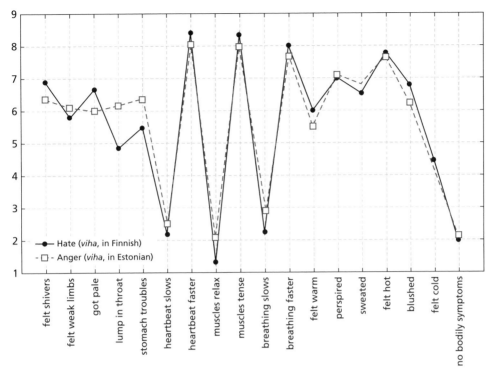

Figure 21.1 Ratings of the word *viha* across the emotion component "Bodily experiences" in Estonian and Finnish. Solid lines show the profile of the emotion term "hate" (*viha* in Finnish); dotted lines show the profile of the emotion term "anger" (*viha* in Estonian). The ICC between the Estonian and the Finnish ratings = 0.97 (*p* <0.001).

Five of the seven features overlapped for the comparison of *viha* vs *suuttuminen* and *viha* vs *viha*. If an Estonian-speaking person uses the word *viha* to describe his/her emotional experience, she or he is more likely than a Finnish-speaking person who uses either the word *viha* ("hate") or *suuttuminen* ("anger") to have an assertive voice (expression), to feel inhibited or blocked, to hand over the initiative to someone else, to stop sensory contact (action tendencies), and to feel at ease (feeling). When experiencing *viha*, Estonian-speaking persons are also believed to have the urge to run away in whatever direction (action tendency) and to be changed in a lasting way (general) compared to Finns experiencing *suuttuminen*. Finally, if a Finnish-speaking person uses the word *viha* to describe his/her emotional experience, she or he is more likely than an Estonian-speaking person experiencing *viha* to speak more slowly (expression) and to control the intensity of one's emotional feeling (regulation).

21.7 **What is anger?**

What are the most likely emotion features related to the experience of anger in Estonian and Finnish? Across all 144 features, the Spearman *R* between the mean ratings of "anger" and *viha* in Estonian and Finnish were *R* = 0.85 and 0.89, respectively (both correlations significant at *p* <0.01). Table 21.3 shows the 15 most characteristic features of the emotion term "anger" for Estonians (*viha*) and Finns (*suuttuminen*) as well as for the emotion term "hate" in Finnish (*viha*). For *viha*

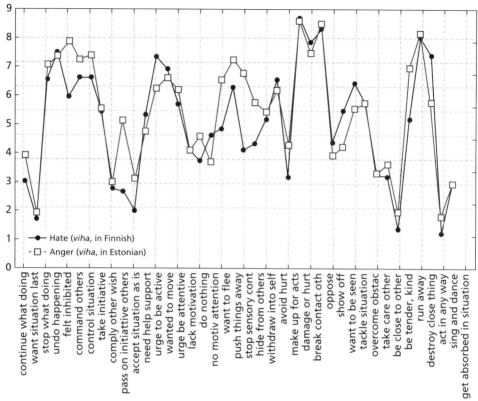

Figure 21.2 Ratings of the word *viha* across the emotion component "Action tendencies" in Estonian and Finnish. Solid lines show the profile of the emotion term "hate" (*viha* in Finnish); dotted lines show the profile of the emotion term "anger" (*viha* in Estonian). The ICC between the Estonian and Finnish ratings = 0.87 (*p* <0.001).

vs suuttuminen and *viha vs viha*, there are 7 and 11 overlapping features in the list of the 15 most frequently associated emotion features in Estonian and Finnish, respectively. This and the above-mentioned Spearman rank-order correlation coefficients confirm earlier findings that the meaning of the emotion term *viha* in Estonian and Finnish is more similar than the meaning of the word "anger" (*viha* vs *suuttuminen*) in the two languages.

If an Estonian or Finnish-speaking person uses the word *viha* to describe his or her emotional experience, what feelings, bodily expressions, or action tendencies are most likely to occur? As can be seen from Table 21.3, when experiencing *viha*, both Finns and Estonians are likely to have an urge to do damage, hit, or say something that hurts; to feel that he or she is treated unjustly; to have an urge to oppose; to be in an intense emotional state; to feel negative; to have an increasing heartbeat; to speak in a louder voice and have (whole body) muscle tension; to have an urge to destroy whatever is close; to press their lips together; and to change the melody of her or his speech. Finnish "anger" (*suuttuminen*), however, is much milder in its meaning. The things Finnish speakers report are most likely to occur when they feel *suuttuminen* are basically the same as what Estonians report when using the word *viha* but not as intense. This also supports the interpretation that dictionaries give about the meaning of these words.

Table 21.2 Mean scores of the different emotion features of the emotion terms "anger" and "hate" for the Estonian and Finnish samples

No	Emotion Component	Anger						Hate		
		Finnish (*suuttuminen*)			Estonian (*viha*)			Finnish (*viha*)		
		LCI	M	UCI	LCI	M	UCI	LCI	M	UCI
	Expression									
#67	had an assertive voice	2.79	4.36	6.07	6.63	7.63	8.41	4.26	5.52	6.65
#74	spoke slower				1.84	2.50	3.16	3.13	4.26	5.22
	Action Tendency									
#80	felt inhibited or blocked	3.71	5.00	6.43	7.41	7.84	8.28	4.48	5.91	7.26
#85	wanted to hand over the initiative to someone else	1.64	2.86	4.00	4.03	5.09	6.16	1.78	2.65	3.83
#96	wanted to prevent or stop sensory contact	3.00	4.00	4.86	5.59	6.72	7.66	2.61	4.09	5.30
#111	wanted to run away in whatever direction	3.07	4.43	5.71	5.91	6.91	7.78			
	Feeling									
#121	felt at ease	1.14	1.50	1.93	1.94	2.72	3.69	1.13	1.39	1.78
	Regulation									
#138	tried to control the intensity of the emotional feeling				3.97	5.09	6.00	6.00	7.13	8.04
	General									
#142	will be changed in a lasting way	2.21	3.21	4.14	4.28	5.22	6.16			

Note: *LCI* = lower confidence interval; *UCI* = upper confidence interval. Means are different at the *p* <0.01 level.

Table 21.3 Means of the 15 most frequently mentioned emotion features for "anger" and "hate" in Estonian and Finnish

No	Anger								Hate			
	#	Cat	Finnish (suuttuminen)	M	#	Cat	Estonian (viha)	M	#	Cat	Finnish (viha)	M
1	38	BR	heartbeat getting faster[EV]	8.50	101	AT	wanted to do damage, hit, or say something that hurts[FS, FV]	8.56	101	AT	wanted to do damage, hit, or say something that hurts[EV]	8.65
2	123	F	felt negative[EV]	8.50	103	AT	wanted to oppose[FV]	8.44	123	F	felt negative[EV]	8.44
3	42	BR	breathing getting faster	8.21	59	E	produced abrupt body movements	8.28	38	BR	heartbeat getting faster[EV]	8.40
4	64	E	increased the volume of voice[EV]	8.07	64	E	increased the volume of voice[FS, FV]	8.22	29	A	treated unjustly[EV]	8.39
5	40	BR	muscles tensing (whole body)[EV]	8.07	29	A	treated unjustly[FS, FV]	8.13	40	BR	muscles tensing (whole body)[EV]	8.35
6	29	A	treated unjustly[EV]	8.07	112	AT	wanted to destroy whatever was close[FV]	8.13	103	AT	wanted to oppose[EV]	8.26
7	116	F	was in an intense emotional state[EV]	8.00	116	F	was in an intense emotional state[FS, FV]	8.13	116	F	was in an intense emotional state[EV]	8.13
8	14	A	caused by somebody else's behavior	7.93	71	E	changed the melody of her or his speech[FV]	8.06	42	BR	breathing getting faster	8.00
9	8	A	in itself unpleasant for the person	7.86	38	BR	heartbeat getting faster[FS, FV]	8.03	112	AT	wanted to destroy whatever was close[EV]	7.96
10	1	BR	blushed	7.64	40	BR	muscles tensing (whole body)[FS, FV]	7.97	46	BR	felt hot	7.78
11	54	E	frowned	7.64	123	F	felt negative[FS, FV]	7.94	54	E	frowned	7.78
12	46	BR	felt hot	7.64	73	E	spoke faster	7.94	64	E	increased the volume of voice[EV]	7.78
13	27	A	suddenly	7.64	136	F	felt nervous	7.88	52	E	pressed lips together[EV]	7.78
14	47	A	violated laws or socially accepted norms	7.64	52	E	pressed lips together[FV]	7.88	102	AT	wanted to break contact with others	7.78
15	101	AT	wanted to do damage, hit, or say something that hurts[EV]	7.64	80	AT	felt inhibited or blocked	7.84	71	E	changed the melody of her or his speech[EV]	7.67

Note: Cat = Emotion Category; A = Appraisal; AT = Action Tendency; BR = Bodily Reaction; E = Expression; F = Feeling. EV = Same feature as for the Estonian "anger" (viha). FS = Same feature as for the Finnish "hate" (viha). FV = Same feature as for the Finnish "anger" (suuttuminen).

21.8 **Discussion**

Although anger is allegedly recognized in nearly all cultures, both facially and vocally, and there are equivalents for the word "anger" in most languages of the world, the term "anger" is still a cultural artefact of one particular language and it may carry different meanings across different languages and cultures (Wierzbicka, 1999). As argued above, some languages do not have lexical and conceptual equivalents of the English term "anger" (e.g., Briggs, 1970) whereas, in other languages, there is more than one term which corresponds to "anger" in English. For instance, in Samoan, there are two terms which denote anger whereas Biblical Hebrew has seven such terms (Pavlenko, 2005). At the same time, there are languages (e.g., Ilongot and Ifaluk) where the same term is used to refer to both "anger" and "sadness" (Lutz, 1988; Rosaldo, 1980). This tells us that the repertoire of emotion concepts may vary across cultures and languages and that English emotion terms are not always easily translatable into other languages. Therefore, when we talk about emotion terms cross-culturally, it is crucial to describe what they actually mean for representatives of a different cultural or linguistic group—or, more specifically, what kind of appraisals, subjective experiences, action tendencies, expressions, and bodily changes accompany them.

Our results showed that the conceptual grid for describing the meaning of "anger" in two closely related Finno-Ugric languages—Estonian and Finnish—is in fact very similar. When feeling anger, both Finns and Estonians are likely to experience an intense negative emotional state, to feel that they have been treated unjustly, and to experience a variety of physiological changes, such as increasing heartbeat, muscle tension, and louder volume of voice. This is consistent with previous results which have shown that increased heartbeat and tense muscles are among the most frequently reported symptoms of anger (for 49% and 43% of anger episodes, respectively) in 27 different countries (Wallbott & Scherer, 1988).

Yet, as shown by our analyses, the meaning of the emotion term *viha* ("anger" in Estonian, "hate" in Finnish) is even more similar than the meaning of the translation of the word "anger" (*viha* in Estonian and *suuttuminen* in Finnish) in the two languages. The most frequently mentioned emotion feature for experiencing *viha* in both Estonian and Finnish is an urge to do damage, hit, or say something that hurts. This finding corresponds well to the cognitive linguistic view of anger, according to which anger needs to be vented or released in order to reduce the intensity of the inner negative emotional pressure (Lakoff, 1987). Thus, our findings seem to suggest that the word *viha* in Finnish may be a conceptually closer equivalent to the English term "anger" than the term *suuttuminen*, which was chosen as the linguistic equivalent for the current study. More specifically, it appears that the Finnish term *suuttuminen* refers to a milder emotion (such as irritation, for instance) than the Finnish or the Estonian *viha*.

In line with previous findings (see Pavlenko, 2005, for more information), our results show that anger, which is referred to with a single term in English, may be lexically differentiated in other languages, such as Estonian and Finnish. In other words, our results show that the semantic field of emotions appears to be differently divided up in English, Estonian, and Finnish. In two closely related languages—Estonian and Finnish—the boundary between the close emotions anger and hate is not drawn in exactly the same place as in English nor is it even in the same place in Finnish and Estonian. In Estonian, only *viha* could be used as a conceptual and lexical equivalent to the English term "anger". In Finnish, however, both "anger" and "hate" could be translated as *viha*. Yet, the common linguistic heritage of Estonian and Finnish can be seen in the meaning of the words— in this case, the word *viha*—even though the languages and the meanings have drifted apart somewhat in the course of the history. Thus, as argued by Wierzbicka (1999a), even an "apparently basic and innocent concept like anger is in fact linked with a certain cultural model and so cannot be taken for granted as a 'culture-free' analytical tool or as a universal standard for describing 'human emotions' " (p. 32). Our findings illustrate how important it is for psychologists to take into account the richness and variability of word meaning. They also show that psychology in general, and the GRID paradigm in particular, may help linguists achieve a fuller understanding of emotion terms.

Acknowledgments

This project was supported by grants from the Estonian Ministry of Science and Education (SF0180029s08 and IUT2-13) and funded in part by the Finnish Academy Centre of Excellence, the Research Unit for Variation, Contacts and Change in English. We are grateful to Hanna Sola, Markku Ojanen, Maarika Pukspuu, Margus Mere, Cristina Soriano, Johnny Fontaine, and Delaney Michael Skerrett for their assistance at different stages of this project.

Chapter 22

Types of anger in Spanish and Russian

Cristina Soriano,[1] Johnny J. R. Fontaine, Anna Ogarkova,
Claudia Mejía Quijano, Yana Volkova, Svetlana Ionova,
and Viktor Shakhovskyy

22.1 Introduction

In the study of emotions in communication and negotiation, anger stands as a particularly relevant category. It identifies contexts of conflict and influences judgment and decision making (Dunn & Schweitzer, 2005; Lerner & Tiedens, 2006; Litvak, Lerner, Tiedens, & Shonk, 2010; Small & Lerner, 2008; Renshon & Lerner, 2011). Its perception has also been shown to modulate negotiation outcomes and practices (Adler, Rosen, & Silverstein, 1998). The experience seems to be intelligible to members of any cultural group. Anger is always included in the list of alleged universal (Hupka et al., 1999), basic (Ekman, 1992, 1999; Ortony & Turner, 1990) or modal (Scherer, 1994, 2005a, 2009c) emotions. Its facial expression is one of the most thoroughly researched and, at least in the version that includes a frown, it appears to be consistently recognized across cultures (Ekman, 1992; Hejmadi et al., 2000; Matsumoto et al., 2010).

Anger is also a salient category at the linguistic level. According to Wierzbicka (1999a: 276), all languages have an "anger-like" word. For instance, Chewong, the language with the smallest known emotion vocabulary, still has an "anger" label, *chan* (Howell, 1981: 133). Some cultures have been claimed not to have a word for this emotion (e.g., Briggs, 1970), but the statement should be interpreted as meaning that the concept typically referred to in English as "anger" is not lexically coded in them. It can still be the case that other experiences of a similar nature (e.g., animosity, reprehension) find their way into their languages. This view is supported by Anna Wierzbicka's research (and that of her colleagues) on dozens of languages around the world, which suggests that two of the defining cognitive assessments for anger-like experiences, namely "I don't want things like this to happen" and "I want to do something because of this," are lexically coded in all languages and, therefore, constitute lexical universals in the emotion domain (Wierzbicka, 1999a: 287). Other anthropological research on emotion lexicons also suggests that anger (or an anger-like construct, to be more specific) is indeed a pervasive category around the world (e.g., Hupka et al., 1999, see also Chapter 3).

In addition to being a type of emotional experience commonly coded in language, anger is a profusely coded one. In other words, anger tends to be extensively lexicalized compared to other emotional families, like pride (Ogarkova, Soriano, & Lehr, 2012). We find extreme examples of

[1] Corresponding author: Cristina Soriano. Swiss Center for Affective Sciences - University of Geneva. 7, Rue des Battoirs, CH-1205 Geneva, Switzerland. Cristina.Soriano@unige.ch

lexicalization in Tahitian, which distinguishes 46 varieties of anger (Levy, 1973), and in Shuswap, with over 30 anger-related words (Kuipers, 1974).

Broad emotion semantic categories are less likely to be internally homogenous, that is, the words in a rich lexical group are less likely to refer to one type of (or very similar subtypes of) emotional experience. Hence, one can expect to find quite some variation within the anger family of a given language compared to other families. Additionally, cross-linguistic variation is also to be expected. As many of the chapters in this volume attest (cf. Parts IV to VII), emotion words capture essential features of the emotional cultures of the speakers of those languages, which can vary considerably. In relation to anger specifically, how people act on their feeling constitutes one of the most important and recognized aspects of cross-cultural variance. For example, Woleanian *song*, Chinese *qi*, Malay *marah,* and Arrente *akiwarre* are all claimed to be prototypical anger-like concepts in their cultures that do not imply immediate retaliation against a wrongdoer (see Chapter 3 for more details and additional examples).

Given the relevance of anger for all cultural groups and the variability that is to be expected in its conceptualization, a linguistic analysis of the domain becomes particularly important. Both linguistics and psychology have addressed this issue. Within linguistics numerous studies have been conducted on anger words in the framework of the Natural Semantic Metalanguage (NSM), which strongly emphasizes the non-equivalence of emotion terms across languages (e.g., see Lorenzano, 2006 for an overview). However, we lack *empirical* evidence demonstrating that those are the most salient anger words in the respective cultural groups,[2] nor is it known if the native speakers of a language are aware of the proposed differences in meaning. Within psychology, in turn, ample empirical evidence is available about the structure of the anger domain in different languages (e.g., Russell & Fehr, 1994; Shaver, Murdaya, & Fraley, 2001), but these studies present some limitations too. First, they frequently disregard potential *country* differences within a language. Second, they primarily employ similarity ratings as an analytic method, which allows them to see how native speakers group the words according to their semantic distance, but do not inform us about the *features* that differentiate the emergent word clusters in a language. For the same reason, when two languages are compared, one cannot know to what extent their respective clusters match.[3]

This limitation has practical consequences. A better understanding of what kind of information is coded in the meaning of emotion words is instrumental for the successful practice of translators and interpreters, for example. In this sense, one of the major contributions of the GRID project reported in this volume is the demonstration that emotion words across languages and cultures include information about the five domains that psychology often quotes as basic components of the emotional experience: appraisals about the causes and consequences of an emotion, the bodily reactions that accompany it, the typical expressive behaviors (e.g., vocal or facial), the behavioral impulses one experiments, and the general subjective feeling (e.g., good/ bad, aroused/ relaxed) one composes on the grounds of this information. The GRID has shown that speakers of very different languages around the world reliably agree on what features from these components are contained in the meaning of a given word. Therefore, translators trying to find the closest

---

[2] For instance, Goddard (1996) looks at Indonesian *marah* as a prototype anger word. However, in Shaver et al. (1992: 217), *marah* is only the 5th term with regards to prototypicality ratings.

[3] For example, in Shaver et al. (1987), the English anger terms are found to fall into six clusters. In Shaver et al. (2001), the Indonesian anger terms fall into seven clusters. No direct comparison is provided of the content of these clusters in the two languages.

equivalent for an emotion word in a different language should take into account their componential semantic profile.

In sum, previous linguistic studies in the NSM tradition on the lexical representation of anger across languages do not provide empirical evidence that the speakers of a language are aware of the described meaning differences between terms, or whether the analyzed words are the most representative in the language. Psychological studies on the contrary do provide empirical, speaker-driven results, but they lack enough detail about the features that distinguish broad groups of words in a given language and they tend to disregard potential country-specific effects. As we shall see in more detail in the following sections, our study tries to overcome these limitations. First, an emotion-situation free-labeling task was used to identify the most representative anger terms in each language investigated, thus guaranteeing that our target words would be both salient (i.e., easily accessible to speakers, frequent in recall) and comparable across languages (as the same set of emotion situations was used). Second, we employed the psycholinguistic GRID-based instrument, which allows us to identify not only clusters of similar terms, but also the componential features that differentiate them. Thirdly, our study was conducted in two separate countries for each language represented, so as to be able to identify potential country-specific differences.

The study reported in this chapter belongs to a larger research initiative on Emotion Language in International Negotiation (ELIN). The goal of the ELIN project was to investigate the conceptualization of conflict-relevant emotions across languages and cultures. One of the research lines was devoted to the semantic analysis of the lexicon of anger, shame, guilt, and pride in the official languages of the United Nations. The GRID methodology was chosen for this purpose and the original questionnaire was modified so as to be able to identify subtle differences between near-synonyms in those semantic domains. In this paper, we report results on anger for two of the most wide-spread languages in the world: Russian and Spanish. Given the relevance of these languages in international communication and the fact that all documents and official communications of the United Nations are either issued in or translated into these two languages, it was relevant to explore to what extent the lexicon of anger was organized around the same types of concepts, and to what extent country variation could make a difference. The specific objectives of the study were (1) to look at the internal organization of the domain in Russian and Spanish (based on salient anger words); (2) to identify the features underlying this structure; (3) to compare the two languages; and (4) to locate possible country differences within them. Due to space constraints, in this paper, we will not tackle cross-lingual differences at term level.

22.2 **Method and instrument adaptation**

The GRID methodology advocates a psycholinguistic approach to the study of meaning in which the native speakers of a language are directly inquired about the meaning of the words in their language (for more details on the GRID methodology, see Chapter 5). The 144 features (i.e., questions) in the original GRID instrument were derived from a broad range of emotion theories suitable to discriminate between a large and varied set of emotion categories representative of the whole emotion domain (Fontaine, Scherer, Roesch, & Ellsworth, 2007, see also Chapter 5). Despite this focus on broad emotion categories (e.g., anger, fear, joy), the GRID paradigm is also applicable to the study of subordinate-level terms, or "subtypes" of a given category, like *anger*, *rage*, and *indignation* in the English category ANGER.[4]

---

[4] In the remainder of the paper, following the convention in cognitive linguistics (CL), small capitals are used for concepts or categories ("domains" in CL) and italics for specific words in a given language.

Feature selection

In order to be able to capture more subtle differences within a domain, a revision of the set of GRID features was necessary. A review of the literature was undertaken to expand the range of potentially relevant semantic aspects to be reflected in the questionnaire. The review revealed that a substantial part of variation between emotion words taps on social aspects of meaning. Five aspects were identified that seemed particularly relevant in emotion term semantics (see Chapter 3 for a more detailed account and other examples of these aspects). The first one is the *social status* (superior, equal, or inferior) of the person who causes an emotional experience with respect to the experiencer. For example, the two prototypical anger words in Russian, *gnev* (justified anger) and *zlost'* (anger) differ with regards to the social status of the wrongdoer: whereas one can experience *zlost'* toward a person with either a lower or a higher social status, *gnev* is more typically experienced by a superior toward his/her inferior. A second important aspect is the *closeness* between the experiencer and the other people involved in the emotion (i.e., whether they belong to the same social group or not). For example, in Pintupi the social world is divided between "kin" and "not-kin" (Myers, 1979: 351) and this leads to different modes of emotional expression associated to the emotion words. A third important aspect is the *focus of the appraisal*, in other words, the specific aspect of the other person (e.g., their behavior, their personality, or their possessions) that elicits the emotional reaction. For example, while *gnev* is always experienced about people or their actions, *zlost'* can refer to being generally angry, not necessarily at a particular person (Pavlenko, 2008). *Social sharing* is another important factor. By social sharing in this context we refer to the likelihood that an emotion is felt by a single person in isolation or by a group of people simultaneously. For example, many Palauan emotion words are inherently about "mutual" feelings among people (e.g., *klsiberreng* "mutual bad or hurt feelings" – Smith & Tkel-Sbal, 1995: 91). The last relevant aspect was *attribution*, namely the likelihood that a given emotional experience is more readily attributed to others (i.e., said to happen to others) than to oneself, or is felt about others rather than about oneself. For example, whereas one can experience *zlost'* about one's own actions or behavior (i.e., as a self-directed emotion), the use of *gnev* in such contexts is very rare.

The above-mentioned aspects (see summary in Table 22.1) were taken into account in the construction of a new GRID-based tool: the ELIN questionnaire (Table SM 1).[5] A number of new features were thus added to tap on these aspects. Features pertinent for SHAME, PRIDE, and GUILT were also part of the questionnaire, as all four emotions were the object of study in the ELIN project. Given that it was uneconomical to add the new features to the already existing GRID instrument (as it would render the rating process too long), we selected the set of GRID features that best characterize the ANGER (and SHAME, PRIDE, and GUILT) prototypical labels in the overall sample of languages included in the GRID study. In order to select them, first an ANOVA analysis was executed on each of the GRID features using a randomized block design with the four emotion terms (anger, irritation, guilt, and shame) being the independent variable and the sample the block variable. If the difference between the emotion terms was significant, a post-hoc test (Sidak) was executed to identify which emotion terms were significantly different from one another on the respective feature. In its final version, the ELIN questionnaire comprises 95 features (46 from GRID and 49 new) from several emotion components: 26 features related to appraisals of the event that caused the emotion, 11 to bodily reactions, 14 to expressions, 14 to action tendencies, 10 to subjective

---

5 All supplementary materials (SM) are available at the GRID website: http://www.affective-sciences.org/ GRID. See Appendix 1 ("Availability") for further details.

Table 22.1 Complementary aspects in the ELIN-GRID questionnaire encoding social nuances in the meaning of emotion terms across languages

SOCIAL ASPECTS	SPECIFICATION	
person causing an emotional experience	social status	superior
		equal
		inferior
	closeness	close person, in-group
		stranger, out-group
focus in appraising the wrongdoer	behavior (action)	
	intrinsic quality	
	possessions	
social sharing	experienced individually	
	experienced with others	
attribution	said of oneself	
	said of others	

feelings, and 3 to emotion regulation strategies. In addition, 17 more features addressed general issues about emotion conceptualization, like social acceptability and frequency (see Table SM 1).

Word selection

A crucial point in the study was the appropriate selection of emotion terms. For that reason a pre-study was carried out (Ogarkova, Soriano, & Lehr, 2012) to empirically identify the most central emotion terms per category. In the study, prototype scenarios or scripts were constructed using a facet approach (Borg & Shye, 1995) and given to participants, who had to free list the emotion labels (noun or adjective) that would best describe the way they would feel in those scenarios. The most salient Spanish and Russian terms (in descending order of frequency) are presented in Table 22.2.

Datasets: languages and countries

The questionnaire was administered to each participant in their mother tongue. Each language was investigated in two countries, to assess the stability of the organization in the ANGER domain and the possible impact of the cultural background in communities with the same language. The two Spanish samples were collected in Spain and Colombia. A slight adaptation was required in the Spanish version of the questionnaire, as two of the words originally identified as central (*cabreo* and *enfado*) were not in common use in Colombia. Consequently, two close terms (*bravo* and *enojo*, respectively) were chosen through discussion by the two authors of this paper with native-speaker competence in Spanish, both of them linguists.[6]

---

[6] Posterior analyses revealed a good semantic profile correlation between *enfado* and *enojo* (Pearson correlation at 0.761**), corroborating their presumed semantic similarity. The correlation between *cabreo* and *bravo*, on the contrary, was very low (0.204*), indicating that these terms are not good translation equivalents.

Table 22.2 Spanish and Russian anger words

Spanish	Russian
rabia [anger]	*razdrazhenie* [irritation]
enfado [anger/ annoyance]	*obida* [resentment/ hurt]
indignación [indignation]	*zlost'* [anger]
cabreo [anger/ angry mood]	*gnev* [wrath, justified anger]
ira [anger/ wrath]	*dosada* [frustration/ vexation]
molesto [angry/ upset]	*vozmuschenie* [indignation]
frustración [frustration]	*negodovanie* [indignation]
irritación [irritation]	*jarost'* [fury]
	serdityj [cross]

Note: words in descending order of frequency of appearance in a situation free-labeling task (Ogarkova et al., 2012). For readability reasons, Russian words are transliterated from Cyrillic.

The Spain sample comprised university students from several regions in the country (N = 45; 39 females; mean age of 22.2, SD = 4.03). The Colombia sample was composed of university students from the University of Antioquía, in Medellín (N = 38; 19 females, mean age of 24.8, SD = 7.44). The two Russian samples were collected in Russia and Ukraine. The Ukrainian native speakers of Russian were recruited at the University Kyiv-Mohyla Academy in Kyiv (N = 41; 29 females; mean age of 26.1, SD = 4.43). The Russia sample was collected at the University of Volgograd (N = 40; 19 females; mean age of 21.2, SD = 2.99).

Procedure

The same procedure was used for the online administration of the ELIN questionnaire as for the administration of the GRID questionnaire (see Chapter 6). Participants were provided with a password and study code to log into the study and fill in the questionnaire at their own pace. Each participant was presented with four to five emotion terms and asked to rate how likely it was that the 95 features were part of the meaning of the words. Features were presented one at a time. The response scale was the same adopted in the original GRID study (1 = "extremely unlikely," 5 = "neither likely, not unlikely," 9 = "extremely likely"). Each lexeme was rated by at least 20 subjects.

22.3 **Analyses and results**

The reliability of the semantic patterns per term across the 95 features was investigated by means of Cronbach's alpha with the participants being treated as variables and the features as observations.[7] For the Spanish ANGER terms in Spain, the reliability ranged from 0.87 to 0.95, with an average of 0.92. For the Colombian Spanish terms, the reliability ranged from 0.87 to 0.94, with an average of 0.91. For the Russian terms in Russia, the reliability ranged from 0.82 to 0.92, with an average

---

[7] The data had first been centered per term per person in order to remove response biases. Centering involved the average score being computed across the 95 questions for each term and the mean score being subtracted from each observed score.

of 0.88. For the Ukrainian Russian terms, the reliability ranged from 0.88 to 0.94, with an average of 0.91.

To have a general idea of how well the ANGER domain in each of the four countries shared the same semantic profile across the 95 features, an average ANGER profile was computed per country across all terms evaluated in that country. These average profiles were then correlated. The correlations were found to be very high (between 0.82 and 0.86), suggesting a good match between the general ANGER category in Russian and Spanish. The highest correlations were found between the countries with the same language, (0.94 between the Spanish samples and 0.90 between the Russian ones).

Variation in the meaning of the ANGER emotion terms within and across countries was investigated in three ways. First, semantic profile similarities were computed between the ANGER terms (based on Pearson correlations). Hierarchical cluster analyses were executed per country and across countries on these profile similarities using average linkage. These analyses identify clusters of terms with comparable meaning. Second, non-metrical multidimensional scaling (MDS) was executed on the same profile similarities per country and across countries. MDS represents psychological (dis)similarities between stimuli (profile similarities between ANGER terms) as distances between points in a geometrical space, such that large similarities are represented by small distances in the spatial representation. The hierarchical cluster analysis and the MDS offer complementary representations of the same profile similarity data, as one offers a categorical representation and the other a dimensional representation. Finally, the identified clusters of the ANGER terms are further explored by investigating (with an analysis of variance) how the individual features differ between them.

For each of the four countries a similar two-cluster structure emerged in the hierarchical structure analysis at the highest level of the dendrogram, as represented in Table 22.3.

The same structure was observed at the highest level of the dendrogram when all terms from all countries were analyzed together (Figure 22.1). The largest cluster contained the bulk of the ANGER terms representing a variety of intensities, from the "explosive" *zlost'*, *gniev*, *jarost'*, and *ira* to the milder *razdrazhenie*, *enfado*, and *irritación*. The other smaller cluster agglutinated lexemes related to FRUSTRATION and RESENTMENT (*obida*, *dosada*, and *frustración*).

Subsequently, non-metrical multidimensional scaling analyses were executed on the terms of each country separately and on all the terms across countries. Each of these analyses revealed comparable structures. One bipolar dimension represented the similarities between the semantic profiles very well (with a dispersion accounted for of more than 0.99). An opposition was observed between the FRUSTRATION and RESENTMENT terms, on the one hand, and all the other terms, on the other hand. This structure was confirmed by an MDS on all terms from all countries. In this case a one-dimensional solution also fitted well (with a dispersion accounted for of 0.98). The single bipolar dimension ranged from various forms of "hot" ANGER (*jarost'*, *zlost'*, *gnev*, *ira*)

Table 22.3 Lexeme clusters per country

	Cluster 1	Cluster 2
Sp	rabia, irritación, ira, indignación, enfado, cabreo	frustración, molesto
Co	rabia, irritación, ira, indignación, enojo, bravo, molesto	frustración
Ru	zlost', gnev, razdrahenie, jarost', negodovanie, vozmuschenie, serdityj	obida, dosada
Ukr	zlost', gnev, razdrahenie, jarost', negodovanie, vozmuschenie, serdityj	obida, dosada

Note: Sp = Spain, Co = Colombia, Ru = Russia, Ukr = Ukraine.

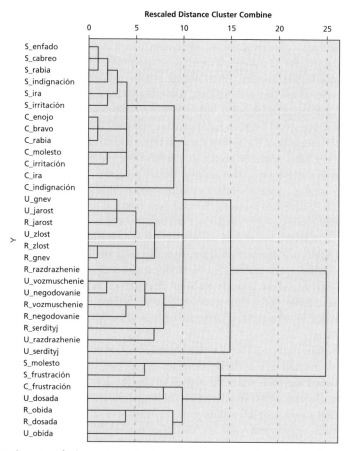

Figure 22.1 Dendrogram of a hierarchical cluster analysis on the profile similarities between anger words across languages and countries.

Note: C = Colombian, R = Russian, S = Spanish, U = Ukrainian.

to FRUSTRATION/RESENTMENT terms (*frustración, obida, dosada*) (Table 22.4). This confirms the results of the cluster analysis, and additionally allows us to see that the ANGER terms within a language can gradually differ on this dimension. For instance, Colombian *indignación* and Spanish *molesto* are closer to the "frustration" end of the scale than Spanish *indignación* and Colombia *molesto*, respectively.

Both the categorical and the dimensional analyses of the profile similarities revealed two clear groups of terms both within and across countries: a group of general ANGER terms and another with FRUSTRATION/RESENTMENT terms. In order to investigate what specific features differentiate these two groups an analysis of variance was executed on each of the 95 features with the ANGER cluster as an independent variable. Because of the high number of statistical tests (the 95 features were individually tested), the results were Bonferroni corrected. Only those features for which the *p*-value was smaller than 0.0005 were retained (see Table 22.5).

The features on which the lexemes in these clusters differ significantly tell us what the nature of the clusters is about. Relative differences emerge at each of the emotion components.

Table 22.4 Coordinates of Spanish and Russian anger words in a one-dimensional representation

Words	Dimension 1
R_jarost'	−0.690
R_gnev	−0.665
U_gnev	−0.612
U_jarost'	−0.587
R_zlost'	−0.566
S_ira	−0.522
C_ira	−0.505
U_zlost'	−0.458
C_bravo	−0.399
C_rabia	−0.378
C_enojo	−0.370
S_rabia	−0.361
S_cabreo	−0.340
C_irritación	−0.330
R_vozmuschenie	−0.310
R_negodovanie	−0.278
U_vozmuschenie	−0.278
U_negodovanie	−0.254
S_irritación	−0.239
S_enfado	−0.216
C_molesto	−0.200
S_indignación	−0.168
U_razdrazhenie	−0.144
R_razdrazhenie	−0.068
R_serdityj	−0.051
C_indignación	0.112
U_serdityj	0.223
S_molesto	0.354
S_frustración	0.928
U_obida	1.199
R_obida	1.404
U_dosada	1.437
C_frustración	1.614
R_dosada	1.719

Note: C = Colombian, R = Russian, S = Spanish, U = Ukrainian.

Table 22.5 Mean centered scores of the significantly differentiating features between the two clusters of anger words

Components and features	Cluster 1	Cluster 2
Appraisal		
was caused by the behavior of a stranger (#65)	0.720	−0.743
affected others (#76)	1.010	−0.049
called for an immediate response or action (#69)	0.699	−0.629
affected the person only (#77)	0.591	1.546
was caused by an intrinsic quality of a stranger (#66)	−0.057	−0.958
involved (serious) damage to others (#73)	1.188	0.109
was caused by someone inferior in social status (#60)	0.608	−0.719
violated laws or socially accepted norms (#71)	0.940	−0.019
happens when other people are present (#92)	1.019	−0.316
Bodily reaction		
had a lump in the throat (#20)	0.488	2.219
felt her/his heartbeat getting faster (#17)	2.003	0.280
felt cold (#15)	−2.494	−0.229
felt hot (#14)	1.234	−0.779
felt her/his breathing getting faster (#18)	1.701	0.044
felt her/his muscles getting tense (#19)	1.618	−0.156
blushed (#11)	1.197	−0.392
Feeling		
felt strong (#3)	−0.028	−2.462
felt weak (#4)	−1.051	1.489
felt socially unworthy (#10)	−0.155	1.796
felt degraded (#9)	0.692	1.977
felt blameworthy (#8)	−1.108	0.331
felt calm (#5)	−3.720	−2.545
felt responsible for what had happened (#7)	−0.913	0.470
Expression		
spoke louder (#22)	2.173	−0.405
covered the face with her/his hands (#29)	−1.699	1.603
adopted a straighter body posture (#30)	0.733	−2.042
pushed her/his chest forward (#31)	0.752	−2.226
had a slumped bodily posture (#32)	−1.923	1.552
lifted the chin (#33)	1.012	−1.750
lowered her/his head (#34)	−1.948	2.046
closed her or his eyes so as to avoid eye contact (#28)	−0.732	1.627

Table 22.5 (continued) Mean score of the significantly differentiating features between the two clusters of anger words

Components and features	Cluster 1	Cluster 2
spoke faster (#23)	1.476	−0.301
showed tears (#26)	−0.463	2.377
Action tendency		
wanted to escape from, or flee the situation (#41)	−0.407	1.889
wanted to apologize (#43)	−2.865	−0.839
wanted to repair the damage/harm s/he had done (#42)	−2.249	−0.290
wanted to be seen, to be in the center of attention (#47)	−0.272	−1.879
wanted to damage, hit, or say something that hurts to whoever was nearby (#38)	1.179	−0.364
wanted to withdraw from people or things (#40)	0.235	1.943
wanted to damage, hit, or say something that hurts to the person who had caused the emotion (#37)	2.120	0.829
Regulation		
hid the emotion from others by smiling (#50)	−1.572	0.681

Note: all $p<0.0005$.

With regards to **Appraisal**, the two clusters of words differ in the typical antecedent events. In cluster 1, the words refer to emotions aroused by the behavior of a stranger (#65), typically inferior in status (#60), who commits a norm violation (#71) causing some damage (#73) to others (#73, #76), all of which requires an immediate reaction (# 69). None of those features apply to the words in cluster 2. More typically in the second cluster the antecedent event affects the person only (#77), rather than others (#76), and is caused neither by a stranger (#65), nor by the violation of a social norm (#71). The words in cluster 2, thus, focus more on an internal state of affairs, and do not involve immediate retaliation (#69).

Concerning **Bodily reactions**, the words in the first cluster depict an anger experience where the person experiences a high state of arousal characterized by faster heartbeat and breathing (# 17, 18), tense muscles (#19), feeling hot (#14), and getting red (# 11). The words in the second cluster denote emotional experiences where the arousal is lower, or less visible (significantly lower increase in heart and breathing rate, no blushing or feeling hot, no tense muscles). The person just feels a lump in the throat (#20), ostensibly an invisible symptom of the emotion.

Coherent with the above are the typical **Feelings** associated with the emotions in the two clusters. The experiencer typically envisioned in cluster 2 feels weak (#4), socially damaged (#9, #10), and to a certain extent responsible for what has happened (# 7, #8). By contrast, no feelings of weakness or responsibility apply to the words in cluster 1.

The ANGER concept in the first cluster is **expressive** – speaking louder (#22) and faster (#23) – and involves body behavior coherent with self-assured, high-power, confrontational emotions, namely a straight body posture (#30), chest pushed forward (#31), and a lifted chin (#33). By contrast, the behavior implied by the words in cluster 2 is avoidant (covering the face #29, avoiding eye contact #28), with expressions coherent with feelings of low-power, like a slumped body posture (#32), lowered head (#34), and tears (#26). The preference for **concealment** is also evidenced in the fact that the emotions in cluster 2 may be hidden behind a smile (#50) and are unlikely to happen when others are present (#92).

Concerning **Action tendencies**, cluster 2 is characterized by a desire to escape the situation (#41), and a comparatively greater inclination to withdraw from people and things (#40) and not to be the focus of attention (#47). By contrast, the reactions in cluster 1 are more likely to involve a desire to damage, hit, or say something that hurts to the person who caused the emotion (#37), or even to anybody else close by (#38). Such indiscriminate aggression tendency is not part of the meaning of the words in cluster 2. In sum, the lexemes of the first cluster refer to an ANGER concept where the prevailing action tendency is approach, and more concretely, aggression. On the contrary, the dominant action tendency in the second cluster is withdrawal.

Finally, although the various words in the domain vary from country to country in their relative positions within the FURY–FRUSTRATION continuum (see Table 22.4), there are no country differences in the clusters they form. The only exception is the word *molesto* (lit. "discomforted"), which belongs to cluster 1 in Colombia and cluster 2 in Spain. In other words, the term is closer to high-power prototypical anger in Colombia than in Spain. In Spain, the word refers to a low-power, more internal and concealed emotion concept, close in meaning to *frustración*. In Colombia, on the contrary, *molesto* is closer in meaning to Colombian *ira* (anger/wrath), than to *frustración*. An analysis of variance (ANOVA) was carried out for the word *molesto* in Spanish and Colombia to identify the features that were differentially rated in the two countries (see Table 22.6).

Table 22.6 Differentiating features between Spanish and Colombian *molesto*

Features	Mean Spain	Mean Colombia	Mean difference
lifted the chin (#33)	4.62	6.83	−2.21**
blushed (#11)	4.57	6.61	−2.04***
was caused by an intrinsic quality of a stranger (#66)	5.48	7.17	−1.69*
felt strong (#3)	3.67	5.33	−1.66*
pushed her/his chest forward (#31)	4.95	6.56	−1.61*
perspired (#12)	4.33	5.89	−1.56*
wanted to be seen, to be in the centre of attention (#47)	3.81	5.28	−1.47***
felt warm (#13)	5.43	6.83	−1.40***
was caused by someone superior, or higher in social status (#61)	5.86	7.17	−1.31***
is experienced by the person only about her/his actions (#81)	6.48	5.33	1.15**
showed tears (#26)	7.43	6.22	1.21*
wanted to apologize (#43)	5.14	3.44	1.70*
wanted to repair the damage/harm s/he had done (#42)	5.95	3.89	2.06*
lowered her/his head (#34)	6.10	3.56	2.54**
had a slumped bodily posture (#32)	5.95	3.33	2.62*

Note: * $p < .05$, ** $p < .01$, *** $p < .001$.

The results indicate that Colombian *molesto* is characterized by perspiration (#12), redness in the face (#11), and a greater feeling of warmth (#13). The person feels strong (#3), and lifting the chin (#33) or pushing the chest forward (#31) are possible expressive behaviors involved in the experience. By contrast, Spanish *molesto* is rather characterized by a slumped body posture (#32), lowered head (#34), and a greater likelihood of tears (#26). The features pertaining to appraisal suggest why this may be the case. While Colombian *molesto* is comparatively more likely to be felt toward a superior (#61) or the annoying features of a stranger (#66), Spanish *molesto* is more likely to be caused by actions carried out by oneself (#81) (hence the more likely tendency to want to repair any caused damage (#42) or apologize (#43)). All in all, Spanish *molesto* seems more likely applicable to cases of self-directed ANGER.

22.4 Discussion and conclusions

Most languages of the world have at least one word referring to an experience comparable to what is denoted in English by the word *anger*. Given both the universality of ANGER codification in human natural languages and its profuse lexicalization, the main research question addressed in this paper was whether the ANGER words in two of the most widespread languages of the world (also official languages of the United Nations), Spanish and Russian, refer to one and the same concept, or whether the lexicon is rather organized around different types of it. We also wanted to explore the stability of this organization across languages and countries.

In the psychological and linguistic literature, anger is generally described as a high-power, expressive, and confrontational emotion triggered by a demeaning offense against the self or relevant others, leading to the experiencer's loss of control and the desire for retribution (Fontaine et al., 2007; Lakoff & Kovecses, 1987; Lazarus, 1991; Scherer, 1986; Scherer, Summerfield, & Wallbott, 1983; Scherer, Wallbott, Matsumoto, & Kudoh, 1988; Wierzbicka, 1999). This is probably true for the prototypical concept of ANGER as an overarching category in the general emotion domain (Shaver, Schwartz, Kirson, & O'Connor, 1987; Russell, 1991b; see also Chapter 28, this volume). However, a closer look at the internal structure of indigenous ANGER categories in Spanish and Russian reveals a more subtle picture. The terms empirically identified as the most salient in the lexicalization of anger experiences in Russian and Spanish do not form one single family, but split into two. The clusters formed by these lexemes are not arbitrary; the features that differentiate them reveal two distinct concepts, or types. On the one hand, the terms in the first and larger cluster refer to a form of ANGER characterized by a feeling of high-power, expressive behavior, and approach (confrontational) tendencies, easily recognizable from earlier descriptions of the ANGER prototype; in the second cluster, we find a less expressive form of ANGER, with feelings of low-power, emotion-concealing behavior, and a preference for withdrawal. Given their systematic differences across components, but especially on subjective feeling, expression and behavior, these two ANGER types can be provisionally labeled "high-power/ active" and "low-power/ passive" anger. The first type agglutinates most of the terms, including the ones typically considered central to the category (like Russian *zlost'* or *gnev* and Spanish *ira* and *rabia)*. The second type includes words related to frustration (*frustración, dosada*) and resentment/hurt (*obida*). In future studies, it would be interesting to test if the semantic profiles of the words in the second cluster are closer than those in the first cluster to low-power words like "disappointment," "despair," or "hurt" (see Chapter 7, Table SM 2).

It is important to note that, contrary to what it may seem, the two clusters in Russian and Spanish do not represent "more intense" and "less intense" types of anger. A feature in the questionnaire explicitly asked about the intensity of the emotion (# 82 – "the emotional experience referred to by the word is an intense emotional state"), but the analysis of variance did not reveal this to be a differentiating feature between the two clusters. What the clusters reflect instead is a difference in the felt power and in the expressive/behavioral features of the emotions. These results are coherent with a previous study by Galati and collaborators (Galati, Sini, Trinti, & Testa, 2008), which identified potency as the second most important dimension (after valence) for the differentiation of the general affective space in Spanish, and they also cohere with the cross-cultural GRID results (see Chapter 7), in which POWER emerges as the second most salient dimension (after VALENCE) in 34 samples from 24 languages and 27 countries around the world. Our analyses further highlight the saliency of power for the specific internal organization of the ANGER domain.

The results have also revealed differences in the meaning of emotion words between speakers of the same language from different cultural groups (cf. also Chapters 20 and 24). The meaning of Colombian *molesto* was found to be closer than Spanish *molesto* to expressive and powerful forms of the emotion like *rabia* or *ira*. This has important consequences for international communication. For example, following his/her representation of the meaning of the word, a Colombian could mistakenly expect more confrontational behavior from a Spaniard describing himself as "molesto," or fail to believe those feelings in the absence of clearer signs of arousal. Similarly, a Spaniard might confusedly wonder about the hidden motives of a red-in-the-face Colombian that "only" claims to be *molesto*.

The ELIN-GRID questionnaire has allowed us to identify a number of differences in the lexical representation of ANGER in Spanish and Russian, with potential consequences in international communication. Not all words in the Russian and Spanish lexicon point to the same underlying concept: two distinct types of ANGER can be identified. It matters which of the two types of word is used, as they convey different information about the various emotion components, notably concerning subjective feeling, expression, and behavior. Additionally, we have shown how the cultural background of the speaker matters as well, as the same word can refer to different concepts in two countries sharing the same language.

Acknowledgments

This research has been carried out with the support of the Swiss Network for International Studies (SNIS) in the framework of the ELIN project.

Chapter 23

What the GRID can reveal about culture-specific emotion concepts: A case study of Russian "toska"

Anna Ogarkova,[1] Johnny J. R. Fontaine, and Irina Prihod'ko

23.1 Introduction

The ways emotional experiences are conceptualized and labeled in natural languages vary across cultures. For instance, an emotion word in one language can cover only a part of the meaning of a comparable word in another language (Stepanova et al., 2006), or two different emotion categories (like English *anger* and *sadness*) can be spanned into one emotion concept in another language (Leff, 1973; Orley, 1970; Rosaldo, 1980). Likewise, comparable concepts in different languages can overlap in their central meanings but differ at the periphery or in the links between the category they label and other categories (Russell, 1991a; Pavlenko, 2008).

Among these and other "asymmetries" in emotion conceptualization (see Chapter 3 for an overview), frequent are the instances of linguistically and culturally untranslatable emotion concepts, otherwise referred to as "culture-specific." These emotion concepts have two major characteristics. The first is their cultural salience, which manifests itself in the frequency of the respective words mentioned in everyday discourse, written language, and self-report (Wierzbicka, 1992b, 1998b; Kitayama et al., 2000). The second trait is their "untranslatability": the words that refer to them in a language either do not have a one-word equivalent in other languages or, if a conventional translation or approximation is possible, detailed specifications are necessary to properly render their meaning in other cultures. Relevant anthropological, ethnographic, and linguistic literature shows that this phenomenon is widespread and does not only relate to "exotic," that is, less studied languages. Quite to the contrary, alongside with many non-Western lingual groups who lexicalize emotional experiences without a one-word designation in Western European languages (e.g., Choi & Han, 2008; Geertz, 1959; Gerber, 1985; Russell, 1991a), cultural peculiarity has been reported for words referring to (Western) European emotion concepts (e.g., Altarriba, 2003; Farrell, 2006; Panayiotou, 2004a, b, 2006; Wierzbicka, 1998b). Of relevance for this chapter, numerous relevant cases are attested for emotion words in the Slavic languages (Gladkova, 2005; Levontina & Zaliznyak, 2001; Pavlenko, 2002a, b; Slaměník & Hurychová, 2006; Stefanskyy, 2005, 2006, 2007a, b, 2009a, b; Wierzbicka, 1998a, b; 2001a).

The many approaches that evolved to account for the meaning of culture-specific emotion words—ranging from the *Natural Semantic Metalanguage* studies to semi-structured interviews

[1] Correspondence concerning this chapter should be addressed to Anna Ogarkova, Swiss Center for the Affective Sciences, 7 Rue des Battoirs, CH-1205, Geneva, Switzerland, e-mail: Anna.Ogarkova@unige.ch

with the native speakers (e.g., Farrell, 2006; Lorenzano, 2006; Lutz, 1982, 1983; Panayiotou, 2004a; Wierzbicka, 2001a)—all have a common denominator. In different phases of the analysis, most of them resort to comparing the culture-specific emotion labels to the prototypical, basic-level ones (Fehr & Russell, 1984; Rosch, 1978), either in the same language or in another language (typically English). At this stage, frequent become the (essentially metaphorical) descriptions of culture-specific emotion terms as "mixtures," "blends," or "combinations" of more translatable, "modal" emotional meanings (cf. Scherer, 1994, 2005a, 2009c). For example, German *Angst* is defined as "roughly a cross between 'anxiety' and 'fear' but with a touch of mystery or existential insecurity" (Wierzbicka, 1998a: 161), the Greek term *stenahorieme* is defined as "a mixture of sadness, discomfort, and suffocation" (Panayiotou, 2004a: 4), Czech *lítost* is said to be "a mixture of the feelings of despair, compassion, remorse and indefinable desire" (Slaměník & Hurychová, 2006: 121).

The GRID methodology is interesting to apply in this context for three reasons. Firstly, GRID targets the semantic profiles of a balanced set of prototypical emotions "[. . .] commonly used in both emotion research and everyday language" (Fontaine et al., 2007: 1050). Thus, comparing the semantic profile of an "untranslatable" emotion term with those of the prototypical emotions (both in the same language and in other languages) can help establish the categorical membership, or memberships, of a "lacunal" emotion word. For instance, if a culture-specific word is described as a "mixture," or "blend" of emotions X and Y, GRID allows verification if indeed it equally strongly correlates with the respective terms, or, alternatively, to which of the semantic profiles it is still closer in meaning.

Secondly and more importantly, GRID can provide a highly granular specification on how a culture-specific term relates to its closest correlate(s) among the prototypical labels. This can be done with the help of relevant analyses both at a more general level, as in considering the positions of emotion terms in the four-dimensional space, and in a more detailed fashion, as in looking at the differences in the emotion components or the (clusters of) individual features in the meaning profiles of emotion terms.

The third advantage, affordable with the GRID method, is the possibility to capture a most salient, or primary meaning of a culture-specific word. By its very design, GRID targets the "invariant," decontextualized lexical meaning, rather than its actualizations in context (Fontaine et al., 2007, cf. Chapter 4) and, thus, can help establish the "default" semantic profile of an emotion word. Although this bias can be critically evaluated by empiricist approaches in cognitive semantics (cf. Geeraerts, 1999), it can be argued to be particularly helpful for the lexicographic representation of the meanings of emotion words (e.g., in the frequently mutually contradictory dictionary definitions).

The present chapter explores the applicability of the GRID method to the study of culture-specific emotion concepts in a case study of Russian *toska*, an emotion term which is frequently said to refer to a "key" emotion concept in the Russian culture (e.g., Levontina & Zaliznyak, 2001; Stepanov, 1997; Uryson, 1997; Wierzbicka, 1992a, 1998b). In what follows, we briefly outline the previous linguistic research on *toska* and the major debates about its meaning (see Section 23.2), which underlie the hypotheses tested in this study (see Section 23.3).

23.2 **Present study**

Prior linguistic research on toska and the hypotheses of the present study

Toska is a salient emotion term in the Russian language. Several studies report its high frequency in Russian corpora, 59 tokens per million words (Zasorina, 1977) as contrasted to 14, 12, and 9 usages per million of its English translation equivalents *yearning, longing and pining* (Kuchera & Francis, 1967, quoted in Wierzbicka, 1992a). Our own corpus search reveals largely the same tendency: while *toska* is used 64.6 times per million words in the Russian National Corpus (henceforth RNC),[2] the frequencies of *yearning, longing and pining* in the British National Corpus (henceforth BNC) are 2.74, 7.57, and 0.4, respectively. In addition, relevant corpora searches show that *toska* is more frequent than other SADNESS[3] words in both Russian (*grust'* "sadness", 22.0, *pečal* "sorrow", 26.1, and *unynie* "gloom", 10.9, RNC), and English (*sadness*, 7.5, *grief*, 17.6, *sorrow*, 5.4, BNC).

Another important aspect is the difficulty of rendering *toska* into other languages. One of the studies reports over 20 of its contextual translations in English, including *yearning, longing, pining, desire, regret, grieving, mourning, weeping, gloom, dismay, boredom, fatigue, exhaustion, suffering, wretchedness, sorrow, anguish, ache, pain, fretting, throes,* and *hyp* (Rudakova, 2002). Another work shows that frequent English correlates of Russian *toska*, in the descending order of frequency, are: *depression, boredom, depressed, anguish, longing, sadness, be/get bored, misery, melancholy,* and that the occasional contextual correlates also include *mental pain, despair, wretchedness, craving (for), urge, anxiety, unhappiness, sorrow, grief,* and *fit* (Anfinogenova, 2006). Rendering *toska* into French appears to be similarly problematic. One of the relevant studies shows that the contextual French approximations of Russian *toska* are *angoisse* "anguish," *tristesse* "sadness," *chagrin* "grief," *anxiété* "anxiety," and *ennui* "boredom"(Dimitrova, 2001). Another study contends that, together with the three most frequent French correlates of the Russian word (*tristesse* "sadness," *nostalgie* "nostalgia," and *angoisse* "anguish"), *toska* is also rendered into French as *affliction* "affliction," *agitation* "restlessness," *amertume* "bitterness," *désespoir* "despair," *détresse* "distress," *tourment* "torture," *douleur* "pain," *inquietude* "worry," *melancolie* "melancholy," *abattement* "despondency," *langueur* "languor," *anxieté* "anxiety," *cafard* "gloomy," *chagrin* "grief," *désir* "desire," *regret* "regret," *trouble* "worry," and *ennui* "boredom" (Vakulenko, 2003). Finally, Russian *toska* appears to have no satisfactory equivalent in German either. Here, it is translated as *Trauer* "sorrow," *Melancholie* "melancholy," *Wehmut* "wistfulness," and *Gram* "grief"(Krasavsky, 2001), or as *Sehnsucht* "yearning," *Traurigkeit* "mournfulness," and *Schwermut* "sorrow, nostalgia"(Syritsa, 2008).

The entirety of the translational correlates of *toska* in Western European languages suggests that its meaning can be approximated using the emotion lexemes from three categories, namely: (1) the words denoting varieties of sadness, sorrow, and grief (e.g., English *mourning*, French *tristesse*, and German *Schwermut*); (2) the words referring to a passionate, restless yearning and desire, as well as anguish and anxiety (e.g., English *longing* and *yearning*, French *angoisse*, and German *Sehnsucht*); and (3) the words denoting boredom and gloom (e.g., English *to be bored*, *gloom*, and French *ennui*). Indeed, several linguists speak about *toska* having three components, or facets, one of which brings it close to fear/anxiety; another to sadness, melancholy and nostalgia; and a third to boredom and revulsion (e.g., Levontina & Zaliznyak, 2001: 300).

However, a major controversy in the views of lexicographers and semanticists about the meaning of *toska* can be assigned to two major positions. The first position is that *toska* is **a "mixture," or "blend" of sadness and anxiety**. This view is shared by several lexicographic sources: in Ozhegov

---

[2] National Corpus of the Russian Language (http://www.ruscorpora.ru) comprises about 180 million words and is one of the most reputable corpora available nowadays for the Russian language.

[3] Throughout this paper, we are using italics (*toska*) to refer to emotion words, no marks (e.g., sadness) to refer to emotional experiences proper. Small capitals (SADNESS) will be used terminologically, to refer to categories of sadness-like experiences in all languages, without implying that they are the same as the English category of SADNESS, or the English word *sadness*.

(1988), a most reputable dictionary of the Russian language, *toska* is defined as "soul-felt anxiety combined with sadness" (Ibid: 656[4]). Other dictionaries define *toska* as a "painful emotional state characterized by yearning, sadness, anxiety, and exhaustion" (Chernyh, 1993, II: 253), or as "languor of the soul, torturous sadness, anxiety, worry, dread" (Dal', 1880).

Many linguists (Levontina & Zaliznyak, 2001: 299–300; Stepanov, 1997; Stefanskyy, 2005, 2006) speak about an interesting parallel between the frequent metaphorical association of Russian *toska* to the idea of squeezing, tightness, or compression, as in *toska szhala serdče* "toska compressed/ squeezed the heart," and the attested etymological links between European ANXIETY words and the words to denote physical tightness or compression (e.g., German *Angst*, French *angoisse*, and English *anguish* derive from Latin *angustia* "tightness"→ Latin *angor* "compression," "anxiety").

Finally, the view on *toska* as a "blend" of sadness and anxiety comes from translation studies. In parallel to the tendency to translate *toska* by both SADNESS and ANXIETY words in European languages, *toska* is used as a contextual translation equivalent of both FEAR/ANXIETY and SADNESS words in other Slavic languages, such as Polish *lek* "fear," *niepokoj* "anxiety, unrest," Czech *uzkost* "anxiety," on the one hand, and Polish *žal* "sorrow," *smutek* "sadness," and Czech *smutek* "sadness," on the other hand (Stefanskyy, 2005, 2006, 2009a).

The second position on the debate about the meaning of Russian *toska* is the view that it is **essentially a SADNESS word** in Russian. For instance, Apresjan and associates (1997) group the Russian words *pečal* "sorrow," *toska*, and *grust'* "sadness" into one category of words denoting "the unpleasant experiences a person undergoes when s/he wants something s/he doesn't have and doesn't believe one can get it." The same view is shared by the editor of the *Russian Dictionary of Synonyms* where *toska* is attributed SADNESS-related synonyms: *unynie* "doom," *melancholia* "melancholy," and *handra* "spleen" (Evgen'eva, 2003). Finally, *grust'* "sadness," *pečal* "sorrow" and *toska* repeatedly emerge in each others' explications in *The Russian Associative Dictionary* based on the free associations of native speakers (Karaulov et al., 2002).

In tune with the lexicographers, Anna Wierzbicka identifies "sadness," "emptiness caused by the absence or unavailability of somebody or something good," "intolerable suffering" as the key semantic components of Russian *toska*. However, her NMS scenarios of *toska* and *grust'* "sadness" suggest that these two emotional experiences are caused by different types of eliciting events: while the main event appraisal in Russian *grust'* "sadness" is a negative event happening in the past, *toska* is elicited by the desire for something good to happen (see Table 23.1).

Table 23.1 NSM scenarios of Russian toska and grust'

TOSKA scenario	**GRUST' scenario**
X thinks something like this:	X thinks something like this:
I want something good to happen	I know: something bad happened now
I do not know what	I don't want things like this happen
I know: it cannot happen	I know I can't do anything
	Because this person thinks this, this person feels something for a short time
(Wierzbicka, 1992b: 172)	(Wierzbicka, 1998a: 14)

---

[4] All definitions translated into English by the first author.

The categorical membership of *toska* as a SADNESS word has also been substantiated in two experimental linguistic studies. The first is a hierarchical clustering study of negative emotion words in Russian based on the native speakers' similarity judgments (Solovyev, 2008). This study shows that *grust'* "sadness," *pečal* "sorrow," and *toska* cluster together and emerge as a distinct group of words, as opposed to five other clusters denoting grief (e.g., *gore* "woe," *skorb'* "mourning"), anguish (e.g., *trevoga* "anxiety," *smyatenie* "agitation"), disappointment (e.g., *ogorchenie* "being upset," *rasstrojstvo* "disappointment"), despair (e.g., *otchayanie* "despair," *beznadezhnost'* "despondency"), and apathy (e.g., *depressiya* "depression," *handra* "spleen"). The second relevant experimental study is a cognitive linguistic investigation of the behavioral profiles (Divjak & Gries, 2006) of SADNESS words in Russian. This study reports that the range and the frequency of distribution of prepositional constructions in which *toska* and Russian SADNESS words appear bear a significantly higher similarity to each other than to the constructional profiles of their non-synonyms (Janda & Solovyev, 2009).

The two positions discussed above—that *toska* is an emotional "blend" of sadness and anxiety or that *toska* is primarily a SADNESS word—underlie the hypotheses tested in this study. Using the GRID approach, we aim to verify whether *toska* bears a significantly closer resemblance to the semantic profile of Russian *grust* "sadness" and other SADNESS words in Russian (Hypothesis 1) or, alternatively, whether it equally strongly correlates with both SADNESS and ANXIETY words (Hypothesis 2).

Among the methods used to capture the meaning of *toska* in previous research, GRID is closest to the experimental approach illustrated in Solovyev (2008). Firstly, both approaches are data-driven (rather than based on non-systematic linguistic evidence); secondly, both methods derive from the native speakers' assessments of the meaning of words (rather than researchers' introspection). At the same time, GRID is a stronger method in this context because it allows the overcoming of two limitations inherent in the technique of hierarchical clustering derived from similarity judgments. The latter technique is a discrete method which offers an "either-or" solution, that is, it can only suggest that a term either belongs to a cluster or does not belong to it. So, if *toska* were a "blended" emotion with a strong overlap with ANXIETY but yet a more pronounced overlap with SADNESS, it would still emerge in the SADNESS cluster. By contrast, GRID allows for assessing the *degree of overlap* with both clusters of words, even if this overlap is less pronounced in one of the cases. The second limitation of Solovyev's study (2008) is that it is based on semantic similarity judgments, and thus does not specify the reasons why *toska* clusters with SADNESS, but not with ANXIETY words. With GRID, however, it is possible to see which (clusters of) rating features, emotion components, or dimensions are responsible for the outcome.

Data

The data used in this chapter come from the Russian GRID sample (*N* = 166, 102 females, mean age 23.7).[5] For comparative purposes, we also use eight more samples from the GRID database. These include four Western European/American datasets: British English (*N* = 201, 124 females; mean age, 21.51), US American English (*N* = 182, 129 females; mean age, 18.5), German (*N* = 120, 92 females; mean age 24.5), and French (*N* = 140, 101 females; mean age, 23.8). The four Slavic samples are Polish (*N* = 187, 131 females; mean age, 24.5), Czech (*N* = 120, 43 females, mean age, 19.28), Slovak (*N* = 128, 107 females, mean age, 22.2), and Ukrainian (*N* = 147, 89 females; mean age, 22.3).

---

[5] The numbers in the Russian, Polish, and Ukrainian samples include the participants who rated the standard set of 24 GRID words, and another group who rated an extra set. The Russian extra set included the word *toska*.

23.3 **Results**

Toska in Russian: a variety of sadness, or a mixture of sadness and anxiety?

Four types of findings affordable with the GRID method—all capturing different levels of granularity of semantic similarity or divergence—provide evidence on the categorical membership of *toska* in Russian.

The first piece of evidence comes from the feature-based hierarchical clustering of Russian emotion words. Here our result fully replicates Solovyev's (2008) finding: *toska* indeed clusters with Russian *grust'* "sadness" and the two words form a distinct outlier cluster in the class of Russian negative emotion terms (see Figure 23.1, **in bold**).

However, using GRID feature ratings as the basis for the hierarchical clustering offers much richer detail than the same technique applied to the graded similarity judgments. With GRID, it is possible not only to see which words cluster together, but also to inspect which features discriminate well between clusters, that is, foreground the most important properties of a cluster (Divjak & Gries, 2008). Here,

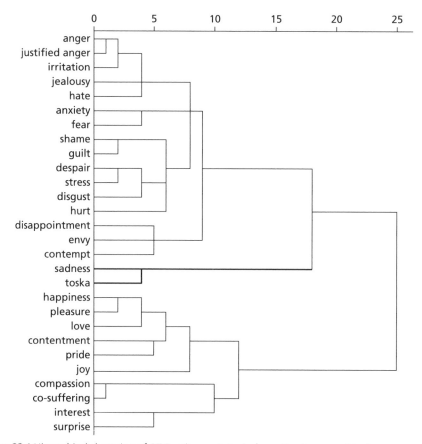

Figure 23.1 Hierarchical clustering of 27 Russian prototypical emotion terms and *toska*.

Note: for better readability, English translations are used for Russian emotion terms (except *toska*). Clustering was performed on centered means, the metric used is squared Euclidean distances with features as variables (Z-normalized) and emotion words as cases.

Table 23.2 Features with the highest *t*-values in the [*grust', toska*] cluster

#	feature	t	#	feature	t
74	spoke slower	2.11	87	needed help and support	1.40
92	wanted to do nothing	1.98	41	breathing slowing down	1.38
98	wanted to withdraw into the self	1.96	75	no change in vocal expression	1.35
63	no change in gestures	1.91	68	fell silent	1.35
61	withdrew from people or things	1.85	65	decreased the volume of voice	1.34
93	had no motivation to pay attention	1.85	49	no bodily symptoms	1.34
37	heartbeat slowing down	1.81	58	no change in facial expression	1.30
119	felt tired	1.75	55	closed the eyes	1.26
91	lacked the motivation to do anything	1.57	102	wanted to break contact with others	1.19
57	showed tears	1.51	97	wanted to disappear or hide	1.19
137	felt weak	1.44	99	wanted not to be hurt	1.18
39	muscles relax	1.43	85	wanted to hand over the initiative	1.08
31	suffered an irrevocable loss	1.42	122	felt powerless	1.00
141	hid the emotion by a smile	1.42			

calculating *t*-values[6] facilitate determining which variables are most strongly represented in a cluster as compared to all other groups. The features with the highest positive *t*-values for the (*grust', toska*) cluster, which are simultaneously negative for the words in all other clusters are shown in Table 23.2. Clearly, these are prototypical features reported for SADNESS experiences across cultures (cf. Folkman & Lazarus, 1986, Lazarus, 1991a), including feelings of weakness and powerlessness (# 119, 137, 87, 122), low degree of AROUSAL (# 37, 39, 41, 74), the overall lack of expressive symptoms (# 75, 49, 58, 68) except for crying (# 57), and, most prominently, withdrawal/avoidance tendencies (# 55, 61, 98, 99, 102, 97).[7]

The second piece of evidence in favor of the view that *toska* is a SADNESS word (Hypothesis 1) comes from computing the correlations of *toska* with all other Russian emotion words. Alongside with showing that *toska* correlates the highest with *grust'* "sadness" (0.88), this analysis also reveals its relatively high correlations with two other SADNESS-related labels (*otčayanie* "despair" and *dosada* "disappointment"), but, at the same time, considerably lower correlations with Russian ANXIETY words *trevoga* "anxiety" and *strah* "fear" (see Table 23.3, **in bold**). This analysis also suggests that, in the ANXIETY group, *toska* is closer to Russian *strah* "fear" (0.46) than to *trevoga* "anxiety" (0.37).

The third analytical procedure where the findings support Hypothesis 1 is the Principal Component Analysis which renders a four-dimensional solution with VALENCE, POWER, AROUSAL, and NOVELTY as defining factors accounting for 75.07% of the total variance in the Russian sample. Here, comparing the dimensional scores of *toska* with those of *grust'* "sadness," on the one hand, and *trevoga* "anxiety" and *strah* "fear," on the other hand, shows that the difference is almost always less pronounced in the former case, which suggests that *toska* is closer to SADNESS than to the ANXIETY/FEAR pole on the four emotion dimensions (see Table 23.4, but see the section that follows).

---

[6] The *t*-values for any feature for a cluster *c* out of *n* clusters are computed as follows: (mean within *c*—mean across all *n* clusters)/standard deviation of the mean across all *n* clusters (see Divjak & Gries, 2006, 2008).

[7] However, certain variability has been attested as to the importance of these SADNESS features in different cultural groups (see, e.g., Vandervoot, 2001).

Table 23.3 Profile correlations of *toska* with 27 prototypical emotion terms in Russian

word	PC	word	PC	word	PC
sadness	**0.88**	disgust	0.45	justified anger	0.02
guilt	0.69	envy	0.39	love	−0.32
disappointment	**0.68**	compassion	0.38	surprise	−0.32
despair	**0.67**	anxiety	**0.37**	contentment	−0.38
shame	0.60	irritation	0.28	pleasure	−0.47
being hurt	0.57	contempt	0.27	pride	−0.49
co-suffering	0.47	jealousy	0.26	happiness	−0.49
fear	**0.46**	hate	0.25	joy	−0.57
stress	0.46	anger	0.19	interest	−0.59

Note: for better readability, English translations are used for Russian emotion terms (except *toska*).

Finally, supporting evidence for Hypothesis 1 comes from the Univariate Analyses of Variance on the component features. For this analysis, we chose *strah* "fear" as the highest correlate of *toska* among ANXIETY/FEAR terms (see Table 23.3) and conducted ANOVA's on *grust'* "sadness," *toska,* and *strah* "fear" feature ratings with the Sidak correction for multiple testing. The results yield a picture largely similar to the one obtained in previous analyses. Overall, significant differences between the three terms were found on 44 features. In 25 of these 44 features (56.7%) there is no difference between *grust'* "sadness" and *toska,* but there *is* a significant difference between *strah* "fear" and *toska* (for the list of these features, see Table 23.5).

The qualitative aspects suggested by these ANOVA results are also revealing: on the vast majority of features (21 out of 25) *toska* was rated significantly lower than *strah* "fear" on prototypical ANXIETY/FEAR characteristics. These include typical antecedents (sudden and unpredictable events, # 12, 3, 30) requiring immediate action (#22), "somatic" reactions such as changes in bodily temperature (#32, 44, 45, 48), heartbeat and breathing increase (#42, 38), restlessness in body movement (# 59), and muscle tension (# 40), as well as "psychic" reactions such as feeling nervous (#136, cf. Magnusson & Stattin, 1978; Taylor, 1953).

Overall, the four types of analyses presented above offer very convincing support to Hypothesis 1 that *toska* is a sadness term and, taken together, conclusively resolve the ambiguity about the categorical membership of this salient Russian emotion term.

"Anxiety" facet in the meaning of Russian toska

Alongside with the robust evidence in support of Hypothesis 1 presented above, the question remains regarding the relatedness of *toska* to ANXIETY/FEAR words in Russian. Three types of

Table 23.4 Dimensional coordinates of Russian SADNESS, Russian ANXIETY words, and *toska*

word	VALENCE	POWER	AROUSAL	NOVELTY
grust' (sadness)	−0.17	−1.30	−2.43	−1.53
toska	−0.12	−0.90	−1.52	−1.43
strah (fear)	−0.42	−0.78	0.93	0.89
trevoga (anxiety)	−0.60	0.15	1.48	−0.09

Table 23.5 Features differentiating *grust'* (sadness) and *toska* from *strah* (fear)

#	feature	*grust'*	*toska*	*strah*
119	felt tired	6.7[a]	6.7[b]	4.1[a,b]
92	wanted to do nothing	6.8[a]	6.3[b]	3.5[a,b]
65	decreased the volume of voice	7.6[a]	6.1[b]	3.7[a,b]
93	no motivation to pay attention	5.5	5.7[b]	3.4[b]
48	felt cold	4.4[a]	5.1[b]	7.7[a,b]
30	in danger	4.4[a]	4.8[b]	7.6[a,b]
12	caused by chance	3.9[a]	4.7[b]	6.8[a,b]
116	was in an intense emotional state	3.7[a]	4.7[b]	7.1[a,b]
136	felt nervous	4.4[a]	4.6[b]	7.7[a,b]
33	felt weak limbs	4.6	4.5[b]	7.0[b]
131	felt calm	4.9[a]	4.4[b]	2.3[a,b]
3	unpredictable	3.0[a]	4.1[b]	6.3[a,b]
40	muscles tensing (whole body)	2.2[a]	4.1[b]	7.4[a,b]
22	required an immediate response	4.2[a]	4.0[b]	7.4[a,b]
42	breathing getting faster	2.8[a]	4.0[b]	7.0[a,b]
1	suddenly	3.5[a]	3.9[b]	7.0[a,b]
95	wanted push things away	4.1	3.8[b]	6.2[b]
34	got pale	5.1[a]	3.8[b]	7.7[a,b]
32	felt shivers	4.2[a]	3.7[b]	7.7[a,b]
28	center of attention	4.7	3.6[b]	6.2[b]
59	produced abrupt body movements	2.2[a]	3.5[b]	5.7[a,b]
44	perspired or had moist hands	2.7[a]	3.5[b]	7.4[a,b]
38	heartbeat getting faster	2.7[a]	3.4[b]	7.7[a,b]
56	opened her or his eyes widely	2.5[a]	3.2[b]	6.9[a,b]
45	sweat	2.2[a]	3.0[b]	6.6[a,b]

Note: *grust'*, *toska*, *strah*—raw mean values; [a] mean difference significant at 0.01 significance level; [b] mean difference significant at 0.01 significance level.

findings specify this link. Firstly, the profile correlations show that *toska* is somewhat closer to FEAR/ ANXIETY words than *grust'* "sadness" is (0.37 vs 0.23 with *trevoga* and 0.46 vs 0.30 with *strah* "fear"). Secondly come the observations on the emotion dimension scores (see Table 23.4). Here, for one thing, *toska* is closer to *strah* "fear" than to *grust'* "sadness" on POWER (score differences 0.12 and 0.4, respectively), suggesting that the experiences of *toska* and *strah* "fear" are relatively less characterized by appraisals of control, feelings of POWER, dominance, and impulses to act (Fontaine et al., 2007: 1051). Furthermore, differences are observed on AROUSAL: while *toska* is clearly at the SADNESS pole on this dimension, it is still closer to *strah* "fear" and *trevoga* "anxiety" than *grust'* "sadness" is (the dimension score differences are 2.45 vs 3.36 and 3.0 vs 3.91, respectively, see Table 23.4). Thus, *toska* denotes an emotional state which implies a higher degree of sympathetic AROUSAL than *grust'* "sadness" does.

Table 23.6 Features where toska is in-between grust' (sadness) and strah (fear)

#	feature	grust'	toska	strah
57	showed tears	7.8[a]	6.7	4.9[a]
98	**wanted to withdraw into her/himself**	**8.6[a]**	**6.7**	**5.0[a]**
74	spoke slower	7.6[a]	6.5	5.1[a]
134	**felt alert**	**4.8[a]**	**6.5**	**7.7[a]**
132	**felt out of control**	**4.7[a]**	**6.4**	**7.1[a]**
61	**withdrew from people or things**	**7.7[a]**	**6.0**	**5.6[a]**
63	no changes in gestures	6.4[a]	5.4	3.8[a]
25	consequences able to live with	6.1[a]	5.1	3.3[a]
54	frowned	6.6[a]	5.1	3.5[a]
113	wanted to act whatever action it might be	2.8[a]	4.4	6.5[a]
15	caused by a supernatural POWER	3.0[a]	4.1	6.2[a]
49	had no bodily symptoms at all	4.7[a]	3.8	2.4[a]
89	**wanted to move**	**2.2[a]**	**3.8**	**5.1[a]**
115	**wanted to get totally absorbed in the situation**	**5.6[a]**	**3.8**	**2.3[a]**
73	spoke faster	2.3[a]	3.7	5.4[a]
46	felt hot	2.1[a]	3.5	5.3[a]

Note: grust', toska, strah—raw mean values; [a] mean difference significant at 0.01 significance level.

Third and finally, among the 44 features where significant differences between *toska, grust'* "sadness," and *strah* "fear" were found (with ANOVA and pairwise comparison with Sidak), on 16 features there is a significant difference between *grust'* "sadness" and *strah* "fear," but *toska* is in-between and does not differ significantly from either of the terms (see Table 23.6). In most of these cases the means of *toska* are closer to those of *grust'* 'sadness' (which substantiates the conclusion that *toska* is more related to SADNESS than to FEAR/ANXIETY). However, 6 features are exceptions from the pattern (see Table 23.6, **in bold**).

Qualitatively, the ratings on these six emotion features suggest two important nuances. Firstly, *toska* appears to be closer to *strah* "fear" than it is to *grust'* "sadness" on the feelings of alertness (# 132), as well as the desire to act/move (# 89). This finding is consonant with the reported quality of "restlessness" of *toska* experience (cf. Stefanskyy, 2005, 2006, 2009a; Wierzbicka, 1992b, 1998b). Secondly, *toska* appears to be farther away from *grust'* "sadness" on several features capturing withdrawal/avoidance tendencies and resignation (#61, 98, 115), which suggests that *toska* does not share some of the key traits of SADNESS to the same degree as the category prototype (*grust'*) does.

Overall, the conclusion that can be drawn from the results presented above is that *toska* is relatively closer to FEAR/ANXIETY than the prototypical Russian SADNESS label (*grust'*) is. However, the shift of *toska* from SADNESS to ANXIETY is fairly subtle, so that what is at stake is not a "symmetrical," comparably strong correlation of *toska* with two emotion categories (Hypothesis 2), but its very substantial overlap with one category (SADNESS), and a very partial relatedness to another one (FEAR/ANXIETY).

Rendering Russian toska in other languages

As discussed in the section on 'Prior linguistic research on toska and the hypotheses of the present study', one of the key characteristics of Russian *toska* is the difficulty of rendering its meaning into other languages, which results in its numerous contextual correlates in other languages, Western European and Slavic alike. By virtue of targeting the "invariant," decontextualized lexical meaning, GRID cannot resolve conclusively the issue of better translation equivalents of Russian *toska* in specific contexts. However, it allows for verification if the pattern in which *toska* relates to SADNESS and FEAR/ANXIETY in Russian fares well cross-linguistically.

To explore this issue, we have computed the profile correlations of *toska* with all the prototypical emotion terms in seven languages: three spoken by Western European populations (UK and US English, French, and German), and four Slavic (Polish, Czech, Slovak, and Ukrainian).

As becomes clear from the results (see Table 23.7), the pattern observed in the Russian data holds very well across all eight different data samples: *toska* invariably correlates highest

Table 23.7 Profile correlations of Russian "toska" with SADNESS and ANXIETY words in Western European and Slavic languages

	LG	L	label	PC		LG	L	label	PC
Sadness	Western European	UK	sadness	**0.77**	Fear	Western European	UK	fear	0.35
		US	sadness	**0.75**			US	fear	0.36
		Fr	tristesse	**0.79**			Fr	peur	0.42
		Ger	Trauer	**0.74**			Ger	Angst	0.43
	Slavic	Pl	smutek	**0.83**		Slavic	Pl	strach	0.43
		Cz	smutek	**0.69**			Cz	strach	0.44
		Sl	smútok	**0.88**			Sl	strach	0.41
		Ukr	smutok	**0.79**			Ukr	strah	0.46
Disappointment	Western European	UK	disappointment	0.77	Anxiety	Western European	UK	anxiety	0.43
		US	disappointment	0.72			US	anxiety	0.37
		Fr	déception	0.73			Fr	anxiété	0.44
		Ger	Enttäuschung	0.68			Ger	Besorgnis	0.47
	Slavic	Pl	rozczarowanie	0.63		Slavic	Pl	niepokój	0.52
		Cz	zklamání	0.73			Cz	nepokoj	0.49
		Sl	sklamanie	0.63			Sl	úzkost'	0.46
		Ukr	shkoda	0.59			Ukr	tryvoga	0.43
Despair	Western European	UK	despair	0.66	Stress	Western European	UK	stress	0.39
		US	despair	0.63			US	stress	0.52
		Fr	désespoir	0.78			Fr	stress	0.26
		Ger	Verzweiflung	0.58			Ger	Stress	0.27
	Slavic	Pl	rozpacz	0.59		Slavic	Pl	stres	0.34
		Cz	beznaděj	0.65			Cz	stres	0.49
		Sl	beznádej	0.63			Sl	stres	0.34
		Ukr	vidchaj	0.56			Ukr	stres	0.47

Note: LG, language group; L, language; PC, profile correlation; UK, British English; US, American English; Fr, French; Ger, German; Pl, Polish; Cz, Czech; Sl, Slovak; Ukr, Ukrainian.

with the prototypical SADNESS words, such as English *sadness*, French *tristesse*, Ukrainian *smutok*, or Polish *smutek*. Moreover, its correlations with other allegedly SADNESS-related words (DISAPPOINTMENT and DESPAIR terms) are remarkably high and are, what is crucial, invariably higher than its correlations with ANXIETY, FEAR, and STRESS words.

23.4 **Conclusion**

This chapter aimed to investigate the applicability and the potential of the GRID method in the research on "culture-specific" emotion concepts, a domain that emphasizes cultural variability in emotion conceptualization and lexicalization and asserts that the indigenous emotion categories play a major role in the cultural construction of emotional reality and cultural socialization processes. Our case study focused on the Russian culture-specific concept of *toska*. The word that labels it in Russian is particularly attractive because of its language saliency and the lack of congruent translation correlates in other European languages, Western European and Slavic alike. Translational ambiguity of *toska* is largely underpinned by the controversy in lexicographers and semanticists' views about its meaning. Here, two principal positions can be discerned: on the one hand, some researchers contend that *toska* is a variety of sadness, and thus pertains to the cluster of SADNESS words in the Russian language, on the other hand, others suggest that *toska* is a "mixture" of sadness and anxiety, and, therefore, has an equally strong relation to both SADNESS and ANXIETY. These two views are the hypotheses tested in the present study.

Our results provide robust support to the view that *toska* bears a significantly higher similarity to SADNESS than to ANXIETY/FEAR words, and does so not only in Russian, but also in seven more languages from three language groups: Germanic (English, German), Romance (French), and Slavic (Czech, Slovak, Polish, and Ukrainian). In the light of this evidence, defining *toska* as "[. . .] anxiety coupled with sadness" (e.g., Ozhegov, 1988: 656) appears to be less appropriate than defining it as a word denoting a SADNESS-related emotional state (Apresjan et al., 1997; Evgen'eva, 2003; Wierzbicka, 1992b, 1998b).

However, the GRID method also shows that Russian *toska* appears to be semantically closer to ANXIETY/FEAR words than the prototypical SADNESS label (*grust'*) is. This shift does not, however, suggest a "symmetrical," that is, a comparably strong correlation of *toska* with both emotion categories. Rather, an "anxious" component in *toska* constitutes a "potentiality," which can get actualized in specific contexts. This, in turn, explains why *toska* can contextually be used as a translation correlate of ANXIETY/FEAR words denoting in other languages for example, French *angoisse* and *anxiété*, English *anxiety* and *anguish*, Polish *lek* and *niepokoj*.

Methodologically, the present study illustrates a high investigative potential of the GRID method in the study of culture-specific emotion concepts. Unlike the discrete methods (e.g., hierarchical clustering or classical dimension studies), where only a very small and abstracted aspect of meaning is tapped on—that of the relative similarity of a set of emotion terms within the domain (Moore et al., 1999; Russell, 1980; Russell & Sato, 1995; Solovyev, 2008)—GRID allows the pinning down of the *reasons* underlying those judgments through considering the (dis)similarities of the words' ratings on a wide range of emotional features. Applied to the study of a disputed categorical membership of a culture-specific term, GRID allows not only to conclusively establish the category to which an emotion label belongs, but also to specify the degree of gradual overlap with the other emotion categories (candidate to be important for its meaning) and to show, in a highly granular fashion, which emotion dimensions or (clusters of) individual features foreground the observed pattern of results.

Further applications of the GRID method in the domain of the research on culture-specific emotion concepts can develop in two directions. Firstly, in addition to the features derived from a range of very diverse emotion theories, more case-relevant features can be included in the instrument so that to capture all the essential characteristics of culture-specific emotion terms. For instance, in the domain of Russian SADNESS words, one of the aspects that differentiates Russian *pečal* "sorrow," *gore* "grief," on the one hand, from Russian *grust'* and *toska,* on the other hand, is the likelihood of respective emotional experiences being elicited by an "identifiable cause" (Wierzbicka, 1998b: 12): while central to the emotional experiences of *pečal* "sorrow" and *gore* "grief," it is said to be a much less salient characteristic of *grust'* "sadness" and *toska*. Thus, including this feature into the rating instrument would allow the verification of its discriminative relevance, and if so, to test whether the difference in its ratings would be congruent with the previous research.

The second direction where GRID could be enhanced in future studies relates to the selection of words to which a culture-specific term is compared. The present study contrasts *toska* to the set of prototypical emotion words. This approach serves the purpose well if the aim is to identify the categorical membership of an untranslatable emotion label. However, this might not be enough to find a best translation equivalent possible (in another language), or a closest synonym available (in the same language) for that word. Future studies including many more relevant terms (e.g., English *yearning* and *anguish*) can definitely be enlightening in this respect.

Chapter 24

Pride is not created equal: Variations between Northern and Southern Italy

Marcello Mortillaro,[1] Pio E. Ricci-Bitti,
Guglielmo Bellelli, and Dario Galati

The majority of cross-cultural studies of emotions analyzed the differences between very dissimilar and geographically separated cultures, while only few studies dealt with regional differences, that is, cultural differences within a single country. Indeed, many countries, due to historical and/or geographical reasons, are not culturally homogeneous and, in principle, their different regions should be analyzed separately when considering cultural aspects. In the light of the economical and historical differences between its North and South regions and the quite recent linguistic unification, Italy may be one of these countries. In the current research, using the GRID data, we wanted to test whether Northern Italians and Southern Italians differ with respect to the meaning of emotion terms. We focused our analysis on pride (*orgoglio*, in Italian) because it is considered extremely sensitive to cultural influences (Eid & Diener, 2001), and it is experienced in very different ways across societies (Hofstede, 1984; Marcus & Kitayama, 1991).

In this chapter, we will first describe the category of self-conscious emotions in order to introduce pride and its main features. Subsequently, we will review some evidence about the cultural variability of pride. Finally, we will present an analysis of the GRID data to determine if and how the meaning of pride differs between Southern and Northern Italians.

24.1 Pride as a positive self-conscious emotion

Shame, pride, embarrassment, and guilt are usually labeled "self-conscious emotions" (Darwin, 1872; Lewis, 1992, 1997). These emotions imply sophisticated cognitive abilities, that is, "thinking what others think of us" (Darwin, 1872, p. 325), that are not necessarily implicated in the experience of primary emotions.[2] Recently, Tracy and Robins (2004a) listed five features which are distinctive of the category of self-conscious emotions. First, the elicitation of self-conscious emotions requires that the person has self-awareness, self-representations, and the capacity of self-evaluation. Indeed, self-conscious emotions imply the evaluation of behavior with respect to a culture dependent set of standards, rules, and goals (Lewis, 1992; Stipek, Recchia, McClintic, & Lewis, 1992). Second,

---

[1] Corresponding author: Marcello Mortillaro. Swiss Center for Affective Sciences - University of Geneva. 7, Rue des Battoirs, CH-1205 Geneva, Switzerland. Marcello.Mortillaro@unige.ch

[2] The so-called primary emotions can occur at different levels of cognitive processing: sensory-motor, schematic, and conceptual (Leventhal & Scherer, 1987). Self-conscious emotions are supposed to occur only in consequence of a conceptual cognitive processing.

several studies proved that self-conscious emotions emerge only when children are 3 years old, that is, when they have awareness of their mental acts and the capacity of self-evaluation. Only at about that age do children experience unspecific emotional states like empathy or embarrassment and even later they start to experience more specific self-conscious evaluative emotions (Lewis, 1992, 2003; Sullivan, Bennet, & Lewis, 2003). Third, self-conscious emotions evolved to promote the attainment of social goals, by helping people in being proper member of groups, and avoiding the occurrence of more negative emotions like anger or contempt (Haidt, 2003). Fourth, self-conscious emotions do not have universal facial expressions, but they are consistently expressed and recognized starting from other nonverbal expressive cues, namely body postures – as is the case for pride (Tracy & Robins, 2004b, 2008) and blushing (Darwin, 1872; Crozier, 2001; Keltner & Harker, 1998).[3] Finally, self-conscious emotions are cognitively complex, because they always require at least three evaluations: about the agency (internal vs external attribution; Weiner, 1986), about the event (success or failure), and about global or specific aspects of the self.

Pride is the prototypical positive self-conscious emotion, which is experienced in consequence of an event appraised as a personal achievement (Lewis, 2003, 2008).[4] Pride is experienced when the person evaluates the event as a success with respect to his/her standards, goals, and rules (achievement) and he/she considers himself/herself personally responsible for the success (Lewis, 1997). The attribution of the success to either the global self, or a specific aspect of it, determines which forms of pride will be experienced. The first form of pride is called "alpha" pride (Tangney, 1990), hubris (Lewis, 1992) or hubristic pride (Tracy & Robins, 2007b). In this form, pride is directed at the global self of the person ("I am good"), is ego-focused, and relates to both arrogance and narcissism (Lewis, 2000; Tracy, Cheng, Robins, & Trzesniewski, 2009). The second form of pride has been called "beta" pride (Tangney, 1990), pride (as opposed to hubris, Lewis, 1992), or authentic pride (Tracy & Robins, 2007b). In this form, pride is directed at the specific behavior ("I did well"), relates to achievement motivation (Stipek, 1998) and to self-esteem (Tracy et al., 2009), and it is morally relevant (Hart & Matsuba, 2007). Both forms of pride evolved as emotions adaptive to attain higher social status (Tracy, Sharif, & Cheng, 2010). Human social status can derive either from agonistic (force threat – dominance) or non-agonistic (excellence in valued domains – prestige) sources (Henrich & Gil-White, 2001). Tracy and colleagues (2010), argue that the physical agonistic behavior, in contemporary human societies, is substituted by more subtle verbal and nonverbal displays. Hubristic pride evolved to foster a reputation of dominance – and thus a higher social status – without the need of physical attacks. Conversely, authentic pride evolved to motivate the attainment of prestige by evidencing one's accomplishments and inhibiting aggression (Tracy et al., 2010).

24.2 **Cultural variability of pride**

Most cross-cultural models describe societies in terms of how much they focus on the individuals (individualism) rather than on the society as a whole (collectivism), assuming the existence of a continuous dimension between the two poles of pure individualism and pure collectivism (Hofstede,

---

[3] Blushing was the theme of the chapter of Darwin's book "The expression of emotions in man and animals" (1872) dedicated to self-conscious emotions. This expressive feature has been regarded as a sign of appeasement (Castelfranchi & Poggi, 1990), as a sign of shame (Keltner & Harker, 1998), or as a sign that something that should be hidden has been exposed (Crozier, 2001).

[4] We label *Positive* those emotions that are elicited by an event appraised as Intrinsically Pleasant and/or Goal Conducive (Scherer, 2001).

1984; Markus & Kitayama, 1991). Individualism and collectivism, indeed, are both present in every society and have been related to two different forms of self: the independent self, more diffused in individualistic societies, is characterized by a unique configuration of inner attributes that define the person with respect to the other members of the society; the interdependent self, more diffused in collectivistic societies, is characterized by the other selves, with the conception that the self is made of its social relationships (Hofstede, 1984; Marcus & Kitayama, 1991; Triandis, Bontempo, Villareal, Asay, & Lucca, 1988). In societies where collectivism prevails, the person is not supposed to be completely independent from the others, but to harmoniously fit in the societal organization of roles and duties. These two cultures, thus, imply different conceptions of what is well-being and which are the elements at the basis of positive emotions (e.g., Galati, Manzano, & Sotgiu, 2006).

Culture influences emotions in many different aspects (e.g., Mesquita, Frijda & Scherer, 1997; Russell, 1991a), and this is even more true for self-conscious emotions because they imply social awareness and cognitive effort (Tangney & Fischer, 1995). Social awareness depends on culture because it entails the set of standards, goals and rules which are culturally determined and learnt through socialization (Lewis, 1992; Mascolo, Fischer, & Li, 2003). Similarly, the cognitive elements of emotions (i.e., appraisal) are influenced by the culture in which the evaluation occurs (Mesquita & Ellsworth, 2001; Roseman, 1991; Scherer, 2001, 2009; Scherer & Brosch, 2009).[5] A recent wave of studies showed that pride, in particular, is deeply intertwined with the culture to which the person belongs; for example, Eid and Diener (2001) found for pride the largest differences between Australia, China, Taiwan, and United States in terms of norms for experiencing emotions (see also Van Osch et al., in this volume). The effect of culture on pride is partly mediated by two societal values, which have different relevance and salience in collectivistic and individualistic cultures: achievement, personal or collective, and honor.

In those societies where individualism prevails, personal achievement is one of the most prominent socially rewarded goals and it plays an important role in determining individuals' self-esteem (Maehr, 1974; Triandis et al., 1988). As a consequence, it is accepted that individuals mark their personal achievements by overtly expressing their pride. Conversely, in those societies where collectivism prevails, self-esteem is dependent on social harmony, and, as a consequence, individuals accept and expect the expression of pride for an achievement that benefits others too and not only the person (Stipek, 1998). The experience of group pride depends on the activation of collective self-representations, which are more salient in societies where collectivism is more diffused (Tracy & Robins, 2008).

Honor – the self-respect judged by the person himself/herself and by others (Pitt-Rivers, 1965) – has been deemed relevant for the experience of pride (Markus & Kitayama, 1991; Rodriguez Mosquera, Manstead, & Fischer, 2000, 2002). Typically, in an individualistic culture, honor is associated to personal achievements and positive feedbacks, whereas in a collectivistic culture honor is associated to behavior that enhances interdependency (Rodriguez Mosquera et al., 2002). A series of studies compared Spanish and Dutch respondents – considered as having, the first, an honor-based and a rather collectivistic culture; and, the second, a rather individualistic culture – with respect to the elicitation, the experience and the communication of pride (Fischer, Manstead, & Rodriguez Mosquera, 1999; Rodriguez Mosquera et al., 2000). On the basis of prototypical descriptions of pride, Fischer and colleagues (1999) found that pride is a more readily salient emotion

---

[5] A thorough discussion of the effects of culture on appraisal goes beyond the goals of the present chapter. A more general description of the effect of culture on appraisal can be found elsewhere (Mesquita and Ellsworth, 2001).

for Spaniards than for Dutch, confirming that an honor-based culture assigns to pride an important position in the emotional domain. Furthermore, Dutch respondents referred the experience of pride to personal achievement and to self-related appraisals, whereas Spaniards reported more frequently other-related appraisals. Finally, Spaniards were more ambivalent toward pride reporting more negative feelings, and a less frequent and more controlled expression. Although differences in terms of antecedents and phenomenological contents were not confirmed in a subsequent study (Rodriguez Mosquera et al., 2000), these findings seem to suggest an important role for honor and personal achievement in pride, and that collectivism-individualism may be a meaningful dimension on which to compare the experience of pride in different cultures. Both theory and evidence suggest that societies in which individualism prevails, value pride higher than those where collectivism is dominant (Eid & Diener, 2001). The different importance given to the values of honor and personal achievement may be at the basis of these variations in the judgment of pride.

The present research

We wanted to use the GRID data to test whether Northern and Southern Italians differ with respect to the implicit meaning of pride. Italy provides a good opportunity for a case study on the existence of regional differences in the implicit meaning of emotion words. All Italians, nowadays, speak the same language but the process of linguistic unification throughout the country took place only recently. One century ago only a small percentage of Italians could speak Italian, while (regional) dialects were the only languages known and spoken. The diffusion of a common Italian language happened only during the twentieth century and even now more than half of Italians use dialect on some occasions (De Mauro, 2005). In consequence of this only recent linguistic integration, it seems possible that the same Italian emotion word could have slightly different variation in meaning when used by Italians from different regions.

In addition to the linguistic argument, some scholars suggested that Northern and Southern Italians differ with regard to some social and cultural aspects (Galasso, 2002; Putnam, 1993). Southern Italians are stereotypically described as being more religious than Northern Italians (Putnam, 1993), as giving family a central position in their lives, and as being more "emotional" and expressive (Galasso, 1997; Pennebaker, Rimé, & Blankenship, 1996). Emotions, indeed, were typically indicated as one of these elements that vary between Northern and Southern Italians, and some studies documented differences between Northern and Southern Italians with respect to their emotional experience (Galati, 1987; Giovannini & Ricci-Bitti, 1986). In particular, differences have been found for the ability of recognizing emotions – with Northern Italians better able to recognize emotions from bodily cues (Brunori, Ladavas, & Ricci-Bitti, 1979; Giovannini, 1983) – and for emotional antecedents, with Northern Italians more centered on the self and Southern Italians on others and their relationships (Galati & Sciaky, 1995). Most of these differences suggest that, in general, Northern Italians have a culture closer to the individualism pole than the Southern Italians, which are thus closer to the collectivism pole than Northern Italians (for a similar position see, Knight & Nisbett, 2007; Ruggiero, 2001; Ruggiero, Hannöver, Mantero, & Papa, 2000).

Furthermore, Southern Italians give more importance to honor than Northern Italians (Galasso, 1997). On this basis, Southern Italians may be more similar than Northern Italians to other Mediterranean societies in the conceptualization of pride (Fischer et al., 1999). On the contrary personal achievement seems more relevant for individualistic societies (Hofstede, 1984) and thus may be more central for Northern Italians (Galati & Sciaky, 1995).

We adopt a multicomponential perspective to the cross-cultural study of emotions (Eid & Diener, 2001) and we predict that the implicit meaning of the word pride will differ between Northern and Southern Italians in terms of three different emotion components: appraisal, subjective feeling, and emotional expression. First, in terms of appraisal, Southern Italians are supposed to be more other-oriented than Northern Italians, thus more frequently implicating "others" in their evaluations (Galati & Sciaky, 1995). We predict that Northern Italians and Southern Italians will differ for the implicit meaning of pride with regard to the social relevance of the eliciting event of pride. In particular, we predict that Northern Italians usually imply from the word pride that the emotion was elicited by an event that was more relevant for the individual than for the community; on the contrary, for Southern Italians, we expect that the meaning of pride implies an emotion elicited by an event that can be equally relevant for the community and/or the self.

Second, pride was related to a different degree of subjective pleasantness, higher for the individualistic cultures with respect to the collectivistic ones (Fischer et al., 1999; Stipek, 1998). Pride, by focusing on the individual and signaling that the person deserves a higher status in the group, may be more ambivalent in collectivistic societies (Fischer et al., 1999; Rodriguez Mosquera et al., 2000). We hypothesize that, similarly, pride is typically a less positive emotion for Southern Italians than for Northern Italians due to the more other-oriented perspective of the firsts. We expect to find this difference in the description of the prototypical meaning of pride at the level of subjective feeling. We predict that Northern Italians estimate more likely than Southern Italians that when a person uses the word pride, he/she refers to a positive subjective feeling, and that this difference in the prototypical subjective feeling is not due to a difference in the appraisal of intrinsic pleasantness. In other words, we hypothesize that both Northern and Southern Italians assume that the word pride refers to a pleasant event. The different degree of pleasantness appears only at the level of subjective feeling, when other emotion components and cognitive evaluations are involved (i.e., the role of others).

Third, it has been suggested that individuals with an interdependent self would exert more control on the expression of pride. Indeed, as found for Spaniards (Fischer et al., 1999), the expression of pride is less overt in collectivistic societies because of its potential of threatening the harmonious functioning of the society. Similarly, the orientation toward others, which is supposedly more present in Southern Italians than in Northern Italians, should be reflected in a different regulation of the expression. We predict that Southern Italians consider more likely than Northern Italians, that pride implies control of the nonverbal expression.

Method

The GRID questionnaire was administered to psychology students of three different Italian universities: two for Northern Italy, University of Turin (n = 168) and University of Bologna (n = 122) – and one for Southern Italy, University of Bari (n = 191). Each participant rated four emotion terms on the 144 items of the questionnaire. For the current research we retained only those participants who rated the word *orgoglio* (pride), yielding a total of 78 respondents (Southern Italy, n = 29; Northern Italy, n = 49).

In order to test our predictions, we considered 13 items of the GRID questionnaire, and, based on them, we computed five variables specifically defined for the testing of our hypotheses (see Table 24.1).

We considered six items related to the Appraisal component. Two items referred to the relevance of the eliciting event for the individual's goals (*i10*) and for those of someone else (*i11*). For testing our first hypothesis, we calculated a variable, *Personal Relevance* (computed as *i10 − i11*, see Table 24.1), that is a measure of how much the prototypical eliciting event implied in pride is specifically relevant for the individual. Positive values indicate that the prototypical elicitor of pride is something more relevant for the goals of the person than for those of someone else – the opposite

Table 24.1 List of GRID items used in the current research and emotional component to which they pertain

Emotion component	Item number	Study variable	Item
Appraisal			
	i6	Pleasantness	[. . .] in itself pleasant for the person
	i7	Pleasantness	[. . .] in itself pleasant for somebody else
	i8	Pleasantness	[. . .] in itself unpleasant for the person
	i9	Pleasantness	[. . .] in itself unpleasant for somebody else
	i10	Personal relevance	[. . .] important and relevant for person's goals
	i11	Personal relevance	[. . .] important and relevant for goals of somebody else
Feeling			
	i118	Pleasant feeling	[. . .] felt good
	i121	Pleasant feeling	[. . .] felt at ease
	i123	Unpleasant feeling	[. . .] felt negative
	i128	Pleasant feeling	[. . .] felt positive
	i133	Unpleasant feeling	[. . .] felt bad
Regulation*			
	i140	Control	[. . .] showed the emotion to other less than s/he felt it
	i141	Control	[. . .] hid the emotion from others by smiling

Note: *Regulation is seen as a moderator of other components.

for negative values. Four items referred to the appraisal of the intrinsic pleasantness of the eliciting event (*i6*, pleasantness for the person; *i7*, pleasantness for somebody else; *i8*, unpleasantness for the person; *i9*, unpleasantness for somebody else). We calculated a single variable, *Pleasantness* (computed as: $(i6 - i8) + (i7 - i9)$, see Table 24.1), that takes into account the pleasantness of the eliciting event for both the self and the others as it was supposed by the raters. Higher values correspond to higher estimation of pleasantness of the prototypical eliciting event.

Five items were taken from the section of the GRID related to the subjective Feeling component of emotion (see Table 24.1). These five items were the ones that had the highest correlation (either negative or positive) with the VALENCE dimension in the analysis reported by Fontaine and colleagues (2007).[6] Three of these items correlated with similar negative strengths to the VALENCE dimension (*i118*, felt good; *i121*, felt at ease; *i128*, felt positive) and they were added to compute a single variable: *Pleasant Feeling*. High values indicate that the meaning of the emotion word typically refers to pleasant subjective feelings. Two other items correlated with similar positive strengths to the VALENCE dimension (*i123*, felt negative; *i133*, felt bad) and they were added to compute a single variable: *Unpleasant Feeling*. High values indicate that the meaning of the emotion word typically refers to unpleasant subjective feelings. We decided to keep pleasantness and unpleasantness separated for the Feeling component, because, beside positive and negative, an emotion can be conceived as neutral in VALENCE (both variables close to the central value of their

---

[6] The strength of the correlations can be found in Fontaine et al., (2007; see Table 24.1, pp. 1052–1054).

range) or as an ambivalent emotion state (both variables with values higher than the central value of their range).

The last two items were related to the likelihood of implying down-regulation strategies of expression in the meaning of pride, namely, "to show the emotion less than what was really felt" (*i139*), and to "hide it by smiling" (*i140*); a fifth variable, *Control*, was computed by adding these two items. High values indicate that the meaning of the emotion word implies that it is likely that people try to conceal the emotion expression.

Results

Means and standard deviations of the GRID items considered in the present study, organized by Region (North vs South), are reported in Table 24.2. Means and standard deviations of the five variables used to test our predictions are reported in Table 24.3, organized by Region.

Table 24.2 Means and standard deviations of the GRID items used in the current study in the North and in the South samples

Item	North (n = 49)		South (n = 29)	
	Mean	SD	Mean	SD
i6	6.73	2.23	5.66	2.45
i7	5.39	2.29	5.34	2.09
i8	3.63	2.51	4.1	2.58
i9	3.96	2.33	4.59	2.68
i10	6.96	2.25	6.07	2.58
i11	5.02	2.63	5.66	2.18
i118	7.33	2.34	5.72	3.05
i121	6.78	2.32	5.14	2.96
i123	3.14	2.46	4.38	3.06
i128	7.47	1.78	5.1	3.14
i133	2.78	1.78	3.66	2.61
i140	5	2.48	5.62	2.34
i141	5.02	2.86	5.38	2.72

Table 24.3 Means and standard deviations of the five variables used in the present study for the North and the South samples

Variable	Computation	North (n = 49)		South (n = 29)	
		Mean	SD	Mean	SD
Personal relevance	i10 – i11	1.94	2.50	0.41	3.03
Pleasantness	(i6 + i7) – (i8 + i9)	4.53	6.39	2.31	4.94
Pleasant feeling	i118 + i121 + i128	21.57	5.90	15.97	7.77
Unpleasant feeling	i123 + i133	5.92	3.49	8.03	5.15
Control	i140 + i141	10.02	4.17	11.00	4.34

24.3 **The relevance of the antecedents of pride**[7]

Our first hypothesis was that Southern Italians and Northern Italians would have partly different prototypical representations of the eliciting event of pride, especially in terms of its relevance. Accordingly, Northern Italians reported significantly higher value (M = 1.94; SD = 2.50) than Southern Italians (M = 0.41; SD = 3.03) for the personal relevance of the typical eliciting event implied from the meaning of pride (see Table 24.3; *Personal Relevance*; MD = 1.52; SE = 0.63; $t(76) = 2.41$, $p < 0.05$). Higher values indicated that the meaning of pride implies an eliciting event appraised as more pertinent to the goals of the individual who experiences pride than to those of someone else. For Northern Italians, the event that is prototypically implied by pride is something relevant for the person with no particular consideration of the event's relevance for others; Southern Italians, on the contrary, did not make this distinction and rated approximately the same the likelihood that the prototypical eliciting event implied by pride is relevant for the person or for someone else. This finding is in line with the hypothesis that Southern Italians are in general more other-oriented than Northern Italians. In collectivistic societies, pride is especially well accepted when it is experienced and shown as a consequence of an event that benefits the group (or the community) to which the person belongs (Stipek, 1998). The difference we found between the prototypical meaning of pride for Northern and Southern Italians may reflect this belief, that for the latter the personal achievement is typically beneficial for the others too. Noticeably, the difference is not the agency at the basis of the success – for both Northern and Southern Italians, pride usually implies an event caused by the individual's behavior (see footnote 6) – but its relevance, more focused on the individual for Northern Italians. Current findings suggest that Southern Italians give more importance to group and societal bonds as elements prototypically implied in pride.

24.4 **The pleasantness of pride**

Our second hypothesis was that Northern and Southern Italians would differ in their prototypical representation of the subjective feeling that is implied by the word pride.

In terms of subjective feeling, Northern Italians, as predicted, reported that the word pride typically stands for an experience that is very likely related to pleasant feelings (see Table 24.2 and Table 24.3) while Southern Italians rated this likelihood significantly lower (see Table 24.3; *Pleasant Feeling*; MD = 5.60; SE = 1.56; $t(76) = 3.60$, $p < 0.01$). Accordingly, the likelihood that the word pride typically refers to an experience related to unpleasant feelings was rated lower by Northern Italians than by Southern Italians (see Table 24.3; *Unpleasant Feeling*; MD = 2.12; SE = 0.98; $t(76) = 2.16$, $p < 0.05$). Subjective feeling supposedly integrates all the other emotion components, being

---

[7] We conducted a preliminary control analysis for the kind of pride that the two groups rated. A different level of collectivism and individualism in the two cultural groups could have led the two groups to rate two different forms of pride, that is, group pride and individual pride. The difference between the two kinds of pride lays in the agency, that is, whether the responsibility for the successful event is attributed to the individual's behavior or to someone belonging to the in-group. For this reason, we compared the two groups for the items concerning agency (i13, "[. . .] caused by the person's own behavior," and i14 "[. . .] caused by someone else's behavior") and we did not find any significant difference between the two groups (*i13*: North, Mean = 6.57; SD = 2.24; South, Mean = 6.17; SD = 2.38; *i14*: North, Mean = 5.24 SD = 2.20; South, Mean = 5.45; SD = 2.20). Both groups rated more likely that the word pride refers to an emotion due to an event caused by the person's behavior: for both groups, pride is typically due to personal achievement.

the component corresponding to the emotional quality perceived by the subject (Scherer, 2001). Even though the subjective feeling typically implied by pride is pleasant for both groups, Northern Italians use the word pride to refer to an emotion exclusively related to subjective pleasant feelings; Southern Italians, conversely, estimate the presence of pleasant feelings only slightly more likely than the presence of unpleasant feelings. The different degree of pleasantness of the subjective feeling inferred from Northern and Southern Italians suggests that in the two Italian regions people see the prototypical meaning of pride as qualitatively different. Northern Italians conceived pride as a desirable positive emotion as it is typical for most Western individualistic societies (Eid & Diener, 2001). On the contrary, Southern Italians did not exclude the presence of negative feelings in the prototypical experience of pride – which, nevertheless, remains positive – as it could be expected for individuals who have a more other-oriented perspective (Fischer et al., 1999; Rodriguez Mosquera et al., 2000; Stipek, 1998). If pride is due to personal achievement, a proud person, typically, demands to be regarded as someone who deserves higher social recognition than what he or she has: individuals who are more other-oriented could fear that asking for this status recognition could lead to social rejection if the request appears unjustified. Southern Italians may be more concerned by the reactions of others, thus including in the prototypical representation of pride negative feelings due to the social risks intrinsic to showing pride to other members of the in-group.

An alternative explanation for this finding would be that the difference in the prototypical subjective feeling is due to a dissimilar prototypical appraisal of intrinsic pleasantness. Indeed, legitimately, one could argue that Southern Italians included in the typical meaning of pride, its use for preserving honor, which is a more salient value for Southern Italians (Galasso, 1997). If this is the case, the more likely presence of unpleasant feelings would be due to the fact that Southern Italians considered possible that the eliciting event of pride was negative (as it is the case when pride happens in response to threats to one's honor). We investigated this hypothesis by analyzing the prototypical appraisal of intrinsic pleasantness in Northern and Southern Italians. Coherently with our explanation, we hypothesized that for both Northern and Southern Italians the prototypical event implied by pride was a positive event, that is, a personal achievement. The analysis confirmed that for both Southern and Northern Italians pride typically implies an intrinsically pleasant eliciting event with no difference between the two groups (see Table 24.3; *Pleasantness*; MD = 2.22, SE = 1.38; $t(76)$ = 1.61, *n.s.*). This finding confirms that the typical elicitor of pride is a positive event (achievement) for Southern Italians too: the difference in the rating of the prototypical subjective feeling of pride, thus, does not seem due to a different prototypical pleasantness of the eliciting event implied by pride. We speculate that a purely positive subjective feeling is considered less likely by Southern Italians, because they include in the representation of pride concerns about potential negative reactions of other members of the in-group.

24.5 **Regulation of pride**

Our third hypothesis concerned the difference between Northern and Southern Italians in the expected degree of regulation of the expression implied by pride. Even though Southern Italians seemed to imply a little more control in the expression of pride, there was no significant difference with Northern Italians (see Table 24.3; *Control*; MD = 0.98, SE = 0.99; $t(76)$ = 0.99, *n.s.*). Previous studies hypothesized that the expression of pride is more controlled in collectivistic societies than in individualistic cultures (Fischer et al., 1999). Contrarily to this hypothesis, we did not find a similar difference between Northern and Southern Italians in our current analysis of the prototypical meaning of pride. For both groups, the meaning of pride does not necessarily imply hiding or deintensifying the expression. We can suggest two possible explanations. A first explanation would be that the meaning of pride does not include any clear and established indication regarding the regulation of its expression (neither exaggeration nor suppression). In other words, it would still be possible that Italians regulate their expression when they are feeling pride, but there is not a socially shared normative prescription at this regard that has become part of the prototypical meaning of pride. Furthermore, this potential regulation of expression can be different between Northern and Southern Italians: for example, Southern Italians may be more sensitive to contextual information. A second explanation is that the experience of pride is socially accepted in both groups and thus the expression, as it could be implied from the meaning of pride, does not need to be regulated.[8] From this perspective, then, both groups can be seen closer to the individualistic pole than to the collectivistic one.

It is worth mentioning, however, that our variable measured whether Southern and Northern Italians differed in terms of the control exerted on the expression that could be implied from the meaning of pride, and not whether the two groups implied a different expressive behavior. Thus, it is still possible that the two groups, from the word pride, imply a different expressive behavior that is not regulated in both groups.

24.6 **Conclusion**

Previous research indicated that Northern and Southern Italians do not have exactly the same emotional culture (Galati & Sciaky, 1995; Giovannini & Ricci-Bitti, 1986; Pennebaker et al., 1996); we investigated whether these differences can be found in the case of pride and if they are similar to those found when comparing cultures positioned differently on the individualism–collectivism dimension (Hofstede, 1984; Markus & Kitayama, 1991). We predicted differences between Northern and Southern Italians in the meaning of pride for three emotion components: appraisal, subjective feeling and regulation of expression. In terms of appraisals, results confirmed that Southern Italians considered more likely than Northern Italians an eliciting event with positive consequences that was relevant for someone different from the individual. This suggests that Southern Italians are similar to other cultures (Spaniards) that consider the other members of the in-group in their prototypical appraisals of pride. Our prediction was confirmed for subjective feeling too: Southern Italians implied more negative feelings from the meaning of pride, while Northern Italians considered pride a clearly pleasant emotion. Contrary to our third prediction, the negative feelings implied by the meaning of pride, were not associated with a higher expectation of regulation strategies by Southern Italians.

All in all, we can conclude that, even though the meaning of pride is largely the same for the two groups, some differences exist. Such differences can be explained on the basis of a more diffused other-oriented perspective among Southern Italians, one of the traits more typical of a collectivistic culture. However, we cannot claim that Northern Italians have an individualistic culture and Southern Italians a collectivistic one. This for three reasons: first, we did not test directly the difference between Northern and Southern Italians in terms of individualistic or collectivistic traits; second, the literature is too scarce for affirming undoubtedly that Northern Italians and Southern Italians are examples, respectively, of individualistic and collectivistic cultures; third, our

[8] This hypothesis seems supported by the responses to the item 144 of the questionnaire. This item concerned the social acceptance of the emotion (i144, "To what extent is it socially accepted to experience this emotional state in your society"). For both Northern (M = 6.55, SD = 1.96) and Southern Italians (M = 6.34; SD = 1.99) pride is a socially well-accepted emotion.

results indicate that also for Southern Italians the meaning of pride has aspects more typical of an individualistic perspective than a collectivistic one (the absence of regulation strategies and the social acceptance implied in the meaning of pride). We would rather suggest that the differences between the two groups are better explained by some specific values (e.g., the importance of the family, the consideration of others in their judgments) rather than an abstract counter-position of individualism with collectivism.

Two methodological considerations can be drawn from the current results. First, cultural differences may be found in terms of emotion components (Eid & Diener, 2001); the GRID questionnaire showed its suitability to perform this fine-grained investigation of prototypical meaning of emotion words. In our current study, differences between Northern and Southern Italians in the implicit prototypical meaning of pride for the Feeling component were not related to a difference for the Appraisal component (namely, intrinsic pleasantness). This shows the importance of adopting a multi-componential approach to emotion research, because each component reflects only one element of the whole emotional episode, and differences in one component are not necessarily replicated in other components (Eid & Diener, 2001; Scherer, 2001). This is especially true for subjective feeling, which integrates all the other components, and thus it is the result of multiple complex interactions between the different components. Second, the fact that we found differences in meanings, despite their evident similarity, indicates how important it is to consider cultural groups on the basis of other criteria than nationality. What we found for Italians – same emotion word, slightly different emotional implications from its meaning – may be found for other countries where, even if the language is the same, regional differences may be present because of historical reasons.

At least two limitations of the current research should be mentioned. First, a common limitation of all studies conducted with questionnaires conducted with is the fact that they are based on people's knowledge about emotions, thus stereotypes may play a role in describing prototypical aspects of emotions. Nevertheless, we think that finding differences in meaning reflects a cultural variability at least in terms of social normative evaluation of what is expected to elicit a particular emotion and/or how it is typically experienced and or expressed. Second, our analyses were based on few ad hoc variables, which disregarded most of the information that is made available by the GRID questionnaire. Focusing only on these variables may mislead toward the over-estimation of the differences that exist between the two groups. We were aware of this limitation but our goal was to analyze a very specific object in terms of very fine-grained elements: the identification of such differences required such a tailored approach.

Future studies should compare the descriptions of the meaning of pride with the reports of concrete personal experiences of pride. In other words, it would be interesting to check the degree of correspondence between frozen representations of affect, as it is the prototypical meaning of emotion word, and specific experiences. Future research should also compare different groups on the basis of some specific values (e.g., personal achievement, honor) or cultural traits (e.g., orientation toward others) going beyond broad categorizations – for example, collectivistic vs individualistic cultures – when analyzing cultural variations of self-conscious emotions. For these emotions, single values, like honor and personal achievement, may play a bigger role than general cultural orientations.

Chapter 25

The meaning of pride across cultures

Yvette M. J. van Osch,[1] Seger M. Breugelmans, Marcel Zeelenberg, and Johnny J. R. Fontaine

The emotion literature suggests that we by now have a pretty good picture of what characterizes the emotion pride. We experience the social emotion pride when we compare ourselves to others after an achievement or the acquirement of desired resources (Tracy & Robins, 2007b). Pride temporarily enhances our feeling of social self-worth and status (Leary, 2007). It motivates us to show a more dominant posture, to draw social attention to achievements, and to put effort in maintaining or even extending the achievement and its positive social consequences (Fredrickson, 2001; Kövecses, 1986; Williams & DeSteno, 2008). However, it may be questioned whether these characteristics are universal across cultures. There have been various suggestions in the cross-cultural literature to the effect that this is not the case. In the current chapter, we use the GRID data to test several hypotheses about cross-cultural differences in pride.

The social aspect of pride is especially important for cross-cultural differences (Kitayama, Markus, & Kurokawa, 2000). On the one hand, pride can be a pleasant emotion (positive VALENCE) because it generally arises from situations that have positive outcomes for oneself. On the other, pride can be a negative, socially disruptive emotion because it distinguishes oneself from other people. It has been argued that cultures that emphasize the autonomy of the individual or the uniqueness of the self (e.g., individualist, or independent cultures) tend to focus on the positive aspects of pride, resulting in an evaluation of this emotion as pleasurable and desirable (Markus & Kitayama, 1991). Cultures that emphasize the social embeddedness of the individual (e.g., collectivist or interdependent cultures) tend to focus on the socially disruptive aspect of pride, resulting in an evaluation of this emotion as undesirable. Pride can thus be seen as either a socially engaging or disengaging emotion, dependent on the construction of the self as either independent or interdependent (Kitayama, Markus, & Matsumoto, 1995).

There is scant empirical evidence for the view that in Asian (interdependent) cultures pride is seen as a more negative and undesirable experience than in Western (independent) cultures. The clearest support comes from a study by Stipek (1998). She found that: "Chinese respondents had a negative view of experiencing and expressing pride in personal accomplishments (...) In contrast, American respondents valued pride and did not, on average, agree that it was inappropriate to experience or express pride in personal accomplishments" (p. 626). Chinese respondents did feel positively toward experiencing pride for achievements that benefit others. A drawback of Stipek's study is that it focused mainly on cross-cultural differences in *antecedents* of pride, the type of events that elicit pride, rather than those concerning the *meaning* of emotion terms. Antecedents

---

[1] Correspondence can be addressed to Yvette van Osch, Tilburg University, Department of Social Psychology, P.O. Box 90153, 5000 LE, Tilburg. The Netherlands. E-mail Y.M.J.vanOsch@uvt.nl

do not necessarily say much about the meaning of the emotion pride or about the way pride is experienced or expressed. Another study by Scollon, Diener, Oishi, and Biswas-Diener (2004) also argued that "pride may be considered pleasant or unpleasant in particular cultures" (p. 321). They found that pride clustered with negative instead of positive emotions for respondents from India. However, this was not the case for respondents from Japan and the United States (US), two groups that should differ on the basis of cross-cultural theories about self-construal. So, it can be tentatively concluded that *theoretically* various differences have been suggested in the meaning of pride across cultures (e.g., Markus & Kitayama, 1991; Kitayama, Markus, & Matsumoto, 1995), but that there is still a lack of *empirical* evidence supporting this claim.

On the basis of cross-cultural studies on emotion experience there is actually little reason to expect broad cross-cultural differences in pride. Many studies have shown very limited cross-cultural variation in the experience of emotions (Matsumoto, Nezlek, & Koopmann, 2007; Scherer & Wallbott, 1994; Wallbott & Scherer, 1986). Many emotion characteristics, such as appraisals (Scherer, 1996), phenomenology (Breugelmans & Poortinga, 2006; Fontaine et al., 2006), body sensations (Breugelmans et al., 2005), facial expressions (Ekman, 1994; Matsumoto et al., 2008), and nonverbal expressions (Tracy & Robins, 2008) show notable cross-cultural similarities. Those differences that are found tend to be item specific or situation specific (e.g., display rules; Ekman, 1973). The discrepancy between these studies and the theoretical expectations with regard to cultural differences in pride, calls for a more thorough analysis of cross-cultural variation in this emotion. The GRID data set provides a unique opportunity for such an analysis.

We investigated the extent of cultural variation in the meaning of pride at three different levels of analysis. At the *Emotion Dimension Level*, we explored the data for cross-cultural similarities and differences at the level of the four basic dimensions of emotional space. These dimensions are VALENCE, POWER, AROUSAL, and NOVELTY (Fontaine, Scherer, Roesch, & Ellsworth, 2007; see Chapter 7). We used several country level indices (see method section of the current chapter) to predict the factor scores of pride from each sample on the four emotion dimensions. Factor scores are the correlations between the variable (i.e., the item; in this case the country level indices) and the factor (i.e., underlying dimension; in this case one of the four emotion dimensions that underlie all emotional meaning). Higher factor scores indicate that an item is stronger related to the emotion dimension; alternatively, it could be said that the higher the factor score of an item, the better it represents the emotion dimension. The most important dimension for potential cross-cultural differences would be the first dimension of VALENCE (positive–negative). Based on cultural theory, it could be expected that a strong endorsement of individualism, which corresponds with an independent self-construal (Oyserman, Coon, & Kemmelmeier, 2002), is related to a more positive meaning of pride. Cultures high in individualism endorse the distinctness of an individual, allow people to "do their own thing," and make the leaving and finding of in-groups easier (Triandis, Bontempo, Villareal, Asai, & Lucca, 1988). Because pride is associated with distinguishing oneself from the in-group, in cultures where uniqueness is valued, the word pride is expected to have a more positive association, than in cultures where conformity is valued. This should express itself as a higher factor loading for pride on the VALENCE dimension for cultures scoring high on individualism.

At the *Pride Aspect Level*, we identified specific items that are most relevant to the emotion pride. The GRID project is aimed at a broad selection of emotions, including 144 emotion features to study 24 emotion terms. Not all 144 emotion features are equally relevant for pride. We selected 22 items that are most relevant for this emotion (see Table 25.1). Item selection was based on an extensive literature review. Pride results from meaningful achievements that are attributed to the self (Leary, 2007; Shaver, Schwartz, Kirson, & O'Connor, 1987), leading to the selection of the items

Table 25.1 Centered mean scores on the 22 pride items for the samples from the US and Japan

Item	US	Japan	Mean difference
Felt in control	1.45	1.51	−0.06
Tried to control intensity of the emotional feeling	−0.28	0.01	−0.29
Consequences able to live with	0.68	0.63	0.05
Center of attention	1.58	1.51	0.07
Important and relevant for person's goals	1.40	1.48	−0.08
Smiled	1.89	1.99	−0.10
Felt positive	1.80	1.41	0.39
Wanted to sing and dance	1.38	0.84	0.54
Wanted the ongoing situation to last or be repeated	1.57	0.42	1.15
Showed the emotion to others less than (s)he felt it	−0.08	0.08	−0.16
Felt good	1.75	1.93	−0.18
Showed the emotion to others more than (s)he felt it	0.88	0.65	0.23
Consequences positive for person	1.30	1.78	−0.48
Moved toward people or things	0.92	−0.47	1.39
Felt powerful	1.78	1.70	0.08
Wanted to show off	1.89	2.06	−0.17
Felt energetic	1.50	1.25	0.25
Wanted to be seen, to be the center of attention	1.91	2.06	−0.15
Felt strong	1.64	1.25	0.39
Had an assertive voice	1.29	1.49	−0.20
Felt dominant	1.77	1.64	0.13
Caused by the person's own behavior	1.25	0.59	0.66

"important and relevant for a person's goals," "felt in control," and "caused by the person's own behavior." People generally feel good about themselves and feel positive about the future when they experience pride (Herrald & Tomaka, 2002; Stipek, 1998; Tracy & Robins, 2007b), leading to the selection of the items "smiled," "felt positive," "felt good," "consequences positive for the person," "consequences able to live with," and "wanted to sing and dance." Pride makes people want to communicate their achievement to others in order to attain status (Leary, 2007; Tracy & Robins, 2007b), leading to the selection of the items "felt dominant," "had an assertive voice," "felt strong," "wanted to show off," "felt powerful," "wanted to be seen," "to be the center of attention," "showed the emotion to others more (and less) than (s)he felt it," "center of attention," "tried to control the intensity of the emotional feeling," and "felt energetic." Pride motivates achievement (Herrald & Tomaka, 2002; Higgins et al., 2001; Verbeke, Belschak, & Bagozzi, 2004; Williams & DeSteno, 2008), and social behavior (Boezeman & Ellemers, 2007; Hart & Matsuba, 2007; Tracy & Robins, 2004b), leading to the selection of the items "wanted the ongoing situation to last or be repeated", and "moved toward people or things."

From a subset of these items we constructed three scales of aspects of pride that, based on theory, are expected to differ across cultures (see method section of the current chapter). First, we composed a *Positivity* scale because the VALENCE of pride is said to differ across cultures (e.g., Scollon et al., 2004). Second, we composed a *Perception of Control* scale because the responsibility for an event is crucial in the elicitation of pride, and is suggested to differ across cultures. For instance, Americans mostly report pride for achievements they themselves controlled (i.e., caused), whereas Chinese also report instances in which the achievement was controlled by someone else (Stipek, Weiner, & Li, 1989). Third, we composed an *Expressivity* scale because cultural norms on the expression of pride are said to differ across cultures (Matsumoto et al., 2008) and are thought to affect pride. Markus and Kitayama (1991) hypothesized that in interdependent cultures the expression of pride may be avoided because it could be interpreted as being proud of one's unique attributes, which is contrary to the ideology of an interdependent culture. Thus, theory would predict cultural differences on all three scales, mainly along the dimensions of individualism; cultures low on individualism should lead to experiences of pride that are less positive, less controllable, and with less expression.

At the *Individual Item Level* we searched for clusters of countries on the basis of their scores across the 22 selected pride items. Thus, we tried to cluster countries according to their pattern of scores on the pride-relevant items. If cross-cultural differences are systematic, we would expect countries with a similar culture to cluster together and those with a different culture to appear in different clusters.

At the *Individual Item Level* we also focused on pride as a specific case comparison between the US and Japan and in a second comparison between a cluster of Western and Asian countries. The US and Japan are by far the most studied countries in cross-cultural comparisons of emotion (Van Hemert, Poortinga, & Van de Vijver, 2007) and are often put forward as the prototypes of interdependent and independent cultures (Markus & Kitayama, 1991). Standardized mean scores of both samples on the 22 pride items were probed for differences between these two cultures. Each sample was treated as one observation. On the basis of theory, we again expected pride to be seen as more negative, less controllable, and less desirable to express in Japan than in the US. In the second analysis, we looked at the extent to which differences between the US and Japan can be generalized to differences between Western countries (independent cultures) and East-Asian countries (interdependent cultures). The same differences in pride were expected between these two clusters as between the two countries.

25.1 **Method**

Data from 27 samples in the GRID data file were used: Canada (French), China (Mandarin), the Czech Republic, England, Estonia, Finland, Germany, Greece, Israel, Italy (samples from Bari and Bologna)[2], Japan, the Netherlands, Poland, Russia, Singapore, Slovakia, Spain (the peninsular samples were Spanish from Southern Spain and the Basque Land, and Basque from the Basque Land), Taiwan, Tunisia, Turkey, Switzerland (French and Romanisch), Ukraine, and the United States. Characteristics of the individual datasets can be found in Chapter 6.

Analyses at the *Emotion Dimension Level* and the *Pride Aspect Level* used several country level indices to explain cross-cultural differences in the factor scores of pride on the four overall factors

---

2 Because the samples in this book were treated as independent samples, we also treated all samples as independent, even though some samples were similar in country and language.

of VALENCE, POWER, AROUSAL, and NOVELTY (see Chapter 7). Due to the quasi-experimental nature of cross-cultural designs, any difference between countries can be attributed to a large number of potential cultural characteristics (Van de Vijver & Leung, 1997). In other words, countries often differ on hundreds of characteristics such as economic level, climate, political system, and values. It is unclear which of these characteristics can explain any cross-cultural differences, when found. In order to be more specific in which country characteristics can explain cross-cultural differences in the meaning of the emotion term pride, we included several economic, political, and psychological variables.

As economic variables, we included the Gross Domestic Product (GDP) and the Human Development Index (HDI). We used the GDP per capita (PPP US$) and HDI value over 2005. GDP is a measure for a nation's annual income and output in regard of the economy. The HDI index indicates how "developed" a country is and takes matters such as literacy, education opportunities, life expectancy, and GDP into account. Both indices were obtained from the United Nations Development Programme (2007), which is a report on human development in the period 2007–2008. GDP and HDI measures were not available for Taiwan.

As a political variable, we included the Gender Empowerment Measure (GEM) from the United Nations Development Programme (2007). The GEM indicates the level of inequality in a country, regarding the opportunities men and women have. GEM measures were not available for Taiwan and Tunisia.

As psychological variables, we included the country-level value scores of Hofstede Schwarz values. Five Hofstede (2001) value dimensions were included: Individualism, Masculinity, Uncertainty Avoidance, POWER Distance, and Long Term Orientation. Data were not available for Tunisia and Ukraine. Schwarz values were obtained from the World Value Survey (2005). These values originated from a shortened version of the Portrait Values Questionnaire. For every value, one item was included. Data for Canada, the Czech Republic, Estonia, Greece, Israel, Italy, Singapore, Slovakia, and Tunisia were not available.

At the *Pride Aspect Level*, we constructed three scales, each representing one of the aspects of pride that were expected to differ across cultures. Selection was done from the 22 pre-selected items that were relevant for pride (see introduction). Items were subsequently selected based on the content of the item and its relation to the three aspects. The scales were: (1) *Positivity*, which comprised the items: "felt positive," "felt good," "consequences positive for person," "consequences able to live with," and "important and relevant for person's goals" (Cronbach's α = 0.66); (2) *Perception of Control*, which comprised the items: "felt in control," "felt powerful," "felt energetic," and "felt strong" (α = 0.72); and (3) *Expressivity*, which comprised the items: "wanted to show off," "wanted to be seen," "to be the center of attention," and "showed the emotions to others more than (s)he felt it" (α = 0.73).

25.2 Results

Level 1: Emotion Dimension Level

Inspection of the factor scores for pride on each emotion dimension revealed that pride in all samples was seen as positive (ranging from 0.32 to 1.49) and powerful (0.52 to 2.31). In all but one sample (Turkey) pride was thought of as predictable (−1.56 to 0.05). On the AROUSAL dimension larger variation was found (−1.22 to 0.24); four samples had a positive score on this dimension (the UK, Singapore, Italy [Bari sample], and Israel). This means that pride in all countries was seen as a positive and potent emotion. Pride is generally also seen as an emotion that is predictable and, for most countries, pride is an emotion that is neutral to low in AROUSAL.

Factor scores of pride on each emotion dimension across samples were correlated with the country level indices. GDP showed a significant relation with the AROUSAL dimension, $r(26) = 0.41, p = 0.04$. This means that the higher the GDP of a country is, the higher the AROUSAL is that is associated with pride. So, in wealthy countries people see pride as an emotion with more AROUSAL than people in less wealthy countries. Uncertainty Avoidance also correlated with the AROUSAL dimension, $r(25) = -0.41, p = 0.04$, indicating that the larger the Uncertainty Avoidance is, the less AROUSAL is associated with pride. In other words, the more people rely on rules on how to behave the less AROUSAL they associate with pride. POWER Distance correlated significantly with the VALENCE dimension, $r(25) = -0.53, p = 0.01$; the larger the POWER Distance (i.e., the inequality of POWER relations) in a culture the more pride is seen as a negative emotion. POWER Distance was also correlated with the POWER dimension, $r(25) = 0.42, p = 0.04$; the larger the POWER Distance in a culture the more pride is seen as a powerful emotion. Finally, POWER Distance was negatively correlated with the AROUSAL dimension, $r(25) = -0.42, p = 0.04$; the larger the POWER Distance the less pride is seen as an emotion with high levels of AROUSAL. Correlations among the country level indices were: $r_{GDP-UncertaintyAvoidance}(24) = -0.25, p = 0.25, r_{GDP-PowerDistance}(24) = -0.66, p > 0.001, r_{UncertaintyAvoidance-PowerDistance}(25) = 0.06, p = 0.79$. GDP and POWER Distance were highly negatively correlated, which means that POWER Distance is less strong in more wealthy countries. Uncertainty Avoidance was unrelated to the other two indices. Even though GDP and POWER Distance were highly correlated, their unique variance related in the opposite direction to the AROUSAL dimension.

Level 2: Pride Aspect Level

Inspection of the sample scores on the three pride aspect scales revealed that the largest variation among samples was on the *Expressivity* scale (0.48 to 2.27) followed by the *Positivity* scale (0.81 to 1.80), and the *Perception of Control* scale (1.15 to 1.93). This means that, across countries, most differences are found on the question to what extent pride is an emotion that should be expressed or rather an emotion that should be kept to oneself. Less variation is found on the question whether pride is a positive or negative emotion, and least variation is found on the question whether pride is an emotion that is related to feelings of control.

Two of the three pride aspect scales were correlated to the country level indices. The *Positivity* scale correlated negatively with POWER Distance, $r(25) = -0.40, p = 0.05$, meaning that the larger the POWER Distance in a country the less positive pride feels. This finding is consistent with findings at the *Emotion Dimension Level* where we found that higher POWER Distance was related to a negative score on the VALENCE dimension of emotions. Significant correlations were also found between the *Perception of Control* scale and the Schwartz values of POWER, $r(17) = -0.51, p = 0.04$, and tradition, $r(17) = -0.49, p = 0.05$, indicating that in countries where social status and prestige are valued, or in countries where dominance over people and resources is valued, pride is seen as an emotion that is to a lesser extent under one's personal control. At the *Emotion Dimension Level* we saw that higher scores on POWER Distance were associated with higher scores on POWER. In contrast, at the *Pride Aspect Level* we see an inverse relationship; the more POWER is valued the less control is perceived. In interpreting these seemingly contradictory results, it is good to keep in mind that POWER Distance refers to the perceived inequality of actual POWER relations in a country, whereas the Schwartz value of POWER refers to the extent to which people want to have POWER and social status. In fact, both country level indices were highly negatively correlated, $r_{PowerDistance-Power}(16) = -0.75, p > 0.01$, meaning that people value the possession of POWER and status less in countries in which POWER is more unequally divided. Possibly, this shows that people adapt their aspirations (wanting to obtain POWER) to the reality of their society (the possibility to obtain POWER). In any case, it does explain the inverse relationship between POWER Distance and pride, and Schwartz' value of POWER and pride. No country level indices were related to the *Expressivity* scale.

Level 3: Individual Item Level with country specific comparisons

Hierarchical cluster analysis was used in order to uncover meaningful clustering between samples on the pride items. Hierarchical cluster analysis combines two cases (samples) with the lowest squared Euclidean distances in subsequent steps, and thus seeks out similarity in scores (Norušis, 2008). The analysis starts out by taking each sample as an individual cluster (in this case, 27 different clusters), and in the final step all samples are in one cluster. In essence, this exploratory analysis will tell you to what extent groups of samples score a similar pattern on the items. Our samples were clustered on all 22 pride items (see introduction). The Agglomeration Schedule did not indicate a good solution; the distance statistic showed the largest drop between a solution with 25 and 26 clusters. With 27 samples in total this means that there is little similarity in patterns on these items across samples according to this fit index, and that almost each sample has a unique pattern. However, inspection of the vertical icicle plot and dendrogram, that both indicate the clusters at subsequent steps revealed an interesting pattern for a solution with nine clusters. The vertical icicle plot and dendrogram indicate, at each step, which samples cluster together. The solution with nine clusters consisted of two clusters of countries plus seven individual countries that each formed their own individual cluster (Czech Republic, Tunisia, Slovakia, Canada, Finland, Turkey, and Italy [Bari sample]). When we for the moment ignored these individual countries for the sake of exploring potentially meaningful clusters, we found on the one hand a Western cluster consisting of US, Switzerland (French sample), Germany, Estonia, Italy (Bologna sample), UK, and the Netherlands (listed in order of subsequent steps in the clustering) and on the other hand an East-Asian cluster consisting of Japan, Taiwan, and China. This latter cluster already appeared in a solution with 12 clusters, so it is quite stable. Even though these clusters are not pure the East versus the West (e.g., Singapore [English sample] could also be included in the Western cluster), it does suggest that there may be distinct cultural clusters that have a somewhat different take on what the word pride means. As representatives of the two clusters, we compared the item scores between Japan and the US (see Table 25.1). Inspection of the differences of item mean values suggests that North-Americans see pride as more positive, want the experience to last longer, celebrate it (sing and dance) more, try to socially connect (move toward others) more, and believe that they themselves are more responsible for the event that caused the person to feel pride. On the other hand, the Japanese see consequences of pride as more positive for the person than respondents from the US.

We also looked at whether similar differences in the meaning of pride would emerge if we compared the Western and Eastern clusters that emerged from the cluster analysis. If the differences between the US and Japan represent general cultural differences, we could expect the findings from this comparison to generalize to a comparison between East-Asian and Western cultural clusters. For each cluster, we computed mean scores for all pride items. We used data from the US, Switzerland (French sample), Germany, Estonia, Italy (Bologna sample), UK, and the Netherlands to compute a "Western score," and data from Japan, Taiwan, and China to compute an "Eastern score." Subsequently, we ran a MANOVA with these two clusters as the independent groups and all pride items as the dependent variables. As can be seen in Table 25.2, seven significant differences were found between the clusters on the items "tried to control the intensity of the emotional feeling," "felt positive," "wanted the ongoing situation to last or be repeated," "wanted to show off," "wanted to be seen, to be the center of attention," "felt strong," and "caused by the person's own behavior."

Table 25.2 Centered mean scores on the 22 pride items for a Western (US, Switzerland [French sample], Germany, Estonia, Italy [Bologna sample], UK, and the Netherlands) and an Eastern Cluster (Japan, Taiwan, and China)

Item	Western	Eastern			
	M (SD)	M (SD)	Mean difference	$F(1,10)$	Partial η^2
Felt in control	1.41 (0.23)	1.61 (0.19)	−0.20	1.72	0.18
Tried to control intensity of the emotional feeling	−0.46 (0.34)	0.16 (0.21)	−0.62	8.50*	0.52
Consequences able to live with	0.43 (0.28)	0.67 (0.05)	−0.24	2.15	0.21
Center of attention	1.56 (0.09)	1.55 (0.04)	0.01	0.10	0.01
Important and relevant for person's goals	1.40 (0.13)	1.11 (0.34)	0.29	4.26	0.35
Smiled	1.90 (0.19)	2.02 (0.04)	−0.12	1.10	0.12
Felt positive	1.83 (0.09)	1.32 (0.08)	0.51	72.94***	0.90
Wanted to sing and dance	1.42 (0.27)	1.20 (0.31)	0.22	1.33	0.14
Wanted the ongoing situation to last or be repeated	1.56 (0.019)	0.78 (0.33)	0.78	24.10**	0.75
Showed the emotion to others less than (s)he felt it	−0.04 (0.20)	0.08 (0.17)	−0.12	0.80	0.09
Felt good	1.84 (0.17)	1.66 (0.26)	0.18	1.83	0.19
Showed the emotion to others more than (s)he felt it	0.66 (0.17)	0.55 (0.09)	0.11	0.96	0.11
Consequences positive for person	1.43 (0.17)	1.65 (0.20)	−0.22	3.31	0.29
Moved toward people or things	0.79 (0.25)	0.29 (0.66)	0.50	3.52	0.31
Felt powerful	1.72 (0.16)	1.74 (0.08)	−0.02	0.03	0.00
Wanted to show off	1.63 (0.20)	2.08 (0.05)	−0.45	14.16**	0.64
Felt energetic	1.64 (0.22)	1.42 (0.15)	0.22	2.26	0.22
Wanted to be seen, to be the center of attention	1.73 (0.20)	2.06 (0.01)	−0.33	7.64*	0.49
Felt strong	1.73 (0.15)	1.35 (0.17)	0.38	13.01**	0.62
Had an assertive voice	1.37 (0.20)	1.22 (0.64)	0.15	0.40	0.05
Felt dominant	1.59 (0.27)	1.81 (0.15)	−0.22	1.77	0.18
Caused by the person's own behavior	1.27 (0.14)	0.85 (0.28)	0.42	10.41*	0.57

Note: * $p < 0.05$, ** $p < 0.01$, *** $p < 0.001$

In the Eastern cluster the intensity of pride was controlled more, pride was more associated with showing off and trying to be the center of attention than in the Western cluster. On the other hand, in the Western cluster, pride was felt as a more positive and stronger emotion, it was a desirable emotion that people wanted to last longer or repeat more than in the Eastern cluster. Furthermore, in the Western cluster, pride was more associated with a person having caused his or her own pride than in the Eastern cluster.

A comparison of the results for the US–Japan and East–West comparison shows substantial overlap in the direction of the differences in the pride items. Interestingly, the largest differences are found in the expression of pride. In contrast to what would be expected from the cultural theory of independent and interdependent selves, in the Eastern cluster, pride was associated more with controlling the emotion, showing off and wanting to be the center of attention. The Eastern cluster did rate the experience of pride as being less positive than the Western sample, which is in line with the cultural theory, but it must be noted that the score was still positive (i.e., pride is a positive emotion). These findings are in line with the results from the pride aspects, which indicated that the largest variation was found in the expressive components of pride, not in its experiential components of perceptions of control and positivity.

25.3 **Discussion**

In this study, we explored the GRID data for cross-cultural differences in the meaning of pride that could be expected on the basis of theories of cultural differences. In general, the results of this study are in line with previous cross-cultural studies on emotions (Matsumoto et al., 2007; Scherer & Wallbott, 1994); the meaning of pride shows strong similarities across cultures. Cross-cultural differences, when found, are mostly located in specific items and specific countries. At the level of *Emotion Dimensions* the data showed that people in most countries thought of pride as positive, powerful, predictable, and not very high in AROUSAL. At the *Pride Aspect Level* minor differences were found. Most variation was found in the expressivity of pride. Minor differences were found in the positivity of pride and the perception of control, based on cultural differences in the Schwartz value of POWER or POWER distribution. Cluster analysis at the *Individual Item Level* hinted at a division between Eastern and Western societies. Some differences were found between the US and Japan on individual pride items; these differences tended to generalize to differences between a cluster of Western and Eastern countries. Even though we did find notable differences at item level, it should be noted that differences were only found on seven of the 22 pride items. Thus, the data should not be interpreted in terms of large-scale differences in the meaning of pride. Evidently, the meaning of pride is to a large extent similar across these cultures. Differences are mainly found indicated in the expressive element of pride.

So, how do these results relate to the cross-cultural differences expected on the basis of cultural theories? The answers to these questions are sobering to researchers who assume strong effects of culture on the emotion of pride. Contrary to what was expected, the individualism–collectivism dimension did not relate at all to the evaluation dimension, nor to any of the other emotion dimensions and pride aspects. If anything, POWER Distance was the strongest correlate of cross-cultural differences in pride, both at the level of *Emotion Dimensions* and at the *Pride Aspect Level*. At the level of individual pride items, more differences were found, albeit in a minority of the comparisons (i.e., 7 out of 22). In line with cultural theories, pride was found to be less positively evaluated in Eastern than in Western cultures (though still positive in an absolute sense). However, most differences were found in items related to expressivity. Surprisingly, Eastern samples associated pride with *more* expression (i.e., showing off and wanting to be the center of attention) than Western samples. This would seem to go against what would be expected on the basis of differences between individualism–collectivism and interdependent–independent cultures. Maybe it is exactly because pride is more expressive in Eastern countries that it is evaluated a bit less positively, but the size of the differences, in any case, does not warrant the expectation of large cross-cultural differences in the meaning of this emotion.

Our findings have implications for theoretical expectations about cross-cultural differences in emotions. In line with numerous studies on the experience of emotions (e.g., Breugelmans & Poortinga, 2006; Matsumoto, Nezlek, & Koopmann, 2007; Scherer & Wallbott, 1994; Wallbott & Scherer, 1986), we found that the characteristics of the emotion pride are to a very large extent universal. Any cross-cultural differences in pride are culture specific and item specific. This implies that theories on cross-cultural differences in emotion should be mainly concerned with a detailed level of emotion. By this, we mean that the cross-cultural variation should be searched for in specific items and specific situations. For example, pride may be experienced and expressed similarly across cultures, but the antecedents of pride as well as its specific behavioral expression may be affected by cultural situation-specific normative scripts (e.g., Yamagishi, Hashimoto, & Schug, 2008). Theories of broad cultural differences in emotion appear to have little rationale in empirical data. This is good news for emotion psychologists in general. Studies of the experience and function of emotions in one cultural setting are most likely to also bear validity for other cultural settings. Of course, this message should not be taken as a licence to conveniently ignore culture in emotion studies. Minor cross-cultural differences in the antecedents or experience of emotion can have major consequences for behavior as well as intercultural communication (Berry, Poortinga, Breugelmans, Chasiotis, & Sam, 2011).

One of the surprising findings of this study is that not individualism–collectivism, but rather POWER Distance is the most important dimension in cross-cultural differences in the meaning of pride. The greater the acceptance of POWER-inequality of a nation, the more negative pride is experienced. These findings seem to link to the idea that control and POWER are important aspects of pride (Lazarus, 1991a). How exactly cultural variables of control and POWER are related to pride is still unknown. We can only speculate that maybe the level of POWER-inequality of a country dictates the way pride is supposed to be experienced. For example, in a country where only a small percentage of the nation has most of the POWER, and where the majority will have no choice but to conform, people would not feel safe or comfortable to distinguish oneself from the group and become visible for the superior minority. Pride, almost by definition distinguishes oneself from the group, which in such societies can be an uncomfortable feeling, leading to insecurity. In any case, the dominance of POWER Distance suggests that any cross-cultural differences in emotion may not have so much to do with a focus on the individual or the collective, but rather with the social stratification and opportunities for social mobility in a country. This strongly suggests that comparisons between East-Asia and Western countries (notably the US) that are so pervasive in the cross-cultural emotion literature are not the best if we are to look for cross-cultural differences. A broader scope on the range of countries that are included in cross-cultural comparisons may open interesting new avenues for the development of theories regarding the relationship between culture and emotion.

One potential limitation of the GRID data file, and hence of the analyses that have been reported in this chapter, is that pride was studied by means of a single emotion term. Some languages distinguish between two terms that have different meanings and stand for two "types" of pride (Tracy & Robins, 2007b). First, pride can be seen as authentic pride, which is the emotion we have been discussing in this chapter. Second, pride can be seen as hubristic or arrogant pride (e.g., Tissari, 2006). Another distinction is one between a morally good version of pride (e.g., the German term *stolz*), and a morally bad version of pride (e.g., the German term *hochmut*; Mulligan, 2009). For instance, in the Basque language a distinction is made between *harrotasuna* and *harrokeria*. Even though *harrotasuna* is supposed to be the morally good version of pride in Basque, it is related to arrogance and haughtiness, and clusters into a negative-anger cluster of emotion words in a hierarchical cluster analysis (Alonso-Arbiol et al., 2006). The morally bad version of pride is often associated with vanity and narcissism, and is more a trait than a temporarily activated emotion state (Kövecses, 1986). People can act in a way that is vain or narcissistic, but this does not imply experiences of a specific emotion of pride. In this study, we focused on the emotion pride (we assume that the word for pride in other languages used in the GRID questionnaire referred to the emotion word for pride) and thus did not distinguish between the two types of pride. However, for the investigation of pride in countries where there are two words for pride, a distinction might be necessary.

An interesting possibility is that claims with regard to cross-cultural differences in pride are related to the morally distinct types of pride (which are denoted by different terms in other languages). As was stated in the introduction, pride can be a positive emotion (because we gain from pride) as well as a negative emotion (because we set ourselves apart from the group). These two sides show parallels with the distinction between a morally good type and a bad type of pride (for a similar discussion on envy see Van de Ven, Zeelenberg, & Pieters, 2009). So, it could be that the hypothesized cross-cultural differences in pride in the literature are caused by a different focus on different aspects of pride rather than on culturally distinct experiences of the emotion. So, if the word pride in, for instance, Japan is more associated with a negative view on pride, whereas in the US the word pride is more associated with a positive view on pride, then the differences we are talking about are not in emotion phenomenology but in semantics. Even so, the results of our analyses suggest that such semantic differences are restricted to specific items or characteristics of pride, not to the meaning of the emotion in general. A more extensive treatise on the two types of pride can be found in Chapter 24.

What does it mean to be proud? We set out to use the GRID data set to test theories with regard to cross-cultural differences in the meaning of pride. In theory, pride was a prime candidate for cross-cultural differences but we found little evidence for pervasive differences in the meaning of this emotion. POWER Distance (but not individualism–collectivism) was found to relate to cultural variation in emotion dimensions. However, none of the country level indices related to the expressivity of pride, which was the pride aspect that showed the largest cultural variation. Most differences that were found were confined to specific items. So, there may be subtle differences in meaning, but by and large pride refers to a similar emotion across cultural groups.

Acknowledgments

The data reported in this chapter was collected by several collaborators. They have also contributed helpful suggestions to the paper, and we would like to thank them for that. They are listed in alphabetical order (see the author index and list of GRID collaborators in this volume for additional details): Itziar Alonso-Arbiol, Roderick Cowie, Michael Eid, Shlomo Hareli, Ursula Hess, Keiko Ishii, Zoltan Kövecses, Barbara Lewandowska-Tomaszczyk, Marcello Mortillaro, Anna Ogarkova, Nataliya Panasenko, Hu Ping, Anu Realo, Klaus Scherer, Yuh-Ling Shen, Cristina Soriano, Diane Sunar, Heli Tissari, Eddie M. W. Tong, Aïda Zitouni. We thank Phoebe Ellsworth and Athanassios Protopapas for providing us with data from the US and Greece.

Chapter 26

Cultural differences in the meaning of guilt and shame

Mia Silfver-Kuhalampi,[1] Johnny J. R. Fontaine,
Let Dillen, and Klaus R. Scherer

26.1 Guilt and shame in cross-cultural and anthropological theorizing: Contradicting predictions

Ever since Ruth Benedict (1946) hypothesized a distinction between guilt and shame cultures, there has been a longstanding tradition in both anthropology and cross-cultural psychology which assumes that guilt and shame differ between cultural groups (Bierbrauer, 1992; Hofstede, 1980; Markus & Kitayama, 1991; Mead, 1952). Despite this long tradition, no cumulative theorizing and supportive empirical findings have been generated with respect to cultural differences in guilt and shame. Rather on the contrary, opposing hypotheses have been formulated in the literature. For instance, Triandis (1988) and Hofstede (1980) hypothesized that guilt would be more salient in individualistic than in collectivistic cultural groups, but Eid and Diener (2001) hypothesized the reverse. They predicted that guilt would be more salient in collectivistic cultural groups than in individualistic cultural groups.

These inconsistent and sometimes even opposite predictions can be attributed to the different ways in which guilt and shame have been defined and differentiated from one another (Fontaine et al., 2006). According to the hypothesis, which states that guilt is more salient in individualistic cultural groups, guilt and shame are differentiated in terms of an internal versus an external orientation. Guilt would be triggered by a violation of internalized standards, while shame would be triggered by an audience (real or imagined) disapproving one's wrongdoing or norm incompatibility (e.g., Ausubel, 1955; Smith, Webster, Parrott, & Eyre, 2002). Based on this definition, it can indeed be expected that guilt is more salient in individualistic cultural groups, where internalized and personal standards are more salient. Shame would be more salient in collectivistic cultural groups that stress one's relationship with the in-group. However, the currently dominant framework in social and personality psychology differentiates guilt and shame in a very different way. According to this view, guilt would be characterized by an action focus: in guilt the person would be oriented toward restoring the wrong done. In contrast, shame would be characterized by a global negative self-focus: in shame the global self would be experienced as weak and inferior (e.g., Tangney & Dearing, 2002; Tracy & Robins, 2004a). From this line of theorizing it makes no sense

[1] Correspondence concerning this article should be addressed to Mia Silfver-Kuhalampi, Department of Social Research (Social Psychology), Faculty of Social Sciences, P.O. Box 54, Unioninkatu 37, 00014 University of Helsinki, Finland. E-mail: mia.silfver@helsinki.fi.

to expect that shame is more salient in collectivistic cultural groups, or that guilt is more salient in individualistic cultural groups. For guilt there is still a third line of theorizing, namely that guilt would be a communal-oriented emotion (Baumeister, Stillwell, & Heatherton, 1994). Through its reparative action tendency the function of guilt would mainly be to restore interpersonal bonds. If guilt is defined in this way, it makes sense to predict that guilt is more salient in collectivistic cultural groups.

While each of these three previous approaches disagree on the defining and differentiation characteristics of guilt and shame, they do share the expectation that the meaning of guilt and shame is comparable across cultural groups. Cultural differences are only expected in the salience or prevalence of these emotions. The inconsistencies in the anthropological and cross-cultural literature have also been explained in a different way: it has been hypothesized that the very meaning of guilt and shame, and how they are differentiated, differs systematically between cultural groups (e.g., Kitayama, Markus, & Matsumoto, 1995; Mesquita & Karasawa, 2004). In the literature, we identified four such hypotheses which we labeled (1) the embarrassment hypothesis, (2) the defensive reaction hypothesis, (3) the standards and law hypothesis, and (4) interpersonal-orientation hypothesis.

26.2 **The embarrassment hypothesis**

Walbott and Scherer (1995) studied emotional experiences in 37 countries around the world in their project called the International Survey on Emotion Antecedents and Reactions (ISEAR). They found that self-reported shame experiences were more acute/short-lived with less trophotropic AROUSAL (lump in the throat, stomach troubles, crying/sobbing), fewer negative influences on self-esteem and relationships, more laughing/smiling, and a higher felt temperature in cultural groups that were collectivistic, high in POWER distance and high in uncertainty avoidance compared to cultural groups that were individualistic, low in POWER distance, and low in uncertainty avoidance as assessed by Hofstede's cultural value dimensions (1980; 2001). The pattern in cultural groups that were collectivistic, high in POWER distance and in uncertainty avoidance resembles the Western concept of embarrassment, which is characterized by sympathetic nervous system activation and the feeling of being at the center of attention (Miller, 2007). For guilt experiences, Wallbott and Scherer (1995) did not find clear cultural differences. In general, guilt appeared to be a more internal experience that reflected the sense of moral transgression, and was often attributed to the self. Shame experiences were found to be more similar to guilt experiences in cultures that are individualistic and low on POWER distance and low on uncertainty avoidance. Based on these findings, we formulated the embarrassment hypothesis: the meaning of shame is more characterized by embarrassment features in cultural groups that are collectivistic, high in POWER distance, and high in uncertainty avoidance compared to cultural groups that are individualistic, low in POWER distance, and low in uncertainty avoidance.

26.3 **The defensive reaction hypothesis**

In Western theorizing, it has been suggested that shame is likely to lead to defensive reactions, whereas guilt would motivate positive social behaviors (e.g., Joireman, 2004; Tangney & Dearing, 2002). Tangney, Stuewig, and Mashek (2007) argue that the connection between shame and defensive reactions can be explained by the painful nature of shame as a negative self-focused emotion. In order to relieve shame, the shamed individual may externalize the blame or withdraw from the shameful situation. Tangney, Stuewig, and Mashek (2007) propose that "in this way, shamed individuals may regain some sense of control and superiority in their life." However, Kitayama, Markus, and Matsumoto (1995) argue that shame relates to defensive reactions only in individualistic cultures, like the U.S. where an independent sense of self is valued. In individualistic cultures, expressing shame to others can be interpreted as a sign of weakness, because it communicates submission. In cultures where interdependence is valued, expressing shame to others is seen as positive. There the concept of self includes a deep sense of connectedness to others. In other words, people in interdependent cultures may not have a similar "sense of control in their life," nor do they expect to have it. Social hierarchies and submission are not seen as humiliating, but as an essential part of social interaction. Moreover, in many Eastern cultures like China and Japan, expressing anger, in general, is considered as highly inappropriate, because it would disrupt harmonious social interaction (e.g., Markus & Kitayama, 1991). In contrast, in cultures with an independent self-construal, anger is often seen as positive and as a justified way to defend one's individual rights.

Consistent with this idea, Fontaine, Poortinga, Setiadi, and Markam (2002) found that guilt and shame were more closely associated with fear in Indonesia than in the Netherlands, whereas these concepts were considered more related to anger in the Netherlands than in Indonesia. Moreover, there are studies suggesting that shame relates to more positive social behaviors in some cultural contexts than others. Bagozzi, Verbeke, and Gavino (2003) studied Dutch and Filipino salespersons' experiences of shame and found that the emotional shame experience was very similar for both groups (painful, self-focused emotion, felt threat to the core self), but the behavioral reactions to it were different: for Filipino employees shame enhanced customer relationship building, where as for Dutch employees shame diminished it. Similarly, Mesquita and Karasawa (2004) emphasize that in the Japanese culture, shame is seen as a valued emotion, and not a threat to the self-esteem. Experiencing shame is seen as a way to maintain social harmony and develop oneself as a person. In Japan, shame is often accompanied by public expressions and apologizing. One of the most frequent responses in shame situations is *gambaru*, that can be translated as a resolve to self-improvement. In accordance with this, Bear, Uribe-Zarain, Manning, and Shiomi (2009) found that Japanese children were less prone to externalize blame compared to American children, and that shame had a much stronger connection to anger among American than Japanese children. Similarly, Rozin (2003) found that Indians were clearly more likely to agree with the statement "shame is more similar to happiness than to anger" than Americans were. Americans considered shame and anger to be similar, because they are both negatively valenced emotions, whereas Indians considered shame and happiness to be similar, because both have positive effects on social interaction, while anger is socially disruptive.

Based on this line of theorizing and these empirical findings, we formulated the *defensive reaction hypothesis*. We hypothesize that the meaning of shame is defined by the presence of defensive reaction features (externalization/aggression and desire to withdraw) in cultural groups with an independent self-construal, whereas in cultural groups with interdependent self-construal defensive reaction features (externalization/aggression and desire to withdraw) are absent from the meaning of shame (Kitayama, Markus, & Matsumoto, 1995; Mesquita & Karasawa, 2004).

26.4 **The standards-orientation hypothesis**

It has also been hypothesized that guilt varies systematically between cultural groups. Markus and Kitayama have hypothesized in 1991 that the violation of internalized moral and legal norms would be much more central for guilt in Western cultural groups characterized by an independent self-construal than in Eastern cultural groups characterized by an interdependent self-construal.

Thus, guilt would be a more internally-oriented emotion in independent cultural groups compared to interdependent cultural groups. Based on this line of theorizing, we formulated the standards-orientation hypothesis, namely that the meaning of guilt is more defined by the violation of internalized standards and laws in more independent cultural groups.

26.5 The interpersonal-orientation hypothesis

In the same article, Markus and Kitayama (1991) also suggested that guilt is much more focused on interpersonal relationships in cultural groups with an interdependent self-construal compared to cultural groups with an independent self-construal. The interpersonal-orientation hypothesis then states that the meaning of guilt is more defined in terms of interpersonal reparative features in more interdependent cultural groups.

The current study investigates whether the meaning of guilt and shame terms differs systematically between cultural groups as expected by the embarrassment, the defensive reaction, the standards and law, and the interpersonal-orientation hypotheses. Moreover, it will be exploratively investigated whether meaning differences between guilt and shame are found in the overall four-factorial structure of VALENCE, POWER, AROUSAL, and NOVELTY that spans the emotion domain (Fontaine, Scherer, Roesch, & Ellsworth, 2007).

26.6 Method

Samples

Data from 34 samples were used: Belgium, Canada (French), Chile, China, Czech Republic, Estonia, Finland, Germany, Greece, Hong Kong, Israel, Italy Bari, Italy Bologna, Italy Turin, Japan, Myanmar, Peru, Poland, Russia, Singapore, Slovakia, South-Africa (Afrikaans), Spain (Basque), Spain (Spanish North), Spain (Spanish South), Switzerland (French), Switzerland (Romanish), Taiwan, The Netherlands, Tunisia, Turkey, United Kingdom, Ukraine, and the United States. Characteristics of the individual samples are described in Chapter 6.

Emotion features

Out of the 142 emotion features in the GRID, those features that best represented the hypotheses were identified and were aggregated into conceptually coherent feature scales. Two features closely matched the embarrassment hypothesis, namely "center of attention" and "blushed." The embarrassment feature scale had an internal consistency of 0.82 (Cronbach's alpha). Six features closely matched the defensive reaction hypothesis, namely "wanted to do damage, hit, or say something that hurts," "wanted to destroy whatever was close," "wanted to flee," "wanted to disappear or hide from others," "wanted to withdraw into her/himself," and "wanted to run away in whatever direction." As there are conceptually two clearly different aspects involved, namely reacting aggressively and withdrawing, two feature scales were constructed for the defensive reaction hypothesis. The aggression feature scale had an internal consistency of 0.69 and the withdrawing feature scale had an internal consistency of 0.88. Two features corresponded to the standards-orientation hypothesis, namely "incongruent with own standards and ideals" and "violated laws or socially accepted norms." The standards-orientation feature scale had an internal consistency of 0.48. Finally, five features closely related to the interpersonal-orientation hypothesis, namely "in itself unpleasant for somebody else," "consequences negative for somebody else," "wanted to take care of another person or cause," "wanted to tackle the situation," and "wanted to make up for what she or he had done." As the first two features related to a cognitive concern for others and the last three to repara-tive behavior, two feature scales were constructed. The first feature scale had in internal consistency of 0.86 and the latter of 0.73.

Besides these ad hoc constructed feature scales, we also analyzed the scores of guilt and shame on the four overall factors of VALENCE, POWER, AROUSAL, and NOVELTY.

Cultural characteristics

In order to understand which cultural features best explain the possible meaning differences, we used the Hofstede (1980; 2001) cultural dimensions. He proposed five dimensions on which cultures may vary, namely Individualism, POWER Distance, Uncertainty Avoidance, Masculin-ity, and Long-Term Orientation. Individualism–collectivism (IDV; high scores indicate indi-vidualism and low scores indicate collectivism) relates to the degree to which individuals are supposed to look after themselves versus the degree to which they are integrated into in-groups. The POWER Distance dimension (PD) refers to the extent to which a society accepts that POWER is unequally distributed among its institutions and people. Uncertainty Avoidance (UA) de-scribes the extent to which members of a society or culture feel uncomfortable with ambiguous situations. Masculinity–femininity (MAS; high scores mean masculine and low scores mean feminine) indicates the degree to which the dominant values in a society are "masculine" ori-ented (such as assertiveness, money, heroism, achievement) or "feminine" oriented (such as high quality of life, caring for others, maintaining relationships). Long-Term Orientation is not included in this study, as scores for this dimension were lacking for too many countries from our sample. The Hofstede scores were not available from Myanmar, Tunisia, and Ukraine. Val-ues of similar countries were used as proxies for these samples. The values of Russia were used for Ukraine, the values of Arab countries were used for Tunisia, and the values of Thailand were used for Myanmar.

Analyses

A stepwise regression analysis with three steps was applied on each of the six feature scales and each of the four overall factors. In a first step, the (effect-coded) differentiation between guilt and shame was entered as a predictor. In the next step, individualism, POWER distance, masculinity, and uncertainty avoidance were entered as predictors. Only the significant predictors were re-tained using a forward selection procedure. In the final step, the interaction between guilt and shame on the one hand and individualism, POWER distance, masculinity, and uncertainty avoid-ance on the other hand were entered as predictors. Only the significant interaction effects were retained using a forward selection procedure. Note that the hypotheses are only tested in the last step as each of the hypotheses implies that guilt and shame are differentiated differently as a func-tion of cultural characteristics. The results are presented step by step.

26.7 **Results**

Step 1. The average differentiation between guilt and shame terms. Four of the six feature scales differed significantly in the first step. Shame was significantly more related to embarrass-ment ($R^2 = 0.65$, $p <0.001$) and to withdrawal ($R^2 = 0.42$, $p <0.001$) than guilt, and guilt was sys-tematically more related to reparation ($R^2 = 0.54$, $p <0.001$) and to concern for others ($R^2 = 29$, $p <0.001$) than shame was. Guilt and shame did not differ significantly on aggression ($R^2 = 0.00$, $p = 0.720$), nor on standards-orientation ($R^2 = 0.04$, $p = 0.103$).

Guilt and shame differed significantly on all four emotion factors: shame was seen as more negatively valenced ($R^2 = 0.12$, $p = 0.003$), less powerful ($R^2 = 0.23$, $p <0.001$), more activated ($R^2 = 0.25$, $p <0.001$), and especially more unpredictable ($R^2 = 0.47$, $p <0.001$) than guilt.

Step 2. Relations of both guilt and shame with the four Hofstede dimensions. The meaning of both guilt and shame related to cultural characteristics for three of the six feature scales, namely for the withdrawal scale ($\Delta R^2 = 0.04$, $p = 0.036$), the embarrassment scale ($\Delta R^2 = 0.07$, $p <0.001$), and the standards-orientation scale ($\Delta R^2 = 0.36$, $p <0.001$). As the withdrawal scale was also involved in an interaction effect in the third step, we only present here the results for the embarrassment and the standards-orientation scales. It was observed that both guilt and shame related more to embarrassment features in more uncertainty avoidant societies ($\beta = 0.27$, $p <0.001$). Moreover, both guilt and shame were more related to a standards-orientation in more uncertainty avoidant societies ($\beta = 0.33$, $p = 0.002$), but were less related to a standards-orientation in more POWER distant ($\beta = -0.24$, $p = 0.019$), and more masculine ($\beta = -0.40$, $p <0.001$) societies.

None of the four overall emotion factors were related to the Hofstede dimensions.

Step 3. The differential meaning of guilt and shame in relation to the Hofstede dimensions. In the final step, a significant interaction effect was not observed for any of the four emotion factors. A significant interaction effect was observed for two of the six feature scales. A significant interaction effect between guilt/shame and POWER distance was observed for withdrawal ($\Delta R^2 = 0.03$, $p <0.041$) and for interpersonal-orientation ($\Delta R^2 = 0.05$, $p <0.024$). To further explore these significant interaction effects, regression analyses were executed separately for guilt and shame. POWER distance was unrelated to withdrawal for guilt ($\beta = -0.01$, $p = 0.948$), but POWER distance was negatively related to withdrawal for shame ($\beta = 0.56$, $p <0.001$). Thus the more POWER distance, the less withdrawal defined the meaning of shame. The opposite effect was observed for concern for others. POWER distance was not related to concern for others for shame ($\beta = 0.22$, $p = 0.223$), but POWER distance was negatively related to concern with others for guilt ($\beta = -0.35$, $p = 0.046$). In more POWER distant cultural groups, guilt is *less* characterized by concern for others.

26.8 Discussion

The overall differentiation between guilt and shame terms

While guilt and shame are closely related emotion terms, we do confirm a systematic differentiation between the terms on average. Shame was generally seen as a more unpleasant, weaker, higher in AROUSAL, and less predictable emotion than guilt. This is consistent with theories describing shame as more painful and more difficult to manage than guilt (Lewis, 1971; Tangney & Dearing, 2002; Tracy & Robins, 2004a). Moreover, when it comes to the guilt- and shame-specific features, guilt and shame turn out to be strongly differentiated. On one hand, guilt is characterized by more concern for others and especially more reparative behavior. This is in line with the theories that define guilt in terms of a moral focus (Lazarus, 1991a) and consider it as a communal-oriented emotion (Baumeister, Stillwell, & Heatherton, 1994). Guilt is focused on the negative consequences of one's behavior for others much more than shame is, and it is related to a strong tendency to set things right. On the other hand, shame is strongly characterized by its external orientation and the tendency to withdraw. This is in line with the old theorizing of Benedict (1946) and Mead (1952), and more recently of Smith, Webster, Parrott, and Eyre (2002) that consider an external orientation as the central feature of shame.

We find no evidence that guilt is more characterized by a focus on (internalized) standards and norms, as predicted by the old internal-external opposition. Apparently, the fact that the expectation of public exposure defines the meaning of shame does not imply the absence of an awareness of the violation of (internal) standards and norms. Moreover, we find no evidence for the position that the meaning of shame would be more related to aggression as predicted by Tangney and colleagues. Together with the finding that shame is related to a strong external orientation, the present findings question the theory that shame is to be defined in terms of a global negative self-focus. The link with aggression was mainly expected as a defensive reaction against the painfulness of the global negative self-focus in shame. However, as the GRID does not contain emotion features that directly operationalize global negative self-focus, the present study gives only indirect indications about the role of a global negative self-focus in the meaning of guilt and shame.

26.9 **Culturally determined meaning shifts in guilt and shame**

The central research question of the present study was whether the meaning of guilt and shame shifted systematically as a function of cultural-level characteristics. To that end, we derived four hypotheses from the literature, namely the embarrassment, the defensive reaction, the standards-orientation, and the interpersonal-orientation hypotheses.

The embarrassment hypothesis. Based on the research of Wallbott and Scherer (1995), it was hypothesized that shame, but not guilt, would be more related to a public exposure experience in more collectivistic, more uncertainty avoidant, and more POWER distant societies. This was not observed. Still, it was observed that the meaning of *both* guilt and shame related more to an experience of public exposure in more uncertainty avoidant cultural groups. This could mean that the community is more actively involved in imposing rule abidance in highly uncertainty avoidant cultural groups.

The defensive reaction hypothesis. Based on the theorizing that negative self-focus is (more) threatening in cultural groups with an independent self-construal, it was hypothesized that shame would be more related to defensive reactions (externalizing aggressive reactions as well as withdrawal) in individualistic cultural groups than in collectivistic cultural groups. The hypothesis was only partially confirmed: The meaning of shame did not vary systematically in terms of externalizing aggressive reactions, nor did withdrawal reactions relate to individualism–collectivism. The predicted effect was only observed for POWER distance: the more POWER distant a society, the less the meaning of shame is defined by withdrawal tendencies. This is consistent with previous studies suggesting that in some cultural contexts behavioral responses in shame situations are less defensive than in others (e.g., Bear et al., 2009; Bagozzi, Verbeke, & Gavino, 2003).

The standards–orientation hypothesis. Based on the theorizing of Markus and Kitayama (1991) that guilt is more about standards and law violation in cultural groups with an independent self-construal, it was hypothesized that guilt is more defined by a standards–orientation in individualistic cultural groups. This was not observed. It was observed though, that the meaning of both guilt and shame substantially varies in terms of standards–orientation: The more uncertainty avoidant, the less masculine, and the less POWER distant the cultural group is, the more *both* guilt and shame refer to a violation of standards and norms.

The interpersonal–orientation hypothesis. Building on the theorizing of Markus and Kitayama (1991) which assumed that guilt is much more interpersonally oriented in cultural groups with an interdependent self-construal, it was predicted that the meaning of guilt is more related to concern for others and to reparation in collectivistic cultural groups. However, no such effect was observed. Reparative behavior did not relate to cultural characteristics, and moreover, individualism–collectivism was not related to concern for others. Still, guilt did differ systematically in meaning with respect to concern for others: in more POWER distant cultural groups the meaning of guilt was *less* related to concern for others.

While none of the hypotheses was fully confirmed, the present analyses did find evidence for some systematic shifts in meaning of guilt, shame, and their differentiation as a function of cultural characteristics. However, none of the meaning shifts were related to the expected individualism–collectivism dimension. Two cultural dimensions accounted for most of the meaning shifts, namely uncertainty avoidance and especially POWER distance. The present study calls for an extension of our cultural focus beyond individualism–collectivism and the way it is currently elaborated in terms of independent and interdependent construal of the self. Especially the role of POWER distance mirrors the findings in the chapter on pride (see Chapter 25): There it was also found that variations in the meaning of pride did not relate to individualism–collectivism, but to POWER distance. Pride was more negative in high POWER distant cultural groups. Here it is observed that shame is less related to withdrawal and that guilt is less related to concern for others in high POWER distant cultural groups. This seems to indicate that the prototypical meaning of self-conscious emotion terms is coloured by their role in preserving the hierarchical social organization. Personal pride can question the existing hierarchical social order. Moreover, in high POWER distant cultural groups, there is a higher acceptance of hierarchies and being judged by more powerful others is inevitable. It can be hypothesized that guilt and shame are more often elicited or purposefully aroused by others after a breach of the hierarchical social relationships with the goal to align the person's behavior again with his social hierarchical position. In such a context, norm violation neither implies a disadvantaged or hurt person, nor is it functional to withdraw from the social situation.

While we found clear evidence for systematic cultural differences in the meaning of guilt and shame, the size of these differences is mostly small. Six of the 10 features that were investigated were unrelated to the cultural variables. For three of the feature scales, the effects were small. Only for one feature scale, namely standards-orientation, a large cultural effect was observed. These findings indicate that the overall meaning of guilt and shame terms, and how they are differentiated, is stable across cultural groups. Cultural effects do not alter the overall meaning of the terms, but lead to shades of variation with respect to specific meaning features. The present study indicates that the meaning of guilt and shame is by and large comparable across cultural groups.

26.10 **Limitations**

An important limitation of the present study is that it only looked at the meaning of translation equivalent terms for guilt and shame. It did not study the emotion processes themselves. It can therefore not be concluded from the present study that the emotion processes, which are labeled by the terms guilt and shame, truly differ between cultural groups. Genuine differences in the emotion processes form only one possible account for the differences in meaning. Another account could be that the prevalence of the specific events that trigger these emotions differs between cultural groups (e.g., a breach of the hierarchical social order is less likely to occur in more egalitarian societies). These differences in prevalence could get encoded into the prototypical decontextualized meaning of these terms.

Another important limitation is that the GRID features do not operationalize all characteristics that are theoretically deemed important for differentiating guilt from shame, like for instance a global negative self-focus (e.g., Tracy & Robins, 2004a; Tangney & Dearing, 2002). Moreover, most feature scales only relied on two features, which makes the scales sensitive to the specific wording of the features. We thus need further research from various theoretical stances that operationalizes these concepts better in order to fully understand the meaning variations in guilt and shame across cultural groups.

The fact that the GRID only studies differences in action *tendencies*, and not in *actual behavior* can also be considered as a limitation from a culture-comparative point of view. Cultural differences in emotion often appear in the domain of emotion regulation and thus in the behavior that is actually observed (Mesquita & Frijda, 1992). For instance, while no cultural differences in the tendency for defensive aggression were found, it is very well possible that cultural groups differ in the actual display of defensive aggressive behavior.

26.11 **Conclusions**

We can conclude that by and large guilt and shame terms are differentiated in very comparable ways across cultural and linguistic groups, with guilt being characterized by a concern for others and a tendency to set things right, and shame being characterized by a tendency to feel exposed and desire to withdraw from the social situation. At the same time, systematic cultural variation in shades of meaning of guilt and shame terms was revealed. This variation, however, could not be attributed to cultural differences on the individualism–collectivism dimension. The present study calls for a broadening of the theorizing of the cultural characteristics that have an impact on guilt and shame and to the function of these two emotions in different social contexts.

Part VI

Linguistic perspectives

Chapter 27

Comparing the Natural Semantic Metalanguage (NSM) approach to emotion and the GRID paradigm

Zhengdao Ye[1]

27.1 Introduction

Three important starting points of the GRID paradigm are that (a) the words and expressions ordinary people use to talk about their emotional experience are central to emotion research, (b) emotions are multicomponential phenomena, and (c) the study of the commonalities of human emotion should be firmly grounded in cross-cultural research (e.g., Scherer, 2005a, Fontaine et al., 2007). Each of these positions finds strong resonance in the Natural Semantic Metalanguage (NSM) approach to emotion (e.g., Wierzbicka, 1972, 1973, 1986, 1990b, 1992a, 1992c, 1994b, 1995b, 1999a, 2004, 2009; Goddard, 1996, 1997a, 1997b, 2001, 2002a; Harkins & Wierzbicka, 2001; Enfield & Wierzbicka, 2002). The aim of this paper is to compare these two approaches to emotions and explore the possibility of a joint effort between them in the common quest for a better understanding of both the universals and culture-specific aspects of the human emotional experience.

The paper will first introduce the NSM approach to emotion, and then discuss the common ground between the GRID paradigm and the NSM approach, while at the same time pointing out the particular area of emphasis within each of them. This is followed by a discussion of how these two approaches can complement each other in a cross-cultural research setting.

27.2 An overview of the Natural Semantic Metalanguage (NSM) approach to emotion

The NSM approach to emotion is a linguistic approach. It is "linguistic" in two senses. Firstly, its research object is primarily the words and expressions ordinary people use to describe and talk about their emotional experience. Secondly, it uses a method rooted in linguistic semantics, the Natural Semantic Metalanguage theory, to address a key methodological issue in cross-cultural emotion research. That is, how meanings and conceptualizations encoded in emotion words and expressions from different languages can be analyzed with both precision and neutrality. NSM theory is able to tackle the issue because it is the only linguistic theory available that offers a set of empirically established lexical and grammatical universals which are intersections

[1] Zhengdao Ye. School of Language Studies, Baldessin Precinct Building (#110), The Australian National University, Canberra ACT 0200 Australia. zhengdao.ye@anu.edu.au

of all languages. Thus, when these universals are employed as a descriptive language to specify and represent meanings of emotion words and expressions, not only is the descriptive tool itself culture-independent but also the meaning description can achieve maximum translatability. That is, the meaning of an emotion term of any language specified in NSM terms can be represented not only by words available in that language but also by words of any other language. Over the course of nearly 40 years of cross-linguistic investigation of typologically different and unrelated languages, 65 or so such universals, which constitute the shared lexical-conceptual core of all languages, have been identified (see Table 27.1; see also Wierzbicka, 1972, 1980, 1996; Goddard & Wierzbicka, 1994, 2002; Peeters, 2006). These universals are also semantic primitives—linguistic units whose meaning cannot be further decomposed—which function as the building blocks for all complex meanings. The search for these universals or semantic primitives can be seen as an effort to realize Leibniz's dream of finding the "alphabet of the human thoughts" (Wierzbicka, 1972, 2001c). Because these 65 or so linguistic universals are instantly taken as conceptual universals, the NSM approach to emotion assumes a similar conceptual stance as does the conceptual metaphor approach to emotion within linguistics (see Chapters 4 and 28), where linguistic analysis is mapped onto conceptual analysis (e.g., Lakoff & Kövecses, 1987; Kövecses, 1990, 2000).

The NSM research program on emotion includes a full-scale study of the language of emotion, which examines how emotions are encoded, described and expressed in languages across cultures. In this process, meaning remains a central issue to an in-depth understanding of any "emotion talk," and NSM has proven to be an effective tool for exploring the emotional worlds of people across languages and cultures. This point will be expounded upon in Section 27.4.

Table 27.1 The Natural Semantic Metalanguage (NSM) – English version

I, YOU, SOMEONE, SOMETHING/THING, PEOPLE, BODY	substantives
KIND, PART	relational substantives
THIS, THE SAME, OTHER/ELSE	determiners
ONE, TWO, SOME, ALL, MUCH/MANY	quantifiers
GOOD, BAD	evaluators
BIG, SMALL	descriptors
THINK, KNOW, WANT, FEEL, SEE, HEAR	mental predicates
SAY, WORDS, TRUE	speech
DO, HAPPEN, MOVE, TOUCH	action, events, movement, contact
BE (SOMEWHERE), THERE IS, HAVE, BE (SOMEONE/SOMETHING)	location, existence, possession, specification
LIVE, DIE	life and death
WHEN/TIME, NOW, BEFORE, AFTER, A LONG TIME, A SHORT TIME, FOR SOME TIME, MOMENT	time
WHERE/PLACE, HERE, ABOVE, BELOW, FAR, NEAR, SIDE, INSIDE	space
NOT, MAYBE, CAN, BECAUSE, IF	logical concepts
VERY, MORE	intensifier, augmentor
LIKE	similarity

In the actual meaning description, apart from using a culture-independent metalanguage, the NSM approach to emotion also involves explicating the "prototypical cognitive scenario," a script-like narrative slot that serves as a standard conceptual reference point linking an emotion with prototypical thoughts and wants associated with this emotion. For example, the meaning of the English emotion term *sad* is explained by reference to the following cognitive scenario (reproduced here from Goddard & Schalley, 2010: 108, modified on the basis of Wierzbicka, 1999a: 60–4):

[A] *Someone X felt sad*
a. someone X felt something bad
like someone can feel when they think like this:
b. "I know that something bad happened
I don't want things like this to happen
I can't think like this: I will do something because of it now
I know that I can't do anything"

In contrast, the cognitive scenario of the English emotion word *unhappy* can be spelt out as follows (ibid):

[B] *Someone X felt unhappy*
a. someone X felt something bad
like someone can feel when they think like this:
b. "some bad things happened to me
I wanted things like this not to happen to me
I can't not think about it"
c. this someone felt something like this, because this someone thought like this

In both of the explications, the first component (a) sets up a prototypical cognitive scenario where the frame indicates that to feel a certain emotion means to feel like a person does who has certain specifiable thoughts (Wierzbicka, 1972, 1973).

The specific thoughts and wants spelt out in component (b) of each explication not only define each emotion term but also distinguish one term from another. At the same time, they show the connections with other related emotions. For example, the conceptual element "something bad happened" present in the explications of both *sad* and *unhappy* shows how these, and other "sad-like" emotion terms, are related. Compared to *sad*, the thought of *unhappy* is personal ("some bad things happen *to me*"). This is supported by linguistic evidence that, unlike *sad*, one cannot feel *unhappy* on account of things that happen to other people. *Unhappy* focuses on thwarted desires ("I wanted things like this not to happen to me"), and as a result, the thought encoded is more active ("I can't not think about it") compared with that of *sad*. It is more about dissatisfaction, rather than resignation ("I know that I can't do anything") (Goddard & Schalley, 2010:18). The absence of the final component in *sad* is meant to account for the implications that *sad* can be "free-floating," whereas *unhappy* actually had some thoughts like this, as is reflected in the language—one can say *I feel sad, I don't know why*, while it would be odd to say *I feel unhappy, I don't know why* (see also Ortony & Clore, 1989).

It is clear from the above comparison that the cognitive scenario provides a kind of standard reference point by which the nature of the associated emotion can be identified and compared. That is, the cognitive scenario, which portrays how the experiencer construes the event, defines the meaning of an emotion and provides a conceptual link permitting shared understanding of that emotion within a speech community.

The specific content of the prototypical cognitive scenario of each emotion term is arrived at through careful examination of the linguistic evidence surrounding the use of the term by ordinary speakers and through a painstaking experimentation process of trial and error. One can test its validity by substituting each component into the term's context of use, owing to the fact that the metalanguage in which the cognitive scenario is written is derived from natural language. In this regard, while what is captured in the cognitive scenario reflects the folk knowledge and understanding of the emotion term in question, it nonetheless can be subject to further experimental tests.

The use of semantic primitives to describe meaning means that there can only be overlaps in components between emotion terms, but no circularity in definitions. Any native English speaker would feel inadequate when describing their *sad* feeling via *unhappy*, or vice versa, due to the slightly different cognitive scenario each emotion is associated with. As succinctly put by Wierzbicka (1992a:292), "To compare concepts with any degree of precision we need to have definitions, which, if they are to have any explanatory POWER, cannot be, directly or indirectly, circular. This in turn requires that they are based on a set of listed indefinables or primitives."

As a universal metalanguage, the NSM is essentially a *tertium comparationis,* a common yardstick that allows meaning to be compared within a language and across languages on some common basis. In the context of emotion research, cross-cultural similarities and differences can therefore be explained via the extent to which the cognitive scenarios overlap and differ from each other. What follows illustrates this point by focusing on two sad-like emotions in Chinese *bēi* ("tragic fatalistic sadness") and *kǔ* ("anguish") (Ye, 2001, 2007a).

Bēi appears in different lists of "basic emotions" proposed in the traditional Chinese texts. It is a momentary feeling that carries a tragic and fatalistic tone, suggesting powerlessness before the laws of nature ("when things like this happen, no one can do anything about it"). *Bēi* has long been linked in Chinese literature and poetry with the season of *qiū* ("autumn"), with *bēiqiū* (lit. "*bēi*-autumn"), which is a lexicalized item, being one of the most enduring themes in Chinese literature. The prototypical cognitive scenario of *bēi* is represented as follows:

> [C] *Someone X felt bēi*
> a. someone X felt something very bad
> like someone can feel when they think like this:
> b. "something bad happened now
> I know that after this good things will not happen anymore
> I don't want things like this to happen
> I want to do something if I can
> I know that I can't do anything because I know that no one can do anything when things like this happen"
> c. this someone felt something like this, because this someone thought like this

Once the meaning of *bēi* is decomposed in NSM, one can see clearly the exact ways in which this Chinese "basic" emotion resembles and departs from its English counterpart *sad*, which is often argued to be a pan-culture basic emotion (e.g., Ekman, 1992).

The ability of NSM to explain seemingly inexplicable culture-specific emotion terms and concepts is demonstrated further in the explication of *kǔ* (anguish; lit. "bitter"), another culturally salient emotion concept in Chinese that is sad-like. The use of *kǔ* reflects a habitual way of describing emotions in Chinese—via tastes (Ye, 2007b). *Kǔ* is an intense and pent-up feeling, which is kept deep inside and which has a distinct facial expression to accompany it, as if cannot contain such an emotion in one's heart. Many *kǔ*-related words, such as *kǔmèn* (bitterness, pain, suffering, agony, anguish; lit. "bitter-sealed"), *kǔtòng* (acute mental suffering, tormented; lit. "bitter-pain"), and *kǔnǎo* (troubled, don't know what to do; lit. "bitter-vexed"), share some of the core semantic features: mental suffering of a person, facing an ongoing situation that they find difficult to speak about or extract themselves from. The explication of *kŭ* can be read as follows:

[D] *Someone X felt something kŭ*
a. someone X felt something very bad
like someone can feel when they think like this:
b. "something bad has been happening to me for a long time
I feel something very bad because of this
I don't want to say this to other people because I don't know how I can say this to other people
if I say it, I don't think that they will know how I feel
they cannot know because something like this is not happening to them"
c. this person felt something like this, because this someone thought like this
d. often, people know how this person feels when they see this person's *liăn* ("face")

Kŭ is an ineffable feeling ("I don't want to say this to other people"). Note that it is not that one *cannot* actively verbalize their feeling, but rather that one chooses not to. Linguistic evidence shows that the experiencer *will* talk about their mental sufferings if they trust the other person or when the other person has had a similar experience (Ye, 2007a). It is not difficult to see that this attitude toward emotion expression has huge implications for psychotherapy practice in the Chinese context (e.g. Leung & Lee, 1996; see also Tsai et al., 2004). Here, undoubtedly, a revelation of the cognitive scenario can inform researchers of the distinct cultural values and attitudes attached to the communication of emotion.

Scherer (2000c:152) points out that "cultural values can strongly affect appraisal." This point is evident from the thoughts revealed in the cognitive scenarios of the above two Chinese emotions. The explications of the typical thought patterns that are linked with a feeling allows researchers to get as close as possible to how people within a culture conceptualize their own experience and to reveal the underlying values and worldviews that shape the culturally distinct ways of conceptualizing emotions. The implication of this strength of the NSM approach for the GRID paradigm will be discussed in Section 27.4.

27.3 Comparing the NSM and the GRID approaches to emotion

Having introduced the NSM approach to emotion and illustrated how it works in practice, it is not difficult to see that the NSM and the GRID approaches share some fundamental assumptions about emotions, especially with regard to the role of ordinary language in emotion research, the nature of emotion, the common goal of uncovering the universal and culture-specific aspects of human emotions, and the need for a culture-sensitive measurement tool in cross-cultural research. The fundamental difference between the two approaches, however, appears to lie chiefly in how they actually go about cross-cultural research, with the NSM approach aiming for what Geertz (1973:5–6, 9–10) calls "thick description" and provision of a culture-internal perspective, and the GRID paradigm for a systematic comparison of the full profile of each emotion. In this regard, the methods that the NSM and the GRID approaches use can be seen as complementary. In order to explore ways that can combine these two approaches, the following discussion will focus on the common ground and the particular emphasis of each approach, as well as the correlations between NSM findings and the componential approach.

Emotion labels and emotion worlds

Both the GRID paradigm and the NSM approach recognize the important role that language plays in emotion research. They both firmly hold the view that ordinary language concepts—the ways in which people think and talk about their emotional experience—are the bedrock of the scientific study of emotion. This is because the study of the psychology of emotion, to a large extent, has to rely on language to access the "raw experience" and its interpretation. The legitimacy of building emotion theory on the basis of folk knowledge has not been unquestioned (e.g., Griffiths, 1997). However, as Scherer (2005a:696) argues compellingly, "the need of much of social science to work with layperson's self-report . . . makes it mandatory to employ lay or native concepts." Furthermore, to be able to empirically test and distinguish emotions, researchers have no other means but "re-course to the study of folk concepts of emotion in order to make headway on the question of the number and nature of discriminable types of emotions" (ibid:707). This view is also widely shared by (other) emotion researchers of various theoretical persuasions (e.g., Davitz, 1969; Averill, 1975; de Rivera, 1977; Frijda, 1986; Russell, 1983; Ortony et al., 1988; Frijda et al., 1995).

For NSM researchers, emotion labels and, in general, the language used to describe experience are probably the most direct and only reliable means researchers have to approach and under-stand the inner world, which is otherwise not readily accessible to an "outsider." In Wierzbicka's (1999a:26) words, "the way people interpret their own emotions depends, to some extent at least, on the lexical grid provided by their native language." (One may *infer* certain emotions and states of mind of other people from bodily symptoms. But to be able to interpret and fully understand what is going on in others' hearts and minds, one has to have recourse to verbal explanation.) This of course does not mean that when a language does not have an emotion term or label its speakers lack corresponding experiences. Rather, the experiences or aspects of experiences that are given linguistic labels are those that are regarded by people of a given culture as relevant, salient or im-portant enough to single out and talk about (Wierzbicka, 1992a, 1995b). As such, folk labels in ef-fect reveal what Jurij Apresjan, the noted Russian lexicographer, calls "a naïve picture of the world" and "a naïve picture of the human being" (Apresjan, 2000:102-4).

Furthermore, in the view of NSM researchers, the clear-cut demarcation made between the folk and the scientific theory appears largely untenable. It is not only difficult for scientific theories to be fully free from the "naïve picture" created by any natural language researchers use, but also a scien-tific theory about human emotion yet with little folk knowledge as its theoretical basis ultimately lacks a "human face" (Wierzbicka, 1992a, 1999a; Goddard, 1997b; Ye, 2004; see also Kövecses, 2000). Goddard & Schalley (2010: 94) point out that, within semantics, an important current thinking on language holds that "ordinary language use involves more or less a seamless integration of linguistic knowledge, cultural conventions, and real world knowledge." Following this insight, it may not be an exaggeration to say that an emotion theory dissociated from ordinary language use runs the risk of being divorced from much of the social reality and cultural contexts where people's emotional life actually takes place and which give rise to the incredible richness of human emotional life.

Multi-componential nature of emotion

The GRID paradigm is based on the assumption that emotion is a multi-componential process (Scherer, 1984b, 2005a). That is, emotion can be conceptualized as encompassing a set of compo-nents including (a) appraisal of the emotion-eliciting event, (b) psychophysiological changes (bod-ily sensations), (c) motor expressions (face, voice, gestures), (d) action tendencies, (e) subjective experiences (feelings), and (f) emotion regulation (Fontaine et al., 2007:1050). These components constitute a comprehensive process model of emotion incorporating a diverse range of emotion theories, such as "the appraisal theory of Scherer (2001), the psychophysiological emotion litera-ture (Stemmler, 2003), the action-tendency theory of Frijda (Frijda et al., 1989), the current-affect theory of Russell (Yik et al., 1999), and the expression-regulation theory of Ekman and Friesen

(1969)" (Fontaine et al., 2007:1051) (cf. also Chapter 5). This component definition of emotion thus allows researchers to establish a detailed "semantic profile" (Scherer, 2005a:695) for each folk concept of emotion named by a natural language, a profile which relates to all of the six process components. By this measure, the multicomponential approach represents one of the most comprehensive approach to emotion, and the GRID is like a rich archive where all of the related information about each named emotion is stored. Based on the cross-linguistic study of a number of European languages and prior findings in emotion literature, the GRID paradigm has identified 24 prototypical emotion terms and 144 features relevant to them (such as "in itself unpleasant for the person," "felt shivers," "frowned," "felt the urge to stop what he or she was doing," "felt bad," "showed the emotion to others more than he or she felt it"). These features belong to different process components and serve as the basis for comparison of "semantic profiles" of named emotions across languages and cultures, and for uncovering the pan-cultural dimensions underlying all emotions (Fontaine et al., 2007, see also Chapter 5).

It is perhaps not difficult to discern conceptual similarities between the semantic primitives of the NSM and the components of the GRID and how this multicomponential model of emotion is reflected in and supported by the NSM explications of emotion terms. In particular, the correspondence between the GRID components and the NSM semantic primitives can be paired as follows: "appraisal"–"think," "psychophysiological changes"–"body," "motor expressions"–"do something with part of one's body," "action tendencies"–"(not) want to do something," "subjective experiences"–"feel." Arguably, in light of the GRID, what is specified in the prototypical cognitive scenario seems to concern mostly the Appraisal, Action tendency, and Feeling components, whereas the roles of the body and motor expressions and emotion regulation are often not immediately visible in the explications. However, it should be borne in mind that the semantic primitive "feel" encompasses both bodily and psychological feelings. Empirical investigation has shown that, across languages, physical and psychological feelings do not appear to be differentiated linguistically (e.g., Goddard & Wierzbicka, 1994). In other words, when someone says something like "I feel something now," it can refer to either bodily or psychological feeling or a combination of both.

Furthermore, the components relating to the body, the motor expressions, and emotion regulation in the GRID paradigm are reflected in another two parallel lines of NSM research on emotion: the study of the language of emotion, that is, how emotions are encoded, described and expressed in language (e.g. Ameka, 1990, 1992; Wierzbicka, 1999a; Harkins & Wierzbicka, 2001; Ye, 2004) and "emotional scripts" (i.e., "cultural norms for emotion expression"; e.g., Wierzbicka, 1994b, 1999a; Ye, 2006b). The related literature is extensive and cannot be detailed here. The examples given here relate to those linguistic descriptions concerning the body. Cross-linguistic investigation using the NSM framework has shown that information about the body appears to be universally encoded in the language of emotion (e.g., Wierzbicka, 1999a; Amberber, 2001; Enfield & Wierzbicka, 2002; Junker & Blacksmith, 2006). In particular, three modes of emotion descriptions involving body part terms are identified to be universal. Emotions can be talked about (in terms of body features) via (a) externally observable (involuntary) bodily changes, (b) sensations, and (c) figurative bodily images. The first two modes of descriptions correspond directly to the "Bodily symptom" component in the GRID paradigm and distinguish the physiology that others can see from that one can feel even if others cannot see it.

In Chinese (Ye, 2002), for example, one can find descriptions of bodily change in facial colour, and bodily processes associated with bones and tendons, trembling and sweating, erection of head and body hairs, and *qi* ("essence of life force and energy/breath") as commonly used references in relation to bodily processes that are understood as signals of inner feelings; whereas conventionally used references in descriptions of bodily sensation include fast heartbeat or the skipping of a heartbeat, feeling hot in the face, in the ears and in the heart, feeling cold, feeling numbness, feeling muscle movement, and feeling pain, dizziness, and impairment of vision. In terms of description involving an imaginary or figurative bodily event, this is typically done in Chinese through a counterfactual grammatical construction *xiàng . . . side* or *rú* ("as if") or a conventional metaphorical phrase involving bodily images which have references to internal organs, such as the "heart," "gallbladder," "soul," "intestine", and "stomach." The prominent role that the body plays in the language of emotions across languages shows the intrinsic link between emotions and the bodily experience, and points to the important place of the "Bodily symptom" component in the process model of emotion. In general, cross-linguistic investigations have shown that all of the six major emotion process components are presented or encoded in language.

The search for commonality and variations in human emotions: the common goal

At the heart of both the GRID paradigm and the NSM approach is the goal of uncovering the commonality and culture-specificity of the human emotional experience. Both approaches believe that this cannot be achieved from one single linguistic or cultural perspective, and that the search for what Franz Boas and others have called "the psychic unity of humankind" can only be achieved through cross-linguistic and cross-cultural investigation. Both approaches also recognize the challenges presented in researching emotions in a cross-cultural setting, especially with regard to the issues of translatability and comparability of the instrument. (e.g., Fontaine et al., 2002; Scherer, 2005a). The GRID paradigm attempts to overcome these problems by systematically measuring and comparing responses to semantic grid profiles. Only when the full semantic profiles of two emotions match can they be said to be equivalent. The NSM approach uses a simple and universal metalanguage to model the associated thoughts of a feeling felt by the experiencer. In an intuitively accessible representation that is simultaneously translatable across languages, the NSM approach also provides a culture-internal perspective on the shared understanding of named emotional experiences within a culture. Therefore, it allows researchers to enter into the subjective experience of the other, assess meaning equivalence between languages, and pinpoint the similarities and variations between ways of conceptualization. Undoubtedly, a joint effort between the GRID and the NSM approach that combines perception of meaning with conceptualization of experience can further deepen our understanding of human emotional experience from outside and from within. The next section will explore the potential for such an effort.

27.4 Combining the GRID and NSM approaches

In many ways, the GRID and NSM methods are complementary in nature. The strength of the GRID paradigm lies in its comprehensiveness and quantitative analysis. One can gain a broad picture of all the information about a named emotion by examining the responses to the proposed 144 features that encompass the six process components ranging from appraisal to physiological changes. One can also gain a general picture of the extent to which the variations of similar emotion concepts across cultures are based on statistical information gathered from responses to questionnaires concerning the features. In contrast, the NSM approach is especially appropriate for conducting fine-tuning, in-depth conceptual analysis and for revealing the conceptualizations encapsulated in an emotion concept—be it in the form of words, phrases, or grammatical constructions. In view of this strength, the NSM can be applied to the GRID paradigm in two ways. Firstly, it can help make sense of culture-specific ways of speaking, which the GRID program would inevitably encounter in a cross-linguistic and cross-cultural context when gathering information from its subjects, and to do so from a culture-internal perspective. Secondly, the conceptual content spelt out in the prototypical cognitive scenarios can be tapped by the GRID paradigm in question-naire design. In particular, it can provide cues with regard to the "Appraisal," "Feeling," and "Action tendency" components. In Section 27.2, the ways in which the NSM can be used to explain culture-specific emotion terms were demonstrated. What follows will illustrate how it can be applied to make sense of meanings and conceptualizations of "emotion talk" in general and how it can con-tribute to an accurate understanding of certain nuanced ways of talking about emotions that may be lacking in a researcher's own language. The first example relates to bodily descriptions while the second relates to the "experiencer construction."

In Section 27.3, the topic of bodily description was touched upon. A key question emerging from an examination of the language relating to the body is how one can determine the correlation be-tween a particular bodily description and the specific emotional state that it refers to and how one can interpret the embodied meaning accurately. The explication of the associated cognitive scenarios of these bodily descriptions holds the key to the answer. Laying out the specific thoughts associated with the bodily description is especially important because similar bodily descriptions in different languages and cultures can have different emotional meaning. For example, "feeling cold in the body" as suggested in the Chinese phrase *liángle bànjié* ("cold over half of one's body") describes the feeling of experiencers who are suddenly made aware of a misfortune that they least expected to happen. It is associated with the following prototypical thoughts: something very bad is happening to me; because of this, I now know what will happen to me; I didn't know before this would happen to me; I didn't know before this that something like this would happen; I wanted something else to happen; I know now that I can't do much. In English, "feeling cold in the body" as reflected in the phrase "sending a shiver down one's spine" is typically linked with the thought that "something bad is happening to someone." It does not have to happen to the experiencer himself. It is clear that the NSM approach can help to decipher the culture-specific interpretations of the link between bodily events and emotions.

The usefulness of the NSM approach for a paradigm like the GRID in understanding the mean-ings of culture-specific emotion talk can be further demonstrated in the following case where the NSM can be applied to elucidate nuanced meanings of experiencer constructions. It has been found that a wide range of languages have a special set of grammatical structures called "experi-encer constructions," which especially encode subjective experience of feeling and convey the par-ticular perspective the experiencer takes when conceptualizing their emotions and sensations, that is, whether the feeling or emotion in question is controllable, wanted or unwanted, or whether it is externally caused or self-generated (e.g. Wierzbicka, 1986, 1999; Ameka, 1990; Bugenhagen, 1990; see also Reh, 1998). For example, according to Ameka (1990), the Ewe language (a Kwa language of West Africa) offers a number of alternatives for saying something like "X was happy," including the following (all from Ameka, 1990:140–1; transcriptions have been slightly modified):

(1a)	*me*	*kpo*	*dzidzo.*	
	1SG	see	happiness	"I was happy."
(1b)	*dzi*	*dzo*	*m.*	
	heart	straight	1SG	"I was happy."
(1c)	*é-*	*dzo*	*dzi*	*ná-m.*
	3SG	straight heart	to 1SG	"It pleased me"
(1d)	*é-*	*dzo*	*dzidzo*	*ná-m.*
	3SG	cause	happiness	to 1SG	"It made me happy."

Each of these ways of saying "I was happy" conveys a slightly different view of the emotional expe-rience and affective situation on the part of the experiencer. In (1a), the experiencer is coded as the subject and is perceived to be an "active" agent who can control his or her feelings; whereas in (1b), the coding of the experiencer as the object reflects the conceptualization of the experiencer that he or she is a "passive" participant in the situation. In (1c), the experiencer is marked as the object of the dative marker *ná-*. The emphasis of this construction is that the experiencer is the "recipient" of the affective state, which has the stimulus (*é-*) in the subject position. The emphasis of (1d) is placed on the causer—the thing, event or person that is responsible for bringing about the "happiness."[2] Such terms as "active" and "passive" are quite vague and do not say much about the exact ways of viewing one's subjective experiences. The different perspectives on how the experiencer comes to have, and view, the feeling in question, as encoded in each of the constructions, can be explained and represented in the following schema:

> (1a') The meaning of the Ewe "subject experiencer" construction:
> X felt something
> X could do something not to feel like this if X wanted to
> (1b') The meaning of the Ewe "object experiencer" construction:
> X felt something
> not because X wanted it
> X couldn't not feel this
> (1c') The meaning of the Ewe "emotional stimulus" construction:
> X felt something
> because X thought something about S ("stimulus")
> not because X wanted to feel this
> (1d') The meaning of the Ewe "emotional causer" construction:
> X felt something
> because S ("person responsible") did something
> not because of anything else

The "experiencer construction" strongly suggests the presence of the "Feeling (subjective experiences)" and "Appraisal" components in the process model of emotion, and reflects the attention people commonly give to aspects of their private experiences. When researchers study the emotional experience of people from a given speech community, the "experiencer construction" itself can tell them a great deal about the aspects of the conceptualization of emotions in question. This is made clear with the aid of a culture-independent metalanguage consisting of semantic primitives.

More than four decades ago, Davitz in his pioneer book *The Language of Emotion* wrote:

> What does a person mean when he says someone is happy or angry or sad? . . . Our question, however, requires a descriptive or definitional answer about how people use language in referring to emotion states (Davitz, 1969:1–2).

The question posed by Davitz must be an *a priori* assumption in any cross-cultural emotion research. It is in its descriptive and definitional strength that the NSM approach can best complement the GRID paradigm, which in turn creates a platform on which NSM researchers can test explications empirically, further informing NSM research in order to fine-tune its analysis. For example, on the one hand, the subtle but important difference made between "I *don't* want

---

[2] According to Ameka (1990), these different constructions are not available to all emotions and sensations. Some predicates, by virtue of their meaning, can only select one single construction. For example, the predicates describing uncontrollable physiological experiences such as *dowuo* ("be hungry") are only compatible with the "object experiencer" construction.

to say this to other people" and "I *can't* say this to other people" in the explication of *kǔ* (anguish; lit."bitterness"), which was discussed in Section 27.2, has bearings on the appraisal-related feature content. On the other, NSM researchers can verify the proposed meaning component to do with willingness to verbalize one's emotions by testing it against the intuitions of a large number of native speakers.

It is clear that there is much scope for the two approaches to cooperate. Such an effort can not only benefit each approach but ultimately contribute to a better and deeper understanding of both the universals and culture-specific aspects of the human emotional experiences.

Chapter 28

Conceptual Metaphor Theory and the GRID paradigm in the study of anger in English and Spanish

Cristina Soriano[1]

28.1 Introduction

Over the past two decades numerous disciplines in the brain and human sciences have experienced the "affective revolution," a shift of focus from the purely cognitive to the affective component of human behavior that has given rise to the growing field of the Affective Sciences (cf. Davidson, Scherer, & Goldsmith, 2003). Emotions have become an issue of particular interest in psychology, linguistics, anthropology, economics, and the neurosciences, to cite just a few of the involved disciplines. This shared interest is fortunate because a cross-disciplinary approach is necessary to address the multifaceted nature of emotion, and because it facilitates result triangulation and disciplinary cross-fertilization. In this paper, we compare two language-based methodologies in the study of emotion conceptualization stemming from psychology and linguistics, respectively: the GRID paradigm presented in this volume (see Chapter 5) and Conceptual Metaphor Theory.

The primary goal of the GRID paradigm is to investigate the meaning of emotion words, because the meanings are expected to reflect people's folk models of the emotions labeled that way. In turn, Conceptual Metaphor Theory (henceforth CMT), looks at the metaphors we use to talk about any given conceptual domain (e.g., emotion) under the assumption that regularities in the figurative language we use to talk about that domain, inform us about the way it is conceptualized.

In this work, we compare the insight provided by the GRID paradigm and CMT using the notion of "semantic focus" as *tertium comparationis*. Semantic foci are here understood as important aspects in the conceptualization of an emotion (e.g., causation, intensity) that are frequently highlighted by the source domains employed in its metaphorical representation. "Source domain" in CMT refers to the conceptual space from which structure and knowledge are borrowed to represent another domain metaphorically (e.g., conceptualizing emotions in terms of "physical forces," or in terms of "disease").

CMT and the GRID paradigm will be compared in their account of anger.[2] In psychology, anger is claimed to be one of the basic or universal emotions (e.g., Ekman, 1984, 1992; Izard, 1977;

---

[1] Cristina Soriano. Swiss Center for Affective Sciences - University of Geneva. 7, Rue des Battoirs, CH-1205 Geneva, Switzerland. Cristina.Soriano@unige.ch

[2] Italics are used in this paper to refer to specific emotion terms in a language (e.g., English *anger*); small capitals are used for concepts and conceptual metaphors (e.g., the English concept ANGER). No specific format is used to refer to the emotion itself.

Johnson-Laird & Oatley, 1989). Linguistics has also observed that an *anger*-like emotion term exists in all languages of the world (Wierzbicka, 1999a). The GRID study itself constitutes empirical evidence of the semantic overlap between English words like *anger* and *irritation* and their closest counterparts in more than 20 other languages all over the world (see Chapters 6 and 7). Thus, a cross-cultural "ANGER" concept[3] seems to exist that is lexically instantiated (in similar, but not identical ways) in many languages. The object of study in this chapter is the cross-cultural category ANGER as instantiated in (American) English and (Spain) Spanish.

The remainder of the paper will be organized as follows. We will first explain the notion of conceptual metaphor in some more detail and introduce the inventory of most representative ones reported in the previous literature for the conceptualization of anger in English and Spanish (Section 28.2). These will be analyzed in terms of their main *semantic foci*, in order to provide a profile of the emotion concept along these parameters (Section 28.3). The same foci will then be investigated using the GRID questionnaire as a testbed for the hypothesized profile (Section 28.4); convergences and discrepancies will be discussed. In subsequent sections we will explore the unique contribution of each methodology, first reviewing some features revealed by the GRID paradigm that escape the scope of metaphor analysis (Section 28.5), and then some aspects captured by metaphor that remain unaccounted for by the GRID data (Section 28.6). We will conclude with a summary of the major findings and an evaluation of the merits and limitations of each approach.

28.2 **Conceptual Metaphor Theory and the study of emotion conceptualization**

Conceptual Metaphor Theory (CMT) is one of the most popular branches of cognitive linguistics.[4] Within this approach, regularities in the figurative expressions we use to talk about a given domain are believed to reflect the way the latter is conceptually represented. For example, across languages anger-related words and expressions appear associated to the idea of "heat." Examples in English include the phrases *hot-headed*, *hot temper*, or *hot under the collar*, but also verbs like *sizzling*, *boiling*, and *steaming*. According to CMT, these regularities in language reveal a conceptual association between the domain/concept ANGER and the domain/concept HEAT. Many of these associations in language seem to be grounded in experience. For example, the association between HEAT and ANGER may be based on the experiential correlation between an anger episode and an increase in body temperature, the later being a well-known physiological response to the emotion (e.g., Ekman, Levenson, & Friesen, 1983). But this conceptual association between HEAT and ANGER is not mere declarative knowledge that "one gets hot when angry." Recent experimental studies have shown that the very cognitive representation of anger is systematically linked to that of heat in such a way that activating one concept automatically activates the other, leading to facilitation effects in their recognition and influencing reasoning (Wilkowski, Meier, Robinson, Carter, & Feltman, 2009). Additional empirical evidence has started to accumulate in the past few years on the psychological reality of many of the conceptual metaphors that were first hypothesized on the grounds of linguistic observation (e.g., Meier & Robinson, 2004; Meier, Robinson, & Clore, 2004; Soriano & Valenzuela, 2009; Williams & Bargh, 2008; Wilkowski et al., 2009; Zhong & Leonardelli, 2008).

---

[3] The cross-cultural concept "ANGER" is understood here as a prototype composed of frequent, but not necessarily sufficient or necessary features across all instantiations.

[4] For an introduction to the basic features and tenets of cognitive linguistics, see Croft and Cruse (2004), Geeraerts and Cuyckens (2008) or – in Spanish –Ibarretxe-Antuñano and Valenzuela (2012).

What is more, since conceptual metaphors are ways of thinking – and not just fancy or anecdotal ways of speaking – the conceptual associations they reflect can also be found in gesture (Cienki & Müller, 2008), images (Forceville, 1996), the rhetoric of publicity (Ungerer, 2000), ritual, social behavior, and even in the objects we make for everyday use (cf. Kövecses, 2000 and Soriano, 2005 for examples of conceptual metaphor in these and other realms).

Conceptual metaphors are conventionally represented in the CMT tradition by means of small capitals in a formula that explicitly relates the two domains at stake. The formula reads "[TARGET DOMAIN] IS [SOURCE DOMAIN]." The most salient conceptual metaphors specific to the representation of anger in English and Spanish are presented in Table 28.1 (cf. Lakoff & Kövecses, 1987; Barcelona, 1989a; Soriano, 2005). This inventory constitutes a revision of the original list proposed by Lakoff and Kövecses (1987).[5]

The metaphor ANGER IS A FLUID IN A PRESSURIZED CONTAINER reflects the conceptualization of the body as a container, and of emotions (anger among them) as substances inside (1). When the intensity of the emotion increases, the fluid rises in the person (2), until there is no more space (3) and it begins to exert pressure on the walls of the container. The person is expected to resist the pressure and keep the anger inside (4). But if the intensity becomes too high, the container breaks (5), that is, the person loses control over the emotion. An alternative and more desirable outcome is to communicate anger in a controlled fashion (6), for example avoiding the indiscriminate "explosion" by reducing the pressure (7).

1   *To feel anger inside, internal anger, anger within*

2   *Rising/towering anger*

3   *Full of anger, brimming with anger*

4   *To contain/refrain/suppress/repress anger, to keep anger bottled up inside oneself*

5   *To explode, to blow up, to blow one's top, to hit the roof*

6   *To learn to bring anger into the open, anger outlets*

7   *To vent, to let off steam*

Anger is also represented as a fire inside the person (8) and the effects of anger (physiological and behavioral manifestations) correspond to the physical effects of the flames: smoke (9), sparks (10), light (11). The anger-fire can "burn" the person (12), and although the big flames typically do not last for a long time (because they "consume" the person and extinguish their fuel), a low-grade intensity "fire" can last for a long time (13).

8   *To kindle somebody's anger, inflammatory remarks, to ignite, to incense*

9   *To fume*

10 *To sparkle with anger (the eyes)*

11 *To blaze, to flare up, to glow with anger*

12 *To burn with anger*

13 *To do a slow burn, to smolder*

---

5   The original inventory in English was offered by Lakoff and Kövecses (1987) in a seminal work that inspired Barcelona's (1989a) analysis in Spanish. Soriano (2005) offers a revision and expansion of their findings in both languages based on a larger data pool and a more systematic methodology of analysis. Examples in this paper are taken both from Lakoff and Kövecses (1987) and Soriano (2005). Due to space constraints, only examples in English are provided, but see Soriano (2005) for these and many other examples in English and Spanish.

Table 28.1 Conceptual metaphors in the representation of anger in English and Spanish

ANGER IS A FLUID IN A PRESSURIZED CONTAINER
ANGER IS FIRE
ANGER IS ILLNESS
ANGER IS INSANITY
ANGER IS AN AGGRESSIVE ANIMAL
ANGER IS AN OPPONENT IN A STRUGGLE
ANGER IS A NATURAL PHYSICAL FORCE
ANGER IS A WEAPON
THE CAUSE OF ANGER IS PHYSICAL NUISANCE
THE CAUSE OF ANGER IS TRESPASSING A LIMIT

The anger-fire is not the only thing that can harm the person and those around. Anger is also conceptualized as an illness. As such, it is represented as damaging for the health of the person (14) and contagious (15, 16). The titles in the current self-help literature on anger management also reflect this view: anger requires healing (17–20) and it can be lethal in the long run (21).

14 *To be sick of it, to fester, to rankle*[6]

15 *"One or two angry people can take pent-up anger or stress and infect a whole room"*

16 *"Young Irish learn their history in school . . . anger becomes contagious"*

17 *Healing Anger: The POWER of Patience from a Buddhist Perspective* (by Dalai Lama, Snow Lion Publications, 1997)

18 *Brothers on the Mend: Guide for Managing & Healing Anger in African American Men* (by Johnson, Pocket Books, 1999)

19 *Healing Our Anger: 7 Ways to Make Peace in a Hostile World* (by Obsatz, Augsburg Fortress Publication, 2000)

20 *Anger Kills* (by Williams & Williams, HarperCollins Publishers, 1994)

21 *"Getting angry is like taking a small dose of some slow-acting poison — arsenic, for example — every day of your life [. . .]. Anger is a toxin to your body"*

Among the disruptions created by anger, one of the most salient ones in our folk model of the emotion is irrational behavior. This is elaborated in the metaphor ANGER IS INSANITY, where the irrational, violent behavior typical of the emotion is conceptualized as a direct result of transient madness (22–24). The anger-insanity, as any other psychological disorder, can be said to require therapy (25, 26).

22 *To be mad, to madden, to drive somebody crazy/berserk*

23 *To be fit to be tied, to be ready for a straightjacket*

24 *To lose one's head, to get out of one's mind*

---

[6] Only etymologically. *To rankle* derives from Middle English *ranclen*, "to fester; become or make inflamed" (*Webster's New World College Dictionary*, 3rd edition).

25 "'I have always found' he said, 'that the best therapy for outrage and anger is action'"

26 "Surely we are entitled to be a little bit uneasy about the potential therapeutic value – to a president afflicted by unfocused anger – of a largely unprovoked, open-ended naval confrontation with Khomeini in the Persian Gulf"

Irrationality and violence, typical of INSANITY, are also elaborated by the metaphor ANGER IS AN AGGRESSIVE ANIMAL. In addition, this metaphor communicates an idea of debasement: the angry person, when out of control, is more similar to an animal than to a rational human being. The metaphor evokes the idea of the "beast inside," the instinctual part of our nature that can override the purely rational and moral one. In a first variant of the metaphor, anger is viewed as an animal (27, 28) that has to be kept in check (29). In the second variant of the metaphor the person is already the animal, and angry human behavior is assimilated to all sorts of aggressive animal behavior (30).

27 Ferocious/fierce/monstrous temper

28 To whip up anger

29 To keep one's anger in check, to unleash one's anger, to fly off the handle (one's anger), unbridled anger

30 To get one's hackles up, to bristle with anger, to ruffle one's feathers, to put one's back up, to bare one's teeth, to bite somebody's head off, to chew somebody out, to snap, to snarl, to growl, to bark

The idea of control is further elaborated by a very recurrent metaphor in which anger is personified as an opponent in a struggle (31–33) (ANGER IS AN OPPONENT IN A STRUGGLE). If anger wins the fight (34), it rules over the person (35).

31 Anger invades the person, to be seized by anger

32 To struggle/wrestle/fight with one's anger

33 To conquer/subdue one's anger

34 To be overcome by anger, to succumb to one's anger, to surrender/yield to one's anger, to take control of the person (anger)

35 Acts dictated by anger, to be governed by anger

When the person is out of control, the feeling of powerlessness is strong. In this case anger is also conceptualized as a natural physical force (ANGER IS A NATURAL PHYSICAL FORCE) (36, 37) that sweeps the person away (38), causing behaviors that are violent and dangerous (39, 40).

36 Wave of indignation, rising tide of anger, inner storm

37 "Act nothing in a furious passion. It's putting to sea in a storm"

38 A wave of anger surged through/washed over him

39 To fulminate against somebody,[7] to thunder, to erupt

40 "Filch's pasty face went brick red. Harry braced himself for a tidal wave of fury"

Finally, anger is a high-power emotion that can help us achieve our goals. Since the prototypical anger scenario involves a wrongdoer that creates a disadvantage for the person, the first goal in anger is to oppose him or her. This whole situation allows us to conceptualize anger as a weapon (ANGER IS WEAPON) that we use against a target (41–43).

---

[7] From Latin fulminare, to strike (said of lightning).

41 *To aim anger at somebody, to be the target of one's wrath, to direct anger at somebody, to focus anger on somebody, to turn anger against somebody, to go ballistic*

42 *"Every woman has a well-stocked arsenal of anger potentially useful against those oppressions, personal and institutional, which brought that anger into being"*

43 *"The unexpressed anger lies within them like an undetonated device, usually to be hurled at the first woman of color who talks about racism"*

The metaphors seen so far provide in some occasions an implicit understanding of what the causes of anger might be *like*: awakening the sleeping beast inside us, kindling an all-consuming fire, etc. But two specific metaphors proposed by Lakoff and Kövecses (1987) tell us what the causes of anger are *about*. In the first one, the cause of anger is metaphorically construed as trespassing a physical limit (THE CAUSE OF ANGER IS TRESPASSING A LIMIT) (44). In the second one, nuisances of any sort are metaphorically represented as physiological harm (THE CAUSE OF ANGER IS A PHYSICAL NUISANCE) (45, 46). Notice that *literal* physical injury is frequently quoted in the expert literature as a cause of anger (Alschuler & Alschuler, 1984; Schimmel, 1979). The difference is that, in folk models, any kind of anger-inducing event or situation can be metaphorically conceptualized as an injury.

44 *This is where I draw the line*

45 *To irritate, to gall, to be a pain, to be a pinprick, to be a thorn in the side/flesh, to nettle, to touch on the raw, to step on somebody's toes/corns, to rub the wrong way, to chafe*

46 *"I think of such incidents puncturing my spirit each day like needle jabs, then multiplied by weeks and years. I sense how my anger would accumulate as a result of the injustices"*

Each of these metaphors picks up and expands different aspects of our folk-understanding of anger. But they do not provide independent characterizations; on the contrary, they converge in a unified picture of the emotion. For example, Barcelona (1989a) and Soriano (2005) have shown for Spanish how the various metaphors contribute to the general anger scenario suggested by Lakoff and Kövecses (1987) in English. In this chapter, we further propose that the metaphors contribute coherent information along a number of relevant *semantic foci* or relevant aspects of emotion. The following section will define those semantic foci and describe the contribution of each metaphor to them.

28.3 **Semantic foci in the metaphorical representation of anger**

Many of the metaphors discussed above are not specific to ANGER, but apply to other emotions as well. According to Kövecses (2000), these common source domains highlight a number of aspects important in most emotion concepts. From the list of aspects suggested by Kövecses (Ibid. pp. 40–46), a subset can be selected that is specifically relevant for ANGER: Intensity, Evaluation (positive/ negative), Difficulty to cope, Control, Desire, and Harm.[8] One more aspect can be added to the original inventory: Causation.

Intensity is an emergent subjective feeling constructed by a person on the grounds of cumulative information from the various emotion components (e.g., appraisals of gravity, high physiological activation, abundant expressive behavior, strong action tendencies etc.) (see Scherer, 2004). However, emotional intensity tends to be most strongly associated to high physiological AROUSAL. In the metaphorical expressions we use to talk about anger, Intensity is implied in the reference to AROUSAL and to the grave effects of the emotion (physiological or behavioral). AROUSAL is often

---

[8] "Passivity" is another relevant semantic aspect in the conceptualization of anger, but it is excluded here because it cannot be directly explored by the current set of questions in the GRID instrument.

metaphorically represented as heat (e.g., *hot anger*) and the disruptive and aggressive effects of anger are metaphorically represented as a strong force. Many metaphors elaborate on these ideas: FIRE (e.g., *burn with anger, flare up*), AGGRESSIVE ANIMAL (e.g., *ferocious anger*), INSANITY (e.g., *to madden*) and NATURAL PHYSICAL FORCE (e.g., *to storm, to erupt*). Together these metaphors forcefully communicate an image of anger as an intense experience.

Evaluation as a semantic focus in this paper refers to the positive or negative connotation that the emotion concept acquires as a result of being represented by metaphors whose source domain is intrinsically positive/pleasant or negative/unpleasant. According to Kövecses (2000), "emotions like anger [...] are not conceptualized as inherently good or bad" (p. 44) (see also Alschuler & Alschuler, 1984). However, none of the source domains in the metaphorical conceptualization of anger in English and Spanish are intrinsically positive (unlike other emotions, like love, which is commonly represented as a "treasure" or as a "valuable commodity" – see Kövecses, 1990). On the contrary, most ANGER source domains are intrinsically bad. The ANGER metaphors tell us the emotion is a physiological and a psychological disorder (ILLNESS and INSANITY), an aggressive beast (ANIMAL), an enemy (OPPONENT) and a harmful tool (WEAPON). NATURAL PHYSICAL FORCE also highlights the negativity of the emotion by elaborating on the powerlessness of the emoter to counteract the uncontrollable force of anger and its high potential for damage to the emoter and others around. Although some authors defend the presence of both positive and negative sensations associated to anger (Schimmel, 1979), most psychology theories tend to consider anger as a negative emotion as well.

The next semantic focus is elaborated by metaphors whose source domain invites the inference that the emotion can harm the person experiencing it and/or other people around. All ANGER metaphors elaborate this idea: anger (metaphorically) damages the person who tries to keep it inside (FLUID IN A PRESSURIZED CONTAINER, e.g., *bursting with anger*), removes one's capacity to behave rationally (INSANITY, e.g., *insane with rage*), burns (FIRE, e.g., *consumed by anger*), makes the person feel ill (ILLNESS, e.g., *I'm sick and tired of this*), causes aggression (AGGRESSIVE ANIMAL, e.g., *to bite somebody's head off*), is violent and unstoppable (NATURAL PHYSICAL FORCE, e.g., *tidal wave of indignation*), and is used to harm others (WEAPON: *aiming one's anger at the wrong person*). In other words, **Harm** to oneself and to others is a salient focus in our metaphorical representation of anger. By contrast, psychological theories of emotion tend to highlight the second aspect only, that is, the aggression to others (Watson, 1929; Frijda, 1986; Mandler, 1984; Rubin, 1986).

Metaphors also tell us about the causes of anger (**Causation** focus), that is, the reason why the emotion comes into existence. According to the metaphors outlined above, the cause can be an event (e.g., trespassing a limit, starting a fire, awakening or whipping up a dormant animal, etc.) or a state of affairs (e.g., being exposed to a constant physical nuisance). The second, however, is less salient, since the majority of metaphorical expressions about causation depict an event. This insight is coherent with a view of emotions as short-lived states, in opposition to moods or affective dispositions (cf. Scherer, 2000c). It is also coherent with appraisal theories of emotion, according to which emotions are elicited upon evaluation of a given event as relevant for one's goals (cf. Scherer, 2001, 2009c; Ellsworth & Scherer, 2003). Without a specific event, we are more likely to experience a general mood than a prototypical emotional episode.

Metaphors not only tell us that anger is typically caused by an event, they also tell us what type of event. Most information is provided by the two metaphors that specialize on anger causation: ANGER IS TRESPASSING and ANGER IS PHYSICAL NUISANCE. The first tells us there has been some kind of violation of rules or standards, and the second that the eliciting event was unpleasant. Additionally, these and other metaphors (like FIRE, AGGRESSIVE ANIMAL, FLUID) suggest that the eliciting event is caused by others, rather than oneself – as hinted by the anomaly of sentences like (47–49).

47 (?) *I kindled my anger*

48 (?) *I awakened my anger*

49 (?) *I filled me with anger*

Another semantic aspect elaborated by the ANGER metaphors is **Desire to act**.[9] Most conceptual metaphors in the system convey the idea that the person experiences a drive to react, to engage in expressive (and sometimes aggressive) behavior (e.g., *to vent contained anger* - FLUID IN A PRESSURIZED CONTAINER; *to rave* – INSANITY; *to erupt, to thunder* – NATURAL PHYSICAL FORCE; *to snap at somebody, to snarl* – ANIMAL; *to go ballistic* – WEAPON; etc).

An additional semantic focus in the metaphorical representation of anger is **Control**, that is, the attempt to regulate the felt intensity or the expression of the emotion. Three metaphors emphasize the need for down-regulation and no (or controlled) expression: PRESSURIZED FLUID, AGGRESSIVE ANIMAL, and OPPONENT. According to the logic of those metaphors, people should exert a counter-pressure against the anger inside them to avoid expression (e.g., *to repress/suppress anger* – PRESSURIZED FLUID), they should tame or keep harnessed the most instinctual part in themselves (e.g., *bridle, keep a grip on anger* – ANIMAL), and they should aim to defeat the emotion in a fight for self-control (e.g., *to struggle/wrestle with one's anger* – OPPONENT). Some accounts of anger in the psychology models include this control component as well (Shaver, Schwartz, Kirson, & O'Connor, 1987; Russell & Fehr, 1994).

A last aspect highlighted by the metaphors in our folk model of the emotion is the difficulty inherent in controlling it. The **Difficulty to cope** focus is implicit in PRESSURIZED FLUID, AGGRESSIVE ANIMAL, and OPPONENT, which foreground the effortful opposition of two competing forces. But two other metaphors in the system take this dimension a step further and present anger as an intrinsically uncontrollable state. Control is not difficult, but rather impossible when the emotion is represented as a force of nature (*wave of indignation, flood of fury, anger storm* – NATURAL PHYSICAL FORCE) or a state of frantic delirium (*to be beside oneself with anger, deranged by anger, to have a fit* – INSANITY).

So far we have described how an analysis in terms of conceptual metaphors of the figurative expressions we use to talk about anger can inform us about the way the emotion is represented in our folk models. We have specifically described how the metaphors coherently highlight seven important aspects of the emotion that we have labeled "semantic foci." An important question at this point is how useful these semantic foci are for the study of emotion at large. A first answer was already proposed by Kövecses (2000: 47): some of the foci – like **Evaluation**, **Intensity**, or **Desire to act** – match Wierzbicka's semantic universals (cf. Wierzbicka, 1995b; see also Chapter 27). This would mean that aspects like evaluation, intensity, or desire to act are universal in emotion conceptualization. But the applicability of these foci outside linguistics and for all emotions also finds (partial) empirical support in the psychological literature on emotion. First, factorial or dimensional analyses of emotion lexicons around the world (e.g., Church, Katigbak, Reyes & Jensen, 1998; Fontaine, Poortinga, Setiadi, & Markam, 2002; Galati, Sini, Tinti, & Testa, 2008, Herrman & Raybeck, 1981, Russell, 1980; Shaver et al., 1987) have yielded the uncontested conclusion that **Evaluation** (also called axiology, VALENCE, or pleasantness) is one of the strongest dimensions underlying our representations of the emotional domain.

---

[9] Kövecses identifies two versions of Desire: desire to react as a result of the emotion, and desire to have the emotion (2000: 45). Given that the latter does not apply to ANGER because this is conceptualized as a negative emotion, Desire in this study only refers to "desire to act" or "reaction".

Secondly, another widely-observed dimension is AROUSAL (also called activation or activity). It refers to the level of "excitement" accompanying the emotion, typically sympathetic activation like increased heartbeat or breathing rate. AROUSAL is related to the semantic focus **Intensity**, although Intensity comprises more than AROUSAL (since "intense" emotions are also those with no physiological excitation, but with strong effects, as is the case for depression). In spite of the lack of perfect match, in as much as Intensity includes AROUSAL, Intensity can be considered a universal meaning focus in the conceptualization of emotion.

Thirdly, **Desire to act** finds its psychological counterpart in Frijda's Action Tendency theory (e.g., Frijda, 1986, 2007a). According to Frijda, emotions are best defined in terms of the actions (or motivational inclinations) they spur. In this sense, Desire to react is another viable candidate to universality. Furthermore, the GRID study reported in this volume (see Chapter 11) has provided evidence that action tendencies are tightly related to POWER or potency, a third and crucial dimension in the representation of the affective domain that is also found cross-culturally.

Three related semantic foci from Kövecses' inventory remain unaccounted for: **Harm, Control,** and **Difficulty** to cope. Kövecses himself suggests that these may not be universal aspects in the metaphorical representation of emotion, but typical of the occidental "emphasis on controlling emotion and regarding the emotions as things that are harmful to the proper functioning of the Western ideal of a rational person" (Kövecses, 2000: 48) (see also Solomon, 1993 for a similar account of Western thought). Kövecses may be right concerning the Western saliency of rationality, but emotional control should also be relevant for non-Western cultures that value interdependence among their members, as in those contexts the appropriate regulation of emotion would be particularly valued as a means to preserve societal harmony.

28.4 **Testing semantic dimensions with the GRID paradigm**

The GRID study reported in this volume employs an online questionnaire for native speakers of a language to rate how likely it is for a number of features to be part of the meaning of emotion words (see Chapter 5 for details). The semantic foci discussed above can be explored using the GRID paradigm because many of the features in the questionnaire refer to such aspects too.[10] Two of the words investigated in the GRID study were related to anger ("anger" and "irritation"). If the metaphor analysis revealed a semantic focus to be relevant for the characterization of anger, we expected the GRID features related to that focus to be perceived as salient in the meaning of the anger words (Hypothesis 1). The GRID scale ranged from 1 (= "extremely unlikely") to 9 (= "extremely likely"), with a middle point 5 (= "neither likely, nor unlikely") (see Chapter 5). The mean rates for the features were zero-centered (substracting five from them) and a t-test was used to determine which of them were salient. A feature was considered salient if it scored significantly above or below 0 (middle neutral point of the scale). Based on the previous metaphor analysis, we also hypothesized that some would be perceived as likely and others as unlikely (Hypothesis 2). Likely features were those scoring significantly above 0 (positive centered mean). Unlikely features were the ones scoring significantly below 0 (negative centered mean). Not all features in the questionnaire were analyzed. A selection was made a priori with those explicitly related to a semantic focus (N = 41). All semantic foci and their corresponding features can be found in Table 28.2 with indication of the expected effect (likely feature or unlikely feature), 0-centered mean rates in each language, and significance level.

....

[10] The features were not included in the questionnaire to address the foci reported in this paper, but they can be easily associated to them. Features were only retained if they referred to the foci under consideration literally.

Table 28.2 Relevance of the features pertaining to the various semantic foci highlighted by metaphor (t-test)

#	Feature	H	0-centered mean	
			Spanish	**English**
	Intensity			
116	the person was in an intense emotional state	P	2.19***	1.88***
	Evaluation			
118	the person felt good	N	−3.13***	−2.49***
128	the person felt positive	N	−2.71***	−2.44***
18	the event had consequences positive for the person	N	−2.94***	−2.24***
19	the event had consequences positive for somebody else	N	−2.21***	−0.75*
50	the person smiled	N	−3.15***	−2.97***
114	the person wanted to sing and dance	N	−3.22***	−2.71***
133	the person felt bad	P	1.79***	1.42***
123	the person felt negative	P	1.79***	2.34***
20	the event had consequences negative for the person	P	2.17***	2.56***
21	the event had consequences negative for somebody else	P	1.33***	1.1***
	Harm			
101	the person wanted to do damage, hit, or say something that hurts	P	3.21***	2.83***
112	the person wanted to destroy whatever was close	P	3.3***	2.69***
62	the person moved against people or things	P	1.76***	1.42***
110	the person wanted to be tender, sweet, and kind	N	−2.91***	−2.42***
	Causation			
26	event incongruent with own standards	P	1.76***	1.85***
27	event that violated laws or socially accepted norms	P	1.28***	1.53***
13	event that was caused by the person's own behavior	N	0.2	0.54
14	event that was caused by somebody else's behavior	P	1.58***	1.93***
6	event that was in itself pleasant for the person	N	−2.71***	−2.08***
7	event that was in itself pleasant for somebody else	N	−1.45***	−0.37
8	event that was in itself unpleasant for the person	P	2.03***	2.25***
9	event that was in itself unpleasant for somebody else	P	1.2***	0.85***
	Desire to act (reaction)			
76	the person wanted to go on with what he/she was doing	N	−1.63***	−1.44***
78	the person felt the urge to stop what he/she was doing	P	1.62***	2.02***
92	the person wanted to do nothing	N	−0.76**	−1.02***
88	the person felt an urge to be active, to do something	P	0.45	1.44***
93	lacked the motivation to pay attention to what was going on	N	0.12	0.2
90	the person felt an urge to be attentive to what was going on	P	0.02	0.36

Table 28.2 (continued) Relevance of the features pertaining to the various semantic foci highlighted by metaphor (t-test)

#	Feature	H	0-centered mean	
			Spanish	**English**
91	the person lacked the motivation to do anything	N	−0.1	−0.37
113	the person wanted to act, whatever action it might be	P	1.94***	1.92***
106	the person wanted to tackle the situation	P	1.17***	0.78*
86	the person wanted to submit to the situation as it was	N	−1.57***	−1.47***
79	the person wanted to undo what was happening	P	0.94***	2.17***
22	event that required an immediate response	P	0.63**	1.32***
	Control			
82	the person wanted to be in control of the situation	P	1.38***	1.88***
138	the person tried to control the intensity of the emotional feeling	P	0.29	0.86**
	Difficulty to cope with the emotion			
122	the person felt powerless	P	1.9***	0.42
132	the person felt out of control	P	2.78***	1.83***
127	the person felt powerful	N	−0.47	−0.25
125	the person felt in control	N	−1.49***	−1.15***

Note: features were considered salient if their mean (zero-centered) deviated significantly from zero (Hypothesis 1): * p <0.05, ** p <0.01, *** p <0.001 two-tailed. H = expected direction of the saliency (Hypothesis 2). P = positive mean expected (likely feature), N = negative mean expected (unlikely feature).

Three groups of native speakers were used in this study: a sample of English speakers from the USA (N = 59), a sample of Spanish speakers from the Basque Land (a Northern region of Spain) (N = 56), and a sample of Spanish speakers from several regions in the South of Spain (N = 30).[11] Two Spanish samples were chosen to provide a geographically varied account of peninsular Spanish, but they were treated as the same language group. The ages of the participants ranged between 13 and 57; mean ages (and SDs) were as follows: 18.37 (0.71) for the USA; 23.21 (6.32) for Northern Spain; 32.46 (13.47) for Southern Spain.

We collapsed responses for the two anger words in the GRID set: *anger* and *irritation* in English, *ira* and *irritación* in Spanish. The responses were collapsed because we were interested in features typical of both terms, as those more likely to be relevant for the ANGER category as a whole than features characteristic of one term only.

Three types of features were identified from the results of the t-test: salient features in both languages, non-salient features in both languages, and features salient for one language only. In order to explore the differences between the two languages, we conducted an additional analysis of variance, a two (English vs Spanish) × two (*anger* vs *irritation*) MANCOVA, with mean rate as covariate in order to control for possible differences in scale use.

The first group of features was the most numerous. Thirty-two out of the 41 selected features were indeed significant in the representation of anger for both languages (Hypothesis 1) and in

---

[11] We would like to thank Phoebe Ellsworth and Itziar Alonso-Arbiol for allowing us to use their US English and Northern Spanish datasets, respectively.

all cases the effect followed the direction predicted by metaphor (Hypothesis 2). In one more case (feature #138), the results seemed not to apply for one of the languages in spite of the trend in the expected direction, but the MANCOVA revealed no statistically significant differences between the samples.

The second group was constituted by three features for which the t-test confirmed the expected saliency and direction in one of the languages only (being non-significant in the other). The MANCOVA confirmed these differences. A main effect of language was found for the feature "felt an urge to be active, to do something" (#88) (p <0.05), more salient in English. In addition, "event was pleasant for somebody else" (#7) (p <0.05) – which was rated as unlikely – and "feeling powerless" (#122) (p <0.001) were more salient in Spanish. For the latter feature, an interaction was also found between language and emotion terms (p <0.05), indicating that Spanish *ira (anger)* was rated as involving a feeling of powerlessness (mean *ira* = 2.37, SD = 0.27), while English *anger* did not entail such a feeling (mean *anger* = −0.18, SD = 0.35).

Finally, a third group emerged with five features that, contrary to expectation, did not reach statistical significance in either language. Three of them belonged to the meaning focus Desire to act (reaction). These are features pertaining to attention deployment (#90, #93) and motivation to act (#91). The other two referred to whether the emotion is caused by the person's own behavior (#13) and whether he/she feels powerful (#127). In both languages, these features did not deviate significantly from the middle point of the scale (neither likely nor unlikely), indicating that they were not perceived as salient in the meaning of the two anger terms.

In summary, Hypothesis 1 concerning saliency was confirmed for 33 out of the 41 features (80.49%) and in all cases the effect followed the direction predicted by metaphor (Hypothesis 2), which indicates that, overall, elicited measures of meaning from naïve judges confirmed the observations of CMT. In terms of semantic foci, our hypotheses concerning Intensity, Evaluation, and Harm were confirmed in their entirety for both languages. In the following section, we explore in more detail some of the differences in saliency observed between the languages and illustrate other insights afforded by the GRID paradigm.

28.5 **GRID-specific insights**

The metaphor systems in English and Spanish for the conceptualization of anger are roughly equivalent (Soriano, 2005). This makes metaphor-based predictions applicable to both languages. So far we have seen how the GRID data can confirm most of them. But the GRID has also revealed differences between the two languages that cannot be immediately observed with a traditional analysis of metaphor of the sort illustrated in 28.2. For example, as we saw in the previous section, the t-test identified three features that are salient in one language but not the other. In addition, the MANCOVA can reveal relative differences between other coherent features that are salient in both languages.

The saliency of English Desire to act and Spanish Harm

One of the differences between the two languages concerns a relatively higher importance in English of features pertaining to the focus Desire to act. In addition to the already identified saliency in English (vs Spanish) on the feature "felt an urge to be active, to do something" (#88), the MANCOVA revealed differences for four other features. In spite of being relevant in both languages, the English ratings were significantly more extreme than the Spanish ones in the features "wanted to undo what was happening" (#79), more likely in English (p = 0.001), "wanted to do nothing" (#92), less likely in English (p <0.05), and "felt the urge to stop what he/she was doing" (#78), for which an interaction effect was also observed (p <0.05) (while in both languages "irritation" was more likely related to this feature than "anger," the difference was small in Spanish and very large in English). Spanish only scored higher on the feature "wanted to tackle the situation" (#106, p = 0.005) and an interaction with the emotion term was also observed (p <0.005): "anger" scored higher than "irritation" in both languages. All in all, more features emerged in the semantic focus Desire to act for which the English lexemes obtained significantly more extreme ratings than the Spanish ones.

Spanish, on the other hand, showed comparatively higher ratings for features related to the focus Harm. The MANCOVA revealed that the languages differed significantly in three features, all of them more likely in Spanish for both emotion terms: "wanted to do damage, hit, or say something that hurts" (#101, p = 0.005), "wanted to destroy whatever was close" (#112, p = 0.001) and "moved against people or things" (#62, p <0.05). A main effect of emotion term was also found in the latter case: "moving against people or things" was more likely for "anger" than "irritation" in both languages (p <0.05). In summary, the results of both the t-test and the MANCOVA reveal a greater saliency in English of features pertaining to a generic desire to react, while in Spanish greater importance is given to the aggressive tendencies of this reaction and the harm they cause.

The saliency of "others" in Spanish

One of the observed differences in Section 28.4 concerns the relative saliency in English vs Spanish of anger-eliciting events that affect "others" (and not only oneself). A traditional analysis of conceptual metaphors does not afford us any insight in this respect. By contrast, the GRID revealed that events that are pleasant for somebody else are more salient in our semantic representation of anger in Spanish than in English. The MANCOVA confirmed this observation and revealed an additional significant difference in the likelihood that anger would be elicited by an event with positive consequences for somebody else (#19, p = 0.01) (more unlikely in Spanish). This greater saliency in Spanish of events and consequences that affect others (rather than the person only) is coherent with the characterization of Spain as a more collectivistic culture in comparison to the more individualistic nature attributed to the United States (Hofstede, 1980). In collectivistic (or interdependent) cultures, the construal of the self involves not only the person, but the closest people in one's core social circle, especially the kin. This means that, in principle, events that affect in-group people should be more likely to be interpreted with the same relevance as if they were happening to oneself. This might explain our results and is only suggested here as a post-hoc explanation requiring further investigation.

Feeling "powerless" in Spanish

Another interesting difference is found for the feeling of powerlessness, more associated to the emotion in Spanish according to the t-test. The MANCOVA confirmed this difference and revealed congruent relative differences in other features in our selection. First, a main effect of language was found for the feature "felt out of control" (#132), likely and salient in both languages but significantly more in Spanish (p = 0.001). Additionally, an interaction between language and term was found for the feature "felt in control" (#125, p <0.05): while unlikely in both languages, Spanish *ira* is less likely to feel in control than English *anger*, although English *irritation* is less in control than Spanish *irritación*. The general saliency of powerlessness in Spanish is also coherent with the results of a previous study in which native speakers of English and Spanish were asked to label what one would feel in a number of emotion-eliciting situations (Ogarkova, Soriano, & Lehr, 2012). For the anger-eliciting contexts, the word "impotence" in Spanish (*impotencia*) was as frequently quoted as the most frequent Spanish anger word in the study (*rabia*). By contrast, *impotence* was hardly ever used in English. Additional research is still necessary to clarify the exact nature of this "powerlessness," that is, what it is that Spanish speakers seem to feel powerless about, according to the meaning of the anger words in their language (cf. also Chapter 22).

28.6 **CMT-specific insights**

In spite of its usefulness, the current GRID questionnaire entails some limitations with respect to metaphor analysis as well. Metaphor highlights the existence of some aspects in our folk-understanding of anger that the current set of questions in the GRID instrument does not tap on. These include, for example, the damage that the emotion can cause *to the experiencer* of anger (an insight best captured by the metaphors ILLNESS, FIRE, or PRESSURIZED FLUID) and the culturally-imposed evaluation of *debasement* that the person incurs if he/she lets the emotion gain control over him/her (as highlighted by the ANIMAL metaphor).

An additional aspect highlighted by metaphor is the *irrationality* involved in the emotion, mostly captured and elaborated by the metaphors INSANITY and ANIMAL. While salient in our folk representations, irrational behavior may not play such a central role in the scientific views of the emotion, as suggested both by the absence of features inquiring about rationality/irrationality in the GRID questionnaire and the figurative ways in which psychologists themselves talk about emotion, in comparison to laymen. In an analysis of English psychology guides and of websites where laypeople turn for advice on their psychological problems, Berger and Jäkel (2009) found that experts hardly talk about anger resorting to the INSANITY metaphor, while the strategy is common among laypeople. This may reflect a tendency in the expert discourse to foreground the general adaptive nature of emotion rather than the possibly negative consequences of appraisal biases and disregulation.

Some other features highlighted by metaphor are only implicit in the GRID questionnaire. One of them is the idea of *utility*. According to metaphor, anger is a tool – and more specifically a weapon – useful to empower the person to reach their goals (WEAPON, FUEL/SOURCE OF ENERGY– cf. Kövecses, 1990). Another aspect fully elaborated by metaphor but only tangentially approached by the GRID is the *necessity for emotional control* or *regulation*. Notice that the anger metaphors reported in this study can be broadly divided into three groups: metaphors that tell us what anger feels like (FIRE, ILLNESS), metaphors that tell us why anger happens (TRESPASSING, PHYSICAL NUISANCE), and metaphors that tell us what anger does (OPPONENT, ANIMAL, NATURAL FORCE, INSANITY, FLUID, WEAPON). The latter are the most abundant type, so it is the dynamics of emotional behavior and its control that these conceptual metaphors mostly elaborate on. By contrast, the current formulation of the GRID questionnaire devotes comparatively less attention to emotion control (only four features) and more to a different type of control: the "potency" or "POWER" to cope with the circumstances in which the emotion has emerged and their consequences (cf. Chapter 5) (for suggestions on expanded versions of the GRID questionnaire see Chapters 3 and 22).

28.7 **Conclusions**

In this paper, we have explored how our folk representation of anger can be studied looking at language in two complementary ways: through key emotion terms and through figurative language. The link between both approaches has been a number of semantic foci or aspects of emotion frequently highlighted by conceptual metaphors across the emotional domain.

On the basis of linguistic observation of figurative language use, we first described the implicit conceptualization of anger in English and Spanish in terms of conceptual metaphors. Building on this model, several hypotheses were proposed on the nature of the concept ANGER in English and Spanish in terms of Causation, Controllability, Desire to act, Evaluation, Harm, Difficulty to cope with the emotion, and Intensity. These semantic foci seem to have a very wide-spread scope and some of them resemble well-established constructs in psychology, like action tendencies and the VALENCE and AROUSAL dimensions. The GRID questionnaire was shown to be able to tap on the same semantic aspects and provide quantitative empirical evidence about them. A number of features from the questionnaire pertaining to the foci were selected and used to test the hypothesized saliency of the various aspects highlighted by metaphor in the meaning of two anger terms in English and Spanish: *anger/ira* and *irritation/irritación*. Most of the hypotheses were confirmed, but the GRID proved also capable of providing additional, more nuanced and language-specific insight about the meaning of the words, for example with respect to the relative saliency of aggression, feelings of POWER, or the emotion's social scope. Metaphor analysis, in turn, was capable of pointing out aspects of ANGER overseen (or underdeveloped) in the current GRID questionnaire, like the irrationality and debasement attached to the emoter, the need for emotional control, and the potential harm to oneself that are implicit in our folk models of the emotion.

Both approaches have advantages and disadvantages. A CMT approach as illustrated in Section 2 is limited in that it can only hint at likely and unlikely features, but it cannot *confirm* what is actually part of the representation of the emotion in the speakers' minds. A statistical corpus-based study of metaphor (cf. Chapters 29 and 30) or a testing tool like the GRID questionnaire are better equipped to provide quantifiable empirical answers in this respect. Conversely, the GRID instrument can only inquire about the features already built in. An examination of language use, like the one afforded by metaphor analysis, is better equipped to *explore* what areas of experience may be relevant in the representation of emotion and thus in the meaning of words.

All in all, both methods have proven to be complementary, supplying converging evidence on a number of aspects concerning the representation of emotion, as well as supplementary approach-specific insight. Semantic foci also proved useful as *tertium comparationis* for a systematic comparison of both methodologies. This common ground or common language is desirable for interdisciplinary communication and cross-fertilization, very much in the spirit of the Affective Sciences, where the close collaboration between disciplines and the use of mutually informative methodologies continues to be the best resource we count on to advance in our understanding of emotion.

Acknowledgments

This research has been carried out with the support of the project "Conceptual metaphors: Language, thought and brain" (ref. P09-SEJ-4772) funded by the Consejería de Innovación, Ciencia y Empresa, Junta de Andalucía, and the European Regional Development Fund (ERDF).

## Chapter 29

English "fear" and Polish "strach" in contrast: The GRID paradigm and the Cognitive Corpus Linguistic methodology

Barbara Lewandowska-Tomaszczyk[1], Paul A. Wilson, and Y. Niiya

29.1 Introduction

The present paper is a contrastive study of the English emotion *fear* and its Polish dictionary equivalent *strach*. Preliminary analyses based on the dimensional structure reported by Fontaine et al. (2007) highlighted potentially interesting differences between these two emotions on the POWER dimension. Fontaine et al. explain that the POWER "dimension is characterized by appraisals of control, leading to feelings of POWER or weakness; interpersonal dominance or submission, including impulses to act or refrain from action; changes in the rate and volume of speech; and parasympathetic symptoms" (2007: 1051). The POWER dimension is particularly relevant to fear, as the GRID features that have relatively high and low loadings on this dimension characterize two of the main fear responses that have been observed in both animals and humans: *fight* and *fright* (the third one – *flight* – will not be considered here). In this paper, we aim to demonstrate how *fear* and *strach* differ in terms of fight and fright response styles.

According to Eilam (2005), the fight response involves a direct attack aimed at the source of fear in order to dissuade it from launching its own offensive, and it occurs when it is not possible to freeze or flee. Placing the fight response in a wider human context, this response style can be witnessed whenever an individual actively confronts a source of danger. He/she then feels powerful, dominant and, if successful, in control of fear. Fontaine et al. (2007) explain that a high level of POWER is characterized by feelings of POWER, interpersonal dominance, and impulses to act. There is clear correspondence then between the fight response and high POWER.

Fright has been demonstrated in both animals and humans in a number of studies. Fiszman et al. (2008) explain that fright "is a reflexive and involuntary defensive response characterized in several species by profound motor inhibition, lack of vocalization, tremors, and analgesia, with evidence of preserved awareness of the environment" (pp 193–194). Fright is a survival mechanism that is used to reduce the likelihood that a predator will continue its attack (Monassi, 1999). Human instances of fright have been described in World War I soldiers (van der Hart et al., 2000)

---

[1] Corresponding author: Barbara Lewandowska-Tomaszczyk. Department of English Language and Applied Linguistics, University of Łódź, Kosciuszki 65, 90–514 Łódź, Poland. E-mail: blt@uni.lodz.pl

and victims of sexual abuse (Heidt et al., 2005). In a broader context, LeDoux and Gorman (2001) explain that in more everyday situations the behavioral correlates of fright are becoming withdrawn, avoidant, and sometimes despondent. An individual with the fright response experiences a paralyzing effect and feels weak, submissive, passive, and controlled by fear. Fontaine et al. (2007) describe low POWER in terms of feelings of weakness and submission, as well as impulses to refrain from action. It is clear that fright corresponds closely to low POWER.

The results of our preliminary analyses showed that whereas *strach* was associated with relatively lower POWER, *fear* was characterized by higher POWER. This led to the more rigorous testing of the comparison between *strach* and *fear* on the POWER dimension using the GRID instrument. However, in addition to the GRID methodology, we employ a cognitive linguistic analysis of Polish and English corpus materials (Lewandowska-Tomaszczyk & Dziwirek, 2009; Dziwirek & Lewandowska-Tomaszczyk, 2010). The equivalents to low and high POWER in the corpus analysis are the fear event scenarios of FRIGHT and FIGHT, respectively (see sections 29.3, 29.4 and 29.5 below).

The two approaches employed are not mutually exclusive, but rather complementary. In what follows we will first present the results with the GRID instrument and then discuss aspects of cognitive linguistics which, combined with corpus data, provide converging and complementary results.

29.2 Semantic profiles analysis: the GRID data

Analyses were performed to compare Polish-speaking participants' ratings of *strach* (21 participants: mean age 23 years, 19 females) with British English-speaking participants' ratings of *fear* (36 participants: mean age 21.5 years, 21 females) on the GRID features that were associated with low and high POWER. First, it was necessary to identify these features. Principal component analyses performed on all the contributing languages in the GRID project has revealed that emotional representation can be divided into four dimensions (VALENCE, POWER, AROUSAL, and NOVELTY, in order of importance – see Chapter 7). Table 29.1 shows the features that loaded on the POWER dimension (with loadings in parenthesis), divided into high-power and low-power features. These are consistent with the FRIGHT and FIGHT event scenarios identified in the corpora (see below).

The means of the low-power features and the high-power features were determined for each subject. A 2 × 2 ANOVA was then performed on these means that had one between-subjects variable (language group: Polish *strach* vs English *fear*). There was also one within-subjects variable that was the dichotomization of features into low vs high POWER (POWER: low-power features vs high-power features – see Table 29.1). There was a significant main effect of POWER, $F(1, 55) = 52.22$, p <0.0001. From Figure 29.1, it can be seen that low-power features were rated as comparatively more likely to occur than high-power features (means of 6.65 and 5.25, respectively). There was also a significant main effect of language group, $F(1, 55) = 6.15$, p <0.05. *Fear* was associated with a higher likelihood of occurrence of the features on the POWER dimension than *strach* (means of 6.2 and 5.71, respectively). There was also a significant interaction between language group and POWER, $F(1, 55) = 10.59$, p <0.01. Contrasts were performed to break down this interaction. There was a significant difference between *strach* and *fear* on the high-power features, $F(1, 55) = 12.12$, p <0.01. Figure 29.1 shows that *fear* was relatively more associated with experiences of higher high-power ratings than *strach* (means of 5.81 and 4.7, respectively). By contrast, there was no significant difference between *strach* and *fear* on the low-power features, $F(1, 55) = 0.45$, p >0.05. Both *strach* and *fear* had lower scores on the high-power features than the low-power features: $F(1, 55) = 43.48$, p <0.0001, for *strach*; $F(1, 55) = 10.7$, p <0.01, for *fear*. Looking at Figure 29.1, it can be seen that

Table 29.1 GRID features defining the POWER dimension

Low-power features	High-power features
Decreased the volume of voice (0.749)	Increased the volume of voice (0.804)
Fell silent (0.708)	Had an assertive voice (0.749)
Felt weak limbs (0.667)	Felt dominant (0.643)
Closed his or her eyes (0.655)	Spoke faster (0.637)
Felt weak (0.645)	Wanted to take initiative him/herself (0.610)
Wanted someone to be there to provide help and support (0.625)	Wanted to act, whatever action it might be (0.550)
Spoke slower (0.624)	Wanted to be in control of the situation (0.501)
Wanted to hand over the initiative to somebody else (0.617)	Wanted to move (0.498)
Felt submissive (0.591)	Wanted to tackle the situation (0.491)
Wanted to make up for what she or he had done (0.591)	
Had a trembling voice (0.583)	
Showed tears (0.569)	
Had a lump in the throat (0.511)	

this difference was more pronounced for *strach* (means of 6.73 and 4.7 for low-power and high POWER, respectively) than *fear* (means of 6.58 and 5.81 for low POWER and high POWER, respectively).

All in all the data suggests that both in English and Polish the concept of fear is conceptualized as involving a sense of low POWER, rather than high POWER. However, for the English participants the mean for the high-power features is higher than for the Polish participants which might mean that the Polish term *strach* is overall lower on POWER than the English word *fear*.

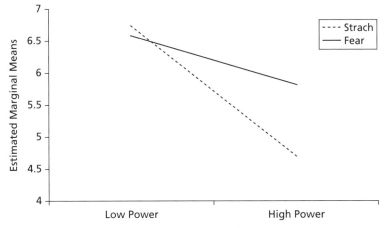

Figure 29.1 Means of strach vs fear on low and high-power features.

29.3 **Cognitive corpus linguistics analysis: Scenarios**

Language materials

Instead of limiting our analysis to the de-contextualized meaning of words (like the GRID does), we also resort to large corpora of English and Polish. Such corpus-based studies describe meaning as being dependent on context, which can be uncovered by means of collocations and their frequencies and also by the conceptual environment pertaining to a word. Based on frequency of occurrence, corpus-based methods let us determine statistically which meanings are most salient.

Corpus studies are carried out most commonly by looking at words and their contexts in large collections of authentic natural language, compiled from written and oral sources. Quantitative data sets are compared to see if an observed phenomenon (e.g., a co-occurrence) is significantly more frequent than another; frequencies of lexical co-occurrences are also used for descriptive purposes and exemplification.

The materials we used come from several sources. First, we used the British National Corpus (100 million words) and a combined Longman and Microconcord corpus (15 million words) of English. Second, for Polish we used two large sources: the second demo version of the National Corpus of Polish (NKJP) (with over 400 million words at the time of the research, and still growing) and the Polish reference PELCRA corpus (93 million words), compiled at the Department of English Language and Applied Linguistics of Lodz University. Additionally, two samplers were also used: a PELCRA Polish Sampler with 14,098,028 words and an English Sampler (Combined Longman and Microconcord English data) with 14,001,641 words. Both large corpora and both samplers are comparable in size and they cover well-balanced language materials of different genres and styles, including written and spoken (ca. 10%) conversational data.

Unlike the GRID instrument, corpus findings do not focus exclusively on nominal concepts, but can be extended to cover adjectives, adverbs, verbs, and their participial forms. This is desirable in the investigation of concepts, which can be manifested in multiple ways (e.g., the important role of prepositions in Polish or English, as in *fear of, fear about, fear from*, or *fear for* – cf. Dziwirek & Lewandowska-Tomaszczyk, 2010). However, to make them comparable to the GRID data, we only used data of the nominal *fear* and *strach* words in the present paper. We conducted automatic analyses of these word frequencies and their lexical collocations (more precisely, the verbs and prepositions that introduce them) in spoken and written texts. The search tools Wordsmith Tools and SlopeQ (http://tnij.org/slopeq1) were applied to generate the word frequencies and (parts of speech-sensitive) collocations. We also manually extracted contexts of relevant words and relevant metaphors (cf. Lakoff & Johnson, 1980; Lakoff & Kövecses, 1987), and annotated the axiological charge of the emotions (positive-negative) in context and their membership to FRIGHT or FIGHT scenarios. Frequencies were counted for the types of scenario and metaphor types.

Emotion Event scenarios

Emotion words, like any other, can be analyzed as isolated concepts, whose meanings can be extracted by means of questionnaires and which adequately describe prototypical emotion category members. On the other hand, one can look at emotion words as they are used in authentic language materials (spoken and written), by different speakers, in numerous contexts and infer their regular patterns of use in terms of canonical or elaborate Emotion Events (EEs). Canonical Emotion Events are patterned in terms of typical scenarios which cover states and activities and involve participants interconnected by relations in a given spatio-temporal context.

Fear words participate in Events with a prototypical scenario involving two actors: a cause or stimulus of fear (see Document SM 1 for examples),[2] felt as a *threat* (prototypically a grammatical object), and an experiencer of fear (typically the grammatical subject). Fear relations in a fear-event can be accounted for by resorting to the concept of *force dynamics*. Force dynamics (cf. Talmy, 1988) describes the ways entities interact in an event where one of them is trying to exert POWER over the other using a physical (prototypically) or a mental force. Fear is conceptualized by assuming a scenario in which fear is perceived as an agonist ("doer") and the experiencer as an antagonist. The outcome of the force dynamics depends on the balance of forces: either the agonist wins and fear overcomes the experiencer, or the experiencer succeeds and fear is con-quered. Other EE participants are also potentially present in extended fear scenarios (e.g., agent, beneficiary).

We propose here that the concepts of *fear* in English and *strach* in Polish are polysemous, as the authentic corpus data we investigate show at least two senses, which can be captured in terms of two different scenarios with different reactions of the experiencer towards fear. The FRIGHT scenario (paralyzing effect, passive, the experiencer feels weak, submissive, and fully controlled by fear; examples 1–4) is expressed in the pattern *Fear overcame Experiencer* and the effect on the experiencer is paralysis. The FIGHT scenario (active challenge, the experiencer feels powerful, dominant, and in control of fear; examples 5–8) involves an active challenge towards the emotion and eventual control over it.

1 *Strach opanował wszystkich w mieście* (Fear overwhelmed everybody in town).

2 *Przez lata rządził nami strach* (For years fear ruled over us).

3 *Those nearest to him fell back in fear. Even Hazel could not have said a word for his life.*

4 *Okonkwo was not a cruel man. But his whole life was dominated by fear.*

5 *Skoczkowie wiedzą, że strach to jest coś, co po prostu trzeba pokonać* (Ski jumpers know that fear is something one has simply to fight).

6 *Zwykle podczas lotu strach rozpuszczam w podwójnym ginie z tonikiem* (Usually during the flight I dilute the fear in double gin and tonic).

7 *Paul fought down his fear.*

8 *Where East Germans conquer fear.*

A number of problems arose with the classification of the examples in the course of the analysis, connected with the nature of language and communication, and in particular with the absence of crisp inter-categorical semantic boundaries. Firstly, not all corpus examples are clear-cut instances of the category fear. In many cases, one does not experience a simple single emotion, but rather a fairly complex, or blended one. Such blended concepts or combinations of emotions occur in both languages, where emotions come in clusters, as in:

9 *Like Mickey Rooney staring down at him, unable to speak, trembling with fear and confusion.*

10 *In fear and trepidation.*

11 *Kipiał we mnie strach i odraza* (Fear and repulsion were boiling in me).

12 *Rozpacz i strach zagłusza szaleńczym treningiem szarych komórek* ([He] dampens despair and fear with mad training of gray matter).

---

2 All supplementary materials (SM) are available at the GRID website: http://www.affective-sciences.org/ GRID. See Appendix 1 ("Availability") for further details.

When two such emotions (e.g., *fear and repulsion)* are mentioned, the combination names a new conceptual/emotional space, which is composed by the two emotions named and an emergent, new conceptual structure that has a value that is different from the two component ones. The combination of *fear* and *repulsion* produces a complex emotion in which fear is not experienced consecutively before or after repulsion, but together with repulsion; both are strong and agitating emotions, and their blended experience does not happen to have a lexicalized label in Polish (or English).

We also note a number of problems with the interpretation of examples including modal and auxiliary verbs, like *he was trying to control his fear* or *he has to overcome his fear*. The former is rather consistent with the FIGHT scenario, but the latter can only be classified as a "potential" FIGHT reaction scenario. The same problems arise with questions and commands.

Negation is a different case. For example, in *"he is not paralyzed by fear"* the FIGHT scenario is not explicitly mentioned. Nevertheless, it is known from semantic analyses of negation (cf. e.g., Lewandowska-Tomaszczyk, 1996) that negative utterances are rich in presuppositional content and there is reason to assume that the example illustrates a FIGHT scenario. A force-dynamic pattern is presupposed in the negative sentence in which fear has a strong force but, against expectation, the experiencer does not yield and succeeds in defeating the emotion. This complex scene is rendered as a negated FRIGHT scenario, but a classification as FIGHT can be performed when the wider context is taken into consideration.

There is still a different problem with the experiencer's reactions in the form of *trembling with fear* or *shaking with fear*. It is possible to be trembling or shaking with fear and still be fighting fear. But it is also possible to be trembling and shaking with fear and being inactive – i.e., FRIGHT. Such cases then, with no additional clues, cannot be unambiguously classified.

Emotion concepts, and fear among them, are frequently described metaphorically or metonymically, which uncovers additional facets of the meanings of *strach* and *fear*, not necessarily unambiguously covered in the GRID features. The properties of such figurative uses, and in particular their source domains, are quite revealing in this respect. They merit special attention and will be described in Section 29.4.

Corpus findings

The first quantitative analyses revealed that the Polish noun *strach* is used more frequently than the English noun *fear* in the corpora consulted, but the difference is negligible (6,292 occurrences of *strach* and 6,028 of *fear*). During the next step, 1,500 *fear* and *strach* examples from each of the *fear/strach* concordances obtained from the BNC and PELCRA were randomly generated, and the concordances that describe reactions to fear in each language were manually excerpted (196 in English and 140 in Polish). In English, there were 78 FRIGHT scenarios (39.8%) and 82 FIGHT scenarios (41.8%), whereas in Polish there were 66 FRIGHT scenarios (47.1%), and 34 FIGHT scenarios (24.3%). These numbers refer to the cases that could be unambiguously interpreted (160 out of the 196 English concordances, and 100 out of the 140 Polish concordances). The remaining examples belonged either to the FLIGHT scenario (not discussed in the present chapter) or were ambiguous as to the interpretation.

The results show that whereas in Polish, FRIGHT is a more frequent scenario than FIGHT, and thus conceptually more salient, there is no significant difference between the two in English. Therefore, it could be conjectured that a (proto)typical reaction to a threatening stimulus is a *fright* response in Polish. The FIGHT scenario, however, is significantly more frequent in the English than in the Polish data. More light will be shed on this issue by the metaphoricity reported in Section 29.4.

Collocational patterns of the fear nouns and VALENCE relations in English and Polish appear to add still another perspective to the fear concept. First of all, collocational patterns reveal typical causes of English *fear*, as reflected by the pattern *fear of* in the English Sampler. They include (*fear of*) *losing, God, consequences, the unknown, men, the future, failure, death, life, revolution, man, pain, the British*, and POWER (see Table SM 1 for more details). It is interesting to note that written corpus data (particularly recent press articles from 2006–2009) include *crime, debt, violence, crisis*, and *unemployment* as directly neighboring the frequencies obtained for "(*fear of*) *death*." A full list of causes observed in the comparable Polish sample can be found in Table SM 2. The first 10 are *death, pain, life, Russia, blood, the night, Germans, love, war*, and *master/God*. Some of the causes, in particular those with the highest frequencies, overlap in both languages. They correspond to more universal concepts such as *death, pain*, or *the future*. Others, like *communism, war, Russia*, and *Germans*, appear more frequently in the Polish data. While one cannot identify significant differences over such a fairly small set of data, the results may be interpreted against the historical background of the communities using the two languages.

The collocational patterns of *fear* and *strach* with other emotion terms uncover the most salient chains or clusters of emotion senses (see Table 29.2). One of our assumptions here is that meanings

Table 29.2 Collocations of "fear" and "strach" with other emotion terms in the English and Polish samplers

Word	N° Texts	Total	Word	N° Texts	Total
ANGER	5	21	WSTYD "shame"	10	14
ANXIETY	4	21	LĘK "anxiety"	11	13
GUILT	4	18	ROZPACZ "despair"	8	12
HATRED	4	12	NIENAWIŚĆ "hate"	7	12
JEALOUSY	3	10	NIENAWISCI "hate" [Gen]	6	10
PITY	3	8	RADOSCI "joy" [Gen]	10	10
PANIC	3	7	RADOŚĆ "joy"	6	8
DESIRE	3	7	NIEPEWNOŚĆ "uncertainty"	6	9
SHOCK	3	7	WOLNOŚĆ "freedom"	6	9
LOATHING	2	6	NIEPOKÓJ "uneasiness/anxiety"	7	9
HORROR	2	6	ODPOWIEDZIALNOŚC* "responsibility"	6	8
RAGE	1	6	OBAWA "weaker fear"	6	8
AGGRESSION	2	5	NIECHĘCI "unwillingness"/"resentment" [Gen]	5	7
GREED	4	5	MIŁOŚCI "love"	5	7
DISTRESS	2	5	ŻAL "sadness, yearning, longing for"	6	7
TERROR	3	5	CIEKAWOŚĆ "interest"	4	6
RESPECT	4	5	PRZERAŻENIE "horror"	4	6
			ROZPACZY "despair" [Gen]	5	6
			NIECHĘĆ "unwillingness"/"resentment" [Gen]	5	6
			NADZIEI "hope" [Gen]	5	5
			PONIŻENIA "humiliation" [Gen]	4	5

Note: [Gen] Genitive

of emotion words are very difficult, if not impossible, to discreetly dissect into crisp notions. Instead, we think that such meanings overlap in some of their aspects and dimensions. Therefore, when people use language, they will have a tendency to mention a number of emotions in a row to convey an enriched and fuller description of their feelings to the interlocutor. Alternatively, some emotions appear as an integrated, blended concept whose input emotions may contain opposing features, as in *love and fear* (see Turner & Fauconnier (1998) for the concept of blending).

One last observation refers to the higher incidence of positive emotions and attitudes in the emotion-word collocations of Polish *strach* compared to English *fear* (e.g., *wolność* "freedom," *radość* "joy," or *strach i nadzieja* "fear and hope").

29.4 Corpus and cognitive linguistic analysis: conceptual metaphors

Although fear and other emotions are experienced by every human being, we believe that their meanings are not effable for explicit semantic characterization by means of necessary and sufficient properties of a given sense. Moreover, cross-linguistic comparisons show also that what is a fairly crisp concept in one language may be considered a blended notion in another (see Turner & Fauconnier, 1998; see also Chapter 36). However, the Principle of Effability, first proposed by the philosopher Katz (1978: 209–216), assumes that any thought a person can have "can be expressed by some sentence in any natural language," so any thought expressed in one language can also be expressed in another. Our position in this respect is rather that parts of the meanings of emotion concepts are accessible via behavioral and experiential properties and conceptualized not as direct meanings but as networks of different kinds of meaning via figurative, frequently, metaphoric forms. Therefore, while we accept and use a meaning description in terms of component features, we also make an attempt to enrich them with the analysis of *mental imagery* expressed in language, predominantly in terms of figurative uses, which frequently involve metaphor. Here we make use of the notion of conceptual metaphor as put forward in cognitive linguistics (see Chapter 4). Conceptual metaphor is a cross-domain mapping in which a conceptual domain is understood as a mental structure of related concepts capturing a body of knowledge. In conceptual metaphors, one of the domains (the "target domain") is understood in terms of another (the "source domain"), which is usually more basic and physically grounded. The source functions as a mapping site for a given target domain. For example, the linguistic metaphor *Tom is a lion* is based on a conceptual metaphor in which the source domain of lions—which includes the wide concept of lions, their looks, behavior, habitat, associations, and evaluation—constitutes a mapping site for the conceptualization of Tom's courageous behavior (the target domain). Emotions too can be mapped onto by a number of source domains, some of which apply to the notion of fear. According to our data, fear can be conceptualized as an opponent or enemy (*fighting against fear*), dirt (*I'm fasting to cleanse myself of fear and helplessness*), a ruler (*a dominion of fear, regime of fear*), an unwanted guest (*fear knocks at my door*), a winner (*fear overcame me*), or a defeated agent (*he killed the fear*).

Emotions can also be represented metonymically. Metonymy foregrounds areas of contiguity or inclusion between two domains. One illustrative example of metonymy is a *pars pro toto* or part-for-a-whole relation, in which one word or phrase is substituted for another with which it is closely associated (such as *crown* for *royalty*, *skirt* for *woman*, *the White House* for the *US presidency*). In the realm of fear, metonymy can be seen in expressions that refer to the physiological effects of the emotion, like *shock of fear*, or in complex metaphor-metonymy scenarios where what is exploited are both processes (metaphor and metonymy), as in "*the failure nevertheless sent a shiver of fear through both markets and the Treasury*," in which *a shiver of fear* is part of the bodily reactions to fear (metonymy). The whole scene is metaphoric, involving a *failure* conceptualized as an agent that *sends* an object (*fear*), possibly an instrument, which is likely to be sharp (and dangerous) and goes *through* (i.e., affects rapidly and violently) the entire object, *markets and the Treasury*.

All the figurative expressions around the lexemes *fear* and *strach* can also be profitably analyzed as instances of the FRIGHT or the FIGHT scenario. Examples of the figurative FRIGHT scenario in Polish and English include the following phrases (for more examples from the corpora see Document SM 2): *umierał ze strachu* (was dying of fear), *dusi ją strach* (fear strangles her), *tortured by fear*, *a straitjacket of fear*, etc. Some figurative examples of FIGHT scenarios in Polish and English include *zagłuszył strach* (he dampened fear), *oddalił strach* (he sent his fear away), *przełamał strach* (he broke fear), *to choke back fear*, *defeat fear*, or *conquer fear*.

The analysis of the figurative expressions in our corpus data reveals that the majority of metaphor source domains are identical in both languages. For the FRIGHT scenario, the main domains used are sickness (madness, paralysis), death, temperature (freezing, cold), immobilization, rule and control. The predominant source domains with reference to the FIGHT scenario come from physical fighting and killing. Other domains involve occasional reference to bodily processes such as swallowing, or physical covering, breaking, and generally destroying.

A more detailed analysis of the metaphors reveals a frequent use of the processes of personification, reification, and spiritualization. In personification *fear* is conceptualized as an animate (human) agent acting upon the passive experiencer (as in *consumed by fear*, *dominated by fear*, *silenced by fear*, *locked by fear*), or where the experiencer is active and *knocks out* fear or *conquers* it. In reification, *fear* is considered an object or an instrument (as in *spit the fear* or *swallow fear*), a medical condition, or a wound (e.g., *to be weakened with fear*). Finally, in spiritualization, fear has a ghost-like nature, as in *possessed by fear* or *haunting fear*. In all cases, the metaphors convey an image of fear affecting the experiencer in the first phase, with possible FRIGHT (and *surrender*) or FIGHT (and *combat*) outcomes.

In sum, there are two co-operating figurative phenomena: (a) a metonymic representation of the emotion in terms of its effects (either potentially real – e.g., shaking – or fully metaphorical – e.g., dying) and (b) a metaphorical representation of the emotion, the most frequent of which is fear as a personified agent against which the experiencer has to fight. In this case, the struggle for emotion regulation can be won by the person (FIGHT scenarios) or by the emotion (FRIGHT scenarios).

Finally, we will look at the frequency of figurative vs literal expressions in FIGHT and FRIGHT scenarios in our Polish and English data (a random selection of 1,500 sentences containing the words *strach* and *fear*, respectively) and the number of figurative types observed (total number of different metaphors or metonymies). This can give us an idea of the relative centrality of FRIGHT and FIGHT reactions associated with *fear* and *strach*. In Polish, we identified 66 instances of FRIGHT sentences, of which 35 were non-figurative and 31 were figurative (the latter comprised 14 different types of figurative scenarios), and 23 FIGHT sentences, of which five were non-figurative and 18 were figurative (the latter comprised nine different types of figurative scenarios). For English, in 78 instances of FRIGHT sentences, there were 33 non-figurative and 45 figurative cases (the latter comprised 22 different types of figurative scenarios), and in 82 FIGHT sentences, there were 38 non-figurative and 44 figurative cases (the latter comprised 10 different types of figurative scenarios). The type-token ratio between the number of figurative uses and their types is shown in Table 29.3 (a full inventory of all figurative scenarios for FIGHT and FRIGHT in Polish and English in our data – a random 1,500 sentence selection – can be found in Document SM 2).

The numbers suggest that the paralyzing effect of fear (i.e., FRIGHT) can be possibly considered the most salient scenario for this emotion (over FIGHT responses) for both Polish and English. FRIGHT has almost twice as many different figurative scenarios than FIGHT in both languages, and

Table 29.3 Type-token relationship between fright and fight in Polish and English

	Polish	**English**
FRIGHT	31 examples – 14 types	45 examples – 22 types
	(2.2 tokens per 1 type)	(2.0 tokens per 1 type)
FIGHT	18 examples – 9 types	44 examples – 10 types
	(2.0 tokens per 1 type)	(4.4 tokens per 1 type)

its type-token ratio is almost identical in them. However, the FIGHT number of instances is higher in English (44 tokens) than in Polish (18 tokens).

29.5 Cognitive corpus interpretation versus GRID data

The comparison of the two methodologies revealed some interesting consistencies. From Table 29.4, it can be seen that the significantly higher ratings on the high (vs low) POWER GRID features of *fear* (mean, 5.81) in comparison with *strach* (mean, 4.7) is congruent with the corpus results, where FIGHT is also more salient for *fear* (41.8%) than *strach* (24.3%) (see Section 29.3 for details of what the percentages refer to). Additionally, both methodologies reveal a more marked Polish preference for low (vs high) POWER reactions. This is shown in the GRID, where the mean difference for low and high-power features in Polish (means of 6.73 and 4.7, respectively) is larger than in English (means of 6.58 and 5.81, respectively). And this effect is even more salient in the corpus results: while the frequencies of FRIGHT and FIGHT scenarios are about the same for English *fear* (39.8% and 41.8%, respectively), FRIGHT is almost twice as frequent as FIGHT in Polish *strach* (47.1% and 24.3%, respectively). In sum, FIGHT/high POWER is higher (than FRIGHT/low POWER) for *fear* than for *strach*. And FRIGHT/low POWER is more salient (than FIGHT/high POWER) in *strach* than in *fear*.

A word of caution regarding the reaction type frequencies (i.e., FRIGHT vs FIGHT) should be added in connection with the corpus methodology. Corpora have their limitations. There are tools available to generate frequencies of individual items and phrases, concordances with expanded contexts, collocations, and keywords. There are also encouraging results of automatic metaphor identification (e.g., Stefanowitch & Gries, 2007). However, when it comes to semantic and pragmatic annotations of meanings in use, particularly in large corpora, adequate corpus tools are practically in *statu nascendi*. This is especially relevant to our discussion of the FRIGHT and FIGHT scenarios. As indicated above, it is not always possible to automatically determine (at least not to the extent needed for the sake of an over-one-billion-item corpus) whether the use of an item, phrase or sentence is unmarked or marked, whether it is jocular, ironic, used as pretence, or whether it is

Table 29.4 Comparison of the corpus and GRID results

	Fear	**Strach**
Corpus Methodology – FRIGHT Scenario (%)	39.8	47.1
Corpus Methodology – FIGHT Scenario (%)	41.8	24.3
GRID Methodology – Low-power features (means)	6.58	6.73
GRID Methodology – High-power features (means)	5.81	4.70

entirely neutral and unmarked. Furthermore, some of the descriptions of the reactions do not refer to the Polish or English experiencers and may involve references to people of different national or ethnic backgrounds. When discussing frequencies of *fear* reactions then, one has to be careful in the interpretation of the data. That was also the reason why we decided to apply manual identification of the fear reactions and used, for the time being, only a small amount of data.

29.6 **Discussion and conclusions**

The GRID methodology proves to be a powerful tool suitable for the cross-linguistic comparison of emotion words. It focuses on concept prototypes and indicates areas of overlap and divergence. The Cognitive Corpus analysis of the material on the other hand provides additional insights in the cross-linguistic construction of emotions.[3]

Our aim of comparing the corpus and GRID methodologies on the responses associated with *strach* and *fear* is only valid insofar as these responses are equivalent in both methodologies. Looking at Table 29.1, it can be seen that the characteristics of the FRIGHT event scenarios (paralyzing effect, passive, the experiencer feels weak, submissive, and fully controlled by fear) are present in the low-power features in the GRID instrument. Likewise, the high-power features in the GRID are consistent with the characteristics of the FIGHT event scenarios (active challenge, the experiencer feels powerful, dominant, and in control of fear).

It is also important to acknowledge that this part of our research relates to conceptualization and semantic content, that is, how people represent things through language; but we cannot extrapolate to how a Polish person actually feels in comparison to an English person when they say they feel *fear/ strach*. It is beyond the scope of this chapter to provide a detailed explanation of the reasons underlying the pattern of results reported here. However, with an eye on future studies it could be hypothesized that the relatively higher FIGHT/high POWER associated with *fear* compared to *strach* is due to *fear* being a weaker emotion than *strach*. If this is true, in our mental representation of the emotions, individuals experiencing *fear* vis-a-vis *strach* would be more likely to display a greater degree of dominance, POWER and activity as they overcome a fearful event. Conversely, the relatively greater FRIGHT/low POWER shown by *strach*, which was especially evident in the corpus data, could point to its relative greater intensity over *fear*, suggesting that individuals feeling *strach* are represented as more passive, weak and submissive than those described as feeling *fear*. This reasoning is consistent with proposals that it is the distance from a predator or danger that determines the type of fear response. For example, the "distance-dependent defense hierarchy" (Gallup, 1974; Ranter, 1977) explains that a moderately close predator induces fleeing, and that fighting occurs in response to an even closer predator/danger, where the intensity of the emotion should be higher, as the danger is more imminent. Bracha (2004) further explains that the fright response occurs when flight or fight are no longer an effective option, suggesting that the predator/danger is very close, even closer than in the scenarios in which fight can be effectively used. Mapping our results onto this pattern, it would seem that *strach* is associated more than *fear* with an imminent or close source of danger. Further work is necessary to test these predictions.

The proximity of the predator or danger is also relevant to determining whether FIGHT and FRIGHT should be considered as separate scenarios or as the same event but separated by points in time. Clearly, an organism can adopt different fear response behaviors depending on the proximity of the threat. However, these different behaviors should not be seen as following a causal pattern, as each to a large extent is dependent on the external situation (i.e., the proximity of the source of danger). Further evidence for viewing *fear* responses as separate scenarios comes from results showing that different fear responses are associated with different neurological structures (Eilam, 2005).

---

[3] See Wilson (2012) for other studies employing the Cognitive Corpus methodology and other methodologies in cross-linguistic analyses of emotions.

It is clear that future work is needed to evaluate more fully the role of the third possible response, fleeing (FLIGHT), in our conceptualization of fear. FLIGHT constituted a fairly large proportion of fear reactions in the corpus data we investigated in both languages. The inclusion of FLIGHT would enable us to gain a more comprehensive understanding of the differences in how *fear* and *strach* are conceptualized.

The results obtained from the two sets of data support the claim that the two research methods are complementary. The GRID methodology accounts mostly for prototypical category members and presupposes the cross-linguistic equivalence of general categories. The Cognitive Corpus method is a combination of a quantitative approach, which analyses frequencies of use of linguistic units, and large amounts of heterogenous linguistic material, and it provides valuable insights on individual linguistic units as well as on their relations with any of the potential cross-linguistic equivalent candidates. The methods employed together provide instruments to gain a better understanding of how emotions are conceptually represented across languages and cultures. The GRID instrument allows us to compare more precisely cross-linguistic differences in the native speakers' models of the prototypical meanings of emotion words and uncover the differences in their profiles and dimensions (in this case, POWER for *fear* and *strach*). Cognitive linguistic tools uncover similarities and differences in cross-linguistic and cross-cultural conceptualizations of members of the same emotion cluster and show both their universal core as well as language-specific differences. What has also been presented is a distinct composition of EEs, particularly from the point of view of the instantiation of the semantic roles of particular event participants. Corpus data and the frequency counts signal the typicality of certain structures and uses, and the marginality of others. It can thus be concluded that both approaches are not only compatible, but also complementary.

Chapter 30

Triangulating the GRID: A corpus-based cognitive linguistic analysis of five Greek emotion terms

Marina Terkourafi,[1] Efthymia C. Kapnoula,
Penny Panagiotopoulou, and Athanassios Protopapas

30.1 Introduction

"Although language is abstracted from human experience, it must correspond to human experience and represent important human concerns." (Fontaine et al., 2007: 1056)

The aim of correlating subjective experience with its lexicalization by means of particular emotion terms in a language is at the heart of the GRID (Fontaine et al., 2007). To achieve this, the GRID builds semantic profiles of prototypical emotion terms by asking questionnaire respondents to rate each term on more than one hundred features capturing several dimensions of variation in emotional experience across languages/cultures (Fontaine et al., 2007:1050).

Problems can, nevertheless, arise if the initial process of translation/back-translation used to identify the translation equivalents of the 24 prototypical emotion terms delivers more than one translation equivalent for the same term in different languages. In our data, this was the case with the Greek terms *lipi* ("sorrow") and *stenokhorja* ("chagrin"), both suggested as translation equivalents of the English term "sadness" by our bilingual translators.

Our search for a solution to this practical problem prompted us to explore an alternative approach to the meaning of emotion terms, namely, a corpus-based cognitive linguistic approach that probes the meaning of emotion terms in context. In this chapter, we present the results of that exploration and compare them with those obtained by the GRID. Our evidence illustrates the different strengths and weaknesses of the two approaches and suggests that they should be seen as complementary. In other words, a more comprehensive picture of the meaning of emotion terms emerges if the two methodologies are used *in tandem*.

[1] Corresponding author: Marina Terkourafi. University of Illinois Urbana Champaign, Department of Linguistics, 4080 Foreign Languages Building, 707 S Mathews Ave, Urbana IL 61801. mt217@illinois.edu

30.2 **Two approaches to the meaning of emotion terms**

A major theme of emotion research to date has been establishing a small set of basic dimensions that underlies the conceptualization of emotions in different languages/cultures. This has led to an important motivation for proposing the GRID methodology, namely "[t]o obtain definitive evidence concerning the optimal low-dimensional space" against which emotions are conceptualized cross-linguistically (Fontaine et al., 2007: 1050). By enabling large-scale comparison of the semantic profiles of prototypical emotion terms based on empirical data, the GRID methodology represents an important step toward reaching this goal and has already made significant contributions to this debate, most notably by revealing that four, rather than two, dimensions are necessary in order to account for variation in emotional experience cross-linguistically (see Chapter 7; see also Fontaine et al., 2007).

To analyse the meaning of emotion terms, the GRID builds on the linguistic semantic tradition of componential analysis (Goodenough, 1956; Lounsbury, 1956) or decompositional semantics (e.g., Jackendoff, 1972; Katz & Fodor, 1963), in which word meanings are analytically broken down into smaller components (or features) intended to capture the atomic elements of their meaning.

Recently, an alternative view of word meaning has emerged within cognitive linguistics, on which there is no easy distinction between lexical meaning and encyclopaedic knowledge (Peeters, 2000; Taylor, 2003). On the cognitive linguistic view, linguistic semantics (encoded meaning) emerges out of pragmatics (use), and word meanings are "a network of shared, conventionalised, and to some extent perhaps idealised knowledge, embedded in a pattern of cultural beliefs and practices" (Taylor, 2003: 86). Moreover, word meanings are dynamic cognitive structures whose meaning can only be understood in the context of other cognitive structures (such as domains, frames, and schemata) that also extend beyond the language system itself (2003: 87). In other words, linguistic semantic information seriously underdetermines word meaning, leaving significant scope for contextual inference to fill in the gap (Récanati, 2004). This view has been gaining ground in linguistic circles and is currently being explored in the rapidly growing field of lexical pragmatics (Wilson & Carston, 2007; Wilson, 2003).

The difference between contextualized and decontextualized approaches to word meaning is also highlighted by the proponents of the GRID. Discussing a distinction (proposed by Robinson & Clore, 2002) "between current emotion, which is episodic, experiential, and contextual, and beliefs about emotions which are semantic, conceptual, and decontextualised," they state that "clearly, by design, our data on semantic profiles belong to the latter category" (Fontaine et al., 2007: 1056). This remark leaves open the possibility that an approach which analyses the meaning of emotion terms in context may be a welcome addition on the side of the GRID and could reveal interesting new generalizations about the meaning of emotion terms.

In setting out to discover what a contextualized approach may have to add to the analysis of emotion terms undertaken by the GRID, we adopt a corpus-based methodology that exploits the increasing availability of natural language corpora as extensive repositories of longer stretches of discourse produced spontaneously by a variety of speakers/authors. In this way, two desiderata of the cognitive linguistic enterprise can be met at once: (a) the study of the meaning of emotion terms in context, and (b) the investigation of a sufficiently diverse pool of informants, since the only prerequisite to considering a piece of (encyclopaedic) knowledge as part of the meaning of a word is that it be "shared by a sufficient number of people" (Taylor, 2003: 93).

Corpus-based methodologies present us with the further opportunity of analysing the meaning of emotion terms by studying the grammatical relationships that they contract with other constituents within the clause. To find out what these relationships can reveal about their semantic structure, we adopt Halliday's framework of systemic functional grammar as applied to emotion research in English (Halliday, 1998) and Greek (Lascaratou, 2007; Terkourafi & Bali, 2007). The central insight of this approach is that grammatical structure re-packages experience into relations within the clause. This is what Halliday calls the "experiential" function of the clause, that is, "its guise as a way of representing patterns of experience" (1994/1985: 106). This is accomplished through grammatical metaphor (ibid.: 340–367), a term coined by Halliday to refer to variation in how meanings are *expressed* rather than in the meanings themselves (ibid: 341).

To understand how grammatical metaphor works, an example by Halliday himself may be useful. In analysing the meaning of *I have a headache*, he explains:

> Here the grammar constructs an entity, a kind of thing, called an *ache*; it then uses a part of the body to assign this ache to a class, *head + ache*, which it constructs into a composite thing called a *headache*. . . . The grammar then sets up a structural configuration of possession [. . .]. Some person (usually the speaker) becomes the owner of this thing [. . .] and someone else can ask them *how's your headache?*, with *you* as possessive Deictic. (Halliday, 1998: 3–4)

But why should the grammar favour wordings like *I have a headache* over *My head aches*? The answer to this second question, according to Halliday, lies in information structure preferences, specifically the default preference in English to present in initial clause position the "theme" of the message (that which is being talked about) and use the rest of the message to say something about it. In *I have a headache*,

> . . . the setting of this unpleasant experience, is not my head, it is me—my self as a whole. So the grammatical Theme of the clause ought to be "me." Therefore, since it is the first element of clause structure [. . .] that is thematic, this "me" has to figure by itself as a nominal group; and the unmarked way of getting a nominal group into thematic position in English, given that the clause is declarative, is to map it onto the Subject. Hence the preferred form of expression will be that with Subject *I*. (Halliday, 1998: 4–5)

Similar considerations lead to equivalent structures in several other languages (e.g., French, Russian, and Chinese) which share the information structure preferences of English: "In all these languages, it is the person rather than the body part which is typically selected as Theme in expressions of pain" (1998: 5).

Grammatical metaphor is thus responsible for meaning attributed to a word in virtue of the grammatical category to which it belongs (Verb, Noun, etc.) and the role this plays in the clause (Subject, Complement, etc.) rather than because of its lexical content. In Halliday's example above, "pain" is conceptualized as a possession in virtue of its lexicalization as a noun that fulfils the grammatical role of complement of the verb "to have." On this view, processes are typically realized by the verbal group of the clause, participants by nominal groups, and circumstances by adverbial or prepositional phrases (for a concise summary of Halliday's process types and their linguistic reflexes, see Lascaratou, 2007: 37–44).

30.3 **Design and methodology of the corpus study**

To explore the potential of a corpus-based methodology to contribute to the analysis of the meaning of emotion terms in context, five Greek emotion terms were selected for analysis. Three of these terms (*aghonia*, "anticipation, anguish," *erotas*, "passion, romantic love," and *siginisi*, "yearning, being touched or moved")[2] were not among the basic set of 24 prototypical emotion terms of the GRID. They were selected because they appear to be specific to Greek, having no precise translational equivalent in English, and were expected to be important and meaningful to Greek respondents based on preliminary frequency counts.[3] The final pair (*lipi*, "sorrow," and *stenokhorja*, "chagrin") were proposed as translation equivalents of the same English term, "sadness," by our bilingual translators. We thus hoped that a corpus-based methodology might help us to shed some more light onto the meanings of these emotion terms for Greek speakers.

These five emotion terms were investigated using both the GRID instrument and a corpus-based methodology. For the needs of the GRID, data collection was carried out on a sample of 40 Greek university students (see Chapter 6). In what follows, we draw on the GRID results for information about the component scores of the five terms on the four dimensions, about term scores on selected individual items from the questionnaire, and about correlations among feature ratings between terms, in order to identify maximally similar and dissimilar terms from the basic set.

For the purposes of the corpus study, occurrences of the five terms were located in the Hellenic National Corpus, a 47 million word written corpus drawn mainly from journalistic sources (HNC, available from hnc.ilsp.gr; Hatzigeorgiu et al., 2000). To ensure comparability with the results of the GRID, which used the citation form of words (i.e., nominative singular in Greek), only nominative singular and accusative singular occurrences of these terms were considered, nominative and accusative being morphologically indistinguishable for feminine nouns in Greek (i.e., four of our terms: *aghonia, siginisi, lipi,* and *stenokhorja*). For the fifth term, *erotas*, which is masculine and so has distinct nominative and accusative forms, we ran separate searches for nominative (*erotas*) and accusative (*erota*) occurrences and included all of these in the analysis.

A number of occurrences thus obtained were unsuitable for our purposes and excluded from further analysis. Specifically, out of the total number of occurrences of the five terms in the corpus we excluded appearances in book or movie titles, or when the terms were the object of lexicographical definition, as these did not represent spontaneous usage by the author. In addition, cases in which the exact same clause was repeated in the corpus, and cases in which *erotas*, "romantic love," referred to the act of lovemaking (as in the collocation *kano erota*, lit. "make love"), rather than the emotion, were also excluded. Our final sample thus consisted of 1,986 tokens of *aghonia*, 1,593 of *erotas* (including accusative *erota*), 707 of *siginisi*, 585 of *lipi*, and 156 of *stenokhorja* (including the alternative spelling *stenakhorja*). Manual annotation and statistical analysis of this sample using SPSS and R was carried out by one annotator in consultation with the other authors, with whom problematic cases were also discussed.

As was mentioned earlier, in Halliday's framework of systemic functional grammar, lexicalization by verb is generally thought to indicate conceptualization as a process, while Noun Phrases (NP) are thought to lexicalize the roles of participants in a process, and Adverbial Phrases (AP) or Prepositional Phrases (PP) optional circumstances surrounding the process. Since the current analysis—in order to yield results comparable with those of the

---

[2] The original Greek spellings of these words are αγωνία, έρωτας, συγκίνηση, λύπη and στενοχώρια. Their Roman transliterations are used throughout this text for the convenience of the readers and do not constitute accurate representations of pronunciation. The canonical pronunciation of these five terms in IPA notation is /aɣoˈnia/, /ˈeɾotas/, /siˈɟinisi/, /ˈlipi/, and /stɛnoˈxoɾja/, respectively.

[3] Notice that in the corpus, all three are more frequent (N = 1,986, 1,593, and 707 respectively) than either of the pair of terms (N = 585 and 156) that correspond to English "sadness," a term that *was* among the 24 terms of the original GRID set.

GRID—focused only on lexicalization of emotions by means of nouns,[4] the relevant grammatical functions out of this list are those that can be fulfilled by nouns, that is, verbal subject, verbal complement (traditional "direct object"), and complement of a preposition (as part of a PP). Moreover, it is well known from the cognitive linguistic literature on transitive clauses as a type of construction (Taylor, 2003: 231–235) that the prototypical transitive clause involves a human agent volitionally acting on a patient whose free will and possibility for autonomous action is correspondingly curtailed, making it appear more object-like as a result. Building on this literature as well as in line with previous work on emotion terms in Greek (Lascaratou, 2007; Terkourafi & Bali, 2007), we took nouns functioning as verbal subjects to indicate the agent of a process (1), while we considered nouns functioning as verbal complements to be potential objects of possession (2), and nouns functioning as part of a PP to indicate optional circumstances associated with the process (quality, location, etc.; 3).

1 *Ki oso pernun i meres o **erotas** mu olo fundoni* ("And as the days pass, my **passion** grows stronger.")

2 *Dhen ekho **aghonia** ghia to melon* ("I have no **anxiety** about the future.")

3 *Tileorasis ki efimeridhes estiazun se thimata apo ti Sumatra os ti Stokholmi ke olos o kozmos skivi **me siginisi** pano apo tin kini tu simfora* ("Television and newspaper reports focus on victims from Sumatra to Stockholm and the entire world bows **with sympathy** over its shared tragic fate.")

In addition, potentially significant dimensions of semantic variation were noted. The relevant indications were provided by the semantics of the verb or by means of (adjectival or adverbial) modification (the relevant clues are indicated in bold in the examples below). Specifically, we coded for intensity (4), duration (5), repetition (6), and potential metaphorical construal of the emotion in physical terms (e.g., as a liquid; 7),[5] as we expected all of these to provide additional insights into the type of eventuality or entity the emotion was conceptualized as.

4 (Intensity): *I **aghonia** ton anthropon ikhe **apokorifothi*** ("**Anticipation** was at its **highest point.**")

5 (Duration): *Omos i **stenokhorja** tu **kratise** ligho* ("But his **chagrin** didn't **last** long.")

6 (Repetition): *I lipi pu **enalasete** me ti khara* ("**Sorrow** that keeps **alternating** with joy.")

7 (Physical construal/liquid): *I **siginisi** ekhi **plimirisi** tis kardhies olon ton theaton* ("**Yearning** has **flooded** the hearts of all the spectators.")

Finally, we assessed each clause for the kind of affect expressed, distinguishing between "very positive," "positive," "negative," "very negative," or "undecided" (8–13). By "affect" we mean the attitude or emotional stance that the speaker adopts or conveys through his/her utterance. At first sight, affect is the only one of our corpus annotation categories that maps relatively straightforwardly onto one of the GRID dimensions, namely "VALENCE"—even here, however, the mapping

---

[4] Lexicalization by noun is of course not the only means of lexicalizing emotional experience (for some other possibilities, see, for instance, Lascaratou's, 2007, and Terkourafi and Bali's, 2007, analyses of various expressions lexicalizing "pain" in Greek).

[5] In coding for metaphorical construal of the emotions, we follow Conceptual Metaphor theory (e.g., Lakoff & Johnson, 1980; Lakoff & Kövecses, 1987), according to which metaphor is a necessary mode of thought that involves the mapping of abstract concepts on to concrete ones and enables us to reason about the former in virtue of this mapping.

should not be assumed a priori but rather subject to confirmation by the empirical data, for it is possible that whether a term is assessed in context or in isolation could drastically alter the affect felt to be expressed by it. To assess affect in a replicable manner, we referred to semantic information expressed by the surrounding linguistic context *excluding* the emotion term itself. Potential sources included other nouns conjoined with or dependent on the emotion term (8, 9, 10, 11), semantic contrast (12), as well as prepositional phrases, adjectives, adverbs, and verbs present in the clause. When the surrounding linguistic context provided conflicting indications (12) or did not provide any indications as to affect (13), this was classified as "undecided."

8 (Very positive): *Etsi kharaktirizi o idhios tin tenia tu epimenondas omos ke **stin aghapi, ton erota kai ti sindrofikotita** pu ta enoni*. ("This is the way that he himself characterizes his movie, insisting also on **the love, the passion and the companionship** that binds it all together.")

9 (Positive): *Thimame **ti siginisi ke ti khara** pu eniosa otan kitaksa ti fotografia aftu tu pedhiu* ("I remember **the yearning and the joy** that I felt when I looked at the photograph of this child.")

10 (Negative): *Dhen prepi na dhiksi **fovo i stenokhorja*** ("He must not show **fear or chagrin.**")

11 (Very negative): *Pote dhen idha toso polus skinothetes ke tosi **aghonia. Apoghnosi** skhedhon*. ("I never saw so many (film) directors and so much **anticipation.** Almost to the point of **despair.**")

12 (Undecided/conflicting cues): ***Aghapes, entiposis, apoghoitefsis kai nostalghies** [. . .] ksana-zondanevun [. . .] me ena lirizmo pu bori na feri tin piitiki **siginisi** os ta dhakria* ("**Passions, impressions, disappointments and yearnings** come to life with a lyricism that can bring poetic **yearning** to the point of tears.")

13 (Undecided/lack of clues): *Simera mia olokliri khora perimeni me **aghonia** tin etimighoria ghia enan mono anthropo* ("Today an entire country is waiting with **anticipation** for the verdict for a single man.")

In summary, the following categories were used to annotate occurrences of the five terms in the sample of sentences selected from the corpus: (a) grammatical function (= subject/object/prepositional phrase), (b) significant dimensions of semantic variation (= intensity/duration/repetition/physical construal), and (c) affect (= very positive/positive/negative/very negative/undecided). A record of all the relevant clues used during the annotation process was kept for the purposes of verification and future analysis. In the next section, we present the results of the corpus analysis and compare them with those of the GRID.

30.4 **Results**

Aghonia (= anguish, anxiety, anticipation, suspense)

We begin by discussing the results for the most frequent of the five terms, *aghonia*. In English, *aghonia* can correspond to "anguish, anxiety" as well as more positively-loaded "anticipation, suspense." In total, 1,986 occurrences of *aghonia* in the corpus were included in the final analysis (for a summary of the results, see Table 1 in Document SM 1)[6]. Some examples are provided below.

---

[6] All supplementary materials (SM) are available at the GRID website: http://www.affective-sciences.org/GRID. See Appendix 1 ("Availability") for further details.

14 *I **aghonia** ke o fovos mu meghalonan* ("My **anguish** and my fear grew bigger.")

15 *S'ola ta pedhia aresi i dhrasi ke i **aghonia** ke to kalo istoriko mithistorima ekhi bolika ke apo ta dhio.* ("All children love action and **suspense**, and a good historical novel has plenty of both.")

16 *Metakinume dhistaktika, ja na min po me **aghonia*** ("I move with hesitation, not to say with **apprehension**.")

In terms of grammatical function within the clause, occurrences of *aghonia* were evenly split between subject (32.2%, 4, 14) and complement (32.4%, 2) positions ($\chi^2(1) = 0.01$, $p = 0.911$), and although there was a slight trend for it to occur as part of a PP (35.4%, 16), this trend was not statistically significant ($\chi^2(1) = 2.67$, $p = 0.102$). This means that if we want to locate the core meaning of *aghonia*, we must look elsewhere.

Some useful indications in this regard are provided by its co-occurrence with lexical items indicating long duration (e.g., verbs *perimeno/anameno*, "to wait"; 28.2%) and high intensity (e.g., *meghali*, "great"; 25.3%), which were relatively more frequent than lexical items indicating physical construal of the emotion (e.g., physical appearance: *emfanis/faneri*, "visible/obvious"; 7.6%) and repetition (e.g., *pali* "again"; 4.1%). These differences were statistically significant (e.g., proportion of intensity vs proportion of physical construal, $\chi^2(1) = 1841.91$, $p <0.0001$), suggesting that duration and intensity are significant dimensions of semantic variation for the conceptualization of *aghonia*. The importance of intensity to the conceptualization of *aghonia* is also supported by its co-occurrence with lexical items indicating verticality (*katakorifo*, "vertical, sheer," *korifonete*, "soars"; 2.6%, 4) suggesting a metaphorical mapping akin to that of heat, which exploits a combination of two conceptual metaphors, INTENSITY IS QUANTITY and MORE IS UP (Lakoff, 1987). Finally, in terms of affect, occurrences of *aghonia* tend to be negatively (52.2%) rather than positively colored (13.4%) or undecided (34.4%): these proportions are significantly unevenly distributed ($\chi^2(2) = 448.91$, $p <0.0001$) and the proportion of negative occurrences is marginally significantly greater than the positive and undecided proportions combined ($\chi^2(1) = 3.72$, $p = 0.054$), whereas the proportion of positive occurrences is significantly less than the negative and undecided proportions combined ($\chi^2(1) = 1064.51$, $p <0.0001$).

Taken jointly, these results suggest that the core meaning of *aghonia* is to indicate a state of excited expectation, with the possibility of negative affect foregrounded in the context of other terms occurring in the same clause (e.g., *apoghnosi*, "despair," 11, *fovos*, "fear," 14). These findings are consistent with the Greek GRID results. Specifically, in the GRID ratings for the 144 emotion features, *aghonia* correlated highly positively with anxiety (*aghkhos*, 0.91), stress (*stres*, 0.89), and fear (*fovos*, 0.86). Moreover, *aghonia* was second only to *stres* on the high end of the AROUSAL dimension (3rd factor), with a factor score of 1.59. The heightened degree of AROUSAL conveyed by *aghonia* is also consistent with its low absolute scores on the other two dimensions, 0.01 on POWER and 0.28 on NOVELTY, while the potential for negative affect is consistent with its somewhat negative score (−0.38) on the VALENCE dimension.

Erotas (= passion, romantic love)

Next we discuss results for *erotas*, another Greek-specific term that may be rendered in English as "romantic love" or "passion." In total, 1,593 occurrences of *erotas* in the corpus were analysed (for a summary of the results, see Table 2 in Document SM 1). In terms of affect, *erotas* occurred predominantly in positively-loaded contexts (54.7%) as opposed to negatively-loaded ones (10.3%), while undecided occurrences of *erotas* were also non-negligible (35%). The difference between positive and non-positive contexts (negative and undecided combined) was statistically significant, $\chi^2(1) = 13.94$, $p = 0.0002$, allowing us to infer that *erotas* is a predominantly positive emotion.

Table 30.1 Grammatical functions of "erotas" in the corpus by type of affect

	Affect		
	Negative	**Undecided**	**Positive**
Verbal subject	**12.00%**	36.00%	52.00%
Prepositional phrase	10.09%	34.63%	55.28%
Complement	7.71%	33.26%	**59.03%**

This is in accordance with the Greek GRID results, where *erotas* correlated positively with love (*aghapi*, 0.88), pleasure (*apolafsi*, 0.77), and joy (*khara* 0.76), and scored positively very high on VALENCE (1.33).

However, a closer look at the corpus data suggests that this is not the end of the story for *erotas*. The most frequent grammatical function of *erotas* is as a verbal complement (40.8%), a proportion that is statistically significantly greater than the proportion of its occurrences as a verbal subject (28.5%), $\chi^2(1) = 34.80$, $p < 0.0001$, or as part of a PP (27.4%).[7] However, occurrences of *erotas* in these three syntactic positions are not equally distributed with respect to affect (see Table 30.1).

As Table 30.1 shows, the proportion of negative affect is significantly higher in subjects than in complements, $\chi^2(1) = 4.90$, $p = 0.027$, while the proportion of positive affect is significantly higher in complements than in subjects, $\chi^2(1) = 5.06$, $p = 0.025$. Examples 17 and 18 illustrate these two possibilities.

17 *Dhioti **o erotas** tifloni ke ine kakos odhighos.* ("Because **romantic love** blinds and is a treacherous guide.")

18 *Latrepses ti zoi, tin aghapi, **ton erota**.* ("You worshipped life, love, **romantic love**.")

The difference in the affect expressed by *erotas* in the two positions is statistically significant and may be interpreted as indicative of two opposing conceptualizations of romantic love in Greek: when conceptualized as an object (18), *erotas* is positively loaded, leading to a view of romantic love as a prized possession, one that can enrich one's life; conversely, when conceptualized as an agent, *erotas* is negatively loaded, with examples such as 17 suggesting an image of romantic love as a perpetrator that torments those afflicted by it.

This second facet of *erotas* is one that cannot be detected from the GRID results in which *erotas* scored positively very high on VALENCE (1.33). How can we reconcile these two findings? One possible suggestion is that the predominance of occurrences of *erotas* in positively-loaded contexts, as seen in the corpus data, may make this the default context for the term, biasing interpretation toward the first of the two conceptualizations presented above. In other words, it is possible that, when presented with the term in isolation, questionnaire respondents implicitly called up a positively-loaded context in which they assessed the term. Nevertheless, this contextual association does not capture the totality of the semantic potential of *erotas*—for this, a contextualized approach is necessary. Indeed, focusing on the positive conceptualization alone could lead to the simplifying assumption that romantic love is always positively conceptualized in Greek, contrary to what we see in the corpus data and leaving us with little to say about its negatively-loaded occurrences.

---

[7] In the remaining 3.3% of occurrences, *erotas* was not integrated into the syntactic frame of the sentence (e.g., enumerations).

An analysis of significant dimensions of semantic variation completes this picture. Here, *erotas* is most frequently characterized by high intensity (17.6%), long duration (14.5%), and physical realization of the emotion (11.5%) but only rarely by repetition (2.8%)—a finding which is statistically significant, with the proportion of repetition being significantly less than the next semantic dimension, the proportion of physical construal, $\chi^2(1) = 90.33$, $p <0.0001$. Moreover, frequent references to the lifecycle of romantic love with verbs such as *ksekino*, "start," *arkhizo*, "begin," *ghenieme*, "be born," and *anthizo*, "blossom," suggest that romantic love in Greek is characterized by an upbeat feeling and a sense of vitality.

These findings provide further support for those of the GRID. Specifically, the intensity and vitality seen in the corpus analysis are consistent with the very high score of *erotas* on AROUSAL (1.44), while the gradually evolving durative aspect of the term is consistent with its very low score on NOVELTY (−1.07). Its intermediate position on the negative side of the POWER dimension (−0.35), on the other hand, suggests that POWER is not a defining feature of this term. Finally, it is worth mentioning that *erotas* is immediately adjacent or next-to-adjacent in scores to *aghapi* ("love") on three of the GRID dimensions (*aghapi* was located at 1.39 on VALENCE, −0.27 on POWER, and −1.63 on NOVELTY), but further toward the high end on AROUSAL (cf. *aghapi* at 0.32), indicating both the similarity between the two terms as well as the crucial distinction between them—a distinction whose significance becomes fully apparent only once the corpus data are taken into account. According to these, the higher degree of AROUSAL that characterizes *erotas* may be attributed to the agentivity associated with negatively-loaded occurrences of *erotas* in subject position.

Siginisi (= sympathy, yearning, being touched or moved by something)

The third term we analyzed was *siginisi*, a Greek-specific term with no obvious English translation; depending on context, *siginisi* may be rendered in English as "sympathy," "yearning," "being touched," or "deeply moved" (3, 7, 9, 12). The lack of an obvious translation for *siginisi* is paralleled by an absence of any immediately recognizable distinct emotional content conveyed by it: in the GRID ratings, *siginisi* did not correlate significantly with any other emotion term; its highest correlation, with compassion (*simbonja*), reached barely 0.55.

In total, 707 occurrences of *siginisi* in the corpus were analysed (for a summary of the results, see Table 3 in Document SM 1). In these, *siginisi* tended to occur in positively affective clauses (57.9%) as opposed to either negatively affective (23.3%) or undecided (18.8%) ones, a difference that was statistically significant, $\chi^2(1) = 17.43$, $p <0.0001$. This indicates that *siginisi* is generally a positively-loaded emotion and agrees with its moderately high score (0.75) on the positive side of the VALENCE dimension in the GRID results.

In terms of grammatical function, in the corpus *siginisi* tended to occur primarily as part of a PP (37.6%, 3) or as a verbal complement (36.4%, 9), and less frequently in subject position (25.6%, 7). The proportion of occurrences of *siginisi* in subject position is significantly less than the proportion of its occurrences as a complement, $\chi^2(1) = 13.19$, $p = 0.0003$, suggesting that *siginisi* tends not to be conceptualized as an agent that acts wilfully on those that experience it.

What *siginisi* does tend to be conceptualized as becomes clearer if we look at the semantic dimensions along which it tends to vary. Here, *siginisi* is mostly characterized by high intensity (35.4%), long duration (16%), and only rarely by repetition (2.8%; significantly less than the duration proportion, $\chi^2(1) = 70.25$, $p <0.0001$). Moreover, when *siginisi* is construed in physical terms (7.8%, 7), this is almost always as a liquid (51 occurrences, or 7.3%), as can be inferred from its co-occurrence with verbs such as *plimirizo*, "overflow;" *ghemizo*, "fill;" and *pnigho*, "drown;" nouns such as *khimari*, "torrents;" and adjectives such as *vathia*, "deep" (which can indicate a liquid by metonymy, as in "deep sea") and *dhiakhiti*, "pervasive, diffuse" (from Greek *dhia* + *kheō* ="pour through"). In this, *siginisi* parallels several other emotions, which are similarly metaphorically conceptualized as contained within the human body.[8]

The metaphorical construal of *siginisi* as a liquid that can overflow its container (i.e., the human body and, by metonymy, its human bearer) is consistent with its very low score on the POWER dimension (−1.03) in the GRID results, suggesting that *siginisi* is an emotion over which Greek speakers feel they have little or no control. However, this result would seem to be at odds with the finding cited just above, based on its grammatical function within the clause, namely that *siginisi* does not tend to be conceptualized as an agent that acts wilfully on those that experience it. Nevertheless, these two results are not necessarily irreconcilable. The key lies in the conceptualization of *siginisi* as a liquid: once we have established that *siginisi* is metaphorically conceptualized in this way, we are in a position to see that *siginisi* is not so much conceptualized as an agent that acts out of free will but rather as a force of nature that simply cannot be resisted. This interpretation gains support from the moderately positive score of *siginisi* on the NOVELTY dimension (0.49) in the GRID results, which underscores the relative unexpectedness of this emotion, as well as by its frequent modification on the intensity dimension in the corpus data: as with all natural phenomena, man has no control over their timing or intensity. In summary, *siginisi* offers a prime example of an emotion term where the corpus and the GRID results combine to yield a fuller picture than what either of them can capture in isolation.

Lipi and stenokhorja (= sorrow and chagrin)

The final pair of terms analysed are *lipi*, "sorrow," and *stenokhorja*, "chagrin." These were selected not because they are in any way specific to Greek but because of their semantic proximity to English "sadness," one of the GRID's 24 prototypical emotion terms, of which both are translation equivalents in Greek. The results of the Greek GRID confirmed this intuition, with *stenokhorja* being highly correlated with *lipi* (0.94) and both being highly correlated with "sadness" from the English sample (0.92 for *stenokhorja* and 0.91 for *lipi*). The relative positions of the two terms along the four basic dimensions also suggest a near identity, as they are adjacent or next-to-adjacent in POWER (both very low: −1.23 for *stenokhorja* vs −1.37 for *lipi*), AROUSAL (both somewhat low: −0.37 vs −0.57, respectively), and NOVELTY (both in the middle region: 0.02 vs −0.22, respectively). There is a minor difference in VALENCE only, where they both occupy the middle region but are separated by five intervening terms along this dimension, with *stenokhorja* (−0.47) being slightly more negative than *lipi* (−0.18).

A comparison of the feature profiles of the two terms using MANOVA over the 144 features by the distinct groups of raters showed them to be statistically indistinguishable: Wilks' lambda = 0.019, $F(1, 80) = 0.641$, $p = 0.785$. In simple between-subject contrasts, only two of the individual features were significantly different for the two terms after Bonferroni correction ($\alpha = 0.000035$), while for 116 features there was no trace of a difference ($p > 0.1$). The two features distinguishing *lipi* from *stenokhorja* were q026 "incongruent with own standards and ideals," with *stenokhorja* scoring higher than *lipi*, and q028 "center of attention," with *lipi* scoring higher than *stenokhorja*. Both of these significant differences were in Appraisal items. The two terms were also identical in the other terms with which they correlated: high positive correlations for *lipi* included being hurt

---

[8]   On the metaphor THE BODY IS A CONTAINER FOR THE EMOTIONS, see Kövecses, 1990.

(*na plighonese* 0.90), disappointment (*apoghoitefsi* 0.88), and despair (*apoghnosi* 0.86), with the corresponding coefficients for *stenokhorja* being 0.94, 0.93, and 0.93, respectively.

Turning to the corpus results, in total, 585 occurrences of *lipi*, and 156 of *stenokhorja* (or *stenak-horja*) were included in the analysis (for a summary of the results, see Table 4 in Document SM 1). An analysis of the affect of the clauses in which the two terms appeared in the corpus data showed them to be nearly synonymous and overwhelmingly negatively loaded (86.8% for *lipi* vs 85.9% for *stenokhorja*, significantly greater than the corresponding alternatives combined, $p < 0.0001$), with undecided occurrences ranking a distant second (11.5% vs 13.5%), and positively-loaded ones being extremely rare (1.7% vs 0.6%).

Where differences between the two terms began to emerge, however, was in their grammatical function within the clause. Here, the preference for *lipi* in complement position was clear (65.6%); only secondarily (and statistically significantly less frequently, $\chi^2(1) = 114.77$, $p < 0.0001$) did *lipi* function as part of a PP (23.8%), and even less frequently as a subject (10.4%). Occurrences of *stenokhorja*, on the other hand, were much more evenly distributed among the three grammatical functions (31.4% in subject position vs 30.8% in complement position, and 38.5% as part of a PP, a distribution not statistically different from uniform, $\chi^2(2) = 1.69$, $p = 0.429$).

Zooming in on occurrences of *lipi* as a verbal complement, we find that in a large majority of cases (77.6%) *lipi* collocates with the verb *ekfrazo*, "express," a finding whose significance becomes obvious when we consider that the next two verbs *esthanome* and *niotho* (both "feel") taken jointly account for only 6.51% of occurrences of *lipi* in complement position. "Express sorrow" (*ekfrazo lipi*), in other words, constitutes a collocation or formula (Wray, 2002) in Greek, frequently found in formal contexts as in (19):

19 *I elvetiki kivernisi **eksefrase** ti vathia tis **lipi** ke ta silipitiria tis stus sigenis ton thimaton* ("The Swiss government **expressed** its deep **sorrow** and its condolences to the relatives of the victims.")

Closer examination of the corpus data reveals that the full form of the collocation is as in (20):

20 *(PRO)$_i$ ekfrazi (ti) (vathia) (POSS)$_i$ lipi (POSS)$_i$ (ghia)*

((PRO)$_i$ expresses (DET) (deep) (POSS)$_i$ sorrow (POSS)$_i$ (for))

Here, PRO stands for pronoun, DET for determiner (here, the definite article), POSS for possessive, the subscript index $_i$ shows referent identity (the person that expresses sorrow is the same as the one that possesses it), and parentheses indicate optional items.

The formula in (20), which may be paraphrased as "X expresses X's deep sorrow for," accounts for over three quarters of occurrences of *lipi*, "sorrow," in the corpus data. In over three quarters of instances, that is, occurrences of *lipi* in the corpus are not part of a novel expression creatively put together by the speaker/author but part of a set phrase. As part of a set phrase, *lipi* in these instances is largely bleached of its full-fledged semantic content (Lehman, 1985), its use driven mainly by situational considerations and the exigencies of particular settings for the expression of certain socially prescribed feelings. This hypothesis is supported by the patterns of semantic variation found with the two terms. Of the two, *stenokhorja* is consistently modified (by means of adjectives, etc.) more than *lipi*, sometimes two to three times as much, scoring 34.6% vs 17.6% for intensity ($\chi^2(1) = 20.33$, $p < 0.0001$), 15.4% vs 5.6% for duration ($\chi^2(1) = 15.12$, $p = 0.0001$), 10.3% vs 3.6% for physical construal ($\chi^2(1) = 10.18$, $p = 0.0014$), and a non-significant 1.9% vs 1.5% for repetition ($\chi^2(1) < 0.001$, $p = 0.985$). In all these ways, *stenokhorja*, "chagrin," offers opportunities for foregrounding the subjectivity of the speaker, something which *lipi* seems ill-suited to achieve by virtue of its situational exigency-driven formulaic outlook.

To the apparent identity of the two terms in the GRID results, the corpus data add an interesting twist. On the one hand, consistent with a slightly more negative position on the VALENCE dimension of the GRID, the corpus analysis indicated that *stenokhorja* is the more creatively used, and so more subjectively loaded, term of the two. On the other hand, and beyond formulaic usage, corpus analysis revealed that the two words, albeit both being potential translation equivalents of English "sadness," are not absolutely synonymous. They are separated by differences in register (formal vs informal) and in semantic strength (degree of foregrounding of the speaker's subjectivity). In fact, these two types of differences are not independent but mutually reinforce each other: decreased subjectivity and emotional detachment are exactly what one might expect to find in formal settings, while the opposite might be expected to be true in informal, more personable circumstances. Since translation equivalence is not only a matter of lexical semantics but also of stylistic and situational appropriateness, a corpus-based methodology seems particularly well-suited in this case to help select the most appropriate translation equivalent each time.

30.5 **Conclusions**

We outlined a corpus-based methodology that builds on Halliday's framework of systemic functional grammar, in particular his notion of grammatical metaphor, to analyse the semantics of emotion terms, and compared our findings to those of the GRID. We investigated two different sets of terms. First, terms deemed to be specific to Greek sociocultural experiences were investigated. Analysis of three such terms (*aghonia*, "anguish," *erotas*, "romantic love," and *siginisi*, "being touched") confirmed the results of the GRID and added new dimensions to their meaning (e.g., the findings regarding two types of romantic love, and metaphorical construal of *siginisi* as a liquid). Second, terms constituting translation equivalents of a single English term were investigated. Here, two terms, *lipi* ("sorrow") and *stenokhorja* ("chagrin"), were compared. The results of the corpus analysis once again confirmed those of the GRID but this time they additionally revealed stylistic and semantic differences between the two terms that remained undetected by the GRID and could be crucial in determining the best translation equivalent of a term in context. In conclusion, we propose that the two methodologies are complementary and that using them *in tandem* can significantly enhance the analytical breadth and depth of future analyses of emotion terms.

Part VII

Special topics

Chapter 31

The GRID study in India

Ahalya Hejmadi[1]

The experience of using the GRID in India was educative, inasmuch as apart from that fact that it yielded data that was incongruent with the findings from other countries, it provided useful pointers about the methodological issues that need careful attention in the future. It provided the first empirical evidence for the emotions of compassion and contentment that are central to the Indian cultural milieu.

The GRID in India was administered in the Hindi language. Hindi, which is an Indo-Aryan language spoken or understood by at least half of the Indian billion plus population, is closely associated with Sanskrit. Many of ancient India's rich tradition of music and drama was in Sanskrit, some dating back to as far as 1500 BC. One of the most notable is the *Natyashastra* (Bharata, 1956), an ancient Indian treatise on the performing arts. While the *Natyashastra* primarily deals with stagecraft, it also contains a description of various emotional states. According to the Natyashastra, emotions are composed of antecedents, consequents, subjective experience, and physiological correlates. Further, separate bodily components are clearly distinguishable for each of these emotions (Hejmadi, Davidson, & Rozin, 2000).

The componential approach of the GRID (Fontaine et al., 2007, Scherer, 2009c) has great utility for comparative studies of emotion, including in the Indian context. The questionnaire covers a broad spectrum of emotion terms, including a few that are common in the Hindi lexicon and have sociocultural relevance. At the present time, there is a lack of detailed empirical evidence accounting for how Indians actually represent these emotions or their basic components, and this gap in knowledge will be well served by an empirical approach such as the GRID study.

Although the length of this chapter does not permit a detailed analysis of all possible emotions or emotion families that could be significant in the Indian psyche, it would be educative to discuss briefly the data pertaining to quintessentially Indian emotions like compassion and contentment. The emotions of compassion and contentment are described in ancient Hindu and Buddhist texts, which inform sociocultural norms in India (Gandhi, 1927, Jeste & Vahia, 2008, Sharma, 1999). The data collected by the GRID study provides the first systematic attempt to collect descriptive data on the emotional meaning and interpretation of compassion and contentment for the Indian population. In particular, it was of interest to compare the data on these emotions to the other positive emotions, for example, pleasure, happiness, and joy. While individual pleasure may definitely be seen as positive, Indians perceive contentment and compassion to be especially positive, and socially desirable. It is also possible that within the category of evaluation, the emotions could be associated with their traditions, passed down by ancestors, and sanctioned by relevant divine texts.

---

[1] Ahalya Hejmadi. University of Maryland, USA and Utkal University, India. 17 Letitia Lane, Media, PA 19063, USA. ahalyahejmadi@gmail.com

31.1 **Method**

Participants

Usable data was collected from 122 adults. Of these, 102 were white-collar postal workers and the remaining were students from a local college. There were 69 females and 53 males with ages ranging from 18 to 51. 65% had passed High school or its equivalent, and 35% were either enrolled in a further course of study or had a bachelor's degree in a subject from an Indian University.

Instruments

The GRID instrument in Hindi was used in this study. The author solicited the help of two Hindi scholars—a teacher of Hindi at a local college and a Hindi translator employed in a Government department—to do the translation and back translation of the Hindi words to their English equivalents. Initially, an attempt was made to computerize the questionnaire, but technical issues while posting the Hindi on to the GRID website, and the availability of computers to record the participant's responses limited our options to using paper and pencil questionnaires. Subsequently, participant data had to be manually entered into the computer.

Procedure

The GRID questionnaire was administered in sessions involving not more than 8 to 10 participants. Typically each session lasted for about an hour. While the postal employees participated in the testing sessions either during their lunch break or at the end of their work shift, the college students were tested between the class breaks. During each testing session, a supervisor initially gave detailed instructions about how to fill up the data sheet and responded to participants' questions.

31.2 **Results**

General

The results from the Indian GRID data indicated that the Indian clusters were incongruent with the typical emotion profiles for most of the other countries and consequently merited a separate explanation than the ones applicable to other countries. Upon further analysis, it was seen that while the overall reliability of the Indian data was somewhat low, there was significant consistency between raters in distinguishing between positive and negative emotions.

The GRID data from India showed that the emotions of sadness, guilt, shame, disappointment, despair, stress, anxiety, fear, jealousy, hate, irritation, anger, surprise, being hurt, disgust, and contempt were consistently reported as being negative. There was equal consistency in reporting compassion, love, contentment, happiness, pride, pleasure, joy, and interest as positive. It was also interesting to note that the participants did not seem to differentiate significantly between the emotions on any of the other dimensions.

There are several possible reasons why this might have occurred. It is relevant to examine the factors that influenced the results, to provide guidelines for future researchers. The section on "future directions" discusses this in some detail.

Compassion and contentment

A novel aspect of this study was the systematic study of the emotions of compassion and contentment, which are significant in Indian sociocultural context, but have hitherto received no actual empirical scrutiny. A closer look at certain features of particular categories showed some interesting results in the categories of evaluation, subjective experience, and the general category of social acceptance and desirability. In comparing the ranking of the positive emotions, compassion and contentment consistently figured in the top three rankings (on a scale of 1–10), especially in the categories of evaluation (in itself, consequences), subjective experience (felt positive), and general social (socially acceptable and frequently experienced) categories. The "influence of ancestors/divinity" was another aspect that showed a higher rating than all of the other emotions studied, pointing out a possibly strong cultural influence. A certain amount of self-other overlap was, in addition, seen in the emotion of compassion. For instance, in the case of the category of evaluation, particularly for the specific question of the emotion in itself being pleasant for self and other, there was no significant difference (t value df. 19, −0.32, p >0.05) between self and other. Similarly, for the "consequences as positive for self and other" feature, there was a significant self-other overlap (t value df. 19, 0.469, p >0.05). This could be an indication that the emotion of compassion is seen by Indians to be agreeable, both to the self and in the case of others. The consequences of being compassionate are not only beneficial to oneself, but also to others in society. The general trend of these emotions shows that there is promise to this particular type of study, and it can reveal important characteristics of emotions that are pre-eminent in particular cultures.

Limitations and future directions

This chapter may not be able to cover all the points, but picks out a few that could be especially useful in the light of sharing with future researchers who might attempt similar studies. Certain factors could have influenced this trend of the data, and may be kept in mind for future researchers. Possible confounds could be as follows.

First, unfamiliarity of participants with data collection and entry, may have had an effect on the data. Using participants who have more experience with questionnaires, who are more motivated, and able to handle the challenge of a longer questionnaire could yield better results in future. Regarding the nature of the participants, who were mainly postal workers, addressing the questionnaire could have proved to be too arduous a task. Some may not have followed the instructions, which may explain the fact that we had to discard about 25% of the questionnaire responses, due to participants not completing the required questions.

Using non-students could pose difficulties in data collection and accuracy of response, so student groups with a higher education level, and an interest and understanding of the concepts would be more effective as participants. Students would also be more capable of distinguishing between particular characteristics and distinctiveness as opposed to mere global distinctions.

Third, possible difficulties with translation and back translation, especially in concepts where Indians may have more than one word in the lexicon or may not distinguish easily (pleasure and joy, despair, disappointment, and sadness, for example). Unfamiliarity with certain emotion terms such as stress, which are not common in everyday language use, could have influenced the results.

Finally, there were difficulties with administration of the instrument, including access of participants in India (and other developing countries) to computers and reliable electrical supply, and using paper and pencil questionnaires vs online versions (perhaps the latter would have yielded more accurate results). Targeting institutions with computer access and student populations may yield more reliable results in the future.

Acknowledgments

I acknowledge the help of the Indian team, without whose help this paper would not be possible. Special thanks are due to Prof. M. Sharma and Mr. P.K. Jain for their assistance in translation, Sudesh Gaikwad, V. Iyer, S. Badami, and P.K. Dash for their tireless work in test administration, discussion, and planning, and Bhanu Pratap and P.K. Dash for data entry.

## Chapter 32

Adaptation of the GRID instrument in Setswana

Cara Jonker,[1] Lerato Mojaki, Deon Meiring, and Johnny J. R. Fontaine

This chapter reports on the adaptation of the short GRID into Setswana. Setswana, spoken by black native communities in the North-West Province of South Africa, required this adaptation because previous applications of the GRID in three other African languages had been unsuccessful. An application of a paper-and-pencil version of the GRID instrument among Tshivenda- and Xitsonga-speaking samples revealed very low inter-rater reliability to a degree such that the data could not be used for further analyses[2]. In a third Sepedi-speaking sample the inter-rater reliability was better, but still moderate, and a two-dimensional structure could be interpreted, with the dimensions VALENCE and POWER structuring the domain (Rauch, 2009).

The Tswana group of people in South Africa are ethno-culturally related to the inhabitants of Botswana, a neighboring country of South Africa. Under the apartheid regime, a separate homeland was created for the Tswana people, namely Bophuthatswana, meaning *The Gathering of the Tswana*. After the abolishment of apartheid, the region was reintegrated into a newly-formed province, today known as the North-West Province. In that province the Tswana group is the dominant cultural group. 3,677,010 Tswanas live currently in the North-western region of South Africa. Setswana, the language spoken by the Tswana, is one of the 11 official languages in South Africa.

Only recently interest has emerged in constructing reliable and valid psychological assessment instruments in the black African languages (Meiring, 2007). This interest is stimulated by new legal requirements since the abolishment of apartheid. The Employment Equity Act—a subdivision of the Labour Act of South Africa—requires psychological measurements for use in clinical and work settings to be reliable, valid, and free from bias (Government Gazette, 1998). In this sense, very little work has been done in the affective domain. Only a recent study of Wissing et al. (2010) aimed at validating a general well-being scale in Setswana. As part of the well-being measures used in the study, the Affectometer-2 (Kamman & Flett, 1983) measured affective well-being as a two-factorial structure of positive and negative affectivity.

The current chapter reports on an attempt to adapt the GRID instrument for use with Setswana-speaking participants.

---

[1] Corresponding author: Cara Jonker. North-West University. School of Human Resource Sciences, Building E3, Office number 217, Hoffman Street, Potchefstroom, South Africa. Cara.Jonker@nwu.ac.za

[2] Because there were serious doubts about the motivation of the participants in these two samples, the samples were excluded from the GRID database reported in this volume.

32.1 **Method**

Adapting the GRID instrument to Setswana

A shortened version of the original GRID instrument with 61 items (a precursor of the CoreGrid presented in Chapter 44) was taken as a starting point for the adaptation of the instrument.

A series of pilot studies were conducted over a period of six months. After each pilot study, suggestions for improvement were made and the questionnaire was adapted accordingly. Several difficulties were observed. Participants in the pilot studies experienced the questionnaire as a highly technical instrument. It was also difficult for them not to rate their own emotion experiences, but to make a judgment of people in their culture based on the meaning of the words. Additionally, they found it tiresome to rate four emotions on each emotion feature and found the method very complex to comprehend. Many participants requested the English translation for the words, as they reported that Setswana emotion terms are often context-bound. They, therefore, requested that the emotion terms be stated in a given situation or scenario. A clear description of each emotion term was also requested by many participants. The reason for this, one participant stated, was that one Setswana emotion term can refer to different English emotion terms. For example, English emotion terms such as *happiness, joy*, and *elation* are translated with only one Setswana emotion term, namely *boitumelo*. Participants noted that the instructions were too long and after reading them they were still confused as to how to proceed. They found the rating scale (a Likert-type scale from 1 to 9) very difficult to interpret. They questioned the omitted descriptive anchors, since only 1 (extremely unlikely), 5 (neither likely nor unlikely), and 9 (extremely likely) were labeled. There was also no clear translation in Setswana for "neither likely nor unlikely."

The English version of the short GRID instrument was first translated into Setswana by the Setswana-speaking researcher who was part of this research team. The translated Setswana version was then checked for correctness and quality of translation by another Setswana native speaker, a lecturer at a higher education institution in the North-West Province. Yet another Setswana translator translated the version back into English to detect possible inconsistencies when compared with the original English version. Changes were also made according to the comments of the participants regarding the translation of words. The pilot studies involved Setswana-speaking students who majored in Setswana as a first language. A group of Setswana-speaking educators also made comments that led to the adjustment of certain words.

One of the translation issues was the wording of the different emotion components in the short GRID. No direct translation for the five emotion components exists in Setswana. After consultation with a variety of language experts and native language speakers, the conclusion was made that the translation of the components worked better as descriptions of the content of the specific emotion component. For example, the component Bodily reaction was changed into a description of words—directly translated from Setswana as: " . . . *changes that you feel inside your body when you experience this emotion.*" Participants also responded better to a five-point rating scale that ranged from 1 (completely disagree) to 5 (completely agree). Better results regarding the administration of the questionnaire were also found when instructions for each section were given verbally in Setswana.

In conclusion, the questionnaire was adapted with regard to instructions, rating scale, and descriptions of the emotion.

Participants

All of the participants (n = 122) were Setswana-speaking and their ethnicity was black. 47% of the participants were males. The average age of the participants was 22.7 years. All of the participants were enrolled at university. Students came from all majors at university. Students from the Faculty of Commerce and Administration were the most represented (24.6%). The place of birth of the largest group of participants was Mafikeng (capital city of the North-West Province) (49.6%). The largest part of the sample (97.4%) resided in the North-West Province during the time of the research study. The participants enrolled in the study on a voluntary basis.

32.2 **Results**

The inter-rater reliability of the sample was measured first (see Table 32.1). Each term was rated on average by 14.63 participants and the Cronbach's alpha ranged from 0.17 to 0.86, with an average of 0.64 when all participants were taken into account. With only the converging participants, whose feature profile correlated at least 0.20 with the average feature profile of the other participants that rated the same emotion term, the Cronbach's alpha ranged from 0.64 to 0.96, with an average of 0.78. While each term was rated on average by 14.63 participants, only 9.25 participants converged on the meaning of each emotion term (see Table 32.1). Thus, with only the converging participants,

Table 32.1 Interrater reliability (Cronbach's alpha) and number of participants with all (A) and with only converging (C) participants

Emotion words	Alpha$_A$	N$_A$	Alpha$_C$	N$_C$
joy	0.76	14	0.79	12
fear	0.45	12	0.66	4
jealousy	0.54	13	0.65	8
despair	0.66	17	0.72	12
love	0.76	16	0.84	12
disappointment	0.55	14	0.70	8
compassion	0.81	14	0.85	10
disgust	0.70	17	0.82	10
guilt	0.63	15	0.71	11
surprise	0.57	11	0.67	7
anger	0.73	13	0.79	10
interest	0.64	17	0.74	8
happiness	0.82	16	0.86	14
contempt	0.69	14	0.79	9
being hurt	0.86	14	0.90	11
irritation	0.76	17	0.82	13
anxiety	0.60	13	0.69	7
pleasure	0.17	13	0.72	3
stress	0.26	13	0.64	3
pride	0.68	17	0.76	9
contentment	0.84	16	0.86	14
shame	0.27	14	0.86	4
sadness	0.77	14	0.96	7
hate	0.86	17	0.87	16

Note: *Alpha$_A$*: Cronbach's alpha across all participants; *N$_A$*: Number of participants per emotion word; *Alpha$_C$*: Cronbach's alpha with only converging participants (participant-rest correlation ≥0.20), *N$_C$*: Number of converging participants.

the reliability was moderate, and much lower than in most of the other samples in the GRID study (see Chapter 6).

A factor analysis (Principal Component Analysis) was executed on the mean centered feature scores per emotion term (computed on the basis of only the converging participants, as has also been done in Parts II and III of this book). Only the first dimension could be well interpreted as a VALENCE dimension, on which positive emotion terms were opposed to negative emotion terms (see Figure 32.1). The first dimension accounted for 16.96% of the total variance. The second dimension, which could be best interpreted without rotation, shared characteristics with the POWER dimension identified by the standard GRID instrument (see Chapter 7). The second factor accounted for an additional 8.71% of the total variance. The negative pole of this factor was characterized by low POWER features (such as "tears" and "wanting to make up for what one has done") (see Table 32.2). On this factor especially the emotion terms *sadness, shame*, and to some extent *fear*, were differentiated from the other emotion terms (see Figure 32.1). Higher dimensional interpretations were not at all interpretable.

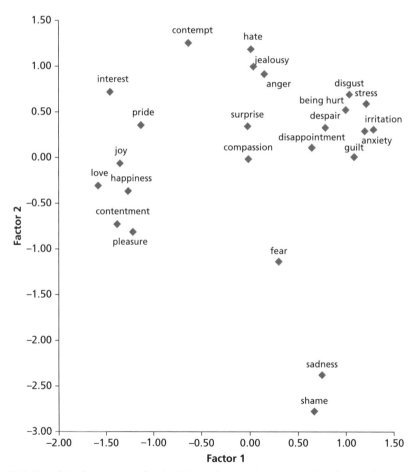

Figure 32.1 Plot of the factor scores for the 24 emotion words on FACTOR 1 and FACTOR 2.

Table 32.2 Loadings of the 61 GRID features in a two-factorial structure

GRID features	F1	F2
felt weak	0.68	0.31
felt tired	0.67	−0.56
felt bad	0.66	−0.09
felt weak limbs	0.60	−0.40
did not want to do anything	0.58	0.06
wanted to disappear or hide from others	0.56	−0.11
felt restless	0.52	0.40
had threatening consequences	0.51	0.29
wanted to do damage, hit, harm, or say something that hurts	0.48	0.16
felt quiet	0.46	0.14
felt their heartbeat getting faster	0.28	−0.11
produced speech disturbances	0.18	0.17
had consequences the person had sufficient POWER to change or control	0.17	0.07
experienced an intense emotional state	0.10	−0.03
lacked the motivation to pay attention to what was going on	−0.20	−0.14
wanted to show off	−0.29	0.03
had the eye brows go up	−0.32	0.17
felt awake	−0.45	0.12
of which the consequences were likely to be positive, desirable for somebody else	−0.45	0.36
showed the emotion to other less than s/he felt it	−0.49	0.28
wanted to be tender and kind	−0.49	−0.13
had consequences a person could live with	−0.51	−0.18
wanted to be seen, to be in the center of attention	−0.51	−0.27
felt strong	−0.52	0.13
wanted to engage in action	−0.54	−0.24
spoke in a firm, forceful voice	−0.62	−0.16
spoke louder	−0.68	0.01
felt good	−0.73	−0.47
smiled	−0.84	−0.04
wanted to destroy whatever was close	0.21	0.79
tried to control the intensity of the emotional feeling	−0.23	0.62
felt hot (puff of heat, cheeks or chest)	−0.08	0.56
wanted someone to be there to provide help or support	−0.08	0.49
involved behavior which was unjust	−0.15	0.47
involved suffering a serious loss	0.15	0.46

Table 32.2 (continued) Loadings of the 61 GRID features in a two-factorial structure

GRID features	F1	F2
spoke in a trembling voice	0.31	0.46
frowned	0.23	0.43
felt cold	0.29	0.42
felt an urge to be active, to do something, anything	−0.35	0.38
that involved behavior which violated laws or socially accepted norms	0.11	0.34
of which the consequences were likely to be negative, undesirable for the person him/herself	−0.27	0.33
sweated	0.18	0.29
experienced the emotion for a long time	0.06	0.29
that was totally (essentially) unpredictable	0.20	0.27
that was caused by the person's own behavior	−0.19	0.21
that was caused by somebody else's behavior	−0.10	0.17
wanted to flee	0.13	0.16
felt their breathing slowing down	0.15	0.16
wanted to make up for what they has done	−0.20	−0.39
had the jaw drop	0.40	−0.41
felt active	−0.27	−0.43
that occurred suddenly	0.45	−0.45
spoke faster	0.35	−0.47
spoke more slower	0.26	−0.49
had stomach troubles	0.45	−0.53
closed their eyes	0.51	−0.54
had tears in the eye	0.35	−0.57
felt their muscles relaxing (whole body)	0.37	−0.58
that was pleasant for people (independently of its possible consequences)	−0.32	−0.64
felt calm	−0.18	−0.68
wanted to be near or close to people or things	−0.54	−0.70

32.3 **Discussion**

Despite an extensive adaptation process, the modified GRID instrument did not give a very clear representation of the meaning structure of emotion terms in Setswana. Only a single VALENCE factor opposing positive to negative emotion terms could be interpreted well. It is not clear whether this deviating structure points to a cultural and linguistic specificity in the meaning structure of emotion terms in Setswana. A more likely alternative explanation is methodological: the four dimensional structure identified for the rest of the samples could not be replicated because the Setswana participants agreed only moderately on the meaning of the emotion terms.

One possible reason for this lack of inter-rater agreement is the lack of standardization of spoken Setswana. Although a standard version of the language exists and is taught at primary school, many different dialects are used in daily language. Differences between the dialects may have caused differences in the meaning of individual emotion terms and of the emotion features on which they were rated. Additionally, despite the adaptation of the instructions and the rating scale, other methodological factors might still have caused problems in the current version of the instrument: especially the format of the instrument, whereby decontextualized emotion terms had to be rated, constitutes a possible source of unreliability.

The results clearly indicate that an assessment instrument that works well in very diverse countries, such as the USA, Russia, and China, need not be universally applicable. These findings underline the necessity to adapt Western measuring instruments for use in other cultural groups in South Africa (Foxcroft, 1997). The present study calls for a further in-depth investigation of how method factors affect the interrater reliability of the meaning profiles of emotion terms in Setswana. Only when reliable meaning profiles can be identified, the question of possible cultural and linguistic differences in the meaning structure of the emotion domain can be properly addressed.

Chapter 33

Comparison of the AROUSAL dimension in Turkey and the USA

Gülcan Akçalan Akırmak,[1] Diane Sunar, and Hale Bolak Boratav

The GRID instrument was designed to investigate the meaning of emotion words across languages and cultures. In the present paper, we analyse the internal structure of the semantic space covered by the GRID terms in Turkish and US English. We analyse the Turkey and USA datasets (see Chapters 5 and 6 for a description of the GRID paradigm and its database). Since most of the psychology research on emotion is published in English, the comparability with the English translation of the emotion terms is of particular interest.

We first present the internal structure analyses for the USA and the Turkey structures separately as well as their congruence after Procrustes rotation. We then focus on one of the four identified factors, AROUSAL, which demonstrates substantial differences between the two cultural groups. The differences are described both in terms of the emotion features that define the AROUSAL factor as well as in terms of the position of the emotion terms on the AROUSAL factor.

33.1 The internal structure of the emotion domain in Turkey and the USA

The results of the Principal Components analyses on the 142 emotion features across the 24 emotion terms, with four factors, accounted for 79.2% and for 81.7% of the total variance in the Turkey sample and in the USA sample respectively. Moreover, VARIMAX rotations revealed the four dimensions of VALENCE, POWER, AROUSAL, and NOVELTY in each of the two samples, although with variations to be discussed below. In each of the two cultural groups the highest loading features (in absolute terms) seem to support this interpretation. For example, the features "wanted to be tender, sweet, and kind," "consequences positive for person," "event in itself unpleasant for the person," and "wanted to destroy whatever was close" have the highest (absolute) loadings on the first factor, VALENCE. In turn, features like "felt submissive," "fell silent," "wanted to be in command of others," and "had an assertive voice" are among the highest loading features on the second factor, POWER. The third factor, AROUSAL, received high loadings from features like "heartbeat getting faster," "perspired, or had moist hands," "had no bodily symptoms at all," and "did not show any changes in vocal expression." Finally, "had eyebrows go up," "had the jaw drop," "suddenly," and "unpredictable" defined the fourth factor, NOVELTY, in both samples.

[1] Corresponding author: Gülcan Akçalan Akırmak. Istanbul Bilgi University, Kazım Karabekir Cad. No:2/13 Eyüp, Istanbul, 34060 Turkey. gakcalan@bilgi.edu.tr

However, when the Turkey structure was orthogonally Procrustes rotated toward the USA structure, the AROUSAL factor showed a considerable difference. While the congruence (Tucker's phi) was 0.90 for VALENCE, 0.88 for POWER, and 0.84 for NOVELTY, the congruence was only 0.77 for AROUSAL, which is substantially below the cut-off value of 0.85 for moderate congruence (see Chapter 5). This low congruence clearly indicates substantial differences on the AROUSAL factor between the Turkey and the USA structures. As this difference in structure was not anticipated, we further explore in this chapter the meaning of the AROUSAL factor in both cultural groups. We first describe and compare the features that define the third factor and then look at the emotion terms that are most differentiated on this factor between both groups.

33.2 The defining features of the AROUSAL factor in the Turkey and USA samples

In total, 16 features had an absolute loading of 0.40 or higher in both cultural groups on the AROUSAL dimension (see Table 33.1). The positive loading features refer to sympathetic AROUSAL (e.g., "heartbeat getting faster" and "perspired") and the negative loading items refer predominantly to the absence of bodily symptoms and the absence of expressive features. The fact that these features define the third dimension in both cultural groups supports the basic interpretation of this dimension as an AROUSAL dimension.

We then looked at those features that differed between the two groups. We only took into account those features with an absolute difference in loading of 0.40 and more. In total, seven features loaded more positively on AROUSAL in the USA than in Turkey (see Table 33.1).

Three of these features came from the Feeling component (namely "was in an intense emotional state," "felt alert," and "felt restless"), and all three loaded higher than 0.40 in the positive direction on AROUSAL for the USA sample while none of them did for the Turkey sample.

Another three of these features were from Action tendencies ("wanted to act, whatever action it might be," "wanted to be in control of the situation," and "wanted to tackle the situation"); only one of these ("wanted to act, whatever action it might be") loaded more than 0.40 on AROUSAL for the USA sample, and only one ("wanted to tackle the situation") loaded more than 0.40 in the negative direction for the Turkey sample, while the remaining item ("wanted to be in control of the situation") did not meet the 0.40 criterion for either sample.

One feature from (vocal) Expression ("produced a short utterance"), while loading less than 0.40 for the USA sample, still differed widely from the negative loading in the Turkey sample (−0.41).

Three features loaded higher on AROUSAL in Turkey than in the USA, of which two were Bodily reaction features ("felt warm" and "blushed"); both of these loaded highly for the Turkey sample but loaded less than 0.40 for the USA sample. Both of these items fit the physiological AROUSAL aspect of the factor. The third item was a regulation feature ("showed the emotion to others more than s/he felt it"), which did not load significantly on AROUSAL for either sample, but was positive for the Turkey sample while being negative for the USA sample.

Since three of the ten differences occurred on items that did not meet the loading criterion of 0.40 for either sample, and another two involved maximum loadings of 0.41 and 0.46, there were only five differences in the actual composition of the factors. Thus the overall conclusion that the four-factor structure is valid for both samples received support.

The features that loaded differently on the third factor between the two cultural groups seem to indicate that the third dimension is somewhat more defined by the Bodily reaction component in the Turkey sample than in the USA one, and that AROUSAL has a somewhat broader meaning in

Table 33.1 Features loading on the AROUSAL factor in the Turkish and the US English structures

	USA	Turkey
Features that define the AROUSAL dimension in both the USA and Turkey		
had no bodily symptoms at all	−0.77	−0.80
did not show any changes in gestures	−0.67	−0.70
did not show any changes in vocal expression	−0.66	−0.69
heartbeat slowing down	−0.79	−0.48
did not show any changes in face	−0.54	−0.69
breathing slowing down	−0.72	−0.42
felt calm	−0.49	−0.43
spoke slower	−0.44	−0.43
felt out of control	0.42	0.43
felt shivers	0.55	0.43
muscles tensing (whole body)	0.60	0.40
breathing getting faster	0.81	0.80
heartbeat getting faster	0.82	0.82
felt hot	0.76	0.91
sweat	0.82	0.88
perspired, or had moist hands	0.87	0.90
Features that define the AROUSAL dimension more in the USA, than in Turkey		
was in an intense emotional state	0.63	−0.03
wanted to act, whatever action it might be	0.51	−0.15
produced a short utterance	0.17	−0.41
felt alert	0.46	−0.07
felt restless	0.57	0.06
wanted to be in control of the situation	0.30	−0.16
wanted to tackle the situation	−0.03	−0.46
Features that define the AROUSAL dimension more in Turkey, than in the USA		
felt warm	0.12	0.83
showed the emotion to others more than s/he felt it	−0.12	0.35
blushed	0.32	0.78

the USA sample, with some feelings and, to a lesser degree, Action tendencies also being associated to it. In other words, this pattern seems to indicate that the third USA factor includes more of a general activation aspect rather than just focusing on physiological AROUSAL, as in the case of the Turkish factor. This finding parallels the debate in the literature on the interpretation of the AROUSAL/activation dimension (e.g., Duffy, 1957).

33.3 **The coordinates of the emotion terms on the** AROUSAL **factor in Turkey and the USA**

We first looked at those emotion terms that were highly differentiated on the third factor in both samples. We looked only at those that had an absolute coordinate of 0.80 or higher (which is comparable to a large effect in the guidelines of Cohen (1992)). In both cultural groups *contentment* and *disappointment* scored 0.80 or more below the mean of the dimension and *love* and *anxiety* scored 0.80 or more above the mean (see Table 33.2). The position of these four terms is congruent with the interpretation of the third factor as an AROUSAL factor.

In a second step, we looked for those emotion terms that showed a large difference (0.80 or larger) in their position on the third factor. In total, four terms showed a large difference, namely *contempt*, *fear*, *sadness*, and *irritation* (see Table 33.2); each of them exceeded the criterion of 0.80 or greater absolute coordinate for one sample but not the other.

While *contempt* is situated in the middle of the AROUSAL dimension for the USA sample, it scores extremely negative in the Turkey sample. For *irritation* the opposite is observed—while it is situated in the middle of the AROUSAL dimension in the USA sample, it scores highly positive in the Turkey sample. In both groups *fear* scores positively, but only in the USA sample it has an extremely high positive score of more than two standard deviations above the mean. In both groups, *sadness* scores negatively, but it is much more negative in the USA than in Turkey. These four discrepancies can be summarized as follows: (1) in the Turkey sample, a strong opposition is observed between *irritation* and *contempt* on the third dimension, while this is not the case in the USA; (2) in the USA sample, a strong opposition is observed between *fear* and *sadness*, while the opposition is much less pronounced in the Turkey sample.

Differences between the position of the Turkish and the US English emotion terms on the AROUSAL factor could be attributed to two different causes, namely to cultural differences in the experience of specific emotions and to linguistic differences in the meaning of those words.

For example, a cultural explanation could be given for the fact that *sadness* was very low on the AROUSAL factor for English speakers, but not for Turkish speakers, since there may be genuine

Table 33.2 Coordinates on the AROUSAL factor of the Turkish and the US English emotion terms

	USA	Turkey
Emotion terms that define the AROUSAL dimension in both the USA and Turkey		
anxiety	1.48	1.04
love	1.28	0.82
disappointment	−1.32	−1.12
contentment	−2.57	−2.03
Emotion terms that define the AROUSAL dimension more in the USA, than in Turkey		
fear	2.28	0.77
contempt	−0.17	−1.95
Emotion terms that define the AROUSAL dimension more in Turkey, than in the US		
irritation	−0.07	1.28
sadnesss	−1.62	−0.35

cultural differences in the expression of sadness. Findings by Matsumoto et al. (2008; 2009) support the idea of differences in the expression of emotions according to cultural values. In a study of emotional display rules in Turkish culture (Boratav et al., 2011), it was found that the expression of sadness had higher endorsement than the other basic emotions, except for happiness and surprise. The possibly higher expressiveness of sadness in the Turkish culture compared to the USA could allow for more AROUSAL to be experienced during sadness episodes, therefore making sadness a more aroused emotion, in general, in Turkey compared to the USA. On the other hand, a linguistic interpretation of the difference between the samples in coordinates of *sadness* is also possible. The Turkish term for "sad" may in some contexts imply something closer to the English word "upset." (Alternative terms would have had implications of grief or mourning.) This linguistic difference could, of course, be a reflection of the cultural experience as well.

The difference observed between *contempt* and *irritation* could also possibly be interpreted as a linguistic effect. For example, the Turkish expression for *contempt* may be more like the English expression "to look down on" while the word for *irritation* may be closer to the English word *anger*. Since both terms occupy middle positions in the dimension in English, but score high values in Turkish, it could be the case that the Turkish lexemes are more sensitive than the English ones to a differentiation between cold and hot types of anger, or conversely that English contains more named gradations among different varieties of anger.

33.4 **Conclusions**

The results of this study support the four-dimensional model uncovered by the GRID paradigm for the meaning of emotion words. For both the USA and Turkey samples, the best factor solution consisted of four factors. However, substantial differences were observed between the USA and Turkey with respect to AROUSAL. The core of this factor had the same meaning in both cultural groups, as it was characterized by features of sympathetic AROUSAL. The factor, however, had a broader meaning in the USA than in Turkey, also including features referring to some subjective feelings and Action tendencies in the USA. Moreover four emotion terms clearly differed with respect to their coordinates on this third dimension, namely *fear*, *sadness*, *contempt*, and *irritation*. The differences between the two cultural groups can be explained both in terms of cultural differences in the experiences of emotions as well as in terms of what is lexicalized in specific languages. Only tentative post-hoc interpretations in this respect could be made, which call for further empirical research.

Acknowledgments

The authors are grateful to Johnny Fontaine for his help with the data analyses and information about the USA data.

Chapter 34

Familiarity and disappointment: A culture-specific dimension of emotional experience in Greece?

Penny Panagiotopoulou,[1] Marina Terkourafi, and Athanassios Protopapas

34.1 Culture and psychological differentiation

Explaining human behavioral reactions has been a longstanding research effort based on psychological constructs—including motivational constructs, such as values—and cognitive constructs, such as social axioms (Bond et al., 2004). Social axioms are generalized beliefs about oneself, the social and physical environment, or the spiritual world, and are in the form of assertions about the relationship between two entities or concepts (Leung et al., 2002: 289). They are built on the individuals' life experience within their culture.

Analysis of social axioms has identified a structure of five factors: (a) Social Cynicism, represents a negative assessment of human nature, lack of trust in social institutions, and rejection of legitimate means in achieving one's goals (e.g., "kind-hearted people usually suffer losses"); (b) Reward for Application, refers to the belief that investment of human resources, knowledge, and planning will lead to positive outcomes (e.g., "hard working people will achieve more in the end"); (c) Social Complexity, refers to the view that there are multiple solutions to a problem, the outcome of events is uncertain, and human inconsistency across situations is acceptable (e.g., "one has to deal with matters according to the circumstances"); (d) Fate Control, refers to the general belief that social events are influenced by impersonal, external forces (e.g., "fate determines one's successes and failures"); and, finally, (e) Religiosity, refers to the view that spiritual forces influence the human world and that religious institutions exert a positive effect on social outcomes (e.g., "religious people are more likely to maintain moral standards").

This social axiom structure varies to some extent across cultures in the relative importance of each factor (Neto, 2006). Replication of the basic structure has also revealed a sixth factor operative in some cultures (e.g., Safdar et al., 2006), including Greece (Gari et al., 2009). For the Greek sample, the sixth factor appears to represent a notion of Competition that derives from the struggle of the individual to address effectively the perceived complexity of societal reality. Competition combines the Social Cynicism dimension with the Social Complexity dimension in a contrasting fashion. The Greek sixth factor's core meaning refers to a possibly competitive and cruel world, in

---

[1] Contact author: Penny Panagiotopoulou, Department of Primary Education, University of Patras 26500 Rio, Patras, Greece. p.panagiotopoulou@gmail.com

which competition may or may not hinder progress, and in which the individual causing cruelty is divinely punished and eventually isolated.

But the most widely known attempt to define culture and subsequently explain human behavior has been based on values and conducted by Hofstede. Individualism-Collectivism, POWER Distance, Uncertainty Avoidance, and Masculinity-Femininity are used as organizing and explanatory constructs in many disciplines. A fifth dimension named Short-term vs Long-term orientation was later added to the initial four (Hofstede, 1980, 1991).

In Hofstede's structure (2001), Greece is placed in the middle of the POWER Distance index and the Individualism index, highest (first) on the Uncertainty Avoidance index, and relatively high on the Masculinity index. Based on the Uncertainty Avoidance ranking, Greeks appear to be facing extreme uncertainty, which entails intolerable anxiety. In addition, Greece has demonstrated a high positive correlation between Uncertainty Avoidance scores and the expression of affect, which is associated with high cultural levels of anxiety (Edelmann et al., 1989).

In this chapter, we discuss a culture-specific factor emerging from the Greek GRID results using a mixed approach from cultural and cross-cultural psychology. The profile of Greece on the four cultural dimensions of Hofstede will constitute the theoretical framework of the cross-cultural aspect of our approach. The culture-specific factor arising from the social axioms survey in Greece will contribute to the cultural-indigenous approach. It may appear as if, in our cross-cultural effort to discuss the Greek culture-specific—hereafter referred to as emic (Pike, 1967; Berry, 1999)—factor of the GRID based on Hofstede's dimensions, we will be committing the ecological fallacy (Hofstede, 1980). However, because the GRID survey in Greece was carried out on a representative and highly reliable sample, we contend that Hofstede's measurements can be used for this purpose (Smith & Bond, 1997).

34.2 **Reliability and dimensions of the Greek GRID data**

The Greek sample comprised 245 students at undergraduate, graduate, and doctoral levels in a wide range of disciplines from several Greek universities[2]. The majority of the respondents were women and the average age was 26 years.

Internal consistency (Cronbach's α) of the Greek item-level raw data was very high, ranging between 0.95–0.98, except for compassion (συμπόνια, 0.90), surprise (έκπληξη, 0.93), and contempt (περιφρόνηση, 0.88) (see Table SM 1)[3], indicating high reliability of the great majority of the ratings. The excellent reliability of the Greek data allows greater confidence in the results of the factor analysis.

The analysis of the Greek GRID centered data has successfully reproduced the general four-factor structure of emotion dimensions found cross-linguistically. However, when the analysis of the Greek raw data was carried out without prior centering, thus allowing response tendencies of potential cultural significance to affect the covariance matrix, an additional fifth factor was reliably extracted.

Specifically, initial factor analysis of the Greek raw (uncentered) data set extracted a four-factor solution. On the basis of the individual feature loadings, the resulting factor structure was judged

---

[2] This number includes both the participants who rated the 24 standard GRID terms, as well as another group who rated an additional set of Greek words.

[3] All supplementary materials (SM) are available at the GRID website: http://www.affective-sciences.org/GRID. See Appendix 1 ("Availability") for further details.

to be poorly interpretable. The total proportion of variance explained was 76.8%. After applying Procrustes rotation toward the original Belgian/Swiss/UK solution (Fontaine et al., 2007), the resulting congruence indices (Tucker's Φ) were very high for the factors VALENCE (0.94) and POWER (0.90) but moderate for AROUSAL (0.84), and low for NOVELTY (0.76).

A subsequent analysis, extracting five factors, resulted in a higher proportion of variance explained (80.9%) and better interpretability of the solution. Due to the high reliability of the data, the five factor structure was deemed acceptable. After Procrustes rotation of this structure, the first four factors were sufficiently congruent to the original Belgian/Swiss/UK four-factor solution, with Φ values of 0.94 (VALENCE), 0.91 (POWER), 0.89 (AROUSAL), and 0.83 (NOVELTY). The corresponding proportions of variance taken up by the four dimensions were 45.8%, 10.5%, 9.5%, and 7.6%, respectively. The remaining 7.4% was accounted for by the additional (fifth) factor, which did not appear in the cross-cultural analysis.

In the remainder of this chapter, we present and discuss this fifth factor as reflecting the reality of life in Greece. In particular, we consider the possibility that the fifth factor is related to the culture and social context of Greece as this emerges from the aforementioned research on social axioms and cultural dimensions.

34.3 **The fifth factor**

Table 34.1 lists the emotion features loading on the fifth factor. There were no negative loadings among them. On this dimension, Greek individuals classify the eliciting events of the ensuing emotion state with respect to "frequency," "suddenness," "unpredictability," "consistency with one's expectations," "relevance to one's goals," "chance cause," "cause someone else's actions," "unavoidability of consequences," "result of irrevocable loss," and "unpleasantness." The emotional state following the eliciting event is characterized by a "slowing down of breathing," "slowing down of the heartbeat," "tiredness," "exhaustion," "submissiveness," "showing tears," "speech disturbances," "dropping of the jaw," as well as by a "desire to tackle the situation," "overcome the obstacle," "take action or initiative," "control the situation," and "seek external support."

Based on this list of defining features, it seems that the emotion dimension defined by the fifth factor concerns the frequent and familiar experience in the Greek cultural setting of unforeseen situations demanding the individual's attention. The situations in question constitute obstacles and are a cause for concern. Individuals are worn out by the constant struggle to maintain balance and progress in the face of potential negative developments. Effective management of such situations is a prerequisite for the individual's evolvement. The individual will either turn to him/herself for support or s/he will attempt to externalize his/her emotions and course of action—the line between the two options is a fine one. Therefore, this factor may be described as the emotional reaction of a Greek when trying to function effectively and adapt to the surrounding social context.

From the cross-cultural perspective, Greeks, living in a country high in Uncertainty Avoidance, "look for structure in their organizations, institutions, and relationships, which makes events clearly interpretable and predictable" (Hofstede, 2001: 148). They may demonstrate a high sense of urgency, engage in dynamic problem solving, and become involved in risky behavior in order to reduce ambiguity. They are used to living in a country with unstructured situations—novel, unknown, surprising, and different from usual—from which uncomfortable feelings ensue.

Additionally, Greece has been traditionally found to be a collectivistic culture, but is currently placed in the middle of the Individualism index (Triandis et al., 1986; Hofstede, 1980, 2001). This placement is indicative of a transition from collectivism to individualism, which results in conflicting schemas in everyday encounters that attract the individuals' attention and emotional reaction.

Table 34.1 Emotional features with highest loadings on the fifth Greek factor, in descending order (only features with loadings of 0.30 or greater are shown)

Emotion feature (emotion component)	Loading
how frequently experienced (general)	0.63
familiar (evaluation)	0.51
enough resources to avoid or modify consequences (evaluation)	0.51
heartbeat slowing down (physical symptoms)	0.51
wanted to tackle the situation (action tendency)	0.49
breathing slowing down (physical symptom)	0.49
caused by somebody else's behavior (evaluation)	0.49
showed tears (expression)	0.48
wanted to overcome an obstacle (action tendency)	0.45
produced a long utterance (expression)	0.43
felt tired (subjective feeling)	0.43
had the jaw drop (expression)	0.41
changed the melody of her or his speech (expression)	0.40
suddenly (evaluation)	0.39
caused by chance (evaluation)	0.38
wanted someone to be there to provide help or support (action tendency)	0.38
wanted to act, whatever action it might be (action tendency)	0.36
consequences avoidable or modifiable (evaluation)	0.36
important and relevant for person's goals (evaluation)	0.36
important and relevant for goals of somebody else (evaluation)	0.35
unpredictable (evaluation)	0.35
wanted to take initiative her/himself (action tendency)	0.34
wanted to be in control of the situation (action tendency)	0.34
felt an urge to be attentive to what is going on (action tendency)	0.34
consequences able to live with (evaluation)	0.33
irrevocable loss (evaluation)	0.33
moved toward people or things (expression)	0.32
inconsistent with expectations (evaluation)	0.32
showed the emotion to others more than s/he felt it (regulation)	0.31
to what extent is it socially accepted (general)	0.31
confirmed expectations (evaluation)	0.31
felt exhausted (subjective feeling)	0.31
wanted to be near or close to people or things (action tendency)	0.31
felt submissive (subjective feeling)	0.30
in itself unpleasant for somebody else (evaluation)	0.30

Note: corresponding feature categories indicated in parentheses. There were no features with high negative loadings (<−0.30) on this factor.

As a traditionally collectivistic culture, Greeks focus on groups, contexts, and relationships; whereas as a budding individualistic culture they are associated with overall higher expressivity norms avoiding inward emotions such as contempt, irritation, or anxiety (Matsumoto et al., 2008). This state of flux may underlie the reduced predictability and increased need for coping expressed in the fifth Greek factor.

The set of emotions best exemplifying the fifth factor is consistent with a mix of individualist and collectivist aspects (see Table 34.2). The emotion terms scoring positively highest included *disappointment*, *sadness*, and *being hurt*, whereas the highest negative scores were found for *disgust*, *guilt*, *shame*, *contempt*, *fear*, *hate*, and *love*. Some of the high-scoring emotion terms refer to engaged emotions (Kitayama et al., 2000), that is, emotions which emphasize vulnerability, interdependence, and closeness with others. Respect for authority and maintenance of social order, social

Table 34.2 Scores of individual emotion terms on the Greek fifth factor

Emotion term	Regressed 5th-factor value
disappointment	1.62
sadness	1.42
being hurt	0.92
interest	0.83
anger	0.72
despair	0.64
anxiety	0.55
compassion	0.54
stress	0.46
contentment	0.45
joy	0.45
irritation	0.32
jealousy	0.24
pleasure	0.17
surprise	−0.06
happiness	−0.33
pride	−0.70
love	−0.70
hate	−0.91
fear	−0.96
contempt	−1.03
shame	−1.53
guilt	−2.09
disgust	−2.19

norms, and social participation, which are features of hierarchical cultures like Greece (Schwartz, 2004), appear to be relevant for the conceptual definition of this factor, because disruptive emotions such as shame, guilt, and fear score negatively high on this factor. However, emotions such us disgust, anger, and hate, which are expressed more in individualistic countries, also score high on this factor (Matsumoto et al., 2007).

Given that competition is salient in individualistic behavior, the rise of individualism is further supported by the finding that competition in interpersonal relations was the main emphasis in the sixth Social Cynicism dimension in the survey of social axioms. In other words, research on social axioms introduced the parameter of Competition as an important functional element for the dimension of Social Cynicism (Gari et al., 2009). Competition, as a dynamic feature of the relationship with out-groups, has been studied in the Greek cultural setting as a contrast to "filotimo," a Greek culture-specific term whose meaning is associated with "cooperation, fairness and altruism" (Triandis & Vassiliou, 1972; Vassiliou & Vassiliou, 1973).

The fifth Greek factor, then, may be related to the special circumstances of the emotional makeup of Greeks living today in a transitional culture resulting in certain frequent emotional conflicts and tensions between old-fashioned collectivism and emerging individualism, between the clearly emic notion of "filotimo" and the enriched notion of Social Cynicism with social axioms referring to competition. If this interpretation is on the right track, then other transitioning cultures with their unique cultural dimensions profile might also exhibit idiosyncratic dimensions in their conceptual space of emotion terms, in addition to the four general cross-cultural dimensions, specifically related to the particulars of their intermediate situation. Inasmuch as dimensions used to describe nations at the cultural level, such as Hofstede's dimensions, do not necessarily align with the same qualitative and quantitative differences among cultural groups at the individual level, there is no guarantee of the stability of the findings from cultures placed highest or lowest on each dimension. Rather, what is implied is the existence of possible emic conditions in the intermediate cultures. Perhaps variation along several cultural dimensions might shed some light onto similarities and differences between languages and cultures along the emotional dimensions, as well as on how these interact and change over time.

## Chapter 35

The meaning of happiness in Japan and the United States

Keiko Ishii[1]

It is well known that there is a strong belief of independent agency in North American cultural contexts, whereas there is a strong belief of interdependent agency in East Asian cultural contexts including Japan (Markus & Kitayama, 1991; Nisbett, Peng, Choi, & Norenzayan, 2001). Research in cultural psychology has suggested that the culturally different views of agency encourage divergent modes of motivation and emotion. Independent agency is likely to associate with a tendency toward personal goal pursuit and control, whereas interdependent agency is likely to associate with a tendency to orient to the goals and desires of surrounding others (e.g., Iyengar & Lepper, 1999). Reflecting this diversity, for people with independent agency (e.g., North Americans), happiness is likely to depend primarily on personal achievement, whereas for those with interdependent agency (e.g., Japanese), happiness is likely to depend primarily on social harmony and adjustment to others (Kitayama, Ishii, Imada, Takemura, & Ramaswamy, 2006; Kitayama, Markus, & Kurokawa, 2000; Kitayama, Mesquita, & Karasawa, 2006).

In order to show additional evidence regarding the difference in the meaning of happiness, data related to happiness from Japanese and Americans in the GRID project were analyzed (see Chapter 6 for details on these data samples). The Visual Hypothesis Testing with Confidence Intervals (see Chapter 5) was used to confirm the significance of cultural differences for each item. For 31 out of 144 emotion features, the confidence intervals were non-overlapping or they were overlapping, but with the means outside the respective confidence intervals (which is referred to as significant and marginally significant differences, respectively) (see Table 35.1 for more details). Results on specific items which are relevant for the framework of independence and interdependence were summarized below.

It would be expected that North Americans regard happiness primarily as personal achievement and control, whereas Japanese regard it primarily as realization of social harmony and adjustment. Consistent with this prediction, "wanted to be in control of the situation" was more related to the meaning of happiness in the US than in Japan ($M = 5.13$ vs 2.74). The difference was significant. Moreover, the same tendency was found in the item "wanted to be in command of others" ($M = 4.55$ vs 3.00), although the difference was marginally significant. On the other hand, "(an event) that confirmed the expectations of the person" was more connected to the meaning of happiness in Japan than in the US ($M = 8.05$ vs 6.03). The difference was significant. The pattern was reversed, however, for the item "(an event) that was inconsistent with the expectations of the person" ($M = 3.16$ vs 4.77), although the difference was marginally significant.

---

[1] Correspondence concerning this chapter should be addressed to: Keiko Ishii, Faculty of Letters, Kobe University, 1-1 Rokkodai-cho, Nada-ku, Kobe 657-8501 E-mail: ishii@lit.kobe-u.ac.jp

Table 35.1 Thirty-one features in which there were differences between Japan and the US regarding the meaning of happiness

Features	Japan	US	
Appraisal (five features)			
confirmed expectations	8.05	6.03	**
inconsistent with expectations	3.16	4.77	*
required an immediate response	3.37	5.00	*
enough resources to avoid or modify consequences	2.53	5.84	**
consequences able to live with	4.95	6.58	*
Bodily reaction (four features)			
heartbeat slowing down	5.37	3.13	*
muscles relaxing	7.53	5.90	*
breathing slowing down	6.05	4.26	*
breathing getting faster	4.05	6.06	*
Expression (eight features)			
had eyebrows go up	3.53	5.87	*
showed tears	7.26	4.94	*
moved against people or things	2.37	3.84	*
did not show any changes in gestures	4.11	2.68	*
decreased the volume of voice	7.21	3.39	**
had a trembling voice	5.53	2.84	*
spoke faster	5.53	7.06	*
spoke slower	6.84	3.55	**
Action tendency (nine features)			
wanted to go on with what he or she was doing	4.37	6.84	*
wanted to be in command of others	3.00	4.55	*
wanted to be in control of the situation	2.74	5.13	**
wanted to move	6.68	5.23	*
wanted to be hurt as little as possible	2.37	4.97	*
wanted to be seen, to be in the center of attention	5.42	6.87	*
wanted to take care of another person or cause	4.47	6.55	*
wanted to be near or close to people or things	4.89	6.97	**
wanted to be tender, sweet, and kind	5.37	7.97	**
Feeling (four features)			
felt submissive	2.58	3.87	*
felt at ease	6.58	7.71	*
felt energetic	6.42	7.97	*
felt alert	3.32	6.94	**
Regulation (one feature)			
showed the emotion to other less than s/he felt it	5.53	3.97	*

Note: * overlapping confidence intervals, ** non-overlapping confidence intervals

In addition, in Japan, compared to the US, a low-arousal state indicated by some Bodily reaction features such as "felt his/her heartbeat slowing down" ($M = 5.37$ vs 3.13), "felt his/her muscles relaxing (whole body)" ($M = 7.53$ vs 5.90), and "felt his/her breathing slowing down" ($M = 6.05$ vs 4.26) and Expression features such as "spoke softer" ($M = 7.21$ vs 3.39) and "spoke slower" ($M = 6.84$ vs 3.55) was associated with the meaning of happiness. The differences on the two Expression features were significant, while those regarding the three Bodily reaction features were marginally significant. In contrast, in the US, compared to Japan, the high-arousal state indicated by some features such as "felt his/her breathing getting faster" ($M = 6.06$ vs 4.05) and "spoke faster" ($M = 7.06$ vs 5.53) was associated with the meaning of happiness, although these differences were marginally significant. The results are consistent with those in Tsai, Knutson, and Fung (2006) and Uchida and Kitayama (2009).

Furthermore, the extent to which the meaning of happiness was connected to love, a socially engaging positive emotion, or pride, a socially disengaging positive emotion, was examined in each culture. Because socially disengaging emotions affirm independent self, while socially engaging emotions affirm interdependent self (Kitayama, Mesquita, et al., 2006), happiness would be more connected to pride than to love in the US, whereas it would be more connected to love than to pride in Japan. Relevant regression coefficients are summarized in Table 35.2. In both cultures, happiness was significantly connected to both love and pride over 144 features. In addition, when regression analyses were performed for each of the five subcategories of the features (i.e., Appraisal, Bodily

Table 35.2 Regression coefficients (β) that predict happiness as a function of pride and love

Culture	Pride	Love
	Over 144 features	
Japan	0.54***	0.42***
US	0.58***	0.41***
	Appraisal	
Japan	0.41**	0.57***
US	0.18 +	0.80***
	Bodily reaction	
Japan	0.14	0.83***
US	0.88***	0.04
	Expression	
Japan	0.44***	0.54***
US	0.71***	0.28*
	Action tendency	
Japan	0.55***	0.34**
US	0.34***	0.68***
	Feeling	
Japan	0.73***	0.29**
US	0.74***	0.26*

Note: *** $p < 0.001$, ** $p < 0.01$, * $p < 0.05$ + $p < 0.10$

reaction, Expression, Action tendancy, and Feeling) in each culture, the same tendency was found in all the subcategories except for the Bodily reaction. For the Bodily reaction features, happiness was significantly connected to pride, not love, in the US, whereas it was significantly connected to love, not pride in Japan, consistent with the prediction. This suggests that cultural differences in predictors of happiness may be limited to a specific type of feature.

In summary, although many features of the meaning of happiness are common between the two cultures, there are also cultural differences reflecting divergent modes of agency (i.e., independence vs interdependence). In the US, happiness was more related to a sense of control and high-arousal states, whereas in Japan, happiness was more related to the fulfillment of other's expectations, as well as low-arousal states. Moreover, overall happiness was connected to both pride and love in both cultures. Regarding the Bodily reaction features, however, happiness was connected more to pride than love in the US, whereas the pattern was reversed in Japan. Further analyses will be needed to examine the details for dimensions, which consist of happiness in the two cultures, as well as to evaluate the validity of previous findings on culture and happiness.

Chapter 36

Happiness and contentment in English and Polish

Paul A. Wilson,[1] Barbara Lewandowska-Tomaszczyk, and Yu Niiya

36.1 **Introduction**

Many studies show that emotion terms do not translate well across languages. For example, Wierzbicka (2009) explains that many languages do not have an equivalent to the English word *happy*. The focus of this study was to investigate the degree to which the American English terms *happiness* and *contentment* correspond to the widely accepted Polish equivalents *szczęście* and *zadowolenie*. Our everyday experience with the two languages as well as the lexicographic material from monolingual and bilingual dictionaries drew our attention to a certain asymmetry between the putative equivalents. For example, according to a leading English–Polish Dictionary (*Oxford–PWN English–Polish and Polish–English Dictionary*, 2002), the Polish equivalent of English *happiness* is *szczęście*, while the entry for *szczęście* offers the English equivalents *happiness* on the one hand and *luck* and *fortune* on the other. The word *contentment* corresponds to *zadowolenie*, while the English equivalents of Polish *zadowolenie* are *satisfaction* and *contentment*. As for definitions in monolingual dictionaries, the Polish *Uniwersalny Słownik Języka Polskiego* (2003) foregrounds an element of pleasure in *zadowolenie* and *satysfakcja*, while Polish *szczęście* has at least three different senses (polysemous): *happiness*, *good fate*, and *good luck*. The *New Oxford Dictionary of English* (2003) explains that *happiness*, "as a derivative of *happy* is used to describe feeling or showing *pleasure* or *contentment*," whereas *content*, and by extension *contentment*, is "a state of peaceful happiness"; *satisfaction* is defined as "fulfilment of one's wishes, expectations, or needs, or the pleasure derived from this."

Considering the vagueness and a certain circularity present in dictionary definitions, the GRID instrument was employed to provide further insight into the differences that might exist between *szczęście* and *happiness*, and between *zadowolenie* and *contentment*. The results are reported within the framework of the universal dimensional structure of emotions identified in the GRID data, which comprises four dimensions: VALENCE, POWER, AROUSAL, and NOVELTY (cf. Chapter 7 for more details).

There is a paucity of evidence on the differences in dimensional patterning that might exist between *szczęście* and *happiness*, and between *zadowolenie* and *contentment*. However, differences between the latter two emotions might be predicted on the basis of the above dictionary definitions

---

[1] Corresponding author: Paul A. Wilson. Department of English Language and Applied Linguistics, University of Łódź, Kosciuszki 65, 90-514 Łódź, Poland. p.wilson@psychology.bbk.ac.uk

that state that *zadowolenie*, in contrast to *contentment*, is associated more with *satisfaction* and *pleasure*. Shaver et al. (1987) showed that *happiness*, *satisfaction*, and *pleasure* were associated with a relatively more positive VALENCE than *contentment*, and from this we can deduce that the elements of satisfaction and pleasure in *zadowolenie* will result in *zadowolenie* being evaluated relatively more positively than its English counterpart, *contentment*. Shaver et al. (1987) also found little difference between *contentment* and *satisfaction* in terms of potency, which is equivalent to the POWER dimension in GRID. We therefore do not expect the relatively greater association between *zadowolenie* and *satisfaction* to produce any significant differences between *zadowolenie* and *contentment* on the POWER dimension in the present study.

The differences between *szczęście* and *happiness* are likely to be fewer than between *zadowolenie* and *contentment*, because, as Shaver et al. (1987) explain, there is more cross-cultural equivalence between basic emotions such as happiness due to their biological grounding. Nevertheless, the element of luck and fortune implicit in *szczęście*, but not in *happiness*, suggests that there will be differences between *szczęście* and *happiness* on some of the four underlying dimensions, although it is difficult to predict in which of the dimensions they might be located.

On the basis of the element of pleasure implicit in *zadowolenie*, and the natural association between pleasure and happiness in general, it can be predicted that there will be a higher correlation between *zadowolenie* and *szczęście* than between their English counterparts, *contentment* and *happiness*.

36.2 **GRID data**

The mean ages and gender ratios of the participants for each of the emotion terms were as follows: *zadowolenie* (20 Polish-speaking participants; mean age 26.1 years, 17 females); *contentment* (30 American English-speaking participants; mean age 18.3 years, 21 females); *szczęście* (20 Polish-speaking participants; mean age 23.5 years, 16 females); *happiness* (32 American English-speaking participants; mean age 18.4 years, 23 females).

Analyses were performed to compare the GRID features that were associated with the four dimensions identified in the GRID data: VALENCE, POWER, AROUSAL, and NOVELTY. Tables SM 1 to 4[2] show the features that loaded on these dimensions following principal component analysis (with VARIMAX rotation). Mean values of the features that loaded on these dimensions were obtained for each participant, producing a mean value of each of the four dimensions for each participant. These mean values of the four dimensions comprised the dependent variables of a MANOVA that had two between-subjects variables (emotion: happiness vs contentment; language: Polish vs American English). There was a significant main effect of language, $F(4, 94) = 7.9$, $p < 0.0001$, showing that the Polish-speaking participants rated the features as comparatively more likely to occur than American English-speaking participants (means of 6.18 and 5.62, respectively). There was also a significant main effect of emotion, $F(4, 94) = 9.9$, $p < 0.0001$, showing that the feature ratings of happiness were associated with a higher likelihood of occurrence than the feature ratings of contentment (means of 6.16 and 5.64, respectively). There was also a significant interaction between language and emotion, $F(4, 94) = 8.46$, $p < 0.0001$. This showed that whereas the feature ratings of contentment were associated with a higher likelihood of occurrence for the Polish-speaking participants compared with the American English-speaking participants (means

---

[2] All supplementary materials (SM) are available at the GRID website: http://www.affective-sciences.org/ GRID. See Appendix 1 ("Availability") for further details.

of 6.13 and 5.15, respectively), there was less difference between the Polish-speaking and American English-speaking participants for happiness (means of 6.23 and 6.09, respectively).

The results for VALENCE showed a significant main effect for language, $F(1, 97) = 10.32$, $p < 0.01$. The Polish-speaking participants rated the VALENCE features as more likely to occur than the American English-speaking participants (means of 7.19 and 6.68, respectively). There was also a significant interaction between language and emotion, $F(1, 97) = 9$, $p < 0.01$. This was broken down with contrasts comparing VALENCE ratings for Polish contentment (*zadowolenie*), English contentment (*contentment*), Polish happiness (*szczęście*), and English happiness (*happiness*). These ratings showed a significant difference between *zadowolenie* and *contentment*, $F(1, 48) = 7$, $p < 0.05$. *Zadowolenie* was characterized by a relatively higher degree of perceived positive VALENCE than *contentment* (means of 7.33 and 6.35, respectively). There were no significant differences between *szczęście* and *happiness* on the VALENCE dimension.

The results for POWER showed a significant main effect for language, $F(1, 97) = 4.39$, $p < 0.05$. The Polish-speaking participants rated the POWER features as more likely to occur than the American English-speaking participants (means of 5.95 and 5.65, respectively). There was also a significant interaction between language and emotion, $F(1, 97) = 22.25$, $p < 0.001$. This was broken down with contrasts comparing POWER ratings for the four words. These ratings showed a significant difference between Polish contentment (*zadowolenie*) and English *contentment*, $F(1, 48) = 25.59$, $p < 0.001$. *Zadowolenie* was relatively more associated with experiences of high POWER than *contentment* (means of 6.14 and 5.18, respectively). There were no significant differences between *szczęście* and *happiness* on the POWER dimension.

The results for AROUSAL showed a significant main effect for language, $F(1, 97) = 17.21$, $p < 0.001$. The Polish-speaking participants rated the AROUSAL features as more likely to occur than the American English-speaking participants (means of 6.1 and 5.11, respectively). There was also a significant main effect for emotion, $F(1, 97) = 34.26$, $p < 0.001$. Happiness was characterized by a relatively higher degree of perceived AROUSAL than contentment (means of 6.3 and 4.9, respectively). Contrasts showed that this effect was similar for both languages. There was a significant difference between *szczęście* and *happiness*, $F(1, 49) = 7.9$, $p < 0.01$. *Szczęście* was relatively more associated with experiences of higher AROUSAL than *happiness* (means of 6.72 and 5.88, respectively). There was also a significant difference between *zadowolenie* and *contentment*, $F(1, 48) = 9.33$, $p < 0.01$. *Zadowolenie* was characterized by a relatively higher degree of perceived AROUSAL than *contentment* (means of 5.47 and 4.33, respectively).

There was a significant main effect of language on the NOVELTY dimension, $F(1, 97) = 7.93$, $p < 0.01$. The Polish-speaking participants rated these features as more likely to occur than the American English-speaking participants (means of 5.49 and 5.03, respectively). There was also a significant interaction between language and emotion, $F(1, 97) = 6.03$, $p < 0.05$. This was broken down with contrasts comparing NOVELTY ratings for the four terms. These ratings showed a significant difference between *zadowolenie* and *contentment*, $F(1, 48) = 12$, $p < 0.01$. *Zadowolenie* was relatively more associated with experiences of higher unpredictability than *contentment* (means of 5.57 and 4.72, respectively). There were no significant differences between *szczęście* and *happiness* on the NOVELTY dimension.

Finally, recall that, on the basis of the common association of *zadowolenie* and *szczęście* with pleasure, it was predicted that there would be a higher correlation between *zadowolenie* and *szczęście* than between *contentment* and *happiness*. Pearson correlations were performed on the mean values of the complete profile of GRID features between *zadowolenie* and *szczęście*, and between *contentment* and *happiness*. Pearson correlations were additionally performed on the mean values of the features that loaded on each of the four dimensions. It can be seen in Table 36.1 that

Table 36.1 Correlations (*zadowolenie–szczęście, contentment–happiness*)

	Zadowolenie–szczęście	*Contentment–happiness*
Complete profile of GRID features	0.742**	0.72**
VALENCE features	0.791**	0.649**
POWER features	0.636**	0.475*
AROUSAL features	0.694**	0.618*
NOVELTY features	0.828**	0.441 (ns)

Note: * correlation is significant at the 0.05 level (two-tailed); ** correlation is significant at the 0.01 level (two-tailed).

the relatively stronger correlation between *zadowolenie* and *szczęście* was more pronounced for these four dimensions than for the complete profile of features.

Summarizing the GRID results, it was found that *zadowolenie* was relatively more associated with experiences of higher VALENCE, POWER, AROUSAL, and NOVELTY than *contentment*. *Szczęście* was characterized by a relatively higher degree of perceived AROUSAL than *happiness*. The higher correlation between *zadowolenie* and *szczęście* than between *contentment* and *happiness* is consistent with the relatively greater degree of pleasure associated with *zadowolenie* than *contentment*.

36.3 **Discussion and conclusions**

As predicted, *zadowolenie* was more positively evaluated than *contentment*. Recall that, according to dictionary definitions, *zadowolenie* is associated with pleasure and satisfaction. When this is considered in the light of Shaver et al.'s (1987) finding that *pleasure* and *satisfaction* are relatively more positively evaluated, it would appear that these elements are responsible for the more positive VALENCE of *zadowolenie* over *contentment*.

Contrary to our prediction that there would be no difference between *zadowolenie* and *contentment* in terms of POWER, it was found that *zadowolenie* was more associated with a higher degree of POWER than *contentment*. A moment's reflection, however, on the GRID features that comprise high POWER (e.g., "increased volume of voice," "feeling dominant," "speaking faster," and "wanting to act, whatever action it might be") indicate that one would expect *zadowolenie*, following the energizing effect of its association with pleasure and elements of happiness, to be relatively more associated with these features than *contentment*. Further research is clearly necessary to gain a better understanding of the relationship between *zadowolenie* and *contentment* in terms of POWER.

Differences between the Polish and English representations of contentment also provide an explanation of the more unpredictable nature of *zadowolenie* relative to *contentment*. This is connected with the fact that the noun *zadowolenie* is used much more frequently in Polish than *contentment* is in English, and also in more varied contexts. The Polish adjectives *zadowlony/-a/-e*, and their grammatical case and number variants, are most frequently rendered as *glad* or *satisfied* and less often as *content*. *Satysfakcja* (i.e., the satisfaction that Polish dictionary definitions associate with *zadowolenie*) occurs more frequently than *contentment* in reactions to specific events. For example, one is more likely to feel *satysfakcja* than *zadowolenie* as a reaction to some personal or professional achievement that may involve some effort to attain. This has an element of unpredictability, as one is never certain of the outcome of such occasions before the event. This can be contrasted with the more long-term, less sudden state of peaceful happiness, tranquillity, or well-being that characterizes *contentment*.

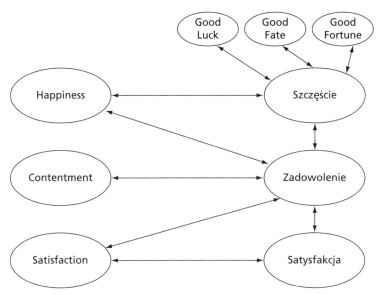

Figure 36.1 Relationship between Polish and English happiness, contentment, and satisfaction.

As predicted on the basis of happiness being more of a basic emotion than contentment (Shaver et al., 1987), there were fewer differences between *szczęście* and *happiness* than between *zadowolenie* and *contentment*. In fact, there was only one notable difference between them, namely the higher ratings of *szczęście* than *happiness* on the AROUSAL features. This is consistent with the polysemy of *szczęście*, between happiness and luck, as luck can be associated with energy and activation. It seems Polish *szczęście* is characterized by higher levels of activation and energy and appears to be a more intense emotion than *happiness*. In this sense, Polish *szczęście* appears to be similar to the French *bonheur*, German *Glück* and Italian *felicità*, which, in comparison to the weaker English *happiness*, express "a common European concept" of an emotion that "fills a human being to overflowing, leaving no room for further desires or wishes" (Wierzbicka, 1992a, p. 299).

A picture which evolves from the discussion presents a fairly complex network of English–Polish correspondences in the domain of happiness and contentment. There exist no one-to-one equivalents in this respect, which, based on the results of our investigation of other emotion concepts across languages, is rather the rule. Attempts to identify one-word equivalents usually fail. A certain approximation toward the complexity of English–Polish equivalence in the domain of happiness and contentment is presented in Figure 36.1.

As can be seen from Figure 36.1, the relationship between *happiness* and *szczęście* is only partial due to the polysemy of the Polish form, which is ambiguous between happiness, good luck, good fate, and good fortune. A Polish speaker using this form most often activates a blend of these meanings rather than one crisp concept. English *happiness* is also partly equivalent to Polish *zadowolenie*, particularly in politeness formulas, whereas Polish *zadowolenie* in turn (which is used in many diverse contexts), also partly corresponds to English *contentment* and *satisfaction*. The latter is a close equivalent to Polish *satysfakcja*, both referring to a scenario in which an experiencer develops this emotion as a result of a positively completed task or achievement.

Chapter 37

Exploring the meaning of pride and shame in Hong Kong-Chinese

Sowan Wong[1] and Dannii Y. Yeung[2]

In the study of cross-cultural emotions, a lot of effort has been put into investigating the similarities/differences of various emotion aspects of individuals from individualistic and collectivistic cultures. Comparisons were usually made between participants from the United States (US) and those from China, Japan, or Taiwan (e.g., Matsumoto, 2005; Stipek, 1998), representing cultural groups that emphasize the independent and interdependent views of self, respectively (Markus & Kitayama, 1991). However, the question remaining is whether the observed patterns of emotion features in collectivistic cultures can be generalized to other cultures like Hong Kong, which is traditionally a Chinese society, but has undergone rapid modernization and a large exposure to the Euro-American cultures due to its history as a British colony.

The cultural framework of a society shapes the meaning and the manifestation of emotions (Markus & Kitayama, 2001). In cultures where the independent view of self is emphasized, individuals' subjective experiences are foregrounded; on the other hand, in cultures where the interdependent self is emphasized, it is the relationship with others that is underlined. However, Kagitcibasi (2006) has postulated a family and cultural model, in which a third type of self is identified, in addition to the autonomous (independent) and relational (interdependent) selves. The third type of self-construal is the autonomous-relational self, which is a combination of relational orientation and autonomy, and is usually found in collectivistic cultures undergoing urbanization and modernization. In these cultures, psychological interdependence in the family is emphasized and preserved; however, individual autonomy becomes increasingly emphasized as it is adaptive to the changing social environment. Given the cultural background of Hong Kong, individuals in this society are more likely to possess this autonomous-relational self, and their emotional experiences will be shaped accordingly.

In order to explore the representation that individuals of Hong Kong make of different emotional experiences, two emotions, pride and shame, were chosen in the present study; and comparisons were also made between the Hong Kong-Chinese participants and their counterparts in the US. Both pride (positive emotion) and shame (negative emotion) involve self-evaluation, and require a perception of personal responsibility (Stipek, 1998); so they may demonstrate how the perception of self may shape the emotional experiences in these two cultures. Previous studies have shown that Chinese participants from mainland China regarded pride as more undesirable, and had lower frequency of this emotion than their counterparts in the US and Australia (Eid & Diener, 2001).

[1] Corresponding author: Sowan Wong. City University of Hong Kong. Kowloon Tong, Hong Kong. E-mail: sowan_w@hotmail.com.

[2] Corresponding author: Dannii Y. Yeung. Department of Applied Social Studies, City University of Hong Kong, Kowloon Tong, Hong Kong. E-mail: dannii.yeung@cityu.edu.hk.

They also reported personal achievement failures as antecedents to shame more frequently than their American counterparts (Stipek et al., 1989). The present study aims to explore the way Hong Kong-Chinese participants represent pride and shame, highlighting the differences of those experiences compared to the American participants.

37.1 **Method**

Participants and procedure

The sample consisted of 148 Hong Kong-Chinese university students aged between 17 and 34 (M = 20.25, SD = 1.68), with 63.6% of them being female. They joined the study as part of the course requirements for an introductory psychology course. There were four data collection sessions, in which participants completed the online survey in a computer room at a local university. Each session was supervised by a research assistant and lasted for about an hour.

37.2 **Results**

The following comparisons of emotion features are made by following visual hypothesis testing with confidence intervals (see Chapter 5 for details). Means for which the confidence intervals were non-overlapping are referred to as significantly different. Means for which the confidence intervals were overlapping, but with the means outside the respective confidence intervals, are referred to as potentially significantly different (see illustrations in the SM figures)[3]. In general, the Hong Kong-Chinese participants reported similar patterns of emotion features as their American counterparts for both pride and shame. The differences of the two cultural groups in the five emotion components (Appraisal, Bodily reaction, Expression, Action Tendency, Feeling) and regulation are highlighted in the following sections.

Comparing features of pride

In terms of appraisal features, the Hong Kong-Chinese respondents evaluated pride as likely to be "pleasant for the person," being caused by "an event that is important and relevant for the person's goals," and involving a situation where the person is "at the center of attention" to a significantly higher extent than did the American respondents. There was a potentially significant difference in evaluating pride as "caused by the person's own behavior" between the two cultural groups, with a higher degree of likelihood reported by the Hong Kong-Chinese (Figure SM 1). Regarding Bodily reaction features, the Hong Kong-Chinese respondents reported a significantly higher likelihood of "feeling warm," and a potentially significant higher likelihood of "blushing" than the American respondents. They also reported a significantly higher likelihood of "moving toward people or things" when expressing the pride emotion.

The Hong Kong-Chinese and American respondents also reported differences in the Action tendencies for the emotion of pride (Figure SM 2). In particular, as compared with the Americans, the Hong Kong-Chinese participants reported a significantly higher likelihood of "wanting to continue what they were doing," "hoping the ongoing situation would last or be repeated," "feeling an urge to be active," and "a desire to be attentive," "to show off," "to be seen," "to tackle the situation," and "to be close to people or things." There was also

---

[3] All supplementary materials (SM) are available at the GRID website: http://www.affective-sciences.org/GRID. See Appendix 1 ("Availability") for further details.

a potentially significant higher likelihood for the Hong Kong-Chinese of "wanting to avoid hurt." In terms of Feelings (Figure SM 3), the Hong Kong-Chinese participants were significantly more likely to report that the person "experienced the emotional state for a long time," "felt good," "at ease," "in control," "powerful," "strong," "alert," and "dominant." They also reported that the person was potentially less likely to "feel submissive" than their American counterparts. There was no significant difference in terms of regulation for the emotion of pride; however, it was regarded as an emotional state that was significantly more "frequently experienced" and more "socially accepted in the society" among the Hong Kong-Chinese than the American respondents.

Comparing features of shame

The feeling of shame was evaluated as stemming from an event that was "incongruent with the person's own standards" and whose "consequences were in principle avoidable or modifiable" to a significantly greater extent for the Hong Kong-Chinese than the American respondents (Figure SM 4). The appraisals that the emotion was "caused by one's own behavior" and the person had "sufficient resources to change the event" were also potentially more likely among the Hong Kong-Chinese respondents. For Bodily reactions, the Hong Kong-Chinese respondents reported a significantly higher likelihood of "feeling a lump in the throat," "having stomach discomfort," and "feeling warm"; while, concerning the Expression component, the American respondents reported a significantly lesser likelihood that the person would "frown," "close eyes," "show tears," and "move against people or things" in their expressions (Figure SM 5). The Hong Kong-Chinese reported a higher likelihood of engaging in Action tendencies like "wanting to undo what was happening" and "wanting to flee" as compared with their American counterparts for the emotion of shame. For Feelings (Figure SM 6), the Hong Kong-Chinese participants reported a potentially greater likelihood that the person "experienced the emotional state for a long time," and "felt nervous"; while the American participants reported a potentially lower likelihood of "feeling powerless" and "feeling bad." In terms of regulation, the Hong Kong-Chinese respondents reported a significantly higher likelihood that the person would "show a weaker degree of shame than actually felt" as compared with their American counterparts.

Measure of self-construal

In addition to the online GRID questionnaire, each participant was also asked to fill in a one-page survey assessing the autonomous and autonomous-relational self (Kagitcibasi, 2006), with nine items measuring each of the two dimensions. Participants rated these items on a seven-point Likert scale (1 = strongly disagree to 7 = strongly agree). Internal reliabilities of the two subscales were satisfactory, with Cronbach's alpha as 0.85 and 0.81 for the autonomous self and the autonomous-relational self, respectively. The mean scores of the two subscales were 3.69 (SD = 0.95) and 5.15 (SD = 0.81), respectively.

37.3 **Discussion**

The results showed that individuals from Hong Kong and from the US exhibited similar patterns of emotional experiences in the semantic profiles of the emotions of pride and shame; however, there were also some significant differences in these experiences that could be explained by the different focus of the autonomous and relational self-construal in the two cultures.

Based on the family and cultural model (Kagitcibasi, 2006), Hong Kong-Chinese are more likely to possess the autonomous-relational self, since Hong Kong is a traditionally collectivistic society, which has undergone a high degree of modernization and urbanization. In fact, the Hong Kong-Chinese participants scored relatively high on the autonomous-relational self, and about half-way of the autonomous self, which shows that both autonomous and relational selves were being endorsed. Although the scores of self-construal for the American participants were not available, it could be reasonably assumed that they should score higher in the autonomous self than the Hong Kong-Chinese participants (Markus & Kitayama, 1991).

For the emotion of pride, the Hong Kong-Chinese participants reported that pride would be appraised as related to one's own goals and behaviors in their culture much more than their American counterparts. Since individuals from Hong Kong focus on both the autonomous and relational selves, the concept of self may encompass more than the individual him/herself, but include other people who are close to the individual. Therefore, what is relevant to oneself for the Hong Kong-Chinese individuals may carry more weight than it does for the American participants. Moreover, as the situation that causes the emotion may affect not only the individual but the close others as well, the emotion is much more empowering and experienced as much more positive to the individuals in Hong Kong. As the positive influences of the situation may affect more than the individual self, the pride emotion motivates the Hong Kong-Chinese to be active, show off to other people, try to make the situation last longer, and at the same time, be close to other people, due to the importance of others in relation to the individual self. It should be noted that in the Chinese translation of the emotion term "pride," the word carries a positive connotation, because it is a term different from a similar but pejorative word meaning "conceited." Possibly because of the positive influences of pride on the individual and others related to the individual, this emotion is regarded as much more socially acceptable, and experienced much more in the society by the Hong Kong-Chinese participants.

For the emotion of shame, given that what an individual does may affect not only him/herself, but also the close others, individuals in Hong Kong may be more sensitive to the consequences of their behavior, and appraise the emotion as caused by one's behavior and incongruent with one's own standards much more than their American counterparts. Moreover, since the negative influences of the situation may also affect the close others, the emotion is regarded as much more negative, and evokes much more nervousness, in terms of subjective feelings and physiological AROUSAL, for the Hong Kong-Chinese. However, the emotion also leads to some rather contradictory reactions among the Hong Kong-Chinese. The situation that causes the emotion is more likely to be appraised as modifiable, and individuals have sufficient resources to deal with the situation. However, probably because of its strong repercussions to the self and others, the individuals want to escape from the emotion more by wanting to undo the situation, to flee, or by showing the emotion less to others.

This exploratory study shows that although the patterns of emotional features of two self-evaluative emotions, pride and shame, were similar for the Hong Kong-Chinese and American participants, the differences observed could be understood through the cultural construction of self as autonomous-relational among the Hong Kong-Chinese. Future research could further investigate how this view of the self of the Hong Kong-Chinese affects their emotional experiences, especially compared to individuals with a more autonomous, or relational view of the self, and shed further light on the cultural construction of emotions.

Chapter 38

The meaning of Dutch "schaamte" as a single term for shame and embarrassment

Yvette M. J. van Osch,[1] Seger M. Breugelmans, and Marcel Zeelenberg

In the English language a common distinction can be made between the emotions of shame and embarrassment. Such a distinction is not evident in the Dutch language, where a single term (*schaamte*) can refer to both feelings of shame and of embarrassment (Breugelmans, 2009). The translation equivalent for embarrassment in Dutch is *gêne*; however, this term is much less commonly used in Dutch than it is in English and is more often seen as a synonym for shyness (e.g., Den Boon & Geeraerts, 2005). In this chapter, we explore the consequences of this difference in the Dutch and English emotion vocabularies for differences in emotional meaning of the terms *shame* and *schaamte*.

Even in the English language, the extent to which *embarrassment* and *shame* refer to different emotion experiences has been debated. Embarrassment has often been thought of as a milder state of shame (Lewis, 1992). Recently, researchers have started to view embarrassment as a distinct emotion (for an overview see: Keltner & Buswell, 1997). Compared to shame, embarrassment results from more trivial events and more often occurs in front of large audiences (Keltner & Buswell, 1996). Embarrassment is also a less intense and painful emotion than shame (Tangney, Miller, Flicker, & Barlow, 1996). Shame refers to more unpleasant experiences than embarrassment. Embarrassment is also more strongly associated with a number of audience-oriented emotion components such as feelings of exposure, blushing, or smiling (Breugelmans, 2009). In both emotions, the "self" is experienced in a negative way, but whereas this is often only the outward appearance of the self in embarrassment, experiences of shame usually involve experiences of the self as being truly flawed, bad, or weak.

The Dutch term *schaamte* can be used to denote both experiences of shame and embarrassment. We explored a number of potential consequences of this distinction for meaning differences between *schaamte* and *shame*. First, we expected *schaamte* to have a less painful and unpleasant meaning than *shame*. Second, we expected *schaamte* to refer to less strong experiences than *shame*.

Third, we expected *schaamte* to be more strongly associated with emotion component items that in English should be more strongly associated with embarrassment than with shame. Fourth, we expected *schaamte* to be more distinct from guilt, another self-conscious emotion that appears

[1] Correspondence can be addressed to Yvette van Osch, Tilburg University, Department of Social Psychology, P.O. Box 90153, 5000 LE, Tilburg, the Netherlands. Email Y.M.J.vanOsch@uvt.nl

to be more closely related to shame than embarrassment (Tangney et al., 1996). We tested these expectations on data from the Dutch and US samples.

38.1 Method

The US data were provided by the editors of this book (see Chapter 6 for details on the dataset). Therefore, we will only describe the Dutch data in this method section.

Participants

In the study, 178 Dutch students (142 female; M_{age} = 19.76, SD = 2.78), participated voluntarily and received partial fulfilment of course credit in exchange. Four students were excluded from analyses because they provided the same response to at least 100 of the 144 features for a single emotion.

Material

Participants completed the Dutch version of the GRID web-based questionnaire. The Dutch translation was adopted from the version made by the Ghent research team for application in Flemish-speaking Belgium. The Flemish–Dutch version was found to be adequate by the native Dutch authors of this chapter.

Procedure

Students were approached through a mailing list of the Social Psychology research laboratory at Tilburg University. They were requested to participate in a study on "the meaning of emotion words." Interested students contacted the first author and received an email containing a link to the Dutch version of the web-based GRID questionnaire. They were instructed to fill-out the questionnaire in one session in a place where they would not be disturbed. Filling out the questionnaire took approximately one hour.

38.2 Results

Differences on VALENCE and POWER dimensions

Scores of shame on the four emotion dimensions (Dimension1 = VALENCE, Dimension2 = POWER, Dimension3 = AROUSAL, and Dimension4 = NOVELTY) were compared across the two samples. The VARIMAX rotated factor scores of shame from the US and Dutch samples showed large differences on the POWER dimension; Dimension2$_{Dutch}$ = 1.75, Dimension2$_{US}$ = −1.33. Whereas the Dutch associate *schaamte* with powerlessness, *shame* in US English was associated with powerfulness. Because these scores were standardized, this result can be interpreted as a large difference, confirming our second expectation. We also found some evidence for our first expectation, in the sense that *schaamte* referred to a less negative emotion than *shame* (Dimension1$_{Dutch}$ = 0.04, Dimension1$_{US}$ = −0.35), although the difference is not very large. Other dimensions showed less variation across samples. (Dimension3$_{Dutch}$ = 0.90, Dimension3$_{US}$ = 0.63, Dimension4$_{Dutch}$ = −1.40, Dimension4$_{US}$ = −1.18).

Differences on emotion features

We compared all 144 emotion features between the Dutch and US data on *schaamte* and *shame* using Visual Hypothesis Testing with Confidence Intervals as described in Chapter 5. Five features in the Appraisal component were different: Dutch subjects were less likely to describe shame events in terms of "familiar events," "events that confirmed the expectations of the person," "events that were caused intentionally," "of which the consequences were predictable," and "in which the person had sufficient resources to cope with the event," than would US subjects. Two features of the Bodily reaction component differed: Dutch subjects reported less "stomach troubles," but also indicated that *schaamte* was less associated with "no bodily symptoms at all." Large differences were found on the features of the Expression component: US participants reported that *shame* was more associated with "raised eyebrows," "tears," "moving against people or things," "short utterences" and "long utterances," "frowning," "loud voice," and a more "assertive voice." For the last four items, the confidence intervals of the Dutch and US data did not overlap at all. The Dutch were more inclined to associate *schaamte* with "soft speech," and "falling silent." Interestingly, the US participants associated *shame* more with both "short utterances" and "long utterances" than did Dutch participants, suggesting that *schaamte* in the Netherlands is less accompanied by speech than in the US.

Eleven features of Action tendency component differed between the Dutch and the US data. US participants associated *shame* more with "wanting the situation to last longer," "taking initiative," "urge to be attentive," "wanting to damage, hit, or say something that hurts," "wanting to be seen," "tackle the situation," "take care of others," "wanting to destroy whatever was close," and "wanting to sing and dance." They also reported more "wanting to move," and "wanting to be close to others." For these last two items, the confidence intervals of the Dutch and US data did not overlap at all.

Eight features of the Feeling component differed. US participants associated *shame* more with "feeling at ease," "feeling in control," "feeling powerful," "feeling positive," "feeling calm," "feeling alert," and "feeling dominant," than did Dutch participants. For the latter item, the confidence intervals of the Dutch and US data did not overlap at all. In contrast, the Dutch associated *schaamte* more with "feelings of submission" than did Americans. No differences between the samples were found on any of the regulation features.

Differences in the relationship with the meaning of guilt

To answer the question whether *schaamte* and guilt (in Dutch: *schuld*) would be more differentiated in Dutch than *shame* and guilt would be in US English, we compared shame and guilt on the 144 emotion features. The Dutch data revealed 44 features that differed between *schaamte* and *schuld*, of which there were nine with no overlap of the confidence intervals for both means. The US data, however, revealed only 19 features that differed between *shame* and *guilt* and for all of these the confidence intervals were overlapping. The most salient differences between *schaamte* and *schuld* in Dutch were that *schaamte* was more associated with "feeling warm," "running away," "feelings of submission," and "showing the emotion than actually felt," and that *schuld* was more associated with a "loud voice" and a "assertive voice," "the urge to be attentive to what is going on," "take care of another person," and "feeling dominant." There was little overlap with the items that were found to differ between *shame* and *guilt* in the US data; only the item "felt warm" was more associated with shame than with guilt in both languages. These results clearly suggest that the terms *guilt* and *shame* are more closely related than the Dutch terms *schuld* and *schaamte*.

38.3 **Discussion**

The Dutch emotion word *schaamte* can be used to refer to experiences that would be labeled *shame* as well as *embarrassment* in the English language. In this chapter, we found a number of consequences of this difference between Dutch and US English for the meanings of *schaamte* and *shame*. This is an important finding for researchers comparing emotion studies across these two languages.

We found *schaamte* to be less unpleasant than *shame* on a dimensional level (expectation 1). However, the evidence for our first expectation is somewhat mixed, since on item-level, *shame* was found to be more related to feeling at ease and positive than *schaamte*. This effect could be caused by the fact that *shame* is experienced with substantially more control than *schaamte*. We found *schaamte* to be less potent than *shame* (expectation 2). In addition, we found a number of emotion components where *schaamte* was associated more strongly with features that in English would be associated with embarrassment (expectation 3). For example, *schaamte* was found to be more associated with events that were unintentional, unexpected, and unfamiliar, that were predictable, and for which enough coping potential was available. This is clearly in line with the violations of social conventional standards that are more often associated with embarrassment than the violations of moral standards that are associated with shame (Keltner & Buswell, 1996). In addition, *schaamte* was associated more with physiological symptoms that tend to most strongly differentiate shame from guilt (see Breugelmans & Poortinga, 2006; Fontaine et al., 2006).

On the other hand, there were also a number of emotion features where *shame* was rated higher than *schaamte*. In general, *shame* was associated more with being strong, being expressive, being assertive, and being vocally present. The meaning of these differences in terms of shame and embarrassment are not clear. However, they could point to the fact that *schaamte* is seen as less potent in Dutch than it is in US English. This is in line with differences between shame and embarrassment in terms of intensity, because *shame* was associated with more positive feelings in the US than *schaamte* was in the Netherlands.

Finally, we found quite some evidence for our fourth expectation that *schaamte* would be more different from the Dutch equivalent of guilt (*schuld*) than *shame* would be in the US sample. The number of emotion features differing between these emotions in the Netherlands clearly surpassed that of the US. We interpret this as evidence for our assumption that *schaamte* is more distant from guilt (*schuld*) than *shame* in the US due to the inclusion of experiences that in English are denoted by *embarrassment*.

Our chapter shows how the GRID data can be successfully used to explore possible differences in the meaning of emotion words, even in languages that are as closely related as English and Dutch. The potential implications of these findings are large. Researchers need to take into account the potential differences in meaning between *schaamte* and *shame* when interpreting findings from studies done in these different languages. When only emotion words are used to measure emotion experiences researchers may be prone to biases in their findings because of the stronger association of *schaamte* with embarrassment. An easy solution would be to measure emotion features from various emotion components in addition to the emotion words, which would allow for testing the equivalence of experiences prior to comparison.

In our view, the findings in this chapter indicate a difference in the meaning of emotion words, not differences in the underlying experiences. Cross-cultural research has shown that emotion experiences can be similar even if different lexical categories are available across languages (e.g., Breugelmans & Poortinga, 2006; Van de Ven, Zeelenberg, & Pieters, 2009). In addition, the same emotion word can be used to refer to different types of experiences within the same language (e.g., Zeelenberg & Breugelmans, 2008, on the difference between regret and guilt). Differences in the meaning of emotion words are important because they may guide participants into different interpretations of the same events, leading to differences in responses that do not necessarily indicate differences in emotion experience. In view of the observation that a single term for embarrassment and shame can also be found in various other languages besides Dutch (e.g., Spanish, Malay; Breugelmans, 2009), the generalizability of data gathered with the English words *shame* and *embarrassment* should be empirically verified.

Chapter 39

Emotion term semantics in Russian–Ukrainian and Ukrainian–Russian bilinguals

Anna Ogarkova,[1] Irina Prihod'ko, and Julia Zakharova

39.1 Introduction

Research on emotions in bilingual populations shows that the interaction of emotion concepts in the mental lexicon of bilinguals can lead to the consolidation of comparable concepts in the two languages, so that the words referring to those concepts become closer in meaning (e.g., Pavlenko, 2005, 2008 for overviews). In this chapter, we aim to verify this contention, focusing on the meaning profiles of emotion terms in two bilingual groups: native speakers (henceforth L1) of Russian and Ukrainian from the same region (city of Kyiv, Ukraine). Given both the evidence cited above and the specific characteristics of our samples, the expectation is that the meaning profiles of emotion terms would exhibit none, or minimal and non-systematic differences between the two bilingual groups.

On the cultural side, the two target groups are indeed very similar: 166 L1 Russian (102 females; mean age, 23.7) and 147 L1 Ukrainian speakers (89 females; mean age, 22.3) come from the same social group (university students), are of the same age (means 22.3 and 23.7, respectively), and have the same culture exposure (all gaining maturity after the collapse of the Soviet Union in 1991 and having lived in Ukraine for all their lives)[2]. A more general reason to expect a high between-group homogeneity is that, although the distribution of L1 Ukrainian and L1 Russian speakers in Ukraine is roughly the same (Khmel'ko, 2004, cf. also the latest all-Ukrainian census http://www.ukrcensus.gov.ua/eng/), about two thirds of the Ukrainian population identify themselves as culturally Ukrainian only (62.9%), and 22% more respondents report to have a "mixed" type of cultural self-identity (Khmel'ko, 2004). This puts the percentage of people who identify themselves as culturally "Russian only" to a scarce 10% (see Table SM 1[3]). Agreeably, many culture scholars argue that the interaction of languages and cultures within the Ukrainian society is a gradual

---

[1] Correspondence concerning this chapter should be addressed to Anna Ogarkova, Swiss Center for the Affective Sciences, 7 Rue des Battoirs, CH-1205, Geneva, Switzerland, e-mail: Anna.Ogarkova@unige.ch

[2] These numbers include the participants who rated the standard set of 24 GRID words, and another group who rated an extra set. In addition to the 24 standard GRID words, two more were added to the questionnaire: "envy" (Russian *zavist'* and Ukraine *zazdrist'*) and "justified anger" (Russian *gnev* and Ukraine *gniv*).

[3] All supplementary materials (SM) are available at the GRID website: http://www.affective-sciences.org/GRID. See Appendix 1 ("Availability") for further details.

consolidation of closely-related languages and cultures, and that the ethnic differences are neither of a fundamental, nor of a confrontational character (e.g., Lanovenko et al., 1998; Masenko, 2004).

Two more linguistic factors contribute to the minimization of the differences between the two groups. Firstly, the languages at stake are typologically very close, as both belong to the same language subfamily (Eastern-Slavic languages) within a broader family of the Slavic languages. Secondly, 21 out of 26 of Russian–Ukrainian emotion word pairs included in the analyses are cognate words—that is, words that have the same etymological origin (see Table 39.1). Although the common origin of words alone does not guarantee a higher similarity in the synchronic meanings of the words (cf. Boster, 2005), the fact that these cognates are simultaneously the *best matches* of the corresponding English terms (the pre-requisite for inclusion into the GRID analyses), suggests a high semantic similarity of the emotion words at stake.

The only parameter that sets our two groups apart is the fact that the participants come from two different "student subcultures" determined by differences in educational styles at the two universities where the participants were recruited. Specifically, the L1 Ukrainian group are students of the National University "*Kyiv-Mohyla academy*," the first university in Ukraine to adopt, back in 1992, the Western system and style of education, including the system of earning credits, free choice of the disciplines to be studied, more individual student work, and overall more emphasis on individual initiative, responsibility, and critical thinking. In addition, the Kyiv-Mohyla academy has been, ever since 1992, an authentically Ukrainian university, promoting patriotism and national pride, as well as freedom of expression and democracy in the classroom. In contrast, the L1 Russian group was recruited from students of Russian philology at Kyiv National Taras Schevchenko University, a most reputed, old, and conservative university in the country. This educational institution relies on more formalistic principles of education promoting little personal choice (with

Table 39.1 Russian and Ukrainian words used in GRID

#	English	Russian	Ukrainian	#	English	Russian	Ukrainian
1	contempt	prezrenie	prezyrstvo	14	pleasure	**udovol'stvie**	**nasoloda**
2	disgust	otvraschenie	vidraza	15	pride	gordost'	gordist'
3	anger	zlost'	zlist'	16	happiness	schast'ye	schastya
4	irritation	razdrazhenie	rozdratuvannya	17	contentment	udovletvorennost'	zadovolennya
5	hate	nenavist'	nenavyst'	18	love	lubov'	lubov
6	jealousy	revnost'	revnoschi	19	disappointment	**dosada**	**shkoda**
7	fear	strah	strah	20	compassion	sochuvstvie	spivchuttya
8	anxiety	trevoga	tryvoga	21	guilt	vina	provyna
9	stress	stress	stres	22	shame	**styd**	**sorom**
10	despair	otchayanie	vidchaj	23	sadness	**grust'**	**smutok**
11	surprise	udivlenie	podyv	24	being hurt	**obida**	**obraza**
12	interest	interes	interest	25	envy	zavist'	zazdrist'
13	joy	radost'	radist'	26	justified anger	gnev	gniv

Note: for better readability, Russian and the Ukrainian emotion terms are transliterated from Cyrillic into Latin letters. In **bold** are the non-cognate words.

almost all academic courses being obligatory for both attendance and the taking of exams), and with an overall more authoritative style of teaching that encourages the students to follow the existing academic regulations, and where emotional control, obedience, and recognition of academic hierarchy are promoted.

39.2 **Results**

Two types of findings confirm our expectation of little between-group variation in L1 Russian and L1 Ukrainian bilinguals. Firstly, the overall correlation of Russian and Ukrainian samples is 0.88, which clearly points to a high between-group similarity. Secondly, the same pattern is suggested by the profile correlations at the term level: the correlations of 26 Russian and Ukrainian emotion terms are considerably high and range from 0.76 to 0.93 (see Table SM 2). The only exception is disappointment words: Russian *dosada* ("disappointment/frustration/vexation") and Ukrainian *shkoda* ("upset/regret/pity") correlate at 0.69, but this exception is more of a translation issue than a case of a genuine semantic divergence. Russian *dosada* is defined in reputed dictionaries as "a feeling of irritation, dissatisfaction that arises from a mishap or an insult" (Ozhegov, 1990; translation by the first author) and can be regarded as an anger word in Russian (Ogarkova, Soriano, & Lehr, 2012). At the same time, *shkoda* is defined as "a feeling of frustration/disappointment about having lost something," and is thus a disappointment/pity word.

However, computing the correlations of the 142 GRID emotion features across the 26 emotion terms reveals 27 features that correlate below 0.7, and thus are clearly deviant in meaning across the samples (see Table 39.2). These features pertain to all emotion components (except Feeling), but are unevenly spread across the GRID feature inventory. For example, deviant features in the Appraisal component constitute 22.5% of the total number of features in this component, Bodily reaction features are deviant in 16.6% of cases, 26.9% of the emotional Expression features correlate very low across the samples. The main regularity, however, is that *all* emotion regulation

Table 39.2 Deviant (C <0.7) features across the 26 emotion terms in L1 Russian and L1 Ukrainian samples

Component	Feature	C	%
Appraisal	familiar event	0.38	22.5
	unpredictable event	0.47	
	caused by chance	0.68	
	caused intentionally	0.39	
	consequences predicable	0.55	
	consequences negative for somebody else	0.69	
	required an immediate response	0.38	
Bodily reaction	felt weak limbs	0.66	16.6
	heartbeat slowing down	0.54	
	breathing slowing down	0.68	

Table 39.2 (continued) Deviant (C <0.7) features across the 26 emotion terms in L1 Russian and L1 Ukrainian samples

Component	Feature	C	%
Expression	did not show any changes in face	0.42	26.9
	did not show any changes in gestures	0.68	
	decreased the volume of voice	0.53	
	produced a short utterance	0.63	
	produced a long utterance	0.65	
	changed the melody of her or his speech	0.50	
	did not show any changes in vocal expression	0.62	
Action tendency	wanted to be in control of the situation	0.26	15.0
	wanted to hand over the initiative to someone else	0.69	
	lacked the motivation to do anything	0.66	
	wanted to be hurt as little as possible	0.55	
	wanted to tackle the situation	0.13	
	experienced the emotional state for a long time	0.46	
Regulation	tried to control the intensity of the emotional feeling	**0.44**	**100**
	showed the emotion to others more than s/he felt it	**0.53**	
	showed the emotion to other less than s/he felt it	**0.13**	
	hid the emotion from others by smiling	**0.43**	

Note: only features with correlations (C) below 0.7 are listed. %, the percentage of low-correlating features in the respective emotion component.

features (100%) correlate below 0.7, and the correlations get indeed very small, ranging from 0.13 on "showed the emotion less than s/he felt it" to maximally 0.53 on "showed the emotion more than s/he felt it." In summary, these findings suggest a consistent, pattern-like deviation in *emotion regulation* as part of the meaning of Russian and Ukrainian emotion terms as rated by the two bilingual student groups.

To investigate the nature of variation on emotional regulation between the two sets of words, a Principal Component Analysis on the four regulation features across the Russian and Ukrainian samples has been conducted. The results clearly point at one bipolar factor: *controlling expression* ("tried to control the intensity of the emotion," "showed the emotion less than s/he felt it," "hid the emotion by a smile", positive pole) versus *enhancing expression* ("showed the emotion more than s/he felt it", negative pole). Comparing the regulation scores of Russian and Ukrainian terms on this factor suggests that the Russian labels for negative emotions score on average higher on the control side (see Table 39.3). Specifically, both the opposing interpersonal terms (*hate, being hurt, irritation, disappointment, jealousy*) and fear-related terms (*shame, despair, fear*) terms score much higher on regulation in Russian. Taken together, these findings suggest two display rules: inhibiting an outright manifestation of socially disruptive emotions (e.g., *hate*) and not showing weakness (e.g., *fear*), both of which appear to be more salient in the meaning profiles of Russian negative emotion terms as compared to the corresponding Ukrainian ones.

Table 39.3 Regulation scores of Russian and Ukrainian emotion terms

Word	Ru	Ukr	Dif	Word	Ru	Ukr	Dif
jealousy	1.91	−0.49	2.40	happiness	−1.17	−1.80	0.63
fear	1.36	−0.72	2.07	contempt	0.86	0.26	0.61
disappointment	1.60	−0.30	1.91	anxiety	0.87	0.37	0.50
irritation	1.12	−0.68	1.80	pleasure	−0.69	−1.03	0.34
being hurt	0.93	−0.87	1.79	interest	0.29	−0.03	0.33
despair	0.58	−0.97	1.55	love	0.33	0.38	−0.05
hate	1.47	0.17	1.30	surprise	0.20	0.43	−0.23
shame	2.00	0.92	1.08	compassion	−1.91	−1.66	−0.25
anger	−1.06	−2.02	0.96	sadness	−0.11	0.27	−0.38
contentment	0.64	−0.24	0.89	guilt	0.11	0.80	−0.69
stress	0.60	−0.28	0.88	joy	−1.53	−0.65	−0.88
pride	−0.17	−1.03	0.86	disgust	−0.03	0.96	−0.99

Note: Dif, difference in the regulation scores of Russian and Ukrainian emotion terms; Ru, Russian; Ukr, Ukrainian. For better readability, English translations of Russian and Ukrainian words are used.

39.3 **Discussion**

The hypothesis tested in this study—on the minimal and unsystematic divergences in how L1 Russian and L1 Ukrainian speakers would rate the emotional terms in their native languages—has only been partially confirmed by our analyses, and only with regard to the overall similarity between the samples and the profile correlations at the term level. The correlations at the feature level reveal a different picture, namely, systematic differences emerge regarding the ways of regulating emotions labeled by several negative emotion words in the two languages. The very pattern of these feature-based deviations suggests that the negative emotion terms (opposing interpersonal terms and fear-related terms) score higher on the control side in the L1 Russian group than in L1 Ukrainian group.

This latter finding can have three *post hoc* interpretations, each illustrating the usefulness of the GRID approach for hypothesis generation and deserving further exploration in future studies. Firstly, the systematic differences in the emotion regulation features can relate to the between-group differences at *the sub-cultural level*. Specifically, the observed divergence can be hypothesized to be a result of a more authoritative and hierarchical academic environment of the L1 Russian group (which encourages repression of negative emotions among students), and the more democratic environment of the L1 Ukrainian group (where freedom of (emotional) expression is being promoted). Testing this hypothesis requires running additional GRID studies in non-student groups, to rule out the possibility that larger cultural differences are at stake.

Secondly, a possibility stands that our findings highlight the existence of *biculturalism* in contemporary Ukraine, where L1 Ukrainian speakers exhibit a closer resemblance to Ukrainian culture, whereas L1 Russian speakers have a more pronounced bias to Russian culture. Verification of this hypothesis requires conducting additional GRID studies in a monolingual Russian group from Russia and in a group of monolingual Ukrainians from Ukraine, with the aim of seeing if monolingual samples would exhibit the same (or more pronounced) divergence with respect to the emotional regulation features. Should this expectation be confirmed, a theoretical challenge would be to interpret the findings. For socially disruptive emotion words (but not for the fear-related ones), the interpretation can elaborate along the individualism/collectivism axis of cultural variation, which suggests more regulatory control over negative other-directed emotions like anger in collectivistic societies (cf. Hofstede, 2001). Although no research has directly compared Russian and Ukrainian populations, previous studies involving a *tertium comparationis*—a Western, typically an Anglo-Saxon society—showed that Russians are more collectivistic than Ukrainians. For instance, several studies show that while Russians remain more collectivistic than British (Tower et al., 1997) and Americans (Realo & Allik, 1999), Ukrainian females display a more pronounced tendency for individualism than American women (Shafiro et al., 2003).

The third hypothesis which our finding generates relates to the processes in the mental lexicons of bilinguals. Here, the possibility is that, rather than dealing with the process of *concept consolidation*, we are observing the process of emotion *concept restructuring* (Pavlenko, 2008: 154). On this hypothesis, the meanings of Russian and Ukrainian emotion words (existing in parallel in the mental lexicon of bilingual speakers) have, under the influence of the principle of language and cognitive economy, gone apart to cover a wider spectrum of the emotion domain. As a result of this differentiation in meaning, one set of negative emotion words (Russian) has come to denote emotional experiences that imply more regulatory effort in their experiencers, whereas another set of words (Ukrainian) has come to embrace the words of roughly the same meaning but diverging from the former set in that they do not imply a heightened emotional control. Testing this hypothesis would require complementary studies with Russian and Ukrainian monolingual samples and two additional studies where Russian and Ukrainian bilinguals rate the emotion words from their second language (L2). The hypothesis would be confirmed if two conditions are simultaneously true: (1) the meaning profiles of emotion words obtained from monolingual speakers do not show a systematic divergence on the emotion regulation, and (2) all L2 ratings confirm the findings of the present study—that is, when, regardless of whether the emotion words are from bilinguals' L1 or L2, Russian negative emotion words diverge from their Ukrainian cognates on emotion regulation. Should confirmatory evidence be obtained for this hypothesis, the challenge would nevertheless remain to explain the mechanisms under which specifically Russian, but not Ukrainian negative emotion words have acquired the connotations of an enhanced emotional control.

Acknowledgments

The authors gratefully acknowledge the valuable assistance of Dr. Tetyana Ogarkova, director and Dr. Volodymyr Yermolenko, deputy director of the *Centre for Intercultural Communication* at the National University "Kyiv-Mohyla academy," in obtaining the L1 Ukrainian sample. We are also grateful to Johnny Fontaine for his invaluable help with the data analyses.

Chapter 40

The vocal expression component in the meanings of Russian, Ukrainian, and US English emotion terms

Julia Zakharova[1] and Anna Ogarkova

40.1 Introduction

One of the major functions of prosody and vocal cues is expressing speakers' emotions. Previous research has generated several views on the relation between prosodic cues and emotional expression (Ekman, 1992; Izard, 1992; Power & Dalgleish, 1997; Scherer, 1986b; Scherer et al., 2001, 2003). Some studies suggest the existence of a number of cross-culturally stable patterns of how emotions are expressed vocally, which enables people to recognize vocal expression from other cultures with accuracy above chance (e.g., Albas, McCluskey, & Albas, 1976; Graham, 2001; Holden & Hogan, 1993; Kramer, 1964; Scherer et al., 2001, 2003; Swan & Smith, 2001; van Bezooijen et al., 1983). More specifically, evidence is available on the universally recognizable vocal signals for communicating the "Big Six," that is, the supposedly basic emotions of anger, fear, disgust, happiness, sadness, and surprise (e.g., Pell, 2006; Sauter et al., 2009). Therefore, reasonably accurate recognition of emotion vocalics of a limited number of affective states does not require that the producer and listener share the same language or culture (Sauter et al., 2009).

At the same time, there is a body of research that suggests that emotional prosody can, to a certain degree, be culture-determined, so that people more accurately recognize emotions expressed vocally by the members of their own cultural group (Erickson, 2006; Matsumoto, 1989; Matsumoto et al., 2002; Scherer et al., 2001). This tendency has been termed an "ethnic bias," or the "in-group advantage" (Elfenbein & Ambady, 2002b; Markham & Wang, 1996), which, on cultural terms, is a result of the match between vocal emotional expression and the emotional concept shared by members of the same cultural group. Alongside cultural explanations, a contributing factor here is also the typological variability of languages in their suprasegmental features, such as accent and tone. While suprasegmental features remain among the least typologically studied phenomena (Dubovskiy, 1979; Pavlenko, 2005), evidence is available that suggests languages vary significantly in the function of pitch, intensity of stress, and rhythmic structure. Consequently, prosodic differences in typologically distant languages can contribute to the misinterpretation of emotional vocal cues in cross-lingual communication. For example, a study of Arabic–English bilingual political discourse has shown that speakers' directives (characterized by a high degree of prosodic interference) cause communicative tension because of incorrect intonation nuances: exaggerated

---

[1] Correspondence concerning this chapter should be addressed to Julia Zakharova, Foreign Languages Department, Internal Affaires Ministry Academy, Trutenko Street 22, Kyiv, Ukraine, e-mail: juza@ukr.net.

politeness, uncertainty, excessive emotionality, rigidity, excessive persistence, and even rudeness (Zakharova, 2005).

The GRID approach is of interest in this research context for two reasons. Firstly, although substantial empirical research is available on actual emotional vocal expression, no systematic attempt has yet been made to investigate if vocal expression, a major emotion component (Scherer, 2005a), is centrally involved in the meaning of emotion *terms* labeling those emotions in language. GRID offers a pioneering possibility to test if indeed the meanings of emotion words vary from language to language on the component of vocal expression, as well as to specify which categories of vocal cues are most discriminative across different language samples. Secondly, GRID-based results are of interest to be tested for convergence with the empirical research on vocal emotional expression. If one assumes that language "must correspond to human experience and represent important human concerns" (Fontaine et al., 2007: 1056), then the meanings of emotion terms in natural languages should overall cohere with the empirical findings about actual emotional experiences, and the vocal characteristics of specific emotions.

This chapter investigates both issues in a contrastive analysis of the emotion terms from three groups: Russian and Ukrainian bilinguals in Ukraine, and English-speaking Americans. Given both the specific characteristics of the samples, and previous research (see below), two expectations are formulated. Firstly, we expect that the ratings of emotion words on the vocal expression features will be more similar between Russian and Ukrainian than between them and English (Hypothesis 1). The second expectation is that the GRID results will largely cohere with prior empirical research on emotional prosodic cues associated to specific emotions in the languages under study (Hypothesis 2).

Hypothesis 1 is underpinned by two factors. The first one derives from the cultural characteristics of the samples under study: the Russian and Ukrainian groups have much more in common with each other than with the US English sample (see Chapters 39 and 41 for more detail). The second factor relates to the language characteristics of the samples, and is two-fold. Firstly, Eastern Slavic languages are typologically very close because both belong to the same subgroup within the Slavic group of languages. Secondly, although several studies have shown that Ukrainian and Russian have somewhat different inventories of speech melody contours (Nikolaeva, 1977: 254–258), these prosodic differences can be expected to be less pronounced for the Russian–Ukrainian bilinguals that constituted our groups. Indeed, phonetic interference effects (e.g., vowel reduction, devocalization of sonants, and several types of palatalization) between the two languages in Ukraine are reported to be very common (Ishchenko, 2009; Khomenko, 2004; Obukhova, 2008; Plyushch, 2000; Stebunova, 2001; Superanskaya, 1999). The factors behind these effects are linked to (a) transparent etymological correlations between Ukrainian and Russian words; (b) orthographic similarities between both languages; (c) processes of removal of phonetic nonconformity between common/cognate word forms; (d) absence of critical attitude of native speakers toward language phonetics (Vovchok, 2002: 35).

The expectation on the convergence of the GRID-based results with empirical findings (Hypothesis 2) is tested against the research results reported by Nushykyan (1986). This study has been chosen as a reference point because it focuses on vocal emotional expression in Russian and Ukrainian (as spoken in Ukraine) and English, and because it includes eight of the GRID emotions (⅓): *joy, surprise, anger, anxiety, contempt, despair, fear,* and *sadness.* Nushykyan shows that in all three languages the vocal expression of anger, joy, despair, and contempt is characterized by a higher speech intensity than in neutral (non-emotional) condition, while the vocal expression of sadness, fear, and anxiety is characterized by a lower speech intensity than in neutral condition (see Figure SM 1)[2]. Thus, our first prediction (**2.1**) is that in all languages *anger, joy, despair, and contempt* will be rated significantly higher on the likelihood of voice increase than on the likelihood of voice decrease (feature # 65 in the GRID inventory), while *sadness, fear,* and *anxiety* will exhibit the opposite pattern (features # 64 and 65). Nushykyan also reports that while Ukrainian and Russian exhibit fairly small differences in pitch contours of vocal emotional expression, the differences between them and English are much more pronounced (Nushykyan, 1986: 64–71). Thus, our second prediction (**2.2**) is that speech melody (feature # 71) will differentiate the Eastern Slavic words from US English more consistently than it differentiates the Russian from the Ukrainian terms.

40.2 **Data**

The data used for analyses come from three GRID samples: L1 Russian ($N = 166$, 102 females, mean age 23.7), L1 Ukrainian ($N = 147$, 89 females, mean age 22.3), and US English sample ($N = 182$, 129 females; mean age 18.5)[3]. The 12 GRID vocal expression features analysed in this chapter fall into five categories: (a) *speech melody*: "the speaker changed the melody of speech" (# 71); (b) *voice loudness*: "the speaker decreased/increased the volume of voice" (# 64, 65); (c) *voice quality*: "the speaker had a trembling/assertive voice/speech disturbances" (# 66, 67, 72); (d) *temporal aspects of speech*: "the speaker spoke slower/faster," "the speaker produced a short/long utterance" (# 69, 70, 73, 74). Two more GRID vocal expression features refer to (e) *presence/absence of vocal cues*: "the speaker did not show any changes in vocal expression," "the speaker fell silent" (# 75, 68). The 24 Russian and Ukrainian words used in GRID are given in Table 41.1 of Chapter 41.

40.3 **Results**

Four types of analyses affordable with the GRID method confirm Hypothesis 1. Firstly, Pearson correlations of 24 emotion terms on 12 vocal expression features in the three samples show that at least 17 emotion terms (70.8%) in Russian and Ukrainian correlate higher with each other than each of them with the English words (see Table 40.1).

Secondly, the same pattern is suggested by the correlations of vocal expression features by the emotions terms: in at least nine cases (75%), they are higher between Russian and Ukrainian than between either of them and English (see Table 40.2).

Thirdly, the analyses at the term by feature level (cf. Visual Hypothesis Testing with Confidence Intervals, Chapter 5) reveal fewer differences between Russian and Ukrainian (38 cases, i.e., 13.2%), as compared to 56 in Russian vs English (20.1%), and 50 in Ukrainian vs English (17.3%) (see Tables SM 1–3). Fourthly and finally, while Russian and Ukrainian are differentiated by one category of vocal cues (*voice loudness*), both Slavic languages differ from English in three categories of vocal cues (*voice loudness, voice quality,* and *speech melody*) (see Tables SM 1–3). Taken together, these results jointly confirm Hypothesis 1: a higher degree of similarity in vocal expression features between Russian and Ukrainian than between the Slavic languages and English.

The convergence between GRID results and empirical research on speech melody (Hypothesis 2, prediction 2.2) has also been confirmed. In line with the empirical findings (Nushykyan, 1986), speech

---

[2] All supplementary materials (SM) are available at the GRID website: http://www.affective-sciences.org/ GRID. See Appendix 1 ("Availability") for further details.

[3] The numbers in the Russian and Ukrainian samples include both the participants who rated the standard set of 24 GRID words, and another group who rated an extra set or words.

Table 40.1 Correlations of English, Russian, and Ukrainian emotion terms on 12 vocal expression features

Emotion term	Ru/Ukr	Ru/En	Ukr/En
contempt	0.69	0.40	0.38
disgust	0.85	0.75	0.80
anger	0.93	0.92	**0.95**
irritation	0.87	**0.93**	0.86
hate	0.76	**0.87**	0.54
jealousy	0.88	**0.90**	0.85
fear	0.87	**0.92**	**0.93**
anxiety	0.80	**0.87**	0.79
stress	0.86	0.80	0.87
despair	0.85	0.65	0.73
surprise	0.73	0.86	**0.73**
interest	0.83	0.81	**0.84**
joy	0.89	0.86	**0.96**
pleasure	0.70	0.57	0.51
pride	0.74	**0.93**	**0.76**
happiness	0.76	0.55	0.75
contentment	0.42	**0.69**	0.06
love	0.92	0.63	0.78
disappointment	0.55	0.48	0.83
compassion	0.85	0.30	0.22
guilt	0.94	0.77	0.88
shame	0.92	0.84	0.89
sadness	0.93	0.90	0.91
being hurt	0.86	0.74	0.85

Note: correlations were computed on the centered means. Underlined and in **bold** are the correlations that are higher in Ukrainian/Russian vs US English than between the Slavic samples.

melody (# 71) distinguishes only one emotion (*hate*) in the Russian–Ukrainian contrast, but discriminates between more terms in the Russian–English (*anxiety, disgust, guilt* and *hate*) and Ukrainian–English comparisons (*contentment, interest, anxiety, guilt,* and *jealousy,* see Tables SM 1–3).

Partial support to the prediction about the convergence of GRID results with previous empirical findings on the voice loudness (Hypothesis 2, prediction 2.1) has also been found. Congruently with the expectation, robust consistencies in all three languages have been found in the tendencies for voice increase in *joy* and *anger,* and voice decrease in *sadness* (see Table 40.3). However, the expected cross-lingual tendencies were not found for four other terms, like voice increase in *despair* (observed for Russian only), *contempt* (only found in English), and *fear* and *anxiety* (no effects in any of the languages).

Table 40.2 Correlations of 12 vocal expression features across 24 emotion terms in English, Russian, and Ukrainian

#	Feature	Ru/Ukr	Ru/En	Ukr/En
64	increased the volume of voice	0.86	0.83	0.79
65	decreased the volume of voice	0.52	0.49	**0.80**
66	had a trembling voice	0.73	0.68	0.53
67	had an assertive voice	0.84	0.81	0.81
68	fell silent	0.83	0.74	0.62
69	produced a short utterance	0.58	0.14	0.29
70	produced a long utterance	0.57	0.49	0.44
71	changed the melody of her or his speech	0.25	**0.52**	**0.48**
72	produced speech disturbances	0.72	0.58	0.38
73	spoke faster	0.78	**0.85**	0.69
74	spoke slower	0.72	**0.84**	0.70
75	did not show any changes in vocal expression	0.64	0.51	0.27

Note: correlations computed on the centered means. Underlined and in **bold** are the correlations that are higher in Ukrainian/Russian vs US English than across the Slavic samples.

Table 40.3 Congruence of empirical research on voice intensity from Nushykyan (1986) and GRID voice loudness vocal cues ("spoke louder" vs "spoke quieter")

	anger	joy	despair	contempt	anxiety	fear	sadness
English	+ +	+ +	–	+	–	–	+ +
Russian	+ +	+ +	+	–	–	–	+ +
Ukrainian	+ +	+ +	–	–	–	–	+ +

Note: + + mark certainly significant cases (CI's do not overlap). + marks probably significant cases (the means of "*spoke louder*" and "*spoke quieter*" for each of the emotion terms are outside each other's CIs); – marks the unconfirmed cases.

40.4 **Conclusion**

Against the rich background of empirical research on vocal emotional expression that focuses on both the universal and the cultural aspects in the domain of emotion vocalics, the present study is a first attempt to focus on vocal expression as one of the constitutive components in the meaning profiles of words labeling emotion experiences in different languages. Methodologically, the GRID method allows it to be checked if indeed the meanings of emotion words can vary on the features capturing vocal variation, and, if so, to specify which of the categories of vocal cues have the highest discriminative potential in cross-lingual comparisons. Another reason why GRID is a methodologically interesting approach is that its findings can be tested for convergence with the empirical research on vocal emotional expression.

The present study investigated two hypotheses. Firstly, we aimed to verify the prediction that the vocal expression component as part of the meaning profiles of emotion terms would exhibit a higher degree of similarity in typologically closer languages spoken by bilinguals from the same geographic region than in a typologically non-related language spoken by a different cultural group (Hypothesis 1). Our second hypothesis was the expectation of a certain convergence between the results of the empirical research on vocal emotional expression and the GRID-based results on emotion word semantics (Hypothesis 2). Both hypotheses were generally confirmed.

This said, the explanatory potential of GRID as regards the vocal emotional expression has its limitations. Specifically, the 12 vocal expression features in the inventory do not allow for the investigation of several other important types of prosodic cues, such as pitch contours, nuclear tones, pitch range and intervals, speech rate values and pauses, average syllable length, and utterance energy. Although the stability of the differences on these categories of vocal variation remains yet to be established, they may as well be part of the meanings of emotion terms.

Chapter 41

Language family similarity effect: Emotion term semantics in Russian, Ukrainian, Czech, Slovak, and Polish

Anna Ogarkova,[1] Nataliya Panasenko,
and Barbara Lewandowska-Tomaszczyk

41.1 Introduction

The idea explored in this chapter resonates with one of the findings reported in the present volume: namely, the study by Alonso-Arbiol, Soriano, and van de Vijver (see Chapter 20) shows that language similarity effects are very strong and can overrule the effects of cultural affinity in geographically close populations. Specifically, it is found that the meaning profiles of the Spanish word *desesperación* (despair) obtained from three different Spanish-speaking groups (Northern and Southern Spanish, and Chilean) have more in common with one another than they do with the semantic profiles of the equivalent Basque term *etsipena* (the other major language in the Basque Land), and the US English *despair*. Our hypothesis is similar because we expect that the meaning profiles of prototypical emotion words in the languages from the same language group (i.e., the Slavic languages) should be closer to each other than each of them is to the corresponding words in a language from a different language group (English, Germanic languages).

A very popular and recurrent idea in the vast linguistic literature on Slavic emotion term semantics is that the emotion words in these languages (and, thus, the emotion concepts linked to them) encode a specific world-view (cf. Weisgerber, 1943, 1950), which is not penetrable by, or is poorly understandable to the outsiders (e.g., Gladkova, 2005; Levontina & Zaliznyak, 2001; Wierzbicka, 1990a). Moreover, this cultural specificity is assumed to characterize not only allegedly "untranslatable" words like Russian *toska* (see Chapter 23) or Czech *litost'* (Kundera, 1980; Russell, 1991a), but also words that have conventional translations in other languages (e.g., Wierzbicka, 1998b).

There are three a priori considerations why GRID can be a promising method in this research context. Firstly, GRID allows for the investigation of a wide selection of emotion terms in several languages at a time, and thus can yield systematic, rather than eclectic evidence. This is particularly valuable in the investigation of the Slavic language family, as previous research on Slavic emotion lexis has been largely unsystematic. Indeed, most of previous work has focused on smaller-scale comparisons between individual lexemes: several studies compared translation equivalents within the group of Slavic languages (e.g., Stefanskyy, 2000, 2004, 2007a, b, 2009a, b), some focused on the

---

[1] Correspondence concerning this chapter should be addressed to Anna Ogarkova, Swiss Center for the Affective Sciences, 7 Rue des Battoirs, CH-1205, Geneva, Switzerland, e-mail: Anna.Ogarkova@unige.ch

emotion terms within just one Slavic language (e.g., Kallimulina, 2006; Levontina, 2004; Slaměník & Hurychová, 2006; Solovyev, 2008), yet another group considered how individual lexemes in a Slavic language diverge from their correlates in a Western language, typically English (e.g., Apresjan, 1997; Krasavskyy, 2001; Wierzbicka, 1986, 2001a). A second advantage of the GRID methodology, in contrast to many linguistic approaches, is that it can provide measurable support to a hypothesis, which makes the semantic conclusions provided by it quantifiable. Finally, GRID helps obtain and analyze psychologically realistic data, which favorably distinguishes it from conventionally "prescriptive" linguistic accounts that are too frequently based on introspection, rather than on genuinely empirical evidence.

Our hypothesis about a higher degree of similarity between the meaning profiles of Slavic emotion words as compared to their correlates in English is underpinned by two factors: a

Table 41.1 English and Slavic emotion terms used in GRID

English	Ukrainian	Russian	Polish	Czech	Slovak
being hurt	obraza	obida	poczucie krzywdy	ublížení	ranené city
sadness	*smutok*	grust'	*smutek*	*smutek*	*smútok*
shame	sorom	styd	wstyd	<u>hanba</u>	<u>hanba</u>
guilt	*provyna*	vina	poczucie winy	*vina*	*pocit viny*
compassion	spivchuttya	socuvstvie	współzucie	<u>slitování</u>	zľutovanie
disappointment	shkoda	dosada	rozczarowanie	*zklamání*	*sklamanie*
love	*lubov*	*lubov'*	miłość	<u>láska</u>	<u>láska</u>
contentment	*zadovolennya*	*udovletvorennost*	*zadowolenie*	spokojenost	opovrhutie
happiness	schastya	schast'ye	szczęście	*štěstí*	*šťastie*
pride	*gordist'*	*gordost'*	duma	pýcha	*hrdosť*
pleasure	nasoloda	udovol'stvie	przyjemność	*potěšení*	*potešenie*
joy	*radist'*	*radost'*	*radość*	*radost*	*radost'*
interest	*interes*	*interes*	zainteresowanie	<u>zájem</u>	<u>záujem</u>
surprise	*podyv*	udivlenie	zdziwienie	<u>překvapení</u>	<u>prekvapenie</u>
despair	vidchaj	otchayanie	rozpacz	<u>beznaděj</u>	<u>beznádej</u>
stress	*stres*	*stress*	*stres*	*stres*	*stres*
anxiety	*tryvoga*	*trevoga*	<u>niepokój</u>	<u>nepokoj</u>	úzkosť
fear	*strah*	*strah*	strach	strach	strach
jealousy	*revnoschi*	*revnost'*	zazdrość	<u>žárlivost</u>	<u>žiarlivosť</u>
hate	*nenavyst'*	*nenavist'*	nienawiść	*nenávist*	*nenávist*
irritation	*rozdratuvannya*	razdrazhenie	irytacja	*podrážděnost*	*podráždenie*
anger	zlist'	zlost'	złość	<u>hněv</u>	<u>hnev</u>
disgust	vidraza	otvraschenie	obrzydzenie	<u>odpor</u>	<u>odpor</u>
contempt	*prezyrstvo*	*prezrenie*	pogarda	<u>opovržení</u>	<u>opovrhnutie</u>

Note: Cognate terms are in *italics*, the cases where English terms have two sets of cognate terms in the Slavic languages, the second set is <u>underlined</u>. For better readability, Russian and Ukrainian emotion terms are transliterated from Cyrillic into Latin letters.

linguistic and a cultural one. The linguistic factor derives from the phylogenetic affinity between the languages at stake. The five Slavic languages considered in the study belong to two subdivisions of the same Slavic family: Eastern (Russian and Ukrainian), and Western (Polish, Czech, and Slovak). Within the Western subfamily, Czech forms a group with the Slovak language, whereas Polish (together with Pomeranian and Silesian) belongs to the Lechitic subgroup. Furthermore, among the 24 prototypical emotion terms included in GRID, six terms (correlates of English *happiness, joy, fear, hate, guilt*, and *stress*) are mutual cognates in *all* five Slavic languages (e.g., happiness: Ru *schast'ye*, Ukr *schastya*, Pl *szczęście*, Cz *štěstí*, and Sl *šťastie*). In addition, 19 terms are mutual cognates in Russian and Ukrainian, 20 terms are cognates in Czech and Slovak, and 14 Polish terms are cognate with at least one word in the other Slavic languages (for details, see Table 41.1).

The cultural factor underpinning our hypothesis derives from the evidence on two cultural dimensions where the Slavic cultures are closer to each other that they are to Anglo-Saxon cultures (US American and British). The most pronounced difference between US American and British, on the one hand, and the Slavic cultural groups, on the other, is found on the individualism/collectivism dimension, where the latter groups are reported to be more collectivistic (Hofstede, 2001). A less clear but still noticeable difference is found on the POWER Distance dimension. This dimension conceptualizes the extent to which a society's level of inequality is endorsed by the followers as much as by the leaders. Relevant indices suggest that in the Slavic cultures societal inequality is comparatively more readily acknowledged (Hofstede, 2001).

41.2 **Results**

The meaning profiles of 24 prototypical emotion words were obtained from 166 Russian-speaking (102 females, mean age 23.7), 147 Ukrainian-speaking (89 females, mean age 22.3), 187 Polish (131 females, mean age 24.5), 120 Czech (43 females, mean age 19.28), and 128 Slovak-speaking participants (107 females, mean age 22.2).[2] The Anglo-Saxon data come from two samples: a British English sample (201 participants, 124 females; mean age 21.51) and US American students (182 participants, 129 females; mean age 18.51).

A confirmation of our hypothesis on the overall distinctiveness of the meaning profiles of the emotion words in the Slavic languages compared to those from UK and US English required that the five Slavic samples would correlate with one another higher than they did with the two English samples. However, given that the Slavic samples were generally less reliable than the English ones, a straightforward comparison was not possible, because a higher correlation of a Slavic sample with English could be due to the overall higher reliability of the English samples.

To resolve this problem of unreliability, we computed the Anglo-Saxon mean value and five mean values for each of the Slavic samples, each time based on the remaining four Slavic languages (i.e., leaving out the Slavic language focused on). Our initial prediction would thus be confirmed if the correlation of each of the Slavic languages with the English average was much lower than with the Slavic average (the language at stake excluded). Pearson correlations indeed showed that for each of the Slavic languages the correlation with the Slavic average was higher than the correlation with the English average, although these differences range from 0.02 to 0.07 and thus are relatively small (see Table 41.2).

---

[2] The numbers in the Russian, Ukrainian, and Polish samples include both the participants who rated the standard set of 24 GRID words, and another group who rated an extra set or words.

Table 41.2 Bivariate correlations of Ukrainian, Russian, Czech, Slovak, and Polish samples with Slavic and Anglo-Saxon mean values across the 24 emotion terms

Language	Slavic mean	Anglo-Saxon mean	Difference
Ukrainian	0.89	0.82	0.07
Russian	0.88	0.83	0.05
Czech	0.77	0.74	0.03
Slovak	0.78	0.76	0.02
Polish	0.89	0.86	0.03

Table 41.3 Partial correlations of Slavic samples with the Slavic and the Anglo-Saxon patterns

	Ukrainian		Russian		Czech		Slovak		Polish	
	Slavic	AS	Slavic	AS	Slavic	AS	Slavic	AS	Slavic	AS
total	0.60	0.12	0.57	0.19	0.35	0.20	0.34	0.25	0.49	0.39
being hurt	0.48	0.09	0.55	0.16	0.41	0.18	**0.34**	**0.38**	**0.37**	**0.42**
sadness	0.67	−0.08	0.59	−0.16	0.37	0.23	**0.19**	**0.58**	0.55	0.44
shame	0.59	0.14	0.48	0.19	0.41	0.21	**0.32**	**0.37**	0.43	0.32
guilt	0.63	0.11	0.59	0.07	0.43	0.15	0.49	0.39	0.45	0.38
compassion	0.73	−0.23	0.71	0.27	**−0.10**	**0.66**	0.68	−0.30	0.72	−0.36
disappointment	0.39	0.01	0.47	0.21	**0.28**	**0.31**	**0.39**	**0.44**	0.46	0.38
love	0.63	0.36	0.71	0.11	0.53	0.13	0.56	0.15	0.54	0.23
contentment	0.78	0.07	0.69	0.48	**0.39**	**0.47**	−0.17	−0.36	0.64	0.42
happiness	0.73	−0.02	0.72	0.05	0.46	0.17	0.52	0.27	0.55	0.43
pride	0.55	0.38	0.62	0.21	0.30	0.07	0.37	0.06	**0.38**	**0.61**
pleasure	0.46	0.22	0.59	0.16	0.36	0.09	0.31	0.36	**0.38**	**0.45**
joy	0.66	0.13	0.61	0.25	0.53	−0.01	0.43	0.34	0.49	0.41
interest	0.58	0.41	0.61	0.19	0.39	0.10	0.49	0.09	0.53	0.42
surprise	0.65	−0.18	0.59	−0.08	0.54	0.19	**0.34**	**0.39**	**0.37**	**0.54**
despair	0.67	−0.00	0.53	0.17	**0.31**	**0.31**	0.47	0.39	0.51	0.24
stress	0.54	0.33	0.43	0.29	0.45	0.00	0.51	0.29	0.51	0.35
anxiety	0.42	0.25	0.52	0.15	0.32	0.13	**0.32**	**0.36**	**0.41**	**0.47**
fear	0.63	0.12	0.45	0.29	0.44	0.02	0.5	0.28	0.58	0.49
jealousy	0.69	0.24	0.60	0.28	0.63	−0.21	0.59	0.13	**0.48**	**0.49**
hate	0.57	0.13	0.52	0.38	0.46	−0.07	0.34	0.27	**0.46**	**0.48**
irritation	0.57	0.09	0.44	0.35	0.33	0.19	0.42	0.13	0.53	0.46
anger	0.53	0.22	0.59	0.30	0.47	0.02	0.42	0.22	0.48	0.38
disgust	0.56	0.29	0.60	0.14	0.39	0.07	**0.22**	**0.39**	0.45	0.35
contempt	0.55	0.19	0.44	0.06	0.39	0.05	**0.15**	**0.54**	0.48	0.45

Note: AS, Anglo-Saxon mean value. Correlations where a Slavic language correlates higher with the Anglo-Saxon mean value than with the Slavic one are in **bold**.

However, additional confirmatory evidence for our hypothesis was obtained from computing the partial correlations between each of the Slavic samples and the Slavic pattern (the language at stake excluded) controlling for the Anglo-Saxon pattern, and, vice versa, between each of the Slavic language samples and the Anglo-Saxon pattern, controlling for the Slavic pattern. These analyses were done for the five Slavic languages both across the entire inventory of GRID terms, and for each emotion term separately (see Table 41.3). These results suggest that the overall partial correlations are always considerably higher for the Slavic languages with their family than with English. A very similar picture emerges also at the term level: in Ukrainian and Russian, the higher similarity effect to the Slavic pattern holds for all the emotion terms; in Czech, Slovak, and Polish, the partial correlations with the Slavic pattern are higher in the majority of cases, from 70% in Polish to 83% of cases in Czech (see Table 41.3 for further details).

41.3 Discussion

This study explored the hypothesis that the meaning profiles of prototypical emotion words in languages from the same language group are closer to each other than each of them is to the corresponding words in a language from a different language group. The hypothesis was generally confirmed, suggesting that there is indeed evidence for particular information that is shared by the Slavic languages but is not captured by the meanings of UK and US English emotion words. The Slavic family similarity effect was found to be stronger for Russian and Ukrainian than for Czech, Slovak, and Polish. This finding may highlight the historical and the present-day developments in the Slavic societies where Czech, Slovak, and Polish can be seen as more "Westernized" European societies (members of European Union), whereas Ukraine (where the Russian and Ukrainian samples were collected) still remains largely a state of post-Soviet historical heritage. Future studies are however needed to determine which terms, features, emotion components, and dimensions contribute most prominently to the observed pattern of results.

Alongside with the confirmatory evidence for our hypothesis, the results also suggest that the observed effect is relatively small. Thus, the emotion domains (represented by a set of prototypical emotion words) can be said to be fairly similar across languages from two language families considered in the present study (Slavic and Germanic). This finding contributes to the universality claim in the studies on emotion lexicons and contradicts previous claims about a remarkable cultural "untranslatability" of Slavic emotion concepts.

Acknowledgments

The authors gratefully acknowledge the valuable assistance of Dr. Tetyana Ogarkova, director and Dr. Volodymyr Yermolenko, deputy director of the *Centre for Intercultural Communication* at the National University "Kyiv-Mohyla academy" for obtaining the Ukrainian sample. We would also like to thank Johnny Fontaine for his invaluable help with the data analyses.

Chapter 42

Cognitive appraisals can differentiate positive emotions: The role of social appraisals

Eddie M. W. Tong[1]

According to appraisal theories of emotions, emotions are influenced by how objective events are subjectively interpreted as a function of personal goals and well-being (Ellsworth & Scherer, 2003). Any given event can be appraised in a large number of ways, along a set of cognitive dimensions known as appraisals. For example, an event can be appraised in terms of its relevance to the person's goals, whether it is blocking those goals, whether it is fair or unfair, who or what caused it, and how much the person can cope with it. More importantly, each emotion is associated with a combination of these appraisals. For example, if an event is appraised as a hindrance to personal goals, as unfair, and as caused by others, the person is likely to feel anger, but if it is appraised as a hindrance to personal goals, as unfair, and as caused by the self, the person could feel guilt.

Numerous studies conducted using different methods, and over diverse cultural samples, have found several appraisal–emotion relationships, which appraisal theories predict (see Ellsworth & Scherer, 2003 for a review). Hence, appraisal theories are among the most successful theoretical models for understanding and predicting emotions. However, several concerns remain unaddressed, and this paper reports a preliminary analysis of one of these issues using the GRID data. One of the persisting problems in appraisal research is the extent to which appraisals can differentiate positive emotions (e.g., joy, hope, interest, gratitude, and contentment). Current evidence suggests that the appraisals that were commonly examined (which are referred to here as classic appraisals) cannot differentiate positive emotions as strongly as they do for negative emotions. Although there are different appraisal theories, they overlap considerably in terms of the appraisals they propose, and examples of these common classic appraisals are NOVELTY, VALENCE, goal significance, coping potential, and compatibility with standards (Ellsworth & Scherer, 2003). In the seminal study by Smith and Ellsworth (1985), participants recalled (in turn) events of 15 emotions and then rated their appraisals of these events. Six emotions were positive (e.g., happiness, interest, pride) and nine were negative (e.g., anger, sadness, fear). Six classic appraisals (pleasantness, effort, certainty, attention, self-other responsibility/control, and situational control) were examined for their ability to differentiate these emotions, as reflected by the locations of the emotions on multi-dimensional appraisal spaces formed by the appraisals. The positive emotions were found to occupy a smaller portion of the spaces than the negative emotions, which seems to suggest that classic appraisals are not as capable of differentiating positive emotions as they do for negative emotions.

[1] Correspondence on this chapter should be addressed to Eddie M. W. Tong, Department of Psychology, National University of Singapore, 9 Arts Link, Room 02-09, Singapore 117570, email: psytmwe@nus.edu.sg

Other studies provide indirect support. In studies that examined current (instead of recalled) emotional experiences, positive emotions were found to correlate more strongly with each other than negative emotions (Barrett, Gross, Christensen, & Benvenuto, 2001; Smith & Ellsworth, 1987). This indicates that positive emotions are more likely to co-occur than negative emotions, which suggests more similarity between different positive emotions than between different negative emotions. Although these findings did not involve appraisals, they can reinforce the impression that positive emotions are less differentiable by appraisals.

Findings like these are incompatible with everyday understanding of positive emotions as experientially different. They also do not sit well with a large literature (outside of appraisal research) that posits positive emotions as conceptually distinct, each with its own set of qualities (for in-depth accounts on individual positive emotions, see Snyder & Lopez, 2002). One approach to this issue is to consider whether appraisal research, in its focus on classic appraisals, has neglected other appraisals that could be strong differentiators of positive emotions. The problem of "missing appraisals" is not new; appraisal theorists have long argued for the need to look beyond the classic appraisals to understand emotions (Reisenzein & Hofmann, 1990; Smith & Ellsworth, 1985).

There is emerging (but largely indirect) evidence that social appraisals might be some of these "missing appraisals" that could discriminate positive emotions strongly. Social appraisals are appraisals of how the situation is affecting another person (Manstead & Fischer, 2001; Parkinson & Simons, 2009). Initial theorizing emphasized how events are appraised in terms of whether they serve or threaten personal goals and well-being and how these self-related appraisals affect emotional experience. However, there is increasing recognition that emotions are also affected by appraisals of how the situation is affecting the goals and well-being of someone else (Manstead & Fischer, 2001). Social appraisals can affect emotions in many ways. First, they can serve as direct inputs in determining emotional responses; for example, we feel joy when a loved one receives praise for a job well done, or relief when he or she escapes a bad predicament. Second, they can disambiguate situations and clarify their emotional meanings, such as those revealed in the classic studies by Schachter and Singer (1962) in which participants appraised others' emotional reactions to understand their own feelings. Third, they can compound or negate the effects of self-related appraisals on emotions; for example, our enjoyment of a promotion can be enhanced when we notice that other people are happy for us, or can be dampened when they do not seem to appreciate our success (Jakobs, Manstead, & Fischer, 1999, 2001).

Social appraisals are already known to be important for positive emotions. For instance, knowing that a situation has helped a loved one is a source of positive emotions such as joy, contentment, pride, and relief (e.g., Isen, 1999; Lazarus, 1991a; Lewis, 1993; Lyubormirsky & Tucker, 1998). Love and gratitude correlate with wanting the best outcomes for the beloved and the benefactor, respectively (Lazarus, 1991a; McCullough, Kilpatrick, Emmons, & Larson, 2001). Compassion occurs when another person is hurt or is suffering (Cassell, 2002). More relevant to the current concern, past studies also suggest that social appraisals could be strong differentiators of positive emotions. In a study by D'Andrade, Boster, and Ellsworth (in preparation), participants indicated their imagined emotional responses to hypothetical situations. Factor analyses of the data revealed a social factor (indicating that one is loved and cared for by another), which most strongly differentiated the positive emotions they examined. In another study by Shaver, Schwartz, Kirson, and O'Connor (1987), hierarchical cluster analyses of similarity ratings of positive emotion terms suggested that positive emotions can be separated according to whether a loved one is involved in the emotional experience. However, no appraisals were measured in these studies. Another study by Tong (2007), more directly examined the discriminatory POWER of appraisals on positive emotions. In this study, participants recalled their experiences of 14 positive emotions (in turn) and then rated their appraisals of these experiences. Social appraisals together with some classic appraisals were found to differentiate these positive emotions close to the level of accuracy with which classic appraisals differentiated negative emotions in past studies (Frijda, Kuipers, & ter Schure, 1989; Scherer, 1997a; Smith & Ellsworth, 1985). However, Tong (2007) examined only positive emotions, leaving unanswered the question of whether social appraisals could also differentiate negative emotions just as strongly.

The current argument does not imply that social appraisals are not important for negative emotions. We do get angry or sad when our loved ones are hurt; we worry about their safety; and we may feel guilty when they commit an inappropriate act. Further, it remains possible that social appraisals could discriminate negative emotions just as strongly. The current critique also does not imply a fundamental flaw in appraisal theories or its studies. What it does imply is the need to go beyond the classic appraisals to include new ones to examine whether there are appraisals that can strongly differentiate positive emotions. In view of the suggested strong discriminatory POWER of social appraisals on positive emotions shown by past studies (D'Andrade et al., in preparation; Shaver et al., 1987; Tong, 2007), social appraisals might be a good candidate to consider for this purpose. Hence, a potentially important question in appraisal research is how strongly do social appraisals differentiate positive emotions and this can be assessed in comparison to the discriminatory POWER of the social appraisals on negative emotions. Evaluation of the discriminatory POWER of the social appraisals on positive emotions is better served by comparing it to the discriminatory POWER on negative emotions, without which the evaluation would be quite arbitrary. Also, differences (if any) in the discriminatory POWER of the social appraisals between the positive and negative emotions could be helpful for the development of theoretical models concerning the differences between these emotions.

The GRID study has the potential to investigate this issue. It examines participants' understanding of the meanings behind the linguistic labels of 24 positive and negative emotions as used in their cultural contexts and was conducted internationally over numerous cultures. Participants rated how much they associated a set of features (e.g., action tendencies, bodily expression) with each emotion label whenever it was used in everyday conversation. Social appraisals were among the features measured and are the focus here. This paper reports the first analysis of the discriminatory POWER of social appraisals over the measured positive and negative emotions. Data from Singapore was chosen for this preliminary assessment, results of which can be used to guide subsequent analyses on the larger GRID dataset. It is possible that the GRID data only reflect cultural beliefs about emotions as reflected in linguistic labels, not actual emotional experiences. However, to some extent, cultural beliefs should also derive substantially from actual experiences and hence there should be some degree of correspondence between meanings associated with cultural labels and actual experiences. Future studies should extend the current research by examining actual experience (especially if the present results do suggest that social appraisals differentiate positive emotions strongly).

One hundred and three undergraduates (85 females, 18 males; mean age = 20.03, SD = 1.58) from the National University of Singapore (NUS) participated in exchange for course credits. They completed the GRID instrument on-line, following the same procedure used in other countries that participated in the GRID project (see Chapter 6). In this measure, 24 emotions were tested and 144 emotion features (e.g., appraisals, bodily expression, facial expression, vocal expression, action tendencies, subjective feelings, and regulatory processes) were measured. The emotions were selected based on frequent usage in research and daily language and the features were drawn from dominant theoretical perspectives of these emotions (see Chapter 5 for details).

The GRID instrument was administered in English, the first-language in Singapore, which all NUS undergraduates are fluent in. Four randomly chosen emotions were selected for each participant. Participants were presented with the label of an emotion (e.g., *anger*) and then rated items that assessed its perceived features. The instruction was "If a person in your cultural group uses the following emotion word to describe an emotional experience, how likely is it that the person experienced an event . . .," which was followed by the items. The items for social appraisals were "that was in itself pleasant for somebody else (independently of its possible consequences)," "that was in itself unpleasant for somebody else (independently of its possible consequences)," "of which the consequences were likely to be positive, desirable for somebody else," and "of which the consequences were likely to be negative, undesirable for somebody else," and "that was important and relevant for the goals or needs of somebody else." These items were chosen because they fit well with the conceptual definition of social appraisals (see Manstead & Fischer, 2001), which concerns whether the situation has harmed or helped someone else and how important is the situation for that person. All items were rated on nine-point scales that ranged from 1 (*extremely unlikely*) to 9 (*extremely likely*). Each item was presented on a separate screen. Participants spent about 15 min completing all questions for each emotion before proceeding to the next until all four emotions were responded to. Although 24 emotions were tested in the GRID study, only 18 (nine positive emotions—compassion, contentment, happiness, interest, joy, love, pleasure, pride, and surprise; nine negative emotions—anger, anxiety, contempt, disgust, fear, guilt, hate, sadness, and shame) were examined here based on two considerations. First, the number of positive and negative emotions should be kept equal for a fair comparison; because only nine positive emotions were examined in the GRID study, only nine negative emotions were selected. Second, the negative emotions were selected to be as similar as possible to those examined by Smith and Ellsworth (1985), which is the study closest to the current purpose; this permitted some (but limited) comparison between the current results and those from Smith and Ellsworth. Despite leaving some emotions out of the analyses, the sample size was maintained at 103.

Discriminant function analysis was employed to test how sensitive the social appraisals were to the differences between the emotions. First, a set of "discriminant functions" (equations comprising the social appraisals) was computed and the extent to which these functions accounted for the variance (i.e., the differences) between the emotions was evaluated using the Wald's λ test. Second, classification indices were computed to evaluate how accurately these functions classified all cases (data units) into their respective emotion categories. For instance, a case that was rated in reference to sadness should be classified as a member of the sadness category. Hence, higher classification accuracy would mean that the social appraisals were more sensitive to the differences between the emotions. All classification indices were computed using the "leave-one-out" method, which classified each case using functions derived from all other cases and hence would provide better estimates of the classification accuracy of the social appraisals. Two discriminant analyses were conducted, one on the positive emotions and the other on the negative emotions. In both analyses, the five social appraisals were entered as predictors. At this point, certain caveats should be mentioned. First, discriminant analysis was developed for analyzing between-participant data, but not within-participant data (not to mention the present form of within-participant data in which each participant responded to a small subset of the 24 emotions). Hence, the consequence of applying discriminant analysis to the current data is not well understood. Also, no technique has been developed to statistically compare classification indices, which means that classification indices are typically interpreted descriptively. These qualitative comparisons, however, provide heuristic indications of the discriminatory POWER of the social appraisals on emotions, which can be useful for future theorizing concerning social appraisals. In summary, the analyses are meant to be preliminary and exploratory, and the interpretations that follow are tentative and should be taken cautiously.

The results indicated that only the functions computed for the positive emotions were significant, Wald's $\lambda = 0.67$, $\chi^2(40) = 35.70$, $p = 0.034$, whereas those computed for the negative emotions were not, Wald's $\lambda = 0.47$, $\chi^2(40) = 43.86$, $p = 0.35$. Hence, the social appraisals were significant differentiators of the positive emotions but not the negative emotions. The "leave-one-out" classification index for the positive emotions was 19.5% whereas that for the negative emotions was 12.8%. Note that the prior probabilities of correctly classifying the emotions by chance were 11.1% for both types of emotions. Hence, not only did the classification index for the positive emotions seem larger than that for the negative emotions, it also appeared to be considerably above chance levels (the classification accuracy of the negative emotions, however, was too close to chance). Thus, the social appraisals seemed to classify the positive emotions more accurately than the negative emotions.

These findings appear promising, but one should be mindful of its limitations. As just mentioned, the data do not reflect actual emotional experiences and there could be analytical problems associated with using discriminant analyses on within-participant data. In addition, the extent to which the same findings can be replicated with other emotions and in other cultures is unknown at this point. Also, the classification indices are not high; the discriminant functions classified the positive emotions correctly only for 19.5% of the cases and the negative emotions only for 12.8% of the cases. They are also largely lower than those produced by the classic appraisals in the study by Smith and Ellsworth (1985), which ranged from 29.2% to 36.5% for the positive emotions and 17.4% to 27.8% for the negative emotions. This might suggest that classic appraisals still do better than social appraisals in differentiating both positive and negative emotions. However, there are differences between the current study and Smith and Ellsworth's that limit comparison, including the number and type of emotions examined and methodological differences (their participants recalled actual emotional experiences whereas the GRID participants responded only to labels). Finally, researchers should also consider the reasons why social appraisals differentiate positive emotions more strongly than negative emotions (assuming this is further replicated).

Despite these reservations, the current results, preliminary as they are, are quite promising. Given the large number of cultures examined in the GRID study, the current question concerning social appraisals could be subjected to a more powerful test with greater precision once the entire data set is available. Although the problems and limitations mentioned are formidable, they can be dealt with using the GRID dataset (e.g., developing disciminant analytical techniques that suit the GRID data), or with another study (e.g., one that examines actual emotional experiences). In addition, the GRID data can test other hypotheses concerning social appraisals. In particular, one could examine whether the relationships between social appraisals and emotions might be more pronounced in collectivistic cultures than in individualistic cultures (Manstead & Fischer, 2001). In summary, further research on social appraisals seems promising, and the GRID data can be used further to examine how social processes influence emotional experiences.

Chapter 43

Where do emotional dialects come from? A comparison of the understanding of emotion terms between Gabon and Quebec

Ursula Hess,[1] Pascal Thibault, and Manon Levesque

"La tournure et la démarche ont autant d'accent que la parole."
Delphine Gay de Girardin

This statement extracted from the 1843 "*Lettres parisiennes du vicompte de Launay*" describes how nonverbal behaviors can communicate information about the origins of an individual just as language does. The goal of the present study is to use the GRID paradigm to help us better understand this process.

Specifically, it has been proposed that there is a universal language of emotion that allows us to generally understand the emotion expressions of people across the globe, but that this language also has dialects, which reflect expressive differences among cultures (Elfenbein & Ambady, 2002a, 2002b; Elfenbein, et al., 2007). These differences are subtle enough to allow good communication across cultures, but are substantive enough to potentially cause communication problems, and hence, just as we are sometimes mistaken when listening to someone who speaks with a different linguistic accent, we are also sometimes mistaken when we interpret expressions by an individual with a different nonverbal accent (Elfenbein & Ambady, 2002b).

The existence of nonverbal dialects within a universal language of emotion raises the question as to where do these dialects come from? Herein we propose that nonverbal dialects are the result of subtle differences in the modal appraisal of emotions, which translate into expressive differences. In what follows, we will first define emotional dialects and then outline our hypothesis that they are based in the appraisal of model emotions. We then present a study using the GRID instrument to test this hypothesis in Quebec and Gabon, two French-speaking countries for which emotion dialects have been demonstrated (Elfenbein et al., 2007).

[1] Corresponding author: Ursula Hess, Department of Psychology, Humboldt University, Rudower Chaussee 18, 12489 Berlin, Germany. Email: Ursula.Hess@psychologie.hu-berlin.de

43.1 **Emotional dialects**

As mentioned above, the concept of nonverbal dialects (Elfenbein & Ambady, 2002a, 2002b, 2003; Marsh et al., 2003) is based on a language metaphor. Thus, just as words may be pronounced differently by individuals from different regions who speak the same language, facial expressions vary subtly from region to region, and just as not all words are pronounced differently, we would not expect all emotion expressions to differ. Specifically, both disgust and surprise share the majority of their features with reflexes closely linked to the typical elicitors of these emotions, the gustofacial reflex for disgust, and the startle reflex for surprise. The possible impact of cultural dialects on such expressions may be muted. Likewise, as Darwin noted (1872/1965), displays of fear are very similar across mammals, hence they should not be expected to vary much across cultural groups.

It should also be noted that the simple fact that members of different ethnic groups differ in decoding accuracy is not necessarily indicative of the presence of an emotional dialect. Rather, emotion decoding accuracy may differ because of relative differences in task difficulty. For example, because of such features as the contrast between sclera and skin color and the presence and absence of an epicantic fold, the raising of the eye lids in fear is much more salient in African than in Asian faces (Beaupré & Hess, 2005) and hence easier to detect in the former than the latter. Yet, individuals who are more familiar with Asian faces can learn to compensate for this difference, thereby improving their decoding accuracy. Hence, to conclude toward the presence of emotional dialect for an emotion, both the encoding and the decoding of the emotion need to be studied, and both differences in expression and in decoding accuracy have to be found.

This was done by Elfenbein and colleagues (Elfenbein et al., 2007), who tested the dialect hypothesis by asking participants from Quebec and Gabon, two countries where the language of education is French, to show an emotion expression such that their friends, that is, members of their own group, would well understand what they were trying to show. That is, Elfenbein and colleagues were not investigating spontaneous expressions, but rather the "within cultural" stereotypical expressions. The resulting expressions were coded using FACS (Facial Action Coding System, Ekman & Friesen, 1978), an anatomically based coding system that describes individual facial actions. The dummy coded FACS codes were submitted for discriminant analysis. For seven out of ten emotions it was possible to correctly classify, based only on the pattern of facial expressions, whether the expresser was from Gabon or Quebec. That is, the expressions were sufficiently different to statistically distinguish between the groups (Elfenbein et al., 2007). Yet at the same time, an accompanying judgment study showed that these expressions were still recognized by members of both groups at well above chance rates, suggesting that they are indeed variants of a recognizable expressive prototype (Elfenbein et al., 2007). In line with the reflections above, expressions of disgust and fear, but also of embarrassment, did not differ between groups (Elfenbein et al., 2007).

What the study by Elfenbein et al. (2007) did not address was the question of the origin of cultural dialects. In fact, generally speaking, the question of *why* emotion expressions take the form they take is actually not one that is typically addressed. Thus, Darwin (1872/1965) in "The expression of the emotions in man and animals," was actually the only person who tried on a scientific basis to comprehensively explain the origins of the specific expressive elements that compose an emotion expression.

43.2 **Facial actions as the output of appraisals**

However, more recently, appraisal theory has made proposals along those lines. Specifically, it has been suggested that the individual elements of facial expressions are a function of appraisal outcomes and their effects on motor behavior (Kaiser & Wehrle, 2001; Pope & Smith, 1994; Scherer,

1992, 2005b; Smith & Kirby, 2001). That is, facial expressions are not so much the output of emotions, but rather the output of appraisals. In particular, specific appraisals are associated with specific action tendencies, which can include information search and adaptive behaviors as well as social messages. Consequently, appraisals are linked to the expressive elements that combine to create facial expressions. This hypothesis also implies that when there are subtle differences in appraisal processes, we might also expect subtle differences in expression. Yet, not all such differences should translate into different expressions as some early appraisal outcomes may be overridden by later ones or different appraisals can lead to the same expressions. For example, empirical evidence links action of the *Corrugator Supercilii* muscle (frown) both to feelings of unpleasantness (Cacioppo et al., 1986) and to perceived goal obstruction (Scherer & Ellgring, 2007b; Smith & Scott, 1997).

Importantly, Scherer (1987, 1994) further suggests that some appraisal patterns are found more frequently across species, but also within cultures because specific environmental challenges, general conditions of life, and constraints of social organization, combine to produce recurring patterns of appraisals. He refers to these recurring patterns as modal (in the statistical sense) emotions. If this were the case, then the exact facial expression that within a culture is prototypically associated with a specific emotion should vary to the degree that modal appraisal patterns vary.

What this implies for cultural dialects is that one reason why members of different cultures show subtly different emotion expressions may be that they have subtly different modal appraisal patterns for the emotion in question. The research described below was conducted to assess this hypothesis with regard to the emotional dialects found in Quebec and Gabon. Specifically, the GRID approach was used to assess appraisal dimensions of emotions in Quebec and Gabon. We expected that emotions for which cultural dialects were found by Elfenbein et al. (2007) would also be appraised differently by the members of the two groups.

43.3 Differences in appraisal dimensions between Quebec and Gabon

Method

Participants

Data was collected from French-speaking university students from the University of Quebec at Montreal in Canada and Omar Bongo University in Gabon. French is the official language in Quebec and the University of Quebec is a French language institution. The language of education in Gabon is French and university students will have spoken French from early childhood on. Hence members of both groups were equivalent in their understanding of the language. The data from 74 Gabonese (35% women) and 90 Quebecers (66% women) with a mean age of 27 years (SD = 11) and 25 years (SD = 4), respectively, who completed the entire GRID questionnaire were retained for analysis.

Material

The GRID questionnaire (see Chapter 5 for details on the questionnaire) was presented in its entirety via a web interface. An additional module of words was added to the GRID, which included the emotions serenity, admiration, nostalgia, and embarrassment. Since the goal of this study was to assess differences in appraisals between Gabon and Quebec and relate these to differences in expressive behavior, only the data from the Appraisal dimension of the emotional experience were analyzed.

Data preparation and analyses

The first step was to verify the reliability of the ratings. For this, interclass correlations were calculated for each emotion for Quebecois and Gabonais participants separately. Data from participants whose ratings had a negative or close to 0 item correlation were removed and data from the retained participants were averaged. The final samples averaged 0.85 (range: 0.66 to 0.93) for the Gabonais participants,[2] and 0.88 (range: 0.75 to 0.94) for the Quebecois participants.

The mean values were factor analyzed separately for each group. Initial factor analyses suggested a comparable three-factor solution for both groups, which explained 60% of the variance for the Gabonais sample and 79% for the Quebecois sample. The factor scores from both groups was then z-transformed and combined; Euclidian distances were calculated to assess the difference in factor space between emotions across all three dimensions.

43.4 **Results**

The factor analysis of the combined data for the appraisal dimensions had a KMO of 0.79 and explained 70% of the variance. The first factor, VALENCE, explained 40% of the variance. Two separate loci of control dimensions emerged, one focused on the internal locus of control, with items such as "was predictable," "was caused by self", which explained 24% of the variance; and a second dimension that was basically the converse, explaining 6% of the variance. In order to facilitate the presentation of the results, and given the relatively small percentage of the variance explained by the 3rd factor, Figure 43.2 shows only the VALENCE and internal locus of control dimensions as these explained most of the variance in the factor analysis.

Elfenbein et al. (2007) found the strongest dialect effect for serenity, which was explained as a calm, tranquil state of mind. All Quebec expressers showed a weak smile when posing this emotion, whereas the Gabonese expressers preferentially showed a neutral facial expression (see Figure 43.1). Because smiles are associated with positive VALENCE (Cacioppo et al., 1986), this suggests

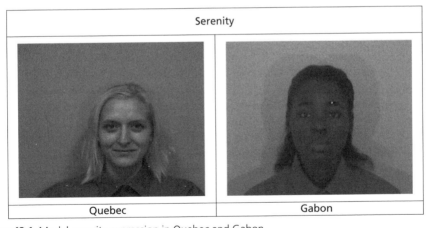

Figure 43.1 Modal serenity expression in Quebec and Gabon.

---

2 For embarrassment and nostalgia, no satisfactory reliability could be established for the Gabonais sample. Analyses in- and excluding these variables lead to highly congruent results, hence the complete set of variables was used for the following analyses.

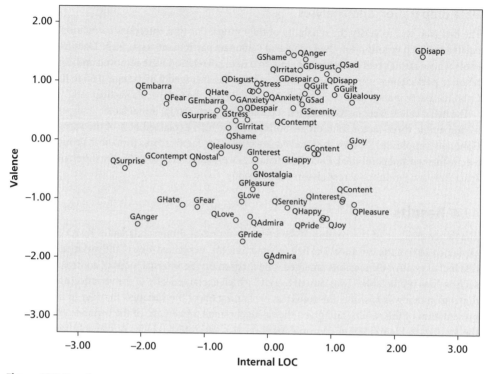

Figure 43.2 Emotion space.

that serenity in Quebec is an emotion that has a more positive VALENCE and hence would load higher on the positive VALENCE axis in the factor analysis—this was indeed the case, with 0.63 for Gabon versus −1.13 for Quebec (with negative factor scores indicating positive VALENCE). Further, inspection of the emotion space (see Figure 43.2) showed that serenity as appraised by Quebecois is more closely surrounded by other positive emotions such as happiness, joy, love, pride, and admiration (mean Euclidian distance = 1.98), than when appraised by Gabonais (mean ED = 2.64). By contrast, in Gabon, serenity is more closely surrounded by such emotions as sadness and even despair (mean ED = 1.05) than is the case in Quebec (mean ED = 2.69).

Several dialect expressions differed with regard to the presence of facial actions that signal POWER potential. Thus, in Quebec, anger and contempt were typically posed with lowered eyebrows and tightened eyes and lips, whereas in Gabon, the expression for anger was preferentially composed of a stare with wide-open eyes, and for contempt with a pout. In turn, according to Kaiser and Wehrle (2001) wide-open eyes are associated with an appraisal of low POWER.

Hence, we would expect that for Gabon compared to Quebec, anger and contempt should load lower on the internal locus of control—again an inspection of the factor scores confirms this to be the case (Anger: −2.05 vs 0.038; Contempt: −1.63 vs 0.038, for Gabon vs Quebec, respectively). In addition, even though anger was situated quite close to hate in both countries (ED = 1.17 for Gabon and ED = 1.50 for Quebec), anger and contempt were relatively closer in emotion space to fear and surprise—emotions for which internal locus of control is low—in Gabon (mean ED = 1.82 and 1.43 for anger and contempt, respectively) compared to Quebec (mean ED = 3.11 and 4.57 for anger and contempt, respectively).

Sadness in Quebec usually involved some brow knitting—a sign of goal obstruction—in Gabon, this was not the case; rather a more submissive or disengaged head gesture was preferentially shown. Congruent with this observation, Quebec sadness was situated closer to other emotions characterized by goal obstruction such as anger (ED = 1.18 for Quebec vs ED = 4.16 for Gabon), whereas for Gabon sadness was very close to serenity (see above), suggesting lower appraisals of goal obstruction in Gabon than in Quebec.

As mentioned above, not all emotion expressions were expected to have a dialect. In particular, no differences were found for fear, disgust and embarrassment. Indeed, the Gabon and Quebec appraisals of disgust and embarrassment are very close (ED = 1.09 for disgust and ED = 1.34 for embarrassment) and the emotions also have similar "neighbors." However, for fear the situation is somewhat more complex. In Gabon and Quebec, fear is appraised similarly with regard to internal locus of control (factor score of −1.61 for Quebec and −1.12 for Gabon), but for Gabon compared to Quebec, fear was higher in positive VALENCE (factor score of 0.62 for Quebec and −1.13 for Gabon, with negative factor scores indicating positive VALENCE), as well as being much closer in locus of control to love (difference in factor scores:0.70 vs 2.54). Fear is related to affiliation (Marsh, Adams, et al., 2005; Marsh, Ambady, et al., 2005), which can explain the closeness to love, but overall the finding suggests a difference in appraisal pattern that is not expressed in a difference in facial expression. Yet, as mentioned above, fear expressions are strongly based on the startle reflex and in this case more subtle appraisal based influences may be overridden in the final expression.

An interesting case was presented by happiness. In their judgment study, Elfenbein et al. (2007) did not find differences in decoding accuracy for happiness. However, they did find strong expressive differences. Whereas 53% of the Quebecois participants showed a Duchenne smile (upturned corners of the mouth combined with wrinkles around the eyes) when asked to pose a clearly recognizable state of happiness, only 23% of the Gabonese did. Inspection of the emotion space suggests that happiness is appraised somewhat less positively in Gabon (factor score on the VALENCE dimension of −0.21 for Quebec versus 1.29 for Gabon, with negative factor scores indicating more positive VALENCE), which would explain differences in intensity, but unlike serenity, happiness was surrounded by other positive emotions in both countries and the Euclidian distance between the two happiness appraisals is relatively small (ED = 1.69). Hence in Gabon, as well as in Quebec, happiness seems to be a positive emotion that is appraised with an absence of goal obstruction.

This is especially pertinent because wrinkles around the eyes have been described as a reliable sign (Ekman & Friesen, 1982; Frank & Ekman, 1993) and even a hard-wired marker for smile authenticity (Williams et al., 2001). That Gabonese do not use this marker when posing happiness suggests either that they are somehow less able to voluntarily contract the *Orbicularis Oculi* muscle that creates the wrinkles around the eye or that the marker is not universal as a sign of true positive feeling. Thibault et al. (2012) confirmed that the latter is indeed the case. In their study, Gabonese did not use the Duchenne marker to assess smile authenticity at all. Interestingly, in the same study, a group of mainland Chinese immigrants to Quebec showed sensitivity to the presence of the Duchenne marker, but only when judging smiles by French-Canadian encoders and not when judging expressions by other Chinese. These findings suggest that the Duchenne marker is not a universal marker of smile authenticity. Specifically, the GRID approach provided converging evidence to the finding by Thibault et al. (2012) that the absence of the marker in Gabonese smiles does not signal a lack of positive VALENCE associated with that happiness expression.

In summary, the GRID approach suggests that differences in emotion expressions between Gabon and Quebec can be linked directly to matching differences in appraisals as reflected by the differences in the local meaning of the French emotion terms and conversely the absence of an expressive difference was found to be matched by congruent appraisals.

Yet, the GRID approach may also be a useful tool to generate hypotheses, which can then be followed up by more detailed research. For example, not all emotions for which cultural dialects were found by Elfenbein et al. (2007) generated clear appraisal predictions based on the AUs. Thus, shame posed by Quebecois was characterized by a frequent unilateral lip curl (AU 14), an expressive element that is more typically described as a characteristic of contempt expressions. By contrast, in Gabon, shame was posed as a more submissive forward head tilt. The inspection of the emotion space showed that in fact, for Quebec, shame was situated closer to contempt in terms of VALENCE (difference in factor scores: 0.35) than was the case for Gabon (difference in factor scores: 1.90), whereas for Gabon, shame was relatively isolated, with the closest other emotions being despair and disgust. These emotions are in fact withdrawing emotions, such as shame is generally considered to be. This allows the hypothesis that in Quebec shame is not strictly based on appraisals of a failure that is attributed to the self and that entrains withdrawing, but seems to suggest some resistance to this acceptance. This hypothesis could be followed up by future research.

In summary, the present analyses provide supportive evidence for the notion that cultural dialects can be traced to differences in appraisals between cultures. Specifically, the GRID approach allowed to confirm differences in cultural appraisal patterns predicted by differences in cultural emotion expression dialects. Thus, serenity was found to be a more positive emotion in Quebec than in Gabon, contempt to be closer related to anger in Quebec than in Gabon and sadness to be associated with less goal obstruction in Gabon than in Quebec. We also could show that expressions of disgust and embarrassment for which no dialects were found, were appraised very similarly, the case for fear, however, was more complex. In addition, the usefulness of the GRID approach to suggest avenues for future studies regarding potential expressive and appraisal differences between cultures was shown for shame and happiness.

A note of caution is necessary, however. As noted above, the reliability of appraisal judgments varied between emotions and this variance was larger in Gabon, where a lack of familiarity with the computerized data collection procedure caused procedural problems. For this reason, the findings were also based on relatively fewer individuals than is the case for other studies reported in this volume. Overall, however, these findings show the POWER of the GRID approach to help us better understand why certain facial expressions are shown in certain cultural contexts.

43.5 **Conclusion**

In summary, in this exploratory study the GRID approach supported the notion that emotional dialects may be caused by differences in the modal appraisal pattern (as reflected in the respective component of the local word meanings) of these emotions in different cultures. Thus, differences between expressions posed by individuals from Quebec and Gabon were congruent with differences in appraisals on the VALENCE and locus of control dimensions. The findings of the present study join a growing literature highlighting the suitability of a componential emotion model over discrete emotion theories that posit rigid neural programs, which include emotion-specific patterns of facial expressions. The present results demonstrated that there are differences in how individuals in Gabon and Quebec conceived of the underlying appraisals of certain emotions; differences that match differences in emotion expression in Gabon and Quebec found by

Elfenbein et al. (2007). Therefore, we consider that the GRID approach constitutes a highly promising methodology to understand where emotional dialects come from.

Acknowledgments

This research was supported by a grant from the Fonds Québécois de Recherche sur la Société et la Culture to Pascal Thibault. The preparation of this manuscript was facilitated by Grant LX0990031 from the Australian Research Council to Ursula Hess.

Part VIII

Taking stock and further development of the GRID paradigm

Chapter 44

CoreGRID and MiniGRID: Development and validation of two short versions of the GRID instrument

Klaus R. Scherer,[1] Johnny J. R. Fontaine, and Cristina Soriano

The development of the GRID instrument has been strongly guided by theoretical considerations. Based on the Component Process Model (see Chapter 1), the five major emotion components that are recognized by most emotion theorists as essential building blocks of emotion processes, namely Appraisals, Bodily reactions, Expression, Action tendencies, and Feelings, have each been operationalized by one or more dominant theories. The empirical evidence across languages and cultural groups presented throughout this book demonstrates that the GRID instrument can, as predicted, be used to establish comprehensive and fine-grained semantic profiles for a representative selection of major emotion words. The 142 features that have been selected to cover major aspects of each of the emotion components allow mapping the meaning of emotion terms into a high-dimensional space, producing precise discriminations, both with respect to other emotion terms in the same language and to similar terms in other languages. However, this high degree of resolution and precision comes at a price with respect to the time and effort needed to generate reliable profiles with large numbers of native language speakers. It takes one participant about one hour to rate only four emotion words. Because the level of precision and detail provided by the GRID instrument is not required for many psycholinguistic research questions, the mere size of the instrument might hamper its future use. Therefore, two shortened versions of the GRID instrument have been developed, namely the CoreGRID and the MiniGRID instruments. The shortening of the original GRID instrument, to which we will further refer in this chapter as the FullGRID instrument, has been strongly guided by the empirical results reported in the previous parts of this book.

Throughout this book, three levels of semantic profiles have been presented that show a different trade-off between informativeness and cognitive economy, namely the feature level, the emotion component factor level, and the overall factor level. At the feature level, each of the 142 features is taken into account to identify the meaning of an emotion term. This is a fine-grained level of analysis, but not very economical. At a higher level, one can look at the component-specific *factors* that capture the semantic overlap of the features within each emotion component. This level is far more economical, as it only comprises 22 factors across the five emotion components (as opposed to 142 features). However, this level of analysis is also less fine-grained. The role that individual

[1] Corresponding author: Klaus R. Scherer. Swiss Center for Affective Sciences—University of Geneva. 7, Rue des Battoirs, CH-1205 Geneva, Switzerland. Klaus.Scherer@unige.ch

features play in the meaning of emotion terms is not fully represented by the emotion component factors. For instance, the feature "blushing" loads highly on the BODY TEMPERATURE factor, but BODY TEMPERATURE as a whole does not capture the particular relevance of "blushing" for the meaning of *shame*. Despite this limitation, in general the emotion component factors form a good level of analysis to identify differences in meaning between emotion terms. The 24 emotion terms can be almost as accurately classified based on only the 22 emotion component factors rather than on the 142 individual features (namely an accuracy of 79.8% vs 82.1%, see Chapters 7 and 13). Finally, among the 22 emotion component factors, there are also strong mutual relationships. They can at the highest level be represented by an overall four-factorial structure: VALENCE, POWER, AROUSAL, and NOVELTY. This highest level is very economical as one only looks at four factors, but it is also the least informative. It gives no information about how the different emotion components contribute to the meaning of the emotion term. Many research questions, however, are only formulated at this general level. As demonstrated in this book, the FullGRID instrument can be used at each of these three levels of analysis.

As a compromise between precision and economy the CoreGRID instrument has been developed, assessing the semantic profiles on the level of *emotion components* but with a much smaller number of features (less than 50% of the features). For research questions which are well served by knowing the dimensional coordinates of emotion words in four-dimensional space, we developed a MiniGRID, consisting of only 16 features. In the following sections, we first present the development of the CoreGRID instrument and then the development of the MiniGRID.

44.1 **Development of the CoreGRID instrument**

The CoreGRID instrument has been developed to assess the 22 emotion component factors (representing Feeling, Bodily reaction, Expression, Action tendency, and Appraisal) with a much smaller number of features than was the case in the FullGRID instrument.

The following guidelines were used to select the features for the CoreGRID from the complete set of 142 in the FullGRID:

1 The starting point was taking the factor structures for each of the emotion components reported in Part III of this book (see Chapters 8 to 12) and selecting features in such a way as to reproduce these emotion component factors as faithfully as possible.

2 Each emotion component factor was to be represented by at least two emotion features.

3 If an emotion component factor was bipolar, at least one feature from both poles was to be included.

4 Emotion component factors that were defined by many features in the FullGRID were also to be represented by a proportionally larger number of features in the CoreGRID instrument.

5 The selected features were to robustly reproduce the overall four-factorial structure of VALENCE, POWER, AROUSAL, and NOVELTY.

6 The CoreGRID features were to represent the major theoretical concerns that informed the original selection of features in the FullGRID instrument. This required new features to be added for three of the emotion components, in order to improve the representation of certain factors from a theoretical approach (based on the hypotheses generated by the current empirical findings, notably in Chapter 8 on the Feeling component and in Chapter 12 on the Appraisal component).

7 The selected features per emotion component were to empirically reproduce the component factor structure identified by the FullGRID. After Procrustes rotation of the emotion component factors in the CoreGRID to the emotion component factors in the FullGRID, the

congruence (Tucker's phi) was to reach at least 0.85 per factor, and the factor scores should correlate at least 0.80.[2]

8   The features of the CoreGRID were to achieve a high accuracy level in classifying the 24 emotion terms by discriminant analysis.

In the remainder of this section, we first present the selection of the features per emotion component (using the feature labels in the full GRID instrument described in this volume) and the congruence of the emotion component structures in the CoreGRID with the emotion component structures in the FullGRID. Then the overall structure of the CoreGRID is investigated. Subsequently, discriminant analyses on the CoreGRID features and emotion component factors are compared with the discriminant analyses on the FullGRID features and factors.

The CoreGRID Feeling component

A four-factorial structure was identified for the Feeling component based on the data obtained with the FullGRID (see Chapter 8). The first factor was a general VALENCE feeling factor with all feeling features having their highest or second highest loading on it. The three remaining factors were subsidiary, as the features that loaded high on these remaining factors also had a high or even higher loading on the first factor. The first subsidiary factor was a POWER feeling factor opposing strength and dominance (and control) to weakness and submissiveness. In the last two subsidiary factors, the expected AROUSAL dimension was split into a tense AROUSAL factor opposing restlessness to calmness and a tiredness factor which was characterized by exhaustion and fatigue. These four feeling factors were descriptively labeled as: BAD VS GOOD, WEAK VS STRONG, CALM VS RESTLESS, and TIRED.

For the CoreGRID Feeling component each pole of the first three factors was represented by one feeling feature. The fourth factor was represented by only one pole of the fourth dimension, namely "feel tired." However, as it was hypothesized in Chapter 8 that the last feeling factor refers to the sleep-wake cycle, a new feature—"felt awake"—was added to operationalize it. Thus, the four feeling factors were operationalized by the following eight feeling features in the CoreGRID:

BAD VS GOOD

- felt bad
- felt good

WEAK VS STRONG

- felt weak
- felt strong

CALM VS RESTLESS

- felt calm
- felt restless

TIRED VS AWAKE

- felt tired
- felt awake (new feature)

---

2   All analyses have been executed on the 142 by 816 data matrix, with the 142 columns representing the 142 features in the FullGRID and the 816 rows representing the 24 emotion terms in the 34 samples (see Chapter 5 for a full description).

Table 44.1 Loadings of the CoreGRID feeling features in a three-factorial Procrustes rotated structure and congruence with FullGRID feeling structure

	BAD VS GOOD	WEAK VS STRONG	CALM VS RESTLESS	TIRED
CoreGRID feeling features				
felt good	0.95	0.20	−0.13	0.06
felt bad	−0.91	−0.29	0.08	−0.12
felt strong	0.82	0.51	−0.07	0.16
felt weak	−0.71	−0.64	0.01	−0.25
felt restless	−0.45	−0.04	0.86	−0.23
felt calm	0.90	0.04	−0.36	−0.14
felt tired	−0.76	−0.10	−0.13	−0.62
Congruence				
Tucker's phi	1.00	0.99	1.00	1.00
$r_{factor\ scores}$	0.97	0.83	0.94	0.88

A factor analysis on the first seven feeling features (omitting "felt awake," as it was a new feature) with Procrustes rotation reproduced the feeling factors of the FullGRID very well, with a Tucker's phi of 0.99 and higher in all cases, and with the factor scores correlating higher than 0.83 (see Table 44.1).

Concerning feeling, there is also emerging evidence of the existence of systematic differences in the modal levels of intensity and duration for specific emotions (Sonnemans & Frijda, 1994; Wallbott & Scherer, 1995; Scherer et al., 2004; Verduyn et al., 2009a, b). In Chapter 8, it was demonstrated that emotion terms are especially differentiated on intensity and duration within the four major emotion clusters of joy, anger, sadness, and fear. These differences might therefore be important when deciding what emotion word out of a family of terms should be used to refer to a specific instance of the emotion—for example, for the anger family there probably are systematic intensity differences between "irritation" and "rage." In order to allow for the documentation of such systematic differences in future research, the following two FullGRID feeling features were maintained in the CoreGRID:

Intensity

- was in an intense emotional state.

Duration

- experienced the emotion for a long time.

Thus the Feeling component, which was operationalized by 22 features in the FullGRID, is represented by 10 features in the CoreGRID.

The CoreGRID Bodily reaction component

On the basis of earlier reports in the literature (Rimé & Giovannini, 1986; Rimé, Philippot, & Cisamolo, 1990; Scherer & Wallbott, 1994, p. 313), a three-factor structure was expected in the Bodily reaction component. After orthogonal Procrustes rotation, this structure was by and large confirmed (see Chapter 9). The three Bodily reaction factors were labeled as follows: DISTRESS SYMPTOMS, AUTONOMIC AROUSAL, and BODY TEMPERATURE. As the Bodily reaction component was particularly important for defining the AROUSAL factor in the overall factor structure, this component—and especially the AUTONOMIC AROUSAL factor—has been more extensively represented in the CoreGRID than the other emotion components. Of the 18 Bodily reaction features in the FullGRID the following 11 were retained in the CoreGRID instrument:

DISTRESS SYMPTOMS

- felt weak limbs
- got pale
- had stomach troubles

AUTONOMIC AROUSAL

- muscles tensing (whole body)
- breathing getting faster
- sweat
- heartbeat getting faster
- heartbeat slowing down
- breathing slowing down

BODY TEMPERATURE

- felt warm
- felt cold

A factor analysis on the 11 Bodily reaction features of the CoreGRID with Procrustes rotation reproduced the Bodily reaction factor structure of the FullGRID very well, with a Tucker's phi of 1.00 in all cases, and factor scores correlating at 0.94 or higher (see Table 44.2).

Table 44.2 Loadings of the CoreGRID bodily reaction features in a three-factorial Procrustes rotated structure and congruence with FullGRID bodily reaction structure

	DISTRESS SYMPTOMS	AUTONOMIC AROUSAL	BODY TEMPERATURE
CoreGRID bodily reaction features			
felt weak limbs	0.90	0.08	−0.06
got pale	0.76	0.26	−0.52
had stomach troubles	0.66	0.41	−0.41
muscles tensing (whole body)	0.27	0.84	−0.14
breathing getting faster	0.13	0.81	0.44
sweat	0.45	0.71	0.20
heartbeat getting faster	0.07	0.61	0.70
heartbeat slowing down	0.28	−0.82	−0.22
breathing slowing down	0.10	−0.92	0.09
felt warm	−0.30	0.08	0.84
felt cold	0.63	0.00	−0.66
Congruence			
Tucker's phi	1.00	1.00	1.00
$r_{factor\ scores}$	0.96	0.98	0.94

The CoreGRID Expression component

As discussed in Chapter 10, facial and vocal expressions were analyzed separately to acknowledge the different nature of these two expression modalities and to extract the most representative factors in each modality. In contrast to the two emotion components described above, we had no prior expectations about the underlying structure of the Expression component for theoretical or empirical reasons, as there have been few attempts in the expression literature to link individual expression features to underlying dimensions or factors. Using the FullGRID, we could empirically identify a stable three-factorial facial expression structure and a two-factorial vocal expression structure. The three facial expression factors were descriptively labeled FROWN VS SMILE, JAW DROP/EYEBROWS UP, and EYES CLOSED/TEARS. The two vocal expression factors were labeled VOCAL ENERGY and FIRM VS PERTURBED SPEECH. For the final selection of the expression features, we relied on both statistical information and on earlier qualitative interpretations of studies on facial and vocal expressions (Goudbeek & Scherer, 2010; Scherer & Ellgring, 2007a; Scherer, Johnstone, & Klasmeyer, 2003). The original 21 facial and vocal expression features included in the FullGRID were reduced to the following 12 in the CoreGRID:

FROWN VS SMILE

- frowned
- smiled

JAW DROP/EYEBROWS UP

- had the jaw drop
- had the eyebrows go up.

EYES CLOSED/TEARS

- closed her or his eyes
- had tears in the eyes.

VOCAL ENERGY

- spoke louder
- spoke faster
- spoke more slowly.

FIRM VS PERTURBED SPEECH

- had an assertive voice
- had a trembling voice
- had speech disturbances

A factor analysis on the CoreGRID facial and vocal expression features largely replicated the original structures in the FullGRID. For facial expression, the Tucker's phi were all 1.00 and the factor score correlations were higher than 0.82 (see Table 44.3). For the vocal expression factors the Tucker's phi were higher than 0.87 and the factor score correlations higher than 0.95 (see Table 44.4).

The CoreGRID Action tendency component

The features in this component were based on the work of Frijda (Frijda, 1987; Frijda, Kuipers, & ter Schure, 1989; Frijda, Markam, Sato, & Wiers, 1995), who has given much attention to the issue

Table 44.3 Loadings of the CoreGRID facial expression features in a three-factorial Procrustes rotated structure and congruence with FullGRID facial expression structure

	FROWN VS SMILE	JAW DROP/EYEBROWS UP	EYES CLOSED/TEARS
CoreGRID facial expressions			
frowned	0.96	−0.03	−0.10
smiled	−0.94	0.07	−0.22
had the jaw drop	−0.12	0.94	−0.02
had eyebrows go up	−0.17	0.70	−0.55
closed her or his eyes	−0.01	−0.05	0.83
had tears	0.03	0.04	0.84
Congruence			
Tucker's phi	1.00	1.00	1.00
$r_{\text{factor scores}}$	0.98	0.82	0.95

of classifying Action tendencies (see Chapter 11). While he and his collaborators have enumerated quite a large number of such Action tendencies, as reflected in the large number of items in the FullGRID, there has been little effort so far to determine the underlying structure or the superordinate categories. In the GRID study, a three-factorial structure was identified comprising one general Action tendency factor on which almost all action tendencies had their highest or second highest loading, and two subsidiary factors. The first factor opposed appetitive versus defensive action tendencies, in line with the recent theorizing by Frijda (2010). On the two subsidiary factors, disengagement action tendencies were opposed to intervention action tendencies, and submit action tendencies were opposed to attack action tendencies, respectively. Each pole of the three factors was represented by the two most appropriate action tendency features. Moreover, for

Table 44.4 Loadings of the CoreGRID vocal expression features in a three-factorial Procrustes rotated structure and congruence with FullGRID vocal expression structure

	VOCAL ENERGY	FIRM VS PERTURBED SPEECH
CoreGRID vocal expression features		
spoke faster	0.88	−0.32
spoke louder	0.78	−0.46
spoke slower	−0.90	0.23
had speech disturbances	0.25	0.88
had a trembling voice	−0.01	0.91
had an assertive voice	0.29	−0.80
Congruence		
Tucker's phi	0.87	0.99
$r_{\text{factor scores}}$	0.94	0.95

its theoretical relevance for fear emotions, two action tendency features were additionally selected, namely "wanted to run away in whatever direction" and "wanted to disappear or hide from others." Thus, the Action tendency component was operationalized in the CoreGRID by 14 features out of the 40 features in the FullGRID:

DEFENSIVE VS APPETITIVE

- wanted the ongoing situation to last or be repeated
- wanted to sing and dance
- wanted to run away in whatever direction
- wanted to disappear or hide from others
- felt the urge to stop what he or she was doing
- wanted to undo what was happening.

DISENGAGEMENT VS INTERVENTION

- wanted to tackle the situation
- wanted to overcome an obstacle
- lacked the motivation to pay attention to what was going on
- wanted to do nothing.

SUBMIT VS ATTACK

- wanted to oppose
- wanted to do damage, hit, or say something that hurts
- wanted to hand over the initiative to someone else
- wanted to comply to someone else's wishes

After orthogonal Procrustes rotation, the selected 14 features accurately reproduced the Action tendency structure of the FullGRID, with a Tucker's phi of 0.99 and higher in all cases and factor score correlations of 0.91 and higher (see Table 44.5).

The CoreGRID Appraisal component

The features in the Appraisal component in the FullGRID were mostly based on the appraisal criteria or checks postulated by appraisal theorists of emotion (as described and justified in Chapter 1 and Chapter 12). Both the scree plot and the stability of the structure across language groups seemed to point to only a two-factor structure in the Appraisal component, namely VALENCE APPRAISAL and NOVELTY APPRAISAL (see Chapter 12). This could be explained by the fact that virtually all appraisal criteria, except the NOVELTY appraisals, are strongly valenced in and of themselves (e.g., having POWER is positive, and violations of norms are bad; see also Chapter 1) and therefore all load on a single factor. This suggests that there is a VALENCE superfactor or general factor and a number of lower order appraisal factors. We computed the superfactor on the basis of four Appraisal features (positive and negative intrinsic pleasantness and goal conduciveness) and regressed this factor on the other theoretically postulated appraisal items. A subsequent factor analysis on the residual scores yielded six factors that corresponded well to the theoretically postulated groups of appraisal checks, namely NOVELTY/CHANCE CAUSE, COPING ABILITY, EXPECTED/FAMILIAR, GOAL RELEVANCE, NORM VIOLATION, and SELF VS OTHER CAUSE. This structure with one VALENCE APPRAISAL superfactor and six specific appraisal factors was also operationalized in the CoreGRID.

Table 44.5 Loadings of the CoreGRID action tendency features in a three-factorial Procrustes rotated structure and congruence with FullGRID action tendency structure

	DEFENSIVE VS APPETITIVE	DISENGAGEMENT VS INTERVENTION	SUBMIT VS ATTACK
CoreGRID action tendency features			
wanted the ongoing situation to last or be repeated	0.93	0.15	0.21
wanted to sing and dance	0.93	0.10	0.22
wanted to run away in whatever direction	−0.86	−0.34	0.09
wanted to disappear or hide from others	−0.87	−0.39	0.01
felt the urge to stop what he or she was doing	−0.91	−0.20	0.16
wanted to undo what was happening	−0.92	−0.10	0.03
wanted to tackle the situation	0.16	0.87	0.04
wanted to overcome an obstacle	−0.10	0.85	0.25
lacked the motivation to pay attention to what was going on	−0.56	−0.57	0.10
wanted to do nothing	−0.58	−0.61	0.00
wanted to oppose	−0.73	0.11	0.57
wanted to do damage, hit, or say something that hurts	−0.66	0.03	0.65
wanted to hand over the initiative to someone else	−0.45	−0.35	−0.69
wanted to comply to someone else's wishes	0.50	0.06	−0.71
Congruence			
Tucker's phi	1.00	0.99	0.99
$r_{factor\ scores}$	0.98	0.91	0.92

The VALENCE APPRAISAL superfactor was operationalized by the following two appraisal features:

VALENCE APPRAISAL

- in itself pleasant for the person
- consequences negative for person

The factor scores derived from these two features correlated almost perfectly with the original VALENCE APPRAISAL factor ($r = 0.99$).

For each of the six specific appraisal factors two features were selected for the CoreGRID. Only the UNEXPECTED/CHANCE factor was represented by four features, because of the importance of NOVELTY appraisals to define the overall NOVELTY factor. Additionally, the COPING ABILITY factor was represented by three features, because of its theoretical importance for the POWER factor. The following 15 appraisal features were selected:

UNEXPECTED/CHANCE

- suddenly
- unpredictable
- caused by chance
- required an immediate response.

COPING ABILITY

- enough resources to avoid or modify consequences
- consequences avoidable or modifiable
- consequences able to live with.

EXPECTED/FAMILIAR

- confirmed expectations
- consequences predictable.

GOAL RELEVANCE

- important and relevant for person's goals
- important and relevant for goals of somebody else.

NORM VIOLATION

- violated laws or socially accepted norms
- incongruent with own standards and ideals.

SELF VS OTHER CAUSATION

- caused by the person's own behavior
- caused by somebody else's behavior

After orthogonal Procrustes rotation, the selected 15 features reproduced the action tendency structure of the FullGRID very well, with a Tucker's phi of 0.98 and higher for all factors and factor score correlations of 0.87 and higher (see Table 44.6).

For theoretical reasons, the three coping ability items reported above were reformulated in the CoreGRID instrument with respect to the FullGRID, and three new appraisal items were added to them. In Chapter 12, it was observed that the appraisal features selected for the coping potential check only moderately predicted the overall POWER and the overall AROUSAL factors. Theoretically the coping ability features should have been the most important predictors of the POWER factor. The fact that this was not observed can be reasonably attributed to the formulation of these features. Therefore it was decided to reformulate the above three COPING POTENTIAL features as follows:

- the person had POWER over the consequences of the event
- the person could control the consequences of the event
- the person could live with the consequences of the event.

In addition, the following two items were added to capture the powerless pole of the dimension:

- the event that caused this emotion was uncontrollable (new feature)
- the person was powerless in the situation (new feature)

Furthermore, one appraisal feature was added to represent dominance:

- the person had a dominant position in the situation (new feature)

As there was only one appraisal item that loaded on the overall AROUSAL factor, namely "required an immediate response," the following feature was added to better capture the potential need for an urgent response:

- there was no urgency in the situation (new feature)

Thus, in the CoreGRID the Appraisal component was operationalized by 21 features. In total, the final version of the CoreGRID instrument contains 68 features (of which four appraisal features

Table 44.6 Loadings of the residual CoreGRID appraisal features in a six-factorial Procrustes rotated structure and congruence with FullGRID appraisal structure

	NOVELTY/ CHANCE CAUSE	COPING ABILITY	EXPECTED/ FAMILIAR	GOAL RELEVANCE	NORM VIOLATION	SELF VS OTHER CAUSE
Residual CoreGRID appraisal features						
suddenly	0.88	−0.10	0.03	0.0-0	−0.02	0.03
unpredictable	0.84	−0.18	−0.12	0.00	0.04	0.11
caused by chance	0.78	−0.10	0.05	0.09	0.10	0.07
required an immediate response	0.66	0.24	−0.29	0.14	0.05	−0.06
enough resources to avoid or modify consequences	−0.05	0.84	0.12	−0.12	0.06	−0.17
consequences avoidable or modifiable	−0.03	0.80	0.18	−0.04	0.25	−0.14
consequences able to live with	0.00	0.71	0.11	0.32	−0.07	0.20
confirmed expectations	−0.24	0.01	0.75	0.32	−0.03	−0.09
consequences predictable	−0.22	0.38	0.71	0.09	−0.11	−0.18
important and relevant for person's goals	0.11	0.00	−0.05	0.89	−0.06	−0.19
important and relevant for goals of somebody else	0.04	0.05	0.13	0.80	−0.02	0.25
violated laws or socially accepted norms	0.11	0.02	0.00	−0.11	0.84	−0.22
incongruent with own standards and ideals	0.06	0.15	−0.06	0.06	0.84	0.22
caused by somebody else's behavior	0.34	0.01	0.34	0.16	0.03	0.70
caused by the person s own behavior	−0.06	0.24	0.36	0.07	0.09	−0.72
Congruence						
Tucker's phi	0.99	0.99	0.98	0.98	0.99	0.99
$r_{factor\ scores}$	0.98	0.99	0.87	0.97	0.98	0.97

and one feeling feature were added anew for theoretical reasons). This represents a substantial re-duction from the original 144 items of the FullGRID, allowing a more economical rating procedure as more words can be processed in a given amount of time. The final CoreGRID instrument with instructions can be found in Appendix 3 of this volume. In the interest of making the chosen fea-tures as comprehensible and easily translatable as possible, we decided to slightly rephrase certain items without changing their meaning, following the suggestions of several English native-speaker advisers[3]. In consequence, the formulation of some items in the new CoreGRID instrument differs from those in the selection lists provided above for each of the components.

In addition to questions about the five components discussed so far (Appraisal, Bodily reac-tion, Expression, Action tendencies, and Feeling), the original FullGRID also included questions concerning emotion regulation. These were not included in the CoreGRID instrument because, although systematic differences have been observed in the regulation features (see Chapter 10),

[3] The authors would like to thank Tony Manstead, Paula Niedenthal, Jenefer Robinson, and Gerhard Stemmler for their valuable input on this matter.

regulation is not regarded as a separate component of emotion by most theorists and it adds very little to the meaning of emotion words over and above the five major emotion components. Rather than being highly constitutive for the semantic profiles of emotion words, regulation is better understood as a modifier that varies across individuals, groups, and contexts.

The overall structure of the CoreGRID instrument

After the selection of the CoreGRID features, it was also investigated whether they reproduced the overall four-factorial structure. A factor analysis on the 63 features with four factors accounted for 67.14% of the total variance. A simple VARIMAX rotation already revealed the expected structure of VALENCE, POWER, AROUSAL, and NOVELTY (see Table 44.7). Moreover, the scores of the emotion

Table 44.7 Loadings of the 63 CoreGRID features in a four-factorial structure after VARIMAX rotation

CoreGRID features	VALENCE	POWER	AROUSAL	NOVELTY
felt good	0.95	0.25	−0.03	0.06
in itself pleasant for the person	0.95	0.20	−0.01	0.08
wanted to sing and dance	0.94	0.20	0.02	0.07
smiled	0.94	0.22	−0.01	0.08
wanted the ongoing situation to last or be repeated	0.93	0.26	−0.04	0.06
felt calm	0.86	0.16	−0.34	−0.05
important and relevant for person's goals	0.85	0.18	0.00	0.03
important and relevant for goals of somebody else	0.79	0.21	−0.12	0.06
felt strong	0.78	0.53	0.09	−0.03
consequences able to live with	0.76	0.22	−0.15	−0.06
confirmed expectations	0.73	0.26	−0.13	−0.24
wanted to comply to someone else's wishes	0.71	−0.16	−0.12	−0.06
felt warm	0.59	0.25	0.42	−0.07
consequences predictable	0.50	0.22	−0.21	−0.41
caused by the person's own behavior	0.48	0.02	−0.06	−0.35
consequences avoidable or modifiable	−0.37	0.09	−0.12	−0.24
wanted to do nothing	−0.52	−0.49	−0.43	−0.14
produced speech disturbances	−0.53	−0.49	0.37	0.11
lacked the motivation to pay attention to what was going on	−0.54	−0.35	−0.36	−0.17
felt restless	−0.57	−0.07	0.36	−0.03
felt cold	−0.58	−0.51	−0.23	0.14
muscles tensing (whole body)	−0.65	0.09	0.60	0.14
felt weak	−0.68	−0.63	−0.16	−0.06
felt tired	−0.68	−0.36	−0.24	−0.20
got pale	−0.70	−0.56	0.04	0.21
had stomach troubles	−0.72	−0.41	0.21	−0.01
wanted to disappear or hide from others	−0.79	−0.50	−0.10	−0.12

Table 44.7 (continued) Loadings of the 63 CoreGRID features in a four-factorial structure after VARIMAX rotation

CoreGRID features	VALENCE	POWER	AROUSAL	NOVELTY
violated laws or socially accepted norms	−0.81	−0.07	−0.03	0.06
wanted to run away in whatever direction	−0.81	−0.45	0.06	−0.02
wanted to undo what was happening	−0.84	−0.27	−0.08	−0.10
wanted to do damage, hit, or say something that hurts	−0.85	0.26	0.03	−0.11
frowned	−0.88	0.18	−0.07	−0.04
wanted to oppose	−0.88	0.25	0.02	−0.10
incongruent with own standards and ideals	−0.89	−0.07	−0.12	0.07
felt the urge to stop what he or she was doing	−0.89	−0.28	−0.02	−0.05
felt bad	−0.91	−0.32	−0.07	−0.10
consequences negative for person	−0.92	−0.19	−0.07	0.01
had an assertive voice	0.28	0.78	−0.01	−0.08
spoke louder	0.11	0.70	0.39	0.20
wanted to tackle the situation	0.22	0.57	0.12	−0.15
wanted to overcome an obstacle	0.08	0.35	0.17	−0.19
wanted to hand over the initiative to someone else	−0.15	−0.60	−0.10	−0.08
had tears	−0.00	−0.62	−0.08	−0.16
had a trembling voice	−0.44	−0.66	0.20	0.04
closed her or his eyes	0.01	−0.69	−0.25	−0.13
felt weak limbs	−0.29	−0.75	0.17	0.20
breathing getting faster	−0.08	0.13	0.89	0.21
heartbeat getting faster	0.23	0.11	0.87	0.18
sweat	−0.36	−0.16	0.72	0.07
spoke faster	0.25	0.51	0.67	0.19
was in an intense emotional state	0.14	−0.17	0.45	−0.07
spoke slower	−0.01	−0.51	−0.67	−0.17
breathing slowing down	0.40	−0.18	−0.69	−0.09
heartbeat slowing down	0.08	−0.29	−0.75	−0.05
unpredictable	0.01	−0.16	0.14	0.79
suddenly	0.16	−0.08	0.19	0.73
had the jaw drop	0.14	−0.00	−0.11	0.73
caused by chance	0.43	−0.00	0.07	0.63
had eyebrows go up	0.18	0.47	0.04	0.59
required an immediate response	−0.09	0.11	0.36	0.50
caused by somebody else's behavior	−0.15	0.28	−0.12	0.40
enough resources to avoid or modify consequences	−0.04	0.19	−0.14	−0.29
experienced the emotional state for a long time	0.26	−0.23	−0.11	−0.58

terms on these CoreGRID factors correlated very highly with the factor scores on the FullGRID overall factors, namely 0.99, 0.96, 0.95, and 0.92 for VALENCE, POWER, AROUSAL, and NOVELTY, respectively. Thus, the CoreGRID faithfully reproduces the overall factor structure of the FullGRID.

Classification accuracy

Finally, the accuracy of the classification of the 24 emotion terms on the basis of the CoreGRID and the FullGRID was compared. The accuracy of the classification was computed on the basis of the 63 CoreGRID features, the 22 CoreGRID emotion component factors, the four overall CoreGRID factors, the 142 FullGRID features, the 22 FullGRID emotion component factors, and the four

Table 44.8 Comparison between the CoreGRID and the FullGRID with respect to the classification accuracy for the 24 emotion words in discriminant analyses based on individual features, emotion component factor scores, and overall factor scores

Emotion words	FullGRID 142 features	CoreGRID 63 features	FullGRID Component factor scores	CoreGRID Component factor scores	FullGRID Overall factor scores	CoreGRID Overall factor scores
being hurt	85.3	82.4	70.6	70.6	41.2	50.0
sadness	88.2	85.3	94.1	94.1	82.4	82.4
shame	91.2	88.2	88.2	82.4	79.4	58.8
guilt	94.1	97.1	91.2	91.2	97.1	97.1
compassion	94.1	91.2	88.2	88.2	79.4	85.3
disappointment	85.3	85.3	79.4	82.4	76.5	82.4
love	97.1	97.1	97.1	91.2	97.1	88.2
contentment	73.5	70.6	70.6	73.5	67.6	67.6
happiness	38.2	47.1	38.2	47.1	58.8	50.0
pride	91.2	94.1	91.2	91.2	82.4	82.4
pleasure	67.6	70.6	61.8	61.8	38.2	29.4
joy	44.1	61.8	64.7	64.7	67.6	61.8
interest	97.1	94.1	91.2	91.2	79.4	88.2
surprise	100.0	100.0	100.0	100.0	100.0	97.1
despair	91.2	70.6	76.5	61.8	35.3	29.4
stress	91.2	85.3	82.4	79.4	70.6	52.9
anxiety	76.5	67.6	70.6	61.8	50.0	41.2
fear	94.1	94.1	91.2	91.2	82.4	79.4
jealousy	91.2	97.1	91.2	100.0	73.5	70.6
hate	79.4	73.5	79.4	85.3	67.6	61.8
irritation	58.8	70.6	61.8	64.7	11.8	38.2
anger	70.6	73.5	70.6	70.6	67.6	67.6
disgust	88.2	85.3	85.3	79.4	94.1	88.2
contempt	82.4	85.3	79.4	79.4	64.7	67.6
Total	82.1	82.0	79.8	79.3	69.4	67.4

overall FullGRID factors. The comparisons of the cross-classified accuracy in the multiple discriminant analyses show there is virtually no loss going from the FullGRID to the CoreGRID on each of the three levels of analysis, namely the level of the individual features, the level of the emotion component factors, and on the level of the four overall factors (see Table 44.8). The loss in overall accuracy is 2% or less. Looking at the accuracy percentages for the individual emotions, the picture shows more variation. For some emotion terms, the discrimination by the CoreGRID features is higher than for the FullGRID features; for other emotion terms the reverse is observed. This suggests that some of the features *not* included in the CoreGRID might in fact facilitate confusions. This is the case for some of the positive emotions, which are often confused among each other in the classification as well as for *irritation*, often confused with *anger*.

All in all the comparisons between the CoreGRID and the FullGRID clearly indicate that both the emotion component factors and the overall factors are adequately reproduced by the CoreGRID, and that the CoreGRID feature patterns allow for almost as good an identification of the associated emotion terms as the one afforded by the FullGRID.

44.2 **Development of the MiniGRID instrument**

The MiniGRID, designed as a rapid screening instrument, was developed to assess the position of emotion terms on the four overall factors VALENCE, POWER, AROUSAL, and NOVELTY with only three to four features per dimension.

The construction of the MiniGRID was based on the following guidelines:

1 The MiniGRID features had to be a subset of the features selected for the CoreGRID.

2 Features from all emotion components (except Feeling, for reasons explained below) were to be represented. The Feeling component was not included for theoretical and pragmatic reasons. From a theoretical standpoint, the Feeling component is an emergent component triggered by activity in the Appraisal, Bodily reaction, Expression, and Action tendency components, which directly determines the feeling dimensions (see Chapter 1 and Chapter 8). The pragmatic reason is that the Feeling component factors add very little to the discriminative POWER of the component factors (see Chapter 13).

3 Features should be selected to represent the information in the four overall dimensions of VALENCE, POWER, AROUSAL, and NOVELTY, as well as possible.

4 The selected features per emotion component should empirically reproduce the overall factor structure of the FullGRID. After Procrustes rotation of the overall factors in the MiniGRID to the overall factors in the FullGRID, the congruence (Tucker's phi) should be at least 0.85 per factor and the factor scores should correlate at least at 0.80.[4]

5 The features of the MiniGRID had to achieve a good accuracy level in classifying the 24 emotion terms by discriminant analysis.

Based on these guidelines, the following 14 features were selected (the minus sign shown after some features indicates that they represent the negative pole of the respective dimension):

VALENCE

- event in itself pleasant for the person
- frowned (−)
- wanted to sing and dance.

---

[4] See note 2.

POWER

- spoke louder
- felt weak limbs (−)
- closed his or her eyes (−)
- wanted to tackle the situation.

AROUSAL

- breathing getting faster
- sweat
- heartbeat getting faster.

NOVELTY

- suddenly
- unpredictable
- caused by chance
- had the jaw drop

As for the CoreGRID, in the interest of documenting systematic differences in intensity and duration in future research, we included the following two GRID features in the MiniGRID, bringing the number of features to 16:

Intensity

- was in an intense emotional state.

Duration

- experienced the emotion for a long time

The complete version of the MiniGRID, together with the suggested instructions, is reproduced in Appendix 4 of this volume (a Word document that can be duplicated directly for paper administration is available in Appendix 5). As described earlier, some of the original features were slightly reworded in the CoreGRID for easier readability. These improved versions were also used in the MiniGRID.

The overall structure of the MiniGRID instrument

A factor analysis was executed on the 14 component-related MiniGRID features (excluding intensity and duration, as these additional items would take too much weight in analysis with only 14 component-related features). A four factor solution accounted for 76.71% of the total variance. After orthogonal Procrustes rotation these four factors were highly congruent with the overall FullGRID factors (see Table 44.9). The Tucker's phi were 1.00, 0.99, 0.99, and 0.99 for VALENCE, POWER, AROUSAL, and NOVELTY, respectively. Moreover, also the factor scores were highly correlated between both versions. The Pearson correlations between them were 0.97, 0.89, 0.91, and 0.87 for VALENCE, POWER, AROUSAL, and NOVELTY, respectively.

Classification accuracy

The accuracy of the classification of the 24 emotion terms on the basis of the 14 component-related MiniGRID features (excluding intensity and duration, for the same reason given above) and the four overall MiniGRID factors has been compared with the accuracy of classification achieved on the basis of the 142 FullGRID features and the four overall FullGRID factors, respectively.

Table 44.9 Loadings of the 14 MiniGRID features in a four-factorial structure after Procrustes rotation

MiniGRID features	VALENCE	POWER	AROUSAL	NOVELTY
in itself pleasant for the person	0.95	0.17	−0.03	0.07
wanted to sing and dance	0.95	0.16	0.00	0.05
frowned	−0.91	0.19	−0.09	−0.06
spoke louder	0.15	0.74	0.32	0.13
wanted to tackle the situation	0.25	0.66	−0.05	−0.17
felt weak limbs	−0.32	−0.72	0.33	0.20
closed her or his eyes	−0.00	−0.82	−0.13	−0.08
breathing getting faster	−0.06	0.27	0.90	0.13
heartbeat getting faster	0.25	0.24	0.88	0.11
sweat	−0.34	−0.06	0.81	0.00
unpredictable	−0.02	−0.08	0.17	0.85
suddenly	0.14	0.03	0.20	0.84
had the jaw drop	0.13	0.06	−0.06	0.72
caused by chance	0.46	0.05	0.07	0.68

The comparison of the accuracy in the multiple discriminant analyses shows there is a loss when going from the FullGRID to the MiniGRID for each of the two levels of analysis (see Table 44.10). However, the accuracy with the MiniGRID is still very high and much higher than the 4.2% that can be expected with random classification. With only 14 features, 69.9% of the terms could still be correctly classified (instead of the 82.1% achieved by the 142 features of the FullGRID), and with the four overall factors of the MiniGRID, 61.4% could still be correctly classified, instead of the 69.4% afforded by the overall factors in the FullGRID. The loss in accuracy is thus relatively minor, given that there are almost ten times fewer features. But, interestingly, in the case of the MiniGRID, there are disproportionally high losses for some of the less frequently studied emotions like *being hurt*, *despair*, and *compassion*, as well as for some of the most common ones, like *anger* and *anxiety*.

Scale scores for the MiniGRID factors

Finally, as the MiniGRID is meant to be used as a screening instrument, we also looked at the simple scale scores to estimate the position of emotion terms on each of the four dimensions. The scale scores are computed as the sum of the respective feature scores. The scales are fairly reliable for each of the four factors. The Cronbach's alpha is 0.93, 0.72, 0.86, and 0.79 for VALENCE, POWER, AROUSAL, and NOVELTY, respectively. Moreover, the scales scores are very highly correlated with the overall factor scores of the MiniGRID (namely 0.99, 0.97, 0.97, and 0.96 for VALENCE, POWER, AROUSAL, and NOVELTY, respectively) and with the overall factor scores of the FullGRID (namely 0.97, 0.89, 0.91, and 0.84 for VALENCE, POWER, AROUSAL, and NOVELTY, respectively). Furthermore, there is almost no loss when the scale scores are used instead of the MiniGRID factor scores in a multiple discriminant analysis (only a loss of 1.1% cross-classified accuracy). Thus, simple scale scores can be used to assess the position of emotion terms in the four-factorial structure.

Table 44.10 Comparison between the MiniGRID and the FullGRID with respect to the classification accuracy for the 24 emotion words in discriminant analyses based on individual features, overall factor scores, and scale scores

Emotion words	FullGRID 142 features	MiniGRID 14 features	FullGRID overall factor scores	MiniGRID overall factor scores	MiniGRID overall scale scores
being hurt	85.3	38.2	41.2	35.3	26.5
sadness	88.2	85.3	82.4	73.5	70.6
shame	91.2	73.5	79.4	50.0	52.9
guilt	94.1	88.2	97.1	88.2	82.4
compassion	94.1	79.4	79.4	67.6	67.6
disappointment	85.3	73.5	76.5	76.5	70.6
love	97.1	94.1	97.1	82.4	82.4
contentment	73.5	61.8	67.6	67.6	61.8
happiness	38.2	50.0	58.8	38.2	32.4
pride	91.2	91.2	82.4	88.2	91.2
pleasure	67.6	64.7	38.2	29.4	32.4
joy	44.1	61.8	67.6	70.6	67.6
interest	97.1	91.2	79.4	85.3	88.2
surprise	100.0	100.0	100.0	100.0	100.0
despair	91.2	41.2	35.3	38.2	32.4
stress	91.2	73.5	70.6	55.9	55.9
anxiety	76.5	52.9	50.0	50.0	47.1
fear	94.1	85.3	82.4	79.4	88.2
jealousy	91.2	73.5	73.5	44.1	44.1
hate	79.4	64.7	67.6	67.6	64.7
irritation	58.8	38.2	11.8	26.5	20.6
anger	70.6	61.8	67.6	67.6	61.8
disgust	88.2	67.6	94.1	38.2	47.1
contempt	82.4	64.7	64.7	52.9	58.8
Total	82.1	69.9	69.4	61.4	60.3

44.3 Conclusions

The analyses on the two short versions of the GRID instrument, the CoreGRID (68 items), and the MiniGRID (16 items), confirm the extraordinary stability of the componential structure of the emotion terms and of the internal factors within each component. The fact that the very high discriminability of the emotion terms is conserved, after a drastic reduction in the number of features used, testifies to the robustness, but also the shared prototypical core of the meaning of major emotion terms. While an individual's emotions might vary widely in a complex manner based on subjective appraisal and salient aspects of the context, the representation of what types of antecedents and responses should be represented in the componential meaning of common emotion terms seems to be highly constrained. This is to be expected, of course, for words in a language constitute a code used for communication in a given culture, which requires conciseness and stability of meaning.

The CoreGRID may become the default instrument for most research purposes in the future. It offers a highly satisfactory trade-off between economy and informational value. With only 68 features, it accurately captures the major factors in each of the emotion components put forward by the Component Process Model, and it affords a very good accuracy in the discrimination of emotion terms on the basis of their feature profile. If one is only interested in identifying the position of a large set of emotion terms in the overall four-dimensional space of VALENCE, POWER, AROUSAL, and NOVELTY, the MiniGRID constitutes a good alternative. However, if one is interested in identifying differences between related emotion terms within or between languages, or is interested in a more exhaustive representation of one or more emotion components, the FullGRID instrument remains the best choice.

Chapter 45

Promises delivered, future opportunities, and challenges for the GRID paradigm

Johnny J. R. Fontaine,[1] Klaus R. Scherer, and Cristina Soriano

The GRID instrument was developed to study the meaning of emotion terms from a theoretical vantage point whereby emotions are considered as processes that synchronize different components—event appraisal and the consequent action tendencies, bodily changes, motor expressions, and subjective experiences reflecting the component changes. Postulating a domain-specific approach to semantics, we proposed to measure the meaning of emotion terms in natural language through probability estimates of profiles of component features that characterize major emotion categories and for which translation-equivalent words exist in many different languages. This approach allows assessment of the meaning of emotion words in a way that is relevant for many theoretical approaches to emotion and that accommodates the perspectives taken by the three main disciplines involved in the study of emotion words: psychology, cultural comparative studies (specifically cultural anthropology and cross-cultural psychology), and linguistics. In this concluding chapter, we discuss, on the basis of the massive data set reported in this volume, the extent to which the GRID instrument is capable of delivering on its promise. In addition, we reflect on the future opportunities afforded by the GRID, its limitations, and its foreseeable challenges. We start by discussing the validity of the GRID as an assessment instrument for meaning. We then examine the implications of the findings for a psychological perspective on emotions, first for the componential approach to emotion (specifically the Component Process Model; Scherer, 2009c; see Chapter 1), which constitutes the theoretical basis of the GRID paradigm, and then for basic emotion and dimensional approaches. We continue by discussing the relevance of the GRID paradigm for the cultural-comparative and linguistic perspectives in the study of emotion categories. We conclude with a discussion of the lexical sedimentation hypothesis in the emotion domain.

45.1 The GRID instrument as an assessment tool

Promises delivered

The GRID instrument was developed to assess the meaning of emotion words in a quantified and standardized way. In the domain of psychological assessment, an extensive formal framework has been developed to evaluate the quality of assessment instruments (e.g., Messick, 1989). Three

---

[1] Corresponding author: Johnny J. R. Fontaine. Department of Personnel, Work and Organisational Psychology. Faculty of Psychology and Educational Sciences. Ghent University. Henri-Dunantlaan 2, 9000 Gent, Belgium. Johnny.Fontaine@UGent.be

major criteria particularly apply in evaluating the quality of the GRID instrument: reliability, construct validity, and generalizability.

The first quality criterion of an assessment instrument is reliability. The question is whether the assessment is reproducible. In the GRID study, we have looked at one form of reliability, namely interrater reliability. We have assessed whether and to what extent reliable componential emotion profiles could be obtained across judges who evaluate the same emotion term (see Chapter 6). For most emotion terms, it was observed that with 20 to 25 judges, it was possible to identify reliable meaning profiles, with Cronbach's alpha exceeding 0.80 and in many cases 0.90. However, this overall observation has to be qualified in two ways. First, the judgments by students were more reliable than the judgments by non-student adults. Second, reliability tended to be higher in Western than in non-Western samples (e.g., see Chapters 6, 31, and 32). Both effects are likely to be method artifacts. As the GRID instrument is web-based, it requires familiarity with a computerized testing environment. Western students are probably more familiar with such a testing environment than are adults and non-Western samples, leading to more reliable responding.

The second quality criterion is construct validity. The question is whether the instrument indeed assesses the intended construct. Three aspects of construct validity are of particular relevance for the GRID instrument: (a) the content aspect of construct validity, (b) the internal structure aspect of construct validity, and (c) trait validity (or replicability across different methods). (a) The content aspect of construct validity deals with the question of whether and to what extent the items and stimuli are representative and relevant for the intended domain of study. Although the GRID instrument does not claim to exhaustively represent the features that can play a role in the meaning of emotion terms, the operationalization of the Component Process Model by different theoretical frameworks for each of the emotion components guarantees the relevance and representativeness of the content of the instrument (see Chapter 5). All components have been operationalized in the questionnaire and, for each component, features were identified that were considered relevant for the emotion domain according to the respective theories. (b) The second aspect relative to construct validity is the internal structure of the instrument. The question is whether the relationships among the stimuli can be represented by a theoretically interpretable internal structure. It was observed that the internal structure of each emotion component separately, as well as the internal structure across all emotion components, could be represented by low-dimensional factor structures, with each of the factors being well interpretable in terms of the respective emotion theories (see Chapters 7–13). (c) The third important aspect of construct validity is trait validity. The question in this case is whether there is a convergence between the GRID method and alternative methods for the assessment of the meaning of emotion words. Besides conceptual relationships with other linguistic approaches (e.g., Chapter 27), converging empirical results were observed between the GRID instrument and similarity approaches (see Chapter 14), metaphor approaches (see Chapter 28), and corpus approaches to the study of meaning (see Chapters 29 and 30). There is thus converging evidence for the construct validity of the GRID instrument.

The final criterion of quality for assessment instruments is population generalizability. The question in this case is whether and to what extent the instrument can be generalized to other contexts, especially to other cultural groups. Overall there is strong evidence for generalizability in the GRID. In virtually all samples, the instrument was adequately completed and empirical evidence was found for equivalence of the internal structure in the four best represented language groups: Germanic, Romance, Slavic, and what we could call East-Asian (i.e., Chinese and Japanese; see Chapters 7–12). This overall conclusion has to be qualified, though; in a few cultural groups, for instance in two Black African samples (see Chapter 32), the instrument did not work sufficiently well to include the data in the analysis. Future investigations will be required to determine whether this can be attributed to methodological factors biasing the assessment, or whether fundamental cultural differences exist in how the emotion domain is cognitively represented in those cultures.

In general, it can be concluded that the GRID instrument is a reliable and valid assessment instrument. Twenty to twenty-five judges can generate reliable meaning profiles that represent all emotion components, and these profiles give rise to coherent and theoretically interpretable internal structures that are replicated across cultural groups and that relate systematically to other methods for the study of the meaning of emotion words.

Future challenges and opportunities

Three important aspects of the GRID instrument can be further developed in the future, namely the selection of emotion terms and emotion features, the types of analyses performed on the GRID data, and the length of the instrument.

Concerning the first aspect, both the terms and the features were carefully selected to represent the variability in the emotion domain. However, future research can extend the use of the GRID instrument by including additional features and additional emotion terms. Studying additional emotion terms, over and above the 24 employed in this study, is an obvious next step, as the goal of the GRID paradigm is to assess the meaning of emotion terms in general. Adding emotion features can also be interesting, since only one or two dominant theories were used for the operationalization of most components. There are many more theories, the operationalization of which could be valuable in the future. However, it can be reasonably expected that adding emotion terms and emotion features will not (or only marginally) affect the overall structures that were discovered with the current instrument, because both the current emotion terms and the current features can be considered as representative for the emotion domain.

A second aspect where development is expected, concerns the methods used in the statistical analysis of the GRID data so far. As the goal was to use the GRID across theoretical approaches and disciplines, only standard analysis methods that are frequently used in the social sciences have been applied (e.g., principal component analysis, regression analysis, and discriminant analysis). Given that the data are extremely rich and show a multilevel structure, with raters being nested in cultural groups, it would be exciting to apply more sophisticated analysis methods, such as multilevel component analysis (e.g., Timmerman, 2006) or network analysis (e.g., Cramer et al., 2012).

Finally, a very important aspect for further development is the length of the instrument. Judges needed about one hour to rate all the features for only four emotion words at a time. This investment in time and effort makes it difficult to use the GRID instrument in certain contexts where many words have to be judged or where rapid results are required (as in applied settings). Because we anticipated this problem, we created two alternative versions for the original GRID instrument, the CoreGRID, which contains 68 items, and the MiniGRID, which contains 16 items (see Chapter 44).

The CoreGRID has been constructed according to the same general principles as the full instrument. With less than half of the items, it still represents the factors identified by the full GRID for all emotion components, as well as the four overall dimensions VALENCE, POWER, AROUSAL, and NOVELTY. In Chapter 44, we showed that the CoreGRID achieves results that are close to the results obtained with the full instrument, at least for the current data set. Therefore, we suggest that the CoreGRID can be used for basic and applied research in which a lower level of comprehensiveness and detail can be tolerated, given that the result closely approaches that of the full version. The use of the full version is recommended for all those cases in which a standard is to be established for a particular language or a particular domain of words—especially in cases in which direct comparison with the current database is intended.

A second, very short, instrument has been developed, the MiniGRID, which differs markedly from the full and the CoreGRID in that it does not attempt to produce a comprehensive semantic profile. Rather, it focuses on the position of words on the four overall dimensions that define the emotion domain: VALENCE, POWER, AROUSAL, and NOVELTY. By choosing the best predictor features from all components, we were able to select a pool of 16 features that allows for the prediction of these overall factors with high accuracy (with correlations exceeding 0.84 between the full and the MiniGRID factor scores). While the MiniGRID cannot be used to establish detailed semantic profiles for specific emotion words, it gives an accurate estimate of the position of a word on the four major dimensions of the emotion space. Thus, it is recommended to be used in all those cases in which this kind of resolution (which is likely to be close to what can be achieved with multidimensional scaling of similarity ratings) is considered sufficient for the research aim or application at hand. Moreover, the MiniGRID features can be used as response items to define the position of an emotion in four-dimensional space in research areas where modal emotion responses are unlikely (e.g., marketing/product research and research in esthetic domains: music, literature, and cinema), or where researchers want to avoid regular emotion words.

We end this section by pointing out that the GRID can also be used in the future to construct or improve new instruments in the emotion domain. For instance, because the GRID instrument represents the emotion domain in a balanced way and gives insight into the relationships between the emotion components, it can be used to improve the assessment of emotional intelligence (see Chapter 19).

45.2 **Psychological perspectives: The componential approach**

Psychologists have a hard time agreeing on the nature and definition of emotion (see Chapters 1 and 2). There is general agreement that (1) emotion episodes have several components (such as bodily reactions, facial/vocal expressions, and subjective feelings); (2) these episodes can be grouped into more or less prototypical categories for which most languages have developed labels; and (3) both nonverbal and verbally labeled emotional experiences can be represented in a lower order dimensional space (e.g., VALENCE, POWER, and AROUSAL). The different theoretical approaches in psychology do not agree, however, on the relative importance of these three elements (i.e., component features, categories and dimensions) and how they map into each other. We maintain that the GRID paradigm can help to clarify this conundrum and we will successively evaluate the relevance of the data gathered in this study for (a) the componential approach (with an emphasis on the Component Process Model) and (b) the basic emotion and dimensional approaches. We will conclude this overview of the relevance of the GRID for the psychological study of emotion with an attempt to integrate the three approaches. In the remainder of this section we will discuss the componential approach. Categorical and dimensional approaches will be discussed in section 45.3.

Promises delivered

The GRID instrument has been developed on the basis of the Component Process Model (CPM) (see Chapters 1 and 5). The basic theoretical proposition of the CPM is that an emotion is a process elicited by a goal-relevant event that consists of a coordinated change in each of the involved human subsystems to prepare a rapid adaptive reaction. The three fundamental hypotheses generated from the CPM were that (1) emotion terms refer to a change in activity in each of the emotion components; (2) each of the components are characterized by their own internal structure, as each of them fulfils its own particular function in the emotion process; and (3) the emotion components

are substantially interrelated, as they synchronize during an emotion process. These three fundamental hypotheses were fully confirmed in the GRID research. (1) It was indeed observed that
emotion terms across languages and cultural groups refer to changes in Appraisals, Bodily reactions, Expressions, Feelings, and Action tendencies, as well as to regulatory efforts to deal with
them (see Chapters 7–13). (2) Moreover, each emotion component was indeed characterized by its
own internal structure (see Chapters 8–12). (3) Finally, the relationships across all features from
each of the emotion components could be represented by a low-dimensional structure, as could
be expected if these emotion components synchronize during an emotion process (see Chapters 7
and 13).

The internal structures of the individual emotion components are especially highlighted in this
section, as the GRID project is the first to systematically study the internal meaning structure of
each individual emotion component on the basis of its respective features. The most important
aspect in the representation of the Appraisal component was whether an event is good or bad for
the person (VALENCE). Beyond this overall VALENCE APPRAISAL factor, six additional appraisal
dimensions could be identified: NOVELTY, COPING ABILITY, CONFIRMATION OF EXPECTATIONS,
GOAL RELEVANCE, NORM VIOLATION, and SELF/OTHER CAUSATION (see Chapter 12). In the representation of the Action tendency component, the GRID revealed a prominent factor opposing APPETITIVE VS DEFENSIVE action tendencies. Two other factors also emerged, one opposing
DISENGAGEMENT to INTERVENTION, and another opposing SUBMITTING to ATTACKING action
tendencies (see Chapter 11). For the Bodily reaction component, three readily interpretable factors emerged, one concerning DISTRESS SYMPTOMS, another AUTONOMIC AROUSAL, and a third
BODY TEMPERATURE (see Chapter 9). For the Expression component, it was observed that the
facial channels and the vocal channels are very different in meaning and internal structure (see
Chapter 10). Three facial expression factors were observed: FROWNING VS SMILING, JAW DROP-
RAISED EYEBROWS, and CLOSED EYES-TEARS. Two different vocal factors emerged: VOCAL ENERGY
and having a FIRM VS PERTURBED SPEECH.

The internal structure of the Feeling component revealed a paradoxical finding (see Chapter 8).
On the one hand, VALENCE dominated the component to a much more important extent than it did
for the other components. On the other hand, a complex four-factorial structure could still be robustly identified across language families. In addition to VALENCE, not one, but two AROUSAL factors emerged (RESTLESSNESS and TIREDNESS), as well as a POWER factor. The structure of the Feeling
component indicates that the models that have dominated the emotion assessment literature—in
particular the positive/negative affect model (Watson & Tellegen, 1985), the pleasure–AROUSAL
model (Russell, 1980), the tense AROUSAL and energetic AROUSAL model (Thayer, 1989), and the
pleasantness–activation model (Larsen & Diener, 1992)—are not just variations that can be represented in a common two-dimensional structure (Yik, Russell, & Feldman Barrett, 1999). At least
when it comes to the meaning of emotion terms, each of them captures only one aspect of the
four-dimensional structure of the Feeling component.

Future challenges and opportunities

The separate analyses on the internal structure of each emotion component generated many
interesting questions for future research. For the Appraisal component, the results invite future research to operationalize the individual appraisal checks with a more comprehensive
number of features and to systematically look at interaction effects between appraisals. Since
many checks were operationalized by only one feature, they could not be identified as separate
factors in the internal structure. The aspects of control, POWER, and adjustment in particular

need to be separated and represented better by appropriate features. Moreover, according to the CPM, the appraisal process is essentially configurational rather than additive: it predicts that separate appraisals will interact with one another in a successive and Gestalt-like way to drive the emotion process. This requires going beyond the linear analysis methods that were predominantly applied in this book and especially looking at interaction effects between appraisals.

A further issue concerns Action tendencies. The analyses of this component revealed that seemingly incompatible responses, such as fleeing and attacking, tended to be similarly related to the meaning of emotion terms. They all shared the same high loading on the APPETITIVE VS DEFENSIVE action tendency factor. A question for future research is whether this observation points to a mere linguistic phenomenon or represents how action tendencies are activated during actual emotion processes. It could be that seemingly incompatible action tendencies are associated in terms of meaning just because they share the same VALENCE. In this case, the association would just be a linguistic phenomenon. However, it may also be that seemingly incompatible emotion action tendencies can be elicited within the same emotion process in order to allow for a rapid change of the eventual behavior as a function of the precise development of the emotional event. For instance, when a prey perceives a predator, it would be adaptive that fight, freeze, and flight responses are conjointly prepared, so that the animal can switch its behavior rapidly depending on the changing distance of the predator. In this case, language would reveal a genuine property of the Action tendency component.

The findings in the Bodily reaction component raise important issues about the underlying processes. Only one of its three factors could be clearly linked to physiological mechanisms; namely AUTONOMIC AROUSAL could be related to sympathetic AROUSAL (e.g., heartbeat going up). It is less clear which physiological mechanisms the other two factors refer to. TEMPERATURE may refer to a homeostatic process where very high and low temperatures point to a basic deregulation of the system. The DISTRESS SYMPTOMS factor seems to refer to a bodily protective reaction in which blood flow is channelled to the essential organs and withdrawn from the periphery (such as the muscles) and the less central organs for immediate survival (such as the stomach). A challenge for future research will be to further explore the meaning of these two latter factors and to validate their interpretation.

For the Expression component, only a few gestural features were included in the questionnaire. Future research is needed to operationalize gestural expressions more extensively and to see how the internal structure relates to vocal and facial expressions.

Finally, an important question emerging from the Feeling component is why a separate TENSE AROUSAL and a separate TIREDNESS factor could still be identified over and above the VALENCE and POWER factors. It may also be useful to investigate the interpretation of TIREDNESS as a wake–sleep cycle factor.

Further research is also desirable to explore alternative operationalizations of the components and their relationships. As mentioned in the previous section, for most of the five emotion components, only one dominant theory was extensively operationalized (see Chapter 5). In future research, it would be interesting to systematically compare different theories for a single component, as was done for the Feeling component in the current GRID instrument (see Chapter 8). For instance, for the Appraisal component, Lazarus's core relational theme appraisal theory (Lazarus, 1991b) and Roseman's structural appraisal theory (Roseman, 2001) could be systematically compared with the CPM.

To keep the results to be discussed manageable, we only investigated the relationship of each emotion component with the overall emotion structure (from which the respective emotion component had been removed) (see Chapters 8–13). Research on how the mutual relationships between emotion components are represented in language would be very timely.

45.3 Psychological perspectives: The basic emotion and dimensional approaches

Promises delivered

Emotion theories start from different vantage points, and thus view the phenomenon under study—emotion—from different angles. This fact alone often accounts for many of the debates since the days of William James. The most obvious, tangible, and accessible approach for studying emotion is to investigate emotion categories, precisely because natural languages contain the kinds of emotion labels we have studied in the GRID. As we saw in the introductory section, many emotion theorists propose going beyond these categories and either looking at specific components, or at dimensions. What we have tried to show in this book is that each of these three approaches (basic emotion, dimensional, and componential) constitutes a valuable vantage point for studying both emotion and its representation in language (see Chapter 2).

In the previous section we separately discussed the componential feature profile approach, because it formed the basis for the development of the GRID instrument (see Chapter 1). The GRID results clearly support the hypothesis that emotion terms can be defined as patterns of features that represent the state of each emotion component during an emotion process. In this section, we discuss whether and to what extent the GRID results are also relevant for the basic emotion and the dimensional approaches in the study of emotion, both of which are prominent in psychology (see Chapter 2).

The basic emotion approach. According to the basic emotion approach, there are a limited number of qualitatively different and biologically rooted emotions. Three hypotheses were developed on the basis of the basic emotion literature (see Chapter 5): (1) basic emotion terms were expected to have a more stable meaning across languages and cultures, as they would refer to universal biologically rooted emotion processes; (2) on the grounds of the similarity sorting literature, emotion terms would cluster into four basic emotion categories (e.g., Fontaine, Poortinga, Setiadi, & Markam, 2002; Shaver, Schwartz, Kirson, & O'Connor, 1987)—joy, anger, fear, and sadness—which represent emotions that are recognized by all basic emotion theorists as basic emotions; and (3) if the emotion domain is organized in terms of qualitatively different and internally coherent emotion processes that are each labeled by different emotion words, then people should infer these emotion processes from each of the emotion labels.

The second and third hypotheses were clearly confirmed. Earlier findings were replicated by using hierarchical cluster analysis on profile similarities from which four large emotion families were identified in the emotion domain: joy, fear, sadness, and anger (see Chapter 7). Moreover, a particular emotion process was indeed inferred from each of the 24 emotion terms. It was possible to correctly assign up to 81% of all emotion terms across all samples to one of the 24 emotion categories on the basis of their feature patterns (see Chapter 7). Thus, across cultural and linguistic groups, the 24 emotion terms tended to be characterized by a stably differentiated meaning profile. The first hypothesis, however, was not confirmed. There was no tendency for presumably basic emotion terms to have a more stable componential pattern than "non-basic" emotion terms (see Chapter 7). In general, emotion terms that referred to interpersonal contexts (such as *being hurt, guilt, shame, love*, and *hate . . .*), which were expected to vary the most across cultures, were not less stable in meaning than the presumed basic emotion terms, which were expected to be more stable (such as *joy* and *fear*).

The dimensional approach. Since much emotion research, especially research using emotion terms, relies on a dimensional model of emotions, the insight afforded by the GRID data on the dimensional approach is particularly relevant for psychology (see Chapter 2). From the dimensional emotion literature (e.g., Shaver et al., 1987), it was expected that the meaning of emotion terms could be represented in a three-dimensional space characterized by the dimensions of VALENCE, POWER, and AROUSAL. As predicted, VALENCE, POWER, and AROUSAL were found to define the emotion structure in that order of importance on the basis of the feature profiles of the emotion terms. Moreover, a fourth smaller factor emerged across language groups—NOVELTY (see Chapter 7).

This low-dimensional representation does not conflict with the componential approach to emotions discussed in the previous section. According to the CPM, the defining characteristic of an emotion process is the synchronization between emotion components (see Chapter 1). This implies that clear relationships are expected between them. In a factor analysis, this coherence between the components would be represented by a low-dimensional factor model. While the GRID data clearly lends itself to a low-dimensional representation, the emerging structure differs in two important ways from the commonly used dimensional models in psychology. These models are two-dimensional and generally represent VALENCE and AROUSAL. In the GRID, not one, but two additional dimensions structure the meaning space, namely POWER and NOVELTY.

The emergence of the POWER factor in research on the meaning of emotion terms is not in itself new (see Chapter 2). A POWER factor was earlier observed across languages in research that studied the perceived similarities between emotion terms (e.g., Shaver et al., 1987). Moreover, extensive work by Osgood and colleagues from the fifties to the seventies had already revealed that the connotative meaning of words is universally organized according to the three dimensions of VALENCE, POWER, and AROUSAL, in that order of importance (Osgood, May, & Miron, 1975). The unique contribution of the GRID research is that VALENCE, POWER, and AROUSAL emerge when people are asked to evaluate the meaning of emotion terms on the basis of features that directly operationalize the emotion process itself. Thus, the present project has revealed not only that Osgood's classic three dimensions are relevant for studying the connotative meaning structure in language, but that they also emerge when emotion terms are exclusively rated on emotion-defining features.

The most surprising finding, however, was that a fourth dimension was identified, which is defined by appraisals of NOVELTY and facial expressions of surprise. This NOVELTY dimension is not an artifact of the GRID method itself. It was demonstrated that people spontaneously use the NOVELTY dimension to evaluate the similarity between emotion terms (thus without making explicit the features on the basis of which the similarity has to be judged) (see Chapter 14).

The GRID data clearly reveal an overall compatibility between the dimensional and the componential approaches in the study of emotion. Furthermore, the data have also demonstrated that the dimensional approach is not incompatible with the basic emotion approach—quite to the contrary. When only the coordinates on the overall four factors were used to assign an emotion term to one of the 24 emotion categories, 69% of the terms could be correctly assigned (compared to 4.2% under random assignment) (see Chapter 7). A four-dimensional representation of the feature profiles thus contains most of the categorical information. Moreover, the categorical representation on the basis of the dimensional information confirms the importance of the POWER and the NOVELTY dimensions. When only VALENCE and AROUSAL are used to assign an emotion term to one of the 24 emotion categories, correct assignment was substantially reduced. With these two dimensions, only 41.2% of the terms could be correctly assigned.

In summary, it can be concluded that the analyses of the GRID data from the componential, the basic emotion, and the dimensional approaches confirmed that each of these approaches offers interesting and worthwhile vantage points from which to study emotion. More importantly, the three approaches not only generate different information about the emotion domain, but they also generate compatible information. The feature profiles of emotion terms can be represented by the same dimensional structure as that identified on the basis of direct similarity ratings of emotion terms, and the similarities between emotion terms on the basis of their respective feature profiles also replicate the categorical cluster structure in the emotion domain. Moreover, the dimensional representation of the features allows us to categorize the 24 emotion terms with a high level of accuracy.

Future challenges and opportunities

The central question for the future will be why the assessment instruments that are commonly used in psychological research to assess emotion and affect have only identified two dimensions so far, while the GRID and similarity research robustly identify three to four dimensions (see also Chapter 14). One possible explanation can be excluded, namely that there is a divergence between the actual emotional experiences of people and the meaning structure that is encoded in language. When the componential emotion profiles are computed on the basis of daily emotional episodes, a four-factorial structure emerged that is highly similar to that identified by GRID for emotion words (see Chapter 15). Throughout the book, two explanations have been suggested for the absence of POWER and NOVELTY in other studies (e.g, Chapter 14). The first is that the VALENCE and the POWER dimension are distinguishable, but not independent. We find evidence for a correlation between both factors when they are obliquely rotated, with a tendency for powerful emotions to be more positively valenced (see Chapter 7). This raises the hypothesis that the existing two-dimensional models do not lack a POWER dimension, but that the POWER dimension is confounded with the VALENCE dimension in those models. A similar account could hold for AROUSAL and NOVELTY, since in a three-dimensional representation of the GRID data, the third dimension was defined by both AROUSAL and NOVELTY features (see Chapter 7). Another possible explanation for the absence of POWER and NOVELTY in earlier studies is that the commonly used models do not make a distinction between emotion terms that refer to synchronized activity between emotion components (such as the terms "anger" and "fear") and feeling terms that refer to the general quality of the emotional experience (such as "good" and "strong"), a distinction that has been made in the GRID instrument (see Chapter 8). In the Feeling component, which is operationalized by terms such as *good/bad*, *strong/weak*, or *restless/calm*, the AROUSAL dimension was observed to be relatively more important than the POWER dimension (two AROUSAL dimensions even emerged in the Feeling component). It could therefore be hypothesized that the AROUSAL dimension is much more salient for general feeling terms than for emotion terms. This would imply that the more an assessment instrument contains general feeling terms, the more AROUSAL is likely to emerge as a second factor in the emotion domain.

It has been repeatedly mentioned that the GRID paradigm is compatible with all of the major theoretical approaches in the psychology of emotion—componential, basic emotion, and dimensional. The current data set facilitates the discussion of the convergence between these approaches. These three approaches refer to different levels of abstraction. Clearly, the component features form the lowest, most detailed level of the conceptual structure. They provide the building blocks for the categorization of emotional experience into labeled emotion prototypes at a mid-level of representation and for the mapping of component feature configurations onto four major dimensions at the highest level of abstraction. The intermediate level categories or labels can, as shown by similarity rating studies, also be mapped into a low-dimensional space. From a statistical point of view, this intermediate step is not necessary: as we have shown, the features map directly into a low-dimensional space. It remains for future research to examine the underlying psychological processes. Concretely, does the proprioception of component changes immediately produce a central representation of a position in low-dimensional space (as the proponents of a "core affect" notion propose; see Chapters 1 and 2), or is there an intermediate step of categorization at a mid-level (albeit possibly in a much larger fuzzy set of possibly nonverbal categories rather than a small set of basic emotions)? One important issue to consider in this context is that, if features are immediately mapped into low-dimensional space, the specific information of the components is lost and unavailable for categorization at the mid-level, should the need arise for such categorization (for example, if one is asked to label an emotional experience after the fact).

45.4 The cultural-comparative perspective in emotion research

Promises delivered

Four major culture-comparative issues have received particular attention in the study of emotion (see Chapter 3). (1) The first issue is the existence of culture-specific emotion words and culture-specific meanings of seemingly equivalent emotion words. Both in cultural anthropological and in cross-cultural psychological research, emotion terms have been reported that seem to be culture-specific and cannot be translated into English, such as Japanese *amae* or Portuguese *saudade*, or that exist in English but the meaning of which has no counterpart in other languages, such as English *sadness* in Tahitian. Furthermore, even when translation-equivalent words exist, their meaning need not be exactly the same in different cultural groups. (2) A second issue at stake is the fact that, according to more relativistic accounts of emotion, not only do emotion terms shift in meaning between cultural and linguistic groups, but fundamental cultural differences can also be expected in the very organization of the emotion domain. (3) Third, it has been hypothesized that cultural groups differ with respect to the salience they give to the somatic component of emotions, with Western cultural groups focusing more on the mental aspects of emotions and non-Western groups focusing more on the somatic aspects. (4) Finally, a whole tradition exists that expects cultural differences in the interpersonal aspects of emotions, with emotions being more intrapersonally oriented in independent cultural groups and more interpersonally oriented in interdependent cultural groups (e.g., Markus & Kitayama, 1991).

These four major cultural issues have been taken into account both in the construction of the GRID instrument and in the analyses of the GRID data (see Chapter 5). First, those aspects that were hypothesized to vary the most between cultural and linguistic groups—the somatic and the interpersonal aspects of the emotion process—were extensively operationalized in the GRID instrument. The somatic aspect was included by default because the GRID was developed on the basis of the CPM, which means that all emotion components were represented in the questionnaire, including the Bodily reaction component. The interpersonal and relational aspects of emotions were operationalized both as interpersonally oriented features (such as the appraisal that the event had negative consequences *for others*), and as emotion terms that were clearly interpersonal in nature (such as *love* and *being hurt*). Second, language- and culture-specific words were added to the basic set of 24 emotion terms in some samples (e.g., *toska* in Russian). Third, most analyses were executed in such a way that no equivalence in meaning between cultural and linguistic groups needed to be assumed: the terms in each linguistic group were treated as separate emotion words, even though they were intended to be translation equivalents. Finally, the possibility that the emotion domain is structured in fundamentally different ways in different communities was explored by investigating whether and to what extent the overall dimensional structure across all samples could be replicated in four language groups, namely Germanic, Romance, Slavic, and East-Asian.

The results of the GRID study have shed valuable light on the four major issues raised above. (1) With respect to the relative equivalence of emotion words, the GRID revealed a striking overall similarity across languages and cultural groups. Although evidence was certainly found for some meaning differences between translation-equivalent words, most of these words shared a comparable profile of features. The 142 feature profiles allowed us to correctly identify the emotion word in 81% of the cases across languages, cultural groups, and samples (see Chapters 7 and 13). Moreover, if only the scores of those words on the four overall factors were taken into account, 69% of the emotion terms could still be correctly identified (see Chapters 7 and 13). Thus, while differences in translation-equivalent words certainly exist, the majority of these words shared highly comparable meaning patterns across cultural and linguistic groups.

(2) No overall differences were found between language groups. The dimensional structures per emotion component and across all emotion components were highly comparable between the Germanic, Romance, Slavic, and East-Asian languages (see Chapters 8–12). At least for these four groups, there was no evidence of fundamental differences in the meaning structure of the emotion domain. A limitation is of course that these groups are not representative of the variation of languages in the world. Nevertheless, the structures were confirmed for the East-Asian group (Chinese and Japanese), one that is very different from the other languages, which are all Indo-European.

No evidence was found for differences between cultural groups either in the role of the somatic component or in the interpersonal orientation of emotions. (3) The somatic component defined the emotion structure in comparable ways across language groups, as can be inferred from the stability of the overall structure across all emotion components (see Chapter 7). The Bodily reaction component played an especially defining role in the overall AROUSAL dimension. Its role, however, is not limited to AROUSAL. Two of the Bodily reaction factors contributed to additional overall dimensions: DISTRESS SYMPTOMS are strongly related to the overall POWER dimension and BODY TEMPERATURE to the overall VALENCE dimension (see Chapter 9). Thus, Bodily reactions play an important role in defining emotion words across all cultural groups.

(4) A similar result was observed for the interpersonal aspects of the emotion domain. Both in typical Western independent and in typical Eastern interdependent cultural groups, an overall POWER dimension emerges characterized by interpersonal features (such as feeling dominant and feeling submissive) (see Chapter 7). Moreover, interpersonal appraisals seem to play in important role in differentiating positive emotions (see Chapter 42). The GRID results seem to indicate that, rather than Western culture, it is Western scientific theorizing that has (over)stressed the intrapersonal aspects of emotion.

The results obtained with the GRID instrument further illustrate the essential complementarity between identifying similarities and identifying differences in the meaning of emotion words. The stability of the overall structures functioned as a *tertium comparationis* (Poortinga, 1997), or point of reference, on which the cultural specificities could be mapped. For instance, the observation that self-conscious emotion words (*pride, guilt,* and *shame*) differ in meaning in high POWER-distant countries compared to low POWER-distant cultures could only be observed because each of the translations for these terms could be represented in one and the same emotion space and their position could be quantified (see Chapters 25 and 26).

The GRID data have revealed both similarities where differences were expected (e.g., the terms *viha* in Finnish and Estonian share a highly similar componential pattern, despite the fact that the predominant meaning of the word *viha* is *hate* in Finnish and *anger* in Estonian; see Chapter 21) and substantial differences between seemingly equivalent terms, even within languages (e.g., the componential pattern of the Spanish term for *despair* in the Basque Country looked much more like the Basque term for *despair* than was the case in the other two Spanish-speaking samples) (see Chapter 20). Differences between translation-equivalent terms were demonstrated both at a feature level (e.g., between Japanese and English *happiness*) (see Chapter 35) and at a dimensional level (e.g., between Polish and English *fear*, see Chapter 29, or between *happiness* and *contentment* in English and Polish, see Chapter 36). Specific differences in the vocal component were analyzed for Russian, Ukrainian, and US English emotion terms (see Chapter 40). The GRID semantic profiles were also used to explore the relationship between partially overlapping words, such as *disgust*, *anger*, and *fear* (see Chapter 17). Additionally, the profiles helped to characterize the meaning of language-specific emotion words, such as the Russian *toska* (see Chapter 23), and to identify the best translation-equivalent where several competing terms were available in a language (see Chapter 41). The GRID results were also used to generate hypotheses about the emergence of emotional dialects between cultural groups in emotional expression (see Chapter 43). Moreover, the GRID could be used to identify culture-driven specificities within a single language; for example, differences in the meaning of *pride* were found between Northern and Southern Italy, consistent with a distinction between collectivistic and individualistic cultures (see Chapter 24). Specificities in the overall dimensional structure were observed and explored in the Turkish sample (see Chapter 33) and the Greek sample (see Chapter 34). The specific meanings of *pride* and *shame* were explored in the Hong Kong Chinese sample (see Chapter 37) and the specific meaning of *shame* in the Dutch sample (see Chapter 38).

Future challenges and opportunities

The GRID has proven to be a useful paradigm in the study of emotion terms within and across languages and cultures, allowing for a feature-based, componential, and dimensional description of the meaning of words. The existence of a stable four-dimensional structure underlying the semantic space, the attestable relevance of all five components, and the richness in detail provided by the 142 features constitute a valuable *tertium comparationis* for comparative research.

An important future challenge for the GRID project will be to extend the number of languages and cultures investigated. The current sample is not fully representative of the cultural and linguistic variety of the world. Special attention should be paid to the emotion terms in Africa, as the few attempts to apply the GRID method there turned out to be problematic (see Chapter 32). Further investigation is needed on whether these difficulties are attributable to methodological problems, mainly due to a lack of familiarity with the instrument (web-based, design, and response scale), or whether there are genuine cultural differences in the conceptualization of the emotion domain.

Another challenge will be to further define criteria for the establishment of "sufficient similarity" between emotion words. One of the major goals of the GRID study, explicitly intended from the start of the project, was to provide a tool for researchers in the area of culture-comparative research on affective phenomena to compare the semantic profiles of supposedly equivalent terms, so as to ensure that comparable concepts are used in different language groups. To this purpose, sufficient similarity could be established, for example, on the grounds of a certain level of profile correlations, or by differentially weighting certain emotion component features, depending on the intended use of the terms.

Finally, while many semantic differences have already been reported, more insight should be gained about the reasons behind them. For example, a point of attention for future research is the relationship between broad cultural dimensions (e.g., POWER distance, individualism–collectivism) and meaning shifts in individual emotion terms.

45.5 **The linguistic perspective in emotion research**

Promises delivered

Within linguistics, lexical meaning can be investigated by adopting a semasiological or an onomasiological approach (see Chapter 4 for further details). Semasiology looks at the meanings of individual words, while onomasiology investigates how concepts are represented lexically, that is, what words are used to label them, also in different languages. The GRID paradigm adopts a synchronic semasiological approach to the study of meaning, but the data also afford onomasiological insight. Both types of contribution are discussed below.

In the GRID, the meaning of emotion words is described as a profile across 142 semantic features concerning five emotion components: Appraisal, Bodily reaction, Expression, Action tendency, and Feeling. For each of the 24 emotion terms, features from all five components were identified that either clearly defined the term or were excluded from its meaning. At the same time, the feature profiles allow us to look into the low-level structural organization of the domain. Across emotion terms, a highly consistent internal semantic structure emerged in terms of four major dimensions: VALENCE, POWER, AROUSAL, and NOVELTY. This underlying dimensional structure obtained from the analysis of semantic features is the same as that obtained in studies based on similarity ratings of emotion terms (see Chapter 14) and on ratings of the characteristics of actual emotional experiences (see Chapter 15). Additionally, as already mentioned, this structure resembles the three dimensions discovered by Osgood and colleagues (1975) for connotative meaning: evaluation (good vs bad), potency (strong vs weak) and activity (active vs passive). In the GRID, VALENCE, POWER, and AROUSAL—akin to evaluation, potency and activity, respectively—also emerge as the three most important dimensions. This congruency allows us to construct compelling hypotheses about why language is universally characterized by three connotative meaning dimensions. It is possible that words of any type (e.g., *table*, *politics*, *future*) acquire a connotative meaning in terms of VALENCE, POWER, and AROUSAL because those dimensions represent the core of affective experience, and words acquire the affective value of the experiences associated with them (i.e., the affective value of the contexts in which the words are used).

The GRID allowed us to identify four major emotion clusters across languages (anger, fear, sadness, and joy, see Chapter 7); in other words, these are four broad emotion concepts that find lexicalization in many languages of the world. Since the terms were selected to represent as accurately as possible the scope of the emotion space, the emerging clusters can be said to represent the main "focal points" in this cross-linguistic semantic space. The GRID also allowed us to explore differences between the lexical realizations of the same general concept. For instance, the analysis of the concept "anger" in Spanish and Russian resulted in the identification of two main types in each language: a high-power and a low-power type of anger (see Chapter 22).

The GRID paradigm was able to reveal basic characteristics of the meaning of emotion words by using small samples of judges (see Chapter 6). Indeed, the most important difference between the GRID and commonly used linguistic methods in the study of emotion semantics is that the GRID directly assesses speakers' linguistic awareness, while typical linguistic methods rely on language use observation, as is the case in corpus studies, frame semantics, metaphor studies, and Natural Semantic Metalanguage. The GRID results were shown to converge with those from other methodologies (see Chapters 14 and 28–30), but also to provide method-specific information about the meaning of emotion words across languages and cultures (chapters in Parts III to V in this volume). The reliability of the speakers' judgments, the overlap in findings across methodologies, and the ability of the GRID to contribute method-specific insight into the study of lexical meaning confirm the utility of the method for linguistic research and make the GRID a suitable instrument for triangulation with other linguistic methods in order to get a more complete account of what is conceptually represented in the speakers' minds.

In summary, the GRID has contributed a number of important insights for linguistics. First, the study demonstrates that informants can be used to investigate meaning and that this method is complementary to others in linguistics based on language use observation (see Chapters 5 and 27–30). Second, lexical meaning has been shown to be encyclopedic: when cued by decontextualized words, people can reconstruct a wealth of information pertaining to varied aspects of emotional experience (e.g., see Chapter 7). Third, the semantic content of emotion words seems to reflect the conceptual representation that we make of emotional experience. This is observed in two ways: (a) the features selected a priori on the basis of psychological theories of emotion proved to be present in the meaning of the words (e.g., see Chapters 5, 7–13); and (b) a highly similar dimensional structure emerged from the GRID feature ratings and from emotional experience self-report (see Chapter 15). Fourth, the semantic content of the words can be profitably described as an "averaged," "modal," or "prototypical" (in the sense of most likely features) representation of emotional experience. Whether some of these features always appear across subjects for the meaning of a term still needs to be investigated, as well as whether such features would be stable across languages and cultures (see Chapter 7). Fifth, the results of the GRID suggest that certain words may be preferred to label an experience because they provide the closest match to the profile of features representing the emotion process (see Chapter 15). And finally, the GRID paradigm emerges as a valuable *tertium comparationis* for emotion semantic description across disciplines because it directly links semantics with psychological accounts of emotion and can be profitably used to describe and compare meaning across lexicogrammatical constructions, languages and cultures (see Chapters 20–26).

Future challenges and opportunities

The GRID has opened the door to a number of exciting possibilities. One of them concerns the long-standing controversy in linguistics about the convenience of the classical definition of meaning (minimal and sufficient features) versus a prototype approach (see Chapter 4). The semantic profiles in the GRID are proposed as probabilistic bundles of features, none of which is a priori expected to always be present across subjects in the meaning of a word. A close investigation of the semantic profile of a given emotion term across a large enough sample could tell us which features are more recurrently present and which differentiate the term better from neighboring categories, and thus whether the patterns would provide evidence of the existence of a subset of necessary and sufficient features in the meaning of the word. The same could be done to explore the issue across languages.

Adopting an onomasiological approach, it would be interesting in the future to investigate which GRID features best define each of the four overall concepts or broad emotion categories identified (anger, fear, sadness, and joy), and how the specific words in those groups relate to one another hierarchically (i.e., which words are more general and more specific with respect to the others and thus higher or lower in the structural hierarchy).

Other avenues for future exploration include the investigation of meaning change in bilinguals (how do their semantic repertoires change with respect to monolinguals?) (see Chapter 39). One could also use the GRID to assess meaning equivalence across different lexico-grammatical constructions used to refer to emotion; for example, the GRID could be used to describe the semantic content of idioms and metaphorical expressions and to find the best match in meaning between them and the available emotion words of a language.

Additionally, the GRID can be applied to investigate semantic variation in other grammatical forms. A commitment for only nouns over adjectives or verbs (or any other grammatical construction) entails some drawbacks for onomasiological research. Corpus linguistic studies of emotion have demonstrated that the nominal and adjectival construals of an emotion need not be the same conceptually (e.g., Glynn 2009, 2010). Additionally, an emotion concept may be preferentially realized in a language as a noun, as an adjective, or as a verb, and this preferential grammatical construal can also inform us about differences in conceptualization. Verbs encode emotions as processes and relationships, thus highlighting their procedural and interpersonal aspects. Nouns and adjectives, in contrast, by construing emotions as "things" and "qualities" pertaining to the person, respectively, are more likely to focus on the experience of the individual. Accordingly, it has been found that, in the self-report of emotion experience, verbs are used more than nouns or adjectives to name the felt emotion in cultures that value interdependence compared to those that emphasize the value of the individual. Conversely, more individualistic cultures prefer the use of adjectives and nouns over verbs (Semin, Görts, Nandram & Semin-Goosens, 2002).

Another exciting extension of the GRID paradigm will be to use the instrument in the study of contextualized examples. Using decontextualized words as cues to reconstruct their meaning misses the potentially important nuances conveyed by grammar. For example, the emotion nouns may more frequently appear as subjects than as objects of the sentence, hinting at an active (vs passive) view of the emotion as a causer of changes, rather than as an object of manipulation. The same could be hinted at by a higher degree of personification (i.e., construal as "living being") over reification (i.e., construal as "material thing") in the figurative uses of the word. The GRID paradigm cannot observe these preferences in construal, but it can describe the differences in meaning that the speakers of a language perceive in them.

Finally, the GRID paradigm could be used to explore the semantic differences between three types of affective labels: emotion words (*anger*, *fear*, *joy*), feeling words that represent the general quality of the emotional experience (*good*, *strong*, *excited*), and words that predominantly make reference to one of the emotion components (*offended*, *aggressive*, *cold*). Several hypotheses are worth investigating, for example, whether "emotion terms" (e.g., *anger*) are more complex semantically than "feeling terms" (e.g., *excited*), or whether their dimensional structure differs. One would also expect "component words" (e.g., *aggressive*) to be semantically less well defined than the canonical emotion words that they can metonymically refer to (e.g., *anger*). Furthermore, their semantic profile could be used to identify the specific emotion words that they are compatible with (*offended* → *anger/hurt/sad*).

Another interesting development would be to investigate whether the sedimentation of emotion terms in language follows a lawful pattern when emotion language is studied diachronically. For instance, a pattern in semantic change could be hypothesized from words that refer to one of the components only versus full-blown emotion words that refer to whole emotion processes.

45.6 **The lexical sedimentation hypothesis**

Promises delivered

The first chapter of this book started with a quote by Austin suggesting that we should examine words to learn more about the phenomenon they refer to—here, the emotions. According to the lexical sedimentation hypothesis, important aspects of human functioning get encoded in language. Correspondingly, many of the hypotheses about the meaning of emotion terms throughout this book were developed on the basis of theories on emotion processes and on the assumption that the respective emotion processes sediment in language (see Chapter 5). Virtually all hypotheses formulated in this way were confirmed (e.g., see Chapter 7). As expected from the CPM (which constituted the basis for the GRID instrument), Appraisals, Action tendencies, Bodily reactions, Expressions and Feelings that refer to the general quality of the emotional experience constituted the very core of the meaning of emotion terms. Each of the components was also observed to be characterized by its own internal structure and the components to be mutually related to a large extent. Moreover, as predicted by the dimensional models, it was observed that the relationships between a very large set of emotion features can be represented by a low-dimensional structure. Furthermore, as predicted by the discrete emotion models, an emotion term can be well identified on the basis of its profile of features. More importantly, these phenomena were observed across diverse linguistic and cultural groups and a strong correspondence was observed between the meaning structure of emotion terms and the experience structure of emotion terms (see Chapter 15). These cross-cultural and cross-linguistic structural similarities, as well as the convergence between meaning and experience, can be best explained as an effect of lexical sedimentation, that is, by hypothesizing the existence of recurrent and fairly homogeneous emotion processes across cultural groups that have been encoded in similar ways in the languages of the world.

The present results do not, however, provide evidence for deterministic relationships between the underlying emotional processes and the emotion vocabulary referring to them, either at the level of the different languages and cultural groups, or at the level of the individual language users. On the contrary, evidence was found for individual, cultural, and linguistic differences in the meaning of emotion terms. What has been observed, though, is a convergent structure that consists of probabilistic relationships between emotion terms and emotion features. This convergent structure across languages and cultures does not exclude the possibility that cultural-linguistic constructivist processes affect the development of emotional language, but it substantially constrains their potential extent. More importantly, the convergent structure can be used as *tertium comparationis* to identify specificities in the lexical representation of individuals, cultural groups, and languages.

Similarly, our observations on the decontextualized meaning of words do not exclude the possibility of more constructivist processes in the process of *labeling* concrete emotional episodes. The meaning of a word, as captured by the GRID, is a highly coherent representational structure that probably emerges from recurrent patterns of features across experiences labeled with that word; but the concrete experience one undergoes at a given moment need not match these prototypical patterns. Arguably, one would tend to choose the label that best matches the componential profile of one's experience, but this leaves room for psychological labeling effects and constructivist processes. Moreover, the adherence to a particular label may well change the represented quality of the experience to some extent. Maybe it is just because emotion terms represent the most probabilistic relationships of features in general that they can have powerful effects when used to label a specific emotional experience.

An important limitation of the GRID paradigm is that all observations reported in this book are based on *associations* between emotion features across a representative set of emotion terms. Such observations cannot confirm any *causal* model for the relationships between the components that constitute the emotional phenomena. For example, the componential, basic emotion, and dimensional theories of emotion differ in the mechanisms that they assume to account for the relationships between the emotion components. Componential emotion theories account for the relationships between the components by resorting to a multidimensional appraisal process, while basic emotion theories account for those relationships by means of a limited set of different and internally coherent affect programs. In turn, the fundamental difference between componential emotion theories and dimensional theories has to do with the status of the dimensions. Componential theories do not exclude the possibility of representing the emotion domain in a low-dimensional space, but they see these dimensions as properties that emerge from complex multicomponential processes. In the dimensional theories, by contrast, the dimensions constitute the core of the emotion construct, with each of the components being more or less likely to become associated with these dimensions.

In conclusion, although the psycholinguistic methodology used throughout the current book allows neither choosing between any causal account of the emotion domain, nor postulating deterministic relationships between emotion processes and emotion language, the methodology does offer clear evidence against a dissociation between emotional experience and language. Lexical sedimentation constitutes a plausible explanation for the observed stability in emotion structures.

Future challenges and opportunities

As we have studied neither a fully representative sample of linguistic and cultural groups in the world, nor an exhaustive set of emotion terms, much empirical research on the lexical sedimentation hypothesis still needs to be done. Further investigation will be necessary to determine whether the current findings can be generalized to other linguistic and cultural groups and to other terms used to label emotional processes. It is important to point out that the lexical sedimentation hypothesis would not be falsified by the observation that expected associations between emotion features do not hold for a specific emotion word in a specific situation in a particular linguistic or cultural group. The lexical sedimentation hypothesis does not imply a deterministic relationship between the actual emotional experiences and their lexicalization in language. Rather, probabilistic relations are expected, with more frequent and salient emotion experiences being more likely to be encoded across languages.

The litmus test for the lexical sedimentation hypothesis eventually consists of studying the convergence between the associations among emotion features as they have been encoded in language and the associations among these emotion features as they emerge during actual emotion processes. In this respect, we are only at the beginning of the journey, as we have just started studying this relationship in one linguistic group (see Chapter 15).

Studying the convergences or divergences between information encoded in language and the actual emotion processes is a gradually evolving research process because the scientific study of emotion semantics and of actual emotion processes are interdependent. On the one hand, studying the actual emotional processes relies almost always (directly or indirectly) on emotion words because participants have to report on their emotional reactions by rating emotion words the stimuli used in emotion research are often emotion words and emotion words often play an indirect role in selecting the stimuli. Thus, a better grasp of the meaning of emotion words would allow for a more focused investigation of the actual emotion processes. For instance, the research reported in the current book suggests the important role of POWER and NOVELTY in the actual emotion experiences (e.g., see Chapters 16 and 18), although both dimensions are absent in the current assessment models.

On the other hand, new insights into the actual emotion processes offer new opportunities to improve our understanding of what emotion words mean in language. The GRID instrument is a good example of this. Developed entirely on the grounds of scientific (psychological) theories of emotion, it provides a new methodology whose findings about emotion term semantics (although necessarily partial) can be immediately related to other findings on emotion experience from neighboring disciplines.

The results reported in this book are evidence that more intense exchanges between psychological research on actual emotion processes and psycholinguistic research on the meaning of emotion terms would benefit both research domains.

45.7 **General conclusion**

At the end of this book, we can conclude that the aim of constructing an instrument capable of studying the meaning of emotion terms from various disciplinary perspectives and theoretical approaches was by and large realized by the GRID instrument. It has been shown that each of these perspectives and approaches reveals specific and complementary information about the emotion domain. We have tried to show that the utility of the GRID paradigm consists, among other things, in the pertinence of the empirical data collected with the instrument to mediate between different disciplinary perspectives and theoretical approaches. The most important contribution of the project, however, is probably not to be found in the questions that have been answered, but in the new research questions that have been raised and in the introduction of a valid interdisciplinary method to address them. We hope that this will lead, in due time, to breaking the deadlock that characterizes much of our current theorizing and research on emotion and will help settle the existing disputes in a more empirical fashion.

Appendix 1

Availability

A number of online materials and facilities are available to the reader of this volume and can be freely used at, or downloaded from, the GRID website at http://www.affective-sciences.org/GRID. These include:

1. Complementary information to the book chapters (tables, figures and additional documents too large to include in the printed volume). These are referred to in the respective chapters as Supplementary Materials ("SM") and labeled according to their type as "Table," "Figure," or "Document" (e.g., Table SM 1).

2. Additional detail on the GRID collaborators and datasets. This includes updated information on:

   - languages in which the instrument is available
   - countries for which data has been collected
   - languages for which data has been collected
   - name and affiliation of all dataset owners and their teams
   - contact information for dataset owners

   Please, note that the GRID is an ongoing project and more datasets are constantly being collected in new languages and countries.

3. Electronic versions of the instruments provided in appendices to this volume: the full GRID instrument (see Appendix 2), the CoreGRID instrument (see Appendix 3), the MiniGRID instrument (see Appendix 4), as well as a paper version of the MiniGRID instrument (see Appendix 5). The original version of the GRID instrument is reproduced in this volume (see Appendix 2); the online version will be continuously updated.

4. Translations of the standard set of 24 GRID words into all available languages

5. A continuously updated list of publications using the GRID paradigm

6. Errata—a listing of errors discovered after the publication of the volume

If you would like to use the GRID, the CoreGRID, or the MiniGRID instruments online, using the web experimentation platform of the Swiss Center for Affective Sciences, please send an email to GRID@unige.ch specifying your name and affiliation, discipline, the language and country you would like to gather data for, and your research goals. You will then receive further information on how to proceed. Please note that a license is required for commercial use of the instrument, so please specify exactly how you wish to use it.

If you use the paper version of the GRID instruments provided in this volume and downloadable from the site, please refer to these in your publications as "GRID instrument" (/"CoreGRID instrument"/"MiniGRID instrument") and include a reference to this volume and the link to our website (http://www.affective-sciences.org/GRID), from where the instrument has been downloaded.

Appendix 2

GRID instrument[1]

Around the world, people use words to describe their ongoing or past emotional experiences. By using a single emotion word, people can convey a lot of information. They can refer to their interpretation of the situation that caused the emotional experience, the bodily symptoms they felt, the way they expressed their emotional experience, the way they wanted to react to the situation, their actual feelings, or the way they tried to regulate their emotion.

In the present study, we would like to examine how languages differ with respect to the information that can be inferred when persons use emotion words to describe their emotional experience. In other words, we are interested in understanding the explicit and implicit meanings of emotion words across languages.

We would like to ask you to define the meaning of four different emotion words, as commonly used in your language, in terms of a set of emotion features. These features are grouped in the following categories.

1 **Evaluation**—features describing the person's evaluation or appraisal of the event, conscious or not.

2 **Bodily symptoms**—features describing the bodily symptoms that tend to occur during the emotional state.

3 **Expressions**—features describing facial and vocal expressions and gestures, that accompany the emotion.

4 **Action tendencies**—features describing tendencies to behave in certain ways that accompany the emotion.

5 **Subjective feeling**—features describing the subjective experience that characterizes the emotion.

6 **Regulation**—features describing ways in which the emotion can be regulated.

7 **General**—some general features of the emotion experienced.

We would like you to focus as much as possible on the meaning of each of the four emotion words among speakers of your language.

Please rate the likelihood of each emotion feature occurring when a particular emotion word is used by speakers of your language to describe an emotional experience.

For each feature, you can use the following nine-point response scale to indicate the likelihood of the feature occurring when a speaker of your native language uses a particular emotion word to describe his/her emotional experience.

Extremely unlikely			Neither likely, nor unlikely				Extremely likely	
1	2	3	4	5	6	7	8	9

[1] The most recently updated version of the GRID questionnaire is available at the GRID website: http://www.affective-sciences.org/GRID

Based on a pilot study, we expect you will need about an hour to complete the questionnaire. Thank you in advance for your time and cooperation.

To be able to compare the results across cultures and languages, we need some background information. Thank you for answering the following questions.

Sex: male/female

How old are you?

Where did you spend most of your life (country)?

Where do you live now (country)?

Educational attainment:

- basic education
- basic education + vocational training
- secondary education
- university/college education.

Are you a student currently enrolled at a university? yes/no

Did you, your parents or your grandparents, migrate to the country where you are residing now?

If yes, what was the country of origin?

Evaluation

This section lists features describing the evaluation or appraisal (conscious or not) of the situation that led to the emotion.

If a speaker of your native language as spoken in your country or region uses the following emotion words[2] to describe an emotional experience, how likely is it that the person experienced an event:

1 that occurred suddenly
2 that was familiar
3 that was essentially unpredictable
4 that confirmed the expectations of the person
5 that was inconsistent with the expectations of the person
6 that was in itself pleasant for the person (independently of its possible consequences)
7 that was in itself pleasant for somebody else (independently of its possible consequences)
8 that was in itself unpleasant for the person (independently of its possible consequences)
9 that was in itself unpleasant for somebody else (independently of its possible consequences)
10 that was important and relevant for the person's goals or needs
11 that was important and relevant for the goals or needs of somebody else
12 that was caused by chance

----

2 In the online study several emotion terms are displayed on screen for the participant to rate.

13   that was caused by the person's own behavior

14   that was caused by somebody else's behavior

15   that was caused by a supernatural POWER (e.g., God, ancestors, ghosts)

16   that was caused intentionally

17   of which the consequences were predictable

18   of which the consequences were likely to be positive, desirable for the person him/herself

19   of which the consequences were likely to be positive, desirable for somebody else

20   of which the consequences were likely to be negative, undesirable for the person him/herself

21   of which the consequences were likely to be negative, undesirable for somebody else

22   that required an immediate response

23   of which the consequences were in principle avoidable or modifiable

24   with consequences that the person would be able to avoid or change (i.e., through her or his own POWER, or helped by others)

25   with such consequences that the person would be able to live with them and adjust to them

26   that was inconsistent or incongruent with the person's own standards and ideals

27   that violated laws or socially accepted norms

28   where the person was at the center of attention

29   where the person was treated unjustly (and felt offended)

30   where the person was in danger (experienced a threat)

31   where the person experienced an irrevocable loss.

Bodily symptoms

This section lists features describing the bodily symptoms that can occur during an emotional experience.

If a speaker of your native language as spoken in your country or region uses the following emotion words[3] to describe an emotional experience, how likely is it that the person:

32   felt shivers (in the neck, or chest)

33   felt weak limbs

34   got pale

35   had the feeling of a lump in his/her throat

36   had stomach discomfort

37   felt his/her heartbeat slowing down

38   felt his/her heartbeat getting faster

39   felt his/her muscles relaxing (whole body)

40   felt his/her muscles tensing (whole body)

41   felt his/her breathing slowing down

42   felt his/her breathing getting faster

---

[3]   See note 2.

43 felt warm (whole body)

44 perspired, or had moist hands

45 sweated (whole body)

46 felt hot (puff of heat, cheeks or chest)

47 blushed

48 felt cold (whole body)

49 had no bodily symptoms at all.

Expressions

This section lists features describing the facial and vocal expressions and gestures that occur during emotional experiences.

If a speaker of your native language as spoken in your country or region uses the following emotion words[4] to describe an emotional experience, how likely is it that the person:

50 smiled

51 felt his/her jaw drop

52 pressed his/her lips together

53 felt his/her eyebrows go up

54 frowned

55 closed his/her eyes

56 opened his/her eyes widely

57 had tears in his/her eyes

58 did not show any changes in his/her face

59 made abrupt body movements

60 moved toward people or things

61 withdrew from people or things

62 moved against people or things

63 did not show any changes in gesture or movements

64 spoke louder

65 spoke softer

66 had a trembling voice

67 had an assertive voice

68 fell silent

69 produced a short utterance

70 produced a long utterance

71 changed the melody of his/her speech

72 had speech disturbances

---

[4] See note 2.

73 spoke faster

74 spoke slower

75 did not show any changes in his/her vocal expression.

Action tendencies

This section lists features describing tendencies to behave in certain ways that may occur during an emotional experience.

If a speaker of your native language as spoken in your country or region uses the following emotion words[5] to describe an emotional experience, how likely is it that the person:

76 wanted to go on with what he/she was doing

77 wanted the ongoing situation to last or be repeated

78 felt the urge to stop what he/she was doing

79 wanted to undo what was happening

80 felt inhibited or blocked

81 wanted to be in command of others

82 wanted to be in control of the situation

83 wanted to take initiative him/herself

84 wanted to comply to someone else's wishes

85 wanted to hand over the initiative to someone else

86 wanted to submit to the situation as it was

87 wanted someone to be there to provide help or support

88 felt an urge to be active, to do something—no matter what

89 wanted to move

90 felt an urge to be attentive to what is going on

91 lacked the motivation to do anything

92 wanted to do nothing

93 lacked the motivation to pay attention to what was going on

94 wanted to flee

95 wanted to keep or push things away

96 wanted to prevent or break off sensory contact (e.g., seeing, hearing, smelling, or touching)

97 wanted to disappear or hide from others

98 wanted to withdraw into him/herself

99 wanted to be hurt as little as possible

100 wanted to make up for what he/she had done

101 wanted to do damage, hit, or say something that hurts

102 wanted to break contact with others

---

[5] See note 2.

103 wanted to oppose

104 wanted to show off

105 wanted to be seen, to be in the center of attention

106 wanted to tackle the situation

107 wanted to overcome an obstacle

108 wanted to take care of another person or cause

109 wanted to be near or close to people or things

110 wanted to be tender, sweet, and kind

111 wanted to run away in whatever direction

112 wanted to destroy whatever was close

113 wanted to act, whatever action it might be

114 wanted to sing and dance

115 wanted to get totally absorbed in the situation.

Subjective feeling

This section lists features describing the subjective experience referred to by the emotion words.

If a speaker of your native language as spoken in your country or region uses the following emotion words[6] to describe an emotional experience, how likely is it that the person:

116 was in an intense emotional state

117 experienced the emotional state for a long time

118 felt good

119 felt tired

120 felt submissive

121 felt at ease

122 felt powerless

123 felt negative

124 felt energetic

125 felt in control

126 felt restless

127 felt powerful

128 felt positive

129 felt exhausted

130 felt strong

131 felt calm

132 felt out of control

133 felt bad

---

[6] See note 2.

134   felt alert

135   felt dominant

136   felt nervous

137   felt weak.

Regulation

This section lists features describing the way in which people can regulate their emotions.

If a speaker of your native language as spoken in your country or region uses the following emotion words[7] to describe an emotional experience, how likely is it that the person:

138   tried to control the intensity of the emotional feeling

139   showed a stronger degree of emotion than he/she actually felt

140   showed a weaker degree of emotion than he/she actually felt

141   hid the emotion from others by smiling.

General

Just three more questions about the emotions referred to by the emotions words.

If a speaker of your native language as spoken in your country or region uses the following emotion words to describe an emotional experience.

142   How likely is it that he/she will be changed in a lasting way (due to the emotional experience)?

143   How frequently is this state generally experienced in your society?

144   To what extent is it socially accepted to experience this emotional state in your society?

Personal information

To be able to compare the results across cultures and languages, we need some background information. Thank you for answering the following questions.

Next you will find the description of two different individuals. Which person do you think resembles you most? Please choose the profile that best characterizes you, even if one or two items do not apply.

- Person A: Likes languages a lot, reads a lot, expresses herself or himself clearly, likes games like cross-words, does not like numbers
- Person B: Is good at Maths, is at ease with abstract symbols, likes strategy games like chess, does not pay much attention to her or his writing style

What is your mother tongue (language you were raised in)?
Which languages do you know (all languages of which you have at least a passive knowledge)?
During the last year, I spoke/read/wrote in this language:

1   on a daily basis

2   at least once a week

3   at least once a month

---

[7]   See note 2.

4 several times a year

5 (almost) never

To be rated for all languages with at least a passive knowledge.

Do you have any comments on the questions or their presentation? Please write them down here.

You are now done with the questionnaire.

We thank you for your participation in this study.

Appendix 3

CoreGRID instrument

Around the world, people use words to describe their ongoing or past emotional experiences. By using a single emotion word, people can convey a lot of information. They can refer to their interpretation of the situation that caused the emotional experience, the bodily symptoms they felt, the way they expressed their emotional experience, the way they wanted to react to the situation, their actual feelings, or the way they tried to regulate their emotion.

In the present study, we would like to examine how languages differ with respect to the information that can be inferred when persons use emotion words to describe their emotional experience. In other words, we are interested in understanding the explicit and implicit meanings of emotion words across languages.

We would like to ask you to define the meaning of different emotion words, as commonly used in your language, in terms of a set of emotion features. These features are grouped in the following categories:

1 **Feelings**—features describing the feeling that characterizes the emotion

2 **Bodily reactions**—features describing the bodily reactions that tend to occur during the emotional state

3 **Expression**—features describing facial and vocal expressions that accompany the emotion

4 **Behavioral tendencies**—features describing tendencies to behave in certain ways that accompany the emotion.

5 **Event evaluation**—features describing the person's evaluation or appraisal of the event, conscious or not.

We would like you to focus as much as possible on the meaning of each of the emotion words among speakers of your language.

Please rate the likelihood of each emotion feature occurring when a particular emotion word is used by speakers of your language to describe an emotional experience.

For each feature, you can use the following nine-point response scale to indicate the likelihood of the feature occurring when a speaker of your native language uses a particular emotion word to describe his/her emotional experience.

Extremely unlikely			Neither likely, nor unlikely				Extremely likely	
1	2	3	4	5	6	7	8	9

Thank you in advance for your time and cooperation.

To be able to compare the results across cultures and languages, we need some background information. Thank you for answering the following questions.

Sex: male/female

How old are you?

Where did you spend most of your life (country)?

Where do you live now (country)?

Educational attainment:

- basic education
- basic education + vocational training
- secondary education
- university/college education

Are you a student currently enrolled at a university? yes/no

Did you, your parents or your grandparents, migrate to the country where you are residing now?

If yes, what was the country of origin?

Feelings

This section lists features describing the feeling referred to by the emotion words.

If a speaker of your native language as spoken in your country or region uses the following emotion words[1] to describe an emotional experience, how likely is it that the person felt:

1 the emotion very intensely
2 the emotion for a long time
3 good
4 tired
5 restless
6 strong
7 calm
8 bad
9 awake
10 weak

Bodily reactions

This section lists features describing the bodily reactions that can occur during an emotional experience.

If a speaker of your native language as spoken in your country or region uses the following emotion words to describe an emotional experience, how likely is it that the person had the following bodily reactions?

11 feeling weak limbs
12 becoming pale
13 stomach disturbance
14 slowed heart rate

---

[1] In the online study several emotion terms are displayed on screen for the participant to rate.

15 rapid heart rate

16 muscles tensing

17 slowed breathing

18 rapid breathing

19 feeling warm

20 sweating

21 feeling cold

Expression

This section lists features describing the facial and vocal expressions that occur during emotional experiences.

If a speaker of your native language as spoken in your country or region uses the following emotion words to describe an emotional experience, how likely is it that the person:

22 smiled

23 had the jaw drop

24 raised the eyebrows

25 frowned

26 closed the eyes

27 had tears in the eyes

28 spoke more loudly

29 spoke in a trembling voice

30 spoke in a firm voice

31 had speech disturbances

32 spoke more rapidly

33 spoke more slowly

Behavioral tendencies

This section lists features describing tendencies to behave in certain ways that may occur during an emotional experience.

If a speaker of your native language as spoken in your country or region uses the following emotion words to describe an emotional experience, how likely is it that the person:

34 wanted the ongoing situation to last or be repeated

35 wanted to stop what he/she was doing

36 wanted to undo what was happening

37 wanted to comply with someone else's wishes

38 wanted to leave the initiative to someone else

39 wanted to overcome an obstacle

40 wanted to do nothing

41 lacked the motivation to pay attention to what was going on

42 wanted to disappear or hide from others

43 wanted to do damage, hit, or say something that hurts

44 wanted to oppose someone or something

45 wanted to tackle the situation

46 wanted to run away in any direction

47 wanted to sing and dance

Event evaluation

This section lists features describing the evaluation or appraisal (conscious or not) of the situation that led to the emotion.

If a speaker of your native language as spoken in your country or region uses the following emotion words to describe an emotional experience caused by an event, how likely is it that

48 the event had consequences that were predictable

49 the event had negative, undesirable consequences for the person

50 the event happened by chance

51 the event involved the violation of laws or socially accepted norms

52 the event occurred suddenly

53 the event required an immediate response

54 the event was caused by somebody else's behavior

55 the event was important for and relevant to the person's goals or needs

56 the event was uncontrollable

57 the event was pleasant for the person

58 the event was unpredictable

59 there was no urgency in the situation

60 the person could control the consequences of the event

61 the event was caused by the person's own behavior

62 the event was important for and relevant to the goals or needs of somebody else

63 the person had a dominant position in the situation

64 the event was inconsistent with the person's own standards and ideals

65 the person had POWER over the consequences of the event

66 the event confirmed the expectations of the person

67 the person was POWERless in the situation

68 the person could live with the consequences of the event

Personal information

To be able to compare the results across cultures and languages, we need some background information. Thank you for answering the following questions.

Next you will find the description of two different individuals. Which person do you think resembles you most? Please choose the profile that best characterizes you, even if one or two items do not apply.

- Person A: Likes languages a lot, reads a lot, expresses herself or himself clearly, likes games like cross-words, does not like numbers
- Person B: Is good at Maths, is at ease with abstract symbols, likes strategy games like chess, does not pay much attention to her or his writing style

What is your mother tongue (language you were raised in)?

Which languages do you know (all languages of which you have at least a passive knowledge)?

During the last year, I spoke/read/wrote in this language:

1 on a daily basis

2 at least once a week

3 at least once a month

4 several times a year

5 (almost) never

To be rated for all languages with at least a passive knowledge.

Do you have any comments on the questions or their presentation? Please write them down here.

You are now done with the questionnaire.

We thank you for your participation in this study.

MiniGRID instrument

Sex M/F

Age

Student Yes/No

Native language

Imagine that a speaker of your native language, as spoken in your country or region, uses one of these emotion words to describe an emotional experience. Please describe, for each of the words[1], the probability for the following reactions to occur. Indicate your response by choosing one of the numbers from 1 (extremely unlikely to occur) to 9 (extremely likely to occur):

Feelings

How likely is it that the person felt the emotion . . .

  1 very intensely

  2 for a long time

Bodily reactions

How likely is it that the person had the following bodily sensations?

  3 weak limbs

  4 rapid heart rate

  5 rapid breathing

  6 sweating

Expression

How likely is it that the person . . .

  7 had the jaw drop

  8 frowned

  9 closed the eyes

 10 spoke more loudly

---

[1] In the online study several emotion terms are displayed on screen for the participant to rate.

Behavioral tendencies

How likely is it that the person . . .

11 wanted to tackle the situation

12 wanted to sing and dance

Event evaluation

How likely is it that the event that caused this emotion . . .

13 occurred suddenly

14 was unpredictable

15 was pleasant for the person

16 happened by chance

Appendix 5

MiniGRID instrument (paper version)

Imagine that a speaker of your native language, as spoken in your country or region, uses one of these emotion words to describe an emotional experience. Please describe, for each of the words, the probability for the following reactions to occur. Indicate your response choosing one of the numbers from 1 (extremely unlikely to occur) to 9 (extremely likely to occur):

Words	Anger	Joy	Sadness	Fear
Reactions				
Feelings. How likely is it that the person *felt the emotion* . . .				
very intensely	1 2 3 4 5 6 7 8 9	1 2 3 4 5 6 7 8 9	1 2 3 4 5 6 7 8 9	1 2 3 4 5 6 7 8 9
for a long time	1 2 3 4 5 6 7 8 9	1 2 3 4 5 6 7 8 9	1 2 3 4 5 6 7 8 9	1 2 3 4 5 6 7 8 9
Bodily reactions. How likely is it that the person *had the following bodily sensations* . . .				
weak limbs	1 2 3 4 5 6 7 8 9	1 2 3 4 5 6 7 8 9	1 2 3 4 5 6 7 8 9	1 2 3 4 5 6 7 8 9
rapid heart rate	1 2 3 4 5 6 7 8 9	1 2 3 4 5 6 7 8 9	1 2 3 4 5 6 7 8 9	1 2 3 4 5 6 7 8 9
rapid breathing	1 2 3 4 5 6 7 8 9	1 2 3 4 5 6 7 8 9	1 2 3 4 5 6 7 8 9	1 2 3 4 5 6 7 8 9
sweating	1 2 3 4 5 6 7 8 9	1 2 3 4 5 6 7 8 9	1 2 3 4 5 6 7 8 9	1 2 3 4 5 6 7 8 9
Expression. How likely is it that the person . . .				
had the jaw drop	1 2 3 4 5 6 7 8 9	1 2 3 4 5 6 7 8 9	1 2 3 4 5 6 7 8 9	1 2 3 4 5 6 7 8 9
frowned	1 2 3 4 5 6 7 8 9	1 2 3 4 5 6 7 8 9	1 2 3 4 5 6 7 8 9	1 2 3 4 5 6 7 8 9
closed the eyes	1 2 3 4 5 6 7 8 9	1 2 3 4 5 6 7 8 9	1 2 3 4 5 6 7 8 9	1 2 3 4 5 6 7 8 9
spoke more loudly	1 2 3 4 5 6 7 8 9	1 2 3 4 5 6 7 8 9	1 2 3 4 5 6 7 8 9	1 2 3 4 5 6 7 8 9
Behavioral tendencies. How likely is it that the person . . .				
wanted to tackle the situation	1 2 3 4 5 6 7 8 9	1 2 3 4 5 6 7 8 9	1 2 3 4 5 6 7 8 9	1 2 3 4 5 6 7 8 9
wanted to sing and dance	1 2 3 4 5 6 7 8 9	1 2 3 4 5 6 7 8 9	1 2 3 4 5 6 7 8 9	1 2 3 4 5 6 7 8 9
Event evaluation. How likely is it that *the event that caused this emotion* . . .				
occurred suddenly	1 2 3 4 5 6 7 8 9	1 2 3 4 5 6 7 8 9	1 2 3 4 5 6 7 8 9	1 2 3 4 5 6 7 8 9
was unpredictable	1 2 3 4 5 6 7 8 9	1 2 3 4 5 6 7 8 9	1 2 3 4 5 6 7 8 9	1 2 3 4 5 6 7 8 9
was pleasant for the person	1 2 3 4 5 6 7 8 9	1 2 3 4 5 6 7 8 9	1 2 3 4 5 6 7 8 9	1 2 3 4 5 6 7 8 9
happened by chance	1 2 3 4 5 6 7 8 9	1 2 3 4 5 6 7 8 9	1 2 3 4 5 6 7 8 9	1 2 3 4 5 6 7 8 9

References

Abele-Brehm, A., & Brehm, W. (1986). On the conceptualization and measurement of mood. *Diagnostica, 32*, 209–28.

Abondolo, D. (2006). *The Uralic Languages: Routledge language family descriptions*. London: Routledge.

Adler, R. S., Rosen, B., & Silverstein, E. M. (1998). Emotions in negotiation: How to manage fear and anger. *Negotiation Journal, 14*, 161–79.

Agbo, M. (2011). The syntax and semantics of Igbo verbs of emotion. In G.C. Batic (Ed.), *Encoding Emotions in African Languages* (pp. 73–82). Muenchen: Lincom GmbH.

Albas, D. C., McCluskey, K. W., & Albas, C. A. (1976). Perception of the emotional content of speech: A comparison of two Canadian groups. *Journal of Cross-Cultural Psychology, 7*, 481–90.

Alonso-Arbiol, I., Gorostiaga, A., & Balluerka, N. (2008 July). GRID approach for the assessment of emotions in Basque and Spanish. Paper presented at the 19th International Congress of the International Association for Cross-Cultural Psychology, Bremen, Germany.

Alonso-Arbiol, I., Shaver, P., Fraley, R. C., Oronoz, B., Unzurrunzaga, E., & Urizar, R. (2006). Structure of the Basque emotion lexicon. *Cognition & Emotion, 20*, 836–65.

Alschuler, C. F., & Alschuler, A. S. (1984). Developing healthy responses to anger: The counselor's role. *Journal of Counseling and Development, 63*, 26–9.

Altarriba, J. (2003). Does cariño equal "liking"? A theoretical approach to conceptual nonequivalence between languages. *International Journal of Bilingualism, 7*, 305–22.

Amberber, M. (2001). Testing emotional universals in Amharic. In J. Harkins & A. Wierzbicka (Eds.), *Emotions in Crosslinguistic Perspective* (pp. 35–69). Berlin: Mouton de Gruyter.

Ameka, F. (1990). The grammatical packaging of experiencers in Ewe: A study in the semantics of syntax. *Australian Journal of Linguistics, 10*, 139–81.

Ameka, F. (Ed.). (1992). Interjections [Special Issue]. *Journal of Pragmatics, 18*(2/3).

Ameka, F. K. (2002). Cultural scripting of body parts for emotions: On "jealousy" and related emotions in Ewe. *Pragmatics & Cognition, 10*, 27–55.

Anderson, N. H. (1989). Information integration approach to emotions and their measurement. In R. Plutchik & H. Kellerman (Eds.), *Emotion: Theory, research, and experience. Vol. 4. The measurement of emotion* (pp. 133–86). New York: Academic Press.

Anfinogenova, A. I. (2006). Variativnost' emotivnyh leksem v anglijskih perevodah p'yes A.P. Chekhova. [Variability of emotion lexemes in the English translations of A.P. Chekhov's plays]. (Unpublished dissertation thesis). Saint-Petersburg State University, Saint-Petersburg.

Angyal, A. (1941). Disgust and related aversions. *Journal of Abnormal and Social Psychology, 36*, 393–412.

Anolli, L. (2005). The detection of the hidden design of meaning. In L. Anolli, S. Duncan, M. Magnusson, & G. Riva (Eds.), *The hidden structure of interaction: From neurons to culture patterns* (pp. 23–50). Amsterdam: IOS Press.

Apresjan, J. (2000). *Systematic lexicography*. New York: Oxford University Press.

Apresjan, J. D., Boguslavskij, O. J., Levontina, I. B., Uryson, E. V., Glovinskaja, M. J., & Krylova, T. V. (Eds.). (1997). *Novyj ob"jasnitel'nyj slovar' sinonimov russkogo jazyka*. [The new explanatory dictionary of synonyms in the Russian language]. Moscow: Jazyki russkoj kul'tury.

Apresjan, V. (1997). "Fear" and "Pity" in Russian and English from a lexicographic perspective. *International Journal of Lexicography, 10*, 85–111.

Araki, H. (1994). *Nihongo ga mieru to eigo mo mieru: shin eigo kyouiku ron.* [Once you understand Japanese, you will understand English, too: A new theory for English education]. Tokyo: Chuo Couron Sha.

Ariel, M. (Ed.). (2002). Literal, minimal, and salient meanings [Special Issue]. *Journal of Pragmatics*, 34.

Aristotle. *Rethorica*. Available online at http://rhetoric.eserver.org/aristotle/

Arnold, M. B. (1960). *Emotion and personality. Vol. 1. Psychological aspects.* New York: Columbia University Press.

Athanasiadou, A. (1998). The conceptualisation of the domain of fear in Modern Greek. In A. Athanasiadou & E. Tabakowska (Eds.), *Speaking of emotions: Conceptualization and expression* (pp. 227–52). Berlin: Mouton de Gruyter.

Aue, T., & Scherer, K. R. (2008). Appraisal-driven somatovisceral response patterning: Effects of intrinsic pleasantness and goal conduciveness. *Biological Psychology*, 79, 158–64.

Aue, T., & Scherer, K. R. (2011). Effects of intrinsic pleasantness and goal conduciveness appraisals on somatovisceral responding: Somewhat similar, but not identical. *Biological Psychology*, 86, 65–73.

Aue, T., Flykt, A., & Scherer, K. R. (2007). First evidence for differential and sequential efferent effects of stimulus relevance and goal conduciveness appraisal. *Biological Psychology*, 74, 347–57.

Austin J. (1956). A plea for excuses. *Proceedings of the Aristotelian Society*, 57, 1–30.

Austin, E. J. (2010). Measurement of ability emotional intelligence: Results for two new tests. *British Journal of Psychology*, 101, 563–78.

Ausubel, D. P. (1955). Relationships between shame and guilt in the socialization process. *Psychological Review*, 67, 378–90.

Averill, J. (1975). A semantic atlas of emotional concepts. *JSAS Catalog of Selected Documents in Psychology.* (Ms. No. 421), 5(330), 1–64.

Averill, J. (1980). A constructivist view of emotion. In R. Plutchik & H. Kellerman (Eds.), *Emotion: Theory, research, and experience* (Vol. 1, pp. 305–40). New York: Academic Press.

Averill, J. (2009). Vocabulary of emotion. In D. Sander & K. R. Scherer (Eds.), *Oxford companion to emotion and the affective sciences* (pp. 403–4). Oxford: Oxford University Press.

Baccianella, S., Esuli, A., & Sebastiani, F. (2010). SentiWordNet 3.0: An enhanced lexical resource for sentiment analysis and opinion mining. In *Proceedings of the Seventh conference on International Language Resources and Evaluation (LREC'10)* (pp. 2200–4).

Bagozzi, R. P., Verbeke, W., & Gavino, J. C., Jr. (2003). Culture moderates the self-regulation of shame and its effects on performance: the case of salespersons in the Netherlands and the Philippines. *Journal of Applied Psychology*, 88, 219–33.

Banse, R., & Scherer, K. R. (1996). Acoustic profiles in vocal emotion expression. *Journal of Personality and Social Psychology*, 70, 614–36.

Bänziger, T., Grandjean, D., & Scherer, K. R. (2009). Emotion recognition from expressions in face, voice, and body: The multimodal emotion recognition test (MERT). *Emotion*, 9, 691–704.

Bänziger, T., Tran, V., & Scherer, K. R. (2003). Dimensionality and similarity ratings of emotion labels: A validation study of French and English labels included in the Geneva Emotion Wheel. Unpublished report to the Gottlieb-Daimler-und- Karl-Benz-Stiftung, University of Geneva.

Bänziger, T., Tran, V., & Scherer, K. R. (2005, June). *The emotion wheel. A tool for the verbal report of emotional reactions.* Poster presented at the International Society of Research on Emotion, ISRE 2005, Bari, Italy.

Barasch, M. (1999). Despair in the medieval imagination. *Social Research*, 66, 565–76.

Barcelona, A. (1986). On the concept of depression in American English: A cognitive approach. *Revista Canaria de Estudios Ingleses*, 12, 7–35.

Barcelona, A. (1989a). Análisis contrastivo del léxico figurado de la ira en inglés y en español. *Actas del VI Congreso Nacional de Lingüística Aplicada. AESLA* (pp. 141–8). Santander: Universidad de Cantabria.

Barcelona, A. (1989b). Being crestfallen/estar con las orejas gachas, o por qué es metafórica y metonímica la depresión en inglés y en español. In J. Santoyo (Ed.), *Actas del XI Congreso de ADEAN*, (pp. 219–25). León: Universidad de León.

Barcelona, A. (1992). El lenguaje del amor romántico en inglés y en español. *Atlantis. Revista de la Asociación Española de Estudios Anglonorteamericanos, 14*(1), 2–27.

Barcelona, A. (1995). Metaphorical models of romantic love in *Romeo and Juliet. Journal of Pragmatics, 24*, 667–88.

Bardzell, S., Bardzell, J., & Pace, T. (2009). Understanding affective interaction: Emotion, engagement, and internet videos. In *Proceedings of 2009 IEEE International Conference on Affective Computing and Intelligent Interaction*.

Barker, K., & Davey, G. C. L. (1997). *Categories of disgust: A factor analysis study*. (Unpublished manuscript). Brighton, UK: University of Sussex.

Barrett, L. F. (2005). Feeling is perceiving: Core affect and conceptualization in the experience of emotion. In L. F. Barrett, P. Niedenthal, & P. Winkielman (Eds.), *Emotion and consciousness* (pp. 255–84). New York: Guilford Press.

Barrett, L. F. (2006a). Are emotions natural kinds? *Perspectives on Psychological Science, 1*, 28–58.

Barrett, L. F. (2006b). Solving the emotion paradox: Categorization and the experience of emotion. *Personality and Social Psychology Review, 10*, 20–46.

Barrett, L. F. (2009). Variety is the spice of life: A psychological construction approach to understanding variability in emotion. *Cognition & Emotion, 23*, 1284–306.

Barrett, L. F., & Russell, J. A. (1999). The structure of current affect. *Current Directions in Psychological Science, 8*, 10–4.

Barrett, L. F., Gross, J., Christensen, T. C., & Benvenuto, M. (2001). Knowing what you're feeling and knowing what to do about it: Mapping the relation between emotion differentiation and emotion regulation. *Cognition & Emotion, 15*, 713–24.

Barrett, L. F., Lindquist, K., & Gendron, M. (2007). Language as context for the perception of emotion. *Trends in Cognitive Sciences, 11*, 327–32.

Barrett, L. F., Tugade, M. M., & Fredrickson, B. L. (2004). Psychological resilience and positive emotional granularity: Examining the benefits of positive emotions on coping and health. *Journal of Personality, 72*, 1161–90.

Bartlett, D. L. (1999). Physiological responses to music and sound stimuli. In D. A. Hodges (Ed.), *Handbook of Music Psychology* (2nd ed., pp. 343–85). San Antonio: IMR.

Bashore, T. R., & van der Molen, M. W. (1991). Discovery of the P300: A tribute. *Biological Psychology, 32*, 155–71.

Batic, G. (2011). Love encoding in Hausa: Sources and conceptual models. In G. C. Batic (Ed.), *Encoding Emotions in African Languages* (pp. 139–51). Muenchen: Lincom GmbH.

Bauer, A. (1973). Das melanesische und chinesische Pidginenglish. Regensburg: Carl.

Baumeister, R. F., Stillwell, A. M., & Heatherton, T. F. (1994). Guilt: An interpersonal approach. *Psychological Bulletin, 115*, 243–67.

Bayer, M., Sommer, W., & Schacht, A. (2010). Reading emotional words within sentences: The impact of arousal and valence on event-related potentials. *International Journal of Psychophysiology, 78*, 299–307.

Bayer, M., Sommer, W., & Schacht, A. (2011). Emotional words impact the mind but not the body: Evidence from pupillary responses. *Psychophysiology, 48*, 1554–62.

Bear, G. G., Uribe-Zarain, X., Manning, M. A., & Shiomi, K. (2009). Shame, guilt, blaming, and anger: Differences between children in Japan and the US. *Motivation and Emotion, 33*, 229–38.

Beatty, A. (2005). Emotions in the filed: What are we talking about? *Journal of the Royal Anthropological Institute, 11*, 17–37.

Beaupré, M. G., & Hess, U. (2005). Cross-cultural emotion recognition among Canadian ethnic groups. *Journal of Cross-Cultural Psychology, 36*, 355–70.

Becher, J. (2003). Experiencer constructions in Wolof. *Hamburger Afrikanistische Arbeitspapiere, 2*, 1–89. Retrieved from http://www.aai.uni-hamburg.de/afrika/HAAP/Becher2003.pdf.

Beck, A., Stevens, B., & Bard, K. (2009). Comparing perception of affective body movements displayed by actors and animated characters. In N. Berthouze, M. Gillies, & A. Ayesh (Eds.), *Proceedings of the symposium on mental states, emotions and their embodiment at the AISB convention 2009* (pp. 10–5). Edinburgh: SSAISB.

Bender, A., Spada, H., Seitz, S., Swoboda, H., & Traber, S. (2007). Anger and rank in Tonga and Germany: Cognition, emotion, and context. *Ethos, 35*, 196–234.

Benedict, R. (1946). *The chrysanthemum and the sword: Patterns of Japanese culture*. Boston: Houghton Mifflin.

Benoist, A., Roussin, M., Fredette, M., & Rousseau, S. (1965). Depression among French Canadians in Montreal. *Transcultural Psychiatric Research Review, 2*, 52–4.

Berger A., & Jäkel O. (2009). ANGER, LOVE and SADNESS revisited: Differences in emotion metaphors between experts and laypersons in the genre psychology guides. *Metaphorik.de, 16*, 87–108. Retrieved from http://www.metaphorik.de/16/BegerJaekel.pdf.

Bernat, E., Patrick, C. J., Benning, S. D., & Tellegen, A. (2006). Effects of picture content and intensity on affective physiological response. *Psychophysiology, 43*, 93–103.

Berry, J. W. (1999). Emics and etics: A symbiotic conception. *Culture & Psychology, 5*, 165–71.

Berry, J. W., Poortinga, Y. H., Breugelmans, S. M., Chasiotis, A., & Sam, D. L. (2011). *Cross-cultural psychology: Research and applications* (3rd ed.). Cambridge: Cambridge University Press.

Berry, J. W., Poortinga, Y. H., Segall, M. H., & Dasen, P. R. (2002). *Cross-cultural psychology: Research and applications* (2nd ed.). Cambridge: Cambridge University Press.

Besemeres, M. (2006). Language and emotional experience: The voice of translingual memoir. In A. Pavlenko (Ed.), *Bilingual minds: Emotional experience, expression, and representation* (pp. 34–58). Clevedon, UK: Multilingual Matters.

Besnier, N. (1990). Language and affect. *Annual Review of Anthropology, 19*, 419–51.

Bharata, K. M. R. (1956). *Natyasastra by Bharatamuni.* (M. R. Kavi, Ed.). Baroda: Gaekwad Oriental Series.

Bierbrauer, G. (1992). Reactions to violation of normative standards: A cross-cultural analysis of shame and guilt. *International Journal of Psychology, 27*, 181–93.

Bilodid, I. K. (1970). *SUM- Slovnyk ukrains'koi movy v 11 tomah.* [Dictionary of the Ukrainian language in 11 volumes]. Kyïv: Naukova dumka.

Bird, A., & Tobin, E. (2008). Natural kinds. In E. N. Zalta (Ed.), *The Stanford Encyclopedia of Philosophy (Summer 2010 Edition)*. Retrieved from http://plato.stanford.edu/archives/sum2010/entries/natural-kinds.

Blanchard, D. C., & Blanchard, R. J. (2005). Stress and aggressive behaviors. In R. Nelson (Ed.), *Biology of aggression* (pp. 275–94). Oxford: Oxford University Press.

Blanchard, R. J., Blanchard, D. C., Takahashi, L. K., & Kelley M. J. (1977). Attack and defensive behaviour in the albino rat. *Animal Behavior, 25*, 622–634.

Block, J. (1957). Studies in the phenomenology of emotions. *Journal of Abnormal and Social Psychology, 54*, 358–63.

Bloom, P. (2004). Descartes' baby: How the science of child development explains what makes us human. New York: Basic Books. BNC: British National Corpus. (n.d.). Available at http://www.natcorp.ox.ac.uk/

Boezeman, E. J., & Ellemers, N. (2007). Volunteering for charity: pride, respect, and the commitment of volunteers. *The Journal of Applied Psychology, 92*, 771–85.

Bond, M. H., Leung, K., Au, A., Tong, K.-K., de Carrasquel, S. R., Murakami, F., Yamaguchi, S., et al. (2004). Culture-level dimensions of social axioms and their correlates across 41 Cultures. *Journal of Cross-Cultural Psychology, 35*, 548–70.

Bondeelle, O. (2011). From body to emotion in Wolof: a phraseology process. In G.C. Batic (Ed.), *Encoding Emotions in African Languages* (pp. 17–34). LINCOM Studies in African Languages 84. Muenchen: Lincom GmbH.

Boratav, H. B., Sunar, D., & Ataca, B. (2011). Emotional display rules and their contextual determinants: A study with Turkish university students. *Turkish Psychology Journal (Türk Psikoloji Dergisi), 27* (67), 90–101. (In Turkish).

Borg, I., & Groenen, P. (1997). Modern multidimensional scaling: Theory and applications. New York: Springer.

Borg, J. S., Lieberman, D., & Kiehl, K. A. (2008). Infection, incest, and iniquity: investigating the neural correlates of disgust and morality. *Journal of Cognitive Neuroscience, 20*, 1529–46.

Borg, I., & Shye, S. (1995). *Facet Theory: Form and Content*. Thousand Oaks, CA: Sage.

Boster, J. S. (2005). Emotion Categories across Languages. In C. LeFebvre & H. Cohen (Eds.), *Categorization in the Cognitive Sciences* (pp. 198–220). Amsterdam: Elsevier.

Bracha, H. S. (2004). Freeze, flight, fight, fright, faint: Adaptationist perspectives on the acute stress response spectrum. *CNS Spectrums, 9*, 679–85.

Bradley, M. M., Codispoti, M., Cuthbert, B. N., & Lang, P. J. (2001). Emotion and motivation I: Defensive and appetitive reactions in picture processing. *Emotion, 1*, 276–98.

Bradley, M. M., Codispoti, M., Sabatinelli, D., & Lang, P. J. (2001). Emotion and motivation II: sex differences in picture processing. *Emotion, 1*, 300–19.

Bradley, M. M., Cuthbert, B. N., & Lang, P. J. (1998). *International Affective Digitized Sounds. Technical Manual and Affective Ratings*. Gainsville: University of Florida, The Center for Research in Psychophysiology.

Bradley, M. M., Greenwald, M. K., & Hamm, A. O. (1993). Affective picture processing. In N. Birbaumer & A. Öhman (Eds.), *The Structure of emotion: Psychophysiological, cognitive, and clinical aspects* (pp. 48–65). Seattle: Hogrefe & Huber.

Bradley, M. M., & Lang, P. J. (1994). Measuring emotion: The self-assessment manikin and the semantic differential. *Journal of Behavior Therapy and Experimental Psychiatry, 25*, 49–59.

Bradley, M. M., & Lang, P. J. (1999). *Affective norms for English words (ANEW): Stimuli, instruction manual, and affective ratings* (Tech. Rep. No. C-1). Gainsville: University of Florida, The Center for Research in Psychophysiology.

Bradley, M. M., Miccoli, L., Escrig, M. A., & Lang, P. J. (2008). The pupil as a measure of emotional arousal and autonomic activation. *Psychophysiology, 45*, 602–7.

Brandt, M. E., & Boucher, J. D. (1986). Concepts of depression in emotion lexicons of eight cultures. *International Journal of Intercultural Relations, 10*, 321–46.

Breckler, S. J. (1984). Empirical validation of affect, behavior, and cognition as distinct components of attitude. *Journal of Personality and Social Psychology, 47*, 1191–205.

Bretherton, I., & Beeghly, M. (1982). Talking about internal states: The acquisition of an explicit theory of mind. *Developmental Psychology, 18*, 906–12.

Breugelmans, S. M. (2009). Embarrassment. In D. Sander & K. R. Scherer (Eds.), *Oxford companion to emotion and the affective sciences* (pp. 138–9). New York: Oxford University Press.

Breugelmans, S. M., & Poortinga, Y. H. (2006). Emotion without a word: Shame and guilt among Rarámuri Indians and Rural Javanese. *Journal of Personality and Social Psychology, 91*, 1111–22.

Breugelmans, S. M., Poortinga, Y. H., Ambadar, Z., Setiadi, B., Vaca, J. B., Widiyanto, P., & Philippot, P. (2005). Body sensations associated with emotions in Rarámuri Indians, rural Javanese, and three student samples. *Emotion, 5*, 166–74.

Briggs, J. L. (1970). *Never in Anger: Portrait of an Eskimo Family*. Cambridge, MA: Harvard University Press.

Briggs, J. L. (1998). *Inuit morality play: The emotional education of a three-year-old*. New Haven, CT: Yale University Press.

Brosch, T., & Scherer, K. R. (2012). Relevance and attention: An appraisal theory perspective on the emotional modulation of attention. Manuscript submitted for publication.

Brosch, T., Sander, D., & Scherer, K. R. (2007). That baby caught my eye . . . Attention capture by infant faces. *Emotion, 7*, 685–9.

Brown, C. H. (1989). Naming the days of the week: A cross-language study of lexical acculturation. *Current Anthropology, 30*, 536–50.

Bruce, K. L., & Bruce, L. P. (2010). Emotions in the Alamblak lexicon. In K. A. McElhanon and G. Reesink (Eds.), *A mosaic of languages and cultures: Studies celebrating the career of K.J. Franklin* (pp. 38–59). Dallas: SIL International.

Brunori, P., Ladavas, A., & Ricci-Bitti, P. E. (1979). Differential aspects in the recognition of facial expression of emotions. *Italian Journal of Psychology, 6*, 265–72.

Bugenhagen, R. D. (1990). Experiential constructions in Mangap-Mbula. *Australian Journal of Linguistics, 10*, 183–215.

Bugenhagen, R. D. (2001). Emotions and the nature of persons in Mbula. In J. Harkins & A. Wierzbicka (Eds.), *Emotions in crosslinguistic perspective* (pp. 73–118). Berlin: Mouton de Gruyter.

Bundgaard, P. F., Østergaard, S., & Stjernfelf, F. (2007). Meaning construction in the production and interpretation of compounds is schema-driven. *Acta Linguistica Hafniensia: International Journal of Linguistics, 39*, 155–77.

Burger, L. K., & Miller, P. J. (1999). Early talk about the past revisited: Affect in working-class and middle-class children's co-narrations. *Journal of Child Language, 26*, 133–62.

Caceido, D. G. & van Beuzekom, M. (2006). "How do you feel?" An assessment of existing tools for the measurement of emotions and their application in consumer products research. Report, Delft University of Technology. Retrieved 13/4/2012 from http://bluehaired.com/corner/wp-content/uploads/2008/10/final-report-assessment-of-existing-tools-for-the-measurement-of-emotions.pdf.

Cacioppo, J. T., Petty, R. E., Losch, M. E., & Kim, H. S. (1986). Electromyographic activity over facial muscle regions can discriminate the valence and intensity of affective reactions. *Journal of Personality and Social Psychology, 50*, 260–8.

Cacioppo, J. T., Tassinary, L. G., & Berntson, G. G. (2000). *Handbook of psychophysiology*. New York: Cambridge University Press.

Cacioppo, J. T., Uchino, B. N., Crites, S. L., Snydersmith, M. A., Smith, G., Berntson, G. G., & Lang, P. J. (1992). Relationship between facial expressiveness and sympathetic activation in emotion: A critical review, with emphasis on modeling underlying mechanisms and individual differences. *Journal of Personality and Social Psychology, 62*, 110–28.

Canli, T., Qiu, M., Omura, K., Congdon, E., Haas, B. W., Amin, Z., Herrmann, M. J., et al. (2006). Neural correlates of epigenesis. *Proceedings of the National Academy of Sciences of the United States of America, 103*, 16033–8.

Cannon, W. (1929). Bodily changes in pain, hunger, fear and rage an account of recent researches into the function of emotional excitement. (2nd ed.). New York: D. Appleton & Co.

Cannon, W. B. (1927). The James-Lange theory of emotions: Critical examination and an alternative theory. *The American Journal of Psychology, 39*, 106–24.

Caplan, D. (1992). Language: structure, processing, and disorders. Cambridge, MA: MIT Press.

Carruthers, P. (2008). Language in cognition. In R. Margolis, R. Samuels, & S. Stich (Eds.), *The Oxford handbook of philosophy of cognitive science*. Oxford: Oxford University Press.

Casasanto, D. & Dijkstra, K. (2010). Motor action and emotional memory. *Cognition, 115*, 179–85.

Cassell, E. J. (2002). Compassion. In C. R. Snyder & S. J. Lopez (Eds.), *Handbook of positive psychology*. New York: Oxford University Press.

Castelfranchi, C., & Poggi, I. (1990). Blushing as discourse: Was Darwin wrong? In R. Crozier (Ed.), *Shyness and embarrassment: A social psychological perspective* (pp. 230–51). New York: Cambridge University Press.

Cattell, R. B. (1943). The description of personality: Basic traits resolved into clusters. *Journal of Abnormal and Social Psychology, 38*, 476–506.

Cattell, R. B. (1966). The scree test for the number of factors. *Mutivariate Behavioral Research*, *1*, 245–76.

Cattell, R. B. (1990). Advances in Cattellian Personality Theory. In L. A. Pervin (Ed.), *Handbook of Personality: Theory and Research* (pp. 101–10). New York: Guilford.

Cervantes, C. A. (2002). Explanatory emotion talk in Mexican immigrant and Mexican American families. *Hispanic Journal of Behavioral Sciences*, *24*, 138–63.

Cervantes, C. A., & Callanan, M. A. (1998). Labels and explanations in mother-child emotion talk: Age and gender differentiation. *Developmental Psychology*, *34*, 88–98.

Chamberlain, A. F. (1895). On the Words for "Anger" in certain languages. A study in linguistic psychology. *The American Journal of Psychology*, *6*, 585–92.

Chamberlain, A. F. (1899). On the words for "Fear" in certain languages. A study in linguistic psychology. *The American Journal of Psychology*, *10*, 302–5. doi:10.2307/1412486.

Chan, D. W. (1990). The meaning of depression: the Chinese word associations. *Psychologia*, *33*, 191–6.

Chapman, H. A., Kim, D. A., Susskind, J. M., & Anderson, A. K. (2009). In bad taste: Evidence for the oral origins of moral disgust. *Science*, *323*, 1222–6.

Chapman, R. M., McCrary, J. W., Chapman, J. A., & Martin, J. K. (1980). Behavioral and neural analyses of connotative meaning: Word classes and rating scales. *Brain and Language*, *11*, 319–39.

Charland, L. C. (1995). Feeling and representing: Computational theory and the modularity of affect. *Synthese*, *105*, 273–301.

Cheetham, W. S., & Cheetham, R. J. (1976). Concepts of mental illness amongst the rural Xhosa people in South Africa. *Australian and New Zealand Journal of Psychiatry*, *10*, 39–45.

Chernyh, P. Y. (1993). *Istoriko-etymologicheskij slovar' russkogo yazyka*. [The etymological dictionary of the Russian language] (Vols. 1–2). Moscow: Rysskij Yazyk.

Choi, S. C., & Han, G. (2008). Shimcheong psychology: A case of cultural emotion for cultural psychology. *International Journal for Dialogical Science*, *3*, 205–24.

Choi, S. C., Kim, U., & Choi, S. H. (1993). Indigenous analysis of collective representations: A Korean perspective. In U. Kim & J. W. Berry (Eds.), *Indigenous psychologies: Research and experience in cultural context* (pp. 193–210). Newbury Park, CA: Sage.

Chomsky, N. (1980). *Rules and Representations*. New York: Columbia University Press.

Chon, K. K. (2002). Cultural aspects of anger. In C. von Hofsten & L. Bäckman (Eds.), *Psychology at the turn of the millennium: Vol. 2: Social, developmental, and clinical perspectives* (pp. 323–46). East Sussex, UK: Psychology Press.

Chon, K. K., Kim, K. H., & Ryoo, J. B. (2000). Experience and expression of anger in Korea and America. *Korean Journal of Rehabilitation Psychology*, *7*, 61–75.

Church, A. T., Katigbak, M. S., Reyes, J. A. S., & Jensen, S. M. (1998). Language and organization of Filipino emotion concepts: Comparing emotion concepts and dimensions across cultures. *Cognition & Emotion*, *12*, 63–92.

Cienki, A. & Müller, C. (Eds) (2008). *Metaphor and gesture*. Amsterdam: John Benjamins.

Clark, H. H., & Clark, E. (1977). *Psychology of language*. New York: Harcourt, Brace, Jovanovich.

Clore, G. L., Ortony, A., & Foss, M. A. (1987). The Psychological foundations of the affective Llexicon. *Journal of Personality and Social Psychology*, *53*, 751–66.

Cohen, J. (1992). A power primer. *Psychological Bulletin*, *112*(1), 155–9, doi:10.1037/0033-2909.112.1.155.

Cohen, D., Hoshino-Browne, E., & Leung, A. K.-Y. (2007). Culture and the structure of personal experience: Insider and outsider phenomenologies of the self and social world. In M. P. Zanna (Ed.), *Advances in Experimental Social Psychology* (Vol. 39, pp. 1–67). San Diego, CA: Academic Press.

Conroy, M. A., & Polich, J. (2007). Affective valence and P300 when stimulus arousal level is controlled. *Cognition & Emotion*, *21*, 891–901.

Conway, A. M., & Bekerian, A. D. (1987). Situational knowledge and emotion. *Cognition & Emotion*, *1*, 145–91.

Corrigan, R. (2007). An experimental analysis of the affective dimensions of deep vocabulary knowledge used in inferring the meaning of words in context. *Applied Linguistics*, *28*, 211–40.

Cowie, R., Douglas-Cowie, E., Savvidou, S., McMahon, E., Sawey, M., & Schröder, M. (2000). FEELTRACE: An instrument for recording perceived emotion in real time. In *Proceedings of the ISCA Tutorial and Research Workshop (ITRW) on Speech and Emotion* (pp. 19–24). Belfast: Textflow.

Cowling, W. R. (2004). Despair: a unitary appreciative inquiry. *Advances in Nursing Science*, *27*, 287–300.

Cowling, W. R. (2008). An essay on women, despair, and healing: A personal narrative. *Advances in Nursing Science*, *31*, 249–58.

Craig, A. D. (2002). How do you feel? Interoception: the sense of the physiological condition of the body. *Nature Reviews Neuroscience*, *3*, 655–66.

Cramer, A. O. J., Van der Sluis, S., Noordhof, A., Wichers, M., Geschwind, N., Aggen, S. H., Kendler, K. S., & Borsboom, D. (2012). Dimensions of normal personality as networks in search of equilibrium: You can't like parties if you don't like people. *European Journal of Personality*, *26*, 414–31.

Crawford, L. E. (2009). Conceptual Metaphors of Affect. *Emotion Review*, *1*, 129–39.

Critchley, H. D., Tang, J., Glaser, D., Butterworth, B., & Dolan, R. J. (2005). Anterior cingulate activity during error and autonomic response. *NeuroImage*, *27*, 885–95.

Crocket, D. B. (2002). Shame, resentment, envy, and pity—A semantic analysis. *Lingua*, *47*, 279–300.

Croft, W., & Cruse, D. A. (2004). *Cognitive Linguistics*. Cambridge: Cambridge University Press.

Crozier, W. R. (2001). Blushing and the exposed self: Darwin revisited. *Journal for the Theory of Social Behaviour*, *31*, 61–72.

Cruse, D. A. (1986). *Lexical semantics*. Cambridge: Cambridge University Press.

Crystal, D. (1997). *The Cambridge Encyclopedia of language* (2nd ed.). Cambridge, UK: Cambridge University Press.

Cumming, G. (2008). Inference by eye: Reading the overlap of independent confidence intervals. *Statistics in Medicine*, *28*, 205–20.

Cumming, G., & Finch, S. (2005). Inference by eye: Confidence intervals and how to read pictures of data. *American Psychologist*, *60*, 170–8.

Curtis, V., & Biran, A. (2001). Dirt, disgust, and disease: Is hygiene in our genes? *Perspectives in Biology and Medicine*, *44*, 17–31.

Cuthbert, B. N., Schupp, H. T., Bradley, M. M., Birbaumer, N., & Lang, P. J. (2000). Brain potentials in affective picture processing: covariation with autonomic arousal and affective report. *Biological Psychology*, *52*, 95–111.

D'Andrade, R., Boster, J., & Ellsworth, P. C. (in preparation). *The structure of feelings*.

Dael, N., Mortillaro, M., & Scherer, K. R. (2012). Emotion expression in body action and posture. *Emotion*, *12*, 1085–101.

Dal', V. I. (1880). *Tolkovij slovar' zhivogo velikorusskogo yazyka*. [Explanatory dictionary of the live great Russian language] (Vols. 1–4). Moscow-St. Petersbrug: Izdanie M.O. Vol'fa. Also available at http://slovari.yandex.ru/dict/dal/.

Dan Glauser, E. S., & Scherer, K. R. (2008). Neuronal processes involved in subjective feeling emergence: Oscillatory activity during an emotional monitoring task. *Brain Topography*, *20*, 224–31.

Danaher, D. (2002). The semantics of pity and zhalost' in a literary context. *Glossos*, *3*. Retrieved from http://www.seelrc.org/glossos/issues/3/danaher.pdf.

Danovitch, J., & Bloom, P. (2009). Children's extension of disgust to physical and moral events. *Emotion*, *9*, 107–12.

Darwin, C. (1872). The origin of species by means of natural selection, or, the preservation of favoured races in the struggle for life. London: John Murray.

Darwin, C. (1965). *The expression of the emotions in man and animals*. Chicago: The University of Chicago Press. (Original work published 1872).

Darwin, C. (1972). *The Expression of the emotion in man and animals*. Oxford, UK: Appleton. (Original work published 1872).

Darwin, C. (1998). *The expression of the emotions in man and animals*. (P. Ekman, Ed.) (3rd ed.). London: HarperCollins. (Original work published 1872).

Davison, A. C., & Hinkley, D. V. (1997). *Bootstrap methods and their application*. Cambridge: Cambridge University Press.

Davidson, R. J., Pizzagalli, D., Nitschke, J. B., & Kalin, N. H. (2003). Parsing the subcomponents of emotion and disorders of emotion: Perspectives from affective neuroscience. In R. J. Davidson, K. R. Scherer, & H. Goldsmith (Eds.), *Handbook of the Affective Sciences* (pp. 8–24). New York and Oxford: Oxford University Press.

Davidson, R. J., Scherer, K. R., & Goldsmith, H. (Eds.). (2003). *Handbook of the Affective Sciences*. New York and Oxford: Oxford University Press.

Davitz, J. R. (1969). *The language of emotion*. New York: Academic Press.

De Mauro, T. (2005). Dialetti [Dialects]. In G. Calcagno (Ed.), *Bianco, rosso e verde: l'identità degli italiani*, [White, red and green: The Italians' identity] (pp. 59–68). Roma-Bari, Italy: Laterza.

De Rivera, J. H. (1977). A structural theory of the emotions. *Psychological Issues, 10*(4), (Monograph No. 40) New York: International Universities Press.

de Saussure, F. (2002). *Ecrits de linguistique générale*. (S. Bouquet & R. Engler, Eds.). Paris: Gallimard.

Deci, E., & Ryan, R. (Eds.). (2002). *Handbook of self-determination research*. Rochester, NY: University of Rochester Press.

Delgado, A. R. (2007). Spanish basic emotion words are consistently ordered. *Quality and Quantity, 43*, 509–17.

Delplanque, S., Grandjean, D., Chrea, C., Coppin, G., Aymard, L., Cayeux, I., Margot, C., et al. (2009). Sequential unfolding of novelty and pleasantness appraisals of odors: Evidence from facial electromyography and autonomic reactions. *Emotion, 9*, 316–28.

Delplanque, S., Silvert, L., Hot, P., Rigoulot, S., & Sequeira, H. (2006). Arousal and valence effects on event-related P3a and P3b during emotional categorization. *International Journal of Psychophysiology, 60*, 315–22.

Delplanque, S., Silvert, L., Hot, P., & Sequeira, H. (2005). Event-related P3a and P3b in response to unpredictable emotional stimuli. *Biological Psychology, 68*, 107–20.

Den Boon, T., & Geeraerts, D. (Eds.). (2005). *Van Dale groot woordenboek van de Nederlandse taal*. Utrecht, The Netherlands: Van Dale Uitgevers.

Dennett, D. (1988). Quining qualia. In A. Marcel & E. Bisiach (Eds.), *Consciousness in modern science* (pp. 42–77). Oxford: Oxford University Press.

Dennett, D. (2001). Are we explaining consciousness yet? *Cognition, 79*, 221–37.

Deonna, J., & Scherer, K. R. (2009). The case of the disappearing intentional object: Constraints on a definition of emotion. *Emotion Review, 2*, 44–52.

Desmet, P. M. A. (2003). Measuring emotion; development and application of an instrument to measure emotional responses to products. In M. A. Blythe, A. F. Monk, K. Overbeeke, & P. C. Wright (Eds.), *Funology: From usability to enjoyment* (pp. 111–23). Dordrecht: Kluwer Academic Publishers.

Dewaele, J., & Pavlenko, A. (2002). Emotion vocabulary in interlanguage. *Language Learning, 52*, 263–322.

Diller, A. V. N., & Juntanamalaga, P. (1990). "Full hearts" & empty pronominals in Thai. *Australian Journal of Linguistics, 10*, 231–55.

Dimitrova, E. V. (2001). *Translyatsija emotivnyh smyslov russkogo kontsepta TOSKA vo francuzskuu linguokul'turu*. [Translation of the emotional meanings of the Russian concept TOSKA into the French lingual culture]. (Unpublished doctoral dissertation). Volgograd State Pedagogical University, Volgograd.

Divjak, D., & Gries, S. (2006). Ways of trying in Russian: clustering behavioral profiles. *Corpus Linguistics and Linguistic Theory, 2*, 23–60.

Divjak, D., & Gries, S. (2008). Clusters in the mind? Converging evidence from near synonymy in Russian. *The Mental Lexicon, 3*, 188–213.

Dobrovol'skij, D., & Piirainen, E. (2005). *Figurative language: Cross-cultural and cross-linguistic perspectives.* Current Research in the Semantics/pragmatics Interface (1st ed., Vol. 13). Amsterdam: Elsevier Science Ltd.

Doi, T. (1981). The Anatomy of dependence: The key analysis of Japanese behavior (2nd ed.). Tokyo: Kodansha International.

Doi, T. (1990). The cultural assumptions of psychoanalysis. In J. W. Stigler, R. A. Shweder, & G. H. Herdt (Eds.), *Cultural psychology: Essays on comparative human development* (pp. 446–53). Cambridge: Cambridge University Press.

Dubovskiy, Y. A. (1979). *Konkretno-yazykovoye i tipologicheskoye v anglijskoj intonatsii.* [Specific linguistic and typological features in English intonation]. Minsk: Minsk Pedagogical Institute of Foreign Languages.

Duffy, E. (1941). An explanation of "emotional" phenomena without the use of the concept "emotion." *Journal of General Psychology, 25,* 283–93.

Duffy, E. (1957). The psychological significance of the concept of "arousal" or "activation." *Psychological Review, 64,* 265–75.

Dunn, J. (2003). Emotional development in early childhood: a social relationship perspective. In R. J. Davidson, K. R. Scherer, & H. H. Goldsmith (Eds.), *Handbook of affective sciences* (pp. 332–46). New York: Oxford University Press.

Dunn, J., & Brown, J. (1994). Affect expression in the family, children's understanding of emotions, and their interactions with others. *Merrill-Palmer Quarterly, 40,* 120–37.

Dunn, J. R. and Schweitzer, M.E. (2005). Feeling and believing: The influence of emotion on trust. *Journal of Personality and Social Psychology, 88,* 736–48.

Durst, U. (2001). Why Germans don't feel "anger." In J. Harkins & A. Wierzbicka (Eds.), *Emotions in crosslinguistic perspective* (pp. 119–52). Berlin: Mouton de Gruyter.

Dziwirek, K., & Lewandowska-Tomaszczyk, B. (2010). *Complex emotions and grammatical mismatches: A contrastive corpus-based study.* Berlin: Mouton de Gruyter.

Dzokoto, V., & Adams, G. (2007). Analyzing Ghanaian emotions through narrative: A textual analysis of Ama Ata Aidoo's novel changes. *Journal of Black Psychology, 33,* 94–112.

Dzokoto, V. A., & Okazaki, S. (2006). Happiness in the eye and the heart: Somatic referencing in West African emotion lexica. *Journal of Black Psychology, 32,* 17–140.

Edelmann, R. J., Asendorpf, J., Contarello, A., Zammuner, V., Georgas, J., & Villanueva, C. (1989). Self-reported expression of embarrassment in five European cultures. *Journal of Cross-Cultural Psychology, 20,* 357–71.

Efron, B., & Tibshirani, R. J. (1993). *An introduction to the bootstrap.* New York: Chapman & Hall.

Eid, M., & Diener, E. (2001). Norms for experiencing emotions in different cultures: Inter- and intranational differences. *Journal of Personality and Social Psychology, 81,* 869–85.

Eilam, D. (2005). Die hard: A blend of freezing and fleeing as a dynamic defense–implications for the control of defensive behavior. *Neuroscience and Biobehavioral Reviews, 29,* 1181–91.

Ekman, P. (1955). Dimensions of emotion. *Acta Psychologica, 11,* 279–88.

Ekman, P. (1972). Universals and cultural differences in facial expression of emotion. In J. R. Cole (Ed.), *Nebraska symposium on motivation* (Vol. 19, pp. 207–83). Lincoln: University of Nebraska Press.

Ekman, P. (1973). Cross-cultural studies of facial expression. In P. Ekman (Ed.), *Darwin and facial expression* (pp. 169–222). New York: Academic Press.

Ekman, P. (1984). Expression and the nature of emotion. In K. R. Scherer & P. Ekman (Eds.), *Approaches to emotion* (pp. 319–44). Hillsdale, NJ: Erlbaum.

Ekman, P. (1992). An argument for basic emotions. *Cognition & Emotion, 6,* 169–200.

Ekman, P. (1994). Strong evidence for universals in facial expressions—A reply to Russells mistaken critique. *Psychological Bulletin, 115,* 268–87.

Ekman, P. (1999). Basic emotions. In T. Dalgleish & M. J. Power (Eds.), *Handbook of cognition and emotion* (pp. 45–60). Sussex, UK: John Wiley & Sons.

Ekman, P. (2003). Emotions revealed: Recognizing faces and feelings to improve communication and emotional life. New York: Times Books.

Ekman, P. (2004). What we become emotional about. In A. S. R. Manstead, N. Frijda, & A. Fischer, (Eds.), *Feelings and emotions: The Amsterdam symposium* (pp. 119–35), Cambridge and New York: Cambridge University Press.

Ekman, P., & Friesen, W. V. (1969). The repertoire of nonverbal behavior: Categories, origins, usage, and coding. *Semiotica*, *1*, 49–98.

Ekman, P., & Friesen, W. V. (1971). Constants across cultures in face and emotion. *Journal of Personality and Social Psychology*, *17*, 124–9.

Ekman, P., & Friesen, W. V. (1975). *Unmasking the face; a guide to recognizing emotions from facial clues.* Englewood Cliffs, NJ: Prentice Hall.

Ekman, P., & Friesen, W. V. (1978). *The Facial Action Coding System: A technique for the measurement of facial movement.* Palo Alto, CA: Consulting Psychologists Press.

Ekman, P., & Friesen, W. V. (1982). Felt, false, and miserable smiles. *Journal of Nonverbal Behavior*, *6*, 238–52.

Ekman, P. and Friesen, W. V. (1986). A new pan-cultural facial expression of emotion. *Motivation & Emotion*, *10*, 159–68.

Ekman, P., Levenson, R.W., & Friesen, W.V. (1983). Autonomic nervous system activity distinguishes between emotions. *Science*, *221*, 1208–10.

Ekman, P., & Oster, H. (1979). Facial expressions of emotion. *Annual Review of Psychology*, *30*, 527–54.

Ekman, P., Sorenson, E. R., & Friesen, W. V. (1969). Pan-cultural elements in facial displays of emotion. *Science*, *164*(3875), 86–8.

Elfenbein, H. A., & Ambady, N. (2002a). Is there an in-group advantage in emotion recognition? *Psychological Bulletin*, *128*, 243–9.

Elfenbein, H. A., & Ambady, N. (2002b). On the universality and cultural specificity of emotion recognition: A meta-analysis. *Psychological Bulletin*, *128*, 203–35.

Elfenbein, H. A., & Ambady, N. (2003). Universals and cultural differences in recognizing emotions. *Current Directions in Psychological Science*, *12*, 159–64.

Elfenbein, H. A., Beaupré, M. G., Levesque, M., & Hess, U. (2007). Toward a dialect theory: Cultural differences in the expression and recognition of posed facial expressions. *Emotion*, *7*, 131–46.

Ellsworth, P. C. (1994). William James and emotion: Is a century of fame worth a century of misunderstanding? *Psychological Review*, *101*, 222–9.

Ellsworth, P. C., & Scherer, K. R. (2003). Appraisal processes in emotion. In R. J. Davidson, K. R. Scherer, & H. H. Goldsmith (Eds.), *Handbook of affective sciences* (pp. 572–95). New York: Oxford University Press.

Enfield, N. J., & Wierzbicka, A. (Eds.). (2002). The body in description of emotion: Cross-linguistic studies pragmatics & cognition. *Pragmatics & Cognition*, *10*(1/2).

Enriquez, V. G. (1992). *From colonial to liberation psychology: The Philippine experience.* Quezon City: University of Philippine Press.

Ethnologue. (n.d.). Retrieved from http://www.ethnologue.com/.

Erickson, D. (2006). Some gender and cultural differences in perception of affective expressions. In *Proceedings of Speech Prosody 2006. ISCA Archive.*

Ertel, S. (1964). Die emotionale Natur des "semantischen" Raumes. *Psychologische Forschung*, *28*, 1–32.

Esuli, A. & Sebastiani, F. (2005). Determining the semantic orientation of terms through gloss analysis. In *Proceedings of CIKM-05, 14th ACM International Conference on Information and Knowledge Management* (pp. 617–24). Bremen.

Esuli, A. & Sebastiani, F. (2006). SENTIWORDNET: A publicly available lexical resource for opinion mining. In *Proceedings of LREC-06, 5th Conference on Language Resources and Evaluation* (pp. 417–22).

Evans, N., & Levinson, S. C. (2009). The myth of language universals: Language diversity and its importance for cognitive science. *Behavioral and Brain Sciences, 32*, 429–48.

Evgen'eva, A. P. (2003). *Slovar' sinonimov russkogo yazyka* [Dictionary of Synonyms of the Russian language] (Vols. 1–2). Moscow: Astrel.

Farrell, P. (2006). Portuguese SAUDADE and other emotions of absence and longing. In B. Peeters (Ed.), *Semantic primes and universal grammar: Empirical evidence from the Romance languages* (pp. 235–58). Amsterdam: John Benjamins.

Fehr, B. (1988). Prototype analysis of the concepts of love and commitment. *Journal of Personality and Social Psychology, 49*, 1416–26.

Fehr, B., & Russell, J. A. (1984). Concept of emotion viewed from a prototype perspective. *Journal of Experimental Psychology: General, 113*, 464–86.

Fehr, B., & Russell, J. A. (1991). The concept of love viewed from a prototype perspective. *Journal of Personality and Social Psychology, 60*, 425–38.

Feld, S. (1990). *Sound and Sentiment: Birds, Weeping, Poetics and Song in Kaluli Expression* (2nd ed.). Philadelphia, PA: University of Pennsylvania.

Feldman-Barrett, L. & Russell, J. A. (1998). Independence and bipolarity in the structure of current affect. *Journal of Personality & Social Psychology, 74*, 967–84.

Fellbaum, C. (1998). *WordNet: An Electronic Lexical Database*. Cambridge, MA: MIT Press.

Ferguson, F. J., & Austin, E. J. (2010). Associations of trait and ability emotional intelligence with performance on Theory of Mind tasks in an adult sample. *Personality and Individual Differences, 49*, 414–8.

Ferguson, F. J., & Austin, E. J. (2011). The factor structures of the STEM and the STEU. *Personality and Individual Differences, 51*, 791–4.

Fernandez-Dols, J. M., Carrera, P., & Casado, C. (2001). The meaning of expression: Views from art and other sources. In L. Anolli, R. Ciceri, & G. Riva (Eds.), *Say not to say: New perspectives on miscommunication* (pp. 122–37). Amsterdam: IOS Press.

Fillenbaum, S., & Rapoport, A. (1971). *Structures in the subjective lexicon*. New York: Academic Press.

Fillmore, C. (1975). An alternative to checklist theories of meaning. *Berkeley Linguistics Society, 1*, 123–31.

Fillmore, C. (1985). Frames and the semantics of understanding. *Quaderni di Semantica, 6*, 222–54.

Fillmore, C. J., Baker, C. F., & Sato, H. (2002). The FrameNet database and software tools. In *Proceedings of the Third International Conference on Language Resources and Evaluation (LREC)* (pp. 1157–60).

Finnish Literature Society. (1951). *Nykysuomen sanakirja*. [Dictionary of Modern Finnish] (Vols. 1–6). Helsinki: WSOY. (Published between 1951 and 1961).

Fischer, A., Manstead, A. S. R., & Rodriguez-Mosquera, P. M. (1999). The role of honor-related vs. individualistic values in conceptualising pride, shame, and anger: Spanish and Dutch cultural prototypes. *Cognition & Emotion, 13*, 149–79.

Fischer, R., & Fontaine, J. J. R. (2011). Methods for investigating structural equivalence. In D. Matsumoto & F. van de Vijver (Eds.), *Cross-cultural research methods in psychology* (pp. 197–215). Cambridge: Cambridge University Press.

Fiszman, A., Mendlowicz, M. V., Marques-Portella, C., Volchan, E., Coutinho, E. S., Souza, W. F., Rocha, V., et al. (2008). Peritraumatic tonic immobility predicts a poor response to pharmacological treatment in victims of urban violence with PTSD. *Journal of Affective Disorders, 107*, 193–7.

Fivush, R. (1989). Exploring sex differences in the emotional content of mother-child conversations about the past. *Sex Roles, 20*, 675–91.

Folkman, S., & Lazarus, R. S. (1986). Stress processes and depressive symptomatology. *Journal of Abnormal Psychology, 95*, 107–13.

Fontaine, J. J. R., Luyten, P., de Boeck, P., Corveleyn, J., Fernandez, M., Herrera, D., Ittzés, A., et al. (2006). Untying the Gordian Knot of Guilt and Shame—The structure of guilt and shame reactions based on situation and person variation in Belgium, Hungary, and Peru. *Journal of Cross-Cultural Psychology, 37,* 273–92.

Fontaine, J. J. R., Poortinga, Y. H., Delbeke, L., & Schwartz, S. H. (2008). Structural equivalence of the values domain across cultures: Distinguishing sampling fluctuations from meaningful variation. *Journal of Cross-Cultural Psychology, 39,* 345–65.

Fontaine, J. J. R., Poortinga, Y. H., Setiadi, B., & Markam, S. S. (2002). Cognitive structure of emotion terms in Indonesia and The Netherlands. *Cognition & Emotion, 16,* 61–86.

Fontaine, J. J. R., Scherer, K. R., Roesch, E. B., & Ellsworth, P. (2007). The world of emotion is not two-dimensional. *Psychological Science, 18,* 1050–7.

Forceville, C. (1996). *Pictorial Metaphor in Advertising.* London: Routledge.

Forster, D. A. (2006). Validation of individual consciousness in Strong Artificial Intelligence: An African Theological contribution. (Unpublished doctoral dissertation). University of South Africa.

Foolen, A. (1997). The expressive function of language: Towards a cognitive semantic approach. In S. Niemeier & R. Dirven (Eds.), *The language of emotions* (pp. 15–31). Amsterdam: John Benjamins.

Foolen, A. (2012). The relevance of emotion for language and linguistics. In A. Foolen, U. M. Lüdtke, T. P. Racine, & J. Zlatev (Eds.), *Moving ourselves, moving others: Motion & emotion in intersubjectivity, consciousness and Language* (pp. 349–69). Amsterdam: John Benjamins.

Foxcroft, C. D. (1997). Psychological testing in South Africa: Perspectives regarding ethical and fair practices. *European Journal of Psychological Assessment, 13,* 229–35.

Frank, M. G., & Ekman, P. (1993). Not all smiles are created equal: The differences between enjoyment and nonenjoyment smiles. *Humor: International Journal of Humor Research, 6,* 9–26.

Fredrickson, B. L. (2001). The role of positive emotions in positive psychology: The broaden-and-build theory of positive emotions. *American Psychologist, 56,* 218–26.

Frijda, N. H. (1986). *The emotions.* Cambridge, UK: Cambridge University Press.

Frijda, N. H. (1987). Emotion, cognitive structure, and action tendency. *Cognition & Emotion, 1,* 115–43.

Frijda, N. H. (2000). The psychologist's point of view. In M. Lewis & J. M. Haviland-Jones (Eds.), *Handbook of Emotions* (2nd ed., pp. 59–74). New York: Guilford.

Frijda, N. H. (2005). Emotion experience. *Cognition & Emotion, 19,* 473–797.

Frijda, N. H. (2007a). *The laws of emotion.* Mahwah, NJ: Lawrence Erlbaum.

Frijda, N. H. (2007b). What might emotions be? Comments on the Comments. *Social Science Information, 46,* 433–43.

Frijda, N. H. (2010). Impulsive action and motivation. *Biological Psychology, 84,* 570–9.

Frijda, N. H., Kuipers, P., & ter Schure, E. (1989). Relations among emotion, appraisal, and emotional action readiness. *Journal of Personality and Social Psychology, 57,* 212–28.

Frijda, N. H., Markam, S., Sato, K., & Wiers, R. (1995). Emotions and emotion words. In J.A. Russell, J.-M. Fernández-Dols, A. S. R. Manstead, & J. C. Wellenkamp (Eds.), *Everyday conceptions of emotion: An introduction to the psychology, anthropology and linguistics of emotion* (1st ed., pp. 121–44). Dordrecht: Kluwer Academic Publishers.

Frijda, N. H., Mesquita, B., Sonnemans, J., & Van Goozen, S. (1991). The duration of affective phenomena or: Emotions, sentiments and passions. In K. T. Strongman (Ed.), *International review of studies on emotion* (pp. 187–225). Chichester: John Wiley.

Frijda, N. H., & Parrott, W. G. (2011). Basic emotions or ur-emotions? *Emotion Review, 3,* 406–15.

Frijda, N. H., & Scherer, K. R. (2009). Emotion definition (psychological perspectives). In D. Sander & K. R. Scherer (Eds.), *Oxford companion to emotion and the affective sciences* (pp. 142–3). Oxford: Oxford University Press.

Frijda, N. H., & Tcherkassof, A. (1997). Facial expressions as modes of action readiness. In J. A. Russell & J. M. Fernandez-Dols, (Eds.), *The psychology of facial expression* (pp. 78–102). Cambridge, UK: Cambridge University Press.

Gaby, A. (2008). Gut feelings: locating intellect, emotion and life force in the Thaaorre body. In F. Sharifian, R. Dirven, & S. Niemeier (Eds.), *Culture, body, and language* (pp. 27–44). Berlin: Mouton de Gruyter.

Galasso, A. (2002). *L'Italia s'è desta: tradizione storica e identità nazionale dal Risorgimento alla Repubblica.* [L'Italia s'è desta: Historical tradition and national identity from the Risorigmento to the Republic]. Florence, Italy: Le Monnier.

Galasso, G. (1997). *L'altra Europa: per un'antropologia storica del Mezzogiorno d'Italia.* [The other Europe: An anthropological history of the Italian Mezzogiorno]. Lecce, Italy: Argo.

Galati, D. (1987). Il riconoscimento di antecedenti situazionali delle emozioni. Confronto tra due contesti culturali: l'Italia Settentrionale e l'Italia Meridionale [Recognition of situational antecedents of emotions. Comparison of two cultural contexts: Northern Italy and Southern Italy]. *Ikon, 14,* 143–58.

Galati, D., & Sciaky, R. (1995). The representation of antecedents of emotions in northern and southern Italy. *Journal of Cross-Cultural Psychology, 26,* 123–40.

Galati, D., Sini, B., Tinti, C., & Testa, S. (2008). The lexicon of emotion in the neo-Latin languages. *Social Science Information, 47,* 205–20.

Galati, D., Manzano, M., & Sotgiu, I. (2006). The subjective components of happiness and their attainment: a cross-cultural comparison between Italy and Cuba. *Social Science Information, 45,* 601–30.

Galli, C., & Zammuner, V. (2006). Concepts of emotion and dimensional ratings of Italian emotion words in pre-adolescents. In *Proceedings of the 28th Annual Conference of the Cognitive Science Society* (p. 2486).

Gallup, G. G. (1974). Animal hypnosis: Factual status of a fictional concept. *Psychological Bulletin, 81,* 836–53.

Gandhi, M. K. (1927). *The story of my experiments with truth.* Gujarat: Navajivan Trust. [Translated into English in 1993].

Gari, A., Panagiotopoulou, P., & Mylonas, K. (2009). Social axioms in Greece: Emic and etic dimensions and their relationships with locus of control. In K. Leung & M. H. Bond (Eds.), *Psychological aspects of social axioms: Understanding global belief systems* (1st ed., pp. 197–216). New York: Springer.

Gatchet, A. S. (1894). The Terrabi Indians. *American Anthropologist, 7,* 218–9.

Geeraerts, D. (1989). Prospects and problems of prototype theory. *Linguistics 27,* 587–612.

Geeraerts, D. (1997). *Diachronic prototype semantics: A contribution to historical lexicology.* Oxford: Oxford University Press.

Geeraerts, D. (1999). Idealistic and empiricist tendencies in cognitive semantics. In T. Janssen & G. Redeker (Eds.), *Cognitive linguistics: Foundations, scope, and methodology* (pp. 163–94). Berlin: Mouton de Gruyter.

Geeraerts, D. (2002). The theoretical and descriptive development of lexical semantics. In L. Behrens & D. Zaefferer (Eds.), *The lexicon in focus. Competition and convergence in current lexicology* (pp. 23–42). Frankfurt am Main: Peter Lang Verlag.

Geeraerts, D. (2009). *Theories of lexical semantics.* Oxford: Oxford University Press.

Geeraerts, D. & Cuyckens, H. (Eds.). (2008). *Handbook of cognitive linguistics.* Oxford: Oxford University Press.

Geeraerts, D., & Gevaert, C. (2008). Hearts and (angry) minds in Old English. In F. Sharifian, R. Dirven, & S. Niemeier (Eds.), *Culture, body, and language* (pp. 319–48). Berlin: Mouton de Gruyter.

Geeraerts, D., & Grondelaers, S. (1995). Looking back at anger. Cultural traditions and metaphorical patterns. In John Taylor & Robert E. MacLaury (Eds.), *Language and the construal of the World* (pp. 153–80). Berlin: Mouton de Gruyter.

Geertz, C. (1959). The vocabulary of emotion: A study of Javanese socialization processes. *Psychiatry, 22,* 225–37.

Geertz, C. (1973). Thick description: Toward an interpretive theory of culture. In C. Geertz (Ed.), *The interpretation of cultures: Selected essays* (pp. 3–30). New York: Basic Books.

Geertz, C. (1984). From a native's point of view: On the nature of anthropological understanding. In R. A. Shweder & R. A. LeVine (Eds.), *Culture theory: Essays on mind, self, and emotion* (pp. 123–36). Cambridge: Cambridge University Press.

Gehm, T., & Scherer, K. R. (1988). Factors determining the dimensions of subjective emotional space. In K. R. Scherer (Ed.), *Facets of emotion: Recent research* (pp. 99–114). Hillsdale, NJ: L. Erlbaum Associates.

Gerber, E. (1975). *The Cultural Patterning of Emotions in Samoa.* (Unpublished doctoral dissertation). University of California, San Diego.

Gerber, E. (1985). Rage and obligation: Samoan emotion in conflict. In G. M. White & J. Kirkpatrick (Eds.), *Person, self, and experience: Exploring Pacific ethnopsychologies* (pp. 121–67). Berkeley: University of California Press.

Gert, B. (2008). The definition of morality. In E. N. Zalta (Ed.), *The Stanford Encyclopedia of Philosophy.* Retrieved from http://plato.stanford.edu/entries/morality-definition.

Geurts, K. L. (2002). On rocks, walks, and talks in West Africa: Cultural categories and an anthropology of the senses. *Ethos, 30,* 178–98.

Gevaert, C. (2002). The Evolution of the lexical and conceptual field of anger in old and middle English. In J. Diaz (Ed.), *A changing world of words: Diachronic approaches to English lexicology and semantics* (pp. 275–99). Amsterdam: Rodopi.

Gibbs, R. W., Jr. (1994). *The Poetics of mind. Figurative thought, language and understanding.* Cambridge, MA: Cambridge University Press.

Gilovitch, T. D., Griffing, D. W., & Kahneman, D. (Eds.). (2001). *Heuristics and biases: The psychology of intuitive judgement.* Cambridge: Cambridge University Press.

Giovannini, D. (1983). Cultura e sesso come variabili intervenienti nel riconoscimento delle emozioni [Culture and gender as intervening variables for emotion recognition]. In G. Attili & P. E. Ricci-Bitti (Eds.), *Comunicare senza parole,* [Communicating without words] (pp. 187–1995). Rome: Bulzoni.

Giovannini, D., & Ricci-Bitti, P. E. (1986). The Italian case: A stereotype confirmed? In K. R. Scherer, H. G. Wallbott, & A. B. Summerfield (Eds.), *Experiencing emotions. A cross-cultural study* (pp. 211–4). Cambridge: Cambridge University Press.

Gladkova, A. (2005). Sočuvstvie and Sostradanie. *Lidil, Revue de linguistique et de didactique des langues, 32,* 35–47.

Gladkova, A. (2010). A linguist's view of 'pride'. *Emotion Review, 2,* 178–9.

Gleitman, L., & Papafragou, A. (2005). Language and thought. In K. J. Holyoak & R. G. Morrison (Eds.), *The Cambridge handbook of thinking and reasoning* (pp. 633–61). Cambridge: Cambridge University Press.

Glynn, D. (2009). Polysemy, syntax, and variation. A usage-based method for Cognitive Semantics. In V. Evans & S. Pourcel (Eds.), *New directions in cognitive linguistics* (pp. 77–106). Amsterdam: John Benjamins.

Glynn, D. (2010). Synonymy, lexical fields, and grammatical constructions. A study in usage-based Cognitive Semantics. H.-J. Schmid & S. Handl (Eds.), *Cognitive foundations of linguistic usage-patterns* (pp. 89–118). Berlin: Mouton de Gruyter.

Gobl, C. & Chasaide, A. N. (2003). The role of voice quality in communicating emotion, mood and attitude. *Speech Communication, 40,* 189–212.

Goddard, C. (1996). The Social Emotions of Malay (Bahasa Melayu). *Ethos, 24*(3), 426–64.

Goddard, C. (1997a). Cultural values and "cultural scripts" of Malay (Bahasa Melayu). *Journal of Pragmatics, 27*(2): 183–201.

Goddard, C. (1997b). Contrastive semantics and cultural psychology: "Surprise" in Malay and English. *Culture & Psychology, 3,* 153–81.

Goddard, C. (1998). *Semantic analysis: A practical introduction.* Oxford: Oxford University Press.

Goddard, C. (2001). Hati: A key word in the Malay vocabulary of emotion. In J. Harkins & A. Wierzbicka (Eds.), *Emotions in crosslinguistic perspective* (pp. 167–196). Berlin: Mouton de Gruyter.

Goddard, C. (2002a). Explicating emotions across languages and cultures: A semantic approach. In S. Fussell (Ed.), *The verbal communication of emotions* (pp. 19–53). Mhawah, NJ: Lawrence Erlbaum Associates.

Goddard, C. (2002b). The search for the shared semantic core of all languages. In C. Goddard & A. Wierzbicka (Eds), *Meaning and universal grammar—Theory and empirical findings*. (Vol. 1, pp. 5–40). Amsterdam: John Benjamins.

Goddard, C. (2005). *The languages of East and Southeast Asia*. Oxford: Oxford University Press.

Goddard, C. (2007). A culture-neutral metalanguage for mental state concepts. In A. C. Schalley & D. Khlentzos (Eds.), *Mental states: Language and cognitive structure* (Vol. 2, pp. 11–35). Amsterdam: John Benjamins Publishing Company.

Goddard, C., & Schalley, A. C. (2010). Semantic analysis. In N. Indurkhya & F. J. Damerau (Eds.), *Handbook of natural language processing* (2nd ed.). New York: Marcel Dekker.

Goddard, C., & Wierzbicka, A. (Eds.). (1994). *Semantic and lexical universals: Theory and empirical findings*. Amsterdam: Benjamins.

Goddard, C., & Wierzbicka, A. (Eds.). (2002). *Meaning and universal grammar: Theory and empirical findings* (Vol. 1–2). Amsterdam: John Benjamins Publishing Company.

Gohm, C. L., & Clore, G. L. (2000). Individual differences in emotional experience: Mapping available scales to processes. *Personality and Social Psychology Bulletin, 26*, 679–97. doi:10.1177/0146167200268004.

Goldie, P. (2004). The life of the mind: Commentary on "Emotions in everyday life." *Social Science Information, 43*, 591–8.

Goodenough, W. H. (1956). Componential analysis and the study of meaning. *Language, 32*, 195–216.

Goodie, J. (2002). The anthropology of the senses and sensations. *La Ricerca Folklorica, 45*, 17–28.

Gordon, P. (2004). Numerical cognition without words: Evidence from Amazonia. *Science, 306*, 496–9.

Gordon, P. (2005). Author's response to "Crying Whorf." *Science, 307*, 1721–2.

Government Gazette, Republic of South Africa, Vol. 400, no19370. Cape Town. 19 October 1998.

Goudbeek, M., & Scherer, K. R. (2010). Beyond arousal: Valence and potency/control in the vocal expression of emotion. *Journal of the Acoustical Society of America, 128*, 3, 1322–36.

Graham, J. L. (2001). The role of feelings of tension during international business negotiations: US executives negotiating with Chinese executives (Working Paper). University of Southern California.

Grandjean, D., Sander, D., & Scherer, K. R. (2008). Conscious emotional experience emerges as a function of multilevel, appraisal-driven response synchronization. *Consciousness and Cognition, 17*, 484–95.

Grandjean, D., Sander, D., Pourtois, G., Schwartz, S., Seghier, M., Scherer, K. R., & Vuilleumier, P. (2005). The voices of wrath: Brain responses to angry prosody in meaningless speech. *Nature Neuroscience, 8*, 145–6.

Grandjean, D., & Scherer, K. R. (2008). Unpacking the cognitive architecture of emotion processes. *Emotion, 8*, 341–51.

Green, D. P., Goldman, S. L. & Salovey, P. (1993). Measurement error masks bipolarity in affect ratings. *Journal of Personality and Social Psychology, 64*, 1029–41.

Green, D. P., Salovey, P., & Truax, K. M. (1999). Static, dynamic, and causative bipolarity of affect. *Journal of Personality and Social Psychology, 76*, 856–67.

Griffin, D., & Gonzalez, R. (1995). Correlational analysis of dyad-level data in the exchangeable case. *Psychological Bulletin, 118*, 430–9.

Griffiths, P. E. (1997). *What emotions really are: The problem of psychological categories*. Chicago: University of Chicago Press.

Griffiths, P. E. (2004). Is wmotion a natural kind? In R. C. Solomon (Ed.), *Philosophers on emotion* (pp. 233–49). Oxford and New York: Oxford University Press.

Griner, L. A., & Smith, C. A. (2000). Contributions of motivational orientation to appraisal and emotion. *Personality and Social Psychology Bulletin, 26*, 727–40.

Grondelaers, S., & Geeraerts, D. (1998). Vagueness as a euphemistic strategy. In A. Athanasiadou & E. Tabakowska (Eds.), *Speaking of emotions: Conceptualization and expression* (pp. 357–74). Berlin/New York: Mouton de Gruyter.

Grygorash, S. M. (2006). Leksyko–semantychne pole iz dominantoju "kohaty" v ukrains'kyh narodnyh pisnyah pro kohannya [The lexico–semantic field of "kohaty" in Ukrainian folk love songs]. *Lingvistychni Studii, 2*, 62–8.

Grygorash, S. M. (2007). *The Vocabulary and frasemics of intimate lyrics (based on the Ukrainian folklore)*, PhD Thesis. Ivano-Frankivsk: Vasyl Stefanyk National University.

Guttman, L. (1954). A new approach to factor analysis: The radex. In P. F. Lazarsfeld (Ed.), *Mathematical thinking in the social sciences* (pp. 258–348). Glencoe, IL: Free Press.

Györi, G. (1998). Cultural variation in the conceptualisation of emotions: A historical study. In A. Athanasiadou, & E. Tabakowska (Eds.), *Speaking of emotions: Conceptualisation and expression* (pp. 99–124). Berlin & New York: Mouton de Gruyter.

Haidt, J. (2003). The moral emotions. In R. J. Davidson, K. R. Scherer, & H. H. Goldsmith (Eds.), *Handbook of affective sciences* (pp. 852–70). Oxford: Oxford University Press.

Haidt, J., McCauley, C., & Rozin, P. (1994). Individual differences in sensitivity to disgust: A scale sampling seven domains of disgust elicitors. *Personality and Individual Differences, 16*, 701–13.

Haidt, J., Rozin, P., Mccauley, C., & Imada, S. (1997). Body, psyche, and culture: The relationship between disgust and morality. *Psychology & Developing Societies, 9*, 107–31.

Halberstadt, J. (2005). Language, emotion attribution, and emotional experience. *Psychological Inquiry, 16*, 18–21.

Halliday, M. A. K. (1994). *An introduction to functional grammar* (2nd ed.). London: Hodder Arnold. (First published 1985).

Halliday, M. A. K. (1998). On the grammar of pain. *Functions of Language, 5*, 1–32.

Hamlin, J. K., Wynn, K., & Bloom, P. (2007). Social evaluation by preverbal infants. *Nature, 450*(7169), 557–9.

Hamm, A., Schupp, H. T., & Weike, A. I. (2003). Motivational organizations of emotions: Autonomic changes, cortical responses, and reflex modulation. In R. J. Davidson, K. R. Scherer, & H. H. Goldsmith (Eds.), *Handbook of affective sciences* (pp. 187–211). Oxford: Oxford University Press.

Harkins, J. (1990). Shame and shyness in the aboriginal classroom. *Australian Journal of Linguistics, 10*, 293–306.

Harkins, J. (2001). Talking about anger in Central Australia. In J. Harkins & A. Wierzbicka (Eds.), *Emotions in Crosslinguistic Perspective* (pp. 197–216). Berlin: Mouton de Gruyter.

Harkins, J., & Wierzbicka, A. (Eds.). (2001). *Emotions in crosslinguistic perspective*. Berlin: Mouton de Gruyter.

Harré, R. (Ed.). (1986). *The social construction of emotions*. Oxford: Oxford University Press.

Harrigan, J. A., Rosenthal, R., & Scherer, K. R. (Eds.). (2005). *The new handbook of methods in nonverbal behavior research*. Oxford: Oxford University Press.

Hart, D., & Matsuba, M. K. (2007). The development of pride and moral life. In J. L. Tracy, W. R. Robins, & J. P. Tangney (Eds.), *The self-conscious emotions: Theory and research* (pp. 114–33). New York: The Guilford Press.

Hasada, R. (2002). "Body part" terms and emotion in Japanese. *Pragmatics & Cognition, 10*, 107–28.

Hasada, R. (2008). Two virtuous emotions in Japanese: *Nasake/joo* and *jihi*. In C. Goddard (Ed.), *Cross-linguistic linguistics* (pp. 331–47). Amsterdam: John Benjamins.

Haspelmath, M. (2001). The European linguistic area: Standard average European. In M. Haspelmath, E. König, W. Oesterreicher, & W. Raible (Eds.), *Language typology and language universals: an international handbook* (Vol. 2, pp. 1492–510). New York: Walter de Gruyter.

Hatzigeorgiou, N., Gavrilidou, M., Piperidis, S., Karayannis, G., Papakostopoulou, A., & Spiliotopoulou, A. (2000). Design and implementation of the online ILSP corpus. In *Proceedings of the Second International Conference on Language Resources and Evaluation (LREC)* (Vol. 3, pp. 1737–40).

Hauser, M. D. (1996). *The evolution of communication*. Cambridge, MA: MIT Press.

Hayes, C. J., Stevenson, R. J., & Coltheart, M. (2007). Disgust and Huntington's disease. *Neuropsychologia*, *45*, 1135–51.

Heider, K. G. (1991). Landscapes of emotion: mapping three cultures of emotion in Indonesia. Cambridge: Cambridge University Press.

Heidt, J. M., Marx, B. P., & Forsyth, J. P. (2005). Tonic immobility and childhood sexual abuse: A preliminary report evaluating the sequela of rape-induced paralysis. *Behaviour Research and Therapy*, *43*, 1157–71.

Hejmadi, A., Davidson, R. J., & Rozin, P. (2000). Exploring Hindu Indian emotion expressions: Evidence for accurate recognition by Americans and Indians. *Psychological Science*, *11*, 183–7.

Henrich, J., & Gil-White, F. J. (2001). The evolution of prestige: Freely conferred deference as a mechanism for enhancing the benefits of cultural transmission. *Evolution and Human Behavior*, *22*, 165–96.

Herbert, C., Junghöfer, M., & Kissler, J. (2008). Event related potentials to emotional adjectives during reading. *Psychophysiology*, *45*, 487–98.

Herbert, C., Kissler, J., Junghöfer, M., Peyk, P., & Rockstroh, B. (2006). Processing of emotional adjectives: Evidence from startle EMG and ERPs. *Psychophysiology*, *43*, 197–206.

Herrald, M. M., & Tomaka, J. (2002). Patterns of emotion-specific appraisal, coping, and cardiovascular reactivity during an ongoing emotional episode. *Journal of Personality and Social Psychology*, *83*, 434–50.

Herrmann, D. J., & Raybeck, D. (1981). Similarities and differences in meaning in six cultures. *Journal of Cross-Cultural Psychology*, *12*, 194–206.

Hiatt, L. R. (1978). Classification of the emotions: An ontogenetic perspective. *Language Sciences*, *6*, 29–156.

Higgins, E. T. (1997). Beyond pleasure and pain. *American Psychologist*, *52*, 1280–300.

Higgins, E. T., Friedman, R. S., Harlow, R. E., Idson, L. C., Ayduk, O. N., & Taylor, A. (2001). Achievement orientations from subjective histories of success: Promotion pride versus prevention pride. *European Journal of Social Psychology*, *31*, 3–23.

Hirschfeld, L. A. (2001). On a folk theory of society: Children, evolution, and mental representations of social groups. *Personality and Social Psychology Review*, *5*, 107–17.

Ho, D. Y., Peng, S., Lai, A. C., & Chan, S. F. (2001). Indigenization and beyond: Methodological relationalism in the study of personality across cultural traditions. *Journal of Personality*, *69*, 925–53.

Ho, D. Y.-F., Fu, W., & Ng, S. M. (2004). Guilt, shame and embarrassment: Revelations of face and self. *Culture & Psychology*, *10*, 64–84.

Hockett, C. F. (1960). The origin of speech. *Scientific American*, *203*, 88–96.

Hofmeister, P. (2005). Psychollocations cross-linguistically and experiencer realization. Unpublished manuscript.

Hofstede, G. (1980). Culture's consequences: International differences in work-related values. Beverly Hills, CA: Sage.

Hofstede, G. (1984). Culture's consequences: International differences in work-related values (2nd ed.). Beverly Hills, CA: Sage.

Hofstede, G. (1991). Cultures and organizations: Software of the mind. London: McGraw-Hill.

Hofstede, G. (2001). Culture's consequences: Comparing values, behaviors, institutions, and organizations across nations. Thousand Oaks, CA: Sage Publications.

Holden, K. T., & Hogan, J. T. (1993). The emotive impact of foreign intonation: An experiment in switching English and Russian intonation. *Language and Speech*, *36*, 67–88.

Howell, S. (1981). Rules not words. In A. Lock & P. Heelas (Eds.), *Indigenous psychologies: The anthropology of the self* (pp. 133–43). San Diego, CA: Academic Press.

Hupka, R. B., Lenton, A. P., & Hutchison, K. A. (1999). Universal development of emotion categories in natural language. *Journal of Personality and Social Psychology*, *77*, 247–78.

Hurtado de Mendoza, A. (2007). *Hacia una aproximación enciclopédica del concepto de vergüenza y el concepto de shame*. Doctoral dissertation, Universidad Autónoma de Madrid.

Hurtado de Mendoza, A. (2008). The problem of translation in cross–cultural research on emotion concepts. *International Journal for Dialogical Science, 3*(1), 241–8.

Iaccino, J. (1989). *Understanding the concept emotion: Support for a prototype perspective.* (ERIC Document Reproduction Service No. ED 299 637). ERIC-CAPS: Office of Educational Research and Improvement, Communication and Reading Skills Database. Lisle: Illinois Benedictine College, Department of Sociology-Psychology.

Ibarretxe-Antuñano, I. (2008). Guts, heart, and liver: the conceptualization of internal organs in Basque. In F. Sharifian, R. Dirven, & S. Niemeier (Eds.), *Culture, body, and language* (pp. 103–28). Berlin: Mouton de Gruyter.

Ibarretxe-Antuñano, I. & Valenzuela, J. (Eds.). (2012). *Lingüística cognitiva.* Barcelona: Anthropos.

Ice, G. H., & Yogo, J. (2005). Measuring stress among Luo elders: Development of the Luo Perceived Stress Scale. *Field Methods, 17*, 394–411.

Ikegami, Y. (2008). The heart: What it means to the Japanese speakers. In F. Sharifian, R. Dirven, & S. Niemeier (Eds.), *Culture, body, and language* (pp. 169–90). Berlin: Mouton de Gruyter.

Isen, A. M. (1999). Positive affect. In T. Dalgleish & M. J. Power (Eds.), *Handbook of cognition and emotion* (pp. 521–39). Chichester, England: Wiley.

Ishchenko, O. (2009). Rytmichna organizatsiya ukrains'koho slova zalezhno vid tempu movlennya [Rythmical Structure of a Ukrainian Word Depending on the Speech Tempo]. *Zagadnienia slowianskiej fonotaktyki.* Torun, Instytut filologii slowianskiej UMK.

Itkonen, E., & Kulonen, U.-M. (Eds.). (2000). *Suomen sanojen alkuperä. Etymologinen sanakirja.* [The origin of Finnish words. Etymological dictionary.] Helsinki: Finnish Literature Society.

Ito, T. A., Larsen, J. T., Smith, N. K., & Cacioppo, J. T. (1998). Negative information weighs more heavily on the brain: The negativity bias in evaluative categorizations. *Journal of Personality and Social Psychology, 75*, 887–900.

Iyengar, S. S., & Lepper, M. R. (1999). Rethinking the value of choice: A cultural perspective on intrinsic motivation. *Journal of Personality and Social Psychology, 76*, 349–366.

Izard, C. E. (1971). *The face of emotion.* New York: Appleton-Century-Crofts.

Izard, C. E. (1977). *Human emotions.* New York: Plenum Press.

Izard, C. E. (1991). *The psychology of emotions.* New York: Plenum Press.

Izard, C. E. (1992). Basic emotions, relations among emotions, and emotion-cognition relations. *Psychological Review, 99*, 561–5.

Izard, C. E. (1993). Four systems for emotion activation: cognitive and noncognitive processes. *Psychological Review, 100*, 68–90.

Izard, C. (1994). Innate and universal facial expressions: Evidence from developmental and cross-cultural research. *Psychological Bulletin, 115*, 288–99.

Izard, C. E. (2007). Basic emotions, natural kinds, emotion schemas, and a new paradigm. *Perspectives on Psychological Science, 2*, 260–80.

Jackendoff, R. (1972). *Semantic interpretation in generative grammar.* Cambridge, MA: MIT Press.

Jackendoff, R. (1983). *Semantics and cognition.* Cambridge, MA: MIT Press.

Jadhav, S. (1996). The cultural origins Western depression. *International Journal of Social Psychiatry, 42*, 269–86.

Jaisser, A. (1990). DeLIVERing an introduction to psycho-collocations with SIAB in White Hmong. *Linguistics of the Tibeto-Burman Area, 13*, 159–77.

Jakobs, E., Manstead, A. S. R., & Fischer, A. H. (1999). Social motives, emotional feelings, and smiling. *Cognition and Emotion, 13*, 321–45.

Jakobs, E., Manstead, A. S., & Fischer, A. H. (2001). Social context effects on facial activity in a negative emotional setting. *Emotion, 1*, 51–69.

James, W. (1884). What is an emotion? *Mind, 9*, 188–205.

James, W. (1890). *The principles of psychology*. New York: Holt.

James, W. (1894). The physical basis of emotion. *Psychological Review*, *1*, 516–29.

Janda, L. A., & Solovyev, V. D. (2009). What constructional profiles reveal about synonymy: A case study of Russian words for SADNESS and HAPPINESS. *Cognitive Linguistics*, *20*, 367–93.

Jänig, W. (2003). The autonomic nervous system and its co-ordination by the brain. In R. J. Davidson, K. R. Scherer, & H. H. Goldsmith (Eds.), *Handbook of affective sciences* (pp. 135–86). Oxford & New York: Oxford University Press.

Jay, T., & Janschewitz, K. (2007). Filling the emotion gap in linguistic theory: Commentary on Potts' expressive dimension. *Theoretical Linguistics*, *33*, 215–21.

Jeste, D. V., & Vahia, I. V. (2008). Comparison of the conceptualization of wisdom in ancient Indian literature with modern views: focus on the Bhagavad Gita. *Psychiatry*, *71*, 197–209.

John, O. P., Angleitner, A., & Ostendorf, F. (1988). The lexical approach to personality: A historical review of trait taxonomic research. *European Journal of Personality*, *2*, 171–203.

Johnson, R., Jr. (1988). The amplitude of the P300 component of the event-related potential. In P. K. Ackles, J. R. Jennings, & M. G. H. Coles (Eds.), *Advances in psychophysiology* Greenwich, CT: JAI Press, (*Vol. 2*, pp. 69–138).

Johnson-Laird, P. N., & Oatley, K. (1989). The language of emotions: An analysis of a semantic field. *Cognition and Emotion*, *3*, 81–123.

Johnstone, T., van Reekum, C. M., Bänziger, T., Hird, K., Kirsner, K., & Scherer, K. R. (2007). The effects of difficulty and gain versus loss on vocal physiology and acoustics. *Psychophysiology*, *44*, 827–37.

Johnstone, T., van Reekum, C. M., Hird, K., Kirsner, K., & Scherer, K. R. (2005). Affective speech elicited with a computer game. *Emotion*, *5*, 513–8.

Joireman, J. (2004). Empathy and the self-absorption paradox II: Self-rumination and self-reflection as mediators between shame, guilt, and empathy. *Self and Identity*, *3*, 225–38.

Jones, A., & Fitness, J. (2008). Moral hypervigilance: The influence of disgust sensitivity in the moral domain. *Emotion*, *8*, 613–27.

Jones, D. (2007). Moral psychology: The depths of disgust. *Nature*, *447*(7146), 768–71.

Junghöfer, M., Bradley, M. M., Elbert, T. R., & Lang, P. J. (2001). Fleeting images: A new look at early emotion discrimination. *Psychophysiology*, *38*, 175–8.

Junker, M.-O., & Blacksmith, L. (2006). Are there emotional universals? Evidence from the Native American language East Cree. *Culture & Psychology*, *12*, 275–303.

Juslin, P. N., & Scherer, K. R. (2005). Vocal expression of affect. In J. Harrigan, R. Rosenthal, & K. Scherer (Eds.), *The new handbook of methods in nonverbal behavior research* (pp. 65–135). Oxford, UK: Oxford University Press.

Kaaya, S. F., Fawzi, M. C. S., Mbwambo, J. K., Lee, B., Msamanga, G. I., & Fawzi, W. (2002). Validity of the Hopkins Symptom Checklist-25 amongst HIV-positive pregnant women in Tanzania. *Acta Psychiatrica Scandinavica*, *106*(1), 9–19.

Kagitcibasi, C. (2006). Theoretical perspectives on family change. In J. Georgas, J. W. Berry, F. J. R. Van de Vijver, C. Kagitcibasi, & Y. H. Poortinga (Eds.), *Families across cultures: A 30-nation psychological study* (pp. 72–89). Cambridge: Cambridge University Press.

Kaiser, S., & Scherer, K. R. (1998). Models of "normal" emotions applied to facial and vocal expressions in clinical disorders. In W. G. Flack & J. D. Laird (Eds.), *Emotions in psychopathology: Theory and research* (pp. 81–98). New York: Oxford University Press.

Kaiser, S., & Wehrle, T. (2001). Facial expressions as indicators of appraisal processes. In K. R. Scherer, A. Schorr, & T. Johnstone (Eds.), *Appraisal processes in emotion: Theory, methods, research* (pp. 285–300). New York, NY: Oxford University Press.

Kalimullina, L. A. (2006). *Semanticheskoje pole emotivnosti v russkon yazyke: synhronnij i diahronicheskij aspecty*. [The lexico-semantic field of emotiveness in the Russian language: synchronic and diachronic aspects]. (Habilitation paper). Bashkirskij University, Ufa.

Kamman, R., & Flett, R. (1983). Affectometer 2: A scale to measure current level of general happiness. *Australian Journal of Psychology, 35,* 259–6.

Kanner, L. (1931). Judging emotions from facial expressions. *Psychological Monographs, 94*(3).

Kant, I. (2001). *Kritik der Urteilskraft.* Hamburg: Meiner. (Originally published 1790).

Karaulov, A. V., Ufimtseva, N., Cherkasova, G., & Karaulov, Y. (Eds.). (2002). *Russian Accosiative Dictionary* (Vols. 1–2). Moscow: Astrel'. Also available at http://tesaurus.ru/dict/dict.php.

Karelson, R., Kullus, V., Raiet, E., Tiits, M., Valdre, T., Veskis, L., Langemets, M., et al. (Eds.). (2009). *Eesti keele seletav sõnaraamat.* [Dictionary of the Estonian language]. Tallinn: Eesti Keele Instituut. Retrieved from http://www.eki.ee/dict/ekss/ekss.html.

Katz, J. J. (1966). *The philosophy of language.* New York: Harper & Row.

Katz, J. J. (1976). A hypothesis about the uniqueness of natural language. In S. R. Harnad, H. D. Steklis, & J. Lancaster (Eds.), *Origins and evolution of language and speech, Annals of the New York Academy of Sciences, 28(Special Issue),* 33–41.

Katz, J. J. (1978). Effability and translation. In F. Guenthner & M. Guenthner-Reutter (Eds.), *Meaning and translation. Philosophical and linguistic approaches* (pp. 191–235). London: Duckworth.

Katz, J. J., & Fodor, J. A. (1963). The structure of a semantic theory. *Language, 39,* 170–210.

Katz, J. J., & Postal, P. M. (1964). *An integrated theory of linguistic descriptions.* Cambridge, MA: MIT Press.

Kayser, J., Tenke, C., Nordby, H., Hammerborg, D., Hugdahl, K., & Erdmann, G. (1997). Event-related potential (ERP) asymmetries to emotional stimuli in a visual half-field paradigm. *Psychophysiology, 34,* 414–26.

Keeler, W. (1983). Shame and stage fright in Java. *Ethos, 11,* 152–65.

Keltner, D., & Buswell, B. N. (1996). Evidence for the distinctness of embarrassment, shame, and guilt: A Study of recalled antecedents and facial expressions of emotion. *Cognition & Emotion, 10,* 155–71.

Keltner, D., & Buswell, B. N. (1997). Embarrassment: Its distinct form and appeasement functions. *Psychological Bulletin, 122,* 250–70.

Keltner, D. & Gross, J. (1999). Functional theories of emotions. *Cognition & Emotion, 13,* 467–80.

Keltner, D., Gruenfeld, D. H., & Anderson, C. (2003). Power, approach, and inhibition. *Psychological Review, 110,* 265–84. doi:10.1037/0033-295X.110.2.265.

Keltner, D., & Haidt, J. (2001). Social functions of emotions. In T. Mayne & G. A. Bonanno (Eds.), *Emotions: Current issues and future directions* (pp. 192–213). New York: Guilford Press.

Keltner, D., & Harker, L. A. (1998). The forms and functions of the nonverbal display of shame. In P. Gilbert & B. Andrews (Eds.), *Interpersonal approaches to shame* (pp. 78–98). Oxford, UK: Oxford University Press.

Khmel'ko, V. (2004). Linguo-etnichna struktura Ukrainy: Regional'ni osoblyvosti ta tendentsii zmin za roky nezalezhnosti [Linguo-enthnic structure of Ukraine: Regional peculiarities and the tendencies of change in the years of independence]. *Naukovi zapysky NAUKMA. Seriya 'Sotsiologichni nauky, 32,* 3–15.

Khomenko, L. M. (2004). Systemno–structurni vidnoshennya v myakyh skladah (akustychnyi aspekt syntaksychnoi phonetyky ukrains'koho movlennya). [Systemic and Structural Relations in Soft Syllables (Acoustic Aspect of the Syntactical Phonetics of Ukrainian Speech).] *Acta Universitatis Nicolai Copernici. Studia Slavica IX,* 25–36. Torun: Instytut filologii słowiańskiej UMK.

Kim, U., Yang, G., & Hwang, K. K. (2006). *Indigenous and cultural psychology: Understanding people in context.* New York: Springer.

Kirk, R. (1996). *Raw feeling: A philosophical account of the essence of consciousness.* Oxford: Oxford University Press.

Kissler, J., Assadollahi, R., & Herbert, C. (2006). Emotional and semantic networks in visual word processing: insights from ERP studies. *Progress in Brain Research, 156,* 147–83.

Kissler, J., Herbert, C., Peyk, P., & Junghöfer, M. (2007). Buzzwords: early cortical responses to emotional words during reading. *Psychological Science, 18,* 475–80.

Kitayama, S., Ishii, K., Imada, T., Takemura, K., & Ramaswamy, J. (2006). Voluntary settlement and the spirit of independence: Evidence from Japan's "Northern frontier". *Journal of Personality and Social Psychology*, *91*, 369–84.

Kitayama, S., & Markus, H. R. (1991). Culture and the self: Implication for cognition, emotion, and motivation. *Psychological Review*, *98*, 224–53.

Kitayama, S., Markus, H. R., & Kurokawa, M. (2000). Culture, emotion, and well-being: Good feelings in Japan and the United States. *Cognition & Emotion*, *14*, 93–124.

Kitayama, S., Markus, H. R., & Matsumoto, H. (1995). Culture, self, and emotion: A cultural perspective on "self–conscious" emotions. In J. P. Tangney & K. W. Fischer (Eds.), *Self-conscious emotions: The psychology of shame, guilt, embarrassment, and pride* (pp. 439–63). New York: The Guilford Press.

Kitayama, S., Mesquita, B., & Karasawa, M. (2006). Culture and emotional experience: Socially engaging and disengaging emotions in Japan and the United States. *Journal of Personality and Social Psychology*, *91*, 890–903.

Klamer, M. (1998). *A grammar of Kambera* (pp. 304–12). Berlin, NY: Mouton de Gruyter.

Kleinginna, P. R., & Kleinginna, A. M. (1981). A categorized list of emotion definitions, with suggestions for a consensual definition. *Motivation & Emotion*, *5*, 345–79.

Kleinman, A., & Kleinman, J. (1985). Somatization: The interconnections in Chinese society among culture, depressive experiences, and the meanings of pain. In A. Kleinman & B. Good (Eds.), *Culture and depression: Studies in the anthropology and cross-cultural psychiatry of affect and disorder*. Berkeley: University of California Press.

Knight, N., & Nisbett, R. E. (2007). Culture, class and cognition: Evidence from Italy. *Journal of Cognition and Culture*, *7*, 283–91.

Kornacki, P. (2001). Concepts of anger in Chinese. In J. Harkins & A. Wierzbicka (Eds.), *Emotions in Cross-linguistic Perspective* (pp. 259–92). Berlin: Mouton de Gruyter.

Koselak, A. (2005). Mépris/dédain, deux mots pour un même sentiment? Synonymie et incompatibilité des noms d'émotions. *Lidil* [Special issue: 'Sémantique des noms et adjectifs d'émotion], *32*, 21–34.

Kövecses, Z. (1986). *Metaphors of anger, pride, and love: A lexical approach to the structure of concepts*. Amsterdam: John Benjamins Publishing Company.

Kövecses, Z. (1990). *Emotion concepts*. New York: Springer-Verlag.

Kövecses, Z. (1991). Happiness, a definitional effort. *Metaphor and Symbolic Activity*, *6*, 29–46.

Kövecses, Z. (1995a). Anger: Its language, conceptualization and physiology in the light of cross-cultural evidence. In J. Taylor & R.E. MacLaury (Eds.), *Language and the cognitive construal of the world* (pp. 181–96). Berlin and New York: Mouton de Gruyter.

Kövecses, Z. (1995b). Metaphor and the folk understanding of anger. In J. Russell, J. M. Fernández-Dols, A. Manstead, & J.C. Wellenkamp (Eds.), *Everyday Conceptions of Emotion* (pp. 49–71). Dordrecht: Kluwer Academic Publishers.

Kövecses, Z. (2000). *Metaphor and emotion: Language, culture, and body in human feeling* (1st ed.). Cambridge: Cambridge University Press.

Kramer, E. (1964). Elimination of verbal cues in judgments of emotion from voice. *Journal of Abnormal and Social Psychology*, *68*, 390–6.

Krasavsky, N. A. (2001). *Emotsional'nie koncepty v russkoj i nemetskoj lingvo-kul'turah*. [Emotion Concepts in the Russian and German lingual cultures]. Volgograd: Peremena.

Kreibig, S. D. (2010). Autonomic nervous system activity in emotion: A review. *Biological Psychology*, *84*, 394–421.

Kreibig, S. D., Gendolla, G. H. E., & Scherer, K. R. (2010). Psychophysiological effects of emotional responding to goal attainment. *Biological Psychology* [Special Issue: The biopsychology of emotion: Current theoretical and empirical perspectives], *84*, 474–87.

Kross, E., Ayduk, O., & Mischel, W. (2005). When asking "why" does not hurt. Distinguishing rumination from reflective processing of negative emotions. *Psychological Science*, *16*, 709–15.

Kučera, H., & Francis, W. N. (1967). *Computational analysis of present-day American English.* Providence: Brown University Press.

Kuipers, A. H. (1974). *The Shuswap language.* The Hague, the Netherlands: Mouton de Gruyter.

Kundera, M. (1980). *The book of laughter and forgetting.* New York: Knopf. (Original work published 1979).

Kuppens, P. (2005). Interpersonal determinants of trait anger: low agreeableness, perceived low social esteem, and the amplifying role of the importance attached to social relationships. *Personality and Individual Differences, 38,* 13–23.

Kuppens, P., & Van Mechelen, I. (2007). Interactional appraisal models for the anger appraisals of threatened self-esteem, other-blame, and frustration. *Cognition & Emotion, 21,* 56–77.

Kuppens, P., Van Mechelen, I., & Meulders, M. (2004). Every cloud has a silver lining: Interpersonal and individual differences determinants of anger-related behaviors. *Personality and Social Psychology Bulletin, 30,* 1550–64.

Kuppens, P., Van Mechelen, I., & Rijmen, F. (2008). Toward disentangling sources of individual differences in appraisal and anger. *Journal of Personality, 76,* 969–1000.

Kuppens, P., van Mechelin, I., Smits, D. J. M., & De Boeck, P. (2003). The appraisal basis of anger: Specificity, necessity, and sufficiency of components. *Emotion, 3,* 254–69.

Kuppens, P., Van Mechelen, I., Smits, D. J. M., De Boeck, P., & Ceulemans, E. (2007). Individual differences in patterns of appraisal and anger experience. *Cognition & Emotion, 21,* 689–713.

Kuwabara, M., & Smith, L. B. (2007). Emotional terms and body parts in two languages. In *Proceedings of the 10th Cognitive Linguistics Conference* (pp. 133–4).

Kuzar, R., & Kidron, Y. (2002). My face is paling against my will: Emotion and control in English and Hebrew. *Pragmatics & Cognition, 10,* 129–57.

Laakso, J. (2001). The Finnic languages. In Ö. Dahl & M. Koptjevskaja-Tamm (Eds.), *Circum-Baltic Languages. Volume I: Past and Present* (pp. 179–212). Amsterdam: John Benjamins.

Lacewing, M. (2007). Do unconscious emotions involve unconscious feelings? *Philosophical Psychology, 20,* 81–104.

Lakoff, G. (1987). Women, fire and dangerous things: What categories reveal about the mind. Chicago: The University of Chicago Press.

Lakoff, G., & Johnson, M. (1980). *Metaphors we live by.* Chicago: University of Chicago Press.

Lakoff, G., & Kövecses, Z. (1987). The cognitive model of anger inherent in American English. In D. Holland & N. Quinn (Eds.), *Cultural models in language and thought* (pp. 195–221). Cambridge: Cambridge University Press.

Lance, C. E., Butts, M. M., & Michels, L. C. (2006). The sources of four commonly reported cutoff criteria: What did they really say? *Organizational Research Methods, 9,* 202–20.

Lanctôt, N., & Hess, U. (2007). The timing of appraisals. *Emotion, 7,* 207–12.

Lang, P. J. (1980). Behavioral treatment and bio-behavioral assessment: Computer applications. In J. B. Sidowski, J. H. Johnson, & T. A. Williams (Eds.), *Technology in mental health care delivery systems* (pp. 119–137). Norwood, NJ: Ablex.

Lang, P. J., Bradley, M. M., & Cuthbert, B. N. (1998). Emotion, motivation, and anxiety: brain mechanisms and psychophysiology. *Biological Psychiatry, 44,* 1248–63.

Lang, P. J., & Bradley, M. M. (2010). Emotion and the motivational brain. *Biological Psychology, 84,* 437–50.

Lang, P. J., Bradley, M. M., & Cuthbert, B. N. (2005). *International affective picture system (IAPS): Instruction manual and affective ratings* (Technical Report A-6). Gainesville, FL: The Center for Research in Psychophysiology, University of Florida.

Lang, P. J., & Davis, M. (2006). Emotion, motivation, and the brain: reflex foundations in animal and human research. *Progress in Brain Research, 156,* 3–29.

Lang, P. J., Greenwald, M. K., Bradley, M. M., & Hamm, A. O. (1993). Looking at pictures: Affective, facial, visceral, and behavioral reactions. *Psychophysiology, 30,* 261–73.

Langacker, R. (1987). The foundations of cognitive grammar: Volume I: Theoretical prerequisites (1st ed.). Stanford: Stanford University Press.

Langacker, R. (1991). Foundations of cognitive grammar: Volume II: Descriptive application. Stanford: Stanford University Press.

Lanovenko, O., Shvalb, Y., & Kubelius, O. (1998). Movni ta sotsiokul'turni chynnyky konsolidatsii ukrains'kogo suspil'stva. [Language and sociocultural factors of the Ukrainian society consolidation]. *Ukrains'ko-Rosijs'ki vidnosyny: humanitarny vymir*, [Ukraine-Russia Relations: humanitarian dimension], 46–54. Kyiv: Logos.

Larsen, J. T., Norris, C. J., & Cacioppo, J. T. (2003). Effects of positive and negative affect on electromyographic activity over zygomaticus major and corrugator supercilii. *Psychophysiology, 40*, 776–85.

Larsen, J. T., Norris, C. J., & Cacioppo, J. T. (2004). *The evaluative space grid: A single-item measure of positiveand negative affect.* (Unpublished manuscript). Texas TechUniversity, Lubbock, TX.

Larsen, J. T., Norris, C. J., McGraw, A. P., Hawkley, L. C., & Cacioppo, J. T. (2009). The evaluative space grid: A single-item measure of positivity and negativity. *Cognition & Emotion, 23*, 453–80.

Larsen, R. J., & Diener, E. (1992). Promises and problems with the circumplex model of emotion. In M. S. Clark (Ed.), *Review of Personality and Social Psychology* (Vol. 8, pp. 25–59). Thousand Oaks, CA: Sage Publications.

Lascaratou, C. (2007). *The language of pain: Expression or description?* Amsterdam: John Benjamins Publishing Company.

Laver, J. (1980). *The phonetic description of voice quality.* Cambridge: Cambridge University Press.

Lazarus, R. S. (1968). Emotions and adaptation: Conceptual and empirical relations. In W. J. Arnold (Ed.), *Nebraska Symposium on Motivation* (pp. 175–270). Lincoln, NE: University of Nebraska Press.

Lazarus, R. S. (1991a). *Emotion and adaptation.* New York: Oxford University Press.

Lazarus, R. S. (1991b). Progress on a cognitive-motivational-relational theory of emotion. *The American Psychologist, 46*, 819–34.

Leary, M. R. (2007). Motivational and emotional aspects of the self. *Annual Review of Psychology, 58*, 317–44.

Leary, T. (1957). *Interpersonal diagnosis of personality.* New York: Ronald Press.

Lebra, T. S. (1983). Shame and guilt: A psycho-cultural view of the Japanese self. *Ethos, 11*, 192–210.

LeDoux, J. E., & Gorman, J. M. (2001). A call to action: Overcoming anxiety through active coping. *American Journal of Psychiatry, 158*, 1953–5.

Lee, S. W. S., & Ellsworth, P. C. (2009). *Two kinds of disgust.* Manuscript in preparation.

Lee, S. W. S., & Schwarz, N. (2009). Clean your dirty mouth—no, not your hands: Modality-specific embodiment of the Morality-Hygiene metaphor. Manuscript in preparation.

Leff, J. P. (1973). Culture and the differentiation of emotional states. *The British Journal of Psychiatry, 123*(574), 299–306.

Lehman, C. (1985). Grammaticalization: Synchronic variation and diachronic change. *Lingua e Stile, 20*, 303–18.

Lehmann, D., & Skrandies, W. (1980). Reference-free identification of components of checkerboard-evoked multichannel potential fields. *Electroencephalography & Clinical Neurophysiology, 48*, 609–21.

Leighton, A. H., Lambo, T., Hughes, T., Leighton, D., Murphy, J., & Macklin, D. (1963). *Psychiatric disorder among the Yoruba.* Ithaca, NY: Cornell University Press.

Lemaître, Y. (1995). *Lexique de Tahitien contemporain.* Paris: IRD Editions.

Lerner, J. S., Tiedens, L. Z. (2006). Portrait of the angry decision maker: How appraisal tendencies shape anger's influence on cognition. *Journal of Behavioral Decision Making, 19*, 115–37.

Leung, K., Bond, M. H., de Carrasquel, S. R., Muñoz, C., Hernández, M., Murakami, F., Yamaguchi, S., et al. (2002). Social axioms. *Journal of Cross-Cultural Psychology, 33*, 286–302.

Leung, P. W. L., & Lee, P. W. H. (1996). Psychotherapy with the Chinese. In M. H. Bond (Ed.), *The handbook of Chinese psychology* (pp. 441–56). Hong Kong: Oxford University Press.

Levenson, R. W. (2003). Autonomic specificity and emotion. In R. J. Davidson, K. R. Scherer, & H. H. Goldsmith (Eds.), *Handbook of the affective sciences* (pp. 212–24). New York and Oxford: Oxford University Press.

Leventhal, H., & Scherer, K. R. (1987). The relationship of emotion to cognition: A functional approach to a semantic controversy. *Cognition & Emotion*, *1*, 3–28.

Levine, N. E. (1988). The dynamics of polyandry: kinship, domesticity, and population on the Tibetan border. Chicago: University of Chicago Press.

Levontina, I. B. (2004). Žalosť, sočuvstvie, sostradanie, učastie. In J. Apresjan et al. (Eds.), *Novyj ob' 'jasnitelnyj slovar'sinonimov russkogo jazyka*, [New Explanatory Dictionary of Russian Synonyms] (2nd ed., p. 327–31). Moskva – Vena: Jazyki slavjanskoj kuľtury – Wiener Slawistischer Almanach.

Levontina, I. B., & Zaliznyak, A. A. (2001). Human emotions viewed through the Russian language. In J. Harkins & A. Wierzbicka (Eds.), *Emotions in crosslinguistic perspective* (pp. 291–336). Berlin: Mouton de Gruyter.

Levy, R. I. (1973). *Tahitians*. Chicago: University of Chicago Press.

Levy, R. I. (1982). On the nature and functions of the emotions: An anthropological perspective. *Social Science Information*, *21*, 511–28.

Levy, R. I. (1983). Introduction: Self and Emotion. *Ethos*, *11*(3), 128–34.

Levy, R. I. (1984). The emotions in comparative perspective. In P. Ekman & K. R. Scherer (Eds.), *Approaches to emotion*. Hillsdale, NJ: L. Erlbaum Associates.

Lewandowska-Tomaszczyk, B. (1996). *Depth of negation—A cognitive semantic study*. Lodz: Lodz University Press.

Lewandowska-Tomaszczyk, B., & Dziwirek, K. (Eds.). (2009). *Studies in cognitive corpus linguistics*. Frankfurt a. Main: Peter Lang GmbH.

Lewis, C. I. (1929). *Mind and the world-order*. New York: C. Scribner's Sons.

Lewis, H. B. (1971). *Shame and guilt in neurosis*. New York: International Universities Press.

Lewis, M. (1992). *Shame: The exposed self*. New York: The Free Press.

Lewis, M. (1993). Self-conscious emotions: Embarrassment, pride, shame, and guilt. In J. M. Haviland-Jones & M. Lewis (Eds.), *Handbook of emotions* (1st ed., pp. 541–68). New York: Guilford Press.

Lewis, M. (1997). The self in self-conscious emotions. In J. G. Snodgrass & R. L. Thompson (Eds.), *The self across psychology: Self-recognition, self-awareness, and the self concept*. New York: New York Academy of Sciences.

Lewis, M. (2000). Self-conscious emotions: Embarrassment, pride, shame, and guilt. In M Lewis & J. M. Haviland-Jones (Eds.), *Handbook of emotions* (2nd ed., pp. 623–36). New York: Guilford Press.

Lewis, M. (2003). The emergence of consciousness and its role in human development. In J. LeDoux, J. Debiec, & H. Moss (Eds.), *The self: From soul to brain* (pp. 1–29). New York: New York Academy of Sciences.

Lewis, M. (2008). Self-conscious emotions: Embarrassment, pride, shame, and guilt. In M. Lewis, J. M. Haviland-Jones, & L. Feldman-Barrett (Eds.), *Handbook of Emotions* (3rd ed., pp. 742–56). New York: Guilford Press.

Li, J., Wang, L., & Fischer, K. (2004). The organisation of Chinese shame concepts? *Cognition & Emotion*, *18*, 767–97.

Lindquist, K. A., & Barrett, L. F. (2008). Constructing emotion: The experience of fear as a conceptual act. *Psychological Science*, *19*, 898–903.

Lindström, E. (2002). The body in expressions of emotion: Kuot. *Pragmatics & Cognition* [Special Issue: The Body in Description of Emotion], *10*, 159–84.

Littmann, E., & Hoeffner, M. (1962). *Woerterbuch der Tigre-Sprache*. Wiesbaden: Franz Steiner Verlag.

Litvak, P. M., Lerner, J. S., Tiedens, L.Z., & Shonk, K. (2010). Fuel in the fire: How anger impacts judgment and decision making. In M. Potegal, G. Stemmler, & C. D. Spielberger (Eds.), *International handbook of anger* (pp. 287–311). New York: Springer.

Locke, E. A. (2009). It's time we brought introspection out of the closet. *Perspectives on Psychological Science*, *4*, 24–5.

Longhi, M. T., Pereira, D. F., Bercht, M., & Behar, P. A. (2009). An experiment to understand how the affective aspects can be detected in virtual learning environments. *CINTED-UFRGS, 7*.

Lorenzano, A. (2006). GALIT: The Filipino emotion word for "anger". In *Proceedings of the Tenth International Conference on Austronesian Linguistics*. Retrieved from http://www.sil.org/asia/philippines/ical/papers/lorenzana-GALIT%20THE%20FILIPINO%20EMOTION.pdf.

Lounsbury, F. G. (1956). A semantic analysis of the Pawnee kinship usage. *Language, 32*, 158–94.

Louw, D. J. (2001). Ubuntu and the challenges of multiculturalism in post-Apartheid South Africa. *Quest: An African Journal of Philosophy, XV*, 15–36.

Lutz, C. (1982). The domain of emotion words on Ifaluk. *American Ethnologist, 9*, 113–28.

Lutz, C. (1983). Parental goals, ethnopsychology, and the development of emotional meaning. *Ethos, 11*, 246–62.

Lutz, C. (1985). Ethnopsychology compared to what? Explaining behaviour and consciousness among the Ifaluk. In G. M. White & J. Kirkpatrick (Eds.), *Person, self, and experience: Exploring Pacific ethnopsychologies* (pp. 35–79). Berkeley: University of California Press.

Lutz, C. (1986). Emotion, thought, and estrangement: Emotion as a cultural category. *Cultural Anthropology, 1*, 287–309.

Lutz, C. (1988). Unnatural emotions: Everyday sentiments on a Micronesian atoll and their challenge to Western theory. Chicago: University Of Chicago Press.

Lyons, J. (1977). *Semantics* (Vol. 1). Cambridge: Cambridge University Press.

Lyubomirsky, S., King, L., & Diener, E. (2005). The benefits of frequent positive affect: Does happiness lead to success? *Psychological Bulletin, 131*, 803–55.

Lyubomirsky, S., & Tucker, K. L. (1998). Implications of individual differences in subjective happiness for perceiving, interpreting, and thinking about life events. *Motivation and Emotion, 22*, 155–186.

Maalej, Z. (2004). Figurative language in anger expressions in Tunisian Arabic: An extended view of embodiment. *Metaphor and Symbol, 19*, 51–75.

MacCann, C., & Roberts, R. D. (2008). New paradigms for assessing emotional intelligence: Theory and data. *Emotion, 8*, 540–51.

MacCann, C., Roberts, R. D., Matthews, G., & Zeidner, M. (2004). Consensus scoring and empirical option weighting of performance based emotional intelligence (EI) tests. *Personality and Individual Differences, 36*, 645–62.

MacKenzie, M., Duffy, E., Jancewicz, B., Junker, M.-O., Moar, E., Neeposh, E., Bobbish-Salt, L., et al. (Eds.) (2006). *The Eastern James Bay Cree dictionary on the Web: English–Cree and Cree–English (Northern and Southern Dialects)*. Retrieved from http://dict.eastcree.org/

MacKinnon, D. P., Krull, J. L., Lockwood, C. M. (2000). Equivalence of the mediation, confounding and suppression effect. *Prevention Science, 1*, 173–81.

Maehr, M. L. (1974). Culture and achievement motivation. *American Psychologist, 29*, 887–96.

Mageo, J. M. (1991). Samoan moral discourse and the Loto. *American Anthropologist, 93*, 405–20.

Magnusson, D., & Stattin, H. (1978). A cross-cultural comparison of anxiety responses in an interactional frame of reference. *International Journal of Psychology, 13*, 317–32.

Mandler, G. (1975). *Mind and emotion*. New York: Wiley.

Mandler, G. (1984). Mind and body: Psychology of emotion and stress. New York: Norton.

Mandler, G. (1990). A constructivist theory of emotion. In N. L. Stein, B. Leventhal, & T. Trabasso (Eds.), *Psychological and biological approaches to emotion*. Hillsdale, NJ: Lawrence Erlbaum Associates.

Manley, R. S., & Leichner, P. (2003). Anguish and despair in adolescents with eating disorders–helping to manage suicidal ideation and impulses. *Crisis, 24*, 32–6.

Manly, B. F. J. (1997). *Randomization, bootstrap and Monte Carlo methods in biology* (2nd ed.). London: Chapman & Hall.

Manstead, A. S. R., & Fischer, A. H. (2001). Social appraisal: The social world as object of and influence on appraisal processes. In K. R. Scherer, A. Schorr, & T. Johnstone (Eds.), *Appraisal processes in emotion: Theory, methods, research* (pp. 221–32). New York: Oxford University Press.

Markham, R., & Wang, L. (1996). Recognition of emotion by Chinese and Australian Children. *Journal of Cross-Cultural Psychology, 27*, 616–43.

Markus, H. R., & Kitayama, S. (1991). Culture and the self: Implications for cognition, emotion, and motivation. *Psychological Review, 98*, 224–53.

Markus, H. R., & Kitayama, S. (2001). The cultural construction of self and emotion: Implications for social behaviours. In W. G. Parrott (Ed.), *Emotions in Social Psychology* (pp. 119–37). Philadelphia, PA: Psychology Press.

Marsella, A. J. (1980). Depressive experience and disorder across cultures. In H. C. Triandis & J. G. Draguns (Eds.), *Handbook of cross-cultural psychology* (Vol. 6, pp. 237–89). Boston: Allyn & Bacon.

Marsh, A. A., Adams, R. B., Jr., & Kleck, R. E. (2005). Why do fear and anger look the way they do? Form and social function in facial expressions. *Personality and Social Psychological Bulletin, 31*, 73–86.

Marsh, A. A., Ambady, N., & Kleck, R. E. (2005). The effects of fear and anger facial expressions on approach- and avoidance-related behaviors. *Emotion, 5*, 119–24.

Marsh, A. A., Elfenbein, H. A., & Ambady, N. (2003). Nonverbal "accents": Cultural differences in facial expressions of emotion. *Psychological Science, 14*, 373–6.

Marshall, L. (1961). Sharing, talking, and giving: Relief of social tensions among Kung Bushmen. *Africa: Journal of the International African Institute, 31*, 231–49.

Marzillier, S., & Davey, G. (2004). The emotional profiling of disgust-eliciting stimuli: Evidence for primary and complex disgusts. *Cognition & Emotion, 18*, 313–36.

Mascolo, M. J., Fischer, K. W., & Li, J. (2003). Dynamic development of component systems of emotions: Pride, shame, and guilt in China and the United States. In R. J. Davidson, K. R. Scherer, & H. H. Goldsmith (Eds.), *Handbook of affective sciences* (pp. 375–408). Oxford: Oxford University Press.

Masenko, L. (2004). Lingual situation in Ukraine. *Nezalezhnij cul'nurologichnij chasopys, 35*, 34–45.

Matisoff, J. (1986). Hearts and minds in South-East asian languages and english: an essay in the comparative lexical semantics of psycho-collocations. *Cahiers de linguistique - Asie orientale, 15*, 5–57.

Matsuki, K. (1995). Metaphors of anger in Japanese. In J. Taylor & R. E. Maclaury (Eds.), *Language and the cognitive construal of the world* (pp. 137–51). Berlin and New York: Mouton de Gruyter.

Matsumoto, D. (1989). Cultural influences on the perception of emotion. *Journal of Cross-Cultural Psychology, 20*, 92–105.

Matsumoto, D. (1990). Cultural similarities and differences in display rules. *Motivation & Emotion, 14*, 195–214.

Matsumoto, D. (2005). Scalar ratings of contempt expressions. *Journal of Nonverbal Behavior, 29*, 91–104.

Matsumoto, D., Franklin, B., Choi, J. W., Rogers, D., & Tatani, H. (2002). Cultural influences on the expression and perception of emotion. In W. Gudykunst & B. Mody (Eds.), *Handbook of International and Intercultural Communication*. Thousand Oaks, CA: Sage Publications, Inc.

Matsumoto, D., Nezlek, J. B., & Koopmann, B. (2007). Evidence for universality in phenomenological emotion response system coherence. *Emotion, 7*, 57–67.

Matsumoto, D., Yoo, S.H., & Chung, J. (2010). The expression of anger across culture. In M. Potegal, G. Stemmler, & C. Spielberger (Eds.), *International Handbook of Anger* (pp. 125–38). New York, Dordrecht, Heidelberg, London: Springer.

Matsumoto, D., Yoo, S. H., & Fontaine, J. (2008). Mapping expressive differences around the world: The relationship between emotional display rules and individualism versus collectivism. *Journal of Cross-Cultural Psychology, 39*, 55–74.

Matsumoto, D., Yoo, S. H., Fontaine, J., & 56 Members of the Multinational Study of Cultural Display Rules. (2009). Hypocrisy or maturity? Culture and context differentiation. *European Journal of Personality, 23*, 251–64.

Matsumoto, D., Yoo, S. H., Fontaine, J., et al. (2009). Hypocrisy or maturity? Culture and context differentiation. *European Journal of Personality, 23*, 1–14.

Matsuyama, Y., Karma, H., Kawamura, Y., & Mine, H. (1978). An analysis of emotional words. *The Japanese Journal of Psychology, 49*, 229–32.

Matthews, G., Derryberry, D., & Siegle, G. J. (2000). Personality and emotion: Cognitive science perspectives. In S. E. Hampson (Ed.), *Advances in personality psychology* (Vol. 1, pp. 199–237). Hove, UK: Psychology Press.

Maxwell, J. S., & Davidson, R. J. (2007). Emotion as motion: Asymmetries in approach and avoidant actions. *Psychological Science, 18*, 1113–9.

Mayer, J. D., Salovey, P., & Caruso, D. R. (2000). Emotional intelligence as zeitgeist, as personality and as a mental ability. In R. Bar-On, & J. D. A. Parker (Eds.), *The handbook of emotional intelligence* (pp. 92–117). New York: Jossey-Bass.

Mayer, J. D., Salovey, P., & Caruso, D. R. (2002). *Mayer–Salovey–Caruso Emotional Intelligence Test (MSCEIT): User Manual*. New York: Multi-Health Systems.

Mayer, J. D., Salovey, P., & Caruso, D. R. (2008). Emotional intelligence: A new ability or eclectic trait. *American Psychologist, 63*, 503–17.

Mayer, J. D., Salovey, P., Caruso, D. R., & Sitarenios, G. (2003). Measuring emotional intelligence with the MSCEIT V2. 0. *Emotion, 3*, 97–105.

McCrae, R. R. (2008). A note on some measures of profile agreement. *Journal of Personality Assessment, 90*, 105.

McCullough, M. E., Kilpatrick, S. D., Emmons, R. A., & Larson, D. B. (2001). Is gratitude a moral affect? *Psychological Bulletin, 127*, 249–66.

McDougall, G. J., Blixen, C. E., & Suen, L.-J. (1997). The process and outcome of life review psychotherapy with depressed homebound older adults. *Nursing research, 46*, 277–83.

McElhanon, K. A. (1977). Body image idioms in Irianese and Papua New Guinean languages. *Irian, 6*, 3–27.

McElhanon, K. A., & McElhanon, N. A. (1970). *Selepet-English dictionary*. Canberra: Australian National University.

McPherson, L., & Prokhorov, K. (2011). Structural correlates of 'liver' expressions in Dogon emotional vocabulary. In G. C. Batic (Ed.), *Encoding emotions in African languages* (pp. 38–56). Muenchen: Lincom GmbH.

Mead, M. (1952). Some anthropological considerations concerning guilt. In M. L. Reymert (Ed.), *Feelings and emotions* (pp. 362–73). New York: McGraw-Hill.

Mead, M. (1961). Coming of age in Samoa; a psychological study of primitive youth for western civilisation. New York: Morrow Quill. (Original work published 1928).

Meier, B., & Robinson, M. (2004). Why the sunny side is up. Associations between affect and vertical position. *Psychological Science, 15*, 243–7.

Meier, B., & Robinson, M. (2005). The metaphorical representation of affect. *Metaphor and Symbol, 20*, 239–57.

Meier, B. P., Robinson, M. D., & Clore, G. L. (2004). Why good guys wear white. Automatic inferences about stimulus valence based on brightness. *Psychological Science, 15*, 82–7.

Meiring, D. (2007). Bias and equivalence of psychological measures in South Africa. The Netherlands: Ladyrinth Publication.

Mervis, C. B., & Crisafi, M. A. (1982). Order of acquisition of subordinate-, basic-, and superordinate-level categories. *Child Development, 53*, 258–66.

Mesquita, B., & Ellsworth, P. C. (2001). The role of culture in appraisal. In K. R. Scherer, A. Schorr, & T. Johnstone (Eds.), *Appraisal processes in emotion: Theory, methods, research* (pp. 233–48). New York: Oxford University Press.

Mesquita, B., & Frijda, N. H. (1992). Cultural variations in emotions: A review. *Psychological Bulletin, 112*, 179–204.

Mesquita, B., Frijda, N. H., & Scherer, K. R. (1997). Culture and emotion. In J. W. Berry, P. R. Dasen, & T. S. Saraswathi (Eds.), *Handbook of cross-cultural psychology, Volume 2: Basic processes and human development* (pp. 255–97). Needham Heights, MA: Allyn & Bacon.

Mesquita, B., & Karasawa, M. (2004). Self-conscious emotions as dynamic cultural processes. *Psychological Inquiry, 15*, 161–6.

Messick, S. (1989). Validity. In R. L. Linn (Ed.), *Educational measurement* (3rd ed., pp. 13–103). New York: Macmillan.

Metslang, H. (2009). Estonian grammar between Finnic and SAE: Some comparisons. *Language Typology and Universals, 62*, 49–71.

Metzinger, T. (2004). Being no one: The self-model theory of subjectivity. Cambridge, MA: MIT Press.

Michelson, K. (2002). Emotions in Oneida. *Pragmatics & Cognition, 10*, 185–206.

Mikołajczuk, A. (1998). The metonymic and metaphorical conceptualization of anger in Polish. In A. Athanasiadou & E. Tabakowska (Eds.), *Speaking of emotions. Conceptualization and expression* (pp. 153–90). Berlin and New York: Mouton de Gruyter.

Mikula, G., Scherer, K. R., & Athenstaedt, U. (1998). The role of injustice in the elicitation of differential emotional reactions. *Personality and Social Psychology Bulletin, 24*, 769–83.

Miller, R. S. (2007). Is embarrassment a blessing or a curse? In J. L. Tracy, R. W. Robins, & J. P. Tangney (Eds.), *The self-conscious emotions—Theory and research* (pp. 245–62). New York: Guilford Publications.

Miller, W. I. (1997). *The Anatomy of disgust*. Cambridge, MA: Harvard University Press.

Mischel, W., & Shoda, Y. (1995). A cognitive-affective system theory of personality: Reconceptualizing situations, dispositions, dynamics, and invariance in personality structure. *Psychological Review, 102*, 246–68.

Mithun, M. (1984). The evolution of noun incorporation. *Language, 60*, 847–94.

Moll, J., de Oliveira-Souza, R., Moll, F. T., Ignácio, F. A., Bramati, I. E., Caparelli-Dáquer, E. M., & Eslinger, P. J. (2005). The moral affiliations of disgust: a functional MRI study. *Cognitive and Behavioral Neurology, 18*, 68–78.

Moltó, J., Montañes, S., Poy, R., Segarra, P., Pastor, M. C., Tormo, M. P., et al. (1998). Un nuevo método para el estudio experimental de las emociones: El International Affective Picture System (IAPS). Adaptación española. *Revista de Psicología General y Aplicada, 52*, 55–87.

Monassi, C. R., Leite-Panissi, C. R., & Menescal-de-Oliveira, L. (1999). Ventrolateral periaqueductal gray matter and the control of tonic immobility. *Brain Research Bulletin, 50*, 201–8.

Moore, C. C., Romney, A. K., Hsia, T. -L., & Rusch, C. D. (1999). The universality of the semantic structure of emotion terms: Methods for the study of inter- and intra-cultural variability. *American Anthropologist, 101*, 529–46.

Moors, A. (2009). Theories of emotion causation: A review. *Cognition & Emotion, 23*, 625–62.

Morgan, R. L., & Heise, D. (1988). Structure of emotions. *Social Psychology Quarterly, 51*, 19–31.

Morice, R. (1978). Psychiatric diagnosis in a transcultural setting: The importance of lexical categories. *British Journal of Psychiatry, 132*, 87–95.

Morris, M. (1998). Morris Student Plus Dictionary: Euskara-Ingelesa English-Basque. Donostia: Klaudio Harluxet Fundazioa.

Mulligan, K. (2009). Moral emotions. In D. Sander & K. R. Scherer (Eds.), *The Oxford companion to emotions and the affective sciences* (pp. 262–4). New York: Oxford University Press.

Mulligan, K., & Scherer, K. R. (2012). Toward a working definition of emotion. *Emotion Review, 4*(4), 345–57.

Mumford, D. B. (1993). Somatisation: A transcultural perspective. *International Review of Psychiatry, 5*, 231–42.

Myers, F. R. (1979). Emotions and the self: A theory of personhood and political order among Pintupi Aborigines. *Ethos, 7*, 343–70.

Myhill, J. (1997). What is universal and what is language-specific in emotion words? Evidence from Biblical Hebrew. *Pragmatics & Cognition, 5*, 79–129.

Na, I.-J. (2007). Love is a seed of tears: Metaphors of love in Korean. *Proceedings of the 10th International Cognitive Linguistics Conference* (Vol. 1, pp. 172–3). Krakow, Poland.

Nabi, R. L. (2002). The theoretical versus the lay meaning of disgust: Implications for emotion research. *Cognition & Emotion, 16*, 695–703.

Naumann, E., Bartussek, D., Diedrich, D., & Laufer, M. E. (1992). Assessing cognitive and affective information processing functions of the brain by means of the late positive complex of the event-related potential. *Journal of Psychophysiology, 6*, 285–98.

Nayak, N., & Gibbs, R. (1990). Conceptual knowledge in idiom interpretation. *Journal of Experimental Psychology, 116*, 315–30.

Needham, R. (1981). *Circumstantial deliveries*. Berkeley: University of California Press.

Neisser, U. (1987). Concepts and conceptual development: Ecological and intellectual factors in categorization. Cambridge: Cambridge University Press.

Nesse, R. M. (1999). The evolution of hope and despair. *Social Research, 66*, 429–69.

Nesse, R. M. (2004). Natural selection and the elusiveness of happiness. *Philosophical Transactions of the Royal Society B: Biological Sciences, 359*, 1333–47.

Neto, F. (2006). Dimensions and correlates of social axioms among a Portuguese sample. *Individual Differences Research, 4*, 340–51.

Nida, E. A. (1958). Analysis of meaning and dictionary making. *International Journal of American Linguistics, 24*, 279–92.

Niedenthal, P., Auxiette, C., Nugier, A., Dalle, N., Bonin, P., & Fayol, M. (2004). A prototype analysis of the French category "emotion." *Cognition & Emotion, 18*, 289–312.

Niedenthal, P. M., Barsalou, L. W., Winkielman, P., Krauth-Gruber, S., & Ric, F. (2005). Embodiment in attitudes, social perception, and emotion. *Personality and Social Psychology Review, 9*, 184–211.

Niemeier, S. (1997). To have one's heart on the right place. Metaphorical and metonymic evidence from the folk model of the heart as the site of emotions in English. In B. Smieja & M. Tasch (Eds.), *Human contact through language and linguistics* (pp. 87–106). Frankfurt am Main: Peter Lang.

Niemeier, S. (2008). To be in control: kind-hearted and cool-headed. The head-heart dichotomy in English. In F. Sharifian, R. Dirven, & S. Niemeier (Eds.), *Culture, body, and language* (pp. 349–73). Berlin: Mouton de Gruyter.

Nikolaeva, T. (1977). *Phrazovaja intonatsija slavyanskih yazikov*. [Phrase Intonation of the Slavic Languages]. Moscow: Nauka.

Nisbett, R. E., Peng, K., Choi, I., & Norenzayan, A. (2001). Culture and systems of thought: Holistic vs. analytic cognition. *Psychological Review, 108*, 291–310.

Nisbett, R. E., & Schachter, S. (1966). Cognitive manipulation of pain. *Journal of Experimental Social Psychology, 2*, 227–36.

Norušis, M. J. (2008). *SPSS 17.0 Statistical procedures companion*. Amsterdam: Benjamins Publishing Company.

Nushykyan, E. (1986). *Typologia intonatsii emotsional'noj rechi*. [Typology of Emotional Speech Intonation]. Kyiv-Odessa: Vyshcha Shkola.

Nuyts J., & Pederson E. (Eds.) (1997). *Language and Conceptualization*. Cambridge & New York: Cambridge University Press.

Oaten, M., Stevenson, R. J., & Case, T. I. (2009). Disgust as a disease-avoidance mechanism. *Psychological Bulletin, 135*, 303–21.

Oatley, K. (2004). *Emotions: A brief history*. Malden, MA: Blackwell Publishing.

Oatley, K., & Duncan, E. (1994). The experience of emotions in everyday life. *Cognition & Emotion, 8*, 369–81.

Oatley, K., & Johnson-Laird, P. N. (1987). Towards a cognitive theory of emotions. *Cognition & Emotion, 1*, 29–50.

Oatley, K., & Johnson-Laird, P. N. (1996). The communicative theory of emotions: Empirical tests, mental models, and implications for social interaction. In L. Martin & A. Tesser (Eds.), *Striving and feeling: Interactions among goals, affect, and self-regulation* (pp. 363–93). Mahwah, NJ: Erlbaum.

Obeyesekere, G. (1981). Medusa's hair: an essay on personal symbols and religious experience. Chicago: University of Chicago Press.

Obukhova, V. N. (2008). Problemy preodoleniya mezhyazykovoi interferentsii v ukrainskoi rechi studentov-philologov v usloviyah russko-ukrainskoho bilingvizma [Problems of Interlingual Interference Negotiation in the Philology Students Ukrainian Speech in the Conditions of Russian-Ukrainian Bilingualism]. *Humanitarni nauky* [The Humanities], *1*, 59–65.

Occhi, D. J. (2008). How to have a HEART in Japanese. In F. Sharifian, R. Dirven, & S. Niemeier (Eds.), *Culture, body, and language* (pp. 191–212). Berlin: Mouton de Gruyter.

OED: Oxford English Dictionary. (n.d.). Retrieved from http://dictionary.oed.com/

Oey, E. (1990). Psycho-collocations in Malay: A Southeast Asian areal feature. *Linguistics of the Tibeto-Burman Area*, *13*, 141–57.

Ogarkova, A. (2003). Verbalization of the concept of LOVE as a culture–specific phenomenon. *Journal of Kyiv National Taras Shevchenko University (Foreign Languages)*, *34*, 62–75.

Ogarkova, A. (2004). Metaphoric representation of the concept of LOVE in Different Types of Discourse. *Language and Conceptual Pictures of the World*, *10*, 466–73.

Ogarkova, A. (2005). *The concept of LOVE in modern English. Cognitive and Discursive Aspects.* (Unpublished doctoral thesis). Kyiv National Taras Shevchenko University, Kyiv.

Ogarkova, A. (2007). Green-eyed monsters: a corpus-based study of the concepts of ENVY and JEALOUSY in modern English. *Metaphorik.de*, *13*, 87–147.

Ogarkova, A., & Borgeaud, P. (2009). (Un)common denominators in research on emotion language. *Social Science Information* [Special Issue], *48*, 523–43.

Ogarkova, A., Soriano, C., & Lehr, C. (2012). Naming feeling: Exploring the equivalence of emotion terms in five European languages. In Wilson, P. A. (ed.) *Dynamicity in Emotion Concepts* (pp. 245–76) (Lodz Studies in Language, vol 27). Frankfurt am Main: Peter Lang.

Öhman, A. (1986). Face the beast and fear the face: Animal and social fears as prototypes for evolutionary analyses of emotion. *Psychophysiology*, *23*, 123–45.

Öhman, A. (2000). Fear and anxiety: Evolutionary, cognitive, and clinical perspectives. In M. Lewis & J. M. Haviland-Jones (Eds.), *Handbook of emotions* (pp. 573–93). New York: Guilford Press.

Olatunji, B. O., Tolin, D. F., Huppert, J. D., & Lohr, J. M. (2005). The relation between fearfulness, disgust sensitivity and religious obsessions in a non-clinical sample. *Personality and Individual Differences*, *38*, 891–902.

Olatunji, B. O., Williams, N. L., Tolin, D. F., Abramowitz, J. S., Sawchuk, C. N., Lohr, J. M., & Elwood, L. S. (2007). The Disgust Scale: Item analysis, factor structure, and suggestions for refinement. *Psychological Assessment*, *19*, 281–97.

Olney, R. K., & Lomen-Hoerth, C. (2005). Exit strategies in ALS: An influence of depression or despair? *Neurology*, *65*, 9–10.

Orley, J. H. (1970). *Culture and mental illness.* East African studies. Nairobi, Kenya: East African Publishing House.

Ortony, A. (1988). Are emotion metaphors conceptual or lexical? *Cognition & Emotion*, *2*, 95–103.

Ortony, A., & Clore, G. L. (1989). Emotions, moods, and conscious awareness. *Cognition & Emotion*, *3*, 125–37.

Ortony, A., Clore, G. L., & Collins, A. (1988). *The cognitive structure of emotions.* Cambridge: Cambridge University Press.

Ortony, A., Clore, G. L., & Foss, M. A. (1987). The referential structure of the affective lexicon. *Cognitive Science*, *11*, 341–64.

Ortony, A., & Turner, T. J. (1990). What's basic about basic emotions? *Psychological Review, 97*, 315–31.

Osgood, C. E. (1964). Semantic differential technique in the comparative study of cultures. *American Anthropologist, 66*, 171–200.

Osgood, C. E. (1966). Dimensionality of the semantic space for communication via facial expressions. *Scandinavian Journal of Psychology, 7*, 1–30.

Osgood, C. E., May, W. H., & Miron, M. S. (1975). *Cross-cultural universals of affective meaning.* Urbana, IL: University of Illinois Press.

Osgood, C. E., Suci, G. J., & Tannenbaum, P. H. (1957). *The measurement of meaning.* Urbana, IL: University of Illinois Press.

Oxford PWN Polish-English English-Polish Dictionary. (2002). Warszawa: PWN.

Oyserman, D., Coon, H. M., & Kemmelmeier, M. (2002). Rethinking individualism and collectivism: Evaluation of theoretical assumptions and meta-analyses. *Psychological Bulletin, 128*, 3–72.

Ozhegov, S. I. (1988). *Slovar' russkogo yazyka.* [The Russian language dictionary] (20th ed.). Moscow: Rysskij Yazyk. Electronic version available at http://www.ozhegov.su/.

Ozhegov, S. I. (Ed.). (1990). *Slovar' russkogo yazyka.* [Dictionary of the Russian language] (22nd ed.). Electronic version available at http://www.ozhegov.su/ (accessed May 2010).

Palazova, M., Mantwill, K., Sommer, W., & Schacht, A. (2011). Are effects of emotion in single words non-lexical? Evidence from event-related brain potentials. *Neuropsychologia, 49*, 2766–75.

Pammi, S., & Schröder, M. (2009). Annotating meaning of listener vocalizations for speech synthesis. In *Proceedings of 2009 IEEE International Conference on Affective Computing and Intelligent Interaction.* doi:10.1109/ACII.2009.5349568.

Panayiotou, A. (2004a). Bilingual emotions: The untranslatable self. *Estudios de Sociolinguistica, 5*, 1–19.

Panayiotou, A. (2004b). Switching codes, switching code: Bilinguals' emotional responses in English and Greek. *Journal of Multilingual and Multicultural Development, 25*, 124–39.

Panayiotou, A. (2006). Translating guilt: An endeavor of shame in the Mediterranian? In A. Pavlenko (Ed.), *Bilingual minds: Emotional experience, expression and representation* (pp. 183–209). Clevedon, UK: Multilingual Matters.

Panayiotou, G. (2008). Emotional dimensions reflected in ratings of affective scripts. *Personality and Individual Differences, 44*, 1795–806.

Panksepp, J. (2005). Affective consciousness: Core emotional feelings in animals and humans. *Consciousness and Cognition, 14*, 19–69.

Paradis, C. (2012). Lexical Semantics. In C. Chapelle (Ed.), *The encyclopedia of applied linguistics.* Oxford: Wiley-Blackwell.

Paradis, M. (1997). The cognitive neuropsychology of bilingualism. In A. De Groot & J. F. Kroll (Eds.), *Tutorials in bilingualism: Psycholinguistic perspectives* (pp. 331–54). Mahwah, NJ: Lawrence Erlbaum.

Parkinson, B. (2004). Auditing emotions: What should we count? *Social Science Information, 43*, 633–45.

Parkinson, B., & Simons, G. (2009). Affecting others: Social appraisal and emotion contagion in everyday decision making. *Personality and Social Psychology Bulletin, 35*, 1071–84.

Partington, A. (1998). Patterns and meanings: using corpora for English language research and teaching. Amsterdam: John Benjamins.

Pasa, S. F., Kabasakal, H., & Bodur, M. (2001). Society, organisations, and leadership in Turkey. *Applied Psychology: An International Review, 50*, 559–89.

Pavlenko, A. (1999). New approaches to concepts in bilingual memory. *Bilingualism: Language and Cognition, 2*(3), 209–30.

Pavlenko, A. (2002a). Bilingualism and emotions. *Multilingua, 21*, 45–78.

Pavlenko, A. (2002b). Emotions and the body in Russian and English. In N. J. Enfield & A. Wierzbicka (Eds.), *The body in description of emotion: Cross-linguistic studies. Pragmatics & Cognition* [Special Issue], *10*, 207–41.

Pavlenko, A. (2005). *Emotions and multilingualism*. Cambridge: Cambridge University Press.

Pavlenko, A. (2008). Emotion and emotion-laden words in the bilingual lexicon. *Bilingualism: Language and Cognition, 11*, 147–64.

Pearsall, J. (1998). *New Oxford Dictionary of English*. Oxford: Claredon Press.

Pederson, E. & Nuyts, J. (1997). Overview: on the relationship between language and conceptualization. In J. Nuyts & E. Pederson (Eds.), *Language and Conceptualization*. (pp. 1–12). Cambridge & New York: Cambridge University Press.

Peeters, B. (Ed.) (2000). *The Lexicon-encyclopedia interface*. Oxford: Elsevier.

Peeters, B. (Ed.) (2006). *Semantic primes and universal grammar: Empirical evidence from the Romance languages*. Amsterdam: John Benjamins Publishing Company.

Peirce, C. S. (1977). *Semiotics and significs: Correspondence between Charles S. Peirce and Lady Victoria Welby*. (C. S. Hardwick, Ed.). Bloomington, IN: Indiana University Press.

Pell, M. (2006). Implicit recognition of vocal emotions in native and non-native speech. Speech Prosody 2006 Conference, Symposium on "Understanding emotions in speech: Neural and cross–cultural evidence." Dresden, Germany.

Pennebaker, J. W., Rimé, B., & Blankenship, V. E. (1996). Stereotypes of emotional expressiveness of Northerners and Southerners: A cross-cultural test of Montesquieu's hypotheses. *Journal of Personality and Social Psychology, 70*, 372–80.

Pérez, R.G. (2008). A cross-cultural analysis of heart metaphors. *Revista Alicantina de Estudios Ingleses, 2*, 25–56.

Pęzik, P. (2011). Providing corpus feedback for translators with the PELCRA search engine for NKJP. *Practical Applications in Language and Computers PALC 2009*. Frankfurt am Main: Peter Lang.

Picton, T. W., & Hillyard, S. A. (1988). Endogenous event-related potentials. In T. W. Picton (Ed.), *Human event-related potentials: EEG handbook* (Vol. 3, pp. 361–426). Elsevier.

Pike, I. L., & Young, A. (2002). Understanding psychosocial health among reproductive age women from Turkana District, Kenya and Mbulu District, Tanzania. *American Anthropological Association Annual Meeting Abstracts*, 479.

Pike, K. L. (1967). Language in relation to a unified theory of the structure of human behavior (2nd ed.). The Hague: Mouton.

Pitt-Rivers, J. (1965). Honour and social status. In J. G. Péristiany (Ed.), *Honour and shame: The values of Mediterranean society*. London: Weidenfeld & Nicolson.

Planalp, S. (1999). Communicating emotion: Social, moral, and cultural processes. Paris: Cambridge University Press.

Plutchik, R. (1980a). A general psychoevolutionary theory of emotion. In H. Kellerman & R. Plutchik (Eds.), *Emotion: theory, research, and experience* (Vol. 1, pp. 3–33). New York: Academic Press.

Plutchik, R. (1980b). *Emotion: A psychoevolutionary synthesis*. New York: Harper & Row.

Plutchik, R. (2001). The nature of emotions: Human emotions have deep evolutionary roots, a fact that may explain their complexity and provide tools for clinical practice. *American Scientist, 89*, 344–50.

Plutchik, R. (2003). *Emotions and life: Perspetives from psychology, biology, and evolution*. Washington, DC: American Psychological Association.

Plyushch, N. (2000). Vymovni normy ukrains'koi literaturnoi movy v umovah ukrains'ko-rosiys'koi dvomovnosti [Ukrainian Pronunciation Standards in the Situation of Ukrainian-Russian Bilingualism]. Proceedings of "Derzhavnist ukrains'koi movy i movnyi dosvid svitu" conference [State Status of the Ukrainian language and World Language Experience], pp. 350–62.

Polich, J. (2007). Updating p300: An integrative theory of P3a and P3b. *Clinical Neurophysiology, 118*, 2128–48.

Poole, F. J. P. (1985). Among the boughs of the hanging tree: Male suicide among the Bimin–Kuskusmin of Papua New Guinea. In F. X. Hezel, D. H. Rubinstein, & G. M. White (Eds.), *Culture, youth and suicide in the Pacific: Papers from an East–West Center Conference* (pp. 152–81). Honolulu, Hawaii: Pacific Islands Studies Program, Center for Asian and Pacific Studies, University of Hawaii at Manoa.

Poortinga, Y. H. (1992). Toward a conceptualization of culture for psychology. In Y. Iwawaki, Y. Kashima, & K. Leung (Eds.), *Innovations in cross-cultural psychology* (pp. 3–17). Amsterdam: Swets & Zeitlinger.

Poortinga, Y. H. (1997). Towards convergence? In J. W. Berry, Y. H. Poortinga, & J. Pandey (Eds.), *Handbook of cross-cultural psychology: Theory and method* (Vol. 1, pp. 347–87). Needham Heights, MA: Allyn & Bacon.

Pope, L. K., & Smith, C. A. (1994). On the distinct meanings of smiles and frowns. *Cognition & Emotion, 8,* 65–72.

Potts, G. F., & Tucker, D. M. (2001). Frontal evaluation and posterior representation in target detection. *Cognitive Brain Research, 11,* 147–56.

Pourtois, G., Grandjean, D., Sander, D., & Vuilleumier, P. (2004). Electrophysiological correlates of rapid spatial orienting towards fearful faces. *Cerebral Cortex, 14,* 619–33.

Power, M. J., & Dalgleish, T. (1997). *Cognition and emotion: From order to disorder.* Hove: Psychology Press.

Priestley, C. (2002). Insides and emotion in Koromu. *Pragmatics & Cognition, 10,* 243–70.

Prinz, J. J. (2004). *Gut reactions: A perceptual theory of emotion.* Oxford: Oxford University Press.

Putnam, R. D. (1993). *Making democracy work: Civic traditions in modern Italy.* Princeton: Princeton University Press.

Quine, W. V. (1965). Meaning and translation. In J. A. Fodor & J. J. Katz (Eds.), *The structure of language: Readings in the philosophy of language* (pp. 460–78). Englewood Cliffs, NJ: Prentice Hall.

Racy, J. (1980). Somatization in Saudi women: A therapeutic challenge. *British Journal of Psychiatry, 137,* 212–6.

Ranter, S. C. (1977). Immobility in invertebrates: What can we learn? *Psychological Review, 1,* 1–14.

Rasmussen, S. J. (2007). Continuing commentary: Revitalizing Shame: Some Reflections on "Changing Idioms of Shame: Expressions of Disgrace and Dishonour in the Narratives of Turkish Women Living in Denmark". *Culture & Psychology, 13,* 231–42.

Rauch, E. (2009). Measuring the Grid in the Sepedi, Xitsonga and Tshivenda language groups in the South African Police Service. (Unpublished master dissertation). North-West University, Potchefstroom, South Africa.

Real Academia Española. (2003). *Diccionario de la lengua española* (22 ed., 1.0 electronic version ed.). Madrid: Espasa Calpe.

Realo, A., & Allik, J. (1999). A cross-cultural study of collectivism: A comparison of American, Estonian, and Russian Students. *Journal of Social Psychology, 139,* 133–42.

Récanati, F. (2004). *Literal meaning.* Cambridge: Cambridge University Press.

Redondo, J., Fraga, I., Padrón, I., & Comesaña, M. (2007). The Spanish adaptation of ANEW (Affective Norms for English Words). *Behavior Research Methods, 39,* 600–5.

Reh, M. (1998). The language of emotion: An analysis of Dholuo on the basis of Grace Ogot's novel Miaha. In A. Athanasiadou & E. Tabakowska (Eds.), *Speaking of emotions: Conceptualisation and expression* (pp. 375–408). Berlin: Mouton de Gruyter.

Reips, U. D. (2000). The Web experiment method: Advantages, disadvantages, and solutions. In M. H. Birnbaum (Ed.), *Psychological experiments on the Internet* (pp. 89–114). San Diego, CA: Academic Press.

Reips, U. D. (2002). Standards for Internet-based experimenting. *Experimental Psychology, 49,* 243–56.

Reisenzein, R. (1994). Pleasure-arousal theory and the intensity of emotions. *Journal of Personality and Social Psychology, 67*(3), 525–39.

Reisenzein, R., & Hofmann, T. (1990). An investigation of dimensions of cognitive appraisal in emotion using the repertory grid technique. *Motivation & Emotion, 14,* 1–26.

Reisenzein, R., & Weber, H. (2009). Personality and emotion. In P. J. Corr & G. Matthews (Eds.), *The Cambridge handbook of personality psychology* (pp. 54–71). Cambridge: Cambridge University Press.

Remington, N. A., Fabrigar, L. R., & Visser, P. S. (2000). Reexamining the circumplex model of affect. *Journal of Personality and Social Psychology, 79,* 286–300.

Renshon, J.B. & Lerner, J. S. (2011). The role of emotions in foreign policy decision making. In D. J. Christie & C. Montiel (Eds.), *Encyclopedia of peace psychology.* Malden, MA: Wiley-Blackwell Press.

Resner, G., & Hartog, J. (1970). Concepts and terminology of mental disorder among Malays. *Journal of Cross-Cultural Psychology, 1,* 369–82.

Revelle, W., & Scherer, K. R. (2009). Personality and emotion. In D. Sander & K. R. Scherer (Eds.), *Oxford companion to emotion and the affective sciences.* Oxford: Oxford University Press.

Ricci-Bitti, P., & Scherer, K. R. (1986). Interrelations between antecedents, reactions, and coping responses. In K. R. Scherer, H. G. Wallbott, & A. B. Summerfield (Eds.), *Experiencing emotion: A cross-cultural study* (pp. 129–41). Cambridge: Cambridge University Press.

Riesman, P. (1977). *Freedom in Fulani social life: An introspective ethnography.* (M. Fuller, Trans.). Chicago: University of Chicago Press. (Original work published 1974).

Rimé, B. (2009). Emotion elicits the social sharing of emotion: Theory and empirical review. *Emotion Review, 1,* 60–85.

Rimé, B., & Giovannini, D. (1986). The physiological patterns of reported emotional states. In K. R. Scherer, A. B. Summerfield, & H. G. Wallbott (Eds.), *Experiencing emotion: A cross-cultural study* (pp. 84–97). Cambridge: Cambridge University Press.

Rimé, B., Philippot, P., & Cisamolo, D. (1990). Social schemata of peripheral changes in emotion. *Journal of Personality and Social Psychology, 59,* 38–49.

RNC: Russian National Corpus. (n.d.). Available at http://www.ruscorpora.ru/index.html.

Robinson, M. D., & Clore, G. L. (2002). Belief and feeling: Evidence for an accessibility model of emotional self-report. *Psychological Bulletin, 128,* 934–960.

Rodriguez Mosquera, P. M., Antony, S. R., Manstead, A. S. R. & Fischer, A. H. (2002): The role of honour concerns in emotional reactions to offences. *Cognition & Emotion, 16*(1), 143–163.

Rodriguez Mosquera, P. M., Manstead, A. S. R., & Fischer, A. H. (2000). The role of honor-related values in the elicitation, experience, and communication of pride, shame, and anger: Spain and the Netherlands compared. *Personality and Social Psychology Bulletin, 26,* 833–44.

Rodriguez Mosquera, P. M., Manstead, A. S. R., & Fischer, A. H. (2002). Honor in the Mediterranean and Northern Europe. *Journal of Cross-Cultural Psychology, 33,* 16–36.

Romney, K., Moore, C., & Rusch, C. D. (1997). Cultural universals: Measuring the semantic structure of emotion terms in English and Japanese. *Proceedings of National Academy of Science of the United States of America (Anthropology), 94,* 5489–94.

Rosaldo, M. (1984). Toward an anthropology or self and feeling. In R. A. Shweder & R. A. LeVine (Eds.), *Culture theory: Essays on mind, self, and emotion* (pp. 137–57). Cambridge: Cambridge University Press.

Rosaldo, M. Z. (1980). *Knowledge and passion: Ilongot notions of self and social life.* Cambridge: Cambridge University Press.

Rosch, E. (1978). Principles of categorization. In E. Rosch & B. Lloyd (Eds.), *Cognition and categorization* (pp. 27–48). Hillsdale, NJ: Lawrence Erlbaum Associates.

Rosch, E. H. (1973a). Natural categories. *Cognitive Psychology, 4*(3), 328–50.

Rosch, E. (1973b). On the internal structure of perceptual and semantic categories. In T. E. Moore (Ed.), *Cognitive development and the acquisition of language* (pp. 111–44). New York: Academic Press.

Rosch, E. (1975). Cognitive representations of semantic categories. *Journal of Experimental Psychology: General, 104,* 192–233.

Rosch, E., Mervis, C. B., Gray, W. D., Johnson, D. M., & Boyes-Braem, P. (1976). Basic objects in natural categories. *Cognitive Psychology, 8,* 382–439.

Roseman, I. J. (1991). Appraisal determinants of discrete emotions. *Cognition & Emotion, 5,* 161–200.

Roseman, I. J. (2001). A model of appraisal in the emotion system: Integrating theory, research, and applications. In K. R. Scherer, A. Schorr, & T. Johnstone (Eds.), *Appraisal processes in emotion: Theory, methods, research* (pp. 68–91). New York: Oxford University Press.

Roseman, I. J., & Smith, C. A. (2001). Appraisal theory: Overview, assumptions, varieties, controversies. In K. R. Scherer, A. Schorr, & T. Johnstone (Eds.), *Appraisal processes in emotion: Theory, methods, research* (pp. 3–34). New York: Oxford University Press.

Roseman, M. (1988). *Head, heart, odor and shadow: The structure of the self and the emotional world.* (Unpublished manuscript). Tufts University, Department of Anthropology, Medford, MA.

Rosenthal, R., & Rosnow, R. L. (2008). *Essentials of behavioral research: Methods and data analysis* (3rd ed.). New York: McGraw-Hill.

Rothbaum, F., & Tsang, B. Y.-P. (1998). Lovesongs in the United States and China. *Journal of Cross-Cultural Psychology, 29,* 306–19.

Royzman, E. B., & Sabini, J. (2001). Something it takes to be an emotion: The interesting case of disgust. *Journal for the Theory of Social Behaviour, 31,* 29–59.

Rozin, P. (2003). Five potential principles for understanding cultural difference in relation to individual differences. *Journal of Research in Personality, 37,* 273–83.

Rozin, P., & Fallon, A. E. (1987). A Perspective on disgust. *Psychological Review, 94,* 23–41.

Rozin, P., Haidt, J., & McCauley, C. R. (1999). Disgust: The body and soul emotion. In T. Dalgleish & M. J. Power (Eds.), *Handbook of cognition and emotion* (pp. 429–45). Chichester, England: Wiley.

Rozin, P., Haidt, J., & McCauley, C. R. (2000). Disgust. In M. Lewis & J. Haviland (Eds.), *Handbook of emotions* (2nd ed., pp. 637–8). New York: Guilford Press.

Rubin, D. C., & Talarico, J. M. (2009). A comparison of dimensional models of emotion: Evidence from emotions, prototypical events, autobiographical memories, and words. *Memory, 17,* 802–8.

Rubin, J. (1986). The emotion of anger: Some conceptual and theoretical issues. *Professional Psychology: Research and Practice, 17,* 115–24.

Rudakova, N. V. (2002). *Toska v anglijskih perevodah A.S. Pushkina.* Presented at the Annual research forum, Kazan': Kazan' State University.

Ruggiero, G. M. (2001). One country, two cultures. In M. Nasser, M. Katzman, & R. Gordon (Eds.), *Eating disorders and cultures in transition* (pp. 127–36). New York: Brunner Routledge.

Ruggiero, G. M., Hannöver, W., Mantero, M., & Papa, R. (2000). Body acceptance and culture: A study in northern and southern Italy. *European Eating Disorders Review, 8,* 40–50.

Russell, J. A. (1978). Evidence of convergent validity on the dimensions of affect. *Journal of Personality and Social Psychology, 36,* 1152–68.

Russell, J. A. (1980). A circumplex model of affect. *Journal of Personality and Social Psychology, 39,* 1161–78.

Russell, J. A. (1983). Pancultural aspects of the human conceptual organization of emotions. *Journal of Personality and Social Psychology, 45,* 1281–8.

Russell, J. A. (1991a). Culture and the categorization of emotions. *Psychological Bulletin, 110,* 426–50.

Russell, J. A. (1991b). In defense of a prototype approach to emotion concepts. *Journal of Personality and Social Psychology, 60,* 37–47.

Russell, J. A. (2003). Core affect and the psychological construction of emotion. *Psychological Review, 110,* 145–72.

Russell, J. A. (2009). Emotion, core affect, and psychological construction. *Cognition & Emotion, 23,* 1259–83.

Russell, J. A., & Carroll, J. M. (1999). On the bipolarity of positive and negative affect. *Psychological Bulletin, 125,* 3–30.

Russell, J. A., & Fehr, B. (1994). Fuzzy concepts in a fuzzy hierarchy: Varieties of anger. *Journal of Personality and Social Psychology, 67,* 186–205.

Russell, J. A., Fernández-Dols, J.-M., Manstead, A. S. R., & Wellenkamp, J. C. (Eds.). (1995). *Everyday conceptions of emotion: An introduction to the psychology, anthropology and linguistics of emotion*. Dordrecht: Kluwer Academic Publishers.

Russell, J. A., Lewicka, M., & Niit, T. (1989). A cross-cultural study of a circumplex model of affect. *Journal of Personality and Social Psychology, 57*, 848–56.

Russell, J. A., & Mehrabian, A. (1977). Evidence for a three-factor theory of emotions. *Journal of Research in Personality, 11*, 273–94.

Russell, J. A., & Sato, K. (1995). Comparing emotion words between languages. *Journal of Cross-Cultural Psychology, 26*, 384–91.

Russell, J. A., Weiss, A., & Mendelsohn, G. A. (1989). Affect Grid: A single-item scale of pleasure and arousal. *Journal of Personality and Social Psychology, 57*, 493–502.

Russo, M. (2010). Lokalizatsiya emotsij v yazykah mira [Localization of emotions in world languages]. *Review of Institut Yazykoznaniya Rossijskoj Akademii Nauk, 2*. Retrieved from www.iling-ran.ru/library/sborniki/for_lang/2010_02/4.pdf.

Sacharin, V., Schlegel, K., & Scherer, K. R. (2012). *Geneva Emotion Wheel Rating Study)* (Report. University of Geneva, Swiss Center for Affective Sciences, Geneva.

Safdar, S., Lewis, J. R., & Daneshpour, M. (2006). Social axioms in Iran and Canada: Intercultural contact, coping and adjustment. *Asian Journal Of Social Psychology, 9*, 123–31.

Salzmann, Z. (1954). The problem of lexical acculturation. *International Journal of American Linguistics, 20*, 137–9.

Samsonovich, A. V., & Ascoli, G. A. (2007). Cognitive map dimensions of the human value system extracted from natural language. In B. Goertzel & P. Wang (Eds.), *Advances in artificial general intelligence:Concepts, architectures and algorithms*. In *Proceedings of the AGI Workshop 2006. Frontiers in Artificial Intelligence and Applications* (Vol. 157, pp. 111–24). Amsterdam: IOS Press.

Sander, D., Grandjean, D., & Scherer, K. R. (2005). A systems approach to appraisal mechanisms in emotion. *Neural Networks, 18*, 317–52.

Santos, J. M. R. dos. (2008). Gaia: Intelligent control of virtual environments. (Unpublished master dissertation) Instituto Superior Tecnico, Universidade Tecnica de Lisboa, Lisboa. Retrieved 13/4/2012 from https://dspace.ist.utl.pt/bitstream/2295/236570/1/Dissertacao%20da%20Tese%20de%20Mestrado%20-%20FINAL%20-%20Revised%20-%20Jorge%20Santos.pdf.

Sarasola, I. (2007). *Euskal Hiztegia*. Donostia: Elkar.

Saucier, G., & Goldberg, L. R. (1996). The language of personality: Lexical perspectives on the five-factor model. In J. S. Wiggins (Ed.), *The five-factor model of personality: Theoretical perspectives* (pp. 21–50). New York: Guilford Press.

Sauter, D., Eisner, F., Ekman, P., & Scott, S. K. (2009). Universal vocal signals of emotion. In N. Taatgen & H. Van Rijn (Eds.), In *Proceedings of the 31st Annual Meeting of the Cognitive Science Society (CogSci 2009)* (pp. 2251–5). Cognitive Science Society.

Sauter, D., Eisner, F., Ekman, P., & Scott, S. K. (2010). Cross-cultural recognition of basic emotions through nonverbal emotional vocalizations. *Proceedings of the National Academy of Sciences of the United States of America, 107*, 2408–12.

Saxena, S., Nepal, M. K., & Mohan, D. (1988). DSM-III axis I diagnoses of Indian psychiatric patients with somatic symptoms. *The American Journal of Psychiatry, 145*, 1023–4.

Schacht, A., & Sommer, W. (2009a). Emotions in word and face processing: Early and late cortical responses. *Brain and Cognition, 69*, 538–50.

Schacht, A., & Sommer, W. (2009b). Time course and task dependence of emotion effects in word processing. *Cognitive, Affective & Behavioral Neuroscience, 9*, 28–43. doi:10.3758/CABN.9.1.28.

Schachter, S., & Singer, J. E. (1962). Cognitive, social, and physiological determinants of emotional state. *Psychological Review, 69*, 379–99.

Schenker, N., & Gentleman, J. F. (2001). On judging the significance of differences by examining the overlap between confidence intervals. *The American Statistician*, 55, 182–6.

Scherer, K R. (1982). Emotion as a process: Function, origin and regulation. *Social Science Information*, 21, 555–70.

Scherer, K. R. (1984a). Emotion as a multicomponent process: A model and some cross-cultural data. In P. Shaver (Ed.), *Review of personality and social psychology: Vol. 5. Emotions, relationships and health* (pp. 37–63). Beverly Hills, CA: Sage.

Scherer, K. R. (1984b). On the nature and function of emotion: A component process approach. In K. R. Scherer & P. Ekman (Eds.), *Approaches to emotion* (pp. 293–317). Hillsdale, NJ: Erlbaum.

Scherer, K. R. (1986a). Emotion experiences across European cultures: A summary statement. In K. R. Scherer, H. G. Wallbott, & A. B. Summerfield (Eds.), *Experiencing emotion: A cross-cultural study* (pp. 173–90). Cambridge: Cambridge University Press.

Scherer, K. R. (1986b). Vocal affect expression: A review and a model for future research. *Psychological Bulletin*, 99, 143–65.

Scherer, K. R. (1987). Towards a dynamic theory of emotion: The component process model of affective states. *Geneva Studies in Emotion and Communication*, 1, 1–98.

Scherer, K. R. (1988a). Criteria for emotion-antecedent appraisal: A review. In V. Hamilton, G. H. Bower, & N. H. Frijda (Eds.), *Cognitive perspectives on emotion and motivation* (pp. 89–126). Dordrecht: Kluwer.

Scherer, K. R. (1988b). On the symbolic functions of vocal affect expression. *Journal of Language and Social Psychology*, 7, 79–100.

Scherer, K. R. (1992). What does facial expression express? In K. Strongman (Ed.), *International review of studies on emotion* (Vol. 2, pp. 139–65). Chichester: Wiley.

Scherer, K. R. (1993). Studying the emotion-antecedent appraisal process: An expert system approach. *Cognition and Emotion*, 7, 323–55.

Scherer, K. R. (1994). Toward a concept of "modal emotions." In P. Ekman & R. J. Davidson (Eds.), *The nature of emotion: fundamental questions* (pp. 25–31). New York: Oxford University Press.

Scherer, K. R. (1996). Current perspectives on appraisal theories of emotion. *International Journal of Psychology*, 31, 4003.

Scherer, K. R. (1997a). Profiles of emotion-antecedent appraisal: Testing theoretical predictions across cultures. *Cognition and Emotion*, 11, 113–50.

Scherer, K. R. (1997b). The role of culture in emotion-antecedent appraisal. *Journal of Personality and Social Psychology*, 73, 902–22.

Scherer, K. R. (1998). Analyzing emotion blends. In A. Fischer (Ed.), In *Proceedings of the 10th Conference of the International Society for Research on Emotions* (pp. 142–8). Würzburg, Amsterdam: Faculty of Psychology.

Scherer, K. R. (1999a). Appraisal theories. In T. Dalgleish & M. Power (Eds.), *Handbook of cognition and emotion* (pp. 637–63). Chichester, UK: Wiley.

Scherer, K. R. (1999b). On the sequential nature of appraisal processes: Indirect evidence from a recognition task. *Cognition and Emotion*, 13, 763–93.

Scherer, K. R. (2000a). Emotion. In M. Hewstone & W. Stroebe (Eds.), *Introduction to social psychology: A European perspective* (3rd ed., pp. 151–91). Oxford: Blackwell.

Scherer, K. R. (2000b). Emotions as episodes of subsystem synchronization driven by nonlinear appraisal processes. In M. D. Lewis & I. Granic (Eds.), *Emotion, development, and self-organization: Dynamic systems approaches to emotional development* (pp. 70–99). New York: Cambridge University Press.

Scherer, K. R. (2000c). Psychological models of emotion. In J. Borod (Ed.), *The neuropsychology of emotion* (pp. 137–62). New York: Oxford University Press.

Scherer, K. R. (2001). Appraisal considered as a process of multilevel sequential checking. In K. R. Scherer, A. Schorr, & T. Johnstone (Eds.), *Appraisal processes in emotion: Theory, methods, research* (pp. 92–120). New York: Oxford University Press.

Scherer, K. R. (2004a). Feelings integrate the central representation of appraisal-driven response organization in emotion. In A. S. R. Manstead, N. H. Frijda, & A. H. Fischer (Eds.), *Feelings and emotions: The Amsterdam symposium* (pp. 136–57). Cambridge: Cambridge University Press.

Scherer, K. R. (2004b). Ways to study the nature and frequency of our daily emotions: Reply to the commentaries on "Emotions in everyday life." *Social Science Information*, 43, 667–89.

Scherer, K. R. (2004c). Which emotions can be induced by music? What are the underlying: Mechanisms? And how can we measure them? *Journal of New Music Research*, 33, 239–51.

Scherer, K. R. (2005a). What are emotions? And how can they be measured? *Social Science Information*, 44, 695–729.

Scherer, K. R. (2005b). Unconscious processes in emotion: The bulk of the iceberg. In P. Niedenthal, L. F. Barrett, & P. Winkielman (Eds.), *The unconscious in emotion* (pp. 312–34). New York: Guilford.

Scherer, K. R. (2009a). Emotions are emergent processes. They require a dynamic computational architecture. *Philosophical Transactions of the Royal Society, Series B*, 364, 3459–74.

Scherer, K. R. (2009b). Psychological theories of emotion. In D. Sander & K. R. Scherer (Eds.), *Oxford companion to emotion and the affective sciences*. Oxford: Oxford University Press.

Scherer, K. R. (2009c). The dynamic architecture of emotion: Evidence for the component process model. *Cognition & Emotion*, 23, 1307–51.

Scherer, K. R. (2010a). Emotion and emotional competence: Conceptual and theoretical issues for modeling. In K. R. Scherer, T. Bänziger, & E. B. Roesch (Eds.), *A blueprint for affective computing: A sourcebook and manual* (pp. 3–20). Oxford: Oxford University Press.

Scherer, K. R. (2010b). The component process model: A blueprint for a comprehensive computational model of emotion. In K. R. Scherer, T. Banziger, & E. Roesch (Eds.), *A blueprint for affective computing: A sourcebook and manual* (pp. 47–70). Oxford: Oxford University Press.

Scherer, K. R., Banse, R., & Wallbott, H. G. (2001). Emotion inferences from vocal expression correlated across languages and cultures. *Journal of Cross-Cultural Psychology*, 32, 76–92.

Scherer, K. R., & Brosch, T. (2009). Culture-specific appraisal biases contribute to emotion dispositions. *European Journal of Personality*, 23, 265–88.

Scherer, K. R., & Ceschi, G. (1997). Lost luggage: A field study of emotion-antecedent appraisal. *Motivation and Emotion*, 21, 211–35.

Scherer, K. R., & Ceschi, G. (2000). Criteria for emotion recognition from verbal and nonverbal expression: Studying baggage loss in the airport. *Personality and Social Psychology Bulletin*, 26, 327–39.

Scherer, K. R., Clark-Polner, E., & Mortillaro, M. (2011). In the eye of the beholder? Universality and cultural specificity in the expression and perception of emotion. *International Journal of Psychology*, 46, 401–35.

Scherer, K. R., & Ekman, P. (Eds.) (1984). *Approaches to emotion*. Hillsdale, NJ: Erlbaum Associates.

Scherer, K. R., & Ellgring, H. (2007a). Are facial expressions of emotion produced by categorical affect programs or dynamically driven by appraisal? *Emotion*, 7, 113–30.

Scherer, K. R., & Ellgring, H. (2007b). Multimodal expression of emotion: Affect programs or componential appraisal patterns? *Emotion*, 7, 158–71.

Scherer, K. R. & Ellsworth, P. C. (2009). Appraisal theories. In D. Sander, & K. R. Scherer (Eds.), *Oxford companion to emotion and the affective sciences* (pp. 45–49). Oxford: Oxford University Press.

Scherer, K. R., Johnstone, T., & Klasmeyer, G. (2003). Vocal expression of emotion. In R. J. Davidson, K. R. Scherer, & H. H. Goldsmith (Eds.), *Handbook of affective sciences* (pp. 433–56). New York: Oxford University Press.

Scherer, K. R., & Meuleman, B. (2013). Human emotion experiences can be predicted on theoretical grounds: Evidence for verbal labeling. *PLoS ONE, 8(3)*: e58166. doi:10.1371/journal.pone.0058166.

Scherer, K. R., & Peper, M. (2001). Psychological theories of emotion and neuropsychological research. In F. Boller & J. Grafman (Eds), *Handbook of Neuropsychology* (Vol. 5, pp. 17–48). Amsterdam: Elsevier.

Scherer, K. R., Schorr, A., & Johnstone, T. (Eds.). (2001). *Appraisal processes in emotion: Theory, methods, research*. Series in affective science. New York: Oxford University Press.

Scherer, K. R., Summerfield, A. B., & Wallbott, H. G. (1983). Cross-national research on antecedents and components of emotion: A progress report. *Social Science Information, 22,* 355–85.

Scherer, K. R., & Wallbott, H. G. (1994). Evidence for universality and cultural variation of differential emotion response patterning. *Journal of Personality and Social Psychology, 66,* 310–28.

Scherer, K. R., Wallbott, H. G., Matsumoto, D., & Kudoh, T. (1988). Emotional experience in cultural context: A comparison between Europe, Japan, and the USA. In K. R. Scherer (Ed.), *Facets of emotion: Recent research* (pp. 5–30). Hillsdale, NJ: Erlbaum.

Scherer, K. R., Wallbott, H. G., & Summerfield, A. B. (Eds.). (1986). *Experiencing emotion: A cross-cultural study.* Cambridge: Cambridge University Press.

Scherer, K. R., Wranik, T., Sangsue, J., Tran, V., & Scherer, U. (2004). Emotions in everyday life: Probability of occurrence, risk factors, appraisal and reaction patterns. *Social Science Information, 43,* 499–570.

Scherer, K. R., & Zentner, K. R. (2001). Emotional effects of music: Production rules. In P. N. Juslin & J. A. Sloboda (Eds.), *Music and emotion: Theory and research* (pp. 361–92). Oxford: Oxford University Press.

Scherer, K. R., Zentner, M. R., & Stern, D. (2004). Beyond surprise: The puzzle of infants' expressive reactions to expectancy violation. *Emotion, 4,* 389–402.

Schieffelin, E. L. (1985). The cultural analysis of depressive affect: An example from New Guinea. In B. Good & A. Kleinman (Eds.), *Culture and depression: Studies in the anthropology and cross-cultural psychiatry of affect and disorder* (pp. 101–33). Berkeley, CA: University of California Press.

Schimmack, U., & Reisenzein, R. (2002). Experiencing activation: Energetic arousal and tense arousal are not mixtures of valence and activation. *Emotion, 2,* 412–7.

Schimmel, S. (1979). Anger and its control in Graeco-Roman and modern psychology. *Psychiatry, 42,* 320–37.

Schlosberg, H. (1952). The description of facial expressions in terms of two dimensions. *Journal of Experimental Psychology, 44,* 229–37.

Schlosberg, H. (1954). Three dimensions of emotion. *Psychological Review, 61,* 81–8.

Schmid, J., & Leiman, J. M. (1957). The development of hierarchical factor solutions. *Psychometrika, 22,* 53–61.

Schnall, S., Haidt, J., Clore, G. L., & Jordan, A. H. (2008). Disgust as embodied moral judgment. *Personality and Social Psychology Bulletin, 34,* 1096–109.

Schneirla, T. C. (1959). An evolutionary and developmental theory of biphasic processes underlying approach and withdrawal. In M. R. Jones (Ed.), *Current theory and research in motivation* (pp. 1–49). Lincoln, NB: University of Nebraska Press.

Scholl, W. (2013). The socio-emotional basis of human interaction and communication: How we construct our social world. *Social Science Information, 52(1),* 3–33.

Schorr, A. (2001). Appraisal: The evolution of an idea. In K. R. Scherer, A. Schorr, & T. Johnstone (Eds.), *Appraisal processes in emotion: Theory, methods, research* (pp. 20–36). New York: Oxford University Press.

Schupp, H., Cuthbert, B., Bradley, M., Hillman, C., Hamm, A., & Lang, P. (2004). Brain processes in emotional perception: Motivated attention. *Cognition & Emotion, 18,* 593–611.

Schupp, H. T., Cuthbert, B. N., Bradley, M. M., Caciopppo, J. T., Ito, T., & Lang, P. J. (2000). Affective picture processing: The late positive potential is modulated by motivational relevance. *Psychophysiology, 37,* 257–61.

Schupp, H. T., Hamm, A. O., & Weike, A. I. (2003). Emotional facilitation of sensory processing in the visual cortex. *Psychological Science, 14,* 7–13.

Schupp, H. T., Stockburger, J., Codispoti, M., Junghöfer, M., Weike, A. I., & Hamm, A. O. (2007). Selective visual attention to emotion. *Journal of Neuroscience, 27,* 1082–9.

Schwartz, S. H. (1992). Universals in the content and structure of values: Theoretical advances and empirical tests in 20 countries. In M. Zanna (Ed.), *Advances in experimental social psychology* (Vol. 25, pp. 1–65). Orlando, FL: Academic Press.

Schwartz, S. H. (2004). Mapping and interpreting cultural differences around the world. In H. Vinken, J. Soeters, & P. Ester (Eds.), *Comparing cultures: Dimensions of culture in a comparative perspective* (pp. 43–73). Leiden: Brill.

Schwibbe, M., Räder, K., Schwibbe, G., Borchardt, M., & Geiken-Pophanken, G. (1992). Zum emotionalen Gehalt von Substantiven, Adjektiven und Verben. In W. Hager & M. Hasselhorn (Eds.), *Handbuch deutschsprachiger Wortnormen*. Göttingen: Hofgrefe.

Scollon, C. N., Diener, E., Oishi, S., & Biswas-Diener, R. (2004). Emotions across cultures and methods. *Journal of Cross-Cultural Psychology, 35*, 304–26.

Seidensticker, T. (1992). *Altarabisc, Herz und sein Wortfeld*. Wiesbaden: Otto Harrassowitz.

Seligman, M. E., Abramson, L. Y., Semmel, A., & von Baeyer, C. (1979). Depressive attributional style. *Journal of Abnormal Psychology, 88*, 242–7.

Semin, G., Gorts, C., Nandram, S., & Semin-Goossens, A. (2002). Cultural perspectives on the linguistic representation of emotion and emotion events. *Cognition & Emotion, 16*, 11–28.

Shafiro, M. V., Himelein, M. J., & Best, D. L. (2003). Ukrainian and U.S. American females. *Journal of Cross-Cultural Psychology, 34*, 297–303.

Sharifian, F., Dirven, R., Yu, N., & Niemeier, S. (Eds.). (2008). Culture, body, and language: Conceptualizations of internal body organs across cultures and languages. Berlin: Mouton de Gruyter.

Sharma, S. (1999). Corporate Gita: Lessons for management, administration and leadership. *Journal of Human Values, 5*, 103–23.

Sharoff, S. (2006). The core lexicon of emotion. *Meaning as use: A communication-centered approach to lexical meaning*. (Unpublished manuscript).

Shaver, P., Schwartz, J., Kirson, D., & O'Connor, C. (1987). Emotion knowledge: Further exploration of a prototype approach. *Journal of Personality and Social Psychology, 52*, 1061–86.

Shaver, P., Wu, S., & Schwartz, J. (1992). Cross-cultural imilarities and differences in emotion and its representation. A prototype approach. In M. S. Clark (Ed.), *Review of Personality and Social Psychology* (Vol. 13, pp. 175–212). Thousand Oaks, CA: Sage Publications.

Shaver, P. R., Murdaya, U., & Fraley, R. C. (2001). Structure of the Indonesian emotion lexicon. *Asian Journal of Social Psychology, 4*, 201–24.

Shiota, M. N., & Keltner, D. (2005). What do emotion words represent? *Psychological Inquiry, 16*, 32–7.

Shore, B. (1982). *Sala'ilua, a Samoan mystery*. New York: Columbia University Press.

Shuman, V., Sander, D., & Scherer, K. R. (2013). Levels of valence. *Frontiers in Psychology, 4*, 00261, *DOI=10.3389/fpsyg.2013.00261 Emotion Science*.

Shweder, R. A., Balle-Jensen, L. A., & Goldstein, W. M. (1995). Who sleeps by whom revisited: A method for extracting the moral goods implicit in practice. In J. J. Goodnow, P. J. Miller, & F. S. Kessel (Eds.), *Cultural practices as contexts for development* (pp. 21–39). San Francisco: Jossey-Bass.

Siahaan, P. (2007). Understanding abstract concepts through body parts in Indonesian. In *Proceedings of the 10th Cognitive Linguistics Conference* (pp. 106–7).

Siahaan, P. (2008). Did he break your heart or your liver? A contrastive study on metaphorical concepts from the source domain ORGAN in English and in Indonesian. In F. Sharifian, R. Dirven, & S. Niemeier (Eds.), *Culture, body, and language: Conceptualizations of internal body organs across cultures and languages* (pp. 45–74). Berlin: Mouton de Gruyter.

Simpson, J., Carter, S., Anthony, S. H., & Overton, P. G. (2006). Is disgust a homogeneous emotion? *Motivation & Emotion, 30*, 31–41.

Sinclair, J. (1991). *Corpus, concordance, collocation*. Oxford: Oxford University Press.

Skrandies, W. (1998). Evoked potential correlates of semantic meaning. A brain mapping study. *Cognitive Brain Research, 6*, 173–83.

Skrandies, W., & Chiu, M. J. (2003). Dimensions of affective semantic meaning-behavioral and evoked potential correlates in Chinese subjects. *Neuroscience Letters, 341*, 45–8.

Slaměník, I., & Hurychová, Z. (2006). Socio-cultural dependency of emotions: Comparative analysis using the prototype approach. In V. Kebza (Ed.), *Psychological aspects of transformation of the Czech society within the context of European integration* (pp. 105–22). Praha: Matfyzpress.

Small, D. A., & Lerner, J. S. (2008). Emotional policy: Personal sadness and anger shape judgments about a welfare case. *Political Psychology*, *29*, 149–68.

Smith, C., & Lazarus, R. (1993). Appraisal components, core relational themes, and the emotions. *Cognition & Emotion*, *7*, 233–69.

Smith, C. A., & Ellsworth, P. C. (1985). Patterns of cognitive appraisal in emotion. *Journal of Personality and Social Psychology*, *48*, 813–38.

Smith, C. A., & Ellsworth, P. C. (1987). Patterns of appraisal and emotion related to taking an exam. *Journal of Personality and Social Psychology*, *52*, 475–88.

Smith, C. A., & Kirby, L. D. (2001). Affect and cognitive appraisal processes. In J. P. Forgas (Ed.), *Handbook of affect and social cognition* (pp. 75–92). Mahwah, NJ: Lawrence Erlbaum.

Smith, C. A., & Scott, H. S. (1997). A componential approach to the meaning of facial expressions. In J. A. Russell & J. M. Fernández-Dols (Eds.), *The psychology of facial expression* (pp. 229–54). New York: Cambridge University Press.

Smith, K. D., & Tkel-Sbal, D. (1995). Prototype analyses of emotion words in Palau, Microneasia. In J. A. Russell, J.-M. Fernandez-Dols, A. S. Manstead, & J. C. Wellenkamp (Eds.), *Everyday conceptions of emotion: an introduction to the psychology, anthropology, and linguistics of emotion* (pp. 85–102). Dordrecht: Kluwer Academic Publishers.

Smith, N. K., Cacioppo, J. T., Larsen, J. T., & Chartrand, T. L. (2003). May I have your attention, please: Electrocortical responses to positive and negative stimuli. *Neuropsychologia*, *41*, 171–83.

Smith, N. K., Larsen, J. T., Chartrand, T. L., Cacioppo, J. T., Katafiasz, H. A., & Moran, K. E. (2006). Being bad isn't always good: Affective context moderates the attention bias toward negative information. *Journal of Personality and Social Psychology*, *90*, 210–20.

Smith, P. B., & Bond, M. H. (1997). *Social psychology across cultures*. New York: Prentice Hall.

Smith, R. H., Webster, J. M., Parrott, W. G., & Eyre, H. L. (2002). The role of public exposure in moral and nonmoral shame and guilt. *Journal of Personality and Social Psychology*, *83*, 138–59.

Smith, R. W. (1997). Visual hypothesis testing with confidence intervals. In *Proceedings of the Twenty-Second Annual SAS Users Group International Conference (SUGI 22)*. Retrieved from http://www2.sas.com/proceedings/sugi22/STATS/PAPER270.PDF

Smith, S. T., & Smith, K. D. (1995). Turkish emotion concepts: A prototype analysis. In J. A. Russell, J.-M. Fernandez-Dols, A. S. Manstead, & J. C. Wellenkamp (Eds.), *Everyday conceptions of emotion: An introduction to the psychology, anthropology, and linguistics of emotion* (pp. 103–20). Dordrecht: Kluwer Academic Publishers.

Snyder, C. R., & Lopez, S. J. (2002). *Handbook of positive psychology*. New York: Oxford University Press.

Solomon, R. C. (1993). *The passions. Emotions and the meaning of life*. Indianapolis, IN: Hackett Publishing Company.

Solomon, R. C. (2003). *Not passion's slave: Emotions and choice*. Oxford: Oxford University Press.

Solovyev, V. D. (2008). Eksperimental'noe izuchenie struktury semanticheskogo polya otricatel'nih emotsij v russkon yazyke [Experimental investigation of the structure of the semantic domain of negative emotions in the Russian language]. *Ucheniye zapiski Kazanskogo universiteta (Gumanitarnie nauki)*, *150*, 239–48.

Sonnemans, J., & Frijda, N. H. (1994). The structure of subjective emotional intensity. *Cognition & Emotion*, *8*, 329–50.

Soriano, C. (2003). Some anger metaphors in Spanish and English. A contrastive review. *Contrastive Cognitive Linguistics*, monograph issue of the *International Journal of English Studies (IJES)*, *3*, 107–22.

Soriano, C. (2005). The conceptualization of anger in English and Spanish: A cognitive approach. (Unpublished doctoral dissertation). University of Murcia, Murcia, Spain.

Soriano, C., & Ogarkova, A. (2009). Linguistics and emotion. In D. Sander & K. R. Scherer (Eds.), *Oxford companion to emotion and the affective sciences* (pp. 240–2). Oxford: Oxford University Press.

Soriano, C., & Valenzuela, J. (2009). Are conceptual metaphors accessible online? A psycholinguistic exploration of the CONTROL IS UP metaphor. In J. Valenzuela, A. Rojo, & C. Soriano (Eds), *Trends in cognitive linguistics: Theoretical and applied models* (pp. 29–49). Frankfurt: Peter Lang.

Spinosa, B. (1677). *Ethica*. Amsterdam, The Netherlands: Rieuwertz.

Stebunova, A. N. (2001). Kharakternye cherty vzaimovliyaniya russkoho i ukrainskoho yazykov v Donbasskom regione [Interference Characteristics of Russian and Ukrainian Languages in Donbass Region]. In *Proceedings of the "Russkiy yazyk:istoricheskiye sud" by i sovremennost" conference*, [Russian Language: Historical Destinies and Contemporaneity] (pp. 314–5).

Stefanowitsch, A. (2004). HAPPINESS in English and German: A metaphorical-pattern analysis. In M. Achard & S. Kemmer (Eds.) *Language, culture, and mind* (pp. 137–49). Stanford, CA: University of Stanford.

Stefanowitsch, A. (2006). Words and their metaphors. A corpus-based approach. In A. Stefanowitsch & S. T. Gries (Eds), *Corpus-based approaches to metaphor and metonymy* (pp. 61–105). Berlin/New York: Mouton de Gruyter.

Stefanowitsch, A., & Gries, S. T. (2007). *Corpus-based approaches to metaphor and metonymy*. Berlin: Mouton De Gruyter.

Stefanskyy, E. E. (2000). Kontsept toski v russkoj, scheshskoj, i pol'skoj lingvokul'turah [The concept of toska in Russian, Czech, and Polish lingual cultures]. *Balkanskaja rusistika, 2*. Retrieved from www.russian. slavica.org/article1772.html.

Stefanskyy, E. E. (2004). Slavyanskij ANGST [Slavic ANGST]. *Proceedings of the conference 'Aksiologicheskaya lingvistika: problemy i perspectivy*, [Axiological linguistics: problems and perspectives] 27 April 2004, 102–105. Volgograd: College.

Stefanskyy, E. E. (2005). Russkaya toska na fone analogichnih kontseptov pol'skogo i česhskogo yazykov [Russian toska and its conceptual correlates in Polish and Czech]. *In Proceedings of the international conference "The Russian language and literature of the XX–XXI centuries"* (pp. 150–60). Samara: Samara State Pedagogical University.

Stefanskyy, E. E. (2006). Scenarii toski v russkoj, pol'skoj, i česhskoj lingvokul'turah [The scripts of "toska" in the Russian, Polish, and Czech lingual cultures]. In *Proceedings of the XXXVth International Philological Conference, Vol. 8 (Lexicology: Slavic studies)* (pp. 30–6). Saint-Petersburg: Saint-Petersburg State University.

Stefanskyy, E. E. (2007a). Concept gneva v russkoj, scheshskoj, i pol'skoj lingvoku'turah [The concept of "anger" in Russian, Polish, and Czech lingual cultures]. *Yazyk na perekrestke kul'tur, 58–71*. Samara: SaGA.

Stefanskyy, E. E. (2007b). Kul'turnie scenarii realizatsii emotsional'nij kontseptov v hudozhestvennom diskurse [Cultural scenarios of the representation of emotion concepts in fiction]. *Vestnik Samarskoj gumanitarnoj akademii, 1*, 172–82.

Stefanskyy, E. E. (2009a). Konceptualizatsija negativnih emotisij v mifologicheskom i sovremennom yazykovom soznanii: na materiale russkogo, pol'skogo, i cheshskogo yazykov. [The conceptualization of negative emotions in the mythological and contemporary mentality: the case of Russian, Polish, and Czech]. (Habilitation paper.). Volgodrad: Volgograd Pedagogical University.

Stefanskyy, E. E. (2009b). Lichnostnoe i kollectivnoe v perezhivanii emotsij v russkoj, scheshskoj, i pol'skoj lingvokul'turah [The individual and the collective in the emotion concepts in Russian, Polish, and Czech lingual cultures]. *Acta Linguistica, 3*, 110–5.

Stemmler, G. (2003). Methodological considerations in the psychophysiological study of emotion. In R. J. Davidson, K. R. Scherer, & H. H. Goldsmith (Eds.), *Handbook of affective sciences*. Oxford: Oxford University Press.

Stepanov, Y. S. (1997). *Konstanty: Slovar' russkoj kul'tury*. [Invariables: Dictionary of the Russian culture] (2nd ed.). Moscow: Jazyki russkoj kul'tury.

Stepanova, O., Sachs, O., & Coley, J. (2006). Envy and jealousy in Russian and English: Labeling and conceptualization of emotions by monolinguals and bilinguals. In A. Pavlenko (Ed.), *Bilingual minds: Emotional experience, expression, and representation* (pp. 209–31). Clevedon: Multilingual Matters.

Sternberg, R. J., & Grigorenko, E. L. (Eds.). (2002). *The general factor of intelligence: How general is it?* Mahwah, NJ: Lawrence Erlbaum Associates.

Stipek, D. (1998). Differences between Americans and Chinese in the circumstances evoking pride, shame, and guilt. *Journal of Cross-Cultural Psychology, 29*, 616–29.

Stipek, D., Recchia, S., McClintic, S., & Lewis, M. (1992). Self-evaluation in young children. *Monographs of the Society for Research in Child Development*, 57, i–95.

Stipek, D., Weiner, B., & Li, K. (1989). Testing some attribution-emotion relations in the people's Republic of China. *Journal of Personality and Social Psychology*, 56, 109–16.

Storm, C., & Storm, T. (1987). A taxonomic study of the vocabulary of emotions. *Journal of Personality and Social Psychology*, 53, 805–16.

Strapparava, C., & Valitutti, (2004). WordNet-Affect: an affective extension of WordNet. In *Proceedings of 4th International Conference on Language Resources and Evaluation (LREC 2004)* (pp. 1083–6).

Strelau, J., & Zawadzki, B. (1997). Temperament and personality: Eysenck's three superfactors as related to temperamental dimensions. In H. Nyborg (Ed.), *The scientific study of human nature: Tribute to Hans J. Eysenck at eighty* (pp. 68–91). New York: Pergamon.

Stubbs, M. (2001). Words and phrases: Corpus studies of lexical semantics. Oxford: Blackwell Publishers.

Subirats, C. and Petruck, M. (2003): Surprise: Spanish FrameNet! In E. Hajicova, A. Kotesovcova, & J. Mirovsky (Eds.), In *Proceedings of CIL 17. CD-ROM*. Prague: Matfyzpress.

Sullivan, M. W., Bennett, D. S., & Lewis, M. (2003). Darwin's view. Self-evaluative emotions as context-specific emotions. *Annals of the New York Academy of Sciences*, 1000, 304–8.

SUM: Slovnyk ukrains'koi movy v 11 tomah. (n.d.). [Dictionary of the Ukrainian language in 11 volumes]. Kyiv: Naukova dumka, 1970–80.

Sunar, D. (2002). Change and continuity in the Turkish middle class family. In E. Ozdalga & R. Liljestrom (Eds.), *Autonomy and dependence in the family: Turkey and Sweden in critical perspective* (pp. 217–37). Istanbul: Swedish Research Institute.

Sunar, D., & Fisek, G. (2005). Contemporary Turkish families. In U. P. Gielen & J. L. Roopnarine (Eds.), *Families in global perspective* (pp. 169–83). Boston: Allyn & Bacon.

Superanskaya, A. (1999). Kak proiznosit' bukvu "G"? [How to Pronounce the Letter "G"?]. *Nauka i zhyzn'*, [Science and Life], (2).

Susskind, J. M., Lee, D. H., Cusi, A., Feiman, R., Grabski, W., & Anderson, A. K. (2008). Expressing fear enhances sensory acquisition. *Nature Neuroscience*, 11, 843–50.

Swan, M., & Smith, B. (Eds.) (2001). *Learner English: A teacher's guide to interference and other problems* (2nd ed.). Cambridge: Cambridge University Press.

Syritsa, G. (2008). K voprosu ob etno-kul'turnoj specifike emotsional'nih konceptov [On the issue of the ethno-cultural specificity of emotion concepts]. *Philologija*, 13, 120–8.

Tabachnick, B. G., & Fidell, L. S. (2007). *Using multivariate statistics* (5th ed.). Boston, MA: Pearson.

Tallon-Baudry, C., Bertrand, O., Delpuech, C., & Pernier, J. (1996). Stimulus specificity of phase-locked and non-phase-locked 40 Hz visual responses in human. *The Journal of Neuroscience*, 16, 4240–9.

Talmy, L. (1988). Force dynamics in language and cognition. *Cognitive Science*, 12, 49–100.

Tanaka-Matsumi, J., & Marsella, A. J. (1976). Cross-cultural variations in the phenomenological experience of depression. *Journal of Cross-Cultural Psychology*, 7, 379–96.

Tangney, J. P. (1990). Assessing individual differences in proneness to shame and guilt: Development of the self-conscious affect and attribution inventory. *Journal of Personality and Social Psychology*, 59, 102–11.

Tangney, J. P., & Dearing, R. L. (2002). *Shame and Guilt*. New York: Guilford Publications.

Tangney, J. P., & Fischer, K. W. (Eds.). (1995). Self-conscious emotions: The psychology of shame, guilt, embarrassment, and pride. New York: The Guilford Press.

Tangney, J. P., Miller, R. S., Flicker, L., & Barlow, D. H. (1996). Are shame, guilt, and embarrassment distinct emotions? *Journal of Personality and Social Psychology*, 70, 1256–69.

Tangney, J. P., Stuewig, J. & Mashek, D. J. (2007). What's moral about the self-conscious emotions? In J. L. Tracy, R. W. Robins, & J. P. Tangney (Eds.), *The self-conscious emotions. Theory and research* (pp. 21–37). New York: Guilford Publications.

Taylor, J. (1995). Linguistic categorization. Prototypes in linguistic theory. Oxford: Oxford University Press.

Taylor, J. A. (1953). A personality scale of manifest anxiety. *Journal of Abnormal and Social Psychology, 48,* 285–90.

Taylor, J. R. (2003). *Linguistic categorization: Prototypes in linguistic theory* (3rd ed.). New York: Oxford University Press.

Taylor, J. R., & Mbense, T. G. (1998). Red dogs and rotten mealies: How Zulus talk about anger. In A. Athanasiadou & E. Tabakowska (Eds.), *Speaking of emotions: Conceptualisation and expression* (pp. 191–226). Berlin/New York: Mouton de Gruyter.

Terkourafi, M., & Bali, P. (2007). Speaking of pain in Greek: Implications for the cognitive permeation of emotions. *Cognition & Emotion, 21,* 1745–79.

Teroni, F., & Deonna, J. (2008). Differentiating shame from guilt. *Consciousness and Cognition, 17,* 725–40.

Termansen, R. E., & Ryan, J. (1970). Health and disease in a British Columbian Indian community. *Canadian Psychiatric Association Journal, 15,* 121–7.

Thayer, R. E. (1989). *The biopsychology of mood and arousal.* New York: Oxford University Press.

Thayer, R. E. (1996). The origin of everyday moods: Managing energy, tension, and stress. New York: Oxford University Press.

The New Oxford Dictionary of English. (2003). Oxford: Oxford University Press.

Thibault, P., Levesque, M., Gosselin, P., & Hess, U. (2012). The Duchenne marker is NOT a universal signal of smile authenticity: But it can be learned! *Social Psychology on Culture as Process (Special Issue), 43,* 215–21.

Timmerman, M. E. (2006). Multilevel component analysis. *British Journal of Mathematical and Statistical Psychology, 59,* 301–20.

Tissari, H. (2001). AFFECTION, FRIENDSHIP, PASSION and CHARITY: A history of four 'love lexemes' since the fifteenth century. *Neuphilologische Mitteilungen, 1,* 49–76.

Tissari, H. (2006). Justified pride? Metaphors of the word pride in English language corpora, 1418–991. *Nordic Journal of English Studies, 5,* 15–49.

Tolman, E. C. (1935). Psychology versus immediate experience. *Philosophy of Science, 2,* 356–80.

Tomkins, S. (1963). Affect, imagery, consciousness: The negative affects (Vol. 2). New York: Springer Publishing Company.

Tomkins, S., & McCarter, R. (1964). What and where are the primary affects? Some evidence for a theory. *Perceptual and Motor Skills, 18,* 119–58.

Tomkins, S. S. (1962). Affect, imagery, consciousness: Vol. 1. The positive affects. New York: Springer.

Tomkins, S. S. (1984). Affect theory. In K. R. Scherer & P. Ekman (Eds.), *Approaches to emotion* (pp. 163–96). Hillsdale, NJ: L. Erlbaum Associates.

Tong, E. M. W. (2007). The cognitive phenomenology of positive emotions: An extensive profiling of the differences and the nature of 14 positive emotions (Unpublished doctoral dissertation).

Tower, R. K., Kelly, C., & Richards, A. (1997). Individualism, collectivism and reward allocation: A cross-cultural study in Russia and Britain. *British Journal of Social Psychology, 36,* 331–45.

Tracy, J. L., Cheng, J. T., Robins, R. W., & Trzesniewski, K. H. (2009). Authentic and hubristic pride: The affective core of self-esteem and narcissism. *Self and Identity, 8,* 196–213.

Tracy, J. L., & Robins, R. W. (2004a). Putting the self into self-conscious emotions: A theoretical model. *Psychological Inquiry, 15,* 103–25.

Tracy, J. L., & Robins, R. W. (2004b). Show your pride: Evidence for a discrete emotion expression. *Psychological Science, 15,* 194–7.

Tracy, J. L., & Robins, R. W. (2007a). Emerging insights into the nature and function of pride. *Current Directions in Psychological Science, 16,* 147–50.

Tracy, J. L., & Robins, R. W. (2007b). The psychological structure of pride: A tale of two facets. *Journal of Personality and Social Psychology, 92,* 506–25.

Tracy, J. L., & Robins, R. W. (2008). The nonverbal expression of pride: Evidence for cross-cultural recognition. *Journal of Personality and Social Psychology, 94,* 516–30.

Tracy, J. L., Shariff, A. F., & Cheng, J. T. (2010). A naturalist's view of pride. *Emotion Review*, *2*, 163–77.

Tran, V. (2004). The influence of emotions on decision-making processes in management teams. Unpublished Ph.D. thesis, University of Geneva [Download http://archive-ouverte.unige.ch/vital/access/manager/Repository/unige:236].

Tran, V., Páez, D., & Sánchez, F. (2012). Emotions and decision-making processes in management teams: A collective level analysis. *Revista de Psicología del Trabajo y de las Organizaciones*, *28*, 15–24.

Trask, R. L. (1996). *The history of Basque*. London: Routledge.

Travis, C. (1998). Omoiyari as a core Japanese value: Japanese style empathy? In A. Athanasiadou & E. Tabakowska (Eds.), *Speaking of emotions: Conceptualization and expression* (pp. 55–82). Berlin: Mouton de Gruyter.

Traxel, W. (1962). Grundzüge eines Systems der Motivierungen. *Archiv für die gesamte Psychologie*, *114*, 143–72.

Traxel, W., & Heide, H. J. (1961). Dimensionen der Gefühle. *Psychologische Forschung*, *26*, 179–204.

Trentacosta, C. J., & Fine, S. E. (2010). Emotion knowledge, social competence, and behaviour problems in childhood and adolescence: A meta-analytic review. *Social Development*, *19*, 1–29.

Triandis, H. C. (1988). Collectivism versus individualism: A reconceptualization of a basic concept of cross-cultural psychology. In G. K. Verma & C. Bagley (Eds.), *Cross-cultural studies of personality, attitudes and ccognition* (pp. 60–95). London: Macmillan.

Triandis, H. C. (1995). *Individualism and collectivism*. Boulder, CO: Westview.

Triandis, H. C., Bontempo, R., Betancourt, H., Bond, M., Leung, K., Brenes, A., Georgas, J., et al. (1986). The measurement of the etic aspects of individualism and collectivism across cultures. *Australian Journal of Psychology*, *38*, 257–76.

Triandis, H. C., Bontempo, R., Villareal, M. J., Asai, M., & Lucca, N. (1988). Individualism and collectivism: Cross-cultural perspectives on self-ingroup relationships. *Journal of Personality and Social Psychology*, *54*, 323–38.

Triandis, H. C., & Vassiliou, V. (1972). A comparative analysis of subjective culture. In H. C. Triandis & V. Vassiliou (Eds.), *The analysis of subjective culture* (pp. 299–335). New York: Wiley-Interscience.

Tsai, J. L., Knutson, B., & Fung, H. H. (2006). Cultural variation in affect valuation. *Journal of Personality and Social Psychology*, *90*, 288–307.

Tsai, J. L., Simeonova, D. I., & Watanabe, J. T. (2004). Somatic and social: Chinese Americans talk about emotion. *Personality and Social Psychology Bulletin*, *30*, 1226–38.

Tschan, F., Semmer, N. K., Messerli, L., & Janevski, C. (2010). Discrete emotions in interactions with superiors: Some are more role-related, some are more relationship related. In T. Rigotti, S. Korek, & K. Otto (Eds.), *Gesund mit und ohne Arbeit* (p. 289–304). Lengerich: Pabst Science Publishers.

Tseng, W.-S., & Hsu, J. (1969). Chinese culture, personality formation and mental illness. *International Journal of Social Psychiatry*, *16*, 5–14.

Tung, M. P. (1994). Symbolic meanings of the body in Chinese culture and "somatization." *Culture medicine and psychiatry*, *18*, 483–92.

Tuovila, S. (2005). *Kun on tunteet: Suomen kielen tunnesanojen semantiikkaa*. [Because we have emotions: On the semantics of Finnish words for emotions]. Oulu: University of Oulu, Department of Finnish, Information Studies and Logopedics. Retrieved from http://jultika.oulu.fi/Record/isbn951-42-7807-0

Turner, M., & Fauconnier, G. (1998). Conceptual integration networks. *Cognitive Science*, *22*, 133–87.

Turpin, M. (2002). Body part terms in Kaytetye feeling expressions. *Pragmatics & Cognition*, *10*, 271–305.

Tybur, J. M., Lieberman, D., & Griskevicius, V. (2009). Microbes, mating, and morality: Individual differences in three functional domains of disgust. *Journal of Personality and Social Psychology*, *97*, 103–22.

Tzeng, O. C. S., Hoosain, R., & Osgood, C. E. (1987). Cross-cultural componential analysis on affect distribution of emotion terms. *Journal of Psycholinguistic Research*, *16*, 443–65.

Uchida, Y., & Kitayama, S. (2009). Happiness and unhappiness in East and West: Themes and variations. *Emotion, 9*, 441–56.

Ungerer, F. (2000). Mutted metaphors and the activation of metonymies in advertising. In A. Barcelona (Ed.), *Metaphor and Metonymy at the Crossroads* (pp. 321–40). Berlin and New York: Mouton de Gruyter.

United Nations Development Programme. (2007). Human Development Report 2007–2008. Fighting climate change: Human solidarity in a divided world. New York: Palgrave Macmillan.

Uniwersalny słownik języka polskiego. (2003). Warszawa: PWN.

Uryson, M. (1997). Toska, unynie, pečal, grust'. In J. D. Apresjan, O. J. Boguslavskij, I. B. Levontina, E. V. Uryson, M. J. Glovinskaja, & T. V. Krylova (Eds.), *Novyj ob"jasnitel'nyj slovar' sinonimov russkogo jazyka*, [The new explanatory dictionary of synonyms in the Russian language] (pp. 1165–70). Moscow: Jazyki russkoj kul'tury.

Ushakov, D. N. (Ed.) (1940). *Tolkovij slovar' russkogo yazyka.* [Explanatory dictionary of the Russian language]. Moscow: Soviet Encyclopedia.

Vainik, E. (2002a). Emotions, emotion terms and emotion concepts in an Estonian folk model. *Trames, 6*, 322–41.

Vainik, E. (2002b). Hot-blooded Estonians. On Estonians' folk category of emotions. *Folklore, 21*, 26–51.

Vainik, E. (2004). Lexical knowledge of emotions: The Structure, variability, and semantics of Estonian emotion vocabulary. (Unpublished doctoral dissertation). Tartu University, Tartu.

Vainik, E. (2007). Body parts in Estonian figurative descriptions of emotions. In *Proceedings of the 10th Cognitive Linguistics Conference* (pp. 105–6).

Vainik, E., & Orav, H. (2005). Welcome to Estonia! From the folk theory of emotions and character traits to brand Estonia. *Folklore, 30*, 7–42.

Vaitl, D. (1996). Interoception. *Biological Psychology, 42*, 1–27.

Vakulenko, E. (2003). Connotations culturelles et émotivité: Un exemple russo-francais. In *Actes des VIemes RJC ED268 "Langage et langues."*

Valitutti, A., Strapparava, C. & Stock, O. (2004). Developing affective lexical resource. *PsychNology Journal, 2*, 61–83.

Van Benthem, J. (1991). Linguistic universals in logical semantics. In D. Zaefferer (Ed.), *Semantic universals and universal semantics*, Groningen-Amsterdam Studies in Semantics (GRASS) (Vol. 12, pp. 17–36). Berlin: Foris.

Van Bezooijen, R., Otto, S. A., & Heenan, T. A. (1983). Recognition of vocal expressions of emotion: A three-nation study to identify universal characteristics. *Journal of Cross-Cultural Psychology, 14*, 387–406.

Van de Ven, N., Zeelenberg, M., & Pieters, R. (2009). Leveling up and down: The experiences of benign and malicious envy. *Emotion, 9*, 419–29.

Van de Vijver, F. J. R., & Leung, K. (1997). *Methods and data analysis for cross-cultural research.* Thousand Oaks, CA: Sage.

Van der Hart, O., van Dijke, A., van Son, M., & Steele, K. (2000). Somatoform dissociation in traumatized World War I combat soldiers: A neglected clinical heritage. *Journal of Trauma & Dissociation, 1*, 33–66.

Vandervoort, D. J. (2001). Cross-cultural differences in coping with sadness. *Current Psychology, 20*, 147–53.

Van Goozen, S., & Frijda, N. H. (1993). Emotion words used in 6 European countries. *European Journal of Social Psychology, 23*, 89–95.

Van Hemert, D. A., Poortinga, Y. H., & Van de Vijver, F. J. R. (2007). Emotion and culture: A meta-analysis. *Cognition & Emotion, 21*, 913–43.

Van Hooff, J. A. R. A. M. (1972). A comparative approach to the phylogeny of laughter and smiling. In R. A. Hinde (Ed.), *Non-verbal communication* (pp. 209–41). Cambridge: Cambridge University Press.

van Reekum, C., Banse, R., Johnstone, T., Etter, A., Wehrle, T., & Scherer, K. R. (2004). Psychophysiological responses to appraisal responses in a computer game. *Cognition & Emotion, 18*, 663–88.

van Reekum, C. M., & Scherer, K. R. (1997). Levels of processing for emotion-antecedent appraisal. In G. Matthews (Ed.), *Cognitive science perspectives on personality and emotion* (pp. 259–300). Amsterdam: Elsevier.

Vassiliou, V. G., & Vassiliou, G. (1973). The implicative meaning of the Greek concept of Philotimo. *Journal of Cross-Cultural Psychology, 4,* 326–41.

Veirman, E., & Fontaine, J. J. R. (2011). The development of feeling and emotion terms from childhood to adolescence. Manuscript in preparation.

Verbeke, W., Belschak, F., & Bagozzi, R. P. (2004). The adaptive consequences of pride in personal selling. *Journal of the Academy of Marketing Science, 32,* 386–402.

Verduyn, P., Delvaux, E., Van Coillie, H., Tuerlinckx, F., & Van Mechelen, I. (2009a). Predicting the duration of emotional experience: Two experience sampling studies. *Emotion, 9,* 83–91.

Verduyn, P., Van Mechelen, I., Tuerlinckx, F., Meers, K., & Scherer, K. R. (2013). The relation between appraised mismatch and the duration of negative emotions: Evidence for universality. *European Journal of Personality.* Article first published online: 14 Jan 2013, DOI: 10.1002/per.1897.

Verduyn, P., Van Mechelen, I., Tuerlinckx, F., Meers, K., & Van Coillie, H. (2009b). Intensity profiles of emotional experience over time. *Cognition & Emotion, 23,* 1427–43.

Vila, J., Sánchez, M., Ramírez, I., Fernández, M. C., Cobos, P., Rodríguez, S., Múñoz, M. A., et al. (2001). El Sistema Internacional de Imágenes Afectivas (IAPS): Adaptación Española. Segunda parte. *Revista de Psicología General y Aplicada, 54,* 635–57.

Violi, P. (2001). *Meaning and experience.* Bloomington: Indiana University Press.

Von Fintel, K., & Matthewson, L. (2008). Universals in Semantics. *The Linguistic Review, 25,* 139–201.

Vovchok, Z. I. (2002). Spetsyfika interferentsii blyz'kosporidnenyh mov [Closely-Related Languages Interference Specificity] *Funktsyonal'naya lingvistika. Itogi i perspektivy. [Functional Linguistics. Results and Prospects]: Conference Proceedings,* Yalta, 34–6.

Vuilleumier, P. (2005). How brains beware: Neural mechanisms of emotional attention. *Trends in Cognitive Sciences, 9,* 585–94.

Vygotsky, L. (1986). *Thought and language.* Cambridge, MA: MIT Press.

Wallace, A. F. C., & Carson, M. T. (1973). Sharing and diversity in emotion terminology. *Ethos, 1,* 1–29.

Wallbott, H. G. (1998). Bodily expression of emotion. *European Journal of Social Psychology, 28,* 879–96.

Wallbott, H. G., & Scherer, K. R. (1986). How universal and specific is emotional experience? Evidence from 27 countries on five continents. *Social Science Information, 25,* 763–95.

Wallbott, H. G., & Scherer, K. R. (1988). How universal and specific is emotional experience? Evidence from 27 countries on five continents. In K. R. Scherer (Ed.), *Facets of emotion: Recent research* (pp. 31–56). Hillsdale, NJ: Erlbaum.

Wallbott, H. G. & Scherer, K. R. (1995). Cultural determinants in experiencing shame and guilt. In J. P. Tangney & K. W. Fischer (Eds.), *Self-conscious emotions: The psychology of shame, guilt, embarrassment and pride* (pp. 465–87). New York: Guilford Publications.

Watkins, E. A. (1938). *A dictionary of the Cree language.* Toronto, Ontario: Church of England in Canada.

Watson, D. & Clark, L. A. (1997). Measurement and mismeasurement of mood: Recurrent and emergent issues. *Journal of Personality Assessment, 68,* 267–96.

Watson, D., Clark, L. A., & Tellegen, A. (1988). Development and validation of brief measures of positive and negative affect: The PANAS scales. *Journal of Personality and Social Psychology, 54,* 1063–70.

Watson, D., & Tellegen, A. (1985). Toward a consensual structure of mood. *Psychological Bulletin, 98,* 219–35.

Watson, D., Wiese, D., Vaidya, J. & Tellegen, A. (1999). The two general activation systems of affect: Structural findings, evolutionary considerations, and psychobiological evidence. *Journal of Personality and Social Psychology, 76,* 820–38.

Watson, J. B. (1929). *Psychology from the Standpoint of a Behaviorist.* Philadelphia: Lippincott.

Watson, J. M. (2004). From interpretation to identification: A history of facial images in the sciences of emotion. *History of the Human Sciences, 17*, 29–51.

Weathers, M. D., Frank, E. M., & Spell, L. A. (2002). Differences in the communication of affect: Members of the same race versus members of a different race. *Journal of Black Psychology, 28*, 66–77.

Weigerber, L. (1943). *Die volkhaften Kräfte der Muttersprache* (3rd ed.). Frankfurt am Main: Moritz Diesterweg.

Weigerber, L. (1950). *Vom Weltbild der deutschen Sprache*. Düsseldorf: Schwann.

Weiner, B. (1982). The emotional consequences of causal attributions. In M. S. Clark & S. T. Fiske (Eds.), *Affect and cognition: the seventeenth annual Carnegie Symposium on Cognition*. Hillsdale, N.J.: L. Erlbaum Associates.

Weiner, B. (1985). An attributional theory of achievement motivation and emotion. *Psychological Review, 92*, 548–73.

Weiner, B. (1986). An attributional theory of motivation and emotion. New York: Springer.

Weinreich, U. (1962). On the semantic structure of language. In J. H. Greenberg (Ed.), *Universals of Language* (pp. 114–71). Cambridge, MA: MIT Press.

Weiss, J. (1977). *Folk psychology of the Javanese of Ponorogo*. (Unpublished doctoral dissertation). Yale University, New Haven.

Werner, O. (1965). Semantics of Navaho medical terms: I. *International Journal of American Linguistics, 31*, 1–17.

Whalen, P. J., & Kleck, R. E. (2008). The shape of faces (to come). *Nature Neuroscience, 11*, 739–40.

Wheatley, T., & Haidt, J. (2005). Hypnotic disgust makes moral judgments more severe. *Psychological Science, 16*, 780–4.

White, G. (1978). Ambiguity and ambivalence in A'ara personality descriptors. *American Ethnologist, 5*, 334–60.

White, G. L., & Mullen, P. E. (1989). *Jealousy: Theory, Research, and Clinical Strategies*. New York, NY: Guilford Press.

White, G. M. (1980). Conceptual universals in interpersonal language. *American Anthropologist, 82*, 759–81.

White, G., & Kirkpatrick, J. (Eds.) (1985). *Person, self, and experience: Exploring Pacific ethnopsychologies*. Berkeley: University of California Press.

Whorf, B. L. (1956). Science and linguistics. In J. B. Carroll (Ed.), *Language, thought, and reality: Selected writings of Benjamin Lee Whorf* (pp. 207–19). Cambridge, MA: MIT Press.

Wiens, S. (2005). Interoception in emotional experience. *Current Opinion in Neurology, 18*, 442–7.

Wierzbicka, A. (1972). *Semantic primitives*. Frankfurt: Athenaeum.

Wierzbicka, A. (1973). The semantic structure of words for emotions. In R. Jakobson, C. H. van Schooneveld, & D. S. Worth (Eds.), *Slavic poetics: Essays in honour of Kiril Taranovsky* (pp. 499–505). The Hague: Mouton.

Wierzbicka, A. (1980). Lingua mentalis: The semantics of natural language. Sydney: Academic Press.

Wierzbicka, A. (1986). Human emotions: universal or culture-specific? *American Anthropologist*, New Series, *88*, 584–94.

Wierzbicka, A. (1990a). Duša (soul), toska (yearning), sud'ba (fate): three key concepts in Russian language and Russian culture. In Z. Saloni (Ed.), *Metody formalne w opisie języków słowiańskich* (pp. 13–32). Białystok: Dzial Wydawn.

Wierzbicka, A. (1990b). Introduction. *Australian Journal of Linguistics* [Special issue on the semantics of emotions], *10*, 133–8.

Wierzbicka, A. (1992a). Talking about emotions: Semantics, culture, and cognition. *Cognition & Emotion, 6*, 285–319.

Wierzbicka, A. (1992b). Semantics, culture, and cognition: Universal human concepts in culture-specific configurations. Oxford: Oxford University Press.

Wierzbicka, A. (1992c). Defining emotion concepts. *Cognitive Science, 16*, 539–81.

Wierzbicka, A. (1994a). "Cultural scripts": A new approach to the study of cross-cultural communication. In M. Pütz (Ed.), *Language contact and language conflict* (pp. 69–88). Amsterdam: John Benjamins.

Wierzbicka, A. (1994b). Emotion, language and "cultural scripts." In S. Kitayama & H. R. Markus (Eds.), *Emotion and Culture: Empirical Studies of Mutual Influence* (1st ed., pp. 130–98). Washington D.C.: American Psychological Association (APA).

Wierzbicka, A. (1995a). Emotion and facial expression: A semantic perspective. *Culture & Psychology, 1*, 227–58.

Wierzbicka, A. (1995b). Everyday conceptions of emotion: A semantic perspective. In J. A. Russell, J.-M. Fernández-Dols, A. S. R. Manstead, & J. C. Wellenkamp (Eds.), *Everyday conceptions of emotion: An introduction to the psychology, anthropology and linguistics of emotion* (pp. 17–49). Dordrecht: Kluwer.

Wierzbicka, A. (1996). *Semantics: Primes and universals.* Oxford: Oxford University Press.

Wierzbicka, A. (1998a). Angst. *Culture & Psychology, 4*, 161–88.

Wierzbicka, A. (1998b). Sadness and Anger in Russian: The non-universality of the so-called "basic human emotions." In A. Athanasiadou & E. Tabakowska (Eds.), *Speaking of emotions: Conceptualisation and expression* (pp. 3–28). Berlin: Mouton de Gruyter.

Wierzbicka, A. (1999a). *Emotions across languages and cultures: Diversity and universals.* Cambridge: Cambridge University Press.

Wierzbicka, A. (1999b). Emotional universals. *Language design, 2*, 23–69.

Wierzbicka, A. (2001a). A culturally salient Polish emotion: Przykro. *International Journal of Group Tensions, 30*, 3–27.

Wierzbicka, A. (2001b). A culturally salient Polish emotion of przykro. In J. Harkins & A. Wierzbicka (Eds.), *Emotions in crosslinguistic perspective* (pp. 337–57). Berlin, NY: Mouton de Gruyter.

Wierzbicka, A. (2001c). Leibnizian linguistics. In I. Kenesei & R. M. Harnish (Eds.), *Perspectives on semantics, pragmatics, and discourse* (pp. 229–53). Amsterdam: John Benjamins Publishing Company.

Wierzbicka, A. (2003). Emotion and culture: Arguing with Martha Nussbaum. *Ethos, 31*, 577–600.

Wierzbicka, A. (2004). "Happiness" in cross-linguistic & cross-cultural perspective. *Daedalus, 133*(2), 34–43.

Wierzbicka, A. (2006). *English. Meaning and Culture.* Oxford: Oxford University Press.

Wierzbicka, A. (2009). Language and metalanguage: Key issues in emotion research. *Emotion Review, 1*, 3–14.

Wiggins, J. S. (1979). A psychological taxonomy of trait-descriptive terms: The interpersonal domain. *Journal of Personality and Social Psychology, 37*, 395–412.

Wiggins, J. S., & Trobst, K. K. (1997). When is a circumplex an "interpersonal circumplex"? The case of supportive actions. In R. Plutchik & H. R. Conte (Eds.), *Circumplex models of personality and emotions* (pp. 57–80). Washington, DC: American Psychological Association.

Wikan, U. (1990). *Managing turbulent hearts.* Chicago: University of Chicago Press.

Wikan, U. (1992). Beyond the words: the power of resonance. *American Ethnologist, 19*, 460–82.

Wilce, J. M. (2009). *Language and emotion.* Cambridge: Cambridge University Press.

Wilkowski, B. M., Meier, B. P., Robinson, M. D., Carter, M. S., & Feltman, R. (2009). Hot-headed is more than an expression: the embodied representation of anger in terms of heat. *Emotion, 9*, 464–77.

Williams, L. A., & DeSteno, D. (2008). Pride and perseverance: The motivational role of pride. *Journal of Personality and Social Psychology, 94*, 1007–17.

Williams, L. E., & Bargh, J. H. (2008). Experiencing physical warmth promotes interpersonal warmth. *Science, 322*, 606–7.

Williams, L. M., Senior, C., David, A. S., Loughland, C. M., & Gordon, E. (2001). In search of the "Duchenne Smile": Evidence from eye movements. *Journal of Psychophysiology, 15*, 122–7.

Wilson, D. (2003). Relevance and lexical pragmatics. *Italian Journal of Linguistics/Rivista di Linguistica, 15*, 273–91.

Wilson, D., & Carston, R. (2007). A unitary approach to lexical pragmatics: relevance, inference and ad hoc concepts. In N. Burton-Roberts (Ed.), *Advances in Pragmatics* (pp. 230–59). London: Palgrave.

Wilson, P. A. (2012). *Dynamicity in emotion concepts.* Frankfurt am Main: Peter Lang GmbH.

Wissing, M. P., Thekiso, S. M., Stapelberg, R., Van Quickelberge, L., Choabi, P., Moroeng, C., et al. (2010). Validation of three Setswana measures for psychological wellbeing. *SA Journal of Industrial Psychology*, *36*, dec. 2010.

Wittgenstein, L. (1953/2001). *Philosophical investigations* (3rd ed.). Oxford: Blackwell Publishing.

Wittgenstein, R. D. (2008). Factors influencing individual readiness fo change in a health care environment. *Dissertation Abstracts International, 69* (01) (UMI No. 3296851). Retrieved from http://gradworks.umi.com/32/96/3296851.html.

Wolfson, I. (2005). *Adjectival participles as emotion words.* (Unpublished master dissertation). Hamline University, Saint Paul, MN.

Wollheim, R. (1999). *On the emotions.* New Haven, CT: Yale University Press.

World Value Survey. (2005). *Official data file v.20081015. World Values Survey Association.* Retrieved from www.worldvaluesurvey.org.

Wranik, T., & Scherer, K. R. (in press). Why do I get angry? A componential appraisal approach. In M. Potegal, G. Stemmler, & C. Spielberger (Eds.), *A handbook of anger: Constituent and concomitant biological, psychological, and social processes.* Cambridge: Cambridge University Press.

Wray, A. (2002). *Formulaic Language and the Lexicon.* Cambridge: Cambridge University Press.

Wundt, W. (1896). Grundriss der Psychologie. Leipzig: Engelmann. [Outline of psychology; translated by C. H. Judd, 1897; online at http://psychclassics.yorku.ca/Wundt/Outlines/index.htm].

Wundt, W. (1905). Grundzüge der physiologischen Psychologie (5th ed.). [Fundamentals of physiological psychology] Leipzig: Engelmann.

Yamagishi, T., Hashimoto, H., & Schug, J. (2008). Preferences versus strategies as explanations for culture-specific behavior. *Psychological Science, 19*, 579–84.

Yavuz, H., & van den Bos, K. (2009). Effects of uncertainty and mortality salience on worldview defense reactions in Turkey. *Social Justice Research, 22*, 384–98.

Ye, Z. (2001). An inquiry into "sadness" in Chinese. In J. Harkins & A. Wierzbicka (Eds.), *Emotions in crosslinguistic perspective* (pp. 359–404). Berlin: Mouton de Gruyter.

Ye, Z. (2002). Different modes of describing emotions in Chinese: Bodily changes, sensations, and bodily images. *Pragmatics & Cognition, 10*, 307–39.

Ye, Z. (2004). The Chinese folk model of facial expressions: A linguistic perspective. *Culture & Psychology, 10*, 195–222.

Ye, Z. (2006a). Why are there two 'joy–like' 'basic' emotions in Chinese? Semantic theory and empirical findings. In P. Santangelo & D. Guida (Eds.), *Love, hatred and other passions: Questions and themes on emotions in Chinese civilisation* (pp. 59–80). Leiden: E.J. Brill.

Ye, Z. (2006b). Why the "inscrutable" Chinese face? Emotionality and facial expression in Chinese. In C. Goddard (Ed.), *Ethnopragmatics: Understanding Discourse in Cultural Context* (pp. 127–70). Berlin/New York: Mouton de Gruyter.

Ye, Z. (2007a). *"I feel ku in my heart": sadness, taste and Chinese attitudes towards emotion.* Paper presented at the XVth Conference of International Society of Researchers on Emotion, Coolum, Australia (11–5July 2007).

Ye, Z. (2007b). Taste as a gateway to Chinese cognition. In A. C. Schalley & D. Khlentzos (Eds.), *Mental states: Language and cognitive structure* (Vol. 2, pp. 109–32). Amsterdam: John Benjamins Publishing Company.

Yik, M. S. M., Russell, J. A., & Barrett, L. F. (1999). Structure of self-reported current affect: Integration and beyond. *Journal of Personality and Social Psychology, 77*, 600–19.

Yoon, K.-J. (2008). The Korean conceptualization of heart: An indigenous perspective. In F. Sharifian, R. Dirven, & S. Niemeier (Eds.), *Culture, body, and language* (pp. 213–46). Berlin: Mouton de Gruyter.

Yu, N. (1995). Metaphorical expressions of anger and happiness in English and Chinese. *Metaphor and Symbolic Activity*, *10*(2), 59–92.

Yu, N. (2002). Body and emotion: Body parts in Chinese expression of emotion. *Pragmatics & Cognition*, *10*, 341–67.

Yuan, J., Zhang, Q., Chen, A., Li, H., Wang, Q., Zhuang, Z., & Jia, S. (2007). Are we sensitive to valence differences in emotionally negative stimuli? Electrophysiological evidence from an ERP study. *Neuropsychologia*, *45*, 2764–71.

Zakharova, J. (2005). Prosodic interference in English discourse (Experimental phonetic research on the speech of Arabic-English bilinguals). (Unpublished doctoral dissertation). Kyiv National Taras Shevchenko University, Kyiv.

Zammuner, V. L. (1998). Concepts of emotion: "Emotioness", and dimensional ratings of Italian emotion words. *Cognition & Emotion*, *12*, 243–72.

Zasorina, L. N. (Ed.). (1977). *Chastotnij slovar' russkogo yazyka*. [Frequency dictionary of the Russian language]. Moscow: Nauka.

Zeelenberg, M., & Breugelmans, S. M. (2008). The role of interpersonal harm in distinguishing regret from guilt. *Emotion*, *8*, 589–96.

Zholkovsky, A., & Mel'cuk, I. (1984). Tolkovo-kombinatornyj slovar' russkogo jazyka [Explanatory combinatorial Dictionary of Modern Russian]. Vienna: Wiener Slawistischer Almanach.

Zhong, C. B., & Leonardelli, G. J. (2008). Cold and lonely. Does social exclusion literally feel cold? *Psychological Science*, *19*, 838–42.

Zhong, C.-B., & Liljenquist, K. (2006). Washing away your sins: Threatened morality and physical cleansing. *Science*, *313*(5792), 1451–2.

Zipf, G. K. (1949). *Human behavior and the principle of least effort*. Cambridge, MA: Addison-Wesley Press.

Name index

Note: "n." after a page reference indicates the number of a note on that page

Subject index

Note: "n." after a page reference indicates the number of a note on that page